Index of Obituaries and Marriages in THE [BALTIMORE] SUN 1861–1865

Joseph C. Maguire, Jr.

HERITAGE BOOKS
2011

HERITAGE BOOKS
AN IMPRINT OF HERITAGE BOOKS, INC.

Books, CDs, and more—Worldwide

For our listing of thousands of titles see our website
at
www.HeritageBooks.com

Published 2011 by
HERITAGE BOOKS, INC.
Publishing Division
100 Railroad Ave. #104
Westminster, Maryland 21157

Copyright © 1991 Maryland Historical Society

All rights reserved. No part of this book may be reproduced or transmitted in any form or by any means, electronic or mechanical, including photocopying, recording or by any information storage and retrieval system without written permission from the author, except for the inclusion of brief quotations in a review.

International Standard Book Numbers
Paperbound: 978-1-58549-203-9
Clothbound: 978-0-7884-8955-6

Dedicated To

My Parents,

Joseph and Ruth Maguire

ACKNOWLEDGEMENTS

I wish to thank the everyone who helped me to complete this project.

Christopher Jeffries, MHS volunteer, was one of the main compilers of the data and has assisted in what seems like countless proofreadings of the manuscript. He has been involved in this almost from the start and has my deepest gratitude.

Several interns have also been involved in this project over the past year and have been of valuable assistance. Dwayne Townsend of Towson State, Susan McGinley of the University of Baltimore and Mary Ramos of the University of Maryland were all exceptional in their work. I thank them and wish them well in future endeavours. My own internships at the University of Baltimore were especially meaningful, and I hope that in this manner I have returned the favor.

Special thanks to my technical consultants, Robert Barnes, Tom Hollowak, Robert Bruger, and anyone else that was in the general vicinity at any given time who offered helpful suggestions. Mr. Barnes has urged me on from the outset.

FOREWORD

Newspapers are a rich mine of source material for the family historian. That they have not been used is due to the fact that until the 1960's most of them were not indexed. Unless the researcher had some idea of the date of death or marriage, he or she would have to turn page after page, hoping to find the long sought marriage notice or obituary.

Louis H. Deilman and Francis S. Hayward had copied items from newspapers in the 18th and early 19th Century and placed their findings on cards which are now at the Maryland Historical Society, but these have not been published. Christopher Johnston and George A. Martin had published some biographical notices from the Maryland Gazette in the Maryland Historical Magazine, but these referred mainly to the inhabitants of Annapolis.

In the last thirty years more and more vital records from newspapers have been abstracted and/or indexed. Thomas L. Hollowak indexed marriages and deaths from the Baltimore Sun, 1837-1850, and marriages only 1851-1860. Walter Arps abstracted obituaries from the same paper for 1851 through 1860. Edward Wright has published abstracts from Harford and Cecil County newspapers, Eastern Shore newspapers, 1790-1834, and Western Maryland newspapers, 1786-1820. This writer has abstracted genealogical items from Maryland newspapers, 1727-1795, marriages and deaths from the Annapolis Maryland Gazette, 1727-1839, and Baltimore newspapers, 1796-1816. Most recently, Karen Green has abstracted all items from the Annapolis Maryland Gazette, 1727-1761.

Joseph Maguire has performed a valuable service in indexing the marriages and deaths from the Baltimore Sun for the years 1861 through 1865. During the Civil War, the Sun was the only newspaper in Baltimore that did not suspend publication for even the shortest time. As a result, the marriages and deaths of the period were reported continuously to the readers of Baltimore--and Maryland.

This publication, containing over 27,000 entries, gives the name of the bride or groom or the deceased, the date of the event, and the date of the issue of the newspaper. In the case of the marriages, there are entries under both the bride's or the groom's name, making an index unnecessary.

Genealogists will find ths index invaluable. It is hoped that it will be followed by a volume for the years 1866-1870.

                                             Robert Barnes
                                             August 1991

PREFACE

Some of the most frequently used references in the library of the Maryland Historical Society have been the volumes listing obituaries and marriages published in old Maryland newspapers. Robert Barnes concentrated on early Maryland newspapers, Tom Hollowak compiled the Sun's deaths and marriages 1837-1850 and deaths only, 1851-1860. Walter Arps concentrated on two series--deaths in the Sun from 1851-1860 and the Sun almanacs for the years 1875 through 1915. However valuable, these sources have left gaps for the years 1816-1837 and 1861-1875. Marriage/obituary indexes available at the Maryland Historical Society, the Maryland Room at the Central Branch of the Enoch Pratt Free Library, and similar repositories only partially satisfy the serious researcher. This book compiles published obituaries and marriages for the Civil War years in Baltimore.

The deaths and burials of prominent people in the community (see, for example, the passing of Francis P. Kenrick, archbishop of Baltimore, in early July 1863 and the death of Congressman Henry Winter Davis at the end of December 1865) supplied front-page news in the Sun for several days. But most period newspapers printed the obituaries and marriages section on page two of period newspapers--where, a bit strangely, one also found references to traveling circuses, visiting troubadors, and sundry amusements. The second page offers the modern reader far more than twigs for the family tree. Indeed, against the backdrop of Civil-War Baltimore, the mere printing of a newspaper testified to a publisher's political skills, for federal authorities looked over every editor's shoulder just as surely as the public hungered for news from the scenes of military action.

Not all such information was readily published as events took place. Like other newspapermen, Arunah S. Abell, owner and publisher of the Sun, had to weigh what was prudent to print and what was not. On April 19, 1861, the Pratt Street Riot resulted in the deaths of a number of Baltimore citizens and members of the 6th Massachusetts Infantry Regiment. In the next day's Sun obituary column only the names of three Baltimoreans--Robert W. Davis, James Clark and Thomas Miles--were included. Even then, James Clark and Phillip Thomas Miles were reported as "William Clarke" and "Phillip Thomas Wiles." John McGann, one of the wounded, died on the 20th, and the notice appeared on the 21st. The 6th Massachusetts Regiment's dead went unmentioned; the paper said nothing of the victims' dying "suddenly" or "unexpectedly." The Sun notices were completely devoid of commentary.

Throughout the war period, the Sun downplayed the deaths of Marylanders who fought for the Confederacy. Although death notices of Rebel officers were fairly frequent, the paper scarcely printed obituaries for all Southern families--perhaps assuming the deaths were common knowledge. Conspicuous by his absence, for instance, was the name of Confederate general Lewis Armistead, nephew of George Armistead who in 1814 had commanded forces at Fort McHenry during the British bombardment. Armistead was killed at Gettysburg, in the front rank of Pickett's Charge. He was quietly buried in St. Paul's Cemetery, next to his uncle.

Overall, Baltimore newspapers published death/marriage information in the same manner as other nineteenth-century prints, and, in keeping with the social conventions of the time, typically excluded blacks, Jews, and the less well-to-do unless they were so prominent in the community that they could not readily be ignored. Notices apparently were based on details furnished by family and friends. Out-of-state newspapers occasionally requested Baltimore newspapers to reprint marriage or death notices. Word of war-related deaths may have come from the War Department in Washington or from various informal sources.

In the entries below, spellings have been corrected if obviously wrong. Name abbreviations such as Wm., Jno., etc., have been expanded. We have included military rank, professional standing, and the marital status of women. All entries appeared on page two of the paper. Two dates appear in the individual entries--the first the date of the event, the second the date of publication.

We hope this compilation will provide a logical extension of and a tribute to the work of past compilers of Maryland newspaper abstracts and indexes and generally cultivate interest in Maryland's past.

                                                        Joseph C. Maguire, Jr.
                                                        October 1991

INDEX OF OBITUARIES AND MARRIAGES IN

THE [BALTIMORE] SUN, 1861-1865

Abbell, Christopher C. died 12/14/65   12/16/65
Abbett, V. Eudora married Noyes, Edward C. 11/09/64   11/10/64
Abbey, Elizabeth (Mrs.) died 07/27/63   08/18/63
Abbot, Matilda died 02/04/65   02/14/65
Abbott, Amanda married Carter, George 01/28/64   01/30/64
Abbott, Clara E. married Myers, Thomas A. 10/09/62   10/11/62
Abbott, Daniel E. R. married Benner, Mary E. C. 04/14/64   04/16/64
Abbott, David M. married Mitchell, Sadie C. 08/03/65   08/09/65
Abbott, Elizabeth A. died 04/29/65   05/01/65
Abbott, Elizabeth A. died 04/29/65   05/02/65
Abbott, Kate Beatty died 12/13/64   12/14/64
Abbott, Mary E. married Frank, Milton B. 01/09/61   01/12/61
Abbott, William died 12/30/64   12/31/64
Abbott, William Martin married Wilkinson, Fannie Virginia 07/11/61
    09/11/61
Abel, Charles T. married Barbour, Amanda E. 04/03/64   05/04/64
Abell, Christian died 07/21/64   07/22/64
Abell, Edward B. died 12/16/61   12/28/61
Abell, Edwin F. married Curley, Maggie 11/25/63   11/26/63
Abell, Eleanora (Mrs.) died 01/06/63   01/10/63
Abell, Mary Louisa died 08/08/61   08/09/61
Abell, Mary M. died 09/06/61   09/07/61
Abell, Susan Elizabeth died 06/01/65   06/02/65
Abell, Thomas P. died 12/13/63   12/18/63
Abell, Virginia F. died 03/02/63   03/12/63
Abendschone, Alois died 09/11/63   09/12/63
Abercrombie, David married Jenness, Addie Hutton 10/10/61   10/11/61
Abercrombie, David, Sr. died 03/05/64   03/07/64
Abernathy, Hattie E. married Tough, William S. 10/25/65   11/01/65
Abey, George died 03/07/65   03/18/65
Abey, George Washington died 06/23/63   06/24/63
Abey, Joseph died 02/01/64   02/03/64
Abey, Joseph C. married Haas, Barbara 08/18/64   09/02/64
Abey, Peter Mowel died 05/04/61   05/06/61
Abey, Samuel married Chance, M. E. 05/22/65   05/31/65
Abey, Sarah F. married Lewis, Charles H. 05/25/65   05/31/65
Abrahams, Nathaniel F. died 05/10/64   05/12/64
Abrahams, S. Maria (Mrs.) died 09/07/63   09/19/63
Abrams, Desdamona married Hirsch, John 11/12/63   11/19/63

Abrams, Mary Frances married Berry, Michael 09/07/65   09/11/65
Abrams, Mary Frances married Barry, Michael 09/07/65   09/12/65
Abrams, Washington, Jr. died 07/27/63   07/28/63
Absolam, Annie married Robbins, David B. 03/09/64   03/22/64
Aburn, Charles Henry died 11/16/61   11/18/61
Aburn, Charles Henry died 11/16/61   11/20/61
Aburn, Eugenia died 03/25/61   03/26/61
Aburn, George Edwin died 01/22/64   01/28/64
Aburn, James B. died 01/26/63   01/27/63
Aburn, Johnson B. died 11/19/62   11/21/62
Aburn, Joshua B. died 11/19/62   11/20/62
Aburn, William Henry Slicer died 04/14/62   04/17/62
Accman, Elizabeth married Franklin, Chase 04/12/64   04/28/64
Achey, Mary L. married Slack, George A. 11/10/63   11/11/63
Achres, Elizabeth married Christner, John 02/18/64   02/25/64
Ackerson, Daniel M. married Chaillou, Victoria Amanda 05/19/64   06/24/
Ackler, Dorothea married Gissler, John A. 02/27/62   03/04/62
Ackler, M. A. married Eckhardt, William 12/29/64   01/02/65
Acomb, Fanny married Jones, John 05/01/62   06/10/62
Acomb, Maggie E. married Bartholow, George E. 04/21/64   05/02/64
Adair, Elizabeth died 07/26/61   07/27/61
Adam, John Edward died 08/14/62   08/15/62
Adam, Maggie D. died 06/21/61   06/22/61
Adams, Anna Margaretta died 10/04/62   10/06/62
Adams, Annie K. married Henney, Daniel H. 03/07/65   03/13/65
Adams, Annie Virginia died 08/21/62   08/25/62
Adams, Anthony F. died 02/24/63   02/25/63
Adams, Catharine (Mrs.) died 11/27/63   12/07/63
Adams, Charles (Cpt.) died 10/07/64   10/08/64
Adams, Charles H. married Bunting, Elizabeth C. 11/30/65   12/02/65
Adams, Charles W. married Neilson, Cynthia J. 05/10/65   05/18/65
Adams, David F. died 11/17/63   11/19/63
Adams, David F. died 11/17/63   12/07/63
Adams, Elizabeth died 04/26/64   04/27/64
Adams, Elwyn died 08/28/62   08/29/62
Adams, Emma died 11/11/63   11/12/63
Adams, Emma R. married West, Salathiel M. 08/03/63   08/08/63
Adams, Eugenie D. (Mrs.) died 03/11/64   03/15/64
Adams, Frank A. married McCabe, William H. 03/16/65   03/24/65
Adams, George L. married Taylor, Sarah A. 12/30/64   01/02/65
Adams, Harriet Anna married Ayers, George W. 04/12/65   10/13/65
Adams, Hattie married Price, Allen 05/21/63   05/23/63
Adams, James died 03/27/65   03/28/65
Adams, James C. died no date   09/13/64
Adams, Jane C. died 12/24/62   12/29/62
Adams, Jane E. married Williams, Isaac J. 04/08/62   04/14/62
Adams, John A. married Carroll, Sarah E. 09/15/62   09/17/62
Adams, John E. died 07/15/62   07/16/62
Adams, John Thomas died 03/22/64   03/23/64
Adams, Joseph died 07/10/64   07/14/64
Adams, Joseph died 11/24/65   11/25/65
Adams, Kate (Mrs.) died 04/18/65   04/22/65
Adams, Louisa died 05/01/63   05/09/63
Adams, Maggie married Aiken, Samuel D. 01/29/63   03/16/63
Adams, Marcellina married Dorsey, Ridgely 08/24/64   08/31/64

Adams, Margaret died 07/01/62   07/03/62
Adams, Mary Florence died 12/02/62   12/05/62
Adams, Mary J. married Snyder, A. 03/15/65   03/16/65
Adams, Richard died 07/15/64   07/19/64
Adams, Samuel died 06/08/63   06/09/63
Adams, Sarah died 01/18/61   01/19/61
Adams, Susan Maria died 12/13/63   12/15/63
Adams, William married Gregg, Mary 03/19/63   04/03/63
Adams, William J. died 04/12/65   04/20/65
Adams, William Samuel died 09/18/61   09/20/61
Adams, William W. died 09/17/62   09/18/62
Addeby, Phebia married McCubbin, Moses 08/27/63   08/29/63
Addison, Augustus E. died 08/05/63   08/15/63
Addison, Charles C. died 05/03/63   05/05/63
Addison, Fannie died 07/14/62   07/16/62
Addison, Francis R. died 10/09/65   10/10/65
Addison, Frank R. married Reese, Sue R. 07/09/63   09/15/63
Addison, George C. died 10/06/63   10/08/63
Addison, John W. married Kolb, Mary E. 11/20/62   12/01/62
Addison, Mary E. married Elmer, William S. 04/05/65   05/06/65
Addison, Mary Lizzie married Elmer, William S. 04/05/65   05/09/65
Addison, Mollie M. married Ingle, Osborne 08/11/64   08/13/64
Addison, Nettie S. married Darneille, Benjamin J. 07/18/61   07/20/61
Addison, Sallie R. married Thorn, Columbus W. 05/11/65   05/29/65
Adelsberger, Daniel G. married Busby, Margaret Mary Josephine 01/29/61
   01/31/61
Aderon, H. Clay married Navy, Virginia 02/09/61   02/15/61
Adieon, Joseph L. (Dr.) died 02/24/62   02/25/62
Adler, Henry married Stern, Hannah 02/24/61   02/26/61
Adler, Henry M. married Floss, Ellen J. 07/16/65   07/18/65
Adler, Lewis H. married Black, Lillie H. 06/04/61   02/27/62
Adler, Maria died 03/14/61   03/19/61
Adolph, Elizabeth died 01/18/65   01/20/65
Adrean, Hannah died 07/24/62   07/25/62
Adrean, Martha Ann married Wyant, Isaac L. 09/26/63   10/14/63
Adriance, James A. married Alloways, Sarah V. 08/08/65   08/10/65
Ady, Henrietta M. (Mrs.) died 07/29/65   07/31/65
Ady, Mary married Roberts, Lewis 03/18/65   04/03/65
Affayroux, Charles Edward died 11/01/62   11/06/62
Affayroux, William Harrison died 11/04/62   11/06/62
Agnew, Catherine died 02/17/63   02/18/63
Agnew, Catherine Ann died 02/18/63   02/19/63
Agnew, James married Grimes, Annie E. 05/23/65   05/24/65
Agnew, Thomas died 08/17/65   08/18/65
Agustes, Henry died 03/31/65   04/01/65
Ahern, Anne Regina died 12/04/61   12/05/61
Ahl, William married Wooden, Sarah A. (Mrs.) 11/05/65   11/07/65
Ahler, George E. married Peregoy, (Miss) 02/19/64   02/23/64
Aigan, Martin died 06/09/65   06/10/65
Aiken, Samuel D. married Adams, Maggie 01/29/63   03/16/63
Aiken, Sarah (Mrs.) died 07/10/65   07/11/65
Aiken, Sarah (Mrs.) died 07/10/65   07/12/65
Aikin, Ambrosia died 10/16/65   10/25/65
Airey, H. Eugenia (Mrs.) died 12/26/64   12/29/64
Airey, Jamina (Mrs.) died 03/08/65   03/10/65

Airey, Jamina (Mrs.) died 03/08/65   03/13/65
Airey, John B. (Cpt.) died 07/20/64   08/08/64
Airey, John Bond died 07/20/64   07/21/64
Airey, John William died 01/31/65   02/02/65
Airey, Sarah died 08/12/65   08/14/65
Airey, William died 04/20/61   04/22/61
Aisquith, George R. died 09/30/63   10/01/63
Aisquith, Mary Elizabeth married Phipps, William 09/27/61   10/08/61
Aitchison, Laura H. married McMillan, William D. 11/12/63   11/13/63
Aitken, Edith M. died 06/19/65   06/22/65
Aitken, J. A. M. married Savin, R. T. 07/10/61   07/13/61
Aitken, Lizzie M. married Balloch, R. A. 05/27/65   05/30/65
Aitken, Robert married Patton, Agnes 10/20/63   10/22/63
Akers, Anna Maria died 02/23/64   02/24/64
Akers, Charles, Jr. died 03/09/61   03/11/61
Akers, Joseph married Sherbert, Annie 08/08/61   08/10/61
Akers, Mary Virginia married Chappell, Thomas S. 12/23/62   12/25/62
Akers, Susan married Davis, Robert W. (Dr.) 05/11/65   05/18/65
Akins, Ellen married Johnson, Oliver 04/28/61   07/10/61
Alban, Sarah L. married Kroh, Charles W. 04/24/62   04/26/62
Albaugh, Charles L. P. died 07/20/61   07/24/61
Albaugh, Daniel (Sgt.) died 02/06/65   04/07/65
Albaugh, Emma Jene married James, William H. 09/24/63   09/30/63
Albaugh, John W. died 03/03/65   03/04/65
Albert, Anne married Cole, Alexander 04/25/63   05/05/63
Albert, Eleanor T. married Bliss, Alexander 10/03/65   10/09/65
Albert, Eliza M. (Mrs.) died 03/05/64   03/07/64
Albert, George died 06/23/61   07/24/61
Albert, Henry J. married Gueraud, Victorine M. 05/30/65   05/31/65
Albert, J. Taylor married Mayer, Dora 01/07/64   01/09/64
Albert, Lawrence died 07/07/61   07/09/61
Albert, Mary E. married Bossle, Joseph C. 06/27/65   06/30/65
Albert, Mary Jane married Bell, John 12/22/64   12/23/64
Albert, Theodore Lyman died 09/03/61   09/07/61
Albertson, Cornelia B. married Harper, J. Sylvester 12/12/65   12/14/65
Albertson, Rebecca T. married Lovejoy, P. R. 08/03/64   08/08/64
Albertson, Sarah died 09/19/65   09/21/65
Albinus, Clarance died 01/19/62   01/21/62
Albison, George C. died 11/28/63   11/30/63
Albridge, Frederick A. married Mastermann, Josephine C. 12/24/65
   12/27/65
Albright, Caroline (Mrs.) died 08/20/64   08/22/64
Albright, Tresay A. married Smith, Oliver N. 07/16/61   07/17/61
Alcock, Marie Louise married Bixler, Benjamin M. 05/28/63   05/30/63
Alden, Luna T. married McCullough, George 01/01/63   01/02/63
Alden, Mary (Mrs.) died 07/23/63   07/24/63
Alder, Julia S. married Keene, Edward A. 10/21/63   10/28/63
Alder, Mary married Brown, Owen J. 10/16/62   10/25/62
Alder, Susannah died 01/02/61   01/11/61
Alderson, C. D. (Lt.) married Arman, Fannie 11/21/62   02/18/63
Alderson, C. Davis married Hopkins, Annie P. 09/29/63   10/06/63
Aldrich, Robert married Cheney, Hester A. 06/23/63   03/28/64
Aldworth, Elizabeth died 12/24/64   12/31/64
Alen, Martin died 10/16/62   10/17/62
Aler, Almira married Wilson, Robert 06/09/63   06/15/63

Aler, Ann (Mrs.) died 02/28/63   03/04/63
Aler, John M. died 01/09/65   01/19/65
Aler, Lucretia married Ziegler, Henry S. 08/29/65   09/05/65
Aler, Martin Washburn died 06/21/65   06/22/65
Aler, Rox A. V. married Reynolds, Alfred D. 04/21/64   05/19/64
Aler, Sylvanus R. married Washborn, Eunice A. no date   11/06/61
Alexander, Catherine died 05/25/63   05/27/63
Alexander, Charles died 01/16/62   01/17/62
Alexander, Charles married Curran, Julia A. 01/06/63   01/08/63
Alexander, Charles Curran died 12/13/65   12/14/65
Alexander, Fanny married Kerr, Edward L. 03/19/64   03/21/64
Alexander, Hannah R. M. married Loane, John T. S. 03/02/63   03/10/63
Alexander, John died 10/08/62   11/22/62
Alexander, John died 01/26/63   01/28/63
Alexander, Levi T. (Rev.) died 12/15/62   12/25/62
Alexander, Mary (Mrs.) died 09/14/64   09/16/64
Alexander, Mary C. married Dryden, James 10/01/61   10/05/61
Alexander, Nannie J. married Armiger, John F. 02/24/63   03/10/63
Alexander, Sarah (Mrs.) married James, John Henry 06/09/64   06/11/64
Alexander, William married Johnson, Sophia 06/07/63   06/09/63
Alford, Mary M. (Mrs.) died 06/08/65   06/09/65
Allan, Henrietta married Allan, William G. 11/22/65   11/25/65
Allan, John died 07/03/63   07/28/63
Allan, Sophia Hanzsche died 08/20/62   08/21/62
Allan, Sophia Hanzsche died 08/20/62   08/22/62
Allan, William G. married Allan, Henrietta 11/22/65   11/25/65
Allard, Edward C. married Switzer, Emily 03/29/64   04/05/64
Allard, George Washington died 11/22/61   11/23/61
Allard, William H. married Mobley, Lydia 05/27/63   05/29/63
Allen, Alice A, married Loney, William A. 01/06/64   01/16/64
Allen, B. McIntyre married Barris, Elizabeth 09/11/65   09/15/65
Allen, Cecelia E. married Ewart, John E. 09/20/61   09/23/61
Allen, Frances married Carter, William 04/02/63   04/04/63
Allen, George W. married Hurst, Louisa E. 10/09/62   10/15/62
Allen, George W. married Williams, Georgennie 11/07/65   11/11/65
Allen, Henry Hoffman died 07/26/62   08/29/62
Allen, James married Stephens, Charlotte Rebecca 01/11/65   01/14/65
Allen, Jane married Thompson, Robert 02/15/63   04/08/63
Allen, Jane H. (Mrs.) died 03/04/65   03/07/65
Allen, Jenny M. married Jenkins, Upton P. 03/03/63   03/10/63
Allen, Joel married Harrod, Georgetta 07/05/65   07/12/65
Allen, John E. married Chase, Harriet 04/20/65   04/27/65
Allen, John L. died 07/23/65   07/26/65
Allen, Joseph S. died 02/10/65   03/28/65
Allen, L. S. (Dr.) married Hoffman, Eurith Sophia 01/10/61   01/31/61
Allen, Margaret P. married Gibson, George 05/14/61   05/16/61
Allen, Naomi Virginia married Culley, Joseph (USN) 08/11/63   08/15/63
Allen, Permelia died 06/13/61   06/14/61
Allen, Robert died 08/09/64   08/10/64
Allen, Sarah A. (Mrs.) died 04/07/63   04/08/63
Allen, Sarah Elizabeth died 06/24/62   06/25/62
Allen, Theodore B. married Everist, Dalcedia 10/19/64   11/04/64
Allen, William died 03/21/62   03/29/62
Allen, William died 02/07/63   02/09/63
Allen, William died 09/08/64   09/10/64

Allen, William H. married Phillips, Elizabeth 11/16/62 12/02/62
Allen, William N. married Harding, Lucie S. 12/07/65 12/14/65
Allen, William P. died 08/03/63 08/04/63
Allenbaugh, Charles T. married Christopher, Willie R. 04/26/64 04/28/6
Allensworth, Robert married Hutchins, Julia 01/09/62 01/10/62
Allers, Emma Virginia died 06/15/61 06/18/61
Allers, Maggie Steibel married Collins, John W. 10/21/63 10/24/63
Alligood, Maria married Bradford, Joseph 01/01/61 01/11/61
Allison, James died 03/05/64 04/04/64
Allison, Janey married White, Robert John 12/26/61 12/28/61
Allmand, William H. died 10/12/64 11/02/64
Allnut, Eva married Chiswell, Edward J. 12/05/65 12/20/65
Allnut, John F. married Marlow, Annie 11/05/63 11/12/63
Allnutt, E. Severn married Barklie, Anna 01/17/64 01/18/64
Allnutt, Franklin Pierce died 10/16/62 10/21/62
Alloways, Sarah V. married Adriance, James A. 08/08/65 08/10/65
Allwell, Arinetta died 11/14/64 11/16/64
Allwell, Wesley died 02/15/64 02/19/64
Allyn, Mollie J. married Field, William (USN) 07/12/64 07/14/64
Almack, Hester A. married Reckert, Charles A. 05/05/63 05/11/63
Almer, John married Rose, Fanny 07/29/65 08/01/65
Alnut, Thomas J. married Credit, Alexina 02/16/65 02/18/65
Alricks, Sophia Ridgely married Haughton, Henry Osburne 12/21/65 12/23/65
Alsop, Augustus married Gross, Mary E. 01/01/63 01/05/63
Alt, Peter married Smith, Mary 11/18/62 01/07/63
Alterhoff, (Miss) married Shultz, Bernhard 07/02/63 09/24/63
Alton, Ella M. married Carter, Charles W. 01/17/61 01/31/61
Altpeter, George married Schukle, Mary C. 01/18/63 01/21/63
Altvater, John H. died 09/24/63 09/26/63
Altvater, Walter B. died 08/25/63 08/26/63
Aluather, C. B. died 02/12/62 02/14/62
Alverda, Mary died 06/16/62 06/17/62
Aman, Sebastian married Kolb, Emma 09/27/63 10/08/63
Ambrose, Colombus died 08/31/61 09/03/61
Ambrose, Joseph White died 10/13/65 10/14/65
Ambrose, Sallie A. married Osborn, George A. 08/28/64 09/05/64
Ambrose, Violetta died 12/03/62 12/10/62
Ament, George Louis married Sheibler, Elizabeth 06/16/63 06/18/63
Ament, Margaret married Killian, George F. 04/04/65 04/06/65
Ames, Annie Janette married Nelson, Thomas F. (USN) 06/14/65 06/17/65
Ames, Daniel died 12/26/62 12/27/62
Ames, Sarah (Mrs.) died 10/23/65 11/08/65
Amey, Frances F. died 08/18/65 08/19/65
Amey, Kate married Comley, James F. 07/28/63 08/29/63
Amey, Rebecca died 01/29/61 01/30/61
Amey, Samuel R. died 10/11/63 10/13/63
Amick, Mary (Mrs.) died 04/03/63 04/04/63
Ammons, Kate married Wilson, William T. 12/24/63 04/13/64
Amos, Annie E. married Kincaid, W. H. (Rev.) 02/13/62 02/14/62
Amos, J. Edwin married Amoss, Lucy V. 02/09/64 02/10/64
Amos, James L. died 05/24/64 05/26/64
Amos, John H. married Woods, Laura J. 08/22/61 09/11/61
Amos, Joseph Robert died 08/27/65 08/30/65
Amos, Kate married Greve, Lewis F. 11/07/64 11/16/64

```
Amos, Nancy died 05/21/61  05/24/61
Amos, Ruth died 04/14/61  04/16/61
Amos, Sarah Jane married Peck, Daniel Coker 06/25/63  06/27/63
Amos, Scott died 03/10/65  03/18/65
Amoss, Alfred P., Jr. married Clark, Lizzie D. 06/08/65  06/13/65
Amoss, Anna R. married Parlett, William J. 12/21/65  12/22/65
Amoss, Lucy V. married Amos, J. Edwin 02/09/64  02/10/64
Amoss, Oliver H. died 04/09/64  04/15/64
Amy, Thomas Edward died 01/02/63  01/03/63
Anadale, Thomas D. died 10/27/64  11/05/64
Anders, Deliah married Balderston, W. A. 02/10/65  02/11/65
Anderson, A. L. married Gibbs, Robert H. 06/04/61  06/06/61
Anderson, Adah May died 06/02/61  06/03/61
Anderson, Allen died 03/20/61  03/22/61
Anderson, Andrew died 07/17/65  07/18/65
Anderson, Andrew married Campbell, Eliza 01/12/65  01/14/65
Anderson, Andrew P. married Gardner, Ann M. 01/22/61  01/24/61
Anderson, Ann Teresa died 01/30/62  02/01/62
Anderson, Annie married Woodward, A. G. 12/19/61  12/30/61
Anderson, Annie married Thompson, William H. 02/17/63  02/27/63
Anderson, Benjamin F. married Guthrie, Mrs. Susan E. 12/26/64  01/10/65
Anderson, Benjamin F. L. died 09/06/62  09/08/62
Anderson, Cassie A. married Kirk, Charles D. 04/02/61  04/03/61
Anderson, Catherine married Dickinson, James 05/10/65  05/12/65
Anderson, Charles died 06/30/62  07/01/62
Anderson, Charles Wesley died 05/04/63  05/05/63
Anderson, Charles Wesley died 05/04/63  05/06/63
Anderson, Clara May died 04/04/64  04/05/64
Anderson, Daniel married Digner, Bridget 06/03/63  08/28/63
Anderson, Eliza died 08/20/62  09/02/62
Anderson, Eliza married Brown, John 08/17/65  08/19/65
Anderson, Elizabeth (Mrs.) died 10/19/64  10/26/64
Anderson, Elizabeth Jane died 05/19/61  05/21/61
Anderson, Ella E. married Anderson, James G. 02/13/62  02/18/62
Anderson, G. E. married Pumphery, Thomas J. 11/29/64  12/08/64
Anderson, George H. died 08/12/64  08/13/64
Anderson, George H. married Kilpatrick, Rachel 04/07/64  04/26/64
Anderson, Henrietta married Perry, Edward 08/23/63  08/26/63
Anderson, Jacob died 01/31/63  02/02/63
Anderson, James G. married Anderson, Ella E. 02/13/62  02/18/62
Anderson, James H. died 05/27/61  06/06/61
Anderson, Jason G. married Ford, Elizabeth W. 07/03/62  07/04/62
Anderson, Jennie died 03/11/62  03/12/62
Anderson, John died 12/02/63  12/03/63
Anderson, John L. married Cadwallader, Lizzie V. 05/20/61  05/28/61
Anderson, John W. married Swann, Bettie A. 04/30/61  05/03/61
Anderson, Joshua V. died 03/04/63  03/07/63
Anderson, Joshua V. died no date   04/20/63
Anderson, Julia died 06/22/64  06/28/64
Anderson, Julia (Mrs.) died 06/22/64  06/23/64
Anderson, Kate married Knipe, B. F. 11/06/64  12/30/64
Anderson, Louisa married Williams, Henry no date  08/31/64
Anderson, Louisa A. died 09/27/63  09/29/63
Anderson, Louisa J. married Morsel, Z. J. 01/20/63  01/23/63
Anderson, Marion married Johnson, Oscar 09/17/61  09/20/61
```

Anderson, Mary A. died 02/12/61   02/13/61
Anderson, Mary Agnes married Trout, Adam M. 11/07/61   12/03/61
Anderson, Mary Ann (Mrs.) died 12/10/64   12/21/64
Anderson, Mary Augusta died 03/09/64   03/11/64
Anderson, Mary C. married Matthews, Oliver 02/25/64   03/05/64
Anderson, Mary L. married Tingstrom, Charles J. 01/02/63   01/22/63
Anderson, Mollie E. married Webb, W. A., Jr. 12/26/65   12/30/65
Anderson, Moses T. married Bond, Frances Isabella 01/05/65   01/07/65
Anderson, Nannie died 06/30/63   07/03/63
Anderson, R. N. married Miles, Susan W. 02/26/61   03/08/61
Anderson, Richard married Hobson, Elizabeth no date   05/06/63
Anderson, Robert N. died 08/18/63   08/21/63
Anderson, Rosella died 04/05/61   04/06/61
Anderson, Rozena married Thompson, Charles 12/10/63   12/23/63
Anderson, Samuel Marryman married Bosley, S. Anna 11/01/64   11/05/64
Anderson, Sarah E. married Kirk, James A. 07/07/63   07/22/63
Anderson, Sarah L. married Hitchcock, Jessie A. 02/19/61   02/23/61
Anderson, Sarah Lizzie died 12/31/61   01/01/62
Anderson, Sophia married Harriday, Jesse 10/26/63   10/28/63
Anderson, Sophie died 02/18/61   02/20/61
Anderson, Susan E. died 09/16/62   09/17/62
Anderson, Thomas married Johnson, Laura 05/15/64   05/19/64
Anderson, Thomas J. died 01/05/64   01/06/64
Anderson, William married DeSwan, Maggie N. 06/16/64   06/23/64
Anderson, William G. married Hershner, Amanda 10/22/63   11/20/63
Anderson, William H. married Young, Josephine F. 01/14/64   01/16/64
Anderson, William S. died 01/19/65   01/21/65
Andrew, Elizabeth V. died 01/08/64   01/09/64
Andrew, Isabella died 03/24/65   03/25/65
Andrew, Sophie B. married Eichelberger, Eccleston 05/19/64   05/24/64
Andrews, Charles H. married Roycroft, Sarah E. 04/04/61   04/06/61
Andrews, Daniel S. married Galloway, Annie 04/26/63   05/02/63
Andrews, Elizabeth (Mrs.) died 09/01/63   09/02/63
Andrews, Ida Lyle died 01/20/63   01/22/63
Andrews, John B. died 07/19/65   07/20/65
Andrews, Lavinia married Girvines, William L. 09/19/65   09/30/65
Andrews, Louisa (Mrs.) died 05/25/64   05/27/64
Andrews, Louisa (Mrs.) died 05/25/64   05/28/64
Andrews, Mary E. married Ashley, Charles C. 02/23/64   03/02/64
Andrews, Mary Rebecca died 09/05/63   09/09/63
Andrews, Matthew married Taylor, Mary E. 10/12/65   10/14/65
Andrews, Miranda married Pritchett, Samuel 08/18/64   08/27/64
Andrews, Robert C. married Whitehouse, Sarah A. 11/25/62   11/27/62
Andrews, Thomas Alvia died 08/28/63   08/29/63
Angel, Maggie married Naill, H. Clay 01/15/63   01/16/63
Angel, Mary Ann married Russell, James 04/04/61   06/03/61
Angell, A. H. married Medairy, M. Kate 02/12/63   02/14/63
Angell, James B. died 11/10/61   11/11/61
Angell, Mary Ann died 05/06/61   05/07/61
Annan, A. M. F. (Mrs.) died 06/20/64   06/28/64
Annesly, Robert died 12/15/64   12/16/64
Annesly, Robert died 12/15/64   12/17/64
Anschutz, Kate married Norwood, Delos M. 11/27/63   12/07/63
Anthony, Amelia (Mrs.) died 10/16/65   10/17/65
Anthony, Anne died 03/04/61   03/05/61

Anthony, Anne died 03/04/61 03/06/61
Anthony, Anne Elizabeth died 08/03/62 08/05/62
Anthony, Emma Beauregard died 04/25/64 05/11/64
Anthony, Evan Reese died 04/11/65 04/13/65
Anthony, Janie married Harkness, Andrew J. 09/29/64 10/11/64
Anthony, Laura Virginia died 01/29/64 01/30/64
Anthony, Mary Eliza died 09/02/64 09/03/64
Anthony, Mary Ellen died 09/15/65 09/19/65
Anzmann, A. married Seymour, H. O. 07/21/64 04/22/65
Anzmann, Joseph A. A. married George, Mary R. J. 04/16/63 04/18/63
Aordin, Catherine died 01/21/62 01/22/62
Apel, Mary C. died 05/30/64 06/02/64
Apple, John H. married Cunningham, R. Virginia 10/22/64 10/29/64
Appleby, Amanda married Carrigan, William J. 06/12/64 06/14/64
Appleby, Ann Maria died 11/30/63 01/11/64
Appleby, Elizabeth died 02/03/65 02/04/65
Appleby, George married Sheridan, Jennie 06/22/65 06/27/65
Appleby, Greenbury R. (Cpt.) died 01/01/64 04/26/65
Appleby, James H. married Rumstine, Mary A. 05/18/63 05/23/63
Appleby, Udora Jeanette died 02/22/64 02/27/64
Appleby, Virginia married Dougherty, Philip H. 01/15/63 01/17/63
Appleby, William H. married Nichol, Matilda 01/27/61 02/11/61
Applegaith, William Sidney died 07/16/64 07/18/64
Applegarth, Ann Maria (Mrs.) died 02/24/65 02/25/65
Applegarth, Mollie E. married Meginniss, C. G. 03/28/65 04/04/65
Applegarth, Robert died 06/23/65 06/27/65
Applegarth, William Thomas died no date 09/01/64
Applegate, Arthur W. married North, Emily 11/26/61 12/10/61
Appler, Ferdinand C. married Thomas, Lizzie C. 05/24/64 06/01/64
Appleton, John W. died 03/27/62 03/28/62
Appold, Levina married McClellan, George F. 01/24/64 01/30/64
Aquivre, Epifanio married Barnard, Mary B. 08/21/62 09/04/62
Arbeltier, Nicholas Prosper died 07/02/62 07/04/62
Archbold, Beckie married Todd, William A. 06/11/63 06/25/63
Archer, Pamelia B. (Mrs.) died 04/01/63 04/09/63
Archer, Roland D. married Hunter, Emma L. 09/21/65 10/03/65
Ardin, David died 10/03/63 03/15/64
Ardisson, Maximin married Fahl, Mary 12/03/63 12/05/63
Arlow, Mollie A. married Welden, William T. 07/30/65 08/02/65
Armacost, Rachel W. died 12/01/63 12/02/63
Armacost, Richard C. died 01/16/61 01/17/61
Armacost, Sarah Virginia died 06/27/62 06/28/62
Arman, Fannie married Alderson, C. D. (Lt.) 11/21/62 02/18/63
Armesworthy, Bebjamin married Bayard, Mary R. 02/04/64 02/06/64
Armesworthy, Biddy L. died 10/19/62 10/21/62
Armiger, Charles W. died 09/29/62 09/30/62
Armiger, Charles Wesley died 09/29/62 10/18/62
Armiger, John F. married Alexander, Nannie J. 02/24/63 03/10/63
Armiger, Joseph married Tanner, Elizabeth 04/10/65 04/27/65
Armiger, Lilly Davis died 11/09/62 11/10/62
Armiger, Margaret (Mrs.) died 07/08/64 07/11/64
Armiger, Mary Lizzie died 08/16/62 08/18/62
Armiger, Robert B. married Chesney, Harriet E. 06/21/64 07/07/64
Armiger, Sarah died 12/26/65 12/28/65
Arminger, B. Franklin married Price, Mary Ann 12/06/60 07/19/61

Armistead, Louisa died 10/03/61   10/15/61
Armitage, Charles B. died 01/16/63   03/31/63
Armitage, Joseph died 03/05/63   03/31/63
Armon, John F. died 06/19/63   06/20/63
Armor, Mary M. (Mrs.) died 03/15/64   03/17/64
Armor, William died 07/10/61   07/11/61
Armour, James died 06/04/63   06/17/63
Armstrong, Ann married McGuire, Patrick 07/14/65   07/17/65
Armstrong, Ann married McGuire, Patrick 07/14/65   07/18/65
Armstrong, Asa died 08/10/63   08/11/63
Armstrong, Daniel S. died 11/09/64   11/11/64
Armstrong, Daniel W. married Waterworth, Hellen Isabella 11/16/63
    11/26/63
Armstrong, David died 02/09/64   02/10/64
Armstrong, Elizabeth married Bowen, Thomas H. 04/27/65   05/02/65
Armstrong, Elizabeth married Bowen, Thomas H. 04/27/65   05/03/65
Armstrong, Hosea died 08/16/63   08/17/63
Armstrong, Ida E. died 10/10/65   10/19/65
Armstrong, Israel married Bailey, Tobeath 12/07/65   12/09/65
Armstrong, James married Thomas, Mahlom 05/18/63   05/20/63
Armstrong, James married Thomas, Maylyum 05/18/63   05/21/63
Armstrong, James died 08/04/65   08/05/65
Armstrong, James C. married Canavan, Eliza 11/02/63   11/13/63
Armstrong, John died 07/20/64   07/22/64
Armstrong, John died 07/20/64   07/25/64
Armstrong, John H. married Ellis, Kate M. 04/26/63   05/02/63
Armstrong, John, Jr. married Salmon, Kate 07/02/63   08/08/63
Armstrong, Kate A. married Johnson, Lewis R. 05/12/65   06/28/65
Armstrong, Laura A. married Thackeray, William A. 03/31/64   04/02/64
Armstrong, Margaret A. (Mrs.) died 09/18/64   09/20/64
Armstrong, Mary A. married Smith, Samuel R. 06/30/64   07/21/64
Armstrong, Mary E. died 01/20/63   01/21/63
Armstrong, Mary E. died 01/20/63   01/22/63
Armstrong, Mary G. married Sommers, James M. 12/07/65   12/13/65
Armstrong, R. D. married Walker, Helena K. 04/30/62   05/02/62
Armstrong, Rebecca married King, Wallace 10/16/61   10/17/61
Armstrong, Robert died 01/06/62   01/07/62
Armstrong, Robert W. married Muller, Eudocia 11/28/65   12/04/65
Armstrong, Samuel S. married Hardy, Mary C. 10/25/65   10/27/65
Armstrong, Sarah died 08/18/62   08/22/62
Armstrong, Sarah E. (Mrs.) died 03/08/63   03/10/63
Armstrong, Thomas married Garrett, Martha Jane 10/16/62   10/17/62
Armstrong, Tillie C. married Trotten, John C. 10/31/65   11/04/65
Armstrong, William married Espey, Eliza 08/29/61   09/17/61
Armsworthy, Catherine (Mrs.) died 04/10/63   04/11/63
Armsworthy, Henry married Griffith, Catherine 06/11/61   06/12/61
Arnold, Albert married Bears, Fannie 03/28/64   04/04/64
Arnold, Alexander married Miller, Elizabeth 07/28/62   04/30/63
Arnold, Ann died 11/10/61   11/12/61
Arnold, C. Albert married Bean, Fannie 03/28/64   04/04/64
Arnold, Clara Virginia died 05/20/64   05/21/64
Arnold, Eliza (Mrs.) died 05/19/64   06/01/64
Arnold, Henry A. married Davis, Fanny 08/08/61   08/24/61
Arnold, Isaiah died 03/03/64   03/17/64
Arnold, John W. married Stansbury, Emma C. 11/17/63   11/19/63

Arnold, Kate E. married Cunningham, Samuel D. 08/28/62 09/23/62
Arnold, Laura married Reese, August 10/22/65 10/24/65
Arnold, Lizzie T. married Justis, William F., Jr. 01/15/61 01/19/61
Arnold, Madora W. married Pierce, George W. 09/26/61 09/30/61
Arnold, Martha Jane married Rea, Joseph B. 12/13/64 12/20/64
Arnold, Mary Jane married Howell, John, Jr. 12/17/63 12/22/63
Arnold, Mary Jane died 11/13/65 11/14/65
Arnold, Sarah Ann married Barton, Charles H. 09/29/62 10/08/62
Arnold, Sarah J. died 04/17/65 04/19/65
Arnold, William David died 03/28/63 03/30/63
Arnold, William H. married Gardner, Susan E. 10/09/64 10/12/64
Arnold, William Henry died 02/26/65 02/28/65
Arnold, William Howard died 11/06/62 11/07/62
Aro, Lewis died 08/14/65 08/15/65
Aro, Lewis Edward died 07/17/65 11/18/65
Arozo, Mariano married Brown, Charlotte Cornelia 04/03/61 04/06/61
Arquit, Joseph (Capt.) died 02/15/62 03/10/62
Arringdale, William L. married Fickey, Carrie 11/28/61 12/03/61
Arrington, Mary Elizabeth married Denmon, Henry 03/03/64 03/11/64
Art, Joseph died 03/11/65 03/16/65
Arthur, Anna died 04/22/61 04/24/61
Arthur, Anna died 06/10/62 06/16/62
Arthur, Anna S. died 04/03/65 04/04/65
Arthur, Charlotte died 10/04/65 10/05/65
Arthur, Fannie A. married Bouis, John H. 12/23/63 12/25/63
Arthur, John died 09/30/65 10/05/65
Arthur, John T. married Miskimon, Mary E. 02/11/64 02/15/64
Arthur, Mary J. married Hills, Luther 09/06/64 09/24/64
Arthur, Thomas married Dormandy, Sarah Jane 04/04/64 09/07/64
Asey, Christian died 07/25/64 07/28/64
Ash, George T. married Beale, Eleanora D. 01/24/61 01/30/61
Ash, John McGowen died 03/21/61 03/23/61
Ashby, Laura A. married Walter, Thomas 04/14/63 04/20/63
Ashby, Richard Henry died 03/21/61 03/22/61
Ashcom, Pamelia A. married Daiger, M. A. 01/15/63 01/17/63
Ashcroft, Lavinia died 10/22/65 10/24/65
Ashcroft, Wellsgette died 06/26/61 06/27/61
Asher, John E. married McKinley, Mary 11/02/65 11/11/65
Ashley, Charles C. married Andrews, Mary E. 02/23/64 03/02/64
Ashley, Rebecca died 05/23/61 05/24/61
Ashman, Mary A. died 01/01/62 02/03/62
Ashman, William died 09/14/63 09/17/63
Ashman, William died 09/14/63 09/18/63
Ashton, Ellen died 07/04/63 08/01/63
Ashton, Thomas married Cornish, Anna 03/26/63 03/28/63
Askew, Florence Mariam died 07/10/62 07/12/62
Askew, Louisa Brun died 07/29/63 07/31/63
Askew, Mary E. married Bull, Nicholas 10/23/62 10/27/62
Askew, Mary Ella died 10/06/63 10/08/63
Askew, Mary Emma H. died 08/28/63 08/29/63
Askew, Thomas B. died 06/10/65 06/14/65
Askey, Lizzie E. married Mitchell, John W. (Cpt.) 05/11/63 05/14/63
Askins, Eleanora married Owens, Basil 10/18/64 10/20/64
Askins, James married Clark, Anna 02/27/62 03/01/62
Askins, W. E. married Carroll, H. E. 04/25/61 09/14/61

Aspril, James L. married Robinson, Emma Elizabeth 09/22/63   10/07/63
Atkins, Edward married Senderling, Sarah A. 06/05/64   06/07/64
Atkinson, Charlotte died 03/29/61   03/30/61
Atkinson, Eliza P. (Mrs.) died 04/17/63   04/20/63
Atkinson, George H. died 02/13/62   02/20/62
Atkinson, Harriet L. married Gibson, Horatio Gates (Cpt.) 03/16/63   03/28/63
Atkinson, James J. (USA) died 12/02/63   12/04/63
Atkinson, John F. died 03/24/65   03/25/65
Atkinson, Lizzie C. married Chalmers, J. Wesley 06/28/63   07/27/63
Atkinson, Lydia M. married Laws, Beverly D. 12/22/63   12/24/63
Atkinson, Robert A. died 12/25/62   12/27/62
Atkinson, Rosina Isabel died 09/06/63   09/08/63
Atkinson, Susannah died 09/09/65   09/11/65
Atkinson, William C. married Nittnacht, Jean 03/04/62   03/05/62
Atkinson, William C. married Mittnacht, Jean 03/04/62   03/06/62
Atlee, James married Ware, Anna M. 10/27/63   10/29/63
Atter, Mary Rebecca married Lazenby, Daniel Langan 12/10/63   12/15/63
Atwell, George A. married Spencer, Mary S. 12/15/65   12/18/65
Atwell, George M. married Rodgers, Hester E. (Mrs.) 11/28/65   12/06/65
Atwell, Isabell died 05/14/63   05/19/63
Atwell, James M. died 05/07/64   05/10/64
Atwell, James R. married Taylor, Lizzie A. 02/15/63   03/04/63
Atwell, Mary died 07/19/63   07/22/63
Atwell, S. Frances married Bowie, William J. 10/13/62   04/20/63
Atwell, Sarah E. married Tucker, John M. 11/06/64   11/08/64
Atwell, William R. married Bassford, Louise V. 04/23/63   05/02/63
Atwood, Catherine died 05/05/61   05/06/61
Aubrey, William George died 12/25/62   12/27/62
Audoun, Horace Fuller died 05/02/65   05/03/65
Audoun, Lewis W. married Price, Annie S. 06/30/64   08/09/64
Auerbach, S. L. married Behrens, Susie 02/22/63   02/24/63
Auerbach, Sivia Rebecca died 06/06/64   06/07/64
Aughenbaugh, Catherine (Mrs.) died 03/21/63   04/20/63
Augustus, Clara Virginia died 03/30/64   04/02/64
Augustus, Frances married Wright, Thomas 12/22/64   12/24/64
Augustus, Victoren P. married Baragars, Adell V. 11/04/62   12/04/62
Aukwood, Emily A. married Hill, C. H. 06/02/64   06/04/64
Aulbah, Catherine died 09/14/61   09/16/61
Auld, Elenor (Mrs.) died 05/22/63   05/25/63
Auld, Hugh died 12/23/61   12/24/61
Auld, Mary died 09/11/61   09/12/61
Auld, Mary died 09/11/61   09/13/61
Auld, Mary A. (Mrs.) married Kreis, George W. 09/30/61   10/04/61
Auld, Thomas (Capt.) married Thompson, Amanda M. 05/23/65   05/26/65
Ault, Mary died 07/01/61   07/03/61
Ault, Sallie E. married Lucas, William George 03/29/64   03/31/64
Austen, Caroline (Mrs.) died 02/07/64   02/13/64
Austin, A. R. married Hoover, Ellen Virginia 05/08/62   05/12/62
Austin, Annie E. died 02/25/62   03/04/62
Austin, Fannie M. married Cruse, William F. 05/15/64   10/17/64
Austin, Fannie M. married Cruse, William F. 05/05/64   10/18/64
Austin, Frances Ellen married Umstattd, Richard S. 01/06/63   01/08/63
Austin, Henry died 04/25/64   04/26/64
Austin, Susie M. married Jay, Samuel I. 05/06/62   05/09/62

12

Austin, Thomas H. B. died 06/26/65   06/27/65
Austin, Thomas S. died 11/17/64   11/19/64
Auston, Nancy A. died 03/18/63   03/19/63
Awbry, Andrew J. married Hull, Mary E. 10/24/61   10/29/61
Axtell, Edgar (Cpl.) married Havercutter, Catharine 01/15/62   01/22/62
Aydelott, Peter died 05/13/61   05/14/61
Aydelott, Mary A. (Mrs.) died 04/10/65   04/12/65
Ayers, Elizabeth (Mrs.) died no date   11/03/65
Ayers, George W. married Adams, Harriet Anna 04/12/65   10/13/65
Ayers, Marietta C. married Gilmor, James 01/03/61   01/07/61
Ayers, Thomas died 04/06/64   04/29/64
Ayler, Ann E. married Smead, James B. 09/10/63   09/22/63
Ayler, Mahala F. married Smead, E. S. 10/24/65   10/26/65
Ayres, Amelia Ann died 05/21/65   05/23/65
Ayres, Eugenie married DeLamar, C. M. 01/02/64   01/28/64
Ayres, James E. married Scarff, Amanda 07/03/64   07/12/64
Ayres, James H. died 01/22/61   01/23/61
Ayres, James H. died 01/22/61   01/24/61
Ayres, Maggie A. married Selby, Joseph E. (Sgt.) 04/07/64   04/13/64
Ayres, Sallie E. married Posterly, Mortimer 11/09/64   11/10/64
Ayres, Sarah Jane married Welman, William A. 05/01/64   05/07/64
Babb, Helen died 07/11/64   07/12/64
Baber, Mary died 06/08/62   06/09/62
Bach, Elizabeth married Driver, Charles F. 01/06/63   01/08/63
Bachs, Jacob died 10/25/62   11/26/62
Backman, Frances died 04/05/65   04/07/65
Backman, John H. died 06/18/61   06/21/61
Bacon, Samuel H. married Sangston, Jennie R. 06/22/65   06/26/65
Badders, Ellen died 12/08/62   12/20/62
Badders, Mary died 08/24/62   08/27/62
Badders, Townsand Bonsall died 11/26/65   11/30/65
Baden, William H. died 01/28/62   01/30/62
Badger, Alice Ann married Carmack, Jehu 12/31/63   01/02/64
Badger, Elisha (Rev.) married Chambers, Catherine 10/10/61   10/12/61
Badger, Frances A. (Mrs.) died 03/13/65   03/14/65
Badger, Jarred married Jones, Elenorah 05/12/61   05/18/61
Badger, Julia Mary Ann died 12/10/63   12/12/63
Badger, Mary Elizabeth married Williams, Arthur 08/08/60   03/09/61
Badger, Mary H. died 06/24/64   06/25/64
Baer, Abraham married Waldanl, Rachel 11/13/64   11/19/64
Baer, Caleb Dorsey died 08/30/63   10/10/63
Baer, Hattie S. married Stevenson, William J. (Rev.) 12/15/64   12/19/64
Bailey, Alfred J. married Lane, Annie E. 12/08/64   12/09/64
Bailey, Ann Maria married Dodson, Peter 08/01/61   08/03/61
Bailey, Ann Maria married Mathewes, Charles H. 08/13/63   08/15/63
Bailey, Eliza D. died 07/09/64   07/11/64
Bailey, Elizabeth A. married Hudson, C. B. 03/07/61   03/08/61
Bailey, Emeline married Turner, James P. 05/17/63   05/19/63
Bailey, George died 01/11/63   01/12/63
Bailey, Harriet Lydia married Needhammer, William 11/12/63   04/18/64
Bailey, Henry married Newman, Henrietta 05/15/64   05/21/64
Bailey, Isabel married Cleary, William 07/08/62   07/26/62
Bailey, John married Sheaf, Catherine A. 06/20/61   06/22/61
Bailey, Lizzie died 07/19/63   07/25/63
Bailey, Louisa married Disney, Alfred J. 02/24/61   05/10/61

```
Bailey, Lydia Ann died 07/27/63   07/28/63
Bailey, Lydia Ann died 07/27/63   07/29/63
Bailey, Margaret married Isaac, John T. 06/26/64  07/02/64
Bailey, Martha married Jones, Denwood 12/26/61   12/28/61
Bailey, Rebecca A. married Stansbury, Daniel L. 06/25/61   06/27/61
Bailey, Robert J. married Ledden, Catharine E. 10/16/64   10/18/64
Bailey, Sarah J. married Cooper, James C. 12/17/63   12/22/63
Bailey, Thomas married Shaffer, Fannie A. 01/07/64   01/09/64
Bailey, Tobeath married Armstrong, Israel 12/07/65   12/09/65
Bailly, Draper died 01/27/63   01/28/63
Bailone, Pascal A. died 03/26/63   03/27/63
Bailone, Pascal A. died 03/26/63   03/28/63
Bailone, Ruth A. died 08/30/62   09/01/62
Baily, Ann Rebecca (Mrs.) married Owings, Basal 12/11/62  01/05/63
Baily, Edwin L. married Plowman, H. Nannie 12/04/62   12/06/62
Baily, Henry died 07/14/62   08/07/62
Baily, Margaret G. died 06/09/62   06/11/62
Baily, Maria Louisa married Cooper, John H. 10/11/63   10/14/63
Baily, Peter married Jackson, Mary F. A. 01/17/61   01/19/61
Baily, William died 09/04/63   09/07/63
Bain, James Francis died 06/01/63   06/02/63
Baird, Esther Thompson (Mrs.) died 08/07/65   08/19/65
Baird, Margaret E. married Warfield, Lancelot 07/05/64   07/12/64
Baird, Margaret P. married Christopher, Francis A. 02/06/65   02/18/65
Baird, Samuel M. died 01/23/64   01/26/64
Baird, Virginia T. died 04/16/62   04/23/62
Baitzell, Elizabeth H. died 08/17/61   08/19/61
Baker, A. C. (Mrs.) married Ford, George M. 03/12/63   03/13/63
Baker, Alfred O. married Bruen, Charlotte 04/07/64   05/06/64
Baker, Amanda married Edwards, Charles H. 01/18/65   02/07/65
Baker, Caroline E. (Mrs.) died 09/08/64   09/09/64
Baker, Charles died no date   10/30/62
Baker, Charles H. married Hoffman, Margaret E. 09/08/64   10/12/64
Baker, Eliza (Mrs.) died 04/15/64   04/18/64
Baker, Emma J. (Mrs.) married Buxton, Brook, Jr. 12/07/65   12/13/65
Baker, Emma Maria died 04/14/65   04/19/65
Baker, Frances Teresa died 10/25/62   10/28/62
Baker, Francis A. died 04/04/65   04/08/65
Baker, Frederick married Clemens, Rosalia 01/04/61   01/07/61
Baker, George married Thompson, Margaret A. 01/27/61   02/07/61
Baker, Georgeanna married Canway, George 01/10/63   02/12/63
Baker, H. B. (Cpt.) married Shekells, Annie 05/09/64   05/11/64
Baker, Henry died 06/05/64   06/06/64
Baker, Henry died 09/30/65   10/02/65
Baker, Ida Frances died 04/17/65   04/19/65
Baker, Jestiner Frances died 04/13/64   04/21/64
Baker, John G. died 08/14/65   08/30/65
Baker, John M. married Deal, Mary J. 01/27/63   04/07/63
Baker, John W. married Nicholson, Mary F. 12/22/64   12/30/64
Baker, Lina A. married Folks, John A. 05/30/61   06/01/61
Baker, Louisa died 10/29/65   11/04/65
Baker, Maria (Mrs.) died 11/16/63   11/18/63
Baker, Marina (Mrs.) died 04/14/65   04/14/65
Baker, Martha died 08/17/61   08/21/61
Baker, Mary C. died 11/10/61   11/13/61
```

```
Baker, Mary M. married Kimball, George S. 03/26/62   04/12/62
Baker, Nathan A. died 10/24/63   10/28/63
Baker, Nelson R. married Peary, S. Elizabeth 09/11/61   09/13/61
Baker, Otho K. died 05/11/64   05/12/64
Baker, Peter died 04/19/63   04/20/63
Baker, Rebecca E. married Boden, John G. 06/06/61   06/11/61
Baker, Sadie A. W. married Norris, Richard (Rev.) 01/01/61   01/02/61
Baker, Sarah died 11/18/65   11/21/65
Baker, Sidney A. (Mrs.) died 03/01/64   03/02/64
Baker, Susan F. married Smith, Jacob A. 10/22/64   10/29/64
Baker, William married Durham, Mina 01/31/65   02/02/65
Baker, William Clare died 06/25/62   06/26/62
Baker, William H. died 08/25/61   08/26/61
Baker, William J. married Norville, Sarah A. 12/14/65   12/18/65
Baker, William Nelson died 07/23/65   07/24/65
Baker, William Worth married Livington, Martha A. 04/03/64   04/15/64
Bakes, Catherine died 10/23/64   10/25/64
Balderston, W. A. married Anders, Deliah 02/10/65   02/11/65
Baldertson, Hannah died 10/29/61   10/31/61
Baldus, Catherine E. died 10/01/62   10/02/62
Baldus, Mary C. R. died 08/02/61   08/05/61
Baldus, Theresa married Wernith, Joseph B. 02/08/64   02/12/64
Baldwin, A. S. (Dr.) married Hyde, Emma 10/20/63   10/21/63
Baldwin, Anne M. died 01/22/61   01/23/61
Baldwin, Charles E. married Vickers, Henrietta 04/05/64   04/06/64
Baldwin, Elva Iola died 08/05/62   08/06/62
Baldwin, Emma (Mrs.) died 01/19/65   01/21/65
Baldwin, John F. died 07/05/64   07/07/64
Baldwin, John T. married Delmas, Frances Almira 07/10/65   07/29/65
Baldwin, John, Sr. died 02/21/63   03/30/63
Baldwin, Joseph married Gerbrick, Josephine 08/06/63   09/15/63
Baldwin, Juliet 'Kate' died 11/01/65   11/07/65
Baldwin, Mary E. married Miller, A. Berkley 10/21/62   10/29/62
Baldwin, Mollie A. married Duvall, Charles S. 01/31/62   02/15/62
Baldwin, Olivia married Mangum, Richard 01/31/64   02/02/64
Ball, Ann Rudolph died 12/02/62   12/03/62
Ball, Anna V. died 02/17/63   02/18/63
Ball, Anna V. died 02/17/63   02/19/63
Ball, Charles Alexander died 12/20/62   12/22/62
Ball, Ellick married Cross, Maggie E. 05/29/64   06/06/64
Ball, George R. married Johnson, Sarah Jane 10/26/62   10/27/62
Ball, George R. died 02/07/63   02/13/63
Ball, George R. died 02/07/63   02/21/63
Ball, Herbert Carey died 12/10/63   12/11/63
Ball, John died 04/05/63   04/07/63
Ball, John D. married Hall, Eliza J. 11/23/64   11/26/64
Ball, John Turner died 04/14/61   04/15/61
Ball, Kate B. married Benson, Jesse C. 06/02/64   06/13/64
Ball, Lizzie Wilmot died 06/29/65   07/01/65
Ball, Margaret died 12/27/62   12/31/62
Ball, Mary died 06/25/65   06/26/65
Ball, Mary died 06/25/65   06/27/65
Ball, Mary Louisa married Magaw, Samuel 11/19/60   01/08/61
Ball, Mary M. died 10/04/62   10/07/62
Ball, Sallie died 05/06/65   05/08/65
```

Ball, Sarah L. married Vance, Joseph L. 07/31/65   08/14/65
Ball, Walter Sr. died 09/25/63   09/26/63
Ball, William died 07/30/63   07/31/63
Ball, William died 07/30/63   08/01/63
Ballard, Bernhard died 11/16/65   11/17/65
Ballard, Elizabeth died 12/25/62   12/27/62
Ballard, Emma N. died 06/19/64   06/22/64
Ballard, Hannah (Mrs.) died 12/20/62   01/08/63
Ballard, Susan died 11/08/64   11/21/64
Ballauf, Charles married Hammill, Jane 12/31/63   01/04/64
Ballauf, Mary E. married Benson, Joseph E. 11/19/63   11/21/63
Balloch, R. A. married Aitken, Lizzie M. 05/27/65   05/30/65
Balls, Emma married Duckworth, Emory 10/03/65   10/14/65
Balls, Robert W. died 11/19/63   11/21/63
Balster, John C. died 09/01/62   09/02/62
Baltzell, Ann Maria died 04/24/63   04/29/63
Baltzell, Emanuel died 09/15/62   09/16/62
Baltzell, John J. died 02/10/65   02/11/65
Baltzell, John J. died 02/10/65   02/11/65
Baltzell, Meredith Oliver died 11/24/61   12/05/61
Baltzell, Philip died 12/02/65   12/04/65
Baltzell, Sarah C. married Connely, Andrew J. 09/17/65   09/27/65
Bamber, Carrie died 07/11/64   07/16/64
Bamberger, John died 08/14/65   08/15/65
Bancroft, John D. married Feldhaus, Minnie 12/29/64   01/02/65
Bancroft, Minnie died 10/31/65   11/01/65
Bandel, Ella Virginia died 03/14/64   03/15/64
Bandel, George S. died 02/13/64   02/15/64
Bandel, George W. married Smith, Mollie L. 02/15/65   02/20/65
Bandel, Grafton J. married Welch, Eliza Jane 01/15/65   02/14/65
Bandel, Marten Dutten died 07/24/62   07/25/62
Bandel, Thomas Jefferson died 08/17/63   08/18/63
Bandell, Emma V. married Hopkins, David C. 03/16/64   03/18/64
Bandell, Maria (Mrs.) died 07/30/64   08/02/64
Bangent, Mary E. married Beckwith, Franklin M. 10/03/64   10/04/64
Banghart, Perry married Mudd, Virginia 10/27/65   11/04/65
Bankard, Charles H. (Lt.) married Lukens, Sidney 06/08/64   06/22/64
Bankard, Elizabeth (Mrs.) died 06/23/65   06/24/65
Bankard, Jacob died 02/14/64   02/15/64
Bankert, Barbara Ellen married Weatherstine, James 10/20/61   06/12/62
Bankert, Jacob married Robinson, Ann R. 06/20/65   06/23/65
Bankes, Charles married Burry, Anna 11/05/63   11/07/63
Banks, Burwell married Govans, Charity 10/06/63   10/08/63
Banks, Charlotte died 12/24/63   12/25/63
Banks, Elizabeth married Whorton, James T. 04/26/63   05/05/63
Banks, Emily J. married Madden, James 08/31/64   11/05/64
Banks, F. Almira died 06/07/64   06/09/64
Banks, George Anderson died 11/16/65   11/17/65
Banks, Georgeanna died 02/13/62   02/17/62
Banks, J. Marion married Carper, Clamanda J. 01/13/63   01/21/63
Banks, Laura D. died 08/17/62   08/18/62
Banks, Lotty H. died 02/05/64   02/06/64
Banks, Margaret married High, Emory 05/09/65   05/15/65
Banks, Margaret W. married Dorsey, Thomas R. 04/25/61   04/27/61
Banks, Mary E. married Biglin, Patrick 01/29/64   01/30/64

Banks, Morton D. married Cross, Amelia A. 04/20/65 04/24/65
Banks, Richard married Williams, Sidney 04/06/64 04/09/64
Banks, Sallie died 05/12/63 05/14/63
Banks, Susie married Goudy, John 04/09/61 04/16/61
Banks, William H. S. married Taylor, Kate 07/25/61 12/18/61
Bannan, Catherine died 06/09/61 06/10/61
Bannan, Hugh died 10/18/61 10/19/61
Bannen, Peter died 02/02/64 02/05/64
Bannon, Jane (Mrs.) died 10/14/63 10/16/63
Bannon, John died 03/19/65 03/20/65
Bannon, Patrick married McAllister, Annie 11/26/65 12/05/65
Bansemer, G. A. married Dent, Henrietta H. 05/26/64 05/28/64
Bansemer, Lulie died 02/09/61 02/12/61
Bansemer, Susan died 05/01/61 05/02/61
Banton, Anna Maria married Jolly, David 04/30/65 05/02/65
Banty, P. S. married Reese, Mattie T. 11/03/64 11/12/64
Baoyer, Mary C. married Stockham, John Q. 06/15/64 06/20/64
Baqyley, Eliza (Mrs.) died 06/14/64 06/16/64
Baragars, Adell V. married Augustus, Victoren P. 11/04/62 12/04/62
Baranger, Catherine married Coulter, John H. 03/03/61 12/25/61
Barbary, Mary died 01/16/61 01/18/61
Barbine, Charles died 03/26/65 03/29/65
Barbine, Eliza died 07/02/62 07/03/62
Barbine, William E. married Maguire, Ellenora 05/07/63 05/09/63
Barbour, Amanda E. married Abel, Charles T. 04/03/64 05/04/64
Barbour, Emma married Miller, Thomas H. 06/04/63 06/27/63
Barbour, James married Jones, Mary 01/12/65 01/13/65
Barbour, James P. married Biddison, Elizabeth A. 10/30/62 02/04/63
Barbour, Lillie A. M. married Riley, E. S., Sr. 08/11/64 08/16/64
Barbour, Lizzie J. (Mrs.) died 11/26/64 11/28/64
Barchus, John Hedges married Lightner, Alice P. 05/25/64 05/27/64
Barclay, Grace Ann died 12/08/63 12/11/63
Barclay, Laura J. married Collins, James E. 11/21/65 11/28/65
Barcroft, Mary died 02/19/63 03/11/63
Bardroff, Daniel Lewis died 06/27/65 06/29/65
Bare, Elizabeth (Mrs.) died 06/17/64 06/18/64
Barenger, Catherine married Sherman, John 08/10/63 08/15/63
Barenstecker, Catharine (Mrs.) died 09/23/64 09/24/64
Bargan, Julia married Stahl, Jacob 11/05/63 11/10/63
Bargar, Julia died 01/15/65 01/16/65
Barickman, Mary Ann married Brennen, James F. 04/02/63 04/13/63
Barke, William H. died 09/07/64 09/09/64
Barker, George Melvin died 11/27/61 11/28/61
Barker, Helena V. (Mrs.) died 01/10/65 01/11/65
Barker, Helena V. (Mrs.) died 01/10/65 01/12/65
Barker, John died 12/17/61 12/19/61
Barker, Joseph H. married Ward, Helena V. 04/22/62 04/28/62
Barker, Joseph W. died 11/30/64 12/08/64
Barker, Mary (Mrs.) died 12/17/63 12/18/63
Barker, Mary A, married Crise, G. W. 02/22/64 03/16/64
Barker, Nathan died 08/06/63 08/08/63
Barker, Thomas died 06/28/62 07/02/62
Barker, William Ward died 03/14/64 03/15/64
Barkley, Mary died 10/28/62 10/31/62
Barklie, Anna married Allnutt, E. Severn 01/17/64 01/18/64

```
Barkman, Mary Elizabeth died 07/20/63  07/23/63
Barks, Francis Marion died 06/02/62  06/04/62
Barksdale, Mary Ann died 06/11/63  07/04/63
Barksdale, Sally Wilurer died 05/31/64  07/21/64
Barley, Ruth A. married Kahn, Adam 01/13/61  01/31/61
Barlow, James T. married Clautice, Salie C. 03/05/62  04/18/62
Barlow, James T. married Clautice, Sallie C. 11/07/64  11/14/64
Barman, Cecelia M. married Taylor, Robert T. 10/07/62  10/10/62
Barn, Elizabeth Isabella died 07/18/62  07/19/62
Barnard, James died 04/26/64  05/07/64
Barnard, John J. married Keech, Kate Hope 11/12/63  11/14/63
Barnard, Mary B. married Aquivre, Epifanio 08/21/62  09/04/62
Barnard, Rollings died 03/07/64  03/09/64
Barnes, Abraham died 04/10/63  04/11/63
Barnes, Ann Rebecca married Boston, Daniel 10/22/63  10/26/63
Barnes, Elizabeth married Barnes, John W. 06/01/65  06/07/65
Barnes, Emy L. married Kershaw, Charles K. (USV) 03/09/64  08/04/64
Barnes, Emy L. married Kershaw, Charles K. (USN) 03/09/64  08/06/64
Barnes, James H. married Dayhoff, Emily J. 06/13/65  07/27/65
Barnes, Jennie married Phillips, B. F. 01/03/61  01/08/61
Barnes, John A. married Ross, Kate 04/28/64  04/30/64
Barnes, John K. (USA) married Brown, Susan 08/01/65  08/04/65
Barnes, John R. married Dawes, Jennie R. 06/02/63  06/06/63
Barnes, John W. married Barnes, Elizabeth 06/01/65  06/07/65
Barnes, Josephine married Moore, Matthew 01/19/62  01/21/62
Barnes, Laura died 03/04/65  03/09/65
Barnes, M. Carrie married Dunning, Joseph H. (Cpt.) 05/10/64  05/13/64
Barnes, Mary H. married Ginn, James J. 10/03/61  10/04/61
Barnes, S. A. married Holges, R. E. 12/28/62  12/30/62
Barnes, Sallie married Murray, James 12/22/64  12/26/64
Barnes, Samuel died 02/04/61  02/05/61
Barnes, Samuel died 11/19/65  11/21/65
Barnes, William J. died 07/01/65  07/03/65
Barnett, Alberta Louisa died 06/09/65  06/10/65
Barnett, Catherine died 03/30/62  03/31/62
Barnett, Dennis married Dorsey, Mary 10/20/64  10/22/64
Barnett, Edward William died 04/24/64  04/26/64
Barnett, Eleanor Achsah died 06/12/65  06/15/65
Barnett, Eugene Marsden died 07/12/63  07/13/63
Barnett, Helen Florence died 12/10/64  12/12/64
Barnett, Julia C. married Marriott, John S. 10/17/62  10/28/62
Barnett, Richard M. married Smith, Sue Melissa 12/29/64  01/02/65
Barnett, Sarah A. married Griffith, John R. (Capt.) 03/17/64  03/19/64
Barnett, William died 10/18/62  10/20/62
Barney, James Henry married Roberson, Emeline 12/11/62  12/13/62
Barney, John Henry died 06/11/63  06/12/63
Barns, Christopher R. died 02/22/63  03/13/63
Barnsby, Mary E. married Jones, Josiah W. 06/09/64  06/14/64
Barnsley, J. D. married Owen, Mary E. 05/24/64  05/27/64
Barnum, Augusta died 08/16/64  08/17/64
Barnum, Augusta died 08/16/64  08/18/64
Barnum, Zenus died 04/05/65  04/06/65
Barnum, Zenus died 04/05/65  04/07/65
Barow, John Ulysses Grant died 07/11/65  07/13/65
Barr, D. Miller (Dr.) married Dickson, Sue 07/28/64  07/30/64
```

Barr, James B. died 04/12/62   05/13/62
Barr, Margaret J. married Cross, Samuel J. 10/23/61   10/25/61
Barr, Mary Elvina married Gaven, William Henry 03/30/63   04/15/63
Barrall, Samuel died 06/24/64   07/26/64
Barranger, F. V. M. married Kupp, Charles L. (Lt.) 09/17/61   11/27/61
Barranger, Louis L., Sr. married Gibbons, Delia 02/12/62   02/14/62
Barrenger, Laura J. married Bayless, John T. 07/03/62   09/23/62
Barrenger, Margaret married Forrester, Barnet 04/15/62   05/23/62
Barrenger, Sarah C. married Sherman, John 08/10/63   08/20/63
Barret, Bridget died 09/10/61   09/11/61
Barrett, Ann Eliza (Mrs.) died 07/06/64   07/07/64
Barrett, Annie Ann married Barrett, Emory 11/01/64   11/10/64
Barrett, Augustus died 02/08/62   02/10/62
Barrett, Charles died no date   07/02/63
Barrett, Eliza died 10/03/62   10/04/62
Barrett, Emory married Barrett, Annie Ann 11/01/64   11/10/64
Barrett, F. Oliver married Post, Sallie L. 11/12/63   11/13/63
Barrett, James married Carroll, Catherine 05/21/63   05/22/63
Barrett, James E. married O'Connell, Annie 02/28/65   03/08/65
Barrett, Jenny died 03/10/62   03/11/62
Barrett, John died 03/13/64   03/16/64
Barrett, Joseph E. died 01/05/63   01/06/63
Barrett, Margaret died 05/19/62   05/21/62
Barrett, Margaret M. married Chambers, George M. 05/19/62   06/07/62
Barrett, Mary E. married Crook, William H. 12/19/61   01/28/62
Barrett, Minet died 08/18/64   08/20/64
Barrett, Minot died 08/18/64   08/24/64
Barrett, Patrick died 07/13/61   07/15/61
Barrett, Sallie A. married Buschman, Victor H. 02/18/64   02/20/64
Barrett, Sally (Mrs.) died 09/24/63   09/28/63
Barrett, Virginia T. died 01/24/63   02/04/63
Barrett, William D. married Cushing, Janet M. 07/19/64   07/26/64
Barrett, William H. married Fitzpatrick, Mary 06/30/64   07/11/64
Barrett, William T. died 12/29/61   01/02/62
Barrington, Isabel married Diggs, James 06/19/62   06/23/62
Barris, Elizabeth married Allen, B. McIntyre 09/11/65   09/15/65
Barroll, Henry died 01/18/65   01/19/65
Barron, John died 04/15/63   04/17/63
Barron, John married Edwards, Frances T. 03/01/64   03/03/64
Barron, Mary E. married Jones, Lewis 12/06/65   12/23/65
Barron, P. D. married Morris, Josephine S. 06/02/63   06/17/63
Barron, Thomas married Fagen, Julia C. 09/07/62   09/11/62
Barrott, Susan (Mrs.) died 02/21/64   02/23/64
Barrow, Alexander H. died 01/02/63   01/03/63
Barrow, Charles Pitt died 10/26/61   10/28/61
Barrow, Thomas married Eager, Julia O. 09/07/62   09/10/62
Barrows, Rebecca A. B. (Mrs.) married Gaffard, William 12/07/64
   12/08/64
Barry, Camilla died 07/13/62   07/14/62
Barry, Casey, Jr. married Barry, Josephine 05/30/65   06/03/65
Barry, Ella Lee died 06/26/64   06/27/64
Barry, George E. died 05/04/61   05/06/61
Barry, H. A. married Patterson, Alice M. 10/12/65   10/24/65
Barry, James B. married McDowell, Belle 06/09/64   06/22/64
Barry, John died 04/27/62   04/29/62

Barry, John S. died 05/30/64   05/31/64
Barry, Josephine married Barry, Casey, Jr. 05/30/65   06/03/65
Barry, Margaret died 09/01/61   09/02/61
Barry, Mary A. died 12/12/63   12/19/63
Barry, Mary C. married Keenan, Thomas 09/20/63   09/25/63
Barry, Matilda died 06/29/62   06/30/62
Barry, Michael married Abrams, Mary Frances 09/07/65   09/12/65
Barry, Nancy E. married Hepburn, William H. 02/06/62   02/07/62
Barry, William died 04/24/64   04/26/64
Barter, Richard H. married Stewart, Rebecca B. 04/23/61   05/01/61
Bartgis, Robert C. died 05/04/64   05/05/64
Bartgis, Robert C. died 05/04/64   05/06/64
Barth, Catherine L. C. married Horn, William 12/26/61   12/28/61
Barth, Christiana Sophia married Briscoe, Alexander M. 05/22/65   10/09/65
Barth, Ernest Clinton died 05/31/64   06/01/64
Barth, Fannie married Leslie, John 12/28/65   12/30/65
Barth, Helen married Souder, C. S. 10/05/65   10/09/65
Barth, Henry Herman died 02/13/63   02/14/63
Bartheson, Alonzo D. married Skinner, Alice 04/20/65   04/26/65
Bartheson, Alonzo D. married Skinner, Alice 04/20/65   04/27/65
Bartholdt, John F. died 07/23/61   07/26/61
Bartholomer, Theodore M. married Maclellan, Kate F. 09/17/62   10/07/62
Bartholomer, Avis Belle died 10/25/62   10/28/62
Bartholow, Avis Isabella died 10/27/62   10/29/62
Bartholow, Emily Frances died 10/17/65   10/18/65
Bartholow, George E. married Acomb, Maggie E. 04/21/64   05/02/64
Bartholow, J. M. C. married Cassard, A. L. 12/06/65   12/11/65
Bartholow, Jesse H. died 07/13/62   07/14/62
Bartholow, Thomas died 10/20/64   10/21/64
Bartis, Martin E. died 06/02/64   06/11/64
Bartlett, Abner T. married Cole, Mary M. 03/03/63   03/06/63
Bartlett, Caroline H. (Mrs.) died 09/27/64   10/05/64
Bartlett, Hannah married Bartlett, J. Thomas 11/26/62   12/01/62
Bartlett, Isaac Cook died 10/25/61   10/26/61
Bartlett, J. Thomas married Bartlett, Hannah 11/26/62   12/01/62
Bartlett, James died 01/07/65   01/09/65
Bartlett, James F., Jr. married Netsel, Annie 02/14/64   02/26/64
Bartlett, Mary (Mrs.) died 05/06/65   05/08/65
Bartlett, Susan married Taylor, Henry T. 11/20/65   12/04/65
Bartlett, William died 01/24/62   01/25/62
Bartlett, William died 01/07/65   01/10/65
Bartlett, William E., Sr. died 08/10/65   08/14/65
Bartlett, William S. married Francis, Charlotte C. 09/14/64   09/20/64
Bartling, Thomas died 07/30/63   07/31/63
Bartol, Emma A. married Hays, John 08/09/64   08/19/64
Barton, Andrew C. married Graham, Elizabeth 05/14/61   05/17/61
Barton, Anna Cecelia died 02/04/64   02/05/64
Barton, Caroline married Miskelly, Joseph 12/31/63   02/17/64
Barton, Charles H. married Arnold, Sarah Ann 09/29/62   10/08/62
Barton, Elizabeth married Tillman, William H. 01/01/63   01/07/63
Barton, Elizabeth (Mrs.) died 10/03/63   10/06/63
Barton, Elizabeth G. died 04/30/65   05/10/65
Barton, Esau died 03/12/63   03/14/63
Barton, George S. died 05/29/62   06/03/62

```
Barton, Ida Malica died 03/16/63   03/17/63
Barton, John S. died 12/22/62   12/24/62
Barton, Joshua died 05/12/64   05/13/64
Barton, Joshua N. married German, Mary C. 08/15/64   08/16/64
Barton, Laura J. married Wooters, James M. 09/01/64   09/03/64
Barton, Lizzie J. married Smith, Thomas H. 07/02/61   07/08/61
Barton, Mary (Mrs.) died 12/13/63   12/15/63
Barton, Mary Ann died 08/26/61   08/27/61
Barton, Matthew Birmingham died 07/08/65   07/12/65
Barton, Philip A. married Oliver, Annie M. F. 01/31/65   02/06/65
Barton, Rebecca Jane died 01/16/61   01/17/61
Barton, Samuel J. married Collier, Annie E. 01/21/65   09/02/65
Barton, Stephen W. married Knight, Susan 04/09/63   04/18/63
Barton, Stephen W. died 03/18/64   03/23/64
Barton, Willard G. married Firoved, Sarah E. 12/30/61   01/04/62
Barton, William married Tiroved, Sarah E. 12/30/61   01/03/62
Barton, William H. died 01/21/64   02/01/64
Barton, William N. married Emerson, S. Lizzie 12/14/65   12/18/65
Barton, Winfield Scott died 08/15/61   08/19/61
Bartow, J. F. married Steele, Annie Key 01/06/64   01/09/64
Bartscher, John married Tomlinson, (Tomlison) Kate 01/05/65   01/07/65
Baryer, Catherine married Schueler, Lewis 12/01/63   12/02/63
Baryey, Ruth A. married Kahn, Adam 01/13/61   01/30/61
Base, Sallie (Mrs.) died 08/20/65   08/30/65
Bash, John H. married Hayes, Lottie 04/22/62   04/25/62
Basil, Henrietta married Saumenig, William A. 05/15/61   05/24/61
Basil, John, Jr. married Crummer, Matilda 07/30/61   07/31/61
Basley, Arabella married Clowdsley, John H. 01/22/62   01/31/62
Basley, Peter died 09/10/62   10/07/62
Bass, Henry J. married Wood, Margaret E. 02/05/63   02/13/63
Bassell, Sarah E. died 08/03/63   08/04/63
Bassett, Richard A. married Williams, Mary 05/12/64   05/14/64
Bassford, Louise V. married Atwell, William R. 04/23/63   05/02/63
Bassford, Thomas R. died 04/19/63   04/20/63
Basshor, Thomas C. married Green, Susan 09/17/61   09/24/61
Basshor, Thomas C. married Wedge, Emma A. 11/16/65   11/21/65
Basshorr, Thomas C. [retract] married Green, Susan [retract] no date
     09/26/61
Bastable, Maria died 07/10/62   07/11/62
Bastianeill, Ulisse J. died 08/16/65   08/17/65
Bastianelli, Charles R. died 02/08/63   02/09/63
Bastianelli, Willie died 10/23/64   10/25/64
Bastianelli, Willie died no date   11/07/64
Bastianielli, Gaetano died 02/23/65   02/25/65
Batchelor, Charles E. died 09/20/63   10/01/63
Batchelor, Charles Henry died 11/07/63   11/11/63
Batchelor, Sarah E. married France, Charles D. 12/12/65   12/16/65
Bateman, Constance died 01/16/62   01/17/62
Bateman, Henry died 03/23/64   03/24/64
Bateman, James Adolphus died 12/16/64   12/17/64
Bateman, James Orlando died 09/06/63   09/07/63
Bateman, John Thomas died 01/22/61   01/24/61
Bateman, Joshua died 05/16/63   05/19/63
Bateman, Sarah Ann married Stephenson, James 08/23/64   08/25/64
Bateman, Sydney A. married Payne, William T. 11/24/64   11/29/64
```

```
Bates, Ann married Dumm, William T. 03/16/64  03/18/64
Bates, Charles W. married Gourley, Sarah 01/12/65  01/25/65
Bates, Ella L. died 06/16/64  06/17/64
Bates, Fannie J. died 07/03/64  07/04/64
Bates, James married Smith, Kate D. 06/09/63  06/15/63
Bates, John Bernard L. died 04/22/62  04/25/62
Bates, Martin married Perine, Sarah Jane 08/23/63  09/12/63
Bates, Mary Louisa (Mrs.) died 12/16/63  12/18/63
Bathran, Eugene H. married Luckett, Mary C. 12/03/61  12/12/61
Bathurst, Ann died 10/07/62  10/11/62
Baton, Anna Maria married Jolly, David 04/30/65  05/02/65
Battarder, Maggy died 07/10/64  07/11/64
Battee, Dennis H. (Rev.) died 03/08/65  03/10/65
Battee, Honoria married Edwards, States 10/25/65  11/04/65
Battee, John S. died 11/13/65  11/15/65
Battee, Joshua W. married Edwards, Amanda M. 11/30/64  12/14/64
Battee, Robert N. died 03/30/61  04/01/61
Battees, John died 11/06/61  11/13/61
Batty, Francis M. died 07/28/63  07/30/63
Batty, Joseph W. married Lynch, Anne S. 08/13/63  08/18/63
Bauer, Margaret Emma died 08/16/62  08/18/62
Bauerfeind, Christoph married Stier, Anna M. (Mrs.) 04/24/64  04/26/64
Bauerschmidt, John married West, Eliza 12/18/64  12/22/64
Baugher, Adolphus Oechs died 02/17/63  02/18/63
Baugher, William Fenwick (CSA) died 09/12/63  10/30/63
Baughman, Francis M. died 07/23/65  07/24/65
Baughman, John W. married Lovejoy, Hettie M. 06/21/65  07/24/65
Baumgardner, William J. died 03/11/63  03/13/63
Baumgarten, Elizabeth (Mrs.) died 12/17/64  12/19/64
Bausmith, Charles married Roberts, Julie 10/25/64  11/04/64
Bausmith, Sallie (Mrs.) died 09/17/63  09/18/63
Bausmith, Sallie (Mrs.) died 09/17/63  09/19/63
Baversack, John W. married Stephenson, Sallie E. 01/06/64  01/23/64
Bawm, Christian J. died 02/08/62  02/14/62
Bawn, Mary Ann died 04/25/65  04/26/65
Bawn, Ruth Elizabeth died 06/13/62  06/14/62
Baxley, Elizabeth Dorsey died 11/07/62  11/11/62
Baxley, James died 05/16/61  05/18/61
Baxter, Annie Olivia married Taylor, Sidney T. 05/05/61  05/11/61
Baxter, Benjamin died 04/07/63  04/11/63
Baxter, Isabella died 01/23/64  01/25/64
Baxter, James A. died 04/09/61  04/17/61
Baxter, Mary C. married Ryan, Samuel 10/20/63  12/05/63
Baxter, W. H. married Rote, Rosetta 02/21/61  02/22/61
Baxter,James Union died 02/26/64  02/27/64
Bay, James died 03/31/63  04/01/63
Bayard, Mary R. married Armesworthy, Bebjamin 02/04/64  02/06/64
Bayer, Caroline C. died 04/21/62  04/22/62
Bayer, Louis died 08/09/63  08/11/63
Bayfield, James H. died 03/10/62  03/12/62
Bayles, Frederick married Trunk, Josephine 05/28/63  06/01/63
Bayless, Georgie B. died 07/19/63  07/21/63
Bayless, John T. married Barrenger, Laura J. 07/03/62  09/23/62
Bayless, William J. died 12/09/65  12/11/65
Bayley, Beckie married McGee, George R. 12/08/63  12/23/63
```

Bayley, Eliza A. died 08/10/64   08/11/64
Bayley, Eliza Jane married Piper, Robert H. 07/07/63   07/11/63
Bayley, Emily died 07/15/62   07/16/62
Bayley, George W. married Weise, Regina 03/08/61   05/08/61
Bayley, George W. died 05/09/64   05/11/64
Bayley, Henry D. died 10/22/64   10/24/64
Bayley, Mary A. E. married Reinhart, George P. 09/18/64   09/21/64
Bayley, William F. died 09/29/62   09/30/62
Bayley, William F. died 09/29/62   10/01/62
Bayley, William T. married Kirsch, Sarah E. 02/08/61   02/12/61
Bayleys, Samuel Smith (Cpt.) married Valiant, Lavinia Bell 02/16/63
   02/20/63
Baylor, Elizabeth (Mrs.) died 01/14/65   01/16/65
Bayly, Henrietta (Mrs.) married Owens, Baziel 12/17/62   12/17/62
Bayly, Marcus Buck married Rogers, Eunice F. 10/22/64   10/29/64
Bayly, Mary Jane died 09/20/62   09/22/62
Bayly, Phillip R. died 11/24/65   11/25/65
Bayly, Sallie Gorsuch died 10/09/64   10/10/64
Baynard, Anna M. married Crooks, Rufus S. 01/28/64   01/30/64
Bayne, John T. married Filius, Sarah E. 05/17/64   05/21/64
Bayne, Lucia married Rodgers, Henry J. (Maj.) 10/12/65   10/16/65
Bayne, Rosa Kate died 08/21/63   09/07/63
Bayne, William C. married McDonald, Mary 12/21/64   01/02/65
Baynes, Alice P. married Twining, D. H. 12/14/65   12/16/65
Baynes, John T. married Filius, Sarah E. 05/17/64   05/20/64
Baynes, John T. married Fillins, Sarah E. 05/17/64   05/19/64
Baynes, Thomas died 10/23/64   10/25/64
Baynes, Thomas, W. died 09/19/62   09/20/62
Baynes, William W. married Seymour, Sarah E. 07/27/65   07/29/65
Bazell, John Milton died 03/12/61   03/14/61
Beach, Bertha J. married McCarriar, James 06/11/61   06/15/61
Beach, John Newton died 04/30/64   05/03/64
Beach, Thomas J. died 05/08/64   05/11/64
Beach, William J. married Sims, Mary E. 06/17/65   06/20/65
Beacham, Mary E. married Stephens, George R. 05/26/64   06/07/64
Beachamp, John Elwood died 11/19/65   11/21/65
Beacher, A. Burre married Burns, Kate Olivia (Mrs.) 07/13/63   07/18/63
Beadenkoph, Kate married Hullan, Thomas 08/23/63   09/04/63
Beal, Maria T. married Kelly, William H. 11/30/65   12/01/65
Beal, William Benjamin died 02/09/61   02/13/61
Beale, A. M. married Porter-Wood, Mary no date   01/14/64
Beale, Eleanora D. married Ash, George T. 01/24/61   01/30/61
Beall, B. L. (Col.) died 08/16/63   08/17/63
Beall, Emma married Dickenson, P. Eugene 06/25/61   06/28/61
Beall, George W. married Syayne, M. E. N. 03/05/61   03/09/61
Beall, John J. married Dodge, Lizzie 06/17/62   06/20/62
Beall, Mary died 10/11/62   10/13/62
Beall, Walter T. (CSA) died 11/27/63   12/03/63
Bealmar, James George died 05/31/65   06/03/65
Bealmear, J. Francis married Hunt, Eliza 06/25/63   06/27/63
Beam, Clinton Davis died 08/14/62   08/16/62
Beam, Margaret S. died 06/01/61   06/06/61
Beam, Mary Jane married Liamond, William 02/09/64   02/12/64
Beam, Sarah C. married Toel, Charles H. 10/19/65   10/23/65
Beam, Sarah E. married Pickering, William J. 03/07/64   10/03/64

Beam, William James died 10/09/64   10/10/64
Beaman, Lucy died 01/19/61   01/21/61
Beamer, Rachel (Mrs.) died 03/15/64   03/18/64
Beaming, Mary died 09/21/61   09/23/61
Bean, Ann R. died 02/14/65   02/15/65
Bean, Fannie married Arnold, C. Albert 03/28/64   04/04/64
Bean, John Henry died 05/26/61   05/28/61
Bean, Joseph H. died 03/22/65   03/23/65
Bean, Joseph H. died 03/22/65   03/24/65
Bean, Kate died 01/13/63   01/15/64
Bean, Mary Ellen married Booz, William Barry 12/03/65   12/06/65
Bean, Rufus S. (Lt.) married Forest, Nannie A. 04/23/64   04/30/64
Beane, Ann (Mrs.) died 08/16/65   08/17/65
Beane, William McKendree died 04/15/62   04/18/62
Beard, Bettie married Hopkins, John J. 01/24/61   01/30/61
Beard, Emily L. died 05/08/65   05/18/65
Beard, Emma F. married Stubbs, Joseph S. 04/07/62   04/08/62
Beard, Fannie married Bennett, Samuel E. 07/21/62   07/22/62
Beard, Franklin died 12/31/63   01/02/64
Beard, Henry Clay married Patterson, Fannie Woodward 09/24/62   09/27/62
Beard, John died 09/19/63   09/25/63
Beard, Lillian died 10/28/61   11/05/61
Beard, Margaret died 11/13/63   11/18/63
Beardsley, John D. (Maj.) married Poole, Susan C. no date   09/13/65
Bears, Fannie married Arnold, Albert 03/28/64   04/04/64
Beatson, George D. married Loane, Millie A. 06/14/64   06/15/64
Beatty, Agnes married Lindsay, James L. 10/17/65   10/19/65
Beatty, Catherine B. died 09/15/61   09/21/61
Beatty, Charlotte Jane (Mrs.) died 01/08/63   01/10/63
Beatty, Edward (Lt.) died 03/24/64   04/25/64
Beatty, George died 10/21/61   10/23/61
Beatty, Mary A. died 03/07/63   03/09/63
Beatty, William J. A. married Sangston, Charlotte Jane 04/22/62
    04/24/62
Beauchamp, Annie E. married Merson, Charles E. 02/11/61   02/20/61
Beauchamp, Grace Webster died 08/09/65   08/10/65
Beauchamp, Isaac (Cpt.) died 05/10/64   05/16/64
Beauchamp, Isaac W. (Capt.) died 02/17/61   02/18/61
Beauchamp, John Elwood died no date   12/18/65
Beauchamp, Leah J. married Davis, Charles L. 03/01/65   03/07/65
Beauchamp, Leah J. married Davis, Charles L. 03/01/65   03/08/65
Beauregard, Samuel died 10/29/62   10/30/62
Beaver, J. Lewis (Cpt.) married Browne, Emma Alice 11/01/64   11/03/64
Beck, Annie Eva died 10/29/61   10/30/61
Beck, Christopher J. died 02/09/65   02/10/65
Beck, Ernest died 08/16/65   08/18/65
Beck, John married Hobbs, Mary E. 06/09/61   06/14/61
Beck, Mary C. married Werkamp, Louis E. 10/06/64   10/14/64
Beckenridge, John C. married Callow, Catherine 03/31/64   04/02/64
Becker, H. L. died 09/25/62   09/26/62
Becker, Louisa Jane married Schneider, Henry 04/07/63   04/11/63
Beckerstith, Mary died 08/02/65   08/04/65
Beckett, Ann R. married Riddle, George W. 01/10/61   01/17/61
Beckett, Margaret R. married Clark, Charles (Dr.) 11/14/61   11/19/61
Beckett, Thomas A. died 03/24/65   03/25/65

Beckham, Charles married McIntosh, Mary 09/25/62   09/27/62
Beckley, John W. married Hayward, Sophia 10/10/65   10/17/65
Beckley, Robert T. married Helmes, Jeanie 05/25/65   06/01/65
Beckly, William Henry died 01/16/62   01/18/62
Beckwith, Franklin M. married Bangent, Mary E. 10/03/64   10/04/64
Beckworth, Sarah Cunningham married Hubbard, Samuel 12/31/60   01/03/61
Beckworth, Thomas married Wheeler, Mary Jane 09/04/61   09/07/61
Bedford, John R. D. married Bosley, Rosalla A. 08/11/64   08/13/64
Bedford, Julia Belle married Fox, F. J. E. 01/03/61   01/12/61
Beeder, Ambrose Jacob died 07/04/61   07/06/61
Beehler, Geoffrey Ernest died 03/22/64   03/23/64
Beeler, Henry S. married Goodman, Susie E. 01/22/63   02/06/63
Beeman, Amelia J. died 11/23/65   11/28/65
Beeman, Josephine married Winchester, H. R. 06/04/63   06/06/63
Beeman, Lucy Amelia died 10/09/65   10/11/65
Beeman, Susan J. married Robinson, James C. 10/06/63   10/08/63
Been, Thomas C. married Phellen, Ellen 02/10/61   02/26/61
Beers, Sophia died 11/17/60   01/11/61
Beers, Thomas R. died no date   11/04/64
Beers, William died 11/13/60   01/11/61
Beeter, Emma Virginia died 02/24/64   02/27/64
Beetly, Anna Pauline died 07/16/64   07/18/64
Begg, Sarah married Richardson, Samuel 02/04/64   02/13/64
Beggs, Agnes died 09/01/64   09/05/64
Behee, Lewis died 03/07/63   03/09/63
Behn, Henry J. T. married Halbach, Louisa M. 06/20/65   06/21/65
Behrans, William Henry died 08/02/65   08/12/65
Behrens, Alice Virginia died 08/12/65   09/06/65
Behrens, Harriet Ann died 08/28/65   09/06/65
Behrens, Marie married Wetzel, Philip 11/23/62   11/26/62
Behrens, Susie married Auerbach, S. L. 02/22/63   02/24/63
Behrens, William L. died 09/02/65   09/06/65
Beil, N. Van married Herrisse, Valeria 06/05/65   06/06/65
Belbson, William R. married Frazier, Martha A. 09/13/65   09/23/65
Bell, Achsah died 01/07/61   01/08/61
Bell, Ann Jane married Harris, Leroy 05/27/63   06/02/63
Bell, Barbara E. died 06/08/65   06/09/65
Bell, Charles Edgar died 04/25/62   04/28/62
Bell, Clara A. married McCurley, Edward 01/14/62   01/20/62
Bell, Clara Virginia died 04/06/64   04/08/64
Bell, Eliza married Suggicks, Raisin 02/11/64   02/13/64
Bell, Elizabeth E. married Fort, Edward S. 09/29/62   10/20/62
Bell, Emma J. died 11/19/62   11/22/62
Bell, George H. married Roberts, Mary Alice 01/27/63   02/02/63
Bell, Harry died 12/11/62   12/15/62
Bell, Harry Burgess died 07/07/64   07/12/64
Bell, Henry died 01/24/63   02/14/63
Bell, John married Bilson, Anna 12/30/62   01/03/63
Bell, John married Butler, Frances Ann 10/01/63   10/03/63
Bell, John died 10/18/65   10/19/65
Bell, John married Albert, Mary Jane 12/22/64   12/23/64
Bell, John A. married Bunting, Maggie T. 01/05/65   01/07/65
Bell, Josiah V. married Mitchell, Cornelia J. 11/30/65   12/04/65
Bell, Kate Madora died 06/30/64   07/01/64
Bell, Laura Emma died 05/28/65   05/29/65

```
Bell, Margaret married Williams, John 05/23/63  06/05/63
Bell, Mary (Mrs.) died 02/08/65  02/10/65
Bell, Mary (Mrs.) died 02/08/65  02/10/65
Bell, Mary E. married Jones, William G. 11/03/63  11/17/63
Bell, Mary E. married Jones, WIlliam G. 12/02/63  12/18/63
Bell, Mary E. A. died 10/15/65  10/17/65
Bell, Mary Ellen S. died 06/17/64  06/18/64
Bell, Milcha (Mrs.) died 11/18/63  11/26/63
Bell, Rebecca A. married Curry, James 02/26/61  03/02/61
Bell, Thaddeus married McCarraher, Mary L. 11/17/64  11/28/64
Bell, Virginia D. died 03/04/61  03/06/61
Bell, W. D. married Gifford, Emily C. 10/23/64  10/25/64
Bell, William A. died 07/22/65  07/24/65
Bell, William Stockley died 08/11/64  08/15/64
Bellis, George Washington died 06/27/64  06/29/64
Bellis, Joseph Ellsworth died 06/28/64  06/29/64
Bellowson, Charles W. married Frybogle, Harriet 06/14/64  06/21/64
Belt, Ann Elizabeth died 06/13/65  06/14/65
Belt, Ann G. died 07/10/61  07/11/61
Belt, Lucretia A. married Reeves, William, Jr. 11/23/64  11/26/64
Belt, Mary Lizzie married Dennis, Emory 06/06/64  06/11/64
Belt, Milcha (Mrs.) died 11/18/63  11/16/63
Belt, S. Sprigg married Moale, Susan P. 06/05/62  06/07/62
Belt, Thomas H. married Johns, Fidelia 10/05/64  10/07/64
Benan, Priscilla J. (Mrs.) died 04/01/63  04/02/63
Benard, Caroline married Proctor, William 11/26/63  12/10/63
Benbury, James died 06/24/65  06/27/65
Benbury, James H. died 10/02/65  10/12/65
Benbury, Joseph H. died 10/02/65  10/03/65
Bendan, John Harrison died 08/13/63  08/14/63
Bendann, Daniel married Lisner, Hannah 01/05/65  01/07/65
Bender, Jacob died no date  06/23/64
Benezet, Annie M. married Mitchell, Charles E. 11/01/64  11/03/64
Benezet, Annie M. married Mitchell, Charles E. 11/02/64  11/04/64
Benezet, George W. married King, Maggie 02/25/64  02/27/64
Benham, Annie married Megraw, John 11/08/64  11/10/64
Benhardt, Andrew married Manley, Elizabeth 03/13/64  03/15/64
Benjamin, Hester married Miller, Banjamin 01/21/64  01/25/64
Benjamin, James W. married Taylor, Rebecca L. 02/12/63  03/04/63
Benneman, John H. died 10/22/64  10/24/64
Benner, Carrie E. died 07/09/65  07/22/65
Benner, Ferdinand C. married Pritchett, Louisa E. 02/19/63  02/24/63
Benner, Jean died 03/31/64  04/01/64
Benner, Mary E. C. married Abbott, Daniel E. R. 04/14/64  04/16/64
Bennet, Frank Barker died 11/04/63  11/05/63
Bennet, Laura E. married Inderrieden, Charles H. 04/02/64  04/04/64
Bennett, Basil C. S. died 03/05/64  03/07/64
Bennett, Charles Gwyn died 12/02/61  12/04/61
Bennett, Conrad F. married Wood, Mary Jane 08/14/64  10/05/64
Bennett, David married Vickers, Mary Virginia 01/07/64  01/14/64
Bennett, Elizabeth J. died 12/12/63  12/17/63
Bennett, Fannie W. died 03/10/64  03/11/64
Bennett, Franklin Ward died 07/25/62  07/26/62
Bennett, G. W. (Lt.) married Ward, Mary A. 02/13/62  02/19/62
Bennett, George H. M. married Moss, Emma J. 05/29/65  05/30/65
```

Bennett, Georgie A. married Ridgaway, Thomas S. 06/03/63 06/09/63
Bennett, Harry married Sefton, Sevilla 03/12/63 03/14/63
Bennett, Helen married Vincent, Thomas B. 11/03/63 07/07/64
Bennett, Jennie H. married Welch, William B. 02/04/64 02/06/64
Bennett, John died 05/27/61 06/01/61
Bennett, John died 08/12/62 08/14/62
Bennett, John died 08/12/62 08/22/62
Bennett, John A. died 07/08/63 07/11/63
Bennett, John A. married Milstead, Annie 01/26/64 02/01/64
Bennett, John E. married Zimmerman, Lizzie 02/19/63 02/25/63
Bennett, John Edward married Dorsey, Amanda R. 04/13/65 05/09/65
Bennett, John Edward married Dorney, Amanda R. 04/13/65 05/10/65
Bennett, Julia Frances died 12/11/63 12/14/63
Bennett, Kate L. Cook married Legg, Edward C. 10/29/63 11/02/63
Bennett, L. Emory married Blake, Annie A. 10/17/61 10/18/61
Bennett, Lewis H. died 04/11/64 04/12/64
Bennett, Livingston M. died 09/00/00 09/07/63
Bennett, Maggie E. died 02/17/64 03/04/64
Bennett, Margaret Marks, Henry 11/06/63 11/28/63
Bennett, Maria S. married Street, E. F. 03/07/64 03/10/64
Bennett, Mary married Fisher, George G. 11/17/64 11/19/64
Bennett, Mary Emily married Benson, Charles J. (Dr.) 09/11/61 09/13/61
Bennett, Mingo died 03/28/63 03/30/63
Bennett, N. S. married Davidson, Maggie A. 02/16/65 03/06/65
Bennett, Samuel E. married Beard, Fannie 07/21/62 07/22/62
Bennett, Thomas died 04/28/62 04/30/62
Bennett, Thomas W. (Cpt.) married Wheeler, Mary Emily 11/03/63 12/08/63
Bennett, Urith died 09/27/61 09/28/61
Bennett, William Clark died 04/08/64 04/09/64
Bennette, Mary A. married Sollers, T. Everist 04/12/64 04/13/64
Bennoch, James Alexander died 06/21/61 07/06/61
Bennoch, Thomas died 07/22/62 07/23/62
Benny, Cornelia married Lare, Edward 08/11/64 08/15/64
Benny, Florence Matilda died 01/04/65 01/07/65
Benson, Agnes A. married Morgan, Walter T. 01/26/64 01/28/64
Benson, Alpha died 08/09/62 08/18/62
Benson, Amos S. died 03/27/63 03/28/63
Benson, Anna died 09/23/61 10/02/61
Benson, Annie died 11/01/61 11/02/61
Benson, Charles J. (Dr.) married Bennett, Mary Emily 09/11/61 09/13/61
Benson, Elenora (Mrs.) died 11/15/64 11/16/64
Benson, Emily married Bowen, Henry 03/29/64 04/20/64
Benson, Harriet (Mrs.) died 04/26/65 04/28/65
Benson, James H. (Capt.) married Caulk, Rosaline 04/13/65 04/17/65
Benson, Jesse C. married Ball, Kate B. 06/02/64 06/13/64
Benson, John B. died 05/17/64 05/18/64
Benson, Joseph E. married Ballauf, Mary E. 11/19/63 11/21/63
Benson, Lorenzo S. died 05/09/62 05/20/62
Benson, Mary (Mrs.) died 08/06/64 08/16/64
Benson, P. V. (M.D.) married Seth, Mollie M. 12/04/62 12/09/62
Benson, William D. married Kelly, Janie 03/04/62 03/06/62
Benson, William H. married Miller, Frances Jane 10/13/63 10/24/63
Benson, William W. married Jenkins, Rachel 10/17/65 10/20/65
Benteen, Cornelia died 08/12/63 08/13/63
Benteen, F. D. died 01/22/64 01/23/64

```
Benteen, Frederick D., Jr. died 01/02/64   01/04/64
Bentley, Ambrose died 06/02/63   06/04/63
Bentley, Edgar died 02/25/64   02/26/64
Bentley, Jane married Riley, Emanuel 01/08/63   01/17/63
Bentley, Julis A. (Mrs.) died 01/24/63   01/26/63
Bently, Elizabeth died 11/29/62   12/08/62
Benton, Arron T. married White, Priscilla 03/08/64   03/10/64
Benton, Mary married McDonald, John (Lt.) 05/07/63   05/11/63
Benton, Sarah C. married Geddes, James A. 07/03/64   07/13/64
Bentz, George married Clark, Ellen 01/14/63   01/24/63
Bentz, George married Clark, Ellen M. A. 01/14/63   01/26/63
Benzinger, Joseph C. (Dr.) married Wahl, Annie V. 09/27/65   09/29/65
Benzinger, Mary Catharine died 10/17/65   10/18/65
Benzinger, Pierre G. B. died no date   09/22/63
Benzinger, Pierre G. B. died no date   09/23/63
Beo, Anne Elizabeth died 06/25/61   06/26/61
Beohm, John married Miller, Louisa E. 06/22/64   06/24/64
Beon, John M. married Bowman, Mary Alice 11/02/65   11/04/65
Berenger, Anastasia died 01/26/61   01/29/61
Beresch, Karl married Bode, Angela 08/21/65   08/25/65
Berg, Adolph (Maj.) married Stevenson, M. A. (Mrs.) 09/14/65   09/15/65
Berg, Albert B. married Conry, Annie S. 06/13/65   06/19/65
Berger, Caroline M. C. married Brown, John W. 05/23/65   05/29/65
Berger, Eliza E. married Hagerman, Martin L. 12/17/63   12/19/63
Berger, M. E. married Maurer, C. M. 03/19/65   06/01/65
Berger, Mary married Sache, Justin 12/25/61   12/27/61
Berger, P. R. married Weyforth, Louisa M. 12/07/65   12/20/65
Bergers, William married Morgan, Eliza B. 04/06/64   04/07/64
Bergin, Ellen Mary died 09/24/65   09/25/65
Bergin, Mary married Delany, Daniel 05/03/63   05/05/63
Bergin, Mary died 09/24/65   09/26/65
Bergman, Henry married Cramer, Hannah 03/05/65   03/17/65
Beringer, Cecilia married Wright, Amassa A. 07/31/65   08/10/65
Berkley, John M. married Frazier, Ellen L. 11/14/65   11/18/65
Berkley, Matilda died 03/13/62   03/14/62
Berlin, Sadie A. married Vermilyn, James H. 11/23/65   11/27/65
Berlin, Sadie A. married Vermilya, James H. 11/23/65   11/28/65
Bernard, C. Kate married Worthington, Rezin H. 02/10/63   02/12/63
Bernard, Lucy A. died 05/26/65   05/27/65
Bernard, Richard married Duvall, Lucy A. 11/26/63   12/10/63
Berrell, Clara A. died 06/18/65   06/20/65
Berrell, Samuel died 07/24/64   07/28/64
Berret, Julius Hopkinson died 03/25/62   03/28/62
Berry, A. M. married Sutton, Nannie 11/07/65   11/11/65
Berry, Alburtus D. married Work, Sallie J. 04/29/64   05/03/64
Berry, Ann E. (Mrs.) died 08/06/65   08/19/65
Berry, B. D. married Hissey, Eliza J. 01/01/61   01/04/61
Berry, Benjamin W. married Wonn, Florence A. 04/13/63   04/21/63
Berry, Caroline died 02/24/65   02/28/65
Berry, Charles H. married Fillinger, Josephine M. 06/19/65   07/18/65
Berry, Clara L. married Fleehearty, John T. 07/30/64   08/02/64
Berry, Eliza T. (Mrs.) died 06/23/64   06/24/64
Berry, George A. died 06/26/65   06/27/65
Berry, J. I. married Wrinn, C. Virginia 02/27/65   03/06/65
Berry, James died 09/13/65   09/16/65
```

Berry, John married Mollowry, Ann 10/11/63 11/09/63
Berry, John died 07/06/65 07/07/65
Berry, John B. N. married Berry, Rosa E. 11/01/64 11/09/64
Berry, Joseph married Chase, Mary A. 12/16/62 12/24/62
Berry, Louisa C. E. died 06/13/61 06/14/61
Berry, Louisa C. E. died 06/13/61 06/15/61
Berry, Mary A. died 12/12/63 12/14/63
Berry, Mary A. married Jenks, H. Frederick 07/18/65 08/10/65
Berry, Mary E. married Johnson, E. Dorsey 06/24/62 06/27/62
Berry, Michael married Abrams, Mary Frances 09/07/65 09/11/65
Berry, Richard died 04/10/61 04/16/61
Berry, Richard died 09/19/63 09/24/63
Berry, Rosa E. married Berry, John B. N. 11/01/64 11/09/64
Berry, Samuel Henry died 01/16/63 01/19/63
Berry, Thomas Edward died 01/02/63 01/05/63
Berry, William died no date 03/04/64
Berryman, John married Downs, Caroline 11/17/63 11/19/63
Bersch, Elizabeth married List, George R. 11/07/65 11/10/65
Bertier, Mary Ann married Smith, Robert F. 06/13/65 06/28/65
Bervard, Mary married Ray, Francis 01/09/62 01/13/62
Bery, Adolph (Maj.) married Stevenson, M. A. (Mrs.) 09/14/65 09/27/65
Beson, Emma married Ludwig, J. Henry 06/22/65 06/23/65
Besser, Catharine Amelia died 02/01/65 02/02/65
Best, J. W. F. married Harris, Sarah V. H. 12/25/60 03/11/61
Betal, Adam died 08/12/63 08/13/63
Betson, George (Dr.) married Covey, Anna V. 11/07/65 11/13/65
Betson, Joseph died 02/15/61 02/18/61
Betton, Alfred J. married Nicholson, Mary Jane 10/14/62 10/23/62
Betton, Wilhelmina D. married Dawes, Joseph D. 11/16/63 11/26/63
Betts, Anna E. died 05/11/62 05/12/62
Betts, Charles Beaufort died 01/29/65 02/01/65
Betts, Juliana (Mrs.) died 12/30/64 12/31/64
Betts, Maggie married Boyd, J. L. 07/05/64 07/07/64
Betts, Solomon (Dr.) married Bowen, Josie 06/07/65 06/10/65
Betts, William died 12/23/61 12/24/61
Beundell, Rose (Mrs.) died 03/16/64 03/19/64
Bevan, Bertha died 02/25/63 02/26/63
Bevan, Eliza E. married Gardner, Samuel 05/23/65 05/25/65
Bevan, Thomas H. died 06/26/63 06/27/63
Bevan, Thomas W. married Sergeant, Kate 05/31/64 06/01/64
Bevans, Harriet V. married Glenn, Samuel 11/28/61 11/30/61
Bevans, John T. died 12/19/62 12/20/62
Bevans, Julia Robinson died 12/17/61 12/19/61
Bevans, Maria married Spencer, David J. 02/07/65 02/11/65
Bevans, William married Sample, Margaret 05/14/63 05/16/63
Bevans, William Alpheus married Caulk, Virginia 07/20/63 08/04/63
Beveridge, Francis Albert died 06/05/64 06/08/64
Bey, Jacob died no date 12/29/63
Bherns, Sarah A. married West, Charles P. 03/29/64 04/02/64
Bias, Caroline (Mrs.) married Nicholson, Isaac 11/28/61 12/03/61
Bias, Horace married Boston, Sarah Ann 09/01/64 09/02/64
Bias, John W. married Wallace, Amelia Ann 06/05/62 06/07/62
Biays, James died 09/29/65 10/04/65
Bickerstaff, Henry died 10/29/64 10/31/64
Bickham, Sarah E. married Nimmo, William T. 04/06/64 05/16/64

```
Biddison, Elizabeth A. married Barbour, James P. 10/30/62   02/04/63
Biddison, Keren H. married Coleman, Richard 09/15/62   02/21/63
Biddison, Martha W. married Cougler, John 03/10/62   03/14/62
Biddison, Mary Helen married Brown, Thomas W. 02/03/63   02/04/63
Biddison, Susanna married Hinkle, Charles 01/01/61   01/09/61
Biddison, Thomas C. married McCauley, Julia A. 09/10/62   09/13/62
Biddle, Emma Virginia died 01/25/61   01/28/61
Biddle, Joseph died 10/28/65   10/30/65
Biddle, Julia G. married Bivons, Andrew 12/25/61   01/03/62
Biddle, Rebecca died 03/20/61   03/21/61
Bideke, Dena married Leach, John H. 12/16/61   12/19/61
Bidell, Richard married Giles, Mary E. 06/30/64   07/02/64
Biden, Mary married Diven, Edward T. 03/24/63   03/30/63
Biden, Mary (Mrs.) died 01/12/63   01/14/63
Bidey, Henry died 05/23/62   05/24/62
Bieghtler, George W. married Kemper, Catherine E. 08/16/64   09/01/64
Bien, Maggie died 01/19/65   01/26/65
Bien, Maggie died 01/19/65   01/27/65
Bier, Susannah Barbara died 04/02/65   04/04/65
Bigger, Margaret Jane married Durkes, John H. 04/14/64   04/19/64
Biggs, Anna married Mason, Charles 07/18/65   07/20/65
Biggs, Mary married Elliott, John 10/11/65   10/14/65
Biggs, Sarah Jane (Mrs.) died 09/23/63   09/25/63
Biggs, Zacharia K. married Reynolds, Mary E. (Mrs.) 01/10/65   01/16/65
Bigham, Marshall M. married Caldwell, Carrie L. 09/28/65   10/06/65
Biglin, Patrick married Banks, Mary E. 01/29/64   01/30/64
Billings, Amanda Traverse died 07/28/64   07/29/64
Billings, Henry J. married Partridge, Jennie E. 04/03/63   04/09/63
Billingslea, Ethlin married Robb, John 02/05/61   02/06/61
Billingslea, Lizzie H. married Reifsnider, John L. 12/10/61   12/11/61
Billingsly, Thomas A. married Dalrymple, Mollie E. 04/13/65   04/15/65
Billington, Harriet Elizabeth died 01/01/64   01/02/64
Billington, James P. married Mace, Emira S. 03/15/65   03/17/65
Billmeyer, Jacob died 05/19/63   05/20/63
Billmire, Georgeanna married Linsted, Henry C. 09/05/65   09/30/65
Billmyer, Catherine (Mrs.) married Marshael, Reuben 01/25/63   01/29/63
Billups, George M. married Dorsey, Rebecca E. 12/01/62   12/04/62
Billups, John R. married Vanhorn, Fanny A. 08/23/64   08/30/64
Billups, Lucy A. (Mrs.) died 02/12/63   02/14/63
Bilmyer, Catherine married Kalb, Jacob 04/28/61   04/30/61
Bilson, Anna married Bell, John 12/30/62   01/03/63
Bilson, Daniel married Weller, Liney D. 12/15/63   03/22/64
Bilson, Estella Eudora died 07/21/65   07/24/65
Bilson, Louisa married O'Donnell, James S. 08/02/63   11/09/63
Bilson, Sallie married Ports, J. William 02/16/65   02/18/65
Bilson, William S. died 05/13/62   05/14/62
Bines, Mary B. married Max, Jacob 09/05/65   12/23/65
Bingham, Jane (Mrs.) died 01/02/64   01/04/64
Binnex, Mary Browning died 12/24/63   01/01/64
Binney, Charles married Youngman, Eliza Jane 03/12/63   03/27/63
Binnie, Mary D. married Wells, Robert H. 11/30/65   12/04/65
Binnix, Maggie married Sherry, P. 03/29/64   03/31/64
Binswanger, Amelia married Treuman, Max 09/27/64   09/29/64
Binyan, John L. died 04/21/65   04/22/65
Binyon, John L. died 04/21/65   04/26/65
```

Birchett, Clara Elizabeth died 11/20/61 11/21/61
Birckhead, Ann (Mrs.) died 07/09/64 07/11/64
Birckhead, Anna Elizabeth died 11/23/63 11/26/63
Birckhead, Joseph Edwin died 11/06/63 11/26/63
Birckhead, Susan (Mrs.) died 03/31/63 04/02/63
Bird, Annie married Grinnage, Eli 02/11/64 02/13/64
Bird, Ferdinand Chatard died 06/21/64 06/22/64
Bird, Frank L. married Richstein, Retta J. 09/12/65 09/15/65
Bird, Gustavas married Hall, Annie L. 01/14/64 01/25/64
Bird, Peter died 06/18/63 06/19/63
Bird, Samuel R. married Norfolk, Celia J. 06/17/62 06/18/62
Bird, Thomas T. died 03/12/64 03/16/64
Birdsal, Marinda married McLaughlin, Henry 09/13/64 10/31/64
Birkey, Maria E. married Sappington, Nicholas J. 01/15/61 01/17/61
Birley, Mayberry Goheen died 09/06/65 09/07/65
Birmingham, Cary Elizabeth died 07/30/62 07/31/62
Birmingham, Elizabeth A. died 12/15/63 01/15/64
Birmingham, Mollie E. married Dudrow, George W. 08/11/64 08/19/64
Birney, Charles married Youngman, Eliza J. 03/12/63 04/07/63
Biscoe, Daniel Campbell died 07/12/62 07/29/62
Biscoe, Elizabeth Ellen died 09/17/62 09/19/62
Biscoe, Isabella married Miller, Charles H. 03/21/64 03/28/64
Biscoe, James Bennett died 10/16/63 10/22/63
Biscoe, James E. married Carman, Maria Agnes 03/01/64 03/10/64
Bishop, Annie D. married Bishop, T. J. 11/21/65 11/22/65
Bishop, D. A. married Tremmea, Florence 01/01/65 03/13/65
Bishop, E. Tracy (M.D.) married Coakley, Mary L. 06/18/62 06/19/62
Bishop, Elizabeth N. died 04/05/63 04/06/63
Bishop, Ella married George, Francisco Primicerio 08/22/65 08/25/65
Bishop, George married Washington, Isabella 01/01/63 01/03/63
Bishop, George died 10/19/64 10/20/64
Bishop, George C. married Hochadel, Adeline 09/03/63 09/09/63
Bishop, Henrietta S. married Simpson, Charles H. 12/24/61 01/15/62
Bishop, Henry married Cole, Elizabeth 09/27/64 09/30/64
Bishop, John Edward died 11/18/61 11/19/61
Bishop, John H. married Huzzy, Emma J. 09/01/61 09/16/61
Bishop, Laura Virginia married Robinson, George 12/18/62 12/23/62
Bishop, Nicholas C. died 08/25/62 08/29/62
Bishop, T. J. married Bishop, Annie D. 11/21/65 11/22/65
Bishop, William married Haight, Joanna 05/02/65 05/13/65
Bishop, William L. married Craig, Frances L. 08/28/65 09/04/65
Bishop, Winchester died 06/12/61 06/14/61
Bisley, Rachell died 06/01/62 06/02/62
Bissell, Susan Reed died 02/28/62 03/08/62
Bissell, William R. (Cpt.) died 07/17/63 07/24/63
Bissett, Charles died 08/08/62 08/09/62
Bitter, Louisa died 11/12/61 11/13/61
Bitzel, Hennie L. married Mason, George E. 12/06/64 12/21/64
Bivons, Andrew married Biddle, Julia G. 12/25/61 01/03/62
Bixler, Benjamin M. married Alcock, Marie Louise 05/28/63 05/30/63
Bixler, David Farragut died 06/14/65 06/16/65
Bixler, William H. H. married Rowe, H. Lizzie 04/06/65 04/08/65
Bizouard, Elizabeth Bonne died 06/24/64 06/25/64
Black, Belle died 12/07/64 12/09/64
Black, Bernard died 11/05/64 12/09/64

Black, Bernard died 11/05/64   12/12/64
Black, Catherine died 09/19/62   09/20/62
Black, Ezelia married Parsons, William 10/24/65   10/26/65
Black, Henry Drakely died 04/08/65   04/19/65
Black, James married Fairbank, Mary E. 03/19/63   03/24/63
Black, Jason C. died 03/30/62   04/01/62
Black, John married McMahon, Mary (Mrs.) 07/12/63   07/15/63
Black, Lewis H. died 09/30/64   10/04/64
Black, Lillie H. married Adler, Lewis H. 06/04/61   02/27/62
Black, Mary Louisa married Gannon, Peter 03/30/62   04/01/62
Black, Sallie H. married Griffith, Israel 12/24/63   12/31/63
Black, Sarah Jane (Mrs.) died 08/22/63   08/24/63
Black, Sophia (Mrs.) married Hamilton, James M. (USN) 10/22/62   02/10/
Black, Susan A. married Williams, Benjamin F. 04/02/63   04/04/63
Black, William married Dickerson, Emelia 12/26/65   12/27/65
Black, William B. died 04/06/65   04/24/65
Blackburn, Edward J. married Chase, Mary Virginia 11/06/64   11/16/64
Blackburn, Thomas F. married Woods, Margaret Ann 03/05/65   04/11/65
Blackburn, Uriah died 05/30/62   06/03/62
Blackiston, Delmer died 09/17/63   09/18/63
Blackiston, Harvey Rowland died 03/28/63   03/30/63
Blacklock, Mary (Mrs.) died 05/02/64   05/10/64
Blacklor, Ann died 11/29/61   11/30/61
Blades, John M. married Guyther, M. C. 11/05/61   11/07/61
Blades, Thomas W. married Norris, Susannah 10/01/62   10/04/62
Blaheney, Edward Charlton died 01/29/65   01/31/65
Blair, Agnes married McCoy, David 02/28/65   03/04/65
Blair, Charles Everett died 06/29/61   07/01/61
Blair, George W. died 06/28/62   06/30/62
Blair, Henry H. married Thomas, Helen M. 06/25/63   06/27/63
Blair, Kate A. B. married McClintock, C. W. 08/11/64   08/26/64
Blair, Thomas G. died 07/01/62   07/02/62
Blair, Wilson L. P. married Delahay, Christina H. 01/26/61   01/28/61
Blake, Anne Elizabeth died 12/18/64   12/20/64
Blake, Annie A. married Bennett, L. Emory 10/17/61   10/18/61
Blake, Catherine M. died 07/11/64   07/16/64
Blake, Edward died 06/26/65   06/30/65
Blake, Frank (Lt., U.S.N.) married Spencer, Sallie E. 05/25/61   05/28/
Blake, George A. H. (Col.) married Wood, Margaret A. (Mrs.) 12/16/63
   12/18/63
Blake, Hester died 11/20/63   11/21/63
Blake, Jane died 04/26/64   04/30/64
Blake, Josiah married Brown, Rachael Ann 03/06/63   03/08/62
Blake, Mary married Truitt, Ambrose 06/18/63   06/20/63
Blake, Mary A. married Whittaker, Lewis F. 08/24/63   08/27/63
Blake, Mary Jane married Hall, Henry 12/22/63   12/24/63
Blake, Thomas died 04/08/61   04/19/61
Blake, Thomas V. died 12/20/62   01/08/63
Blake, William F. died 09/12/65   09/15/65
Blake, William Henry died 05/04/63   05/05/63
Blakeney, Mary Margaret died 11/25/65   11/27/65
Blakney, Charles E. died 09/02/61   09/03/61
Blamire, Charles Bruce McCord died 09/15/65   09/16/65
Blamire, Edward Eugene died 10/11/63   10/12/63
Blamire, Edward Eugene died 10/11/63   01/08/64

Blanch, Elizabeth died 07/10/61   07/15/61
Blanchard, Edward Philpot died 09/26/63   10/01/63
Blanche, Ada married Murray, Thomas S. 11/21/65   11/24/65
Bland, Martha E. died 01/18/65   01/19/65
Blandon, Elizabeth died 03/09/62   03/11/62
Blandy, Albert Bledsoe died 10/21/64   10/25/64
Blandy, Albert Bledsoe died 10/21/64   10/26/64
Blaney, Harry died 09/20/65   09/21/65
Blaney, Lily died 08/19/63   08/20/63
Blaney, J. Murray married Leyburn, Jane 09/24/61   12/13/61
Blankford, Jacob married McIntosh, Elizabeth A. 10/31/61   11/02/61
Blass, William H. died 01/12/65   01/14/65
Blatchley, Lydia married Lee, Charles E. 01/13/64   01/19/64
Blatchley, Peter died 12/03/61   12/04/61
Blatchley, Robert S. died 01/18/64   01/19/64
Blaumont, Charles E. married Mortimer, May E. 08/27/62   09/04/62
Blaylock, Statia A. (Mrs.) died 10/02/64   10/04/64
Bleakley, James B. married Mahon, Mary 02/07/61   02/14/61
Bleany, Charles K. married Harman, Mary E. 08/11/64   08/20/64
Blessing, John married Reese, Mary C. 07/16/65   07/18/65
Blessing, Louisa (Mrs.) died 02/05/63   02/07/63
Blessing, Mary L. died 01/01/65   01/02/65
Blew, Robert W. married Wyatt, Sallie Z. 01/10/61   01/12/61
Blew, Robert W. married Wyatt, Sallie Z. 01/10/61   01/11/61
Bliss, Alexander married Albert, Eleanor T. 10/03/65   10/09/65
Blizzard, Annie E. died 02/19/65   02/21/65
Blizzard, Elizabeth (Mrs.) died 04/04/63   04/07/63
Blizzard, Joel married Myerly, Clementine 11/02/65   11/03/65
Blizzard, Lizzie A. died 04/07/61   04/10/61
Blochburn, Margaret died 02/13/65   02/14/65
Blocher, Henry W. married Shurles, Laura V. 11/21/65   11/29/65
Block, Edward married Dallam, Mary A. 03/25/62   03/27/62
Block, Finley married Hickey, Rose Alphonso 06/29/64   07/15/64
Block, Henrietta married Murphy, William 10/07/61   10/12/61
Block, Henrietta married Wells, John 04/19/64   04/25/64
Block, Henrietta [retract] married Murphy, William [retract] no date
    10/15/61
Block, Henry married Mickel, Elizabeth 01/18/61   01/21/61
Blom, Christian died 01/01/62   01/03/62
Blondel, Emma J. married Virtue, A. M. 11/16/62   01/10/63
Blondheim, Kate married Seligman, Adolph 07/25/64   07/28/64
Blood, Phylura S. died 03/17/61   03/21/61
Blood, Phylura S. died no date   03/23/61
Bloodgood, Harry married Smith, Helena 09/08/64   09/14/64
Bloodsworth, Emma B. died 01/06/64   01/08/64
Bloodsworth, Henry died 01/13/63   01/14/64
Bloomer, Frederick died 04/22/62   04/25/62
Bloomer, Howard Wyatt died 03/06/61   03/08/61
Bloomer, William F. married White, Annie W. 08/17/63   08/19/63
Blue, Alice married Smith, Jacob 01/04/65   01/07/65
Blufford, William H. married Simmonds, Rachel 07/27/65   07/29/65
Blum, Jennie died 11/21/63   11/23/63
Blundan, Jane married Smith, James 01/16/62   01/18/62
Blundell, Catherine died 06/22/65   06/24/65
Blundell, Rose (Mrs.) died 03/16/64   03/18/64

Blundelle, Ellie died 10/25/63 10/26/63
Blunt, Bettie died 08/25/63 08/31/63
Blunt, Ella died 08/23/63 08/31/63
Blunt, Mary A. married Rusk, John G. 11/22/63 11/24/63
Blunt, Samuel died 08/29/63 08/31/63
Blunt, Sarah married Peregoy, John H. 12/28/62 12/30/62
Blunt, Sarah A. (Mrs.) died 12/11/63 12/31/63
Blunt, William H. married Dorsey, Lizzie M. 03/28/61 04/06/61
Blunt, William H. married Dorsey, Lizzie M. 03/28/61 04/08/61
Bly, Marion (Mrs.) died 03/06/63 03/07/63
Bly, William H. married Chaney, Mary L. 02/24/63 02/28/63
Boardman, Mary A. died 09/04/65 09/12/65
Boarman, George S. died 06/07/64 06/09/64
Boarman, Henrietta (Mrs.) died no date 03/09/63
Boarman, Loretta M. Leonora died 09/12/64 09/16/64
Boarman, William J. died 04/08/64 04/13/64
Bobart, Thomas W. married Edwards, Sarah A. 02/03/61 02/05/61
Bobb, John D., Jr. (Lt.) married McDonald, Mary H. 09/19/64 10/03/64
Bobeth, Matilda H. married Schmidt, Henry D. 03/27/62 04/04/62
Boblits, Jacob married Fillius, Olivia A. 07/04/65 07/10/65
Boblitz, George Wesley died 08/02/64 08/04/64
Boche, Charles M. married Elliott, Henrietta 08/03/64 08/04/64
Bode, Angela married Beresch, Karl 08/21/65 08/25/65
Boden, Elizabeth R. (Mrs.) died 05/26/63 05/27/63
Boden, John G. married Baker, Rebecca E. 06/06/61 06/11/61
Boden, John H. died 03/20/63 04/24/63
Bodensick, David died 08/14/63 08/15/63
Bodensick, E. Sophia married Brown, Cornelius A. 04/27/64 08/06/64
Bodensick, William T. married Stall, Lizzie A. 01/19/64 02/01/64
Bodine, John W. married Watkins, Eugenia E. 12/19/65 12/23/65
Boehm, Charles T. married Saurwein, Kates S. 10/10/61 10/11/61
Boehn, Susanna S. died 08/20/65 08/22/65
Boesche, Mary W. (Mrs.) died 11/27/63 11/28/63
Boesche, William Henry married Oetter, Margaret, Sophia 01/08/65
   01/10/65
Boeschi, Henry William married Meyer, Mary Williamina 11/30/62 12/10/
Boggess, William B. F. married Wright, Marcelline 09/28/63 10/07/63
Boggs, Augustus A. married Davis, Laura A. 12/14/65 12/21/65
Boggs, Harmanus died 06/27/63 06/29/63
Boggs, Margaret A. married Fisher, William 04/18/65 04/20/65
Boggs, William H. died 07/23/63 07/27/63
Bogle, Robert died 12/03/64 01/05/65
Bogue, Henry, Sr. died 12/02/63 12/04/63
Bogue, John Augustine died 12/25/65 12/28/65
Bogue, Maria died 08/08/61 08/09/61
Bogue, Michael died 08/25/65 08/26/65
Bogue, Robert H. died 08/07/62 08/09/62
Bohager, Samuel F. married McAdams, Rose E. 03/27/64 03/31/64
Bohanan, Laura A. married Bond, Julius A. 10/25/64 10/26/64
Bohen, Walter J. died 08/30/65 09/26/65
Bohlayer, John died 02/14/61 02/16/61
Bohrer, Benjamin S. died 04/16/62 04/17/62
Bohrer, Mary L. died 04/08/62 04/09/62
Boice, John F. died 03/31/65 04/01/65
Bokee, George M. died 04/01/64 04/02/64

Bokee, John Cramer died 07/03/63 07/04/63
Bokee, Margaret died 12/23/61 12/24/61
Bokee, Margaret Ann died 12/23/61 12/25/61
Bokee, W. A. died 10/28/64 10/29/64
Boland, Bridget (Mrs.) died 04/22/63 04/25/63
Boland, Catherine (Mrs.) died 01/22/63 01/24/63
Boland, Grace Mary died 04/09/63 04/25/63
Boland, Mary married Mooney, Richard 09/03/63 09/07/63
Bolderston, Amelia Emma married Dawson, William H. 11/01/64 11/07/64
Boldin, Samuel R. married Hennick, Josephine 11/22/64 12/05/64
Bolgiano, Anna Rawvey died 07/02/64 07/04/64
Bolgiano, Edward married McElroy, Catherine 05/14/61 05/16/61
Bolgiano, Elmira Grace died 06/28/64 06/29/64
Bolgiano, Frank W. married Ebaugh, Sallie T. 09/27/64 10/03/64
Bolgiano, Gilbert C. married Kirk, Ella E. 06/11/61 06/27/61
Bolgiano, Harry Ellsworth died 03/03/63 03/04/63
Bolgiano, Joseph A. married Walton, Mary E. 05/28/63 06/01/63
Bolgiano, Kate (Mrs.) died 08/28/63 08/29/63
Bolgiano, Laura Virginia died 01/24/61 01/26/61
Bolin, Joseph C. married Hill, Mary R. 07/24/64 07/30/64
Boller, Elizabeth (Mrs.) died 02/06/63 02/09/63
Boller, William married Messer, Annie Margaret 04/14/63 04/15/63
Bollman, Charles A. married Freburger, Sarah R. 12/06/64 12/14/64
Bollman, Margaret A. died 01/03/62 01/06/62
Bollmarr, John W. married DeMangin, Mary H. 06/16/64 06/28/64
Bolster, William H. died 03/03/64 03/15/64
Bolt, Edward J. died 10/10/64 10/12/64
Bolton, Anna L. married Phillips, Richard 05/09/65 05/15/65
Bolton, Henrietta died 02/13/63 02/14/63
Bolton, John H. married Taylor, Mary V. 05/07/63 05/11/63
Bolton, John H. (Dr., USA) married Hartzell, Frances A. 12/16/63 12/17/63
Bombarger, Milford Sylvester died 11/21/63 11/23/63
Bombarger, Willie Alfred died 02/07/63 02/09/63
Bomberger, Charles Edward died 12/19/63 12/21/63
Bommen, Clemen married Reed, Patsey 09/10/63 09/12/63
Bon, Charlotte died 10/07/64 10/08/64
Bond, Addie married Forwood, William Stump (Dr.) 05/06/63 05/07/63
Bond, Alice died 06/01/61 06/03/61
Bond, Anna Helena married Oehm, Francis F. 12/15/64 12/17/64
Bond, Benjamin married Simmonds, Sarah J. 12/24/61 12/25/61
Bond, Caroline married Turner, George 06/09/61 06/11/61
Bond, Caroline died 04/07/61 04/13/61
Bond, Catherine died 04/07/63 04/08/63
Bond, Edward F. died 09/04/64 09/17/64
Bond, Elizabeth died 01/22/61 01/23/61
Bond, Elizabeth died 01/22/61 01/24/61
Bond, Ellen L.(Mrs.) married Nichols, Zachariah 10/09/64 10/11/64
Bond, Emory died 08/11/62 08/12/62
Bond, Frances Isabella married Anderson, Moses T. 01/05/65 01/07/65
Bond, George W. married Reason, Ann Rebecca 12/21/62 12/23/62
Bond, Harriet A. married Kriete, August W. 09/27/65 10/05/65
Bond, Howard B. married Munnikhuysen, Mittie 01/15/61 01/18/61
Bond, Ida M. died 03/05/63 03/06/63
Bond, J. Oliver died 10/23/64 02/14/65

```
Bond, John W. died 12/12/62   12/15/62
Bond, John W. married Chase, Clementine G. 07/07/64   07/08/64
Bond, Joshua married Jackson, Naoma 10/29/63   10/31/63
Bond, Julius A. married Bohanan, Laura A. 10/25/64   10/26/64
Bond, Lambert W. died 06/24/61   06/25/61
Bond, Laura Jane C. married Gray, John H.W. 01/05/65   01/07/65
Bond, Laura Sophia (Mrs.) died 01/07/64   01/08/64
Bond, Laura Virginia died 07/23/63   07/27/63
Bond, Lewis Cass died 10/13/63   10/14/63
Bond, Lydia died 01/20/62   01/21/62
Bond, Margaret died 04/06/63   04/07/63
Bond, Marion Virginia died 12/27/64   12/29/64
Bond, Mary married Williams, Alexander 02/13/62   02/15/62
Bond, Mary (Mrs.) died 10/15/64   10/17/64
Bond, Mary C. died 08/30/62   09/01/62
Bond, Mary S. married Stokes, John 10/28/65   11/04/65
Bond, Rebecca married Guy, William 11/05/63   11/07/63
Bond, Sallie A. married Wright, J. Thomas 02/02/65   02/04/65
Bond, Stephen N. died 08/19/61   08/20/61
Bond, T. Beall married Jarvis, Hattie B. 11/13/65   11/15/65
Bond, Thomas died 08/29/61   09/02/61
Bond, Thomas Burgee died 08/15/64   08/22/64
Bond, Virginia D. (Mrs.) died 11/04/63   11/05/63
Bond, William died 07/20/63   07/22/63
Bond, Willie D. died 11/14/62   11/17/62
Bonday, Mary A. married Rummel, Charles V. (USN) 10/26/65   10/30/65
Bone, Ann Laura died 03/01/62   03/03/62
Bone, Mary Martha (Mrs.) died 10/16/63   10/20/63
Bone, William married Gill, Annie W. 05/11/65   05/18/65
Bone, William W. married Buckingham, Mary M. 03/27/62   03/29/62
Bonhage, Wilhemine (Mrs.) died 08/11/65   08/14/65
Bonine, Maria Louisa died 09/19/62   09/20/62
Bonn, Florence Maud died 08/01/64   08/04/64
Bonn, Florence Mead died 08/02/64   08/03/64
Bonn, Francis Cooper died 12/27/62   01/09/63
Bonn, Therine died 01/01/65   01/03/65
Bonner, Albert Sidney died 06/04/63   06/06/63
Bonner, Hugh died 11/16/64   11/21/64
Bonnett, Willie Isedore died 10/14/64   10/15/64
Bonsail, R. F. married Young, Laura 02/04/64   02/08/64
Bonsf, John died 09/08/64   09/09/64
Bontz, Jacob D. married Hunt, Joanna 01/01/63   01/03/63
Booker, Laura married Carroll, Jams A. 05/26/63   05/29/63
Booker, Virginia H. married Farmer, William A. 02/23/64   02/24/64
Bookman, Elenora (Mrs.) died 05/19/63   05/20/63
Bool, Mary A. married Dempster, Geoffrey E. 03/22/64   03/30/64
Boon, Benjamin died 04/05/64   04/06/64
Boon, Margaret C. died 02/07/62   02/08/62
Boon, Virginia Roberta died 01/17/65   01/18/65
Boon, Virginia Roberta died 01/17/65   01/19/65
Boone, Annie R. married Graham, James R. 04/20/65   04/25/65
Boone, Catherine Virginia died 08/14/62   08/15/62
Boone, Charles married Jenning, Hester 02/16/65   02/18/65
Boone, Denis married Pinkney, Ann 09/17/65   09/23/65
Boone, Edward Augustus died 01/09/65   01/10/65
```

Boone, Emma Jane married Brooks, John 11/02/65 11/04/65
Boone, Franky died 06/29/65 07/01/65
Boone, Gardiner S. died 06/21/62 06/23/62
Boone, Harriet Ann (Mrs.) died 04/02/63 04/04/63
Boone, James Nicholas died 10/31/61 11/04/61
Boone, Joshua married Richards, Hester A. 11/17/61 11/19/61
Boone, Maggie S. married Shitele, Charles W. 11/08/64 11/12/64
Boone, Margaret (Mrs.) died 12/21/64 12/24/64
Boone, Mary E. married Merriken, Franklin (Esq.) 12/29/63 01/01/64
Boone, Thomas C. married Gambril, Mary A. 03/08/64 03/09/64
Boone, William died 01/14/61 01/31/61
Boone, William Joseph died 02/28/65 03/01/65
Booper, Harriet died 10/02/62 10/04/62
Boose, Elizabeth Ann married Jenkins, Philip 10/20/63 10/22/63
Booser, George S. died 06/01/63 06/02/63
Booth, Elizabeth died 11/03/62 11/04/62
Booth, Elizabeth died 11/02/62 11/05/62
Booth, Henrietta died 11/03/62 11/05/62
Booth, Henry A. married Harris, Frances B. 09/21/63 10/08/63
Booth, James H. died 01/29/64 01/30/64
Booth, James Lawrence Coe died 09/16/64 09/17/64
Booth, Maria E. married Watts, William K. 11/10/63 11/16/63
Booth, Mary died 09/28/62 10/06/62
Booth, Mary A. died 05/06/64 05/07/64
Booth, Mary Emma died 09/10/64 09/17/64
Booth, Mary H. (Mrs.) died 06/25/64 06/29/64
Booth, Mollie J. died 01/29/65 01/30/65
Booth, Teresa died 07/26/61 07/29/61
Booth, William married Deaver, Sallie R. 07/30/61 07/31/61
Boothes, Jonathan C. died 03/28/64 03/29/64
Bootman, John W. married Sapp, Martha 02/23/65 02/25/65
Booz, Edward G. married Jordan, Matilda 08/21/64 08/25/64
Booz, Henry P. married Silver, Mary E. 09/24/65 09/27/65
Booz, Mary Elizabeth died 12/05/63 12/07/63
Booz, Thomas H. died 11/21/64 11/24/64
Booz, William Barry married Bean, Mary Ellen 12/03/65 12/06/65
Booz, Willie Edwin died 10/23/61 10/25/61
Booze, Aliceann died 04/27/65 04/29/65
Booze, Elizabeth died 07/22/62 07/23/62
Booze, Lizzie Emma died 11/09/62 11/11/62
Boozer, George S. died 06/01/63 06/03/63
Bopp, Charles L. married Kalvelage, Annie M. 08/16/64 08/17/64
Bopp, Kate married Dorm, Jacob 08/25/63 08/31/63
Bopp, Lawrence married Lloyd, Mary 01/07/62 01/09/62
Borain, William H. married Williamson, Elizabeth A. 02/25/64 03/09/64
Borderly, Margaret A. married Ridgeway, William H. 02/04/64 02/05/64
Bordley, Ellen Barron died 09/18/63 09/19/63
Bordley, Hester married Shipley, Richard 10/21/62 10/22/62
Bordley, Maggie V. married Robinson, John W. 06/11/65 06/14/65
Bordley, Sallie W. (Mrs.) died 10/30/63 11/03/63
Borgalt, Sarah A. (Mrs.) died 11/11/64 11/12/64
Borgono, Manuella married Heuisler, Joseph G. no date 03/18/65
Bork, Johanna married Chalan, Joseph 05/16/63 05/18/63
Borland, Margaret E. died 06/30/63 07/07/63
Bornheim, Hannah married Emerich, Lewis 11/13/64 11/15/64

```
Bornkeim, Hannah married Emerich, Lewis 11/13/64   11/15/64
Bortle, Lysander married Oursien, Matilda P. 12/15/64   12/17/64
Borum, Sallie F. married Fogle, John H. 08/15/65   08/18/65
Bose, Matilda died 06/02/64   06/04/64
Bose, William married Gilder, Elizabeth E. 01/17/61   01/18/61
Boshamer, John C. married McLean, Mary G. 12/07/63   12/15/63
Boshammer, Conrad died 10/08/64   10/10/64
Boshammer, John C. married McLean, Mary G. 12/07/63   12/24/63
Bosler, Nellie died 11/01/61   11/02/61
Bosley, Benjamin died 01/23/64   01/28/64
Bosley, Catherine Stinner died 11/03/63   11/04/63
Bosley, Elizabeth (Mrs.) died 07/07/64   07/09/64
Bosley, Ellenor died no date   07/08/61
Bosley, Emma E. married Lambert, John 03/09/65   03/29/65
Bosley, John C. married Montgomery, Annie T. 05/01/62   05/08/62
Bosley, John Scott died 06/23/65   06/28/65
Bosley, Matilda died 03/27/63   03/31/63
Bosley, Olivia R. married Doe, William R. 06/20/62   10/15/62
Bosley, Peter died 09/10/62   10/08/62
Bosley, Priscilla Ann died 07/07/63   08/01/63
Bosley, Rebecca E. married Wooden, John Lee 04/20/62   04/23/62
Bosley, Rosalla A. married Bedford, John R. D. 08/11/64   08/13/64
Bosley, S. Anna married Anderson, Samuel Marryman 11/01/64   11/05/64
Bosley, Susan M. died 06/17/62   05/20/62
Bosley, William married Evans, Nellie T. 06/19/61   06/22/61
Bosley, William died 06/24/62   06/26/62
Bosley, William died 01/29/63   01/30/63
Bosley, William died 02/17/63   02/19/63
Bosley, William H. married Foose, Ann 11/30/65   12/04/65
Bosman, James E. died 03/21/65   03/24/65
Bosnal, T. S. married Huff, Sarah S. 12/27/65   12/30/65
Boss, Isaac died 12/15/61   12/16/61
Boss, Isaac died 12/15/61   12/17/61
Boss, Margaret died 11/17/64   11/18/64
Boss, Margaret died 11/17/64   11/19/64
Boss, Mary died 07/26/65   07/27/65
Boss, Mary died 07/26/65   07/28/65
Boss, Sophia died 06/21/64   06/22/64
Bosserman, Minnie married Lockwood, Elison J. 12/09/60   07/13/61
Bossle, Joseph C. married Albert, Mary E. 06/27/65   06/30/65
Bossle, Lizzie died 01/27/65   01/30/65
Bosson, Franklin H. died 07/09/65   07/10/65
Bosson, James W., Jr. married Brady, Mary Catherine 09/08/63   09/12/63
Bosson, Mary Jane died 09/06/63   09/07/63
Bostick, Cecelia died 03/26/65   03/30/65
Bostick, Joseph died 01/16/64   01/21/64
Bostick, Sarah F. married Sakers, John S. 09/29/64   10/11/64
Boston, Abram married Butler, Isabella M. 09/04/62   09/06/62
Boston, Amelia died 06/21/62   06/23/62
Boston, Charles H. H. died 11/10/61   11/12/61
Boston, Daniel married Barnes, Ann Rebecca 10/22/63   10/26/63
Boston, Daniel died 07/19/65   07/20/65
Boston, Elizabeth Ann died 07/30/64   08/03/64
Boston, Harriet died 10/27/61   11/02/61
Boston, John B. died 08/14/62   08/15/62
```

```
Boston, John B. died 08/14/62  08/16/62
Boston, Joseph married Carr, Martha no date  12/22/64
Boston, Nelson married Butler, Harriet A.  04/03/63  04/04/63
Boston, Priscilla married Mahorney, Henson  10/13/64  10/14/64
Boston, Sarah Ann married Bias, Horace  09/01/64  09/02/64
Boston, William T. married Cole, Eliza  12/24/62  12/30/62
Boswell, B. S. married Gault, Lucy  12/12/61  12/23/61
Boswell, Ellen J. (Mrs.) died 09/17/63  09/19/63
Boswell, Fannie married Clark, William A.  02/03/65  02/07/65
Boswell, George Arthur died 06/09/65  06/13/65
Boswell, Matilda A. married Jones, James M.  12/07/65  12/12/65
Boswell, Milton A. married Taliaferro, Susie P.  03/29/64  04/05/64
Boswell, Otho, Jr. died 07/14/65  07/17/65
Bosworth, John married Tippett, Margaret  07/26/63  07/28/63
Boteler, Andrew K. married Smith, Eleanor DeF.  01/04/65  01/06/65
Boteler, Arthur died no date  04/04/65
Boteler, Charles J. married Shaw, Leila E.  07/01/62  07/07/62
Boteler, Charlotte R. married Johnson, George M.  06/30/64  07/04/64
Boteler, Edward D. married Cole, Mittie  01/06/63  01/10/63
Boteler, Eleanor Amelia died 08/29/63  08/31/63
Boteler, Ellen A. married Green, Harrison, B.  11/26/63  12/09/63
Boteler, Emma T. married Carter, John W.  03/22/64  03/23/64
Boteler, Emma T. married Coster, J. W.  03/22/64  03/31/64
Boteler, Mattie W. married Garrott, William M.  11/19/63  12/07/63
Botrell, John died 02/04/62  02/05/62
Botte, Simon died 11/20/61  11/21/61
Bottimore, Amelia (Mrs.) died 04/13/65  04/15/65
Bottomer, Thomas died 11/13/63  11/14/63
Bottomore, Jane A. married Grooms, Thomas  05/07/63  05/19/63
Bottrell, Fannie died 01/17/62  01/18/62
Boucher, Maria Josephine died 07/03/63  07/04/63
Boucher, Mary Agnes (Mrs.) died 11/15/64  11/17/64
Boucher, William married Giles, Fannie  05/15/65  05/16/65
Bouchet, Anna M. married Kimball, Ephraim C.  12/03/63  12/08/63
Bouchet, James H. died 03/03/62  03/04/62
Bouchet, John M. married Brown, Lizzie  07/26/64  08/02/64
Bouis, Clara B. died 05/02/65  05/03/65
Bouis, Florence M. died 10/31/65  11/01/65
Bouis, John H. married Arthur, Fannie A.  12/23/63  12/25/63
Bouis, Maria Helen died 05/07/64  05/09/64
Boulden, Jarred C. married Johnson, Kate E.  05/23/61  05/28/61
Boulden, Jesse C. married Johnson, Kate E.  05/23/61  05/25/61
Boulder, Jared C. died 10/16/64  10/18/64
Bouldin, Alexina married Stevens, F. P.  09/27/64  09/30/64
Bouldin, Belle V. married Cadden, J. R.  04/04/65  04/15/65
Bouldin, Harriet died 05/10/64  05/12/64
Bouldin, John L. died 10/07/64  10/08/64
Bouldin, Richard E. married Gough, Martha C.  02/04/64  02/06/64
Bouldin, Spencer died 03/16/65  03/17/65
Boult, Jeanette N. married Cathell, Daniel W.  11/19/63  11/23/63
Boulton, Maggie married Freeburger, Alexander  10/05/62  10/06/62
Bountz, Jacob T. married Hunt, Joanna  01/01/63  01/02/63
Bourguet, Marie A. married Heut, Augustin, Jr.  04/09/61  05/10/61
Bourke, John W. married Raborg, Henrietta S.  11/14/61  11/16/61
Boury, Edward De Larue died 01/23/63  01/30/63
```

Boury, Mollie F. married Mattingly, John H. 01/08/61   01/09/61
Bouse, Thomas J. married Hasleys, Annie Augusta 01/29/65   02/04/65
Bouse, Thomas J. married Haslup, Annie Augusta 01/19/65   02/06/65
Boush, Jerry married Carr, Gustine 05/11/63   05/12/63
Boutwell, Minson W. married Freeman, Mary A. 03/14/64   03/17/64
Bouzer, Alfred died 05/07/62   05/09/62
Bowdle, Sheldon Slater died 10/26/63   10/28/63
Bowdle, Sheldon Slater died 10/26/63   10/29/63
Bowdoin, Lavinia T. E. died 04/16/64   04/18/64
Bowen, A. Evan married Richardson, Tillie B. 08/02/62   04/04/63
Bowen, Annie M. died 12/27/63   08/09/64
Bowen, Annie M. died 12/27/63   08/10/64
Bowen, Clara Bell died 09/18/65   09/20/65
Bowen, Cora Elizabeth died 07/03/63   07/04/63
Bowen, Edward married Raves, Emma 12/25/62   12/29/62
Bowen, Edward Parker died 04/27/62   05/05/62
Bowen, Elizabeth A. married Delcher, James A. 04/19/65   05/10/65
Bowen, Elizabeth C. married Wood, Benjamin F. 03/08/64   03/11/64
Bowen, Emily married Ross, James 12/20/61   12/31/61
Bowen, Emma A. married Reed, George B. W. 09/09/62   09/25/62
Bowen, Emma J. died 04/25/61   04/30/61
Bowen, Henry married Benson, Emily 03/29/64   04/20/64
Bowen, Hettie died 12/12/63   12/14/63
Bowen, Jesse died 03/10/64   03/11/64
Bowen, Jesse N. married Hall, Mary A. 06/07/64   06/13/64
Bowen, John F. died 05/16/62   05/17/62
Bowen, John H. married Thomas, Desdemona 12/16/62   12/23/62
Bowen, John L. married Phillips, Jennie 04/02/63   05/20/63
Bowen, Josie married Betts, Solomon (Dr.) 06/07/65   06/10/65
Bowen, Louisiana C. died 07/28/61   11/20/61
Bowen, Marion A. died 07/30/64   08/09/64
Bowen, Marion A. died 07/30/64   08/10/64
Bowen, Martha Jane died 11/24/62   11/25/62
Bowen, Martha Jane died 11/24/62   11/26/62
Bowen, Mary married Spencer, W. A. R. 08/11/64   06/09/65
Bowen, Mary E. married Rodgers, Joseph 09/19/61   09/21/61
Bowen, Mary J. died no date   09/30/63
Bowen, Thomas H. married Armstrong, Elizabeth 04/27/65   05/02/65
Bowen, Thomas H. married Armstrong, Elizabeth 04/27/65   05/03/65
Bowen, William H. married Butler, Margret A. 06/04/63   08/13/63
Bower, Edward Lewis died 04/08/62   04/09/62
Bower, Elizabeth married Stocksdale, E. C. 01/17/65   01/18/65
Bower, Kate Peck died 10/29/61   10/31/61
Bower, Lewis M. married Coriell, Mary E. 01/28/62   01/31/62
Bowers, Ann Virginia died 04/01/61   04/04/61
Bowers, Elizabeth died 07/07/61   07/08/61
Bowers, Elizabeth died 03/07/64   03/08/64
Bowers, Esther Gruber died 10/12/64   10/14/64
Bowers, George L. died 06/30/65   07/03/65
Bowers, George W. (Capt.) died 06/13/62   06/14/62
Bowers, Isabella F. married Gralle, A. K. 04/18/61   04/22/61
Bowers, Mary Ann (Mrs.) died 08/09/63   08/10/63
Bowers, William married Smith, Elizabeth 06/16/64   07/11/64
Bowersox, David M. married Paxton, Zelia E. 08/17/62   08/29/62
Bowerstock, Austin married Curtis, Emma 12/31/62   01/07/63

Bowes, Ann Jane died 12/15/63 12/17/63
Bowes, William M. died 01/15/63 01/17/63
Bowhan, John W. died 05/01/62 05/02/62
Bowie, Charles married Richardson, Isabella W. 01/29/61 01/31/61
Bowie, Charles T. died 11/27/62 12/08/62
Bowie, David H. married Rannelbarger, Sallie E. 07/07/64 07/09/64
Bowie, M. Augusta married Lindsley, Cleland 01/25/65 01/27/65
Bowie, M. M. (Mrs.) died 12/16/63 12/18/63
Bowie, Sarah J. married Yearly, Aquilla A. 07/12/65 08/24/65
Bowie, William J. married Atwell, S. Frances 10/13/62 04/20/63
Bowin, Margaret H. married Carter, Thomas 12/01/64 12/14/64
Bowles, Martha died 02/01/61 02/11/61
Bowling, Henry J. died 11/26/65 11/28/65
Bowling, James T. married Crozier, Maggie A. 03/16/65 03/17/65
Bowling, John J. married Neale, Susannah Evelina 10/22/65 10/27/65
Bowling, Sophia C. died 08/06/65 08/08/65
Bowlings, Susia married Mitchell, George W. (Cpt.) 12/16/63 12/19/63
Bowly, Francis R. died 05/19/62 05/21/62
Bowly, Mary married Richardson, Geoffrey I. 03/08/64 03/10/64
Bowly, Samuel H. died 02/12/61 02/15/61
Bowman, Emma married Jackson, Jeremiah 01/22/65 01/28/65
Bowman, Henry C. married Roberts, Sarah B. 05/18/65 05/26/65
Bowman, Jane (Mrs.) married Davis, John 05/01/64 05/09/64
Bowman, Mary Alice married Beon, John M. 11/02/65 11/04/65
Bowman, Mary Alice married Brown, John M. 11/02/65 11/10/65
Bowman, Mary E. married Upperman, Thomas 02/18/64 02/23/64
Bowman, Sophie married Winemuller, L. F. 10/25/63 11/20/63
Bowne, Mary E. married Farenger, Benjamin F. 11/03/64 02/09/65
Bowser, Ellen died 06/21/62 07/11/62
Bowser, Samuel B. married Shenck, Lilly 03/05/63 03/12/63
Bowyer, Joanna married Cook, William V. 12/17/63 12/19/63
Bowyer, Mary Fanny died 07/02/62 07/09/62
Bowyer, Susan Ann died 09/20/65 09/21/65
Bowzer, Alfred died 05/07/62 05/08/62
Boxald, George H. died 06/07/61 06/10/61
Boxold, Mary Ann Ellis died 06/27/65 06/28/65
Boxwell, Lizzie Jane died 06/18/61 06/19/61
Boyce, Anne Jane died 09/05/62 09/06/62
Boyce, Frederick W. married Davis, Laura V. 08/18/64 08/26/64
Boyce, James married Moore, Elizabeth 09/27/61 10/01/61
Boyce, Joshua died 10/21/62 10/22/62
Boyd, Amelia died 04/07/62 04/14/62
Boyd, Annie C. married Jamison, John 05/19/64 05/21/64
Boyd, Augusta Viola died 09/29/65 10/04/65
Boyd, Benjamin F. married Schaefer, Elizabeth 06/26/65 07/04/65
Boyd, Catherine (Mrs.) married Haswell, John 12/29/64 12/31/64
Boyd, Charles W. died 08/21/61 09/13/61
Boyd, Edward G. died 10/12/62 10/14/62
Boyd, Elizabeth died 04/30/62 05/02/62
Boyd, Elizabeth died 09/07/64 09/13/64
Boyd, Elizabeth A. married Meyers, Nelson B. 10/19/65 10/24/65
Boyd, Ella Therese died 02/23/61 02/25/61
Boyd, Florence Virginia died 06/07/64 06/09/64
Boyd, George S. died 11/10/64 11/11/64
Boyd, Henrietta married Dodd, John 05/26/63 05/27/63

Boyd, Henry C. died no date 03/31/62
Boyd, J. L. married Betts, Maggie 07/05/64 07/07/64
Boyd, James Increase died 04/29/65 05/01/65
Boyd, John E. married Stewart, Elizabeth A. 02/17/61 02/20/61
Boyd, John, Jr. died no date 10/22/63
Boyd, John, Jr. died no date 09/22/63
Boyd, Joseph died 02/11/65 02/13/65
Boyd, Joseph C. died 08/06/61 08/07/61
Boyd, Joseph C. died 08/06/61 08/08/61
Boyd, Joseph E. married Rolston, Annie M. W. 06/16/63 06/17/63
Boyd, Joseph H., Jr. died 05/04/62 05/05/62
Boyd, Margaret A. married Stetten, Robert A. 07/16/63 07/21/63
Boyd, Margaret Ann (Mrs.) died 01/05/63 01/06/63
Boyd, Mary (Mrs.) died 02/22/65 02/28/65
Boyd, Mary E. married Carroll, D. H. 07/06/65 07/15/65
Boyd, Robert died 07/03/64 07/07/64
Boyd, Robert Lee died 11/30/65 12/01/65
Boyd, Sarah died 11/18/64 11/22/64
Boyd, Vianna A. died 11/09/62 11/11/62
Boyd, William Frank died 05/31/63 06/01/63
Boyd, William Henry died 01/22/63 01/26/63
Boyer, Bill Everett died 07/14/64 07/16/64
Boyer, John married Driscoll, Lucy 11/01/64 11/04/64
Boyer, John W. died 12/19/64 12/20/64
Boyer, Margaret married McQuinn, John S. 04/21/64 05/05/64
Boyer, Rachel A. married Harmon, John F. 02/25/64 03/03/64
Boyer, Willie died 09/12/61 09/13/61
Boylan, Mary died 06/28/64 06/29/64
Boylan, Mary died 03/08/65 03/10/65
Boylan, Mary (Mrs.) died 03/08/65 03/09/65
Boyle, Arthur P. died 06/24/63 07/28/63
Boyle, Cornelia married Watts, Nathaniel S. 02/09/64 02/11/64
Boyle, Eugene died 09/23/63 09/25/63
Boyle, Francis A. married Hemmick, Annie A. 10/19/65 10/31/65
Boyle, James died 08/01/62 08/02/62
Boyle, James A. married Hooper, Julia A. 09/01/62 09/06/62
Boyle, John J. died 07/10/65 07/11/65
Boyle, John James died 07/10/65 07/11/65
Boyle, John S. died 03/11/62 03/13/62
Boyle, Joshua Y. married Caldwell, Margaret A. 09/16/62 09/26/62
Boyle, Lizzie Jane died 07/25/63 07/28/63
Boyle, Maggie Caldwell died 01/26/64 01/28/64
Boyle, Mary married Fester, John 03/01/63 03/05/63
Boyle, Mary married Kilmartin, Bernard no date 11/30/64
Boyle, Mary (Mrs.) died 06/11/63 06/17/63
Boyle, Mary E. married Braden, George W. 02/12/61 02/19/61
Boyle, Mary Olivia (Mrs.) died 11/18/63 11/19/63
Boyle, Molley died no date 06/20/63
Boyle, Mollie died 06/19/63 07/28/63
Boyle, Susan married Pearson, William 04/18/64 04/21/64
Boyle, Susan (Mrs.) died 01/27/64 02/01/64
Boyle, William Matthew died 01/24/64 01/30/64
Boylen, Ellen (Mrs.) died 06/23/63 06/25/63
Boyne, Mary A. died 01/15/63 01/21/63
Boze, Michael died 08/04/63 08/05/63

Bozman, Edward married Warrick, C. (Mrs.) 11/10/64 11/12/64
Bozman, Frances (Mrs.) died 03/05/65 03/06/65
Braby, Harriet married Jones, William 08/10/65 08/25/65
Bracheley, Anna Winfred died 05/14/62 05/15/62
Bracken, John F. married Toner, Annie E. 05/15/65 05/29/65
Brackenridge, Susan married Ruberg, William. 08/19/63 09/08/63
Brackett, Mary (Mrs.) died 05/04/63 05/07/63
Bracklinridge, Thomas died 09/14/62 09/15/62
Brackson, Mary E. married Broson, David W. 01/16/62 04/01/62
Bradbury, John T. died 02/28/64 09/13/64
Braddock, Laura married Wason, James 02/14/65 02/15/65
Braden, George W. married Boyle, Mary E. 02/12/61 02/19/61
Braden, George Washington died 03/17/63 03/24/63
Bradenbaugh, Charles died 04/16/62 04/17/62
Bradey, Joseph A. (Rev.) married Heron, Mary D. 12/28/64 12/31/64
Bradford, Alexander married Macfarlan, Harriet 05/17/62 05/19/62
Bradford, George K. died 12/26/63 01/26/64
Bradford, George K. died no date 03/08/64
Bradford, H. Harrison married Shekell, Annie W. 06/22/65 06/27/65
Bradford, Isaiah died 03/02/61 03/04/61
Bradford, James T. married Wells, Josephine 11/16/65 11/18/65
Bradford, Joseph married Alligood, Maria 01/01/61 01/11/61
Bradford, Rosa married Morrow, Thomas G. 09/08/63 09/12/63
Bradley, A. H. married Gates, Sallie M. 11/08/64 11/14/64
Bradley, A. Thomas married Hughes, Mary A. C. 04/09/63 04/15/63
Bradley, Bridget (Mrs.) died 07/07/63 07/11/63
Bradley, Euphpasia died 09/19/65 09/21/65
Bradley, John F. married Hutchins, Harriet L. 10/23/64 10/29/64
Bradley, Mary A. C. (Mrs.) died 10/13/64 10/14/64
Bradley, Mary Ann died 02/22/61 02/23/61
Bradley, Nannie R. married Clarkson, William W. 03/07/65 05/22/65
Bradley, Philip died 03/28/62 03/29/62
Bradley, Samuel died 07/30/64 08/03/64
Bradley, Thomas B. married Coniken, Hannah E. 07/02/63 07/03/63
Bradley, William Edgar died 10/29/65 10/31/65
Bradley, Wilson married Walter, Sarah E. 08/30/64 08/31/64
Bradon, George Washington died 03/16/63 03/19/63
Brads, Ella Cecilia married Brooks, Christopher C. 01/15/61 01/16/61
Bradshaw, John J. married Tomlinson, Helen A. 01/05/65 01/07/65
Bradshaw, John Julius (Cpt.) married Everhart, Lucille V. 12/26/62
    01/30/63
Bradt, Henry Walter married Gardiner, Ida 08/16/65 08/19/65
Brady, Andrew died 02/05/64 02/06/64
Brady, Anna married Smith, Henry 09/13/65 09/18/65
Brady, Bettie M. married Hauptman, George W. 10/13/63 10/15/63
Brady, Catharine married Umbrage, Joseph 04/06/63 04/13/63
Brady, Curtis P. married Kern, Eleanora 03/03/63 03/06/63
Brady, Frances M. married Westervelt, J. Franklin 01/30/63 02/04/63
Brady, Greenbury died 11/01/64 11/03/64
Brady, James T. died 06/15/65 06/16/65
Brady, John died 09/08/61 09/09/61
Brady, Lawrence Eugene died 10/17/64 10/19/64
Brady, Margaret married Mullen, Timothy 04/27/62 04/29/62
Brady, Margaret married Shields, James 06/22/62 06/24/62
Brady, Martha C. married Kavanagh, James J. 04/17/65 04/26/65

Brady, Mary married Knock, Patrick 12/03/63   01/05/64
Brady, Mary Catherine married Bosson, James W., Jr. 09/08/63   09/12/63
Brady, Mary Frances died 06/03/64   06/07/64
Brady, Patrick married Kenan, Anna 01/12/62   01/13/62
Brady, Samuel married Stiver, Bridget M. (Mrs.) 08/31/64   09/03/64
Brady, Thomas married Kavanaugh, Kate M. A. 08/21/64   08/23/64
Brady, William Granger died 08/02/63   08/08/63
Bradyhouse, Arabella married Wheeden, Thomas J. 07/22/62   09/05/62
Bradyhouse, Frances (Mrs.) died 11/04/63   11/06/63
Bradyhouse, Frances E. (Mrs.) died 11/04/63   11/05/63
Bradyhouse, Thomas married Dunn, Mathilda A. 10/31/64   11/01/64
Bradyhouse, William Elbert died 10/18/61   10/19/61
Brafman, Dora died 04/07/62   04/08/62
Braid, Charles married Dalrymple, Janette S. 11/24/63   11/28/63
Brainard, Eugenie S. married Watkins, Nicholas A. 02/26/65   03/16/65
Brainard, Rufus A. married Elder, Clay 02/09/65   03/06/65
Brainard, Virginia E. married Walters, John W. 01/26/65   01/27/65
Bramble, Amanda F. died 05/05/62   05/06/62
Bramble, Barzilla married Jones, Derinda L. C. 06/16/63   06/18/63
Bramble, Grason married Smith, Mary E. 07/05/65   07/15/65
Bramble, Harriet Elizabeth married Claypoole, George W. 04/12/64
   04/15/64
Bramble, Martha Louisa died 08/29/64   08/30/64
Bramble, Solomon Lewis died 10/02/65   10/03/65
Bramble, Zorah E. married Krager, Elizabeth E. 09/25/62   10/15/62
Brampton, Samuel Thomas married Johnston, Caroline 02/18/61   02/21/61
Bramwell, Cecilia married Howser, Gassaway S. 01/16/62   01/18/62
Bramwell, George died 06/02/63   06/04/63
Branan, Eleanor E. married Haberman, Frederick 06/01/65   06/20/65
Branan, Fletcher Webster died 08/20/63   08/22/63
Branan, James A. died 11/11/64   11/15/64
Brandenburg, Frederick William married Seibel, Gertrude E. 06/07/64
   06/10/64
Brandt, Barbara E. married Sutton, Samuel 06/08/63   06/09/63
Brandy, Michael Thomas died 01/23/64   01/27/64
Branin, Ann died 10/27/63   10/29/63
Brannan, Bernard died 10/07/61   10/08/61
Brannan, Charles H. S. married Dixon, Margaret M. 02/07/61   02/19/61
Brannan, Eliza (Mrs.) died 08/02/63   08/03/63
Brannan, James A. married Hall, Emily C. 09/25/60   01/30/61
Brannan, John E. died 11/08/64   11/10/64
Brannan, Laura married Smith, R. Stump 12/16/62   12/18/62
Brannan, Minnie died 07/10/65   07/12/65
Brannan, Randall B. died no date   03/27/61
Brannan, Rebecca married Bugel, Joseph S. 06/15/65   06/20/65
Brannan, Sue married Gorrell, Henry S. 01/01/61   01/03/61
Brannan, Thomas died 10/02/64   10/03/64
Brannan, Thomas married Smith, F. Gist (Mrs.) 01/01/65   02/28/65
Brannan, Virginia Richmond died 09/14/63   09/16/63
Brannen, Frances died 11/11/61   11/13/61
Brannon, Elizabeth died 09/27/65   09/29/65
Brannon, Elizabeth (Mrs.) died 09/27/65   09/28/65
Brannon, Mary died 04/18/65   04/19/65
Brannon, Rebecca (Mrs.) died 03/13/65   03/14/65
Branon, Eliza married Carle, John H. 04/06/63   06/26/63

Branon, Michael died 02/24/63 02/25/63
Bransby, George Washington died 11/28/63 12/02/63
Bransby, Sarah Addison died 11/27/63 12/02/63
Bransby, Susannah (Mrs.) died 06/09/63 06/11/63
Branscombe, Robert W. (Cpt.) died 08/27/64 10/03/64
Branscombe, Robert W. (Cpt.) died 08/23/64 10/04/64
Branson, Isabella (Mrs.) married Williams, Levi 05/01/64 05/06/64
Branson, Mary died 11/04/62 11/05/62
Brant, Martha A. married Rothrock, Thomas 12/10/61 02/07/62
Brashear, William G. married Pattison, Mary E. 03/02/65 03/06/65
Brashears, Alexander died 02/27/64 03/01/64
Brashears, Elizabeth D. married Hopkins, William E. 01/03/61 01/08/61
Brashears, Rebecca A. died 10/26/61 10/28/61
Brass, Ann married Dawalt, Alexander 09/25/65 09/27/65
Brass, James H. married Preiter, Louisa M. 03/28/65 04/05/65
Bratt, Ada died 07/17/62 07/19/62
Bratt, Florence Augusta died 08/16/61 08/19/61
Bratt, John Thomas died no date 03/24/65
Bratt, John Thomas married Bratt, Martha Ellen 09/18/65 09/22/65
Bratt, Martha Ellen married Bratt, John Thomas 09/18/65 09/22/65
Bratt, Samuel died 04/28/65 05/03/65
Bratt, Sarah A. married Latimer, James 09/24/62 09/27/62
Bratt, Thomas died 06/01/64 06/02/64
Bratt, Wesley Charles died 01/11/64 01/12/64
Braul, Louise died 02/07/65 02/08/65
Brawner, Catherine Louise M. died 04/30/61 05/01/61
Bray, William A. died 12/12/63 12/15/63
Brayshaw, Mary died 04/04/61 04/18/61
Brayshaw, Mary married Childs, John P. 11/12/65 11/14/65
Brazier, Robert died 06/09/63 06/11/63
Brazier, Sarah (Mrs.) died 12/15/65 12/16/65
Brazier, William H. died 09/17/65 09/18/65
Bready, Ellen died 09/08/61 09/09/61
Bready, G. C. married Putts, Mary M. 11/03/62 11/06/62
Brecht, Ernest F. married Tustin, Clara E. 07/06/64 07/09/64
Brecht, Ernest F. R. married Tustin, Clara E. 07/06/64 07/11/64
Brecht, Theodore C. married Voss, Louisa A. 06/12/62 06/17/62
Breck, Charles J. married Valen, Francina T. 01/03/64 01/08/64
Breckenridge, John C. married Callow, Catherine 03/31/64 04/02/64
Breckenridge, Mary C. (Mrs.) died 10/08/64 10/10/64
Breckenridge, Philip married Thornton, Julia 10/23/64 10/26/64
Bredemeyer, Bettie (Mrs.) died 09/15/65 09/16/65
Breen, J. C. died 01/02/64 02/03/64
Breen, James C. married Bryant, Mary E. 01/02/63 06/05/63
Breen, Maggie married Lafevre, Charles E. 11/23/65 12/02/65
Bregel, Elizabeth married Scherer, Frederick H. 12/25/62 12/30/62
Bregel, Margaret A. married Kerndl, Charles 04/15/62 04/23/62
Bregel, Mary Rebecca married Tadgenhorst, Frederick William 08/14/64
    08/17/64
Brehme, Ottomar Traugott died 05/04/65 05/05/65
Bremer, Henry married Easter, A. M. 05/09/61 05/22/61
Bremer, William Louis died 09/04/63 09/05/63
Brenaman, Charles H. married Richardson, Sadie M. 11/21/63 12/01/63
Brenan, Adele married Coonan, M. J. 01/08/63 01/09/63
Brenan, Bridget Minna died 10/17/63 10/19/63

Brenan, Francis Xavier died 06/23/65 06/26/65
Brenen, Cecelia died 06/17/64 06/23/64
Brengle, E. Jane married Tyler, R. Bradley (Dr.) 11/15/65 11/30/65
Brengle, James S. married Gaw, M. Annie 04/27/65 05/02/65
Brennan, Frances M. (Mrs.) died 12/28/63 12/30/63
Brennan, Lewis Oliver died 07/17/64 07/19/64
Brennan, Mary died 10/27/65 10/31/65
Brennen, James F. married Barickman, Mary Ann 04/02/63 04/13/63
Brenner, Sarah married Myers, Lewis 09/21/64 09/22/64
Brenner, Sarah married Myers, Lewis 09/21/64 09/23/64
Brent, Anna died 10/11/62 12/01/62
Brent, Catherine R. married Brooks, Albert J. 04/06/62 04/29/62
Brent, Florence C. married Wilson, James (USA) 07/24/63 07/27/63
Brent, Robert died 01/08/64 01/26/64
Brent, William L. married Corbin, Julie A. 04/02/63 04/28/63
Bresnahan, Catherine married Dengel, Philip H. 04/06/63 04/08/63
Breuhl, Annie E. married Denty, Louis 08/10/64 08/17/64
Breuning, Annie married Thoman, John 11/26/63 11/28/63
Brevitt, Joseph W. married Walker, Rachel 12/02/62 12/06/62
Brewer, Catharine died no date 11/22/62
Brewer, Charles died 07/19/61 07/20/61
Brewer, D. R. (Dr.) married O'Dell, Alexina 12/26/65 12/30/65
Brewer, Fanny A. married Buckley, Charles R. 11/29/62 01/01/63
Brewer, G.G. married Sullivan, Julia M. 04/10/61 04/17/61
Brewer, George G. died 06/09/61 06/10/61
Brewer, Henry Nicholas died 10/16/64 10/21/64
Brewer, Jennie married Thompson, J. C. 12/10/62 01/30/63
Brewer, Jennie married Thompson, S. C. 12/10/62 01/31/63
Brewer, Josephine M. died 06/03/64 06/07/64
Brewer, Marbury married Strandley, Albina D. 04/30/62 05/03/62
Brewer, Sarah Rebecca died 03/07/65 03/09/65
Brewer, Vincent married Reid, Ellen E. (Mrs.) 02/19/63 02/25/63
Brewerton, Henry (USA) married Courtenay, Sarah 04/20/64 04/21/64
Brewster, Sarah Emily died 10/05/65 10/07/65
Brian, Deborah died 12/10/62 12/11/62
Brian, Edward died 02/25/63 02/26/63
Brian, Edward died 02/25/63 02/27/63
Brian, George Marion died 01/19/64 01/21/64
Brian, Hannah married Hill, William Henry 10/25/64 10/27/64
Brian, Jennie E. married Hickman, W. H. 12/01/64 12/03/64
Brian, Olevia died 10/22/64 10/28/64
Brian, William Joseph died 05/09/61 05/10/61
Brice, Abraham married Pratt, Rebecca 02/07/65 02/11/65
Brice, Ann (Mrs.) married Gray, George W. 08/26/64 08/27/64
Brice, Annie M. M. married Marden, Jesse, Jr. 11/10/64 11/11/64
Brice, George Alfred died 07/08/63 07/09/63
Brice, Julia P. died 11/20/65 11/22/65
Brice, Lydia A. married Jackson, James 08/17/65 08/18/65
Brice, Thomas married Bunting, Martha 11/18/64 11/19/64
Bricherd, Lydia Olive died 03/13/65 03/15/65
Briddell, Emily married Fredenberg, John 09/01/64 09/08/64
Bridener, Martin died 03/20/64 03/21/64
Bridge, Richard Durand died 03/20/65 02/21/65
Bridge, Stephen L. married Wroten, Martie 09/25/62 10/06/62
Bridges, Mary L. died 06/22/61 06/28/61

Bridges, W. J. married Jones, Sue H. 12/11/62   12/16/62
Brien, Joseph married Brien, Mary P. 06/25/64   10/11/64
Brien, Mary P. married Brien, Joseph 06/25/64   10/11/64
Brierly, Elizabeth married Hiser, Nicholas 08/31/65   09/05/65
Briggerhard, Frederick died 10/12/61   10/14/61
Briggs, Daniel married Kone, Henrietta 11/21/61   11/22/61
Briggs, Lizzie died 02/28/63   03/02/63
Briggs, Mary Elizabeth died no date   03/17/63
Briggs, Sarah A. died 03/29/61   04/01/61
Briggs, Susan died 07/04/61   07/06/61
Briggs, Thomas H. died 08/06/65   08/07/65
Bright, Charles Marion died 07/26/65   07/27/65
Bright, Elizabeth died 03/31/63   04/02/63
Bright, Francis C. married Dorsey, Anne 11/26/63   11/28/63
Bright, Francis C. married Dorsey, Anna (Mrs.) 11/26/63   11/30/63
Bright, Harriet married Daws, Henry 08/23/64   08/29/64
Bright, Inez Irene died 02/04/64   02/06/64
Bright, Israel C. died 04/12/64   04/13/64
Brightman, Henry E. died 05/26/63   05/28/63
Brightman, William P. died 01/21/65   01/24/65
Bril, Gertrude Blanche died 10/28/65   11/08/65
Brine, G. W. married Winters, H. A. 07/06/65   07/08/65
Brinker, John H. died 05/10/63   05/20/63
Brinkman, C. Henry married Stoll, Elenora 10/10/65   10/13/65
Brinson, Mary J. married Mason, William, Jr. 02/21/61   03/18/61
Brinston, Thomas died 11/16/62   12/04/62
Brisco, Laura E. died 10/26/62   10/20/63
Brisco, Susan died 11/19/63   12/01/63
Briscoe, Alexander M. married Barth, Christiana Sophia 05/22/65
   10/09/65
Briscoe, Andrew J. died 02/28/64   04/05/64
Briscoe, Charles A. married Foy, Mary C. 10/05/65   10/11/65
Briscoe, Henry H. died 03/26/62   03/27/62
Briscoe, John H. married Coleman, Sarah C. 04/13/64   04/16/64
Briscoe, Julia Ann died 11/18/62   01/03/63
Briscoe, Lewis J. married Reigart, John M. 05/02/65   05/11/65
Briscoe, Mary married Moore, David 10/23/62   10/25/62
Briscoe, Mary married Moore, David 10/23/62   10/27/62
Briscoe, Mary A. married Ealey, William H. 10/24/61   10/25/61
Briscoe, Neanie Talley died 06/22/63   06/27/63
Briscoe, W. H. died 12/12/65   12/14/65
Briscoe, William R. died 07/31/65   08/01/65
Briscoe, William T. married Fardwell, Sarah 09/12/65   09/23/65
Bristow, Columbus W. married Tatman, Mary Elizabeth 03/08/64   03/09/64
Bristow, Richard married Tatman, Sarah Jane 12/08/61   12/24/61
Brittain, Thomas died 06/27/64   06/28/64
Britton, Mary Jane died 12/16/62   12/18/62
Britton, Richard N. married Smith, Mary J. 09/05/64   09/13/64
Broad, Jane (Mrs.) died 08/18/64   08/19/64
Broadbeck, William married Sherrer, Barbara 08/21/61   08/23/61
Broadbeck, William married Sherrer, Barbara 08/21/61   08/24/61
Broadbelt, J. Eddie died 12/13/65   12/16/65
Broadbent, Celia E. married Stambaugh, John P. 09/20/64   09/22/64
Broadbent, Isabella married Marshall, William H. 12/17/62   12/30/62
Broadbent, John Scotti died 09/30/65   10/02/65

Broadbent, Joseph Ferdinand married Denmead, Jane 07/16/63   07/18/63
Broadbent, Mattie married Cleary, Thomas 10/10/65   11/01/65
Broadbent, Stephen married Murray, M. Alice 10/25/64   10/26/64
Broadfoot, William J. (CSA) died 08/04/63   08/08/63
Brocchus, Jane M. (Mrs.) died 11/04/63   11/07/63
Brock, John M. married Hafermatz, Elizabeth 03/10/61   03/11/61
Brocon, John J. died 06/30/64   07/07/64
Brodbeck, Maria J. died 03/30/61   04/01/61
Broderick, (Mrs. Thomas) died 01/30/61   01/31/61
Broderick, Daniel V. died 06/02/62   06/06/62
Broderick, John died 10/07/65   10/09/65
Broderick, John T. married Burgan, Sarah J. 10/31/61   11/06/61
Broderick, Margaret died 07/23/62   07/24/62
Broderick, Thomas died 06/21/64   06/22/64
Broderick, William, Sr. died 04/18/64   04/20/64
Broderick, William, Sr. died 04/18/64   04/21/64
Broderick, Willie P. died 07/13/63   07/15/63
Broders, Laura married Harrison, H. T. 09/26/63   09/30/63
Brodreck, William died 11/15/62   11/17/62
Broharn, Sarah J. (Mrs.) married Reister, Peter P. 11/08/65   11/10/65
Brohawn, William married Wood, Harriet 01/16/65   01/24/65
Brohawn, William married Woods, Harriet 01/16/65   01/24/65
Brokel, Mary married Patrick, Thomas L. (Dr.) 06/21/64   06/28/64
Brome, Rebecca (Mrs.) died 12/18/64   12/19/64
Bromel, Amanda married Wittey, Albert 11/07/65   11/18/65
Bromwell, Alvien L. married Brooks, Anna P. Belle 09/28/65   10/04/65
Bromwell, C. O. (Lt., C.S.A.) married Staum, Mary Frances 02/04/62
    02/07/62
Bromwell, Fanny A. died 10/08/63   10/12/63
Bromwell, James died 07/26/64   07/27/64
Bromwell, Willie died 07/28/64   07/29/64
Bronn, Anna Maria died 02/09/62   02/10/62
Brook, Elias married Sutton, Sarah 04/02/62   04/04/62
Brook, John F. died 01/11/65   01/16/65
Brook, Thomas H, died 03/28/64   04/06/64
Brooke, Charles died 12/29/61   01/06/62
Brooke, Eliza died 11/02/64   11/04/64
Brooke, Emily E. died 11/10/62   12/04/62
Brooke, Hester Matilda died 12/02/62   12/04/62
Brooke, J. William died 08/13/62   08/14/62
Brooke, Margaret H. married Magruder, W. E. (Rev.) 05/24/64   05/31/64
Brooke, Roger died 12/31/60   01/07/61
Brookes, Albert married Bryan, Sarah E. 01/21/64   01/23/64
Brookhart, John died 07/20/62   07/22/62
Brooks, Albert Dyre married Jolly, Mary Latilda 04/08/64   04/09/64
Brooks, Albert J. married Brent, Catherine R. 04/06/62   04/29/62
Brooks, Anna (Mrs.) died 03/02/63   03/03/63
Brooks, Anna (Mrs.) died 03/02/63   03/04/63
Brooks, Anna P. Belle married Bromwell, Alvien L. 09/28/65   10/04/65
Brooks, Annie married Price, Thomas 12/24/61   12/27/61
Brooks, Cecilia (Mrs.) married Spencer, Edward N. 11/07/60   07/13/61
Brooks, Celia C. married Onion, James H. 10/20/64   10/21/64
Brooks, Charles E. married McMullan, Mary Virginia 07/03/65   07/24/65
Brooks, Charles S. died 10/10/64   10/24/64
Brooks, Christopher C. married Brads, Ella Cecilia 01/15/61   01/16/61

Brooks, Cornelia (Mrs.) died 01/26/63   01/11/65
Brooks, David died 11/10/64   09/11/65
Brooks, Edward E. died 10/08/62   10/16/62
Brooks, Edward Joseph married Henry, Mary Jane 09/15/65   09/18/65
Brooks, Eliza D. married Finegin, Joseph 02/16/62   03/10/62
Brooks, Eliza Jane married Williams, John 02/07/65   02/10/65
Brooks, Elizabeth died 05/23/63   05/27/63
Brooks, Francis married Francis, Margaret A. 10/30/61   02/01/62
Brooks, George B. married Hickman, Catherine 02/21/65   04/03/65
Brooks, George D. married Maxwell, Maggie J. 07/01/62   07/11/62
Brooks, George W. died 11/28/61   11/30/61
Brooks, Harrison married Williams, Elizabeth 09/18/62   09/20/62
Brooks, Henrietta married Brooks, Thomas E. 08/24/64   08/25/64
Brooks, Isabella married Thompson, James 01/18/65   02/22/65
Brooks, John died 10/12/63   10/13/63
Brooks, John married Boone, Emma Jane 11/02/65   11/04/65
Brooks, John Nelson married Williams, Ellen Ann 08/28/62   08/30/62
Brooks, Lilly Jane died 10/22/63   10/26/63
Brooks, Lizzie Anthony married Tyler, Daniel M. 09/02/62   09/05/62
Brooks, Lizzie J. married Hobday, Edward 08/14/64   08/16/64
Brooks, Margaretta married Smith, Matthew N. 02/25/64   02/27/64
Brooks, Mary died 07/26/61   08/01/61
Brooks, Mary A. married Frederick, William 05/04/64   07/18/65
Brooks, Mary C. married Opel, John T. 09/29/63   10/01/63
Brooks, Mary Catharine (Mrs.) died 01/23/65   01/24/65
Brooks, Mary E. married Gray, George W. 01/03/61   01/19/61
Brooks, Mary E. married Fitsmire, John A. 01/16/63   01/17/63
Brooks, Mary Elizabeth married Thomas, Joseph 07/04/65   07/11/65
Brooks, Mary Louise died 09/30/64   10/01/64
Brooks, Mora B. (Mrs.) married Fox, Orlando B. 11/18/63   11/25/63
Brooks, Oliver E. died 06/28/64   06/29/64
Brooks, Oliver P. died 10/09/62   10/16/62
Brooks, Priscilla married Hubbard, Thomas J. 10/12/65   10/14/65
Brooks, Robert married McMullan, Virginia 07/03/65   07/06/65
Brooks, Samuel D. married Hamilton, Adeline R. 10/10/65   10/12/65
Brooks, Sarah A. (Mrs.) died 02/01/65   02/03/65
Brooks, Sarah A. (Mrs.) died 02/01/65   02/03/65
Brooks, Thomas D. married Watts, Jennie 12/13/64   12/19/64
Brooks, Thomas E. married Brooks, Henrietta 08/24/64   08/25/64
Brooks, William married Farnandis, Catharine 11/16/65   11/18/65
Brooks, William H. married Hollin, Bridget 08/07/65   08/10/65
Brooks, William T. married Espy, Susie 09/11/62   09/23/62
Brooks, William Thomas died 12/02/63   12/03/63
Brooks, William Worth died 08/24/61   08/26/61
Brooks, Zedekiah married Lucas, Mary J. 08/18/64   08/20/64
Broom, Ellen Ophelia died 08/14/63   08/15/63
Broom, Ellen Ophelia died 08/14/63   08/18/63
Broom, Fannie married Mitchell, John W. 08/06/63   09/17/63
Broom, George W. married West, Harriet A. 03/08/64   03/10/64
Broome, Susanna married White, Walter W. 05/03/62   06/09/62
Brophy, Anastasia (Mrs.) died 12/03/65   12/04/65
Broson, David W. married Brackson, Mary E. 01/16/62   04/01/62
Brossine, Louise married Cook, Henry 10/29/63   11/24/63
Brossine, Louise married Cook, Henry 10/29/63   11/25/63
Brossine, Louise married Cook, Henry 10/29/63   11/26/63

```
Brotherton, Martha B. married Lowman, Thomas J. 10/03/61   10/04/61
Brotherton, Phoebe T. (Mrs.) died 07/28/64   08/03/64
Brotten, Mary Jane died 01/23/63   01/24/63
Brotzel, Jacob married Marthlas, Freddie 12/24/61   01/01/62
Broughton, Ella Virginia died 08/27/64   09/05/64
Broughton, Isaac W. died 03/29/62   03/31/62
Broughton, Letitia died 02/14/61   02/16/61
Broughton, Robert Daniel died 06/27/63   06/29/63
Broum, Francis Edgar died 03/06/64   03/08/64
Brow, Jane (Mrs.) died 03/15/63   03/19/63
Brower, Philip died 08/27/61   08/29/61
Brown, A. Virginia married Tilyard, Philip T. 02/25/62   03/01/62
Brown, Absalom married Sewell, Ellen R. 07/06/62   07/14/62
Brown, Adolphus F. D. died 10/10/63   11/05/63
Brown, Alexander J. married Clark, Maria 10/22/64   10/29/64
Brown, Alfred C. married Donohue, Anne E. 11/03/63   11/06/63
Brown, Alice Johnson died 10/15/64   10/17/64
Brown, Amanda E. died 05/10/65   05/11/65
Brown, Amelia Rebecca died 02/18/64   02/20/64
Brown, Andrew died 03/08/64   03/10/64
Brown, Angeline married Kelley, William H. 06/12/65   06/13/65
Brown, Ann B. (Mrs.) died 08/08/63   08/10/63
Brown, Ann Maria married Young, Samuel 10/30/62   11/01/62
Brown, Anna Maria died 02/09/62   02/11/62
Brown, Annetha married Hill, William A. 01/02/61   01/07/61
Brown, Annie married Reynolds, John 06/11/61   07/27/61
Brown, Annie Paulleane died 07/28/65   08/01/65
Brown, Archibald married Reilly, Jane 02/07/61   03/25/61
Brown, Arthur died 02/13/63   02/17/63
Brown, Augustus married Patterson, Amelia 04/06/64   04/07/64
Brown, Aulay, Sr. died 10/23/64   10/24/64
Brown, B. Benton married Gaither, Louisiana 10/15/61   10/22/61
Brown, Barbara Ann died 03/09/64   03/10/64
Brown, Benjamin H. married Walters, Viginia 06/10/62   06/12/62
Brown, Bridget died 08/23/62   08/26/62
Brown, Catherine Ann died 02/06/63   02/11/63
Brown, Charles married Copper, Rachel 04/17/64   04/19/64
Brown, Charles Ford died 10/29/64   10/31/64
Brown, Charles H. H. died 10/02/64   10/03/64
Brown, Charles P. died 01/02/65   01/04/65
Brown, Charles Pitts died 05/21/61   05/22/61
Brown, Charles Powers died 07/31/62   08/01/62
Brown, Charles W. married Hopwood, Susan J. 04/11/61   04/18/61
Brown, Charles W. married Tevis, Josephine A. 11/10/62   12/05/62
Brown, Charlotte C. married Walker, Thomas H. 03/12/62   04/14/62
Brown, Charlotte Cornelia married Arozo, Mariano 04/03/61   04/06/61
Brown, Clara married Coye, John 02/22/63   02/25/63
Brown, Claudius G. married Thompson, Isabella D. 01/10/61   01/15/61
Brown, Cornelius died 03/09/64   03/10/64
Brown, Cornelius A. married Bodensick, E. Sophia 04/27/64   08/06/64
Brown, D. H. married Cephas, Eliza 07/13/65   07/15/65
Brown, Edward married Turner, Marion 10/01/61   11/06/61
Brown, Edward died 01/24/63   01/26/63
Brown, Edward died 03/18/65   03/22/65
Brown, Edward died 03/18/65   03/23/65
```

Brown, Edward Curtis died 07/04/61   07/06/61
Brown, Edward H. died 12/21/63   01/26/64
Brown, Edward Hilert died 07/11/65   07/12/65
Brown, Edwin Walter died 04/19/63   04/20/63
Brown, Eleanor Estelle died 10/05/65   10/07/65
Brown, Elijah died 05/15/63   05/16/63
Brown, Eliza married Howard, Henry 05/09/61   05/11/61
Brown, Eliza died no date   10/25/64
Brown, Eliza (Mrs.) died 11/11/63   11/12/63
Brown, Eliza J. married Chapman, John W. 09/19/65   09/27/65
Brown, Elizabeth died 02/04/61   02/05/61
Brown, Elizabeth died 02/04/61   02/06/61
Brown, Elizabeth died 06/02/63   06/03/63
Brown, Elizabeth married Miller, John H. 05/21/63   05/23/63
Brown, Elizabeth A. married Shipley, Christopher C. 12/24/62   01/01/63
Brown, Elizabeth Ann married Davis, John H. W. 12/13/64   12/17/64
Brown, Elizabeth Merriken died 08/10/65   08/12/65
Brown, Ellen D. married Heffner, John R. 07/15/62   07/16/62
Brown, Emma died 09/10/61   09/13/61
Brown, Emma died 04/20/63   04/21/63
Brown, Emma died 04/20/64   04/22/63
Brown, Emma married Laughlin, Brian O. 01/30/65   02/01/65
Brown, Emma F. married Drummond, John H. 04/31/63   06/03/63
Brown, Emma Marion married Neuwieler, John C. 09/29/64   10/05/64
Brown, Felix E. (Dr.) married Milburn, Clara M. 10/26/65   11/02/65
Brown, Fenix married Lightburn, Jane 04/22/61   04/24/61
Brown, Florence M. died 06/06/64   06/08/64
Brown, Floretta died 07/25/62   07/26/62
Brown, Frances Virginia died 07/23/63   07/24/63
Brown, Francis died 03/27/65   03/28/65
Brown, Geoffrey J. married Taylor, Julia 01/31/64   02/02/64
Brown, George F. married Clark, Margaret A. 08/13/60   01/03/61
Brown, George H. married Robinson, Ellen J. 06/26/62   06/28/62
Brown, George Nathaniel died 09/01/64   09/02/64
Brown, George O. married Cole, Sarah P. 02/22/65   02/25/65
Brown, George W. married Mondowny, Mary Ellen 11/17/63   11/19/63
Brown, George W. died 03/02/65   03/04/65
Brown, Harriet married Brown, John H. 01/10/61   01/11/61
Brown, Harriet S. married Turner, Thomas T. 10/10/65   10/11/65
Brown, Harry Howard died 02/14/61   02/15/61
Brown, Harry Wickham died 06/13/64   06/14/64
Brown, Henry G. died 01/08/62   01/10/62
Brown, Henry G. died 01/08/62   02/04/62
Brown, Henry Lee Beauregard died 03/07/63   03/09/63
Brown, Hester J. married Edwards, Sanford 03/06/64   03/08/64
Brown, Hiram died 05/18/64   05/19/64
Brown, Isaiah died 12/27/62   12/29/62
Brown, Isaiah married Pirres, Sarah E. 05/05/62   05/07/62
Brown, J. Henry married Sigler, Emma A. 03/03/63   03/06/63
Brown, James died 11/04/63   11/05/63
Brown, James A. married Daughaday, Laura V. 11/07/64   12/22/64
Brown, James Edward died 09/23/63   09/24/63
Brown, James M. died 09/15/63   09/17/63
Brown, James M. married Woodcock, Rebecca 02/17/63   03/12/63
Brown, James M. married Eubank, Annie M. (Mrs.) 04/19/65   05/04/65

Brown, James W. died 03/05/63   03/07/63
Brown, Jane (Mrs.) died 03/15/63   03/20/63
Brown, Jane Dorson died 08/11/64   08/17/64
Brown, John died 01/23/62   01/24/62
Brown, John died 01/23/62   01/25/62
Brown, John married Carson, Mary June 03/14/65   03/23/65
Brown, John married Anderson, Eliza 08/17/65   08/19/65
Brown, John Cumming died 12/25/64   12/29/64
Brown, John F. married Grimes, Ella B. (Mrs.) 08/27/63   09/30/63
Brown, John H. married Brown, Harriet 01/10/61   01/11/61
Brown, John Henry died 02/20/62   02/25/62
Brown, John Henry died 07/25/63   07/27/63
Brown, John J. married Corner, Lizzie M. 04/13/64   04/18/64
Brown, John M. married Bowman, Mary Alice 11/02/65   11/10/65
Brown, John Maurice died 08/12/62   08/15/62
Brown, John N. died 03/05/65   03/06/65
Brown, John N. died 03/05/65   03/07/65
Brown, John T. married Butcher, Emma 02/05/61   02/12/61
Brown, John W. married Loks, Monty 12/10/61   12/12/61
Brown, John W. died 06/29/62   07/31/62
Brown, John W. married Gambrill, Abbey 01/04/65   01/09/65
Brown, John W. married Berger, Caroline M. C. 05/23/65   05/29/65
Brown, John Wesley died 12/13/62   12/15/62
Brown, Joseph married Williams, Mary E. 06/18/63   06/19/63
Brown, Joseph M. married Sutter, Josephine 10/16/62   10/23/62
Brown, Josephine married Weaver, James E. 02/16/63   02/17/63
Brown, Julia Cecelia died 05/12/62   05/15/62
Brown, Kate E. married Lawrenson, Richard S. 12/08/63   12/12/63
Brown, Katie married Wickert, Samuel C. 08/15/65   08/24/65
Brown, Lemuel died 09/12/63   09/14/63
Brown, Lewis M. married Coates, Mary Frances 03/26/61   03/27/61
Brown, Lizzie married Bouchet, John M. 07/26/64   08/02/64
Brown, Louis married Cooney, Annie 04/14/65   04/22/65
Brown, Louisa died 11/30/63   12/05/63
Brown, Louisa H. married Forsyth, Samuel J. 12/22/64   02/21/65
Brown, Lucinda died 02/02/62   02/04/62
Brown, Luke married King, Esther Ann 12/15/64   12/17/64
Brown, Lydia died 03/30/64   03/31/64
Brown, Lydia died 02/08/65   02/09/65
Brown, Lydia A. died 08/01/61   08/02/61
Brown, M. A. married Taylor, W. J. 11/10/65   11/11/65
Brown, Margaret died 05/02/62   05/03/62
Brown, Margaret A. (Mrs.) died 12/29/63   01/05/64
Brown, Margaret Ann (Mrs.) died 12/28/63   12/30/63
Brown, Margaret Jane married Langley, William A. 12/25/61   12/31/61
Brown, Maria (Mrs.) died 05/16/65   05/17/65
Brown, Mary married Ruff, William Henry 02/02/62   02/04/62
Brown, Mary died 05/30/63   06/01/63
Brown, Mary married Shelley, George K. 01/16/63   01/22/63
Brown, Mary married Cooper, Hamilton 12/27/63   12/29/63
Brown, Mary died 11/19/65   11/20/65
Brown, Mary died 11/19/65   11/21/65
Brown, Mary married Miller, George W. 07/07/64   07/11/64
Brown, Mary A. married Moudy, William (USN) 10/16/65   11/28/65
Brown, Mary A. (Mrs.) died 08/09/63   09/12/63

Brown, Mary Agnes died 05/28/63   05/29/63
Brown, Mary Ann married Gourley, Joseph 05/02/65   05/06/65
Brown, Mary E. married Wiley, James F. (USN) 07/20/63   07/24/63
Brown, Mary E. married Guyton, William L. 10/10/63   02/01/64
Brown, Mary E. married Langford, Freeborn 06/01/65   06/03/65
Brown, Mary Grace died 11/05/61   11/18/61
Brown, Mary H. married Osburn, Emory W. 10/25/64   11/03/64
Brown, Mary J. died 09/11/62   09/13/62
Brown, Mary J. married Burke, William H. 11/10/63   11/14/63
Brown, Mary M. died 11/08/65   11/10/65
Brown, Mary Margaret died 09/10/61   09/11/61
Brown, Mary Porter died 03/28/62   05/17/62
Brown, Mary Rosensteel died 03/05/61   03/09/61
Brown, Michael married Cull, Eliza 06/24/65   06/29/65
Brown, Milton married Ockerme, Mary A. no date   08/05/63
Brown, Olivia died 09/06/62   09/16/62
Brown, Olivia died 09/16/62   09/17/62
Brown, Olivia Elizabeth died 09/07/62   09/15/62
Brown, Owen J. married Alder, Mary 10/16/62   10/25/62
Brown, Pembroke Womble died 06/16/64   06/18/64
Brown, Polly married Donnelly, Frank 07/28/64   07/30/64
Brown, Rachael Ann married Blake, Josiah 03/06/63   03/08/62
Brown, Rachel died 04/07/64   04/09/64
Brown, Rachel Ann died 10/29/63   11/03/63
Brown, Rachel S. (Mrs.) died 06/17/64   06/18/64
Brown, Raymond Reid died 07/07/65   07/08/65
Brown, Rebecca married Buchanan, James C. 03/07/61   03/09/61
Brown, Rebecca married Edwards, Richard 06/14/64   06/16/64
Brown, Richard married Preston, Ann L. 08/01/64   08/03/64
Brown, Robert died 08/13/61   08/21/61
Brown, Robert died 12/17/65   12/19/65
Brown, Robert H. married Thompson, Mary Louise 10/27/64   11/05/64
Brown, Robert M. married Hall, Josephine S. 06/05/63   06/15/63
Brown, Samuel, Jr. died 07/17/61   07/19/61
Brown, Samuel, Sr. died 08/17/61   08/19/61
Brown, Sarah A. married Stone, J. H. 03/06/61   03/07/61
Brown, Sarah A. W. (Mrs.) died 04/24/65   04/26/65
Brown, Sarah Ann died 03/26/62   03/27/62
Brown, Sarah Jane married Essworth, Daniel 03/06/61   03/16/61
Brown, Shadrick married Poole, Nancy 01/28/64   01/30/64
Brown, Susan married Barnes, John K. (USA) 08/01/65   08/04/65
Brown, Susanna died 09/19/61   10/05/61
Brown, Susannah (Mrs.) died 11/28/64   11/29/64
Brown, Susannah (Mrs.) died 11/28/64   11/30/64
Brown, Susie married Low, Aaron 07/16/63   07/27/63
Brown, Thomas died 03/12/64   03/14/64
Brown, Thomas W. married Biddison, Mary Helen 02/03/63   02/04/63
Brown, William married Wilson, Mary Ellen 06/05/62   06/07/62
Brown, William died 01/31/63   02/03/63
Brown, William died 05/18/65   05/19/65
Brown, William married Curley, Mary Jane 02/14/65   02/16/65
Brown, William Cornelius died 02/16/62   02/18/62
Brown, William D. (Capt.) died 07/10/63   07/31/63
Brown, William H. died 03/27/61   03/29/61

```
Brown, William W. married Hanynie, Elizabeth 08/26/63   11/10/63
Brown, William Ward died 01/02/61   01/03/61
Brown, Zachariah died 04/24/61   04/25/61
Brown, Zachariah married Parker, Elizabeth 03/17/63   03/21/63
Browne, Clara E. married Cissel, Wilbur F. 08/30/64   09/10/64
Browne, Emma Alice married Beaver, J. Lewis (Cpt.) 11/01/64   11/03/64
Browne, Mary A. (Mrs.) died 08/09/63   08/12/63
Browne, Mary Ann died 07/01/65   07/03/65
Browne, Robert A. died 05/05/64   06/27/64
Browning, Agnes married Wolf, George W. 07/27/65   07/29/65
Browning, Edward married Swain, Mary Louisa 10/22/63   12/09/63
Browning, Emma L. married Jones, Hamilton 12/07/65   12/11/65
Browning, Eugena C. married Jacob, John F. 04/16/61   05/01/61
Browning, Margaret died 04/06/61   04/11/61
Browning, Margaret T. died 07/10/61   07/18/61
Browning, Martha died 02/18/63   02/28/63
Browning, Martha died 02/18/63   03/02/63
Browning, Mary Ellen died 10/28/62   11/01/62
Browning, Mary Jane died 06/15/62   06/16/62
Browning, Samuel died 04/02/64   04/04/64
Browning, Samuel died 04/01/64   04/05/64
Brownley, David Greves died 02/20/63   02/27/63
Brownley, Elizabeth Copenhaver died 05/20/61   05/27/61
Brownley, Judith died 01/13/62   01/14/62
Brownley, Martha (Mrs.) died 04/16/65   04/18/65
Brownley, Sarah K. died 02/03/62   02/04/62
Brownley, Thomas J. married Griffith, Jennie A. 03/12/63   03/14/63
Brownson, E., Jr. married Heath, Mary Louisa 12/06/63   12/08/63
Bruce, Florence Pauline died 06/21/64   06/22/64
Bruce, Helen E. V. died 08/15/62   08/16/62
Bruce, Helen E. V. died 08/15/62   08/18/62
Bruce, James Duff died 07/04/63   07/14/63
Bruce, John H. R. died 07/06/63   07/22/63
Bruce, Robert married Eastmond, Maria 04/11/62   05/13/62
Bruce, Robert died 03/16/64   03/17/64
Bruce, Robert A. died 09/29/64   10/13/64
Bruch, Anna Maria (Mrs.) died 02/01/65   02/03/65
Bruch, Anna Maria (Mrs.) died 02/01/65   02/03/65
Bruchey, David H. married Cromer, Georgia 06/04/65   06/06/65
Bruchey, John F. died 01/10/64   01/11/64
Bruck, Kate Wilamine died 08/04/64   08/06/64
Bruefer, Mary married Fisher, Henry 03/09/63   03/10/63
Bruehl, Ellen M. married Hinrichs, Christopher J. 03/05/63   03/09/63
Bruen, Charlotte married Baker, Alfred O. 04/07/64   05/06/64
Bruff, Frances Emily (Mrs.) died 10/29/63   10/31/63
Bruff, William W. married Porter, Ellenora 01/24/61   01/25/61
Bruggmann, John J. died 09/30/65   10/02/65
Brumell, Eliza died 04/13/65   04/14/65
Brummel, A. O. (Lt., C.S.A.) married Staum, M. F. 02/10/62   02/20/62
Brummel, Joseph (Q.M.C.) married High, Sophia E. 12/24/61   01/10/62
Brummel, Sarah Ida Matilda died 12/22/62   12/24/62
Brun, Francis P. died 07/23/63   07/25/63
Brun, Mary Amice died 02/13/65   02/15/65
Brun, Mary Amice died 02/13/65   02/24/65
Brundage, John Thomas died 01/26/62   02/03/62
```

Brundage, Maggy Boyd died 09/02/65 09/05/65
Brundige, Henry died 10/10/65 10/14/65
Brundige, James died 12/07/62 12/09/62
Brundige, James died 05/01/64 05/05/64
Brundige, James died no date 05/06/64
Brundige, John T. B. W. died 09/19/64 09/21/64
Brundige, William married Wiley, Rebecca 09/25/61 09/28/61
Brundon, Samuel married Pinkny, Frances 06/02/61 06/05/61
Brundon, Samuel married Pinkny, Francis 05/12/61 06/04/61
Brune, Annie Caroline died 07/29/64 07/30/64
Brune, John Christian died 12/07/64 12/31/64
Brune, William F. married Smith, Marianne 06/05/62 06/11/62
Brunfield, Nathan married Wall, A. J. 11/16/65 11/24/65
Bruning, M. Minnie married Jensen, J. F. P. (Lt.) 03/19/62 03/22/62
Brunner, Andrew B. (Maj.) died 01/05/64 01/06/64
Brunner, Daniel died 10/15/61 10/16/61
Brunner, Edward Evans died 09/08/64 09/14/64
Brunt, Annie married Holtzman, E. Kent 04/11/61 04/15/61
Brurein, John Francis died 05/22/64 05/23/64
Bruscup, George R. married Millburn, Catherine M. 10/16/62 10/18/62
Bruscup, Mary Jane died 01/31/63 02/02/63
Bryan, Amanda H. (Mrs.) died 06/12/63 06/13/63
Bryan, Arthur L. married Wilson, Emma Roalla 05/26/64 06/07/64
Bryan, Catharine (Mrs.) died 12/24/64 12/26/64
Bryan, Catherine married Petticord, George W. 03/12/61 03/29/61
Bryan, Charles H. married Mercer, Eleanor 10/23/64 10/25/64
Bryan, David A. died 08/17/64 11/07/64
Bryan, David Alexander died 10/17/64 10/21/64
Bryan, Elizabeth Charity died 03/02/63 03/03/63
Bryan, Ellsworth died 08/17/64 09/02/64
Bryan, James died 07/19/65 07/20/65
Bryan, Lewis G. died 08/14/63 08/18/63
Bryan, Lucretia died no date 10/19/65
Bryan, Maria E. died 06/29/62 07/03/62
Bryan, Sarah E. married Brookes, Albert 01/21/64 01/23/64
Bryan, Thomas A. married Higgins, Maria E. 04/22/61 04/24/61
Bryant, Mary E. married Breen, James C. 01/02/63 06/05/63
Bryant, Mary Elizabeth married Helen, Franklin 05/04/62 05/31/62
Bryant, Recharda S. married Robinson, George W., Jr. 10/08/63 10/09/63
Bryce, Robert died 04/15/65 04/17/65
Bryce, Robert James died 08/24/62 08/26/62
Bryon, James R. died 08/10/64 08/12/64
Bryon, Thomas married Chambers, Julia A. 05/15/65 05/23/65
Buchanan, Elizabeth Ferree died 11/28/65 11/29/65
Buchanan, Ester S. died 12/23/65 12/29/65
Buchanan, Henrietta died 09/05/65 09/06/65
Buchanan, James C. married Brown, Rebecca 03/07/61 03/09/61
Buchanan, James Hollis married Gittings, Henrietta 03/30/64 03/31/64
Buchanan, Jarret married Cooper, Sarah 06/30/64 07/02/64
Buchanan, John E. died 11/08/61 11/09/61
Buchanan, Johnny died 01/08/61 01/11/61
Buchanan, Mary Ellen died 09/10/63 09/12/63
Buchanan, P. Carr died 05/23/61 05/31/61
Buchanan, Robert S., Jr. died 05/06/61 05/09/61
Buchanan, Thomas McKean died 01/14/63 01/31/63

Buchheimer, John William died 02/03/63   02/05/63
Buchnan, Mary died 10/01/62   10/02/62
Buck, Alexander Benson died 03/11/65   03/14/65
Buck, Belle married Kennedy, Herbert M. 01/28/63   02/02/63
Buck, Benjamin Herr died 09/09/65   09/18/65
Buck, Catherine married Thomas, Levin 11/01/63   11/03/63
Buck, David died 09/11/63   09/15/63
Buck, H. Best married Hoover, Emily C. 11/30/65   12/11/65
Buck, Henry Edward died 02/20/65   02/21/65
Buck, Jacob John died 10/15/63   10/16/63
Buck, James died 11/01/65   11/03/65
Buck, John Edward died 04/04/65   04/05/65
Buck, Joseph W. married Lemcke, Laura V. E. 11/16/65   12/06/65
Buck, Mary Elizabeth married Keaser, Robert J. 07/05/64   07/07/64
Buck, Minnie W. married Snead, John E. 01/31/61   02/04/61
Buck, Sarah A. (Mrs.) married Crone, William C. 09/07/61   10/08/61
Buck, William H. married Tuckers, Sallie S. 03/17/64   03/22/64
Buckannan, John married Malsburry, Harriet 04/06/65   04/08/65
Buckey, D. married Norris, M. Lizzie 11/19/61   11/21/61
Buckingham, Alfred married Multz, Annie M. 06/09/64   07/16/64
Buckingham, Allen married Jessopp, Arietta W. 08/11/64   08/30/64
Buckingham, Amelia died 01/31/65   02/01/65
Buckingham, George L. married Stone, Mary D. 06/16/64   06/25/64
Buckingham, H. Virginia married McCauley, Alexander T. 10/21/63
    10/24/63
Buckingham, James Holbrook died 05/02/65   05/03/65
Buckingham, James V. married Lawrence, Emma J. 03/10/64   04/01/64
Buckingham, Margaret Jane died 02/08/64   02/09/64
Buckingham, Mary M. married Bone, William W. 03/27/62   03/29/62
Buckingham, William died 05/17/61   05/23/61
Buckler, Annie Stuart died 01/05/61   01/07/61
Buckler, D. Z. married Harvey, Mary E. 04/28/64   04/29/64
Buckler, Eliza (Mrs.) died 02/23/63   02/24/63
Buckler, George W. died 03/18/64   03/22/64
Buckler, James Walter died 03/17/64   03/18/64
Buckler, John died 11/22/63   11/24/63
Buckler, John died 08/21/65   08/23/65
Buckler, John, Jr. died 10/03/63   10/05/63
Buckler, Thomas H. (Dr) married White, Eliza 11/21/65   11/23/65
Buckles, Henry S. married McQuade, Elizabeth 05/06/65   05/09/65
Buckley, Annie married Murry, Hubart 01/08/61   01/11/61
Buckley, Charles R. married Brewer, Fanny A. 11/29/62   01/01/63
Buckley, Charlie died 09/26/65   09/27/65
Buckley, David Z. died 07/25/64   07/26/64
Buckley, Elizabeth died 02/02/63   02/03/63
Buckley, Ellen Vincent died 08/12/63   08/13/63
Buckley, George died 05/27/64   10/25/64
Buckley, Josephine married Morsell, William 07/27/65   08/01/65
Buckley, Michael died 07/28/62   07/29/62
Buckley, Michael died 08/13/62   08/15/62
Buckley, Sarah Ann (Mrs.) died 05/13/63   05/14/63
Buckman, C. B. died 07/05/65   07/06/65
Buckman, Samuel died 09/23/64   09/24/64
Buckmiller, Fannie A. married Watkins, Gassaway 09/17/63   09/23/63
Buckmiller, Frances Ann died 06/22/65   06/23/65

```
Bucksbaum, Judea died 05/30/61   05/31/61
Budd, Caroline married Coy, John H. 02/01/63   02/09/63
Buehler, Kate Olivia died 07/09/63   07/10/63
Bufter, Mary Ann married Hoover, Abraham 08/01/65   08/09/65
Bugel, Joseph S. married Brannan, Rebecca 06/15/65   06/20/65
Buher, Adam died 03/13/62   03/14/62
Buhrman, Emory (Rev.) married Chenoweth, Ada E. 10/27/63   10/29/63
Bulack, Elizabeth Victoria died 03/02/62   03/03/62
Bulett, Elizabeth married Sheaff, Joseph 03/18/61   03/25/61
Bull, Caroline married Horn, Alexander 11/30/65   12/05/65
Bull, Emmanuel died 01/09/65   01/11/65
Bull, Fannie A. died 07/14/64   07/16/64
Bull, Francis married Plummer, J. M. 11/05/63   12/08/63
Bull, H. Fannie married Hampson, James S. 01/20/63   02/22/63
Bull, Harriet (Mrs.) died 08/28/63   09/03/63
Bull, James C. died no date   03/08/65
Bull, Kate D. married Sanders, George W. 10/27/63   10/29/63
Bull, Lydia married Lukehart, Samuel L. 12/19/61   12/21/61
Bull, Mary died 08/07/65   08/10/65
Bull, Mary C. married Champlin, J. H. 12/05/65   12/13/65
Bull, Nicholas married Askew, Mary E. 10/23/62   10/27/62
Bull, Randolph died no date   10/19/65
Bull, Thomas Nelson married McCullough, Mary 03/09/62   03/12/62
Bull, Thomas W. died 01/01/64   01/11/64
Bull, Virginia married Miles, B. F. (Rev.) 12/26/61   01/08/62
Bullen, Clara died 02/26/62   02/28/62
Bullen, William W. married Dunnock, Sarah E. 06/22/65   06/24/65
Bullin, William died 08/31/63   09/01/63
Bullock, Hannah E. married Hoover, William H. 01/07/63   01/12/63
Bullock, Herbert died 01/21/62   01/23/62
Bullock, Rhoda Mary died 03/31/63   04/01/63
Bullock, Samuel J. died 12/18/61   12/20/61
Bullymore, Frank C. married Seidenstricker, Henry A. 11/19/63   11/28/63
Bulock, Samuel J. died 12/18/61   01/23/62
Bultz, Rosine died 07/08/61   07/09/61
Bump, Mary E. married Russell, John S. 08/02/65   08/11/65
Bunce, Edward died 08/30/64   08/31/64
Bunce, Mary (Mrs.) died 09/24/63   09/25/63
Bunch, Ellen C. married Keppler, George W. 01/03/65   01/19/65
Bunter, William died 01/17/64   01/18/64
Bunting, Anna M. married Simpson, Henry C. 11/17/64   11/22/64
Bunting, David G. died 11/30/62   12/02/62
Bunting, David W. died 09/20/63   09/22/63
Bunting, E. married Rinehart, Louis 01/27/65   09/02/65
Bunting, Eben B. married Sisco, Laura J. 06/03/61   06/10/61
Bunting, Elizabeth C. married Adams, Charles H. 11/30/65   12/02/65
Bunting, George R. married Howes, Maggie H. 10/31/65   11/02/65
Bunting, Maggie T. married Bell, John A. 01/05/65   01/07/65
Bunting, Martha married Brice, Thomas 11/18/64   11/19/64
Bunting, Rose Ann died 09/30/62   10/02/62
Bunting, Smith K. died 03/20/65   03/21/65
Bunting, Willey died 06/25/63   06/27/63
Bunting, William married Duvall, Mary Eugenia 12/23/62   12/25/62
Bunton, Edward F. died 09/24/63   10/01/63
Bunton, Edward F. died 09/24/63   10/03/63
```

```
Burch, Eveline married Hill, William B. 08/01/61   02/12/62
Burch, George D. married Harrod, Mary Grace 05/07/63   06/09/63
Burch, James A. married Duff, Mary Letitia 12/17/63   12/19/63
Burch, James C. (Dr.) married Long, Mary P. 06/03/63   06/09/63
Burchall, William married Turner, Matilda 09/02/62   09/29/62
Burchinal, Jeremiah L. W. died 04/07/65   04/08/65
Burchinal, Joseph Thomas died 04/18/65   04/20/65
Bures, James Alexander died 06/04/61   06/05/61
Burgan, Cassandra married King, Alexander R. 11/04/63   01/19/64
Burgan, Charity V. died 05/01/61   05/03/61
Burgan, Charity V. died 05/01/61   05/04/61
Burgan, Deborah died 12/09/61   12/10/61
Burgan, Lizzie A. married Dilworthy, John 06/03/63   06/04/63
Burgan, Mary R. married Getz, John M. 06/18/61   06/26/61
Burgan, Robert James died 05/22/64   05/23/64
Burgan, Sarah J. married Broderick, John T. 10/31/61   11/06/61
Burgee, Singleton F. died 01/21/64   01/22/64
Burgen, John J. married Kenney, Agnes 06/04/63   06/12/63
Burger, Marie M. married McNeale, William 12/25/61   12/30/61
Burger, Marie M. married Neale, William Marshall 12/25/61   12/31/61
Burgers, Laura V. married Galloway, William 06/02/64   06/06/64
Burgess, Basil died 11/24/62   11/25/62
Burgess, Caleb W. married Cable, Mary A. 04/27/65   06/01/65
Burgess, Charles H. married Colladay, Mary E. W. 05/05/64   05/09/64
Burgess, Henrietta R. married Hines, V. Burgess 03/02/64   03/19/64
Burgess, John died 12/10/61   04/21/62
Burgess, Laura V. married Gallaway, William 06/01/64   06/07/64
Burgess, Mary (Mrs.) died 11/11/63   11/24/63
Burgess, Mary Emma died 02/07/64   02/08/64
Burgess, Owen D. married Cook, Elizabeth 03/28/61   04/15/61
Burgess, Sarah Clymer died 08/18/63   08/19/63
Burgess, Sarah S. married Macneal, James B. 04/21/64   04/23/64
Burgess, Stephen died 03/11/61   03/12/61
Burgess, William H. married Lee, Emily A. E. 04/29/62   05/02/62
Burgess, William Vinton died 12/13/65   12/15/65
Burgunder, Rebecca married Newberger, G. 03/10/61   03/13/61
Burgy, William Corwin married Scrivener, Rosie M. 06/14/64   06/16/64
Burk, Elender P. B. died 09/12/65   09/13/65
Burk, Margaret Ann died 06/18/64   06/21/64
Burk, Mary married Cross, William 07/05/62   07/10/62
Burk, Mary married Cross, William 07/05/62   07/11/62
Burk, Mary married Cross, William 07/05/62   07/12/62
Burk, Mary married Cross, William 07/05/62   07/15/62
Burk, Mary A. (Mrs.) died 10/26/64   10/27/64
Burk, Mary P. married Willmore, William 04/07/65   04/12/65
Burke, Catharine (Mrs.) married Stephenson, Joseph B. 09/08/64   09/12/
Burke, Catharine Gertrude died 01/14/62   01/15/62
Burke, Elender P. B. (Mrs.) died 09/12/65   09/14/65
Burke, Henrietta B. married Rosan, C. J. 01/27/63   01/30/63
Burke, Jacob W. married Wolford, Kate L. 12/01/64   12/03/64
Burke, Jerome died 02/14/64   02/16/64
Burke, Johanna T. married Myers, James A. 10/18/65   10/24/65
Burke, John died 03/09/64   03/10/64
Burke, John Henry died 04/24/63   04/25/63
Burke, Johnny died 12/28/63   12/29/63
```

Burke, Joseph F. married Cartier, Mollie E. 04/30/63   05/07/63
Burke, Laura M. died 03/05/61   03/08/61
Burke, M. Cornelia married Mason, William E. 09/29/64   10/20/64
Burke, Margaret died 01/08/64   01/09/64
Burke, Margaret married Jones, Jeffra 03/26/63   03/28/63
Burke, Martha Ann married Guineman, Samuel 09/07/65   11/04/65
Burke, Mary (Mrs.) died 09/18/63   09/19/63
Burke, Mary M. married Switser, John W. 06/23/64   06/30/64
Burke, Oliver married Mackenhamer, Jennie 03/27/62   06/20/62
Burke, Richard H. died 05/05/64   05/06/64
Burke, Richard Vincent died 05/24/63   05/25/63
Burke, Sarah G. died 02/01/62   02/03/62
Burke, Secilia died 02/15/63   02/16/63
Burke, Thomas died 01/04/65   01/06/65
Burke, Thomas Francis died 04/15/64   04/16/64
Burke, William H. married Brown, Mary J. 11/10/63   11/14/63
Burke, William H. died 02/02/64   02/03/64
Burke, William H. died 05/03/65   05/04/65
Burket, Frederick married Willingham, Mary A. 10/01/65   11/14/65
Burks, Mary E. married Eccleston, Robert E. (Sgt.) 05/03/63   05/06/63
Burley, Isaac died 12/26/63   12/28/63
Burley, Julia A. married Slater, Hamilton 12/30/62   01/01/63
Burlin, Robert L. married Short, Nellie C. 04/21/64   05/23/64
Burly, Charlotte G. married Pearce, James Henry 09/26/61   10/01/61
Burly, Louisa married Taylor, Benjamin 03/07/61   03/08/61
Burman, Jeremiah Clay died 02/20/62   02/25/62
Burman, Lewis married Weaver, Christena 01/01/63   01/06/63
Burman, William Ross died 09/17/62   10/23/62
Burmingham, William C. married Hamilton, Sarah A. 07/16/63   07/25/63
Burn, Sarah died 08/12/65   08/14/65
Burne, Clement Rawlesee died 09/18/62   09/23/62
Burnes, John died 01/06/65   01/07/65
Burnes, Joseph died 08/01/64   08/03/64
Burnes, Mary J. married Carter, William 03/17/64   03/23/64
Burneston, Louisa A. married Dutton, Frederick W. 08/30/64   09/05/64
Burneston, Matilda (Mrs.) died 12/14/64   12/16/64
Burneston, Thomas died 10/15/62   10/20/62
Burnett, Annie C. married Cooper, Henry S. S. 06/28/65   07/29/65
Burnett, Henry H. married Hollies, Lydia Hemsworth 05/31/65   06/03/65
Burnett, Maggie married Keller, Otho J. 02/17/64   02/19/64
Burnett, William T. married Simmont, M. Amelia 06/20/64   06/24/64
Burneys, William G. married Ford, Matilda H. 11/27/64   11/29/64
Burnham, Ann Elmirah died 02/26/61   03/04/61
Burnham, Keziah (Mrs.) died 11/01/64   11/03/64
Burnham, Louise married Nace, William L. 04/08/63   04/14/63
Burnham, Olivia died 07/17/63   07/22/63
Burnham, William T. (Capt.) died 10/09/61   10/10/61
Burnham, William T. (Capt.) died 10/09/61   10/11/61
Burns, Amos married Gore, Barbara Marcella 05/04/65   05/09/65
Burns, Dennis died 07/14/62   07/16/62
Burns, Edward died 04/30/62   05/01/62
Burns, Edward died 04/30/62   05/02/62
Burns, Edward married Hall, Elizabeth 06/04/63   06/06/63
Burns, Edwin C. married Cavanaugh, Sarah A. 12/04/64   12/07/64
Burns, Elizabeth J. married Champayne, William K. 04/11/64   04/16/64

Burns, Francis (Rev.) died 04/19/63   04/21/63
Burns, Francis E. died 07/17/63   07/18/63
Burns, George died 02/08/64   02/09/64
Burns, George married Donovan, Kate 11/17/64   11/18/64
Burns, George W. married Lockington, Jennie M. 03/27/62   03/29/62
Burns, James married Crawford, Mary A. 01/04/62   03/03/62
Burns, Jennie M. (Mrs.) died 10/04/63   10/06/63
Burns, John H. married Smith, Maria 12/14/62   12/16/62
Burns, John H. married Eckhardt, Louisa P. 04/23/63   04/25/63
Burns, Kate married Rigney, James 09/17/63   10/07/63
Burns, Kate Olivia (Mrs.) married Beacher, A. Burre 07/13/63   07/18/63
Burns, Laura Virginia died 10/01/64   10/03/64
Burns, Maggie E. married West, George P. 04/23/63   04/27/63
Burns, Martin died no date   12/05/62
Burns, Martin E. married Farr, Julia A. 12/29/61   12/31/61
Burns, Mary A. married Roberts, John B. 04/07/64   04/11/64
Burns, Mary Susannah died 10/03/61   10/04/61
Burns, May died 02/22/62   02/24/62
Burns, Rachel A. married Burns, Richard 10/25/64   10/29/64
Burns, Rachel Agnes married Killen, Thomas 03/14/62   03/18/62
Burns, Richard married Burns, Rachel A. 10/25/64   10/29/64
Burns, Sarah died 01/27/64   01/30/64
Burns, Sarah E. married Gambrill, William B. 11/16/64   11/24/64
Burns, Thomas (1st Sgt.) married Corns, Lizzie F. 12/11/62   12/15/62
Burns, Thomas (Lt.) died 10/28/64   11/01/64
Burns, William Henry died 10/24/62   10/27/62
Burns, Willie Crane died 05/20/63   05/21/63
Burnside, William died 02/03/64   02/04/64
Burr, Jennie married Harrison, Sprague 10/10/64   10/12/64
Burrie, Solomon died 10/01/64   10/03/64
Burrier, Lizze S. married Pruett, James A. 11/09/65   11/15/65
Burrier, Margaret Jane died 05/24/63   05/25/63
Burris, Isaac F. married Fisk, Phebe P. 01/20/63   01/29/63
Burrough, Edward E. married Emery, Lizzie J. 12/27/64   12/30/64
Burrough, Horace married Emory, Mary Juliet 06/06/65   06/09/65
Burrow, Frederick, married Giles, Emily A. 12/29/63   01/12/64
Burrow, Grace Victoria died 07/10/62   07/23/62
Burrows, William married Sheeman, Hannah L. 01/18/64   02/27/64
Burrs, William T. died 07/13/63   07/15/63
Burry, Anna married Bankes, Charles 11/05/63   11/07/63
Bursh, Mary Grace (Mrs.) died 03/18/64   03/31/64
Burt, A. P. married Ellis, Mary E. 09/03/61   09/10/61
Burten, Elizabeth married Deaver, Joseph 08/29/65   09/02/65
Burton, Charles M. died 06/27/65   06/28/65
Burton, Charles M. died 06/27/65   06/29/65
Burton, Emma Turner died 06/24/64   07/01/64
Burton, George W. married Clark, Julia A. 01/08/61   01/10/61
Burton, Martha C. married Vermillion, John T. 12/13/64   12/21/64
Burton, Oliver Welsey died 11/29/63   12/01/63
Burton, Stephen J. married Mass, Sarah Jennings 05/29/65   06/17/65
Burton, Thomas married Hammond, Sarah Elizabeth 10/02/62   10/24/62
Burton, Virginia Gertrude died 03/04/65   03/10/65
Burwick, Johanna married Smith, John Henry 05/17/65   05/24/65
Busby, Ellen married Kegler, John G. 06/07/64   06/14/64
Busby, Margaret Mary Josephine married Adelsberger, Daniel G. 01/29/61

```
                   01/31/61
Busch, Abram V. married Riggin, Alice 12/25/62   02/10/63
Busch, George E. married Sprole, Sarah Jane 02/20/65   02/24/65
Busch, Hannah (Mrs.) died 07/25/63   07/28/63
Busch, Julia A. (Mrs.) died 08/16/64   08/13/64
Busch, William H. married Owings, Mary C. 04/08/61   04/13/61
Buschman, Victor H. married Barrett, Sallie A. 02/18/64   02/20/64
Buschmann, Christopher died 06/23/62   06/24/62
Buschmann, Christopher died 06/23/62   06/25/62
Buschmann, Frederica C. died 12/05/64   12/06/64
Buschmann, Frederica C. died 12/05/64   12/07/64
Busey, Norval H. married Laley, Emma V. 11/22/64   11/24/64
Bush, Amelia Virginia died 02/14/65   02/15/65
Bush, Elizabeth M. died 08/23/61   08/24/61
Bush, Eugene died 12/18/64   01/04/65
Bush, George Washington died 02/09/65   02/11/65
Bush, Maurice died 10/06/63   10/07/63
Bush, Rosanna M. H. died 12/09/61   12/10/61
Bush, S. Kate married Howard, O. H. 01/15/61   02/04/61
Busick, Anna (Mrs.) died 10/05/63   10/07/63
Busk, J. Alexius married Hamilton, Eleanor 01/13/63   01/30/63
Bussard, Priscilla died 02/13/61   02/14/61
Busse, L. V. married Thoman, Mary B. 02/10/63   02/11/63
Butcher, Emma married Brown, John T. 02/05/61   02/12/61
Butcher, James H. (Cpt.) died 04/15/64   04/16/64
Butlee, Thomas married Kane, Mary Ann 09/01/64   09/21/64
Butler, Abraham died 01/17/64   01/19/64
Butler, Ann died 01/14/63   01/15/63
Butler, Ann died 10/24/65   10/26/65
Butler, Elenora married Giles, Nathaniel 04/04/65   04/07/65
Butler, Elijah married Thompson, Louisa 06/30/63   07/02/63
Butler, Eliza married Hindes, Hughy 07/10/65   07/12/65
Butler, Ella M. married Price, J. T. 10/24/65   10/28/65
Butler, Ellen Amelia died 11/11/64   11/12/64
Butler, Frances Ann married Bell, John 10/01/63   10/03/63
Butler, Harriet died 02/09/65   02/10/65
Butler, Harriet A. married Boston, Nelson 04/03/63   04/04/63
Butler, Isaac died no date   06/06/61
Butler, Isabella M. married Boston, Abram 09/04/62   09/06/62
Butler, James H. (Dr.) married Griffin, Kate 11/24/64   11/28/64
Butler, James Henry married Hawkins, Maria 03/03/61   12/12/61
Butler, James Henry died 07/12/65   07/14/65
Butler, Jane P. (Mrs.) married Hunt, Henry A. 12/21/65   12/28/65
Butler, Jemima P. died 07/08/63   07/09/63
Butler, John married Woods, Josephine 10/29/63   10/31/63
Butler, John married Jones, Sarah Amanda 11/16/64   11/17/64
Butler, John C. married Wilson, Ellen Ann 07/10/62   07/12/62
Butler, John H. died 02/08/62   02/10/62
Butler, Kate M. died 10/08/65   10/09/65
Butler, Katie M. died no date   10/11/65
Butler, Lee died 01/13/65   01/14/65
Butler, Leonard married Mason, Rebecca 10/06/63   10/08/63
Butler, Lewis married Lee, Martha A. 07/30/63   08/01/63
Butler, Lizzie married Coleman, K. 10/25/63   10/27/63
Butler, Louise died 01/30/63   02/20/63
```

Butler, Margret A. married Bowen, William H. 06/04/63   08/13/63
Butler, Mary A. died 06/05/64   06/07/64
Butler, Mary A. (Mrs.) married Reilley, Peter 10/14/61   10/19/61
Butler, Mary Ann died 09/27/62   09/29/62
Butler, Mary Grimes died 12/08/65   12/09/65
Butler, Mary V. married Grinage, John 03/28/61   04/09/61
Butler, Michael died 02/18/63   02/20/63
Butler, Peter married McDearmott, Mary 06/19/64   06/25/64
Butler, William H. married Wells, Mary Frances 02/26/63   02/28/63
Butler, William Isiah married Carr, Ann Elizabeth 04/16/61   07/26/61
Butler, William T. married McElhaney, Kate 02/16/63   02/20/63
Butt, John died 12/28/62   12/30/62
Butter, Ann died 10/24/65   10/25/65
Button, Almira married Collgate, Charles E. 08/13/61   08/14/61
Button, Emery V. married Haupt, Lizzie 01/19/64   01/28/64
Button, James Alonzo died 10/24/63   10/26/63
Button, Martha married Smith, Robert 01/12/65   01/18/65
Button, Sarah Jane married Smith, Thomas H. 12/17/61   12/18/61
Butts, George Wilmot died 10/02/65   10/05/65
Buxbaum, Elizabeth (Mrs.) died 12/23/63   12/24/63
Buxbaum, Elizabeth (Mrs.) died 12/23/63   12/25/63
Buxensten, Otto married Henaman, Hannah 02/19/63   03/16/63
Buxton, Brook, Jr. married Baker, Emma J. (Mrs.) 12/07/65   12/13/65
Byer, Lizzie V. married Ways, Charles Edward 09/09/63   09/10/63
Byer, Mary Helen died 01/16/62   03/22/62
Byerly, Mary Ann married Hesse, William F. 03/10/63   03/12/63
Byers, Irene S. married Miller, J. Poulson 11/05/63   11/07/63
Byers, James F. married Richards, Mary A. 02/04/64   02/05/64
Byers, John T. married Snyder, Anna E. 12/21/63   12/21/63
Byers, Rosella died 04/26/64   04/27/64
Byles, Carrie L. married Coffey, Silas D. 11/01/64   11/03/64
Byram, S. D. married Harris, Lannie L. 01/12/63   01/13/63
Byran, S. V. married Harris, L. 01/12/63   01/23/63
Byrd, F. Marion married Owens, Bettie A. 01/21/64   01/29/64
Byrd, Sarah K. married Wollop, William G. H. 11/14/61   12/14/61
Byrd, Thomas T. married Neilson, Emily 05/20/61   04/23/61
Byrely, James T. married Rumstine, Ellen 05/07/63   05/23/63
Byrn, Edward died 10/23/64   11/05/64
Byrn, George V. died 06/04/64   06/06/64
Byrne, Andrew died 12/13/63   12/15/63
Byrne, Ann died 07/19/62   08/02/62
Byrne, Bridget died 12/25/63   12/26/63
Byrne, Catherine died 08/27/61   08/28/61
Byrne, Catherine died 09/15/63   09/16/63
Byrne, Catherine (Mrs.) died 02/10/64   02/11/64
Byrne, Christopher Joseph died 07/13/62   07/16/62
Byrne, Edward died 12/12/65   12/13/65
Byrne, Eliza died 10/26/65   10/27/65
Byrne, Elizabeth died 10/12/62   10/13/62
Byrne, Elizabeth Rosala died 07/08/64   07/09/64
Byrne, James died 04/22/61   04/23/61
Byrne, Marcus Frederick died 11/17/64   11/19/64
Byrne, Margaret died 01/06/61   01/07/61
Byrne, Mary died 08/07/63   08/08/63
Byrne, Michael died 05/20/64   05/23/64

Byrne, Peter A. died 08/27/61 08/28/61
Byrne, Philip died 10/14/63 10/16/63
Byrne, Philip died 10/14/63 10/17/63
Byrne, Sydney Mary died 03/04/63 03/07/63
Byrner, Patrick Francis died 12/11/62 12/12/62
Byrnes, Alice died 07/08/64 07/11/64
Byrnes, Edmund married Finnigan, Mary 04/07/61 07/10/61
Byrnes, Ellen died 07/18/64 07/20/64
Byrnes, John died 08/01/65 08/08/65
Byrnes, Martin married Diffely, Mary A. 07/06/62 07/26/62
Byrnes, Mary A. (Mrs.) died 07/17/63 07/18/63
Byrnes, Mary Ann (Mrs.) died 01/05/64 01/15/64
Byrnes, Michael married Keiley, Margaret K. 11/20/64 12/02/64
Byrnes, Philip died 04/10/64 04/11/64
Byron, Walter Wood died no date 10/19/63
Byus, Laura Estelle married Pattison, A. Augustus 12/02/63 12/04/63
Cable, George S. married Reynolds, Virginia 10/29/63 10/31/63
Cable, Mary A. married Burgess, Caleb W. 04/27/65 06/01/65
Cacy, Eliza A. married Smith, George E. 09/14/65 09/15/65
Cacy, Samuel C. died 12/09/61 12/16/61
Caddemore, John R. died 01/02/65 01/04/65
Cadden, J. R. married Bouldin, Belle V. 04/04/65 04/15/65
Cadow, William Morse died 08/08/65 08/12/65
Cadwallader, Abel married Conley, Olivia 03/28/65 04/03/65
Cadwallader, Able died 03/10/61 03/13/61
Cadwallader, Emma L. married Raynolds, Stephen P. 04/28/64 05/03/64
Cadwallader, Lizzie V. married Anderson, John L. 05/20/61 05/28/61
Cadwallader, S. E. married Hanes, Virginia 05/19/64 05/24/64
Cadwell, Mary E. married Moran, George W. 10/17/65 10/21/65
Cafferty, Catherine died 01/19/61 01/21/61
Cahill, Joseph N. (USN) died 04/15/64 04/18/64
Cahill, Richard died 03/18/63 07/28/63
Cain, A. J. married Smith, Emma R. 05/25/61 08/12/61
Cain, Catherine died 07/25/62 07/26/62
Cain, Charlotte (Mrs.) died 11/07/63 11/11/63
Cain, Edty T. died 12/19/65 12/20/65
Cain, Joseph died 04/21/64 04/22/64
Cain, Mary E. married Hudson, William H. 04/14/64 04/16/64
Cain, Priscilla married Williams, Benjamin 01/15/63 01/17/63
Cain, William H. married Glass, Annie E. 06/01/65 06/13/65
Caine, Mary (Mrs.) died 06/20/64 06/21/64
Calahan, Tabitha E. married Mears, John F. 11/12/61 11/16/61
Calanan, Bridget died 08/31/61 09/02/61
Calder, Jane married Norris, Joseph T. 07/06/65 07/20/65
Calder, Rosanna (Mrs.) died 12/15/64 12/16/64
Calder, William Edward died 09/11/63 09/12/63
Caldwell, A. Palladio married Gibson, Clara A. 11/25/64 12/23/64
Caldwell, Carrie L. married Bigham, Marshall M. 09/28/65 10/06/65
Caldwell, Charles Harrison died 03/17/65 03/20/65
Caldwell, Eliza J. died 02/14/65 02/15/65
Caldwell, Elizabeth died 02/10/63 02/11/63
Caldwell, Jane married Murphy, John P. 05/25/65 05/25/65
Caldwell, Jane married Murphy, John 05/28/65 06/03/65
Caldwell, John (Dr.) married Love, Anna R. 01/05/64 01/07/64
Caldwell, Maranda died 10/23/65 10/25/65

Caldwell, Margaret A. married Boyle, Joshua Y. 09/16/62 09/26/62
Caldwell, Reuben T. married Ridgeway, Georgie 01/13/64 01/19/64
Calhoun, James married Pratt, Sarah Elizabeth 05/15/62 05/17/62
Calhoun, Margaretta (Mrs.) died 12/14/64 12/16/64
Calhoun, Margaretta A. (Mrs.) died 12/14/64 12/15/64
Calhoun, Mary married Nelson, John 10/20/63 10/22/63
Calk, John H. married Higgins, Henrietta 03/21/61 03/23/61
Callaghan, Margarette died 02/27/63 02/28/63
Callaghan, Thomas married Lynch, Annie 02/18/62 02/20/62
Callahan, Ellen married Kerns, Bernard 09/25/64 09/28/64
Callahan, Martin died 11/30/64 12/02/64
Callahan, Thomas died 04/21/62 04/23/62
Callahan, Thomas died 12/09/62 12/10/62
Callan, Christopher B. died 07/25/65 07/26/65
Callan, Elizabeth died 05/15/64 05/16/64
Callan, Julia Ann died 07/29/61 07/30/61
Callan, Owen T. married Standiford, Amanda E. 05/21/62 05/23/62
Callanan, Martin died 09/26/61 09/28/61
Callaway, George F. married Dunn, Hannah 09/03/62 09/10/62
Callaway, Martha E. married Kirkwood, George H. 04/08/62 04/12/62
Calle, Blair Eugene died 01/03/62 01/06/62
Callenber, William H., Jr. married Ferguson, Rozella V. 07/21/63 07/23/63
Callender, Anne (Mrs.) died 12/18/64 12/19/64
Callender, George W. married Payne, Marion 11/20/62 12/12/62
Callender, George W. died 09/06/63 09/08/63
Callender, Sarah died 08/12/62 08/16/62
Callis, Eugene died 12/10/65 12/11/65
Callow, Catherine married Beckenridge, John C. 03/31/64 04/02/64
Callow, Catherine married Breckenridge, John C. 03/31/64 04/02/64
Callow, Katie P. married Swain, J. Francis 07/03/65 07/17/65
Callow, Samuel died 01/25/63 01/26/63
Calloway, Samuel died 04/25/62 04/26/62
Callwell, John married Smith, Harriet Ann Ophelia 04/10/60 03/26/61
Calnan, Mary Ellen died 03/28/64 03/29/64
Caltrider, Barbara (Mrs.) died 05/02/64 05/07/64
Calvert, John B. married Kelmling, Bianca Baptista 09/14/64 09/16/64
Calvert, Mary C. married Solter, George L. 09/19/61 10/12/61
Calvert, William Thomas married King, Ann Rebecca 07/30/63 09/08/63
Calvin, George W. died 10/20/62 10/22/62
Calwell, James married Limbach, Martha 08/25/65 09/09/65
Calwell, James R. married Lochary, Mary 12/08/63 12/12/63
Calwell, Mary Tyson (Mrs.) died 12/31/62 01/05/63
Calwell, William H. died 04/24/63 05/02/63
Cameron, Rachael died 08/24/65 08/25/65
Cameron, Rachel died 08/24/65 08/26/65
Camp, James L. married Mann, Sarah 04/06/65 04/10/65
Camp, Joseph died 03/20/64 03/21/64
Camp, Sarah B. died 03/27/61 03/28/61
Campbell, Ann died 12/27/62 12/29/62
Campbell, Ann M. (Mrs.) died no date 10/07/63
Campbell, Ann Maria died 09/08/62 09/16/62
Campbell, Benjamin F. married Murphy, Annie 04/18/65 04/19/65
Campbell, Charles Jordan died 08/19/62 08/20/62
Campbell, Daniel died 02/18/64 02/19/64

Campbell, Edward died 04/01/62   04/02/62
Campbell, Eliza married Ellis, Charles N. 02/13/62   02/14/62
Campbell, Eliza married Anderson, Andrew 01/12/65   01/14/65
Campbell, Francis Walter died 02/07/63   02/09/63
Campbell, Harry died 09/29/61   09/30/61
Campbell, James G. died 10/01/65   10/02/65
Campbell, Jane (Mrs.) died 09/14/64   09/15/64
Campbell, Jane (Mrs.) died 09/14/64   09/16/64
Campbell, Jane (Mrs.) died 12/20/65   12/21/65
Campbell, John married McCollum, Nancy 04/06/63   04/08/63
Campbell, John married Lynch, Annie 08/18/63   08/31/63
Campbell, Joseph S. died 01/02/63   01/05/63
Campbell, Josua Jackson died 06/18/64   06/21/64
Campbell, Lucie J. married Mewburn, Joseph P. 01/27/64   02/02/64
Campbell, Marshal (Lt. Com.) died 02/22/65   02/23/65
Campbell, Marshal (Lt. Com.) died 02/22/65   02/24/65
Campbell, Mary married Stevers, Joseph 12/10/61   12/18/61
Campbell, Mary Elizabeth died 05/15/61   05/16/61
Campbell, Nathaniel died 04/26/65   04/27/65
Campbell, Rebecca died 02/10/64   02/12/64
Campbell, Rose Ann married Lusby, James 11/28/65   11/30/65
Campbell, Sarah married Sykes, William 07/24/62   07/26/62
Campbell, Sarah married Lynch, William 11/24/64   12/09/64
Campbell, Thomas married McFrederick, Kate R. 08/07/62   09/02/62
Campbell, Thomas K. (Lt.) died 09/23/64   09/27/64
Campbell, William died 04/14/61   04/15/61
Campbell, William died 08/08/62   08/09/62
Campen, John married Schneider, Charlotte 03/02/62   03/04/62
Camper, Clara J. married Trott, Nathaniel J. 12/02/62   05/13/63
Camper, Isaac L. died 04/26/61   05/02/61
Campher, George W. married Smith, Emily J. 07/04/65   07/06/65
Campher, James E. married Dickson, Laura O. 05/25/65   05/27/65
Campher, James R. died 07/22/65   07/29/65
Camron, B. F. died 06/04/61   06/05/61
Canavan, Agnes married Dagney, Daniel 11/23/63   11/30/63
Canavan, Eliza married Armstrong, James C. 11/02/63   11/13/63
Canavan, Jamine H. married Platt, Thomas Mitchell 01/13/62   01/18/62
Canby, Charles died 07/10/65   07/13/65
Canby, William L. died 11/16/63   12/05/63
Cancannon, Timothy Alexis died 04/13/62   04/15/62
Candie, E. R. married Fitzpatrick, George H. 11/29/64   11/30/64
Cane, Charles died 04/17/64   04/18/64
Cane, John married Williams, Mary Elizabeth 12/06/64   12/08/64
Canfield, William J. died 03/21/61   03/22/61
Cannon, Alfred D. married Skillen, Mary 11/10/61   11/28/61
Cannon, Amanda married Jenkins, James H. 10/31/61   11/05/61
Cannon, C. K. married Franklin, Sallie W. 11/12/61   11/22/61
Cannon, Elizabeth died 02/22/62   02/25/62
Cannon, James married Schley, Elizabeth (Mrs.) 10/07/64   10/17/64
Cannon, Kate L. died 02/25/65   02/27/65
Cannon, Louisa J. married Kone, William W. 10/26/62   10/29/62
Cannon, Mary A. married Wallis, William H. 08/13/62   08/27/62
Cannon, Mary E. married Murray, Oliver P. 10/27/61   10/29/61
Cannon, Rosan Arnett died 10/27/63   10/29/63
Cannon, Sallie W. died 05/22/62   05/24/62

Canon, George D. married Gardiner, Delilah M. 06/09/64 06/10/64
Canon, Jane E. died 11/05/65 11/06/65
Canon, Lemelia O. died 03/18/65 03/22/65
Canon, Susie married Hanson, B. H. 01/23/62 01/25/62
Canon, William N. died 05/09/63 05/15/63
Canox, Carie married Reister, Jonathan D. 08/23/65 08/25/65
Canter, Lucinda Varona died 07/29/63 07/31/63
Canter, Lydia R. married Sothoron, Levin J. 12/08/63 12/11/63
Canway, George married Baker, Georgeanna 01/10/63 02/12/63
Caples, Elizabeth (Mrs.) died 05/26/65 05/27/65
Caples, Mary Elizabeth married Day, George no date 08/08/63
Cappeau, Mary E. (Mrs.) died 07/19/65 07/21/65
Cappeau, Serah (Mrs.) died 10/01/65 10/03/65
Caprise, Josephine died 03/11/62 03/14/62
Capron, Richard J. married Lee, Laura 08/24/64 08/27/64
Capron, Richard J. married Lee, Laura 08/24/64 08/30/64
Carback, Charles died 10/09/62 10/13/62
Carback, David A. died 10/10/62 10/13/62
Carback, John died 02/22/64 02/23/64
Carback, Mary J. married Cunningham, Edward T. 10/24/65 10/31/65
Carback, R. C. married Fuller, Mary E. 11/24/64 12/02/64
Carback, Sarah died 10/12/62 10/13/62
Carback, William C. died 02/17/61 02/18/61
Carback, William George died 12/31/62 01/02/63
Carbery, Joseph F. married Howard, Annie E. 05/03/61 05/06/61
Cardwell, Mary married Clarke, Sylvester 07/06/62 07/08/62
Carelton, Elizabeth Agnes married Horstman, Joseph D. 08/31/64 09/03/6
Carey, Andrew N. died 07/20/62 07/21/62
Carey, Anna Maria died 07/21/62 07/23/62
Carey, David F. married O'Connell, Nellie 11/24/63 12/01/63
Carey, Elizabeth (Mrs.) died 12/04/63 12/05/63
Carey, Francis died 11/20/62 11/21/62
Carey, John W. married Frank, Jennie S. 03/26/65 03/30/65
Carey, Johnnie Michael died 05/17/64 06/11/64
Carey, Peter died 02/11/61 02/12/61
Carey, Thomas J. died 07/06/64 07/09/64
Carey, William married Finagan, Maggie 04/05/63 04/08/63
Cariss, Maggie married Griffin, Robert B., Jr. 11/05/63 11/12/63
Carland, Thomas married Gettier, Sarah 06/11/63 06/23/63
Carle, Emma May died 07/08/64 07/09/64
Carle, John H. married Branon, Eliza 04/06/63 06/26/63
Carleton, Elizabeth Agnes married Horstman, Joseph D. 08/31/64 09/07/6
Carlier, Henry married Gaussoin, Elise A. C. 10/23/65 10/24/65
Carlile, James H., Jr. died 10/22/63 10/23/63
Carlin, Christopher died 09/15/63 09/17/63
Carlin, James S. (Dr.) married Staylor, Mary C. 06/02/64 06/06/64
Carlin, James S. (M.D.) married 12/31/63 01/02/64
Carling, Mary died no date 09/11/65
Carlisle, Agness died 11/19/62 11/21/62
Carlisle, George Casper died 10/20/62 10/25/62
Carlisle, Sarah married Pyne, James F. 10/19/65 10/23/65
Carlon, Margaret died 12/29/62 12/31/62
Carmack, Henry C. died 12/30/63 01/09/64
Carmack, Jehu died 11/30/62 12/01/62
Carmack, Jehu died 11/30/62 12/02/62

```
Carmack, Jehu married Badger, Alice Ann 12/31/63   01/02/64
Carmack, Laura A. married Roberts, George S. 04/17/62   04/19/62
Carman, Caleb C. married Foard, Anna E. 11/30/65   12/15/65
Carman, Elizabeth (Mrs.) died 12/14/63   12/15/63
Carman, Jacob Samuel died 10/11/62   10/17/62
Carman, Joseph D. married Cruser, Mary 05/17/63   05/19/63
Carman, Louisa married Gordon, William E. 03/06/61   03/29/61
Carman, Maria Agnes married Biscoe, James E. 03/01/64   03/10/64
Carman, Mary J. married Millan, John G. 05/24/63   05/27/63
Carman, Robert R. married Griffin, Mary E. 05/07/63   05/21/63
Carmichael, Eliza (Mrs.) died 07/19/64   07/21/64
Carmichael, Elizabeth (Mrs.) died 12/12/64   12/14/64
Carmichael, Elizabeth E.(Mrs.) died 12/12/64   12/13/64
Carmichael, Emily Jane died 07/15/64   07/20/64
Carmichael, J. E. married Smith, Margaret C. 11/26/62   12/13/62
Carmichael, Kate died 10/31/61   11/02/61
Carmichael, William married Hoff, Maggie E. 11/02/65   11/04/65
Carmine, Catharine married DeHaven, John David 12/11/64   12/17/64
Carmine, Charles G. married Carrigan, Maggie A. 12/21/65   12/22/65
Carmine, Samuel B. married Ward, Margaret (Mrs.) 01/25/63   01/27/63
Carmine, Thomas Francis died 12/06/63   12/07/63
Carmody, John died 08/10/64   08/11/64
Carmody, William died 07/24/65   07/25/65
Carnan, John Donel died 09/25/65   09/26/65
Carnay, Maria died 09/14/65   09/15/65
Carnes, Andrew J. married Henderson, Marie M. 07/07/64   07/11/64
Carnes, Mary died 01/16/62   01/18/62
Carney, Darby died 01/15/63   01/17/63
Carney, Ellen died 01/15/61   01/16/61
Carney, Jane (Mrs.) died 04/29/65   05/01/65
Carney, Kate married Smith, Joseph 01/06/64   01/09/64
Carney, Sarah died 10/12/62   10/14/62
Carney, Sarah married Gosnell, John 08/29/65   09/01/65
Carney, Thomas died 06/14/65   06/15/65
Caroll, Isabella E. married Croggen, William E. 09/10/65   09/12/65
Caromine, Josiah P. died 10/11/63   10/13/63
Carpenter, Kate Morfit died 10/31/62   11/01/62
Carpenter, Minerva V. (Mrs.) died 03/06/63   03/11/63
Carpenter, Rebecca died 04/22/61   04/23/61
Carper, Clamanda J. married Banks, J. Marion 01/13/63   01/21/63
Carper, Mary L. married Elder, John H. 02/28/65   04/12/65
Carr, Ann died 02/11/61   02/15/61
Carr, Ann (Mrs.) died 07/27/64   07/29/64
Carr, Ann Eliza died 12/11/61   12/18/61
Carr, Ann Elizabeth married Butler, William Isiah 04/16/61   07/26/61
Carr, Arthur married Hardesty, Mary E. 06/10/62   06/13/62
Carr, Augusta Bells died 01/24/64   01/26/64
Carr, Benjamin M. married Willis, Lizzie A. 11/06/65   11/14/65
Carr, Catharine married Jager, John 07/10/64   07/15/64
Carr, Edward married Sinz, Henreeta 03/25/63   04/02/63
Carr, Eliza A. married Ensor, Daniel A. 07/18/65   07/20/65
Carr, Elizabeth married Guista, Stephen 11/04/61   11/08/61
Carr, Ellen died 12/09/61   12/10/61
Carr, George Washington died 06/30/61   07/02/61
Carr, Gustine married Boush, Jerry 05/11/63   05/12/63
```

```
Carr, Helen married Maller, James N. 05/19/64   05/25/64
Carr, Henry married Gould, Annie E. 09/14/61   12/25/61
Carr, Jane died 09/29/64   09/30/64
Carr, John died 02/11/64   02/12/64
Carr, John died 02/11/64   02/13/64
Carr, John died 07/16/65   07/17/65
Carr, Josephine Gustina died 03/19/62   03/21/62
Carr, Julia married Compton, Vernon 11/13/61   11/14/61
Carr, Laura Virginia died 02/22/64   02/24/64
Carr, Lewis died 07/13/64   07/20/64
Carr, Lily S. died 06/27/63   06/29/63
Carr, Margaret died no date   09/05/62
Carr, Margaret married Lockard, Lorenzo D. 04/14/64   04/19/64
Carr, Margaret Virginia married Williams, James T. 07/04/65   07/07/65
Carr, Martha married Boston, Joseph no date   12/22/64
Carr, Martha J. died 08/04/61   08/05/61
Carr, Mary A. died 04/18/63   04/20/63
Carr, Mary B. married Doolittle, H. Clay 10/31/64   11/23/64
Carr, Mary Elizabeth died 08/24/65   08/25/65
Carr, Mary Ellen married Ringold, Daniel Thomas 11/07/61   11/11/61
Carr, Mary Estelle died 01/08/63   01/09/63
Carr, Mary N. died 11/04/62   11/05/62
Carr, Mary N. died 11/04/62   11/06/62
Carr, Matilda married Parkhill, Robert 10/25/65   10/26/65
Carr, Patrick Lawrence died 09/02/63   09/04/63
Carr, Samuel Morgan died 10/08/65   10/10/65
Carr, Sarah H. died 04/15/62   04/18/62
Carr, Theresa married McKitrick, James 12/18/65   12/23/65
Carr, Uriah married Wall, Jane O. 11/16/65   11/24/65
Carr, William died 09/05/62   09/06/62
Carr, William H. married Reed, Martha J. 12/24/62   12/27/62
Carr, William Henry died 03/01/64   03/04/64
Carr, William T. married Sprigg, M. Louisa 11/07/65   11/09/65
Carr, Willington Washington died 05/06/62   05/07/62
Carrey, Anne Joseph died 06/09/64   06/11/64
Carrick, B. Franklin married Lewis, Adeline V. Lewis 03/03/63   03/06/6
Carrick, Charles Thomas F. died 03/10/65   04/08/65
Carrick, George W. married Myers, Lucretia A. 11/01/65   11/23/65
Carrick, William J. married Miller, Virginia 11/01/64   11/02/64
Carrigan, Elmira (Mrs.) died 07/06/63   07/08/63
Carrigan, Harry Tremain died 07/08/63   07/09/63
Carrigan, Hugh married Lilly, Sallie F. 10/07/62   10/09/62
Carrigan, Maggie A. married Carmine, Charles G. 12/21/65   12/22/65
Carrigan, William J. married Appleby, Amanda 06/12/64   06/14/64
Carrman, Ann Rebecca died 04/23/62   05/03/62
Carrol, Laura died 09/10/62   09/11/62
Carrol, Thomas married Krews, Mary E. 08/22/65   09/05/65
Carroll, Albert H. (Lt.) died 08/07/62   09/22/62
Carroll, Annie R. died 08/05/62   08/06/62
Carroll, C. T. married Milligan, Susan H. 12/08/63   12/09/63
Carroll, Catherine married Barrett, James 05/21/63   05/22/63
Carroll, Catherine M. married Duffy, James 02/04/63   02/07/63
Carroll, Charles died 12/02/62   12/03/62
Carroll, Charles died 12/02/62   12/04/62
Carroll, D. H. married Boyd, Mary E. 07/06/65   07/15/65
```

Carroll, Eabert P. married Fitzgerald, Mary A. 06/08/62 06/13/62
Carroll, Edward died 07/29/65 07/29/65
Carroll, Eliza A. (Mrs.) married Phelps, Joseph R. 04/20/65 04/22/65
Carroll, Elizabeth married Langley, Edward 09/26/61 11/26/61
Carroll, Ellen married Frazer, Henry 12/24/61 12/25/61
Carroll, H. E. married Askins, W. E. 04/25/61 09/14/61
Carroll, Henry married Ockmay, Sarah Ann 03/21/61 03/25/61
Carroll, Henry married Reed, Rebecca 07/16/63 07/18/63
Carroll, James married Woods, Anna 03/07/61 03/08/61
Carroll, James Brown died 08/03/64 08/06/64
Carroll, James Thomas died 06/05/63 06/06/63
Carroll, Jams A. married Booker, Laura 05/26/63 05/29/63
Carroll, Jane married McCallister, William J. 02/09/63 04/08/63
Carroll, Jane (Mrs.) died 09/02/63 09/03/63
Carroll, Janey married Stratton, Thomas H. 07/21/63 09/02/63
Carroll, Joanna (Mrs.) died 02/14/64 02/15/64
Carroll, John died 02/02/62 02/03/62
Carroll, John married Spalding, Ella M. 04/09/63 04/13/63
Carroll, John Francis died 01/17/65 01/18/65
Carroll, Judith Carter (Mrs.) died 01/13/63 01/14/63
Carroll, Maria married Fogarty, James 03/03/62 03/04/62
Carroll, Mary A. married Flamm, George 07/20/65 07/22/65
Carroll, Mary Ann died 08/16/65 08/17/65
Carroll, Michael died 01/08/64 01/09/64
Carroll, Mortimer married Dolan, Kate 11/27/62 12/13/62
Carroll, Nannie Ellen died 03/16/64 03/17/64
Carroll, P. H. married Mortimer, Thomazine L. 03/26/65 05/18/65
Carroll, Robert married Ryan, Mary A. 04/29/65 05/02/65
Carroll, Sallie married Cradock, Thomas 10/22/62 10/23/62
Carroll, Sarah E. married Adams, John A. 09/15/62 09/17/62
Carroll, Susan J, (Mrs.) died 12/05/64 12/06/64
Carroll, Thomas died 02/08/65 02/09/65
Carroll, W. Augustus died 08/31/64 09/01/64
Carroll, W. Augustus died 08/31/64 09/02/64
Carroll, William died 02/10/65 02/11/65
Carroll, William P. married Vernetson, Sue 12/04/61 03/04/62
Carroll, William P. married Rawlings, Ada E. 09/05/65 09/23/65
Carse, Margaret married McIlvaney, Richard 09/22/62 09/25/62
Carson, David E. died 05/03/62 05/05/62
Carson, Hannah Trumbull died 06/09/63 06/10/63
Carson, Henrietta M. married Ehrman, Charles H. 12/19/65 12/25/65
Carson, John L. died 10/08/61 10/21/61
Carson, Mary died 07/11/63 07/13/63
Carson, Mary June married Brown, John 03/14/65 03/23/65
Carson, Sarah died 08/18/64 08/24/64
Carson, Thomas E. (Rev.) married Keene, Mary A. 04/30/63 05/08/63
Carter, (Mrs. Francis) died 02/14/63 02/17/63
Carter, Annie married Thompson, L. S. B. 10/29/61 11/22/61
Carter, Asbury died 10/31/62 11/01/62
Carter, Caroline (Mrs.) died 06/12/63 06/13/63
Carter, Caroline Elizabeth died 03/02/62 03/04/62
Carter, Carrie Emma died 02/17/65 02/20/65
Carter, Charles W. married Alton, Ella M. 01/17/61 01/31/61
Carter, Clement died 11/14/62 11/15/62
Carter, D. J. married Royston, Ciscelia 11/16/65 12/02/65

```
Carter, Edwardeena married Clough, James 01/29/64  01/30/64
Carter, Eliza married Hill, John E. 12/22/63  01/12/64
Carter, Elizabeth died 11/03/61  11/04/61
Carter, Ella married George, Samuel K., Jr. 06/18/63  06/20/63
Carter, Ellen married McHarry, Robert 11/30/65  12/05/65
Carter, Emily (Mrs.) died 01/22/64  01/25/64
Carter, George married Abbott, Amanda 01/28/64  01/30/64
Carter, George W. died 12/02/63  12/04/63
Carter, Hannah J. married Ostlip, Samuel W. 11/08/64  11/14/64
Carter, Harry died 07/16/65  07/21/65
Carter, James E. died 07/14/63  07/17/63
Carter, James W. married Hall, Margaret Ann 09/21/64  09/23/64
Carter, John died 08/01/62  08/02/62
Carter, John W. married Boteler, Emma T. 03/22/64  03/23/64
Carter, John William died 01/16/61  01/17/61
Carter, Josephine married Rusk, William 01/05/64  01/14/64
Carter, Josephine married Whittle, John T. 11/17/64  11/23/64
Carter, Martha V. married Dickson, James A. 09/26/61  09/28/61
Carter, Mary Anna died 11/12/65  11/17/65
Carter, Mary C. (Mrs.) died 10/16/64  10/17/64
Carter, Richard married MacDonald, Mary L. 04/22/65  05/13/65
Carter, Richard R. died 01/14/61  01/15/61
Carter, Robert E. died 04/02/63  04/06/63
Carter, S. Lizzie married Hughey, T. Cook 09/09/63  09/10/63
Carter, Thomas married Bowin, Margaret H. 12/01/64  12/14/64
Carter, Valentine died 04/13/63  04/14/63
Carter, William married Allen, Frances 04/02/63  04/04/63
Carter, William married Burnes, Mary J. 03/17/64  03/23/64
Carter, William H. married Cook, Mary W. 04/15/62  04/17/62
Carter, William H. married Dodson, Julia A. 09/12/64  09/14/64
Carter, William J. married Wasson, Wilthia A. 04/17/65  08/18/65
Carter, William James M. married Ringrose, Olivia 11/30/62  12/05/62
Carter, Willie B. married Fuller, Annie 01/26/65  02/06/65
Cartey, Alray B. died 12/25/65  12/27/65
Cartier, Mollie E. married Burke, Joseph F. 04/30/63  05/07/63
Caruthers, Virginia married Millan, N. M. 02/21/65  02/27/65
Carvalho, Sarah N. (Mrs.) died 03/20/64  03/25/64
Carver, Mary M. (Mrs.) died 07/24/65  08/01/65
Carver, William Milton died 05/06/61  05/08/61
Carvey, Mary married Garrigan, Peter 08/18/64  08/22/64
Carville, Edmund died 10/21/65  10/25/65
Cary, Sarah A. (Mrs.) died 11/01/64  11/02/64
Cary, Sarah Jane married Long, Henry C. 11/09/64  11/12/64
Casby, Mary married Miskimon, Phillip 01/11/64  01/16/64
Case, Lilian Y. died 05/11/63  05/13/63
Case, Mary J. died 08/04/63  08/05/63
Casey, (Mrs.) died 01/07/64  01/08/64
Casey, Annie died 08/03/64  08/04/64
Casey, Annie died 08/03/64  08/23/64
Casey, Fanny A. married Leddon, John W. 06/21/65  07/14/65
Casey, Francis W. died 02/04/62  02/06/62
Casey, Martin J. died 12/25/63  12/26/63
Casey, Mary married Gordon, Bartholomew 02/07/64  02/08/64
Casey, Mary Ellen died 02/17/65  02/18/65
Casey, Thomas J. married Dolly, Margaret A. 09/01/61  09/03/61
```

Casey, William died 01/18/65   01/20/65
Casher, Joseph died 08/09/65   08/10/65
Cashmyer, Ellen Theresa died 09/28/65   09/29/65
Cashmyer, Henry married Zinkland, Mary E. 10/18/64   10/21/64
Caskey, John C. married Long, Addie 10/14/64   02/22/65
Caskey, Mary E. married Tolley, Jeremiah 10/30/65   11/14/65
Caspari, Harriet died 02/25/61   02/26/61
Cass, Louis F. died 10/28/61   10/29/61
Cass, Rina married Lineweaver, P. L. 05/19/64   05/21/64
Cassady, Bartholomew died 06/08/62   06/10/62
Cassady, Francis S. died 08/14/64   08/16/64
Cassady, John G. died 10/28/62   10/29/62
Cassady, John G. died 10/28/62   10/30/62
Cassady, John Granville died 04/02/63   04/07/63
Cassady, Joseph F. died 04/06/61   04/08/61
Cassady, Lilly, died 03/25/63   03/27/63
Cassady, Mary J. died 07/05/63   07/07/63
Cassady, Mary J. died 07/05/63   07/06/63
Cassander, John Gilda died 02/03/61   02/05/61
Cassard, A. L. married Bartholow, J. M. C. 12/06/65   12/11/65
Cassard, Emily married Tyler, G. B. (Gen.) 11/21/65   11/24/65
Cassard, Ernest died 06/30/62   07/01/62
Cassard, George Carleton married Resor, Maggie 11/30/65   12/16/65
Cassard, John died 07/09/62   07/12/62
Cassard, John married Rous, Lucy Chase 10/08/63   10/13/63
Cassard, Sarah (Mrs.) died 12/31/63   01/02/64
Cassel, Kate T. (Mrs.) died 07/24/65   07/27/65
Cassell, Edward A. married Ing, Catharine T. 09/23/64   11/28/64
Cassell, Elizabeth died 04/30/61   05/01/61
Cassell, Leonard married Fairbanks, Eliza A. 08/06/63   08/08/63
Cassell, Mary E. married Jones, Cornelius 04/01/61   04/04/61
Cassell, Mary Elizabeth died 10/15/61   10/21/61
Cassell, Sallie A. E. died 05/02/61   05/06/61
Cassell, Sallie J. married Lytle, William B. 06/24/62   07/01/62
Casselman, W. C. married McDaniel, Laura A. no date   09/19/61
Cassely, Catherine died 09/19/62   09/27/62
Cassidy, Anne died 09/13/61   09/14/61
Cassidy, Emily married Follansbee, George 01/17/61   01/22/61
Cassidy, Emily married Follansbee, George 01/17/61   01/23/61
Cassidy, Esther died 08/15/61   08/16/61
Cassidy, James P. died 06/14/63   06/15/63
Cassidy, James P. died 06/14/63   06/16/63
Cassidy, John Joseph died 10/21/61   10/22/61
Cassidy, Maggie married Rosenteel, John L. 12/03/61   12/05/61
Cassidy, Maggie [retract] married Rosenteel, John L. [retract] no date   12/06/61
Cassidy, Mary died 12/01/63   12/03/63
Cassidy, Mary Elizabeth died 10/11/61   10/12/61
Cassidy, Morgianna died 02/21/63   02/24/63
Cassidy, Patrick died 08/02/65   08/04/65
Cassidy, William married McLaughlin, Mary Ellen 01/01/63   03/03/63
Cassin, Roberta E. married Shriver, John L. 10/19/65   11/01/65
Cassour, Mary died 04/08/64   04/09/64
Castenstine, Moses died 05/30/64   05/31/64
Caster, Robert married Johnson, Ruth 12/15/63   12/19/63

```
Castle, P. A. (Lt.) married Murphy, Fannie 10/19/64   10/20/64
Caston, Alfred H. married Taylor, Mary E. 04/18/61   04/23/61
Castor, John August died 02/03/62   02/05/62
Castor, Noel F. married Johnson, Jane 04/04/61   04/09/61
Caswell, Susan H. (Mrs.) died 02/03/63   02/04/63
Casy, Francis W. died 02/04/62   02/05/62
Cathcart, George H. married Diven, Susannah 05/21/61   05/23/61
Cathcart, George H. died 07/30/64   08/03/64
Cathell, Daniel W. married Boult, Jeanette N. 11/19/63   11/23/63
Cathell, Josephine died 08/12/62   08/13/62
Cather, Annie E. died 02/10/63   02/11/63
Cather, Susie married Lebon, Charles E. 09/00/00   02/05/64
Cathers, John died 10/09/63   10/16/63
Caton, Edward (Rev.) died 06/26/62   06/28/62
Caton, Honora died 12/06/63   12/08/63
Caton, John died 09/28/62   09/29/62
Caton, Julia married Cornet, William F. 05/15/62   05/19/62
Cator, Elizabeth died 05/07/65   05/09/65
Cator, John F. died no date   06/06/63
Cator, John Thomas died 05/22/63   05/26/63
Cator, John Thomas died 05/22/63   08/14/63
Cator, Mary (Mrs.) died 12/22/64   12/24/64
Cator, William D. married Gibson, Anna E. 01/02/62   01/07/62
Cator, William W. (Capt.) died 02/03/65   02/13/65
Caughey, John H. died 08/24/62   08/26/62
Caughy, John H. died 08/24/62   08/25/62
Caugly, Patrick died 03/08/62   03/10/62
Caulfield, Cecelia (Mrs.) died 03/03/63   03/05/63
Caulfield, Ellen (Mrs.) died 06/18/63   06/19/63
Caulk, C. J. married White, Cornelia E. 12/22/63   01/07/64
Caulk, Elizabeth died 01/20/61   01/21/61
Caulk, Jacob H. married Foreman, Sarah E. 07/31/65   10/31/65
Caulk, James died 10/24/61   10/26/61
Caulk, James T. died 08/09/64   08/10/64
Caulk, John R. died 12/30/64   12/31/64
Caulk, Rosaline married Benson, James H. (Capt.) 04/13/65   04/17/65
Caulk, Sargent died 09/29/64   10/25/64
Caulk, Virginia married Bevans, William Alpheus 07/20/63   08/04/63
Caulk, William J. married Young, Laura V. 03/12/63   09/29/63
Caution, Jesse James died 07/15/61   07/16/61
Caution, Samuel James died 10/14/63   10/15/63
Caution,Ann Louisa married Holladay, James H. 09/18/62   09/20/62
Cavanagh, James died 05/06/61   05/07/61
Cavanaugh, Charles M. died 10/24/64   10/25/64
Cavanaugh, Charles M. married England, Annie J. 05/19/64   05/23/64
Cavanaugh, James died 01/06/61   01/07/61
Cavanaugh, John Thomas died 04/26/64   04/28/64
Cavanaugh, Martin died 09/10/64   09/12/64
Cavanaugh, Sarah A. married Burns, Edwin C. 12/04/64   12/07/64
Cavanaugh, Thomas died 01/15/63   01/17/63
Cavano, Mary J. married Grimm, Henry S. 11/21/65   12/25/65
Cave, Charles H. died 03/04/64   03/05/64
Cavenau, Charles died 12/27/63   12/28/63
Cavenau, Charles died 12/27/63   12/29/63
Cavey, Joseph married Forrest, Sarah Jane 09/17/65   09/20/65
```

Cazier, Robert J. died 04/01/61   04/03/61
Cazier, Thomas C. died 04/23/63   04/25/63
Cecil, Julius D. married Dodson, Susan C. 01/17/61   01/21/61
Cecil, William died 12/05/64   12/07/64
Cee, Emory G. married Goodwin, Sarah F. 05/18/64   06/02/64
Censur, Benjamin Luther died 11/02/62   11/04/62
Cephas, Eliza married Brown, D. H. 07/13/65   07/15/65
Cerney, Ellen married Daly, Eugene 03/02/62   03/07/62
Chabot, G. H. died 10/02/63   10/03/63
Chace, Charles Ephraim died 10/31/64   11/02/64
Chace, Tilly died 03/03/62   03/05/62
Chaille, Ellen died 11/17/63   11/18/63
Chaillou, Victoria Amanda married Ackerson, Daniel M. 05/19/64   06/24/64
Chairs, Maria died 06/16/64   06/18/64
Chairs, William B. married Walker, Fanny A. 05/06/62   05/15/62
Chalan, Joseph married Bork, Johanna 05/16/63   05/18/63
Chalfant, Anna M. married Thomas, Henry P. 12/24/63   12/31/63
Chalk, Harriett (Mrs.) died 03/04/65   03/07/65
Chalk, Lizzie A. married Herring, Wilton S. 03/03/64   03/21/64
Chalmers, J. Wesley married Atkinson, Lizzie C. 06/28/63   07/27/63
Chalmers, Maggie A. married Rinker, George E. 10/10/65   10/18/65
Chamberlaine, Henry died 12/30/63   01/07/64
Chamberlin, Charles L. (USI) died 09/09/64   12/05/65
Chamberlin, Emma married Mettee, William H. 08/19/62   08/21/62
Chambers, Bessie died 05/22/62   05/28/62
Chambers, Catherine married Badger, Elisha (Rev.) 10/10/61   10/12/61
Chambers, Catherine Matilda died 11/17/63   11/18/63
Chambers, Christiana E. married Hitchcock, Levi 12/19/65   12/27/65
Chambers, Clara B. married Edwards, Edward J. 11/24/64   11/29/64
Chambers, Ellen Marion died 07/19/63   07/21/63
Chambers, Emily married Harris, Asbury 07/20/65   07/21/65
Chambers, George M. married Barrett, Margaret M. 05/19/62   06/07/62
Chambers, John S. married Knight, Eugenia 02/26/65   03/14/65
Chambers, Julia A. married Bryon, Thomas 05/15/65   05/23/65
Chambers, Martha (Mrs.) died 02/07/64   02/09/64
Chambers, Mary Ann married Reed, Noah R. 11/24/63   12/05/63
Chambers, Mary Florence died 02/21/64   02/22/64
Chambers, Robert M. died 08/14/64   08/18/64
Chambers, Robert M. married Vest, Lucy A. 12/07/65   12/23/65
Chambers, Samuel Joseph died 08/01/64   08/06/64
Chambers, William married Waters, Elizabeth 06/24/62   06/28/62
Chambers, William W. married Personette, Georgeanna 01/01/62   01/03/62
Champayne, William K. married Burns, Elizabeth J. 04/11/64   04/16/64
Champhor, Jacob married Gibson, Mary Jane 12/08/60   03/20/61
Champlin, J. H. married Bull, Mary C. 12/05/65   12/13/65
Chance, Frances A. (Mrs.) died 11/25/63   11/28/63
Chance, Janie Muth died 03/02/65   03/10/65
Chance, Janie Muth died 03/02/65   03/11/65
Chance, M. E. married Abey, Samuel 05/22/65   05/31/65
Chance, Marinas married Hinds, Margaret (Mrs.) 11/07/64   11/26/64
Chance, Mary Jane died 03/19/62   03/20/62
Chance, Mary Jane died 03/19/62   03/21/62
Chanceaulme, Celestine died 10/09/65   10/10/65
Chanceaulme, Edward W. died 10/17/62   09/13/65
Chanceaulme, Martin F. died 10/27/63   10/28/63

```
Chandlee, Clara L. married Leadbeater, Edward S. 10/10/61   10/17/61
Chandlee, William G. died 10/27/64   12/01/64
Chandler, Anna Eliza died 09/23/61   09/24/61
Chandler, David M. died 08/13/62   08/30/62
Chandler, Elizabeth died 02/06/64   02/08/64
Chandler, Harriet J. died 08/14/61   08/16/61
Chandler, Harriett I. died 08/14/61   08/15/61
Chandler, Mary Tyler died 02/14/62   02/21/62
Chandler, Robert J. married Rinerman, C. Miranda 08/29/65   09/12/65
Chandler, Walter S. died 09/25/62   09/26/62
Chandler, Walter S. died 09/25/62   09/27/62
Chandley, John H. married Wilson, Susannah 01/01/65   01/19/65
Chaneay, Winfield Ellsworth died 12/06/64   12/08/64
Chaney, Averrean died 02/12/64   02/17/64
Chaney, Celone married Geoghegan, William C. 05/12/62   05/14/62
Chaney, Emma married Pilson, John T. 04/13/65   05/13/65
Chaney, George W. married Ferguson, Margaret A. 07/05/63   07/07/63
Chaney, Isabel died 07/21/62   07/22/62
Chaney, Laura B. married Dowdall, Charles C. 08/21/63   08/25/63
Chaney, Lizzie married Garmhausen, Frederick C. 08/18/63   08/26/63
Chaney, Louis married Lisle, Sally 10/21/62   01/20/63
Chaney, Mary L. married Bly, William H. 02/24/63   02/28/63
Chaney, Rosener M. died 03/12/65   03/15/65
Chaney, Sarah J. (Mrs.) married Cooper, Thomas J. 10/03/65   10/07/65
Chaney, Sue married Houck, A. E. 02/02/65   02/06/65
Chaney, Zachariah died 01/17/61   01/18/61
Chanler, Thomas M. married Hamilton, Elizabeth 04/12/64   04/15/64
Channel, Alfred M. married Marck, Josephine S. 01/07/64   01/19/64
Chapin, Charles died 09/14/63   11/20/63
Chaplain, Olivia married Franklin, John F. 02/16/65   02/18/65
Chaplin, Isabella married Thilghman, Francis 03/17/63   03/21/63
Chapman, George R. married Welch, Martha E. 05/23/64   06/10/64
Chapman, John W. married Brown, Eliza J. 09/19/65   09/27/65
Chapman, Rebecca (Mrs.) died 09/16/63   09/18/63
Chapman, Sallie died 04/23/63   04/24/63
Chapman, Theodore Cole died 10/24/62   10/25/62
Chappel, Elizabeth C. died 01/05/62   01/07/62
Chappell, George W. married Keene, Eliza J. (Mrs.) 01/22/63   01/26/63
Chappell, Mary died 06/27/64   06/29/64
Chappell, Mary Virginia died 12/25/63   12/28/63
Chappell, Mary Virginia died 12/25/63   12/29/63
Chappell, Samuel Merwin died 11/02/61   11/04/61
Chappell, Thomas S. married Akers, Mary Virginia 12/23/62   12/25/62
Charles, Benjamin married Rhule, Martha 12/06/65   12/09/65
Charles, Elenora died 07/31/62   08/01/62
Charles, Frederick died 10/02/62   10/03/62
Charlton, Anna J. C. married Gallagher, E. G. (Lieut.) 08/05/61
    08/07/61
Charlton, J. W. married Farrow, Mollie C. 03/06/65   03/10/65
Chase, Algernon Sydney died 02/27/64   03/01/64
Chase, Ann Louisa (Mrs.) died 12/03/63   12/04/63
Chase, Clementine G. married Bond, John W. 07/07/64   07/08/64
Chase, Daniel died 02/13/64   02/15/64
Chase, Delos married Saunders, Mary A. 01/09/65   01/11/65
Chase, Edward Linzee died 05/02/64   05/03/64
```

```
Chase, Eliza Jane died 03/10/65   03/14/65
Chase, Elizabeth died 09/12/64   09/13/64
Chase, Elizabeth (Mrs.) died 03/10/65   03/13/65
Chase, Ellen died 05/06/64   05/07/64
Chase, Emily F. married Warren, Gouverneur K. (USA) 06/17/63   06/18/63
Chase, George A. died 12/12/62   12/13/62
Chase, George Thomas married Gant, Arabella 12/23/60   01/03/61
Chase, Harriet married Allen, John E. 04/20/65   04/27/65
Chase, James Henry died 12/18/63   12/19/63
Chase, John J. died 08/12/63   08/14/63
Chase, Joseph Hammon died 08/23/62   08/27/62
Chase, Josiah married White, Sarah A. 12/29/64   01/02/65
Chase, Lucy died 03/23/62   03/24/62
Chase, Mary died 02/12/62   02/14/62
Chase, Mary died 03/18/63   03/23/63
Chase, Mary A. married Berry, Joseph 12/16/62   12/24/62
Chase, Mary Augusta (Mrs.) died 01/27/64   01/28/64
Chase, Mary Virginia married Blackburn, Edward J. 11/06/64   11/16/64
Chase, Samuel married Murdoch, Mary 01/29/63   01/31/63
Chase, Samuel W., Jr. married Reed, Caroline M. 03/12/63   04/07/63
Chase, Sophia died 01/14/61   01/15/61
Chase, Sue V. married Prout, Joseph R. 12/15/64   12/17/64
Chase, Thorndick died 10/05/64   10/06/64
Chase, William died 10/24/61   10/25/61
Chason, Joseph L. married Mulen, Isabelle G. W. 06/12/61   06/19/61
Chassaing, Josephine died 06/26/64   07/04/64
Chassaing, Josephine F. died 06/26/64   07/22/64
Chasteau, Louis Armand died 07/27/62   07/29/62
Chatard, Jean Marie F. (Mrs.) died 05/20/63   05/21/63
Chatard, Kate M. married Ward, William H. 09/28/63   10/05/63
Chayton, Edward C. married Hutchinson, Laura V. 01/19/63   02/06/64
Chaytor, George died 08/03/65   08/07/65
Cheffins, Eli C. married Dempsey, Arabella C. 09/02/64   09/03/64
Cheney, Hester A. married Aldrich, Robert 06/23/63   03/28/64
Chenoweth, Ada E. married Buhrman, Emory (Rev.) 10/27/63   10/29/63
Chenoweth, Ann Amelia died 03/17/63   03/18/63
Chenoweth, James T. died 05/17/63   05/20/63
Chenoweth, Robert married Nichols, Rebecca M. 01/20/63   01/29/63
Chenoweth, Sarah J. married Shipley, Peter A. 05/21/63   05/28/63
Chenowith, Elleanor D. married Von Trobler, Henry Graf (Lt.) 05/23/65
    05/27/65
Chenowith, Johanna died 10/28/65   10/30/65
Chenowith, Mary E. married Morey, George F. 04/16/65   05/06/65
Cherry, Charles Eugene died 02/01/63   02/02/63
Cherry, Charles Eugene died 02/01/63   02/03/63
Cherry, James W. died 02/25/63   10/20/63
Cherry, M. Jerome (Dr.) died 09/24/64   09/26/64
Cherry, Sarah A. (Mrs.) died 10/24/63   10/26/63
Cheseborough, Andronicus married Coflin, Emma F. 05/10/64   05/12/64
Cheseldine, Eleanor C. died 05/02/61   05/03/61
Cheshire, Eugenia married McDowell, G. B. 09/18/65   09/19/65
Chesley, James A. (Dr.) died 04/09/63   04/28/63
Chesley, John W. married Watts, S. E. 08/31/65   11/28/65
Chesnet, Annie Mary married Gray, Augustus 07/31/65   10/04/65
Chesney, Benjamin died 03/18/65   03/21/65
```

Chesney, Edwin O. died 08/25/62   08/26/62
Chesney, George Harvey died 05/29/64   05/31/64
Chesney, Harriet E. married Armiger, Robert B. 06/21/64   07/07/64
Chesney, Jesse T. died 07/11/62   07/12/62
Chesney, John T. died 07/01/61   07/02/61
Chesney, Mary Caroline died 06/04/62   06/06/62
Chesney, Mary Elizabeth died 05/09/63   05/11/63
Chester, Annie married King, Walter W. 12/18/62   02/14/63
Chester, Dawson A. married Cooper, Mary E. 03/30/65   04/01/65
Chester, John married Kurtz, Louisa 10/25/61   10/26/61
Chester, Sarah E. married Tully, Charles E. 05/08/64   06/07/64
Chester, William died 10/31/64   11/01/64
Chestnut, Anna Cassandra died 08/09/62   08/11/62
Chestnut, Charles died 11/20/62   11/24/62
Chestnut, Maggie J. married Sanders, Charles L. 10/10/65   10/11/65
Chestnut, Samuel died 05/19/61   05/23/61
Chestnut, Washington R. married Ely, Fannie 12/30/62   01/02/63
Chew, Ambrose married Travers, Charlotte 08/17/63   08/19/63
Chew, Benjamin died 03/07/64   03/08/64
Chew, Claudia May died 11/08/65   11/10/65
Chew, Driscilla died 06/04/62   06/05/62
Chew, Isabella E. married Steward, William L. 05/15/62   05/19/62
Chew, Mary V. (Mrs.) died 09/07/63   09/09/63
Chew, Samuel died 07/18/64   07/19/64
Chew, Samuel (Dr.) died 12/25/63   12/26/63
Chew, Sutton married King, Hannah 09/28/62   09/30/62
Chew, William B. married Hanson, Helen S. 08/08/61   08/13/61
Chicken, David married Ferguson, Maggie 06/01/64   06/07/64
Chickering, Ella died 06/14/65   06/16/65
Chickering, Eunice Gleason died 06/23/63   06/26/63
Child, Edmund died 09/12/63   09/15/63
Child, James W. married Hunt, Mary Isabelle 10/12/65   10/13/65
Child, Mary died 09/01/61   09/03/61
Child, T. C. married Nield, Mary A. 09/29/64   11/11/64
Child, William W. married Hoff, Julia B. 05/09/64   05/12/64
Childs, Andrew J. died 12/25/65   12/29/65
Childs, Ann (Mrs.) died 08/10/63   08/24/63
Childs, Charles A. died 04/07/64   04/08/64
Childs, Elizabeth (Mrs.) died 09/15/63   09/21/63
Childs, George T. married Degaw, Harriet A. 04/27/63   05/07/63
Childs, George W. married Vickers, Emma 10/30/62   10/31/62
Childs, George W. married Vickers, Emma 10/30/62   11/01/62
Childs, George W. married Vickers, Emma 10/30/62   11/03/62
Childs, Henry married Williams, Margaret 05/11/65   05/17/65
Childs, J. N. married Hardesty, Maggie H. 11/01/65   11/17/65
Childs, Jerine died 05/02/64   05/03/64
Childs, John P. married Brayshaw, Mary 11/12/65   11/14/65
Childs, John W. married Crandall, Bettie S. 06/30/65   07/06/65
Childs, Letitia (Mrs.) died 09/26/63   10/07/63
Childs, Mary Elizabeth died 08/30/61   08/31/61
Childs, Samuel G. died 05/25/65   05/29/65
Childs, William died 07/26/62   07/30/62
Childs, William H. married Johnston, Sallie 02/22/65   07/18/65
Childs, Zachariah W. married Payne, Mary Catherine 05/05/63   05/08/63
Chinewaeth, Elizabeth died 11/06/63   11/09/63

Chipley, Emily O. married Morgan, Edward 09/20/64 10/01/64
Chisner, James Maulden (Sgt.) died 10/15/64 11/29/64
Chisolm, Sarah died 03/06/63 03/13/63
Chiswell, Edward J. married Allnut, Eva 12/05/65 12/20/65
Chivarl, Alexander B. died 09/02/63 09/07/63
Chiveral, James died 12/18/60 03/14/61
Choate, Solomon died 03/06/61 03/08/61
Choen, Margaret died 02/09/63 02/13/63
Chrismer, Alexander D. married Salisbury, Augusta J. 07/17/65 07/22/65
Chrismer, Isabella B. married Crouch, William J. 06/02/62 06/03/62
Christ, Henry married Strott, Katherine 05/14/65 05/19/65
Christee, James married Ware, Caroline C. 12/13/64 02/21/65
Christhilf, George H. died 03/01/64 03/03/64
Christhilf, Rachel (Mrs.) died 03/29/64 04/02/64
Christian, William died 12/13/64 01/04/65
Christie, Jas. J. married Rider, Emma Z. 01/03/65 01/06/65
Christner, John married Achres, Elizabeth 02/18/64 02/25/64
Christon, James married Martin, Sally 01/21/64 01/23/64
Christopher, Francis A. married Baird, Margaret P. 02/06/65 02/18/65
Christopher, Grace Anne married Markley, Samuel 10/31/65 11/01/65
Christopher, Harriet died 01/12/65 01/14/65
Christopher, James (Capt.) died 03/13/64 03/15/64
Christopher, Sarah died 03/17/64 03/18/64
Christopher, Willie R. married Allenbaugh, Charles T. 04/26/64 04/28/64
Christy, F. G. (Lt.) married Goldman, Hannah 09/28/64 10/10/64
Chritzman, H. G. (Dr.) married Newcomer, Emma A. 12/24/63 12/25/63
Chubb, Emily married McFarland, C. Dodd 11/02/65 11/04/65
Chubbs, Anthony died 05/11/62 05/12/62
Church, Charles Henry died 12/17/62 12/18/62
Church, Clara married Regester, Samuel W. 10/04/64 10/06/64
Church, Edward James died 01/17/65 03/11/65
Church, Mary F. married Miller, Edward G. 07/07/64 08/01/64
Church, Samuel T. (Dr.) died 07/13/64 07/18/64
Church, Sarah E. married Clements, John W. 10/01/60 05/06/61
Church, Susan A. married Gray, William M. 05/19/63 05/21/63
Church, W. C. married Metcalf, Mary E. 04/02/63 04/03/63
Cinnamond, Catherine M. died 04/24/61 04/25/61
Cinnamond, Joseph M. died 03/05/64 03/22/64
Cinnamond, Moorehead died 02/23/61 02/25/61
Cisco, Edward L. died 10/01/64 12/28/64
Cissel, B. Albert died 12/07/63 12/11/63
Cissel, Harriet E. (Mrs.) died 09/04/63 09/07/63
Cissel, Sarah Ardella died 04/26/65 04/27/65
Cissel, Wilbur F. married Browne, Clara E. 08/30/64 09/10/64
Cissel, Willie died 07/15/64 07/18/64
Cissell, M. Sophia (Mrs.) died no date 03/29/64
Clabaugh, Ada Stella died 11/05/62 11/06/62
Clabaugh, E. married Dickerson, E. A. 09/27/64 09/28/64
Clabaugh, Emma married Tumbleson, William T. 08/30/65 11/02/65
Clabaugh, James Addison died 06/14/63 06/16/63
Clabaugh, Katie died 06/06/64 06/08/64
Clabby, Pat died 11/06/64 11/07/64
Clabby, Patrick died 11/06/64 11/08/64
Clackner, Elizabeth died 01/16/61 01/18/61
Clackner, George W. died 10/22/64 12/09/64

```
Claflin, Ira W. (Cpt.) married Stuck, Jane 04/21/63   04/25/63
Clagett, Anna married Hardesty, Richard T. 06/01/65   06/22/65
Clagett, Elizabeth W. died 06/17/65   06/19/65
Clagett, Georgeanna died 05/20/63   05/22/63
Clagett, Grace died 09/18/65   09/19/65
Clagett, J. Thomas married Tucker, Mollie G. 11/09/65   11/11/65
Clagett, John married Hollifield, Sarah E. 10/24/61   10/26/61
Clagett, Leonard Obermeyer died 12/15/62   12/16/62
Clagett, Mary C. married Cowman, Philip E. 07/14/63   08/08/63
Clagett, Mary C. married Cowman, Philip E. 07/14/63   08/10/63
Clagett, Priscilla J. married Snyder, Walter 06/13/65   06/15/65
Clagett, Samuel A. married Snyder, Eliza 04/25/65   04/27/65
Claggett, Sarah E. married Talbot, H. Oden 02/05/63   02/10/63
Claiborn, Ferdinand Leigh died 07/31/62   08/02/62
Clairage, Emily L. died 07/12/64   07/13/64
Clamoren, Camille married Dorsey, Edward 11/29/64   12/01/64
Clampitt, William H. married Clark, Emma G. 10/28/61   01/15/62
Claney, Catherine married Rice, Robert 02/09/64   02/16/64
Clap, Harriet Virginia died 09/24/64   09/28/64
Clapsaddle, Ella married Stokes, George W. 11/27/64   11/29/64
Clapsaddle, Michael died 06/24/63   06/26/63
Clara, Emma Clara died 03/16/61   03/20/61
Clark, Albert (Cpl.) died 08/29/63   09/15/63
Clark, Albert (USA) died 08/29/63   08/31/63
Clark, Albert H. died 12/06/63   12/08/63
Clark, Anna married Askins, James 02/27/62   03/01/62
Clark, Annie H. married Iglehart, Milton 01/29/61   02/04/61
Clark, Aseneth S. married Lowry, William H. 08/30/64   09/01/64
Clark, Bellie Ross died 05/24/62   05/26/62
Clark, Bridget died 05/03/63   05/04/63
Clark, Catherine died 07/18/65   07/19/65
Clark, Charles (Dr.) married Beckett, Margaret R. 11/14/61   11/19/61
Clark, Charles Truscott died 01/13/61   01/18/61
Clark, Eliza died 08/14/65   09/02/65
Clark, Elizabeth (Mrs.) died 03/06/65   03/08/65
Clark, Elizabeth Jane died 10/13/64   10/17/64
Clark, Ella died 02/10/64   02/12/64
Clark, Ellen married Bentz, George 01/14/63   01/24/63
Clark, Ellen M. A. married Bentz, George 01/14/63   01/26/63
Clark, Elmira Isadora (Mrs.) died 05/27/64   06/13/64
Clark, Emma G. married Clampitt, William H. 10/28/61   01/15/62
Clark, Emma V. married Graham, R. H. 02/18/64   03/03/64
Clark, Fannie A. died 12/23/62   12/24/62
Clark, Frances (Mrs.) died 03/14/63   03/16/63
Clark, George T. died 01/05/62   01/07/62
Clark, George T. died 01/05/62   01/11/62
Clark, George T. married Mart, Mary 01/21/64   05/06/64
Clark, Grason Aloysius died 11/01/63   11/11/63
Clark, Harriet died 07/07/65   07/08/65
Clark, Henry died 02/19/63   03/11/63
Clark, Henry died 09/02/63   09/04/63
Clark, Hugh Humphries died 12/14/65   12/28/65
Clark, Isabella married Martien, Joseph 03/24/64   03/25/64
Clark, Isabella M. died 12/22/61   12/23/61
Clark, John died 03/27/61   03/28/61
```

```
Clark, John died 07/06/63   07/08/63
Clark, John S. died 10/29/62   10/31/62
Clark, John S. died 09/20/65   09/21/65
Clark, John W. married Rork, Sara R. 01/19/65   01/24/65
Clark, Joseph (Sgt.) died 09/17/62   09/30/62
Clark, Julia A. married Burton, George W. 01/08/61   01/10/61
Clark, Laura A. married Groh, Joseph M. 06/19/65   08/01/65
Clark, Leonard married Morris, Arabelle 10/14/63   10/23/63
Clark, Lizzie D. married Amoss, Alfred P., Jr. 06/08/65   06/13/65
Clark, Lizzie J. died 08/12/61   08/15/61
Clark, Louisa married Walters, J. Blake 06/06/65   06/07/65
Clark, Louisa married Wroth, Edward W. 09/21/65   09/30/65
Clark, M. M. (Major) died 05/10/61   05/11/61
Clark, Margaret A. married Brown, George F. 08/13/60   01/03/61
Clark, Margaret E. died 08/14/64   08/15/64
Clark, Margaret P. (Mrs.) died 12/02/64   12/03/64
Clark, Maria married Brown, Alexander J. 10/22/64   10/29/64
Clark, Marine died 08/20/64   08/25/64
Clark, Mary A. married McCart, James 01/12/62   06/13/62
Clark, Mary A. married Wonder, Henry 01/11/63   01/14/63
Clark, Mary C. married Odell, Greenleaf N. 04/21/64   04/25/64
Clark, Mary E. married Hoy, Thomas 12/24/62   12/30/62
Clark, Matilda F. married Deets, W. H. 11/21/64   11/22/64
Clark, Matthew married McWilliams, Kate 05/09/61   05/13/61
Clark, Molly Bell Everett died 05/22/62   05/23/62
Clark, Nancy (Mrs.) died 11/12/63   02/06/64
Clark, Richard P. died 02/17/64   02/22/64
Clark, Samuel G. died 09/05/63   09/11/63
Clark, Sarah (Mrs.) died 10/12/64   10/14/64
Clark, Sarah Edmond died 05/24/63   05/25/63
Clark, Sarah Elizabeth married Weller, Daniel 07/10/65   07/25/65
Clark, Susan S. married Miller, Chanlur 01/22/62   01/28/62
Clark, Thomas Kirwan died 06/06/63   06/08/63
Clark, Thomas S., Jr. married Hope, Nettie C. 10/08/62   10/10/62
Clark, William died 02/09/64   02/12/64
Clark, William died 04/28/65   05/03/65
Clark, William married Kelly, Nancy 03/30/64   04/01/64
Clark, William A. married Boswell, Fannie 02/03/65   02/07/65
Clarke, Austin Stroud died 10/05/63   10/06/63
Clarke, Catherine Ann (Mrs.) died 08/04/63   08/06/63
Clarke, Charles died 10/15/62   10/16/62
Clarke, Charles H. married Ritter, Margaret E. 10/05/65   10/09/65
Clarke, Edward married Gray, Irene 08/10/63   09/01/63
Clarke, Eleaeor Georgett died 02/25/61   03/06/61
Clarke, Frances Ann died 01/23/61   01/24/61
Clarke, George died 01/24/61   03/06/61
Clarke, George C. married Price, Mollie E. 12/14/65   12/21/65
Clarke, Grace T. died 11/16/62   11/18/62
Clarke, H. F. (Maj. U.S.A.) married Taylor, Belle 09/24/61   10/11/61
Clarke, Henry Clay died 08/28/63   08/29/63
Clarke, Isaac died 08/08/61   08/10/61
Clarke, James married Drugan, Annie 05/26/63   06/16/63
Clarke, Joseph S. married Gers, Laura V. 06/13/65   06/15/65
Clarke, Kate married Humphreys, Thomas H. 11/18/61   11/27/61
```

Clarke, Kate Thornton died 01/04/62 01/06/62
Clarke, Mary married Murtaugh, John 05/03/63 05/07/63
Clarke, Mary died 04/03/65 04/05/65
Clarke, Mary F. married Watson, John 10/27/64 10/31/64
Clarke, Mary S. married Hutchins, William H. 10/19/65 10/20/65
Clarke, Michael died 12/08/61 12/09/61
Clarke, Rachel died 09/30/61 10/05/61
Clarke, Sylvester married Cardwell, Mary 07/06/62 07/08/62
Clarke, Thomas died 04/20/64 04/25/64
Clarke, Tillie F. married Deets, William H. 11/21/64 11/28/64
Clarke, William died 06/01/64 06/03/64
Clarke, William F. died 10/28/65 10/30/65
Clarke, William P. married Phelps, Ann S. 11/29/64 12/01/64
Clarke, William R. died 04/19/61 04/20/61
Clarker, Mary A. Z. married Crosswell, J. W. (Cpt.) 12/14/65 12/22/65
Clarkson, William W. married Bradley, Nannie R. 03/07/65 05/22/65
Clarriage, James M. died 01/24/64 01/25/64
Classen, B. H. married Winchester, Ella A. 07/14/64 07/15/64
Classen, Gussie Marie died 08/17/63 08/18/63
Clathey, Annie L. died 10/03/63 10/05/63
Claude, Adele married Robinson, J. B. (Dr.) 10/26/65 11/07/65
Claude, Marian H. married Howes, Charles F. 06/15/65 06/23/65
Clautice, Francis married Moore, Mary C. 11/24/63 11/28/63
Clautice, James W. died 02/17/62 02/21/62
Clautice, John W. died 04/06/64 04/07/64
Clautice, Joseph married Greenfield, Annie no date 05/16/65
Clautice, Joseph married Greenfield, Annie A. 12/29/64 05/19/65
Clautice, Mary Ellen died 06/09/64 06/10/64
Clautice, Salie C. married Barlow, James T. 03/05/62 04/18/62
Clautice, Sallie C. married Barlow, James T. 11/07/64 11/14/64
Clautice, Sarah died 02/06/62 02/07/62
Clautice, Sarah F. died 02/06/62 02/08/62
Claxton, Rodolphine (Mrs.) died 09/05/63 09/07/63
Clay, Henry married Jackson, Henrietta 01/05/65 01/07/65
Claypoole, Benjamin B. married Lynch, Roseanna 11/05/63 11/18/63
Claypoole, Ellen G. (Mrs.) died no date 06/06/65
Claypoole, George W. married Bramble, Harriet Elizabeth 04/12/64 04/15/64
Claypoole, James V. married McCormick, Ella G. 09/13/64 09/15/64
Claypoole, Julia A. married Rasin, J. Freemay 03/04/62 03/11/62
Clayton, Amelia M. married Doyle, James 11/13/65 11/15/65
Clayton, Amos died 05/03/64 05/05/64
Clayton, Catherine Ann died 05/07/61 05/08/61
Clayton, Dobbin died 12/09/64 12/14/64
Clayton, George Dobbin died 12/09/64 12/15/64
Clayton, Hezekiah married Gibson, Henrietta 09/06/65 09/16/65
Clayton, James D. married Johnson, Annie M. 05/11/64 05/13/64
Clayton, John died 11/30/64 12/14/64
Clayton, John died 11/30/64 12/15/64
Clayton, John Randall died 12/08/64 12/14/64
Clayton, John Randall died 12/08/64 12/15/64
Clayton, Lelia Anna died 06/23/63 06/24/63
Clayton, Mary Emma died 06/15/61 06/18/61
Clayton, William C. died 05/05/65 05/06/65
Cleary, M. Jennie married Johnson, William B. 12/05/65 12/19/65

Cleary, Thomas married Broadbent, Mattie 10/10/65 11/01/65
Cleary, William married Bailey, Isabel 07/08/62 07/26/62
Cleasy, Louisa C. (Mrs.) died 01/04/63 01/13/63
Cleaveland, Mary Jane married Lowe, Charles E. 02/23/65 02/25/65
Clemancs, Annie E. married McCarthey, Charles 12/25/64 01/10/65
Clemens, Rosalia married Baker, Frederick 01/04/61 01/07/61
Clements, Mary Camilla died 07/27/62 07/31/62
Clements, Ambrose James died 07/21/61 07/27/61
Clements, Charlotte (Mrs.) died 04/15/63 04/29/63
Clements, James died 03/02/61 04/03/61
Clements, John W. married Church, Sarah E. 10/01/60 05/06/61
Clements, Joshua died 03/19/64 03/24/64
Clements, W. Diles married O'Donoghue, Eleanor 10/06/64 10/21/64
Clements, William Seth died 10/22/61 11/01/61
Clements, William Seth died 02/04/65 02/06/65
Clemm, John Reese (Lt.) died 05/19/63 05/20/63
Clemm, Laura J. M. married Royer, W. Harry 10/04/64 10/07/64
Clemm, Maria (Mrs.) died 07/04/64 07/06/64
Clemmens, Elizabeth A. married Martin, Joseph F. 05/08/64 05/10/64
Clemmens, James D. married Hanson, Ella 09/13/63 10/03/63
Clemments, Caroline married Ferree, Alexander 06/01/63 06/04/63
Clemmons, Annie B. married Meinkranz, Theodore 02/28/64 03/05/64
Clemmons, William died 12/31/63 01/01/64
Clendenin, Martha E. married Rusling, S. C. 05/04/64 05/12/64
Clendinen, Alex (Dr.) died 04/12/61 04/13/61
Clenighen, Robert married Fryer, Jennie Olive 09/14/65 09/16/65
Clephane, Mary A. married Spier, T. Hamilton 05/22/61 05/25/61
Cleveland, George W. died 07/13/65 07/15/65
Clickner, Ada Parthenia died 03/14/63 03/16/63
Cliff, Lizzie M. died 03/07/64 03/08/64
Clifford, John died 01/11/65 01/12/65
Clifford, Mary Ann died 02/24/64 02/25/64
Clifford, Sylvester, Sr. died 04/14/64 04/16/64
Clifford, William died 08/17/63 08/18/63
Clifford, William H. married Gruver, Mary E. 01/12/64 01/14/64
Clift, John W. died 09/19/64 09/23/64
Clifton, Arthur died 01/24/62 03/11/62
Clifton, Cranville Wood died 05/28/65 06/05/65
Clifton, John Junius died 08/11/65 08/14/65
Cline, Emma Virginia died 08/23/62 08/26/62
Cline, George W. married Hayes, Louisa A. 01/30/65 02/02/65
Cline, Mary E. (Mrs.) married Robinson, George F. (USA) 03/17/63
    03/26/63
Cline, Michael B. died 03/24/64 03/26/64
Clinton, Robert John died 01/22/62 01/24/62
Clive, Daniel H. married McAfee, Martha J. 12/08/63 12/10/63
Cloake, Thomas died 04/18/64 04/18/64
Clocker, Charles H. died 08/05/63 08/06/63
Clocker, Mary A. Lavinia married Croswell, John W. (Cpt.) 12/14/65
    12/25/65
Cloffenstein, John C. married Leedy, Mary E. 09/28/62 10/03/62
Clokey, Emeline died 03/20/61 03/22/61
Clokey, Mary Lizzie died 02/12/63 02/23/63
Clokey, Robert William died 02/17/63 02/23/63
Close, Christian died 05/18/65 05/19/65

```
Clotworthy, Francis William died 07/27/64   07/28/64
Clotworty, Charles A. married Leister, R. Alice 11/10/63   11/16/63
Clough, Elizabeth married Hilberts, Charles A. 03/17/61   03/19/61
Clough, James married Carter, Edwardeena 01/29/64   01/30/64
Clough, John J. married Lowman, Marion 11/27/62   12/10/62
Clowdsley, John H. married Basley, Arabella 01/22/62   01/31/62
Clunet, Janet (Mrs.) died 12/23/63   12/25/63
Clunet, Victor S. married Farlow, Hattie E. 08/08/62   03/15/64
Clyde, Kitty married Keenan, J. F. 12/12/64   12/28/64
Coady, Daniel J. died 01/30/62   01/31/62
Coahly, Martha married Towson, Henry C. 01/10/65   01/12/65
Coakley, Daniel married McCambridge, Ann Jane 02/12/61   02/16/61
Coakley, Daniel married McCambridge, Ann Jane 02/12/61   02/15/61
Coakley, Daniel married McCambridge, Ann Jane 02/12/61   02/14/61
Coakley, Mary L. married Bishop, E. Tracy (M.D.) 06/18/62   06/19/62
Coal, Gertrude Dorsey died 06/30/64   07/02/64
Coal, Mary married Smith, James 06/02/64   06/07/64
Coale, Alfred married Harrison, Lizzie 12/06/64   12/13/64
Coale, Edward died 09/15/65   09/16/65
Coale, Elizabeth A. died 03/27/62   04/14/62
Coale, Mary Elizabeth married Hicks, William H. 07/23/62   07/25/62
Coale, William Edward died 04/24/65   04/26/65
Coale, William J. M. died 01/05/63   01/06/63
Coales, Ann died 08/08/65   08/11/65
Coates, Alexander died 06/04/64   06/06/64
Coates, Ann died 08/08/65   08/12/65
Coates, Ellen C. died 11/19/65   11/20/65
Coates, Mary Frances married Brown, Lewis M. 03/26/61   03/27/61
Coath, Sallie E. married Wright, Willard H. 11/16/65   11/20/65
Coath, Thomas J. died 01/07/64   01/08/64
Coats, Agnes died 08/10/62   08/11/62
Coats, Arthur H. died 08/30/64   08/31/64
Cobb, George A. died 04/06/62   04/07/62
Cobey, Jane married Price, Louis 11/12/61   11/16/61
Coblens, Hannah married Schwab, Morris 10/22/65   10/23/65
Coblens, Hannah married Schwab, Morris 10/22/65   10/25/65
Coblens, Lewis married Keyser, Julia 04/14/65   05/16/65
Coburn, Henry married Fuller, Elizabeth 11/30/63   12/08/63
Coburn, John Wesley died 04/24/64   04/26/64
Coburn, Mary Wilhelmina died 11/24/63   11/25/63
Cochan, John E. married Coffin, Mary E. 12/13/64   12/16/64
Coche, Mary Barnes died 09/11/62   09/15/62
Cochran, Alexander died 11/06/62   11/08/62
Cochran, Charles Oscar died 12/14/63   12/15/63
Cochran, Ella V. married Sears, Jason S. 11/26/63   03/15/64
Cochran, Harry W. married Myers, Ellie M. 02/16/64   02/24/64
Cochran, John C. died 03/21/64   03/22/64
Cochran, Mary E. (Mrs.) married Jones, John P. 04/07/64   04/11/64
Cochran, Mileacent (Mrs.) died 02/17/64   02/20/64
Cockey, Charles E. married Legg, Fanny 11/20/61   11/21/61
Cockey, Charles E. died 03/03/62   03/11/62
Cockey, Emma Virginia died 06/19/65   06/20/65
Cockey, Ginnie married Lodge, William J. (M.D.) 04/24/62   05/02/62
Cockey, Josephine A. married Hart, Barnet 09/22/64   10/03/64
Cockey, Joshua married Door, Ann Maria 02/28/61   03/02/61
```

Cockey, Mary V. married Tolson, H. M. 05/19/64 05/27/64
Cockey, S. Groff died 04/25/64 04/28/64
Cockey, Samuel Owings died 11/22/62 11/24/62
Cockey, William died 02/15/62 02/25/62
Cockrill, James Veasy died 04/29/63 05/02/63
Codd, Edward J. married Tunis, Emma M. 05/31/65 06/30/65
Codd, Mary V. married Windsor, Glendy S. 09/26/65 10/04/65
Codling, James J. died 12/09/65 12/11/65
Codling, James J. died 12/09/65 12/12/65
Codori, John A. married Stein, Sophia C. 12/17/61 12/19/61
Coe, Edward D. died 05/03/63 05/08/63
Coe, Margaret Ellen (Mrs.) died 12/19/65 12/23/65
Coffey, Silas D. married Byles, Carrie L. 11/01/64 11/03/64
Coffield, Josephine E. married Hall, Edward 07/09/61 07/11/61
Coffin, Mary E. married Cochan, John E. 12/13/64 12/16/64
Coffman, Mary V. married Durham, Jerome 01/08/65 01/18/65
Coffman, Sarah (Mrs.) died 01/21/65 01/26/65
Cofield, Aloysious died 02/02/61 02/11/61
Cofield, Aloysious died 02/02/61 02/12/61
Coflin, Emma F. married Cheseborough, Andronicus 05/10/64 05/12/64
Cofran, John L. died 03/05/62 03/08/62
Coggins, Anna Maria died 01/30/61 01/31/61
Coggins, Emma married Neely, Joseph 11/09/65 11/11/65
Coggins, Sarah C. married Piper, William T. 07/07/64 07/13/64
Coghlan, Abraham died 11/08/62 11/26/62
Cogswell, Nathaniel died 10/22/63 10/27/63
Cohen, Agnes died 01/29/61 01/31/61
Cohen, Edward married Myers, Caroline 12/06/65 12/09/65
Cohen, Fanny married Nachman, Adolph 03/09/64 03/12/64
Cohen, Matilda I. married Korte, Frederick 02/24/63 04/07/63
Cohen, Medes married Nathan, Justina 10/18/65 10/26/65
Cohen, Rebecca married Jackson, Eugene J. 02/08/65 02/10/65
Cohen, Rebecca married Jackson, Eugene J. 02/08/65 02/11/65
Colbart, Susie F. married Loker, George T. 04/28/63 04/29/63
Colbert, Augustus F. married Cole, Elizabeth S. 04/18/61 04/23/61
Colbert, Catherine died 05/25/65 05/27/65
Colbert, Harry Augustus died 06/03/64 06/04/64
Colbert, Mary A. married Wolfe, George 06/04/61 06/20/61
Colbert, Mary C. married Solter, George L. 09/19/61 10/14/61
Colbert, Mary Catharine died 08/08/63 08/11/63
Colburn, Edward died 08/07/63 08/15/63
Colburn, Jamesanna L. (Mrs.) died 10/28/63 10/29/63
Colburn, Jamesanna L. (Mrs.) died 10/28/63 10/30/63
Colburn, Nathaniel Knight died 04/24/65 04/25/65
Colby, Acca L. married Purdy, Warren G. 03/13/65 03/17/65
Cole, Alexander married Albert, Anne 04/25/63 05/05/63
Cole, Alice Gertrude died 09/04/62 09/26/62
Cole, Ann Eliza died 02/10/64 02/11/64
Cole, Anna Maria married Sheares, Harman F. 11/07/65 11/16/65
Cole, Charles B. married Stockton, Mary E. A. 05/02/65 05/04/65
Cole, Edward J. died 12/08/61 12/21/61
Cole, Edward J. died 12/08/61 12/24/61
Cole, Edwin Curtis died 09/30/65 10/02/65
Cole, Eliza married Boston, William T. 12/24/62 12/30/62
Cole, Eliza Ann (Mrs.) died 10/28/64 10/29/64

```
Cole, Eliza Jane (Mrs.) married Hitzelberger, Peter 10/26/63   10/29/63
Cole, Elizabeth married Disney, R. P. 12/12/61   12/23/61
Cole, Elizabeth married Bishop, Henry 09/27/64   09/30/64
Cole, Elizabeth (Mrs.) died 12/17/64   12/20/64
Cole, Elizabeth S. married Colbert, Augustus F. 04/18/61   04/23/61
Cole, Emily married Johnson, Daniel 01/05/65   01/07/65
Cole, Emma Estelle died 04/13/65   04/14/65
Cole, Fannie R. married Dryden, J. Meredith 10/10/65   10/12/65
Cole, Frederick died 01/29/61   01/30/61
Cole, George B. died 09/21/65   09/22/65
Cole, Harriet married Eareckson, C. Federal 11/26/62   12/01/62
Cole, Henry Mankin died 05/25/64   05/26/64
Cole, J. Columbus married McNew, Susan 02/19/62   02/27/62
Cole, Jacob died 04/08/64   04/11/64
Cole, John died 01/27/65   01/30/65
Cole, John M. died 10/18/65   11/06/65
Cole, John T. married Goldsmith, Lilie 05/26/64   05/30/64
Cole, John W. married Sroud, Elizabeth Ann 01/10/65   01/14/65
Cole, Joseph died 09/25/63   09/26/63
Cole, Joseph B. died 05/19/65   05/20/65
Cole, Julia married Herkles, Lloyd 12/22/64   12/24/64
Cole, Julia A. married Cromwell, Sedwick T. 12/11/62   12/12/62
Cole, Martha married Kirk, Samuel E. 11/17/63   11/19/63
Cole, Mary A. married Wise, John H. 10/10/61   10/12/61
Cole, Mary A. married Scott, James A. 04/05/65   04/08/65
Cole, Mary A. (Mrs.) died 03/28/64   03/30/64
Cole, Mary Clara Elizabeth died 12/03/63   12/07/63
Cole, Mary M. married Bartlett, Abner T. 03/03/63   03/06/63
Cole, Mary Watts married Royston, John Henry B. 02/19/63   02/20/63
Cole, Matilda A. married Yearly, John T. 03/12/65   03/17/65
Cole, Mittie married Boteler, Edward D. 01/06/63   01/10/63
Cole, Noah H. married Disney, Sophia 03/11/62   03/15/62
Cole, Rachel Malcolm died 01/17/63   01/20/63
Cole, Sarah L. married Hunt, John H. 03/26/61   03/29/61
Cole, Sarah P. married Brown, George O. 02/22/65   02/25/65
Cole, Thomas M. married Willham, Elmira 01/29/63   01/31/63
Cole, William married Neville, Martha E. 03/26/61   03/29/61
Cole, William died 01/23/63   01/24/63
Cole, William H. married Tuttle, Marian V. 06/19/65   06/20/65
Colegate, Mary died 03/16/62   03/22/62
Coleham, Thomas died 11/27/64   11/28/64
Colehan, Michael died 01/30/61   01/31/61
Colehouer, Frederick J. died 08/27/64   08/30/64
Colehouse, William Henry died 04/03/63   04/07/63
Colein, William H. married Yates, Mary E. 06/09/64   06/16/64
Coleman, Anna R. married McCleary, William J. 02/02/65   11/07/65
Coleman, Charles R., Jr. married Griffith, Emma 09/25/62   09/26/62
Coleman, Charles W. died 10/12/63   10/14/63
Coleman, Eliza (Mrs.) died 12/16/65   12/18/65
Coleman, Elizabeth B. married Fenemore, Isaac 01/15/62   02/22/62
Coleman, George Luther died 07/28/63   07/29/63
Coleman, George T. died 09/24/61   09/26/61
Coleman, George Thomas died 07/12/64   07/13/64
Coleman, Hiram Abiff died 03/10/61   03/12/61
Coleman, Joseph Edward died 10/03/62   10/07/62
```

Coleman, K. married Butler, Lizzie 10/25/63   10/27/63
Coleman, Laura Virginia died 05/06/63   06/08/63
Coleman, Leighton married DuPont, Alexis 07/30/61   08/01/61
Coleman, Leonora married Ely, John B. 09/03/62   09/10/62
Coleman, Lizzie Ellen died 10/27/63   10/29/63
Coleman, Mollie M. E. died 05/08/64   05/10/64
Coleman, Nancy M. married Hermann, Amos T. 01/12/63   01/20/63
Coleman, Patrick died 07/08/64   07/09/64
Coleman, Richard married Biddison, Keren H. 09/15/62   02/21/63
Coleman, Sallie married Gayle, Joseph R. 03/13/64   03/17/64
Coleman, Sarah C. married Briscoe, John H. 04/13/64   04/16/64
Coleman, Sarah Jane died 04/10/62   04/12/62
Coleman, W. W. married Hiss, Ellen G. 05/25/64   05/26/64
Coleman, William E. died 02/07/65   02/23/65
Coleman, William E. died 02/07/65   03/04/65
Coleman, William H. married Sanders, Sarah E. 11/04/62   11/06/62
Coleman, Willie died 07/31/62   08/01/62
Coles, William married Coot, Mary 12/23/63   11/21/63
Colfer, Harry died 02/23/65   02/24/65
Colfer, Omaha died 03/17/62   03/26/62
Colimas, Andrew Levy died 09/19/62   09/20/62
Coll, Ann (Mrs.) died 12/28/63   12/29/63
Coll, Hannah died 08/20/64   08/22/64
Colladay, Charles R. married Nicodemus, Mary A. 11/26/62   12/02/62
Colladay, Mary E. W. married Burgess, Charles H. 05/05/64   05/09/64
Colladay, Virginia A. R. died 08/04/61   08/17/61
Collan, Elizabeth died 04/14/64   04/15/64
Collegate, Charles E. died 02/12/65   02/14/65
Collenberg, Louisa S. died 10/01/62   10/02/62
Collett, Sophia L. married Johnson, John W. 01/01/63   01/05/63
Colley, Ursula W. married Dickinson, John, Jr. 12/24/61   01/04/62
Collgate, Charles E. married Button, Almira 08/13/61   08/14/61
Collier, Andrew J. married Lewis, Sarah J. 12/06/63   03/30/64
Collier, Annie E. married Barton, Samuel J. 01/21/65   09/02/65
Collier, Ellen (Mrs.) died 05/01/64   05/02/64
Collier, Frank M. married Harding, Drusilla 11/13/64   11/18/64
Collier, Maria Louisa died 11/30/65   12/04/65
Collimore, E. V. married Steadman, H. B. 11/28/61   02/12/62
Collins, Annie H. died 09/29/63   09/30/63
Collins, Annie M. (Mrs.) died 02/26/63   02/28/63
Collins, Caroline V. married Harvey, Edward A. 04/05/63   04/06/63
Collins, Catherine (Mrs.) died 04/01/65   04/03/65
Collins, Charles B. died 08/10/62   08/16/62
Collins, Charles E. married Smith, Susie R. 07/12/65   07/21/65
Collins, Charles H. married Thompson, Margaret 11/06/64   11/08/64
Collins, Delia A. married Lang, John M 10/01/61   10/03/61
Collins, Elijah died 11/05/64   11/15/64
Collins, Elizabeth married Webster, George W. 11/23/63   11/28/63
Collins, Ellen died 06/15/63   06/18/63
Collins, Emma married Webster, Daniel E. 03/15/63   04/07/63
Collins, Estelle L. married Lilly, Edward A. 06/17/61   07/22/61
Collins, Hugh J. married McCusker, Jane 09/17/65   10/07/65
Collins, James E. married Barclay, Laura J. 11/21/65   11/28/65
Collins, Jane (Mrs.) died 07/26/63   07/27/63
Collins, Joe Stephen died 04/04/64   04/05/64

Collins, Johanna (Mrs.) died 12/22/64 12/24/64
Collins, John H. married Griffith, Janette 11/05/65 11/07/65
Collins, John W. married Allers, Maggie Steibel 10/21/63 10/24/63
Collins, Laura R. married Lee, Jesse W. 04/08/62 04/10/62
Collins, Martha J. died 09/26/62 10/07/62
Collins, Mary died 06/12/61 06/13/61
Collins, Mary died 05/13/64 05/14/64
Collins, Mary died 08/02/65 08/03/65
Collins, Mary died 08/02/65 08/04/65
Collins, Mary Ann married Greene, Thomas 09/12/65 10/02/65
Collins, Michael died 12/18/64 12/19/64
Collins, Patrick died 07/17/64 07/19/64
Collins, Robert married Walker, Amelia Jane 02/06/62 02/08/62
Collins, Sarah Ann (Mrs.) died 05/23/63 05/25/63
Collins, Sarah Elizabeth died 08/22/61 08/23/61
Collins, Seamore married Hall, Harriet A. 06/02/64 06/04/64
Collins, Susannah (Mrs.) married McNeal, George 11/07/65 11/18/65
Collins, Thomas died 11/19/62 11/21/62
Collins, Timothy M. married Halpin, Sarah J. 11/26/65 12/09/65
Collins, William E. married Preston, Sarah Ann 02/16/64 02/18/64
Collins, William H. H. married Rollins, Emma A. 03/23/62 04/29/62
Collinson, Mary Mortimer died 06/19/65 07/08/65
Collinson, William J. married Stallings, Hester Ann 07/06/65 07/10/65
Collison, Mary E. married McMahon, Michael J. 12/02/62 12/20/62
Collison, Sarah A. married Kearney, Charles 02/12/63 02/21/63
Colloday, Edward died 08/08/64 08/09/64
Collopy, Anne M. married St. Germain, Isaac 01/21/62 01/27/62
Colohan, Mary (Mrs.) died 08/10/63 08/11/63
Coloney, J. B. (Maj.) died 10/09/64 10/12/64
Colston, William Edward (Lt.) died 01/10/64 01/20/64
Coltart, Sarah Helen died 11/03/62 11/04/62
Colter, Virginia married Reinhardt, Charles 02/03/65 02/22/65
Colton, Emma Jane Colton died 03/03/61 03/05/61
Colton, James Louis died 02/02/63 02/04/63
Colton, Jane Monacha died 02/02/63 02/04/63
Colton, Mary Catharine died 02/02/63 02/04/63
Colton, Mary Catherine died 02/02/63 02/03/63
Colton, Susan married Gallagher, Hugh 02/05/65 02/07/65
Coltor, Richard died 03/16/63 03/18/63
Coltrider, Amanda married Rineman, John 01/28/63 02/07/63
Combash, John married Hall, Sarah 10/27/65 10/31/65
Combs, Elijah died 11/23/62 03/03/63
Comegys, Henry C. married Grove, Linnie 07/17/61 07/22/61
Comegys, John P. married Mitchell, Georgeanna 12/30/62 01/03/63
Comegys, Jonathan died 10/16/65 10/17/65
Comegys, Lemuel died 03/04/65 03/07/65
Comegys, Philip T. died 11/28/61 12/02/61
Comfort, H. J. (Rev.) married Miller, Maggie A. 10/06/64 10/22/64
Comfort, Margaret A. (Mrs.) died 03/13/65 03/14/65
Comfort, Margaret A. (Mrs.) died 03/13/65 03/15/65
Comings, John died 08/10/63 08/11/63
Comley, James F. married Amey, Kate 07/28/63 08/29/63
Compton, Lillie died 03/29/65 04/01/65
Compton, Owen died 05/30/64 06/02/64
Compton, Rachel K. married Weatherby, Samuel S. 03/30/65 04/10/65

Compton, Vernon married Carr, Julia 11/13/61   11/14/61
Comte, Ann (Mrs.) died 09/05/65   09/06/65
Conain, Lewis died 02/18/65   02/20/65
Conant, Samuel W., Jr. married Hussey, Martha S. 03/11/61   03/16/61
Conaway, Eliza J. (Mrs.) died 02/16/63   03/24/63
Conaway, James F. died 01/16/62   01/17/62
Conaway, James F. died 01/16/62   01/18/62
Conaway, John S. married Jackson, Rachel T. 03/17/65   03/23/65
Conaway, Leah E. died 08/11/62   08/12/62
Concannon, Bernard died 01/05/63   01/06/63
Condon, Pierce M. died 02/28/65   03/02/65
Cone, John W. married Isreal, Virtie 05/25/65   07/31/65
Conelley, Mary Young (Mrs.) died 12/14/65   12/15/65
Conelly, John T. married Loney, Mary Louisa 10/06/63   10/08/63
Conen, Abraham died 02/06/64   02/08/64
Coniken, Hannah E. married Bradley, Thomas B. 07/02/63   07/03/63
Conine, Alfred S. died 06/09/64   06/11/64
Conkline, Antoine Leon died 09/19/63   09/21/63
Conkline, Marie Victoire B. died 02/20/65   02/24/65
Conkling, Caroline (Mrs.) married Wyse, John 09/15/64   09/24/64
Conkling, Caroline (Mrs.) married Wyse, John 09/15/64   09/26/64
Conkling, Milly Cole died 04/07/63   04/09/63
Conlan, John died 03/28/64   04/04/64
Conley, Annie died 03/10/62   03/11/62
Conley, Bridget died 12/26/62   12/27/62
Conley, Calinda (Mrs.) married Proctor, J. T. A. 08/04/64   12/24/64
Conley, Caty died 06/10/63   06/11/63
Conley, Dominick C. married Slorp, Eliza J. 08/09/65   08/25/65
Conley, Olivia married Cadwallader, Abel 03/28/65   04/03/65
Conley, Rebecca (Mrs.) died 06/16/64   06/21/64
Conley, Sarah M. married Kreamer, Nicholas 11/08/64   11/11/64
Conley, William died 02/09/64   02/13/64
Conley, William H. died 02/09/64   02/11/64
Conlon, John died 11/27/63   12/03/63
Conlon, Mary H. died 01/07/64   01/09/64
Conlon, Phebe died 07/23/63   07/24/63
Conn, Anna Virginia died 06/27/65   06/29/65
Conn, Clay A. married DeCormis, Edward, Jr. 11/14/65   11/15/65
Conn, George married Eckert, Missouri 05/01/64   05/07/64
Conn, Jane died 11/15/64   11/18/64
Conn, Laura V. married Granger, Charles 02/04/64   02/09/64
Conn, Marab J. died 10/15/61   10/16/61
Conn, Sallie E. died 09/17/63   10/03/63
Conn, Silas W. married Owings, Sophia R. 01/15/63   01/22/63
Connaughton, Mary Catherine died 08/24/63   08/25/63
Connell, Dennis died 05/26/64   05/27/64
Connell, Francis A. married Fortune, Mary M. 07/08/63   07/10/63
Connell, Mary Francis died 05/09/64   05/11/64
Connelly, Edward died 01/23/62   01/24/62
Connelly, Edward died 01/23/62   01/25/62
Connelly, John died 08/03/63   09/02/63
Connelly, John died 10/15/64   10/18/64
Connely, Andrew J. married Baltzell, Sarah C. 09/17/65   09/27/65
Connely, Francis Elias died 06/13/61   06/14/61
Conner, Arthur died 07/31/63   08/01/63

Conner, Charles Wesley died 06/08/64   06/10/64
Conner, James died no date   09/11/61
Conner, John died 07/24/63   07/25/63
Conner, John Thomas died 02/02/62   02/04/62
Conner, Mary E. married Smith, G. R. 06/27/65   06/29/65
Conner, Mary L. died 08/25/62   08/27/62
Conner, William Small died 12/03/61   12/10/61
Conner, Wyvill Hooper died 11/26/61   12/10/61
Connery, John died 02/18/65   02/20/65
Connish, Charles H. died 01/28/65   01/30/65
Connolly, Charles F. died 08/24/64   08/26/64
Connolly, James died 12/25/64   12/28/64
Connolly, John married Tracey, Ellen 09/08/62   09/11/62
Connolly, John died 11/13/64   11/16/64
Connolly, John Landon (Dr.) died 09/15/63   09/29/63
Connolly, John Thomas died 04/07/61   04/08/61
Connolly, John W. died 03/02/61   04/03/61
Connolly, John William died 01/07/64   01/08/64
Connolly, Mary A. married Potter, B. F. 09/14/65   09/19/65
Connolly, Michael died 11/14/62   11/15/62
Connolly, Nancy died 02/27/62   03/01/62
Connolly, Sallie A. died 12/25/62   12/27/62
Connoly, Margaret Teresa died 10/11/63   10/13/63
Connoly, Mary Elizabeth died 01/11/63   01/15/63
Connoly, Patrick died 02/14/64   02/15/64
Connoly, Samuel T. died 07/22/63   07/23/63
Connoly, Samuel T. died 07/22/63   08/04/63
Connor, Ann died 04/20/62   04/21/62
Connor, Anne (Mrs.) died 01/07/64   01/08/64
Connor, Catherine (Mrs.) died 10/05/65   10/06/65
Connor, Daniel died 03/30/64   03/31/64
Connor, Elizabeth C. married Rigney, John C. 12/25/64   01/02/65
Connor, John died 09/27/63   09/29/63
Connor, Lucinda J. married Swain, James W. 06/20/65   06/24/65
Connor, Margaret (Mrs.) died 07/31/64   08/01/64
Connor, Mary A. married Manly, John S. 04/23/63   04/24/63
Connor, Patrick died 12/21/65   12/22/65
Connor, Patrick died 12/21/65   12/23/65
Connor, Royer died 02/03/65   02/04/65
Conoley, Martin died 11/01/64   11/03/64
Conrad, Christopher F. died 02/19/65   02/21/65
Conrad, David died 03/14/63   03/19/63
Conrad, J. M. M. married Simms, Mary J. 12/12/65   12/14/65
Conrad, Nannie A. died 06/24/64   06/30/64
Conrad, Sarah died 09/02/61   09/04/61
Conrad, Susannah (Mrs.) died 02/23/64   02/24/64
Conrad, William married Zimmerman, Adelaide 11/19/63   11/24/63
Conradt, C. G. died 12/23/63   12/25/63
Conradt, George B. married Poulson, Clara 04/02/63   04/03/63
Conradt, George M. died 08/04/63   08/05/63
Conradt, George M., Sr. died 11/19/61   11/21/61
Conry, Annie S. married Berg, Albert B. 06/13/65   06/19/65
Conry, Jane died 09/29/63   09/30/63
Conry, John Thomas died 12/17/63   12/19/63

Conry, Mary married Cunio, Andrew 05/20/61 07/26/61
Conry, Peter died 06/26/64 06/27/64
Considine, Michael died 03/29/63 03/31/63
Constable, Elizabeth died 06/05/62 06/06/62
Constable, Isabel S. married Gittings, Samuel 11/07/61 11/11/61
Constable, Isabel S. married Skinner, Truman 11/12/63 11/14/63
Constable, Nellie married Hilberg, John A. 01/17/65 01/18/65
Constance, Joseph married Slee, Sarah R. 12/18/62 01/28/63
Constantine, Bridget married Flaherty, John 11/29/60 06/18/61
Constantine, John Morrow died 02/10/62 02/11/62
Contee, Alice Lee died 09/21/64 09/23/64
Contee, Eleanor Russell died 02/14/63 02/19/63
Conway, Catherine died 01/17/61 01/19/61
Conway, Columbus L. died 09/17/61 09/19/61
Conway, Ella Mary died 12/23/61 12/24/61
Conway, Ella Mary died 12/22/61 12/25/61
Conway, James married Cooper, Almira 12/01/64 12/07/64
Conway, Jessie died 07/28/64 07/29/64
Conway, John died 05/01/64 05/02/64
Conway, John Patrick died 03/05/65 03/06/65
Conway, John Wesley died 10/29/65 10/30/65
Conway, Julia (Mrs.) died 01/08/63 01/09/63
Conway, Mary E. married Spence, John E. 02/06/62 02/28/62
Conway, Michael married McNulty, Kate 02/23/62 02/27/62
Conway, Sarah E. died 04/21/65 05/09/65
Conway, Thomas died 12/20/65 12/21/65
Conway, William W. married Warfield, Margaretta 09/24/65 09/26/65
Conyers, Walter married Miller, Henrietta 05/11/61 09/05/61
Coogan, Anastasia E. married McGinn, Bernard 04/17/65 04/27/65
Coogan, Charles Clement died 08/11/63 08/12/63
Cook, Alexander died 03/22/64 03/24/64
Cook, Anne (Mrs.) died 07/24/63 07/25/63
Cook, Annie M. married McGeehan, Edward J. 05/23/65 05/25/65
Cook, Benjamin died 01/06/64 01/08/64
Cook, Camillia Helen died 05/21/63 04/05/64
Cook, Catherine (Mrs.) died 04/26/65 04/28/65
Cook, Cecilia Priscilla died 01/30/63 01/31/63
Cook, Christian A. died 09/06/61 09/07/61
Cook, David W. died 08/19/65 08/21/65
Cook, Edmund died 06/30/61 07/01/61
Cook, Elizabeth married Burgess, Owen D. 03/28/61 04/15/61
Cook, Elizabeth (Mrs.) died 03/08/63 03/11/63
Cook, Elizabeth (Mrs.) died 09/24/63 09/26/63
Cook, Francis married Score, Martha 03/07/61 03/11/61
Cook, G. W. (Dr.) died 04/02/65 04/06/65
Cook, George Olive died 08/23/63 08/24/63
Cook, George William Jefferson died 11/25/64 11/26/64
Cook, Harriet R. married High, George W. 11/13/65 11/16/65
Cook, Henrietta married Savournin, William H. 02/04/62 02/06/62
Cook, Henry married Brossine, Louise 10/29/63 11/24/63
Cook, Henry married Brossine, Louise 10/29/63 11/25/63
Cook, Henry married Brossine, Louise 10/29/63 11/26/63
Cook, Ida Elizabeth died 08/03/62 08/05/62
Cook, James E. married Dolphin, Mary A. D. 09/14/64 09/22/64
Cook, Jefferson M. married Linsted, Emma 10/11/64 10/13/64

```
Cook, Johanna (Mrs.) died 10/09/64   10/10/64
Cook, John K. married McMillin, Margaret Jane Grundy 07/04/61   07/18/6
Cook, Lewis E. married Parlett, Elizabeth A. 07/02/63   07/31/63
Cook, Lewis E. died 04/01/64   10/26/64
Cook, Lizzie A. died 06/07/61   06/08/61
Cook, Louisa (Mrs.) died 06/23/63   06/25/63
Cook, Mahala married Kreile, Frederick 03/31/61   04/03/61
Cook, Margaret Jane Grundy died 07/09/64   07/11/64
Cook, Margaret M. died 11/08/61   11/09/61
Cook, Maria V. married Fuller, J. Warren 01/29/63   02/07/63
Cook, Martin married Hoffman, Eliza Ann 05/07/61   05/16/61
Cook, Martin died 01/03/64   01/05/64
Cook, Mary A. married Deaver, Robert M. 11/25/63   12/01/63
Cook, Mary Elizabeth died 09/20/61   09/21/61
Cook, Mary Elizabeth married Gable, Benjamin F. 10/19/63   10/22/63
Cook, Mary Francis died 08/03/64   08/04/64
Cook, Mary W. married Carter, William H. 04/15/62   04/17/62
Cook, Nathan married Waters, Hattie A. 12/15/63   12/18/63
Cook, William married Waters, Susan A. 04/09/61   05/10/61
Cook, William died 01/26/63   02/04/63
Cook, William F. died 09/09/61   09/14/61
Cook, William H. died 07/18/65   07/19/65
Cook, William H. married McFall, Rose 03/03/64   03/15/64
Cook, William V. married Bowyer, Joanna 12/17/63   12/19/63
Cook, William V. married Martin, Annie E. 11/20/65   12/05/65
Cooke, Benjamin E. married Gillespie, Louisa 09/02/62   01/08/63
Cooke, Charles E. T. died 05/02/61   05/03/61
Cooke, Charles W. S. died 02/28/64   02/29/64
Cooke, Frank died 09/20/62   09/22/62
Cooke, Harry Reamer died 06/19/63   06/20/63
Cooke, Jane (Mrs.) died 03/04/64   03/05/64
Cooke, John died 07/01/64   07/06/64
Cooke, Mary (Mrs.) died no date   10/06/63
Cooke, Mary Hammond died 03/08/65   03/23/65
Cooke, Molly Agnes died 06/16/63   06/20/63
Cooke, Ophelia (Mrs.) died 03/01/64   03/02/64
Cooke, Sarah (Mrs.) died 03/20/63   03/21/63
Cooke, Septimus John died 02/21/65   03/04/65
Cooke, Thomas married Stanford, Emily Kate 04/06/65   04/11/65
Cooke, Warren E. married Scharf, Sallie H. 07/14/64   07/16/64
Cooke, William died 09/15/61   09/17/61
Cookesey, Thomas Neilson married Smith, Rose 08/13/65   08/16/65
Cooksay, Mary Elizabeth died 08/15/64   08/17/64
Cookseu, Helen M. married Mitchell, Thomas J. 12/10/61   12/11/61
Cooksey, George H. married Cooksey, Margaret D. 05/26/63   06/13/63
Cooksey, Margaret D. married Cooksey, George H. 05/26/63   06/13/63
Cooksey, Thomas H. married Meekins, Marcella 10/22/63   10/26/63
Cooley, Mary (Mrs.) died 01/28/64   01/30/64
Coombes, Richard J. married Pasterfield, Martha A. 09/18/64   09/20/64
Coombs, Fannie E. married Zimmerman, H. T. 05/04/65   05/06/65
Coombs, John Thomas died 05/27/61   10/18/61
Coombs, Lydia A. died 10/26/62   10/27/62
Coon, George died 02/28/65   03/03/65
Coonan, Dr. Jonathan married Gross, Kate T. 01/01/65   01/11/65
Coonan, M. J. married Brenan, Adele 01/08/63   01/09/63
```

Coonan, Michael died 01/10/63 01/12/63
Cooney, Ann Jane died 10/26/63 10/27/63
Cooney, Ann Jane died 10/26/63 10/28/63
Cooney, Annie married Brown, Louis 04/14/65 04/22/65
Cooney, Mary died 01/13/64 01/18/64
Cooney, Richard died 08/13/63 08/14/63
Cooney, Thomas J. married Nugent, Mary A. 02/08/64 02/16/64
Cooper, Adderly married Lowell, Rose 06/14/64 07/06/64
Cooper, Almira married Conway, James 12/01/64 12/07/64
Cooper, Ann Eliza died 06/23/65 06/26/65
Cooper, Anna M. married Griffin, Edward 09/01/63 09/03/63
Cooper, E. O. (Cpt.) died 08/08/63 08/10/63
Cooper, Edward married Hamilton, Julia 12/21/63 12/22/63
Cooper, Elizabeth (Mrs.) died 04/21/65 04/27/65
Cooper, Ellen Jane married McCluskling, James 08/04/64 08/13/64
Cooper, Ellen Jane married McCluskling, James 08/04/64 08/15/64
Cooper, Frances M. died 06/02/61 06/04/61
Cooper, George C. married Miller, Mary F. 05/11/63 05/13/63
Cooper, George F. married Montgomery, Sarah A. 10/26/65 10/27/65
Cooper, George W. died 03/26/62 03/28/62
Cooper, H. died 11/06/61 11/07/61
Cooper, Hamilton married Brown, Mary 12/27/63 12/29/63
Cooper, Harriet (Mrs.) died 03/28/65 03/30/65
Cooper, Harriet Ann married Grace, Alexander 04/16/61 04/19/61
Cooper, Helen M. married Griffith, John A. 03/30/64 04/01/64
Cooper, Henry died 10/29/62 10/31/62
Cooper, Henry S. S. married Burnett, Annie C. 06/28/65 07/29/65
Cooper, Hester M. married Wilson, John H. 12/22/62 12/24/62
Cooper, James married Martin, Mary E. (Mrs.) 11/28/61 11/30/61
Cooper, James married Hargrove, Mary E. 12/14/65 12/20/65
Cooper, James C. married Bailey, Sarah J. 12/17/63 12/22/63
Cooper, John died 06/29/64 06/30/64
Cooper, John H. married Baily, Maria Louisa 10/11/63 10/14/63
Cooper, Joshua E. married Hand, Hennie H. 12/06/64 12/08/64
Cooper, Levin married Gipson, Sophia 11/10/64 11/12/64
Cooper, Lucinda died 03/26/64 03/29/64
Cooper, Margaret Louisa died 06/04/63 06/05/63
Cooper, Maria L. married King, Lemuel B. 10/17/64 11/17/64
Cooper, Martha L. died 10/16/62 10/18/62
Cooper, Mary (Mrs.) died 06/30/64 07/01/64
Cooper, Mary Catherine married Marine, William 11/21/61 11/22/61
Cooper, Mary E. married Whiton, Henry 02/22/65 02/25/65
Cooper, Mary E. married Chester, Dawson A. 03/30/65 04/01/65
Cooper, Mary Elizabeth died 11/12/65 11/13/65
Cooper, Mary Ellen married Johnson, Thomas 12/08/64 12/10/64
Cooper, Mary Jane married Williams, Asa 04/09/63 04/16/63
Cooper, Mary Louisa died 05/09/65 05/10/65
Cooper, Mary Louisa (Mrs.) died 12/14/65 12/15/65
Cooper, Mary Louisa (Mrs.) died 12/14/65 12/16/65
Cooper, Matthew H. (Capt.) died 01/18/62 01/20/62
Cooper, Minie Payne died 06/14/64 06/21/64
Cooper, Nelson died 02/27/62 03/01/62
Cooper, Nelson died 02/27/62 03/03/62
Cooper, Phebe died 10/03/61 10/04/61
Cooper, Samuel married Irwin, Charlotte 02/25/64 02/27/64

Cooper, Samuel R. married Hopkins, Lizzie S. 06/28/64   07/08/64
Cooper, Sarah married Buchanan, Jarret 06/30/64   07/02/64
Cooper, Sarah Ann died 08/13/65   08/15/65
Cooper, Sarah Catherine married Pindell, Philip M. 04/04/64   04/07/64
Cooper, Susan A. H. married Richter, Charles A. 08/10/61   08/19/61
Cooper, Thomas J. married Chaney, Sarah J. (Mrs.) 10/03/65   10/07/65
Cooper, William H. married Hedrick, Elizabeth A. 07/13/65   07/15/65
Coopper, Tommy died 02/10/62   02/11/62
Coot, Mary married Coles, William 12/23/63   11/21/63
Cope, Anne Clara died 04/17/64   04/20/64
Cope, William Albert died 02/03/64   02/04/64
Copeland, Mary Ann married Reese, Charles 04/09/63   04/11/63
Copes, Richard H. died 09/29/64   10/27/64
Copes, William V. died 10/20/64   10/27/64
Copper, Joshua T. died 07/20/64   08/29/64
Copper, Rachel married Brown, Charles 04/17/64   04/19/64
Copper, Rebecca married Deshon, J. Westly 04/19/64   04/21/64
Coppuck, Clifford J. died 07/31/62   08/07/62
Coppuck, Clifford J. died 07/31/62   08/08/62
Coram, Joseph died 10/25/65   10/27/65
Corbell, Hiram died 09/21/65   09/22/65
Corbell, Hiram died 09/21/65   09/23/65
Corbett, Abraham died 04/07/64   04/08/64
Corbett, Lydia Jane died 03/09/64   03/10/64
Corbin, Cornelia married Jenkins, John T. 09/08/63   09/11/63
Corbin, Julie A. married Brent, William L. 04/02/63   04/28/63
Corbitt, Lawrence died 10/01/63   10/02/63
Corbitt, Ruth died 04/19/62   04/29/62
Corbitt, T. died 09/13/63   09/14/63
Corcoran, Christopher married Fowble, Cynthia 06/01/65   06/03/65
Corcoran, Ellen married Davis, George W. 01/08/61   04/12/61
Corcoran, Sarah F. married Gregory, John T. 04/28/64   05/02/64
Cord, Carrie H. married Fox, Charles G. 10/12/65   11/15/65
Cord, Francis Marion died 04/14/64   04/16/64
Cordery, James Collier died 01/06/62   01/07/62
Cordray, Mary Bell married Jewett, Charles H. 07/28/64   07/30/64
Cordray, William Bayley died 07/08/61   07/11/61
Corea, Joseph E. died 07/03/61   07/04/61
Corey, Albert William Jackson died 06/15/65   06/16/65
Corey, James Beauregard died 07/30/63   07/31/63
Corey, Michael F. died 10/22/64   10/24/64
Coriell, Mary E. married Bower, Lewis M. 01/28/62   01/31/62
Cork, Christianna R. died 11/23/62   12/01/62
Corkran, Alexander M.(MD, USA) died 07/29/63   07/30/63
Corkran, Francis Spey died 06/13/65   06/15/65
Corletto, Charles W. died 09/03/63   12/11/63
Cormack, Archibald married Harris, Laura 10/01/61   10/03/61
Cornel, Elizabeth married Williams, Henry 06/12/62   06/13/62
Cornelius, Dorothy (Mrs.) died 01/19/64   01/23/64
Cornelius, Elenora died 08/03/62   08/04/62
Cornelius, Fanny married Webb, George H. 12/18/62   12/22/62
Cornelius, J. W. (Rev.) married Dungan, E. D. 11/03/64   11/08/64
Cornelius, Sarah Jane married Crawford, Robert N. 05/30/61   06/01/61
Cornell, Mark J. married Yerkes, Fannie 12/18/61   12/23/61
Cornell, Mary married Taylor, William H. 05/02/61   05/04/61

Cornell, Theodore died 01/13/63 01/14/64
Cornell, William died 09/30/65 10/04/65
Cornell, William C. died 05/04/64 05/05/64
Corner, Anna Maria married Phelan, Daniel L. 02/21/65 03/01/65
Corner, John died 10/30/63 11/02/63
Corner, Lizzie M. married Brown, John J. 04/13/64 04/18/64
Corner, Mary S. married Reed, J. Harris 02/20/61 02/25/61
Corner, William H. married Cromwell, Camilla 01/15/62 01/21/62
Cornes, John died 12/27/64 12/29/64
Cornet, William F. married Caton, Julia 05/15/62 05/19/62
Cornish, Anna married Ashton, Thomas 03/26/63 03/28/63
Cornish, David died 12/14/63 12/15/63
Cornish, Joseph married McGlocklin, Sarah 05/19/64 05/21/64
Cornish, Lucy married Jones, James A. 04/02/61 04/08/61
Cornor, Anna Maria married Phelan, Daniel L. 02/21/65 02/28/65
Cornor, Mary J. married Hardesty, T. Edward 10/11/63 11/10/63
Cornor, William E. married Norris, Mary E. 07/08/62 07/16/62
Cornprobst, Bernard died 03/05/62 03/07/62
Corns, John died 12/27/64 12/28/64
Corns, Lizzie F. married Burns, Thomas (1st Sgt.) 12/11/62 12/15/62
Cornthwait, Edwin Willis died 06/29/64 06/30/64
Cornthwait, Henrietta C. married Stauffer, George W. 05/01/61 05/06/61
Cornthwait, Ida May died 06/21/65 06/26/65
Cornthwait, James H. died 01/08/65 01/10/65
Cornthwait, Mary died 01/10/64 01/11/64
Cornthwaite, Deborah died 04/14/63 04/15/63
Cornthwaite, Robert died 09/17/64 09/19/64
Correar, Clara M. died 06/27/64 06/28/64
Correar, Harry Sherman died 06/04/65 06/05/65
Corrigan, Alice died 07/30/65 07/31/65
Corrigan, Francis married Doyle, Mary 11/24/61 12/05/61
Corrigan, James P. died 08/05/63 08/06/63
Corrigan, Julia died 12/20/63 12/22/63
Corrigan, Mary Ann died 09/19/61 09/21/61
Corse, Hettie S. married Janney, Edward W. (Dr.) 04/13/64 04/16/64
Corse, Robert S. married Norris, Rachel S. 02/24/64 02/29/64
Corvaizier, Eugene P. married Creacy, Mary Jane 04/23/60 01/19/63
Cosgrove, Ann (Mrs.) died 04/16/64 04/18/64
Cosgrove, Francis M. died 09/08/64 09/10/64
Cosgrove, James H. married Murphy, Eliza 02/24/62 03/11/62
Cosgrove, Patrick died 09/10/62 09/11/62
Coskery, Henry J. married Sitler, Bettie 12/09/65 12/12/65
Coskery, Sophia died 01/15/63 01/16/64
Cosley, George W. died 04/15/63 04/17/63
Cosley, Jennie F. married Hall, G. W. 02/02/65 02/10/65
Coss, George M. married Davenport, Phoebe 10/18/62 11/04/62
Coss, George M. died 07/20/64 07/25/64
Coss, Martha Rausse died 11/29/64 12/05/64
Coss, Rina married Lineweaver, P. L. 05/19/64 05/23/64
Costallo, Roseann died 02/27/63 02/28/63
Costello, Elizabeth married Nicoll, William 10/12/62 10/14/62
Costello, Emma married Horn, Philip C. 05/12/62 05/13/62
Costello, Francis Hugh died 02/29/64 03/02/64
Costello, James J. died 07/24/62 07/25/62
Costello, Margaret died 03/31/63 04/01/63

Coster, Carrie Virginia died 10/26/62 10/28/62
Coster, Elizabeth (Mrs.) died 02/04/64 02/05/64
Coster, J. W. married Boteler, Emma T. 03/22/64 03/31/64
Coster, John Henry died 02/28/65 03/01/65
Coster, Joseph L. died 01/19/61 01/26/61
Coster, Nora Lovena died 08/09/61 08/10/61
Costigan, C. I. Dorsey died 11/10/62 12/18/62
Costigin, Kate married Dorsey, Vernon 04/24/62 04/29/62
Costlo, Roseann died 08/31/65 09/01/65
Coswell, William H. S. died 05/01/65 05/06/65
Cotanch, Geoffrey W. died 02/01/64 02/03/64
Cotman, Catherine married Sybry, Bassesto 02/08/64 02/10/64
Cotter, James died 01/02/63 01/03/63
Cotter, John Joseph died 05/29/62 05/31/62
Cotter, Nicholas died 04/03/61 04/05/61
Cotter, Richard died 01/26/64 02/03/64
Cottingham, Ann Jane died 01/01/63 01/03/63
Cottingham, Margaret (Mrs.) died 04/11/64 04/12/64
Cottingham, Sarah F. married Wonn, James G. 06/08/64 06/18/64
Cottman, Elizabeth died 12/30/61 01/02/62
Cottrell, Henry died 05/15/62 05/23/62
Cottrell, J. (Cpt.) married Henschell, Louise (Mrs.) 12/08/63 12/11/6
Cottrell, Jane (Mrs.) died 11/20/64 12/08/64
Cottrell, Jeremiah married Wilkins, Mary E. 10/15/64 05/25/65
Cottrell, Mary A. died 10/03/61 10/05/61
Couchman, Emma J. married Welffel, Henry L. 03/14/64 03/29/64
Couchman, George died 06/24/63 06/25/63
Couchman, Keziak died 03/07/65 03/08/65
Coughlan, Bridget died 06/21/61 06/22/61
Coughlan, Elizabeth (Mrs.) died 08/16/63 08/17/63
Coughlan, Sarah died 12/28/60 01/19/61
Coughlin, Ellen married McMahon, Peter 11/22/64 11/30/64
Coughlin, John married Crowley, Mary 11/07/65 11/10/65
Cougler, John married Biddison, Martha W. 03/10/62 03/14/62
Coulan, Drew J. married Dunn, Veronica T. 01/08/65 01/16/65
Coulbourn, Elizabeth A. married Stubbs, Richard P. 03/10/64 03/14/64
Coulson, Andrew died 01/06/65 01/07/65
Coulter, A. W. married Taylor, Ellen J. 03/09/64 03/14/64
Coulter, Alice Virginia died 09/23/65 09/25/65
Coulter, Catharine died 10/17/65 10/18/65
Coulter, Catherine A. died no date 10/23/65
Coulter, D. Mifflin married Gibson, Sophia Finley 10/12/64 10/13/64
Coulter, Henry S. (Dr.) died 05/07/62 05/09/62
Coulter, Henry S. (Dr.) died 05/07/62 05/12/62
Coulter, John died 09/25/61 10/07/61
Coulter, John H. married Baranger, Catherine 03/03/61 12/25/61
Coulter, Julia Ann married Hamilton, John 04/08/62 04/21/62
Coulter, Margaret married Smith, James 06/04/62 06/20/62
Coulter, Robert A. married Rae, Annie V. 04/21/62 04/26/62
Coulter, Samuel died 03/17/63 03/20/63
Coulter, Sarah C. died 04/13/65 04/15/65
Councell, Joel F. died 05/26/62 05/28/62
Councilman, Martha Ann married McCormick, Alexander 12/31/63 01/12/64
Councilman, Robert married Felton, Mary Jane 12/22/64 12/26/64
Councilman, William died 10/30/61 10/31/61

Counselman, Elizabeth (Mrs.) died 10/07/64   10/12/64
Counselman, J. Henry married Willis, Mary F. 05/17/65   05/18/65
Countess, Olevia died 10/18/61   10/22/61
Coupland, Eliza (Mrs.) died 10/26/64   10/28/64
Coupland, Louisa married Flannery, James J. 12/04/64   12/07/64
Coursey, E. Henry, Jr. married Davis, Amanda 11/17/63   11/21/63
Coursey, John W. died 02/18/61   02/20/61
Coursey, William H. married Smith, Julia Ann 03/24/64   03/30/64
Coursley, George married Norwood, Jennie 10/21/62   10/24/62
Courtenay, Sarah married Brewerton, Henry (USA) 04/20/64   04/21/64
Courtney, Ann Barr died 12/16/62   12/17/62
Courtney, Anne Burr died 12/16/62   12/18/62
Courtney, Catherine died 02/05/65   02/07/65
Courtney, George married Martin, Fannie A. 09/28/65   10/30/65
Courtney, Hugh M. died 02/16/64   02/17/64
Courtney, James died 01/16/61   01/22/61
Courtney, James Thornton died 06/10/64   06/11/64
Courtney, Mary married Riordan, Michael 02/08/63   02/17/63
Courtney, Mary married Desveraux, Francis 09/16/63   01/05/64
Courtney, Patrick (Rev.) died 03/06/63   03/07/63
Courtois, Clementine married Eschbach, Louis A. 10/11/65   10/12/65
Cousino, William J. married Fenwick, Lizzie R. 04/21/64   04/25/64
Cousins, Mary E. married Durding, Leander A. 01/04/62   01/08/62
Cousix, John George died 05/25/63   05/27/63
Covell, Joel died 03/03/61   03/07/61
Cover, John died 08/09/64   09/08/64
Covey, Anna V. married Betson, George (Dr.) 11/07/65   11/13/65
Covey, Isabella married Goslin, Thomas H. 11/07/65   11/13/65
Cowan, Almira V. married Pryer, Edward 02/19/61   06/03/61
Cowan, Charles H. married Stewart, Louie Harrison 07/02/61   07/09/61
Cowan, Eliza Jane married Krebs, Henry W. 12/05/61   12/07/61
Cowan, Robert J. died 05/09/64   05/11/64
Cowan, Sallie E. married Trott, James 04/22/62   04/24/62
Cowan, Sophie married Meekins, Thomas 09/17/61   10/30/61
Coward, Ann died 03/17/61   03/27/61
Coward, Mary S. died 01/25/63   02/02/63
Cowles, George William died 02/12/65   02/14/65
Cowles, John W. died 12/16/63   12/18/63
Cowman, Charles Stewart died 08/25/62   08/28/62
Cowman, Harry W. died 04/14/62   04/16/62
Cowman, Mary Anna died 01/26/61   01/28/61
Cowman, Philip E. married Clagett, Mary C. 07/14/63   08/08/63
Cowman, Philip E. married Clagett, Mary C. 07/14/63   08/10/63
Cox, Annie E. died 11/01/63   11/03/63
Cox, Annie Jackson died 08/20/64   08/27/64
Cox, Annie M. died 10/27/65   10/28/65
Cox, Charles C. died 04/07/65   04/08/65
Cox, Elias died 08/30/62   09/01/62
Cox, Elisha married Hanley, Kate 07/09/63   09/14/63
Cox, Francis Waters died 09/01/65   09/02/65
Cox, Isaac married Wilson, Elvira Z. 05/17/64   05/20/64
Cox, James E. married Ferguson, Ursula C. 08/06/65   08/21/65
Cox, James G. died 08/24/63   08/31/63
Cox, Joal S. married Rogers, Sarah E. 04/17/63   05/05/63
Cox, John died 04/22/65   04/25/65

```
Cox, Julyelma S. married Ebaugh, Francis A. 06/26/62   07/07/62
Cox, Madison married Todd, Rose (Mrs.) 09/09/65   09/12/65
Cox, Maria married Sargent, Oliver B. 11/13/65   11/18/65
Cox, Mary Agnes died 02/07/61   02/08/61
Cox, Mary Jane died 01/12/62   01/13/62
Cox, Mary Jane died 01/27/65   01/28/65
Cox, Mary Lizzie married Keene, John H. 06/29/64   07/02/64
Cox, Mary Lizzie married Keenem, John H. 07/02/64   07/04/64
Cox, Moses died 10/09/65   10/10/65
Cox, Moses died 10/09/65   10/11/65
Cox, Percy Christopher died 07/08/63   07/09/63
Cox, Peregrine married Hooper, Mary A. 02/07/65   02/09/65
Cox, Susan died 10/02/62   10/03/62
Cox, Sylvester L. married White, Rebecca M. 04/28/64   05/05/64
Cox, Walter died 08/21/63   08/22/63
Cox, Welszetta died 08/01/65   08/02/65
Cox, William A. married Ward, Virginia I. 04/19/64   04/21/64
Cox, William B. died no date   10/21/62
Cox, William Slater died 06/28/64   06/29/64
Coxon, Francis married Hallsworth, Jane 05/17/63   05/22/63
Coy, John H. married Budd, Caroline 02/01/63   02/09/63
Coye, John married Brown, Clara 02/22/63   02/25/63
Coyle, Bernard F. married Lawrenson, Mary A. 02/23/63   03/18/63
Coyle, Louisa Vinton married Dukehart, George Dobbin 08/04/64   08/08/6
Coyle, Mary A. S. died 03/24/62   03/25/62
Coyle, Peter A. died 02/06/65   03/08/65
Coyle, Peter A. died 02/06/65   03/09/65
Coyle, Thomas married Hanihan, Mary A. 06/11/61   06/12/61
Coyne, Bridget died 06/15/62   06/16/62
Cozine, Abraham V. died 02/17/61   02/28/61
Cozine, John T. (Corp.) died 12/10/61   12/12/61
Cozzins, Stephen died 08/11/63   08/12/63
Crabbe, Arthur Farnandis died 03/14/62   03/15/62
Cracroft, Mary C. married Robinson, Benjamin N. 02/02/64   03/04/64
Craddick, Joseph N. married Hubbard, Annie E. 10/15/63   10/20/63
Cradock, Thomas married Carroll, Sallie 10/22/62   10/23/62
Craft, Charles H. died 11/17/64   11/19/64
Craft, Eleanor died 07/23/65   07/25/65
Craft, Jacob died 11/26/62   11/27/62
Craft, Jacob married Donohou, Mary 09/29/63   12/31/63
Craft, Mary (Mrs.) died 09/05/65   09/07/65
Craft, Rosanna died 05/28/62   05/30/62
Craft, Rosanna died 05/28/62   05/31/62
Crager, Peter died 01/06/62   01/07/62
Cragg, Annie married Milroy, Alexander 10/22/61   11/04/61
Craig, Alexander married Duncan, Agnes 07/23/63   07/28/63
Craig, Daniel B. died 11/03/65   11/04/65
Craig, Frances L. married Bishop, William L. 08/28/65   09/04/65
Craig, Horatio E. died 04/23/65   04/24/65
Craig, Horatio E. died 04/23/65   04/25/65
Craig, J. Morrel married Davis, Fannie S. 10/17/65   10/24/65
Craig, James L. died 11/04/65   11/16/65
Craig, John died 02/05/61   02/06/61
Craig, John married Gregg, Annie Jane 02/18/64   02/23/64
Craig, Louisa died 12/09/62   12/09/62
```

Craig, Richard R. died 08/20/62   08/22/62
Craig, Robert died 08/23/62   08/25/62
Craig, Robert R. married Keenan, Sarah 09/17/63   09/24/63
Craig, Seldon (Cpt.) married Moore, Virginia C. 04/19/64   04/28/64
Craig, William F. married Dudley, Emily V. 07/26/65   08/08/65
Craig, William W. died 08/15/65   08/16/65
Craigen, William J. (Dr.) married Pue, Rebecca D. 10/13/64   10/19/64
Crain, Robert (Dr.) married Morgan, Nelly 06/01/64   06/04/64
Cramblitt, Henry died 08/23/61   08/28/61
Cramblitt, Jennie married Murphy, John T. 07/09/62   08/27/62
Cramblitt, Mary Ann (Mrs.) died 06/18/63   06/19/63
Cramblitt, Sophia J. married Dahoff, John H. 06/03/61   06/29/61
Cramer, Hannah married Bergman, Henry 03/05/65   03/17/65
Crandall, Bettie S. married Childs, John W. 06/30/65   07/06/65
Crandel, Margaret A. married Jackson, Charles H. 06/14/61   07/29/61
Crandell, Isabel F. married Whittington, William F. 12/20/64   12/26/64
Crandell, Mary E. married Glover, Joshua L. 11/03/64   11/05/64
Crandell, Priscilla died 04/11/61   04/12/61
Crane, A. F. married Woods, Lizzie D. 06/08/64   06/09/64
Crane, Ann Elizabeth died 08/05/63   08/06/63
Crane, Benjamin died 10/27/64   10/28/64
Crane, Benjamin died 10/27/64   10/29/64
Crane, Charles married De Cormis, Mary E. 07/02/63   07/03/63
Crane, George H. married Rew, Anna S. 11/30/64   12/02/64
Crane, Maria Louisa married Woods, Daniel C. 11/23/65   11/28/65
Crane, Mary A. married Devries, William R. 03/02/65   03/07/65
Crane, Mary Clement (Mrs.) died 02/23/63   02/24/63
Crane, W. B. (Dr.) died 02/19/65   02/22/65
Crangle, John died 12/15/62   12/17/62
Crangle, John died no date   12/18/62
Crangle, Mary L. married McCahan, George L. 04/30/61   05/04/61
Crangle, Michael married Murphy, Winnefred 07/24/65   07/26/65
Cranmer, Mary E. married Rolfe, Chester E. 02/11/64   02/12/64
Cranwell, Charles Bassatt died 04/06/63   04/07/63
Crapin, Mary (Mrs.) died 06/02/65   06/05/65
Craumer, George E. married McAtee, John H. 12/12/65   12/15/65
Craumer, Jacob died 06/29/64   07/06/64
Crawford, A. A. married Haller, F. Virginia 06/14/64   06/21/64
Crawford, Andrew J. married Haller, Frances Virginia 06/14/64   06/20/64
Crawford, Anna married Sherlock, William 12/09/61   12/12/61
Crawford, John D. married Jenkins, Josephine 01/31/63   02/03/63
Crawford, Josie married Maynard, George W. 12/25/62   12/27/62
Crawford, Maggie married Hamilton, John 03/27/62   04/30/62
Crawford, Mary A. married Burns, James 01/04/62   03/03/62
Crawford, Mary V. married Douglas, August 06/25/62   06/27/62
Crawford, Minnie F. married Crawford, Richard H. no date   06/18/64
Crawford, Parthenia S. married Passano, Joseph 04/07/63   04/10/63
Crawford, Richard H. married Crawford, Minnie F. no date   06/18/64
Crawford, Robert N. married Cornelius, Sarah Jane 05/30/61   06/01/61
Crawford, Sarah Eliza died 03/25/63   03/26/63
Crawford, Sarah Elizabeth died 04/22/62   04/26/62
Crawford, Sue married Hopkins, Egbert D. 12/21/65   12/23/65
Crawford, Susan died 04/03/64   04/05/64
Crawford, Thomas A. married Heavel, Julia A. 10/23/62   10/25/62
Crawford, William died 07/11/63   08/03/63

Crawford, William Henry married Meyers, Harriet Ann 12/18/62   12/20/62
Cray, Richard R. died 08/20/62   08/23/62
Craycroft, Ann died 01/17/61   01/25/61
Craycroft, Susan Schley died 09/07/65   09/12/65
Creacy, Mary Jane married Corvaizier, Eugene P. 04/23/60   01/19/63
Creagan, Margaret married Danaher, Henry M. C. 06/23/64   06/24/64
Creager, Barbara C. married Swormstedt, Richard 06/19/64   06/21/64
Creager, George U. married Sands, Sallie S. 03/19/61   03/27/61
Cream, Mary died 10/31/62   11/01/62
Cream, Maurice married McDonough, Lizzie 10/15/62   11/01/62
Creamer, Margaret (Mrs.) died 06/29/63   07/01/63
Creamer, Mary died 10/24/61   10/25/61
Creamer, Sallie E. married Marsh, C. H. 11/24/63   11/28/63
Credit, Alexina married Alnut, Thomas J. 02/16/65   02/18/65
Creighton, Augustus W. died 02/26/61   02/27/61
Creighton, Julia died 11/20/61   11/22/61
Creighton, Mary Adaline died 11/29/61   11/30/61
Creighton, Peter died 08/04/65   08/05/65
Creighton, Robert H. married Gable, Sarah Jane 08/04/61   08/13/61
Crem, Sarah C. married Vickers, John 12/24/62   01/05/63
Creney, Thomas Spence died 03/06/65   03/29/65
Creny, Mary Jane died 12/06/63   12/07/63
Crew, George T. married Tall, Isabella 06/19/65   06/24/65
Crew, Raymond died 08/28/64   08/29/64
Crey, Henry married Sullivan, Mary E. 01/15/65   01/18/65
Cridler, John Washington died 01/08/64   01/22/64
Crighton, Malcolm married Kennedy, Antoinette 06/15/65   06/17/65
Cripps, Mollie E. died 08/13/65   08/14/65
Cripps, Mollie E. died 08/13/65   08/15/65
Cripps, William Marcellus died 11/26/63   12/02/63
Crise, G. W. married Barker, Mary A, 02/22/64   03/16/64
Crise, Josie E. married Turner, William J. 01/19/65   01/20/65
Crisp, Charles married Harrington, Catharine 07/05/63   07/07/63
Crisp, Edward F. married Weisoff, Martha 10/27/64   11/03/64
Crisp, Edward T. married Neihoff, Martha 10/27/64   11/04/64
Crisp, Georgianna married Ebsworth, David 12/26/61   12/31/61
Crisp, John M. died 03/24/65   03/29/65
Crisp, William E. married Dryden, Martha 02/11/61   02/20/61
Criss, Otto Von Hein died 08/13/61   08/14/61
Cristener, Mary Ann died 01/12/61   01/15/61
Crittenden, Thomas died 01/17/62   01/25/62
Crittendon, John died 02/01/64   02/22/64
Croboot, Benjamin Franklin died 05/08/64   05/10/64
Crock, C. Louise married Hill, William B. 10/20/64   10/24/64
Crockard, Sarah A. married McFern, Edward 11/03/64   11/14/64
Crocken, Ann Eliza married Whitlock, William 10/05/63   10/08/63
Crocken, James J. died 09/18/65   09/19/65
Croft, Charles Bolithe died 09/15/62   09/22/62
Croft, James died 11/14/64   11/16/64
Crogan, A. E. married Stewart, C. D. 12/29/64   12/30/64
Croggen, William E. married Caroll, Isabella E. 09/10/65   09/12/65
Croghan, St. George(Col., CSA) died 10/00/00   12/09/62
Cromer, Georgia married Bruchey, David H. 06/04/65   06/06/65
Cromer, Hermie E. married Shannan, William 03/09/65   03/13/65
Cromey, John H. married Reed, Anne 06/09/63   06/12/63

```
Cromwell, Camilla married Corner, William H. 01/15/62   01/21/62
Cromwell, Caroline R. died 08/18/63   08/19/63
Cromwell, Catharine married Williams, Solomon 11/15/65   11/18/65
Cromwell, Charles Henry died 05/03/64   05/04/64
Cromwell, Clara died 09/12/65   09/14/65
Cromwell, Edward Clarence died 03/16/62   03/20/62
Cromwell, Frank T. married Phelps, Isabel C. 02/06/62   02/08/62
Cromwell, George died 09/20/64   09/22/64
Cromwell, George W. married Young, Mary R. 02/28/61   03/19/61
Cromwell, George W. married Young, Mary R. 02/28/61   03/18/61
Cromwell, Jacob G. married Michael, Mary M. 05/17/65   05/19/65
Cromwell, John Edward died 11/15/64   11/17/64
Cromwell, Julia A. (Mrs.) died 10/29/63   10/31/63
Cromwell, Louis married Mumma, Georgeanna 12/14/65   12/21/65
Cromwell, Lydia Ann died 08/15/65   08/18/65
Cromwell, Maggie E. married Shanklin, J. W. 09/21/64   09/26/64
Cromwell, Margaret married Langley, Francis W. 02/18/64   02/19/64
Cromwell, Mary died 08/08/65   08/09/65
Cromwell, Mary C. married Moore, John W. 12/23/63   01/14/64
Cromwell, Mary Eugenia died 09/30/61   10/02/61
Cromwell, Medora died 03/19/62   03/20/62
Cromwell, Oliver died 09/28/61   10/15/61
Cromwell, Oliver H. died 08/31/61   09/02/61
Cromwell, Randolph S., Sr. died 07/02/65   07/11/65
Cromwell, Richard married Kennedy, Mary J. 01/31/61   02/04/61
Cromwell, Sedwick T. married Cole, Julia A. 12/11/62   12/12/62
Cromwell, Sophia (Mrs.) died 04/12/65   04/14/65
Cromwell, Walter Young died 06/01/65   06/03/65
Cromwell, William Rowland died 03/11/62   03/13/62
Crone, William C. married Buck, Sarah A. (Mrs.) 09/07/61   10/08/61
Cronin, Mary (Mrs.) died 10/03/63   10/05/63
Cronin, Phillip married Wilson, Kate 02/15/64   02/18/64
Cronmiller, Thomas L. (Dr.) died 09/23/64   09/30/64
Cronon, Harry died 10/26/61   11/05/61
Crook, Amelia Jane died 06/04/62   06/07/62
Crook, Andrew Daniel died 01/11/64   01/12/64
Crook, Anna Mathilda died 01/17/65   01/18/65
Crook, Anna Matilda died 01/17/65   01/19/65
Crook, Charles died 10/26/64   11/28/64
Crook, Daniel died 07/10/64   07/13/64
Crook, Emma (Mrs.) died 11/22/63   11/24/63
Crook, F. M. married Royster, E. Augusta 02/20/65   02/24/65
Crook, Francis A., Jr. married Kaufman, Mary 01/22/63   01/27/63
Crook, George Robert died 05/17/65   05/25/65
Crook, James H. died 07/02/65   08/05/65
Crook, James L. married Forsythe, Emily V. 06/27/65   06/29/65
Crook, James, Jr. died 07/02/63   07/03/63
Crook, Joseph died 02/26/64   02/27/64
Crook, Mary died 12/10/65   12/11/65
Crook, Matilda married Mitchell, George 03/28/61   03/30/61
Crook, Sarah Ann died 05/10/62   05/14/62
Crook, Sarah Anna (Mrs.) died 04/14/64   04/15/64
Crook, William H. married Barrett, Mary E 12/19/61   01/28/62
Crook, Wilson Brown died 09/02/61   09/06/61
Crooks, Eliza Ann (Mrs.) died 08/10/63   08/12/63
```

Crooks, Rufus S. married Baynard, Anna M. 01/28/64   01/30/64
Crookshanks, Charles died 06/02/65   06/05/65
Cropley, Richard L. married Jones, Beccie 10/02/62   10/09/62
Cropp, Jennie F. married Reynolds, O. B. 03/18/63   04/08/63
Cropp, Jennie F. married Reynols, J. R. 03/18/63   06/16/63
Cropp, William died 08/30/65   08/31/65
Cropper, Samuel J. married Saunders, Sarah E. 12/19/61   12/23/61
Cropper, Samuel J. died 05/09/62   05/10/62
Cropper, Sarah E. married Jones, Jeremiah 04/06/65   04/11/65
Cropper, William P. (Capt.) died 07/20/63   08/19/63
Crosbie, Ellen died 02/04/65   02/06/65
Crosby, Alexander L. married Harrison, Sarah Baxter 10/25/65   11/01/65
Crosby, Emma Virginia died 04/22/63   04/24/63
Crosby, George W. married Trine, Sarah 04/21/61   04/29/61
Crosby, Lorane C. died 03/05/64   03/08/64
Crosby, Mary A. married Gillingham, Daniel 09/03/63   09/05/63
Crosby, Mary A. (Mrs.) married Lyles, Samuel 12/28/65   12/29/65
Crosby, Mary Elizabeth died 12/18/62   12/19/62
Crosby, Patrick died 12/07/62   12/08/62
Croshaw, Mary A. married Elder, Zachariah 10/31/61   11/02/61
Crosly, Samuel (Capt.) married McCleary, Mattie A. 02/07/65   02/21/65
Cross, (Mrs. J. L.) died 02/11/62   02/12/62
Cross, Amelia A. married Banks, Morton D. 04/20/65   04/24/65
Cross, Anne Eliza Ritchie died 09/10/65   09/15/65
Cross, Birtie married Williams, James W. 09/21/64   09/26/64
Cross, Edward died 08/30/64   08/31/64
Cross, Edward died 08/30/64   09/01/64
Cross, Elizabeth died 05/17/62   05/19/62
Cross, Elizabeth married Shamburg, Josh 02/18/64   02/19/64
Cross, Elizabeth Jane died 09/27/65   09/28/65
Cross, Eugenia married Selby, Nicholas A. 11/22/64   11/29/64
Cross, Fielder died 11/17/61   11/22/61
Cross, J. H. (Cpt.) married Foster, E. 05/05/63   05/07/63
Cross, James A. married Maher, Anney 02/07/64   02/10/64
Cross, James Wesley married Westwood, Mary Lizzie 04/05/65   05/09/65
Cross, Maggie E. married Ball, Ellick 05/29/64   06/06/64
Cross, Mary Ann married Geyer, Lemuel F. 06/30/64   07/02/64
Cross, Richard died 04/01/63   04/03/63
Cross, Robert H. died 10/22/63   11/24/63
Cross, Sadie V. married Krout, William B. 08/09/64   08/10/64
Cross, Samuel J. married Barr, Margaret J. 10/23/61   10/25/61
Cross, Sarah M. married Wood, Francis M. 09/22/63   10/01/63
Cross, Sarah M. married Wallace, Hugh M. 05/26/64   06/03/64
Cross, Sophie married Ray, William G. 01/27/63   01/31/63
Cross, Thomas died 02/18/63   02/21/63
Cross, William married Burk, Mary 07/05/62   07/10/62
Cross, William married Burk, Mary 07/05/62   07/11/62
Cross, William married Burk, Mary 07/05/62   07/12/62
Cross, William married Burk, Mary 07/05/62   07/15/62
Cross, Willie H. died 04/03/64   04/04/64
Crossley, Joseph married Thorne, Caroline Elizabeth 12/29/64   12/30/64
Crossmore, Mary Ann (Mrs.) died 04/01/65   04/05/65
Crosson, Mary E. died 12/27/62   12/30/62
Crosswell, J. W. (Cpt.) married Clarker, Mary A. Z. 12/14/65   12/22/65
Croswell, Jane E. died 02/04/64   02/06/64

Croswell, John W. (Cpt.) married Clocker, Mary A. Lavinia 12/14/65 12/25/65
Crothers, Elizabeth (Mrs.) died 06/29/63 07/27/63
Crothers, Samuel married Young, Emma 01/11/64 01/13/64
Crotty, Ann Nora died 12/18/63 12/19/63
Crotty, Daniel died 11/04/61 11/05/61
Crouch, David died 11/12/62 11/14/62
Crouch, David died 11/12/62 11/15/62
Crouch, Elizabeth (Mrs.) died 07/31/65 08/01/65
Crouch, Julia Ann died 05/04/65 05/05/65
Crouch, Martha married Riggins, Charles 08/16/64 09/07/64
Crouch, William J. married Chrismer, Isabella B. 06/02/62 06/03/62
Croumer, Margaret A. died 02/10/65 02/11/65
Crouse, Isaac died 11/12/61 11/14/61
Crouse, Jesse B. married Stansbury, Lucinda 09/10/63 09/14/63
Crow, Catherine died 05/07/65 05/08/65
Crow, Dennis died 11/16/64 11/17/64
Crow, Isabella married Kidd, Moses 12/25/62 12/27/62
Crow, Lily died 09/12/61 09/24/61
Crow, Mary Jane married Shamer, Theodore 11/29/64 12/07/64
Crow, Nathaniel Jefferson died 01/07/63 01/08/63
Crowder, Willie A. died 08/21/64 08/24/64
Crowe, Malachi married McNamara, Mary Ann 05/11/62 05/14/62
Crowe, Margaret (Mrs.) died 01/31/64 02/02/64
Crowe, Mary Ann (Mrs.) died 12/10/63 12/12/63
Crowe, Michael died 02/03/65 02/04/65
Crowl, Andrew S. died 01/21/63 01/22/63
Crowl, Isabel married Taylor, Mortimer 06/29/65 07/06/65
Crowley, Blanche died 08/11/63 08/12/63
Crowley, Catherine (Mrs.) died 12/05/64 12/06/64
Crowley, George E. died 06/20/65 06/22/65
Crowley, Kate I. died 02/13/64 02/16/64
Crowley, Mary married Coughlin, John 11/07/65 11/10/65
Crowley, William H. died no date 06/28/64
Crowther, William James died 08/11/61 08/12/61
Croxall, Robert M. died 08/23/65 08/28/65
Croxall, Thomas died 10/21/61 10/26/61
Crozen, Sarah R. (Mrs.) married Wilcox, John H. 08/06/65 08/22/65
Crozier, Eliza (Mrs.) died 01/23/64 01/25/64
Crozier, Maggie A. married Bowling, James T. 03/16/65 03/17/65
Cruett, John W. married Rawlings, Sarah C. 12/03/63 12/07/63
Crum, Louisa M. married Kirkley, Joseph W. 10/17/64 10/19/64
Crumbaugh, William Stump died 01/14/63 01/16/63
Crumbine, Emanuel married Riall, Morgiana K. 10/31/65 11/04/65
Crumlish, Ellen died 03/11/62 03/13/62
Crummer, Mary died 08/06/65 08/07/65
Crummer, Matilda married Basil, John, Jr. 07/30/61 07/31/61
Crummer, Susan died 11/18/64 11/21/64
Crumunell, Martha A. married Jones, Jacob 11/06/63 11/07/63
Crure, John Henry died 03/31/62 04/02/62
Cruse, Andrew J. married Morine, Amanda Virginia 02/07/61 04/11/61
Cruse, John H. married Frampton, Josephine K. 07/15/64 08/24/64
Cruse, Joseph A. married Spelman, Annie R. 08/13/61 08/20/61
Cruse, William F. married Austin, Fannie M. 05/15/64 10/17/64
Cruse, William F. married Austin, Fannie M. 05/05/64 10/18/64

Cruser, Elizabeth D. married Ingham, George S. 04/27/63   04/28/63
Cruser, Mary married Carman, Joseph D. 05/17/63   05/19/63
Cruser, Sarah (Mrs.) died 08/10/64   08/11/64
Cuddy, Helen died 08/08/64   08/09/64
Cuddy, J. W. C. (Dr.) married Graham, Laura C. 03/17/63   03/18/63
Cuddy, John Preston died 07/23/65   07/25/65
Cuffe, Patrick Henry died 07/20/61   07/22/61
Culbertson, Ellen A. married Kennedy, William 06/04/63   06/05/63
Culbertson, James R. died 04/21/61   04/22/61
Cull, Eliza married Brown, Michael 06/24/65   06/29/65
Cullen, Mary (Mrs.) died 05/04/63   05/05/63
Cullen, Patrick died 08/10/63   08/11/63
Culley, Albert W. died 10/11/62   10/14/62
Culley, Joseph (USN) married Allen, Naomi Virginia 08/11/63   08/15/63
Culley, Langley B. died 01/17/63   01/19/63
Culley, Robert H. died 01/19/61   01/21/61
Culley, Robert J. married Norris, Mary F. 04/26/64   05/09/64
Cullimare, Jane (Mrs.) died 04/07/64   04/15/64
Cullington, Daniel married Sturley, Mary 09/13/64   09/19/64
Cullison, Eliza married Wilkinson, George W. 09/04/61   09/05/61
Cullison, Elizabeth married Ginnevan, Charles 06/15/62   06/18/62
Cullison, Jesse M. married Tanzey, Ann Jane 11/19/61   11/30/61
Cullison, Maria (Mrs.) died 04/23/65   04/24/65
Cullison, Owen died 01/08/63   01/09/63
Cullom, Anne E. married Greenland, William 06/21/64   07/09/64
Cullum, J. W. H. died 08/19/65   08/21/65
Culnan, Maggie married Johns, William H. 11/17/63   12/14/63
Culpepper, D. W. married Skinner, Fannie 09/23/65   09/26/65
Culvert, Willie died 05/06/65   05/10/65
Cumming, Augustus John died 07/16/65   07/18/65
Cumming, Margaret (Mrs.) died 10/27/64   10/28/64
Cumming, St. Augustus J. died 02/16/63   02/17/63
Cumming, Veirs died 06/19/64   06/27/64
Cumming, William A. married Veirs, Kate 10/28/62   10/31/62
Cummings, John died 02/01/63   02/02/63
Cummings, S. H. (Rev.) married Merriken, Lou 12/22/63   12/24/63
Cummings, Simon died 05/21/63   05/22/63
Cummins, Daniel G. married Kelly, Bridget C. 11/12/63   11/24/63
Cummins, Henry married Davage, Eliza Jane 11/26/63   11/30/63
Cummins, Mary (Mrs.) died 05/07/64   05/09/64
Cummins, Robert Keys married Paterson, Margaret M. 06/02/64   06/13/64
Cummins, Robert Paterson died 11/09/65   11/13/65
Cunan, Thomas F. died 07/11/64   07/12/64
Cundiff, A. T. (Cpt.) married Moore, Henrietta 05/13/63   05/23/63
Cunio, Andrew married Conry, Mary 05/20/61   07/26/61
Cunningham, Ann Eliza (Mrs.) died 12/15/65   12/16/65
Cunningham, Bridget (Mrs.) died 03/09/63   03/11/63
Cunningham, Cassandra died 07/31/62   08/01/62
Cunningham, Daniel M. (Cpt) died 07/30/65   08/02/65
Cunningham, Edward T. married Carback, Mary J. 10/24/65   10/31/65
Cunningham, Eliza Sopia died 05/06/62   05/10/62
Cunningham, Emma Peirre died 07/21/61   07/24/61
Cunningham, Eveline (Mrs.) died 12/28/63   01/02/64
Cunningham, George A. died 11/07/64   11/08/64
Cunningham, George A. died 01/26/65   01/28/65

```
Cunningham, George Andrew died 08/16/64   08/17/64
Cunningham, Geroge R. died 11/07/64   11/09/64
Cunningham, Isaac William died 06/02/62   06/05/62
Cunningham, James M. married Robinson, Ruth 09/03/61   03/08/62
Cunningham, John Francis V. died 02/16/65   02/17/65
Cunningham, Joseph S. married McCabe, Kate A. 05/28/63   10/29/63
Cunningham, Mary died 02/04/62   02/05/62
Cunningham, Mary died 02/04/62   02/06/62
Cunningham, Mary died 05/09/62   05/10/62
Cunningham, Mary E. died 03/20/65   03/21/65
Cunningham, Mary E. married Hall, John W. 03/01/65   03/04/65
Cunningham, R. Virginia married Apple, John H. 10/22/64   10/29/64
Cunningham, Samuel Clark died 03/05/64   03/07/64
Cunningham, Samuel D. married Arnold, Kate E. 08/28/62   09/23/62
Cunningham, Sarah Elizabeth died 12/01/61   12/02/61
Cunningham, Susan Virginia died 08/12/63   08/13/63
Cunningham, Thomas Mason died 08/29/61   09/02/61
Cunningham, William died 08/09/62   08/12/62
Cunningham, William M. died 04/03/65   04/06/65
Cunningham, William M. died 04/03/65   04/07/65
Cunningham, Zayda Cushing died 03/06/64   03/08/64
Curbon, Mary (Mrs.) died 11/22/63   11/23/63
Curlett, Erneste died 01/21/61   01/22/61
Curlett, John G. died 12/30/60   01/02/61
Curlett, Mary E. married Holte-Martin, Gullermo 02/09/64   02/11/64
Curley, Felix died 11/15/61   11/16/61
Curley, Florence R. married Kinsley, Samuel G. 02/18/64   02/22/64
Curley, Francis Tyler died 07/26/63   07/27/63
Curley, James F. married Kinsley, Kate 11/03/63   01/30/64
Curley, Maggie married Abell, Edwin F. 11/25/63   11/26/63
Curley, Mary Jane married Brown, William 02/14/65   02/16/65
Curley, Sallie E. V. married Schaefer, John F. 11/15/65   11/29/65
Curley, Walter died 08/10/63   08/13/63
Curnel, Margarite died 01/20/62   01/21/62
Curran, Catherine died 09/21/61   09/23/61
Curran, James died 06/24/63   07/16/63
Curran, Julia died 04/05/64   04/07/64
Curran, Julia A. married Alexander, Charles 01/06/63   01/08/63
Curran, Lizzie A. married Jamison, Robert A. 02/17/63   03/02/63
Curran, Nicholas F. married McDonald, Elizabeth J. 02/16/65   02/21/65
Currans, Oliver E. married Ferguson, Bell 03/10/63   03/30/63
Curren, Daniel married Lallor, Kate 09/21/65   09/30/65
Curren, Lizie died 07/26/65   07/28/65
Curren, Mary died 01/31/65   02/01/65
Currens, Belle died 02/04/64   02/05/64
Currey, James H. (Dr.) married Warfield, Martha 04/23/61   04/26/61
Curry, Eliza J. married Rowe, J. A. 03/21/61   04/02/61
Curry, Ellen (Mrs.) died 06/03/63   06/05/63
Curry, James married Bell, Rebecca A. 02/26/61   03/02/61
Curry, Parmilia F. married Penn, Matthew J. A. 10/06/63   10/09/63
Curry, Robert F. married Price, Ruth Ann 07/01/63   07/03/63
Curry, Robert F. died 09/06/65   09/07/65
Curry, Sarah E. died 09/09/61   09/10/61
Cursey, William married Reilly, Rose Anna 12/09/62   12/12/62
Cursey, William E. died 04/02/64   04/22/64
```

Curtain, Henry G. married Robinson, Louisa 02/18/63   02/25/63
Curtis, Emma married Bowerstock, Austin 12/31/62   01/07/63
Curtis, John A. married Fawkes, Fannie E. 01/09/62   01/11/62
Curtis, Patrick died 04/23/65   04/24/65
Curtis, Robert married Locks, Margaret (Mrs.) 10/16/62   10/18/62
Curtis, Robert married Jackson, Eliza 04/28/64   04/30/64
Curtis, Willie Ellsworth died 02/16/65   02/20/65
Curtiss, F. (Sgt.) married Tear, Alice R. 03/12/64   04/20/64
Curtus, Abram died 08/28/61   08/30/61
Curvel, J. Mahlon died 09/14/65   09/15/65
Curvel, John died 03/22/65   03/23/65
Curvill, Annie died 08/13/61   08/14/61
Curvill, Frank Jacob died 10/23/61   10/30/61
Curville, Harry died 10/23/64   10/29/64
Cushaw, Ida May died 05/26/63   05/28/63
Cushing, Frances died 03/13/65   03/15/65
Cushing, Hannah Burr (Mrs.) died 03/22/65   03/23/65
Cushing, Janet M. married Barrett, William D. 07/19/64   07/26/64
Cushing, Joseph Edmands died 11/27/62   12/20/62
Cushing, Robert Henry (CSA) died 07/03/63   07/29/63
Cushing, Robert M. married Dulany, Olivia 04/08/63   04/11/63
Cushley, John A. married Kiely, Mary F. 05/14/65   10/16/65
Cusick, Adolpha E. married Walker, Leonard R. 01/11/65   01/13/65
Cutaiar, Albina Griffin died 08/26/62   08/27/62
Cutaiar, Francis married Scott, Mary J. 09/14/65   09/16/65
Cutaiar, Francis married Scott, Mary 09/14/65   09/18/65
Cutalar, Louisa C. Love died 12/31/63   01/01/64
D'Almaine, Fannie died 10/05/64   10/08/64
D'Arcy, Paul, Jr. died 10/09/61   10/14/61
D'Eberstein, Peter Frederick died 12/10/63   12/11/63
D'unger, Robert (Dr.) married Keene, Laura R. 11/29/61   02/14/62
Dable, Charles Franklin died 09/06/63   09/07/63
Dade, Ruth (Mrs.) died 03/11/64   03/17/64
Dadisman, Jacob married McCafferty, Susannah M. 04/26/64   04/28/64
Daffin, Benjamin married Husband, Sarah Ann 03/06/62   03/08/62
Daffin, Emma Matilda died 04/07/64   04/08/64
Daffy, Edward married McMillan, Emma C. 12/05/61   12/09/61
Dafter, James died 01/25/64   02/09/64
Dagney, Daniel married Canavan, Agnes 11/23/63   11/30/63
Dahl, Louisa married Wallaes, John V. 06/15/62   06/19/62
Dahme, Estelle Iola died 10/18/63   11/30/63
Dahme, Lulie Madden died 11/28/63   11/30/63
Dahne, Florence Estelle died 05/22/61   05/24/61
Dahoff, John H. married Cramblitt, Sophia J. 06/03/61   06/29/61
Daiger, Augustus W. died 07/08/64   07/09/64
Daiger, Francis married McDermott, Kate R. 01/14/64   01/15/64
Daiger, Henry F. died 08/18/64   08/20/64
Daiger, James V. married Smith, Anna M. 10/17/65   10/20/65
Daiger, John Hughes died 05/28/63   05/29/63
Daiger, Joseph F. died 12/03/62   12/04/62
Daiger, M. A. married Ashcom, Pamelia A. 01/15/63   01/17/63
Daigers, Rachel Mary (Mrs.) died 08/03/64   08/08/64
Daigor, Rachel Barbara died 02/11/65   02/13/65
Dail(e)y, Susie married O'Hara, John 04/28/65   05/04/65
Dail, Daniel died 11/28/63   11/30/63

Dail, Daniel H. died 01/08/65   01/09/65
Dail, Julia died 10/21/61   10/22/61
Daile, Mary died 10/23/61   10/24/61
Dailey, Annie married Kearney, Edward 09/05/65   09/14/65
Dailey, Francis died 12/14/65   12/16/65
Dailey, Henry Reid died 07/16/63   07/18/63
Dailey, Sarah A. married Phillips, John E. 08/26/64   11/01/64
Daily, Bartholomew married Rabbitt, Margaret 02/17/63   02/20/63
Daily, Francis died 12/14/65   12/15/65
Daily, George died 11/03/64   11/09/64
Daily, George F. died 02/13/62   02/14/62
Daily, Harry Mott died 01/01/64   01/02/64
Daily, Margaret died 08/07/64   08/08/64
Daily, Mary Conner (Mrs.) died 10/05/63   10/06/63
Daily, Peter died 01/21/65   01/23/65
Daily, Thomas Satterfield died 05/07/63   05/09/63
Dakers, Margaret Ann died 06/07/65   06/12/65
Dale, M. Francis married Ligget, Charles M. 04/23/62   05/10/62
Daley, Amanda J. married Moore, H. P. (Cpt.) 09/29/64   10/05/64
Daley, Elizabeth died 02/22/62   02/24/62
Daley, Elizabeth (Mrs.) died 05/30/64   06/01/64
Dall, Austin died 09/30/62   10/01/62
Dall, James died 03/17/63   03/18/63
Dallam, Cecelia Plowden died 02/19/65   02/22/65
Dallam, Cecelia Plowden (Mrs.) died 02/19/65   02/21/65
Dallam, Edward B. married Jenkens, Cecilia P. 01/07/64   01/08/64
Dallam, John Paca married Thomas, Mary Goldsborough 10/09/62   10/13/62
Dallam, Mary A. married Block, Edward 03/25/62   03/27/62
Dalley, Octavia (Mrs.) died 10/02/64   10/03/64
Dally, Rebecca married Vanvorst, William H. 06/23/63   07/03/63
Dalrymple, Carrie Veeder died 09/25/63   09/28/63
Dalrymple, Charles W. (Rev.) died 01/08/61   01/09/61
Dalrymple, Elizabeth died 12/16/61   12/17/61
Dalrymple, Janette S. married Braid, Charles 11/24/63   11/28/63
Dalrymple, Mary S. died 04/18/63   04/20/63
Dalrymple, Mollie E. married Billingsly, Thomas A. 04/13/65   04/15/65
Dalson, Mary Virginia died 03/05/61   03/06/61
Dalton, Catherine died 10/01/61   10/02/61
Dalton, Edward died 08/04/63   08/05/63
Dalton, Elmira died 12/22/61   12/24/61
Dalton, James died 08/10/65   08/12/65
Dalton, Jane Ellen died 05/04/64   05/06/64
Dalton, Julia died 10/15/65   10/16/65
Dalton, Mary Lorelto died 05/23/64   05/30/64
Daly, Augustine died 01/19/63   01/20/63
GDaly, Eugene married Cerney, Ellen 03/02/62   03/07/62
Daly, Jane Elizabeth (Mrs.) died 07/13/65   07/14/65
Daly, John died 04/27/62   04/28/62
Daly, Michael B. (USA) died 05/03/63   09/08/63
Daly, Owen died 12/20/63   12/22/63
Dalyrymple, Eldridge R. A. died 03/22/63   03/26/63
Damer, Alcinda died 11/27/60   03/29/61
Damer, Alcinda died 03/27/61   04/02/61
Dammann, Clarence Eugene died 03/04/61   03/05/61
Dampman, Albert married Demoss, Lizzie 05/19/64   05/21/64

Dams, Ernest W. died 06/24/65   06/26/65
Danaher, Henry M. C. married Creagan, Margaret 06/23/64   06/24/64
Dandelet, Charles John died 08/25/64   08/26/64
Daneker, Mary A. married Davis, Charles H. 12/22/64   12/30/64
Danels, Joseph D. died 03/23/65   03/24/65
Danels, Joseph D. died 03/23/65   03/25/65
Daniel, Sophia Delahoy died 06/24/61   06/25/61
Daniels, James died 02/02/62   02/05/62
Daniels, William B. died 01/21/63   02/07/63
Daniels, William B. (Cpt.) died 01/21/63   01/24/63
Danna, John married Parker, Julia F. 03/07/65   04/15/65
Dannehey, Mary Virginia died 07/01/61   07/02/61
Danneman, Elvira W. died 01/23/63   01/24/63
Dannerson, Jemima died 08/01/63   08/03/63
Dansbury, Frances Ann married Holland, Joseph 10/30/62   11/01/62
Danskin, Osceola died 03/18/61   03/20/61
Danskin, Rosalia died 02/12/62   02/13/62
Danskin, Washington A., Jr. died 05/20/61   05/21/61
Danson, Ida died 06/02/63   06/04/63
Daran, Frances (Mrs.) married Holliday, William 08/11/64   08/13/64
Darbaugh, Daniel married McMullen, Mary Ann 01/14/64   01/19/64
Darby, Harrison D. married Shaw, Lucretia M. 11/22/64   01/14/65
Darby, Lucretia M. (Mrs.) died 12/14/64   01/14/65
Darby, William S. died 02/03/65   02/04/65
Dare, Catherine died 09/24/62   09/26/62
Darey, Clothilda Hall died 12/27/61   12/28/61
Darison, Thomas R. died 08/20/62   08/21/62
Darley, Julia A. C. married Keedy, Samuel H. (Dr.) 11/09/65   11/14/65
Darley, Julia A. C. married Keedy, Samuel H. (Dr.) 11/09/65   11/15/65
Darley, Louisa E. died 06/25/65   06/26/65
Darley, Mary E. married Wolfersberger, John B. 10/18/64   10/19/64
Darley, Mary E. married Wolfersberger, John P. 10/18/64   10/20/64
Darling, Emaline died 06/14/61   06/15/61
Darling, James died 06/30/65   07/01/65
Darling, Louis died 11/10/62   11/13/62
Darling, W. H. married Hudson, Sarah Anne 09/03/61   09/05/61
Darly, Rufus T. married Matthews, Emily France 04/10/62   04/11/62
Darne, Mary A. (Mrs.) died 08/22/63   09/01/63
Darneille, Benjamin J. married Addison, Nettie S. 07/18/61   07/20/61
Darraugh, Mary Ann died 12/16/65   12/18/65
Darraugh, Regina died 08/10/65   08/11/65
Darraugh, Sarah (Mrs.) died 09/24/63   09/25/63
Darrell, Charles died 12/08/62   12/13/62
Darrell, Lydia Hollingsworth died 03/18/61   03/21/61
Darrell, Mary Hurst died 09/20/64   10/08/64
Darrington, Mary A. (Mrs.) died 11/12/64   11/14/64
Dart, Willie Andrew died 06/22/62   06/24/62
Dashiell, Ellen J. married Smith, Richard G. 12/05/64   12/23/64
Dashiell, Jessie died 03/11/61   03/21/61
Dashiell, John V. married Evans, Anna R. 01/10/61   01/21/61
Dashiell, Margaret P. married Grant, Joseph W. 03/02/62   03/06/62
Dashiell, Mary B. married Thompson, James C. 11/14/65   11/15/65
Dashiell, Mary D. died 01/19/63   01/21/63
Dashiell, Mary D. died 01/19/63   01/22/63
Dashiell, Mary Emma married Sheppard, Charles F. 11/11/63   11/14/63

```
Dashiell, Monteray H. married Rideway, Thomas 10/16/61   11/01/61
Dashiell, Parker died 02/21/62   02/22/62
Daughaday, Job S. died 09/05/62   09/06/62
Daughaday, Laura V. married Brown, James A. 11/07/64   12/22/64
Daugherty, Charles died 04/28/61   04/29/61
Daugherty, James died 06/30/63   07/01/63
Daugherty, Margaret married Hoffman, Charles H. 12/07/64   12/10/64
Daugherty, Thomas married Taylor, Mary Jane 12/02/60   01/23/61
Daughton, Joseph L. died 02/11/64   02/16/64
Daumas, Louise died 06/18/65   06/24/65
Davage, Belinda married Pierce, John 05/09/61   05/11/61
Davage, Eliza Jane married Cummins, Henry 11/26/63   11/30/63
Davenport, Charles E. married Tuxworth, Laura V. 06/14/64   06/20/64
Davenport, Mary died 09/18/61   09/19/61
Davenport, Phoebe married Coss, George M. 10/18/62   11/04/62
Davey, Henry married Pic, Mary 01/17/61   01/23/61
Davey, James died 10/22/62   10/25/62
Davey, Patrick died 06/12/65   06/14/65
David, Esther died 07/25/62   07/26/62
David, Esther died 07/25/62   07/29/62
David, Joseph (Captain) died 01/08/61   01/19/61
Davidson, A. E. married Shreck, Addie E. 09/26/65   09/27/65
Davidson, Cora Virginia died 08/27/65   08/28/65
Davidson, Edward married Peregoy, Henrietta (Mrs.) 06/09/64   09/19/64
Davidson, Elizabeth died 12/06/65   12/07/65
Davidson, Frances Ann married Snyder, William 01/13/63   01/15/63
Davidson, Frances J. married Thomas, Sterling W. 11/29/63   01/12/64
Davidson, Harriet Almedah died 02/06/65   02/07/65
Davidson, James B. married Hamblett, Mary F. 02/06/65   03/28/65
Davidson, Lydia (Mrs.) died 12/27/61   01/02/62
Davidson, Maggie A. married Bennett, N. S. 02/16/65   03/06/65
Davidson, Nelson died 02/28/61   03/01/61
Davidson, Robert J. married Harris, Mary Elizabeth 11/23/63   12/01/63
Davidson, Sarah married Hook, R. Edwin 09/20/64   09/24/64
Davidson, T. W. married Joines, Jennie E. 03/14/65   03/16/65
Davidson, Thomas died 11/16/65   11/17/65
Davidson, Thomas died 11/16/65   11/18/65
Davidson, William married Kidd, Elizabeth (Mrs.) 03/27/64   04/20/64
Davies, Catharine Jane married Pridham, W. F. (Cpt.) 12/05/64   12/08/64
Davies, James married Stephenson, Anna 03/13/64   03/15/64
Davige, Charles H. married Griffith, Henrietta 02/04/65   02/11/65
Davis, Abel died 01/28/61   02/01/61
Davis, Amanda married Coursey, E. Henry, Jr. 11/17/63   11/21/63
Davis, Amanda W. married Linthicum, Abner 04/05/64   04/07/64
Davis, Andrew Thomas died 09/03/61   09/04/61
Davis, Ann Eliza died 02/01/62   02/03/62
Davis, Annie A. married Whittier, Curtis A. 11/08/65   11/10/65
Davis, Archibald T. died 04/03/63   04/04/63
Davis, Benjamin died 09/12/63   09/14/63
Davis, Benjamin D. married Wilson, Ann E. 12/31/60   05/02/61
Davis, Benjamin M. married Sprigg, Jane E. 05/26/64   05/28/64
Davis, Catherine (Mrs.) died 05/02/65   05/09/65
Davis, Catherine E. died 07/08/61   07/10/61
Davis, Charles F. died 09/02/62   10/04/62
Davis, Charles H. married Daneker, Mary A. 12/22/64   12/30/64
```

Davis, Charles L. married Beauchamp, Leah J. 03/01/65   03/07/65
Davis, Charles L. married Beauchamp, Leah J. 03/01/65   03/08/65
Davis, David married Fossett, Mary Elizabeth 02/02/62   02/07/62
Davis, Dennes (Rev) died 01/22/64   01/23/64
Davis, Edward died 10/05/63   01/30/64
Davis, Edward married Turner, Sarah E. 10/22/65   10/27/65
Davis, Edwin R. married Lewis, Sarah E. 09/21/64   09/26/64
Davis, Edwin R. married Lewis, Sarah F. 09/25/64   09/28/64
Davis, Eliza died 11/15/64   11/16/64
Davis, Eliza J. married Slack, George S. 10/05/63   10/15/63
Davis, Elizabeth died 02/18/61   02/19/61
Davis, Fannie A. married Hannock, A. M. (Maj.) 02/24/62   02/27/62
Davis, Fannie S. married Craig, J. Morrel 10/17/65   10/24/65
Davis, Fanny married Arnold, Henry A. 08/08/61   08/24/61
Davis, Francis J. died 12/19/64   12/20/64
Davis, Frederick, Jr. died 06/26/64   06/27/64
Davis, George A. married Hazard, Emma Jane 12/21/62   12/23/62
Davis, George Henry died 02/01/63   02/02/63
Davis, George W. married Webb, Rachel A. 12/25/61   12/27/61
Davis, George W. married Corcoran, Ellen 01/08/61   04/12/61
Davis, George W. D. died 09/02/64   09/06/64
Davis, Hamilton died 01/16/61   01/17/61
Davis, Henrietta Swan died 07/24/65   07/26/65
Davis, Henry married Whiter, Rachel 02/17/61   02/19/61
Davis, Henry died 07/27/64   07/28/64
Davis, Isaac died 03/29/63   03/30/63
Davis, Isaac died 03/29/63   03/31/63
Davis, Isabella died 08/29/65   08/30/65
Davis, Jackson V. B. died 01/21/65   01/23/65
Davis, James H. married Stockett, Carrie 11/16/65   11/28/65
Davis, Jane (Mrs.) died 03/29/63   03/31/63
Davis, Janie E. married Lemmon, B. Franklin 01/24/61   01/28/61
Davis, John died 03/23/62   03/24/62
Davis, John married Percon, Ellen 06/16/62   06/19/62
Davis, John died 07/03/63   07/04/63
Davis, John died 08/02/64   08/04/64
Davis, John married Bowman, Jane (Mrs.) 05/01/64   05/09/64
Davis, John married Roberts, Justina 02/22/65   03/07/65
Davis, John A. married Hancock, Rachel A. 04/02/65   04/07/65
Davis, John H. W. married Brown, Elizabeth Ann 12/13/64   12/17/64
Davis, John J. married Kennedy, Anna 08/21/62   08/23/62
Davis, John Jefferson died 02/20/64   02/22/64
Davis, John P. died 03/24/61   03/26/61
Davis, John T. died 09/26/62   10/06/62
Davis, John T. died 03/26/63   04/10/63
Davis, John Thomas died 09/26/65   09/28/65
Davis, Joseph died 06/28/63   07/01/63
Davis, Joseph W. died 01/20/64   01/23/64
Davis, Josephine married Lindsey, Benjamin 02/22/63   02/26/63
Davis, Josiah H. died 05/01/62   05/07/62
Davis, Laura A. married Boggs, Augustus A. 12/14/65   12/21/65
Davis, Laura V. married Boyce, Frederick W. 08/18/64   08/26/64
Davis, Lucy A. died 02/24/65   03/01/65
Davis, Lyle J. (Mrs.) married Rush, D. G. 12/27/64   01/10/65
Davis, M. R. married Palmer, William C. 03/07/61   03/13/61

Davis, Margaret Ann married Trautfelter, Henry 06/09/61 06/11/61
Davis, Mary A. married Hackett, George A. 03/28/61 03/30/61
Davis, Mary Ann (Mrs.) died 10/30/63 11/06/63
Davis, Mary Catherine died 07/24/64 07/26/64
Davis, Mary Ella died 08/12/65 08/14/65
Davis, Mary Ellen died 06/04/63 06/05/63
Davis, Mary J. married Winter, Gabriel 02/13/62 02/18/62
Davis, Mary Jane married King, Joseph 08/28/62 08/29/62
Davis, Mary Jane married Dicus, Jacob L. 03/08/63 03/10/63
Davis, Matilda Elizabeth died 08/11/62 08/12/62
Davis, Michael married Mettam, Rebecca R. 10/08/63 10/14/63
Davis, Miles married Rinehart, Susan 12/20/64 01/04/65
Davis, Phineas C. died 02/12/64 02/16/64
Davis, Reverdy P. married Rea, E. J. 07/16/63 04/26/64
Davis, Robert died 07/19/62 07/21/62
Davis, Robert W. died no date 04/20/61
Davis, Robert W. (Dr.) married Akers, Susan 05/11/65 05/18/65
Davis, Rowena E. R. married Kenney, James T. 11/25/62 12/01/62
Davis, Ruth died 10/03/63 10/15/63
Davis, Samuel died 06/17/62 06/19/62
Davis, Sarah Ann died 12/11/63 12/14/63
Davis, Sarah S. married Horner, William C. 07/05/64 08/02/64
Davis, Sarah V. married Decker, Andrew J. 09/22/62 09/25/62
Davis, Susan married Laneden, George L. 04/28/64 04/30/64
Davis, Susan (Mrs.) died 11/20/63 11/25/63
Davis, Thomas B. married Magruder, Josephine H. 11/24/63 11/26/63
Davis, Thomas B. married Magruder, Josephine H. 11/24/63 12/03/63
Davis, Thomas Jefferson died 08/28/63 08/29/63
Davis, Thomas R. married Murphy, Sallie E. 07/07/63 07/28/63
Davis, Wilbur F. died 05/17/65 05/19/65
Davis, William married Gibb, Hannah 01/04/64 01/14/64
Davis, William married Gorsuch, Sallie 06/01/65 06/12/65
Davis, William Henry died 07/25/62 08/01/62
Davis, William T. married Haines, Sarah A. 05/18/63 06/13/63
Davis, William T. died 06/29/65 06/30/65
Davis, William Wise died 07/14/63 07/18/63
Davis, Willie Harrison died 09/05/65 09/06/65
Davis, Wilmer S. died 11/14/65 11/15/65
Davison, Frank died 08/08/65 08/11/65
Davison, Helen M. (Mrs.) died 04/05/64 04/09/64
Davison, Jane Elizabeth died 12/06/63 12/10/63
Dawalt, Alexander married Brass, Ann 09/25/65 09/27/65
Dawes, Jennie R. married Barnes, John R. 06/02/63 06/06/63
Dawes, Joseph D. married Betton, Wilhelmina D. 11/16/63 11/26/63
Dawes, Wenona died 03/08/65 03/09/65
Daws, Henry married Bright, Harriet 08/23/64 08/29/64
Dawson, Ann died 05/20/62 05/21/62
Dawson, Emma J. married Oram, James D. 12/24/63 01/04/64
Dawson, Hugh married McColgan, Joanna 01/23/64 01/28/64
Dawson, Jane S. (Mrs.) died 04/13/65 05/04/65
Dawson, Josephine B. married Seibold, Lewis P. 10/02/61 02/13/62
Dawson, Martha M. married Waters, Thomas 12/06/64 12/30/64
Dawson, Mary Elizabeth died 02/22/63 02/24/63
Dawson, Michael died 12/26/61 12/27/61
Dawson, Susan (Mrs.) died 06/04/63 06/16/63

Dawson, Thomas E. married Spicer, Elizabeth L. 12/03/63   12/05/63
Dawson, Thomas E. married Spicer, Elizabeth E. 12/03/63   12/08/63
Dawson, Thomas I. died 06/01/64   06/15/64
Dawson, Thomas L. married Shinnick, Georgia A. 08/04/63   08/19/63
Dawson, William H. married Bolderston, Amelia Emma 11/01/64   11/07/64
Day, Charles S. married Phillips, Harriet E. 07/06/65   07/08/65
Day, George married Caples, Mary Elizabeth no date   08/08/63
Day, Ida Jane died 11/17/62   11/18/62
Day, Jacob died 08/06/61   08/07/61
Day, James Henry died 01/23/61   01/25/61
Day, Janette Frances died 05/01/62   06/05/62
Day, Jeanette Frances died 05/01/62   05/02/62
Day, Juliet S. married Overacre, John W. 12/25/65   12/30/65
Day, Margaret married Smith, William H. 08/06/65   08/08/65
Day, Mary D. married Hunphreys, Richard 12/06/65   12/23/65
Day, Mary S. died 08/08/65   08/11/65
Day, Rhoda M. died 08/07/61   08/08/61
Day, Sarah E. died 12/11/62   12/12/62
Day, William married Mcauley, Charlotte 04/25/64   05/02/64
Dayhoff, Emily J. married Barnes, James H. 06/13/65   07/27/65
De Beet, Duncan H. married Keys, Emma E. 12/02/61   12/04/61
De Cormis, Mary E. married Crane, Charles 07/02/63   07/03/63
De Coursey, Ann (Mrs.) died 10/03/65   10/05/65
De Coursey, Eliza Bond died 11/13/65   11/15/65
de Dorsner, Albine Valerie married Slingluff, C. Bohn 09/29/64   11/11/
De La Roche, Sophie E. B. died 10/30/64   11/01/64
De Le Reinthrie, Margaret died 11/30/65   12/02/65
De Loughery, M. Edwardina married McDonnell, Eugene 09/01/63   09/02/63
De Moss, Emma married Matthews, Benjamin F. 06/22/65   07/07/65
De Moss, Mary J. married Smith, John H. 07/04/65   07/10/65
De Pass, Mary A. died 01/03/63   01/05/63
De Serra, Ann (Mrs.) died 03/04/63   03/06/63
De Vaughn, Mary S. married Hughes, John 02/25/62   03/01/62
Deacey, Catharine married Spillane, James 06/14/64   06/17/64
Deacker, Lewis married Smith, Elizabeth C. 08/23/64   09/01/64
Deacon, Edith Harriet married Durham, James 11/15/64   11/18/64
Deacon, Louisa married Hardy, John (U.S.N.) 08/08/65   08/09/65
Deady, Emma Jane died 09/22/65   09/23/65
Deady, John L. married Jones, Mary Augusta 07/13/63   07/16/63
Deal, Anna M. married McBurney, Louis 10/16/64   10/17/64
Deal, George J. died 06/08/64   06/09/64
Deal, George J. died 06/08/64   06/10/64
Deal, John H. married Mayo, Virginia G. O. M. 07/14/63   07/16/63
Deal, Mary D. married Nones, Henry S. 07/14/62   07/25/62
Deal, Mary J. married Baker, John M. 01/27/63   04/07/63
Deal, Mary R. (Mrs.) married Matthews, Isaac H. 11/28/65   12/05/65
Deal, Richard Henry married Webb, Elizabeth C. 06/08/64   06/09/64
Deal, Theophilus N. died 09/21/64   09/24/64
Deal, Virginia G. O. (Mrs.) died 04/07/65   04/08/65
Deal, William C. married Duncan, Eliza J. 02/21/61   02/25/61
Deale, Hannah E. married Larimore, Richard F. 06/05/62   06/07/62
Deale, Mary Ann died 08/01/61   08/02/61
Dean, G. Albert (USN) married Gorton, Emma V. 12/20/64   12/22/64
Dean, Henrietta married Gray, Shadrach 02/02/65   03/03/65
Dean, Ira married Forrest, Mary 11/10/64   11/18/64

Dean, John married Parr, Rachel 03/01/64 03/07/64
Dean, Rebecca (Mrs.) died 01/13/65 01/14/65
Dean, Sarah P. married Englehart, D. 11/04/61 12/24/61
Dean, William died 09/01/64 09/02/64
Dean, William married Kaufman, M. E. J. 05/11/65 05/16/65
Dean, William H. married Reilly, Josephine 03/28/64 03/30/64
Deane, Elizabeth Ann died 09/06/64 09/08/64
Deaner, Lizzie married Koechling, Charles W. (Dr.) 09/19/65 09/27/65
Dearing, Notley W. died 03/12/63 03/13/63
Deaver, Elizabeth (Mrs.) died 11/07/63 11/16/63
Deaver, George died 05/22/63 06/10/63
Deaver, Henry Jerome died 12/23/65 12/25/65
Deaver, John died 11/20/63 11/21/63
Deaver, Joseph married Burten, Elizabeth 08/29/65 09/02/65
Deaver, Maria J. married Grey, John M. 11/22/63 11/30/63
Deaver, Mary E. married Hubbard, James 05/03/64 05/04/64
Deaver, Mary Elizabeth died 02/21/61 02/22/61
Deaver, Mary J. married Lusby, Edward L. 03/23/63 04/08/63
Deaver, Michael A. died 03/10/61 03/13/61
Deaver, Robert M. married Cook, Mary A. 11/25/63 12/01/63
Deaver, Sallie R. married Booth, William 07/30/61 07/31/61
Deaver, Stephen died 07/05/63 07/06/63
Deaver, William O. died 01/10/61 01/11/61
Debach, Sophia (Mrs.) died 12/28/64 12/31/64
DeBarry, Joseph died 01/14/62 01/16/62
DeBaufre, Anna M. died 06/29/64 06/30/64
Debbing, Anna Henrietta B. died 01/28/65 01/31/65
DeBeaufre, Ann (Mrs.) died 07/11/65 07/13/65
Debow, Christian married Pasterfield, Martha A. 12/13/65 12/23/65
Debow, Elizabeth A. (Mrs.) died 03/03/65 03/04/65
DeBow, Emily E. married Trimmer, Abraham 12/20/60 01/03/61
Debow, Ida Virginia died 08/16/63 08/17/63
Debow, Mary Ann died 12/09/62 12/16/62
Debring, Annie Philemona died 07/06/64 07/07/64
Debring, Mary married Ostendorf, Henry 05/13/62 05/15/62
DeButts, Sophie (Mrs.) died 04/01/64 04/02/64
DeCaindry, Alice died 01/18/63 01/21/63
DeCamp, Lizzie died 07/16/62 07/17/62
DeCamp, Sidney died 12/03/62 12/04/62
Decker, Andrew J. married Davis, Sarah V. 09/22/62 09/25/62
Decker, Jane died 04/08/62 04/09/62
Decker, John Wesley died 01/03/63 01/05/63
Decker, Louis N. married Smith, Elizabeth C. (Mrs.) 08/23/64 09/23/64
Decker, Sarah died 02/06/61 02/08/61
DeCormis, Edward, Jr. married Conn, Clay A. 11/14/65 11/15/65
Decormis, George died 02/19/64 02/20/64
DeCorms, Sarah C. married Kersler, Thomas V. 01/19/65 01/20/65
Deeble, Cornelia Adams died 05/10/64 05/13/64
Deegan, Finton died 06/13/63 06/15/63
Deegan, Robert died 04/12/63 04/14/63
Deegan, William P. married Morgan, Alice 01/24/61 01/28/61
Deems, George married Ritter, Addie 11/02/65 11/08/65
Deems, Ida Frances died 11/21/65 11/23/65
Deems, Laura Virginia married Williams, Daniel V. 05/04/63 05/12/63
Deems, Mary Bell died 12/30/63 01/01/64

Deets, Clemintine died 03/16/64   03/26/64
Deets, Mary married Straesburgh, Harry 12/25/62   01/16/63
Deets, W. H. married Clark, Matilda F. 11/21/64   11/22/64
Deets, William H. married Clarke, Tillie F. 11/21/64   11/28/64
DeFord, Eugene died 07/20/63   07/22/63
Deford, George H. married Douglas, Mary F. 12/30/61   02/03/62
DeFord, George H. died 07/03/65   07/26/65
DeFord, George H. died 07/03/65   07/27/65
Deford, Harriet died 10/20/65   10/21/65
Deford, Julia A. married Ray, Hollis F. 11/21/65   11/23/65
Deford, Katie died 05/29/65   06/01/65
Deford, Mary E. married Pamphellion, William H. 08/06/65   08/10/65
Degaw, Harriet A. married Childs, George T. 04/27/63   05/07/63
Degen, Solomon married Pflounbacher, Mina 03/13/61   03/14/61
DeGoey, Charles L. M. died 10/11/64   10/12/64
DeGoey, Ella Virginia died 10/14/62   10/16/62
DeGoey, Mary Isabella died 03/03/61   03/05/61
DeGoey, Mary Theotine (Mrs.) died 09/01/63   09/03/63
DeGoey, Susan M. married Williams, Edward 09/15/63   09/16/63
DeGoey, William W. married Fryer, Elizabeth I. 07/26/63   08/10/63
Degollado, Mariano married Jordan, Otella 02/02/64   02/03/64
DeHaven, John David married Carmine, Catharine 12/11/64   12/17/64
Dehn, August married Moffitt, Elizabeth 06/04/63   06/06/63
Deitch, Elizabeth (Mrs.) died 02/18/63   02/25/63
Deiter, David died 07/03/65   07/11/65
Deiter, Valentine died 11/21/61   11/22/61
Deitz, George William died 08/29/62   09/03/62
Deitz, Mary Cornelia died 09/05/62   09/12/62
Delafield, Mary married Hull, Joseph J. 12/09/62   12/17/62
Delahay, Christina H. married Blair, Wilson L. P. 01/26/61   01/28/61
DeLamar, C. M. married Ayres, Eugenie 01/02/64   01/28/64
DeLaMatyr, Edward B. married Frost, Annie E. 01/24/65   01/28/65
Delaney, Louis Mitchel died 01/18/65   02/18/65
Delaney, Mary Ann died 02/01/65   02/02/65
Delano, William J. died 10/23/64   04/22/65
Delany, Daniel married Bergin, Mary 05/03/63   05/05/63
Delany, Eliza died 05/26/65   05/27/65
Delany, James J. married Fran, Mary H. 03/09/65   03/13/65
Delawder, Andrew N. married Kerr, Margaret C. 02/20/62   02/24/62
Delcamp, Mary A. married Haile, Charles D. 04/21/63   04/22/63
Delcher, Alice died 10/19/62   10/20/62
Delcher, James A. married Bowen, Elizabeth A. 04/19/65   05/10/65
Delcher, Mary E. married Green, John 11/19/64   12/22/64
Deleny, William T. died 07/28/61   07/29/61
DeLeue, Albert married Nelson, Lizzie 06/08/65   07/03/65
Delevie, Isaac S. married Switzer, Betsy 01/18/63   01/20/63
Dell, Thomas E. married Mills, Amelia 03/31/63   04/08/63
Della, Albert Hersey died 04/25/63   04/28/63
Della, Ella died 07/29/63   07/31/63
Delmann, Herman died 07/17/64   07/19/64
Delmas, Frances Almira married Baldwin, John T. 07/10/65   07/29/65
Delphey, Hannah Virginia died 08/12/64   08/13/64
Delphey, Mary Ann (Mrs.) died 04/20/65   04/21/65
Delphey, Mary Ann (Mrs.) died 04/20/65   04/22/65
Delvechu, James died 04/19/63   04/20/63

DeMangin, Mary H. married Bollmarr, John W. 06/16/64   06/28/64
Demelman, Hannah died 01/09/65   01/11/65
Demelman, Hannah (Mrs.) died 01/09/65   01/12/65
Dement, Eliza Genevieve died 11/17/64   11/24/64
Demitz, Mary E. married Wilcox, John R. 10/30/64   11/01/64
Demoss, Lizzie married Dampman, Albert 05/19/64   05/21/64
Demott, William married Matthews, Georgeanne 02/04/64   02/10/64
Dempsey, Arabella C. married Cheffins, Eli C. 09/02/64   09/03/64
Dempsey, Emma Frances died 09/23/64   10/04/64
Dempsey, John Adam died 07/26/62   07/31/62
Dempsey, John F. married Martin, Mary A. 02/12/63   02/14/63
Dempsey, Mary Elizabeth married Griffith, James F. 05/20/62   06/02/62
Dempsey, Timothy died 01/25/64   01/27/64
Dempster, Geoffrey E. married Bool, Mary A. 03/22/64   03/30/64
Dempster, James F. died 04/13/63   04/14/63
Demuth, John died 09/25/62   09/26/62
Denason, John R. died 12/01/62   12/02/62
Denby, Mary Jane married Jones, John 04/16/61   04/19/61
Dengel, Philip H. married Bresnahan, Catherine 04/06/63   04/08/63
Denham, L. J. married Frere, Carrie C. 07/25/65   07/27/65
Denins, Catherine (Mrs.) died 09/04/64   09/06/64
Denison, George W. died 10/07/65   10/10/65
Denison, John died 09/04/65   09/06/65
Denison, John R. married Megary, Jane 12/23/60   01/05/61
Denison, Mary L. married Russell, J. L. 12/08/64   12/17/64
Denison, Matilda Mary died 05/27/62   05/28/62
Denisson, Mary Eliza married Ridgley, William 05/28/63   05/30/63
Denmead, Adam died 08/09/64   08/11/64
Denmead, Adam died 08/09/64   08/12/64
Denmead, Benjamin married Hutchins, Margaret E. 01/09/62   01/10/62
Denmead, Emma died 09/23/64   09/24/64
Denmead, Florence E. died 04/18/64   04/20/64
Denmead, Jane married Broadbent, Joseph Ferdinand 07/16/63   07/18/63
Denmead, Pleasant L. died 09/06/63   09/08/63
Denmead, W. C. married Lewis, Mary A. 11/09/65   11/23/65
Denmeade, Mary J. married Morgan, George H. 02/16/65   02/22/65
Denmon, Henry married Arrington, Mary Elizabeth 03/03/64   03/11/64
Denney, Eliza C. (Mrs.) married Jordan, John B. 02/07/65   02/11/65
Denney, John married McGowan, Susan 01/01/63   06/09/63
Denney, John died no date   06/28/64
Denney, Kate S. married Trannear, Patrick Henry 07/12/63   07/23/63
Dennig, Milton A. C. died 07/23/64   07/26/64
Dennis, Alfred married Whittington, Mary Elizabeth 05/06/65   05/08/65
Dennis, Ann Rebecca Jane died 03/15/64   03/16/64
Dennis, Benjamin died 06/00/00   06/07/65
Dennis, Charles Wallace died 05/03/63   05/09/63
Dennis, Emory married Belt, Mary Lizzie 06/06/64   06/11/64
Dennis, George R. married McPherson, Fannie 06/09/64   06/11/64
Dennis, George W. married Goodman, Susie 05/26/64   05/28/64
Dennis, George Walter died 10/14/64   10/15/64
Dennis, James M. married Miller, Genyra C. 08/24/62   08/26/62
Dennis, Josiah married Weaver, Julia 10/12/63   11/06/63
Dennis, Martha E. died 03/16/61   03/18/61
Dennis, Mary married Johnson, William 04/21/64   04/23/64
Dennis, Mary A. (Mrs.) died 05/21/64   05/24/64

```
Dennis, Mary Ellen died 03/24/63   03/26/63
Denny, Annie Laurie died 11/24/61   12/04/61
Denny, Catherine (Mrs.) married Hardesty, James H. 05/03/64   05/23/64
Denny, Etta married Hoban, Frederick H. 06/14/65   06/17/65
Denny, Frances Ella died 05/27/65   05/29/65
Denny, Henrietta Clay died 01/10/61   01/11/61
Denny, Jennie Newman died 10/01/63   10/09/63
Denny, Joseph died 09/09/62   09/11/62
Denny, Mary Elizabeth died 08/15/64   08/16/64
Denny, R. Augustus married Stuart, Lizzie 04/26/65   04/28/65
Denny, Thomas died 09/20/61   09/21/61
Denson, William I. M. died 03/30/65   03/31/65
Denson, William I. M. died 03/30/65   04/01/65
Dent, Henrietta H. married Bansemer, G. A. 05/26/64   05/28/64
Dent, Samuel Shrigley died 04/16/61   04/17/61
Dentry, Henry H. married Stewart, Elizabeth A. 02/03/63   02/05/63
Dentry, Mary A. married Martin, Edward 09/25/62   09/29/62
Denty, Louis married Breuhl, Annie E. 08/10/64   08/17/64
Denvier, Caroline died 07/29/65   07/31/65
Denvir, Rose M. married Pleasants, Charles 12/08/64   01/04/65
Depass, John married Remley, Isabella 03/09/65   03/13/65
Depkin, John George died 06/01/61   06/03/61
Depper, John married Gould, Mary 03/15/65   03/17/65
Deppish, Mary died 04/24/64   04/25/64
Derenberger, Elizabeth died 05/05/61   05/06/61
Derenberger, Elizabeth died 05/05/61   05/07/61
Derenberger, Elizabeth died 01/21/64   01/22/64
Deronceray, Charles died 09/27/64   09/28/64
Derr, Daniel I. died 02/15/62   02/26/62
Derr, Sarah A. died 04/18/65   04/19/65
Derr, Willie died 11/12/64   11/15/64
Derry, James S. married Ward, Emily Jane 03/06/62   03/08/62
Derry, John Alexander died 12/17/65   12/19/65
Derry, Mathias married Watts, Martha 06/16/61   06/24/61
Dersch, Casper S. married Hagan, Louisa A. 11/01/64   11/02/64
Des Forger, Julia Winans died 03/02/62   03/04/62
Deshields, Nicholas Leak died 06/18/61   06/20/61
Deshon, Ida C. married Ridgely, N. G. (Dr.) 09/06/64   09/08/64
Deshon, J. Westly married Copper, Rebecca 04/19/64   04/21/64
DeSilver, R. Wilson died 10/24/63   10/29/63
Despeaux, John J. died no date   11/01/65
Desveraux, Francis married Courtney, Mary 09/16/63   01/05/64
DeSwan, Maggie N. married Anderson, William 06/16/64   06/23/64
Deu, John died 05/08/65   05/10/65
Deuber, William died 10/10/64   10/12/64
DeValin, Frank died 10/04/62   10/06/62
DeValin, George B. died 04/26/63   06/04/63
Devalis, Emily married Pattison, John R. 12/21/65   12/29/65
Devery, Joseph died 06/06/65   06/07/65
Devillin, Mary E. married Kirby, George J. 10/05/61   11/25/61
Devinney, John died 09/15/64   09/16/64
Devinney, Mary Ann married Patterson, Robert 01/15/63   01/17/63
DeVoe, Ann Maria married Gallup, Daniel 04/19/64   04/30/64
Devries, Christian married Wilson, Maria 01/01/62   01/02/62
Devries, Martha died 09/11/62   09/12/62
```

Devries, Martha (Mrs.) died 05/12/63 05/13/63
Devries, William R. married Crane, Mary A. 03/02/65 03/07/65
Dew, Elizabeth (Mrs.) died 10/08/64 10/10/64
Dew, Ellen S. married Moffitt, Samuel S. 03/31/62 04/07/62
Dew, John died 05/08/65 05/11/65
Dew, Theodore W. married McMaines, Sarah 07/03/65 07/11/65
Dewees, Mary Eliza died 10/16/63 10/17/63
Dewint, Mary M. died 04/26/62 04/28/62
Dewling, Isiah (Dr.) married Wheatley, Mary A. 08/01/65 08/12/65
Dewling, Margaret A. married Jones, James L. 12/26/61 12/28/61
Diamond, Sarah M. (Mrs.) died 02/25/65 02/27/65
Diamond, Sarah M. (Mrs.) died 02/25/65 02/28/65
Diamond, William Smith died 06/04/65 06/05/65
Dibb, Anna E. (Mrs.) died 03/27/63 03/28/63
Dibb, James married Schneades, Anna Margaret 06/09/64 06/11/64
Dibb, John William died 07/11/64 07/23/64
Dick, Lenie married Halliday, Robert J. 09/22/64 09/27/64
Dickehut, Hannah died 04/24/62 04/25/62
Dickel, John Charles died 10/17/62 10/18/62
Dickel, Mary Annie died 06/05/64 06/06/64
Dickenson, P. Eugene married Beall, Emma 06/25/61 06/28/61
Dicker, John J. married Jones, Laura V. 02/04/64 02/11/64
Dickerson, Anna Maria married Griffin, William 06/30/62 07/03/62
Dickerson, E. A. married Clabaugh, E. 09/27/64 09/28/64
Dickerson, Emelia married Black, William 12/26/65 12/27/65
Dickerson, Emma A. married Wilson, J. Webster 06/29/65 07/01/65
Dickerson, Eugenia married Young, James 09/22/64 09/24/64
Dickerson, Isaac W. married Mathaney, Virginia E. 02/18/64 02/20/64
Dickerson, Josiah F. married Newman, Mary Elizabeth 06/25/65 06/27/65
Dickerson, Richard died 09/16/65 09/18/65
Dickerson, Sarah Jane died 07/22/65 07/31/65
Dickerson, William died 03/21/64 03/23/64
Dickey, Sarah died 06/18/64 06/20/64
Dickinson, Ann Maria married Miller, Leonard D. 04/19/64 04/30/64
Dickinson, Eugene Duvall died 09/17/64 09/19/64
Dickinson, George W. died 04/20/61 04/30/61
Dickinson, James married Anderson, Catherine 05/10/65 05/12/65
Dickinson, John, Jr. married Colley, Ursula W. 12/24/61 01/04/62
Dickson, Catherine died 03/04/63 03/10/63
Dickson, Eliza C. died 02/11/61 02/16/61
Dickson, James A. married Carter, Martha V. 09/26/61 09/28/61
Dickson, Jane (Mrs.) died 03/29/63 04/01/63
Dickson, Laura O. married Campher, James E. 05/25/65 05/27/65
Dickson, M. Ann E. married Grant, J. Hope 10/15/62 10/20/62
Dickson, Mary Anna died 09/23/63 09/24/63
Dickson, Sue married Barr, D. Miller (Dr.) 07/28/64 07/30/64
Dicus, Jacob L. married Davis, Mary Jane 03/08/63 03/10/63
Didemann, John married Gottlieb, Amalia 10/19/62 10/20/62
Didier, Henry D. married Skinner, Ella V. 04/26/65 04/29/65
Dieckmann, Margaret C. married Jones, Charles W. 04/17/65 04/27/65
Diederly, Robert E. died 06/26/64 06/28/64
Dieffenbach, Ferdinand (Dr.) died 03/02/61 03/08/61
Dieffenderfer, Robert E. married Hook, Annie E. 09/09/62 09/13/62
Dieffenderfer, Robert E. married Hook, Annie E. 09/09/62 09/15/62
Diehn, Christopher died 01/31/65 02/02/65

Diekle, Susanna (Mrs.) died 05/09/64 05/10/64
Dielman, Henry died 12/25/63 01/16/64
Diels, Susan Virginia died 06/16/65 06/17/65
Diering, Caroline (Mrs.) died 08/28/63 08/29/63
Dierker, Elizabeth married Imhoff, Herman 09/01/64 09/08/64
Dies, John G. married Loman, Ann Rebecca 01/12/62 01/15/62
Dieter, Daniel died 05/26/62 05/28/62
Dietz, Louis Blake died 07/11/64 07/12/64
Dietz, William A. died 08/08/62 08/13/62
Diffely, Mary A. married Byrnes, Martin 07/06/62 07/26/62
Diffenbaugh, Joseph Wesley died 02/21/64 02/23/64
Diffenbaugh, Marinda (Mrs.) died 06/25/63 06/26/63
Diffendarfer, Susanna married Young, Thomas 05/09/64 05/11/64
Diffenderfer, Ann died 08/07/65 08/09/65
Diffenderfer, Charles F. married Winn, Emma E. 09/08/64 09/10/64
Diffenderfer, Emma G. married Masterman, Charles S. 04/28/64 05/02/64
Diffenderfer, John A. died 06/22/64 06/23/64
Diffenderfer, Joseph T. married Wakeland, Rebecca A. 01/13/61 01/22/6
Diffenderfer, Louis A. died 06/15/61 06/17/61
Diffenderfer, Sallie married Evans, Henry 05/31/65 06/01/65
Diffenderffer, Charles (Dr.) died 07/07/64 07/08/64
Diffenderffer, Mary Laura died 11/28/61 12/02/61
Diffenderffer, Sarah A. (Mrs.) married Trotton, Thomas 11/30/65
    12/04/65
Diffey, Alexander died 10/16/63 10/19/63
Diffey, Francis Marion died 01/29/63 01/31/63
Diffey, Mary Ann died 08/02/62 08/11/62
Diffey, Oliver died 11/04/63 11/06/63
Diffley, Ellen Jane died 08/15/63 08/17/63
Diffley, Kate V. married McMahon, William Monahan no date 07/07/63
Digens, Ann died 09/01/62 09/16/62
Diggs, Ann E. (Mrs.) died 01/10/63 01/12/63
Diggs, Annie M. died 05/22/65 05/23/65
Diggs, Annie M. died 05/22/65 05/24/65
Diggs, Annie M. E. married Harvey, John E. 05/19/63 05/22/63
Diggs, Beverly (Cpt.) died 10/10/62 10/11/62
Diggs, Charles Barrington died 06/17/63 06/18/63
Diggs, Charlotte died 04/13/63 04/14/63
Diggs, Cyrus M. married Perry, Margaret 03/22/64 03/23/64
Diggs, Edward G. married McLaughlin, Hattie E. 01/28/62 01/19/62
Diggs, Elizabeth S. married Ruark, Emanual W. 01/30/61 01/31/61
Diggs, Florene Elizabeth died 09/04/63 09/07/63
Diggs, J. Wesley S. married Mitchell, Mary E. 11/29/65 12/01/65
Diggs, James married Barrington, Isabel 06/19/62 06/23/62
Diggs, Joseph Meades died 07/26/62 08/04/62
Diggs, Richard H. died 10/07/65 10/09/65
Diggs, Wesley S. married Mitchell, Mary E. 11/29/65 12/02/65
Diggs, William B. married McDermott, Annie M. 07/03/63 07/27/63
Dignan, John died 07/21/65 07/22/65
Digner, Bridget married Anderson, Daniel 06/03/63 08/28/63
Digs, Aaron married Jones, Elizabeth Ann 06/23/61 06/26/61
Dilehay, Thomas T. married Soden, Georgeanna 04/16/63 04/25/63
Dill, George E. A. married Thompson, Emma Belle 11/29/64 12/03/64
Dillahay, Jane died 06/09/62 07/16/62
Dillaway, Theodore Stanislaus died 05/28/65 05/29/65

Dillehunt, George R. married Moore, Helena S. 02/15/65 02/17/65
Dillehunt, Mary Emma died 05/04/64 05/05/64
Dillehunt, Sarah J. died 11/17/63 11/18/63
Dillen, Sallie M. married Rynehart, William H. 02/23/64 02/25/64
Dillihunt, Mary Elizabeth married Smith, Samuel E. 01/01/63 01/13/63
Dillon, Martha died 01/28/64 07/08/64
Dillon, Mary Ann married McCann, Terrence 05/02/64 05/24/64
Dillon, Sarah E. married Ford, Charles A. 12/11/63 12/16/63
Dillow, John R. married Nally, Martha E. 06/06/65 06/07/65
Dillow, William died 06/22/62 06/26/62
Dilson, Mary Frances married Dorsey, C. R. 09/20/64 09/21/64
Dilworthy, John married Burgan, Lizzie A. 06/03/63 06/04/63
Diment, Jane S. married Jackson, Joseph H. 03/26/61 06/11/61
Dingle, Eve Rosanna died 03/04/61 03/05/61
Dinkel, Josephine married Hyson, Joseph 12/24/63 12/30/63
Dinkel, Mary Elizabeth married Whiteford, Alfred H. (Dr.) 12/15/62
    01/24/63
Dinsmore, David married Humphries, Mary Ann 04/11/61 04/20/61
Dippell, Sophia M. died 06/04/65 06/06/65
Dipple, Margaret Amelia married Laughlin, William H. 07/11/64 11/22/64
Dipple, Mary L. married Kahlert, Frederick W. 11/30/65 12/02/65
Disney, Alfred J. married Bailey, Louisa 02/24/61 05/10/61
Disney, Andrew J. married Warfield, Ann M. 09/20/63 09/22/63
Disney, David T. died 12/15/63 12/16/63
Disney, Elizabeth M. (Mrs.) died 11/13/63 11/18/63
Disney, G. F. married Warfield, Achsah 12/08/63 12/10/63
Disney, Gerrard Summerfield died 04/18/65 04/19/65
Disney, James Alexander died 08/27/61 08/28/61
Disney, James Alexander died 08/27/61 08/29/61
Disney, James R. died 05/06/61 05/08/61
Disney, John W. died 04/09/61 04/10/61
Disney, Louisa E. married Downs, James T. 12/05/61 12/07/61
Disney, Lucy A. married Skinner, John B. 04/28/64 05/11/64
Disney, Mary died 02/24/62 02/25/62
Disney, R. P. married Cole, Elizabeth 12/12/61 12/23/61
Disney, Rachel (Mrs.) died 08/06/64 11/14/64
Disney, Randolph died 05/01/61 05/02/61
Disney, Sarah A. died 07/24/62 07/25/62
Disney, Snowden died 08/23/62 09/04/62
Disney, Solomon (Capt.) died 05/12/63 05/14/63
Disney, Sophia married Cole, Noah H. 03/11/62 03/15/62
Disney, Wesley married Warfield, Margaret S. 03/26/61 03/30/61
Disosway, I. C. (Lt.) married Lybre, Mary A. 07/08/63 07/09/63
Disosway, William Wilkins (Lt) died 10/13/63 10/28/63
Ditman, Nelson R. died 02/27/63 03/03/63
Ditman, Rachel died 10/09/65 10/10/65
Dittman, Charles W. married Lamb, Martha 02/05/63 02/07/63
Dittus, Gottlieb Frederick died 01/09/65 01/10/65
Dittus, John Frederick died 07/28/65 07/29/65
Diven, Edward T. married Biden, Mary 03/24/63 03/30/63
Diven, George E. married Reckerd, Sarah J. 10/01/63 10/21/63
Diven, John, Sr. died 09/10/65 10/07/65
Diven, Mary E. married Hammersley, George W. 09/22/64 09/27/64
Diven, Susannah married Cathcart, George H. 05/21/61 05/23/61
Divens, John married Harris, Mary 10/15/65 10/18/65

Divers, Mary Matilda (Mrs.) died 03/30/65 03/04/65
Divine, Agnes married Segerman, William H. 01/28/64 02/05/64
Dix, Ann Elizabeth married Williams, George R. 10/29/65 11/04/65
Dix, Ann Rebecca died 09/05/62 09/09/62
Dix, John T. married White, Alphasis E. 11/16/64 11/17/64
Dix, William H. married Thomas, Maggie 03/24/61 04/01/61
Dixon, Alverdi married Snowden, Rezin 05/25/62 05/27/62
Dixon, Anna Mariah died 10/31/62 11/01/62
Dixon, Anne V. (Mrs.) died 10/25/64 10/26/64
Dixon, Caleb died 08/17/62 08/18/62
Dixon, David married Tobin, Mary 01/19/64 01/25/64
Dixon, Ellenora married Thompson, W. A. 07/13/64 07/18/64
Dixon, Fannie E. married Evans, John (USN) 09/02/64 09/07/64
Dixon, George W. C. died 05/05/63 05/06/63
Dixon, James M. died 02/19/63 02/21/63
Dixon, Jennie B. married La Rue, Lawrence P. 02/20/61 02/23/61
Dixon, John Alford married Hoke, Emma D. 09/12/64 05/18/65
Dixon, Johnna Gates died 02/23/61 02/27/61
Dixon, Joseph Wesley died 06/12/63 07/10/63
Dixon, Kate H. died 11/29/61 12/02/61
Dixon, Lydia Ann died 03/17/61 03/18/61
Dixon, Malachi B. died 08/25/61 08/28/61
Dixon, Margaret M. married Brannan, Charles H. S. 02/07/61 02/19/61
Dixon, Patrick married Mitchell, Rose Anna 02/07/61 02/13/61
Dixon, Robert H. died 08/09/63 08/12/63
Dixon, Robert W. died 11/30/61 12/02/61
Dixon, William Gwynn died 07/04/63 07/10/63
Dobbin, James T. died 12/07/64 12/08/64
Dobbin, Jane Susanna Holbrooks died 01/08/63 01/10/63
Dobbin, Robert A. died 08/15/62 08/16/62
Dobbins, Amelia V. died 12/05/62 02/14/63
Dobbins, Chola E. married Fisher, William H. 08/18/63 08/20/63
Dobbins, James died 04/17/62 04/18/62
Dobbins, Sarah died 11/28/61 11/30/61
Dobbs, Ann Elizabeth married Smith, B. E. 05/08/62 05/20/62
Dobbyn, George W. F. died 01/16/61 01/21/61
Dobler, Charles Henry D. died 09/04/63 09/05/63
Dobler, Magdalena (Mrs.) died 03/15/63 03/16/63
Dobler, Margaretta Gulielma died 03/04/62 03/05/62
Dobson, Robert Henry died 09/06/64 09/17/64
Dobson, William Henry died 06/17/65 06/21/65
Dobson, William P. died 01/30/64 02/03/64
Docwra, M. F. died 02/10/62 02/11/62
Docwra, Marian F. died 02/10/62 02/13/62
Docwra, Marion F. died 02/10/62 02/12/62
Dodd, Andrew J. married Litsinger, Anna M. 07/29/63 10/05/63
Dodd, Ann Rebecca died 05/09/61 05/11/61
Dodd, John married Boyd, Henrietta 05/26/63 05/27/63
Dodd, John W. died 04/23/64 04/25/64
Dodd, Robert died 12/14/62 01/06/63
Dodds, L. D. (Lt.) died 07/30/64 08/24/64
Dodge, A. W. (Dr.) married Murray, Maggie 09/29/63 10/10/63
Dodge, Asaph married Pentz, Laura L. 10/03/65 10/07/65
Dodge, Lizzie married Beall, John J. 06/17/62 06/20/62
Dodler, Ella Cecilia died 05/31/65 06/05/65

Dodson, Ann died no date 01/04/62
Dodson, Julia A. married Carter, William H. 09/12/64 09/14/64
Dodson, Maggie A. married Owens, Thomas A. 02/05/63 02/10/63
Dodson, Peter married Bailey, Ann Maria 08/01/61 08/03/61
Dodson, Robert M. died 04/10/63 04/18/63
Dodson, Susan C. married Cecil, Julius D. 01/17/61 01/21/61
Doe, William R. married Bosley, Olivia R. 06/20/62 10/15/62
Doenges, George married Schott, Dorothea 06/05/65 06/08/65
Doenges, Mary C. married Lewin, John H. 11/29/63 12/18/63
Doft, John Oliver died 12/19/63 12/21/63
Doft, Mary E. married Knight, George P. 05/26/63 07/04/63
Doged, John Whitridge died 07/15/62 07/16/62
Doggett, Annie R. married Norman, Joseph 01/22/63 01/24/63
Dohm, Annie Britania died 03/09/63 03/11/63
Dohm, Charles Franklin died 12/09/61 03/07/62
Dohm, Sue M. died 05/27/65 05/29/65
Dolan, Bridget died 11/15/62 11/17/62
Dolan, Joanna died 04/11/61 04/12/61
Dolan, John Francis died 07/15/64 07/16/64
Dolan, Kate married Carroll, Mortimer 11/27/62 12/13/62
Dolan, Walter James died 05/31/63 06/01/63
Doleman, William died 05/16/62 05/17/62
Doll, J. J. died 08/31/63 09/04/63
Doll, Sue M. married Eschbach, E. R. 11/09/64 11/11/64
Dolliver, William T. (USN) married Kemp, Margaret A. 11/30/65 12/05/65
Dolly, Margaret A. married Casey, Thomas J. 09/01/61 09/03/61
Dolphin, Francis died 10/15/63 10/16/63
Dolphin, Mary A. D. married Cook, James E. 09/14/64 09/22/64
Donahue, B. O. married Owens, Ann 04/19/61 05/28/61
Donahue, Richard Lawson died 12/17/62 12/18/62
Donahue, Sarah A. E. died 08/22/63 08/24/63
Donahue, William Westwood died 04/23/65 05/06/65
Donaldson, Alexander married Kierchoff, Elizabeth 07/18/65 07/19/65
Donaldson, Caroline married Parker, Foxhall A. (USN) 10/20/63 10/22/63
Donaldson, George F. married Harris, Mary F. 12/22/64 12/23/64
Donaldson, Jane died 11/04/63 11/06/63
Donaldson, Lucretia died 11/23/61 12/02/61
Donaldson, Samuel Johnston died 11/25/65 11/27/65
Donaldson, Sidnor S. died 10/01/61 10/02/61
Donally, Cornelius married Quinn, Mary 02/27/62 03/15/62
Donat, J. M. married Howard, Lizzie 07/09/65 08/01/65
Donat, Julia (Mrs.) died 12/31/62 01/02/63
Done, Mary died 07/26/63 07/27/63
Dongee, James H. died 01/17/65 01/19/65
Donn, John W. married McElderry, Annie 10/26/65 10/28/65
Donnell, Ann T. died 11/15/62 11/17/62
Donnelly, Ambrose married Keegan, Bridget 01/21/64 01/22/64
Donnelly, Ann (Mrs.) died 02/14/64 02/16/64
Donnelly, Annie died 09/27/65 09/28/65
Donnelly, Daniel died 01/10/64 01/12/64
Donnelly, Eliza J. married Healey, John 10/08/61 10/10/61
Donnelly, Emma P. married Williams, William J. 03/22/63 03/27/63
Donnelly, Essie married Linch, John 02/18/61 02/21/61
Donnelly, Frank married Brown, Polly 07/28/64 07/30/64
Donnelly, James married Sable, Annie R. 02/04/61 02/05/61

Donnelly, James Patrick died 08/29/63   09/02/63
Donnelly, John married Murphy, Margaret 02/07/64   02/11/64
Donnelly, Mary J. married Kagan, Patrick 09/11/64   09/23/64
Donnelly, Mary Rozalia died 07/14/62   07/16/62
Donnelly, Peter died 04/17/63   04/18/63
Donnelly, Richard died 08/14/63   09/02/63
Donnelly, Thomas died 10/19/62   10/20/62
Donnely, John died 11/02/63   11/04/63
Donney, Kate Glossbrewer died 12/03/64   12/05/64
Donnolly, Teresia M. married Roland, Thomas, Jr. 04/13/64   04/18/64
Donoghue, Ellen married Leary, John 06/28/63   07/01/63
Donohou, Mary married Craft, Jacob 09/29/63   12/31/63
Donohue, Anne E. married Brown, Alfred C. 11/03/63   11/06/63
Donohue, Bridget died 08/02/65   08/03/65
Donohue, Chicora Maybel died 09/10/63   09/12/63
Donohue, Margaret died 09/05/64   09/07/64
Donohue, Mary Jane died 09/14/63   09/15/63
Donovan, Daniel G. married Isetts, Margaret 03/31/63   04/01/63
Donovan, Joseph S. died 04/15/61   04/16/61
Donovan, Kate married Burns, George 11/17/64   11/18/64
Doody, Catherine (Mrs.) died 06/15/63   06/16/63
Dooley, Annie died 05/09/64   05/10/64
Doolittle, H. Clay married Carr, Mary B. 10/31/64   11/23/64
Door, Ann Maria married Cockey, Joshua 02/28/61   03/02/61
Dopman, Mary M. married Roome, Theodore E. 12/09/62   02/14/63
Dorbacker, William died 08/15/63   08/17/63
Dorgan, Elizabeth died 12/12/62   12/13/62
Dorm, Jacob married Bopp, Kate 08/25/63   08/31/63
Dorman, Adaline married Murphy, Joseph W. 09/27/65   09/29/65
Dorman, Eliza (Mrs.) died 09/19/64   09/20/64
Dorman, J. Franklin married Peterson, Carrie 04/04/61   05/28/61
Dorman, John died 06/15/63   06/17/63
Dorman, Olivia A. died 05/03/63   05/04/63
Dorman, Olivia A. died 05/03/63   05/05/63
Dorman, William died 11/27/65   11/30/65
Dormandy, Sarah Jane married Arthur, Thomas 04/04/64   09/07/64
Dorney, Amanda R. married Bennett, John Edward 04/13/65   05/10/65
Dorrell, W. B. (Lt. Col.) died 06/18/64   06/29/64
Dorrell, W. B. (Lt. Col.) married McGowan, Addie V. 01/21/64   02/15/64
Dorritee, Elizabeth (Mrs.) died no date   05/15/65
Dorritee, Garet A. died 03/06/64   03/08/64
Dorriter, Thomas A. died 07/15/65   07/17/65
Dorrman, Ellen R. married Lewis, John A. 06/15/65   06/16/65
Dorry, John (Cpt.) died 05/24/64   05/28/64
Dorry, John Campbell died 09/10/62   10/13/62
Dorschel, Albert Edward died 10/24/64   10/27/64
Dorsery, Ann Elizabeth died 09/10/62   09/16/62
Dorset, Ann A. (Mrs.) died 12/25/63   12/26/63
Dorsett, Mary Eleanor died 09/20/64   09/22/64
Dorsey, Aden A. H. died 09/07/63   09/09/63
Dorsey, Amanda married Oliver, Dolphus 11/15/64   11/17/64
Dorsey, Amanda R. married Bennett, John Edward 04/13/65   05/09/65
Dorsey, Ann Howard died 11/10/65   11/28/65
Dorsey, Anna (Mrs.) married Bright, Francis C. 11/26/63   11/30/63
Dorsey, Anna Clare married Mohun, Richard B. 05/05/63   05/07/63

Dorsey, Anne married Bright, Francis C. 11/26/63   11/28/63
Dorsey, Arthur Brooke died 01/12/63   01/14/64
Dorsey, C. R. married Dilson, Mary Frances 09/20/64   09/21/64
Dorsey, Caroline married Wilson, Daniel 02/08/65   02/10/65
Dorsey, Catherine V. (Mrs.) died 03/12/65   03/29/65
Dorsey, Charles DeWarfield died 03/30/63   04/04/63
Dorsey, Charles H. died 06/23/65   06/24/65
Dorsey, Charles W. died 05/24/64   05/26/64
Dorsey, Charlotte married Willis, Edward 02/19/63   02/26/63
Dorsey, Cornelius died 05/13/65   05/15/65
Dorsey, Dan B. died 09/10/65   09/21/65
Dorsey, Edward died 07/21/61   07/23/61
Dorsey, Edward married Clamoren, Camille 11/29/64   12/01/64
Dorsey, Edward H. died 06/08/63   06/10/63
Dorsey, Edwin (Dr., Rev.) died 11/20/63   11/21/63
Dorsey, Elizabeth died 05/17/65   05/22/65
Dorsey, Elizabeth married Trundle, James Otho 02/18/64   02/22/64
Dorsey, Elizabeth Warner died 11/19/61   11/23/61
Dorsey, Ellen Elizabeth died 11/28/61   11/30/61
Dorsey, Ellen V. married Harding, Charles A. 11/25/63   11/28/63
Dorsey, Emma died 03/21/63   03/26/63
Dorsey, Emma L. married Forrest, Andrew J. 06/20/64   07/02/64
Dorsey, Enoch died 01/18/64   01/23/64
Dorsey, Frances died 10/17/61   10/21/61
Dorsey, Frances E. married Goldsborough, John W. 12/09/62   12/11/62
Dorsey, George W. married Hammett, Maria (Mrs.) 04/21/64   04/23/64
Dorsey, Harriet Ann (Mrs.) died 09/05/63   09/10/63
Dorsey, Isabela A. married Houston, John 12/22/64   12/23/64
Dorsey, J. H. T. Jerome died 12/28/61   12/30/61
Dorsey, J. W. married Watkins, Ellen E. 05/27/62   05/28/62
Dorsey, James died 02/08/61   02/09/61
Dorsey, James W. A. died 11/19/61   11/20/61
Dorsey, John T. W. died 02/03/61   02/05/61
Dorsey, Jonathan M. married Stockdale, Julia 02/10/63   02/18/63
Dorsey, Joseph I. married Wheeler, M. A. (Mrs.) 04/09/61   04/13/61
Dorsey, Lizzie M. married Blunt, William H. 03/28/61   04/06/61
Dorsey, Lizzie M. married Blunt, William H. 03/28/61   04/08/61
Dorsey, Lorenzo died 03/09/62   03/11/62
Dorsey, Margaret A. died 11/23/61   11/25/61
Dorsey, Maria L. married Kemp, Simon J. 11/16/65   11/21/65
Dorsey, Marian B. married Gassaway, Louis G. 03/04/62   03/17/62
Dorsey, Marion died 11/14/63   11/24/63
Dorsey, Mary married Barnett, Dennis 10/20/64   10/22/64
Dorsey, Mary A. married Lancaster, Ebenezer 01/01/61   01/09/61
Dorsey, Mary A. died 02/10/61   02/15/61
Dorsey, Mary Ann died 12/16/61   12/17/61
Dorsey, Mary C. married Saville, Alexander 04/08/62   04/09/62
Dorsey, Mary J. married Stuart, John A. 01/01/61   01/03/61
Dorsey, Mary M. married Semmes, A. A. 02/09/64   02/10/64
Dorsey, Medora A. married Sullivan, Philip T. 06/02/64   06/07/64
Dorsey, Nellie M. married Worthington, Otis A. 11/16/65   11/20/65
Dorsey, Nettie married Worthington, Nicholas (Cpt.) 05/15/62   05/16/62
Dorsey, Nettie Cox died 04/13/65   04/14/65
Dorsey, Rachael Ann married Smith, William H. 01/30/62   02/01/62
Dorsey, Rebecca E. married Billups, George M. 12/01/62   12/04/62

Dorsey, Richard H., Jr. married McFadden, Martha 02/01/63 02/17/63
Dorsey, Ridgely married Adams, Marcellina 08/24/64 08/31/64
Dorsey, Samuel A. married Edwards, Mary E. (Mrs.) 11/01/64 11/03/64
Dorsey, Samuel H. died 04/07/64 04/08/64
Dorsey, Samuel H. died 04/07/64 04/12/64
Dorsey, Sarah Rebecca married Miller, George Alexandria 11/22/63 12/01/63
Dorsey, Susan M. died 03/31/65 04/29/65
Dorsey, Thomas died 03/31/65 05/19/65
Dorsey, Thomas died 10/21/65 10/23/65
Dorsey, Thomas E. married Moran, Sarah V. 06/18/63 06/20/63
Dorsey, Thomas N. married Litchfield, Mary L. 11/06/65 11/15/65
Dorsey, Thomas N. married Litchfield, Mary L. 11/06/65 11/18/65
Dorsey, Thomas R. married Banks, Margaret W. 04/25/61 04/27/61
Dorsey, Thomas Riggs died 06/25/65 06/28/65
Dorsey, Truman died 03/31/65 04/29/65
Dorsey, Vernon married Costigin, Kate 04/24/62 04/29/62
Dorsey, William married Russell, Louisa 02/09/64 02/10/64
Dorsey, William H. married German, Ruhamah B. 02/10/63 02/16/63
Dorsey, William H. G. died 10/24/62 10/25/62
dos Santos, Cecelia died 08/29/62 10/16/62
Dotter, Joseph married Mayberry, Mary 04/13/63 04/20/63
Dotterweich, Frederick died 11/08/62 11/10/62
Dotterweih, Frederick married Pickett, Susie 06/08/65 06/12/65
Doubleday, Charlotte M. died 02/12/63 02/21/63
Doud, John Bradford died 10/24/65 10/28/65
Doud, Oliver B. married Walker, Sarah O. 05/07/63 05/25/63
Doud, Oliver B. married Walker, Sarah Olivia 05/07/63 05/26/63
Doud, Sophia Virginia died 05/26/61 05/30/61
Dougass, Elizabeth A. married Rarrick, Charles H., Jr. 04/19/64 04/21/64
Doughaday, Joseph died 04/15/62 04/16/62
Dougherty, Bridget died 04/01/63 04/02/63
Dougherty, Charles H. married Roney, Louisa 10/22/64 10/29/64
Dougherty, Elizabeth A. died 08/08/64 08/09/64
Dougherty, Emma Virginia died 05/03/63 05/11/63
Dougherty, Fannie married Lutts, Charles J. 01/07/64 01/09/64
Dougherty, James died 04/24/63 04/25/63
Dougherty, James Thomas died 12/27/65 12/28/65
Dougherty, John died 02/08/63 02/10/63
Dougherty, Mary died 04/10/63 04/11/63
Dougherty, Mary (Mrs.) died 04/05/63 04/06/63
Dougherty, Mary (Mrs.) died 07/07/64 07/08/64
Dougherty, Mary (Mrs.) died 07/07/64 07/21/64
Dougherty, Mary (Mrs.) died 07/07/64 07/22/64
Dougherty, Mary (Mrs.) died 08/07/64 08/08/64
Dougherty, Philip died 02/03/65 02/04/65
Dougherty, Philip H. married Appleby, Virginia 01/15/63 01/17/63
Dougherty, Thomas B. married Shell, Annie 12/28/61 01/11/62
Dougherty, William married Henderson, Agnes Ophelia 02/07/64 02/11/64
Dougherty, William C. married Petherbridge, Emma J. 05/18/65 05/20/65
Dougherty, William H. married Prince, Sarah E. 12/23/60 02/19/61
Douglas, August married Crawford, Mary V. 06/25/62 06/27/62
Douglas, Caroline married Shepard, James W. 12/31/60 11/09/61
Douglas, Joseph died 10/04/62 11/05/62

```
Douglas, Louis died 11/04/62   11/05/62
Douglas, Mary F. married Deford, George H. 12/30/61   02/03/62
Douglas, Sarah Elizabeth J. died 08/14/65   08/16/65
Douglas, Solomon married Glenn, Deborah 02/26/61   06/18/61
Douglas, William H. died 09/19/64   10/17/64
Douglas, William H. died 09/19/64   10/22/64
Douglass, Edward L. died 09/28/64   10/05/64
Douglass, Fannie E. died 07/31/65   08/01/65
Douglass, Mary married Stime, Joseph C. 05/17/63   05/20/63
Douglass, Mary L. died 03/12/65   03/14/65
Douglass, Sarah married Stine, Joseph C. 05/17/63   05/22/63
Douglass, William died 06/15/64   06/17/64
Douw, Harriet Van Rensalaer died 08/31/62   09/03/62
Dove, Emma married Williams, Thomas H. 03/23/64   03/25/64
Dove, Maggie V. married Yeaton, J. W. (Lt.) 04/14/64   04/19/64
Dove, Martha G. (Mrs.) died 02/24/64   03/04/64
Dove, Milton Harvey died 08/04/64   08/06/64
Dove, Sarah A. married Prime, William T. 05/17/65   05/19/65
Dowd, Patrick died 08/03/64   08/04/64
Dowdall, Charles C. married Chaney, Laura B. 08/21/63   08/25/63
Dowden, Benjamin married Dunbar, Jane R. (Mrs.) 02/26/63   05/07/63
Dowell, George E. married Nalls, Emma D. 10/12/65   10/23/65
Dowell, John Thomas died 04/27/64   04/28/64
Dowell, John Thomas died 04/27/64   04/29/64
Dowell, Kate Virginia died 03/07/65   03/08/65
Dowell, Zora (Mrs.) died 08/04/63   08/10/63
Dowling, Elizabeth married Weger, John 10/02/61   11/04/61
Dowling, Elizabeth (Mrs.) died 08/11/63   08/12/63
Dowling, James died 05/22/61   05/24/61
Downe, William H. married Hartlove, Laura A. 06/25/65   07/01/65
Downes, Elizabeth died 02/28/61   03/01/61
Downes, William H. (Dr.) married Richards, Mary F. 04/30/65   05/04/65
Downey, Ann Maria died 09/14/65   09/15/65
Downey, Charles Henry (USA) married Hopple, Mary Ann 11/27/63   11/30/63
Downey, Florence P. died 12/19/64   12/20/64
Downey, John died 01/06/65   01/14/65
Downey, Kate Glosbrenner died 12/03/64   12/07/64
Downey, Maggie married Long, John 01/17/64   01/18/64
Downey, Mary Elizabeth died 01/17/65   01/19/65
Downey, Matilda (Mrs.) died 02/18/64   02/20/64
Downey, Michael Joseph died 07/20/64   07/22/64
Downey, Michael Joseph died 07/20/64   07/28/64
Downey, Molly died 07/25/64   07/28/64
Downey, Sarah (Mrs.) died 03/07/64   03/08/64
Downing, James L. died 05/07/62   05/09/62
Downly, William died 02/13/61   02/14/61
Downs, Caroline married Berryman, John 11/17/63   11/19/63
Downs, Charles Summerfield died 01/29/64   02/01/64
Downs, Elizabeth married Revels, James 04/09/62   04/11/62
Downs, Elizabeth A. died 01/26/61   01/28/61
Downs, Henry married Jordan, Mary E. 06/04/62   06/07/62
Downs, Henry (Pvt.) died 04/26/64   04/28/64
Downs, Henry C. married Fairbanks, Elizabeth 11/27/62   12/01/62
Downs, Isaiah died 11/20/64   11/22/64
Downs, James married Lee, Fanny 08/18/62   08/20/62
```

Downs, James T. married Disney, Louisa E. 12/05/61   12/07/61
Downs, Mary A. married Robinson, Dorsey 06/23/64   06/30/64
Downs, S. Dickinson married Dutrow, Emma L. 09/22/61   12/28/61
Downs, Samuel Francis died 03/29/62   03/31/62
Downs, Thadeus L. married White, Deborah W. 12/19/64   01/09/65
Downs, Wilbur Reese died 11/27/65   11/29/65
Downs, William died 01/14/63   01/15/64
Downs, William H. married Underwood, Sallie C. 05/12/64   05/20/64
Downs, William H. married Underwood, Sallie C. 05/12/64   05/16/64
Downy, Margaret Ann Louisa died 11/18/62   11/20/62
Doyle, Catharine married McGuirk, Patrick 01/02/65   08/02/65
Doyle, Eliza married Nelligan, Maurice 05/22/64   05/28/64
Doyle, Ellen died 08/15/61   08/16/61
Doyle, Emma E. married Wilderman, Robert B. 03/18/63   03/21/63
Doyle, Hugh Henry died 01/05/65   03/20/65
Doyle, James married Clayton, Amelia M. 11/13/65   11/15/65
Doyle, James A. died 08/03/65   08/04/65
Doyle, James E. married Smith, Margaret A. 04/11/61   04/16/61
Doyle, Manie died 06/20/65   06/22/65
Doyle, Mary married Corrigan, Francis 11/24/61   12/05/61
Doyle, Mary died 07/06/61   07/13/61
Doyle, Mary died 06/20/65   06/24/65
Doyle, Mary A. married Farr, Stewart A. 12/25/62   01/06/63
Doyle, Mary Agnes died 08/15/61   08/16/61
Doyle, Michael A. died 07/05/64   07/06/64
Doyle, Michael E. married Keenan, Mary 01/03/65   01/05/65
Doyle, Michael H. married Omelea, Eliza 03/30/65   05/22/65
Doyle, Thomas G. married Postlethwaite, Charlotte C. 07/25/65   08/02/6
Doyle, Walter John died 08/23/63   08/24/63
Drach, Elender Lamotte (Mrs.) died 10/31/64   11/04/64
Drakeley, Sherman died 08/04/62   08/05/62
Drakely, Henry died 03/17/65   03/23/65
Drakerley, Truman H. died 06/20/65   06/22/65
Drane, Ann Jane died 02/06/65   02/07/65
Drane, Daniel died 07/09/61   07/10/61
Draney, F. M. married Wheeler, Salome H. 03/16/65   04/06/65
Drean, Hugh died 08/13/63   08/14/63
Drean, James died 04/11/61   04/12/61
Drebbing, Augustus L. died 11/04/61   11/05/61
Drechsler, Charles Frederick died 02/26/65   03/02/65
Drepel, Ida Celestia died 04/09/65   04/10/65
Dressel, Anna Amelia died 02/12/65   02/14/65
Dressel, Elizabeth married Walter, Frederick Lewis 10/13/63   11/03/63
Dressel, Werner Edward died 08/01/65   08/03/65
Drew, George W. died 04/07/64   04/19/64
Drew, John Francis died 07/06/65   07/07/65
Drew, Michael died 01/01/61   01/02/61
Drexel, Ida Celestia died 04/09/65   04/11/65
Drill, Jane Morrison died 06/24/64   06/25/64
Drill, Nellie died 08/05/64   08/09/64
Drinkhouse, Henrietta died 08/16/61   08/22/61
Driscol, Denis died 09/24/62   09/25/62
Driscoll, Lucy married Boyer, John 11/01/64   11/04/64
Driver, Auguste married Gieske, Gustavus 06/04/64   06/06/64
Driver, Charles F. married Bach, Elizabeth 01/06/63   01/08/63

Driver, Eleanora died 07/28/65   07/29/65
Driver, John Francis married Eves, Mary Ann 03/29/61   04/09/61
Droghan, Thomas died 10/18/63   10/20/63
Droham, Charley died 09/17/62   09/18/62
Drohan, Florence Amelia died 09/25/62   09/27/62
Drohan, John Meyers died 02/03/65   02/06/65
Drohan, Thomas died 10/19/63   10/19/63
Droney, Mary Lizzie died 02/25/64   02/26/64
Drost, George Washington died 01/14/63   01/15/63
Drost, George Washington died 01/14/63   01/16/63
Druery, George Washington died 05/06/64   05/07/64
Drugan, Annie married Clarke, James 05/26/63   06/16/63
Drummond, John H. married Brown, Emma F. 04/31/63   06/03/63
Drummond, May Blanche died 06/18/65   06/23/65
Drummond, Nancy died 10/22/62   10/23/62
Drury, David M. married Featherall, Biddy 06/07/65   06/12/65
Drury, Fanny married Pindell, R. M. 09/10/63   09/15/63
Drury, J. Thomas married Jenison, Marion M. 11/18/62   11/27/62
Drury, Jerome Ashley died 07/24/65   08/03/65
Drury, Jerome Ashly died 07/24/65   08/01/65
Drury, Jerome Ashly died 07/24/65   08/02/65
Drury, John T. died 07/06/65   07/07/65
Drury, John T. died 07/06/65   07/08/65
Drury, Susan E. (Mrs.) married Wartman, Edmund W. 06/20/61   06/21/61
Drury, William A. married Marines, Suzannah E. 01/01/65   01/03/65
Dryden, Aurelia (Mrs.) died 09/29/65   09/30/65
Dryden, Ellen died 08/13/61   08/14/61
Dryden, J. Meredith married Cole, Fannie R. 10/10/65   10/12/65
Dryden, James married Alexander, Mary C. 10/01/61   10/05/61
Dryden, Martha married Crisp, William E. 02/11/61   02/20/61
Dryden, Mary A. R. married Reese, M. F. 06/16/62   06/17/62
Dryden, Samuel T. died no date   08/04/65
Drysdale, Leila died 11/24/65   11/28/65
Du Val, Charles C. died 08/29/65   08/30/65
Du Vall, Charles Curtis died 08/29/65   09/20/65
DuBois, William R. died 04/02/64   04/06/64
Ducatel, Louise married McNally, Henry R. 01/14/63   01/16/63
Duck, Sarah E. married Ellicott, Samuel 09/18/62   09/23/62
Duckworth, Emory married Balls, Emma 10/03/65   10/14/65
Dudeslugs, Charles L. died 07/01/62   07/10/62
Dudgan, Abel S. died 10/27/63   10/30/63
Dudley, Emily V. married Craig, William F. 07/26/65   08/08/65
Dudley, Emma V. married Klockgether, Albert A. 01/03/65   01/05/65
Dudley, Wiliam Harker died 03/22/65   03/24/65
Dudley, William Harker died 03/22/65   03/23/65
Dudrow, George W. married Birmingham, Mollie E. 08/11/64   08/19/64
Duer, Elizabeth Ann died 04/08/62   04/10/62
Duer, Laura A. married Stanley, Charles A. 11/15/64   11/18/64
Duering, Catherine E. (Mrs.) died 02/15/63   02/17/63
Dueur, Orlando married Reckert, Sarah Rebecca 02/04/64   02/08/64
Duff, Francis Lusby died 07/31/61   08/02/61
Duff, George B. died 12/11/64   12/15/64
Duff, Josephine died 03/11/62   03/12/62
Duff, Maggie Mary died 11/01/64   11/02/64
Duff, Mary Letitia married Burch, James A. 12/17/63   12/19/63

Duffey, Ellize died 07/08/64   07/09/64
Duffey, Julia Ann married Smith, Albert Colburn 01/27/64   01/29/64
Duffin, Abraham B. died 03/08/62   03/10/62
Duffin, Martin Luther married Govens, Elizabeth 12/29/64   12/31/64
Duffy, Ann died 08/09/62   08/11/62
Duffy, Bernard died 02/06/61   02/07/61
Duffy, Bernard died 02/06/61   02/08/61
Duffy, Bridget Maria died 01/17/61   01/18/61
Duffy, Catherine (Mrs.) died 07/27/64   07/29/64
Duffy, Catherine A. married Harding, James 03/09/65   03/15/65
Duffy, Elizabeth Ellen married Winters, John 09/24/64   09/26/64
Duffy, Hugh died 02/26/65   02/27/65
Duffy, James married Carroll, Catherine M. 02/04/63   02/07/63
Duffy, Mary died 11/14/65   11/16/65
Duffy, Mary A. married Kelly, William B. 04/11/64   04/20/64
Duffy, Thomas died 02/15/63   02/17/63
Dufur, George J. married Madden, Hannah M. 12/22/64   12/28/64
Dugan, James married Lennon, Rosa 01/17/64   02/13/64
Dugas, Anna Louisa (Mrs.) died 01/13/63   01/14/64
Duggan, Rose died 02/17/65   02/18/65
DuHamel, Mary E. married Moulton, James F., Jr. 08/06/63   08/12/63
Duhurst, Henry P. died 01/10/62   01/11/62
Duke, Augustus died 06/06/64   06/09/64
Duke, Martha V. died 12/06/63   12/08/63
Duke, William T. died 06/07/62   06/09/62
Dukehart, G. married Harmon, Lillie E. 04/02/65   04/04/65
Dukehart, George Dobbin married Coyle, Louisa Vinton 08/04/64   08/08/6
Dukehart, Isabella (Mrs.) died 10/17/63   10/20/63
Dukehart, Susan B. married Hanway, Franklin 10/17/61   10/18/61
Dukehart, Thomas M. (USN) married Krebs, Mary R. 11/12/63   11/14/63
Dukehart, William died no date 02/19/61
Dukes, Elizabeth died 12/09/61   12/12/61
Dukes, I. Reyner married Gould, M. Helen 06/09/64   06/16/64
Dukes, Lucy Ann died 04/02/61   04/05/61
Dulaney, Eliza J. married Tillery, John A. 02/19/65   02/24/65
Dulaney, William H. (Dr.) married Toldridge, Augusta A. 09/07/65
     09/11/65
Dulany, Eliza V. married Miller, Jacob H. 02/12/63   02/17/63
Dulany, Grafton L. died 05/20/63   05/21/63
Dulany, John died 08/13/62   08/14/62
Dulany, Olivia married Cushing, Robert M. 04/08/63   04/11/63
Duleany, Edward died 12/23/61   12/24/61
Duley, Sarah E. married Wells, James Z. 07/20/63   07/29/63
Dull, Elizabeth Ann died 04/07/64   04/09/64
Dull, Emma S. married Rutter, Andrew C. 11/05/63   11/17/63
Dull, Thomas H. died 08/31/64   09/02/64
Duma, Margaret died 09/25/62   09/26/62
Dumm, William T. married Bates, Ann 03/16/64   03/18/64
Dumphy, Edmond died 03/25/62   03/26/62
Dun, Elizabeth died 11/25/62   11/27/62
Dun, Ellen married McEwan, Hugh 10/00/00   01/17/61
Dunagan, Susan (Mrs.) died 05/07/63   05/08/63
Dunan, Laurette P. died 05/10/65   05/11/65
Dunbar, Fanny (Mrs.) died 07/02/64   07/11/64
Dunbar, Jane R. (Mrs.) married Dowden, Benjamin 02/26/63   05/07/63

Dunbracco, Maggie Vickers died 10/14/65 10/16/65
Duncan, Agnes died 09/13/63 09/15/63
Duncan, Agnes married Craig, Alexander 07/23/63 07/28/63
Duncan, Charles Henry died 03/24/64 03/26/64
Duncan, Eliza died 12/03/63 12/04/63
Duncan, Eliza (Mrs.) died 03/26/64 03/28/64
Duncan, Eliza J. married Deal, William C. 02/21/61 02/25/61
Duncan, Eliza R. died 09/24/61 11/26/61
Duncan, James G. died 09/25/61 09/30/61
Duncan, James George died 09/25/61 10/01/61
Duncan, James George died 09/25/61 10/02/61
Dungan, E. D. married Cornelius, J. W. (Rev.) 11/03/64 11/08/64
Dungan, Emily died 04/28/63 05/08/63
Dungan, Fannie died 04/28/65 05/01/65
Dungan, Susana married Snyder, John Henry 06/25/61 06/26/61
Dungan, Thomas M. (Cpt.) died no date 08/15/64
Dunham, Mary J. married King, Andrew 02/01/64 02/03/64
Dunhell, George B. died 02/19/65 02/22/65
Dunigan, Catherine Isabella died 10/20/63 11/18/63
Dunigan, Thomas A. died 07/01/62 07/02/62
Dunigan, William H. died 01/07/61 01/09/61
Dunigan, Willie died 04/08/62 04/10/62
Dunkell, Rebecca T. married Nicholson, Drew J. 09/21/65 09/23/65
Dunkerly, John died 06/11/64 06/13/64
Dunkle, Mary married Hoffman, Jacob 06/07/65 06/09/65
Dunlap, A. H. married Thompson, Kate 12/15/64 12/16/64
Dunlap, Carrie died 08/26/61 08/29/61
Dunlap, Charles Henry died 09/04/61 09/07/61
Dunlap, John married McCoy, Margaret 02/28/65 04/14/65
Dunlap, Mary Jane died 08/27/64 08/29/64
Dunlap, S. B. (Rev.) died 05/14/61 05/15/61
Dunlevy, M. Raphie married Sullivan, Thomas E. 07/02/61 07/04/61
Dunn, Ann (Mrs.) died 01/01/63 01/02/63
Dunn, Ann Maria married Jenkins, Busirus 06/29/65 07/01/65
Dunn, Catherine died 03/17/63 03/18/63
Dunn, Charles died 07/27/62 07/30/62
Dunn, Edward Klein died 09/05/62 09/16/62
Dunn, George W. died 06/16/61 06/17/61
Dunn, Hannah married Callaway, George F. 09/03/62 09/10/62
Dunn, Hannah married Thomas, Griffith 03/08/65 03/11/65
Dunn, James died 09/30/63 10/02/63
Dunn, Joseph married Kerner, Elizabeth Jane 01/01/62 01/08/62
Dunn, Josephine A. married Seibert, Newton W. 07/07/65 07/15/65
Dunn, Kate died 07/12/61 07/13/61
Dunn, Margaret died 04/26/65 04/29/65
Dunn, Mary Ellen died 01/07/63 01/08/63
Dunn, Mathilda A. married Bradyhouse, Thomas 10/31/64 11/01/64
Dunn, Matilda died 03/07/61 03/08/61
Dunn, Matthew died 07/25/65 07/26/65
Dunn, Michael married Garvey, Alice 01/01/63 01/09/63
Dunn, Robert died 02/22/61 02/23/61
Dunn, Susan H. married Ross, Robert Irvin 10/24/61 11/18/61
Dunn, Susanna married Smith, William 03/30/61 04/01/61
Dunn, Thomas died 04/20/64 04/21/64
Dunn, Veronica T. married Coulan, Drew J. 01/08/65 01/16/65

Dunnett, William married Hush, Sarah 10/12/65 10/16/65
Dunning, Ellen A. married Kuhlman, F. W. 08/02/64 08/08/64
Dunning, Joseph H. (Cpt.) married Barnes, M. Carrie 05/10/64 05/13/64
Dunning, William S. died 07/30/65 08/01/65
Dunnock, Eliza Jane married Johnson, C. W. 11/02/65 11/11/65
Dunnock, Sarah E. married Bullen, William W. 06/22/65 06/24/65
Dunphy, Mary died 07/16/64 07/19/64
Dunsmore, Kate died 06/05/64 06/06/64
Dunster, Fanny Ann died 08/01/61 08/02/61
Dupliex, Clara died 05/03/62 05/06/62
DuPont, Alexis married Coleman, Leighton 07/30/61 08/01/61
Dupre, Frank married Rogesen, Ann 05/12/62 05/14/62
Duran, Garret V. died 08/28/63 09/01/63
Durand, Eliza R. married Jackson, James W. 12/26/64 12/28/64
Durand, John Edwin died 08/12/61 08/13/61
Durborrow, Sidney D. died 12/16/64 03/29/65
Durding, Leander A. married Cousins, Mary E. 01/04/62 01/08/62
Durham, David married Harker, Mary (Mrs.) 04/05/64 04/13/64
Durham, Dorcas died 05/29/62 06/03/62
Durham, James married Deacon, Edith Harriet 11/15/64 11/18/64
Durham, James E. died 04/05/64 06/14/64
Durham, Jerome married Coffman, Mary V. 01/08/65 01/18/65
Durham, Lewis Oliver died 04/11/64 04/12/64
Durham, Martha L. married Feast, L. 04/08/65 04/18/65
Durham, Mina married Baker, William 01/31/65 02/02/65
Durham, Zacharias died 01/27/65 01/31/65
Durhan, Mary (Mrs.) died 08/31/63 09/05/63
Durhm, Mary E. (Mrs.) died 05/21/64 05/23/64
Durkes, John H. married Bigger, Margaret Jane 04/14/64 04/19/64
Durkin, Ellen died 11/14/62 11/15/62
Durnell, Frances T. died 05/17/64 05/19/64
Durr, Charles L. married Stewart, Isabella 08/10/63 08/18/63
Durrell, Charles married Falls, Letitia M. 09/08/63 09/09/63
Durrenberger, Christian died 01/04/65 01/06/65
Dushane, Anna M. married Hynson, William George 02/28/65 03/03/65
Dushane, John died 07/06/61 07/08/61
Dushane, John died 04/19/64 04/20/64
Dushane, Nathan T. (Col.) died 08/21/64 08/24/64
Dushane, Stuart Caldwell died 06/26/61 06/29/61
Dushane, V. married Harwood, Louise V. 10/10/65 10/14/65
Dutrow, Emma L. married Downs, S. Dickinson 09/22/61 12/28/61
Dutrow, Emma Olevia died 06/25/61 06/28/61
Dutrow, Emma V. died 05/03/61 05/04/61
Dutrow, Ida Bell died 09/29/63 10/01/63
Duttan, Charles married Hicks, Sarah 04/20/65 04/22/65
Dutten, Robert J. died 03/28/65 04/14/65
Dutton, Annie Virginia died 06/03/64 06/06/64
Dutton, Belle M. died 08/03/63 08/04/63
Dutton, Belle M. died no date 08/05/63
Dutton, Elizabeth Galt died 03/05/62 03/13/62
Dutton, Fannie G. married Reisdorph, S. A. 09/27/64 10/03/64
Dutton, Frederick W. married Burneston, Louisa A. 08/30/64 09/05/64
Dutton, John Robert died 08/18/64 09/03/64
Dutton, Nannie J. married Stidham, J. F. (Rev,) 06/28/64 06/30/64
Duval, C. P. married Hyde, Mary 12/16/62 01/19/63

Duval, Mary married Jenkins, J. W. 07/16/61 07/18/61
Duval, Peter married Hess, Delia Estelle 06/05/61 06/06/61
Duval, Rena R. married Pettinos, J. W. (Dr.) 03/08/63 03/26/63
Duval, Sarah died 10/04/64 10/15/64
Duvall, A. T. Hawkins died 07/19/62 07/26/62
Duvall, A. T. Hawkins died 07/19/62 07/31/62
Duvall, Anne Maria (Mrs.) died 02/10/65 02/22/65
Duvall, Archibald died 02/09/63 02/10/63
Duvall, Basil died 03/20/62 03/26/62
Duvall, Catharine died 08/25/64 09/01/64
Duvall, Charles died 10/18/62 10/22/62
Duvall, Charles married Tucker, Florence E. 06/16/63 06/25/63
Duvall, Charles S. married Baldwin, Mollie A. 01/31/62 02/15/62
Duvall, Eli died 08/09/61 08/10/61
Duvall, Ella married Freeland, Edward H. 04/11/63 04/14/63
Duvall, Emma Gertrude died 01/25/62 01/27/62
Duvall, Emma Inglehart died 04/08/63 04/09/63
Duvall, Frank died 03/14/65 03/21/65
Duvall, Lemuele died 01/26/62 01/27/62
Duvall, Lemuele died 01/26/62 01/28/62
Duvall, Lucy A. married Bernard, Richard 11/26/63 12/10/63
Duvall, Maria died 03/16/62 04/12/62
Duvall, Mary E. married Heath, Charles L. 09/08/62 09/29/62
Duvall, Mary E. married Sangston, George E. 01/20/63 01/28/63
Duvall, Mary Eugenia married Bunting, William 12/23/62 12/25/62
Duvall, Sallie P. married Hammond, Charles V. 06/10/62 06/12/62
Duvall, Sarah (Mrs.) died 10/04/64 10/31/64
Duvall, Thomas married Todd, Patience Ann 06/20/62 07/04/62
Duvall, Thomas Franklin died 05/13/62 05/14/62
Duvall, Thomas J. married Eagleston, Sarah Frances 09/16/62 09/19/62
Duvall, V. B. married Webb, Mary C. 10/10/65 10/14/65
Duvall, W. B. W. died 09/26/62 10/11/62
Duvall, William Fensley died 07/18/64 07/19/64
Duvall, William J. married Fisher, Sarah E. 06/16/64 06/20/64
Duvall, William W. married Thomson, Jane Kerr 03/31/64 04/16/64
Duwees, George W. died 10/28/61 10/30/61
Duyer, Albert married Tucker, Susan R. 01/02/65 01/11/65
Duyer, Cyrus married Sheckells, Catharine 05/02/64 05/04/64
Duyer, Mary (Mrs.) died 02/09/63 02/11/63
Dwyer, James died 06/23/61 06/25/61
Dwyer, Laura L. married Fout, George C. 07/19/65 07/22/65
Dwyer, Mathew died 08/16/64 08/20/64
Dyer, Charles Franklin died 12/14/65 12/16/65
Dyer, Julia Ann (Mrs.) died 03/02/64 03/03/64
Dyer, Levin married Gaines, Lear Ann 04/16/63 04/18/63
Dyer, Mary died 08/01/65 08/02/65
Dyer, Mary died 08/01/65 08/03/65
Dyer, Sarah Lizzie died 09/18/63 09/19/63
Dyer, William R. died 10/04/63 10/08/63
Dykes, Mary A. died 01/08/61 01/15/61
Dyser, Mathias died 08/20/61 08/30/61
Eachus, Elizabeth J. died 06/17/61 06/18/61
Eager, Julia O. married Barrow, Thomas 09/07/62 09/10/62
Eaggleston, Elizabeth died 01/27/62 01/29/62
Eagleston, Abraim married Meade, Mary C. 01/01/61 01/03/61

Eagleston, Marion Virginia married Seebold, Philip D. 01/05/63   01/20/
Eagleston, Sarah Frances married Duvall, Thomas J. 09/16/62   09/19/62
Eagleston, Sariah A. (Mrs.) died 12/27/65   12/28/65
Eagleston, Sariah A. (Mrs.) died 12/27/65   12/29/65
Eakle, Hiram S. died 02/14/63   02/17/63
Ealey, William H. married Briscoe, Mary A. 10/24/61   10/25/61
Eames, Mary Augusta died 08/03/64   08/04/64
Earechson, Mary Jane died 02/13/65   02/14/65
Eareckson, C. Federal married Cole, Harriet 11/26/62   12/01/62
Eareckson, Mollie J. died 06/13/65   06/16/65
Eareckson, R. A. (Dr.) married Rose, E. Sophia 11/21/61   11/28/61
Earhart, George W., Jr. married Lepper, Lucy 12/15/64   12/17/64
Earhart, Hadie M. married Walker, Thomas S. 04/21/64   04/22/64
Earhart, Harry Lee died 03/29/61   04/02/61
Earicks, Antoinette Eliza died 10/29/65   11/13/65
Earicks, Robert Charles died 10/25/65   11/13/65
Earland, Francis died 11/29/62   12/01/62
Earle, Henry married Norfolk, Mary A. 01/03/65   01/05/65
Earle, Mary J. married Maker, John K. 09/04/62   09/09/62
Earlougher, Henson died 02/19/65   02/22/65
Earlougher, Josephine married Hendley, James D. 12/12/63   12/24/63
Earlougher, Sarah (Mrs.) died 10/30/63   11/06/63
Early, Annie Oswald died 09/20/65   09/21/65
Early, John D., Jr. married Rieman, Martha G. 04/27/65   04/29/65
Early, Mary E. married Goble, Edward A. 08/22/64   08/24/64
Earnest, Rachel died 11/21/61   11/22/61
Earns, Mary Ann married Hess, Joseph 09/28/65   09/29/65
Earp, Albert Long died 01/04/63   01/10/63
Earp, David Amos Henry died 05/28/62   05/29/62
Earp, Marion Monkia died 10/21/62   10/24/62
Earwicker, Mary A. died 05/21/61   05/25/61
East, Caleb J. married Keirie, Marion Annie 07/11/64   07/14/64
East, Henry married Mark, Mary 06/16/64   06/18/64
East, Mary Ann died 10/27/61   10/28/61
East, Mary Ann (Mrs.) died 10/02/63   10/03/63
Easter, A. M. married Bremer, Henry 05/09/61   05/22/61
Easter, Hamilton married Haviland, Anna 07/23/61   07/26/61
Easter, James H. married Mortimer, Mary W. 06/12/62   06/13/62
Easter, John died 07/26/64   09/19/64
Easter, Mary A. died 11/08/61   11/11/61
Easter, Mortimer died 06/27/64   06/28/64
Easter, Sarah Elizabeth (Mrs.) died 12/20/64   12/24/64
Easterly, Elizabeth A. (Mrs.) married Gray, Stephen 08/24/63   09/02/63
Eastman, Annie Mary died 11/15/65   11/16/65
Eastman, Henry William died 06/07/65   06/08/65
Eastman, L. M. (M.D.) married Gormley, Mary A. 09/23/62   10/10/62
Eastman, Lewis Alvin died 08/11/65   08/12/65
Eastmond, Maria married Bruce, Robert 04/11/62   05/13/62
Easton, Charles P. died 01/19/64   02/04/64
Easton, Howard A. died 08/29/62   09/30/62
Eastwood, Anna married Henderson, Arthur B. 12/06/62   12/11/62
Eaton, Ellenor (Mrs.) died 05/30/64   06/01/64
Eaton, Maggie E. married Smith, John H. 02/11/63   04/04/63
Eaverson, G. W. married Wilcox, Cora L. 07/25/61   08/17/61
Eaverson, George W. died 10/25/64   10/26/64

```
Eaverson, J. Harry Shyrock died 06/28/65  06/29/65
Ebaugh, Francis A. married Cox, Julyelma S. 06/26/62  07/07/62
Ebaugh, Mary married Stambaugh, Henry 03/27/62  04/01/62
Ebaugh, Sallie T. married Bolgiano, Frank W. 09/27/64  10/03/64
Eberhart, Charles W. married Hewett, Virginia 02/10/61  02/13/61
Eberhart, Frederick, Jr. died 10/05/64  11/12/64
Ebert, Ann A. (Mrs.) died 03/03/63  03/05/63
Ebert, Anne A. (Mrs.) died 03/03/63  03/04/63
Ebrman, Sarah E. (Mrs.) died 06/17/63  06/18/63
Ebston, Sallie E. died 12/27/64  12/31/64
Ebsworth, Charles Thomas died 12/01/64  12/03/64
Ebsworth, David married Crisp, Georgianna 12/26/61  12/31/61
Ebsworth, Maria Myring died 01/18/61  01/22/61
Eccleston, Charles E. married Grape, Maggie E. A. 10/15/63  10/17/63
Eccleston, Robert E. (Sgt.) married Burks, Mary E. 05/03/63  05/06/63
Eckel, William J. married Graham, Mary 04/24/62  07/24/62
Ecker, John T. died 02/03/62  02/11/62
Eckert, Missouri married Conn, George 05/01/64  05/07/64
Eckert, William Charles died 03/22/63  03/23/63
Eckharat, Katharine died 01/16/62  01/18/62
Eckhardt, Louisa P. married Burns, John H. 04/23/63  04/25/63
Eckhardt, T. Conrad married Gunther, Sophie 06/29/62  07/04/62
Eckhardt, William married Ackler, M. A. 12/29/64  01/02/65
Eckhart, Elizabeth died 09/07/62  09/09/62
Eckles, Elizabeth (Mrs.) married Morrison, Parker 10/23/64  10/26/64
Eckman, William died 03/02/62  03/03/62
Edds, Isaac married Patterson, Martha 10/18/63  10/20/63
Eddy, Mary (Mrs.) died 04/15/64  04/16/64
Edel, Josiah died 05/22/64  05/23/64
Edelen, James married Iglehart, Mary E. 11/16/65  11/21/65
Edelman, John F. married Hauper, Mary A. (Mrs.) 09/03/63  09/05/63
Eden, Ella D. G. married Wilkerson, Albert F. 01/19/65  01/24/65
Eden, Jane (Mrs.) died 02/22/65  03/03/65
Edes, Samuel C. died 01/20/65  01/23/65
Edes, William H. died 01/17/65  01/19/65
Edes, William H. died 01/17/65  01/20/65
Edgar, James Thomas died 08/13/62  08/14/62
Edgar, William died 06/26/63  07/01/63
Edmonds, John Milton died 12/24/61  01/13/62
Edmonds, Lily Taylor died 04/23/63  04/24/63
Edmonds, Rebecca A. (Mrs.) died 04/27/64  04/28/64
Edmonds, Samuel married Pouder, Julia C. 10/15/63  10/21/63
Edmonds, William Shannon died 06/23/65  06/24/65
Edmondson, Horace L. died 05/01/64  05/03/64
Edmondson, Mary married Steuart, Thomas E. 10/15/64  11/05/64
Edmonson, Ellen Jane died 01/12/61  01/14/61
Edmonson, John died 04/10/61  04/13/61
Edmonson, Martha Ellen died 11/30/65  12/22/65
Edmonston, Americus died 06/20/62  06/24/62
Edmunds, Mary D. (Mrs.) died 12/24/64  12/26/64
Edmunds, Mary L. married Frush, Moreau F. (Dr.) 05/16/64  05/18/64
Edwards, Amanda M. married Battee, Joshua W. 11/30/64  12/14/64
Edwards, Avarilla died 06/21/65  06/22/65
Edwards, Charles H. married Baker, Amanda 01/18/65  02/07/65
Edwards, Charles R. married Mety, Annie M. 03/10/63  03/12/63
```

Edwards, Charlotte married Stepney, William 10/08/63   10/10/63
Edwards, Edward J. married Chambers, Clara B. 11/24/64   11/29/64
Edwards, Frances T. married Barron, John 03/01/64   03/03/64
Edwards, Joseph Francis died 06/04/62   05/11/62
Edwards, Laura Virginia died 01/25/64   01/27/64
Edwards, Lizzie died 08/20/61   08/22/61
Edwards, Maggie died 01/01/62   01/03/62
Edwards, Mary Alice married Wilson, John A. 11/23/65   11/24/65
Edwards, Mary E. (Mrs.) married Dorsey, Samuel A. 11/01/64   11/03/64
Edwards, Mary Helen died 11/13/65   11/15/65
Edwards, Nettie Foster died 05/01/64   05/03/64
Edwards, Richard married Brown, Rebecca 06/14/64   06/16/64
Edwards, Richard G. married McLean, Mary E. 11/07/61   11/13/61
Edwards, Richard William died 06/06/64   06/07/64
Edwards, Robert H. M. died 01/27/63   01/28/63
Edwards, Samuel married Hawkins, Mary E. 12/03/63   12/05/63
Edwards, Samuel M. died 11/05/63   11/07/63
Edwards, Sanford married Brown, Hester J. 03/06/64   03/08/64
Edwards, Sarah died 12/18/61   12/20/61
Edwards, Sarah A. married Bobart, Thomas W. 02/03/61   02/05/61
Edwards, Sarah Ann married Smith, Edward 12/11/62   12/13/62
Edwards, Sarah C. married Slee, Joseph 03/06/64   03/09/64
Edwards, States married Battee, Honoria 10/25/65   11/04/65
Edwards, Susan married Gray, Thomas 11/18/64   11/19/64
Edwards, Thomas died 05/05/64   08/09/64
Edwards, Thomas B. married Robinson, Matilda E. 07/02/63   07/07/63
Edwards, Thomas J. died 09/23/63   12/07/63
Edwards, Thomas J. married Harryman, Mary E. 06/01/64   10/06/64
Effingham, George died 09/06/62   09/12/62
Egan, James married Hallauhan, Hanorah 11/06/64   11/08/64
Egan, Michael married McDermott, Mary 04/05/63   04/08/63
Egan, Thomas died 06/14/65   06/15/65
Egan, William J. married Walter, Annie M. 04/13/64   04/20/64
Ege, A. G. married Raite, Lizzie E. 10/29/63   10/30/63
Ege, Michael M. died 04/17/64   04/21/64
Egen, Thomas died 08/02/63   08/03/63
Egerton, Julia C. married Semmes, Robert D. 02/21/61   02/23/61
Egerton, Lela Virginia died 11/26/65   11/27/65
Egerton, William A. married Sanderson, Ellen 02/10/61   02/18/61
Egeston, Charles Calvert died 05/27/62   05/28/62
Egger, Anna Elizabeth died 12/17/64   12/19/64
Egger, Pauline died 05/27/61   05/28/61
Eggleston, Benjamin died 12/03/64   12/08/64
Eggleston, Frances S. died 05/12/62   05/21/62
Eggleston, Jane died 03/07/64   03/12/64
Eglinton, Elizabeth died 03/24/65   03/25/65
Ehlen, John H. died 01/08/64   01/09/64
Ehlers, A. Giles (Mrs.) died 01/12/64   01/13/64
Ehlers, John D. married Gravenstine, Donna E. 12/16/65   12/20/65
Ehlers, Lizzie A. died 09/14/65   09/20/65
Ehlers, Mary C. died 01/21/62   01/22/62
Ehlies, Ella died 09/05/63   09/08/63
Ehlies, J. Henry married Neely, Maggie 06/25/61   07/10/61
Ehlies, W. Henry married Neely, Maggie 06/25/61   07/11/61
Ehrhard, Albert N. died 12/20/63   12/21/63

Ehrhart, Annie R. married Gardner, Augustus M. 09/02/62   09/04/62
Ehrman, Charles H. married Carson, Henrietta M. 12/19/65   12/25/65
Ehrman, Priscilla (Mrs.) died 08/13/63   08/14/63
Ehrmer, John P. died 07/05/64   07/06/64
Eicheberger, Thomas S. married Lee, Mary E. 10/08/63   10/10/63
Eichelberger, Burdie died 08/24/65   08/26/65
Eichelberger, Eccleston married Andrew, Sophie B. 05/19/64   05/24/64
Eichelberger, Frank T. married Tolsin, Alice C. 05/20/64   05/23/64
Eichelberger, Frank T. married Tolson, Alice G. C. 05/20/64   05/24/64
Eichelberger, Itie died 06/14/63   06/16/63
Eichelberger, John W. married Huratty, Rosa 06/25/63   06/27/63
Eichelberger, Nannie died 05/01/63   05/04/63
Eichelberger, Robert died 06/04/65   06/05/65
Eichelberger, Sarah W. (Mrs.) died 03/06/64   03/08/64
Eichelberger, Willie died 04/17/61   04/18/61
Eichman, J. C. married Marden, Rosana 05/29/62   05/31/62
Eichner, Charles died 03/30/63   03/31/63
Eichner, Lottie R. died 08/16/64   08/18/64
Eichner, William C. died 05/14/64   08/18/64
Eickel, Harry died 01/25/64   01/26/64
Eickel, Mary Regina died 04/20/65   04/21/65
Eickhoff, Theodore died 08/02/63   08/03/63
Eigelberner, John William died 01/20/65   01/23/65
Eigelberner, Mary Ann (Mrs.) died 03/31/65   04/01/65
Eillinger, Catherine A. married Gaver, George E. 06/06/65   06/10/65
Einhorn, Mary married Williams, George M. 01/18/64   01/20/64
Einstein, Meyer died 05/14/63   05/16/63
Eisel, Amanda (Mrs.) died 09/12/64   09/14/64
Eisenbrandt, M. Katarina died 09/13/61   09/14/61
Eisenhardt, Willie Wigley died 07/04/63   07/07/63
Eisenhart, John married Weigley, Katherine 12/20/60   01/04/61
Eisler, Margaret A. died 06/09/63   06/10/63
Elbert, Margaret married Morgan, George 10/23/62   10/25/62
Elder, Clay married Brainard, Rufus A. 02/09/65   03/06/65
Elder, Francis S. died 10/16/61   10/18/61
Elder, Harry Owen died 09/27/63   09/30/63
Elder, John H. married Carper, Mary L. 02/28/65   04/12/65
Elder, John J. died 12/06/65   12/07/65
Elder, Margaretta M. married Moale, Henry 10/28/62   11/01/62
Elder, Rachel Amelia died 05/02/64   05/04/64
Elder, Robert Franklin died 05/19/64   05/25/64
Elder, Sarah F. married Wittig, John H. 08/23/64   08/26/64
Elder, William Henry died 10/31/65   11/01/65
Elder, Zachariah married Croshaw, Mary A. 10/31/61   11/02/61
Elderkin, James W. died 11/18/63   11/19/63
Eldridge, Willie died no date   01/03/61
Elems, Ann Mariah died 11/09/62   11/12/62
Elfresh, Laura V. married Price, Levi 02/19/63   02/21/63
Elkins, Charles H. married Linthicum, Sarah C. 12/04/64   12/08/64
Ellander, Benjamin died 05/25/65   06/27/65
Ellen, Mary married Henry, James 08/27/61   08/28/61
Ellender, Charity died 12/30/61   01/01/62
Ellender, Charity died 12/30/61   01/02/62
Ellicott, B. H. died 09/27/63   09/30/63
Ellicott, Samuel married Duck, Sarah E. 09/18/62   09/23/62

Ellingsworth, William died 07/28/62 07/29/62
Elliot, George W. married Kerr, Ann 03/07/65 04/05/65
Elliot, Laura L. died 09/24/61 09/26/61
Elliot, William F. died 04/21/62 05/19/62
Elliot, William T. married Sanderson, Rachel E. 02/21/61 03/23/61
Elliott, A. James married Miller, Emma V. 10/27/64 11/01/64
Elliott, A. V. (Maj.) married Hayes, Ada H. 02/23/65 02/28/65
Elliott, Catherine died 02/05/65 02/06/65
Elliott, Catherine died 02/05/65 02/06/65
Elliott, Eleanor died 11/07/64 11/08/64
Elliott, Eleanor died 11/07/64 11/09/64
Elliott, Eliza married Shurtter, George 01/23/63 11/20/63
Elliott, Elizabeth died 03/22/61 03/23/61
Elliott, Elizabeth died 05/09/62 05/12/62
Elliott, Elizabeth A. (Mrs.) died 05/02/64 05/04/64
Elliott, George Gilbert died 05/30/64 05/31/64
Elliott, Grace Beauregard died 08/20/64 08/24/64
Elliott, Henrietta married Boche, Charles M. 08/03/64 08/04/64
Elliott, Jane died 04/10/61 04/12/61
Elliott, John married Biggs, Mary 10/11/65 10/14/65
Elliott, Josephine married Keepner, Elijah 06/17/65 06/21/65
Elliott, Josephine E. married Keepner, Elijah 06/17/65 06/20/65
Elliott, Julia A. married Stone, William E. 06/13/65 06/15/65
Elliott, Kate E. died 08/11/65 08/12/65
Elliott, Laura H. married Walker, George F. 11/27/62 12/01/62
Elliott, Laura V. married Jackson, Charles R. no date 09/16/65
Elliott, Margaret E. married Green, John R. 11/21/63 12/05/63
Elliott, Margaret J. married Langlois, H. C. 09/05/65 09/29/65
Elliott, Mary Ann Reside died 01/31/61 02/02/61
Elliott, Mary Ann Reside died 01/31/61 02/11/61
Elliott, Mary Catherine died 09/20/64 09/23/64
Elliott, Mary Ellen married Verlanders, Daniel 01/01/61 01/28/61
Elliott, Millard Fillmore died 05/25/65 05/26/65
Elliott, Sarah married White, Daniel 06/26/64 06/28/64
Elliott, Sarah J. married Williams, George W. 11/29/63 12/08/63
Elliott, Thomas C. died 12/07/61 12/09/61
Elliott, Wilhelmina married Todd, John W. 12/11/65 12/13/65
Elliott, William B. died 12/08/63 12/09/63
Elliott, William Charles died 01/16/62 01/17/62
Elliott, William Edward died 08/10/64 08/15/64
Elliott, William Edward died 08/11/64 08/16/64
Elliott, William H. died 05/13/64 05/14/64
Elliott, William H. married Uhler, Sarah A. 12/26/65 12/30/65
Elliott, William H. N. married Sheeler, Cordelia A. 10/26/65 11/01/65
Elliott, William S. died 01/25/61 01/26/61
Ellis, Charles N. married Campbell, Eliza 02/13/62 02/14/62
Ellis, James A. (Lt.) married Willis, Georgeanna 11/11/61 02/25/62
Ellis, James N. married McDonnell, Susan Jane 05/06/62 05/21/62
Ellis, Kate married Franklin, Benjamin H. 05/27/64 06/02/64
Ellis, Kate M. married Armstrong, John H. 04/26/63 05/02/63
Ellis, Mary E. married Burt, A. P. 09/03/61 09/10/61
Ellis, Sarah (Mrs.) died 04/15/65 04/18/65
Ellis, Sarah Catherine died 05/10/63 05/12/63
Ellis, Sarah Ellen died 10/15/65 10/16/65
Ellis, William H. died 10/04/64 10/28/64

```
Ellis, Willis Albert died 02/25/64    02/27/64
Ellsworth, Clara died 11/26/62    11/27/62
Ellsworth, Elmer died 07/10/62    07/11/62
Ellsworth, Fannie died 06/17/62    06/20/62
Ellsworth, George Washington died 06/14/62    06/17/62
Ellsworth, Mary Myring died 01/18/61    01/21/61
Ellsworth, William died 03/12/65    03/14/65
Elmer, Elizabeth (Mrs.) died 10/31/65    11/02/65
Elmer, J. C. (Dr.) died 10/16/63    11/10/63
Elmer, Susan Marian died 08/05/61    08/19/61
Elmer, William S. married Addison, Mary E. 04/05/65    05/06/65
Elmer, William S. married Addison, Mary Lizzie 04/05/65    05/09/65
Elmes, Thomas married Emory, Jane 04/05/65    04/06/65
Elseroad, Susan died 05/09/61    05/11/61
Elsroad, Lennie married Ott, George F. 01/31/61    04/05/61
Elsworth, Isabella died 01/27/63    01/29/63
Elton, Mary Elizabeth died 04/21/63    04/22/63
Elton, Mary Elizabeth died 04/21/63    04/23/63
Ely, Caroline married Rentz, George F. 11/30/65    12/04/65
Ely, Fannie married Chestnut, Washington R. 12/30/62    01/02/63
Ely, Hugh (Gen.) died 12/14/62    12/16/62
Ely, James Henry died 09/16/63    09/17/63
Ely, John B. married Coleman, Leonora 09/03/62    09/10/62
Ely, John C. (Col.) died 11/20/64    11/21/64
Ely, John C. (Col.) died 11/20/64    11/22/64
Ely, Laura Jane married Fales, Nathaniel A. 05/13/62    05/16/62
Ely, Margaret M. (Mrs.) died 04/03/65    04/04/65
Ely, Mary Elizabeth married Weber, George H. 05/04/63    05/07/63
Ely, Mary Jane married Noyes, Henry 11/19/61    11/21/61
Ely, Thomas died 02/24/62    03/03/62
Ely, William died 06/14/62    06/17/62
Emerich, John married Kerr, Catherine 03/20/64    03/21/64
Emerich, Lewis married Bornheim, Hannah 11/13/64    11/15/64
Emerick, Thomas H. married Hall, Carrie 02/16/64    02/19/64
Emerine, Susan died 07/19/64    07/21/64
Emerson, Jane Watson died 06/30/61    07/20/61
Emerson, S. Lizzie married Barton, William N. 12/14/65    12/18/65
Emerson, Sophia Elizabeth married Vollow, William H. 03/29/64    04/07/64
Emerson, W. L. married Smith, S. A. 06/21/63    06/26/63
Emerson, William died 03/26/64    03/28/64
Emery, Elizabeth married Trimble, William P. 01/01/61    01/02/61
Emery, Eva V. married Gray, Edward 12/26/61    12/31/61
Emery, Lizzie J. married Burrough, Edward E. 12/27/64    12/30/64
Emery, Sallie Armitage died 07/26/62    07/28/62
Emge, John married Harrers, Barbara 01/18/63    01/20/63
Emich, Andrew H. died 12/29/63    12/30/63
Emich, Peter died 03/04/61    03/06/61
Emich, Peter died 03/04/61    03/07/61
Emmart, Ann (Mrs.) died 02/19/65    02/21/65
Emmart, Edith Boyston died 08/19/65    08/21/65
Emmart, George died 11/12/65    11/13/65
Emmart, Henry died 06/22/61    07/01/61
Emmart, John married Simmering, Delphine 03/12/63    04/28/63
Emmart, Mary died 03/15/65    03/17/65
Emmart, Sarah (Mrs.) died 01/05/63    01/06/63
```

```
Emmelrich, John W. died no date   10/27/65
Emmert, A. D. married Shaw, Laura 02/10/64   02/16/64
Emmert, George died 11/12/65   11/14/65
Emmert, John Samuel died 06/11/65   06/12/65
Emmert, William Wirt died 10/07/65   10/11/65
Emmich, Thomas S. died 05/01/64   05/02/64
Emory, A. Walsh (Dr.) died 04/09/65   04/10/65
Emory, Ann (Mrs.) died 08/11/64   08/13/64
Emory, Anna Berry died 01/26/61   01/31/61
Emory, Anna M. (Mrs.) died 02/03/64   02/22/64
Emory, Arthur married Kirby, Mary Gordon 01/17/65   01/18/65
Emory, Campbell Dallas married Tilton, Clara 12/29/64   01/02/65
Emory, Elijah died 08/30/62   09/22/62
Emory, Hannah Kate died 12/16/62   01/08/63
Emory, Isabel married Emory, John R. 12/20/64   01/05/65
Emory, Jacob married Malory, Gruey 08/10/65   08/11/65
Emory, Jane married Elmes, Thomas 04/05/65   04/06/65
Emory, John R. married Emory, Isabel 12/20/64   01/05/65
Emory, Mary A. W. married Murray, J. Thomas (Rev.) 06/14/64   06/21/64
Emory, Mary Juliet married Burrough, Horace 06/06/65   06/09/65
Emory, Oram died 02/13/64   02/22/64
Emory, Samuel William died no date   11/14/62
Emory, Sarah Hood died 09/22/61   09/28/61
Emory, T. Lane married Holmes, Selda 11/03/64   11/14/64
Emrich, Elizabeth (Mrs.) died 07/28/64   07/29/64
Emrick, Mollie C. died 12/25/62   12/27/62
Emrier, John died 06/26/63   06/27/63
Endley, Francis died 09/10/65   09/11/65
Eney, Benjamin F. died 05/10/61   05/11/61
Engel, Daniel married Zile, Thirza Ann 10/22/63   10/24/63
Engel, Kate married Wittig, Frederick W. 09/12/65   09/15/65
Engel, Minnie A. married Kennedy, John J. 04/16/65   07/19/65
Engelinger, Isabella married Lieberman, Lewis 10/12/64   10/13/64
Engels, Charity died 06/01/65   06/03/65
England, Annie J. married Cavanaugh, Charles M. 05/19/64   05/23/64
England, Mary E. married Smith, Eli 12/08/64   12/14/64
England, Richard died 10/02/64   09/06/65
England, Susan J. married Holland, Oliver S. 12/15/63   01/09/64
Englebach, Annie married Melchior, Louis 08/04/64   08/08/64
Englehart, D. married Dean, Sarah P. 11/04/61   12/24/61
Englehart, Moses died 05/30/62   06/12/62
Englemeyer, Isabelle married Lieberman, Louis 10/12/64   11/15/64
Engler, Augustus C. married Newman, Elizabeth A. 02/14/61   02/19/61
Englert, Philip married Newmyer, Mary J. 11/12/65   11/16/65
Engles, Harriet died 07/26/65   07/28/65
English, James died 06/22/61   06/25/61
English, Mary Ann (Mrs.) died 04/27/65   04/28/65
English, Mary Ann (Mrs.) died 04/27/65   04/29/65
English, Ramuel R. married Gosdon, Sallie 08/27/62   09/09/62
Ennalls, John W. died 11/30/63   12/01/63
Ennalls, Laura married Gore, S. R. 02/26/63   03/31/63
Ennis, Elizabeth (Mrs.) died 06/10/64   06/11/64
Ennis, George married White, Maria Jane 04/06/65   04/08/65
Ennis, Mary Amelia died 11/15/63   11/17/63
Ennis, Matilda E. married Nevin, Thomas 09/26/61   12/28/61
```

Ennis, Susan L. (Mrs.) died 12/11/64   12/13/64
Ennis, Terresa married How, William 09/20/63   09/22/63
Enright, Mary married Shanahan, Martin 09/24/63   09/26/63
Enright, Willie Ernest died 07/29/64   08/02/64
Ensey, Catherine Virginia died 06/18/62   06/20/62
Ensey, Jacob Norris died 02/25/65   02/27/65
Ensey, Lot died 08/20/64   08/22/64
Ensey, Marcellus P. married Knight, Annie E. 10/08/62   10/16/62
Ensley, Samuel Smith R. died 09/12/61   09/13/61
Ensley, William A. died 11/10/65   11/13/65
Ensor, Arabella Ensor died 10/11/65   10/18/65
Ensor, Daniel A. married Carr, Eliza A. 07/18/65   07/20/65
Ensor, Elizabeth died 05/07/61   05/09/61
Ensor, Franklin A. died 11/08/61   11/10/63
Ensor, John Franklin died 07/30/64   08/03/64
Ensor, Lizzie Jane died 06/07/65   06/08/65
Ensor, Luke C. married Gorsuch, Artage (Mrs.) 10/18/64   10/20/64
Ensor, Mary Ann married Gillingham, James 04/21/61   08/17/61
Ensor, Thomas E. married Wise, Mary T. 01/01/61   01/08/61
Ensor, Washington G. (Pvt.) died 01/00/00   03/22/65
Entwisle, Jennie married Wilson, Albert A. 06/01/61   05/29/62
Entz, Andrew married Orrick, Mollie A. 11/22/65   11/24/65
Entz, Lizzia A. married Glocker, Emanuel J. 12/01/64   12/05/64
Entz, Williamina T. married Miles, Charles M. 06/05/62   06/11/62
Eppley, Julius A. married Sumwalt, Margaret A. 01/28/61   02/02/61
Epron, John Lewis died 06/29/65   06/30/65
Erben, Franklin H. died 09/13/63   09/15/63
Erdman, Catherine Virginia died 12/29/63   12/31/63
Erdman, Catherine Virginia died 12/29/63   01/01/64
Erdman, Isabella Reid died 12/04/63   12/05/63
Erdman, Mary Ann died 06/23/64   06/24/64
Erdman, Mary Louisa died 04/03/63   04/06/63
Erdman, Matthias died 04/28/64   04/29/64
Erek, Charles Winfield died 07/05/64   07/06/64
Erkridge, J. Emory married Halbert, Lizzie 04/06/63   04/07/63
Ermy, Alonzo married Wilson, Mary A. 02/14/61   02/19/61
Ermy, Sermena married Scott, Robert 08/09/64   08/11/64
Ernest, Catharine died 10/09/62   10/11/62
Ernest, Charlotte died 09/28/63   10/02/63
Erney, Mary Theresa died 10/02/62   10/17/62
Erskine, Romulus Riggs died 05/20/63   05/26/63
Ertingen, Baron Otto DeLeutrum married France, Emma 04/24/62   05/15/62
Ervin, George Washington died 08/23/61   08/28/61
Eschbach, E. R. married Doll, Sue M. 11/09/64   11/11/64
Eschbach, Francis F. married Herbstritt, Josephine 10/16/63   10/27/63
Eschbach, Harry Beauregard died 07/18/62   07/22/62
Eschbach, Louis A. married Courtois, Clementine 10/11/65   10/12/65
Eschbach, Margaret V. married Ohlendorf, William G. 10/11/65   10/12/65
Eschbach, Mary Thresia married Ohlendorf, Joseph C. 09/24/61   09/25/61
Esenhart, John August married Mockhoff, Catherine 03/09/63   03/16/63
Eskridge, M. W. married Newton, J. W. (Capt.) 02/14/61   02/19/61
Eslin, Sarah E, (Mrs.) died 08/20/63   08/21/63
Espey, Edward A. Slicer died 07/30/64   08/01/64
Espey, Eliza married Armstrong, William 08/29/61   09/17/61
Espey, Hannah died 10/04/63   10/05/63

Espey, John died 08/03/63   08/04/63
Espey, Kate Ellsworth died 08/08/64   08/18/64
Espey, Rebecca Ann died 02/23/61   02/25/61
Espy, Ella Sherman died 09/28/65   10/02/65
Espy, Margaret married Fowler, John (Capt.) 11/19/61   11/21/61
Espy, Susie married Brooks, William T. 09/11/62   09/23/62
Essender, Agatha married Hughes, John L. 09/15/61   12/12/61
Essender, Mary died 10/29/65   10/30/65
Essex, Maggie M. died 09/15/63   09/19/63
Essex, Robert died 10/06/62   10/16/62
Essworth, Daniel married Brown, Sarah Jane 03/06/61   03/16/61
Estes, Harriet C. died 03/09/64   03/16/64
Etchberger, Fannie A. married Hancock, John F. 02/06/62   02/10/62
Etchberger, Frances Ann (Mrs.) died 07/19/65   07/20/65
Etchison, Bowie died 10/24/62   10/29/62
Etchison, Frank died 10/22/62   10/25/62
Etchison, Josephine F. married Warner, Luther F. 05/29/62   05/31/62
Etchison, Lysander married Price, Anna Corilla 02/12/61   02/18/61
Etheridge, James Freeman died 03/13/64   03/14/64
Etheridge, James Freeman died no date   04/13/64
Etting, Barnard G. died 07/30/62   07/31/62
Etting, Sally died 06/02/63   06/03/63
Etting, Samuel died 05/18/62   05/20/62
Ettinger, Robert B. died 09/27/63   10/10/63
Etzel, Mary Anna died 08/03/65   09/04/65
Eubank, Annie M. (Mrs.) married Brown, James M. 04/19/65   05/04/65
Evan, Benjamin died 04/12/64   04/13/64
Evans, Alice L. died 12/24/62   12/25/62
Evans, Amos died 03/04/65   03/06/65
Evans, Andrew J. married Tracey, Fannie A. 08/04/64   08/08/64
Evans, Anna Maria died 08/25/65   08/29/65
Evans, Anna R. married Dashiell, John V. 01/10/61   01/21/61
Evans, Archibald Buchanan died 03/17/63   03/20/63
Evans, Charlotte died 12/02/64   12/05/64
Evans, David died 02/06/64   02/22/64
Evans, Eliza L. L. married Horney, Samuel 09/29/63   10/01/63
Evans, Elizabeth died 09/16/62   09/17/62
Evans, Ella married Knight, William 06/10/63   02/24/64
Evans, Ellen Frances died 11/24/65   11/25/65
Evans, Emily (Mrs.) died 12/12/64   12/14/64
Evans, Emily (Mrs.) died 12/12/64   12/15/64
Evans, F. S. (Rev.) married McGilton, Margaret C. G. 10/22/61   10/23/6
Evans, Francis Marion died 01/12/65   01/14/65
Evans, Frank Stratton died 05/27/65   05/30/65
Evans, Franklin married Williams, Emma 09/06/60   07/06/61
Evans, George E. died 08/10/62   08/11/62
Evans, George W. (Cpt.) married Waller, Annie H. 04/18/64   04/20/64
Evans, Georgie married Whinna, Robert 02/16/64   02/19/64
Evans, Greenbury died 10/01/65   10/02/65
Evans, Henrietta married Simmons, Thomas E. 08/13/62   08/15/62
Evans, Henrietta B. (Mrs.) died 08/10/63   08/11/63
Evans, Henry married Diffenderfer, Sallie 05/31/65   06/01/65
Evans, Hugh W. died 12/05/63   12/07/63
Evans, Ida married Williams, H. S. 01/25/65   02/07/65
Evans, James married Porter, Henrietta (Mrs.) 10/01/65   10/05/65

Evans, James G. died 07/13/65   07/15/65
Evans, Jane died 12/28/62   12/30/62
Evans, Job died 01/19/64   01/21/64
Evans, John (USN) married Dixon, Fannie E. 09/02/64   09/07/64
Evans, John Hiram died 11/10/65   11/18/65
Evans, John Randolph died 10/31/64   11/01/64
Evans, John T. died 01/19/64   05/02/65
Evans, John Thomas died 01/19/64   01/20/64
Evans, Joseph V. died 02/10/62   03/05/62
Evans, M. A. (Mrs.) married Tucker, Charles C. 11/29/64   11/30/64
Evans, Mary died 12/04/61   12/05/61
Evans, Mary Edverdenia died 08/12/64   08/16/64
Evans, Maybury married Lampley, Susan V. 04/03/62   04/07/62
Evans, Nellie T. married Bosley, William 06/19/61   06/22/61
Evans, Oliver A. died 04/21/63   04/22/63
Evans, Rachel (Mrs.) died 01/28/63   02/02/63
Evans, Richard Franklin died 07/13/61   07/15/61
Evans, Richard J. died 03/21/64   03/22/64
Evans, Rosetta (Mrs.) died 11/20/64   11/21/64
Evans, Sarah died 08/28/62   08/29/62
Evans, Sevile (Mrs.) died 05/01/64   05/06/64
Evans, Theodore W. died 03/02/64   03/03/64
Evans, Thomas B. married Myer, Maggie 10/16/61   10/18/61
Evans, Thomas Henry died 12/02/64   12/05/64
Evans, Virginia R. married Shane, John H. (Lt) 03/11/64   03/22/64
Evans, William married Hale, Margaret A. C. 03/30/65   04/14/65
Evans, William H. married Lupton, Susannah 08/09/64   08/22/64
Evans, Willie Harper died 02/29/64   03/02/64
Everest, James E. died no date   11/01/64
Everett, Ann Eliza died 09/11/61   09/12/61
Everett, Ann Jane died 11/17/62   11/18/62
Everett, Rachel Adeline died 09/18/65   09/22/65
Everett, William married Kemps, Lizzie 12/28/63   01/02/64
Everhart, Ann Maria (Mrs.) died 02/23/64   02/25/64
Everhart, Louisa H. married Mann, B. N. 03/20/62   03/24/62
Everhart, Lucille V. married Bradshaw, John Julius (Cpt.) 12/26/62
   01/30/63
Everhart, O. T. (Dr.) married Shelly, Annie C. 10/18/64   10/19/64
Everhart, Sue married Nixdorff, T. S. 11/15/64   11/22/64
Everheart, Christina married Shirley, William Henry 05/04/62   05/06/62
Everist, Dalcedia married Allen, Theodore B. 10/19/64   11/04/64
Everist, Hester Ann died 12/28/62   12/30/62
Everist, John Wesley died 10/11/63   10/12/63
Everist, Mary E. married Frederick, George A. 01/10/65   01/12/65
Everit, Willie Ellsworth died 02/13/62   02/14/62
Everitt, John Henry died 08/04/61   08/06/61
Everitt, Mary Virginia died 09/04/65   09/06/65
Everitt, Richard O. married Johnson, Elizabeth S. 03/04/63   03/09/63
Evers, Daniel died 08/31/62   09/01/62
Everson, Michael married Lowrey, Laura 09/20/64   10/04/64
Everst, William A. died 08/21/64   11/01/64
Eves, Mary Ann married Driver, John Francis 03/29/61   04/09/61
Ewalt, Emma Boon died 10/24/62   10/25/62
Ewalt, John H. married Walker, Louisa 02/16/65   02/20/65
Ewart, John E. married Allen, Cecelia E. 09/20/61   09/23/61

Ewell, Thomas died 06/12/62   06/13/62
Ewing, E. E. married McMurphy, Emma 07/13/65   07/15/65
Ewing, Robert died 07/01/62   07/03/62
Ewing, William married Smith, Cornelia 01/14/62   01/17/62
Ewing, William Wesley died 07/11/65   07/12/65
Eyanson, Carrie died 06/25/63   06/26/63
Eyerly, Jacob Smith died 05/16/64   05/17/64
Faber, Edward A. R. died 10/01/62   11/27/62
Fackler, Mary married Sinn, John H. 06/23/63   06/24/63
Facts, Rebecca married Randall, Soloman 05/16/61   05/18/61
Fagan, Ella died 08/01/64   08/02/64
Fagel, Charles married Lindemann, Augusta J. 02/09/64   02/12/64
Fagen, Julia C. married Barron, Thomas 09/07/62   09/11/62
Fagen, Mary Ann married Miller, George H. 11/24/62   12/01/62
Faherty, Mary (Mrs.) died 01/03/63   01/05/63
Faherty, Mary J. died 08/10/63   08/14/63
Faherty, Mary J. died 08/10/63   08/15/63
Fahey, Martin died 12/13/62   12/15/62
Fahey, Mary Ann died 01/09/61   01/10/61
Fahey, Sarah Elizabeth died 04/04/61   04/06/61
Fahl, Mary married Ardisson, Maximin 12/03/63   12/05/63
Fahlen, Charles married Ohlendorf, Johanna 06/11/61   06/12/61
Fahnestock, Joseph D. died 06/19/63   06/20/63
Fahnestock, Mary died 01/30/63   01/31/63
Fahnestock, Peter died 11/17/64   11/18/64
Fahnestock, Sarah (Mrs.) died 09/11/63   09/12/63
Fahnstock, Jesse died 04/10/62   04/11/62
Faid, John married Raymond, Catharine Celia 11/10/65   12/19/65
Fair, John died 09/27/65   09/28/65
Fairall, Charles T. died 08/02/65   08/08/65
Fairall, Galena Olevia died 07/26/64   08/02/64
Fairall, Mary Ellen died 06/30/64   07/02/64
Fairbane, Henry died 06/18/65   06/19/65
Fairbank, Charles E. married Hale, E. J. V. 01/30/62   07/21/62
Fairbank, George V. died 05/28/64   05/30/64
Fairbank, John L. Y. died 02/06/63   02/09/63
Fairbank, Joshua M. married Pumphrey, Josephine L. 05/12/64   05/14/64
Fairbank, Mary E. married Black, James 03/19/63   03/24/63
Fairbank, Mary P. married Innerarity, J. W. G. 08/10/65   08/28/65
Fairbank, Thomas Edwin died 05/25/64   11/07/64
Fairbank, Virginia married Wall, Olin M. 06/27/64   06/29/64
Fairbank, William J. married Pumphrey, Mary C. 10/15/61   10/17/61
Fairbanks, Eliza A. married Cassell, Leonard 08/06/63   08/08/63
Fairbanks, Elizabeth married Downs, Henry C. 11/27/62   12/01/62
Fairbanks, James died 10/28/63   10/30/63
Fairley, Thomas married Gettier, Rose H. 04/14/63   04/24/63
Faithful, Lydia died 10/01/61   10/02/61
Falconar, A. Smith married Poultney, Nannie T. 11/12/63   11/16/63
Falconar, Catherine died 04/06/61   04/09/61
Falconer, Caroline died 07/23/63   07/24/63
Falconer, John died 12/04/61   12/05/61
Falconer, Jonathan died 03/11/65   03/13/65
Falconer, Maskil died 11/07/65   11/08/65
Fales, Bettie married Wagner, John 07/16/63   08/17/63
Fales, France Gorton died 11/05/63   11/06/63

```
Fales, James G. died 02/02/63   02/03/63
Fales, Lawrence H. married Reed, Annie 02/20/62   03/18/62
Fales, Lawrence H. died 09/19/64   09/21/64
Fales, Nathaniel A. married Ely, Laura Jane 05/13/62   05/16/62
Fales, William George married Holton, Kate C. 09/11/65   09/14/65
Faley, Rosanna died 04/27/62   04/29/62
Falk, Mary married Williams, Asa 03/14/64   03/24/64
Falkner, Clementine (Mrs.) died 05/26/64   05/27/64
Fallon, Daniel J. married Patterson, Rebecca M. 10/10/65   10/17/65
Fallon, Mallachi married Mahoney, Hannah 01/15/65   01/21/65
Falls, Letitia M. married Durrell, Charles 09/08/63   09/09/63
Falls, Moor married Hamilton, Emilie V. 10/07/63   10/10/63
Falls, Sally (Mrs.) died 08/04/64   08/06/64
Falls, Willie Baily died 03/19/62   03/22/62
Fanning, Eliza married Litsinger, Richard 03/16/65   03/22/65
Fanoll, Bedelia died 06/28/62   06/30/62
Fantom, Mary Ann died 06/05/61   06/06/61
Fardwell, Sarah married Briscoe, William T. 09/12/65   09/23/65
Fardwell, William died 12/25/63   02/16/64
Farenger, Benjamin F. married Bowne, Mary E. 11/03/64   02/09/65
Faring, Eleanora (Mrs.) died 01/23/64   01/25/64
Faringer, Catharine (Mrs.) died 01/17/63   01/21/63
Faringer, Jacob Alonzo died 03/28/65   03/31/65
Faringer, John J. died 01/12/65   03/20/65
Faris, Benjamin Gurney died 06/19/65   06/20/65
Farland, Mary Carter died 06/01/64   06/02/64
Farless, Benjamin married Middleton, Isadore A. 06/29/65   07/07/65
Farlow, Hattie E. married Clunet, Victor S. 08/08/62   03/15/64
Farlow, William H. died 09/16/64   09/17/64
Farmer, James A. died 03/27/65   03/30/65
Farmer, William died 03/21/62   03/22/62
Farmer, William A. married Booker, Virginia H. 02/23/64   02/24/64
Farnan, Michael died 09/27/63   09/29/63
Farnandis, Catharine married Brooks, William 11/16/65   11/18/65
Farnandis, Walter died 01/23/65   01/24/65
Farnandis, Walter died 01/23/65   01/25/65
Farnen, Catherine died 04/03/62   04/05/62
Farnen, Mary died 05/26/62   05/27/62
Farquar, William P. married Nicholson, Maggie E. 03/17/65   03/21/65
Farquhar, John C. married Pickering, Amanda E. 07/23/63   08/22/63
Farquhar, Mary E. married Hershey, B. J. (Dr.) 02/19/61   02/20/61
Farr, Julia A. married Burns, Martin E. 12/29/61   12/31/61
Farr, Stewart A. married Doyle, Mary A. 12/25/62   01/06/63
Farrall, Catherine Ruth Wilks died 03/09/61   03/12/61
Farrar, James married Ford, Laura E. 03/12/63   03/17/63
Farrel, Patrick died 11/30/64   12/01/64
Farrell, Catherine died 07/28/62   07/29/62
Farrell, David died 01/17/65   01/18/65
Farrell, Dennis O. died 07/31/64   08/02/64
Farrell, John married McCarty, Ellen T. 02/16/63   02/20/63
Farrell, Martin married Ryan, Catherine 11/24/61   11/26/61
Farrell, Matthew died 06/02/64   06/03/64
Farrelly, Matthew died 04/28/61   04/29/61
Farren, Isabella died 08/11/62   08/13/62
Farren, Willis H. married Wrighton, Sarah A. 01/11/64   01/19/64
```

Farrenger, M. A. married Pryor, Richard W. 08/06/65   08/08/65
Farrow, Joseph (Rev.) died 04/30/61   05/03/61
Farrow, Mary married Gassaway, William A. 01/21/64   01/22/64
Farrow, Mollie C. married Charlton, J. W. 03/06/65   03/10/65
Farson, Clara Ross died 02/17/63   02/20/63
Farson, George W. married Prather, Emma H. 12/29/63   01/01/64
Farson, Jessie died 05/21/64   05/27/64
Farson, Samuel P. died 03/18/64   03/19/64
Faucett, Michael died 12/16/62   12/17/62
Faucett, William died 08/24/63   09/28/63
Faulkner, Elleanor (Mrs.) died 03/31/63   04/03/63
Faulkner, Patrick died 08/03/64   08/04/64
Faulkner, Sarah died 03/30/61   04/01/61
Fauntleroy, Ann Magill died 06/24/62   07/09/62
Fauth, Mary died 01/20/64   01/22/64
Fauth, Mary A. died 01/20/64   01/21/64
Favier, Mary J. married Herring, William E. no date   12/29/65
Favier, Peter A. married Pryor, Laura E. 04/02/65   06/27/65
Favre, Francois H. married Preadasell, Caroline Elizabeth 09/06/65   09/07/65
Fawcett, Charles died 08/08/62   08/09/62
Fawcus, Mary Ann married Miller, William E. 07/17/65   09/26/65
Fawkes, Fannie E. married Curtis, John A. 01/09/62   01/11/62
Fay, George married Lare, Sophia E. 10/25/65   11/09/65
Fay, Joseph (Lt.) died 08/29/64   09/01/64
Fay, Rose A. married Gurry, James H. 04/13/63   04/30/63
Fay, Sarah J. married Smith, James F. 10/25/65   11/09/65
Fay, Virginia married Riley, Harry E. 06/02/64   06/13/64
Fearis, John died 11/03/61   11/05/61
Fearis, Thomas died 04/16/64   04/18/64
Feast, Clara Ellen died 04/16/65   04/18/65
Feast, L. married Durham, Martha L. 04/08/65   04/18/65
Featherall, Biddy married Drury, David M. 06/07/65   06/12/65
Fedricks, Harry Albert died 06/07/65   06/08/65
Fee, Caleb married Lees, Anna 12/17/61   12/19/61
Feelemyer, Sarah M. died 08/24/64   08/25/64
Feelemyer, Wilbur Barton died 07/25/65   07/29/65
Feeney, James married McGee, Rosanna 05/04/65   05/10/65
Fehely, Catherine died 07/09/62   07/10/62
Fehl, John Harmon died 01/31/65   02/15/65
Feig, Anna Rebecca died 12/20/62   12/23/62
Feig, George A. married Hancock, Laura A. 06/03/62   06/11/62
Feige, Louise died 05/03/65   05/05/65
Feinour, Edward married Mitchell, Margaret Jeanette 10/14/62   10/16/62
Feistel, Pelena A. married Schaeffer, John C. 09/07/65   09/18/65
Feldhaus, Minnie married Bancroft, John D. 12/29/64   01/02/65
Felkner, Alvan B. married Jones, Ruth Eliza 07/19/64   07/21/64
Fell, J. Casper died 06/19/63   06/24/63
Fellemeyer, Josephine married Gross, Henry S. 05/14/63   05/16/63
Felter, Margaret died 05/30/62   05/31/62
Felton, Mary Jane married Councilman, Robert 12/22/64   12/26/64
Feltz, Elizabeth married McManus, John 10/06/63   11/09/63
Fenby, Alice died 12/17/62   12/19/62
Fendrice, Francis married Gable, Mary E. 05/11/65   05/27/65
Fendrich, Mary died 04/21/62   04/22/62

142

Fenemore, Isaac married Coleman, Elizabeth B. 01/15/62   02/22/62
Fenhagen, Mary Cathell died 12/22/64   12/23/64
Fennall, Walter died 11/12/61   11/14/61
Fennell, Maurice Gale died 05/04/63   05/05/63
Fennelly, M. E. married McClintock, John M., Jr. 01/02/61   01/03/61
Fennema, Dedrick died 02/07/64   02/09/64
Fennen, Bernard died 02/10/63   02/11/63
Fenner, Richard S. died 01/29/65   02/03/65
Fenner, Richard S. died 01/29/65   02/03/65
Fennesy, Thomas died 06/01/64   06/02/64
Fenney, Bridget died 04/15/64   04/16/64
Fennimore, William married Merryman, Mary Lizzie 05/06/63   05/07/63
Fennin, Mary Catherine died 03/31/61   04/01/61
Fensley, Willie died 01/24/64   01/25/64
Fenton, Dennis died 04/10/63   04/11/63
Fenton, Harrison married Saunders, Rachel Ann 06/30/64   07/02/64
Fenton, Michael died 11/10/61   03/24/62
Fenton, Michael died 08/29/64   08/31/64
Fentriss, Cary married Hollins, Emily Jane 03/13/64   03/17/64
Fenwick, Annie Louisa (Mrs.) died 02/22/64   02/27/64
Fenwick, Lizzie R. married Cousino, William J. 04/21/64   04/25/64
Ferciot, Maria Louisa married Mossinger, Gustavus (Dr.) 05/05/64   05/09/64
Ferguson, Bell married Currans, Oliver E. 03/10/63   03/30/63
Ferguson, Catherine Ann married Viese, John 11/16/65   10/21/65
Ferguson, David B. died 12/29/63   01/08/64
Ferguson, Eliza married Griffith, John R. 11/24/63   11/25/63
Ferguson, Elizabeth Ann died 10/01/62   10/02/62
Ferguson, George died 08/02/63   08/03/63
Ferguson, Georgeanna T. died 04/25/63   04/28/63
Ferguson, Henry died 01/23/64   01/25/64
Ferguson, Henry Slicer died 02/05/63   02/07/63
Ferguson, Isabella died 04/26/63   04/28/63
Ferguson, James D. died 05/05/61   05/06/61
Ferguson, John died 01/01/62   01/02/62
Ferguson, Kate married Rankin, William 09/14/65   09/29/65
Ferguson, Louisa died 09/26/65   09/27/65
Ferguson, Lydia married Griffith, Charles R. 10/04/64   10/07/64
Ferguson, Maggie married Chicken, David 06/01/64   06/07/64
Ferguson, Maggie J. married Martin, S. Henson 08/30/64   09/03/64
Ferguson, Margaret A. married Chaney, George W. 07/05/63   07/07/63
Ferguson, Robert Moox died 05/05/64   05/07/64
Ferguson, Rozella V. married Callenber, William H., Jr. 07/21/63   07/23/63
Ferguson, Samuel Edwin died 09/18/63   09/19/63
Ferguson, Samuel L. died 06/20/62   06/23/62
Ferguson, Ursula C. married Cox, James E. 08/06/65   08/21/65
Ferguson, William died 02/28/63   03/02/63
Ferguson, William died 11/17/64   11/19/64
Fergusson, Laura died 02/25/62   02/26/62
Ferlemeyer, Charlie David died 07/19/65   07/22/65
Ferrat, John R. married Odend'Hal, Mary Ann 01/14/61   01/15/61
Ferree, Alexander married Clemments, Caroline 06/01/63   06/04/63
Ferree, Sallie Ann died 12/28/62   12/30/62
Ferreira, Augustus G. (Capt.) died 08/09/62   08/11/62

```
Ferrel, Nicholas died 03/24/65  03/25/65
Ferrell, Joshua (Cpt.) died 05/24/64  05/25/64
Ferrell, Joshua (Cpt.) died 05/24/64  05/26/64
Ferry, Mollie E. married Surdall, Charles A. 11/28/65  12/01/65
Ferry, Mollie E. married Sindall, Charles A. 11/28/65  12/02/65
Fesba, Eliza married Handy, Alexander 01/20/63  01/22/63
Fesler, Edward A. married Sutton, Cornelia A. B. 03/12/63  03/17/63
Fester, John married Boyle, Mary 03/01/63  03/05/63
Fetters, John F. married Suton, Ann (Mrs.) 06/07/64  06/09/64
Fetting, John died 02/05/61  02/06/61
Fibbs, Georgianna K. died 02/04/65  02/07/65
Fick, Eva (Mrs.) died 12/15/65  12/16/65
Fickey, Carrie married Arringdale, William L. 11/28/61  12/03/61
Fiddis, Benjamin W. married Whitaer, Susan A. 09/25/63  10/06/63
Field, George Miltenberger died 03/18/65  03/21/65
Field, Grace died 08/19/63  08/20/63
Field, John H. died 01/27/61  01/28/61
Field, Lilian died 11/10/64  11/14/64
Field, Mary E. married Wilson, George H. 12/25/65  12/27/65
Field, Susan (Mrs.) died 03/01/64  03/03/64
Field, William (USN) married Allyn, Mollie J. 07/12/64  07/14/64
Fields, Annie R. married Wyant, William J. 02/17/61  03/06/61
Fields, Caroline (Mrs.) died 06/24/63  06/26/63
Fields, Catharine married Richards, Joshua 01/26/65  01/28/65
Fields, Edward died 12/13/63  12/14/63
Fields, Frances V. married Grobaker, Valentine 05/01/64  05/06/64
Fields, John married Gittings, Rosa S. 04/20/64  04/26/64
Fields, Maria married Tibbals, John G. 11/24/64  12/01/64
Fields, William died 09/11/61  09/12/61
Fields, William married Freeburger, Julia (Mrs.) 06/16/65  06/20/65
Fife, Helen E. married Morgan, John T. 11/01/61  04/19/62
Fifer, Alexina E. married King, Francis 03/15/63  04/01/63
Fifer, Caroline Lafemy died 08/11/61  08/12/61
Fifer, George F. died 10/18/65  10/20/65
Filbert, Catherine died 01/30/62  01/31/62
Filbert, George married Flamm, Kate 04/05/61  12/07/61
Filbert, Ida Rebecca died 07/04/65  07/06/65
Files, Ida Jane died 11/16/64  11/17/64
Files, Mary Ann married Lafielt, Jeremiah 01/05/62  01/07/62
Filgate, Thomas married Kelly, Bridget A. (Mrs.) 04/27/65  04/29/65
Filius, Sarah E. married Baynes, John T. 05/17/64  05/20/64
Filius, Sarah E. married Bayne, John T. 05/17/64  05/21/64
Fillinger, Frances E. married Hobbs, John A. 04/17/65  05/13/65
Fillinger, Josephine M. married Berry, Charles H. 06/19/65  07/18/65
Fillins, Sarah E. married Baynes, John T. 05/17/64  05/19/64
Fillius, Olivia A. married Boblits, Jacob 07/04/65  07/10/65
Fillmore, Willie died 10/21/61  10/24/61
Filton, John married Talbot, Alice 10/20/62  10/21/62
Finagan, Maggie married Carey, William 04/05/63  04/08/63
Finch, Eliza A. G. died 11/06/65  11/07/65
Finch, Mary Ann died 03/14/64  03/16/64
Findlay, John V. L. married MacKenzie, Mary C. 06/16/63  06/18/63
Finegan, Eliza D. B. (Mrs.) died 04/21/64  04/22/64
Finegan, Hanora married Morrisroe, Andrew 01/20/62  09/04/62
Finegin, Joseph married Brooks, Eliza D. 02/16/62  03/10/62
```

Fineren, Margaret died 12/23/62   12/24/62
Fingan, Arthur married Triplet, Hannah A. T. 10/07/64   10/08/64
Finigan, Charles died 03/06/64   03/07/64
Finigan, John died 08/31/62   09/02/62
Finigan, Owen married McKitrick, Mary 10/23/64   10/25/64
Finigan, Patrick died 11/08/63   11/09/63
Fink, Harry died 06/19/64   06/21/64
Finley, Alice Agnes died 10/17/65   10/23/65
Finley, Catherine W. (Mrs.) died 05/27/64   05/28/64
Finley, Eliza White died 03/23/61   03/26/61
Finley, Ella M. married Wylie, George M. 03/08/64   03/10/64
Finley, John F. married McDonough, Mary 04/16/63   04/22/63
Finley, Kate Gregoria died 05/25/62   05/26/62
Finley, Lizzie Millicent died 06/07/64   06/08/64
Finley, Margaret married Holscher, John J. 10/23/63   01/06/64
Finley, Martha Elsie married Thomas, S. Drew 02/25/63   02/27/63
Finley, Rose Ann died 06/05/64   06/06/64
Finley, Samuel Walter died 01/21/65   01/27/65
Finley, Sarah Augusta died 02/13/62   02/17/62
Finley, Sarah Augusta died 10/08/62   10/14/62
Finley, Sarah Jane died 05/30/64   06/06/64
Finley, Thomas Francis died 03/15/61   03/18/61
Finley, William Francis died 07/18/63   07/20/63
Finn, Hugh B. died 01/07/64   01/08/64
Finn, John F. died 02/01/61   02/02/61
Finn, Mary married Shea, Daniel 07/20/64   09/23/64
Finnan, Francis Patrick died 12/13/65   12/15/65
Finnegan, Mary died 04/04/62   04/05/62
Finney, Alex married McIlhenny, Jane 04/18/61   04/20/61
Finney, George J. married Webster, Lou L. 04/26/65   04/27/65
Finney, Hugh married Long, Maggie H. 06/06/64   06/09/64
Finney, John Henry died 04/16/63   04/18/63
Finnigan, Mary married Byrnes, Edmund 04/07/61   07/10/61
Fiquet, Ann (Mrs.) died 07/21/65   08/01/65
Firor, John E. married Mayn, Annie M. 02/10/64   02/15/64
Firoved, Anderson H. married Pickett, Lucy E. 07/07/63   07/13/63
Firoved, Catherine died 03/21/64   03/22/64
Firoved, Hannah Emily died 04/26/64   04/28/64
Firoved, John married Gould, Mary 02/21/65   03/17/65
Firoved, Lydia (Mrs.) died 02/23/63   02/24/63
Firoved, Sarah E. married Barton, Willard G. 12/30/61   01/04/62
Fischer, Caroline M. died 10/25/62   10/27/62
Fischer, Catherine A. married Mason, Joseph T. 03/29/64   03/30/64
Fischer, D. C. S. died 01/27/64   01/28/64
Fischer, Peter died 06/13/62   06/14/62
Fischer, Samuel died 02/27/64   03/02/64
Fish, Ann M. died 06/16/62   06/18/62
Fish, Charles married Fuller, Louisa 05/05/64   05/23/64
Fish, Charles H. married Fisher, Clara D. 01/15/65   01/21/65
Fish, Lizzie Jane died 09/22/63   09/24/63
Fishach, George B. died 09/24/61   01/28/62
Fishach, John Harry Lee died 01/24/62   01/28/62
Fishach, Kate married Sage, George D. 04/25/63   04/28/63
Fishack, William A. died 12/21/62   12/23/62
Fisher, Adam died 10/06/64   10/07/64

Fisher, Alcester A. married Osmonde, Julian 12/24/63 12/31/63
Fisher, Alfred married Haney, Mary 01/01/61 01/03/61
Fisher, Amelia C. died 02/02/62 02/04/62
Fisher, Ann (Mrs.) died 03/17/64 04/11/64
Fisher, Carvel died 06/01/65 06/02/65
Fisher, Catherine L. married Rhine, John W. 03/24/63 03/25/63
Fisher, Charles C. died 10/07/63 10/08/63
Fisher, Chester Quiler married Harter, Kate 06/21/64 07/12/64
Fisher, Christina Johanna died 12/04/61 12/05/61
Fisher, Clara D. married Fish, Charles H. 01/15/65 01/21/65
Fisher, E. Jane married Swigert, D. Amos 12/25/62 12/27/62
Fisher, Elenore (Mrs.) died 06/07/64 06/09/64
Fisher, Elizabeth A. (Mrs.) died 02/19/64 02/20/64
Fisher, Frances A. died 01/30/62 02/01/62
Fisher, Frederick Charles died 10/02/62 10/06/62
Fisher, George G. married Bennett, Mary 11/17/64 11/19/64
Fisher, Henry married Bruefer, Mary 03/09/63 03/10/63
Fisher, Henry W. married Snyder, Mary 12/18/61 12/30/61
Fisher, Herman E. married Latham, Virginia 05/14/63 05/16/63
Fisher, J. Harmanus married Winchester, Lucy 10/11/64 10/12/64
Fisher, Jane Alricks died 07/26/62 07/28/62
Fisher, John died 04/11/63 04/13/63
Fisher, John H. married Mitchell, Margaret J. 09/07/64 09/10/64
Fisher, Lewis married Hammock, Emma L. (Mrs.) 12/11/64 12/13/64
Fisher, Louisa T. (Mrs.) died 12/04/64 12/05/64
Fisher, Louiza T. (Mrs.) died 12/04/64 12/06/64
Fisher, Lucinda J. married Keefer, Edward P. 09/05/65 09/11/65
Fisher, Margaret died 05/03/61 05/04/61
Fisher, Mary died 11/12/61 11/21/61
Fisher, Mary Ann died 11/30/63 12/01/63
Fisher, Mary Anna married Parrott, Frank 06/03/62 06/06/62
Fisher, Mary E. married Mason, Garville S. 11/24/63 12/22/63
Fisher, Mary Juliet died 04/08/64 04/09/64
Fisher, Parks married Schley, Nettie 06/08/65 06/10/65
Fisher, Richard D. married Winchester, Margaret 11/25/62 11/27/62
Fisher, Robert A. married Pigman, Anna B. 01/16/65 01/18/65
Fisher, Sallie R. died 12/21/62 12/22/62
Fisher, Sallie R. died 12/21/62 12/23/62
Fisher, Sarah E. married Duvall, William J. 06/16/64 06/20/64
Fisher, Thomas died 02/23/65 02/24/65
Fisher, Thomas died 02/23/65 02/25/65
Fisher, William married Boggs, Margaret A. 04/18/65 04/20/65
Fisher, William H. died 07/30/62 08/02/62
Fisher, William H. married Dobbins, Chola E. 08/18/63 08/20/63
Fisherty, Mary Elizabeth died 02/11/61 02/16/61
Fishpau, Margaret A. (Mrs.) died 07/21/64 07/23/64
Fishpaw, John L. died 11/05/62 11/07/62
Fisk, Phebe P. married Burris, Isaac F. 01/20/63 01/29/63
Fiske, Lucy A. married Morison, Frank 10/10/65 10/16/65
Fiske, Phebe P. married Purvis, Isaac F. 01/20/63 01/30/63
Fitch, Marcellus L. married Hands, Jennie E. 08/06/63 08/08/63
Fitchett, Zetville married Fowler, William T. 10/19/63 10/26/63
Fitsmire, John A. married Brooks, Mary E. 01/16/63 01/17/63
Fitzchew, Elizabeth married Taylor, Jacob 12/17/63 12/19/63
Fitzgerald, Catherine died 10/28/63 10/29/63

```
Fitzgerald, Eleanora (Mrs.) died 01/19/63   01/21/63
Fitzgerald, Elizabeth (Mrs.) died 03/04/64   03/09/64
Fitzgerald, H. B. married Magness, Lee 08/30/64   08/31/64
Fitzgerald, James died 11/22/63   11/26/63
Fitzgerald, John B. died 07/05/64   07/06/64
Fitzgerald, John Edwin died 11/17/63   01/08/64
Fitzgerald, Margaret married Heffernan, Hugh 01/07/61   01/19/61
Fitzgerald, Maria K. married Moale, Fred L. 07/09/61   07/10/61
Fitzgerald, Mary A. married Carroll, Eabert P. 06/08/62   06/13/62
Fitzgerald, Mary Ellen died 10/14/62   11/03/62
Fitzgerald, Michael married Fitzpatrick, Mary 01/24/64   01/28/64
Fitzgerald, Richard G. died 10/27/65   10/28/65
Fitzgerald, Washington C. died 01/29/61   03/07/61
Fitzgibbon, Joseph D. died 07/14/64   07/15/64
Fitzharris, Catherine E. died 01/18/62   01/22/62
Fitzhugh, Sally Ellicot died 12/16/63   12/28/63
Fitzpatrick, Alice died 08/17/64   08/18/64
Fitzpatrick, Catharine died 09/04/63   09/05/63
Fitzpatrick, Catherine married McGuirk, Bernard 05/07/63   05/12/63
Fitzpatrick, Elizabeth died 09/07/65   09/08/65
Fitzpatrick, George H. married Candie, E. R. 11/29/64   11/30/64
Fitzpatrick, John died 08/14/64   08/15/64
Fitzpatrick, Mary married Hinuff, Jacob Brown 02/01/63   06/16/63
Fitzpatrick, Mary married Fitzgerald, Michael 01/24/64   01/28/64
Fitzpatrick, Mary married Barrett, William H. 06/30/64   07/11/64
Fitzpatrick, Mary married Woodruff, S. S. 10/25/64   12/03/64
Fitzpatrick, Michael died 05/03/61   05/04/61
Fitzpatrick, Patrick married Tangney, Kate 04/20/62   05/01/62
Fitzpatrick, Patrick died 08/11/63   08/12/63
Fitzpatrick, Thomas died 12/27/66  01/23/61
Fitzsimmons, Christopher died 07/29/61   07/30/61
Fitzsimmons, Richard died 08/14/64   08/15/64
Fitzwilson, Virginia E. died 06/19/65   06/21/65
Fizpatrick, Mary W. (Mrs.) married Peter, P. Orange 05/20/62   09/11/62
Flack, Isabella married Manner, Claiborne H. 02/22/61   09/03/61
Flaharty, James L. died 12/16/64   12/17/64
Flaharty, Margaret Ensor died 08/13/65   08/16/65
Flaherty, Andrew J. married Muir, Virginia 06/01/64   06/17/64
Flaherty, Honora Mary died 11/01/63   11/03/63
Flaherty, John married Constantine, Bridget 11/29/60   06/18/61
Flaherty, John Edward died 10/18/64   10/19/64
Flaherty, Margaret Elizabeth died 10/04/64   10/06/64
Flaherty, Mary (Mrs.) died 06/21/64   06/22/64
Flaherty, Mary Ann died 02/10/65   02/11/65
Flaherty, Mary Ann died 09/27/65   09/29/65
Flaherty, Mary Elizabeth died 02/11/61   02/18/61
Flaherty, Mary J. (Mrs.) died 01/18/64   01/19/64
Flaherty, Sarah A. married McNeal, James H. 12/30/61   01/23/62
Flamm, George married Carroll, Mary A. 07/20/65   07/22/65
Flamm, Kate married Filbert, George 04/05/61   12/07/61
Flanagan, Carrol Augusta died 09/11/64   09/12/64
Flanagan, Elizabeth Ann (Mrs.) died 09/30/63   10/01/63
Flanagan, Elizabeth Ann (Mrs.) died 09/30/63   10/02/63
Flanagan, George L. died 11/29/64   11/30/64
Flanagan, George L. died 11/29/64   12/01/64
```

```
Flanagan, Jane Rockaway died 06/22/64   07/25/64
Flanagan, Jane Rockaway died 06/22/64   07/04/64
Flanagan, Luke died 08/09/62   08/11/62
Flanagan, Luke died 08/09/62   08/12/62
Flanagan, M. J. married Walton, Frank 06/02/64   06/04/64
Flanagan, Martha Wilson (Mrs.) died 08/10/64   08/11/64
Flanagan, Mary died 04/19/61   04/20/61
Flanagan, Mary died 04/21/64   04/22/64
Flanagan, Mary Stella died 07/01/64   07/04/64
Flanagin, Patrick married Quigley, Jane 07/24/64   07/30/64
Flanegan, Mary died 10/17/65   10/19/65
Flanery, Michael died 10/26/65   10/27/65
Flanigan, Thomas married Tansey, Anne 01/05/64   01/09/64
Flannagan, Charles A. died 12/24/61   12/28/61
Flannagan, Mary Josephine died 12/24/61   12/28/61
Flannery, Bridget died 12/27/61   12/28/61
Flannery, James J. married Coupland, Louisa 12/04/64   12/07/64
Flannigain, Lemuel died 12/05/61   12/06/61
Flannigain, Lemuel died 12/05/61   12/07/61
Flannigan, Sarah married Tormey, F. D. 11/17/64   11/18/64
Fleck, Joseph died 04/25/65   04/26/65
Fledderman, Charles Lewis died 08/19/65   08/21/65
Fledderman, John Gerhart died 03/29/63   03/31/63
Fleeharty, Anna M. (Mrs.) died 01/07/63   01/09/63
Fleeharty, Thomas J. married Manns, Fannie 01/10/61   01/12/61
Fleehearty, Edith died 11/22/63   11/24/63
Fleehearty, John T. married Stevens, Annie M. 07/20/60   04/09/61
Fleehearty, John T. married Berry, Clara L. 07/30/64   08/02/64
Fleeshell, Georgeanna married Jacobs, John B. 06/01/65   06/08/65
Fleicher, Mary E. died 01/27/62   01/28/62
Fleicher, Samuel married Sanderson, Emily P. 01/22/61   02/02/61
Fleischman, Samuel S. married Goodman, Cecelia 10/30/64   10/31/64
Fleishell, John N. died 09/14/65   09/16/65
Fleishell, Margaret R. died 04/21/62   04/22/62
Fleishell, Mary A. died 10/05/65   10/06/65
Fleishman, Israel married Stein, Bertha 11/05/65   11/07/65
Fleishman, Moses died 08/30/65   08/31/65
Fleishman, Simon died 03/17/61   03/18/61
Fleming, Eliza married Starr, John 02/01/65   02/23/65
Fleming, Elizabeth (Mrs.) died 05/03/63   05/05/63
Fleming, Francis died 09/17/63   10/24/63
Fleming, Henry Bolton died 12/30/62   12/31/62
Fleming, John C. died 01/21/65   01/28/65
Fleming, Mary Anne married Phalan, Joseph 03/09/64   03/02/65
Fleming, Mary Anne married Phalin, Joseph 03/09/64   03/04/65
Fleming, Michael died 03/22/64   03/23/64
Fleming, Samuel Wyatt died 08/24/62   08/25/62
Flemming, Ann Augusta died 01/24/62   01/25/62
Flemming, Charles H. married Russell, Isabel R. 04/07/64   05/17/64
Flemming, James H. died 12/28/61   12/30/61
Flemming, Kate married Wilkinson, E. H. 08/31/63   09/15/63
Flemming, Margaret married Hiring, Christopher J. 05/26/65   05/27/65
Fletcher, Alice Ann Thompson died 07/06/64   07/07/64
Fletcher, Annie Augusta married Smith, John Summerfield 02/18/64
    02/19/64
```

Fletcher, Julia Ann married Thompson, Stephen 02/02/63   03/06/63
Fletcher, Kate F. married O'Rourke, William 10/09/64   10/13/64
Fletcher, Margaretta J. married Stevenson, John H. 10/06/63   10/12/63
Fletcher, Rebecca died 11/29/65   12/01/65
Fletcher, Solomon D. married Hartigan, S. Rebecca 06/26/65   08/10/65
Fletcher, Thomas B. married Flood, Mary Ann no date   02/03/62
Flincheam, Amelia married Hoover, Thomas S. 09/26/65   10/05/65
Flinckom, Martha married Johnson, Marius 12/25/64   12/28/64
Flinn, Catherine (Mrs.) died 08/31/63   09/02/63
Flinn, Lawrence died 12/02/62   12/03/62
Flinspach, Mary Ellen died 03/25/62   03/27/62
Flint, Carrie married Lycett, George no date   02/15/65
Flint, Edward died 02/16/64   02/24/64
Flint, Thomas died 09/04/62   09/05/62
Flint, Thomas died 09/04/62   09/06/62
Flood, Joseph died 11/05/62   11/06/62
Flood, Mary Ann married Fletcher, Thomas B. no date   02/03/62
Floss, Ellen J. married Adler, Henry M. 07/16/65   07/18/65
Flowers, Benjamin B. married Magness, Sarah A. 06/08/65   06/16/65
Floyd, George M. married Rowles, Eliza Ann 08/29/61   09/03/61
Floyd, George Marion died 08/24/65   08/25/65
Floyd, Mary Ann married Wilkie, Robert 12/13/64   12/15/64
Floyd, Philenea died 03/07/61   03/08/61
Floyd, Robert F. died 01/12/64   02/04/64
Floyd, Robert L. (Rev.) married Newell, Matilda C. (Mrs.) 10/15/61   10/22/61
Floyd, William J. died 12/26/63   12/29/63
Floyd, William Joseph died 07/29/61   07/30/61
Fluhart, Mary A. died 05/29/64   06/01/64
Fluharty, Lillian May died 07/15/64   07/16/64
Fluharty, Maggie L. married Hubbard, Alonzo F. 12/29/64   01/02/65
Fluharty, Thomas J. married Manns, Fannie 01/10/61   01/15/61
Flynn, Alice married Rodier, Albert 04/20/63   04/22/63
Flynn, Catharine died 09/03/63   09/04/63
Flynn, Catherine died 03/03/64   03/04/64
Flynn, John died 10/26/63   10/27/63
Flynn, John T. married Woolen, M. E. 06/24/62   06/25/62
Flynn, Kate died 12/27/61   12/28/61
Flynn, Lewis married Reid, Sallie 03/07/65   03/28/65
Flynn, Mary Celestial died 07/17/63   07/18/63
Fmich, Nicholas, Sr. died 12/01/62   12/03/62
Foard, Anna E. married Carman, Caleb C. 11/30/65   12/15/65
Foard, George H. died 04/10/62   04/12/62
Foard, Thomas died 10/21/63   10/31/63
Foard, William A. died 05/18/63   05/12/63
Foble, Anna M. died 12/10/61   12/11/61
Foble, Mary E. died 09/27/65   09/28/65
Foekemmer, Mary A. married Smyser, William H. 07/05/64   07/07/64
Fogarity, John died 05/21/63   05/22/63
Fogarty, James married Carroll, Maria 03/03/62   03/04/62
Fogle, John H. married Borum, Sallie F. 08/15/65   08/18/65
Foige, Adolph married Wright, Joanna 05/14/65   05/23/65
Foldridge, William H. died 05/08/65   05/09/65
Foldridge, William H. died 05/08/65   05/10/65
Foley, Annie died 05/14/64   05/16/64

```
Foley, Daniel died 05/05/61   05/06/61
Foley, Francis died 10/23/61   10/24/61
Foley, Francis died 10/23/61   10/25/61
Foley, John died 04/19/64   04/20/64
Foley, John Thomas died 07/31/65   08/03/65
Foley, Johnny died 10/18/63   10/20/63
Foley, Julia S. married Norfolk, Joseph S. 06/14/65   06/16/65
Foley, Kate died 05/25/64   05/26/64
Foley, Laura M. died 11/02/63   11/03/63
Foley, Mary Frances died 06/23/62   06/28/62
Foley, William F. died 01/01/64   01/04/64
Folks, Ellie died 04/15/64   04/16/64
Folks, John A. married Baker, Lina A. 05/30/61   06/01/61
Follansbee, George married Cassidy, Emily 01/17/61   01/22/61
Follansbee, George married Cassidy, Emily 01/17/61   01/23/61
Follen, Martha R. married Stansbury, George H. 02/29/64   03/04/64
Foltz, Mary A. (Mrs.) died 01/21/65   01/23/65
Fontaine, John L. married Wilson, Belle, H. 09/07/64   09/10/64
Fonville, Henriette (Mrs.) died 11/27/63   11/28/63
Foos, Andrew J. married Lyles, Martha Ann 02/27/62   03/03/62
Foos, Andrew J. died 01/04/64   01/06/64
Foos, Charles Alfred died 02/02/65   02/04/65
Foos, Charles H. died 02/12/63   02/13/63
Foos, George Theodoric died 09/08/65   09/09/65
Foos, George Wallace died 09/06/64   09/10/64
Foos, Henry died 07/09/65   07/10/65
Foos, Joshua J. died 12/06/64   12/07/64
Foos, Martha married Lancaster, Isaac T. 08/04/62   12/11/62
Foos, Martha (Mrs.) died 05/09/64   05/10/64
Foos, William Augustus died 08/14/62   08/16/62
Foos, William L. died 08/31/61   09/02/61
Foos, William Lindergreen died 05/16/64   05/17/64
Foose, Ann married Bosley, William H. 11/30/65   12/04/65
Foose, Augustine married Jones, Asa L. 02/27/61   03/19/61
Foose, Sarah E. died 12/07/61   12/09/61
Foot, John P. married Gulrick, Sarah 01/03/61   01/11/61
Foot, William married Franklin, Rosena 04/17/65   04/29/65
Foote, Josephine C. married Reese, George S. 09/11/61   09/13/61
Fopless, Thomas Robinson died 08/09/63   08/10/63
Forbes, Allie married Root, G. Denison 06/25/63   07/01/63
Forbes, Eliza J. married Fusselbaugh, John S. 07/30/63   08/20/63
Forbes, Ella Florence died 01/04/65   01/18/65
Forbes, J. Harry married Grafton, Annie M. 04/22/62   04/23/62
Force, Elizabeth A. C. (Mrs.) died 10/21/63   10/24/63
Ford, Amelia H. (Mrs.) died 09/12/63   09/14/63
Ford, Ann died 05/04/62   05/06/62
Ford, Ann married Patrick, George C. 07/16/65   08/05/65
Ford, Cassandra (Mrs.) died 03/16/65   03/18/65
Ford, Charles A. married Dillon, Sarah E. 12/11/63   12/16/63
Ford, Daniel White died 06/18/62   06/20/62
Ford, Elizabeth A. married Ryan, James A. 11/19/65   11/22/65
Ford, Elizabeth W. married Anderson, Jason G. 07/03/62   07/04/62
Ford, George M. married Baker, A. C. (Mrs.) 03/12/63   03/13/63
Ford, George W. died 06/12/61   06/14/61
Ford, John married Roberts, Margret Ann 01/04/63   01/06/63
```

Ford, John H. married Robertson, Anna M. 07/11/65   07/15/65
Ford, John Robert died 07/07/63   07/08/63
Ford, Kate B. married Stevens, Daniel G. 09/30/63   10/01/63
Ford, Laura married Hearn, William L. 11/21/65   11/24/65
Ford, Laura E. married Farrar, James 03/12/63   03/17/63
Ford, Lewis Marion died 04/10/64   04/11/64
Ford, Lewis Marion died 04/10/64   04/12/64
Ford, Mary married Meek, James 10/30/62   11/01/62
Ford, Mary A. married Kelly, William L. 05/26/64   05/28/64
Ford, Mary V. married Shipley, Bradley J. 01/07/62   01/09/62
Ford, Matilda H. married Burneys, William G. 11/27/64   11/29/64
Ford, Richard C. married Stevens, Lottie C. 09/17/61   12/04/61
Ford, Robert married Perry, Mary Francis 01/21/64   01/26/64
Ford, Sample (Dr.) married Wall, Jude Kyle 10/05/64   10/06/64
Ford, Samuel married Phipps, Martha Ann 09/22/63   09/26/63
Ford, Sarah A. died 06/23/63   06/25/63
Ford, Sarah Jane died 11/02/64   11/24/64
Ford, Thomas D. died 01/23/64   01/25/64
Ford, Walter died 01/04/65   01/16/65
Ford, William died 01/01/63   01/02/63
Ford, William H. married Reese, Martha Ann 09/20/65   09/25/65
Ford, William R. died 09/27/64   11/05/64
Foreman, Ann M. died 02/18/63   02/20/63
Foreman, Ann M. died 02/18/63   02/21/63
Foreman, Catherine J. married Foreman, Henry C. no date   01/31/61
Foreman, Henry C. married Foreman, Catherine J. no date   01/31/61
Foreman, Mary died 03/23/61   03/26/61
Foreman, Mary Ann married Johnson, Charles Alexander 10/31/65   11/24/65
Foreman, Mary Jane (Mrs.) died 05/28/63   05/29/63
Foreman, Rebecca died 02/07/62   02/08/62
Foreman, Sarah E. married Caulk, Jacob H. 07/31/65   10/31/65
Foreman, Susan (Mrs.) died 05/27/64   05/28/64
Forest, Nannie A. married Bean, Rufus S. (Lt.) 04/23/64   04/30/64
Forewood, Hannah J. married Sperver, John 11/22/64   11/23/64
Forit, Philip P. died 07/17/63   07/18/63
Forman, Alexander D. died 02/01/65   02/03/65
Forman, Harriet E. married Kerr, John M. 06/24/63   07/02/63
Forman, Joseph R. died 10/03/64   10/04/64
Forney, Isaac H. died 06/16/62   07/23/62
Forney, Martha married Jennings, Joseph 01/03/61   01/08/61
Forney, May died 08/27/63   08/31/63
Forney, Olivia died 07/02/63   07/04/63
Forney, Susan Roxillina died 06/08/65   06/10/65
Forrest, Andrew J. married Dorsey, Emma L. 06/20/64   07/02/64
Forrest, J. L. married Henry, Emma C. (Mrs.) 01/26/65   01/28/65
Forrest, John died 09/09/64   09/10/64
Forrest, Joseph T. (Capt.) died 05/24/63   07/09/63
Forrest, Mary married Dean, Ira 11/10/64   11/18/64
Forrest, Matthias died 07/11/64   07/12/64
Forrest, Sarah Ann died 07/01/65   07/03/65
Forrest, Sarah Jane married Cavey, Joseph 09/17/65   09/20/65
Forrestal, Mary died 01/13/63   01/15/63
Forrester, Barnet married Barrenger, Margaret 04/15/62   05/23/62
Forrester, Barnett died 02/06/64   02/08/64
Forrester, Charles married Marryman, Dorcass 01/05/64   01/09/64

Forrester, George Biddison died 01/09/61 01/10/61
Forrester, John J. married Mills, Margret 10/01/63 10/03/63
Forrester, John Turner died 03/04/63 03/05/63
Forrester, Leathe Anne (Mrs.) died 02/01/64 02/02/64
Forrester, Perry died 05/29/62 05/31/62
Forster, Mary C. married Rae, Robert 04/07/64 11/28/64
Forsyth, Jennia S. married Reaney, Alexander J. 02/20/61 03/21/62
Forsyth, Lydia died 02/04/62 02/12/62
Forsyth, Maggie married Moore, William W. 03/29/63 04/10/63
Forsyth, Manuel Thomas married Horner, Averilla 10/21/62 10/22/62
Forsyth, Martha died 09/28/65 09/29/65
Forsyth, Robert Burns died 12/18/61 12/23/61
Forsyth, Samuel J. married Brown, Louisa H. 12/22/64 02/21/65
Forsyth, Virginia married Reaney, Alexander J. 02/20/62 03/20/62
Forsythe, Emily V. married Crook, James L. 06/27/65 06/29/65
Forsythe, Matilda Cripps died 06/30/62 07/25/62
Forsythe, William H. died 12/03/64 12/05/64
Fort, Ann (Mrs.) died 10/09/64 10/11/64
Fort, Edward S. married Bell, Elizabeth E. 09/29/62 10/20/62
Fortie, George died 09/26/64 09/27/64
Fortie, John C. married Harper, Mary E. 04/17/64 04/19/64
Fortman, Mary married Krenitz, Charles Frank 05/31/65 06/03/65
Fortner, Josephine (Mrs.) died 10/15/63 10/17/63
Fortune, Emeline married Johnson, John 07/02/62 07/04/62
Fortune, Mary M. married Connell, Francis A. 07/08/63 07/10/63
Fortune, Thomas died 04/28/64 04/30/64
Forwood, William Stump (Dr.) married Bond, Addie 05/06/63 05/07/63
Fosler, Adella Eugene died 06/06/64 06/08/64
Fosler, Mary S. married Shea, George 12/08/64 12/20/64
Foss, Edwin died 10/08/61 10/09/61
Foss, John Jefferson Davis died 11/25/63 11/26/63
Foss, Margaret died 08/03/65 08/04/65
Fossett, Jennie married Seibert, Edward 11/27/62 12/04/62
Fossett, Mary Elizabeth married Davis, David 02/02/62 02/07/62
Foster, Addison married Maloney, Eliza Ann 01/03/65 01/07/65
Foster, Amanda A. married Letournau, George W. 05/19/61 05/28/61
Foster, Clifton died 04/04/61 04/05/61
Foster, E. married Cross, J. H. (Cpt.) 05/05/63 05/07/63
Foster, Edward F. married Weishampel, Tillie 12/13/64 12/19/64
Foster, Elizabeth (Mrs.) died 06/09/64 06/10/64
Foster, Elizabeth (Mrs.) died 02/18/65 02/20/65
Foster, Eugenia died 07/20/64 07/25/64
Foster, G. Nelson married Wheat, Alice D. 12/10/61 12/19/61
Foster, Janette married Mister, Thomas R. 01/04/63 01/07/63
Foster, John Tucker married Stonebraker, Mary Jane 03/01/64 03/02/64
Foster, Mahlon died 12/01/65 12/04/65
Foster, Marion died 12/01/65 12/05/65
Foster, Mary died 01/12/63 01/14/64
Foster, Mary Ellen died 08/24/65 08/25/65
Foster, Mattie married Maltby, L. U. 02/10/64 02/11/64
Foster, Uriah L. P. married Powers, Mary 10/24/65 12/12/65
Foster, William H. (Sgt.) died 08/25/64 09/10/64
Fouke, Clara Virginia died 08/29/63 09/18/63
Foulds, Kate married Wilson, John G. 09/01/63 09/02/63
Foulkes, Elizabeth A. (Mrs.) died 09/25/64 09/29/64

Foulkes, George H. died 01/29/65 01/31/65
Foulkes, George H. died 01/29/65 02/01/65
Fountain, John T. died 02/09/63 02/11/63
Fountain, Marcy, Jr. married Thawley, Annie E. 01/20/63 01/27/63
Fountain, Margaret married Judson, Charles C. (Rev.) 07/22/61 07/27/61
Fountain, Mary died 02/25/64 02/27/64
Fountin, Orpha H. married Ward, Thomas H. 12/31/61 01/02/62
Fout, George C. married Dwyer, Laura L. 07/19/65 07/22/65
Fout, Philip P. died 06/17/63 07/18/63
Foutz, Debbie married Sefton, John W. 11/13/61 11/15/61
Fowble, Cynthia married Corcoran, Christopher 06/01/65 06/03/65
Fowble, William married Frazier, Juliana M. 07/27/64 07/30/64
Fowble, William H. died 11/05/64 11/07/64
Fowler, Amanda married Joiner, Daniel 02/25/64 02/27/64
Fowler, Ann Jane (Mrs.) married Fowler, Robert 04/28/64 04/30/64
Fowler, Charles V. died 01/23/62 01/27/62
Fowler, Charlotte M. married White, Marcellus (Cpt.) 05/24/63 05/26/63
Fowler, Daniel D. married Maloney, Sarah 05/01/64 05/04/64
Fowler, David Q. married Smith, Laura V. 01/23/61 01/26/61
Fowler, H. Sophia died 08/25/61 09/12/61
Fowler, Harry C. died 02/14/64 02/19/64
Fowler, Henry (Cpt.) died 06/28/64 06/29/64
Fowler, James O. married Leitch, Katie E. 07/30/63 08/01/63
Fowler, John married Holtz, Kate 12/24/61 08/16/62
Fowler, John (Capt.) married Espy, Margaret 11/19/61 11/21/61
Fowler, John B. married Palmer, Elizabeth B. 12/17/63 12/19/63
Fowler, John E. died 10/01/63 10/03/63
Fowler, Malvina (Mrs.) died 04/27/64 04/28/64
Fowler, Margaret Josephine died 03/17/64 03/23/64
Fowler, Martha Elizabeth died 02/09/64 02/11/64
Fowler, Martha P. died 06/10/61 06/11/61
Fowler, Mary E. married Jackson, Charles 05/18/65 06/02/65
Fowler, Matilda C. died 07/07/61 07/09/61
Fowler, Rachel married Stinchcomb, Nelson P. 11/30/62 12/02/62
Fowler, Robert married Fowler, Ann Jane (Mrs.) 04/28/64 04/30/64
Fowler, Samuel B. died 03/15/61 03/18/61
Fowler, Sarah died 08/11/61 08/12/61
Fowler, Thomas married Johns, Rebecca 11/24/63 11/28/63
Fowler, Thomas D. died no date 05/09/65
Fowler, William R. married Tayman, Mollie J. 05/10/64 05/12/64
Fowler, William T. married Fitchett, Zetville 10/19/63 10/26/63
Fowler, William W. married Miskell, Ann (Mrs.) 03/15/63 03/18/63
Fowley, William married Tierney, Mary 04/07/61 04/10/61
Fox, Charles G. married Cord, Carrie H. 10/12/65 11/15/65
Fox, Eliza E. married Jones, Edward D. 03/28/64 04/04/64
Fox, Elizabeth Jane died 07/01/63 07/02/63
Fox, F. J. E. married Bedford, Julia Belle 01/03/61 01/12/61
Fox, George died 01/26/62 01/27/62
Fox, George (Sgt.) died 06/26/64 08/03/64
Fox, Luther died 03/20/62 03/21/62
Fox, Luther died 03/20/62 03/22/62
Fox, Margaret died 12/08/61 12/10/61
Fox, Orlando B. married Brooks, Mora B. (Mrs.) 11/18/63 11/25/63
Fox, Rebecca died 12/12/61 12/13/61
Fox, William Henry Harrison died 08/22/62 10/11/62

Foxwell, Love Adelaide died 12/27/64 12/28/64
Foxwell, Love Adelaide died 12/27/64 12/30/64
Foxwell, Martha Lucinda died 01/02/65 01/03/65
Foxwell, Sarah F. married Han, John F. 08/14/62 08/23/62
Foy, Amanda died 04/14/62 04/16/62
Foy, Harriet died 08/07/64 08/08/64
Foy, Isaac William married Turk, Maggie J. 08/20/63 08/26/63
Foy, Joseph F. died 05/10/64 06/10/64
Foy, Margaret C. (Mrs.) died 12/19/63 12/21/63
Foy, Margaret C. (Mrs.) died 12/19/63 12/22/63
Foy, Mary A. (Mrs.) married Hull, J. D. 12/09/63 05/03/64
Foy, Mary A. (Mrs.) married Hall, J. D. 12/09/63 05/04/64
Foy, Mary Ann died 02/18/63 02/19/63
Foy, Mary C. married Briscoe, Charles A. 10/05/65 10/11/65
Fraley, Harry married Strasbaugh, Susan 12/21/65 11/28/65
Frames, Edward J. married Heffner, Rebecca 03/12/62 03/17/62
Frames, James F. married Van Meter, Sallie E. 07/02/61 07/04/61
Frampton, Henry Thomas died 06/03/62 06/04/62
Frampton, John Thomas died 04/04/64 04/07/64
Frampton, Josephine K. married Cruse, John H. 07/15/64 08/24/64
Frampton, Thomas F. died 06/03/62 06/26/62
Frampton, Thomas Henry died 08/26/61 09/06/61
Fran, Mary H. married Delany, James J. 03/09/65 03/13/65
France, Ambrose M. married Griffin, Laura V. 02/28/64 03/26/64
France, Charles D. married Batchelor, Sarah E. 12/12/65 12/16/65
France, Elenore died 03/21/65 03/22/65
France, Elizabeth (Mrs.) died 02/04/64 02/06/64
France, Emma married Ertingen, Baron Otto DeLeutrum 04/24/62 05/15/62
France, John died 11/10/63 11/11/63
France, Richard Oliver died 08/31/65 09/13/65
Frances, Eliza Jane died 10/09/62 10/10/62
Francis, Amanda died 02/09/64 03/25/64
Francis, Amelia Lerew died 04/14/64 04/15/64
Francis, Charlotte C. married Bartlett, William S. 09/14/64 09/20/64
Francis, Elizabeth died 05/01/61 05/02/61
Francis, Georgina Clara died 01/02/63 01/03/63
Francis, Helen married McJilton, William D. 03/23/65 03/24/65
Francis, James died 06/30/62 07/01/62
Francis, John A. married Rock, Elizabeth 04/24/62 04/29/62
Francis, Joseph David died 06/15/62 06/16/62
Francis, Margaret died 06/16/61 06/18/61
Francis, Margaret A. married Brooks, Francis 10/30/61 02/01/62
Francis, Noah married Smith, Hester 12/24/65 12/28/65
Franck, George C., Jr. died 07/06/64 07/08/64
Franck, Martin V. B. married Phelan, Lizzie T. 11/23/63 12/02/63
Frank, Christian L. died 08/05/64 08/06/64
Frank, Elizabeth (Mrs.) died 01/25/63 01/27/63
Frank, Hannah married Rosenstock, S. 01/20/64 02/25/64
Frank, Jennie S. married Carey, John W. 03/26/65 03/30/65
Frank, John A. died 07/15/64 07/21/64
Frank, Lucy, Elizabeth died 11/29/63 12/01/63
Frank, Milton B. married Abbott, Mary E. 01/09/61 01/12/61
Frank, Oscar W. married Hall, Kate L. 10/08/63 10/12/63
Frankel, Leopold married Lansburgh, Henrietta 02/10/61 02/13/61
Frankenstein, Joseph died 05/01/64 05/03/64

Frankland, Anna married Hardester, John T. 12/30/63   02/08/64
Frankland, Ellen (Mrs.) died 01/10/65   01/11/65
Frankland, S. Elizabeth married Gibson, William J. 09/14/65   09/16/65
Franklin, Anne R. married Schley, Winfield Scott (USN) 09/10/63
    09/11/63
Franklin, Benjamin H. married Ellis, Kate 05/27/64   06/02/64
Franklin, Charles C. married Morgan, Eliza J. 06/11/61   06/15/61
Franklin, Chase married Accman, Elizabeth 04/12/64   04/28/64
Franklin, Elias died 10/26/64   11/04/64
Franklin, Elizabeth Ann married Wilt, John W. 12/29/64   01/02/65
Franklin, Emeline died 07/21/61   07/23/61
Franklin, George married Morsell, Rosanna 07/26/65   08/09/65
Franklin, George B. married Stanley, Medora 03/31/64   04/04/64
Franklin, George R. married Justice, Mary E. 05/10/64   05/11/64
Franklin, Jesse married Ward, Frances Ann 11/14/61   11/16/61
Franklin, John F. married Chaplain, Olivia 02/16/65   02/18/65
Franklin, Mary E. died 09/02/65   09/04/65
Franklin, Mary J. married Sorrell, William 10/06/64   10/07/64
Franklin, Mary V. married Jones, J. G. 11/27/65   12/16/65
Franklin, Rosena married Foot, William 04/17/65   04/29/65
Franklin, Sallie W. married Cannon, C. K. 11/12/61   11/22/61
Frankln, H. J. died 07/21/61   07/23/61
Franz, Mary married Hermes, Henry 05/30/65   06/05/65
Franz, Mary married Herbes, Henry 05/30/65   06/06/65
Fraser, Alexander Crawford died 09/05/64   09/06/64
Fraser, James A. died 06/10/63   06/12/63
Fraser, John died 09/11/63   11/07/63
Fraser, Lena died 11/02/63   11/03/63
Frasier, Frances Virginia G. married Krauss, Charles T. 07/08/63
    07/11/63
Fray, Elizabeth Ann (Mrs.) died 10/14/63   10/15/63
Fray, Emanuel Robert died 06/13/64   06/14/64
Fray, Samuel died 12/07/64   12/08/64
Fray, William married Tracy, Ann Elizabeth 08/14/62   09/17/62
Frazer, Henry married Carroll, Ellen 12/24/61   12/25/61
Frazer, James married Nicelson, Eliza A. Becker 05/16/64   05/18/64
Frazer, Meely (Mrs.) died 01/05/63   01/07/63
Frazier, Basil died no date 05/10/64
Frazier, Caroline died 08/10/61   08/12/61
Frazier, Charles Nickles died 04/22/65   04/24/65
Frazier, Ellen L. married Berkley, John M. 11/14/65   11/18/65
Frazier, Emma Turner died 09/27/63   09/29/63
Frazier, George Marion died 02/04/65   02/07/65
Frazier, James Edward died 04/01/62   04/03/62
Frazier, John died 03/10/64   03/14/64
Frazier, John Lemuel Rusk died 03/17/63   03/18/63
Frazier, Juliana M. married Fowble, William 07/27/64   07/30/64
Frazier, Lizzie A. married Sanders, George E. 12/23/62   12/27/62
Frazier, Martha A. married Belbson, William R. 09/13/65   09/23/65
Frazier, Sarah A. (Mrs.) died 12/08/62   01/13/63
Frazier, William A. died 02/07/64   02/08/64
Freburger, Francis Marion died 08/23/64   08/24/64
Freburger, Isabella Virginia died 11/23/63   11/24/63
Freburger, Mary E. married Sewell, Joseph 11/14/65   11/16/65
Freburger, Maurice Clinton died 01/13/63   01/14/63

Freburger, Sarah R. married Bollman, Charles A. 12/06/64   12/14/64
Fredenberg, John married Briddell, Emily 09/01/64   09/08/64
Frederick, Eliza died 03/30/64   03/31/64
Frederick, George A. married Everist, Mary E. 01/10/65   01/12/65
Frederick, Henry C. married McMillian, Mary A. 05/18/65   08/17/65
Frederick, James Laurence died 07/29/65   07/31/65
Frederick, John died no date 03/20/65
Frederick, John L. died 09/20/64   09/21/64
Frederick, Mary A. married Poston, Daniel T. 12/25/64   01/02/65
Frederick, Peter died 06/08/63   06/10/63
Frederick, Robert died 02/27/62   02/28/62
Frederick, Robert died 02/27/62   03/01/62
Frederick, Samuel Stork died 11/24/63   11/25/63
Frederick, Samuel Taylor died 02/14/61   02/15/61
Frederick, Sarah Elizabeth died 12/04/61   12/05/61
Frederick, Simon died 07/00/00   10/06/64
Frederick, William married Brooks, Mary A. 05/04/64   07/18/65
Frederick, William Clinton died 09/07/65   09/08/65
Fredricks, Agnes Eugenia married Sauerbrey, Ernst A. (Lt.) 02/02/63   02/04/63
Free, Ann Eliza died 04/12/61   04/13/61
Free, Emma Permelia died 03/23/63   03/25/63
Free, Milton died 12/01/62   12/03/62
Freeburger, Alexander married Boulton, Maggie 10/05/62   10/06/62
Freeburger, Julia (Mrs.) married Fields, William 06/16/65   06/20/65
Freeburger, Lydia died 08/27/61   08/28/61
Freederick, William A. died 06/09/65   06/10/65
Freedy, Alfred married Rider, Surfeener 03/16/61   05/22/61
Freeland, Edward married Griffin, Emma C. 09/18/62   09/20/62
Freeland, Edward H. married Duvall, Ella 04/11/63   04/14/63
Freeland, Helen Augusta married Scott, James M. 02/08/65   02/28/65
Freeland, Susan died 03/20/61   03/23/61
Freeling, Henry married Howard, Mary 01/28/64   01/30/64
Freeman, Ann (Mrs.) died 12/12/65   12/13/65
Freeman, Christine L. (Mrs.) died 03/25/64   03/26/64
Freeman, Ellenora married Pully, James 09/02/62   09/06/62
Freeman, Father died 02/28/62   03/01/62
Freeman, James died no date   04/11/64
Freeman, James married Grierson, Jane E. 10/19/64   10/21/64
Freeman, James B. died 07/23/63   07/24/63
Freeman, Josiah D. died 12/30/61   01/02/62
Freeman, Lizzie L. married Tull, J. Emory (Dr.) 03/02/65   03/04/65
Freeman, Martha A. died 11/17/65   11/18/65
Freeman, Mary A. married Boutwell, Minson W. 03/14/64   03/17/64
Freeman, Mary Shipley died 12/24/62   12/25/62
Freeman, Puella married Toy, Richard H. 04/11/61   04/18/61
Freeman, William married Wyatt, Nancy A. 07/26/65   09/19/65
Freeman, William H. died 03/23/63   03/24/63
Freeman, William Walsh died no date   12/03/62
Freemon, Minty (Mrs.) married Parris, Dennis 04/12/63   04/18/63
Freeze, Margaret married Rice, Stephen 01/06/61   01/22/61
Freeze, Mary J. married Rice, Peter 04/10/64   05/30/64
Freise, John died 06/04/65   06/05/65
Freitag, George married Greenzbach, Emma 01/12/65   01/16/65
French, Eleanor Elizabeth married Harris, George M. no date   02/26/61

French, Ellen A. married Shadrick, William R. 12/28/62 02/24/63
French, Emma Gertrude died 02/06/63 02/10/63
French, Mary C. (Mrs.) died 10/04/63 10/06/63
French, Robert died 01/18/61 01/22/61
French, William, Sr. died 03/12/63 03/14/63
Frere, Carrie C. married Denham, L. J. 07/25/65 07/27/65
Fresch, Christina married Murray, Frederick F. 02/27/65 03/02/65
Freshorn, Jacob H. died 03/31/62 04/03/62
Freshour, Greenbury died 03/29/65 03/30/65
Freshour, Jacob H. died no date 04/08/62
Fretwell, Charles A. L. died 03/20/64 03/23/64
Freund, Charlotte Elizabeth died 04/04/65 04/07/65
Freund, Henry died 04/05/65 04/07/65
Frew, James died 01/01/65 01/02/65
Frew, James died 01/01/65 01/03/65
Frew, James Stuart died 08/06/65 08/07/65
Frey, Catherine died 01/06/65 01/07/65
Frey, Edward S. died 11/22/61 11/23/61
Frey, Franklin Cornelius died 03/09/65 03/10/65
Frey, Franklin Cornelius died 03/10/65 03/11/65
Frey, Jacob K. died 11/24/61 11/25/61
Frey, John W. married McComas, Mary E. 12/22/64 12/26/64
Frey, Lewis married Gray, S. Virginia 12/07/65 12/13/65
Frey, Lizzie S. married Sisco, J. Edward 12/17/61 12/18/61
Frey, Louisa C. married Nelker, J. F. 11/15/64 11/26/64
Frey, Margaret C. married Lunn, William F. 10/14/62 10/20/62
Frey, Mary died 10/06/62 10/09/62
Frey, Susan died 12/24/62 12/25/62
Frick, Frank married Lurman, Jenny D. 01/01/61 01/04/61
Friell, Andrew died 03/07/64 03/08/64
Frien, Robert Gilmor died 09/17/62 09/18/62
Friend, Elizabeth died 12/14/63 12/16/63
Friese, Lizzie Georgette died 11/05/62 11/07/62
Fringer, Mary A. died 10/07/61 10/08/61
Frisbie, E. G. married Lingenfelder, Amelia 10/20/63 10/21/63
Frisbie, William died 06/10/65 06/12/65
Frisby, Dinah died 09/05/63 09/07/63
Frisby, George W. died 01/11/63 01/15/63
Frisby, Margaret died 08/18/61 08/27/61
Frisby, Mary E. (Mrs.) died 01/12/63 01/14/64
Frisby, Richard died 07/26/62 07/29/62
Frisby, William G. died 11/21/65 11/22/65
Frisby, William H. married Giles, Mary Priscilla 12/30/60 01/02/61
Frisby, William H. married Johnson, Sarah 09/22/64 09/24/64
Frisch, John N. died 08/31/63 09/02/63
Frisch, Matilda died 07/04/63 07/06/63
Frisly, Samuel died 09/16/62 09/17/62
Frisry, Lizzie B. died 10/08/65 10/10/65
Fritz, Lizzie married Koppelman, George 11/10/64 11/15/64
Frizell, John C. married Wright, Carrie A. 10/08/61 10/15/61
Frizzell, Isaac died 05/27/61 06/07/61
Frizzell, Rachel died 04/23/64 04/25/64
Froakman, William married Ulm, Elizabeth 08/26/64 08/27/64
Frost, Annie E. married DeLaMatyr, Edward B. 01/24/65 01/28/65
Frost, Carrie (Mrs.) died 07/20/63 07/27/63

Frost, Carrie B. married Townsend, Jeremiah 01/27/63   01/30/63
Frost, James A. died 03/29/61   04/06/61
Frost, Maggie Elizabeth died 08/01/63   08/06/63
Frost, Mary died 11/20/61   11/21/61
Frothingham, Charles L. died 05/03/63   05/05/63
Frush, Charles E. married Leas, Sallie E. 08/25/63   08/27/63
Frush, Moreau F. (Dr.) married Edmunds, Mary L. 05/16/64   05/18/64
Frush, Moreau Forrest (Dr.) died 04/06/65   04/07/65
Fry, Gantlett died 07/11/63   07/13/63
Fry, Joetta Amos died 04/10/65   04/12/65
Fry, John Walter died 12/08/63   12/16/63
Fry, Rebecca L. (Mrs.) died 09/24/65   09/26/65
Fry, Thomas died 04/01/63   12/16/63
Fry, William O. died 08/21/63   08/22/63
Frybogle, Harriet married Bellowson, Charles W. 06/14/64   06/21/64
Fryer, Elizabeth I. married DeGoey, William W. 07/26/63   08/10/63
Fryer, Jane Olive died 01/19/61   01/21/61
Fryer, Jennie Olive married Clenighen, Robert 09/14/65   09/16/65
Fryer, Joseph P. died 06/08/64   06/08/64
Fugitt, Carrie Louise died 07/05/62   07/09/62
Fugitt, George T. died 03/10/65   03/13/65
Fulford, Nelson Stocksdale died 08/19/63   08/24/63
Fulham, Catherine (Mrs.) died 02/22/64   03/16/64
Fuller, Annie married Carter, Willie B. 01/26/65   02/06/65
Fuller, Charles F. died 07/17/61   07/18/61
Fuller, Charles W. married Sewell, Laura V. 07/29/63   07/31/63
Fuller, Elizabeth married Coburn, Henry 11/30/63   12/08/63
Fuller, Ella Grace died 09/19/63   09/25/63
Fuller, Ellender died 02/07/61   02/08/61
Fuller, F. married Stewart, Ella R. 01/14/64   01/15/64
Fuller, Isabella A. died 05/22/63   05/23/63
Fuller, J. Warren married Cook, Maria V. 01/29/63   02/07/63
Fuller, Josiah died 09/03/65   09/08/65
Fuller, Josiah, Jr. died 09/03/65   09/09/65
Fuller, Lizzie W. died 07/17/61   07/18/61
Fuller, Louisa married Fish, Charles 05/05/64   05/23/64
Fuller, Lucy Bradford died 11/27/65   11/29/65
Fuller, Maria Elizabeth married Swift, Chaney H. 03/26/63   04/03/63
Fuller, Mary E. married Carback, R. C. 11/24/64   12/02/64
Fuller, Mary Elizabeth died 10/05/63   10/06/63
Fuller, Sallie Margaret died 12/20/61   12/24/61
Fuller, Sarah L. (Mrs.) married Hunter, J. T. 03/17/63   03/25/63
Fuller, William H. married Thomas, Minty 05/02/61   05/08/61
Fullerton, George W. died 07/29/61   08/17/61
Fullum, James married Tuxford, Mary Ann 01/18/63   01/20/63
Fullum, James married Tuxford, Mary A. 01/15/63   01/23/63
Fulton, Clinton Palmer died 10/01/64   10/03/64
Fulton, David Mercer died 08/31/61   09/04/61
Fulton, Emma W. married Nicholson, George T. L. 11/17/63   11/19/63
Fulton, James married Oster, Kate 01/19/64   02/09/64
Fulton, John Bell died 10/01/61   03/05/62
Fulton, Mabel died 12/27/65   12/28/65
Fulton, Mabel died 12/27/65   12/29/65
Fulton, Margaret Ann died 02/14/64   02/15/64
Fulton, Matilda Jane died 02/27/62   03/05/62

Fulton, Robert died 04/03/63   04/04/63
Fulton, Robert John died 07/17/64   07/18/64
Fulton, Susan died 09/14/63   09/15/63
Funk, Grace Alverda died 11/15/63   11/16/63
Funk, Rosina M. died 08/29/64   08/30/64
Fuqua, Sarah C. died 02/12/61   02/21/61
Furlong, Elizabeth died 01/02/65   01/03/65
Furlong, George Weber died 05/03/63   05/04/63
Furlong, Johny died 01/24/64   01/25/64
Furst, Elizabeth Eugenia died 08/19/65   08/21/65
Fury, John Shivers died 03/09/64   03/10/64
Fuss, John died 09/04/64   09/05/64
Fussel, Jacob died 06/22/62   06/24/62
Fusselbaugh, Amanda M. died 10/27/61   10/29/61
Fusselbaugh, John S. married Forbes, Eliza J. 07/30/63   08/20/63
Fusselbaugh, John Summerfield died 12/30/64   12/31/64
Fusselbaugh, Robert G. died 12/10/64   12/12/64
Fusselbaugh, William died 09/16/62   09/17/62
Fussell, Clarissa died 04/28/63   04/30/63
Fussell, Joseph S. died 12/06/64   02/27/65
Gable, Benjamin F. married Cook, Mary Elizabeth 10/19/63   10/22/63
Gable, John married Weis, Henrietta 06/11/61   06/15/61
Gable, Mary E. married Fendrice, Francis 05/11/65   05/27/65
Gable, Sarah Jane married Creighton, Robert H. 08/04/61   08/13/61
Gabler, August died 05/10/63   05/18/63
Gadd, Dally married Short, Perry 06/25/62   07/07/62
Gadd, Emily A. died 10/02/65   10/04/65
Gadd, John died 05/01/65   05/03/65
Gaddes, Alexander died no date   10/18/65
Gaddess, Alexander died 03/31/65   06/29/65
Gaddess, Virginius married Tuxworth, Anna E. 12/13/64   12/17/64
Gade, Kate T. married Watkins, James S. 12/26/61   12/30/61
Gaehle, Lewis married Kammerer, Amelia 09/01/63   09/05/63
Gaehle, William died 04/28/61   04/30/61
Gaertling, Julia died 07/01/64   07/02/64
Gaertling, Mary died 05/22/64   05/23/64
Gaertling, Michael died 01/06/63   01/08/63
Gaertling, Rosina died 11/11/62   11/12/62
Gaffard, William married Barrows, Rebecca A. B. (Mrs.) 12/07/64
     12/08/64
Gaffney, Michael died 01/22/65   01/23/65
Gafford, Ann died 03/26/61   03/28/61
Gafford, Samuel D. died 01/04/61   01/05/61
Gafford, Samuel L. married Mosher, Lizzie W. 10/22/61   10/24/61
Gage, Rebecca V. died no date   01/04/62
Gahagan, Annie married O'Roke, John 09/19/65   09/21/65
Gahring, George J. married Levy, Lizzie A. 06/02/64   06/09/64
Gaierty, Patrick married Matthews, Julia 02/11/61   06/08/61
Gaillard, E. M. married Graves, R. H. 09/08/63   12/28/63
Gaillion, Johnnie died 07/25/65   09/01/65
Gaines, Ann E. died 10/12/61   10/14/61
Gaines, Ann Louisa married Johnson, Samuel 12/04/62   12/10/62
Gaines, Henrietta married Johnson, Thomas 07/08/62   07/12/62
Gaines, Lear Ann married Dyer, Levin 04/16/63   04/18/63
Gaines, Rosella died 07/06/62   07/08/62

Gaines, William R. married Wilkins, Georgeanna 12/13/64   12/16/64
Gains, Mason married Smith, Hettie 02/22/64   02/26/64
Gaither, Alice died 12/20/63   12/22/63
Gaither, Carie Lee died 02/08/65   02/13/65
Gaither, Charles K. died 06/15/65   06/17/65
Gaither, Denis married Mewshaw, Rachel 05/29/62   05/31/62
Gaither, Eliza died 06/13/64   06/14/64
Gaither, Ellijah married Weeks, Elizabeth A. 01/05/64   01/15/64
Gaither, Henrietta M. died 11/06/61   12/11/61
Gaither, Joseph A. died 08/17/63   08/19/63
Gaither, Josephine married Isaacs, John H. 10/24/65   10/31/65
Gaither, Lizzie J. died 03/13/62   04/16/62
Gaither, Louisiana married Brown, B. Benton 10/15/61   10/22/61
Gaither, Margaret Matilda died 06/15/64   06/16/64
Gaither, Maria L. died 09/25/62   10/16/62
Gaither, Mary Ann married Weeks, William A. 02/19/61   02/27/61
Gaither, Mary M (Mrs.) died 03/19/63   03/21/63
Gaither, Rea Y. married Higgins, W. D. 05/18/65   08/12/65
Gaither, Samuel C. died 05/18/61   05/20/61
Gaither, Thomas B. married Porter, Lucretia D. 04/25/65   04/29/65
Galagher, Ann (Mrs.) died 08/02/65   08/03/65
Galagher, Rosann died 06/03/64   06/08/64
Galbraith, George died 08/13/62   08/14/62
Galbraith, J. Clifton married Hall, Sophia L. 05/13/62   05/24/62
Gale, Ananias died 01/04/64   01/08/64
Gale, Charles H. married Redmond, Charlotte E. 11/20/65   12/16/65
Gale, George died 11/08/63   11/13/63
Gale, George G. died 02/27/64   03/11/64
Gale, Grafton L. D. married Jones, Leah O. 07/16/63   07/18/63
Gale, Henrietta (Mrs.) died 04/28/65   04/29/65
Gale, Henry K. died 07/22/62   07/23/62
Gale, Rosa Bell died 08/21/64   08/25/64
Gallagher, Ann died 04/30/61   05/01/61
Gallagher, E. G. (Lieut.) married Charlton, Anna J. C. 08/05/61   08/07/61
Gallagher, Elizabeth (Mrs.) died 02/26/64   02/27/64
Gallagher, Emma died 04/08/64   04/09/64
Gallagher, Emma Veronica T. died 12/24/61   12/25/61
Gallagher, Estelle died 12/18/61   12/20/61
Gallagher, Estelle Jane died 12/18/61   12/25/61
Gallagher, Francis married O'Brien, Jane 01/01/62   04/26/62
Gallagher, Francis P. died 01/29/61   01/30/61
Gallagher, Hugh married Murtugh, Catherine no date 05/29/62
Gallagher, Hugh married Colton, Susan 02/05/65   02/07/65
Gallagher, Jane died 12/05/65   12/07/65
Gallagher, John died 08/10/64   08/12/64
Gallagher, Joseph married Mullen, Ellen 05/14/63   05/23/63
Gallagher, Kate died 08/12/61   08/15/61
Gallagher, Margaret T. died 05/16/61   05/25/61
Gallagher, Mary died 02/07/61   02/11/61
Gallagher, Mary E. (Mrs.) died 07/18/65   07/19/65
Gallagher, Mary E. (Mrs.) died 07/18/65   07/20/65
Gallagher, Mary Lavinia married O'Neill, John F. 06/27/65   06/30/65
Gallagher, Patrick (Cpl.) died 08/30/64   09/03/64
Gallagher, Rachel Adelaide died 12/26/62   12/27/62

```
Gallagher, Susan married McMahon, Michael 06/26/64   03/07/65
Gallaher, B. Frank died 01/09/62   01/16/62
Gallaher, Eliza Ariss died 08/21/63   08/24/63
Gallaher, Francis P. died 01/29/61   01/31/61
Gallaher, S. G. R. died 07/16/62   07/17/62
Gallaway, Adelia Douglas died 07/21/63   07/24/63
Gallaway, Mary married Gosnell, William T. 12/28/62   01/02/63
Gallaway, William married Burgess, Laura V. 06/01/64   06/07/64
Gallion, John J. died 11/07/64   12/30/64
Gallion, Josephine died 02/24/62   03/03/62
Galloway, Amanda Lee died 02/21/63   03/03/63
Galloway, Annie married Andrews, Daniel S. 04/26/63   05/02/63
Galloway, Edward Carey died 06/01/61   06/04/61
Galloway, Gorgge died 02/29/64   03/02/64
Galloway, Maggie J. married Griffith, Lewis 08/28/65   08/29/65
Galloway, Martha A. married Watson, Thomas 08/10/65   08/17/65
Galloway, Mary E. died 06/29/65   07/24/65
Galloway, Sarah died 07/22/65   07/24/65
Galloway, William married Burgers, Laura V. 06/02/64   06/06/64
Galloway, William J. died 03/07/65   03/18/65
Gallup, Daniel married DeVoe, Ann Maria 04/19/64   04/30/64
Gallup, Joseph E. died 10/01/62   10/03/62
Gallup, Lizzie A. married Nelson, George A. 01/03/61   01/10/61
Gallup, Mary L. died 04/22/65   05/04/65
Gallup, Robert died no date   12/11/61
Galoway, Mary Ida died 09/10/64   09/12/64
Galoway, Sophia married Green, William 09/24/63   09/26/63
Galt, Henrietta married Walters, Joseph T. 09/07/65   09/14/65
Galt, Margaret E. married Motter, J. Taylor 11/28/65   11/30/65
Galt, Mary C. married Goldsborough, Charles 11/07/65   11/13/65
Galt, Sterling M. died 10/24/65   11/01/65
Galvin, Susan (Mrs.) died 02/03/63   02/04/63
Galway, Honoria married McCoulough, John 04/19/61   04/24/61
Gamble, Elizabeth L. married Spence, Thomas B. 09/29/65   10/24/65
Gamble, Rosa J. married Lewis, C. W. 03/11/63   03/14/63
Gambrall, George (USN) died 10/09/63   11/03/63
Gambril, Mary A. married Boone, Thomas C. 03/08/64   03/09/64
Gambrill, (Mrs. George E.) died 01/16/63   01/21/63
Gambrill, Abbey married Brown, John W. 01/04/65   01/09/65
Gambrill, Benjamin Franklin died 12/17/62   02/12/63
Gambrill, Charles A. married Hook, Emma L. 02/24/62   02/27/62
Gambrill, Charles Edward died 12/26/61   12/27/61
Gambrill, Charles Edward died 12/26/61   12/28/61
Gambrill, Flaviller Homes died 03/31/63   04/14/63
Gambrill, George married Spedden, Emily 04/14/64   04/16/64
Gambrill, H. D. married Schley, Ellen E. 11/25/62   11/27/62
Gambrill, Janie married Tyson, Robert 06/04/63   06/06/63
Gambrill, John Wesley died 05/22/63   05/25/63
Gambrill, William B. married Burns, Sarah E. 11/16/64   11/24/64
Gammia, Rebecca A. died 02/01/64   02/03/64
Gammie, Mary Ida died 12/15/63   12/19/63
Gannon, Joseph died 04/05/64   04/06/64
Gannon, Peter married Black, Mary Louisa 03/30/62   04/01/62
Gant, Arabella married Chase, George Thomas 12/23/60   01/03/61
Gant, Emily W. married Sparrow, Lewis G. 02/12/61   02/13/61
```

Gantt, Mary died 06/09/61   06/11/61
Gar, William H. E. (USN) married Mass, Ellen M. 04/08/64   04/27/64
Garash, John Benjamin married Ringrose, Mary Bell 03/29/63   04/09/63
Gardener, William J. died 01/07/65   01/09/65
Gardiner, Ann Gain (Mrs.) died 05/18/63   07/28/63
Gardiner, Delilah M. married Canon, George D. 06/09/64   06/10/64
Gardiner, Ida married Bradt, Henry Walter 08/16/65   08/19/65
Gardner, Ann died 01/22/65   01/24/65
Gardner, Ann (Mrs.) died 01/22/65   01/23/65
Gardner, Ann M. married Anderson, Andrew P. 01/22/61   01/24/61
Gardner, Annie J. married Tagart, Samuel 07/21/64   07/22/64
Gardner, Augustus M. married Ehrhart, Annie R. 09/02/62   09/04/62
Gardner, Daniel Ray died 12/18/65   12/19/65
Gardner, Daniel Ray died 12/18/65   12/20/65
Gardner, Edward Everett died 02/19/64   02/20/64
Gardner, Elizabeth married Standclif, John David 12/06/63   12/09/63
Gardner, George died 09/25/62   09/26/62
Gardner, George W. died 02/15/65   02/21/65
Gardner, George Washington died 02/15/65   02/22/65
Gardner, Harry died 03/23/61   03/26/61
Gardner, Jane Julia died 09/24/62   09/29/62
Gardner, John M. died 09/15/65   09/16/65
Gardner, John McClellan died 06/22/64   06/23/64
Gardner, Marcella C. died 07/26/61   07/27/61
Gardner, Martha R. married Morrow, Silas 04/09/62   04/10/62
Gardner, Mary E. married Ogle, James M. 12/26/61   12/30/61
Gardner, Mary Elizabeth died 07/17/63   07/20/63
Gardner, Mary L. married Valiant, James B. 03/28/64   04/02/64
Gardner, Mary V. married Livingston, W. Edwin 10/17/65   10/19/65
Gardner, Mollie A. married Kerr, James W. 10/13/63   10/16/63
Gardner, Nellie married Walcott, Orville D. 10/25/64   05/30/65
Gardner, Rosalie died 04/23/65   04/26/65
Gardner, Samuel married Bevan, Eliza E. 05/23/65   05/25/65
Gardner, Susan E. married Arnold, William H. 10/09/64   10/12/64
Gardner, William died 03/24/63   03/25/63
Gardner, William K. died 12/08/60   02/05/61
Garey, Garland died 02/05/61   02/07/61
Garey, J. Wesley died 02/17/62   02/19/62
Garey, Minnie A. married Holton, H. Benton 08/27/61   09/12/61
Garing, Laura Jane died 12/03/61   12/04/61
Garland, Mary Florence died 02/04/64   02/06/64
Garland, Thomas T. H. died 05/26/65   06/06/65
Garmhausen, Frederick C. married Chaney, Lizzie 08/18/63   08/26/63
Garmhausen, Margaret M. died 05/26/65   05/27/65
Garner, Benjamin R. married Rawlings, Mary Zora 02/09/64   03/04/64
Garner, Emily married Rion, Thomas 11/26/63   11/28/63
Garner, Hellen married Hunt, James H. 02/16/64   03/04/64
Garreet, Hezekiah married Manoka, Sarah J. 04/22/62   04/23/62
Garretson, George W. died 09/05/62   09/11/62
Garrett, Amelia married Gees, Thomas B. 05/03/64   05/06/64
Garrett, John died 04/21/61   04/23/61
Garrett, Maggie J. married Ijams, Charles H. 08/17/63   08/26/63
Garrett, Martha Jane married Armstrong, Thomas 10/16/62   10/17/62
Garrett, Mary Sadonia died 05/14/65   05/16/65
Garrett, Thomas married Harris, Ellen 03/05/63   03/07/63

Garrett, William married Lewis, Caroline 07/02/61   07/03/61
Garrett, William Thomas died 01/28/63   03/03/63
Garrigan, Catharine died 04/27/64   04/29/64
Garrigan, Peter married Carvey, Mary 08/18/64   08/22/64
Garrish, Emma Willietta died 09/14/64   09/15/64
Garrison, Arthur married Lewis, Jane 12/09/62   12/11/62
Garrison, Elizabeth (Mrs.) died 06/01/64   06/02/64
Garrison, Ellen died 05/26/62   05/28/62
Garrison, John Henry married Guyton, Mary J. C. 02/05/61   02/07/61
Garrison, Thomas died 12/09/62   12/10/62
Garrison, William died 10/14/63   10/16/63
Garrott, John Dawson (Dr.) died no date   07/23/63
Garrott, William M. married Boteler, Mattie W. 11/19/63   12/07/63
Garthwaite, Elizabeth married Sanners, Johachan B. 11/09/63   11/19/63
Gartrids, Amanda E. married Webb, Levi 09/03/65   09/05/65
Garvey, Alice married Dunn, Michael 01/01/63   01/09/63
Garvey, Ann (Mrs.) died 12/17/62   12/19/62
Garvey, James, Jr. married McCann, Jane Stewart 01/20/63   03/16/63
Garvey, John Buchanan died 01/08/61   01/09/61
Garvey, Johnny Buchanan died 01/08/61   01/11/61
Garvey, Mary died 06/26/64   06/27/64
Garvey, Mary Rosina died 12/11/64   12/12/64
Garvey, Mary Rosina died 12/11/64   12/13/64
Garvey, Rose E. married Van Daniker, Joseph 06/14/65   07/04/65
Gary, Alberta G. died 05/20/64   05/21/64
Gashinn, Samuel S. died 01/21/62   01/23/62
Gaskins, Charles H. married Homer, Mary 11/10/61   11/12/61
Gaskins, James Edward died 08/12/65   08/14/65
Gaskins, Sewell A. died 03/10/62   04/03/62
Gaskins, Sue died 01/23/61   01/29/61
Gassaway, Henry married Lawrance, Julia A. 04/29/63   05/02/63
Gassaway, Louis G. married Dorsey, Marian B. 03/04/62   03/17/62
Gassaway, Samuel B. married Greenhow, Maria F. 09/24/63   10/07/63
Gassaway, William A. married Farrow, Mary 01/21/64   01/22/64
Gaston, Isabella died 01/16/62   01/17/62
Gatch, Anna W. married Stevenson, Washington 06/02/63   06/04/63
Gatch, Benjamin W. died 12/16/64   09/07/65
Gatch, Elmira V. married Reding, George 05/02/62   05/03/62
Gately, Bridget died 09/11/62   09/13/62
Gately, Patrick died 04/22/61   04/23/61
Gates, Barbara Ellen married Young, Joseph Simon 02/06/62   02/07/62
Gates, Emma Virginia died 02/24/62   02/25/62
Gates, Lloyd V. died 04/28/63   04/30/63
Gates, Mary Florence died 12/25/64   12/26/64
Gates, Sallie M. married Bradley, A. H. 11/08/64   11/14/64
Gathter, John R. married Glasco, Mary E. 09/15/64   09/17/64
Gaule, Stephen died 09/27/61   09/28/61
Gaule, Stephen died 07/26/65   07/27/65
Gauline, Amanda M. (Mrs.) died 04/09/64   04/19/64
Gault, Alice Virginia died 06/02/64   06/03/64
Gault, George Henry died 10/29/61   10/30/61
Gault, Lucy married Boswell, B. S. 12/12/61   12/23/61
Gault, Richard married O'Brien, Bridget 08/08/58 01/11/65
Gault, Richard married O'Brien, Bridget 08/08/58 01/12/65
Gault, Richard married O'Brien, Bridget 08/08/58 01/13/65

Gaunt, Joseph died 03/31/64 04/04/64
Gaussoin, Elise A. C. married Carlier, Henry 10/23/65 10/24/65
Gautlow, Mary E. married Kerr, Thomas 12/28/63 01/02/64
Gaven, John died 04/07/61 04/08/61
Gaven, William Henry married Barr, Mary Elvina 03/30/63 04/15/63
Gaver, George E. married Eillinger, Catherine A. 06/06/65 06/10/65
Gaviett, Daniel died 12/29/61 01/03/62
Gavin, Margaret Agness died 02/16/63 02/18/63
Gaw, M. Annie married Brengle, James S. 04/27/65 05/02/65
Gawthrop, Cornelia married Lilley, Andrew E. 06/25/62 06/27/62
Gay, Mary A. (Mrs.) died 07/09/64 07/11/64
Gayle, John Edward died 01/08/61 01/16/61
Gayle, Joseph R. married Coleman, Sallie 03/13/64 03/17/64
Gayle, Lillian died 08/19/64 08/20/64
Gayleard, Mary A. married Webb, James 12/10/61 12/25/61
Gaynor, John Augustine died 07/01/61 07/03/61
Gaynor, Nicholas died 07/24/61 07/26/61
Gazam, Marguerite De Loche married Stow, Louis 10/19/65 10/21/65
Geager, Joseph R. died 05/07/62 05/08/62
Geb, George W. died no date 03/12/62
Gebb, Mary A. married Oliver, Francis 11/18/63 11/20/63
Gebhard, Charles E. died 03/15/64 03/16/64
Geddes, James A. married Benton, Sarah C. 07/03/64 07/13/64
Geddes, James Alexander died 09/15/64 09/16/64
Geddes, Jane (Mrs.) died 10/21/64 10/22/64
Geddis, Margaret Ann died 10/20/63 10/28/63
Geddis, Robert died 02/23/63 02/24/63
Gedz, Sophia (Mrs.) died 05/20/63 05/23/63
Gees, B. Franklin married Slicer, Mary A. 12/01/63 12/02/63
Gees, Emma Elizabeth died 08/10/62 08/12/62
Gees, Mary died 02/27/62 02/28/62
Gees, Mary died 02/27/62 03/01/62
Gees, Mary Ann married Goodman, John J. 01/19/65 01/21/65
Gees, Thomas B. married Garrett, Amelia 05/03/64 05/06/64
Geiger, Charles Alexander died 08/25/62 08/28/62
Geiger, Kate died 11/30/64 12/01/64
Geiger, Sophie married Sands, Augustus 01/22/65 04/01/65
Geiger, Wilhelmine Virginia died 08/14/65 08/15/65
Geigh, Ida May died 04/01/62 04/02/62
Gein, J. F. married Halsey, M. H. S. 02/27/63 03/12/63
Geisendaffer, John P. died 05/22/61 05/29/61
Gelbach, Christianna died 01/27/61 01/29/61
Gelbach, George married Smith, Julia A. 10/03/65 10/07/65
Gelbee, Catherine died no date 03/14/64
Gellis, Ellen N. died 02/03/63 02/04/63
Gelston, Mary Frances died 10/05/63 10/07/63
Gelston, Nannie S. died 05/19/64 05/21/64
Gemeny, Minnie died 12/28/62 12/30/62
Gemeny, Wilber Hartman died 12/28/62 12/30/62
Gemundt, Marie Louis died 12/29/64 12/31/64
Genals, Louisa married Smoots, William H. 11/14/61 11/16/61
Genkins, Hugh died 12/17/61 12/19/61
Gennett, John A. married Mules, Wilmima A. 04/20/65 04/21/65
Genrous, Elizabeth married Wilkerson, John H. 08/23/64 08/30/64
Gent, A. J. married Holmes, Mary E. 01/20/63 01/22/63

Gent, Henry married Harris, E. 06/16/63   07/20/63
Gentry, Haden married McElroy, Annie A. 01/03/65   01/18/65
Gentry, J. H. married Hoover, M. Victoria 11/30/65   12/12/65
Gentry, Willie died 04/28/65   04/29/65
Geoghegan, James A. married Shenckel, Rosalie 05/03/63   05/07/63
Geoghegan, Lizzie S. married Lilly, Henry A. 12/17/60   01/17/61
Geoghegan, William C. married Chaney, Celone 05/12/62   05/14/62
George, Alfred Everett died 08/07/61   08/08/61
George, Archibald died 01/03/62   01/04/62
George, Carrie died 05/03/62   06/07/62
George, Carville Swope died 12/03/64   12/05/64
George, Elizabeth died 07/21/65   07/25/65
George, Francisco Primicerio married Bishop, Ella 08/22/65   08/25/65
George, James died 12/02/63   12/04/63
George, John S. died 01/23/63   01/24/63
George, John Shamburg died 01/04/65   01/05/65
George, Maggie married Mottu, Theodore 08/20/61   08/21/61
George, Mary F. married Timanus, Luther 05/29/61   06/01/61
George, Mary R. J. married Anzmann, Joseph A. A. 04/16/63   04/18/63
George, Mollie died 01/05/62   01/07/62
George, Samuel K., Jr. married Carter, Ella 06/18/63   06/20/63
George, Thomas Howard died 10/05/64   10/07/64
George, Virginia Carrie died 12/05/63   12/08/63
George, William died 02/13/62   02/14/62
George, William F. married Walker, Harriet A. 04/28/64   06/21/64
Gephart, Henry died 07/10/63   07/15/63
Geraghty, Michael F. died 01/21/65   01/23/65
Gerber, Carrie Louisa died 01/08/62   01/10/62
Gerber, Christian died 08/27/63   08/28/63
Gerber, John Christian died 05/08/64   05/09/64
Gerbrich, Maddue Morselle married McKeever, William T. 01/19/65
    01/23/65
Gerbrich, Rachel P. married Kline, John 09/27/64   09/29/64
Gerbrick, Josephine married Baldwin, Joseph 08/06/63   09/15/63
Gerbrick, Mattie A. married Roby, Willie F. 10/09/64   10/13/64
Gerdts, E. V. (Lt.) married Jordan, Maggie 06/19/65   06/28/65
Gere, E. Gussie married Shipley, J. Lester (Rev.) 10/26/65   10/27/65
Gerhard, Mary Magdalene died 10/06/61   10/07/61
Gerlach, George C. married McClennahan, Susie A. 11/10/65   11/15/65
German, Charles Henry died 09/28/63   09/29/63
German, Elizabeth A. died 10/24/61   10/26/61
German, Ella Carroll died 11/27/63   11/28/63
German, Georgianna E. died 10/03/65   10/04/65
German, Hester died 12/27/63   01/07/64
German, J. Francis died 10/09/63   10/10/63
German, Jacob died 01/06/64   01/08/64
German, John died 08/11/65   08/12/65
German, Margaret died 10/21/61   10/22/61
German, Mary C. married Barton, Joshua N. 08/15/64   08/16/64
German, Mary E. married Marriott, Thomas 12/26/65   12/29/65
German, Robert Clinton died 02/01/61   02/06/61
German, Ruhamah B. married Dorsey, William H. 02/10/63   02/16/63
German, Thomas E. A. married Vanhorn, Annie 08/15/61   08/17/61
Gerral, Michael F. (Cpt.) died 09/07/64   10/10/64
Gers, Laura V. married Clarke, Joseph S. 06/13/65   06/15/65

165

Gessford, James W. married Kerr, Susannah 01/18/65   01/25/65
Gessford, Susannah married Hilleary, John Alexander 10/21/62   10/23/62
Gethins, Thomas married Shia, Emeline 01/22/63   01/23/63
Gettier, Charles H. died 05/26/63   05/28/63
Gettier, Elizabeth (Mrs.) died 04/09/64   04/11/64
Gettier, George died 08/06/61   08/07/61
Gettier, J. M. married Shugars, Mary G. 03/10/64   03/16/64
Gettier, Jacob died 02/19/64   02/20/64
Gettier, John L. married Traband, M. Virginia 06/29/65   08/01/65
Gettier, Laura Virginia died 06/08/61   06/13/61
Gettier, Mary (Mrs.) died 05/28/63   05/29/63
Gettier, Rose H. married Fairley, Thomas 04/14/63   04/24/63
Gettier, Sallie Estelle died 09/06/63   09/08/63
Gettier, Sarah married Carland, Thomas 06/11/65   06/23/65
Gettier, William Eugene died 08/09/64   08/10/64
Gettier, Wilson Jacob died 05/14/62   05/16/62
Gettiet, William H. married Reisinger, Amelia 10/18/64   10/29/64
Gettings, Willey Harker died 05/27/63   05/29/63
Gettslich, Ernest died 04/08/63   04/10/63
Getty, Rose A. died 11/25/64   11/28/64
Getty, Virginia A. married Ostendorf, J. A. 07/02/62   07/04/62
Getz, Belle married Seligman, Ike J. 08/26/63   08/27/63
Getz, Catherine S. died 06/09/65   06/10/65
Getz, John married Joseph, Maggie 02/01/64   02/04/64
Getz, John M. married Burgan, Mary R. 06/18/61   06/26/61
Getz, Sophia (Mrs.) died 05/20/63   05/25/63
Getzendanner, Phineas D. married Weeks, Sarah A. V. 12/28/65   12/30/65
Geyer, Lemuel F. married Cross, Mary Ann 06/30/64   07/02/64
Ghequiere, Sarah S. (Mrs.) died 04/10/64   04/19/64
Gibb, Hannah married Davis, William 01/04/64   01/14/64
Gibb, S. E. (Mrs.) married Little, E. C. 05/22/61   06/04/61
Gibbens, Mary C. died 02/05/61   02/06/61
Gibbes, Henrietta Ann died 10/08/65   10/12/65
Gibbin, Alice Ellen died 11/09/65   11/10/65
Gibbon, John died 06/16/63   06/20/63
Gibbond, J. H. S. married Waring, Sue A. 10/05/65   10/07/65
Gibbons, Daniel P. died 05/15/62   05/16/62
Gibbons, Daniel P. died 05/15/62   05/17/62
Gibbons, Delia married Barranger, Louis L., Sr. 02/12/62   02/14/62
Gibbons, Emma J. married Leech, David 10/27/64   10/31/64
Gibbons, J. Thomas married Kenney, Sue E. 12/26/64   12/29/64
Gibbons, John died 11/06/62   11/08/62
Gibbons, Laura S. married Vaughen, William P. 07/07/65   08/30/65
Gibbons, Robert A. married Mitchell, Henrietta L. 04/05/64   04/13/64
Gibbons, William J. T. married Waddell, Isabella 11/18/64   11/19/64
Gibbs, A. S. married Habbiston, Lizzie 01/02/62   02/01/62
Gibbs, Ella died 07/29/65   07/31/65
Gibbs, Hannah A. (Mrs.) died 12/15/65   12/19/65
Gibbs, Henrietta E. (Mrs.) died 11/05/65   11/11/65
Gibbs, Jacob A. died 06/23/63   06/24/63
Gibbs, James died 02/24/63   02/26/63
Gibbs, Josephine married Marshall, William E. Bruce 11/24/63   12/05/63
Gibbs, Mary Ann married White, William Joseph 06/18/63   06/20/63
Gibbs, Robert H. married Anderson, A. L. 06/04/61   06/06/61
Gibney, Elizabeth died 02/25/61   02/27/61

Gibney, Ellen died 08/27/63   08/28/63
Gibney, Michael died 06/07/62   06/09/62
Gibson, Anna E. married Cator, William D. 01/02/62   01/07/62
Gibson, Anne E. married Godfrey, Samuel 02/02/64   02/02/64
Gibson, Charles William died 02/25/61   02/27/61
Gibson, Clara A. married Caldwell, A. Palladio 11/25/64   12/23/64
Gibson, Edmund died 02/08/61   02/15/61
Gibson, Elizabeth A. married Sullivan, Edward 01/18/63   01/19/63
Gibson, Elizabeth C. died 09/01/61   09/03/61
Gibson, Frederick (Rev.) married Semmes, Kate Middleton 12/26/65   12/28/65
Gibson, George married Allen, Margaret P. 05/14/61   05/16/61
Gibson, George died 03/20/62   03/21/62
Gibson, Henrietta married Clayton, Hezekiah 09/06/65   09/16/65
Gibson, Henry married Wooshe, Caroline (Mrs.) 11/05/63   11/06/63
Gibson, Henry Allen died 11/11/63   11/12/63
Gibson, Horatio Gates (Cpt.) married Atkinson, Harriet L. 03/16/63   03/28/63
Gibson, Isabella A. married Lowry, Stephen A. 01/29/62   01/31/62
Gibson, Isabella R. married Hennaman, Herman 10/27/62   11/04/62
Gibson, Ishmael H. married Waddy, Mary A. 11/03/64   11/05/64
Gibson, James died 06/01/63   06/05/63
Gibson, James (Capt.) died no date 06/28/62
Gibson, James R. died 03/27/63   03/28/63
Gibson, John married Sheeler, Anthony 08/15/60   02/06/61
Gibson, John died 02/17/61   02/19/61
Gibson, Laura A. married King, George W., Jr. 01/31/61   02/02/61
Gibson, Louisi (Mrs.) died 10/08/65   10/11/65
Gibson, M. Jacob died 03/30/64   03/31/64
Gibson, Maria (Mrs.) married Myers, William 01/15/65   01/18/65
Gibson, Mary (Mrs.) died 12/15/64   12/16/64
Gibson, Mary Ann married Johnson, Thomas T. 10/03/64   10/08/64
Gibson, Mary Jane married Champhor, Jacob 12/08/60   03/20/61
Gibson, Mollie A. married Jackson, Thomas D. 02/17/64   02/20/64
Gibson, Peary married Williams, Frances 12/17/63   12/29/63
Gibson, Rebecca married Jackson, Philip 04/11/61   04/13/61
Gibson, Robert A. (Rev.) died 12/27/64   12/29/64
Gibson, Sarah Allen died 01/08/61   01/09/63
Gibson, Sophia Finley married Coulter, D. Mifflin 10/12/64   10/13/64
Gibson, William F. died 10/31/62   11/06/62
Gibson, William H. married Taylor, Carrie A. 10/20/64   10/21/64
Gibson, William Henry died 05/16/62   05/30/62
Gibson, William J. married Frankland, S. Elizabeth 09/14/65   09/16/65
Giddings, Eliza married Sinclair, John 12/05/64   05/08/65
Giddings, Mary M. married Taylor, William H. 06/19/62   06/21/62
Gidelman, Maurice B. died 03/29/62   03/31/62
Gidley, David married Marshall, Hester 09/12/61   09/14/61
Giese, Mary Ann died 03/07/65   03/13/65
Gieske, Gustavus married Driver, Auguste 06/04/64   06/06/64
Gifford, Emily C. married Bell, W. D. 10/23/64   10/25/64
Gigg, William D. married Paddington, Isabella 02/08/64   02/09/64
Gilbert, Abraham A. died 01/31/64   02/15/64
Gilbert, Hannah S. married Grier, J. Richard 10/04/64   10/22/64
Gilbert, Isaac Wilson married March, Emma 11/19/63   11/21/63
Gilbert, Joseph Musgrave died 01/03/65   01/05/65

Gilbert, Joseph Musgrave died 01/03/65   01/10/65
Gilbert, Leuvenia (Mrs.) died 12/06/64   12/09/64
Gilbert, Pacca Thomas married Niles, Sarah Jane 04/16/63   04/18/63
Gilbert, Virginia Julia died 02/17/64   02/18/64
Gilbert, William B. died 12/24/63   12/28/63
Gilchrist, Barnard died 08/05/62   08/07/62
Gildea, John died 03/20/62   03/26/62
Gilder, Elizabeth E. married Bose, William 01/17/61   01/18/61
Giles, Arrietta died 03/08/61   03/09/61
Giles, Elvira G. married Orrell, Edward N. 03/13/62   03/15/62
Giles, Emily A. married Burrow, Frederick, 12/29/63   01/12/64
Giles, Fannie married Boucher, William 05/15/65   05/16/65
Giles, Harriet married Mayes, Joseph 10/03/63   10/06/63
Giles, John R. died 03/05/61   03/06/61
Giles, Mary E. married Bidell, Richard 06/30/64   07/02/64
Giles, Mary Priscilla married Frisby, William H. 12/30/60   01/02/61
Giles, Nathaniel married Butler, Elenora 04/04/65   04/07/65
Gilhooley, Ann died 04/12/63   04/13/63
Gilhooley, Mary (Mrs.) died 02/13/63   02/14/63
Gilkenson, Martha E. married Rodgers, Samuel 03/21/65   08/08/65
Gill, Alexander R. died 05/26/62   06/13/62
Gill, Andrew died 09/21/64   09/22/64
Gill, Andrew B. married Tipton, Ellen M. 10/23/62   10/25/62
Gill, Annie W. married Bone, William 05/11/65   05/18/65
Gill, Bryson Jerome died 03/01/65   03/03/65
Gill, E. Aggie married Gill, N. Rufus 02/06/61   07/09/61
Gill, Elisha H. died 05/29/64   05/30/64
Gill, Elizabeth J. K. died 08/12/62   08/13/62
Gill, George H. married Selecman, Maggie A. 08/02/63   08/19/63
Gill, Hanora died 05/11/63   05/12/63
Gill, John C. died 08/21/63   08/22/63
Gill, John G. married Schenner, Ernestine 04/25/65   04/27/65
Gill, Lawrence married Hogan, Isabella 05/31/63   06/04/63
Gill, M. Louisa (Mrs.) died 11/23/63   11/25/63
Gill, Mary A. died 03/26/63   04/01/63
Gill, Mary E. married Whitaker, Dorsey H. 07/04/65   07/20/65
Gill, Mary Lilly died 08/23/65   08/24/65
Gill, Michael died 08/12/63   08/13/63
Gill, N. Rufus married Gill, E. Aggie 02/06/61   07/09/61
Gill, William E. married Scott, Eliza Jane 10/14/62   10/20/62
Gill, William Ensor married Scott, Eliza Jane 10/14/62   10/23/62
Gill, William Fountain (Dr.) died 12/19/64   12/20/64
Gill, William McCurdy died 08/06/62   08/07/62
Gillaran, Ellen died 05/02/62   05/02/62
Gillard, Kate died 08/01/65   08/03/65
Gillen, Rebecca married Hulett, D. F. (Cpt.) 11/02/65   11/07/65
Gilleran, Catherine died 10/23/64   10/24/64
Gillerin, Margaret died 09/01/61   09/02/61
Gillespie, Louisa married Cooke, Benjamin E. 09/02/62   01/08/63
Gillespie, Mary Ann died 12/29/62   12/30/62
Gillespie, Willie died 02/26/65   03/08/65
Gillet, George M. died 04/06/65   04/07/65
Gilley, Isaac F. (Cpt.) died 09/20/63   09/23/63
Gilliard, Mary Ann married Young, Richard 08/13/63   08/15/63
Gilliard, Thomas A. died 01/06/65   01/07/65

Gilligan, Rosalinda died 07/31/63   08/01/63
Gillin, (Mrs. James) died 09/04/64   09/05/64
Gillin, John died 02/04/61   02/05/61
Gillin, Mary died 01/16/61   01/17/61
Gillin, Michael died 04/02/62   04/03/62
Gillingham, Daniel married Crosby, Mary A. 09/03/63   09/05/63
Gillingham, George H. died 10/10/64   10/12/64
Gillingham, James married Ensor, Mary Ann 04/21/61   08/17/61
Gillingham, Kate Barclay died 11/01/61   11/02/61
Gillingham, Mary C. died 02/07/62   02/10/62
Gillingham, Sammie Lewis died 05/19/64   05/20/64
Gillis, Sarah E. married Hall, William G. 09/10/63   09/12/63
Gillispie, Mary married Woodward, Robert O. 09/10/64   09/13/64
Gillott, Julia married Hutchins, Clarence 10/22/64   10/29/64
Gilman, Charles died 09/09/61   09/11/61
Gilmon, Margaret married Holmes, Thomas 04/11/61   04/24/61
Gilmor, James married Ayers, Marietta C. 01/03/61   01/07/61
Gilmore, John Thomas died 12/19/64   12/20/64
Gilmore, Lina married Mann, Benjamin F. 05/17/64   05/19/64
Gilmore, Nancy C. (Mrs.) married Young, James 05/12/64   05/14/64
Gilmour, Andrew M. died 02/04/63   02/05/63
Gilmour, Frank M. died 06/13/65   06/14/65
Gilmour, Racher married Herbert, James N. 06/01/65   06/07/65
Gilner, Annie died 01/02/64   01/04/64
Gilpatrick, Norton married Lawrence, Kate S. 05/10/65   05/12/65
Gilpen, Albert G. married Poe, Fannie Elliott 06/01/65   06/08/65
Gilpin, Ella married Wilson, John E. 10/19/65   10/23/65
Gilpin, William Gover died 09/30/62   10/08/62
Gilston, Juliette T. died 03/19/64   03/21/64
Gimper, William F. married Spellman, Almira 08/25/65   08/26/65
Ginn, Cora I. died 10/07/65   10/26/65
Ginn, Helen Catherine died 08/12/62   08/13/62
Ginn, James J. married Barnes, Mary H. 10/03/61   10/04/61
Ginn, Joseph Eugene died 04/03/64   04/05/64
Ginn, Samuel H. H. died 08/24/63   09/22/63
Ginnevan, Charles married Cullison, Elizabeth 06/15/62   06/18/62
Ginton, Sarah Jane (Mrs.) died 04/12/64   04/20/64
Gipson, John Henry married Smith, Elizabeth 01/15/65   01/17/65
Gipson, Mary A married Wheeler, James H. 01/10/65   01/23/65
Gipson, Sophia married Cooper, Levin 11/10/64   11/12/64
Girvin, James M. married Whitmore, Anna Mary 11/10/64   11/12/64
Girvin, William Clendy died 06/13/65   06/14/65
Girvines, William L. married Andrews, Lavinia 09/19/65   09/30/65
Gisriel, Carrie Magdaline died 10/17/62   10/22/62
Gisriel, Francis Joseph died 07/17/61   07/19/61
Gisriel, Genevia Sophia died 09/29/62   10/01/62
Gissel, William T. died 11/13/62   11/14/62
Gissler, John A. married Ackler, Dorothea 02/27/62   03/04/62
Gist, Julia C. died 03/12/65   03/13/65
Gist, Martha (Mrs.) died 04/05/65   04/06/65
Gist, William (Col.) died 02/01/62   02/10/62
Gittinger, Louis C. married Myers, Jennie 12/10/63   12/17/63
Gittings, Albert C. died 11/04/62   11/06/62
Gittings, Henrietta married Buchanan, James Hollis 03/30/64   03/31/64
Gittings, Henry M. died 10/31/62   02/27/63

```
Gittings, Margaret S. died 02/09/64   02/11/64
Gittings, Martin V. married Neblett, Mary A. 05/15/62   05/20/62
Gittings, Mary M. died 12/23/61   12/25/61
Gittings, Rosa S. married Fields, John 04/20/64   04/26/64
Gittings, Samuel married Constable, Isabel S. 11/07/61   11/11/61
Givens, Nancy (Mrs.) died 12/15/64   12/21/64
Glade, Mary Jane died 12/06/62   12/10/62
Gladfelter, Jane R. married Tayler, William A. 07/15/62   07/19/62
Glaen, Emma Jane died 01/16/63   03/26/63
Glaeser, Helena died 07/17/62   07/19/62
Glanding, Mary M. married Lynch, George W. 10/20/64   10/22/64
Glanville, Blanche died 01/26/62   01/28/62
Glanville, Thomas died 02/19/64   11/07/64
Glanville, W. Allen died 04/04/62   04/05/62
Glasco, Mary E. married Gathter, John R. 09/15/64   09/17/64
Glaskow, Alexander died 08/22/65   08/23/65
Glass, Annie E. married Cain, William H. 06/01/65   06/13/65
Glass, David died 11/16/64   11/19/64
Glass, George died 02/06/63   02/09/63
Glasspoole, Henry married Grant, Mary Jane 04/07/64   04/19/64
Gleason, David A. died 03/27/64   04/01/64
Gleeson, Isabel, W. died 02/23/62   02/25/62
Gleeson, John P. (Cpt.) died 10/02/63   11/21/63
Gleeson, William E. died 03/01/62   03/04/62
Gleichman, Louis died 10/23/64   10/24/64
Gleim, Henry married Smith, Annie L. 09/01/64   10/11/64
Glen, Thomas died 02/16/63   02/18/63
Glendly, Eleanor (Mrs.) died 12/03/63   12/08/63
Glenn, Andrew died 12/06/65   12/09/65
Glenn, Deborah married Douglas, Solomon 02/26/61   06/18/61
Glenn, George William died 01/20/65   01/23/65
Glenn, Rosa married Hollingsworth, William G. 10/28/63   11/10/63
Glenn, Samuel married Bevans, Harriet V. 11/28/61   11/30/61
Glenn, Samuel B. married Yerkes, Sarah Lenora 03/31/63   04/02/62
Glenn, William Albert died 08/18/65   09/01/65
Glenn, William W. married Jenkins, Elizabeth 04/14/61   05/07/61
Glennen, Julia died 04/08/63   04/09/63
Glenville, W. Allen married Young, Linnie 09/26/61   10/08/61
Glessner, Rebecca L. died 01/15/62   01/16/62
Gline, Sarah Alice died 06/03/61   06/05/61
Glinnen, Cornelius died 11/10/62   11/11/62
Glocker, Emanuel J. married Entz, Lizzia A. 12/01/64   12/05/64
Glodell, Rose Jean died 07/05/64   07/06/64
Glos, John died 07/24/63   07/25/63
Glover, Joshua L. married Crandell, Mary E. 11/03/64   11/05/64
Gluck, Ellenora died 11/11/61   11/13/61
Gluelett, James married Trott, Isabell 01/12/63   01/20/63
Gneison, Clementina Elizabeth died 03/27/64   03/28/64
Goadding, Alfred died 01/29/64   02/03/64
Goar, Lydia died 09/25/63   09/26/63
Goble, Edward A. married Early, Mary E. 08/22/64   08/24/64
Gobright, Covington G. died 05/15/64   05/16/64
Gobright, Matilda A. (Mrs.) died 11/04/63   11/06/63
Goddard, George died 12/25/61   12/27/61
Goddwin, Richard B. died 06/23/64   06/23/64
```

Godfrey, Henry Dashiell died 12/02/65 12/04/65
Godfrey, Samuel married Gibson, Anne E. 02/02/64 02/02/64
Godison, Richard J. died 08/27/62 08/30/62
Godman, Charlotte Lee died 01/03/64 01/08/64
Godman, John D. died 01/01/63 01/03/63
Godman, Thomas E. married Lankford, Isabel F. 10/07/61 11/07/61
Godmar, Sarah H. married White, Thomas B. 02/18/65 05/02/65
Godwin, Benener married Knight, S. W. 07/22/63 08/21/63
Godwin, James died 09/18/65 09/26/65
Godwin, Jeremiah (Capt.) died 03/14/64 03/18/64
Godwin, Walter E. died 08/09/63 08/12/63
Gofford, William died 08/09/62 08/16/62
Goforth, Sarah N. (Mrs.) died 01/26/65 01/27/65
Goheen, Mary died 02/13/64 02/15/64
Gohegan, Phi'n married Pierce, Margaret A. 12/19/64 01/09/65
Going, Alvah died 08/22/62 09/25/62
Golden, Bridget died 08/23/62 08/25/62
Golden, Catherine died 01/28/62 01/29/62
Golden, Delia died 03/12/62 03/13/62
Golden, James died 12/15/62 12/16/62
Golden, James married Lookingland, Elizabeth (Mrs.) 11/28/64 12/01/64
Golden, John died 08/04/61 08/05/61
Golden, Mary T. J. married McComas, John S. 03/01/64 03/04/64
Golden, Thomas died 08/25/61 08/26/61
Golderman, Jacob married Siegle, Frances S. 01/31/64 02/04/64
Goldman, Hannah married Christy, F. G. (Lt.) 09/28/64 10/10/64
Goldsborough, Anna A. married Johnston, Frank H. 04/18/65 04/20/65
Goldsborough, Benjamin married White, Henrietta 12/10/63 12/12/63
Goldsborough, Charles married Galt, Mary C. 11/07/65 11/13/65
Goldsborough, Charles E. married Kemp, Emily B. 10/01/61 10/07/61
Goldsborough, Charles H.(M.D.) died 08/17/62 08/23/62
Goldsborough, Emilie J. married Nicholson, Charles G. 06/04/61 06/11/61
Goldsborough, Eugene Y. died 02/21/65 02/23/65
Goldsborough, Gertrude married Zimmerman, William S. 10/14/65 12/09/65
Goldsborough, Howes died 07/03/62 07/04/62
Goldsborough, James N. married Johnston, Emilie A. 07/17/61 07/18/61
Goldsborough, John W. married Dorsey, Frances E. 12/09/62 12/11/62
Goldsborough, Louis D. married Thompson, M. Virginia 12/03/63 12/07/63
Goldsborough, William J. died 08/03/63 08/04/63
Goldsmith, Charles died 12/18/63 12/19/63
Goldsmith, John B. married Mitchel, Sarah Jane 06/16/63 08/01/63
Goldsmith, Lilie married Cole, John T. 05/26/64 05/30/64
Goldsmith, Sarah Virginia married Pollack, Lewis 08/15/61 08/16/61
Goldsmith, Solomon married Strauss, Sophia 08/27/65 09/02/65
Goldsmith, William died 08/26/63 08/28/63
Golibart, Francis Walter died 08/08/62 08/12/62
Golibart, Julian J. died 04/08/64 06/11/64
Golibart, Sallie Pitt died 10/26/61 10/28/61
Golibart, Simon I. died 10/15/61 10/16/61
Goll, James B. died 09/29/62 09/30/62
Goll, Kate married Helfrich, Samuel D. 02/09/65 02/18/65
Goll, Mary Catherine died 01/02/64 01/21/64
Gomber, Sarah A. married Shower, Theodore A. 06/04/61 06/19/61
Gombert, Anne G. (Mrs.) married Newberth, John M. 10/04/64 10/08/64
Gontran, William Conrad died 01/27/64 01/28/64

Gontrum, John Albert died 02/28/65   03/01/65
Gontrum, William N. married Miller, Josephine 10/30/65   11/04/65
Good, Mary died 08/17/65   08/21/65
Good, Thomas G. married Hodgkin, Ada 01/10/65   01/11/65
Goodacre, Daniel M. married Murry, Belle 09/25/64   10/03/64
Goode, Catherine died 08/12/65   08/15/65
Goode, John B. died 05/28/64   05/31/64
Goodenow, Sophia W. married Tyler, George G. 10/18/65   10/21/65
Goodfellow, Charles M. married Kelso, Maria D. C. 11/13/65   11/20/65
Goodhand, Benenia A. married Wittman, William W. 01/10/61   01/14/61
Goodhand, Coroline H. died 09/13/61   11/11/61
Goodin, Ann (Mrs.) died 09/28/64   09/29/64
Goodman, Cecelia married Fleischman, Samuel S. 10/30/64   10/31/64
Goodman, Edward C. died 02/22/64   02/23/64
Goodman, Florence married Marshall, William no date 04/22/64
Goodman, Harriet Ann married Nelson, Horace B. 12/13/64   12/15/64
Goodman, John J. married Gees, Mary Ann 01/19/65   01/21/65
Goodman, Marmaduke married Worick, Elizabeth Madora 06/19/65   07/14/65
Goodman, Rebecca Gertrude died 12/06/65   12/12/65
Goodman, Susie married Dennis, George W. 05/26/64   05/28/64
Goodman, Susie E. married Beeler, Henry S. 01/22/63   02/06/63
Goodman, William married Orem, Sarah Ann 06/28/65   06/30/65
Goodman, William V. (Cpt.) married Myers, Annie 05/15/62   05/17/62
Goodrich, Henry died 05/25/61   05/28/61
Goodrick, Mollie L. married King, Calvin J. 01/26/64   01/28/64
Goodridge, Eleanor died 04/24/61   04/25/61
Goodwin, Beth A. married Linton, James L. 07/31/65   08/02/65
Goodwin, Edward D. died 06/09/65   06/12/65
Goodwin, Ellen (Mrs.) died 10/17/63   10/20/63
Goodwin, Emma Jane married Tutcheon, Theodore 11/10/64   11/15/64
Goodwin, John E. married Hobbs, Nannie 11/15/64   11/18/64
Goodwin, Mary married Rocks, Patrick 04/20/62   04/26/62
Goodwin, Mary R. married Smith, Samuel E. 10/07/64   03/06/62
Goodwin, Sarah F. married Cee, Emory G. 05/18/64   06/02/64
Gootee, George S. married Wingate, Annie M. 11/16/65   11/23/65
Gorden, Harriet A. married Wallace, Andrew J. 10/16/62   10/29/62
Gordon, Alexander B. died no date 12/10/61
Gordon, Annie Louise died 06/08/64   06/09/64
Gordon, Bartholomew married Casey, Mary 02/07/64   02/08/64
Gordon, Bridget Lanahan died 07/26/63   07/27/63
Gordon, Charles C. died 07/30/64   08/06/64
Gordon, Charles E. (Cpl.) died 07/30/64   07/29/65
Gordon, Fannie married Verdi, Ciro S. (Dr.) 04/28/63   04/29/63
Gordon, George married Trusty, Henrietta E. 04/07/63   05/02/63
Gordon, George H. died 02/21/63   02/25/63
Gordon, George Henry died 07/08/65   07/11/65
Gordon, James died 05/31/61   06/03/61
Gordon, Joseph died 09/10/65   09/14/65
Gordon, Joseph died 11/13/65   11/14/65
Gordon, Kate Mahala died 07/12/61   07/13/61
Gordon, Louisa married Seibold, George W. 03/21/61   07/25/61
Gordon, Mary died 10/17/65   10/18/65
Gordon, Sarah E. married Newgent, Walter H. 01/01/61   01/02/61
Gordon, William E. married Carman, Louisa 03/06/61   03/29/61

Gordon, William H. died 12/11/65 12/12/65
Gore, A. Washington married Neal, Mattie 01/05/65 01/10/65
Gore, Barbara Marcella married Burns, Amos 05/04/65 05/09/65
Gore, Henry H. married Whalon, Annie R. 06/28/63 07/03/63
Gore, Jennie married Price, Jessie 09/19/61 09/25/61
Gore, S. R. married Ennalls, Laura 02/26/63 03/31/63
Gore, Teresa (Mrs.) died 02/29/64 03/08/64
Gorman, Anne (Mrs.) died 02/08/64 02/09/64
Gorman, Emily A. (Mrs.) died 11/21/63 11/23/63
Gorman, Hester died 12/27/63 01/08/64
Gorman, John A. died 08/07/64 08/12/64
Gorman, Kate died 01/14/61 01/16/61
Gorman, Margaret died 10/21/61 10/23/61
Gorman, Margaret died 10/21/61 11/04/61
Gorman, Nicholas died 11/02/61 11/04/61
Gorman, Peter died 06/06/62 06/09/62
Gorman, Robert Clinton died 02/01/61 02/05/61
Gormley, Mary A. married Eastman, L. M. (M.D.) 09/23/62 10/10/62
Gorrell, Henry S. married Brannan, Sue 01/01/61 01/03/61
Gorsuch, Angeline died 06/22/61 06/25/61
Gorsuch, Annie May died 08/10/62 08/13/62
Gorsuch, Artage (Mrs.) married Ensor, Luke C. 10/18/64 10/20/64
Gorsuch, Charles B. died 07/29/62 07/30/62
Gorsuch, Charles B. died 07/29/62 08/01/62
Gorsuch, Charles Leonard died 09/09/61 09/10/61
Gorsuch, Charles Leonard died 09/09/61 08/13/62
Gorsuch, Dickenson married Johnson, Susanna H. 05/20/62 05/23/62
Gorsuch, Ebenezer married Gosnell, Maria 09/18/64 09/28/64
Gorsuch, Hannah J. died 08/15/61 08/17/61
Gorsuch, Ida Catherine died 04/08/64 04/11/64
Gorsuch, James married Plummer, Sarah Jane 12/16/62 12/20/62
Gorsuch, James D. married Thompson, Isabella B. 04/12/64 04/14/64
Gorsuch, Julia Anne married McCormick, John H. 04/29/62 05/01/62
Gorsuch, Maggie A. married Keppel, Lemuel A. 12/27/65 12/30/65
Gorsuch, Marian F. died 10/12/64 11/12/64
Gorsuch, Mary Frances died 08/01/65 08/02/65
Gorsuch, Pleasance Coleman died 11/29/65 12/05/65
Gorsuch, Sallie married Davis, William 06/01/65 06/12/65
Gorsuch, Thomas died 12/14/64 12/15/64
Gorsuch, Thomas died 12/14/64 12/21/64
Gorsuch, Washington married Norris, Mary Jane 05/17/64 05/20/64
Gorten, William A. died 01/08/61 01/09/61
Gortman, William H. died 09/09/62 09/10/62
Gorton, Emma V. married Dean, G. Albert (USN) 12/20/64 12/22/64
Gorton, Marie Louise married Saffell, Celsus L. 11/16/64 11/22/64
Gosden, Bettie died 09/11/62 09/30/62
Gosdon, Sallie married English, Ramuel R. 08/27/62 09/09/62
Goslee, Susie J. married Watts, Henry R. (Dr., USN) 09/21/64 09/23/64
Goslee, William H. died 04/09/62 04/10/62
Goslen, Margaret died 01/17/61 01/24/61
Goslin, Thomas H. married Covey, Isabella 11/07/65 11/13/65
Gosnell, Charles Warner died 10/12/63 10/13/63
Gosnell, Clara A. M. married Hall, Richard B. 03/03/63 03/04/63
Gosnell, John married Carney, Sarah 08/29/65 09/01/65
Gosnell, Lizzie Wray died 02/27/62 02/28/62

Gosnell, Maria married Gorsuch, Ebenezer 09/18/64 09/28/64
Gosnell, Maria married Norwood, Ebenezer 09/18/64 09/30/64
Gosnell, Mary E. married Troxell, John G. 04/04/65 04/10/65
Gosnell, Mary Emma married Parsons, William 09/04/64 09/10/64
Gosnell, Mordicae married Simmons, Margaret 05/05/61 05/18/61
Gosnell, Oliver Coulson died 04/30/61 05/02/61
Gosnell, Robert Bruce died 11/11/61 11/12/61
Gosnell, Sarah Mary died 05/22/62 05/23/62
Gosnell, Susie married Warfield, Thomas 09/27/65 10/14/65
Gosnell, William T. married Gallaway, Mary 12/28/62 01/02/63
Goss, Annie C. married Ruark, Peter M. 11/23/65 11/25/65
Goss, Job died 02/02/65 02/04/65
Goss, Rebecca Ann died 08/07/65 08/08/65
Goss, William R. married Miles, Emma V. 05/14/62 05/16/62
Goss, Winfield S. married Stewart, Eliza W. 11/26/63 12/01/63
Gosweiler, Solomon married Leaib, Louisa 09/01/63 10/10/63
Gotchmer, Mary E. married Jones, Andrew 11/16/64 11/18/64
Gott, Annie married Sloane, John Joseph 09/11/62 09/23/62
Gott, James died 08/06/62 08/07/62
Gott, Jane E. died 05/23/65 05/24/65
Gotte, William died 08/26/63 08/27/63
Gottlieb, Amalia married Didemann, John 10/19/62 10/20/62
Gottlieb, Bertha married Hax, Peter 12/08/61 12/10/61
Gotty, Augustus died 02/01/64 02/02/64
Goudy, Ida Henrietta died 08/23/62 08/28/62
Goudy, John married Banks, Susie 04/09/61 04/16/61
Goudy, Stephen died 09/05/63 09/15/63
Gough, Charles E. died no date 02/22/62
Gough, James married Scott, Mary Ellen 02/15/63 03/07/63
Gough, Jonathan R. died 10/22/63 10/24/63
Gough, Louis died 07/30/64 08/02/64
Gough, M. E. married Morgan, J. F. (M.D.) 04/22/62 04/23/62
Gough, Martha C. married Bouldin, Richard E. 02/04/64 02/06/64
Gould, Annie E. married Carr, Henry 09/14/61 12/25/61
Gould, Columbus W. died 11/30/64 12/02/64
Gould, Fanny (Mrs.) died 04/13/64 04/23/64
Gould, James A. died 06/10/64 06/11/64
Gould, John R. married Kidd, Amelia 02/04/64 02/05/64
Gould, Joseph Warren died 08/10/63 08/13/63
Gould, Kate A. died 06/10/62 06/11/62
Gould, M. Helen married Dukes, I. Reyner 06/09/64 06/16/64
Gould, Mary married Depper, John 03/15/65 03/17/65
Gould, Mary married Firoved, John 02/21/65 03/17/65
Gould, Mary Frances (Mrs.) died 04/09/63 04/10/63
Gould, Robert H. married Hughes, Margaret Ann 02/17/64 02/20/64
Gould, W. H. H. married Stone, Sarah E. 08/21/62 08/29/62
Gould, William Reynolds died 04/14/64 04/15/64
Goulden, Thomas Ambrose died 07/17/63 07/18/63
Gouley, Julie E. C. married Pritchard, Irvin S. 07/12/65 07/19/65
Gourley, Anne married Guy, Joseph 12/24/61 01/20/62
Gourley, Joseph married Brown, Mary Ann 05/02/65 05/06/65
Gourley, Sarah married Bates, Charles W. 01/12/65 01/25/65
Govans, Charity married Banks, Burwell 10/06/63 10/08/63
Govens, Elizabeth married Duffin, Martin Luther 12/29/64 12/31/64
Gover, E. L. married Nason, Mary E. no date 07/29/64

```
Gover, Edward L. married Nason, Mary E. 07/20/64   07/30/64
Gover, Margaret C. (Mrs.) died 04/18/63   04/21/63
Gover, Miriam died 04/18/63   04/22/63
Gover, Samuel H. died 03/08/64   03/09/64
Gover, William L. died 03/01/64   03/02/64
Gowens, George H. died 12/08/64   12/13/64
Gowens, George Henry married Irvin, Jane Catharine 01/13/62   01/16/62
Grabau, Adaline Walker died 06/30/65   07/10/65
Grabau, Adeline Walker died 06/30/65   07/11/65
Grace, Aaron D. married Kimble, Sarah E. 02/06/61   02/09/61
Grace, Aaron O. married Kimble, Sarah E. 02/06/61   02/11/61
Grace, Alexander married Cooper, Harriet Ann 04/16/61   04/19/61
Grace, Ann M. died 06/22/62   06/23/62
Grace, Cecilia Catharine died 05/09/62   05/12/62
Grace, Thomas E. married Preston, Susan R. 05/19/64   05/23/64
Grace, William Boyer died 01/17/65   01/18/65
Gracey, George Cooper died 10/16/63   10/19/63
Gracey, John A. died 06/02/63   06/04/63
Gracey, Mary Elizabeth died 12/26/65   12/29/65
Gradwohl, E. C. married Wetzer, Sarah 02/07/64   02/08/64
Grady, James died 01/12/63   01/14/63
Grady, John died 06/06/64   06/07/64
Grady, Mary married Sheridan, Michael 03/23/63   03/23/63
Grady, Michael died 07/20/62   07/22/62
Grady, Patrick died 10/29/63   10/30/63
Grafflin, Clara died 06/30/65   07/03/65
Grafton, Annie M. married Forbes, J. Harry 04/22/62   04/23/62
Grafton, Eliza married Watkins, John no date 10/18/65
Grafton, Isabella H. died 06/06/62   10/08/62
Grafton, Julia B. (Mrs.) died 02/16/64   02/17/64
Graham, Amanda M. married Hogg, Edmond A. 07/24/61   10/22/61
Graham, Annie married Hartzell, M. I. 09/05/61   10/18/61
Graham, Carrie E. married Wilson, George W. 10/26/64   11/01/64
Graham, Charles McDougal died 08/01/65   08/02/65
Graham, Elizabeth married Barton, Andrew C. 05/14/61   05/17/61
Graham, Ella died 01/10/63   02/19/63
Graham, Ellis J. C. died 08/07/61   08/10/61
Graham, George R. (Cpt.) married Tuckey, Mary L. 10/09/62   10/14/62
Graham, James died 06/23/64   07/04/64
Graham, James R. married Boone, Annie R. 04/20/65   04/25/65
Graham, James T. died 08/10/64   08/11/64
Graham, John married McGahan, Rozine 10/22/61   10/24/61
Graham, John married Scott, Georgeanna 02/09/63   03/10/63
Graham, Josiah died 06/16/61   06/19/61
Graham, Laura C. married Cuddy, J. W. C. (Dr.) 03/17/63   03/18/63
Graham, Marian Ann married Harig, John F. 01/05/63   01/08/63
Graham, Mary married Eckel, William J. 04/24/62   07/24/62
Graham, Mary Eva died 07/28/65   08/01/65
Graham, Matilda (Mrs.) died 07/22/63   07/25/63
Graham, Michael died 05/01/64   05/02/64
Graham, R. H. married Clark, Emma V. 02/18/64   03/03/64
Graham, William died 11/30/64   12/02/64
Graham, William married Thompson, Mary A. 11/30/65   12/02/65
Grahame, Bessie L. died 12/29/63   01/07/64
Grahem, Isabella died 08/04/61   08/05/61
```

Grain, Noah died 07/24/64 07/25/64
Grainger, Annie Virginia died 06/17/61 06/18/61
Grainger, Daniel W. died 08/04/65 08/05/65
Grainger, Mary Frances married Pardoe, William 07/21/64 07/23/64
Gralle, A. K. married Bowers, Isabella F. 04/18/61 04/22/61
Gramblitt, Virginia G. married Willson, William T. 04/10/64 04/20/64
Grammer, Gottlieb Christopher died 03/16/65 03/17/65
Grammer, Julius Probasco died 07/17/65 07/18/65
Granderson, Ann Maria died 12/13/62 12/15/62
Granger, Charles married Conn, Laura V. 02/04/64 02/09/64
Granger, Levin married Joiner, Martha A. 10/20/64 10/22/64
Granger, Rachel E. died 12/15/61 12/16/61
Granger, Rachel E. died 12/15/61 12/17/61
Granger, Thomas married Keenan, Mary 09/28/63 10/02/63
Granger, Thomas died 06/27/64 06/30/64
Granger, Thomas died 06/27/64 07/01/64
Graniss, Freeman Rowe died 07/17/65 07/25/65
Granniss, John R. married Helm, Annie M. 05/11/64 05/13/64
Grant, Caroline (Mrs.) died 04/21/63 04/23/63
Grant, Edward died 08/16/61 09/12/61
Grant, Edward died 02/08/62 02/11/62
Grant, Harriet Chesnut married Stockton, Richard D. 07/10/65 08/10/65
Grant, Ida Mary died 08/29/63 08/31/63
Grant, J. Hope married Dickson, M. Ann E. 10/15/62 10/20/62
Grant, John B. died 01/19/62 01/20/62
Grant, Joseph W. married Dashiell, Margaret P. 03/02/62 03/06/62
Grant, Maria died 06/27/62 06/28/62
Grant, Maria B. died 06/12/61 06/13/61
Grant, Mary Jane died 12/31/62 01/02/63
Grant, Mary Jane married Glasspoole, Henry 04/07/64 04/19/64
Grant, Mary Josephine died 09/07/61 09/12/61
Grant, Minia married Russell, John 08/13/64 09/03/64
Grant, Pierce died 08/10/61 08/15/61
Grape, Ella died 07/23/62 07/24/62
Grape, Maggie E. A. married Eccleston, Charles E. 10/15/63 10/17/63
Grapevine, Catherine died 10/04/63 10/09/63
Grason, Mary Rebecca married Matthews, Lewis 06/04/63 06/06/63
Grasson, Samuel married Moore, Rosetta (Mrs.) 08/30/64 09/01/64
Gravenstine, Donna E. married Ehlers, John D. 12/16/65 12/20/65
Gravenstine, Maritia Paige died 07/27/64 07/29/64
Graves, Allie B. married Knotts, Will H. 09/01/63 09/07/63
Graves, Alverda B. married Knotts, William H. 09/01/63 09/03/63
Graves, Ann (Mrs.) died 06/28/64 08/02/64
Graves, R. H. married Gaillard, E. M. 09/08/63 12/28/63
Graves, Thomas W. died 01/29/65 01/30/65
Gray, Adams (Capt.) died 04/08/65 04/10/65
Gray, Alice Ann died 10/15/63 10/16/63
Gray, Ann (Mrs.) died 02/15/65 02/16/65
Gray, Augustus married Chesnet, Annie Mary 07/31/65 10/04/65
Gray, Betty H. died 07/28/61 08/02/61
Gray, Charity died 01/02/64 01/04/64
Gray, Edward married Emery, Eva V. 12/26/61 12/31/61
Gray, Eliza W. died 07/27/65 07/29/65
Gray, Frank died 11/14/65 11/16/65
Gray, George W. married Brooks, Mary E. 01/03/61 01/19/61

Gray, George W. married Brice, Ann (Mrs.) 08/26/64   08/27/64
Gray, H. H. died 02/11/64   02/13/64
Gray, Horatio N. married Hotchkiss, Emma P. 03/07/61   03/13/61
Gray, Irene married Clarke, Edward 08/10/63   09/01/63
Gray, Isabella A. married Kalling, Lewis 06/23/64   07/09/64
Gray, J. Albert died 09/16/65   09/18/65
Gray, James E. died 12/03/64   12/05/64
Gray, James Franklin died 09/06/62   10/10/62
Gray, James L. married Hay, M. Louisa 12/02/62   12/04/62
Gray, James Mason died 11/05/63   11/09/63
Gray, John died 12/09/64   12/10/64
Gray, John died 02/20/65   02/22/65
Gray, John Edward died 12/24/65   12/25/65
Gray, John H.W. married Bond, Laura Jane C. 01/05/65   01/07/65
Gray, Jonathan Jones died 05/24/64   05/25/64
Gray, Lizebella died 05/12/64   05/13/64
Gray, Lucinda married Moore, Samuel 03/06/61   03/07/61
Gray, Lucy died 12/12/64   12/14/64
Gray, Margaret married Harper, James 10/23/64   11/10/64
Gray, Mary A. (Mrs.) died 12/08/64   12/09/64
Gray, Mary Ann died 04/04/65   04/06/65
Gray, Mary Ann N. (Mrs.) died 04/04/65   04/05/65
Gray, Mary E. (Mrs.) died 04/03/63   04/08/63
Gray, Mary Jane died 03/16/61   03/18/61
Gray, Matilda married Hardy, Randolph 05/03/63   05/06/63
Gray, Priscilla (Mrs.) died 07/19/64   08/04/64
Gray, S. Virginia married Frey, Lewis 12/07/65   12/13/65
Gray, Sallie M. married Johnston, James 12/30/64   02/01/65
Gray, Sarah Elizabeth died 01/06/64   01/08/64
Gray, Shadrach married Dean, Henrietta 02/02/65   03/03/65
Gray, Stephen married Easterly, Elizabeth A. (Mrs.) 08/24/63   09/02/63
Gray, Teresa died 07/22/63   07/23/63
Gray, Thomas married Edwards, Susan 11/18/64   11/19/64
Gray, Thomas Baily died 03/05/63   03/07/63
Gray, Wilhelmina died 12/07/62   12/08/62
Gray, William died 11/02/63   11/03/63
Gray, William died 04/19/64   04/20/64
Gray, William died 04/19/64   04/21/64
Gray, William Leonard died 12/01/65   12/02/65
Gray, William M. married Church, Susan A. 05/19/63   05/21/63
Graydon, Margaret died 06/18/62   06/19/62
Grays, Alexander married Moorsbury, Mary Jane 01/10/61   01/12/61
Grays, Bernard died 07/16/64   07/19/64
Grayson, Janie (Mrs.) died 03/31/64   04/01/64
Greacen, George died 05/31/62   06/02/62
Gream, Harriet married Joyce, William 09/12/61   09/14/61
Greasley, Julia C. married Knipp, John C. 05/23/65   05/29/65
Greason, John married Kraft, Belle B. 10/18/64   10/20/64
Greason, Maggie J. married Smiley, John (Lt.) 01/08/63   01/12/63
Greason, Margaret Ann died 02/07/64   02/13/64
Greatfield, Emma Frances died 07/06/64   07/07/64
Greatfield, Sarah Eleanora died 08/25/65   08/26/65
Greaver, Frank Hough died 06/29/64   07/21/64
Greaver, Kate (Mrs.) died 06/29/64   07/21/64
Greble, Mary S. married Roberts, William, Jr. 10/31/64   11/02/64

Greble, Mary S. married Roberts, William, Jr. 10/31/64   11/03/64
Green, Adelaide died 06/05/63   06/06/63
Green, Alice B. married Robbins, K. R. (Lt.) 10/19/65   10/31/65
Green, Andrew died 08/00/65   08/28/65
Green, Andrew died 08/27/65   08/29/65
Green, Ann Rebecca died 06/28/64   06/29/64
Green, Anna Kate died 06/10/65   06/12/65
Green, Catherine Ann (Mrs.) died 04/16/63   04/18/63
Green, Charles Bennett died 04/08/62   04/10/62
Green, David D. died 01/03/64   01/05/64
Green, Eli H. died 12/14/65   12/15/65
Green, Eliza Ann died 05/29/61   05/30/61
Green, Elizabeth died 03/07/62   03/11/62
Green, Francis married Lehma, Virginia 02/02/64   02/06/64
Green, Francis A. married White, Harriet M. 06/18/61   06/20/61
Green, George T. married Horney, Agnes V. 02/19/63   02/23/63
Green, George W. died 05/13/63   05/14/63
Green, Giles T. died 07/25/63   08/04/63
Green, Hannah Ann died 09/23/65   09/25/65
Green, Harriet A. E. married Wayman, Bishop 05/17/64   05/23/64
Green, Harriet M. (Mrs.) died 01/14/63   01/15/63
Green, Harrison, B. married Boteler, Ellen A. 11/26/63   12/09/63
Green, Henrietta died 06/01/62   06/02/62
Green, James (Capt.) died 01/12/64   01/13/64
Green, James H. married Nesbitt, Mary 01/05/64   02/17/64
Green, James Morris married Ridge, Mary Ellen 02/04/64   02/11/64
Green, James P. married Posterfield, Martha Ann 12/19/61   12/24/61
Green, Jane A. (Mrs.) died 04/04/64   04/06/64
Green, Jenney died 05/23/63   05/29/63
Green, Jesse E. died 11/02/62   11/05/62
Green, John died 03/15/61   03/16/61
Green, John died 04/05/65   04/06/65
Green, John married Delcher, Mary E. 11/19/64   12/22/64
Green, John R. married Elliott, Margaret E. 11/21/63   12/05/63
Green, John W. died 08/15/63   08/17/63
Green, Joshua J. married Smith, Susan J. 04/21/64   05/06/64
Green, Lizzie E. married Wagner, George J. 09/11/60   07/15/61
Green, Lucinde died 05/01/62   05/02/62
Green, Margaret died 02/25/61   02/26/61
Green, Margaret Ann died 02/20/62   02/21/62
Green, Martha A. married Taylor, John H. H. 06/11/63   06/13/63
Green, Martha A. married Taylor, John H. H. 06/11/63   06/18/63
Green, Martha Abbie died 01/04/63   01/06/63
Green, Mary died 04/16/63   04/22/63
Green, Mary died 04/16/63   04/23/63
Green, Mary (Mrs.) died no date 12/17/63
Green, Mary (Mrs.) died 12/16/63   12/18/63
Green, Mary A. (Mrs.) died 05/09/63   05/11/63
Green, Mary Ann died 11/06/62   11/07/62
Green, Mary E. married Potter, Flavius (USA) 07/14/63   07/16/63
Green, Mary Joseph died 10/27/65   10/30/65
Green, Mary L. (Mrs.) died 09/29/63   09/30/63
Green, Mary V. married McCahan, Harry 02/09/64   02/10/64
Green, Nathan G. B. married Wardell, Maggie 01/17/61   01/25/61
Green, Rebeca Jane died 01/06/64   01/08/64

Green, Richard died 05/21/61   05/22/61
Green, Richard died 05/21/61   05/23/61
Green, Richard C. died 09/24/63   09/26/63
Green, Robert died 09/14/64   09/16/64
Green, Rose Ann died 08/23/64   08/24/64
Green, Sarah G. married Palagano, D. 11/24/63   11/28/63
Green, Sarah Jane died 03/31/61   04/02/61
Green, Susan married Basshor, Thomas C. 09/17/61   09/24/61
Green, Susan [retract] married Basshorr, Thomas C. [retract] no date   09/26/61
Green, William married Galoway, Sophia 09/24/63   09/26/63
Green, William died 04/14/65   04/15/65
Green, William (Corp.) died 08/07/63   08/10/63
Green, Willie H. died 02/17/63   02/19/63
Greenawalt, Cinderubed married Stites, John A. 07/23/63   07/30/63
Greene, Charles H. married Pifer, Adeline D. 09/10/62   09/12/62
Greene, Elenora B. died 09/19/65   09/26/65
Greene, Samuel S. married Reinhardt, Amelia 10/26/63   11/07/63
Greene, Thomas married Collins, Mary Ann 09/12/65   10/02/65
Greener, Caroline married Reynolds, George W. 10/15/63   10/20/63
Greener, David died 12/14/61   02/01/62
Greener, Henry married Masters, Mary Amanda 03/21/61   03/25/61
Greener, Mary May died 06/29/65   06/30/65
Greenfield, Annie married Clautice, Joseph no date   05/16/65
Greenfield, Annie A. married Clautice, Joseph 12/29/64   05/19/65
Greenfield, Charles N. died 10/31/61   11/14/61
Greenfield, Harriet Amanda married Lester, Joseph M. 10/08/63   10/24/63
Greenfield, Isaiah died 03/11/64   03/15/64
Greenfield, Phillip C. married Gurdon, Susan M. 06/01/65   06/05/65
Greenfield, Rhoda Harriet died 06/29/63   07/01/63
Greenfield, Winifred (Mrs.) died 04/28/64   04/29/64
Greenhow, Maria F. married Gassaway, Samuel B. 09/24/63   10/07/63
Greenland, William married Cullom, Anne E. 06/21/64   07/09/64
Greenleaf, Albert C. married Snowden, Marie Jane 01/30/62   02/05/62
Greenlee, John married Wright, Margarette 04/25/61   04/27/61
Greenly, Willy E. died 12/01/65   12/02/65
Greensfelder, B. married Myer, Hannah (Mrs.) 12/29/63   12/31/63
Greenwahl, L. H. married Westfall, Sallie E. 03/15/64   03/22/64
Greenway, Mary H. died 06/24/61   06/28/61
Greenwell, Alethia married Tucker, William B. 11/28/63   12/03/63
Greenwell, Mary A. married Spedden, Levin 12/22/62   12/30/62
Greenwood, Angeline A. married Shirden, James 02/18/64   02/24/64
Greenwood, Araminta died 01/27/61   02/09/61
Greenwood, Aurilla died 03/10/65   03/11/65
Greenwood, Frances Jane died 11/06/62   11/07/62
Greenwood, Harriet A. married Mann, Samuel S. (Lt.) 10/16/65   10/18/65
Greenzbach, Emma married Freitag, George 01/12/65   01/16/65
Greer, Alexander died 10/04/61   10/07/61
Greer, Ella married Shreeves, S. J. (USA) 11/02/63   11/05/63
Greer, John died 11/09/64   11/10/64
Greer, Randall died 01/21/64   01/22/64
Greet, William died 07/09/63   07/15/63
Greg, Andrew A. died 10/27/65   11/01/65
Gregg, Annie Jane married Craig, John 02/18/64   02/23/64
Gregg, Mary married Adams, William 03/19/63   04/03/63

Gregg, Thomas C. married Kennard, Clara Virginia 02/24/61   02/26/61
Gregory, Amos died 07/12/61   07/13/61
Gregory, Ann R. died 07/22/65   07/24/65
Gregory, Clara Cecelia died 01/21/65   01/23/65
Gregory, John B. died 06/05/65   06/15/65
Gregory, John T. married Corcoran, Sarah F. 04/28/64   05/02/64
Gregory, William died 10/24/65   10/25/65
Gregory, William died 10/24/65   10/26/65
Greist, William F. married Thompson, Eliza C. 05/05/64   05/09/64
Grenage, Emeline married Preston, Henry 07/31/64   08/03/64
Grendlemeyer, John died 02/19/63   02/21/63
Gresham, James W. died 07/02/62   07/04/62
Greve, Lewis F. married Amos, Kate 11/07/64   11/16/64
Greves, David R. died 05/13/64   05/14/64
Grey, John M. married Deaver, Maria J. 11/22/63   11/30/63
Greylish, Elizabeth (Mrs.) died 03/08/65   03/09/65
Griard, A. B. married Oakes, Mollie C. 11/09/65   11/10/65
Grice, Charlotte E. married Wright, James B. 04/24/62   04/25/62
Grice, Edward G. married Hubbard, Jennevia 05/25/65   05/29/65
Grice, George W. died no date 01/17/63
Grice, Joseph T. P. married Price, M. Evlean 09/07/65   09/08/65
Gridley, Sarah D. (Mrs.) died 01/10/63   01/16/63
Grier, J. Richard married Gilbert, Hannah S. 10/04/64   10/22/64
Grierson, Clementina E. died 03/27/64   04/01/64
Grierson, Jane E. married Freeman, James 10/19/64   10/21/64
Griest, George Collins died 09/24/65   09/25/65
Griest, Mary L. died 12/26/62   12/27/62
Grieves, H. G. died 12/29/64   01/06/65
Grieves, Mary T. died 01/23/63   01/24/63
Griffin, Catherine (Mrs.) died 07/14/64   07/15/64
Griffin, Columbus L. died 06/02/63   06/06/63
Griffin, Edward married Cooper, Anna M. 09/01/63   09/03/63
Griffin, Emily J. died 02/18/65   02/20/65
Griffin, Emily J. died 02/18/65   02/21/65
Griffin, Emma C. married Freeland, Edward 09/18/62   09/20/62
Griffin, Georgeanna married Murkelroy, John J. 04/21/63   07/25/63
Griffin, J. B. died 02/11/61   02/12/61
Griffin, Jane died 03/30/65   04/01/65
Griffin, Jane (Mrs.) died 06/29/64   07/01/64
Griffin, Kate married Butler, James H. (Dr.) 11/24/64   11/28/64
Griffin, Laura V. married France, Ambrose M. 02/28/64   03/26/64
Griffin, Maria F. married Howe, Frank T. 08/06/64   08/15/64
Griffin, Martha E. married League, William F. 02/15/65   03/02/65
Griffin, Martha E. married League, William F. 02/15/65   03/03/65
Griffin, Mary died 11/18/62   11/19/62
Griffin, Mary A. died 02/29/64   03/01/64
Griffin, Mary Ann died no date 04/18/61
Griffin, Mary E. married Carman, Robert R. 05/07/63   05/21/63
Griffin, Mary Louise died 05/04/64   05/05/64
Griffin, Mary Margaret died 08/05/64   08/08/64
Griffin, Matthew died 02/05/64   03/11/64
Griffin, Michael died 06/30/62   07/02/62
Griffin, Patrick died 05/05/61   05/06/61
Griffin, Robert B., Jr. married Cariss, Maggie 11/05/63   11/12/63
Griffin, Robert James died 09/04/62   09/09/62

Griffin, Sarah married Mason, William 05/15/62 05/17/62
Griffin, Thomas J. married White, Maggie A. 05/21/63 10/13/63
Griffin, Thomas M. died 08/15/61 08/16/61
Griffin, William married Dickerson, Anna Maria 06/30/62 07/03/62
Griffing, George Shaffner died 05/31/63 06/02/63
Griffith, Barzillia married Thompson, Mary Geneeve 04/02/61 04/06/61
Griffith, Catherine married Armsworthy, Henry 06/11/61 06/12/61
Griffith, Charles R. married Ferguson, Lydia 10/04/64 10/07/64
Griffith, Edwin L. married Travers, Ada 02/10/63 02/13/63
Griffith, Elizabeth A. died 12/27/64 12/29/64
Griffith, Emma married Coleman, Charles R., Jr. 09/25/62 09/26/62
Griffith, Evelina A. died 08/13/61 08/19/61
Griffith, G. S. married Michael, Ella 06/14/64 06/22/64
Griffith, George Milton died 08/05/64 08/06/64
Griffith, Henrietta married Davige, Charles H. 02/04/65 02/11/65
Griffith, Henry G. died 12/27/61 12/28/61
Griffith, Israel died 08/09/62 08/12/62
Griffith, Israel married Black, Sallie H. 12/24/63 12/31/63
Griffith, J. Howard died 06/17/64 06/18/64
Griffith, James F. married Dempsey, Mary Elizabeth 05/20/62 06/02/62
Griffith, James Fields died 05/19/61 05/22/61
Griffith, Janette married Collins, John H. 11/05/65 11/07/65
Griffith, Jennie A. married Brownley, Thomas J. 03/12/63 03/14/63
Griffith, John (Capt.) died 11/28/61 11/30/61
Griffith, John A. died 10/04/62 10/08/62
Griffith, John A. married Cooper, Helen M. 03/30/64 04/01/64
Griffith, John K. married McCabe, Margaret 09/17/60 01/18/61
Griffith, John Knox died 06/23/62 06/26/62
Griffith, John R. married Ferguson, Eliza 11/24/63 11/25/63
Griffith, John R. (Capt.) married Barnett, Sarah A. 03/17/64 03/19/64
Griffith, Joseph A. died 07/10/62 07/11/62
Griffith, Lewis married Galloway, Maggie J. 08/28/65 08/29/65
Griffith, Lizzie died 07/31/63 08/18/63
Griffith, Louis P. married Roder, Mathilde Regine 04/26/64 04/28/64
Griffith, Nicholas R. died 01/22/64 01/28/64
Griffith, Rayburns died 03/26/64 03/31/64
Griffith, Rebecca died 11/05/64 11/10/64
Griffith, Richard H. died 02/16/64 02/18/64
Griffith, Ruth Hammond died 09/11/63 09/17/63
Griffith, Sarah Belle died 12/24/62 12/25/62
Griffith, Susan died 03/19/65 03/20/65
Griffith, Susan M. (Mrs.) died 12/25/64 12/26/64
Griffith, Thomas married Snyder, Amanda 10/31/61 11/02/61
Griffith, Washington died 10/27/64 11/02/64
Griffith, Wilbur F. died 04/30/62 05/02/62
Griffith, William died 03/23/61 03/25/61
Griffith, William E. married Wilson, Fannie R. 05/08/62 05/12/62
Griggs, Mary (Mrs.) died 01/20/64 01/21/64
Grillard, William H. (Rev.) died 06/25/63 06/27/63
Grim, Mary Ida died 05/05/64 05/09/64
Grimes, Ann died 05/03/62 05/05/62
Grimes, Annie E. married Agnew, James 05/23/65 05/24/65
Grimes, Barbara E. married Partington, Richard M. 06/30/64 07/02/64
Grimes, Charles E. married Sitler, Susie 11/23/65 11/28/65
Grimes, Ella B. (Mrs.) married Brown, John F. 08/27/63 09/30/63

Grimes, Emily J. (Mrs.) died 08/24/63 08/28/63
Grimes, Mary died 12/23/65 12/27/65
Grimes, Mary Ann married Wallace, Charles H. 08/08/64 08/25/64
Grimes, Mary E. married Wright, John A. 06/18/65 07/21/65
Grimes, Oliver married Hammond, Jennie 09/12/64 10/20/64
Grimes, Samuel (Dr.) died 09/01/64 09/02/64
Grimes, Sarah R. married Lewis, John 04/29/64 04/30/64
Grimes, William died 01/11/61 01/19/61
Grimm, Henry S. married Cavano, Mary J. 11/21/65 12/25/65
Grimper, Sarah A. (Mrs.) died 06/23/63 06/24/63
Grinage, Eliza died 07/26/61 07/27/61
Grinage, John married Butler, Mary V. 03/28/61 04/09/61
Grinnage, Eli married Bird, Annie 02/11/64 02/13/64
Grinnell, Charles E. married Washburn, Elizabeth T. 07/11/65 07/25/65
Grinville, Ellen Jane married Yeates, Edward John 08/16/64 08/18/64
Grissam, Elijah died no date 08/14/65
Grobaker, Valentine married Fields, Frances V. 05/01/64 05/06/64
Grogan, Robert married White, Amanda M. J. 02/19/65 02/21/65
Groh, Joseph M. married Clark, Laura A. 06/19/65 08/01/65
Groome, Maria S. married Knight, William M. 04/27/64 05/13/64
Grooms, Ann died 07/17/61 07/18/61
Grooms, Charles Thomas died 07/30/63 07/31/63
Grooms, Edward died 09/02/63 09/04/63
Grooms, Thomas married Bottomore, Jane A. 05/07/63 05/19/63
Gropy, Anna Amelia died 05/28/65 05/30/65
Groscup, Charles Christopher died 09/26/65 10/04/65
Gross, Charles married Lockerman, Margaret 03/27/64 05/09/64
Gross, Charles married Lockwood, Margaret 03/27/64 05/07/64
Gross, E. Alice died 07/06/61 07/08/61
Gross, Henry S. married Fellemeyer, Josephine 05/14/63 05/16/63
Gross, John J. married Toomy, Mary Statia 05/26/64 05/30/64
Gross, Kate T. married Coonan, Dr. Jonathan 01/01/65 01/11/65
Gross, Louisa married Horwitz, Benjamin F. 12/18/62 12/22/62
Gross, Mary married Jones, John T. 02/12/63 02/14/63
Gross, Mary Ann married Hueston, John F. 06/08/65 06/10/65
Gross, Mary E. married Alsop, Augustus 01/01/63 01/05/63
Gross, S. L. married Wade, B. L. 03/13/63 09/03/63
Gross, William H. died 04/12/63 04/15/63
Grosscup, Annie married Henrix, Edward 10/29/63 11/13/63
Grossman, Mary Ann married Malone, John 12/31/62 01/09/63
Grote, John H. died 05/09/61 05/11/61
Grove, Elizabeth M. died 03/28/64 03/29/64
Grove, Franklin died 05/07/61 05/13/61
Grove, Linnie married Comegys, Henry C. 07/17/61 07/22/61
Grove, Lydia A. married Grove, William 11/19/63 11/20/63
Grove, Martin died 02/05/63 02/06/63
Grove, Mary L. (Mrs.) married Hall, Albert S. 09/24/63 09/26/63
Grove, William married Grove, Lydia A. 11/19/63 11/20/63
Grover, Charles Eldridge died 11/14/62 11/17/62
Groverman, A., Jr. married Knowles, Lydia P. 12/01/63 12/05/63
Groverman, Amelia Handy (Mrs.) died 05/02/63 05/04/63
Groverman, Henry died 06/22/63 06/25/63
Groves, George Edward died 02/20/64 02/26/64
Groves, M. A. married Partridge, N. C. 07/09/63 07/22/63
Grow, Mary A. married Walton, George W. 03/29/63 05/02/63

Grubb, William Henry died 12/29/64   01/03/65
Grubbs, Mary Elizabeth died 01/07/65   01/10/65
Grumbine, Emanuel married Riall, Margie A. 10/31/65   11/09/65
Gruver, Elmira married Leman, Walter J. 12/15/64   12/21/64
Gruver, Laura Virginia died 08/09/61   08/10/61
Gruver, Mary E. married Clifford, William H. 01/12/64   01/14/64
Guard, Charles H. married Richter, Mary C. 06/26/62   06/30/62
Gude, Emma died 03/11/63   03/14/63
Gude, Frederick died 07/03/61   07/04/61
Gude, Frederick died 07/03/61   07/06/61
Gude, Laura Amelia died 08/23/62   08/29/62
Gude, Mary Elizabeth died 09/25/65   10/02/65
Gueraud, Victorine M. married Albert, Henry J. 05/30/65   05/31/65
Guest, George H. died 02/03/64   02/08/64
Guest, Krozer died 02/06/65   02/10/65
Guest, Richard S. married Taylor, Virginia P. 04/15/62   04/17/62
Guest, Samuel married Houlton, Mary L. 11/10/63   11/19/63
Guilfoyle, Amelia (Mrs.) died 04/02/63   04/11/63
Guilfoyle, Patrick died 08/16/63   08/17/63
Guillon, Decoline died 11/09/64   11/12/64
Guillou, Acelie (Mrs.) died 04/15/65   04/17/65
Guillou, Victor married Laroque, Acelie M. 10/09/62   10/11/62
Guinea, James died 04/08/64   04/15/64
Guineman, Samuel married Burke, Martha Ann 09/07/65   11/04/65
Guinn, Sarah Jane married Hall, Perry 12/31/60   01/04/61
Guire, W. James married Walter, Mary A. 12/21/63   12/24/63
Guishard, Phebe B. died 07/16/63   07/17/63
Guista, Stephen married Carr, Elizabeth 11/04/61   11/08/61
Guldener, Charlie F. died 03/28/63   03/31/63
Guley, Sarah died 10/27/61   10/28/61
Gulrick, Sarah married Foot, John P. 01/03/61   01/11/61
Gunby, Francis A. (Cpt.) died 12/17/64   12/31/64
Gunnell, Charles E. married Washburn, Elizabeth T. 07/11/65   07/24/65
Gunsalles, Elize Ann died 05/10/62   06/11/62
Gunther, Anton Louis died 06/18/65   06/19/65
Gunther, Charles Augustus died 06/19/65   06/21/65
Gunther, Mary Carolina died 07/03/65   07/06/65
Gunther, Sophie married Eckhardt, T. Conrad 06/29/62   07/04/62
Gunther, Virginia May died 05/18/62   05/20/63
Guntrom, Catharine Augusta died 02/04/64   02/05/64
Gurdon, Susan M. married Greenfield, Phillip C. 06/01/65   06/05/65
Gurney, Ellen died 03/31/61   04/01/61
Gurry, James H. married Fay, Rose A. 04/13/63   04/30/63
Gurry, Mary died 11/12/65   11/13/65
Guston, Ann M. (Mrs.) died 09/16/65   09/30/65
Guthridge, John F. married Old, Mary J. (Mrs.) 05/02/65   05/03/65
Guthrie, Mrs. Susan E. married Anderson, Benjamin F. 12/26/64   01/10/65
Guttle, Sophia married Zentgraf, Adelbert 10/29/65   10/31/65
Guy, Indiana F. married Manson, John G. 12/30/62   12/31/62
Guy, Joseph married Gourley, Anne 12/24/61   01/20/62
Guy, Joseph married Hollins, Elizabeth 03/13/65   03/15/65
Guy, Sallie Ella died 07/04/64   07/06/64
Guy, William died 02/22/62   02/24/62
Guy, William married Bond, Rebecca 11/05/63   11/07/63
Guyer, Albert died 05/26/64   05/27/64

Guynn, Thomas A. married McGuirk, Mary E. 03/01/65 03/04/65
Guyther, M. C. married Blades, John M. 11/05/61 11/07/61
Guyther, Mary Evelina died no date 07/04/64
Guyton, Elisha J. married Suter, Laura 03/01/64 03/04/64
Guyton, Mary J. C. married Garrison, John Henry 02/05/61 02/07/61
Guyton, Sarah died 02/27/63 03/05/63
Guyton, William L. married Brown, Mary E. 10/10/63 02/01/64
Gwin, Mollie E. married Handy, Edward J. 11/18/63 11/20/63
Gwinn, Eliza (Mrs.) died 01/19/65 01/21/65
Haas, Barbara married Abey, Joseph C. 08/18/64 09/02/64
Habbersett, Joseph Hardesty died 04/11/63 04/13/63
Habbiston, Lizzie married Gibbs, A. S. 01/02/62 02/01/62
Haberman, Frederick married Branan, Eleanor E. 06/01/65 06/20/65
Habernagle, Margretta E. died 07/27/64 07/28/64
Hable, Lewis died 07/10/65 07/11/65
Hachtel, Eva Margaret died 10/10/65 10/14/65
Hack, Elizabeth died 10/17/65 10/19/65
Hack, F. W. died 08/01/61 08/02/61
Hack, Henry C. married Thompson, Annie R. 01/17/63 01/21/63
Hack, Henry C. (Lt.) married Soule, Lucy D. 06/14/61 05/19/62
Hack, Henry C. (Lt.) married Soule, Lucy D. 06/14/61 05/20/62
Hack, Lucy D. died 06/14/62 06/17/62
Hack, William A. married Ulrich, Augusta Cecelia 10/08/63 10/13/63
Hacker, Henry died 11/14/63 11/16/63
Hacket, Elizabeth died 03/05/65 03/06/65
Hacket, Robert Clinton married Hobs, Mary Catherine 06/04/65 06/22/65
Hackett, Charles died 08/25/65 08/26/65
Hackett, Edward Pennington died 01/26/63 01/28/63
Hackett, Elizabeth died 03/05/65 03/07/65
Hackett, George A. married Davis, Mary A. 03/28/61 03/30/61
Hackett, Henrietta died 03/25/61 03/27/61
Hackett, Louisa C. married Patterson, Robert 07/21/64 07/22/64
Hadaway, Edward K. died 11/02/65 11/04/65
Haddaway, Mary Ann (Mrs.) died 09/14/64 10/17/64
Haddaway, Mary Ann (Mrs.) died 10/14/64 10/18/64
Hadley, Ann Maria died 04/16/63 04/17/63
Hadley, John W. married Scarborough, Susannah 10/05/65 10/09/65
Haeusser, Carl Ernst died 02/18/61 02/22/61
Hafermatz, Elizabeth married Brock, John M. 03/10/61 03/11/61
Haffcke, Ida died 05/02/65 05/03/65
Haffner, Valentine died 07/18/62 07/19/62
Hagadorn, F. L. (Gen.) married Lunar, Catherine S. 08/25/62 09/04/62
Hagaman, William P. married Litsinger, Mary J. 07/25/65 08/08/65
Hagan, James Henry died 06/11/63 06/12/63
Hagan, Louisa A. married Dersch, Casper S. 11/01/64 11/02/64
Hagan, Mary Ann (Mrs.) died 02/21/64 02/24/64
Hagan, Robert Edward died 10/01/65 10/02/65
Hagan, W. E. died 12/06/64 12/09/64
Hagany, Sallie G. married Harrington, E., Jr. 02/28/65 03/03/65
Hagerman, Martin L. married Berger, Eliza E. 12/17/63 12/19/63
Hagerty, Edward (M.D.) died 09/26/65 09/29/65
Hagerty, Jennie died 08/23/64 08/24/64
Hagger, Charles E. E. died 05/01/64 05/02/64
Hagner, Geneva died 09/21/64 09/23/64
Hagner, Mary R. (Mrs.) died 11/16/64 11/17/64

Hagner, Mattie married Reisner, Albert W. 02/14/65 02/21/65
Hagner, Rebecca Jane married Rilby, Patrick F. 12/20/63 02/05/64
Hags, Nathaniel W. S. died 04/20/63 04/22/63
Hague, James G. died 05/15/63 05/16/63
Hague, Martha died 06/22/62 06/24/62
Hahn, Anna Catherine (Mrs.) died 06/04/64 06/07/64
Hahn, C. Otto married Tennant, Annie C. 03/02/65 03/07/65
Hahn, Caroline married Hahn, Henry G. 12/25/61 12/31/61
Hahn, Henry G. married Hahn, Caroline 12/25/61 12/31/61
Hahn, Joanna D. married Sikes, Columbus H. 04/06/65 04/14/65
Hahn, John D. died 02/15/65 02/18/65
Hahn, Ruth Ann (Mrs.) died 08/09/63 08/11/63
Haig, Albert A. died 11/19/64 11/24/64
Haight, Cornelia died 12/24/62 12/25/62
Haight, Elizabeth (Mrs.) died 07/17/64 07/19/64
Haight, Joana (Mrs.) died 01/17/65 01/18/65
Haight, Joanna married Bishop, William 05/02/65 05/13/65
Haight, William B. married Lawder, Emma V. 03/02/61 05/23/61
Haile, Charles D. married Delcamp, Mary A. 04/21/63 04/22/63
Haines, Margaretta died 03/01/63 03/03/63
Haines, Sarah A. married Davis, William T. 05/18/63 06/13/63
Haislett, Amney E. married Thompson, David P. 02/28/64 04/13/64
Hakesley, William Bandel died 12/18/63 12/21/63
Halbach, Louisa M. married Behn, Henry J. T. 06/20/65 06/21/65
Halbert, Lizzie married Erkridge, J. Emory 04/06/63 04/07/63
Halbert, Sarah R. married Sickel, Edward 06/26/61 06/28/61
Hale, Anna G. (Mrs.) died 12/13/64 12/15/64
Hale, E. J. V. married Fairbank, Charles E. 01/30/62 07/21/62
Hale, Elizabeth died 03/17/64 03/22/64
Hale, George C. died 04/24/65 04/27/65
Hale, Jonathan H. married Simmons, Anna 06/27/65 06/29/65
Hale, Margaret A. C. married Evans, William 03/30/65 04/14/65
Hales, Patsia (Mrs.) died 06/28/65 06/29/65
Haley, Robert M. died 02/03/65 02/06/65
Halfpenny, John died 09/30/61 10/07/61
Halfpenny, Matilda married Taylor, Thomas 09/28/61 10/07/61
Halfpenny, Peter James S. died 08/26/65 09/02/65
Hall, A. Frederick Winfield died 09/12/64 09/13/64
Hall, Albert S. married Grove, Mary L. (Mrs.) 09/24/63 09/26/63
Hall, Andrew died 08/15/65 08/16/65
Hall, Anna died 11/07/61 11/08/61
Hall, Anna E. married Kremeberg, J. George 04/25/64 04/28/64
Hall, Annie L. married Bird, Gustavas 01/14/64 01/25/64
Hall, Annie R. died 05/18/64 05/20/64
Hall, Arthur W. died 08/09/65 08/10/65
Hall, B. D. married Mullikin, Ann D. 06/30/63 07/07/63
Hall, Ben Howard married McAleese, Mary Jane 02/04/62 02/07/62
Hall, Benjamin married Smith, Sarah 09/25/64 09/20/64
Hall, Caroline died 09/04/63 09/05/63
Hall, Carrie married Emerick, Thomas H. 02/16/64 02/19/64
Hall, Cecelia married Russell, W. L. 07/10/62 07/16/62
Hall, Charles A. married Lehman, Sophie 05/29/64 06/01/64
Hall, Charles A. D. married Jones, Alipha E. 12/10/63 12/15/63
Hall, David married Long, Elizabeth 03/27/64 03/29/64
Hall, David E. married Welsh, Marcilla 07/05/63 12/25/63

Hall, E. Thornton died 03/18/64   03/25/64
Hall, Edward married Coffield, Josephine E. 07/09/61   07/11/61
Hall, Edward married Hogans, Elizabeth 08/02/64   08/04/64
Hall, Elias died 08/17/63   08/18/63
Hall, Eliza J. married Ball, John D. 11/23/64   11/26/64
Hall, Eliza S. died 03/04/65   03/06/65
Hall, Eliza S. died 03/04/65   03/07/65
Hall, Elizabeth died 02/01/64   02/04/64
Hall, Elizabeth married Burns, Edward 06/04/63   06/06/63
Hall, Elizabeth (Mrs.) died 03/14/65   03/16/65
Hall, Elizabeth Ann married Williams, Robert 05/25/64   05/27/64
Hall, Elizabeth C. (Mrs.) married Stuart, Harry C. 05/05/64   05/12/64
Hall, Elizabeth Madora died 04/16/63   04/27/63
Hall, Ella Hartman died 07/05/63   07/06/63
Hall, Emily C. married Brannan, James A. 09/25/60   01/30/61
Hall, Emily Marion married Wyatt, Andrew 12/31/60   01/11/61
Hall, Emma J. married Rogers, William 08/24/65   08/26/65
Hall, Eugene S. died 01/14/64   01/23/64
Hall, Ferdinand Chatard died 09/26/63   09/29/63
Hall, Florence J. died 03/21/65   03/25/65
Hall, G. W. married Cosley, Jennie F. 02/02/65   02/10/65
Hall, George W. S. married Smith, Adelia M. 04/30/61   05/04/61
Hall, George Washington died 02/19/65   02/21/65
Hall, Harriet A. married Collins, Seamore 06/02/64   06/04/64
Hall, Harry S. died 05/12/63   05/13/63
Hall, Henry married Blake, Mary Jane 12/22/63   12/24/63
Hall, Henry O. (Lt.) married Willig, Mary 05/06/63   05/07/63
Hall, Ibbie died 01/28/65   02/01/65
Hall, J. D. married Foy, Mary A. (Mrs.) 12/09/63   05/04/64
Hall, James Owen Law died 05/02/65   05/08/65
Hall, James W. died 10/12/61   12/07/61
Hall, John A. died 09/25/64   10/03/64
Hall, John M. died 04/19/64   04/20/64
Hall, John N. (Cpt.) died 10/30/63   11/12/63
Hall, John Thomas died 03/09/63   03/11/63
Hall, John W. died 12/03/62   12/31/62
Hall, John W. married Cunningham, Mary E. 03/01/65   03/04/65
Hall, Josephine S. married Brown, Robert M. 06/05/63   06/15/63
Hall, Julia died 11/04/64   11/05/64
Hall, Kate died 10/06/63   10/07/63
Hall, Kate L. married Frank, Oscar W. 10/08/63   10/12/63
Hall, Laura A. married Wissman, John H. 05/06/61   06/08/61
Hall, Laura Jane died 03/14/62   03/15/62
Hall, Margaret died no date 09/05/61
Hall, Margaret Ann married Carter, James W. 09/21/64   09/23/64
Hall, Margaret H. married Mills, Richard B. 12/30/61   01/10/62
Hall, Margaret Jane married Washington, George 11/13/64   11/15/64
Hall, Maria died 11/05/61   11/06/61
Hall, Maria died 11/05/61   11/07/61
Hall, Maria Gertrude died 01/21/65   01/24/65
Hall, Mary died 05/26/62   05/27/62
Hall, Mary died 10/11/65   10/18/65
Hall, Mary A. married Bowen, Jesse N. 06/07/64   06/13/64
Hall, Mary C. married Janney, Samuel A. 03/12/63   03/19/63
Hall, Mary E. married Herbert, Samuel 04/14/61   04/16/61

Hall, Mary E. married Wheeden, James B. 10/03/65 10/06/65
Hall, Mary Ida died 05/31/65 06/01/65
Hall, Mary L. married Russel, James 01/19/65 01/21/65
Hall, Nannie died 09/21/64 09/28/64
Hall, Nathaniel died 06/25/62 06/26/62
Hall, Perry married Guinn, Sarah Jane 12/31/60 01/04/61
Hall, R. G. married Spencer, J. E. 11/09/65 11/15/65
Hall, Richard married Kaufman, Indiana 09/22/63 09/25/63
Hall, Richard B. married Gosnell, Clara A. M. 03/03/63 03/04/63
Hall, Sarah married Combash, John 10/27/65 10/31/65
Hall, Sarah J. died 08/28/65 09/04/65
Hall, Sarah Jane died 07/06/61 07/12/61
Hall, Sophia died 11/28/62 12/02/62
Hall, Sophia died 12/20/62 12/22/62
Hall, Sophia married Williams, Charles 06/30/64 07/02/64
Hall, Sophia L. married Galbraith, J. Clifton 05/13/62 05/24/62
Hall, Susan A. died 03/19/65 03/23/65
Hall, Susie C. died 05/05/62 05/08/62
Hall, Susie C. died 05/08/62 05/09/62
Hall, Thomas A. married Tucker, Mary E. 11/24/64 12/01/64
Hall, Thomas H. married Iglehart, Rosalie 06/15/64 06/18/64
Hall, William A. married Mettee, Mary E. 10/29/63 11/03/63
Hall, William G. married Gillis, Sarah E. 09/10/63 09/12/63
Hall, William H. died 05/01/64 05/02/64
Hall, William J. H. married Hollingsworth, Harriet Ann 10/26/63
    10/31/63
Hall, William W. married Kirby, Isabella V. 05/20/62 09/10/62
Hall, William Wilmot died 06/12/65 06/16/65
Hall, William Winder Polk died 08/03/62 08/05/62
Hallauhan, Hanorah married Egan, James 11/06/64 11/08/64
Hallen, William A. died 01/13/63 01/15/64
Haller, F. Virginia married Crawford, A. A. 06/14/64 06/21/64
Haller, Frances Virginia married Crawford, Andrew J. 06/14/64 06/20/64
Halliday, Robert J. married Dick, Lenie 09/22/64 09/27/64
Hallock, Nathaniel died 02/13/64 02/15/64
Halloran, Kate died 03/01/65 03/02/65
Hallsworth, Jane married Coxon, Francis 05/17/63 05/22/63
Halpen, Daniel died 05/28/61 05/29/61
Halphin, Alice Ann died 02/23/65 02/25/65
Halpin, Mary (Mrs.) died 11/19/63 11/20/63
Halpin, Sarah J. married Collins, Timothy M. 11/26/65 12/09/65
Halsey, M. H. S. married Gein, J. F. 02/27/63 03/12/63
Ham , Ellen A. (Mrs.) died 01/27/63 01/28/63
Ham, Ann Catherine died 02/25/61 02/27/61
Ham, Ann Mary died 12/30/60 01/02/61
Ham, Elizabeth (Mrs.) died 04/21/63 04/23/63
Haman, James died 02/16/63 02/17/63
Hambleton, James (Capt.) died 01/21/63 06/04/63
Hambleton, John R. died 04/24/63 04/29/63
Hamblett, Mary F. married Davidson, James B. 02/06/65 03/28/65
Hamel, Elizabeth (Mrs.) died 02/11/65 02/13/65
Hamel, Elizabeth Laura died 07/07/63 07/08/63
Hamelin, Emeline M. died 07/31/63 08/01/63
Hamer, Bethia died 12/24/62 12/25/62
Hamer, Lizzie A. married Taylor, M. S. (Dr.) 01/15/61 01/18/61

Hamer, Margaret died 08/16/62 08/19/62
Hamill, Elizabeth married Stewart, Charles M. 03/19/61 03/21/61
Hamill, Emily J. died 02/04/62 02/05/62
Hamill, Kate married Strong, Henry (Lt.) 07/16/65 07/27/65
Hamill, Mary A. married Prenier, Henry L. E. 05/18/65 05/31/65
Hamill, Olivia A. married Hamill, Robert W. 04/09/61 04/23/61
Hamill, Robert died 04/05/65 04/06/65
Hamill, Robert J. B. married Ratcliffe, Mary C. 02/09/63 02/12/63
Hamill, Robert W. married Hamill, Olivia A. 04/09/61 04/23/61
Hamill, William J. died 11/22/61 11/23/61
Hamilton, Adeline R. married Brooks, Samuel D. 10/10/65 10/12/65
Hamilton, Alice Ann (Mrs.) died 11/18/64 11/19/64
Hamilton, Annie Elizabeth died 05/13/65 05/15/65
Hamilton, Beale Duvall (Cpt.) died 07/21/63 07/25/63
Hamilton, Bridget died 01/20/62 01/21/62
Hamilton, Carrie married Sheppard, Thomas D. 07/05/64 07/07/64
Hamilton, Catherine died 01/19/65 01/20/65
Hamilton, Catherine died 01/19/65 01/21/65
Hamilton, Charles died 11/04/61 11/05/61
Hamilton, Edward died 10/28/61 10/29/61
Hamilton, Edward died 03/31/65 04/01/65
Hamilton, Eleanor married Busk, J. Alexius 01/13/63 01/30/63
Hamilton, Eliza R. married Uhler, John R. (Dr.) 04/19/64 04/20/64
Hamilton, Elizabeth died no date 02/14/62
Hamilton, Elizabeth married Chanler, Thomas M. 04/12/64 04/15/64
Hamilton, Elizabeth (Mrs.) died 01/15/65 01/17/65
Hamilton, Emilie V. married Falls, Moor 10/07/63 10/10/63
Hamilton, George died 05/18/64 05/19/64
Hamilton, George D. died 04/05/64 04/07/64
Hamilton, Harriet died 09/09/62 09/11/62
Hamilton, Harry Ellsworth died 01/25/64 01/26/64
Hamilton, Helen died no date 07/20/61
Hamilton, Henry married Harper, Amelia E. J. 10/07/62 10/09/62
Hamilton, James (Pvt.) died 09/03/64 09/10/64
Hamilton, James A. married Scanlan, Maggie A. 05/08/62 06/04/62
Hamilton, James A. died 11/25/63 11/26/63
Hamilton, James M. (USN) married Black, Sophia (Mrs.) 10/22/62 02/10/
Hamilton, James, Jr. died 12/06/65 12/16/65
Hamilton, Johm A. died 01/29/63 01/31/63
Hamilton, John married Coulter, Julia Ann 04/08/62 04/21/62
Hamilton, John married Crawford, Maggie 03/27/62 04/30/62
Hamilton, John married Sullivan, Sue E. 02/09/64 02/11/64
Hamilton, Josie married Suter, Frederick 10/22/63 10/24/63
Hamilton, Julia married Cooper, Edward 12/21/63 12/22/63
Hamilton, Julia Elizabeth died 01/28/61 01/30/61
Hamilton, Kate died 03/01/61 03/02/61
Hamilton, Kate Revere died 07/08/65 07/10/65
Hamilton, Lucinda J. married Hudgen, John 09/11/65 09/13/65
Hamilton, Margaret Jane married Wagonfield, Frederick 05/12/62 05/23/
Hamilton, Mary died 05/20/63 05/21/63
Hamilton, Mary Ann died 12/07/62 12/09/62
Hamilton, Mary Ellen died 01/06/61 01/08/61
Hamilton, Orman married McDermott, Mary E. 11/24/63 11/28/63
Hamilton, Rebecca died 04/16/65 04/17/65
Hamilton, Rebecca died 04/16/65 04/18/65

Hamilton, Ruth married Solomon, Benjamin D. 09/28/65 10/16/65
Hamilton, Samuel H. died 03/25/64 03/31/64
Hamilton, Sarah A. married Zupp, Reuben 03/26/63 04/07/63
Hamilton, Sarah A. married Burmingham, William C. 07/16/63 07/25/63
Hamilton, Sarah E. died 07/02/62 07/03/62
Hamilton, Sarah Elizabeth married Sayre, William H. 01/02/62 01/08/62
Hamilton, Thomas E. died 09/03/64 09/05/64
Hamilton, Tobitha W. married Mullikin, Beale D. 12/12/65 12/16/65
Hamilton, William died 03/21/64 03/23/64
Hamilton, William Campbell died 10/05/63 10/28/63
Hamilton, William H. died 11/15/64 04/07/65
Hamilton, William H. married Wickham, Mary Ann 11/16/65 11/25/65
Hamilyon, Ruth married Solomon, Benjamin D. 09/28/65 10/16/65
Hamlin, George P. married Spring, Elizabeth 11/01/61 01/14/62
Hamman, Elizabeth married Kraft, William H. 05/15/64 05/17/64
Hammand, Henry J. died 06/23/65 06/24/65
Hammer, Andrew died 09/10/65 09/11/65
Hammer, Andrew died 09/10/65 09/14/65
Hammer, Frank H. died 09/12/63 11/28/63
Hammer, Ida A. died 02/11/64 02/12/64
Hammer, James V. married Stine, Sallie J. 03/08/64 03/10/64
Hammer, Jane A. (Mrs.) died 10/26/64 10/29/64
Hammer, Mary A. M. married Mullan, Samuel E. 10/05/63 10/07/63
Hammerslaugh, Julius married Rose, Henny 08/24/62 08/30/62
Hammersley, George W. married Diven, Mary E. 09/22/64 09/27/64
Hammett, Ferdinand died 12/27/64 12/28/64
Hammett, Maria (Mrs.) married Dorsey, George W. 04/21/64 04/23/64
Hammill, Jane married Ballauf, Charles 12/31/63 01/04/64
Hammill, Mary McClelland died 12/24/63 12/25/63
Hammock, Emma L. (Mrs.) married Fisher, Lewis 12/11/64 12/13/64
Hammon, Susana married Oswinkle, Joseph 02/08/64 02/10/64
Hammond, Agnes married Harris, David 12/01/63 12/07/63
Hammond, Anna Catherine died 02/23/65 02/25/65
Hammond, Camille married Ridgely, Gustavus W. 11/11/63 11/12/63
Hammond, Charles died 11/21/65 11/22/65
Hammond, Charles V. married Duvall, Sallie P. 06/10/62 06/12/62
Hammond, Elizabeth died 10/17/65 11/04/65
Hammond, Eveline died 07/06/65 07/21/65
Hammond, Ida died 01/14/63 01/15/64
Hammond, Jennie married Grimes, Oliver 09/12/64 10/20/64
Hammond, John, Sr. died 06/17/65 06/19/65
Hammond, Julia Ann (Mrs.) died 02/05/65 02/10/65
Hammond, Louisa married Hawkins, Alexander 12/11/62 12/13/62
Hammond, Mary Ann died 03/06/62 03/08/62
Hammond, Mollie A. died 11/03/64 11/04/64
Hammond, Oliver E. died 03/27/62 04/09/62
Hammond, Robert married Wittington, Elizabeth 10/10/61 10/12/61
Hammond, Sarah (Mrs.) died 01/12/65 01/13/65
Hammond, Sarah Elizabeth married Burton, Thomas 10/02/62 10/24/62
Hammond, Thomas W. married Murray, Alice A. 10/19/65 10/23/65
Hammond, William (Rev. Dr.) died 02/09/65 02/16/65
Hammond, William Z. died 08/29/63 08/31/63
Hammonds, John H. married Harris, Sarah E. 06/04/63 06/06/63
Hamner, Grace Beauregard died 08/15/63 08/19/63
Hampon, Elizabeth M. (Mrs.) died 10/01/64 10/03/64

Hampson, James S. married Bull, H. Fannie 01/20/63   02/22/63
Hampton, Laura Marcella died 09/07/65   09/09/65
Hamsley, William H. died 11/11/61   11/12/61
Han, John F. married Foxwell, Sarah F. 08/14/62   08/23/62
Hanan, Henry N. died 09/09/63   09/10/63
Hanan, James died 01/09/64   01/11/64
Hanan, John died 11/11/65   11/13/65
Hanan, John S. married Pinkney, Emily M. 11/17/63   11/19/63
Hance, James died 07/17/65   07/18/65
Hance, Mary Albins died 07/11/62   07/12/62
Hance, Patrick died 07/31/63   08/01/63
Hanck, Frederick married Raine, Sophia 10/19/62   10/21/62
Hancock, John A. married Harmon, Susie C. 11/24/63   11/25/63
Hancock, John F. married Etchberger, Fannie A. 02/06/62   02/10/62
Hancock, Lallie E. married Welch, Benjamin G. 01/11/64   01/16/64
Hancock, Laura A. married Feig, George A. 06/03/62   06/11/62
Hancock, Mary Elizabeth died 12/03/62   12/09/62
Hancock, Rachel A. married Davis, John A. 04/02/65   04/07/65
Hancock, Stephen W. died 12/28/62   12/30/62
Hancock, Virginia Quarles died 05/25/63   07/20/63
Hancock, William died 03/11/62   03/13/62
Hand, (Mrs. Henry) died 06/23/64   07/04/64
Hand, Charles C. married McAfee, Sallie 07/23/61   07/29/61
Hand, Hennie H. married Cooper, Joshua E. 12/06/64   12/08/64
Hand, Mary (Mrs.) died 06/23/64   06/24/64
Hand, Stewart Jennings died 09/09/65   09/13/65
Hand, Susan (Mrs.) married Michael, Jacob 05/11/63   05/18/63
Hand, William W. (Dr.) died 01/27/64   01/28/64
Handley, Andrew George died 08/08/63   08/11/63
Handley, Catharine married Mason, William G. 10/26/65   10/28/65
Handley, James died 08/03/64   08/04/64
Handley, Valentine died 09/21/63   09/23/63
Hands, George died 08/11/61   08/12/61
Hands, George died 08/11/61   08/14/61
Hands, Haddie W. married Neily, J. Wilson 02/22/65   02/24/65
Hands, Jane died 07/30/62   08/01/62
Hands, Jennie E. married Fitch, Marcellus L. 08/06/63   08/08/63
Hands, Matilda died 09/10/65   09/14/65
Hands, Rachel D. (Mrs.) died 09/05/64   09/09/64
Hands, Sarah M. married Warfield, Charles A. 11/17/64   11/21/64
Handy, Alexander married Fesba, Eliza 01/20/63   01/22/63
Handy, Edward J. married Gwin, Mollie E. 11/18/63   11/20/63
Handy, Edward Lloyd died 07/09/65   07/10/65
Handy, Edward Lloyd died 07/09/65   07/12/65
Handy, Henrietta G. died 01/19/62   02/18/62
Handy, Isaac died 03/04/63   03/07/63
Handy, John married Samson, Serina 04/17/61   04/20/61
Handy, Julia A. died 01/09/65   01/12/65
Handy, Thomas P. married Poultney, Maria 10/31/65   11/02/65
Hane, Annie L. died 12/22/62   12/23/62
Hanes, Frank M. married Shields, Maggie A. 12/01/63   12/08/63
Hanes, Lida A. married Showalter, Harry 12/14/65   12/21/65
Hanes, Mary E. married Shipley, Samuel (Sgt.) 02/18/63   02/25/63
Hanes, Virginia married Cadwallader, S. E. 05/19/64   05/24/64
Haneway, Charles Lindsey died 06/08/64   07/02/64

Haney, James K. P. married High, Josephine 08/31/65 09/05/65
Haney, Mary married Fisher, Alfred 01/01/61 01/03/61
Haney, Novella married Reese, Thomas H. 08/28/64 09/07/64
Hanihan, Mary A. married Coyle, Thomas 06/11/61 06/12/61
Hank, Nannie Serena died 06/08/63 06/10/63
Hank, Sally V. married Meakin, J. W. 03/17/63 03/23/63
Hankin, James married Leach, Mary 04/07/64 04/09/64
Hanlan, Mary Elizabeth died 06/02/63 06/03/63
Hanlay, Martin married Mahan, Anna 09/12/64 09/13/64
Hanleu, Edward died 07/31/61 08/01/61
Hanley, Bedilia Ann died 10/09/64 10/11/64
Hanley, Kate married Cox, Elisha 07/09/63 09/14/63
Hanley, Tallulah died 07/05/64 07/16/64
Hanlin, Catharine (Mrs.) died 08/16/63 08/17/63
Hann, Emma D. died 08/22/63 09/21/63
Hann, Margaret Barbara married Mathews, John E. 10/09/64 10/12/64
Hann, Susan married Michael, Jacob 05/11/63 05/19/63
Hanna, John died 06/25/62 08/09/62
Hanna, Robert M. (Cpt.) married Morrison, Margaret E. 01/03/63 01/05/63
Hanna, Robert M. (Cpt.) married Morrison, Maggie E. 01/03/63 01/06/63
Hannal, Alfred M. (Capt.) married March, Josephine S. 01/14/64 01/15/64
Hannam, Mary died 04/27/62 04/29/62
Hannam, Uriah G. died 05/02/64 05/05/64
Hannick, J. C. married Winthrop, Eliza V. 06/03/62 06/10/62
Hannock, A. M. (Maj.) married Davis, Fannie A. 02/24/62 02/27/62
Hannon, Ellen died 03/26/62 03/28/62
Hannon, Michael died 11/05/63 11/06/63
Hanrahan, Michael died 12/30/61 01/01/62
Hanrahan, Thomas died 01/04/64 01/05/64
Hansell, Mara died 01/03/61 01/04/61
Hanson, A. B. married Middleton, Annie E. 12/01/64 12/02/64
Hanson, B. H. married Canon, Susie 01/23/62 01/25/62
Hanson, Bridget died 04/03/65 04/05/65
Hanson, Clara married Ways, Leonard Thomas 12/07/63 01/09/64
Hanson, Ella married Clemmens, James D. 09/13/63 10/03/63
Hanson, George M. died 06/10/64 06/11/64
Hanson, Helen S. married Chew, William B. 08/08/61 08/13/61
Hanson, Henrietta M. died 07/23/65 07/24/65
Hanson, James H. married Price, Sarah J. 07/27/65 09/19/65
Hanson, John P. died 08/19/61 08/21/61
Hanson, M. A. married Hinkson, F. 01/10/61 01/24/61
Hanson, Mary Amanda died 11/05/63 11/07/63
Hanson, Mary E. married Stiffler, John N. 12/07/65 12/16/65
Hansow, P. W. married Hopper, Sallie M. 12/08/63 12/15/63
Hanway, Franklin married Dukehart, Susan B. 10/17/61 10/18/61
Hanway, Franklin died 08/28/64 08/30/64
Hanway, Mary Elizabeth died 06/27/62 06/28/62
Hanynie, Elizabeth married Brown, William W. 08/26/63 11/10/63
Hapner, Ann Rebecca married Smith, Jacob Henry 09/22/63 09/24/63
Happersett, George Buchanan died 04/17/61 04/19/61
Harback, Charles Adrian died 12/05/64 12/08/64
Harcourt, J. Milton Whitney died 02/09/62 02/11/62
Harcum, Ann married Waters, Gilbert 03/01/65 03/04/65
Hardcastle, Edwin L. died 08/08/64 08/10/64
Hardcastle, Jane E. died 09/23/64 09/26/64

Harden, Henrietta died 06/14/64 06/15/64
Harden, James D. married Hiner, Emily 02/12/61 02/14/61
Harden, James, Sr. died 12/03/63 12/04/63
Harden, Joseph H. M. died 06/23/64 06/24/64
Harden, Mary Ann died 01/20/65 01/24/65
Hardester, John T. married Frankland, Anna 12/30/63 02/08/64
Hardester, Margaret died 03/23/63 03/25/63
Hardester, Mary died 12/29/61 12/31/61
Hardester, Mary Jane (Mrs.) died 12/28/64 12/30/64
Hardester, William B. married Parsons, Almira G. 09/02/61 09/04/61
Hardester, William David died 03/21/63 03/25/63
Hardesty, Achsah died 11/09/62 11/10/62
Hardesty, Charles R. died 07/09/62 07/11/62
Hardesty, Emma J. died 03/09/63 03/10/63
Hardesty, Emma J. died 03/09/63 03/14/63
Hardesty, James H. married Denny, Catherine (Mrs.) 05/03/64 05/23/64
Hardesty, John Edward died 01/03/65 01/07/65
Hardesty, Maggie H. married Childs, J. N. 11/01/65 11/17/65
Hardesty, Margaret H. married Placide, W. H. 01/13/63 01/16/63
Hardesty, Margaret H. married Placide, W. William H. 01/15/63 01/23/63
Hardesty, Marietta married Minnick, J. M. E. 08/05/61 08/10/61
Hardesty, Mary E. married Carr, Arthur 06/10/62 06/13/62
Hardesty, Richard married Talbott, Maggie 07/05/62 07/07/62
Hardesty, Richard C. died 03/23/63 03/26/63
Hardesty, Richard C. married Harris, Mary C. (Mrs.) 01/24/65 01/25/65
Hardesty, Richard T. married Clagett, Anna 06/01/65 06/22/65
Hardesty, Richard W. married Wood, Rachel S. 01/01/61 01/02/61
Hardesty, Sophia A. married Stevens, Granger F. 04/24/62 04/29/62
Hardesty, T. Edward married Cornor, Mary J. 10/11/63 11/10/63
Hardesty, Thomas H. married Starr, Anna J. 11/07/61 12/09/61
Hardesty, William G. died 04/24/61 04/25/61
Hardesty, William G. died 04/24/61 04/26/61
Hardesty, Willie died 03/13/63 03/16/63
Hardey, William died 10/17/65 10/18/65
Harding, Charles A. married Dorsey, Ellen V. 11/25/63 11/28/63
Harding, Drusilla married Collier, Frank M. 11/13/64 11/18/64
Harding, Eliza married Nickerson, George B. 06/11/65 06/30/65
Harding, Granville Snethen died 03/19/64 04/09/64
Harding, James married Duffy, Catherine A. 03/09/65 03/15/65
Harding, Lucie S. married Allen, William N. 12/07/65 12/14/65
Harding, Matilda died 12/22/64 12/23/64
Harding, Miranda married Latchford, George G. 10/23/65 10/25/65
Harding, Nicholas died 07/20/65 07/22/65
Harding, Nolan R. died 09/26/65 09/30/65
Harding, Rachel died 07/08/64 07/19/64
Harding, Richard A. died 04/12/65 04/14/65
Harding, Zachariah died 01/23/62 01/25/62
Hardister, Mary Jane (Mrs.) died 12/28/64 12/29/64
Hardisty, Harriet Ann died 05/22/62 05/31/62
Hardwick, Arthur James died 11/08/62 11/10/62
Hardy, Amelia Jane married Lee, Samuel J. 02/04/62 02/27/62
Hardy, Benjamin F. died 11/04/63 11/06/63
Hardy, Edward died 02/12/64 02/13/64
Hardy, George L. (Cpt.) died 09/07/64 09/08/64
Hardy, George M. married Madary, Ellen S. 10/19/65 10/21/65

```
Hardy, Henry died 11/29/65   11/30/65
Hardy, Hugh A. died 01/25/63   01/26/63
Hardy, John (U.S.N.) married Deacon, Louisa 08/08/65   08/09/65
Hardy, Martha died 06/12/62   06/17/62
Hardy, Mary C. married Armstrong, Samuel S. 10/25/65   10/27/65
Hardy, Mary E. married Pearson, James H. 12/21/65   12/23/65
Hardy, Randolph married Gray, Matilda 05/03/63   05/06/63
Hardy, Sarah (Mrs.) died 01/16/64   01/20/64
Hardy, Thomas died 03/18/61   03/22/61
Hardy, William G. died 06/06/63   06/08/63
Hare, (Mrs. John) died 12/25/62   12/27/62
Hare, Mary Ann died 08/10/62   08/14/62
Hare, P. (Mrs.) died 10/31/65   11/01/65
Hare, Patrick O. married Hennery, Bridget 01/24/64   01/25/64
Hare, William died 11/02/65   11/03/65
Harford, Georgeanna A. married Younger, William 02/11/64   02/13/64
Harford, Mary A. died 09/04/65   09/19/65
Harford, Thomas B. married Harper, Mary F. 07/11/61   11/05/61
Hargest, John Quincy Adams died 11/11/65   11/14/65
Hargrove, Mary E. married Cooper, James 12/14/65   12/20/65
Haries, George died 07/31/65   08/01/65
Harig, Albert A. died 11/19/64   11/26/64
Harig, Ellenora Rebecca (Mrs.) died 06/24/63   06/26/63
Harig, John F. married Graham, Marian Ann 01/05/63   01/08/63
Harison, Euphamia died 08/01/62   08/05/62
Harken, Mary A. married Hubner, John 09/24/63   09/26/63
Harker, Charlotte died 08/26/61   08/29/61
Harker, Mary (Mrs.) married Durham, David 04/05/64   04/13/64
Harker, Sarah Lizzie died 07/29/63   07/30/63
Harkin, Henrietta married Welslager, James T. 01/11/64   01/12/64
Harkins, William Henry died 03/18/61   03/19/61
Harkness, Andrew J. married Anthony, Janie 09/29/64   10/11/64
Harkness, Sarah J. married Henry, John J. 11/12/61   11/15/61
Harkness, Thomas died 08/07/62   08/09/62
Harkness, Thomas died 08/07/62   09/27/62
Harlen, David W. died 10/17/65   10/23/65
Harley, Augusta J. died 03/09/63   03/10/63
Harlow, (Mrs.) died 08/12/65   08/14/65
Harlow, Catherine died 10/09/63   10/10/63
Harlow, Kendrick Warren died 07/04/61   07/06/61
Harmager, Anna Mary Benondine died 09/03/62   09/06/62
Harman, Ann E. died 10/04/63   10/06/63
Harman, Barzillai W. died 03/23/64   04/12/64
Harman, John died 03/19/62   03/20/62
Harman, John died 06/26/62   06/27/62
Harman, John A. died 09/30/63   11/21/63
Harman, Lavinia died 05/10/63   05/11/63
Harman, Mary E. married Bleany, Charles K. 08/11/64   08/20/64
Harman, Milton Melville died 10/19/63   10/20/63
Harman, Sarah A. married Kirkwood, Charles H. 08/29/61   09/02/61
Harman, Susan married Smith, John 11/26/63   11/28/63
Harmon, Francis D. died 01/29/62   02/01/62
Harmon, George married Oelegrath, Louisa 01/20/63   01/27/63
Harmon, Henrietta (Mrs.) married Spence, John 10/25/64   10/29/64
Harmon, John F. married Boyer, Rachel A. 02/25/64   03/03/64
```

Harmon, Lillie E. married Dukehart, G. 04/02/65 04/04/65
Harmon, Susie C. married Hancock, John A. 11/24/63 11/25/63
Harmond, Mary E. died 09/16/61 09/23/61
Harner, Mary died 07/19/61 07/20/61
Harney, E. Rhodes died 10/05/65 10/06/65
Harney, E. Rhodes died 10/05/65 10/07/65
Harp, Sarah J. married Owings, John 02/28/64 03/01/64
Harper, Amelia E. J. married Hamilton, Henry 10/07/62 10/09/62
Harper, Augusta Eccleston died 03/01/65 03/07/65
Harper, Catherine A. (Mrs.) died 04/07/65 04/11/65
Harper, Catherine Carroll died 02/12/61 02/14/61
Harper, J. Sylvester married Albertson, Cornelia B. 12/12/65 12/14/65
Harper, James married Gray, Margaret 10/23/64 11/10/64
Harper, John Lloyd died 07/22/65 07/25/65
Harper, John P. died no date 02/13/65
Harper, John W. married Hatton, Catherine E. 03/05/61 03/07/61
Harper, Margaret married Linton, Jacob 02/08/64 02/09/64
Harper, Margaret Elizabeth died 03/03/62 03/04/62
Harper, Martha died 11/06/62 11/07/62
Harper, Mary E. married Fortie, John C. 04/17/64 04/19/64
Harper, Mary E. married Norries, Esrom 08/08/65 09/06/65
Harper, Mary F. married Harford, Thomas B. 07/11/61 11/05/61
Harps, Frank H. married Kuhn, Minnie A. 11/24/65 12/12/65
Harrers, Barbara married Emge, John 01/18/63 01/20/63
Harrick, Kate married McKnezie, Francis 01/07/64 01/09/64
Harriday, Jesse married Anderson, Sophia 10/26/63 10/28/63
Harries, William married Lockhart, Maggie J. 05/05/63 06/13/63
Harries, Willie J. died 12/26/64 12/28/64
Harrigan, Ella died 10/29/62 11/01/62
Harrington, Catharine married Crisp, Charles 07/05/63 07/07/63
Harrington, Catherine married Peterson, Peter 08/13/65 08/15/65
Harrington, Deborah Z. died 07/01/64 07/02/64
Harrington, E., Jr. married Hagany, Sallie G. 02/28/65 03/03/65
Harrington, Eliza (Mrs.) died 08/01/65 08/03/65
Harrington, Ellen F. died 05/25/62 05/30/62
Harrington, Emily T. married Porter, Lucius P. 10/22/62 10/28/62
Harrington, Honora died 06/14/64 06/16/64
Harrington, Maggie died 12/08/64 12/10/64
Harrington, Mary Jane died 07/24/65 07/26/65
Harrington, Matilda (Mrs.) died 08/05/65 08/07/65
Harrington, Samuel (Capt.) died 01/31/62 02/01/62
Harrington, Thomas (Capt.) died 03/14/63 03/21/63
Harrington, William S. married Muffitt, Louisa 03/31/61 04/30/61
Harris, Asbury married Chambers, Emily 07/20/65 07/21/65
Harris, Caroline married Shepard, Jacob S. 12/29/64 12/30/64
Harris, Daniel died 12/02/62 12/03/62
Harris, David married Hammond, Agnes 12/01/63 12/07/63
Harris, E. married Gent, Henry 06/16/63 07/20/63
Harris, Elenor died 10/28/63 10/30/63
Harris, Elizabeth died 10/19/61 10/26/61
Harris, Elizabeth (Mrs.) died 01/27/65 01/30/65
Harris, Ellen married Garrett, Thomas 03/05/63 03/07/63
Harris, Ellenora died 08/16/63 08/17/63
Harris, Emily died 05/18/64 05/24/64
Harris, Frances B. married Booth, Henry A. 09/21/63 10/08/63

Harris, Frederick A. died 07/31/64 08/02/64
Harris, George died 01/18/61 01/19/61
Harris, George married Stevenson, Mary Jane (Mrs.) 11/05/63 11/07/63
Harris, George married Wirth, Casalina 05/22/65 06/01/65
Harris, George Beauregard died 08/23/63 08/24/63
Harris, George M. married French, Eleanor Elizabeth no date 02/26/61
Harris, George W. died 03/15/62 03/31/62
Harris, Harry L. died 01/17/65 01/21/65
Harris, Helen E. died 11/09/62 11/10/62
Harris, Isabel died 03/29/65 04/01/65
Harris, James died 04/12/64 04/14/64
Harris, James A. married Jones, Mary Henrietta 05/24/64 05/26/64
Harris, Jane A. (Mrs.) died 07/16/64 07/19/64
Harris, Jerome Bradford died 01/08/61 01/09/61
Harris, L. married Byran, S. V. 01/12/63 01/23/63
Harris, Lannie L. married Byram, S. D. 01/12/63 01/13/63
Harris, Laura married Cormack, Archibald 10/01/61 10/03/61
Harris, Leroy married Bell, Ann Jane 05/27/63 06/02/63
Harris, Margaret died 07/27/62 07/28/62
Harris, Margaret H. (Mrs.) died 02/20/63 02/23/63
Harris, Mary married White, Alexander 12/24/63 01/04/64
Harris, Mary married Divens, John 10/15/65 10/18/65
Harris, Mary A. married Knell, Frank L. 12/08/63 12/15/63
Harris, Mary C. (Mrs.) married Hardesty, Richard C. 01/24/65 01/25/65
Harris, Mary Elizabeth married Davidson, Robert J. 11/23/63 12/01/63
Harris, Mary F. married Donaldson, George F. 12/22/64 12/23/64
Harris, Mary Leslie married Stoddard, Frederick S. 12/21/64 12/29/64
Harris, Mary Stewart died 03/03/63 03/10/63
Harris, Matthias died 12/10/63 12/12/63
Harris, Mollie died 12/18/64 12/19/64
Harris, Samuel M. married Inman, Emma 01/04/64 01/06/64
Harris, Sarah A. died 07/05/64 07/06/64
Harris, Sarah E. married Hammonds, John H. 06/04/63 06/06/63
Harris, Sarah V. H. married Best, J. W. F. 12/25/60 03/11/61
Harris, Sophia died 01/15/63 01/17/63
Harris, Stephen married Robertson, Julia (Mrs.) 12/14/65 12/16/65
Harris, Susan A. died 08/22/65 08/23/65
Harris, Susanna died 10/11/61 10/12/61
Harris, Tabitha Keith died 02/11/64 02/13/64
Harris, Thomas died 01/06/62 01/07/62
Harris, William died 03/30/65 03/31/65
Harris, William John died 11/27/65 11/29/65
Harrisk, John E. married Redmond, Helen R. 03/04/62 03/10/62
Harrison, A. C. Braddie married Spencer, Edward 11/25/61 11/28/61
Harrison, Alexander married Hazard, Eliza M. 03/11/64 03/15/64
Harrison, Anna Caroline died 08/23/65 08/24/65
Harrison, Anne M. (Mrs.) died 08/09/63 08/11/63
Harrison, Benjamin B. died 05/04/62 05/04/62
Harrison, Benjamin F. married Hunt, Martha 03/22/63 04/28/63
Harrison, Benjamin F. died 02/20/64 02/22/64
Harrison, Caroline died 12/28/60 01/10/61
Harrison, Charles A. died 11/28/63 11/30/63
Harrison, Charles Henry died 02/06/62 02/07/62
Harrison, Clara Ella died 06/22/64 06/25/64
Harrison, Elizabeth died 03/13/63 03/14/63

Harrison, Ellen K. died 01/09/61 01/10/61
Harrison, Elnorna Virginia married Williams, Robert C. M. 06/02/61 01/02/62
Harrison, Frederick, Sr. died 11/18/64 12/22/64
Harrison, George Oliver died 01/02/62 01/03/62
Harrison, George W. married Phillips, Lizzie 12/06/60 02/12/61
Harrison, H. T. married Broders, Laura 09/26/63 09/30/63
Harrison, James Price died 04/08/63 04/13/63
Harrison, James Price died 04/08/63 04/15/63
Harrison, James S. married Pryor, Anna S. (Mrs.) 05/12/64 05/14/64
Harrison, James T. married Pryor, Anna S. 05/12/64 05/16/64
Harrison, John married Trail, Eleonora L. 10/20/61 10/21/61
Harrison, Lizzie married Coale, Alfred 12/06/64 12/13/64
Harrison, Lorri May died 05/07/65 05/11/65
Harrison, Mary Amanda died 12/19/61 12/21/61
Harrison, Mary E. (Mrs.) died 02/14/63 02/16/63
Harrison, Mary L. died 03/13/62 03/18/62
Harrison, Mary M. (Mrs.) died 07/11/63 07/14/63
Harrison, Milton Eugene died 02/10/61 02/12/61
Harrison, Robert V. married Ritteau, Margaret 09/04/64 09/20/64
Harrison, Sarah Ann died 04/28/62 04/29/62
Harrison, Sarah Baxter married Crosby, Alexander L. 10/25/65 11/01/65
Harrison, Sarah W. died 07/18/62 07/19/62
Harrison, Sprague married Burr, Jennie 10/10/64 10/12/64
Harrison, Susan died 12/12/64 12/14/64
Harrison, William died 12/06/61 12/07/61
Harrison, William H. married Hunter, Ann Louisa 11/01/64 11/07/64
Harrison, William Henry married Sindall, Mary E. 08/09/65 08/12/65
Harrison, Willie died 03/05/64 03/30/64
Harrod, Georgetta married Allen, Joel 07/05/65 07/12/65
Harrod, Henry died no date 08/23/61
Harrod, Henry died 08/12/61 08/24/61
Harrod, John S. died 10/13/64 10/14/64
Harrod, Mary Grace married Burch, George D. 05/07/63 06/09/63
Harrold, Margaret (Mrs.) died no date 12/09/65
Harrop, Charles married Pascoe, Elizabeth 12/15/64 12/16/64
Harry, William O. married Swadaner, Henrietta 05/21/61 05/23/61
Harryman, Benjamin B. married McNulty, Ellen 03/13/64 03/25/64
Harryman, David died 04/02/64 04/04/64
Harryman, Eliza J. married Wright, Joseph H. 10/13/63 10/15/63
Harryman, Elizabeth (Mrs.) died 10/17/65 10/18/65
Harryman, Joshua died 09/14/64 09/15/64
Harryman, Mary E. married Edwards, Thomas J. 06/01/64 10/06/64
Harryman, S. E. married Marlow, S. D. 11/23/64 11/28/64
Harryman, William died 09/06/63 09/08/63
Harsh, Moses married Rosenfeld, Adaline 10/16/65 10/21/65
Harshberger, Wiliam H. died 03/21/61 03/22/61
Hart, Barnet married Cockey, Josephine A. 09/22/64 10/03/64
Hart, Catharine married Thornton, Frederick 09/10/63 09/12/63
Hart, Eveline married Kennedy, Henry C. 01/30/63 02/07/63
Hart, Francis married Stein, Elizabeth 01/07/63 01/19/63
Hart, S. F. died 07/19/65 07/21/65
Hart, William H. died 09/22/63 01/08/64
Hart, William Henry died 09/22/63 09/23/63
Harteley, Elizabeth died 04/04/61 04/06/61

Harten, Margaret Young (Mrs.) died 03/19/64 03/21/64
Harter, Kate married Fisher, Chester Quiler 06/21/64 07/12/64
Hartigan, Michael died 05/13/64 05/14/64
Hartigan, S. Rebecca married Fletcher, Solomon D. 06/26/65 08/10/65
Hartin, Agnes married McGowan, Thomas 10/17/64 10/20/64
Hartley, Charles L. married Scott, Martha E. 03/22/64 03/29/64
Hartley, Florence died 03/02/65 03/07/65
Hartley, James G. died 10/18/63 10/23/63
Hartley, Lucy died 02/21/65 03/07/65
Hartley, Martha E. (Mrs.) died 10/05/64 10/07/64
Hartley, Mary Tacy died 03/20/62 05/28/62
Hartley, Thomas died 04/25/63 04/28/63
Hartley, Thomas H. married Hobbs, Martha 07/08/62 07/15/62
Hartley, William H. died 06/08/63 06/09/63
Hartley, Yacy died 08/19/64 08/24/64
Hartlove, Ann Yougober died 07/29/63 07/30/63
Hartlove, Catherine died 04/15/61 04/17/61
Hartlove, Elizabeth Ann married Sinkskey, John E. 06/04/61 01/03/62
Hartlove, George Wesley died 07/23/61 07/24/61
Hartlove, Laura A. married Downe, William H. 06/25/65 07/01/65
Hartlove, William H. married Ruley, Zenetter 12/15/63 01/28/64
Hartman, Alice died 08/06/63 08/08/63
Hartman, Bernard A. married Markley, Barbara E. 10/11/64 10/29/64
Hartman, Douisa died 04/09/62 04/12/62
Hartman, George F. married Higgins, Ella M. L. 02/04/63 02/11/63
Hartman, George H. married Higdon, Mary A. 02/06/65 02/11/65
Hartman, John C. died 11/10/62 11/12/62
Hartman, John, Jr. died 11/24/64 11/26/64
Hartman, Julia married Ireland, Wilson 11/18/64 11/22/64
Hartman, Rosa died 01/08/62 01/10/62
Hartman, William James died 10/20/64 10/21/64
Hartmeyer, Charles married Young, Caroline E. 06/29/65 07/08/65
Hartner, Henry died 01/26/65 01/28/65
Hartz, Hannah Hogan died 12/27/64 12/28/64
Hartzell, Frances A. married Bolton, John H. (Dr., USA) 12/16/63 12/17/63
Hartzell, George Winfield died 11/18/65 11/20/65
Hartzell, John died 06/21/62 06/25/62
Hartzell, L. L. married Jones, Lizzie 11/23/63 12/23/63
Hartzell, M. I. married Graham, Annie 09/05/61 10/18/61
Hartzell, Mary Alexine married Switzer, William 12/31/61 01/03/62
Harvey, Archibald died 11/13/63 11/14/63
Harvey, Charles A. married Thompson, Mary E. 02/07/61 02/16/61
Harvey, Edward A. married Collins, Caroline V. 04/05/63 04/06/63
Harvey, Ellen Virginia died 01/17/61 01/18/61
Harvey, Eugenia married Mackin, Robert 08/16/64 08/18/64
Harvey, Hattie died 04/01/63 04/04/63
Harvey, Hattie died 04/01/63 04/09/63
Harvey, Hester Ann married Perks, John 02/05/64 03/25/64
Harvey, John E. married Diggs, Annie M. E. 05/19/63 05/22/63
Harvey, Kate died 12/19/65 12/23/65
Harvey, Mary died 06/27/62 06/28/62
Harvey, Mary C. married Mason, Philip H. 10/03/65 10/11/65
Harvey, Mary E. married Buckler, D. Z. 04/28/64 04/29/64
Harvey, Rachel J. died 05/17/65 05/18/65

Harvey, Susan married Raynor, John 01/02/65 01/05/65
Harvey, Thomas J. died 02/17/62 02/18/62
Harwood, Florence married Knight, Charles P. 10/17/65 10/21/65
Harwood, Henry died 03/12/63 03/14/63
Harwood, Louise V. married Dushane, V. 10/10/65 10/14/65
Harwood, Margaret died 03/02/61 03/07/61
Hasford, Sarah (Mrs.) died 09/13/64 09/14/64
Hashagen, John D. married Wilkens, Anna H. 09/12/61 09/14/61
Haskins, Jacob married Henson, Maria 11/01/63 11/03/63
Haslam, Samuel died no date 04/14/62
Haslett, Deborah V. married McNear, Frank B. 12/24/64 01/12/65
Haslett, Robert H. married Hazard, Eliza 05/23/65 05/25/65
Haslett, Thomas died 01/28/61 01/29/61
Haslett, William V. died 02/23/61 02/25/61
Hasleys, Annie Augusta married Bouse, Thomas J. 01/29/65 02/04/65
Haslup, Annie Augusta married Bouse, Thomas J. 01/19/65 02/06/65
Haslup, Esther M. died 08/12/65 08/14/65
Haslup, Henrietta died 05/10/63 05/12/63
Haslup, Henrietta (Mrs.) died 05/10/63 05/11/63
Haslup, John married Warfield, Ellen L. 11/24/63 12/17/63
Haslup, John Q. died 04/11/63 04/13/63
Haslup, Marion J. died 11/25/64 11/28/64
Haslup, Marion J. died 11/25/64 11/29/64
Haslup, Oliver W. died 10/15/61 10/17/61
Haslup, R. Eugenia married Johnson, A. L. 04/23/63 04/25/63
Haslup, Robert W. died 08/31/62 09/01/62
Haslup, Ruth died 09/27/61 09/28/61
Haslup, Susanna married McGee, Robert 02/07/61 02/12/61
Haslup, Walter Montgomery died 03/30/63 03/31/63
Haslup, Willie Rudolph died 09/19/62 09/20/62
Hasson, Elizabeth (Mrs.) died 03/24/63 03/26/63
Hasson, Isabella married Moor, Gustavus 02/28/65 03/03/65
Hasson, John died 12/29/61 12/30/61
Hasson, Theresa died 03/27/61 04/03/61
Hastings, Ernest Mary died 07/31/62 08/08/62
Hastings, F. William Mary died 07/20/63 07/22/63
Hastry, John Thomas died 01/19/64 01/20/64
Haswell, John married Boyd, Catherine (Mrs.) 12/29/64 12/31/64
Haswell, John Henry Clay died 01/16/65 02/02/65
Hatch, Elizabeth C. died 04/14/62 04/16/62
Hatcheson, Martha Ann died 04/14/65 04/15/65
Hatcraft, Elizabeth married King, Mardon 12/22/61 07/10/62
Hatden, Alloysius died 09/07/65 09/23/65
Hatter, Charles William married Porter, A. E. 05/10/64 05/11/64
Hatton, Ann Maria died 07/09/61 07/10/61
Hatton, Annie M. married Vancourt, John W. 01/23/62 02/07/62
Hatton, Caroline Virginia died 10/24/61 10/26/61
Hatton, Catherine E. married Harper, John W. 03/05/61 03/07/61
Hatton, Margaret Ann married Warner, Asa 02/14/61 02/16/61
Hatty, Mary died 05/27/61 05/28/61
Haubard, Annie Mary (Mrs.) died 07/25/63 07/28/63
Haubert, Harman V. died 02/12/63 02/14/63
Haubert, Randolph Harrison died 07/05/63 07/06/63
Hauenner, Nowal Wilson died 04/19/62 04/25/62
Haugh, Rachel (Mrs.) died 02/10/63 02/11/63

Haughrey, Sarah Jane died 04/08/61 04/11/61
Haughton, Henry Osburne married Alricks, Sophia Ridgely 12/21/65 12/23/65
Hauhn, Mary died 08/18/65 08/19/65
Haul, Elizabeth Elennore married Witz, William 10/01/61 10/05/61
Hauper, Mary A. (Mrs.) married Edelman, John F. 09/03/63 09/05/63
Haupt, Edward J. married Howard, Mary H. 08/13/62 08/18/62
Haupt, Ellanore died 05/19/64 05/21/64
Haupt, John C. married Stetyenbach, Louisa P. 02/21/64 02/24/64
Haupt, Lizzie married Button, Emery V. 01/19/64 01/28/64
Haupt, Mabell died 11/12/61 11/14/61
Haupt, Mary E. married Phillips, William H. (USA) 10/14/63 10/16/63
Haupt, Mary Jane married Macauley, Robert Vinton 06/09/63 06/16/63
Haupt, Mary Josephine died 12/31/61 01/02/62
Hauptman, Ann M. (Mrs.) died 04/02/65 04/04/65
Hauptman, Charles A. died 09/18/62 09/15/62
Hauptman, George W. married Brady, Bettie M. 10/13/63 10/15/63
Hauptman, John died 06/05/64 06/06/64
Hauptman, Thomas died 01/10/63 01/12/63
Hauptmann, Garrett married Shafler, Virginia S. 11/24/64 11/26/64
Hauptmann, Josephine died 10/12/62 10/14/62
Haurand, Lizzie married Kesmodel, Martin 12/25/64 12/31/64
Haurand, Louisa (Mrs.) died 01/12/64 01/13/64
Haurand, William died 10/14/64 10/15/64
Hause, James Ida died 11/21/65 11/22/65
Hause, Lafayette V. died 07/08/63 07/29/63
Hause, Lafayette V. died 07/08/63 07/30/63
Hause, Mary Adelle died 11/04/61 11/06/61
Hause, Mary Jane (Mrs.) died 01/14/65 01/16/65
Haussdoerffer, John married Taylor, Lizzie C. 12/01/60 01/28/61
Haussdoerffer, John married Taylor, Lizzie C. 12/01/60 01/29/61
Hauthorn, George died 02/01/63 02/03/63
Havelock, Henry died 03/09/64 03/12/64
Havenner, Elizabeth (Mrs.) died 03/11/65 03/14/65
Havenner, Elizabeth (Mrs.) died 03/11/65 03/15/65
Havercutter, Catharine married Axtell, Edgar (Cpl.) 01/15/62 01/22/62
Havez, Jean Constant married Watts, Alice 10/03/63 10/05/63
Haviland, Anna married Easter, Hamilton 07/23/61 07/26/61
Hawkins, Alexander married Hammond, Louisa 12/11/62 12/13/62
Hawkins, Ann (Mrs.) died 12/19/65 12/21/65
Hawkins, Ann G. died 04/10/61 04/13/61
Hawkins, Catharine married Henry, David 07/11/64 07/12/64
Hawkins, Catherine married Kelley, Barney 02/26/65 03/03/65
Hawkins, Charles married Woodland, Eliza J. 04/28/64 04/30/64
Hawkins, Charles Irvin died 10/19/65 10/20/65
Hawkins, Eliza A. married Wheeler, John 07/03/65 07/06/65
Hawkins, Ellenora married Williams, Joseph L. 07/06/65 07/12/65
Hawkins, Gertrude Virginia married Moore, Thomas 07/21/64 07/26/64
Hawkins, Jane R. died 07/23/65 07/24/65
Hawkins, John W. died 12/06/63 12/10/63
Hawkins, Maria married Butler, James Henry 03/03/61 12/12/61
Hawkins, Martha married Huber, William H. 09/13/63 09/15/63
Hawkins, Martha died 05/01/65 05/04/65
Hawkins, Mary married Walstrom, Charles E. 12/15/62 01/12/63
Hawkins, Mary (Mrs.) died 11/19/64 11/23/64

Hawkins, Mary E. married Edwards, Samuel 12/03/63   12/05/63
Hawkins, Sue died 06/07/64   06/08/64
Hawley, Annie Severn died 04/10/64   04/16/64
Hawley, Eliza Jane (Mrs.) died 05/22/63   05/23/63
Hawley, Herbert died 03/27/64   03/28/64
Hawley, Margaret Ann died 05/11/65   05/16/65
Hawley, R. K. married Knight, Virginia Freeman 04/23/63   04/25/63
Hawthorn, Sallie E. married Kelley, John B. 09/13/65   09/30/65
Hax, Amalia Mary Louise died 08/18/63   08/19/63
Hax, Peter married Gottlieb, Bertha 12/08/61   12/10/61
Hay, Eleanor died 11/18/61   11/19/61
Hay, George Keyser died 07/26/63   07/27/63
Hay, Gwynn died 12/19/65   12/20/65
Hay, Lizzie J. married Mitchell, William (Capt.) 01/15/62   01/18/62
Hay, Lizzie J. married Mitchell, William (Cpt.) 01/15/62   01/20/62
Hay, M. Louisa married Gray, James L. 12/02/62   12/04/62
Haydem, William Graham died 01/08/64   01/11/64
Hayden, Antoinette married Hess, Frank W. (Maj.) 02/13/65   02/15/65
Hayden, Eliza died 07/24/62   07/26/62
Hayden, Elizabeth died 01/15/64   01/18/64
Hayden, John F. (Capt.) died 01/18/64   01/21/64
Hayden, John Frances married Ogle, Victoria 10/10/65   10/14/65
Hayden, Maria J. died 04/22/64   04/23/64
Hayden, Oscar G. married Young, Mary Elizabeth 02/04/65   02/17/65
Haydon, John Henry died 10/13/61   10/14/61
Hayes, Ada H. married Elliott, A. V. (Maj.) 02/23/65   02/28/65
Hayes, Edward married Kone, Mary A. 05/11/65   05/16/65
Hayes, John Thomas died 09/30/62   10/02/62
Hayes, Lottie married Bash, John H. 04/22/62   04/25/62
Hayes, Louisa A. married Cline, George W. 01/30/65   02/02/65
Hayes, Margaret died 03/20/64   03/21/64
Hayes, Mary J. married Robinson, James W. 06/22/65   06/26/65
Hayes, Mary J. married Robinson, James M. 06/22/65   06/27/65
Hayes, William died 01/29/63   01/31/63
Hayes, William died 08/24/65   08/25/65
Hayman, Mary married Shaw, Daniel W. 09/07/62   09/13/62
Hayne, George W. died 01/22/63   01/23/63
Hayne, George W. died 01/22/63   01/24/63
Hayne, John Nelson died 02/05/63   02/06/63
Hayne, Phrona died 01/17/63   01/19/63
Hayne, William died 06/27/64   06/29/64
Hayne, Willie died 01/16/63   01/19/63
Haynes, Emma married Miller, Franklin A. 05/23/65   06/01/65
Haynes, Mary Ann died 03/11/65   03/13/65
Haynie, Winfield William died 11/24/62   11/26/62
Hays, Charles Augustus died 03/20/63   03/21/63
Hays, Emma Arabella died 06/19/61   06/21/61
Hays, John married Bartol, Emma A. 08/09/64   08/19/64
Hays, Kate married Steel, Samuel 05/26/61   06/08/61
Hays, Lawrence died 03/11/63   03/12/63
Hays, Leonard died 04/25/64   05/18/64
Hays, Lewis C. died 07/28/65   08/02/65
Hays, Patrick married Mason, Maria 01/18/63   01/20/63
Hayward, Clementine Elizabeth died 09/21/62   09/22/62
Hayward, Elizabeth E. died 06/26/62   06/28/62

Hayward, Henry died 06/26/63 06/29/63
Hayward, Josephine L. died 06/03/63 06/04/63
Hayward, Matilda married Washington, Felix 01/20/63 01/22/63
Hayward, Sophia married Beckley, John W. 10/10/65 10/17/65
Hayward, Thomas married Williams, Anna 01/28/61 01/30/61
Hazard, Eliza married Haslett, Robert H. 05/23/65 05/25/65
Hazard, Eliza M. married Harrison, Alexander 03/11/64 03/15/64
Hazard, Emma Jane married Davis, George A. 12/21/62 12/23/62
Hazard, George W. (Capt.) died 08/14/62 08/15/62
Hazard, Priscilla died 12/29/61 12/31/61
Hazelhurst, Fannie married Jenkins, Benjamin W. 10/03/65 10/05/65
Hazelton, Mary died 03/14/64 03/15/64
Hazle, Emma Virginia died 10/26/63 10/30/63
Hazle, Richard Edward died 10/26/63 10/30/63
Hazlitt, Amanda died 02/07/64 02/09/64
Hazlitt, James, Jr. died 03/29/61 03/30/61
Head, Mary W. married Smith, Clementus R. 04/04/65 04/11/65
Headington, James V. died 12/14/62 12/15/62
Heafleich, Agnes V. (Mrs.) died 04/16/63 04/18/63
Heaflich, Elizabeth died 05/27/63 05/28/63
Heagerty, (unnamed son) died 01/09/63 01/10/63
Heagy, Annie V. married Spear, P. Forney 10/22/63 10/23/63
Heagy, Ida Maria died 09/06/65 09/07/65
Heagy, Susan H. died 06/13/62 06/24/62
Heagy, Willie died 06/20/64 06/21/64
Heald, Howard Orne died 08/21/64 08/23/64
Heald, Mary Rebecca died 02/01/62 02/03/62
Heald, Samuel W. married Shipley, Julia E. 11/03/62 12/05/62
Healey, John married Donnelly, Eliza J. 10/08/61 10/10/61
Healey, Mary Agness died 08/14/65 08/15/65
Healey, Mathew died 05/24/64 05/25/64
Healy, Bridget died 07/08/61 07/19/61
Healy, John Olive died 06/12/63 06/13/63
Healy, Josephine N. married Welch, John 03/03/64 03/21/64
Healy, Michael died 10/15/65 10/16/65
Heaney, Daniel died 09/20/64 09/21/64
Heany, Francis died 07/06/65 07/08/65
Heany, John died 12/05/65 12/07/65
Heaps, Annie Rebecca married Tuer, Thomas 05/23/65 05/25/65
Heard, Emma Celestia died 08/26/65 08/29/65
Heard, William F. married Murray, Maggie 09/12/65 09/16/65
Heard, Willie Albert died 05/16/62 05/17/62
Hearn, Alfred J. died 08/09/65 09/02/65
Hearn, Samuel C. married Miller, Maria C. 12/13/64 12/16/64
Hearn, Samuel C. married Miller, Ridie 12/13/64 12/15/64
Hearn, Sarah T. married Iglehart, William A. 11/30/65 12/04/65
Hearn, William L. married Ford, Laura 11/21/65 11/24/65
Heath, Charles L. married Duvall, Mary E. 09/08/62 09/29/62
Heath, Francis Henry died 09/23/64 09/27/64
Heath, John died 07/07/61 07/09/61
Heath, Margaret A. (Mrs.) married Yelhall, Irven 09/18/64 09/20/64
Heath, Mary (Mrs.) died 12/27/64 12/28/64
Heath, Mary Louisa married Brownson, E., Jr. 12/06/63 12/08/63
Heath, S. P. (Cpt.) married Smith, Maggie 04/23/63 04/29/63
Heathcote, Mary Elizabeth died 01/07/62 01/08/62

Heaton, William T. died 02/13/62 02/14/62
Heavel, Julia A. married Crawford, Thomas A. 10/23/62 10/25/62
Heavey, P. J. died 10/16/63 10/17/63
Heavy, D. died no date 10/22/64
Hebb, George Thomas died 12/13/64 12/14/64
Hebb, Joseph died 03/26/63 03/28/63
Hebb, Thomas A. died 12/08/61 02/25/62
Hebbern, Elizabeth died 02/11/61 02/12/61
Hebbern, Lydia died 02/11/61 02/13/61
Hebbern, Samuel died 08/20/63 08/21/63
Hebden, Mamie died 09/02/64 09/05/64
Hecht, Isaac married Roswald, Blemma 07/06/62 07/08/62
Heckel, Henry married Kessler, Mary A. 06/22/65 06/24/65
Heckman, John A. died 08/26/65 08/30/65
Heckrotee, William George died 12/10/62 12/11/62
Heckrotte, Margaret Ann died 12/18/62 12/19/62
Heddinger, Stella Muth died 06/03/65 06/05/65
Heddrick, Andrew Jackson died 05/24/64 05/25/64
Hedges, Alice Lightner died 04/04/62 04/05/62
Hedges, Frank Walter died 05/24/64 05/26/64
Hedian, P. J. died 05/14/65 05/16/65
Hedian, Thomas married Myers, Annie Heiniken no date 04/25/62
Hedian, Willie Myers died 03/12/64 03/14/64
Hedier, P. J. died 05/14/65 05/15/65
Hedley, Joseph M. died 03/03/64 03/05/64
Hedley, William F. died 09/12/63 09/14/63
Hedley, William F. married Skillman, Rebecca (Mrs.) 06/11/63 06/13/63
Hedren, Judson died 09/03/65 09/09/65
Hedrick, William died 10/24/65 11/04/65
Hedrick, Elizabeth A. married Cooper, William H. 07/13/65 07/15/65
Heeps, Mary Emma died 04/29/62 05/01/62
Heffernan, Hugh married Fitzgerald, Margaret 01/07/61 01/19/61
Heffner, Edward married Hunter, Ellen 08/03/65 08/07/65
Heffner, John R. married Brown, Ellen D. 07/15/62 07/16/62
Heffner, John T. married Trundle, Mattie J. 04/08/62 04/11/62
Heffner, Rebecca married Frames, Edward J. 03/12/62 03/17/62
Hegan, Mary Ann died 02/09/61 02/11/61
Hegarthy, Mary died 02/08/64 02/09/64
Heiflich, Jacob D. died 05/04/63 05/05/63
Heighe, B. M. died 11/20/61 11/21/61
Heighe, George died 03/11/64 03/14/64
Heighe, William J. died 02/27/65 02/28/65
Heighe, William J. died 02/27/65 03/01/65
Heigle, Anna R. married Scott, George 01/18/63 01/24/63
Heil, Ferdinand Martin died 05/09/64 05/10/64
Heilbrun, Michael died 03/10/61 03/13/61
Heilbrun, Michael died 03/10/61 03/12/61
Heilner, Samuel married Savage, Isabel 07/23/65 08/16/65
Heim, Gesine died 06/20/61 06/21/61
Heimes, Alena died 07/13/65 07/14/65
Heinecker, Charles H. C. died 05/06/64 12/11/65
Heiner, Elias (Rev.) died 10/20/63 10/21/63
Heiner, Elias (Rev.) died 10/20/63 10/22/63
Heinzelman, Henry J. died 07/27/62 07/28/62
Heird, Samuel C. married Meads, Catherine L. 04/20/63 04/23/63

202

Heis, Wilhelmine H. L. married Wittler, Henry F. W. 06/07/63   06/29/63
Helen, Franklin married Bryant, Mary Elizabeth 05/04/62   05/31/62
Helfrich, Mary T. married Smuck, J. Summerfield 11/09/65   11/11/65
Helfrich, Samuel D. married Goll, Kate 02/09/65   02/18/65
Hellen, B. Johnson (Dr.) died 07/02/64   07/04/64
Hellen, Thomas W. died 11/07/61   11/09/61
Helm, Annie M. married Granniss, John R. 05/11/64   05/13/64
Helm, Charlotte M. married Ketchum, Frederick M. 05/29/64   06/06/64
Helm, Isabella died 07/19/64   07/20/64
Helm, Isabella died 07/19/64   07/21/64
Helmes, Jeanie married Beckley, Robert T. 05/25/65   06/01/65
Helmlin, Emma married Mowell, Joseph 08/21/62   12/08/62
Helmling, Annie R. (Mrs.) died 12/03/63   12/11/63
Helmling, Charlie J. died 12/05/64   12/08/64
Helmling, Jacob died 08/19/61   09/02/61
Helmling, John died 07/21/65   07/24/65
Helmling, John died 12/04/65   12/09/65
Helmling, Marian Virginia married Laynor, George 02/08/63   03/10/63
Helmling, Sophy V. N. died 07/17/61   07/25/61
Helmling, W. Harry married Maffitt, Annie R. 01/01/62   01/04/62
Hemlick, Jacob married Scott, Susan 02/05/64   09/19/64
Hemling, Joseph D. died 08/23/65   08/24/65
Hemmick, Annie A. married Boyle, Francis A. 10/19/65   10/31/65
Hemmick, S. E. W. (Mrs.) died 02/25/63   02/27/63
Hempstone, Fannie married Johnson, E. M. (Dr.) 01/12/65   01/18/65
Hemsley, William died 04/13/62   04/21/62
Hen, William died 09/18/62   09/15/62
Henaman, Hannah married Buxensten, Otto 02/19/63   03/16/63
Henchy, George died 02/01/63   02/02/63
Henck, Louisa R. died 03/02/61   03/05/61
Henck, Sallie V. married Meakin, Joshua W. 03/17/63   03/24/63
Henderson,   Benetta Frank died 06/29/61   07/01/61
Henderson, Agnes Ophelia married Dougherty, William 02/07/64   02/11/64
Henderson, Amelia (Mrs.) died 04/23/63   04/25/63
Henderson, Arthur B. married Eastwood, Anna 12/06/62   12/11/62
Henderson, Benjamin F. died 02/18/61   02/20/61
Henderson, Benjamin F. (Capt.) died 02/18/61   02/19/61
Henderson, Catharine died 05/25/62   05/30/62
Henderson, Catherine A. married Pardoe, Robert A. 03/21/65   03/28/65
Henderson, Elizabeth Eugenia died 03/08/62   03/10/62
Henderson, Ellen married Whitridge, John A. 01/06/63   01/08/63
Henderson, Emma died 10/04/65   10/05/65
Henderson, Emma died 10/04/65   10/06/65
Henderson, Emma G. married Myers, Andrew C. 08/08/65   08/21/65
Henderson, George A. married Lewis, Annie R. 11/19/65   11/21/65
Henderson, Gerard died 07/29/65   08/02/65
Henderson, Gerard Irvine died 08/14/62   08/16/62
Henderson, James T. died 02/13/63   02/18/63
Henderson, John married Mason, Emeline J. 06/10/62   06/11/62
Henderson, John married Spencer, Maria Victoria 06/16/63   06/18/63
Henderson, John M. married Robinson, Hannah 04/06/65   04/08/65
Henderson, Jove died 12/12/63   06/25/64
Henderson, Marie M. married Carnes, Andrew J. 07/07/64   07/11/64
Henderson, Mary E. married Schock, Wilton G. 09/24/64   09/27/64
Henderson, Samuel A. married Reese, E. E. 06/01/63   06/03/63

Henderson, Samuel S. married Stoops, Josephine 02/01/64 02/06/64
Henderson, Sarah died 05/25/62 05/30/62
Henderson, Virginia died 08/04/64 08/06/64
Henderson, William died 07/22/63 08/11/63
Henderson, William Ward married Hollingsworth, Flora 12/10/63 12/16/63
Hendley, James D. married Earlougher, Josephine 12/12/63 12/24/63
Hendren, John died 08/07/61 08/08/61
Henebury, Roseana died 08/05/62 08/06/62
Henigan, Ann Conley (Mrs.) died 01/22/64 01/23/64
Henkel, Ferdinand died 01/01/65 01/02/65
Henkel, William died 04/22/64 04/25/64
Henkle, Georgeiana married Markland, James H. 01/15/63 01/24/63
Henley, Mary died 02/01/65 02/04/65
Henley, Mary died 02/01/65 02/10/65
Hennaman, Herman married Gibson, Isabella R. 10/27/62 11/04/62
Hennery, Bridget married Hare, Patrick O. 01/24/64 01/25/64
Henney, Daniel H. married Adams, Annie K. 03/07/65 03/13/65
Hennick, Francis Marion married Neuberth, Mary C. 04/21/63 04/23/63
Hennick, Josephine married Boldin, Samuel R. 11/22/64 12/05/64
Hennick, Josias G. married Hodge, Mollie J. 09/09/61 09/12/61
Hennick, William George died 03/25/65 03/27/65
Hennicks, Amanda J. married Squires, John H. 09/26/64 09/28/64
Hennicks, George C. died 03/07/64 03/08/64
Hennicks, Zachary Taylor died 01/05/64 01/07/64
Henning, Margaret died 02/07/65 02/09/65
Henning, Virginia A. married Jones, James H. 02/26/63 02/28/63
Henninghausen, Louis married Lange, Louise 09/17/63 09/18/63
Hennixman, George died 04/24/65 04/26/65
Henrich, Patrick died 02/10/65 02/11/65
Henrick, Mary died 09/30/62 10/01/62
Henrix, Edward married Grosscup, Annie 10/29/63 11/13/63
Henrix, Ridie H. married Sangston, B. Whitely 07/08/63 07/10/63
Henry, Alexander died 03/05/64 03/07/64
Henry, Alfred died 06/08/62 06/09/62
Henry, Catherine died 05/25/65 05/26/65
Henry, Daniel died 10/25/62 11/01/62
Henry, Daniel married Logan, Sarah 01/26/62 01/30/62
Henry, David died 11/17/61 12/02/61
Henry, David died 06/21/65 07/03/65
Henry, David married Hawkins, Catharine 07/11/64 07/12/64
Henry, Emma C. (Mrs.) married Forrest, J. L. 01/26/65 01/28/65
Henry, Florence Eugenie died 08/14/63 08/15/63
Henry, James married Ellen, Mary 08/27/61 08/28/61
Henry, James died 12/30/62 01/01/63
Henry, Jane died 02/19/61 02/21/61
Henry, Jane died 02/19/61 02/22/61
Henry, John J. married Harkness, Sarah J. 11/12/61 11/15/61
Henry, John J. died 11/06/64 11/08/64
Henry, Joseph M. married Phester, Kate 11/15/65 11/17/65
Henry, Margaret married McGinn, John 07/24/63 08/11/63
Henry, Mary D. (Mrs.) died 12/18/65 12/19/65
Henry, Mary E. (Mrs.) died 06/11/65 06/13/65
Henry, Mary Elizabeth died 01/21/65 01/25/65
Henry, Mary H. (Mrs.) died 08/15/63 08/20/63
Henry, Mary Jane married Brooks, Edward Joseph 09/15/65 09/18/65

```
Henry, Morton P. married McKee, Annie 12/14/65  12/16/65
Henry, Phebe died 11/21/63  12/05/63
Henry, Sarah Elizabeth died 08/02/64  08/08/64
Henry, Susannah (Mrs.) died 06/24/63  06/25/63
Henry, Susannah (Mrs.) died 06/24/63  06/26/63
Henry, Susie married Zeigler, George W. 10/11/64  10/15/64
Henry, Theodore A. V. married Woolford, Eliza Ann 04/17/64  04/14/64
Henry, William died 01/31/64  02/01/64
Henry, Willie James died 08/06/61  08/13/61
Henschell, Louise (Mrs.) married Cottrell, J. (Cpt.) 12/08/63  12/11/63
Hensel, William Henry died 07/17/62  07/19/62
Henshaw, Carrie died 04/29/62  05/03/62
Henshaw, Charles died 02/07/61  02/25/61
Hensler, Charles A. died 11/21/65  12/05/65
Henson, Clara married Ward, Perry 10/07/62  10/11/62
Henson, Eliza married Stanly, Moses 05/18/65  05/20/65
Henson, Eliza Ann married Hicks, Charles 12/15/63  12/19/63
Henson, Maria married Haskins, Jacob 11/01/63  11/03/63
Henson, Mary married Russell, John 12/01/63  12/02/63
Henson, Nathaniel died 12/14/65  12/21/65
Henson, Robert married Welch, Elizabeth 05/22/62  05/24/62
Henson, Augustus died 06/02/63  06/03/63
Henthorn, John died 04/07/65  04/08/65
Henthorn, John Thomas died 01/09/62  01/10/62
Hepburn, Eliza Stith (Mrs.) died 11/01/64  11/08/64
Hepburn, Eliza Stith (Mrs.) died 11/01/64  11/09/64
Hepburn, Janette S. married Small, Edward C. 05/03/64  05/09/64
Hepburn, William H. married Barry, Nancy E. 02/06/62  02/07/62
Hepburn, William Henry died 09/07/62  09/09/62
Hera, Fanny French died 02/27/63  03/02/63
Herbert, James N. married Gilmour, Racher 06/01/65  06/07/65
Herbert, John Decalb died 02/28/61  03/01/61
Herbert, Martha A. married Kelly, John 02/02/65  02/03/65
Herbert, Mary Ann (Mrs.) died 10/09/63  01/26/64
Herbert, Mary E. died 01/26/62  01/28/62
Herbert, Samuel married Hall, Mary E. 04/14/61  04/16/61
Herbert, Sarah (Mrs.) died 12/25/65  12/27/65
Herbes, Henry married Franz, Mary 05/30/65  06/06/65
Herbstritt, Josephine married Eschbach, Francis F. 10/16/63  10/27/63
Hergesheimer, Christopher died 03/21/62  03/22/62
Hergesheimer, E. Eugenia married James, Morgan 02/24/63  03/02/63
Heritage, Willie B. died 12/28/63  12/30/63
Herkles, Lloyd married Cole, Julia 12/22/64  12/24/64
Herlod, A. G. died 10/06/64  10/08/64
Herman, Catherine (Mrs.) died 01/12/65  01/14/65
Hermann, Amos T. married Coleman, Nancy M. 01/12/63  01/20/63
Hermann, Jacob died 02/05/61  02/06/61
Hermann, John died 11/12/63  11/13/63
Hermes, Henry married Franz, Mary 05/30/65  06/05/65
Heron, Mary D. married Bradey, Joseph A. (Rev.) 12/28/64  12/31/64
Herpel, Anna Catherine (Mrs.) died 03/07/63  03/09/63
Herpel, John H. married Young, Mary Francis 07/16/63  07/18/63
Herr, Narcissa (Mrs.) died 02/20/65  02/21/65
Herring, Anna Day died 03/22/63  03/25/63
Herring, Emogine E. married Mask, John Q. A. 11/14/64  11/15/64
```

Herring, Lizzie Sylvester died 08/07/61   08/15/61
Herring, Malcolm L. married Magee, Josephine R. 04/30/63   05/04/63
Herring, William Bartlett died 07/05/65   07/12/65
Herring, William E. married Favier, Mary J. no date   12/29/65
Herring, Wilton S. married Chalk, Lizzie A. 03/03/64   03/21/64
Herrisse, Valeria married Beil, N. Van 06/05/65   06/06/65
Hersey, John (Rev.) died 11/17/62   11/25/62
Hersh, Alexander O. married Lawder, Emma V. 03/09/65   03/15/65
Hershey, B. J. (Dr.) married Farquhar, Mary E. 02/19/61   02/20/61
Hershner, Amanda married Anderson, William G. 10/22/63   11/20/63
Herzog, Conrad died 06/05/64   06/06/64
Heslen, Sallie died 04/23/63   04/30/63
Hess, Charles married Jacob, Magdalena 10/08/63   10/17/63
Hess, Delia Estelle married Duval, Peter 06/05/61   06/06/61
Hess, Frank W. (Maj.) married Hayden, Antoinette 02/13/65   02/15/65
Hess, George H. married Sims, Agnes C. 07/24/62   07/26/62
Hess, J., Jr. married Miller, M. A. 10/23/65   10/25/65
Hess, Joseph died 08/04/61   08/05/61
Hess, Joseph married Hill, Belinda 12/17/63   12/19/63
Hess, Joseph married Earns, Mary Ann 09/28/65   09/29/65
Hesse, William F. married Byerly, Mary Ann 03/10/63   03/12/63
Hessler, Michael married Kerchner, Ann Caroline 07/04/65   07/10/65
Hetzler, Julia Ann died 02/03/64   02/05/64
Heubeck, George E. died 03/22/63   03/31/63
Heubeck, John H. died 03/22/63   03/31/63
Heuisler, Joseph Anthony died 02/24/62   02/26/62
Heuisler, Joseph G. married Borgono, Manuella no date   03/18/65
Heulse, Oscar Barton died 06/07/63   06/08/63
Heursch, Emma V. married Storrey, William J. 08/21/65   08/23/65
Heuser, Alice Augusta died 06/22/63   06/24/63
Heuser, Alice Augusta died 06/22/63   06/25/63
Heut, Augustin, Jr. married Bourguet, Marie A. 04/09/61   05/10/61
Hevener, Susan married Lantz, Samuel 11/27/65   12/04/65
Heveren, Stephen Asbury died 08/31/62   09/08/62
Hevern, Bernard Lidiard died 12/23/64   12/28/64
Hevern, Harriet married Jones, William 12/31/61   01/02/62
Hevern, John married Lidard, Susie 05/19/63   05/22/63
Heveron, Edmond A. died 02/09/65   02/11/65
Hewett, Florence married Hildreth, George H. 01/06/63   01/10/63
Hewett, Horatio Harrison died 09/17/63   09/19/63
Hewett, Maggie Eudora died 07/22/62   07/23/62
Hewett, Virginia married Eberhart, Charles W. 02/10/61   02/13/61
Hewitt, A. Stephen Douglas died 09/16/65   09/19/65
Hewitt, Alexander C. married Webb, Carrie 03/04/61   03/07/61
Hewitt, Elizzie married Rogers, R. J. 08/27/63   08/31/63
Hewitt, Frances F. married Stites, James 11/01/64   11/04/64
Hewitt, Mary (Mrs.) died 07/26/64   07/27/64
Hewitt, Mary A. (Mrs.) died 06/22/64   06/29/64
Hewitt, Mary R. married Lane, William 02/18/63   03/16/63
Hewlett, John Q. died 11/05/64   11/07/64
Hewlett, Samuel Kempton died 07/11/65   07/15/65
Hewsling, Alexandrine married Lambert, George W. 11/01/61   01/14/62
Hibbitts, John J. died 01/19/62   01/20/62
Hibner, Jane Matilda died 02/17/61   02/18/61
Hibner, William Frederick married Whittle, Caroline M. 12/25/62

                10/22/63
Hickey, James died 11/02/63   11/03/63
Hickey, Martin died 10/05/64   10/06/64
Hickey, Michael J. died 12/19/61   12/20/61
Hickey, Rose Alphonso married Block, Finley 06/29/64   07/15/64
Hickey, William died 08/08/62   08/09/62
Hickman, Catherine married Brooks, George B. 02/21/65   04/03/65
Hickman, George W. married Morgan, Sarah E. 08/03/65   08/05/65
Hickman, W. H. married Brian, Jennie E. 12/01/64   12/03/64
Hickox, Samuel B. died 08/09/63   08/15/63
Hicks, Charles married Henson, Eliza Ann 12/15/63   12/19/63
Hicks, Elizabeth died 07/29/62   07/31/62
Hicks, Richard C. died 12/18/64   12/20/64
Hicks, Samuel married Turner, Anna M. 10/20/64   10/21/64
Hicks, Sarah married Duttan, Charles 04/20/65   04/22/65
Hicks, William H. married Coale, Mary Elizabeth 07/23/62   07/25/62
Hieatzman, Maud Alice died 10/13/65   10/14/65
Hieller, Columbus Conrad died 03/05/65   03/06/65
Hiestand, Sarah M. married Rafferty, Hugh 11/14/65   11/28/65
Higdan, Robert married Reesides, Annie 02/28/65   03/11/65
Higdon, Mary A. married Hartman, George H. 02/06/65   02/11/65
Higdon, Mary Jane (Mrs.) died 04/10/63   04/11/63
Higgins, Ann Eliza died 07/21/62   08/06/62
Higgins, Bertha died 05/12/63   05/18/63
Higgins, Catherine D. married Lenney, Daniel 08/30/63   10/03/63
Higgins, Edward died 10/30/64   10/31/64
Higgins, Eliza (Mrs.) died 03/20/65   03/24/65
Higgins, Ella M. L. married Hartman, George F. 02/04/63   02/11/63
Higgins, Emily T. married Williams, George F. 12/03/64   12/05/64
Higgins, Henrietta married Calk, John H. 03/21/61   03/23/61
Higgins, James died 01/08/63   01/09/63
Higgins, John died 09/23/65   09/27/65
Higgins, Maria E. married Bryan, Thomas A. 04/22/61   04/24/61
Higgins, Mary Mortimer died 10/15/61   11/04/61
Higgins, Ranson died 11/06/65   11/14/65
Higgins, Richard Francis died 10/18/61   11/04/61
Higgins, Richard W. died 04/26/63   04/28/63
Higgins, Rozelma died 10/15/61   11/04/61
Higgins, Rufus M. died 01/09/61   02/05/61
Higgins, Susan A. died 04/14/61   04/15/61
Higgins, Thomas Theodore died 01/20/64   01/23/64
Higgins, W. D. married Gaither, Rea Y. 05/18/65   08/12/65
Higgins, Walter died 09/19/65   09/22/65
Higgins, William Erasmus died 12/30/62   01/02/63
High, Alfred married Huggins, Mary A. 11/24/62   12/25/62
High, Anne M. married Stevenson, William W. 01/14/63   01/29/63
High, Charlie L. died 03/11/62   03/12/62
High, Cora Martin died 08/16/62   08/18/62
High, Edgar Martin died 04/10/65   04/11/65
High, Edward Lewis died 01/26/61   01/29/61
High, Ellenora died 06/02/62   06/03/62
High, Emory married Banks, Margaret 05/09/65   05/15/65
High, George Daniel Reese died 12/29/62   12/31/62
High, George R. married Jenkins, Sarah Gertrude 12/15/64   12/17/64
High, George W. married Cook, Harriet R. 11/13/65   11/16/65

High, James died 08/27/63   08/29/63
High, James H. died 03/20/65   03/23/65
High, Jane (Mrs.) died 05/23/64   06/01/64
High, Joseph died 01/22/65   01/24/65
High, Josephine married Haney, James K. P. 08/31/65   09/05/65
High, Mary Ann (Mrs.) died 03/30/64   03/31/64
High, Mary Louisa died 10/07/62   10/13/62
High, Sarah died 08/07/61   08/08/61
High, Sophia died 12/08/63   12/10/63
High, Sophia E. married Brummel, Joseph (Q.M.C.) 12/24/61   01/10/62
High, William H. died 06/05/64   06/06/64
High, William T. married Wherrett, Henrietta V. 06/17/62   07/08/62
Hight, William married Johnson, Louisa (Mrs.) 10/08/65   10/10/65
Higins, Mary Ann (Mrs.) died 06/27/64   06/28/64
Hilberg, Frederick died 02/14/65   02/16/65
Hilberg, John A. married Constable, Nellie 01/17/65   01/18/65
Hilbert, Henry, Jr. died 10/09/63   10/10/63
Hilbert, Henry, Sr. died 09/17/64   09/19/64
Hilbert, James A. died 09/09/63   09/10/63
Hilbert, John H. married Howard, Sophia 07/11/64   07/16/64
Hilbert, Stella died 08/20/63   08/21/63
Hilberts, Charles A. married Clough, Elizabeth 03/17/61   03/19/61
Hildebrand, S. W. died 02/13/63   02/14/63
Hildebrandt, Margaret E. died 08/16/61   08/20/61
Hildreth, George H. married Hewett, Florence 01/06/63   01/10/63
Hildt, George J. married Kreis, Mary 05/23/65   05/24/65
Hildt, John died 04/04/62   04/30/62
Hildt, Mary died 08/26/62   09/16/62
Hill, Alexander died 04/20/63   04/21/63
Hill, Belinda married Hess, Joseph 12/17/63   12/19/63
Hill, C. H. married Aukwood, Emily A. 06/02/64   06/04/64
Hill, Catharine died 06/16/61   06/18/61
Hill, Edward Snowden died 07/09/65   07/15/65
Hill, Eleanor died 03/15/64   03/16/64
Hill, Franklin Amasa died 06/08/63   06/10/63
Hill, Generva Slack died 06/20/65   06/27/65
Hill, George B. Westcott died 02/21/65   02/22/65
Hill, George C. married Stevens, Helen M. 10/15/63   10/16/63
Hill, Henry married Smuthers, Anna 10/30/64   11/01/64
Hill, Jessie married Watson, Martha A. (Mrs.) 11/13/61   11/15/61
Hill, Joann died 09/02/61   09/04/61
Hill, John married Stewart, Maggie M. 11/07/65   11/09/65
Hill, John E. married Carter, Eliza 12/22/63   01/12/64
Hill, John Thomas married Victoria, Catherine 04/05/64   04/14/64
Hill, Julian married Smith, James 03/19/63   03/20/63
Hill, Mary R. married Bolin, Joseph C. 07/24/64   07/30/64
Hill, Minty Jane married Isaacs, Tobious 06/15/65   06/17/65
Hill, Susan died 01/25/62   01/27/62
Hill, William married Thomas, Mary Jane 05/03/64   05/05/64
Hill, William A. married Brown, Annetha 01/02/61   01/07/61
Hill, William B. married Burch, Eveline 08/01/61   02/12/62
Hill, William B. married Crock, C. Louise 10/20/64   10/24/64
Hill, William Henry married Brian, Hannah 10/25/64   10/27/64
Hillan, Daniel died 07/20/62   07/21/62
Hilleary, Clement Truman died 02/12/61   02/14/61

Hilleary, John Alexander married Gessford, Susannah 10/21/62   10/23/62
Hilleary, Margaret A. (Mrs.) died 01/24/63   01/26/63
Hilleary, Tilghman died 04/07/63   05/05/63
Hilleary, William T. married Jackson, Mary E. 10/02/64   10/25/64
Hilliard, Jeremiah died 10/15/61   10/16/61
Hilliard, Robert married Sampson, Julia 12/16/62   01/06/63
Hillman, Eliza Jane died 06/29/63   07/11/63
Hillman, Esther (Mrs.) died 05/24/64   05/28/64
Hillman, Mary Ann married Rouse, William 11/24/64   11/28/64
Hills, Luther married Arthur, Mary J. 09/06/64   09/24/64
Hillyard, Mary Killan died 08/17/62   08/20/62
Hilstorf, Henry C. died 03/04/64   03/07/64
Hilton, Edward married White, Johanna M. 03/17/63   04/04/63
Hilton, Priscilla (Mrs.) died 04/01/63   04/07/63
Hilton, William W. died 02/03/61   02/05/61
Hincher, Sarah Jane died 12/24/64   12/28/64
Hinder, Jane (Mrs.) died 05/17/64   05/19/64
Hinder, R. A. (Mrs.) died 06/10/64   06/11/64
Hinder, Sarah married Ray, William 05/22/62   05/24/62
Hindes, Daniel B. married Wright, Harriet E. 09/11/64   09/13/64
Hindes, Hughy married Butler, Eliza 07/10/65   07/12/65
Hindes, Mamie Julia died 12/16/65   12/18/65
Hindes, Rosella died 01/22/64   01/25/64
Hindle, John married Kilpaugh, Jane (Mrs.) 10/06/64   11/05/64
Hindman, Annie S. died 10/03/63   10/05/63
Hindman, Oliver J. died 10/13/63   10/15/63
Hinds, Margaret (Mrs.) married Chance, Marinas 11/07/64   11/26/64
Hineker, David Lee died 07/11/64   07/14/64
Hiner, Emily married Harden, James D. 02/12/61   02/14/61
Hiner, Harriet F. died 09/05/63   09/07/63
Hiner, Harriet F. died 09/05/63   09/08/63
Hiner, Sarah J. died 09/01/65   09/02/65
Hines, Emma Lou died 11/15/63   11/17/63
Hines, John C. died 07/20/65   07/22/65
Hines, Julius married Weglein, Ricka 12/30/63   12/31/63
Hines, Kezia (Mrs.) died 07/22/64   07/23/64
Hines, Susie J. married Traband, George W. 05/04/65   05/06/65
Hines, V. Burgess married Burgess, Henrietta R. 03/02/64   03/19/64
Hingerty, Elizabeth died 01/07/61   01/08/61
Hings, Maria married Johnson, Benjamin 10/06/63   12/12/63
Hinkle, Charles married Biddison, Susanna 01/01/61   01/09/61
Hinkley, Edward Otis married Keemple, Anne Maria 06/11/61   06/14/61
Hinks, Albert Dunning died 07/18/62   07/21/62
Hinks, Annie died 09/08/61   09/10/61
Hinks, Charles D. died 12/11/63   12/12/63
Hinks, Charles M. died 11/05/62   11/06/62
Hinks, Charles M. died 11/05/62   11/07/62
Hinks, Hollingsworth died 12/06/63   12/07/63
Hinks, Hollinsworth died 12/06/63   12/08/63
Hinkson, F. married Hanson, M. A. 01/10/61   01/24/61
Hinman, Luther died 02/08/65   02/09/65
Hinman, Mary died 07/08/65   07/21/65
Hinmas, Mary died 07/08/65   07/10/65
Hinrichs, Christopher J. married Bruehl, Ellen M. 03/05/63   03/09/63
Hinton, Ann E. married Trim, W. C. 07/27/65   08/08/65

Hinton, Mary Washington died 12/05/64 12/16/64
Hinton, Matilda (Mrs.) died 09/03/63 09/05/63
Hinton, Theodore married Reynolds, Sallie 02/09/64 02/19/64
Hinton, William F. died 05/05/62 05/06/62
Hintze, F. E. B. (Dr.) died 10/12/65 10/14/65
Hinuff, Jacob Brown married Fitzpatrick, Mary 02/01/63 06/16/63
Hipsley, Sallie E. married Rennie, David P. 10/18/65 10/26/65
Hiring, Christopher J. married Flemming, Margaret 05/26/65 05/27/65
Hirsch, John married Abrams, Desdamona 11/12/63 11/19/63
Hirsch, William died 09/23/65 09/25/65
Hirst, William (Rev.) died 08/10/62 08/11/62
Hiser, Frances Theresa died 09/05/62 09/06/62
Hiser, Nicholas married Brierly, Elizabeth 08/31/65 09/05/65
Hisey, John A. married Shipley, Caroline 01/10/65 01/12/65
Hislop, Elizabeth (Mrs.) died 09/23/63 09/25/63
Hiss, Charles D. died 04/16/63 04/21/63
Hiss, Ellen G. married Coleman, W. W. 05/25/64 05/26/64
Hiss, Ida Bell died 12/11/61 12/12/61
Hiss, Janie C. died 07/05/64 07/06/64
Hiss, Sallie A. married Soper, Samuel J. 10/16/61 10/17/61
Hiss, Stevenson died 07/12/65 07/13/65
Hiss, William George died 01/30/61 02/01/61
Hissey, Eliza J. married Berry, B. D. 01/01/61 01/04/61
Hissey, Elizabeth (Mrs.) died 03/09/64 03/12/64
Hissey, George Whitridge died 07/12/65 07/14/65
Hissey, Oliver M. died 05/04/63 05/06/63
Hissey, William died 07/25/65 07/27/65
Hissey, William Henry died 07/22/65 07/25/65
Hitchcock, Ann Rosella died 11/25/63 11/26/63
Hitchcock, James B. died 04/03/63 04/04/63
Hitchcock, Jessie A. married Anderson, Sarah L. 02/19/61 02/23/61
Hitchcock, Levi married Chambers, Christiana E. 12/19/65 12/27/65
Hitchcock, Martha A. married Landerman, William H. 02/02/65 02/04/65
Hitchcock, Mary Ann died 12/14/62 12/20/62
Hitchens, Mary Eliza married Thompson, Henry 04/20/65 04/22/65
Hitchins, August married Oliver, Sarah Elizabeth 02/07/61 02/09/61
Hiteshew, William Franklin died 03/05/63 03/19/63
Hitselberger, John died 04/05/65 04/06/65
Hitselberger, John died 04/05/65 04/07/65
Hitzel, Ellen J. (Mrs.) died 11/06/65 11/11/65
Hitzelberger, Alice Lentz died 12/05/61 12/07/61
Hitzelberger, Joseph K. died 03/22/65 03/28/65
Hitzelberger, Joseph K. married Kepler, Mary Eliza 04/04/64 04/11/64
Hitzelberger, Mary Elizabeth died 11/06/63 11/07/63
Hitzelberger, Peter married Cole, Eliza Jane (Mrs.) 10/26/63 10/29/63
Hitzelberger, William E. died 07/31/64 08/01/64
Hitzelberger, William J. died 09/09/62 09/23/62
Hoar, Patrick died 04/11/64 04/12/64
Hoar, Patrick died 04/11/64 04/13/64
Hoban, Frederick H. married Denny, Etta 06/14/65 06/17/65
Hobarth, John F. died 06/13/65 06/14/65
Hobbbs, Catherine died 03/13/61 03/15/61
Hobbes, Mary Lizzie died 02/08/62 02/13/62
Hobbs, Ann Lavenia (Mrs.) died 10/11/65 10/16/65
Hobbs, Ann Rebecca died 10/25/63 10/27/63

Hobbs, Columbia E. married Pole, Charles H. 10/11/63 10/16/63
Hobbs, Eleanor Louisa (Mrs.) died 02/18/64 02/23/64
Hobbs, George W., Jr. died 07/29/61 07/31/61
Hobbs, John died 08/28/63 02/23/64
Hobbs, John A. married Fillinger, Frances E. 04/17/65 05/13/65
Hobbs, John D. died 09/17/65 09/18/65
Hobbs, Josephine (Mrs.) died 05/28/64 05/31/64
Hobbs, Laura A. married Seymour, William S. 10/26/64 10/27/64
Hobbs, Laura Jane died 10/28/64 10/29/64
Hobbs, Martha married Hartley, Thomas H. 07/08/62 07/15/62
Hobbs, Mary Celenia died 03/08/65 03/09/65
Hobbs, Mary E. married Beck, John 06/09/61 06/14/61
Hobbs, Nannie married Goodwin, John E. 11/15/64 11/18/64
Hobbs, Olympia (Mrs.) died 01/28/64 02/01/64
Hobbs, Valary V. married White, Cyrus B. 10/28/65 10/31/65
Hobbs, William H. H. married Owen, Laura A. 12/18/62 12/24/62
Hobbs, William P. T. died 12/28/64 12/22/64
Hobbs, Willie Howard died 05/26/62 05/27/62
Hobby, Mary (Mrs.) died 02/25/65 03/07/65
Hobby, Ruth Ella died 07/28/64 07/29/64
Hobday, Edward married Brooks, Lizzie J. 08/14/64 08/16/64
Hoblitzell, Oliver married Woodside, Eliza J. 05/09/61 05/16/61
Hoblitzwell, William Woodside died 12/13/64 12/14/64
Hobs, Mary Catherine married Hacket, Robert Clinton 06/04/65 06/22/65
Hobson, Elizabeth married Anderson, Richard no date 05/06/63
Hobson, George Withington married Schroeder, Henrietta M. 04/03/61
    04/08/61
Hochadel, Adeline married Bishop, George C. 09/03/63 09/09/63
Hockrite, Mary (Mrs.) died 12/11/64 12/12/64
Hoddinott, Charles married Hooper, Mary S. (Mrs.) 01/19/65 02/14/65
Hoddinott, Henrietta C. (Mrs.) died 01/01/64 01/04/64
Hoddinott, Mary A. married Merritt, John G. 03/14/63 03/14/63
Hodge, Annie E. married Robb, Leander A. 09/08/64 09/20/64
Hodge, Mollie J. married Hennick, Josias G. 09/09/61 09/12/61
Hodges, Anna S. married Knapp, Samuel C. 11/30/62 12/02/62
Hodges, Annie R. married Price, Alfred Lee 11/25/64 12/05/64
Hodges, Ellen Stewart died 02/24/64 02/26/64
Hodges, George Jones died 09/18/64 09/19/64
Hodges, J. Chapman (Cpt.) married Webster, Sophie 11/24/63 11/28/63
Hodges, J. Wilson married Stayman, Ada 10/12/65 10/14/65
Hodges, James Evan died 10/31/62 11/04/62
Hodges, John died 01/25/64 02/09/64
Hodges, John Fresbey married Wilson, Harriet 11/23/65 11/25/65
Hodges, Joseph Henry died 09/22/64 09/23/64
Hodges, Leonard Sellman died 01/20/63 01/24/63
Hodges, Robert Emory died 12/09/64 12/10/64
Hodges, Robert R., Jr. died 10/28/64 10/31/64
Hodges, Thomas E. married Lock, Mary E. 09/12/65 09/15/65
Hodgkin, Ada married Good, Thomas G. 01/10/65 01/11/65
Hodgkinson, Sarah Ann died 03/13/63 03/14/63
Hodgman, William married Thompson, Elizabeth 11/28/64 01/02/65
Hodgson, Joseph married Soffell, Martha M. 06/19/64 06/24/64
Hodson, Lizzie H. married Stanton, D. L. (Lt. Col.) 02/09/65 02/24/65
Hoenes, Albert Frederick married Schrivner, Margaret 01/08/61 02/09/61
Hoenes, Albert Frederick died 08/08/65 08/09/65

Hoes, Grunderson died 08/16/63   08/19/63
Hofer, Charles married Hook, Adeline 04/06/64   04/07/64
Hoff, Joseph Perkins died 03/24/61   03/26/61
Hoff, Julia B. married Child, William W. 05/09/64   05/12/64
Hoff, Maggie E. married Carmichael, William 11/02/65   11/04/65
Hoff, Mary E. married Pancoast, N. F. 02/21/61   02/25/61
Hoff, S. Emma married Snowden, Samuel 05/14/63   05/18/63
Hoffer, Charles married Hook, Adeline 04/06/64   04/07/64
Hofferth, Frederick died 06/10/62   06/12/62
Hoffman, Alfred (Maj., CSA) died 08/09/63   08/31/63
Hoffman, Ann (Mrs.) died 07/17/65   07/17/65
Hoffman, Bessie Fuller died 07/07/64   07/08/64
Hoffman, Charles H. married Daugherty, Margaret 12/07/64   12/10/64
Hoffman, Charles McLelan died 04/17/65   04/26/65
Hoffman, Daniel died no date   11/28/63
Hoffman, Edith May died 09/03/62   09/04/62
Hoffman, Eliza Ann married Cook, Martin 05/07/61   05/16/61
Hoffman, Elizabeth died 05/26/64   11/22/64
Hoffman, Elizabeth (Mrs.) died no date   10/14/63
Hoffman, Eurith Sophia married Allen, L. S. (Dr.) 01/10/61   01/31/61
Hoffman, Frederick died 11/10/63   11/11/63
Hoffman, Frederick died 11/10/63   11/12/63
Hoffman, George L. died 01/31/65   02/01/65
Hoffman, H. F. (Capt.) died 06/17/61   06/18/61
Hoffman, Harry May died 10/02/62   10/03/62
Hoffman, Jacob married Dunkle, Mary 06/07/65   06/09/65
Hoffman, Lewis died 09/11/62   09/12/62
Hoffman, Maranda A. married Poisal, Francis A. (Lt.) 10/01/63   10/05/6.
Hoffman, Margaret E. married Baker, Charles H. 09/08/64   10/12/64
Hoffman, Mary E. married Keister, William H. 10/22/63   10/23/63
Hoffman, Mary Frances died 07/05/64   07/06/64
Hoffman, Mildred Lee died 10/21/63   10/22/63
Hoffman, Samuel Owings died 10/01/63   10/05/63
Hoffman, William Henry married Wittler, Rosina 05/13/62   05/16/62
Hoffman, William Henry died 04/30/65   05/04/65
Hoffman, William J. died 02/09/64   02/10/64
Hoffmeister, Johanna married Zimmernam, Charles 08/25/61   09/03/61
Hoffmeister, John married Volker, Elizabeth 10/20/63   10/22/63
Hoffmeister, William died 07/05/64   07/06/64
Hoffna, Martha A. married Mantz, William H. 02/28/65   03/02/65
Hogan, Catharine died 06/02/65   06/03/65
Hogan, Isabella married Gill, Lawrence 05/31/63   06/04/63
Hogan, John died 05/23/63   05/26/63
Hogan, John died 08/07/64   08/08/64
Hogan, John F. died 03/09/64   03/10/64
Hogan, John J. married O'Keefe, Kate A. 07/14/61   08/01/61
Hogan, Mary Ann died 10/26/64   10/27/64
Hogan, Sarah (Mrs.) died 11/30/63   12/02/63
Hogan, Sylvester J. died 10/04/65   10/06/65
Hogan, Therese died 08/18/64   08/19/64
Hogans, Elizabeth married Hall, Edward 08/02/64   08/04/64
Hogans, Henry C. married Limbury, Alice 03/30/65   04/04/65
Hogg, Clara married Simes, William D. 11/03/63   11/06/63
Hogg, David died 09/22/62   09/23/62
Hogg, Edmond A. married Graham, Amanda M. 07/24/61   10/22/61

Hogg, Ellen F. married Knight, Thomas 09/06/64   12/29/64
Hogg, James died 11/28/65   11/30/65
Hogg, James H. died 09/22/65   09/23/65
Hogg, James M. died 04/19/63   04/21/63
Hogg, John died 03/04/61   03/06/61
Hogg, John died 03/28/64   04/02/64
Hogg, Martha (Mrs.) died 01/29/64   02/04/64
Hogister, Mary married Perkins, William 06/02/62   06/06/62
Hoheberger, Willy died 02/18/62   02/20/62
Hohenthal, Herman married Rosenfeld, Rachel 10/15/65   10/21/65
Hohn, Edward A. married Smith, Emma Amelia 08/23/64   08/25/64
Hohn, Margaret (Mrs.) died 03/31/65   04/04/65
Hohnberger, Mary Frances died 02/25/62   02/26/62
Hoit, Emma died 08/14/65   08/17/65
Hoke, Emma D. married Dixon, John Alford 09/12/64   05/18/65
Hokfland, Charles H. married Thurlow, Mary E. 12/25/64   12/28/64
Holcombe, Kitta married Richardson, Howard, Jr. 10/04/65   10/17/65
Holden, Catherine died 05/09/63   05/11/63
Holden, Daniel L. married Pentz, Martha A. 09/12/65   09/14/65
Holden, Estella died 07/06/61   07/16/61
Holden, James Kane died 02/17/62   02/18/62
Holden, Joseph K. died 09/27/64   11/02/65
Holden, Laura V. married Smiley, Joseph 11/25/63   11/30/63
Holden, Mary died 05/22/63   05/23/63
Holden, Patrick died 03/15/64   03/17/64
Holges, R. E. married Barnes, S. A. 12/28/62   12/30/62
Holladay, James H. married Caution, Ann Louisa 09/18/62   09/20/62
Hollan, James married Wright, (Mrs.) 05/01/62   05/03/62
Holland, Calvin died 03/10/64   04/04/64
Holland, Catherine died 05/04/61   05/07/61
Holland, George Albert died 03/17/62   03/18/62
Holland, Henry Stewart died 10/07/63   10/10/63
Holland, Jane E. (Mrs.) died 07/30/65   07/31/65
Holland, John T. died 03/22/64   03/26/64
Holland, John W. (Pvt.) died 06/19/64   09/10/64
Holland, Joseph married Dansbury, Frances Ann 10/30/62   11/01/62
Holland, Joshua died 11/30/64   12/01/64
Holland, Julia died 03/28/61   03/30/61
Holland, Laura S. died 05/25/61   05/29/61
Holland, Lucy Ann married Johnson, Samuel 06/01/62   06/03/62
Holland, Maggie A. married Sellman, James T. 04/10/62   05/06/62
Holland, Marion Estelle died 07/15/65   07/22/65
Holland, Mary J. died 08/08/61   08/09/61
Holland, Mollie E. died 08/08/61   08/10/61
Holland, Oliver S. married England, Susan J. 12/15/63   01/09/64
Holland, Richard H. died 06/11/62   06/12/62
Holland, William Thomas Lee died 10/01/65   10/05/65
Holler, John Benny died 07/20/64   07/22/64
Holley, Mary Catherine died 09/04/64   09/05/64
Holliday, Alice died 05/27/65   05/31/65
Holliday, Annie Holmes died 09/25/64   09/30/64
Holliday, Mary E. married Murray, Albert A. 10/17/65   10/19/65
Holliday, Thomas died 09/12/62   09/13/62
Holliday, William married Daran, Frances (Mrs.) 08/11/64   08/13/64
Hollies, Lydia Hemsworth married Burnett, Henry H. 05/31/65   06/03/65

Hollifield, Laura R. married Walters, Benjamin 02/25/64   03/03/64
Hollifield, Sarah E. married Clagett, John 10/24/61   10/26/61
Hollin, Bridget married Brooks, William H. 08/07/65   08/10/65
Hollingshead, E. R. married Kraft, J. W. 06/04/63   06/10/63
Hollingshead, James married Sumstrom, Lizzie 06/15/65   06/17/65
Hollingsworth, Alfred T. died 06/20/65   06/27/65
Hollingsworth, Ann D. died 03/22/61   03/23/61
Hollingsworth, Emily C. died 12/23/61   12/27/61
Hollingsworth, Flora married Henderson, William Ward 12/10/63   12/16/63
Hollingsworth, Harriet Ann married Hall, William J. H. 10/26/63   10/31/63
Hollingsworth, Helen M. died 02/10/61   02/14/61
Hollingsworth, Louisa married Robinson, William H. 02/14/65   02/15/65
Hollingsworth, Mary died 11/30/64   12/02/64
Hollingsworth, Mary (Mrs.) died 07/30/64   08/01/64
Hollingsworth, T. H. Benton married Sharp, Mary H. G. 11/13/62   12/01/6
Hollingsworth, William G. married Glenn, Rosa 10/28/63   11/10/63
Hollingsworth, Zebulon died 04/03/61   04/05/61
Hollins, Elizabeth married Guy, Joseph 03/13/65   03/15/65
Hollins, Emily (Mrs.) died 03/10/63   03/11/63
Hollins, Emily Jane married Fentriss, Cary 03/13/64   03/17/64
Hollins, George N., Jr. died no date   10/11/62
Hollins, Sterett died 08/14/61   09/02/61
Hollins, William Berry died 10/17/63   10/21/63
Hollins, William Stricker died 06/14/61   06/17/61
Hollinshead, William Alexander died 07/19/63   07/20/63
Hollis, Ann (Mrs.) died 07/17/65   07/19/65
Hollis, Ella A. married Michael, Louis D. 01/12/64   01/30/64
Hollis, Jane died 04/07/62   04/22/62
Hollitt, Emma married Schimp, Martin P. 07/24/65   07/26/65
Holloran, Michael married Roddy, Sarah (Mrs.) 06/14/64   06/17/64
Holloway, Emma A. married Rogers, William F. 01/01/61   01/02/61
Holloway, Fanny married Thorner, Francis 06/29/64   07/08/64
Holloway, Frank died 10/23/62   10/25/62
Holloway, George R. died 02/12/63   02/20/63
Holloway, James H. married Miller, M. M. 11/02/65   12/07/65
Holloway, Margaret A. (Mrs.) died 11/02/64   11/22/64
Holloway, Robert died 07/20/63   07/21/63
Holloway, Robert died 07/20/63   07/22/63
Holloway, William married Hopkins, Sarah A 01/11/64   01/23/64
Holly, George A. died 04/22/62   04/23/62
Holly, George Andrew died 04/22/62   04/24/62
Hollyday, William M., Jr. died 10/17/64   10/22/64
Holmes, A. S. married Lathe, Laura J. 01/18/63   02/03/63
Holmes, Anna Pamelia (Mrs.) died 12/27/63   12/28/63
Holmes, Charles H. married Lefanne, Mary Virgina 05/05/64   05/07/64
Holmes, David W. died 07/30/64   12/06/64
Holmes, Eliza died 08/27/62   08/29/62
Holmes, George married Johnston, Mary J. 06/24/62   06/25/62
Holmes, George Ann died 12/23/62   12/25/62
Holmes, James married Petticord, Ruth (Mrs.) 01/19/65   01/23/65
Holmes, Joseph W. died 01/05/65   01/07/65
Holmes, Laura J. married Pearce, Jacob M. 04/10/61   04/11/61
Holmes, M. Scott died 07/31/64   08/01/64
Holmes, Margareta A. died 08/14/65   08/15/65

Holmes, Mary died 05/10/62   05/13/62
Holmes, Mary E. married Gent, A. J. 01/20/63   01/22/63
Holmes, Mary E. married Jones, Benjamin F. 05/11/64   05/21/64
Holmes, Mary Emily died 02/17/64   02/22/64
Holmes, Mary Louisa (Mrs.) died 01/08/63   01/10/63
Holmes, Robert S. died 10/02/65   10/03/65
Holmes, Robert S. died 10/02/65   10/04/65
Holmes, Sadie C. died 08/12/64   09/17/64
Holmes, Samuel died 05/25/63   05/28/63
Holmes, Samuel married Ogle, Mary E. 10/28/63   11/04/63
Holmes, Sarah married Howson, Neils W. 01/23/65   02/02/65
Holmes, Sarah C. died 08/12/64   08/13/64
Holmes, Selda married Emory, T. Lane 11/03/64   11/14/64
Holmes, Thomas married Gilmon, Margaret 04/11/61   04/24/61
Holmes, William died 08/02/62   08/05/62
Holms, George L. married Smith, Cordelia J. 12/12/64   12/14/64
Holscher, John J. married Finley, Margaret 10/23/63   01/06/64
Holshor, Margaret J. died 03/16/64   03/18/64
Holson, Harriet married Oler, Henry 07/31/65   08/02/65
Holt, Albert A. married Rodgers, Annie M. no date   12/29/64
Holt, William died 10/27/62   10/30/62
Holte-Martin, Gullermo married Curlett, Mary E. 02/09/64   02/11/64
Holter, Agnes Jane married McKim, R. 02/25/64   05/17/64
Holthaus, Herman H. died 08/12/61   08/13/61
Holton, Annie H. married Renoff, George W. 06/13/64   10/04/64
Holton, Charles A. (Lt. Col.) died 12/04/63   02/02/64
Holton, H. Benton married Garey, Minnie A. 08/27/61   09/12/61
Holton, Jane A. married Oursler, John E. 04/25/64   09/27/64
Holton, Kate C. married Fales, William George 09/11/65   09/14/65
Holton, Maria Olevia died 08/09/62   09/03/62
Holtz, Ann Elizabeth married Williams, Denny 05/24/63   12/15/63
Holtz, David married McCauley, Martha W. 10/20/64   10/22/64
Holtz, Emmanuel died 01/17/64   01/18/64
Holtz, John C. married Oldham, Olivia R. 04/30/65   05/03/65
Holtz, Kate married Fowler, John 12/24/61   08/16/62
Holtzman, E. Kent married Brunt, Annie 04/11/61   04/15/61
Holtzman, Eliza died 05/29/63   05/30/63
Holtzman, George died 02/21/64   02/22/64
Holtzman, Israel married Reed, Rebecca E. 04/13/62   04/16/62
Holwey, Philip died 06/05/62   06/06/62
Holyland, Charles married Thurlow, Mary E. 12/25/64   12/29/64
Holyland, Charles J. died 10/22/65   10/23/65
Homann, Adam married Kelley, Mary C. 08/22/61   09/07/61
Homer, Ida Wilhelmina Dorothea died 06/25/61   06/26/61
Homer, Mary married Gaskins, Charles H. 11/10/61   11/12/61
Homer, Robert H. married O'Laughlin, Stacia M. 02/24/64   02/29/64
Homillur, M. B. married King, Mary Jane 02/08/64   02/09/64
Homsher, Rebecca married Martin, John W. 12/29/64   12/30/64
Honey, Bertha Hammond died 02/20/64   02/29/64
Honnet, Jacob died 07/12/64   07/14/64
Hood, Elizabeth A. married Randall, John W. 01/05/64   01/15/64
Hood, Thomas married Schaefer, Eliza A. V. 05/02/65   05/25/65
Hoofnagel, Lydia Maria married Murphy, James 03/19/65   07/06/65
Hoofnagle, Charles Henry died 01/23/61   01/26/61
Hoofnagle, John Henry died 09/26/61   09/28/61

Hook, Adeline married Hoffer, Charles 04/06/64   04/07/64
Hook, Annie E. married Dieffenderfer, Robert E. 09/09/62   09/13/62
Hook, Annie E. married Dieffenderfer, Robert E. 09/09/62   09/15/62
Hook, E. Marion married Kenly, William L. 05/12/61   06/19/61
Hook, E. Marion married Kenly, William L. 05/12/61   06/20/61
Hook, Emma L. married Gambrill, Charles A. 02/24/62   02/27/62
Hook, Frances died 07/02/64   07/06/64
Hook, Frances died 07/02/64   07/07/64
Hook, Helen Marie died 11/17/61   11/18/61
Hook, John F. died 06/18/65   06/26/65
Hook, Lydia J. died 06/07/61   06/08/61
Hook, Marcus R., Sr. died 11/12/61   11/13/61
Hook, Mary died 04/25/61   04/26/61
Hook, Mary E. married Smith, Thomas N. (Sgt.) 05/26/63   06/02/63
Hook, R. Edwin married Davidson, Sarah 09/20/64   09/24/64
Hook, Samuel J. married Hooker, Mary Ann 09/12/65   10/06/65
Hook, Solomon A. died 08/25/61   09/20/61
Hook, Thomas D. married Wright, Lydia 01/11/65   02/16/65
Hook, William Franklin died 04/15/62   04/17/62
Hooker, Jesse died 11/09/62   11/26/62
Hooker, Mary Ann married Hook, Samuel J. 09/12/65   10/06/65
Hooper, Amos died 09/02/64   09/03/64
Hooper, Annie E. (Mrs.) married Young, James E. 03/28/64   07/06/64
Hooper, Benjamin T. married Meekins, Mary E. 10/22/63   10/28/63
Hooper, Charles H. married Johnson, Ellen M. 02/23/64   02/24/64
Hooper, Charlotte died 08/26/61   08/27/61
Hooper, Edwin Eugene married Love, Marion F. 02/21/65   03/09/65
Hooper, Eliza A. (Mrs.) died 12/18/65   12/19/65
Hooper, Eliza A. (Mrs.) died 12/18/65   12/20/65
Hooper, Elizabeth (Mrs.) died 11/17/63   11/18/63
Hooper, Elizabeth (Mrs.) died 12/18/64   12/19/64
Hooper, Elizabeth A. died 11/11/64   11/17/64
Hooper, Elizabeth Ann married Joiner, William F. 04/13/65   04/15/65
Hooper, Florence E. died 11/26/62   11/27/62
Hooper, Frances J. (Mrs.) died 02/28/63   03/02/63
Hooper, George W. died 05/18/64   05/19/64
Hooper, Helen Augusta died 02/17/64   02/20/64
Hooper, James E. married McWilliams, Manie 01/07/62   01/14/62
Hooper, John P. died 08/07/61   08/08/61
Hooper, John Wesley (Cpt.) married Jones, Frances A. 11/24/63   11/25/63
Hooper, Joseph J. married Lightner, Virginia 08/16/64   09/07/64
Hooper, Julia A. married Boyle, James A. 09/01/62   09/06/62
Hooper, Lizzie died 01/20/63   01/22/63
Hooper, Lizzie W. died 01/20/63   01/23/63
Hooper, Margaret Jellerson died 09/05/62   09/08/62
Hooper, Mary died 12/13/61   12/17/61
Hooper, Mary (Mrs.) died 08/02/63   08/20/63
Hooper, Mary A. married Cox, Peregrine 02/07/65   02/09/65
Hooper, Mary E. died 08/05/63   08/06/63
Hooper, Mary S. (Mrs.) married Hoddinott, Charles 01/19/65   02/14/65
Hooper, Pilkington J. died 07/07/62   07/08/62
Hooper, Rebecca married Jones, Isaiah A. 10/09/61   10/11/61
Hooper, Robert, Jr. died 05/29/63   05/30/63
Hooper, Samuel E. married Hunter, C. 01/17/65   07/20/65
Hooper, Samuel T. married Rhinehart, Mary C. 05/14/62   05/16/62

Hooper, Sarah A. died 05/21/61 06/08/61
Hooper, William died 06/15/61 06/17/61
Hooper, William died 10/29/63 10/31/63
Hooper, William married Puhl, Mary Elizabeth 02/15/63 02/17/63
Hooper, William H. died 08/02/62 08/05/62
Hooper, William Thomas died 02/18/62 02/20/62
Hooper, Willie died 12/29/63 01/04/64
Hooper, Willie H. died 02/12/62 02/15/62
Hoopes, Edwin O. married Tyler, Lucy B. 11/20/62 11/26/62
Hoopes, William married Russell, Virginia 11/20/61 12/07/61
Hoopper, Caroline (Mrs.) died 10/24/64 10/31/64
Hoopper, Sarah (Mrs.) died 02/08/65 02/09/65
Hoopper, Sarah (Mrs.) died 02/08/65 02/09/65
Hoover, Abraham married Bufter, Mary Ann 08/01/65 08/09/65
Hoover, Cecilia (Mrs.) died 12/17/63 12/19/63
Hoover, Ellen Virginia married Austin, A. R. 05/08/62 05/12/62
Hoover, Emily C. married Buck, H. Best 11/30/65 12/11/65
Hoover, M. Victoria married Gentry, J. H. 11/30/65 12/12/65
Hoover, Thomas S. married Flincheam, Amelia 09/26/65 10/05/65
Hoover, William died 12/28/64 12/30/64
Hoover, William H. married Bullock, Hannah E. 01/07/63 01/12/63
Hoover, William H. married Regelein, Rose A. 04/20/65 04/28/65
Hope, Catherine died 03/25/61 03/26/61
Hope, Herman died 06/09/62 06/10/62
Hope, Nettie C. married Clark, Thomas S., Jr. 10/08/62 10/10/62
Hope, Sarah Elizabeth died 07/18/61 07/19/61
Hoper, Grafton S. died 11/08/65 11/11/65
Hopkins, Ann Elizabeth died 08/21/65 08/22/65
Hopkins, Anna J. Ellsworth died 11/25/64 11/29/64
Hopkins, Anna M. died 03/29/64 03/30/64
Hopkins, Annie P. married Alderson, C. Davis 09/29/63 10/06/63
Hopkins, Augusta Leavenworth died 03/10/64 03/12/64
Hopkins, Basil B. died 07/26/64 07/26/64
Hopkins, Charles E. H. died 11/14/65 11/15/65
Hopkins, Columbus J. died 08/28/62 09/03/62
Hopkins, David C. married Bandell, Emma V. 03/16/64 03/18/64
Hopkins, David M. died 02/26/61 03/07/61
Hopkins, Egbert D. married Crawford, Sue 12/21/65 12/23/65
Hopkins, Elanor (Mrs.) died 12/18/65 12/19/65
Hopkins, Elizabeth (Mrs.) died 09/30/64 10/03/64
Hopkins, Gerard died 07/16/64 07/23/64
Hopkins, Harriet (Mrs.) died 07/28/65 07/29/65
Hopkins, Harry Moreland died 01/15/61 01/18/61
Hopkins, Henrietta A. died 08/20/61 08/21/61
Hopkins, Ida Margaret died 02/13/62 02/14/62
Hopkins, J. Chandlee died 02/13/63 02/17/63
Hopkins, John J. married Beard, Bettie 01/24/61 01/30/61
Hopkins, John J. died 09/29/63 10/01/63
Hopkins, John S. died 03/03/63 03/04/63
Hopkins, Joseph Orem died 05/15/62 05/16/62
Hopkins, Joseph Orem died 05/15/62 05/17/62
Hopkins, Joseph R. married McCausland, Maria 01/05/65 01/06/65
Hopkins, Josephine H. married West, George W. 03/22/64 03/24/64
Hopkins, Kate married Walton, T. O. (Dr.) 01/29/63 02/12/63
Hopkins, Levin died 03/20/61 03/22/61

Hopkins, Lizzie S. married Cooper, Samuel R. 06/28/64 07/08/64
Hopkins, Margaret (Mrs.) died 11/05/64 11/07/64
Hopkins, Martha died 06/22/64 06/23/64
Hopkins, Mary Anne married O'Brien, James L. 08/15/63 08/24/63
Hopkins, Mary C. (Mrs.) died 02/12/64 02/13/64
Hopkins, Mary J. died 05/14/61 05/16/61
Hopkins, Mary M. married Moore, John T. 12/02/62 12/03/62
Hopkins, Priscilla married Smith, James R. 04/28/64 04/30/64
Hopkins, S. Harris married Laws, Mary C. 04/30/63 05/05/63
Hopkins, Sarah A married Holloway, William 01/11/64 01/23/64
Hopkins, Sarah B. died 05/11/65 05/15/65
Hopkins, Susan died 03/10/63 03/11/63
Hopkins, Thomas E. died 02/18/63 02/26/63
Hopkins, Thomas S. died 07/25/64 07/27/64
Hopkins, William Cooper died no date 08/05/63
Hopkins, William E. married Brashears, Elizabeth D. 01/03/61 01/08/61
Hopkins, William H. married Jones, Annie A. 04/11/65 04/14/65
Hopkins, Willy died 09/13/61 09/17/61
Hopkinson, Mary A. died 08/12/65 08/14/65
Hopper, Sallie M. married Hansow, P. W. 12/08/63 12/15/63
Hopper, Virginia Frances married Hunter, George W. 02/22/65 02/24/65
Hopple, Mary Ann married Downey, Charles Henry (USA) 11/27/63 11/30/63
Hopps, Rebecca married Roder, John E. 09/12/65 09/14/65
Hopps, William Thompson died 08/25/62 08/26/62
Hoppy, Mary married Zoeller, Mathias 05/21/61 06/12/61
Hopwood, Susan J. married Brown, Charles W. 04/11/61 04/18/61
Horan, John Edward died 07/05/63 07/07/63
Horist, Patrick A. married Wilderman, Alice M. 06/26/62 06/30/62
Horn, Alexander married Bull, Caroline 11/30/65 12/05/65
Horn, Annie E. married Pabst, A. 01/16/62 01/28/62
Horn, John Lewis died 02/20/64 02/23/64
Horn, Maggie Hughes died 09/30/64 10/03/64
Horn, Philip C. married Costello, Emma 05/12/62 05/13/62
Horn, Priscilla M. died 05/19/62 05/20/62
Horn, William married Barth, Catherine L. C. 12/26/61 12/28/61
Horner, Averilla married Forsyth, Manuel Thomas 10/21/62 10/22/62
Horner, Ellen died 12/13/61 12/14/61
Horner, Emma J. married Sumwalt, Charles L. K. (Col.) 01/29/63 02/10/6
Horner, Fannie married Larmer, J. William 03/10/63 03/12/63
Horner, Harry Turner died 11/03/65 11/04/65
Horner, Hester died 09/09/65 09/11/65
Horner, Medora died 03/15/61 03/16/61
Horner, William died 03/05/62 03/06/62
Horner, William died 03/15/63 03/17/63
Horner, William C. married Davis, Sarah S. 07/05/64 08/02/64
Horner, Wilson G. died 10/28/64 10/29/64
Horney, Agnes V. married Green, George T. 02/19/63 02/23/63
Horney, Charles T. married Irons, Elizabeth A. 12/14/63 12/19/63
Horney, Elizabeth (Mrs.) died 02/20/63 02/21/63
Horney, James W. died 07/08/64 07/09/64
Horney, John Baptist Robelet died 01/11/61 01/23/61
Horney, John Baptist Robelet died 02/17/62 02/28/62
Horney, Mary died 03/30/64 03/31/64
Horney, Mary Charlotte married Whiteford, Samuel B. 03/07/65 03/10/65
Horney, Mary Lizzie married Woolen, James R. 06/24/62 06/25/62

Horney, Sallie E. married Redman, Thomas V. 12/25/65 12/30/65
Horney, Samuel married Evans, Eliza L. L. 09/29/63 10/01/63
Horney, Thomas married King, Elizabeth 04/28/61 05/08/61
Hornung, John J. died 11/16/63 11/17/63
Horsey, Sarah Ann died 08/08/61 08/31/61
Horstman, Joseph D. married Carelton, Elizabeth Agnes 08/31/64 09/03/64
Horstman, Joseph D. married Carleton, Elizabeth Agnes 08/31/64 09/07/64
Horsy, George W. married Smith, Hennie 06/23/63 06/25/63
Horvison, Sally (Mrs.) died 07/30/63 08/01/63
Horwitz, Benjamin F. married Gross, Louisa 12/18/62 12/22/62
Horwitz, Orville married Rives, Maria 11/07/61 11/13/61
Hosbach, Anna Laura died 02/26/64 02/27/64
Hosemann, Louis C. H. married Zurharst, E. (Mrs.) 08/14/64 08/29/64
Hosford, James H. died 12/30/64 01/12/65
Hoshall, Florence Sidney died 11/13/62 11/15/62
Hoshell, Mary Ellen married Kelly, Hugh 06/07/65 06/13/65
Hosman, William P. B. died 05/28/64 05/30/64
Hossefross, Mary died 11/10/62 11/11/62
Hossefrosse, George H. died 03/16/64 03/19/64
Hotchkiss, Emma P. married Gray, Horatio N. 03/07/61 03/13/61
Houck, A. E. married Chaney, Sue 02/02/65 02/06/65
Houck, Amanda (Mrs.) married Stewart, Andrew 04/21/64 04/23/64
Houck, Andy Carr died 12/28/63 12/30/63
Houck, Frederick married Raine, Sophia 10/19/62 10/22/62
Hough, Joseph P. died 03/21/63 03/31/63
Hough, William T. married Miller, Sue L. 04/13/64 04/14/64
Houlihan, Elizabeth died 11/27/64 11/29/64
Houlton, Catherine died 05/14/62 05/16/62
Houlton, Mary L. married Guest, Samuel 11/10/63 11/19/63
Houlton, Ruth died 04/25/62 04/26/62
Houlton, William died 04/21/63 04/22/63
Houlton, William Jr. died 06/08/63 06/09/63
Hounberger, Sarah Elizabeth died 06/21/65 06/22/65
Hour, Henry died 07/26/64 07/27/64
Housch, Rosena M. died 05/23/64 05/24/64
House, Charles H. married McBride, Mattie W. 12/12/61 12/14/61
House, Edwin married Nicholson, Emma F. 07/23/61 07/26/61
House, John A. died no date 03/14/64
House, Louisa A. died 09/13/61 09/14/61
House, Samuel A. married Sullivan, Mary E. 10/10/61 10/16/61
Houseman, Laura A. married Ulery, E. G. 03/19/61 03/26/61
Houser, Kate F. married Jones, Henry A. 11/07/63 11/13/63
Housh, Justina died 08/13/62 08/15/62
Housnick, Francis married Rice, Lewis 09/05/64 09/08/64
Houston, Agnes died 02/11/62 02/13/62
Houston, Agnes died 06/24/65 06/26/65
Houston, Anne Williamson died 04/27/62 04/30/62
Houston, Eliza Jane died 07/20/63 07/21/63
Houston, John married Dorsey, Isabela A. 12/22/64 12/23/64
Houston, Joseph H. died 04/09/64 04/11/64
How, William married Ennis, Terresa 09/20/63 09/22/63
Howard, Amanda G. married Kone, William H. 11/30/65 12/01/65
Howard, Amanda M. died 07/07/61 07/09/61
Howard, Annie E. married Carbery, Joseph F. 05/03/61 05/06/61
Howard, B. W. married Orendorff, Kate 06/21/64 06/23/64

Howard, Beal died 01/30/61 02/04/61
Howard, Charles married Lansey, Ellenor 12/08/61 12/16/61
Howard, Charles R. (Rev.) died 03/01/62 03/01/62
Howard, Cornelia A. died 12/28/62 12/29/62
Howard, Eliza married Orem, Joshua 09/20/64 10/06/64
Howard, Elizabeth Gray died 11/14/62 11/17/62
Howard, Elizabeth R. died 01/18/64 01/27/64
Howard, Elizabeth S. married Orem, Joshua 09/20/64 09/27/64
Howard, Ellen Key married Morgan, Charlton H. 12/07/65 12/11/65
Howard, Ellen Key married Morgan, Charlton H. 12/07/65 12/12/65
Howard, Ellenor (Mrs.) died 07/24/63 07/25/63
Howard, Emma died 06/01/64 06/02/64
Howard, Fannie married Larrabee, William F. 11/17/64 11/19/64
Howard, Fannie M. died 11/05/62 11/11/62
Howard, Frank Richardson died 10/31/64 11/01/64
Howard, George Eugene married White, Letitia 05/02/65 05/08/65
Howard, George Eugene married White, Letitia V. 05/02/65 05/09/65
Howard, Hamilton P. (Dr.) died 12/29/63 12/31/63
Howard, Henry married Brown, Eliza 05/09/61 05/11/61
Howard, Isaac married Winder, Lucinda 12/22/64 01/04/65
Howard, Jacob married Smith, Sarah 06/05/65 06/08/65
Howard, Jeremiah married Miles, Mary Ann 05/01/62 05/03/62
Howard, John C. died 01/28/65 01/30/65
Howard, John C. died no date 05/19/65
Howard, John R. died 01/02/63 01/16/64
Howard, John R. Kenly died 08/01/64 08/10/64
Howard, Lizzie married Robinson, Richard B. 12/24/64 01/19/65
Howard, Lizzie married Donat, J. M. 07/09/65 08/01/65
Howard, Louisa married Nathan, Adam 08/17/65 08/19/65
Howard, Margaret married Richardson, Francis A. 01/15/61 01/16/61
Howard, Margaret died 06/12/62 06/17/62
Howard, Margaret A. married Smith, George W. 09/09/62 09/17/62
Howard, Mary married Freeling, Henry 01/28/64 01/30/64
Howard, Mary Amelia married Sewell, William H. C. 03/31/62 04/30/62
Howard, Mary Ann (Mrs.) died 11/17/64 11/19/64
Howard, Mary E. married Knapp, James 04/21/61 04/26/61
Howard, Mary H. married Haupt, Edward J. 08/13/62 08/18/62
Howard, Nettie (Mrs.) died 12/11/63 12/24/63
Howard, O. H. married Bush, S. Kate 01/15/61 02/04/61
Howard, Robert died 05/12/65 05/13/65
Howard, Samuel Johnston died 11/20/64 11/26/64
Howard, Sophia married Hilbert, John H. 07/11/64 07/16/64
Howard, Thomas J. died 02/09/61 02/11/61
Howard, Virginia A. died 05/14/61 05/20/61
Howard, William H. (Col.) married Wayson, Eliza W. 01/28/62 01/31/62
Howard, William Henry died 03/02/62 03/04/62
Howard, William Henry married Treasman, Mary 10/01/63 10/05/63
Howard, William Henry died 04/29/64 04/30/64
Howe, Frank T. married Griffin, Maria F. 08/06/64 08/15/64
Howe, Mary Ellen died 09/06/63 09/07/63
Howell, Alice R. married Kirkwood, E. C. (Lt.) 02/05/62 02/06/62
Howell, Frances died 06/08/62 06/25/62
Howell, John A. died 12/14/64 12/19/64
Howell, John, Jr. married Arnold, Mary Jane 12/17/63 12/22/63

```
Howell, Louis died 02/01/65  02/09/65
Howell, Margaret H. died 02/23/61  02/26/61
Howell, Margaretta married Ragan, Richard 11/18/61  11/22/61
Howell, Matilda died 11/29/61  12/02/61
Howell, William died 01/09/63  01/16/64
Howes, Charles F. married Claude, Marian H. 06/15/65  06/23/65
Howes, Ezra C. (Capt.) died 08/07/62  07/08/62
Howes, Ezra C. (Capt.) died 08/07/62  08/09/62
Howes, Maggie H. married Bunting, George R. 10/31/65  11/02/65
Howes, Mary E. married Johnson, William E. 06/05/64  06/25/64
Howit, George H. married Mullen, Sarah 01/06/62  01/14/62
Howland, William H. died 04/25/63  04/28/63
Howman, Charles Stew died 08/25/62  08/27/62
Howser, Frank T. married Mussetter, Sarah A. 04/30/62  05/02/62
Howser, Gassaway S. married Bramwell, Cecilia 01/16/62  01/18/62
Howser, Milton L. married Jones, Annie E. 05/01/61  09/03/61
Howset, Irene died 09/09/65  09/22/65
Howson, E. E. (Mrs.) died 04/04/64  04/06/64
Howson, Neils W. married Holmes, Sarah 01/23/65  02/02/65
Hoy, Thomas married Clark, Mary E. 12/24/62  12/30/62
Hoyt, Lillian L. died 07/29/61  07/31/61
Hoyt, Stella died 06/24/64  06/25/64
Hubard, James R. (Rev.) married Taylor, Sallie 06/01/64  06/13/64
Hubard, Jeannett (Mrs.) died 08/24/65  08/31/65
Hubbard, Alice Virginia died 03/13/65  03/15/65
Hubbard, Alonzo F. married Fluharty, Maggie L. 12/29/64  01/02/65
Hubbard, Annie E. married Craddick, Joseph N. 10/15/63  10/20/63
Hubbard, Buran, married Wright, Mary A. 04/28/63  05/04/63
Hubbard, Dorothy E. died 03/30/65  04/01/65
Hubbard, Eliza married Richardson, Henry 11/12/63  11/14/63
Hubbard, Elizabeth A. died 08/18/61  08/20/61
Hubbard, Henrietta married McGuire, John E. no date  07/06/64
Hubbard, Henry died 05/31/61  06/01/61
Hubbard, James married Deaver, Mary E. 05/03/64  05/04/64
Hubbard, James F. married Slemaker, Eliza 12/07/65  12/13/65
Hubbard, Jennevia married Grice, Edward G. 05/25/65  05/29/65
Hubbard, Maggie M. married Shutt, John W. 03/09/63  03/12/63
Hubbard, Mary A. married Packie, Alexander, Jr. 07/14/65  08/15/65
Hubbard, Mary Jane married Johnson, George 02/16/62  02/18/62
Hubbard, Samuel married Beckworth, Sarah Cunningham 12/31/60  01/03/61
Hubbard, Samuel died 12/31/62  01/01/63
Hubbard, Solomon died 12/26/61  12/27/61
Hubbard, Susan. (Capt.) died 01/21/64  01/22/64
Hubbard, Thomas J. married Brooks, Priscilla 10/12/65  10/14/65
Hubbard, William Albert died 08/14/65  08/26/65
Hubbard, William Bond died 11/30/63  12/01/63
Hubbard, William Henry died 10/12/62  10/13/62
Hubbel, Augustus married McClaskey, Hetty 01/05/62  06/30/62
Hubbel, Esther Jane died 12/28/62  12/30/62
Hubbel, Joseph Augustin died 08/20/63  08/21/63
Hubbel, William Augustus died 03/31/63  04/02/63
Hubbell, Clark married Nichols, Adele 11/08/63  11/10/63
Hubbell, Walter died 08/01/61  08/02/61
Huber, Harry E. died 07/04/62  07/07/62
Huber, Lavina married Sheckels, John 03/14/64  03/17/64
```

Huber, William H. married Hawkins, Martha 09/13/63 09/15/63
Hubner, John married Harken, Mary A. 09/24/63 09/26/63
Hubter, John H. died 02/24/64 02/29/64
Hudgen, John married Hamilton, Lucinda J. 09/11/65 09/13/65
Hudgins, Mary E. married Ripley, William W. 04/02/63 04/07/63
Hudgins, William H. (Sgt.) died 07/30/64 08/09/64
Hudson, Alverta died 09/13/64 09/14/64
Hudson, C. B. married Bailey, Elizabeth A. 03/07/61 03/08/61
Hudson, Charles Henry died 02/07/62 02/10/62
Hudson, David D. married Lee, Emma S. 08/17/65 08/30/65
Hudson, Edward married Pearson, Sarah E. 09/21/64 09/27/64
Hudson, Elijah G. died 02/16/64 02/18/64
Hudson, Elijah G. died 02/16/64 03/01/64
Hudson, Emeline married Wilson, Jeremiah 10/05/62 10/15/62
Hudson, Henry married Weidner, Maggie A. 06/13/64 06/15/64
Hudson, James married Thomas, Mary 10/27/63 10/29/63
Hudson, James T. died 02/07/64 02/09/64
Hudson, Joel Mellard died 08/04/65 08/05/65
Hudson, John L. married Matthews, Emily H. 09/05/61 09/07/61
Hudson, S. E. married Mayfield, William F. 12/08/64 12/23/64
Hudson, Sarah Ann died 07/25/61 07/26/61
Hudson, Sarah Anne married Darling, W. H. 09/03/61 09/05/61
Hudson, William H. married Cain, Mary E. 04/14/64 04/16/64
Hueston, John died 08/07/65 08/09/65
Hueston, John F. married Gross, Mary Ann 06/08/65 06/10/65
Huff, Andrew J. died 01/10/64 01/11/64
Huff, Sarah S. married Bosnal, T. S. 12/27/65 12/30/65
Huffington, Amanda married Martin, H. W. 08/31/64 09/12/64
Huffington, Isabel S. married Phillips, John W. 03/17/63 03/24/63
Huffman, Christener died 12/04/61 12/05/61
Huffman, Sarah L. died 08/31/61 09/02/61
Hufnagel, John married Kramer, Henrietta 02/11/62 02/13/62
Huges, Henrietta died 01/18/65 01/20/65
Hugg, Benjamin F. married Tucker, Susanna G. 04/12/64 04/15/64
Hugg, John died 05/22/65 05/23/65
Hugg, John H. married Jones, Susie M. 05/12/64 05/14/64
Hugger, Annette J. died 09/02/62 09/03/62
Huggins, Jessie married Popplien, Andrew 04/24/65 04/28/65
Huggins, Mary A. married High, Alfred 11/24/62 12/25/62
Hugh, Evan died 09/18/65 10/02/65
Hughes, Anna died 08/25/64 08/26/64
Hughes, Catharine died 04/18/65 04/19/65
Hughes, Edward died 04/03/62 04/04/62
Hughes, Edward Seibert died 06/14/63 06/16/63
Hughes, Elizabeth A. died 11/03/61 11/05/61
Hughes, Elizabeth A. died 11/03/61 01/20/62
Hughes, Ellen married McCormack, Archibald 02/19/63 02/21/63
Hughes, Emily J. married Meads, James T. 01/08/63 01/13/63
Hughes, Evan R. married Ijams, Jerusa A. 01/19/64 02/02/64
Hughes, George Washington died 03/14/62 05/02/62
Hughes, Georgeanna married Miller, Jeremiah 12/02/62 12/05/62
Hughes, Isabel Byron died 10/11/62 10/14/62
Hughes, James died 11/10/63 11/11/63
Hughes, James married Leckie, Levinia M. 03/16/63 03/23/63
Hughes, James Henry died 11/29/65 12/01/65

Hughes, James Henry died 11/29/65   12/02/65
Hughes, Johanna S. B. married Woolford, Littleton W. 12/28/65   12/30/65
Hughes, John married Williams, Susan 02/23/62   02/25/62
Hughes, John married De Vaughn, Mary S. 02/25/62   03/01/62
Hughes, John married Leon, Sarah 07/02/63   07/10/63
Hughes, John L. married Essender, Agatha 09/15/61   12/12/61
Hughes, Joseph married Swainscott, Emaline no date   01/28/61
Hughes, Laura married McKaig, William H. 10/25/65   11/01/65
Hughes, Lydia died 11/25/62   11/26/62
Hughes, Margaret Ann married Gould, Robert H. 02/17/64   02/20/64
Hughes, Margaretta H. married Shaw, Alexander J. (Cpt.) 05/07/63
    05/09/63
Hughes, Mary died 06/19/65   06/20/65
Hughes, Mary (Mrs.) died 08/12/64   08/13/64
Hughes, Mary A. C. married Bradley, A. Thomas 04/09/63   04/15/63
Hughes, Mary Ann married White, William 06/02/61   06/04/61
Hughes, Michael died 08/07/65   08/08/65
Hughes, Peter married Martin, Mary 01/07/64   01/16/64
Hughes, Samuel died 01/07/62   01/08/62
Hughes, Sarah died 04/26/62   04/28/62
Hughes, Sarah (Mrs.) died 07/14/65   07/15/65
Hughes, Sarah Amanda married Lytle, Nicholas D. 12/01/63   12/04/63
Hughes, Sarah E. married Jolly, Stephen 02/17/63   02/21/63
Hughes, Susan P. died 05/07/63   05/15/63
Hughes, T. A. Augusta married Oliver, Nathan E. 02/25/63   06/20/63
Hughes, Thomas married McEldowney, Bessie 03/24/64   03/25/64
Hughes, Thomas L. died 04/06/62   04/07/62
Hughes, Thomas S. married Siller, Sallie A. 06/08/65   06/12/65
Hughes, William married McGall, Mary L. 04/30/63   05/02/63
Hughes, William H. married Reather, Jennie 03/10/61   03/11/61
Hughes, William H. died 10/25/65   10/26/65
Hughes, William H. married Smith, Mary E. 08/09/64   08/12/64
Hughes, William W. married Kerlinger, Eliza A. 03/26/63   03/28/63
Hughey, T. Cook married Carter, S. Lizzie 09/09/63   09/10/63
Hughlett, Charles died 10/05/64   10/27/64
Hughlett, Mary E. married Wells, Joseph D. 11/30/65   12/04/65
Hugo, Samuel B. (Dr.) died 03/01/61   03/23/61
Huke, John died 10/08/64   10/10/64
Huleit, Caroline married Plowman, James T. 07/16/65   08/24/65
Hulett, D. F. (Cpt.) married Gillen, Rebecca 11/02/65   11/07/65
Hull, Aaron died 04/18/64   04/20/64
Hull, Agatha died 06/22/64   06/24/64
Hull, Alfred Clement died 09/16/65   09/18/65
Hull, J. D. married Foy, Mary A. (Mrs.) 12/09/63   05/03/64
Hull, John died 12/08/64   12/17/64
Hull, John Anthony died 09/01/63   09/03/63
Hull, Joseph J. married Delafield, Mary 12/09/62   12/17/62
Hull, Margaret Jane married Washington, George 11/13/64   11/15/64
Hull, Mary E. married Awbry, Andrew J. 10/24/61   10/29/61
Hull, Tilghman Newton died 02/20/62   02/22/62
Hull, William Edwin died 09/11/62   09/12/62
Hullan, Thomas married Beadenkoph, Kate 08/23/63   09/04/63
Hullings, Elizabeth married Reynolds, Chauncey A. 06/09/64   06/11/64
Hulse, Harry died 10/21/61   10/22/61
Hulse, John died 03/20/63   03/21/63

Hultz, Anna May died 11/05/63 11/06/63
Humes, James Spilman died 10/04/63 10/07/63
Humes, Matilda Virginia died 04/30/63 05/02/63
Humes, Priscilla W. died 12/04/62 12/09/62
Hummer, Cassandra married Waidner, John Jacob 03/19/61 03/21/61
Humphreys, Charles K. died 08/04/64 08/06/64
Humphreys, Clara Fritz died 02/20/61 02/22/61
Humphreys, E. J. died 10/18/62 10/20/62
Humphreys, Harry Walter died 04/06/64 04/08/64
Humphreys, Hugh died 10/16/63 10/17/63
Humphreys, Marin Welch died 03/15/64 03/16/64
Humphreys, Thomas H. married Clarke, Kate 11/18/61 11/27/61
Humphries, Humphrey died 07/05/64 07/07/64
Humphries, Mary Ann married Dinsmore, David 04/11/61 04/20/61
Humphrys, Elizabeth married Nuttall, John H. 12/17/65 12/19/65
Humrichouse, Ann L. Ringrose died 10/15/62 10/20/62
Humrichouse, Frederick Vachel died 10/17/62 10/20/62
Hungerford, Frances Ann (Mrs.) died 08/31/63 09/01/63
Hungerford, William S. (Dr.) died 09/09/63 09/10/63
Hungerford, William S. (Dr.) died 09/09/63 09/11/63
Hunley, Margaret (Mrs.) died 06/08/63 06/09/63
Hunphreys, Richard married Day, Mary D. 12/06/65 12/23/65
Hunt, Ann Rebecca (Mrs.) died 05/22/64 05/23/64
Hunt, Annie Lee died 07/01/65 07/04/65
Hunt, Charles (Cpt.) married Moore, Mary Jane 10/12/64 10/15/64
Hunt, Eliza married Bealmear, J. Francis 06/25/63 06/27/63
Hunt, Elizabeth C. married Hunt, Henry C. 04/28/64 04/30/64
Hunt, Elizabeth C. married Hunt, Henry C. 04/28/64 05/02/64
Hunt, Emma May died 07/01/63 07/03/63
Hunt, Henry A. married Butler, Jane P. (Mrs.) 12/21/65 12/28/65
Hunt, Henry C. married Hunt, Elizabeth C. 04/28/64 04/30/64
Hunt, Henry C. married Hunt, Elizabeth C. 04/28/64 05/02/64
Hunt, James H. married Garner, Hellen 02/16/64 03/04/64
Hunt, Joanna married Bountz, Jacob T. 01/01/63 01/02/63
Hunt, Joanna married Bontz, Jacob D. 01/01/63 01/03/63
Hunt, John H. married Cole, Sarah L. 03/26/61 03/29/61
Hunt, Martha married Harrison, Benjamin F. 03/22/63 04/28/63
Hunt, Mary Isabelle married Child, James W. 10/12/65 10/13/65
Hunt, Mollie married McCubbin, William F. 11/05/63 11/07/63
Hunt, Sallie A. married Petty, John S. 12/21/65 12/22/65
Hunt, Samuel C. died 08/13/61 09/13/61
Hunt, Samuel Chew died 08/13/61 08/17/61
Hunt, Stephen died 10/10/61 11/12/61
Hunt, Thomas H. married Linthicum, Vachel J. 02/14/61 02/16/61
Hunt, Thomas J. died 08/12/64 08/22/64
Huntemuller, H. William married Schumacher, Mary R. 07/01/62 07/03/62
Hunter, Ann Louisa married Harrison, William H. 11/01/64 11/07/64
Hunter, C. married Hooper, Samuel E. 01/17/65 07/20/65
Hunter, Elizabeth died 05/28/61 05/29/61
Hunter, Ellen married Heffner, Edward 08/03/65 08/07/65
Hunter, Ellen (Mrs.) died no date 10/23/63
Hunter, Emma L. married Archer, Roland D. 09/21/65 10/03/65
Hunter, George W. married Hopper, Virginia Frances 02/22/65 02/24/65
Hunter, Helena died 01/03/61 01/05/61
Hunter, Hugh Erskine died 06/22/62 06/25/62

Hunter, Ida Isabel died 07/19/65   07/20/65
Hunter, J. T. married Fuller, Sarah L. (Mrs.) 03/17/63   03/25/63
Hunter, Jane died 03/23/61   03/25/61
Hunter, Jane died 08/02/63   08/03/63
Hunter, John died 10/29/64   10/31/64
Hunter, Joseph James died 04/03/65   04/05/65
Hunter, Laura died 11/21/64   11/22/64
Hunter, Marion died 04/18/62   04/23/62
Hunter, Mary E. died 11/06/65   11/07/65
Hunter, Mary M. married Wheeler, Charles W. 07/31/65   08/09/65
Hunter, Peter G. died 10/11/61   10/14/61
Hunter, Richard died 12/27/62   12/29/62
Hunter, William Henry died 09/04/61   09/06/61
Hunting, Eben B. married Sisco, Laura J. 06/03/61   06/11/61
Huppman, Nicholas died 03/05/63   03/06/63
Huppman, Nicholas died 03/05/63   03/07/63
Huppmann, Rachel died 02/26/61   02/27/61
Huratty, Rosa married Eichelberger, John W. 06/25/63   06/27/63
Hurdle, Georgeanna married Nicholson, Joshua W. 06/13/65   06/27/65
Hurley, Charles A. died 07/16/62   07/21/62
Hurlock, Alfred S. married Stephens, Anna S. 12/02/62   12/03/62
Hurlock, Fred S. married Stephens, Anna S. 12/02/62   12/04/62
Hurnell, Christopher died 10/12/63   10/13/63
Hurst, Louisa E. married Allen, George W. 10/09/62   10/15/62
Hurst, Ann (Mrs.) died 11/24/64   12/06/64
Hurst, Annie died 02/15/64   02/19/64
Hurst, Catherine (Mrs.) married Martin, John 03/17/63   03/23/63
Hurst, John J. married Webster, M. Augusta 05/16/65   05/25/65
Hurst, L. Castle died 04/15/62   04/18/62
Hurst, Mary E. B. married Purnell, L. B. 12/14/65   12/18/65
Hurst, Sarah B. married Morgan, DeWitt C. 05/11/65   05/13/65
Hurst, Susan E. (Mrs.) died 12/09/63   12/14/63
Hurtt, Ann E. died 06/02/62   06/04/62
Hurtt, Blanche (Mrs.) died 08/09/64   08/12/64
Hurtt, Edward (Dr.) died 08/02/61   08/07/61
Hurtt, Henry N. died 03/05/62   03/06/62
Hurtt, Mattie J. married Ross, Christopher 02/18/64   02/27/64
Hurtt, Robert Washburn died 01/13/65   01/16/65
Hurtt, Thomas D. (Dr.) died no date   12/22/62
Hurtt, Tilly married Swift, John 12/13/65   12/15/65
Husband, Adelaide A. married Jefferis, E. Phillips 07/13/61   07/19/61
Husband, Mary L. married Shipley, Joseph 08/11/63   08/22/63
Husband, Sarah Ann married Daffin, Benjamin 03/06/62   03/08/62
Husbeck, Joseph married Whiteside, Eliza J. 05/12/64   05/19/64
Hush, Josephine died 06/25/64   07/02/64
Hush, Sarah married Dunnett, William 10/12/65   10/16/65
Huskisson, Nellie died 03/30/62   04/02/62
Huskisson, Willy died 03/30/62   03/31/62
Hussey, Azalia married Thomas, John L., Jr. 01/14/63   01/16/63
Hussey, John died 02/18/62   02/19/62
Hussey, Martha S. married Conant, Samuel W., Jr. 03/11/61   03/16/61
Hussey, Martin married Plunket, Mary 07/24/62   07/26/62
Hussey, Sophia W. married Morgan, William F. 11/09/62   11/26/62
Hussing, Catherine Margaret died 03/15/61   03/16/61
Huster, John Francis died 08/30/61   09/02/61

Huster, Maggie V. married Rupley, Charles P. 12/11/62 12/15/62
Huster, Mary Jane died 07/18/64 07/19/64
Huster, William Andrea died 07/11/64 07/19/64
Hut, Rebecca married Mills, Rufus 02/04/64 02/06/64
Hutchands, Amanda A. died no date 03/13/65
Hutcheson, Robert died 10/04/63 10/06/63
Hutchings, J. T. married Owings, Jane 10/11/64 10/12/64
Hutchings, Merab died 01/15/63 01/16/64
Hutchins, Clara died 01/16/61 01/21/61
Hutchins, Clarence married Gillott, Julia 10/22/64 10/29/64
Hutchins, Emily J. (Mrs.) died 08/31/64 09/01/64
Hutchins, Harriet L. married Bradley, John F. 10/23/64 10/29/64
Hutchins, Joshua died 05/01/64 05/02/64
Hutchins, Julia married Allensworth, Robert 01/09/62 01/10/62
Hutchins, Margaret E. married Denmead, Benjamin 01/09/62 01/10/62
Hutchins, N. J. (Dr.) died 05/30/64 05/31/64
Hutchins, R. C. (Cpt.) died 09/21/64 10/07/64
Hutchins, Robert H. married Martin, Kate A. 09/28/62 10/01/62
Hutchins, Sarah A. married Stinner, Benjamin F. 10/15/65 11/27/65
Hutchins, Sarah E. died 09/18/62 09/19/62
Hutchins, Sheadrick V. married Powell, Harriett E. 06/22/65 06/29/65
Hutchins, William Everett died 10/21/62 10/27/62
Hutchins, William H. married Clarke, Mary S. 10/19/65 10/20/65
Hutchinson, Henry L. B. died 03/26/61 04/04/61
Hutchinson, Laura V. married Chayton, Edward C. 01/19/63 02/06/64
Hutchinson, Mary Jane died 07/02/65 07/03/65
Hutson, Callie C. married Martin, William R. 12/17/63 12/29/63
Hutson, George Oliver died 05/05/64 05/06/64
Hutson, Joseph died 09/26/63 09/28/63
Hutton, Caroline married Roberts, Joseph 02/26/61 02/27/61
Hutton, Eliza A. died 02/22/62 02/26/62
Hutton, Ellen Salome married Ingle, Christopher 02/11/62 02/15/62
Hutton, George Nichloas died 08/04/64 08/08/64
Hutton, George Nicholas died 08/04/64 08/06/64
Hutton, John Henry died 07/04/64 07/07/64
Hutton, Nancy died 03/05/65 03/07/65
Hutton, Susan R. married Irving, Ambrose M. 10/01/62 10/03/62
Hutton, William Rich died 02/13/61 02/15/61
Huzza, Anna C. married Ritter, G. M. 11/11/61 12/05/61
Huzza, John W. died 07/11/62 07/12/62
Huzzy, Emma J. married Bishop, John H. 09/01/61 09/16/61
Hyatt, Alpheus died 03/06/65 03/07/65
Hyatt, Ida married Weaver, A. Ward (Lt. Com.) 02/13/64 02/19/64
Hyatt, Mary E. married Shield, John J. 03/16/63 03/19/63
Hyatt, Robert V. married McKnew, Annie 08/11/64 08/13/64
Hyatt, Sarah Elizabeth (Mrs.) married Riddle, A. P. 04/21/63 04/25/63
Hyatt, Susan died 08/10/62 08/12/62
Hyde, Catherine married Hyde, Richard L. 02/11/64 03/04/64
Hyde, Clara Virginia died 04/27/63 04/28/63
Hyde, Cornelia married Norris, J. Alexander 11/16/65 11/27/65
Hyde, Cornelia married Norris, Joseph A. 11/16/65 11/29/65
Hyde, Elizabeth married Porter, Joseph 08/15/65 08/18/65
Hyde, Elizabeth married Porter, Joseph T. 08/15/65 08/24/65
Hyde, Emma married Baldwin, A. S. (Dr.) 10/20/63 10/21/63
Hyde, Harriet A. (Mrs.) died no date 10/28/64

Hyde, Henry K. died 12/18/64   12/20/64
Hyde, Hetty Gibbons died 05/13/62   05/14/62
Hyde, John died no date   03/14/63
Hyde, John G. died 05/14/64   05/23/64
Hyde, Lizzie died 05/04/63   05/05/63
Hyde, Lucretia died 09/27/64   09/29/64
Hyde, Lydia A. married Wood, Joseph W. 12/26/65   12/28/65
Hyde, M. E. E. married Jeffers, James W. 09/12/65   09/28/65
Hyde, Margaret (Mrs.) died 09/17/65   09/19/65
Hyde, Mary married Duval, C. P. 12/16/62   01/19/63
Hyde, Nathaniel married Smith, Sarah (Mrs.) 06/28/63   03/29/65
Hyde, Nathaniel S. married Smith, Sarah (Mrs.) 06/28/63   03/30/65
Hyde, Nathaniel S. married Smith, Sarah (Mrs.) 03/28/65   03/31/65
Hyde, Richard L. married Hyde, Catherine 02/11/64   03/04/64
Hyde, Sarah (Mrs.) died 07/30/65   08/01/65
Hyland, Lambert W. died 09/08/62   09/11/62
Hynes, Thomas married Shields, Sarah 05/18/65   05/20/65
Hynson, Benjamin Price died 08/25/63   08/27/63
Hynson, John Ringgold died 11/28/64   11/30/64
Hynson, William George married Dushane, Anna M. 02/28/65   03/03/65
Hyser, Margaret Elizabeth died 12/31/63   01/02/64
Hyser, William died 03/04/64   03/07/64
Hyson, Emma Alverta died 09/15/63   09/16/63
Hyson, Joseph married Dinkel, Josephine 12/24/63   12/30/63
Ibbott, Frederick married Wilkinson, Mary 02/15/61   03/26/61
Iceman, John died 12/03/63   12/04/63
Iglehart, Joel died 10/20/63   11/02/63
Iglehart, Mary E. married Edelen, James 11/16/65   11/21/65
Iglehart, Milton married Clark, Annie H. 01/29/61   02/04/61
Iglehart, Rosalie married Hall, Thomas H. 06/15/64   06/18/64
Iglehart, Rufus married Slack, Mary E. 11/02/65   11/05/65
Iglehart, William A. married Hearn, Sarah T. 11/30/65   12/04/65
Igo, Emily A. died 10/13/63   10/15/63
Igo, Eva died no date   12/05/62
Igo, Isabel died 03/05/61   03/06/61
Ijams, Charles Dewitt Clinton died 06/20/65   06/21/65
Ijams, Charles H. married Garrett, Maggie J. 08/17/63   08/26/63
Ijams, Howard B. died 09/12/63   09/14/63
Ijams, Jerusa A. married Hughes, Evan R. 01/19/64   02/02/64
Ijams, Josephine married Mouland, John H. 04/23/61   05/04/61
Ijams, Oliver died 01/11/64   01/12/64
Ilgenfritz, Jackson married Nicholson, Georgiana 03/31/61   04/03/61
Ilgenfritz, Samuel Weiser died 12/03/64   12/05/64
Imhoff, Herman married Dierker, Elizabeth 09/01/64   09/08/64
Imhoff, Margaret married Paul, John 04/09/65   04/12/65
Immore, John E. (Cpt.) died 08/24/62   08/25/62
Inderreiden, Charles H. married Bennet, Laura E. 04/02/64   04/04/64
Ing, Catharine T. married Cassell, Edward A. 09/23/64   11/28/64
Ing, Edward Thomas White died 06/07/64   06/08/64
Ing, Sarah C. married Taylor, John 02/18/64   02/19/64
Ingals, Sarah married Polton, George H. 02/28/62   03/04/62
Ingder, Peter G. died 04/15/65   05/31/65
Ingersoll, Sallie T. married Young, John T. 01/01/62   01/04/62
Ingham, George S. married Cruser, Elizabeth D. 04/27/63   04/28/63
Ingle, Christopher married Hutton, Ellen Salome 02/11/62   02/15/62

```
Ingle, Elija (Mrs.) died 03/04/65  03/06/65
Ingle, Mary C. died 05/30/63  06/03/63
Ingle, Osborne married Addison, Mollie M. 08/11/64  08/13/64
Ingman, Eden D. died 01/10/63  01/19/63
Ingman, Harriet E. married Magness, James E. 06/02/62  06/04/62
Inks, John E. married Schroeder, Henrietta E. 10/09/65  10/11/65
Inloes, Alfred G. died 02/16/63  04/02/63
Inloes, Alfred G. died 02/16/63  04/07/63
Inloes, Alfred G. died 02/16/63  04/03/63
Inloes, Elizabeth married Powell, Samuel S. 01/06/64  01/08/64
Inloes, Frank died 12/13/62  12/15/62
Inman, Emma married Harris, Samuel M. 01/04/64  01/06/64
Innerarity, J. W. G. married Fairbank, Mary P. 08/10/65  08/28/65
Innes, Charles Gidley died 05/07/63  05/08/63
Innis, James died 07/16/63  07/17/63
Iocket, Catherine married Keilholtz, Jacob 01/31/61  02/04/61
Ireland, Daisy Lane died 01/11/63  01/26/63
Ireland, Elizabeth died 01/19/62  01/29/62
Ireland, Elizabeth Chew died 04/04/64  04/12/64
Ireland, Emily Jane died 03/23/63  03/25/63
Ireland, Hans died 08/29/61  08/30/61
Ireland, Jane married Johnston, James N. 10/06/64  10/10/64
Ireland, John B. married Micheals, Clementine C. 06/23/63  06/26/63
Ireland, Richard E. married Lyles, Elizabeth C. 12/06/65  12/12/65
Ireland, Wilson married Hartman, Julia 11/18/64  11/22/64
Ironmonger, Mary J. died 12/13/61  12/16/61
Irons, Elizabeth A. married Horney, Charles T. 12/14/63  12/19/63
Irvan, Euphania died 03/25/65  04/01/65
Irven, Letitia B. (Mrs.) died 01/11/63  01/14/63
Irvin, Jane Catharine married Gowens, George Henry 01/13/62  01/16/62
Irvin, Laura V. married Wilson, Richard S. 05/19/61  05/21/61
Irvine, A. Smith married Whittimore, Donna A. B. 06/27/61  07/08/61
Irving, Alice married Taylor, George M., Jr. 09/05/65  09/07/65
Irving, Ambrose M. married Hutton, Susan R. 10/01/62  10/03/62
Irving, Edward married Underwood, Sarah F. 01/19/65  01/27/65
Irving, George R. died 10/10/62  10/11/62
Irving, John Ellsworth died 07/26/63  07/28/63
Irving, William T. died 07/10/65  07/13/65
Irwin, Alexander died 11/13/65  11/14/65
Irwin, Ann (Mrs.) died 12/27/63  12/28/63
Irwin, Ann M. married Wethered, George Y. 10/01/61  10/03/61
Irwin, Charlotte married Cooper, Samuel 02/25/64  02/27/64
Irwin, Honoria A. married Todd, William J. 09/02/62  09/04/62
Irwin, James L. married Wheeler, Laura V. 11/03/62  11/05/62
Irwin, Julia died 03/18/61  03/19/61
Isaac, John T. married Bailey, Margaret 06/26/64  07/02/64
Isaac, Willie G. died 06/12/63  06/13/63
Isaacs, Francis Brent died 03/19/62  04/01/62
Isaacs, John H. married Gaither, Josephine 10/24/65  10/31/65
Isaacs, Sarah Jane married Strang, Edgar G. 01/24/65  02/02/65
Isaacs, Tobious married Hill, Minty Jane 06/15/65  06/17/65
Isett, Mary A. H. married Keifel, John G. 01/30/61  03/09/61
Isetts, Margaret married Donovan, Daniel G. 03/31/63  04/01/63
Israel, Jacob died 05/10/62  05/12/62
Israel, Nicholas died 03/16/63  03/18/63
```

Israel, Sarah died 04/03/62   04/04/62
Israel, Sarah died 04/03/62   04/05/62
Israel, Stephen B. died 06/02/64   06/04/64
Isreal, Virtie married Cone, John W. 05/25/65   07/31/65
Ives, Sarah Jan (Mrs.) died 01/29/64   02/02/64
Jackson, Alice married Locks, Israel 09/05/65   09/07/65
Jackson, Amanda (Mrs.) died 09/23/64   09/24/64
Jackson, Andrew C. died no date   04/17/61
Jackson, Ann Maria married Stokes, Henry 02/05/63   02/07/63
Jackson, Catharine married Robinson, Alexander 06/26/62   06/28/62
Jackson, Catherine E. married Johnson, William W. 03/19/65   03/21/65
Jackson, Charles married Fowler, Mary E. 05/18/65   06/02/65
Jackson, Charles E. died 08/18/64   08/26/64
Jackson, Charles F. died 09/22/61   09/25/61
Jackson, Charles Frederic died 09/22/61   09/24/61
Jackson, Charles H. married Crandel, Margaret A. 06/14/61   07/29/61
Jackson, Charles R. married Elliott, Laura V. no date   09/16/65
Jackson, Christina died 03/09/61   03/11/61
Jackson, Eliza married Curtis, Robert 04/28/64   04/30/64
Jackson, Eliza Ann married Stewart, Charles J. 04/06/63   04/08/63
Jackson, Eugene J. married Cohen, Rebecca 02/08/65   02/10/65
Jackson, Eugene J. married Cohen, Rebecca 02/08/65   02/11/65
Jackson, George married Ross, Elizabeth 03/02/65   03/25/65
Jackson, Hannah died 12/21/65   12/22/65
Jackson, Henrietta married Clay, Henry 01/05/65   01/07/65
Jackson, Henry J. died 02/27/65   03/14/65
Jackson, Hester died 09/24/64   09/26/64
Jackson, Hezekiah married Parker, Selena 11/19/63   11/21/63
Jackson, J. K. P. married Wamsley, Laura J. 06/25/63   07/01/63
Jackson, J. Stewart married Pickering, M. Cecelia 01/03/64   05/25/64
Jackson, James married Brice, Lydia A. 08/17/65   08/18/65
Jackson, James Henry died 07/17/62   07/18/62
Jackson, James R. died 10/10/64   10/12/64
Jackson, James W. married Durand, Eliza R. 12/26/64   12/28/64
Jackson, Jasper M. (Col.) died 09/02/65   09/07/65
Jackson, Jeremiah married Bowman, Emma 01/22/65   01/28/65
Jackson, John Francis died 07/16/64   07/20/64
Jackson, Jonathan died 12/06/62   12/08/62
Jackson, Joseph died 12/26/65   12/28/65
Jackson, Joseph E. died 11/19/63   11/21/63
Jackson, Joseph H. married Diment, Jane S. 03/26/61   06/11/61
Jackson, Julia Francis died 02/05/64   02/08/64
Jackson, Lucy married Myers, William H. 12/26/65   12/28/65
Jackson, Maria (Mrs.) died 01/14/63   01/16/63
Jackson, Mary died 02/12/62   02/15/62
Jackson, Mary E. married Jones, Thomas F. 11/27/62   12/01/62
Jackson, Mary E. married Hilleary, William T. 10/02/64   10/25/64
Jackson, Mary F. A. married Baily, Peter 01/17/61   01/19/61
Jackson, Mary J. married Lester, George 05/05/63   05/07/63
Jackson, Matilda died 09/10/65   09/12/65
Jackson, Molly Elliott died 03/28/62   03/29/62
Jackson, Naoma married Bond, Joshua 10/29/63   10/31/63
Jackson, Philip married Gibson, Rebecca 04/11/61   04/13/61
Jackson, Rachel T. married Conaway, John S. 03/17/65   03/23/65
Jackson, Randall died 07/31/61   08/02/61

Jackson, Rebecca (Mrs.) died 03/02/64   03/05/64
Jackson, Reuben R. died 07/19/65   07/20/65
Jackson, Robert married Lee, Martha 09/19/61   10/05/61
Jackson, Robert Henry Slicer died 10/07/63   10/08/63
Jackson, Samuel J. married Williams, Ellen 01/02/62   01/14/62
Jackson, Samuel S. married Longfield, Louisa 08/13/63   08/20/63
Jackson, Thomas D. married Gibson, Mollie A. 02/17/64   02/20/64
Jackson, Virginia A. married Ryan, William H. 07/23/63   07/30/63
Jackson, William Harper died 07/21/62   07/22/62
Jackson, William T. died 11/09/65   11/10/65
Jackson, Willie died 09/05/65   09/07/65
Jacob, Alice died 08/19/64   08/25/64
Jacob, Elizabeth died 02/22/62   04/01/62
Jacob, John F. married Browning, Eugena C. 04/16/61   05/01/61
Jacob, Magdalena married Hess, Charles 10/08/63   10/17/63
Jacob, Richard Isaac married Murray, Indiana 09/04/62   09/06/62
Jacobs, Alverdo A. married McKlee, Curtis 01/06/63   01/07/63
Jacobs, Benjamin L. (CSA) died 10/01/63   10/06/63
Jacobs, Deborah died 05/17/61   05/31/61
Jacobs, Hamutal E. (Mrs.) died 02/21/64   03/01/64
Jacobs, Hetty S. died 11/10/61   11/14/61
Jacobs, Jennie died 02/07/62   02/17/62
Jacobs, John B. married Fleeshell, Georgeanna 06/01/65   06/08/65
Jacobs, Martha married Merritt, William H. 01/19/64   01/23/64
Jacobs, Mathias married Sanders, Eliza 05/02/65   05/05/65
Jacobs, Molly died 01/07/62   02/17/62
Jacobs, Richard died 06/29/61   07/03/61
Jacobs, Samuel died 05/27/62   05/29/62
Jacobs, Willie died 01/07/62   02/17/62
Jacobsen, Henry died 02/11/62   02/12/62
Jacobsen, Henry G. died 01/03/61   01/04/61
Jacobson, Charles married Muller, Kate 10/02/63   10/10/63
Jaeger, Louisa (Mrs.) died 10/16/64   10/17/64
Jager, John married Carr, Catharine 07/10/64   07/15/64
Jaiser, Carlis married Towsen, Elizabeth 09/29/63   10/03/63
Jakes, Frederick died 08/19/65   08/21/65
Jakes, Frederick L. died 11/13/63   11/20/63
Jakes, Philip Thomas died 12/29/62   05/09/63
Jamart, Michael Auguste died 03/09/65   03/10/65
Jamason, Margery Ann (Mrs.) died 10/21/64   10/22/64
James, Achsah died 06/28/62   07/15/62
James, Arabell St. Clair died 05/14/65   05/15/65
James, Elizabeth married Melcher, George W. 11/07/65   11/23/65
James, Emelie A. married Smith, Alan P. 10/15/62   10/17/62
James, Fanny C. married McCormick, Harry C. 08/09/64   11/01/64
James, Helen Isadore died 11/25/62   11/26/62
James, Hester A. married Tucker, George W. 08/13/62   04/21/65
James, James died 02/05/63   02/06/63
James, John Henry married Alexander, Sarah (Mrs.) 06/09/64   06/11/64
James, John T. married McDaniel, M. Louisa 01/02/62   01/08/62
James, Louisa Beauregard died 12/01/62   12/02/62
James, Margaret (Mrs.) married Noblet, John 01/16/65   01/25/65
James, Mary E. married Knell, J. Henry 11/16/62   12/02/62
James, Morgan married Hergesheimer, E. Eugenia 02/24/63   03/02/63
James, Peter died 06/02/61   06/03/61

James, R. F. married Odend'Hal, Kate Estelle 01/14/61 01/15/61
James, Rebecca A. married Short, Joseph A. 05/04/65 05/08/65
James, Richard J. married McFaud, Mary V. 11/22/63 11/24/63
James, Robert died 02/25/64 02/26/64
James, Samuel died 11/20/61 11/21/61
James, Sarah Ellen died 10/11/63 10/13/63
James, Sophia married Jones, Isa 02/14/61 02/19/61
James, Sophia died 09/15/62 09/16/62
James, William H. married Albaugh, Emma Jene 09/24/63 09/30/63
James, William H. died 10/08/65 10/10/65
James, William Thomas died 09/23/62 09/24/62
Jameson, H. Gates (M.D.) died 03/29/65 03/31/65
Jameson, Hammond died 02/18/64 02/24/64
Jameson, John married Jones, Maria E. 05/25/65 05/27/65
Jameson, Joseph died 03/23/65 03/25/65
Jameson, Sarah Mc. (Mrs.) died 08/13/65 08/15/65
Jameson, Susannah married Jones, J. Wesley 07/12/65 07/15/65
Jamieson, Andrew married Murdoch, Lousia C. 05/24/65 05/27/65
Jamieson, Robert died 08/11/63 08/12/63
Jamison, Albert died 08/01/65 08/05/65
Jamison, Caecelius C. died 09/08/63 09/10/63
Jamison, Catherine (Mrs.) died 01/10/63 01/12/63
Jamison, Daniel married Owens, Sallie 07/23/65 07/27/65
Jamison, John died 09/06/65 09/21/65
Jamison, John married Boyd, Annie C. 05/19/64 05/21/64
Jamison, Lucinda married Martin, Oliver 07/30/61 08/01/61
Jamison, Robert A. married Curran, Lizzie A. 02/17/63 03/02/63
Janes, Caroline Jarvis (Mrs.) died 10/02/64 10/04/64
Janes, William N. died 03/03/63 03/07/63
Janney, Edward W. (Dr.) married Corse, Hettie S. 04/13/64 04/16/64
Janney, Samuel A. married Hall, Mary C. 03/12/63 03/19/63
Jans, Caroline Jarvis died 10/02/64 10/03/64
January, Daniel died 01/01/64 01/02/64
Janvier, P. died 02/26/65 02/28/65
Jarboe, Catharine C. (Mrs.) died 01/20/63 01/21/63
Jarboe, Catherine C. (Mrs.) died 01/20/63 01/22/63
Jarboe, John W. died 08/28/65 08/30/65
Jarrett, A. Bond married Streett, Isabell A. 06/27/61 06/28/61
Jarrett, Jane L. died 06/03/65 06/05/65
Jarvis, Fanny married Yeatman, James H. 10/19/65 10/23/65
Jarvis, Fanny married Yeatman, James H. 10/19/65 10/25/65
Jarvis, Hattie B. married Bond, T. Beall 11/13/65 11/15/65
Jay, Edward died 06/23/64 07/02/64
Jay, Ella B. died 11/22/65 11/23/65
Jay, Kate F. married Kilmon, Thomas E. 11/07/65 11/15/65
Jay, Mary Virginia died 10/18/65 10/19/65
Jay, Samuel Edward died 12/19/65 12/20/65
Jay, Samuel I. married Austin, Susie M. 05/06/62 05/09/62
Jay, Stephen H. died 01/02/64 01/04/64
Jay, William A. died 04/26/65 04/27/65
Jean, Charles W. died 02/15/65 03/25/65
Jean, Marcella died 08/04/62 08/05/62
Jean, Marcella Isabel married Joyles, Edward J. 03/04/62 03/06/62
Jean, Nancy died 04/07/62 04/08/62
Jean, William F. D. married Phelps, Celia E. 09/17/63 09/19/63

Jeanes, Jacob died 03/15/63   03/27/63
Jeanneret, Z. married Treuxsein, Erwina 07/11/63   07/14/63
Jefferis, E. Phillips married Husband, Adelaide A. 07/13/61   07/19/61
Jeffers, Benjamin died 05/11/65   05/18/65
Jeffers, Benjamin died 05/04/65   05/19/65
Jeffers, Cornelia E. died 08/28/62   09/01/62
Jeffers, James W. married Hyde, M. E. E. 09/12/65   09/28/65
Jefferson, David died 09/14/62   09/19/62
Jefferson, Isabelia died 09/28/63   09/30/63
Jefferson, John B. died 12/29/61   12/31/61
Jefferson, John B. H. married Pascal, Addie A. 04/05/65   04/08/65
Jefferson, Steven died 09/29/64   09/30/64
Jefferson, Susanna (Mrs.) died 10/17/63   10/19/63
Jeffery, Andrew died 05/07/64   05/09/64
Jeffres, Timothy P. died 03/31/63   04/07/63
Jeffrey, Thomas died 09/10/65   09/13/65
Jeffries, Ann Eliza (Mrs.) died 01/27/63   02/21/63
Jeffries, Ettie J. married Porter, F. E. 06/27/65   06/30/65
Jeffries, Lizzie L. married Tucker, John A. 05/11/65   05/20/65
Jenison, Marion M. married Drury, J. Thomas 11/18/62   11/27/62
Jenkens, Cecilia P. married Dallam, Edward B. 01/07/64   01/08/64
Jenkens, Henrietta (Mrs.) died 11/05/63   11/07/63
Jenkins, Anne died 01/04/63   01/07/63
Jenkins, Benjamin W. married Hazelhurst, Fannie 10/03/65   10/05/65
Jenkins, Bennedick died 02/03/63   02/04/63
Jenkins, Busirus married Dunn, Ann Maria 06/29/65   07/01/65
Jenkins, Charley Aloysius died 09/24/63   09/28/63
Jenkins, Chloe died 06/13/62   06/14/62
Jenkins, Clarisa (Mrs.) died 05/11/64   05/13/64
Jenkins, Daniel died 02/23/65   02/25/65
Jenkins, David B. died 06/14/61   06/19/61
Jenkins, E. Courtney married Treadwell, Fanny 11/08/65   11/14/65
Jenkins, Elizabeth married Glenn, William W. 04/14/61   05/07/61
Jenkins, Elizabeth C. married Walsh, Coza G. 11/03/63   11/07/63
Jenkins, Felix (Dr.) married Jenkins, Nannie 05/07/61   05/16/61
Jenkins, George F. died 12/25/63   12/29/63
Jenkins, Georgiana married Myers, Henry L. 08/30/64   09/01/64
Jenkins, Henrietta died 04/10/64   04/12/64
Jenkins, Henrietta (Mrs.) died 11/13/64   11/14/64
Jenkins, Henry died 12/05/63   12/08/63
Jenkins, Henry married Roberts, Cecelia C. M. 09/13/64   01/11/65
Jenkins, Hugh died 12/01/63   12/03/63
Jenkins, Hugh, Jr. died 06/12/63   06/13/63
Jenkins, J. Carrell died 05/22/65   05/23/65
Jenkins, J. W. married Duval, Mary 07/16/61   07/18/61
Jenkins, James died 08/14/64   08/15/64
Jenkins, James H. married Cannon, Amanda 10/31/61   11/05/61
Jenkins, Jane married Wright, John 02/11/64   02/13/64
Jenkins, Jane (Mrs.) died 09/07/64   09/09/64
Jenkins, John Henry died 06/25/62   06/26/62
Jenkins, John T. married Corbin, Cornelia 09/08/63   09/11/63
Jenkins, Josephine married Crawford, John D. 01/31/63   02/03/63
Jenkins, Josias died 01/14/63   01/16/64
Jenkins, Louis F. died 06/30/64   07/01/64
Jenkins, Louisa died 12/24/64   12/26/64

```
Jenkins, Mark W. died 12/05/64    01/02/65
Jenkins, Mary died 04/01/65    04/06/65
Jenkins, Mary Adelaide V. died 12/09/63    12/12/63
Jenkins, Mary E. married Young, R. W. 10/26/65    11/01/65
Jenkins, Mary Rebecca died 04/14/64    04/16/64
Jenkins, Nannie married Jenkins, Felix (Dr.)    05/07/61    05/16/61
Jenkins, Philip married Boose, Elizabeth Ann 10/20/63    10/22/63
Jenkins, Rachel married Benson, William W. 10/17/65    10/20/65
Jenkins, Richard L. married Sasscer, Henrietta M. 10/23/62    10/24/62
Jenkins, Samuel died 01/11/62    01/17/62
Jenkins, Sarah (Mrs.) died 03/19/64    03/29/64
Jenkins, Sarah C. married Sinclair, J. E. 12/10/61    12/18/61
Jenkins, Sarah Gertrude married High, George R. 12/15/64    12/17/64
Jenkins, Sarah Lilly died 09/03/65    09/05/65
Jenkins, Thomas married Regan, Catherine A. 01/11/63    02/03/63
Jenkins, Thomas C. R. died 06/24/64    06/29/64
Jenkins, Thomas W. married Rooke, Teresa W. 02/02/65    02/09/65
Jenkins, Upton P. married Allen, Jenny M. 03/03/63    03/10/63
Jenks, H. Frederick married Berry, Mary A. 07/18/65    08/10/65
Jenks, John N. married Myers, Mary 02/14/64    02/15/64
Jenness, Addie Hutton married Abercrombie, David 10/10/61    10/11/61
Jenning, Hester married Boone, Charles 02/16/65    02/18/65
Jennings, Edward died 06/14/61    06/15/61
Jennings, Elizabeth (Mrs.) died 02/07/63    02/09/63
Jennings, Joseph married Forney, Martha 01/03/61    01/08/61
Jennings, Martha Ellen died 11/09/62    11/11/62
Jennings, Mary Elizabeth married Jones, Bennett 12/24/63    12/28/63
Jennings, Minnie Ann married Walter, Lewis 05/16/64    05/19/64
Jennings, Patrick J. died 06/13/63    07/09/63
Jennings, Patrick J. died 06/13/63    05/30/65
Jennings, Samuel K. died no date    08/19/62
Jennings, William died 02/27/63    03/12/63
Jensen, J. F. P. (Lt.) married Bruning, M. Minnie 03/19/62    03/22/62
Jerome, John H. T. died 01/27/63    01/28/63
Jervis, Edward Nathaniel died 11/21/62    11/22/62
Jervis, James married Madison, Hester A. 12/02/60    01/09/61
Jesse, George R. married Maynard, Camilla F. 06/14/64    07/20/64
Jessop, Ann R. (Mrs.) died 11/01/63    11/06/63
Jessop, Ann Rebecca died 11/01/63    11/03/63
Jessopp, Arietta W. married Buckingham, Allen 08/11/64    08/30/64
Jester, Amanda married Sanborn, D. M. (Dr.) 04/30/63    05/04/63
Jewel, Arkansas A. married O'Neal, James P. 06/27/61    06/29/61
Jewett, Charles H. married Cordray, Mary Bell 07/28/64    07/30/64
Jewett, Eliza (Mrs.) died 06/03/64    06/07/64
Jobes, Edwin S. married Rainier, Caroline 01/02/65    01/07/65
Joeckel, Martin died 04/26/64    04/27/64
Joeckel, Martin died 04/26/64    04/28/64
Johannes, Charles W. married Langdorf, Mary 12/27/64    01/06/65
Johns, Fidelia married Belt, Thomas H. 10/05/64    10/07/64
Johns, George W. married Skinner, Emily 08/02/65    08/04/65
Johns, Kensey married Rynehart, Sarah Jane 05/22/65    05/25/65
Johns, L. H. (Rev.) died 06/28/64    06/29/64
Johns, Lizzie married Keech, Edward P. 11/21/65    11/22/65
Johns, Rebecca married Fowler, Thomas 11/24/63    11/28/63
Johns, William H. married Culnan, Maggie 11/17/63    12/14/63
```

Johns, William H. died 11/11/65 11/13/65
Johnson, A. L. married Haslup, R. Eugenia 04/23/63 04/25/63
Johnson, Africa M. S. L. died 03/20/64 06/13/64
Johnson, Alfred died 02/25/65 03/06/65
Johnson, Ann married Johnson, James 08/24/62 08/26/62
Johnson, Ann died 05/06/64 05/07/64
Johnson, Ann Maria married Owens, John 12/18/62 12/19/62
Johnson, Anna married Linnonburg, Daniel 12/05/61 12/07/61
Johnson, Anne married Poe, John Prentiss 03/02/63 03/05/63
Johnson, Annie Eloise died 08/13/63 08/14/63
Johnson, Annie M. married Clayton, James D. 05/11/64 05/13/64
Johnson, Augustus married Whims, Sarah A. 10/12/63 10/13/63
Johnson, Benjamin married Hings, Maria 10/06/63 12/12/63
Johnson, C. W. married Dunnock, Eliza Jane 11/02/65 11/11/65
Johnson, Caroline married O'Donnell, E. Lewis 12/20/65 12/22/65
Johnson, Caroline (Mrs.) died 09/05/63 09/08/63
Johnson, Catharine married Joyce, Elijah 12/22/62 01/05/63
Johnson, Catherine died 08/22/62 08/23/62
Johnson, Charles married Waters, Lavenia 07/05/64 07/09/64
Johnson, Charles Alexander married Foreman, Mary Ann 10/31/65 11/24/6
Johnson, Charles Edward died 09/24/61 09/28/61
Johnson, Charles Edward died 08/19/63 08/20/63
Johnson, Charles J. died 04/09/65 04/11/65
Johnson, Daniel married Williams, Henrietta 10/16/62 10/20/62
Johnson, Daniel married Cole, Emily 01/05/65 01/07/65
Johnson, E. Dorsey married Berry, Mary E. 06/24/62 06/27/62
Johnson, E. M. (Dr.) married Hempstone, Fannie 01/12/65 01/18/65
Johnson, Edward married Warfield, Ann Eliza 09/03/62 09/06/62
Johnson, Edward P. died 01/14/64 01/18/64
Johnson, Eliza J. married Quebec, James H. 07/31/62 08/27/62
Johnson, Elizabeth (Mrs.) died 01/26/63 01/27/63
Johnson, Elizabeth (Mrs.) died 12/30/63 12/31/63
Johnson, Elizabeth (Mrs.) married Lee, James 12/06/64 12/08/64
Johnson, Elizabeth H. married Scott, Josephine R. 04/14/63 11/11/63
Johnson, Elizabeth S. married Everitt, Richard O. 03/04/63 03/09/63
Johnson, Ellen married Johnson, Oliver 04/28/61 07/06/61
Johnson, Ellen M. married Hooper, Charles H. 02/23/64 02/24/64
Johnson, Emily (Mrs.) married Wheatly, James R. 08/09/63 08/18/63
Johnson, Emma Eudora died 08/11/64 08/15/64
Johnson, Fannie A. died 05/22/61 05/24/61
Johnson, Fannie L. (Mrs.) died 01/16/65 01/18/65
Johnson, Finley married Stansbury, Julia A. 09/21/63 09/26/63
Johnson, Flora married Todd, Henry D. (USN) 09/28/65 10/04/65
Johnson, Florence M. died 02/09/63 02/10/63
Johnson, Frances Jane married Rigley, Samuel 10/06/64 10/08/64
Johnson, Frederick A. J. died 06/16/63 06/17/63
Johnson, Freeman P. died 11/15/61 11/20/61
Johnson, George married Hubbard, Mary Jane 02/16/62 02/18/62
Johnson, George married Tasco, Maria 09/03/63 09/25/63
Johnson, George died 09/19/64 10/25/64
Johnson, George M. married Boteler, Charlotte R. 06/30/64 07/04/64
Johnson, George W. died 08/01/63 08/03/63
Johnson, George W. died 11/27/65 11/29/65
Johnson, George W. married Stone, Almeda 06/08/65 06/10/65
Johnson, Gershom married McCahan, Mollie C. 06/29/64 07/06/64

Johnson, H. L. (Mrs.) married Popalus, Joseph 05/15/63   05/19/63
Johnson, Henrietta died 06/03/64   06/04/64
Johnson, Henry married Johnson, Sarah J. 10/31/61   11/01/61
Johnson, Henry died 11/30/62   12/02/62
Johnson, Henry (Capt.) died 08/04/65   08/05/65
Johnson, Henry Clay married Ozmon, Mary M. 02/13/62   02/14/62
Johnson, Hezekiah died 07/23/65   07/25/65
Johnson, Hiram died 09/05/62   09/06/62
Johnson, Isaac died 01/22/64   01/23/64
Johnson, Isaac Larue married Lear, Bettie O'Neal 06/09/63   06/18/63
Johnson, J. Smith married Lewis, Emma 06/22/65   06/26/65
Johnson, Jacob G. died 03/16/64   03/18/64
Johnson, James married Johnson, Ann 08/24/62   08/26/62
Johnson, James married Johnson, Louisa 04/21/63   04/23/63
Johnson, James died 01/18/65   01/20/65
Johnson, James died 10/31/65   11/08/65
Johnson, James W. married Richmond, Sarah E. 01/28/64   02/22/64
Johnson, James Washington died 01/06/65   01/09/65
Johnson, Jane married Castor, Noel F. 04/04/61   04/09/61
Johnson, Jefferson Davis died 09/26/61   10/01/61
Johnson, John married Fortune, Emeline 07/02/62   07/04/62
Johnson, John married Lane, Elizabeth 05/08/63   05/13/63
Johnson, John Henry married Sharpe, Mary A. 01/20/65   01/23/65
Johnson, John Henry Washington died 10/20/63   10/22/63
Johnson, John L. (Capt.) married Travers, Elizabeth O. 12/26/61   12/28/61
Johnson, John W. married Collett, Sophia L. 01/01/63   01/05/63
Johnson, Joseph died 03/23/62   03/24/62
Johnson, Joseph died 03/02/64   03/03/64
Johnson, Joseph E. died 12/15/63   12/17/63
Johnson, Joseph G. married Maxwell, Annie C. 05/18/63   05/26/63
Johnson, Josephine R. died 05/24/64   05/25/64
Johnson, Josephine R. (Mrs.) died 02/19/64   02/20/64
Johnson, Joshua M. married Watt, Caroline 12/10/63   12/23/63
Johnson, Julia Ann died 10/02/65   10/03/65
Johnson, Julia R. married Thompson, Frederick 10/06/64   10/14/64
Johnson, Kate E. married Boulden, Jarred C. 05/23/61   05/28/61
Johnson, Kate E. married Boulden, Jesse C. 05/23/61   05/25/61
Johnson, Kiziah died 03/21/62   03/24/62
Johnson, L. C. married Wright, W. B. (Rev.) 01/01/63   01/02/63
Johnson, L. O. married Wright, W. B. (Rev.) 01/01/63   01/03/63
Johnson, Laura married Anderson, Thomas 05/15/64   05/19/64
Johnson, Lewis R. married Armstrong, Kate A. 05/12/65   06/28/65
Johnson, Libbie married Worthington, J. Edward 01/17/65   01/25/65
Johnson, Louisa married Johnson, James 04/21/63   04/23/63
Johnson, Louisa (Mrs.) married Hight, William 10/08/65   10/10/65
Johnson, Louisa A. married Vail, John K. 10/22/65   10/25/65
Johnson, Madison married Shriver, Mary 10/20/64   10/22/64
Johnson, Margaret died 12/09/61   12/10/61
Johnson, Margaret Ann died 08/25/64   08/27/64
Johnson, Margaret Ann died 09/09/65   09/11/65
Johnson, Maria married Trusty, Robert 11/11/63   11/24/63
Johnson, Marion married Mitchell, Rebecca 10/26/65   10/31/65
Johnson, Marius married Flinckom, Martha 12/25/64   12/28/64
Johnson, Martha Ann married Mallonnee, William H. 09/25/62   09/30/62

Johnson, Martha Ellen died 12/06/65   12/27/65
Johnson, Mary E. married Reeves, Aaron T. 03/14/61   03/16/61
Johnson, Mary J. married Thomas, Adam 08/20/61   08/24/61
Johnson, Mary Letitia married Williams, George 03/12/61   03/14/61
Johnson, Mattie F. died 03/25/64   03/30/64
Johnson, Mildred died 10/23/61   10/28/61
Johnson, Oliver married Akins, Ellen 04/28/61   07/10/61
Johnson, Oliver married Johnson, Ellen 04/28/61   07/06/61
Johnson, Oliver died 06/12/61   07/06/61
Johnson, Oscar married Anderson, Marion 09/17/61   09/20/61
Johnson, Pamelia A. (Mrs.) died 02/13/63   02/18/63
Johnson, Patrick died 09/04/62   09/06/62
Johnson, Priscilla S. died 06/10/65   06/12/65
Johnson, Rachel Ann married Surudy, Hamilton 10/10/61   10/12/61
Johnson, Rebecca married Tabbs, George 11/03/64   11/30/64
Johnson, Rebecca Jane died 07/18/64   07/19/64
Johnson, Richard married Lee, Jane 08/11/63   08/12/63
Johnson, Richard married Nugent, Agnes 10/02/64   10/04/64
Johnson, Richard A. married Skinner, Julia A. 02/11/64   02/16/64
Johnson, Robert (Cpt.) married Meek, Martha Eliza 11/03/64   11/05/64
Johnson, Rudolph married Simes, Elizabeth 12/08/62   12/29/62
Johnson, Ruth married Caster, Robert 12/15/63   12/19/63
Johnson, Samuel married Holland, Lucy Ann 06/01/62   06/03/62
Johnson, Samuel married Gaines, Ann Louisa 12/04/62   12/10/62
Johnson, Sarah married Frisby, William H. 09/22/64   09/24/64
Johnson, Sarah C. married Sweeney, John W. 05/18/61   05/21/61
Johnson, Sarah C. married Miller, Joseph W. 08/17/65   08/22/65
Johnson, Sarah J. married Johnson, Henry 10/31/61   11/01/61
Johnson, Sarah Jane married Ball, George R. 10/26/62   10/27/62
Johnson, Sidney married Parton, John W. 07/04/61   07/06/61
Johnson, Sophia married Alexander, William 06/07/63   06/09/63
Johnson, Stephen married Mitchell, Josephine 12/25/63   01/02/64
Johnson, Susanna H. married Gorsuch, Dickenson 05/20/62   05/23/62
Johnson, Theodore, C. died 12/22/62   05/25/63
Johnson, Thomas married Gaines, Henrietta 07/08/62   07/12/62
Johnson, Thomas died 06/02/64   06/03/64
Johnson, Thomas married Cooper, Mary Ellen 12/08/64   12/10/64
Johnson, Thomas married Powell, Ann E. 02/10/64   02/13/64
Johnson, Thomas C. married Sharpe, Mary Elizabeth 04/21/62   04/23/62
Johnson, Thomas J. died 11/05/65   11/07/65
Johnson, Thomas S. J. died 11/20/64   01/13/65
Johnson, Thomas T. married Gibson, Mary Ann 10/03/64   10/08/64
Johnson, Walter M. died 11/27/65   11/28/65
Johnson, Willard Bates died 11/11/64   11/15/64
Johnson, William married Dennis, Mary 04/21/64   04/23/64
Johnson, William married Sorrell, Emily Jane 08/26/64   08/31/64
Johnson, William A. married Stewart, Emma 03/16/65   03/18/65
Johnson, William B. married Cleary, M. Jennie 12/05/65   12/19/65
Johnson, William B. C. died 06/30/64   05/02/65
Johnson, William E. married Howes, Mary E. 06/05/64   06/25/64
Johnson, William Fell died 04/15/62   04/17/62
Johnson, William Gerard died 09/08/63   09/10/63
Johnson, William H. married Loehmeyer, Helena 09/13/63   09/21/63
Johnson, William T. (Rev.) married Wheeler, Annie 12/25/65   12/29/65
Johnson, William W. married Jackson, Catherine E. 03/19/65   03/21/65

Johnson, William W. married Williams, Martha H. 06/01/65　06/05/65
Johnson, Willie H. died 12/06/65　12/07/65
Johnston, Caroline married Brampton, Samuel Thomas 02/18/61　02/21/61
Johnston, Carrie V. married Spaulding, James C. 06/05/65　06/09/65
Johnston, Christiana (Mrs.) died 09/14/63　09/16/63
Johnston, Elizabeth married Sinclair, William 07/03/63　07/29/63
Johnston, Emilie A. married Goldsborough, James N. 07/17/61　07/18/61
Johnston, Frank H. married Goldsborough, Anna A. 04/18/65　04/20/65
Johnston, Frederick William died 08/01/62　08/05/62
Johnston, Helen Lindsay died 08/28/63　09/19/63
Johnston, Helen Lindsay died 08/28/63　09/22/63
Johnston, Henry died no date　11/04/61
Johnston, James died 10/03/65　10/04/65
Johnston, James married Gray, Sallie M. 12/30/64　02/01/65
Johnston, James N. married Ireland, Jane 10/06/64　10/10/64
Johnston, John J. died 11/09/64　11/10/64
Johnston, Mary Ann died 08/21/65　08/22/65
Johnston, Mary Elizabeth died 12/11/62　12/13/62
Johnston, Mary J. married Holmes, George 06/24/62　06/25/62
Johnston, Merriken B. died 09/03/65　09/05/65
Johnston, Rachel married Spindle, Dandridge 02/25/64　03/01/64
Johnston, Sallie married Childs, William H. 02/22/65　07/18/65
Johnston, Thomas died 08/05/62　08/06/62
Johnston, Thomas Jefferson died 02/02/62　08/05/62
Johnston, William died 06/15/62　06/23/62
Johnston, William J. died 09/28/63　09/30/63
Johnston, Willie Nusem died 09/02/65　09/04/65
Johson, William married Roberts, Margaret S. 10/06/65　10/10/65
Joice, Stephen Merryman died 02/28/61　03/01/61
Joiner, Daniel married Fowler, Amanda 02/25/64　02/27/64
Joiner, Martha A. married Granger, Levin 10/20/64　10/22/64
Joiner, William F. married Hooper, Elizabeth Ann 04/13/65　04/15/65
Joines, Jennie E. married Davidson, T. W. 03/14/65　03/16/65
Joines, Matilda M. died 08/12/61　08/13/61
Jolce, Grace died 02/08/61　02/19/61
Jolley, Elizabeth (Mrs.) died 11/18/64　11/21/64
Jollie, Catherine McDougal died 07/29/63　08/03/63
Jolly, Anna Mary died 01/28/64　01/29/64
Jolly, David married Baton, Anna Maria 04/30/65　05/02/65
Jolly, David married Banton, Anna Maria 04/30/65　05/02/65
Jolly, Elizabeth A. died 02/26/64　02/29/64
Jolly, Mary Latilda married Brooks, Albert Dyre 04/08/64　04/09/64
Jolly, Stephen married Hughes, Sarah E. 02/17/63　02/21/63
Jonas, Jacob died 11/22/64　11/23/64
Jones, Achias Anna A. married Reed, Richard 12/22/64　12/24/64
Jones, Alfred I. married Stinchcomb, Sarah E. 07/14/62　07/22/62
Jones, Alfred T. married Parker, Josephine V. 09/27/65　09/29/65
Jones, Alice married Moore, Henry D. 08/30/64　08/31/64
Jones, Alice A. married Young, Edward G. 03/03/63　03/09/63
Jones, Alipha E. married Hall, Charles A. D. 12/10/63　12/15/63
Jones, Amelia A. married Stubbins, Thomas G. 10/20/62　10/22/62
Jones, Andrew married Gotchmer, Mary E. 11/16/64　11/18/64
Jones, Ann E. (Mrs.) died 02/16/64　02/29/64
Jones, Ann Rebecca Hanna died no date　07/07/62
Jones, Ann Treasia died 06/26/64　06/27/64

```
Jones, Anna married Jones, Joshua 06/28/64   07/02/64
Jones, Anna Louisa died 02/16/62   02/21/62
Jones, Anna M. married Saunders, George 09/04/64   09/06/64
Jones, Annie A. married Hopkins, William H. 04/11/65   04/14/65
Jones, Annie E. married Howser, Milton L. 05/01/61   09/03/61
Jones, Asa L. married Foose, Augustine 02/27/61   03/19/61
Jones, Asbury died 06/04/64   06/07/64
Jones, B. Franklin married Long, Anne E. 03/28/64   03/30/64
Jones, Basil died 04/20/64   04/22/64
Jones, Beccie married Cropley, Richard L. 10/02/62   10/09/62
Jones, Benjamin F. married Holmes, Mary E. 05/11/64   05/21/64
Jones, Bennett married Jennings, Mary Elizabeth 12/24/63   12/28/63
Jones, Caroline V. died 11/03/65   11/06/65
Jones, Carry May died 09/13/64   09/14/64
Jones, Catharine died 03/19/65   03/22/65
Jones, Catherine (Mrs.) died 05/10/63   05/12/63
Jones, Charles died 05/30/65   06/01/65
Jones, Charles Ellmer died 07/31/62   08/01/62
Jones, Charles H. married Redmond, Josephine M. 07/11/61   07/26/61
Jones, Charles Henry died 04/08/62   04/10/62
Jones, Charles W. married Linthicum, Ozelab M. 03/07/61   03/16/61
Jones, Charles W. married Dieckmann, Margaret C. 04/17/65   04/27/65
Jones, Clara Ann Elizabeth died 05/08/65   05/11/65
Jones, Clemantine died 11/21/61   11/22/61
Jones, Cornelius married Cassell, Mary E. 04/01/61   04/04/61
Jones, Cornelius Washington died 12/02/64   12/05/64
Jones, D. S. died 11/15/62   11/17/62
Jones, Denwood married Bailey, Martha 12/26/61   12/28/61
Jones, Derinda L. C. married Bramble, Barzilla 06/16/63   06/18/63
Jones, Edmund died 01/11/64   01/13/64
Jones, Edward died 11/17/64   11/23/64
Jones, Edward D. married McIlvain, Elizabeth 06/06/62   07/19/62
Jones, Edward D. married Fox, Eliza E. 03/28/64   04/04/64
Jones, Edward R. died 02/17/61   02/19/61
Jones, Elenorah married Badger, Jarred 05/12/61   05/18/61
Jones, Eli died 09/01/64   09/03/64
Jones, Elisha married Tracey, Susanna 12/03/63   02/17/64
Jones, Eliza died 12/06/65   12/09/65
Jones, Elizabeth (Mrs.) died 01/24/64   01/26/64
Jones, Elizabeth Ann married Digs, Aaron 06/23/61   06/26/61
Jones, Elizabeth E. (Mrs.) died 09/21/63   09/22/63
Jones, Ella married Mallalieu, W. H. Harrison 10/10/65   10/18/65
Jones, Emma died 10/31/61   11/02/61
Jones, Emmer Jane married Sprows, William Henry 04/02/63   04/04/63
Jones, Eugene A. married Williamson, Annie E. 07/25/64   07/27/64
Jones, Fanny died 05/19/63   05/20/63
Jones, Frances A. married Hooper, John Wesley (Cpt.) 11/24/63   11/25/6
Jones, Frederick died 06/12/63   06/13/63
Jones, George Edwin died 03/06/63   03/07/63
Jones, George H. died 12/27/64   12/31/64
Jones, George W. married Kelty, Mary Elizabeth 02/03/63   02/09/63
Jones, George W. died 04/20/64   04/21/64
Jones, Georgeanne married Konig, Lloyd 12/11/62   12/16/62
Jones, Grace Elma died 10/13/65   10/16/65
Jones, Grace Elma died no date   10/24/65
```

Jones, Hamilton married Browning, Emma L. 12/07/65 12/11/65
Jones, Harry H. died 07/05/65 07/08/65
Jones, Henry married Martin, Sarah Sophia 12/05/64 02/07/65
Jones, Henry A. married Houser, Kate F. 11/07/63 11/13/63
Jones, Henry C. married Owen, Lizzie J. 01/29/63 02/07/63
Jones, Henry Clinton died 05/11/65 05/15/65
Jones, Henry O. married McNulty, Rosy 06/08/63 06/12/63
Jones, Isa married James, Sophia 02/14/61 02/19/61
Jones, Isaac died 07/14/62 07/18/62
Jones, Isaac died 01/11/64 01/13/64
Jones, Isaac H. died 04/20/64 04/23/64
Jones, Isaiah married Smith, Clara Augusta 06/01/65 06/03/65
Jones, Isaiah A. married Hooper, Rebecca 10/09/61 10/11/61
Jones, J. G. married Franklin, Mary V. 11/27/65 12/16/65
Jones, J. H. married Stansbury, Eliza 01/17/62 01/18/62
Jones, J. W. married Stansbury, Eliza 01/17/62 01/20/62
Jones, J. Wesley married Jameson, Susannah 07/12/65 07/15/65
Jones, Jacob married Crumunell, Martha A. 11/06/63 11/07/63
Jones, James died 02/07/65 02/09/65
Jones, James (M.D.) died 05/30/62 12/10/62
Jones, James A. married Cornish, Lucy 04/02/61 04/08/61
Jones, James H. married Henning, Virginia A. 02/26/63 02/28/63
Jones, James H. died 03/31/65 04/01/65
Jones, James L. married Dewling, Margaret A. 12/26/61 12/28/61
Jones, James M. married Boswell, Matilda A. 12/07/65 12/12/65
Jones, James W. died 03/22/64 03/23/64
Jones, Jason J. married Powell, Henrietta 05/24/63 06/10/63
Jones, Jeffra married Burke, Margaret 03/26/63 03/28/63
Jones, Jeremiah married Cropper, Sarah E. 04/06/65 04/11/65
Jones, Johannah married Russell, William Henry 09/06/64 09/07/64
Jones, John married Denby, Mary Jane 04/16/61 04/19/61
Jones, John married Rainer, Eliza 07/01/61 07/11/61
Jones, John died 02/16/62 02/17/62
Jones, John married Acomb, Fanny 05/01/62 06/10/62
Jones, John married Jones, Mary A. (Mrs.) 01/07/65 01/19/65
Jones, John B. married Lanehart, Mary Ann 09/19/61 09/21/61
Jones, John D. died 02/25/61 02/28/61
Jones, John J. married Wright, Mary E. 06/10/62 06/12/62
Jones, John P. died 11/27/65 11/29/65
Jones, John P. married Cochran, Mary E. (Mrs.) 04/07/64 04/11/64
Jones, John T. married Gross, Mary 02/12/63 02/14/63
Jones, Josephine married Mantle, William 01/17/61 01/18/61
Jones, Joshua married Jones, Anna 06/28/64 07/02/64
Jones, Josiah W. married Barnsby, Mary E. 06/09/64 06/14/64
Jones, Julia Ann Rebecca died 03/28/64 03/30/64
Jones, Julia M. married Mellor, James B. 06/01/63 07/03/63
Jones, Kate Anna died 06/05/64 06/06/64
Jones, Laura V. married Dicker, John J. 02/04/64 02/11/64
Jones, Leah O. married Gale, Grafton L. D. 07/16/63 07/18/63
Jones, Lewis married Barron, Mary E. 12/06/65 12/23/65
Jones, Lizzie married Hartzell, L. L. 11/23/63 12/23/63
Jones, M. Grace died 09/22/65 09/23/65
Jones, Madossa married Potter, Abraham S. 07/16/62 07/22/62
Jones, Maggie died 12/05/64 12/08/64
Jones, Manie M. married Watts, Columbus 05/18/65 05/20/65

Jones, Margaret Ann died 05/15/63   05/20/63
Jones, Margaretta married McCoy, Edmunds 01/14/62   01/17/62
Jones, Maria E. married Jameson, John 05/25/65   05/27/65
Jones, Mary died 12/23/62   12/25/62
Jones, Mary died 01/18/64   01/19/64
Jones, Mary married Kattington, Edward L. 10/25/64   10/29/64
Jones, Mary married Barbour, James 01/12/65   01/13/65
Jones, Mary A. married Shrote, John E. 02/22/65   03/29/65
Jones, Mary A. (Mrs.) died 10/05/64   10/19/64
Jones, Mary A. (Mrs.) married Jones, John 01/07/65   01/19/65
Jones, Mary Ann died 03/15/62   03/17/62
Jones, Mary Anna died 01/22/61   01/24/61
Jones, Mary Anne died 06/15/65   06/19/65
Jones, Mary Augusta married Deady, John L. 07/13/63   07/16/63
Jones, Mary E. married Shields, John William 02/11/61   03/20/61
Jones, Mary E. died 10/01/61   10/08/61
Jones, Mary E. died 10/01/61   10/09/61
Jones, Mary E. died 03/12/62   03/13/62
Jones, Mary E. died 10/07/64   10/17/64
Jones, Mary E. married Lodd, William H. (Capt.) 04/11/65   04/13/65
Jones, Mary E. (Mrs.) died 10/07/64   10/08/64
Jones, Mary Elizabeth died 05/18/65   05/19/65
Jones, Mary Henrietta married Harris, James A. 05/24/64   05/26/64
Jones, Mary Jane died 03/27/65   03/28/65
Jones, Mary S. died 05/20/65   05/22/65
Jones, Mary V. married Skinner, William J. 10/26/63   11/11/63
Jones, Matilda T. (Mrs.) died 08/14/65   08/15/65
Jones, Miley (Mrs.) died 11/07/64   11/08/64
Jones, Moses married Keys, Susan 06/26/62   07/01/62
Jones, Norval Wadsworth died 03/03/63   03/05/63
Jones, Owen D. died no date   09/13/61
Jones, Owen D. married Mason, Annie E. 06/20/65   06/23/65
Jones, P. T. W. married Tucker, Mary J. 02/14/61   02/18/61
Jones, Rachel married Selby, James H. 04/12/64   04/15/64
Jones, Reason died 01/13/64   01/19/64
Jones, Rebecca married Tipton, John H. 05/11/63   06/16/63
Jones, Richard died 09/10/64   08/12/64
Jones, Richard F. married Loveday, Anna 02/18/61   02/21/61
Jones, Robert died 08/25/62   08/26/62
Jones, Robert H. died 04/04/61   04/05/61
Jones, Ruth Eliza married Felkner, Alvan B. 07/19/64   07/21/64
Jones, Ruthey Ann died 06/18/63   06/20/63
Jones, S. Virginia married Morgan, Charles C. 06/08/63   06/10/63
Jones, Samuel George married Ward, Sophia T. 12/20/64   12/24/64
Jones, Sarah died 11/09/61   11/12/61
Jones, Sarah Amanda married Butler, John 11/16/64   11/17/64
Jones, Sarah Ann married White, Charles H. 08/21/62   08/25/62
Jones, Sarah Elizabeth Lloyd died 11/20/62   11/21/62
Jones, Sarah Ellen died 10/11/63   10/14/63
Jones, Sarah Rebecca died 02/06/63   02/09/63
Jones, Stephen married Posey, Chloe M. 03/27/65   03/30/65
Jones, Sue H. married Bridges, W. J. 12/11/62   12/16/62
Jones, Susan (Mrs.) died 03/08/63   03/09/63
Jones, Susan A. married Sterrett, Norman B. 04/05/64   04/15/64
Jones, Susannah died 03/27/64   03/28/64

```
Jones, Susie M. married Hugg, John H. 05/12/64  05/14/64
Jones, T. F. died no date   10/25/62
Jones, Thomas died 03/09/62  03/13/62
Jones, Thomas married Shinton, Annie E. 06/16/64  06/18/64
Jones, Thomas A. married Travers, Rose Ann 08/15/64  09/06/64
Jones, Thomas D. married Reed, Amelia 10/26/64  10/29/64
Jones, Thomas F. married Jackson, Mary E. 11/27/62  12/01/62
Jones, Thomas H. married Thomas, Mary E. 04/08/61  04/10/61
Jones, Thomas M. married Smith, Annie E. 10/31/64  11/02/64
Jones, Thomas W. married Thomas, Mary E. 04/08/61  04/13/61
Jones, Virginia A. married McCarthy, John 05/23/64  06/01/64
Jones, Walter R. died 12/20/62  12/23/62
Jones, William married Hevern, Harriet 12/31/61  01/02/62
Jones, William married McFadden, Sarah 08/19/62  09/04/62
Jones, William died 02/23/64  02/25/64
Jones, William died 08/30/65  08/31/65
Jones, William married Braby, Harriet 08/10/65  08/25/65
Jones, William Edgar died 05/05/65  05/06/65
Jones, William G. married Bell, Mary E. 11/03/63  11/17/63
Jones, William H. died 06/19/64  06/25/64
Jones, William M. married Williams, Hester A. R. 03/16/64  07/06/64
Jones, William T. died no date   10/04/61
Jones, William T. married Wood, Sarah A. 09/17/65  10/18/65
Jones, Willie Ann died 02/23/62  02/24/62
Jordan, Alexander married Niser, Elizabeth 11/20/64  11/22/64
Jordan, Charles Lee died 07/27/65  08/02/65
Jordan, Elizabeth died 01/03/64  01/05/64
Jordan, Ellen Virginia died 07/31/65  08/02/65
Jordan, Herman died 10/11/65  10/17/65
Jordan, James died 05/10/63  05/11/63
Jordan, James A. married Robinson, Mollie R. 12/18/61  12/20/61
Jordan, James B. died 09/25/63  09/30/63
Jordan, James H. married McCabe, Frances Ann 12/01/64  12/03/64
Jordan, John (Rev.) died 01/30/64  02/01/64
Jordan, John B. married Denney, Eliza C. (Mrs.) 02/07/65  02/11/65
Jordan, John E. married Luiz, M. Lizzie 12/22/62  12/29/62
Jordan, Johnna married Uhlhorn, Francis A. 12/26/61  12/27/61
Jordan, M. W. married Rohan, Elizabeth (Mrs.) 06/19/64  06/22/64
Jordan, Maggie married Gerdts, E. V. (Lt.) 06/19/65  06/28/65
Jordan, Martha married Mullan, William H. 12/13/64  12/19/64
Jordan, Mary E. married Downs, Henry 06/04/62  06/07/62
Jordan, Matilda married Booz, Edward G. 08/21/64  08/25/64
Jordan, Otella married Degollado, Mariano 02/02/64  02/03/64
Jordan, Rachel (Mrs.) died 06/09/63  06/10/63
Jordan, Rachel A. married Meachen, Thomas G. 11/15/64  12/14/64
Jordan, Richard J. married Thompson, Margaret M. 03/21/65  03/25/65
Jordan, Samuel died 08/19/65  08/21/65
Jordan, William, Sr. died 01/23/65  01/24/65
Jordon, William Benjamin died 03/16/64  03/18/64
Jory, John J. died 08/14/65  08/15/65
Jory, John, Sr. died 01/08/65  01/10/65
Joseph, Barbara Ann died 01/28/61  01/29/61
Joseph, John F. married Kelley, Annie 12/30/64  01/05/65
Joseph, Maggie married Getz, John 02/01/64  02/04/64
Joseph, Rebecca died 01/28/63  01/30/63
```

```
Josephthal, Moriz married Wise, Theresa 10/11/63   10/20/63
Jourdan, Ellen died 08/11/62   08/12/62
Journey, Mary (Mrs.) died 07/26/64   07/27/64
Joy, Edward died 06/23/64   07/04/64
Joy, Elizabeth (Mrs.) died 02/13/63   02/19/63
Joyce, Catharine (Mrs.) died 08/14/63   08/20/63
Joyce, Clara Estella died 06/15/64   06/16/64
Joyce, Delia Agnes died 06/14/64   06/15/64
Joyce, Delia Agnes died 06/14/64   06/16/64
Joyce, Elijah married Johnson, Catharine 12/22/62   01/05/63
Joyce, Eugenia Thomas died 08/23/65   08/28/65
Joyce, Grace died 02/08/61   02/09/61
Joyce, James A. A. married Shrote, Sarah Elizabeth 01/15/63   01/24/63
Joyce, John married Mulligan, Mary 05/13/63   05/19/63
Joyce, Josephine A. married Pettebone, J., Jr. 03/28/61   04/12/61
Joyce, Mollie E. married Mitchell, Jarrett, T. 04/03/64   04/23/64
Joyce, Robert Henry died 02/22/64   02/23/64
Joyce, S. H. married Nolan, Jane 12/07/65   12/18/65
Joyce, Thomas died 04/21/65   04/22/65
Joyce, Thomas died 04/21/65   04/24/65
Joyce, William married Gream, Harriet 09/12/61   09/14/61
Joyes, Helen Jean died 07/17/64   07/19/64
Joyes, Mary Anne died 05/03/62   05/05/62
Joyles, Edward J. married Jean, Marcella Isabel 03/04/62   03/06/62
Joynes, Edmund died 05/26/64   05/27/64
Judik, C. Josephine married Sawyer, William 11/21/65   11/23/65
Judik, Lidie married Smith, William H. V. 04/18/64   04/20/64
Judlin, Henry died 11/17/64   11/18/64
Judson, Charles C. (Rev.) married Fountain, Margaret 07/22/61   07/27/6
Jump, Charles H. married Thierrouch, Sallie D. 08/06/63   08/10/63
Jurnia, Mary E. married McGuiggen, James S. M. 09/25/64   09/27/64
Jury, Caroline Florance died 01/26/63   02/02/63
Jury, Eliza Jane died 02/11/62   02/12/62
Jury, Joseph M. married Warfield, Margaret Jane 09/15/62   09/17/62
Justice, Charles Thomas died 07/22/63   07/24/63
Justice, Emma C. married Penn, Jacob, Sr. 10/19/65   10/21/65
Justice, J. (Rev.) married Wheeler, Elizabeth J. 01/31/61   02/05/61
Justice, Mary E. married Franklin, George R. 05/10/64   05/11/64
Justis, Kate Isabella died 02/12/62   02/13/62
Justis, William F., Jr. married Arnold, Lizzie T. 01/15/61   01/19/61
Kabernagel, Louisa married Thiem, John 10/11/64   10/18/64
Kagan, Patrick married Donnelly, Mary J. 09/11/64   09/23/64
Kahler, Amalia F. died 05/30/62   05/31/62
Kahler, Jacob died 06/16/63   06/17/63
Kahlert, Frederick W. married Dipple, Mary L. 11/30/65   12/02/65
Kahlert, Gottfried died 03/16/64   03/19/64
Kahmer, John Casper died 08/20/64   08/23/64
Kahn, Adam married Baryey, Ruth A. 01/13/61   01/30/61
Kahn, Adam married Barley, Ruth A. 01/13/61   01/31/61
Kain, Patrick died 08/04/61   08/05/61
Kaiser, Lizzie married McGahan, John J. 05/01/65   05/06/65
Kaiser, Lizzie married McGahan, John J. 05/01/65   05/08/65
Kakman, Richard Henry died 02/06/63   02/07/63
Kalb, David married Long, Elizabeth 03/27/64   03/30/64
Kalb, Jacob married Bilmyer, Catherine 04/28/61   04/30/61
```

Kalb, Kate A. died 03/02/62 03/04/62
Kalbfus, Catherine (Mrs.) died 02/25/64 02/27/64
Kalbus, Louis married Mitchell, Mary Ann 04/12/62 04/14/62
Kalkman, Alexander E. died 10/29/63 11/02/63
Kall, Ann Florentine died 02/07/64 02/08/64
Kalling, Annie E. married Wendroth, Adolphus 04/03/64 04/04/64
Kalling, Lewis married Gray, Isabella A. 06/23/64 07/09/64
Kalmey, Mary E. died 05/14/62 05/17/62
Kalvelage, Annie M. married Bopp, Charles L. 08/16/64 08/17/64
Kalvelage, Henry died 03/05/65 03/08/65
Kammerer, Amelia married Gaehle, Lewis 09/01/63 09/05/63
Kan, Rebecca (Mrs.) died 01/23/65 01/25/65
Kane, Adam died 07/10/64 07/12/64
Kane, Helen Elinda Estelle died 09/25/63 09/26/63
Kane, James married McCourt, Ann 04/07/61 04/09/61
Kane, John died 11/28/65 11/29/65
Kane, Mary Ann married Butlee, Thomas 09/01/64 09/21/64
Kane, Michael died 01/24/64 01/26/64
Kane, Patrick died 05/17/63 05/18/63
Kann, Isabella died 11/13/62 11/14/62
Kann, Jacob married Lewyt, Caroline 05/18/62 05/19/62
Karen, Anna M. married Wolf, Henry C. 11/29/63 11/04/63
Karmrod, Mary (Mrs.) died 12/29/64 12/30/64
Karney, Laura Teresa died 02/25/62 03/07/62
Karthaus, F. K. married Keidel, George (Dr.) 12/27/60 01/04/61
Kating, Rachel died 03/30/62 04/01/62
Kattelman, Charles married Letmate, Mathilda 11/03/61 11/08/61
Katting, Rachael died 03/30/62 03/31/62
Kattington, Edward L. married Jones, Mary 10/25/64 10/29/64
Katzenberger, Josephine married Muth, M. Joseph 01/19/64 01/21/64
Katzenburger, Louis E. married Mallen, Rose M. 02/09/63 02/10/63
Kauffelt, James B. died 07/17/64 07/18/64
Kauffman, A. V. married Winer, W. 03/25/63 03/27/63
Kauffman, Amelia married Smith, A. C. 11/15/64 11/18/64
Kauffman, J. C. married Young, Isabella 01/03/61 02/12/61
Kauffman, Marion W. married Meads, Mary J. 09/14/62 09/16/62
Kauffman, Sarah (Mrs.) died 01/25/65 01/27/65
Kauffman, Virginia died 10/14/63 10/15/63
Kauffman, Warner Meeds died 11/10/64 11/12/64
Kaufman, Alice V. married Stup, Joseph C. 03/36/65 03/28/65
Kaufman, Indiana married Hall, Richard 09/22/63 09/25/63
Kaufman, Joseph married Stern, Rosa 12/01/61 12/02/61
Kaufman, Louis died 07/27/63 07/28/63
Kaufman, Louis died 07/27/63 07/29/63
Kaufman, M. E. J. married Dean, William 05/11/65 05/16/65
Kaufman, Mary married Crook, Francis A., Jr. 01/22/63 01/27/63
Kaufman, Rettie H. married Quell, William F. 09/12/64 09/14/64
Kaufmann, Mary Catherine died 08/03/63 08/06/63
Kaughman, Catherine (Mrs.) died 09/18/63 09/19/63
Kavanagh, James J. married Brady, Martha C. 04/17/65 04/26/65
Kavanaugh, Anne died 03/19/62 03/20/62
Kavanaugh, Dennis died 03/23/63 03/24/63
Kavanaugh, John died 11/02/63 11/04/63
Kavanaugh, Kate M. A. married Brady, Thomas 08/21/64 08/23/64
Kavanaugh, T. P. married Kuhn, Minnie 11/11/65 11/16/65

Keach, Rachel I. (Mrs.) died 12/09/64 12/10/64
Keagle, George P. married Pollard, Helen 10/10/64 10/22/64
Kean, Helen M. P. died 06/02/65 06/03/65
Kean, James G. died 04/11/65 04/19/65
Keane, Jane died 06/16/63 06/17/63
Kearfott, Robert W. died 12/24/64 12/29/64
Keargott, Robert W. died 12/24/64 12/28/64
Kearnes, Thomas died 12/18/62 12/19/62
Kearney, Catherine (Mrs.) died 03/31/64 04/02/64
Kearney, Charles married Collison, Sarah A. 02/12/63 02/21/63
Kearney, Edward married Dailey, Annie 09/05/65 09/14/65
Kearney, Ellenora died 03/14/65 03/15/65
Kearney, Ellenora died 03/14/65 03/16/65
Kearney, George died 01/05/64 01/06/64
Kearney, Rose died 11/18/61 11/19/61
Keaser, Robert J. married Buck, Mary Elizabeth 07/05/64 07/07/64
Keating, Martha J. married Roberts, Harry T. 02/16/63 02/19/63
Keating, Thomas J. married Webster, Sallie F. 06/12/62 06/13/62
Keating, William James died 11/21/64 11/22/64
Kech, Rose married Keech, William S. 11/12/63 11/14/63
Keck, Emily J. married Williams, Jesse W. 04/14/64 05/03/64
Keech, Edward P. married Johns, Lizzie 11/21/65 11/22/65
Keech, John R. (Rev.) died 12/16/61 12/17/61
Keech, Kate Hope married Barnard, John J. 11/12/63 11/14/63
Keech, Samuel C. died 11/04/64 11/09/64
Keech, William S. married Kech, Rose 11/12/63 11/14/63
Keedy, Samuel H. (Dr.) married Darley, Julia A. C. 11/09/65 11/14/65
Keedy, Samuel H. (Dr.) married Darley, Julia A. C. 11/09/65 11/15/65
Keefe, Jeremiah D. died 05/01/64 05/02/64
Keefe, John married Scharf, Laura V. 10/02/64 10/04/64
Keefer, Annie C. married Sevier, Charles E. 12/27/60 01/18/62
Keefer, Edward P. married Fisher, Lucinda J. 09/05/65 09/11/65
Keegan, Bridget married Donnelly, Ambrose 01/21/64 01/22/64
Keegan, John died 01/29/63 01/30/63
Keemple, Anne Maria married Hinkley, Edward Otis 06/11/61 06/14/61
Keen, Aquilla D. died 03/31/61 04/02/61
Keen, Edward M. died 07/30/65 07/31/65
Keen, George B. married Murphy, Mollie 10/03/61 10/04/61
Keen, George Rartol died 05/06/65 05/20/65
Keen, Lizzie married Michael, James H. 02/12/63 02/13/63
Keen, Millicent L. married Peters, C. George (Lt.) 11/24/64 12/07/64
Keen, Sallie J. married Meakin, Nathaniel 01/22/63 01/26/63
Keen, William married Mitchell, Sarah E. 05/24/64 06/03/64
Keenan, Daniel died 04/19/64 04/20/64
Keenan, Daniel died 04/19/64 04/21/64
Keenan, Daniel married Turner, Kate M. 01/15/65 10/05/65
Keenan, George P. died 08/26/61 08/27/61
Keenan, J. F. married Clyde, Kitty 12/12/64 12/28/64
Keenan, Margaret married McColgan, James 08/27/65 09/13/65
Keenan, Mary married Granger, Thomas 09/28/63 10/02/63
Keenan, Mary married Doyle, Michael E. 01/03/65 01/05/65
Keenan, Owen died 06/12/65 06/13/65
Keenan, Samuel died 07/09/63 07/15/63
Keenan, Sarah died 03/09/61 03/11/61
Keenan, Sarah married Craig, Robert R. 09/17/63 09/24/63

Keenan, Thomas married Barry, Mary C. 09/20/63   09/25/63
Keenan, William married Ryan, Mary E. 05/02/62   05/05/62
Keenan, William H. died 10/11/63   10/12/63
Keenan, William H. died 10/11/63   10/13/63
Keenan, William J. died 12/03/65   12/06/65
Keene, Benjamin R. died 09/02/63   09/03/63
Keene, Edward A. married Alder, Julia S. 10/21/63   10/28/63
Keene, Eliza J. (Mrs.) married Chappell, George W. 01/22/63   01/26/63
Keene, H. Augusta died 04/02/64   04/04/64
Keene, John H. married Cox, Mary Lizzie 06/29/64   07/02/64
Keene, Laura R. married D'unger, Robert (Dr.) 11/29/61   02/14/62
Keene, Mary A. married Carson, Thomas E. (Rev.) 04/30/63   05/08/63
Keene, Susan T. died 11/21/65   11/22/65
Keenem, John H. married Cox, Mary Lizzie 07/02/64   07/04/64
Keener, David (M.D.) died 07/30/61   07/31/61
Keener, George P. died 06/14/63   06/16/63
Keenright, Catherine (Mrs.) died 07/30/64   08/01/64
Keepner, Elijah married Elliott, Josephine E. 06/17/65   06/20/65
Keepner, Elijah married Elliott, Josephine 06/17/65   06/21/65
Keerl, George H. (Mrs.) died 04/13/65   04/15/65
Keerl, Richard Dobbs Spaight died 04/29/62   05/20/62
Kees, Bettie A. died 11/02/61   11/04/61
Kees, Francis Augustine died 04/12/62   04/14/62
Keese, Elizabeth Jane (Mrs.) died 01/09/63   01/10/63
Keferstein, Emile J. married Moelich, Bertha F. 03/26/63   03/31/63
Kegler, Barbara died 12/05/61   12/07/61
Kegler, John A. married Thompson, Mary Rosalia 01/10/65   01/20/65
Kegler, John G. married Busby, Ellen 06/07/64   06/14/64
Kehoe, Catharine died 08/16/63   08/17/63
Keidel, George (Dr.) married Karthaus, F. K. 12/27/60   01/04/61
Keifal, Martha L. married Rodenhi, Thomas S. 04/23/64   07/18/64
Keifel, Henry died 12/02/62   12/03/62
Keifel, Isabel married Sheffer, Jesse 12/10/61   12/12/61
Keifel, John G. married Isett, Mary A. H. 01/30/61   03/09/61
Keil, Caroline died 01/08/65   01/11/65
Keiley, Margaret K. married Byrnes, Michael 11/20/64   12/02/64
Keilholtz, Jacob married Iocket, Catherine 01/31/61   02/04/61
Keirie, Marion Annie married East, Caleb J. 07/11/64   07/14/64
Keirle, Emilie died 04/05/61   04/06/61
Keisle, Robert W. married Wirt, Elizabeth (Mrs.) 08/08/65   08/10/65
Keister, William H. married Hoffman, Mary E. 10/22/63   10/23/63
Keith, Charles A. died 04/14/64   04/16/64
Keith, George W. married Kelso, Sarah E. 02/11/63   02/14/63
Keithly, Jane (Mrs.) died 02/05/65   02/10/65
Keizer, Lewis R. married Rusk, Hester H. 12/26/65   12/28/65
Keizer, Lewis R. married Rusk, Hester A. 12/26/65   12/29/65
Kelbaugh, Jehu D. died 09/05/63   09/07/63
Kelbaugh, John D. died 11/02/62   11/03/62
Keleher, John died 10/25/62   12/04/62
Keley, Sebastian died 09/01/64   09/03/64
Kell, Mary Ann died 03/01/62   03/08/62
Kell, Peter married Sullivan, Honorah F. 01/14/62   04/23/62
Kelledy, Larence died 09/29/65   09/30/65
Keller, Alice Vernon died 03/05/64   03/08/64
Keller, Andrew J. married Miller, Amelia J. 03/08/63   04/30/63

Keller, Catherine (Mrs.) died 02/17/64 02/18/64
Keller, Conrad died 01/31/62 02/06/62
Keller, George married Nugent, Lizzie 07/06/64 12/03/64
Keller, George J. married Pool, Matilda 05/31/64 06/07/64
Keller, Harry M. married Woodruff, Jennie H. 04/13/64 04/19/64
Keller, Henry died 02/16/65 02/06/65
Keller, Jacob J. married Scott, Lizzie 12/29/64 01/14/65
Keller, John H. married Zimmerman, Corrilla 03/31/63 05/18/63
Keller, Margaret died 03/17/64 03/18/64
Keller, Otho J. married Burnett, Maggie 02/17/64 02/19/64
Keller, Sarah M. died 08/30/63 09/01/63
Keller, Thomas Henry died 05/24/64 05/26/64
Kelley, Alexander died 02/03/65 02/04/65
Kelley, Annie married Joseph, John F. 12/30/64 01/05/65
Kelley, Barney married Hawkins, Catherine 02/26/65 03/03/65
Kelley, Catherine (Mrs.) died 02/18/63 02/19/63
Kelley, Charcillar died 12/12/61 12/13/61
Kelley, Charles D. married Rouch, Elizabeth 04/19/63 04/21/63
Kelley, Charles M. died 08/01/63 08/05/63
Kelley, Elisha F. married Talbott, Lizzie 10/31/61 11/06/61
Kelley, Henry H, died 01/19/64 01/20/64
Kelley, John died 08/25/64 08/30/64
Kelley, John B. married Hawthorn, Sallie E. 09/13/65 09/30/65
Kelley, John J. died 01/25/62 02/11/62
Kelley, Maggie died 05/22/63 05/23/63
Kelley, Mary C. married Homann, Adam 08/22/61 09/07/61
Kelley, Oliver J. married Perigoy, A. J. 12/24/61 12/25/61
Kelley, Patrick died 10/14/62 10/15/62
Kelley, Thomas died 11/22/61 11/23/61
Kelley, William died 12/09/62 12/10/62
Kelley, William H. married Brown, Angeline 06/12/65 06/13/65
Kelliher, John died 05/11/65 05/13/65
Kellman, Elizabeth died 04/23/62 04/30/62
Kellman, Mary Augusta died 07/14/64 07/20/64
Kelly, Anna Isabel died 03/26/65 03/28/65
Kelly, Bridget died 01/11/61 01/12/61
Kelly, Bridget died 10/18/63 10/19/63
Kelly, Bridget A. (Mrs.) married Filgate, Thomas 04/27/65 04/29/65
Kelly, Bridget C. married Cummins, Daniel G. 11/12/63 11/24/63
Kelly, Catherine married Spradling, John W. 10/03/61 10/09/61
Kelly, Catherine died 05/16/62 05/17/62
Kelly, Catherine married Lacey, James J. 06/29/62 07/07/62
Kelly, Catherine (Mrs.) died 02/10/63 02/11/63
Kelly, Catherine (Mrs.) died 05/09/64 05/10/64
Kelly, Cicelia married Suter, George A. 12/26/64 12/31/64
Kelly, Ellen married Wigley, George 07/08/63 07/16/63
Kelly, Ellen M. (Mrs.) died 07/27/64 07/29/64
Kelly, Francis died 04/06/64 04/08/64
Kelly, Francis (Mrs.) died 01/20/64 01/22/64
Kelly, Francis P. died 04/03/64 04/04/64
Kelly, Hugh married Hoshell, Mary Ellen 06/07/65 06/13/65
Kelly, Ida Amelia died 08/25/62 08/26/62
Kelly, James died 10/08/62 10/10/62
Kelly, James died 10/13/62 10/15/62
Kelly, James died 11/18/63 11/21/63

Kelly, James died 12/06/64   12/07/64
Kelly, James married Reilley, Rose A. 04/20/65   04/28/65
Kelly, James Edward died 04/02/64   04/04/64
Kelly, James Francis died 01/15/62   01/16/62
Kelly, Janie married Benson, William D. 03/04/62   03/06/62
Kelly, John died 08/03/62   08/05/62
Kelly, John died 09/26/62   09/30/62
Kelly, John died 02/25/64   02/26/64
Kelly, John died 11/17/65   11/18/65
Kelly, John married Herbert, Martha A. 02/02/65   02/03/65
Kelly, John C. married Williams, Louisa J. 05/09/64   05/11/64
Kelly, Joseph died 07/27/65   07/27/65
Kelly, Lewis S. died 09/05/65   09/09/65
Kelly, Maggie died 11/19/63   11/20/63
Kelly, Margaret died 01/10/62   01/16/62
Kelly, Margaret died 11/28/65   11/30/65
Kelly, Margaret (Mrs.) died 03/27/64   03/28/64
Kelly, Martin died 12/14/62   01/24/63
Kelly, Martin, Sr. died 07/12/64   07/13/64
Kelly, Mary died 02/16/61   02/18/61
Kelly, Mary married Landry, Elias 10/15/63   10/20/63
Kelly, Mary A. married Rearden, William H. 02/02/64   02/08/64
Kelly, Mary Ann died 12/21/62   12/23/62
Kelly, Mary Catharine died 01/07/62   01/08/62
Kelly, Mary Christina died 01/13/62   01/15/62
Kelly, Mary Christina died 01/13/62   01/16/62
Kelly, Mervin Leaf died 05/27/61   05/28/61
Kelly, Michael died 07/28/65   07/31/65
Kelly, Nancy married Clark, William 03/30/64   04/01/64
Kelly, Nelly died 06/15/65   06/17/65
Kelly, Patrick died no date   02/17/65
Kelly, Peter died 11/01/62   11/03/62
Kelly, Priscilla married Schafer, Daniel R. 10/06/63   10/07/63
Kelly, Robert married Koning, Catharine 04/29/62   05/03/62
Kelly, Sarah Elizabeth (Mrs.) died 10/05/63   10/06/63
Kelly, Thomas died 04/26/61   04/27/61
Kelly, Thomas died 02/24/64   02/26/64
Kelly, Thomas A. died 09/01/65   09/02/65
Kelly, Varina D. died 04/16/65   04/17/65
Kelly, William B. married Duffy, Mary A. 04/11/64   04/20/64
Kelly, William E. died 04/06/65   04/07/65
Kelly, William H. married Beal, Maria T. 11/30/65   12/01/65
Kelly, William J. S. died 04/27/64   05/14/64
Kelly, William L. married Ford, Mary A. 05/26/64   05/28/64
Kelly, William O. married Stafford, Catherine 12/30/60   01/03/61
Kelly, William Q. S. died 04/27/64   05/13/64
Kelly, William Thomas died 01/03/61   01/04/61
Kelly, William Thomas died 12/19/64   12/20/64
Kelmling, Bianca Baptista married Calvert, John B. 09/14/64   09/16/64
Kelsey, Frank Nelson died 02/27/64   02/29/64
Kelso, J. Russell married Richardson, Florence 11/07/61   11/08/61
Kelso, Maria D. C. married Goodfellow, Charles M. 11/13/65   11/20/65
Kelso, Sarah E. married Keith, George W. 02/11/63   02/14/63
Kelty, George W. died 08/14/64   08/17/64
Kelty, Mary Elizabeth married Jones, George W. 02/03/63   02/09/63

Kemp, Ann Liza (Mrs.) died 01/14/63   01/20/63
Kemp, Catherine Ann married Myers, O. A. 09/10/61   09/11/61
Kemp, Ella married Wolf, Edmond J. (Rev.) 12/13/65   12/14/65
Kemp, Ellen died 10/10/65   10/11/65
Kemp, Ellen (Mrs.) died 10/10/65   10/12/65
Kemp, Emily B. married Goldsborough, Charles E. 10/01/61   10/07/61
Kemp, Emily V. died 10/03/65   10/05/65
Kemp, Georgia Gibson died 01/29/64   01/30/64
Kemp, Grace died 05/27/62   05/28/62
Kemp, Joseph H. married Wrightson, Rebecca 11/01/65   11/18/65
Kemp, Laura P. died 04/18/63   04/20/63
Kemp, Margaret A. married Dolliver, William T. (USN) 11/30/65   12/05/6
Kemp, Mary died 07/15/64   07/18/64
Kemp, Mary E. married Smith, G. W. 10/31/65   11/07/65
Kemp, Mary V. married Smith, James H. 03/03/64   04/12/64
Kemp, Nannie Dora died 10/29/63   10/31/63
Kemp, Oliver married Noll, Katee 11/14/65   11/17/65
Kemp, Richard married Shaw, Bell S. 10/03/65   10/05/65
Kemp, Simon died no date   07/28/65
Kemp, Simon J. married Dorsey, Maria L. 11/16/65   11/21/65
Kemp, Thomas E. married Patterson, Binnie G. 11/21/65   11/25/65
Kemp, William A. died 02/29/64   03/02/64
Kemp, William H. (Lt.) died 08/07/64   09/02/64
Kemp, William T. (Dr., USN) died 03/31/64   04/12/64
Kemper, Catherine E. married Bieghtler, George W. 08/16/64   09/01/64
Kemper, Hugh Fisher died 03/18/65   03/28/65
Kemper, John married Stallings, Maggie 09/18/64   09/20/64
Kemple, Alice Rebecca died 06/19/65   06/20/65
Kemps, Lizzie married Everett, William 12/28/63   01/02/64
Kempton, Maria Louisa died 07/23/62   07/25/62
Kempton, Moses died 07/12/64   07/13/64
Ken, Jason married Walker, Mary A. 09/01/64   10/01/64
Kenan, Anna married Brady, Patrick 01/12/62   01/13/62
Kendall, George died 07/05/63   07/07/63
Kendall, James Custus died no date   08/19/65
Kendall, Mary Ann died 01/13/65   01/14/65
Kendall, Thomas (Dr.) died 10/16/63   01/13/64
Kendell, Charles married Oursler, Maggie 07/30/62   09/22/62
Kenedy, Julia Cecilia died 06/07/65   06/08/65
Kengston, Maria Louisa died 07/23/62   07/24/62
Kenly, Edward died 04/29/61   04/30/61
Kenly, Edward died 04/29/61   05/01/61
Kenly, William L. married Hook, E. Marion 05/12/61   06/19/61
Kenly, William L. married Hook, E. Marion 05/12/61   06/20/61
Kennard, Anna R. died 06/15/65   06/19/65
Kennard, Anne married McKinney, James 08/23/65   08/25/65
Kennard, Clara Virginia married Gregg, Thomas C. 02/24/61   02/26/61
Kennard, John R. married Worthington, Emma 01/29/64   03/26/64
Kennard, Joseph Willis died 04/06/63   04/07/63
Kennard, Lewis E. married Scott, R. V. 01/26/65   01/31/65
Kennard, Lewis E. (Lt.) married Scott, R. V. 01/26/65   02/01/65
Kennard, Marion A. married Peck, John D. 10/25/63   10/28/63
Kennard, S. Louisa married Webb, Nathaniel H. 05/19/63   05/20/63
Kennard, Sarah Louisa died 10/04/62   10/07/62
Kennard, Virginia Floral died 07/05/65   07/08/65

Kenne, Ann (Mrs.) died 08/22/65 08/23/65
Kennedy, Amelia T. died 11/28/64 11/30/64
Kennedy, Anna married Davis, John J. 08/21/62 08/23/62
Kennedy, Antoinette married Crighton, Malcolm 06/15/65 06/17/65
Kennedy, Catherine died 09/11/62 09/12/62
Kennedy, Dennis died 08/02/64 08/03/64
Kennedy, Elizabeth married Magill, Charles J. 09/04/64 09/30/64
Kennedy, Elizabeth LePage died 07/08/63 07/10/63
Kennedy, Fanny Howell (Mrs.) died 10/31/64 11/01/64
Kennedy, George A. died 08/19/64 08/20/64
Kennedy, Georgie Virginia died 05/17/64 05/18/64
Kennedy, Henry C. married Hart, Eveline 01/30/63 02/07/63
Kennedy, Herbert M. married Buck, Belle 01/28/63 02/02/63
Kennedy, Hugh T. died 05/24/64 05/25/64
Kennedy, John died 12/22/62 12/23/62
Kennedy, John J. married Engel, Minnie A. 04/16/65 07/19/65
Kennedy, Joseph M. died 03/01/63 03/31/63
Kennedy, Kate married Quinn, Mathew E. 08/14/64 08/22/64
Kennedy, Levi married Stewart, Isabella 04/19/63 04/21/63
Kennedy, Mary Ann died 03/28/64 04/02/64
Kennedy, Mary E. (Mrs.) died 12/17/65 12/18/65
Kennedy, Mary J. married Cromwell, Richard 01/31/61 02/04/61
Kennedy, Philip Clayton (Cpt.) died 08/30/64 09/01/64
Kennedy, Philip Clayton (Cpt.) died 08/31/64 09/02/64
Kennedy, Philip Pendleton died 08/01/64 08/03/64
Kennedy, Rebecca P. (Mrs.) died 05/29/63 06/02/63
Kennedy, Sarah H. died 12/11/62 12/12/62
Kennedy, William married Culbertson, Ellen A. 06/04/63 06/05/63
Kennedy, William T. H. married Sunstrom, Rachel 11/25/62 02/25/63
Kennedy, William W. married McDonough, Susie 05/27/62 05/29/62
Kennel, John W. died 07/27/62 09/02/62
Kenney, Agnes married Burgen, John J. 06/04/63 06/12/63
Kenney, Guillema M. died 05/13/62 05/14/62
Kenney, James T. married Davis, Rowena E. R. 11/25/62 12/01/62
Kenney, Joseph P. died 05/27/62 05/28/62
Kenney, Joseph P. died 05/27/62 05/29/62
Kenney, Mary died 12/29/61 12/30/61
Kenney, Mary Frances died 02/07/63 02/10/63
Kenney, Sue E. married Gibbons, J. Thomas 12/26/64 12/29/64
Kenney, Thomas died 10/27/64 10/28/64
Kenny, Emily A. C. (Mrs.) died 05/11/64 05/14/64
Kenny, Hannah Jane died 05/24/64 05/25/64
Kenny, John Francis died 12/14/64 12/15/64
Kenny, Mary married Parlet, Henry J. 05/28/62 06/04/62
Kenny, Michael died 08/03/63 08/05/63
Kenny, Thomas Steel died 08/15/61 08/21/61
Kenny, William married Seward, Charlotte 10/08/61 11/06/61
Kensett, Amelia Wheeler died 11/17/64 11/18/64
Kensett, Amelia Wheeler died 11/17/64 11/19/64
Kensett, Thomas H. married Reese, Mary A. R. (Mrs.) 10/19/65 10/20/65
Kent, Charles F. died 04/27/65 04/29/65
Kent, Daniel died 05/22/62 05/28/62
Kent, George A. died 08/19/64 08/20/64
Kent, Mary (Mrs.) died 05/19/63 05/20/63
Kent, Sallie O. M. died 12/19/62 12/20/62

Kent, William Jessie married Simpson, Mary C. 05/10/65 05/16/65
Keogh, Annie Virginia died 02/05/64 02/06/64
Kepler, Elizabeth Ann married Owens, Philip 05/08/64 07/23/64
Kepler, Mary Eliza married Hitzelberger, Joseph K. 04/04/64 04/11/64
Kepler, Samuel, Jr. (Dr.) married Risteau, Kate V. 05/02/61 05/04/61
Kepler, Susan died 06/27/61 06/28/61
Kepler, Susan Aletheia died 12/30/62 01/01/63
Keppel, Lemuel A. married Gorsuch, Maggie A. 12/27/65 12/30/65
Keppler, George W. married Bunch, Ellen C. 01/03/65 01/19/65
Kerby, George S. died 06/01/64 06/06/64
Kerchner, Ann Caroline married Hessler, Michael 07/04/65 07/10/65
Kerchner, Mary died 06/17/61 06/18/61
Kerchner, Mary Catherine died 06/29/61 07/01/61
Kerley, John died 08/18/65 08/19/65
Kerlinger, Annie Wilson died 06/05/65 06/07/65
Kerlinger, Eliza A. married Hughes, William W. 03/26/63 03/28/63
Kerlinger, Sarah Catherine died 01/22/62 01/23/62
Kermode, John died 10/08/65 10/10/65
Kern, Eleanora married Brady, Curtis P. 03/03/63 03/06/63
Kernan, James married Reed, Ann V. 10/26/65 10/28/65
Kernan, James married Reed, Ann V. 10/26/65 10/30/65
Kernan, Julia E. (Mrs.) died 03/08/63 03/16/63
Kernan, Lottie died 08/07/64 08/10/64
Kerndl, Charles married Bregel, Margaret A. 04/15/62 04/23/62
Kerner, Elizabeth Jane married Dunn, Joseph 01/01/62 01/08/62
Kerner, M. H. married Ladenslager, Georgie 12/02/62 12/04/62
Kerney, Augustus died 03/30/62 04/01/62
Kerney, Catharine died 01/02/62 01/06/62
Kerney, M. J. died 03/16/61 03/18/61
Kerney, Mary A. married McLaughlin, William 12/28/62 01/19/63
Kerngood, Tobias married Mastbaum, Julia G. 06/24/63 06/29/63
Kerns, Bernard married Callahan, Ellen 09/25/64 09/28/64
Kerns, Thomas died 08/08/61 08/10/61
Kerr, Agnes E. married Snyder, Henry 10/09/61 10/12/61
Kerr, Ann married Elliot, George W. 03/07/65 04/05/65
Kerr, Catherine married Emerich, John 03/20/64 03/21/64
Kerr, Edward L. married Alexander, Fanny 03/19/64 03/21/64
Kerr, Haddie I. D. died 12/11/61 12/12/61
Kerr, James W. married Gardner, Mollie A. 10/13/63 10/16/63
Kerr, Jane Eliza died 04/01/61 04/02/61
Kerr, John M. married Forman, Harriet E. 06/24/63 07/02/63
Kerr, Margaret C. married Delawder, Andrew N. 02/20/62 02/24/62
Kerr, Robert died 05/08/61 05/09/61
Kerr, Susannah married Gessford, James W. 01/18/65 01/25/65
Kerr, Thomas married Gautlow, Mary E. 12/28/63 01/02/64
Kerr, William John died 04/21/61 04/22/61
Kershaw, Charles K. (USN) married Barnes, Emy L. 03/09/64 08/06/64
Kershaw, Charles K. (USV) married Barnes, Emy L. 03/09/64 08/04/64
Kershaw, George H. died 05/22/63 06/04/63
Kersler, Thomas V. married DeCorms, Sarah C. 01/19/65 01/20/65
Kerwin, Ann died 02/07/61 02/08/61
Kerwin, Mary E. married McKanna, Thomas 07/02/65 07/07/65
Kesmodel, Louise died 08/10/63 08/11/63
Kesmodel, Martin married Haurand, Lizzie 12/25/64 12/31/64
Kesmodle, Elizabeth (Mrs.) died 06/08/63 06/09/63

Kesmodle, Elizabeth (Mrs.) died 06/08/63   06/10/63
Kessler, John died 03/22/65   03/24/65
Kessler, Lanah (Mrs.) died 02/11/64   02/12/64
Kessler, Lizzie married Welsh, Napoleon B. 08/09/64   08/10/64
Kessler, Maggie married Taylor, John S. 05/14/63   05/16/63
Kessler, Margaretta (Mrs.) died 01/02/63   01/03/63
Kessler, Mary A. married Heckel, Henry 06/22/65   06/24/65
Ketchum, Frederick M. married Helm, Charlotte M. 05/29/64   06/06/64
Kettering, Peter died 06/10/63   06/11/63
Kettlewell, Edward Randolph died 10/20/64   12/07/64
Kettlewell, John died 09/12/63   09/14/63
Key, Eliza Scott died 09/29/62   10/01/62
Key, Fanny died 02/12/63   02/14/63
Key, Josephine married Stephenson, John R. 05/01/65   05/05/65
Key, Marshall P. died 03/20/62   03/22/62
Key, Willie died 02/24/65   03/01/65
Keyes, Hester Ann married Tilghman, Richard 09/15/64   09/17/64
Keys, Annie Stewart Newman died 02/02/62   02/08/62
Keys, Catharine died 02/09/62   02/11/62
Keys, Emma E. married De Beet, Duncan H. 12/02/61   12/04/61
Keys, Frank Albert died 12/21/63   12/23/63
Keys, Hanson H. married Williams, Elizabeth A. 11/25/62   12/01/62
Keys, Mary Ann E. married Zolhnoffer, Fred 07/18/62   07/21/62
Keys, Mary Fickey died 08/11/64   08/13/64
Keys, Mary Fickey died 08/11/64   08/16/64
Keys, Priscilla Taylor died 02/13/65   02/15/65
Keys, Robert Taylor died 02/19/64   02/20/64
Keys, Susan married Jones, Moses 06/26/62   07/01/62
Keys, William died 09/19/63   09/21/63
Keys, William W. married Willing, Christiana 06/06/65   06/08/65
Keyser, George D. died 03/06/64   03/08/64
Keyser, George D. died 03/06/64   03/09/64
Keyser, H. Irvine married Washington, Mary A. 11/17/64   11/19/64
Keyser, James died 05/10/63   05/11/63
Keyser, John Wyman died 08/19/61   08/21/61
Keyser, Julia married Coblens, Lewis 04/14/65   05/16/65
Keyser, Margaret married Shilling, John Charles 11/25/63   11/28/63
Keyser, Mary Brent died no date   08/19/62
Keyser, Mary Catharine married Maynard, James F. 12/10/62   12/12/62
Keyser, William W. died 04/13/63   04/16/63
Keyser, William W. married Walker, Alice 06/13/64   06/14/64
Keyworth, Isabella A. married McKeever, Joseph E. 02/11/62   02/12/62
Khue, Baszal M. married Needhaven, Josephine 07/29/63   08/04/63
Kibler, Alice Trevister died 03/22/62   03/24/62
Kidd, Amelia married Gould, John R. 02/04/64   02/05/64
Kidd, Charles Henry I. died 07/22/61   07/29/61
Kidd, Elizabeth (Mrs.) married Davidson, William 03/27/64   04/20/64
Kidd, James died 05/01/61   05/03/61
Kidd, James W. died 03/17/62   03/18/62
Kidd, Joshua H. died 10/06/64   10/07/64
Kidd, Juliana died 07/30/63   08/01/63
Kidd, Lewis died 12/11/65   12/13/65
Kidd, Moses married Crow, Isabella 12/25/62   12/27/62
Kidd, Sarah E. married McCallister, Archibald 05/04/65   05/08/65
Kidd, Sarah Ruth died 10/01/62   10/02/62

Kidd, William P. died 08/12/63   08/13/63
Kiel, Philip P. died 03/24/65   03/31/65
Kiely, Mary married Cushley, John A. 05/14/65   10/16/65
Kienzle, Sophia E. married Wagner, John 06/26/64   06/28/64
Kierchoff, Elizabeth married Donaldson, Alexander 07/18/65   07/19/65
Kierle, Mary Jane died 06/04/62   05/05/62
Kiernan, Bernard died 12/19/62   12/20/62
Kile, Rachel (Mrs.) died 01/13/65   01/16/65
Kilgour, John died 12/14/64   12/15/64
Killalea, Margaret died 05/31/61   06/01/61
Killard, Alicia married Moran, Charles 06/18/65   06/20/65
Killelea, Michael died 06/19/64   06/21/64
Killen, Bridget (Mrs.) died 07/24/64   07/25/64
Killen, Joseph died 11/15/64   11/16/64
Killen, Thomas married Burns, Rachel Agnes 03/14/62   03/18/62
Killian, George F. married Ament, Margaret 04/04/65   04/06/65
Killian, Matthew died 07/16/62   07/17/62
Killin, Anne B. married Trego, James D. 01/23/61   01/26/61
Killman, William T. married Short, Ann G. 07/14/64   07/15/64
Killmon, John died 01/03/62   01/04/62
Killmon, Thomas T. married Preston, Anna Nora 08/19/60   10/07/62
Kilmartin, Bernard married Boyle, Mary no date   11/30/64
Kilmer, Harry C. married March, Annie L. 05/12/63   05/14/63
Kilmer, John W. married Nugent, A. Jane 10/07/62   10/10/62
Kilmon, Thomas E. married Jay, Kate F. 11/07/65   11/15/65
Kilpatrick, Laura V. died 02/19/61   02/21/61
Kilpatrick, Mary Ann died 08/31/62   09/02/62
Kilpatrick, Rachel married Anderson, George H. 04/07/64   04/26/64
Kilpatrick, Samuel Joseph died 01/15/63   01/17/63
Kilpatrick, Susan died 01/20/62   01/22/62
Kilpaugh, Jane (Mrs.) married Hindle, John 10/06/64   11/05/64
Kilroe, James died 01/27/61   01/28/61
Kimball, Elizabeth Middleton died 11/27/61   11/28/61
Kimball, Ephraim C. married Bouchet, Anna M. 12/03/63   12/08/63
Kimball, George S. married Baker, Mary M. 03/26/62   04/12/62
Kimball, John W. married Long, Mary Ophelia 03/06/61   03/14/61
Kimball, Lydia died 05/01/62   05/02/62
Kimball, Mary E. married Vansant, James H. 11/05/63   11/17/63
Kimball, Mary Ophelia died 12/28/61   12/30/61
Kimberly, Cornelia R. married Potts, Richard C. 04/11/61   04/13/61
Kimberly, Mary died 04/07/65   04/10/65
Kimberly, Nathaniel died 03/04/63   03/06/63
Kimberly, Nathaniel died 03/04/63   03/07/63
Kimble, Sarah E. married Grace, Aaron D. 02/06/61   02/09/61
Kimble, Sarah E. married Grace, Aaron O. 02/06/61   02/11/61
Kimble, William married Weeks, Rebecca 01/24/62   02/04/62
Kimburg, Mary died 04/07/65   04/08/65
Kimerly, Mary died 05/30/64   06/01/64
Kimmel, Catherine (Mrs.) died 10/07/65   10/10/65
Kimmelresh, Louise married Lansburgh, Gustave 01/04/65   01/09/65
Kincaid, W. H. (Rev.) married Amos, Annie E. 02/13/62   02/14/62
Kindig, Susan J. married Powell, James H. 10/20/63   10/27/63
Kine, Rosina married Meyer, Georgie 01/17/62   01/23/62
Kine, Rosina married Meyer, George 01/17/62   01/24/62
Kines, Dolly Jane died 11/18/63   11/19/63

King, Albert T. married Widerman, Barbara E. 05/31/65 06/07/65
King, Alexander K. married Reed, Anne 07/02/62 07/12/62
King, Alexander R. married Burgan, Cassandra 11/04/63 01/19/64
King, Amanda M. (Mrs.) died 12/18/64 12/20/64
King, Amelia J. died 07/25/65 07/26/65
King, Amos Patterson died 07/31/62 08/01/62
King, Andrew married Dunham, Mary J. 02/01/64 02/03/64
King, Ann Rebecca married Calvert, William Thomas 07/30/63 09/08/63
King, Bell died 09/17/64 09/19/64
King, Benjamin B. married Pell, Theresa C. 04/18/61 07/31/61
King, Bridget (Mrs.) died 02/05/64 02/06/64
King, Calvin J. married Goodrick, Mollie L. 01/26/64 01/28/64
King, Catherine died 05/13/62 05/14/62
King, Charlotte L. died 09/11/65 09/12/65
King, Darby died 03/20/64 03/21/64
King, David died 05/21/65 05/24/65
King, Elizabeth married Horney, Thomas 04/28/61 05/08/61
King, Elizabeth (Mrs.) died 09/01/63 09/03/63
King, Emma Agnes (Mrs.) died 08/21/65 08/23/65
King, Esther Ann married Brown, Luke 12/15/64 12/17/64
King, Francis married Fifer, Alexina E. 03/15/63 04/01/63
King, George married Waters, Elizabeth A. 01/24/64 01/26/64
King, George B. died 11/10/61 11/12/61
King, George R. died 07/13/63 07/14/63
King, George R. died 07/13/63 07/15/63
King, George W. married McGlothlan, Elizabeth 08/26/64 08/31/64
King, George W., Jr. married Gibson, Laura A. 01/31/61 02/02/61
King, Hannah married Chew, Sutton 09/28/62 09/30/62
King, Harriet J. died 06/02/65 06/03/65
King, Harry Lee died 07/15/65 07/18/65
King, Heisler Mervin died 12/09/61 12/12/61
King, Hester died 12/22/62 12/23/62
King, John C. married Petticord, Catharine 09/25/65 10/03/65
King, Joseph married Davis, Mary Jane 08/28/62 08/29/62
King, Joseph A. married McElvaney, Mary E. 12/20/63 12/24/63
King, Joseph, Jr. died 10/29/65 10/30/65
King, Katie Ashley died 06/17/64 06/18/64
King, Lemuel B. married Cooper, Maria L. 10/17/64 11/17/64
King, Lizzie died 05/09/65 05/10/65
King, Louisa A. married Nunn, Stephen E. 07/06/62 07/24/62
King, Maggie married Benezet, George W. 02/25/64 02/27/64
King, Mardon married Hatcraft, Elizabeth 12/22/61 07/10/62
King, Margaret A. died 06/18/62 06/19/62
King, Margaret A. died 06/18/62 06/20/62
King, Margaret Ann died 06/04/61 06/05/61
King, Marie Christine died 02/05/65 02/07/65
King, Mary (Mrs.) died 08/02/63 08/03/63
King, Mary E. married Smith, Nicholas M. 04/23/63 04/27/63
King, Mary Jane married Homillur, M. B. 02/08/64 02/09/64
King, Mary L. married Spaulding, Alva E. 06/22/65 06/27/65
King, Mollie died 05/11/65 05/12/65
King, Samuel R. married Warner, Maggie V. 10/19/63 11/16/63
King, Sarah C. married Ricktor, Samuel 04/09/65 06/05/65
King, Sophia (Mrs.) died 02/05/64 02/12/64
King, W. H. died 01/19/62 01/21/62

King, Wallace married Armstrong, Rebecca 10/16/61   10/17/61
King, Walter W. married Chester, Annie 12/18/62   02/14/63
King, William died 07/13/62   07/14/62
King, William F. died 12/03/62   12/05/62
King, William H. married Mullikin, Olivia 10/26/65   10/30/65
Kingston, Catharine married Marin, George W. 02/19/64   02/24/64
Kinidy, Mary Catherine died 11/06/61   11/07/61
Kinkade, J. Nixon (Lt.) married Rhoderick, Susie 11/19/63   11/30/63
Kinnear, William James died 03/11/63   03/12/63
Kinnemon, Rebecca D. married Tregoe, George W. 10/15/61   10/18/61
Kinsey, Alfred died 07/11/64   07/12/64
Kinsey, Emma died 07/05/62   07/07/62
Kinsey, Johnm married Price, Mary A. 11/22/62   11/27/62
Kinsley, Kate married Curley, James F. 11/03/63   01/30/64
Kinsley, Samuel G. married Curley, Florence R. 02/18/64   02/22/64
Kinstendorff, Jane died 02/22/61   03/13/61
Kipp, John died 02/14/62   02/15/62
Kipp, John W. died 07/14/62   07/15/62
Kirby, Alice C. married Ross, William 04/15/62   05/15/62
Kirby, Amanda married Newkirk, Edward V. 09/08/63   09/17/63
Kirby, Charles A. died 10/14/62   10/17/62
Kirby, Edward Elsworth died 07/04/65   07/06/65
Kirby, Emma R. married Sowders, Harman B. 03/25/63   03/28/63
Kirby, Frances married O'Neill, H. E. (Sgt.) 11/12/63   12/29/63
Kirby, George J. married Devillin, Mary E. 10/05/61   11/25/61
Kirby, Isaac (Capt.) died 01/26/62   01/28/62
Kirby, Isabella V. married Hall, William W. 05/20/62   09/10/62
Kirby, James died 03/15/64   03/17/64
Kirby, James H. married Love, Mary Louisa 12/26/62   02/14/63
Kirby, James S. married Meredith, Emma F. 03/03/63   03/10/63
Kirby, John died 07/05/61   07/06/61
Kirby, John F. died 06/08/63   06/18/63
Kirby, L. Lavinia A. died 03/12/65   03/14/65
Kirby, L. Lavinia A. (Mrs.) died 03/12/65   03/13/65
Kirby, Laura E. married Lloyd, Thomas 01/06/64   01/13/64
Kirby, M. E. married Reed, J. L. 04/25/65   05/29/65
Kirby, Mary Gordon married Emory, Arthur 01/17/65   01/18/65
Kirby, Richard H. married McComas, Olevia J. 07/05/64   07/06/64
Kirby, Richard Henry married Tydings, Hannah Ann 10/10/61   10/29/61
Kirby, Samuel died 02/28/61   03/01/61
Kirby, Thomas Edward married Reilly, Rosetta Virginia 09/27/64   10/01/
Kirby, William died 09/15/61   10/12/61
Kirk, Albina P. (Mrs.) died 12/23/65   12/25/65
Kirk, Charles D. married Anderson, Cassie A. 04/02/61   04/03/61
Kirk, Elijah married Sheridan, Lizzie 02/21/65   03/04/65
Kirk, Ella E. married Bolgiano, Gilbert C. 06/11/61   06/27/61
Kirk, George married Orem, Catherine 06/05/63   06/16/63
Kirk, Harriet J. died 10/08/61   10/09/61
Kirk, James A. married Anderson, Sarah E. 07/07/63   07/22/63
Kirk, Julia married Stevenson, James 08/09/65   08/12/65
Kirk, Margaret A. married Smith, William H. 06/02/63   06/03/63
Kirk, Mary died 02/08/63   02/10/63
Kirk, R. Edwin married Starr, Sydney A. 06/19/62   06/24/62
Kirk, Samuel E. married Cole, Martha 11/17/63   11/19/63
Kirk, Sarah Elizabeth died 12/01/65   12/04/65

Kirk, Washington died 10/20/64   10/22/64
Kirk, William married Tyson, Anne 06/11/61   06/12/61
Kirkamp, Harmon died 03/30/62   04/01/62
Kirkland, Carrie Estelle died 09/09/61   09/10/61
Kirkland, Harry died 08/18/64   09/08/64
Kirkland, Harry died 09/04/64   09/09/64
Kirkland, Sarah Webster died 09/03/62   09/05/62
Kirkland, Sarah Webster Adreon died 06/08/64   06/09/64
Kirkley, Joseph W. married Crum, Louisa M. 10/17/64   10/19/64
Kirkpatrick, A. S. married Stevens, Annie 04/14/62   04/15/62
Kirkpatrick, Eliza Jane died 03/30/65   03/31/65
Kirkpatrick, Emma V. married Phillips, Henry M. 03/23/63   12/28/63
Kirkpatrick, James died 04/16/63   04/17/63
Kirkpatrick, James died 04/16/63   04/18/63
Kirkwood, Charles H. married Harman, Sarah A. 08/29/61   09/02/61
Kirkwood, E. C. (Lt.) married Howell, Alice R. 02/05/62   02/06/62
Kirkwood, George H. married Callaway, Martha E. 04/08/62   04/12/62
Kirkwood, May died 03/18/65   03/22/65
Kirkwood, Philip died 01/04/65   01/05/65
Kirsch, Sarah E. married Bayley, William T. 02/08/61   02/12/61
Kirwan, George W. (Cpt.) died 08/15/63   08/17/63
Kirwan, John died 08/05/63   08/13/63
Kirwan, Lelia Lockerman died 01/15/63   02/24/63
Kirwin, Emily Jane died 02/03/65   02/06/65
Kitchen, James Willis died 05/21/65   05/23/65
Kitrick, Thomas died 09/25/63   09/26/63
Kitron, Sarah Ann died 05/22/62   05/23/62
Kitson, Harry Erskine died 10/27/63   10/28/63
Kitson, John Goodacre died 11/05/63   11/06/63
Kitts, Elizabeth (Mrs.) died 07/25/63   07/31/63
Klages, Diedrich died 09/08/63   09/09/63
Klages, George died 11/07/63   11/09/63
Klass, Margaret died 09/01/62   09/02/62
Klassen, Martin died 06/04/63   06/06/63
Kleff, Arnold married Voshell, Gertrude 01/26/64   01/27/64
Kleibacker, Mary C. married Strodtman, J. H. 12/05/65   12/12/65
Klein, Henry died 04/17/61   04/18/61
Klein, Madison C. died 08/29/62   09/01/62
Klepf, W. Arnold died 06/13/62   06/14/62
Klessell, Augusta E. married Seebode, Albert W. 06/08/65   06/17/65
Kline, Francis M. died 01/14/61   01/16/61
Kline, George F. died 06/08/64   06/20/64
Kline, John married Gerbrich, Rachel P. 09/27/64   09/29/64
Kline, Mary married Smith, Henry 08/10/64   08/11/64
Klinefelter, Victor H. married Turner, Susie J. 12/15/64   12/17/64
Klingle, J. Pierce married Tiernan, Laura C. 10/17/65   10/20/65
Klockgether, Albert A. married Dudley, Emma V. 01/03/65   01/05/65
Kloke, Anthony A. died 05/01/62   05/03/62
Kloke, Catharine died 10/15/65   10/17/65
Kloke, John Joseph died 04/13/62   04/15/62
Kloman, Wilhelmina Fredericka died 10/29/64   10/31/64
Klopfenstein, Philip married Nelker, Henrietta 08/30/65   09/08/65
Klunge, Marion Estella died 07/31/61   08/01/61
Klunk, Harriette Louisa died 06/24/65   06/27/65
Klunk, Louisa May (Mrs.) died 07/15/64   07/16/64

```
Kmelrem, Mary Elizabeth died 05/04/62   05/12/62
Knabe, William died 05/21/64   05/23/64
Knap, Susannah died 06/14/64   06/15/64
Knapp, F. H. (Capt.) married Parsons, Nellie W. 03/04/65   05/04/65
Knapp, James married Howard, Mary E. 04/21/61   04/26/61
Knapp, Samuel C. married Hodges, Anna S. 11/30/62   12/02/62
Knapp, Susie E. married Thompson, Joseph 12/02/62   12/20/62
Knauff, Robert E. died 07/01/64   07/02/64
Knauff, Sarah E. married Rowe, Thomas N. 02/10/63   04/27/63
Kneass, Margie died 01/22/62   01/25/62
Kneidert, Henry died 12/05/63   12/08/63
Knell, Frank L. married Harris, Mary A. 12/08/63   12/15/63
Knell, J. Henry married James, Mary E. 11/16/62   12/02/62
Knickman, Caroline died 06/15/65   06/17/65
Knight, Albert died 06/19/61   06/20/61
Knight, Albert died 09/08/65   09/21/65
Knight, Andrew died 08/04/65   08/05/65
Knight, Annie E. married Ensey, Marcellus P. 10/08/62   10/16/62
Knight, Anthony died 05/12/64   05/14/64
Knight, Austin died 06/12/65   06/13/65
Knight, Charles D. married Porter, Sarah E. 12/29/63   01/06/64
Knight, Charles P. married Harwood, Florence 10/17/65   10/21/65
Knight, Columbus married Wills, Almira 07/02/62   07/07/62
Knight, Edward A. (Rev.) died 09/18/62   09/20/62
Knight, Elizabeth (Mrs.) died 01/14/65   01/16/65
Knight, Eugenia married Chambers, John S. 02/26/65   03/14/65
Knight, George H. died 09/19/65   09/26/65
Knight, George P. married Doft, Mary E. 05/26/63   07/04/63
Knight, George Thomas died 11/21/63   11/23/63
Knight, John died 03/15/61   03/16/61
Knight, John died 05/20/63   05/21/63
Knight, Joseph C. died 07/13/65   07/15/65
Knight, Joseph Henry died 12/05/63   12/07/63
Knight, Mary Clara died 12/14/65   12/15/65
Knight, Rosa V. died 03/29/65   03/30/65
Knight, S. R. (Mrs.) died 11/29/65   12/01/65
Knight, S. W. married Godwin, Benener 07/22/63   08/21/63
Knight, Sarah died 07/20/61   07/22/61
Knight, Sarah Elizabeth died 08/07/63   08/08/63
Knight, Susan married Barton, Stephen W. 04/09/63   04/18/63
Knight, Thomas married Wilson, Mary V. 04/30/63   05/04/63
Knight, Thomas married Hogg, Ellen F. 09/06/64   12/29/64
Knight, Virginia Freeman married Hawley, R. K. 04/23/63   04/25/63
Knight, William married Evans, Ella 06/10/63   02/24/64
Knight, William M. married Groome, Maria S. 04/27/64   05/13/64
Knight, William Stansbury died 06/02/64   06/04/64
Knighton, Francis married Mayberry, Fannie L. 08/09/65   08/28/65
Knighton, John F. married Pentz, Maggie A. 11/17/64   11/18/64
Knipe, Anna Maria died 02/15/62   02/17/62
Knipe, B. F. married Anderson, Kate 11/06/64   12/30/64
Knipe, Charles died 10/22/65   10/26/65
Knipp, John C. married Greasley, Julia C. 05/23/65   05/29/65
Knipp, Phillip died 01/15/63   01/16/64
Knock, Patrick married Brady, Mary 12/03/63   01/05/64
Knode, Annie V. married Merrill, James A. (USN) 12/08/63   12/11/63
```

Knorr, Elizabeth (Mrs.) died 10/10/65 10/11/65
Knorr, Lizzie married Matthews, William J. 02/22/64 03/21/64
Knorr, William died 07/16/61 07/18/61
Knorr, William Henry died 01/16/61 01/19/61
Knott, Bernard J. died 04/06/65 04/07/65
Knott, Charles married McQuilliams, Rose 05/19/64 05/28/64
Knotts, Will H. married Graves, Allie B. 09/01/63 09/07/63
Knotts, William H. married Graves, Alverda B. 09/01/63 09/03/63
Knoup, John M. died 06/04/65 06/07/65
Knowles, George G. married White, Mary E. 04/28/64 05/09/64
Knowles, Lydia P. married Groverman, A., Jr. 12/01/63 12/05/63
Knox, Christiana married Tress, John 10/01/65 10/14/65
Knox, Julius W. married Reuter, Sophia H. 07/21/61 07/24/61
Knox, Margaret married McCain, Edward 09/22/58 03/27/61
Knuff, Margaret (Mrs.) died 10/18/63 10/24/63
Koachling, Matilda Mary died 07/21/61 07/22/61
Kockling, Lucy G. M. (Mrs.) died 12/03/63 12/05/63
Koechling, Caroline married Lartz, John 05/23/65 05/31/65
Koechling, Charles W. (Dr.) married Deaner, Lizzie 09/19/65 09/27/65
Koefoed, Charles J. died 03/25/61 04/23/61
Koeford, Margaret E. (Mrs.) died 05/04/64 05/06/64
Koehler, George L. died 03/08/62 03/10/62
Koestner, Nicholas died 03/24/63 03/25/63
Kohl, Margaret (Mrs.) died 12/19/64 12/20/64
Kohler, Frederick died 05/02/64 05/04/64
Kolb, Emma married Aman, Sebastian 09/27/63 10/08/63
Kolb, Mary married Prout, John W. 11/13/64 11/16/64
Kolb, Mary E. married Addison, John W. 11/20/62 12/01/62
Kolb, Mary E. died 05/18/63 05/19/63
Kolbourn, George C. died 08/29/63 08/31/63
Koller, Cora C. died 04/15/62 04/15/62
Koller, Fanny V. died 04/14/62 04/15/62
Koller, Henry V. died 08/31/63 09/01/63
Kone, Daniel died 01/01/62 01/02/62
Kone, Henrietta married Briggs, Daniel 11/21/61 11/22/61
Kone, Mary A. married Hayes, Edward 05/11/65 05/16/65
Kone, William H. married Howard, Amanda G. 11/30/65 12/01/65
Kone, William W. married Cannon, Louisa J. 10/26/62 10/29/62
Konig, George H. H. died 07/20/65 07/25/65
Konig, Lloyd married Jones, Georgeanne 12/11/62 12/16/62
Koning, Catharine married Kelly, Robert 04/29/62 05/03/62
Konkel, Henry died 04/15/65 04/17/65
Koockogey, George A. W. died 10/24/64 10/28/64
Kopp, Emelia C. died 05/21/65 05/22/65
Koppelman, George married Fritz, Lizzie 11/10/64 11/15/64
Koppelman, Mary died 12/27/62 12/29/62
Korte, Frederick married Cohen, Matilda I. 02/24/63 04/07/63
Koster, Albert died 08/15/61 08/16/61
Kothe, William Henry died 07/20/62 07/22/62
Koutz, Mary Margaret died 04/06/62 04/09/62
Kraber, Mary Ann married Rain, Charles H. B. 01/02/61 01/04/61
Kracht, Christian F. died 01/26/62 01/27/62
Kraeger, Charlotte Sophie died 02/22/64 02/24/64
Kraft, Belle B. married Greason, John 10/18/64 10/20/64
Kraft, Elizabeth died 12/10/61 12/11/61

Kraft, J. W. married Hollingshead, E. R. 06/04/63   06/10/63
Kraft, Julia Ann died 07/16/61   07/27/61
Kraft, Philip J. died 12/30/62   12/31/62
Kraft, Philip J. died 12/30/62   01/01/63
Kraft, Susannah E. K. married Mills, Franklin L. 12/12/65   12/14/65
Kraft, William H. married Hamman, Elizabeth 05/15/64   05/17/64
Krager, Elizabeth E. married Bramble, Zorah E. 09/25/62   10/15/62
Krager, Florence Genevia died 05/04/62   05/09/62
Krager, Frederick Francis died 06/25/63   06/26/63
Krager, John Lewis died 03/03/63   03/05/63
Krager, Margaret (Mrs.) died 06/01/64   06/03/64
Krager, Susanna died 10/30/62   10/31/62
Kramer, Henrietta married Hufnagel, John 02/11/62   02/13/62
Kramer, Mary Elizabeth died 08/23/63   08/26/63
Kramer, Mary Elizabeth died 08/23/63   08/27/63
Kramer, S. R. married Thompson, Levie Georgia 03/06/61   03/11/61
Krantz, A. A. married Martin, A. R. 05/21/63   02/05/64
Kratt, Sophie M. died 08/30/61   08/31/61
Krauss, Charles T. married Frasier, Frances Virginia G. 07/08/63   07/11/63
Krauss, George Washington died 02/27/65   03/03/65
Krauss, Sophia J. died 10/24/65   10/28/65
Kreamer, Elizabeth (Mrs.) died 08/08/64   08/12/64
Kreamer, Nicholas married Conley, Sarah M. 11/08/64   11/11/64
Krearner, Andrew married Leightner, Mage 11/20/65   11/27/65
Krebs, Edwin F. (Mrs.) died 05/16/64   09/27/64
Krebs, Elizabeth H. (Mrs.) died 06/10/63   06/13/65
Krebs, George C. died 08/14/64   08/15/64
Krebs, Henry W. married Cowan, Eliza Jane 12/05/61   12/07/61
Krebs, Hester G. married Smith, Charles F. 11/14/61   11/16/61
Krebs, Jacob Emory married Mead, Rachel M. 09/15/63   09/17/63
Krebs, Martha married Wilson, George B. 04/21/63   04/23/63
Krebs, Mary Adda Elizabeth died 11/28/63   12/04/63
Krebs, Mary R. married Dukehart, Thomas M. (USN) 11/12/63   11/14/63
Krebs, Susan D. (Mrs.) died 05/16/64   05/18/64
Krebs, William Lemuel died 10/10/63   10/13/63
Kregel, Mary A. died 07/23/61   08/15/61
Kreile, Frederick married Cook, Mahala 03/31/61   04/03/61
Kreis, George J. married Nagel, Mary C. Bopp 02/21/65   02/23/65
Kreis, George W. married Auld, Mary A. (Mrs.) 09/30/61   10/04/61
Kreis, Mary married Hildt, George J. 05/23/65   05/24/65
Kreitman, Lena (Mrs.) died 03/23/65   03/25/65
Krekel, Henry died 07/31/64   08/01/64
Kremeberg, J. George married Hall, Anna E. 04/25/64   04/28/64
Kremelberg, Mathilde married Tesdorpf, J. H. 06/24/63   06/27/63
Kremer, J. Clinton died 04/14/63   04/16/63
Kremer, James C. died 11/06/62   11/07/62
Kremer, Joseph died 07/07/65   07/08/65
Kremer, Martha Ella died 06/28/61   06/29/61
Kremer, Mary E. married Sterling, Christopher C. 12/27/64   01/02/65
Kremer, William V. married Scharf, Adelaide Yost 07/14/64   07/16/64
Krems, James B. B. died 04/05/62   04/07/62
Krenitz, Charles Frank married Fortman, Mary 05/31/65   06/03/65
Kretchmer, Mary E. died 12/21/65   12/23/65
Kretzer, John M. died 10/09/65   10/13/65

Kretzet, John M. died 10/09/65 10/12/65
Krews, Mary E. married Carrol, Thomas 08/22/65 09/05/65
Krider, Charles A. died no date 12/10/63
Krider, Charles A. died no date 12/11/63
Kriel, Wallian L. died 07/27/65 07/28/65
Kries, Charlotte died 08/14/64 08/15/64
Kriesman, William died 09/20/61 09/23/61
Kriete, August W. married Bond, Harriet A. 09/27/65 10/05/65
Kriettman, Walter James died 07/02/62 07/03/62
Kroger, Margaret (Mrs.) died 06/01/64 06/02/64
Kroh, Charles A. died 05/14/63 05/18/63
Kroh, Charles W. married Alban, Sarah L. 04/24/62 04/26/62
Kroh, Mary E. married Spicer, John W. 10/24/64 10/27/64
Kronau, John Milton died 07/30/61 08/02/61
Krouse, Nimrod S. died 05/11/62 05/14/62
Krout, William B. married Cross, Sadie V. 08/09/64 08/10/64
Krozer, Charles J. died 01/11/61 01/16/61
Krug, Louisa A. married Nunn, Stephen E. 07/06/62 07/25/62
Kuhlman, F. W. married Dunning, Ellen A. 08/02/64 08/08/64
Kuhlman, William died 08/09/63 08/13/63
Kuhn, Ann Maria died 05/14/61 05/16/61
Kuhn, Catherine died 03/06/62 03/08/62
Kuhn, Catherine (Mrs.) died 08/22/65 08/23/65
Kuhn, Eugene Walter died 01/31/62 02/01/62
Kuhn, John Alphonsus died 01/20/65 01/30/65
Kuhn, John J. married Wheat, Ann Elizabeth 05/31/63 06/08/63
Kuhn, Mary Elizabeth died 08/09/64 08/10/64
Kuhn, Minnie married Kavanaugh, T. P. 11/11/65 11/16/65
Kuhn, Minnie A. married Harps, Frank H. 11/24/65 12/12/65
Kunkel, Charles married Stoss, Elizabeth 07/30/65 08/03/65
Kunsman, William H. married Lowry, Harriet D. 02/21/61 03/04/61
Kunsman, William H. died 04/02/64 04/05/64
Kupp, Charles L. (Lt.) married Barranger, F. V. M. 09/17/61 11/27/61
Kurns, James Nash died 06/05/65 06/06/65
Kurty, Ellenora died 10/13/62 10/15/62
Kurtz, Benjamin (Rev.) died 12/29/65 12/30/65
Kurtz, Charles H. died 09/12/64 09/13/64
Kurtz, Henry died 10/28/64 10/29/64
Kurtz, Louisa married Chester, John 10/25/61 10/26/61
Kurtz, Martin married Meads, Sarah Ellen 05/07/63 05/08/63
Kurtz, Mary died 09/21/65 09/22/65
Kurtz, Mary C. (Mrs.) died 03/08/65 03/10/65
Kurzmaul, Elizabeth H. married Muirs, William E. 08/18/64 08/22/64
Kurzmaul, William F. married Scheese, Mary Louisa 12/15/63 12/19/63
Kuszmaul, Lawrence died 07/05/65 07/06/65
Kuszmaul, Lawrence died 07/05/65 07/07/65
Kyne, Willie T. died 01/26/65 01/28/65
Kyper, George died 01/18/62 01/20/62
Kyper, John died 12/05/64 12/07/64
Kyper, Louisa A. married Weirauch, George M. 09/07/65 09/18/65
Kyper, Mary Wilhelmina died 06/27/61 06/29/61
La Motte, France Louisa died 11/27/64 12/03/64
La Rue, Lawrence P. married Dixon, Jennie B. 02/20/61 02/23/61
Laake, Henry Bernard died 05/03/63 05/19/63
Labroquere, Catharine M. died 07/27/63 07/29/63

Lacey, Emma L. married Sutton, Samuel V. 02/25/62 03/05/62
Lacey, James J. married Kelly, Catherine 06/29/62 07/07/62
Lacey, Sandy (Dr.) died 07/07/65 07/12/65
Lackenmayer, Charles Lewis died 11/27/63 11/28/63
Lackland, Dennis died 03/31/64 04/13/64
Lacross, Mary J. married Langvill, William H. 07/23/63 07/30/63
Lacy, Mary A. married O'Leary, William F. 10/13/61 10/15/61
Ladenslager, Georgie married Kerner, M. H. 12/02/62 12/04/62
Laeth, George W. married Wilson, Mary E. 05/10/64 05/17/64
Lafalonierre, Ann Clare died 01/09/62 01/10/62
Lafayette, Franklin died 04/06/64 04/07/64
Lafever, Elizabeth died 11/24/61 11/25/61
Lafever, William died 02/22/64 02/23/64
Lafevre, Charles E. married Breen, Maggie 11/23/65 12/02/65
Lafferty, Margaret M. died 08/14/61 08/15/61
Laffy, Maggie died 06/23/65 07/01/65
Lafielt, Jeremiah married Files, Mary Ann 01/05/62 01/07/62
Lague, Sarah A. (Mrs.) married Thomas, Joseph E. 08/31/64 09/01/64
Laib, Amelia married Matthews, John J. 07/09/61 07/10/61
Laib, Eliza L. died 07/30/64 08/02/64
Laing, John Randolph died 03/15/63 03/16/63
Lake, Mary Francis married Wallace, William H. 04/18/61 05/01/61
Lakey, Margaret died 12/03/62 12/05/62
Laley, Emma V. married Busey, Norval H. 11/22/64 11/24/64
Lallor, Kate married Curren, Daniel 09/21/65 09/30/65
Lalor, Laurence married McCormick, Annie 06/15/62 06/16/62
Lamaitre, Christiana (Mrs.) died 04/26/65 04/28/65
Lamar, M. T. married Wood, Lizzie 10/22/64 10/29/64
Lamb, Charlie E. died 02/27/64 02/29/64
Lamb, John H. married Pruett, Amanda M. 03/02/62 03/18/62
Lamb, Martha married Dittman, Charles W. 02/05/63 02/07/63
Lambden, George T. (Lt.) died 06/30/62 07/17/62
Lambden, George T. (Lt.) died 06/30/62 07/18/62
Lambdin, (Mrs. E. O.) married McLane, Charles S. 01/16/65 01/19/65
Lambdin, Fanny died 03/06/64 03/07/64
Lambdin, Kate McClellan died 08/12/63 08/14/63
Lambdin, Mannie J. married Thomas, Will R. 06/23/65 07/07/65
Lambdin, Richard Nea died 04/26/64 04/27/64
Lambdin, William D. died 07/12/61 07/13/61
Lambdin, William K. married Lowe, Maria Louisa 12/04/61 12/07/61
Lambdin, William S. died 07/09/64 07/11/64
Lambdin, William Wallace (Dr.) died 07/03/63 07/20/64
Lambe, Patrick died 02/25/65 02/27/65
Lambert, Alexandrine (Mrs.) died 02/20/64 04/20/64
Lambert, George W. married Hewsling, Alexandrine 11/01/61 01/14/62
Lambert, Harry died 03/28/64 04/01/64
Lambert, Joanna married Ruark, John 12/24/65 12/27/65
Lambert, John married Bosley, Emma E. 03/09/65 03/29/65
Lambert, Lizzie A. married Wells, George R. 06/12/65 06/15/65
Lambert, Lizzie A. married Wells, George R. 06/12/65 06/16/65
Lambert, Margaret A. married Parks, Francis S. 09/11/61 09/13/61
Lambert, Robert H. died 12/04/62 12/05/62
Lambert, Robert H. died 07/25/65 07/26/65
Lambert, William H. died 12/03/65 12/04/65
Lambert, William H. died 12/03/65 12/05/65

Lamborn, Samuel H. died 05/19/64   05/24/64
Lambright, Laura V. married McFadden, George W. 07/24/62   08/19/62
Lambright, William married Sweeting, Mary A. 02/27/65   03/02/65
Lamdin, Daniel H. died 04/04/61   04/06/61
Lamdin, J. F. (USN) married Morsell, Lou 09/09/61   09/11/61
Lamdin, Maud died 12/29/64   12/31/64
Lame, George W. died 08/22/65   08/25/65
Lamkin, John Albert died 12/22/63   03/08/64
Lampley, Susan V. married Evans, Maybury 04/03/62   04/07/62
Lanahan, Margaret died 08/02/65   08/03/65
Lancaster, Andrew J. married Weaver, Susannah 01/31/64   02/04/64
Lancaster, Ebenezer married Dorsey, Mary A. 01/01/61   01/09/61
Lancaster, Isaac T. married Foos, Martha 08/04/62   12/11/62
Lancaster, John Henry married Shank, Mary A. 05/31/61   06/03/61
Lancaster, Joseph O. died 05/11/64   08/17/64
Lancaster, Joseph O. (Sgt.) died 05/11/64   08/18/64
Lancaster, Thomas died 01/16/61   01/17/61
Landeman, Jacob died 12/31/61   01/01/62
Landers, Annie married Nixon, Patrick 01/14/64   01/22/64
Landers, Annie Ruark died 11/29/65   11/30/65
Landers, Edward died 04/18/65   04/19/65
Landers, Francis Patrick Henry died 03/09/62   03/10/62
Landers, Nicholas John died 01/29/65   01/30/65
Landers, Nicholas John died 01/29/65   01/31/65
Landis, Julia Robinson died 01/02/62   01/04/62
Landis, Katy Robinson died 01/08/62   01/09/62
Landon, George married Lynch, Sallie J. 05/07/63   05/08/63
Landon, Joseph W. married Pole, Margaret E. 10/31/65   11/01/65
Landry, Elias married Kelly, Mary 10/15/63   10/20/63
Landwer, Harman H. died 09/23/62   09/25/62
Lane, Annie E. married Bailey, Alfred J. 12/08/64   12/09/64
Lane, Elizabeth married Johnson, John 05/08/63   05/13/63
Lane, George A. married Salgee, Sarah A. 05/09/65   05/12/65
Lane, Harry R. died 01/03/63   01/17/63
Lane, James died 07/09/64   07/11/64
Lane, James L. died 08/26/61   08/27/61
Lane, James Wesley married Stevens, Mary Susan 09/06/65   09/09/65
Lane, Laura Virginia died 07/07/64   07/13/64
Lane, Lloyd married Wells, Amanda E. 09/09/60   08/13/61
Lane, Olevia Bell died 08/24/61   08/27/61
Lane, Rachel A. R. married Scott, John W. 12/17/63   12/19/63
Lane, Samuel H. died 03/31/65   11/16/65
Lane, Sylvester C. married Steward, Annie L. 08/16/64   08/18/64
Lane, Virginia Celes died 01/28/65   01/31/65
Lane, William married Hewitt, Mary R. 02/18/63   03/16/63
Lane, William H. died 02/16/65   02/18/65
Laneden, George L. married Davis, Susan 04/28/64   04/30/64
Lanehart, Mary Ann married Jones, John B. 09/19/61   09/21/61
Laney, William Roberts died 09/29/62   10/03/62
Lang, Christian died 06/27/61   06/29/61
Lang, John M married Collins, Delia A. 10/01/61   10/03/61
Lang, Mary C. married Thomson, William 01/21/61   01/24/61
Langan, Thomas died 01/27/63   01/28/63
Langdon, William Edward died 10/06/65   10/10/65
Langdorf, Mary married Johannes, Charles W. 12/27/64   01/06/65

Lange, Hanna R. died 09/18/61 09/19/61
Lange, Louise married Henninghausen, Louis 09/17/63 09/18/63
Langford, Eliza Jane died 03/01/62 03/05/62
Langford, Freeborn married Brown, Mary E. 06/01/65 06/03/65
Langford, Sarah A. died 07/19/63 07/21/63
Langheld, George Frederick died 03/12/62 03/13/62
Langley, Edward married Carroll, Elizabeth 09/26/61 11/26/61
Langley, Francis W. married Cromwell, Margaret 02/18/64 02/19/64
Langley, John W. married Size, Elizabeth 03/05/65 06/01/65
Langley, Joseph died 06/17/63 06/18/63
Langley, William A. married Brown, Margaret Jane 12/25/61 12/31/61
Langley, Zilah A. married White, Henson (Cpt.) 06/30/63 07/07/63
Langlois, H. C. married Elliott, Margaret J. 09/05/65 09/29/65
Langvill, William H. married Lacross, Mary J. 07/23/63 07/30/63
Langville, George W. died 01/12/64 03/09/64
Langville, George Washington died 12/26/62 12/29/62
Langville, Thomas Jefferson died 12/25/62 12/29/62
Langville, William T. J. married Willey, Eliza A. 05/18/65 05/23/65
Lanier, Henry Johns died 01/31/62 02/03/62
Laning, William M. died 03/18/63 03/20/63
Lankford, Isabel F. married Godman, Thomas E. 10/07/61 11/07/61
Lannan, Robert died 05/05/61 05/10/61
Lannay, Amelia died 10/14/61 10/15/61
Lannay, Louis F. married Marshall, M. Jane 04/03/62 04/04/62
Lanpher, Caleb C. died 11/23/61 11/25/61
Lanpher, Fanny died 05/13/65 05/15/65
Lanpher, Wade Stubbs died 01/05/63 01/07/63
Lanpher, Willie Florence died 01/04/63 01/05/63
Lansburgh, Gustave married Kimmelresh, Louise 01/04/65 01/09/65
Lansburgh, Henrietta married Frankel, Leopold 02/10/61 02/13/61
Lansburgh, S. M. died 08/25/62 08/26/62
Lansdale, Edwin Parker died 06/30/63 07/01/63
Lansdale, Florence died 02/12/65 02/13/65
Lansdale, Jennie died 08/03/65 08/05/65
Lansey, Ellenor married Howard, Charles 12/08/61 12/16/61
Lansfield, Wilmer died 12/31/63 01/06/64
Lant, Henrietta Ann died 03/24/62 03/25/62
Lantz, Cassie N. died 02/05/65 02/07/65
Lantz, David died 01/22/63 02/04/63
Lantz, Elizabeth married Seipp, Frederick 08/27/63 09/23/63
Lantz, Samuel married Hevener, Susan 11/27/65 12/04/65
Lantz, Sarah Ann died 02/15/65 02/17/65
Lany, Mary Jane married McDonell, James 08/01/65 09/11/65
Lapouraille, Alfred P. died 11/28/63 11/30/63
Larduskey, Galena died 04/13/64 04/18/64
Lare, Annie E. married Webb, Henry A. 05/19/64 05/20/64
Lare, Edward married Benny, Cornelia 08/11/64 08/15/64
Lare, Rebecca died 06/14/61 06/15/61
Lare, Sophia E. married Fay, George 10/25/65 11/09/65
Large, James died 12/04/62 12/06/62
Larimore, Richard F. married Deale, Hannah E. 06/05/62 06/07/62
Larken, William died 08/09/61 08/10/61
Larkin, Malvina died 08/04/62 08/05/62
Larkin, Willie died 08/13/65 08/15/65
Larkin, Willie died 12/18/65 12/20/65

Larkins, Elizabeth died 08/22/62 08/23/62
Larmer, J. William married Horner, Fannie 03/10/63 03/12/63
Larmour, Mary Anne Howard died 02/21/62 02/22/62
Larmour, William B. died 07/13/61 07/15/61
Laroque, Acelie M. married Guillou, Victor 10/09/62 10/11/62
Laroque, Alexis died 08/31/65 09/01/65
Laroque, Francis E. died 05/11/63 05/14/63
Laroque, Francis Edward (Dr.) died 02/15/61 02/18/61
Laroque, John M. died 03/26/64 03/28/64
Laroque, Joseph Bizourd died 01/20/64 01/22/64
Larrabee, Maggie married Mellor, John B. 11/05/63 11/07/63
Larrabee, William F. married Howard, Fannie 11/17/64 11/19/64
Larracy, Elizabeth died 03/17/64 03/22/64
Larracy, Matthew G. died 01/22/62 01/23/62
Lartz, John married Koechling, Caroline 05/23/65 05/31/65
Lary, Mary died 09/07/65 09/08/65
Lascom, William died 04/03/62 05/05/62
Lash, Maria died 12/26/61 12/30/61
Latchford, George G. married Harding, Miranda 10/23/65 10/25/65
Latchford, Margaret (Mrs.) died 03/04/65 03/06/65
Latchford, Margaret A. died 04/02/62 04/03/62
Latchford, Sarah Jane (Mrs.) died 09/21/63 09/23/63
Latham, Ann Elizabeth died 08/23/63 08/24/63
Latham, Harry died 03/23/63 03/24/63
Latham, Virginia married Fisher, Herman E. 05/14/63 05/16/63
Lathe, Laura J. married Holmes, A. S. 01/18/63 02/03/63
Latimer, James married Bratt, Sarah A. 09/24/62 09/27/62
Latimer, Marcus B. married Lowe, Susie B. 05/12/64 05/14/64
Latore, William Henry died 10/08/65 10/09/65
Latrobe, (Mrs. Ferdinand C.) died 09/05/65 09/07/65
Latrobe, Ferdinand C. married Swann, Louisa 12/26/61 12/28/61
Latsch, Catharine (Mrs.) died 10/19/63 10/20/63
Latta, Maria died 04/12/62 04/17/62
Latz, John Joseph died 04/07/62 04/08/62
Laudeman, Frederick Edward died 04/12/64 04/13/64
Lauderman, Eliza J. (Mrs.) died 08/08/64 08/09/64
Lauderman, William H. married Hitchcock, Martha A. 02/02/65 02/04/65
Lauer, Catherine Josephina died 07/10/63 07/11/63
Laughlen, Jane Eliza died 09/20/64 09/21/64
Laughlin, Ann E. (Mrs.) died 06/27/63 06/29/63
Laughlin, Brian O. married Brown, Emma 01/30/65 02/01/65
Laughlin, William H. married Dipple, Margaret Amelia 07/11/64 11/22/64
Lauman, Louis Simon died 02/18/64 02/19/64
Laurence, Elizabeth died 04/20/64 04/22/64
Laurence, Richard D. died 06/16/63 06/26/63
Laurenson, Charles Carroll died 04/23/65 04/27/65
Lautter, Mary Komrad died 07/06/65 07/08/65
Lavake, Maria E. married Warwick, John G. 01/05/65 01/06/65
Lavery, Joseph married Start, Katherine 05/20/61 05/22/61
Lavinder, Fleming J. died 07/03/62 07/08/62
Lavine, Maurice died 09/04/65 09/06/65
Law, Sarah F. (Mrs.) died 07/24/65 07/25/65
Lawden, Manda (Mrs.) died 11/28/64 11/29/64
Lawder, Ann Jane died 08/13/62 08/15/62
Lawder, Emma V. married Haight, William B. 03/02/61 05/23/61

Lawder, Emma V. married Hersh, Alexander O. 03/09/65   03/15/65
Lawder, Henry Clay died 03/07/65   03/08/65
Lawder, Manada (Mrs.) died 11/28/64   11/30/64
Lawn, Henry died 07/01/64   07/04/64
Lawrance, Julia A. married Gassaway, Henry 04/29/63   05/02/63
Lawrason, Zelia M. (Mrs.) died 07/06/64   08/04/64
Lawrence, Emma J. married Buckingham, James V. 03/10/64   04/01/64
Lawrence, George Meade died 10/02/64   10/07/64
Lawrence, Harold Dorsey died 05/12/64   05/13/64
Lawrence, John W. married Pierpont, Sarah E. no date   10/16/62
Lawrence, Julius Herbert died 12/28/62   12/29/62
Lawrence, Kate S. married Gilpatrick, Norton 05/10/65   05/12/65
Lawrence, Libbie A. died 11/22/64   11/23/64
Lawrence, Margaret died 09/16/61   09/17/61
Lawrence, Margaret died 03/15/64   03/16/64
Lawrence, Oren S. (Lt.) married Maguire, Sarah 04/27/63   04/28/63
Lawrence, Oren S. (Lt.) married Maguire, Sarah 04/27/63   05/02/63
Lawrence, Sarah E. died 12/24/62   12/27/62
Lawrence, William G. died 08/11/63   08/12/63
Lawrenson, Emma V. married Smiley, James 08/26/62   09/02/62
Lawrenson, Fida S. married Roberts, J. Harvey 12/22/64   12/24/64
Lawrenson, Mary A. married Coyle, Bernard F. 02/23/63   03/18/63
Lawrenson, Richard S. married Brown, Kate E. 12/08/63   12/12/63
Laws, Beverly D. married Atkinson, Lydia M. 12/22/63   12/24/63
Laws, Mary C. married Hopkins, S. Harris 04/30/63   05/05/63
Laws, William Patrick died 02/18/65   02/20/65
Lawson, Aaron died 01/25/64   01/30/64
Lawson, Ellen died 10/27/62   10/29/62
Lawson, Robert S. died 09/18/63   09/19/63
Lawson, S. Allen married Morton, Alice 11/22/65   11/23/65
Lawson, Wendel B. died 08/26/65   08/28/65
Lawton, Ann E. married Madgrick, Thomas 11/20/62   12/10/62
Lawton, Charles Francis died 01/26/63   01/29/63
Lawton, George W. died 11/25/63   11/28/63
Lawton, Richard married Pamphilion, Margaret 05/19/61   05/22/61
Layfield, J. Robert died 07/24/61   07/30/61
Layfield, Pricilla A. married Wells, Peter F. 05/15/61   05/16/61
Layfield, Pricilla A. married Wells, Peter F. 05/15/61   05/17/61
Layfield, Sallie H. W. died 07/16/62   07/23/62
Layfield, Sarah E. died 03/12/65   03/12/65
Layfield, William died 04/26/65   04/27/65
Layfield, William D. O. died 10/27/65   10/30/65
Laynor, George married Helmling, Marian Virginia 02/08/63   03/10/63
Layshu, Matilda died 06/28/61   06/29/61
Layton, George B. McClellan died 12/02/63   12/04/63
Lazenby, Daniel L. died 02/28/61   03/01/61
Lazenby, Daniel Langan married Atter, Mary Rebecca 12/10/63   12/15/63
Lazenby, S. H. (Mrs.) died 02/12/63   02/13/63
Lazenly, James William died 10/14/62   10/16/62
Le Bron, Robert Aitken died 10/15/64   10/17/64
Leace, Mary Jane married Martin, John 09/07/65   09/08/65
Leach, Caleb died 11/01/65   11/02/65
Leach, Henry J. died 08/18/65   08/19/65
Leach, J. Holland (Sgt.) married Penn, Lucy Elizabeth 12/01/63   12/08/
Leach, John Bernard died 08/09/63   08/10/63

Leach, John H. married Bideke, Dena 12/16/61   12/19/61
Leach, Mary married Hankin, James 04/07/64   04/09/64
Leach, William died 08/10/63   08/11/63
Leadbeater, Edward S. married Chandlee, Clara L. 10/10/61   10/17/61
League, Alice Ann died 07/06/62   07/07/62
League, Alice Virginia married Smith, William Henry 12/17/62   12/19/62
League, E. L. married Somerville, M. 08/25/64   08/30/64
League, E. L. married Sommerville, M. 08/25/64   08/31/64
League, George B. died 09/04/63   09/05/63
League, John H. died 03/22/64   03/25/64
League, John Wesley married McKinley, Mary Frances 06/22/65   06/24/65
League, Robert Leander Bolton died 07/14/63   07/15/63
League, Thomas C. died 10/22/61   10/23/61
League, Thomas M. died 11/25/65   12/16/65
League, Virginia died 01/28/65   02/07/65
League, William F. married Griffin, Martha E. 02/15/65   03/02/65
League, William F. married Griffin, Martha E. 02/15/65   03/03/65
League, William H. married Michael, S. Jane 02/28/65   06/15/65
Leahey, Thomas died 02/15/64   02/17/64
Leahy, William died 05/22/65   05/23/65
Leaib, Louisa married Gosweiler, Solomon 09/01/63   10/10/63
Leake, Alice Ann died 04/02/65   04/04/65
Leake, Josephine L. died 09/24/64   10/05/64
Leakin, Sheppard A. died 09/08/64   09/10/64
Leakin, William Andrew died 07/27/65   07/31/65
Leapin, Francis married Rodgers, Kate 11/03/61   12/09/61
Lear, Bettie O'Neal married Johnson, Isaac Larue 06/09/63   06/18/63
Lear, Wiliam L. married Rourke, Mary Ann 08/18/64   10/08/64
Leary, Augustus M. died 10/04/64   10/05/64
Leary, Bridget died 07/16/62   07/17/62
Leary, Bridget died 07/16/62   07/18/62
Leary, Durias H. married Wells, Emma E. 04/08/63   04/11/63
Leary, Eliza died 10/28/61   10/29/61
Leary, Elizabeth died 06/18/62   06/19/62
Leary, Hannah died 07/13/62   07/15/62
Leary, Jeremiah died 10/20/62   10/22/62
Leary, John married Donoghue, Ellen 06/28/63   07/01/63
Leary, John died 05/03/65   05/04/65
Leary, Lydia Frances died 02/18/65   02/20/65
Leary, Margaret E. married McLain, John 10/27/63   10/28/63
Leary, Mary (Mrs.) died 11/01/63   10/03/63
Leary, Mary (Mrs.) died 12/26/63   12/28/63
Leas, Sallie E. married Frush, Charles E. 08/25/63   08/27/63
Leate, George A. died 04/09/63   04/10/63
Leavy, Patrick died 11/14/64   11/15/64
Lebon, Charles E. married Cather, Susie 09/00/00   02/05/64
Lebon, Marcellina M. L. married Rosenstein, Simon 11/08/62   01/01/63
LeBrun, Mary Jane died 04/08/64   04/09/64
Lecates, Elijah died 01/25/63   02/14/63
Leche, Lt. David H. died 12/28/62   01/08/63
Leckie, Levinia M. married Stuchell, James 03/16/63   03/21/63
Leckie, Levinia M. married Hughes, James 03/16/63   03/23/63
Leckler, Sarah (Mrs.) died 01/19/64   01/22/64
Lecount, Rachel A. married Moonyer, William M. 08/31/62   09/04/62
Ledden, Catharine E. married Bailey, Robert J. 10/16/64   10/18/64

Leddon, Anna R. married Penn, Jacob, Jr. 11/26/63 12/07/63
Leddon, John W. married Casey, Fanny A. 06/21/65 07/14/65
Leddon, Margaret died 07/20/63 07/22/63
Ledger, Lewis died 04/18/64 04/19/64
Ledley, Alice died 02/06/63 02/07/63
Ledley, Eddy L. C. died 05/15/64 05/17/64
Ledley, Elizabeth Ann died 07/24/64 07/25/64
Ledley, Harry I. E. died 04/04/65 04/05/65
Ledley, Maybell died 10/21/63 10/27/63
Ledley, Willie George died 04/22/65 04/25/65
LeDoyen, Frances Virginia S. died 08/25/64 08/26/64
Ledsinger, George Washington died 07/21/64 07/23/64
Lee, Alice married Parker, James H. 06/25/61 06/26/61
Lee, Andrew D. G. died 05/09/64 05/10/64
Lee, Ann Elizabeth died 10/09/63 10/10/63
Lee, Ann Grant died 07/07/65 07/11/65
Lee, Archibald died 10/29/62 10/30/62
Lee, Archibald died 10/28/62 10/31/62
Lee, Bessie married Perine, William P. 12/26/61 12/28/61
Lee, Caroline married Sutton, John 06/05/62 06/07/62
Lee, Catharine married Watts, Alexander 01/29/65 01/31/65
Lee, Charles E. married Blatchley, Lydia 01/13/64 01/19/64
Lee, Elisha died 05/21/61 05/27/61
Lee, Eliza (Mrs.) died 04/10/64 04/11/64
Lee, Elizabeth A. died 04/13/61 04/15/61
Lee, Elizabeth C. died 09/23/61 09/25/61
Lee, Ellen died 01/23/63 01/24/63
Lee, Emily A. E. married Burgess, William H. 04/29/62 05/02/62
Lee, Emma S. married Hudson, David D. 08/17/65 08/30/65
Lee, Fanny married Downs, James 08/18/62 08/20/62
Lee, George W. married Saterfield, Anna E. 11/01/61 12/05/61
Lee, James married Johnson, Elizabeth (Mrs.) 12/06/64 12/08/64
Lee, James H. died 10/25/65 10/26/65
Lee, Jane married Johnson, Richard 08/11/63 08/12/63
Lee, Jesse W. married Collins, Laura R. 04/08/62 04/10/62
Lee, John died 10/27/61 10/28/61
Lee, John Henry married Stevens, Rachel Ann 05/23/61 05/25/61
Lee, Josephine B. died 07/24/63 07/25/63
Lee, Laura married Capron, Richard J. 08/24/64 08/27/64
Lee, Laura married Capron, Richard J. 08/24/64 08/30/64
Lee, Lucy D. (Mrs.) died 05/20/63 05/21/63
Lee, Martha married Jackson, Robert 09/19/61 10/05/61
Lee, Martha A. married Butler, Lewis 07/30/63 08/01/63
Lee, Martha A. (Mrs.) died 04/16/64 04/18/64
Lee, Mary Ann Elizabeth died 06/19/65 06/20/65
Lee, Mary E. married Eicheberger, Thomas S. 10/08/63 10/10/63
Lee, Mary Elizabeth died 03/09/64 03/17/64
Lee, Nathaniel died 09/27/64 09/28/64
Lee, Patrick died 12/10/62 12/12/62
Lee, Rebecca died 10/06/61 10/18/61
Lee, Samuel H. died 09/18/65 09/19/65
Lee, Samuel J. married Hardy, Amelia Jane 02/04/62 02/27/62
Lee, Sarah Rebecca died 10/06/61 10/19/61
Lee, Stephen Louis died 08/21/63 09/03/63
Lee, William married Orem, Josephine V. 06/30/64 07/07/64

Lee, William T. died 10/21/64 10/29/64
Leech, David married Gibbons, Emma J. 10/27/64 10/31/64
Leeds, Edward W. married Price, Fannie 08/22/65 09/08/65
Leeds, Elizabeth (Mrs.) died 06/11/65 06/13/65
Leedy, Mary E. married Cloffenstein, John C. 09/28/62 10/03/62
Leef, Emily J. married Smith, W. D. 12/24/62 01/19/63
Leef, Fannie married Rogers, James S. 01/14/64 01/26/64
Leef, Joshua C. died 09/06/61 09/11/61
Leeke, Anna M. (Mrs.) died 08/13/63 08/14/63
Leeke, Elizabeth (Mrs.) died 09/01/65 09/02/65
Leeke, Lizzie R. (Mrs.) died 02/22/63 02/24/63
Lees, Anna married Fee, Caleb 12/17/61 12/19/61
Leescey, Julia married Moor, Daniel 06/11/63 06/15/63
Leese, William S. died 04/01/63 04/03/63
Leeson, Thomas died 01/01/62 01/07/62
Leetch, Eliza died 11/29/64 11/30/64
Lefanne, Mary Virgina married Holmes, Charles H. 05/05/64 05/07/64
Leffingwell, W. H. married Lewis, Laura R. 10/05/63 10/06/63
Leffler, Ann Jane (Mrs.) died 08/11/64 08/12/64
Leffler, Ann N. died 03/17/63 03/19/63
Leffler, Anna died 07/31/64 08/01/64
Legates, Kate B. died 11/14/62 11/15/62
Legburn, Minice married Reily, Charles 02/26/62 03/01/62
Legg, Edward C. married Bennett, Kate L. Cook 10/29/63 11/02/63
Legg, Fanny married Cockey, Charles E. 11/20/61 11/21/61
Legg, John W. died 07/04/62 07/07/62
Legg, Matilda (Mrs.) died 09/19/65 09/20/65
Legg, Susan A. married Shaws, William B. 11/10/64 11/12/64
Legg, William married White, Anna Elizabeth 05/26/63 05/27/63
LeGourde, Aggie died 01/10/64 01/13/64
Legrand, Isabella Victoria died 05/23/63 05/27/63
Legrand, John C. (Hon.) died 12/28/61 12/30/61
Lehma, Virginia married Green, Francis 02/02/64 02/06/64
Lehman, Clara died 01/22/63 01/24/63
Lehman, Isaac B. (Corp.) died 07/20/64 07/28/64
Lehman, Isaac B. (Corp.) died 07/19/64 07/29/64
Lehman, Isaac B. (Corp.) died 07/19/64 07/30/64
Lehman, John Christian died 11/18/62 11/19/62
Lehman, John Christian died 11/18/62 11/20/62
Lehman, Nicholas died 03/29/63 03/31/63
Lehman, Nicholas T. died 08/21/62 08/25/62
Lehman, Sophie married Hall, Charles A. 05/29/64 06/01/64
Lehmann, Johanna Rosina (Mrs.) died 07/23/63 07/24/63
Lehmayer, Henrietta died 06/13/65 06/15/65
Lehr, Charles Boninger died 08/10/62 08/14/62
Lehr, Charles Boninger died 08/10/62 08/15/62
Leidy, Philip married Polk, Nellie Maury 02/15/65 02/17/65
Leightner, Mage married Krearner, Andrew 11/20/65 11/27/65
Leinsy, Daniel died 07/07/62 07/08/62
Leinsz, Henry died 08/05/63 08/06/63
Leinsz, Magdalene died 04/19/62 04/21/62
Leis, Thomas married Whitcraft, Hannah no date 07/06/64
Leisburger, Marks married Steigerwald, Betty 03/26/65 03/27/65
Leishear, Catherine married Northcraft, Francis 04/22/63 04/28/63
Leishear, Jane P. (Mrs.) died 11/19/64 11/21/64

```
Leister, R. Alice married Clotworty, Charles A.  11/10/63   11/16/63
Leitch, Katie E. married Fowler, James O.  07/30/63   08/01/63
Leitch, Mary Amelia died 12/03/65   12/04/65
Leitch, William F. died 10/10/65   10/18/65
Leitringer, Matilda (Mrs.) died 05/26/64   05/28/64
Leitz, Rebecca (Mrs.) died 12/12/63   12/14/63
Lelly, James died 06/11/65   06/13/65
Leman, Walter J. married Gruver, Elmira  12/15/64   12/21/64
Lemcke, Detluf H. died 11/19/63   11/20/63
Lemcke, Laura V. E. married Buck, Joseph W.  11/16/65   12/06/65
Lemcke, Sophia married Rausch, John H.  09/15/64   09/17/64
Lemley, John Jacob died 12/31/61   01/01/62
Lemley, Mary S. died 01/20/61   01/21/61
Lemly, Elizabeth B. died 11/25/65   11/27/65
Lemmon, Ann Maria (Mrs.) died 06/26/64   06/28/64
Lemmon, B. Franklin married Davis, Janie E.  01/24/61   01/28/61
Lemmon, Elizabeth Ellen married Nily, A., Jr.  04/23/63   04/25/63
Lemmon, John S. died 11/22/64   11/24/64
Lemmon, Richard died 01/28/63   01/29/63
Lemmon, Robert died 12/05/61   12/06/61
Lemmon, Robert died no date   07/21/63
Lemmon, Robert (Lt., C.S.A.) died 07/02/63   07/18/63
Lemmon, Sarah died 03/14/63   03/16/63
Lemmon, Sarah Ellen married Miller, Jonathan  11/12/61   11/14/61
Lemmon, William P. died 03/08/64   03/10/64
Lenaghan, Bridget died 01/16/61   01/18/61
Lendrum, Maria died 02/22/65   02/23/65
Lendrum, Upton died 09/13/65   09/14/65
Lenhardt, Peter died 05/02/63   05/04/63
Lennan, Henry died 08/16/63   08/18/63
Lennard, John Joseph died 08/02/63   08/03/63
Lennen, Mary died 10/19/65   10/21/65
Lenney, Daniel married Higgins, Catherine D.  08/30/63   10/03/63
Lennon, Patrick died 05/01/61   05/02/61
Lennon, Rosa married Dugan, James  01/17/64   02/13/64
Lenty, Laura married Wentworth, Joseph B.  08/14/64   08/19/64
Len[---], Albert Gorsuch died 11/00/63   11/07/63
Leon, Sarah married Hughes, John  07/02/63   07/10/63
Leonard, Angelina (Mrs.) married Osborne, Henry  09/30/64   10/03/64
Leonard, Augusta C. married Marquette, John N.  01/03/61   01/14/61
Leonard, Bridget died 08/04/62   08/05/62
Leonard, Charles H. married Ysadora, Melvina  06/10/64   06/11/64
Leonard, John Henry married Sanks, Elizabeth  01/01/62   01/03/62
Leonard, John W. R. married Upperman, Laura V.  04/08/63   06/08/63
Leonard, Jonathan H. married Newman, Ann Matilda  04/22/63   04/28/63
Leonard, Maria died 08/20/63   08/21/63
Leonard, Michael died 10/19/64   10/18/64
Leonard, Thomas died 11/12/64   11/14/64
Leonard, William H. married Merson, Jane R.  04/08/61   04/18/61
Leonhardt, William died 08/00/00   08/07/61
Leoplod, Jenny married Oppenheimer, D. S.  11/06/64   11/09/64
Lepper, Lucy married Earhart, George W., Jr.  12/15/64   12/17/64
Lepson, William Henry died 10/07/61   10/08/61
Lerew, Matilda J. married Meixsel, Joseph H.  06/28/64   06/29/64
Lervellyn, Thomas died 12/04/65   12/16/65
```

Leslie, H. Clay (U.S.N.) married Moore, Maggie A. 08/08/65   08/11/65
Leslie, John married Barth, Fannie 12/28/65   12/30/65
Leslie, William died 03/15/62   03/19/62
Lessner, Rebecca married Weisner, Eberhart 03/31/61   04/09/61
Lesson, Maurice died 03/17/64   03/19/64
Lester, George married Jackson, Mary J. 05/05/63   05/07/63
Lester, J. Thomas married Wilhelm, Mollie M. 06/13/62   07/01/62
Lester, Jemima R. married Richstein, William F. 03/19/62   03/20/62
Lester, Joseph M. married Greenfield, Harriet Amanda 10/08/63   10/24/63
Lester, Thomas married Summers, Sarah 01/13/62   01/16/62
Letmate, Mathilda married Kattelman, Charles 11/03/61   11/08/61
Letournau, George W. married Foster, Amanda A. 05/19/61   05/28/61
Letournau, Mary W. died 11/03/65   11/04/65
Lettercurb, Agnes died 11/24/65   11/30/65
Leutbacher, Charles died 05/24/63   05/25/63
Levell, Edward F. married Loughran, Mary J. 05/25/62   05/27/62
Levenworth, Lizzie died 09/25/61   10/02/61
Levering, Eliza A. died 11/05/65   11/07/65
Levering, Martha died 01/02/65   01/04/65
Leverton, Juliaetta died 03/14/63   03/17/63
Levi, Eliza died 10/24/62   10/28/62
Levi, James Himan died 07/15/64   07/16/64
Levis, Amelia married Russell, S. B. 10/23/61   11/01/61
Levy, Leffman died 11/07/63   11/09/63
Levy, Lizzie A. married Gahring, George J. 06/02/64   06/09/64
Levy, Margaret died 04/05/61   04/06/61
Levy, Mary Ann died 02/13/64   02/15/64
Levy, Minie F. died 02/09/65   02/10/65
Levy, Sabrah (Mrs.) died 02/05/62   02/08/62
Lewin, John C. married Robinson, D. Jane 12/12/61   12/18/61
Lewin, John H. married Doenges, Mary C. 11/29/63   12/18/63
Lewin, W. H. married Smute, Kata A. 01/28/64   02/02/64
Lewis, A. J. (Lt.) married Robinson, Anna 03/02/65   05/12/65
Lewis, Abraham died 08/26/64   08/27/64
Lewis, Adeline V. Lewis married Carrick, B. Franklin 03/03/63   03/06/63
Lewis, Amelia married Russell, S. B. 10/23/61   10/30/61
Lewis, Ann Rebecca died 05/14/61   05/15/61
Lewis, Annie E. married Remick, John H. 09/25/64   09/27/64
Lewis, Annie R. married Henderson, George A. 11/19/65   11/21/65
Lewis, C. W. married Gamble, Rosa J. 03/11/63   03/14/63
Lewis, Caroline married Garrett, William 07/02/61   07/03/61
Lewis, Charles H. married Abey, Sarah F. 05/25/65   05/31/65
Lewis, Charles J. died 09/09/65   09/12/65
Lewis, Charles O. married Wells, Rebecca 01/08/61   01/18/61
Lewis, Charles Rankin died 09/17/64   09/19/64
Lewis, Edward died 06/15/65   06/17/65
Lewis, Edwin Martin died 10/16/63   10/17/63
Lewis, Elizabeth (Mrs.) died 07/12/63   07/15/63
Lewis, Elizabeth A. married Smith, Thomas A. 10/08/63   10/10/63
Lewis, Elizabeth D. (Mrs.) married Young, George W. 10/19/65   10/26/65
Lewis, Emma married Johnson, J. Smith 06/22/65   06/26/65
Lewis, Emma Florence died 12/18/65   12/19/65
Lewis, Emma Jane died 11/07/62   11/11/62
Lewis, Eugene R. died 07/21/63   07/23/63
Lewis, Francis married Nicholas, Matilda 11/21/61   11/22/61

Lewis, G. Columbus (Cpt.) died 07/27/65   07/28/65
Lewis, Harriet Virginia died 02/16/65   02/17/65
Lewis, Harriet Virginia died 02/16/65   02/18/65
Lewis, Jacob S. married Simpson, Barbara R. 06/22/65   06/28/65
Lewis, James T. died 12/02/62   12/10/62
Lewis, Jane died 04/07/61   05/24/61
Lewis, Jane married Garrison, Arthur 12/09/62   12/11/62
Lewis, Jennie Bell died 08/09/62   08/12/62
Lewis, John married Miles, Ann Rebecca 11/27/61   11/30/61
Lewis, John died 05/04/63   05/05/63
Lewis, John died 06/25/64   07/06/64
Lewis, John married Grimes, Sarah R. 04/29/64   04/30/64
Lewis, John married Vansant, Sarah E. 09/01/64   09/03/64
Lewis, John A. married Dorrman, Ellen R. 06/15/65   06/16/65
Lewis, John F. married Thamert, Elizabeth 03/16/62   03/22/62
Lewis, John N., Jr. died 06/02/61   06/03/61
Lewis, John T. died 11/11/62   11/12/62
Lewis, John W. married Taylor, Lavinia C. 04/14/64   04/16/64
Lewis, Joseph B. died 09/30/61   10/09/61
Lewis, Laura R. married Leffingwell, W. H. 10/05/63   10/06/63
Lewis, Martha R. married Linthicum, Franklin A. 08/21/62   08/23/62
Lewis, Mary A. died 10/17/65   10/19/65
Lewis, Mary A. married Lungren, John T. 10/03/65   10/07/65
Lewis, Mary A. married Denmead, W. C. 11/09/65   11/23/65
Lewis, Mary Ann (Mrs.) died 02/02/63   02/11/63
Lewis, Mary E. married Remmell, John H. 11/17/64   11/18/64
Lewis, Mary Elizabeth died 08/28/63   08/31/63
Lewis, Mary Ellen died 02/17/65   02/18/65
Lewis, Priscilla Gover died 04/05/62   04/07/62
Lewis, Sallie C. died 02/03/65   02/06/65
Lewis, Samuel D. married Parker, Harriet 01/02/62   01/08/62
Lewis, Sarah Ann died 10/19/63   10/21/63
Lewis, Sarah E. married Davis, Edwin R. 09/21/64   09/26/64
Lewis, Sarah F. married Phillips, J. A. 06/14/63   08/21/63
Lewis, Sarah F. married Davis, Edwin R. 09/25/64   09/28/64
Lewis, Sarah J. married Collier, Andrew J. 12/06/63   03/30/64
Lewis, Sarah R. married Merrill, Richard S. 10/24/65   10/28/65
Lewyt, Caroline married Kann, Jacob 05/18/62   05/19/62
Leyburn, Jane married Blaney,J. Murray 09/24/61   12/13/61
Leydecker, May Capitola E. died 03/29/64   03/31/64
Leypold, John died 10/19/63   10/24/63
Liamond, William married Beam, Mary Jane 02/09/64   02/12/64
Lichfield, Christann (Mrs.) died 09/07/65   09/18/65
Lidard, Susie married Hevern, John 05/19/63   05/22/63
Liddard, Eliza Ann died 01/24/64   01/25/64
Liddel, James E. married Warnick, Caroline M. 03/14/64   05/18/64
Lidiard, Eliza Ann (Mrs.) died 02/24/64   02/27/64
Lidiard, Moses died 12/28/63   12/29/63
Lidiard, Tacy died 02/06/63   02/07/63
Lieb, Reguina died no date   02/13/65
Lieber, George died 08/17/62   08/21/62
Lieberman, John William died 08/08/63   08/10/63
Lieberman, Lewis married Engelinger, Isabella 10/12/64   10/13/64
Lieberman, Louis married Englemeyer, Isabelle 10/12/64   11/15/64
Lieter, John died 01/08/64   01/09/64

Lieutaud, Dennis Claude died 06/12/63   06/18/63
Lieutaud, Rosalie A. married Mullan, Edward B. 01/01/63   01/05/63
Ligget, Charles M. married Dale, M. Francis 04/23/62   05/10/62
Light, Mary died 04/13/61   04/16/61
Lightburn, Jane married Brown, Fenix 04/22/61   04/24/61
Lightner, Alice P. married Barchus, John Hedges 05/25/64   05/27/64
Lightner, Catharine (Mrs.) died 12/27/61   01/01/62
Lightner, David Samuel died 08/25/65   08/26/65
Lightner, Maggie A. died 04/04/61   04/06/61
Lightner, Virginia married Hooper, Joseph J. 08/16/64   09/07/64
Likes, Mary Catharine (Mrs.) died 06/20/64   06/21/64
Lilley, Andrew E. married Gawthrop, Cornelia 06/25/62   06/27/62
Lillibridge, William H. H. died 05/15/65   05/18/65
Lillts, Henry, (Gen., C.S.A.) died 09/19/62   10/20/62
Lilly, Alonzo, Jr. married Wright, Josephine A. 10/12/64   10/13/64
Lilly, Anastasia died 03/30/64   04/11/64
Lilly, Anna Josephine died 12/28/60   01/19/61
Lilly, Charles R. married Taylor, Mary J. 10/20/64   11/09/64
Lilly, Edward A. married Collins, Estelle L. 06/17/61   07/22/61
Lilly, Estelle Louisa died 04/16/65   04/17/65
Lilly, George W. died 04/21/65   04/22/65
Lilly, Henry died 07/22/62   07/28/62
Lilly, Henry A. married Geoghegan, Lizzie S. 12/17/60   01/17/61
Lilly, Josephine A. died 11/03/65   11/04/65
Lilly, Sallie F. married Carrigan, Hugh 10/07/62   10/09/62
Limbach, Martha married Calwell, James 08/25/65   09/09/65
Limberry, Delia died 03/17/61   03/19/61
Limbury, Alice married Hogans, Henry C. 03/30/65   04/04/65
Linaweaver, Catherine died 01/05/61   01/07/61
Linaweaver, Elizabeth (Mrs.) died 05/25/63   05/26/63
Linch, John married Donnelly, Essie 02/18/61   02/21/61
Lincoln, Elnathan died 07/25/61   07/27/61
Lincoln, Elnathon died 07/25/61   07/26/61
Lincoln, John died 06/25/64   07/01/64
Lind, Catherine died 01/13/62   01/14/62
Lind, Edmond G. married Murdoch, Margaret 04/28/63   05/02/63
Lindemann, Augusta J. married Fagel, Charles 02/09/64   02/12/64
Lindemann, Edward C. died 08/08/65   08/09/65
Lindemann, Edward C. died 08/08/65   08/10/65
Linden, Maria Ann (Mrs.) died 12/06/63   12/28/63
Linderman, Christopher died 02/07/65   02/09/65
Lindon, C. M. died 03/31/61   04/01/61
Lindsay, James died 01/31/64   02/05/64
Lindsay, James L. married Beatty, Agnes 10/17/65   10/19/65
Lindsay, James M. died 10/21/64   11/05/64
Lindsay, John D. died 12/14/63   01/12/64
Lindsay, Mollie died 07/26/65   07/28/65
Lindsay, Sallie died 08/24/63   08/27/63
Lindsey, Benjamin married Davis, Josephine 02/22/63   02/26/63
Lindsey, Laura A. married Setchel, (Prof.) 12/15/63   12/22/63
Lindsley, Cleland married Bowie, M. Augusta 01/25/65   01/27/65
Lineberger, Francis M. married Mewshaw, Louisa 04/26/63   04/30/63
Lineweaver, Ann Virginia died 05/26/64   06/25/64
Lineweaver, P. L. married Cass, Rina 05/19/64   05/21/64
Lineweaver, P. L. married Coss, Rina 05/19/64   05/23/64

```
Lineweaver, Willie T. died 12/20/62  12/23/62
Lingenfelder, Amelia married Frisbie, E. G. 10/20/63  10/21/63
Lingenfelder, Frederick died 09/19/62  09/20/62
Lingenfelder, J. Louis died 10/13/61  10/21/61
Linhard, Ferdinand A. died 06/05/63  06/06/63
Linhard, John H. died 10/01/63  10/02/63
Linhard, Philip died 04/19/62  04/21/62
Link, Elizabeth married Lynch, Lewis S. M. 04/17/65  04/19/65
Link, Terrence married McCall, Mary 04/17/65  04/22/65
Link, Terrence married McCall, Mary 04/17/65  04/24/65
Linn, Bernard Thomas died 08/25/63  08/26/63
Linn, William died 11/24/62  11/26/62
Linnonburg, Daniel married Johnson, Anna 12/05/61  12/07/61
Linsay, Emilia married Simmons, Isaac G. 04/11/64  04/13/64
Linsted, Emma married Cook, Jefferson M. 10/11/64  10/13/64
Linsted, Henry C. married Billmire, Georgeanna 09/05/65  09/30/65
Linthicum, Abner married Davis, Amanda W. 04/05/64  04/07/64
Linthicum, Amelia died 04/16/63  04/30/63
Linthicum, Franklin A. married Lewis, Martha R. 08/21/62  08/23/62
Linthicum, George W. married Webb, Kate T. 02/14/61  02/25/61
Linthicum, Gussie married Marshall, William G., Jr. 04/11/61  04/16/61
Linthicum, Harriet (Mrs.) died 05/06/63  05/08/63
Linthicum, Hattie Mabel died 07/29/62  07/31/62
Linthicum, John R. died 06/11/61  06/13/61
Linthicum, Ozelab M. married Jones, Charles W. 03/07/61  03/16/61
Linthicum, Sallie Estelle died 06/18/63  06/20/63
Linthicum, Sarah C. married Elkins, Charles H. 12/04/64  12/08/64
Linthicum, Theodore (Dr.) died 10/29/61  11/08/61
Linthicum, Thomas Jefferson died 12/15/64  12/16/64
Linthicum, Vachel J. married Hunt, Thomas H. 02/14/61  02/16/61
Linton, Fanny G. married Patterson, Isaac M. 09/17/63  09/18/63
Linton, Jacob married Harper, Margaret 02/08/64  02/09/64
Linton, James L. married Goodwin, Beth A. 07/31/65  08/02/65
Linton, Sarah Ann (Mrs.) died 09/29/64  09/30/64
Linton, Sarah Virginia died 12/26/63  12/28/63
Linville, Augustus C. married Wolfe, Catharine 04/30/63  05/02/63
Linzey, Charles Webb died 06/19/64  06/21/64
Linzey, Olevia Ann (Mrs.) died 11/09/64  11/10/64
Linzie, Mary married Shuts, Henry 08/02/64  08/04/64
Lipp, Edward McColgan died 07/01/63  07/06/63
Lipp, Edward McColgan died 07/01/63  07/04/63
Lipp, John died 08/27/65  08/28/65
Lippey, Charles Francis died 09/17/63  09/19/63
Lippey, George died 03/27/65  03/28/65
Lippey, Willie died 03/14/64  04/04/64
Lippincott, Ezra married Sutton, Anna 06/17/62  06/24/62
Liscum, Jehial died 02/13/62  02/15/62
Lish, Letitia F. died 07/16/65  07/18/65
Lishear, Albert F. married Steverson, Margaret M. 10/27/65  11/29/65
Lisle, Sally married Chaney, Louis 10/21/62  01/20/63
Lisner, Hannah married Bendann, Daniel 01/05/65  01/07/65
List, George R. married Bersch, Elizabeth 11/07/65  11/10/65
Litchfield, Mary L. married Dorsey, Thomas N. 11/06/65  11/15/65
Litchfield, Mary L. married Dorsey, Thomas N. 11/06/65  11/18/65
Litsinger, Anna M. married Dodd, Andrew J. 07/29/63  10/05/63
```

Litsinger, Elizabeth married Seiderstricker, William D. 06/30/64 07/15/64
Litsinger, Mary J. married Hagaman, William P. 07/25/65 08/08/65
Litsinger, Richard married Fanning, Eliza 03/16/65 03/22/65
Littig, Jane M. died 10/16/62 10/17/62
Littig, Philip, Jr. died 03/24/65 03/25/65
Littiston, Thomas married Whiteloch, Ellen H. 01/14/65 02/02/65
Little, A. M. married Schelley, J. F. 01/17/61 12/19/61
Little, Albert Lumsden died 04/23/65 04/24/65
Little, Ann died 05/03/62 05/07/62
Little, Annie Francis died 08/14/62 08/16/62
Little, Annie R. married Showacre, Michael S. 10/20/62 10/25/62
Little, E. C. married Gibb, S. E. (Mrs.) 05/22/61 06/04/61
Little, Edwin died 04/17/61 04/23/61
Little, Elizabeth died 12/24/61 12/25/61
Little, Ellen P. married Simpson, Richard F. 02/11/63 02/26/63
Little, Francis M. died 08/08/65 08/22/65
Little, Frankie Ellsworth died 07/10/65 07/14/65
Little, Hannah (Mrs.) died 03/28/63 03/30/63
Little, James, Sr. died 06/04/65 06/05/65
Little, Mary Elizabeth died 12/07/65 12/11/65
Little, Robert died 12/16/64 12/17/64
Little, Robert P. married Turner, Alice 03/19/63 03/21/63
Little, Stephen married Nickol, Janett F. 10/15/60 05/30/61
Little, Thomas died 11/20/65 11/21/65
Little, Thomas Allen married McAdow, Sarah Jane 02/05/63 03/07/63
Little, William B. married Vandaniker, Kate 05/02/64 05/06/64
Little, Willie G. died 05/07/65 05/09/65
Littleton, Elizabeth V. married Price, Richard E. 03/20/62 03/21/62
Littleton, Marion married Smith, Richard A. 09/24/62 10/15/62
Littleton, Suselia (Mrs.) died 06/01/63 06/02/63
Litton, Elizabeth A. died 11/09/61 12/19/61
Livezy, George died 03/12/65 03/13/65
Livezy, George died 03/12/65 03/14/65
Livingston, Helen Roberta died 04/09/62 04/12/62
Livingston, Mary J. married Merriken, William 11/19/63 11/16/63
Livingston, W. Edwin married Gardner, Mary V. 10/17/65 10/19/65
Livington, Martha A. married Baker, William Worth 04/03/64 04/15/64
Livsey, William Joseph died 12/20/61 12/27/61
Lloyd, Eliza Jane died 08/25/62 08/30/62
Lloyd, Eugenia (Mrs.) married McDonald, F. T. (Lt.) 11/10/64 11/18/64
Lloyd, Evan died 09/09/64 09/10/64
Lloyd, Fannie married McCauley, George E. 09/26/65 09/27/65
Lloyd, Fannie L. died 03/18/65 03/21/65
Lloyd, J. Murray died 06/21/61 06/28/61
Lloyd, John Henry died 06/15/63 06/17/63
Lloyd, Lucy M. married Wonderly, Joseph D. 08/30/63 09/01/63
Lloyd, Maria married Wilson, William J. 04/08/63 04/29/63
Lloyd, Mary married Bopp, Lawrence 01/07/62 01/09/62
Lloyd, Mary Henry died 07/01/64 07/02/64
Lloyd, Rebecca T. married McNeal, William 06/06/63 06/25/63
Lloyd, Thomas married Kirby, Laura E. 01/06/64 01/13/64
Lloyd, Thomas (Col.) died 01/13/62 01/14/62
Lloyd, Thomas (Col.) died 01/13/62 01/15/62
Lloyd, William H. died 07/12/62 03/23/63

```
Lloyd, William J. married Ritter, Helen Mar 01/03/65   01/04/65
Loane, Edmund Jackson died 08/22/64   08/25/64
Loane, Elizabeth (Mrs.) died 03/10/63   03/11/63
Loane, Elizabeth (Mrs.) died 03/10/63   03/12/63
Loane, Ellie died 02/24/61   02/26/61
Loane, John T. S. married Alexander, Hannah R. M. 03/02/63   03/10/63
Loane, Millie A. married Beatson, George D. 06/14/64   06/15/64
Lobby, Bridget Ann E. (Mrs.) died 10/31/64   11/05/64
Lochary, Mary married Calwell, James R. 12/08/63   12/12/63
Locher, Elizabeth died 12/09/61   12/11/61
Locher, Mary died 11/20/65   11/22/65
Locher, Mary (Mrs.) died 11/20/65   11/21/65
Lock, Mary E. married Hodges, Thomas E. 09/12/65   09/15/65
Lockard, Lorenzo D. married Carr, Margaret 04/14/64   04/19/64
Lockbaum, Frederick died 01/12/63   01/14/64
Locke, Charles Edward Emmitt died 11/13/62   11/15/62
Locke, Mary A. (Mrs.) died 11/04/63   11/05/63
Locke, Priscilla (Mrs.) died 05/31/63   06/01/63
Locke, Sarah M. married Richards, John M. 06/24/65   06/28/65
Lockerman, Edward died 09/17/62   09/18/62
Lockerman, Edward died 09/17/62   09/19/62
Lockerman, Keziah married Quallion, Mordica 05/22/61   05/25/61
Lockerman, Margaret married Gross, Charles 03/27/64   05/09/64
Lockhart, Maggie J. married Harries, William 05/05/63   06/13/63
Lockington, Jennie M. married Burns, George W. 03/27/62   03/29/62
Lockington, Joshua died 10/15/61   10/16/61
Lockington, Margaret died 10/12/61   10/14/61
Locks, Israel married Jackson, Alice 09/05/65   09/07/65
Locks, Margaret (Mrs.) married Curtis, Robert 10/16/62   10/18/62
Lockwood, Elison J. married Bosserman, Minnie 12/09/60   07/13/61
Lockwood, Elizabeth C. died 08/03/65   08/09/65
Lockwood, Ella C. died 12/15/64   12/17/64
Lockwood, Ella C. died 12/16/64   12/23/64
Lockwood, John died 02/09/65   02/11/65
Lockwood, Margaret married Gross, Charles 03/27/64   05/07/64
Lockwood, Mary Ellen died 07/17/63   07/18/63
Lockwood, Mollie B. died 12/17/64   12/23/64
Lodd, William H. (Capt.) married Jones, Mary E. 04/11/65   04/13/65
Lodge, William J. (M.D.) married Cockey, Ginnie 04/24/62   05/02/62
Loehmeyer, Helena married Johnson, William H. 09/13/63   09/21/63
Loflin, Annie died 11/06/62   11/07/62
Loftis, Nathaniel died 03/14/63   03/16/63
Loftus, Eliza J. married McMahon, James 12/31/63   01/09/64
Logan, Charles Wesley died 11/13/63   11/16/63
Logan, Ellen married Lushbaugh, Martin L. 07/13/65   07/15/65
Logan, Hugh M. died 09/03/63   09/04/63
Logan, Hugh M. died 09/03/63   09/05/63
Logan, Margaret died 04/08/62   04/09/62
Logan, Mary died 03/01/65   03/02/65
Logan, Sarah married Henry, Daniel 01/26/62   01/30/62
Logemann, Margaret died 02/02/61   02/04/61
Logue, Ann died no date   12/16/62
Logue, Everett Parks died 10/31/63   11/25/63
Logue, Mary Edwards died 08/29/65   08/30/65
Logue, Michael died 08/07/62   08/08/62
```

Logue, Michael died 05/29/65   05/30/65
Lohrfink, Lewis died 10/27/64   10/28/64
Lohrfink, Wilhelmina died 10/06/64   10/07/64
Loker, (Mrs. James B.) died 02/06/62   02/07/62
Loker, George T. married Colbart, Susie F. 04/28/63   04/29/63
Loker, James B. (Mr.) died 02/06/62   02/08/62
Loker, John W. married Moore, Missouri 11/28/62   12/01/62
Loker, Michael J. (Cpt.) died 08/14/61   08/16/61
Loks, Monty married Brown, John W. 12/10/61   12/12/61
Lollas, Patrick married McKewen, Anne 09/07/63   09/11/63
Loman, Ann Rebecca married Dies, John G. 01/12/62   01/15/62
Lomax, William H. married Walker, Virginia 04/26/64   05/19/64
Lombard, Isabella married Stewart, Walter H. 12/24/65   12/29/65
Londrigan, Mary died 03/24/64   03/26/64
Lonegan, Mary died 09/22/62   09/23/62
Lonenburger, Margaret Frances died 05/31/63   06/01/63
Loney, E. Catherine married Perry, Thomas (Hon.) 12/04/61   12/07/61
Loney, Edward M. died 01/15/63   01/16/63
Loney, Martha Ann died 08/01/62   08/05/62
Loney, Mary Louisa married Conelly, John T. 10/06/63   10/08/63
Loney, Rebecca (Mrs.) died 03/13/64   03/14/64
Loney, William A. married Allen, Alice A, 01/06/64   01/16/64
Long, Addie married Caskey, John C. 10/14/64   02/22/65
Long, Alice Virginia died 12/26/63   01/06/64
Long, Alpheus died 07/21/64   07/22/64
Long, Ann died 09/29/61   09/30/61
Long, Anne E. married Jones, B. Franklin 03/28/64   03/30/64
Long, C. A. (Mrs.) married Ports, C. J. 12/01/64   12/20/64
Long, Conrad died 08/02/65   08/04/65
Long, Eliza (Mrs.) died 11/10/65   11/11/65
Long, Elizabeth married Hall, David 03/27/64   03/29/64
Long, Elizabeth married Kalb, David 03/27/64   03/30/64
Long, Elizabeth (Mrs.) died 05/11/63   05/13/63
Long, Elizabeth (Mrs.) married Robbins, Milbe 01/01/63   01/05/63
Long, George died 03/11/63   03/13/63
Long, Henry C. married Cary, Sarah Jane 11/09/64   11/12/64
Long, Jeannette Duncan died 11/20/62   11/22/62
Long, John married Wagner, Emma 04/06/63   04/08/63
Long, John married Downey, Maggie 01/17/64   01/18/64
Long, John D. died 07/06/61   07/08/61
Long, John G. died no date   08/13/63
Long, Leonard A. married Stall, Addie E. 12/14/63   12/16/63
Long, Louisa L. (Mrs.) died 01/25/65   01/27/65
Long, Maggie H. married Finney, Hugh 06/06/64   06/09/64
Long, Mariana married Stearns, John (Dr.) 04/04/65   04/06/65
Long, Mary Louisa died 08/01/63   08/08/63
Long, Mary Ophelia married Kimball, John W. 03/06/61   03/14/61
Long, Mary P. married Burch, James C. (Dr.) 06/03/63   06/09/63
Long, Modest V. died 10/12/62   10/15/62
Long, Susan H. (Mrs.) died 05/14/63   05/16/63
Long, Upton T. married Meyers, Louise 09/17/63   10/10/63
Long, William Lewis married Orem, Ann Rebecca 08/29/61   09/05/61
Longcope, William died 07/06/61   07/08/61
Longfield, Louisa married Jackson, Samuel S. 08/13/63   08/20/63
Longley, Joshua married Owens, Elizabeth A. 09/09/63   09/11/63

Longley, Joshua died 07/31/65 08/01/65
Longley, Maria E. died 04/05/62 04/07/62
Longley, Mary Laura Virginia died 02/18/62 02/21/62
Longridge, J. E. married Young, Mary M. 08/08/64 08/16/64
Lookingland, Elizabeth (Mrs.) married Golden, James 11/28/64 12/01/64
Loper, Annie Pierce (Mrs.) died 04/07/64 12/01/64
Lord, John D. married Williams, Jannett R. 02/07/61 02/13/61
Lord, Luther married Warner, Mary R. 05/31/65 06/01/65
Lore, Seth died 08/14/63 08/19/63
Lott, William married Springer, Mary E. 07/16/65 08/05/65
Louden, Mary Priscilla died 11/18/63 12/02/63
Loudenslager, Ann died 11/07/61 11/09/61
Loughran, Mary J. married Levell, Edward F. 05/25/62 05/27/62
Loughran, Patrick died 11/07/63 11/09/63
Louis, Julius married Opperhein, Hannah 01/05/65 02/08/65
Louis, Millie died 04/02/61 04/03/61
Louis, Thisble died 02/03/65 02/04/65
Lourey, Dellia died 10/01/63 10/02/63
Lourey, Robert J. died 08/20/63 08/21/63
Loury, Grafton Dulany died 06/15/64 06/16/64
Loushbaugh, Eleanor Rose (Mrs. died 02/01/65 02/03/65
Love, Amelia H. married Perry, Ancel F. C. 07/11/64 07/13/64
Love, Anna R. married Caldwell, John (Dr.) 01/05/64 01/07/64
Love, Elizabeth (Mrs.) died 07/01/63 07/03/63
Love, George B. died 04/19/65 04/25/65
Love, Harry Lincoln died 08/31/63 09/01/63
Love, J. E. (CSA) died 08/22/63 08/27/63
Love, Joseph died 05/09/64 05/11/64
Love, Joseph H. married Worthington, Annie H. 10/04/64 10/07/64
Love, Marion F. married Hooper, Edwin Eugene 02/21/65 03/09/65
Love, Mary Louisa married Kirby, James H. 12/26/62 02/14/63
Love, Mary W. Johns (Mrs.) died 06/27/64 06/28/64
Love, William died 12/14/63 12/18/63
Loveaire, H. F. married O'Reilly, Bessie 06/16/64 06/17/64
Loveaire, Harry F. married O'Reilly, Bessie 06/16/64 06/18/64
Loveaire, Harry F. married O'Reilly, Bessie 06/16/64 06/20/64
Loveday, Anna married Jones, Richard F. 02/18/61 02/21/61
Loveday, Perry died 01/10/63 01/14/64
Loveday, William Henry died 11/20/61 12/04/61
Lovegrove, Lydia died 06/23/65 06/24/65
Lovegrove, Rachel M. died 11/15/63 11/17/63
Lovejoy, Hettie M. married Baughman, John W. 06/21/65 07/24/65
Lovejoy, P. R. married Albertson, Rebecca T. 08/03/64 08/08/64
Lovel, William Elbert died 07/18/65 08/09/65
Lovell, Solomon G. died 10/05/65 10/11/65
Lovering, Charlotte Frances died 01/17/62 01/18/62
Lovering, Elizabeth Jane died 05/06/62 05/07/62
Lovering, Elizabeth Jane died 05/06/62 05/08/62
Lovering, George Augustus married Lovering, Julia P. 07/27/65 08/08/6
Lovering, Julia P. married Lovering, George Augustus 07/27/65 08/08/6
Lovett, Corneluis died 12/03/65 12/04/65
Lovey, Henry D. married McEvers, Anna 04/26/64 04/28/64
Low, Aaron married Brown, Susie 07/16/63 07/27/63
Low, Aaron (Cpt.) died 08/01/64 08/23/64
Low, Pauline E. married Powell, William T. 09/24/65 11/08/65

Lowe, Annie married Rieman, Joseph M. 10/03/61   10/08/61
Lowe, Charles E. married Cleaveland, Mary Jane 02/23/65   02/25/65
Lowe, Elizabeth Ann (Mrs.) died 01/04/63   01/06/63
Lowe, Elizabeth Benson died 04/26/61   04/27/61
Lowe, Henry died 12/20/61   12/23/61
Lowe, Henry died 09/27/62   11/06/62
Lowe, John (Dr.) died 11/10/65   11/23/65
Lowe, Kate (Mrs.) married Robinson, Henry S. 09/07/64   11/14/64
Lowe, Maggie B. died 08/26/62   08/27/62
Lowe, Maria Louisa married Lambdin, William K. 12/04/61   12/07/61
Lowe, Patrick died 07/25/61   07/26/61
Lowe, Susie B. married Latimer, Marcus B. 05/12/64   05/14/64
Lowe, Thomas W. died 11/09/62   11/10/62
Lowell, Rose married Cooper, Adderly 06/14/64   07/06/64
Lowenberg, Henry died 07/20/61   07/24/61
Lowenstine, Amelia married Wineberg, Samuel 10/11/63   10/13/63
Lowery, Mary Ann died 09/21/63   09/29/63
Lowery, R. B. married Webster, Susie 08/07/62   08/18/62
Lowery, Timothy died 08/26/63   08/28/63
Lowman, Marion married Clough, John J. 11/27/62   12/10/62
Lowman, Thomas J. married Brotherton, Martha B. 10/03/61   10/04/61
Lowndes, Charles married Tilghman, Kate 09/25/62   10/03/62
Lownds, James died 10/23/65   11/04/65
Lownds, Jane Carson (Mrs.) died 12/04/63   12/05/63
Lowrey, Benjamin F. married Ryrie, Johanna 03/15/64   03/18/64
Lowrey, John H. married Tarleton, Mary E. 09/11/64   09/27/64
Lowrey, Laura married Everson, Michael 09/20/64   10/04/64
Lowrey, Sarah C. married Robinson, Alphonso 09/24/63   09/28/63
Lowry, George N. died 08/29/63   08/31/63
Lowry, Grafton Dulany died 08/29/62   08/30/62
Lowry, Harriet D. married Kunsman, William H. 02/21/61   03/04/61
Lowry, Jane died 04/25/62   04/29/62
Lowry, Mary J. married Morrell, Seaman V. 12/17/65   12/19/65
Lowry, Robertia Elizabeth died 04/04/63   04/06/63
Lowry, Stephen A. married Gibson, Isabella A. 01/29/62   01/31/62
Lowry, Thomas died 11/08/62   11/10/62
Lowry, William H. married Clark, Aseneth S. 08/30/64   09/01/64
Lowry, William Palmer married Sewell, Maggie M. 06/18/65   06/10/65
Lowry, Willie L. died 09/23/65   09/25/65
Lowther, Maggie L. married Newcomer, Jessie 08/01/65   08/04/65
Lowther, Sadie Jones died 08/28/63   08/29/63
Lowthers, Emma S. married Turner, Walter B. 09/15/64   09/16/64
Loyd, John T. died 02/16/61   02/18/61
Luber, Eugene N. married Pettigrew, Maria Looclace 05/09/61   05/22/61
Lucas, Amelia Maccubbin died 06/16/64   06/18/64
Lucas, Deborah B. (Mrs.) died 12/27/65   12/30/65
Lucas, Deborah E. died 12/27/65   12/29/65
Lucas, Eliza M. (Mrs.) died 07/21/63   07/23/63
Lucas, Ellie J. married Merryman, Joseph P. 11/17/63   11/20/63
Lucas, George married Ridgly, Fannie 04/07/64   04/15/64
Lucas, John D. married Thompson, Sallie E. 04/30/62   05/03/62
Lucas, Kate B. married White, Thomas H. 05/09/65   05/11/65
Lucas, Margaret died 06/27/62   06/28/62
Lucas, Mary J. married Brooks, Zedekiah 08/18/64   08/20/64
Lucas, William George married Ault, Sallie E. 03/29/64   03/31/64

Lucas, William V. married McIntyre, Margaret E. 12/12/65 12/13/65
Luckett, Mary C. married Bathran, Eugene H. 12/03/61 12/12/61
Ludden, Adeline died 03/04/62 03/05/62
Ludwig, Augusta (Mrs.) died 09/23/64 09/24/64
Ludwig, Catharine (Mrs.) died 09/24/63 09/26/63
Ludwig, J. Henry married Beson, Emma 06/22/65 06/23/65
Ludwig, John married Wudmuller, Eliza (Mrs.) 02/01/65 02/04/65
Luhn, Gustave J. married Medley, Harriet E. 01/08/63 01/16/63
Luits, Josephine married Primrose, Samuel F. 04/15/61 07/06/61
Luiz, M. Lizzie married Jordan, John E. 12/22/62 12/29/62
Lukehart, Samuel L. married Bull, Lydia 12/19/61 12/21/61
Lukens, Sidney married Bankard, Charles H. (Lt.) 06/08/64 06/22/64
Lumpkin, Catherine Wyatt died 06/26/64 06/27/64
Lumpkin, Susia Garrett died 12/17/65 12/18/65
Lumpkin, Thomas died 07/13/63 07/21/63
Lumsdon, Charles Clark died 11/27/62 12/01/62
Lunar, Catherine S. married Hagadorn, F. L. (Gen.) 08/25/62 09/04/62
Lungren, John T. married Lewis, Mary A. 10/03/65 10/07/65
Lunn, William F. married Frey, Margaret C. 10/14/62 10/20/62
Lupton, Susannah married Evans, William H. 08/09/64 08/22/64
Lurman, Jenny D. married Frick, Frank 01/01/61 01/04/61
Lurty, Thomas W. married Skillman, Laura V. 06/16/61 06/28/61
Lusby, Ann (Mrs.) died 07/18/63 07/20/63
Lusby, Charles A. married Swyrp, Cornelia A. (Mrs.) 02/26/63 04/02/63
Lusby, Charles Robert died 09/12/65 09/14/65
Lusby, Edward L. married Deaver, Mary J. 03/23/63 04/08/63
Lusby, Eleathe A. died 07/16/65 07/18/65
Lusby, Henry married Yerby, Mary V. 11/21/64 11/24/64
Lusby, Henry W. died 12/23/63 12/28/63
Lusby, Henry W. died 12/23/63 12/29/63
Lusby, Ida Elizabeth died 12/17/64 12/26/64
Lusby, James married Campbell, Rose Ann 11/28/65 11/30/65
Lusby, Patience died 08/19/63 08/20/63
Lushbaugh, Martin L. married Logan, Ellen 07/13/65 07/15/65
Lushborough, Kate Ella died 11/22/64 11/24/64
Lusk, Mary M. married Smith, Walter D. 11/26/63 11/30/63
Lustnauer, Charles died 03/18/65 03/20/65
Lutin, Sarah married Ringll, Lenard 06/13/61 06/14/61
Luttman, Clara died 07/12/64 07/15/64
Lutton, Benjamin Eli died 07/27/64 11/05/64
Lutts, Charles J. married Dougherty, Fannie 01/07/64 01/09/64
Lutts, John F. died 03/19/64 03/21/64
Lutts, Josephine married Primrose, Samuel F. 04/15/61 07/10/61
Lutts, Josephine married Primrose, Samuel F. 04/15/61 07/11/61
Lutts, Mary B. died 01/28/62 01/29/62
Lutz, Fannie M. married Wentz, Henry C. 07/21/63 07/27/63
Lutz, Mary (Mrs.) died 04/25/65 04/27/65
Lybre, Mary A. married Disosway, I. C. (Lt.) 07/08/63 07/09/63
Lycett, George married Flint, Carrie no date 02/15/65
Lycett, Willis Romaine died 07/11/62 07/12/62
Lyell, Elizabeth died 08/07/61 08/08/61
Lyeth, Emeline died 10/30/65 10/31/65
Lyeth, Emeline died 10/30/65 11/01/65
Lyeth, Emeline, Elizabeth died 06/16/65 06/19/65
Lyford, M. (Mrs.) died 11/24/65 11/29/65

Lyle, Margaret (Mrs.) died 09/22/63   09/23/63
Lyle, Margaret Jane died 10/19/64   11/01/64
Lyles, Elizabeth C. married Ireland, Richard E. 12/06/65   12/12/65
Lyles, Henry married Rutter, Susanna (Mrs.) 10/04/64   10/19/64
Lyles, Martha Ann married Foos, Andrew J. 02/27/62   03/03/62
Lyles, Richard H. died 12/18/65   12/20/65
Lyles, Samuel married Crosby, Mary A. (Mrs.) 12/28/65   12/29/65
Lyles, Thomas married Scott, Susan Jane 09/30/62   10/07/62
Lyman, Mary (Mrs.) died 11/09/65   11/11/65
Lynch, Ann Rebecca (Mrs.) died 01/11/63   01/13/64
Lynch, Anne S. married Batty, Joseph W. 08/13/63   08/18/63
Lynch, Annie married Callaghan, Thomas 02/18/62   02/20/62
Lynch, Annie married Campbell, John 08/18/63   08/31/63
Lynch, Charles E. married Stansbury, Eloise 04/23/63   05/02/63
Lynch, Elizabeth died 01/31/65   02/02/65
Lynch, George W. married Glanding, Mary M. 10/20/64   10/22/64
Lynch, Hester (Mrs.) died 01/23/65   01/24/65
Lynch, James C. died 08/31/63   09/01/63
Lynch, John died 10/03/63   10/05/63
Lynch, Joseph S. married Sanner, Emma J. 06/14/65   07/19/65
Lynch, Lewis S. M. married Link, Elizabeth 04/17/65   04/19/65
Lynch, Rachel Williams died 10/25/61   10/26/61
Lynch, Roseanna married Claypoole, Benjamin B. 11/05/63   11/18/63
Lynch, Sallie J. married Landon, George 05/07/63   05/08/63
Lynch, Susan died 03/12/61   03/13/61
Lynch, William married Campbell, Sarah 11/24/64   12/09/64
Lynch, William F. died 10/17/65   10/19/65
Lynd, John D. died 04/06/63   04/07/63
Lynde, C. R. (Mrs.) died no date   03/30/61
Lynn, Michael married O'Brien, Mary 02/19/65   02/25/65
Lyoh, Upton Berryman died 01/21/61   01/22/61
Lyon, Ellen died 05/20/64   05/23/64
Lyon, Harriet died 03/16/63   03/18/63
Lyon, Jacob T. died 01/20/62   01/23/62
Lyon, Joseph A. died 06/30/61   01/23/62
Lyon, Robert died 02/27/65   03/01/65
Lyon, Robert died 02/27/65   03/10/65
Lyon, Sarah Ann died 01/08/62   01/11/62
Lyon, Sarah Ann died 01/08/62   01/23/62
Lyon, William B. died 04/25/65   04/27/65
Lyons, Daniel married Thomas, Annie T. 11/22/64   11/24/64
Lyons, Ella May died 10/26/64   10/28/64
Lyons, Ellen (Mrs.) died 11/06/64   11/07/64
Lyons, James died 11/16/62   11/17/62
Lyons, Jane died 10/25/64   10/26/64
Lyons, Johanna (Mrs.) died 01/01/63   01/03/63
Lyons, Sarah (Mrs.) died 07/10/64   07/13/64
Lysher, Edmund Franklin L. died 12/30/64   12/31/64
Lytle, Jennie Olive married Savin, Marcus D. 04/23/63   04/27/63
Lytle, Nicholas D. married Hughes, Sarah Amanda 12/01/63   12/04/63
Lytle, Robert A. died 10/13/64   10/20/64
Lytle, William B. married Cassell, Sallie J. 06/24/62   07/01/62
M'Crea, Mary (Mrs.) died 03/10/64   03/11/64
M'Laughin, John died 12/17/64   12/20/64

```
Mabee, Thaddeus died 06/19/64  06/20/64
Mac, Thomas A. married Price, Mary A. 01/05/62  01/07/62
Macartney, John Irby died no date  06/10/61
Macartney, Kerana E. married Stebbing, Jesse 04/28/64  05/07/64
Macartney, Mary E. died 03/02/64  03/11/64
Macaulay, Elizabeth died 01/24/62  01/25/62
Macauley, Robert Vinton married Haupt, Mary Jane 06/09/63  06/16/63
MacCrea, Josephine died 10/11/65  10/14/65
Maccubbin, Agnes L. died 05/01/64  05/02/64
Maccubbin, Agnes L. died 05/01/64  05/03/64
Maccubbin, Agnes L. died 05/01/64  05/05/64
Maccubbin, George W. died 11/21/61  11/22/61
Maccubbin, Henry W. died 12/28/63  12/30/63
Maccubbin, Maggie E. married Neilson, Joseph E. 04/04/64  04/07/64
Maccubbin, Mary Ann (Mrs.) died 01/11/63  01/12/63
Maccubbin, Thomas O. died 12/15/63  12/16/63
Maccubbins, Fannie F. died 10/24/64  10/25/64
Maccubin, Frank W. died 10/23/62  12/06/62
Maccubin, Mary Roberta died 10/29/62  12/06/62
Maccubin, Willie R. died 10/25/62  12/06/62
Macdonald, Catharine died 07/01/63  07/02/63
MacDonald, Mary L. married Carter, Richard 04/22/65  05/13/65
Mace, Elizabeth died 07/09/65  07/10/65
Mace, Emira S. married Billington, James P. 03/15/65  03/17/65
Mace, John Wesley married Woolford, Kate 01/14/62  01/21/62
Mace, Lydia Claudine died 10/11/64  10/12/64
Mace, Stephen T. died 04/02/64  04/04/64
Maceney, Susan died 09/30/63  10/02/63
Macfarlan, Harriet married Bradford, Alexander 05/17/62  05/19/62
Macfarran, William died 05/11/65  05/18/65
Macferran, William died 05/11/65  05/17/65
Machen, Lewis H. died 08/11/63  08/13/63
Macher, Frances A. died 08/05/62  08/07/62
Macher, J. S. married Ridgaway, A. C. 12/15/64  12/24/64
Macher, James P. died 10/28/62  10/30/62
Macher, Mary C. died 04/16/65  04/18/65
Macher, Robert Emory died 07/03/63  07/04/63
Machlin, R. L. died no date  02/11/65
Machrill, William Richardson married Victoire, Mary 03/29/65  03/30/65
Mack, William J. married Wattles, Kate A. 11/18/63  02/13/64
Mackay, Sarah Ann died 02/16/61  02/18/61
Mackenhamer, Jennie married Burke, Oliver 03/27/62  06/20/62
MacKenzie, Mary C. married Findlay, John V. L. 06/16/63  06/18/63
Mackenzie, Thomas G. (Dr.) married Owings, Laura 02/17/63  02/28/63
Mackenzie, Thomas G. (Dr.) married Owings, Laura 02/17/63  03/03/63
Mackey, Alexander died 01/16/62  01/17/62
Mackey, Mannie L. married Meany, Charles F. 08/01/65  08/02/65
Mackey, Margaret died 10/06/62  10/07/62
Mackey, Mary L. married Meaney, Charles F. 08/01/65  08/03/65
Mackey, Nancy died 09/29/64  09/30/64
Mackin, Bernard died 11/29/62  12/01/62
Mackin, Mary (Mrs.) died 10/01/63  10/03/63
Mackin, Mary Ann died 04/20/64  04/21/64
Mackin, Robert married Harvey, Eugenia 08/16/64  08/18/64
Mackintosh, Alexander Smith died 01/24/61  01/28/61
```

Macklin, John died 12/12/65 12/13/65
Macklin, John died 12/12/65 12/14/65
Mackubin, Julianna R. M.(Mrs.) died 10/10/65 10/13/65
MacLaskey, Mary married Mortimer, Henry W. 08/07/65 08/12/65
Maclellan, Kate F. married Bartholomer, Theodore M. 09/17/62 10/07/62
Macleod, Lydia Ann died 03/31/62 04/01/62
Maclin, J. J. married Pindell, M. Alice 01/10/65 02/07/65
MacNeal, Ella A. married Murray, John D. 04/06/64 04/08/64
Macneal, James B. married Burgess, Sarah S. 04/21/64 04/23/64
MacNeil, Ella A. married Murray, John D. 04/06/64 04/08/64
Macrae, Ellen Douglass died 09/30/62 10/02/62
Macubbin, Augusta M. married Prettyman, William E. 04/19/64 05/02/64
Macubin, Edmond died 11/12/65 11/15/65
Madary, Ellen S. married Hardy, George M. 10/19/65 10/21/65
Madden, Caroline died 04/21/64 04/25/64
Madden, Hannah M. married Dufur, George J. 12/22/64 12/28/64
Madden, James married Banks, Emily J. 08/31/64 11/05/64
Madden, Jeremiah died 09/22/62 09/23/62
Madden, John died 07/18/62 07/19/62
Madden, Peter died no date 08/05/63
Madden, Richard William died 12/19/61 12/20/61
Madden, William T. died 08/13/65 08/22/65
Maddigan, Willie died 10/11/65 10/13/65
Maddocks, John B. married Rhoads, Annie J. 01/04/63 03/10/63
Maddox, Lucinda married Waters, Isaac 12/11/62 12/23/62
Maddox, Mary (Mrs.) died 02/24/63 02/26/63
Maddox, Mary E. A. died 03/09/62 03/11/62
Maddox, Rachel (Mrs.) died 10/11/63 10/12/63
Maddox, Rachel (Mrs.) died 10/11/63 10/13/63
Maddox, Robert H. died 03/12/62 03/14/62
Madenan, Elizabeth died 12/30/63 12/31/63
Mades, Amelia (Mrs.) died 04/08/65 04/10/65
Madgrick, Thomas married Lawton, Ann E. 11/20/62 12/10/62
Madigan, Mary married Reilly, Edward E. 12/02/62 12/05/62
Madigan, Thomas married Mahony, Mary F. 09/06/63 11/05/63
Madinger, Mary Barbary died 01/16/61 01/17/61
Madison, Elizabeth (Mrs.) died 12/11/63 12/25/63
Madison, Hester A. married Jervis, James 12/02/60 01/09/61
Madison, Mary Ann died 04/24/61 04/25/61
Maffit, Clayland S. died 10/22/65 10/26/65
Maffit, Samuel S. died 05/24/64 05/26/64
Maffitt, Annie R. married Helmling, W. Harry 01/01/62 01/04/62
Magaw, Samuel married Ball, Mary Louisa 11/19/60 01/08/61
Magaw, Samuel J. married Taylor, Rachal A. 01/10/61 01/21/61
Magee, E. J. married Wylie, Robert 09/30/63 10/02/63
Magee, Harry L. G. died 03/10/63 03/12/63
Magee, Hugh R. died 11/06/65 11/07/65
Magee, Janeia E. died 12/25/62 01/03/63
Magee, Josephine Florence died 12/28/62 01/03/63
Magee, Josephine R. married Herring, Malcolm L. 04/30/63 05/04/63
Magee, William P. died 01/20/63 01/22/63
Mager, Peter A. died 04/18/64 04/20/64
Magers, Elizabeth married Norris, William 04/22/62 04/23/62
Magers, Frances P. died 04/21/62 04/23/62
Magers, Margaret Ann died 12/06/63 12/08/63

Magers, Mary Loretto died 09/24/63 09/25/63
Magers, Minnie S. died 06/07/65 06/09/65
Magess, Louis Lawrence died 05/08/62 05/09/62
Magill, C. J. married Renhoe, E. M. 04/02/64 04/28/64
Magill, Charles J. married Kennedy, Elizabeth 09/04/64 09/30/64
Magill, Mary Ann died 05/19/61 05/20/61
Magilley, William married Stewart, Kate 10/05/62 10/22/62
Maglenn, John died 11/13/63 11/14/63
Magness, Actia (Mrs.) died 04/22/65 04/24/65
Magness, James E. married Ingman, Harriet E. 06/02/62 06/04/62
Magness, Lee married Fitzgerald, H. B. 08/30/64 08/31/64
Magness, Mary Lurecia died 08/25/63 08/27/63
Magness, Sarah A. married Flowers, Benjamin B. 06/08/65 06/16/65
Magness, Sarah Jane married Pyne, William H. 01/30/62 02/03/62
Magness, Thomas M. married Woodland, Susie F. 04/14/65 04/18/65
Magorian, John died 06/02/63 06/04/63
Magraw, Elizabeth (Mrs.) died 05/05/63 05/07/63
Magraw, John James died 06/11/62 06/12/62
Magraw, W. M. F. died 04/07/64 04/08/64
Magruder, Edward P. died 12/11/63 12/14/63
Magruder, John Meade married Nicholson, Emily Erving 06/29/65 07/03/6
Magruder, Josephine H. married Davis, Thomas B. 11/24/63 11/26/63
Magruder, Josephine H. married Davis, Thomas B. 11/24/63 12/03/63
Magruder, Laura Victoria died 08/23/63 08/24/63
Magruder, Sarah married Ray, John R. 03/31/64 04/02/64
Magruder, W. E. (Rev.) married Brooke, Margaret H. 05/24/64 05/31/64
Maguire, Ellenora married Barbine, William E. 05/07/63 05/09/63
Maguire, John A. died 12/26/65 12/28/65
Maguire, John F. married Stapleton, Mollie E. 06/02/64 06/09/64
Maguire, Lucinda died 01/15/63 01/16/63
Maguire, M. Bernard died 11/04/64 11/05/64
Maguire, Patrick married Rooney, Ann 05/02/61 05/14/61
Maguire, Sarah married Lawrence, Oren S. (Lt.) 04/27/63 04/28/63
Maguire, Sarah married Lawrence, Oren S. (Lt.) 04/27/63 05/02/63
Maguire, Susanna married Witts, William 06/01/65 07/26/65
Mahan, Ann died 12/04/64 12/06/64
Mahan, Anna married Hanlay, Martin 09/12/64 09/13/64
Mahan, Edward died 09/19/63 09/22/63
Maher, Anney married Cross, James A. 02/07/64 02/10/64
Maher, Josephine married Wellmore, Edward H. 06/23/64 06/30/64
Mahn, Elizabeth (Mrs.) died 03/10/64 03/12/64
Mahon, Anne (Mrs.) died 03/29/64 03/30/64
Mahon, James died 04/14/62 04/15/62
Mahon, James died 04/14/62 04/16/62
Mahon, John married Patterson, Kate 05/28/65 06/01/65
Mahon, Mary married Bleakley, James B. 02/07/61 02/14/61
Mahon, Theodosia (Mrs.) died 01/08/63 01/10/63
Mahoney, Hannah married Fallon, Mallachi 01/15/65 01/21/65
Mahoney, Katie died 10/26/63 10/27/63
Mahony, Mary F. married Madigan, Thomas 09/06/63 11/05/63
Mahony, Timothy died 11/25/65 11/27/65
Mahool, Eliza died 02/14/62 02/17/62
Mahool, W. Harrison died 02/01/62 02/04/62
Mahorney, Henson married Boston, Priscilla 10/13/64 10/14/64
Mahorney, Maria married Peters, John R. 07/26/63 08/08/63

```
Mahorney, Nancey died 08/01/65   08/02/65
Mahrer, Henry married O'Neill, Margaret A. 01/12/64   03/11/64
Mahtison, Alexander married Robinson, Mary E. 10/30/64   11/01/64
Maihl, Mart died 12/08/62   12/09/62
Maihl, Thomas married Robertson, Sallie M. 10/24/65   10/27/65
Mailhouse, Mary Emma Bertha died 09/24/64   09/26/64
Mainley, Thomas died 10/11/65   10/12/65
Mainster, Israel died 09/04/62   09/06/62
Mainster, Robert Anderson died 05/17/64   05/19/64
Mainster, Sarah (Mrs.) died 01/23/65   02/10/65
Maitland, Benjamin, Jr. died 12/31/60   01/02/61
Maitland, Eliza died 06/06/62   06/11/62
Maitland, Frances died 08/03/63   08/04/63
Maitland, John Wilkes died 08/11/63   08/12/63
Maitland, John Wilkes died 08/11/63   08/13/63
Maker, John K. married Earle, Mary J. 09/04/62   09/09/62
Malcolm, James died 05/10/64   05/11/64
Maldin, Frederick A. died 09/06/61   09/07/61
Male, Mary E. married Walsh, Henry E. 10/27/62   11/03/62
Male, William died 06/26/65   07/17/65
Mallalieu, W. H. Harrison married Jones, Ella 10/10/65   10/18/65
Mallen, Patrick died 02/10/63   02/11/63
Mallen, Rose M. married Katzenburger, Louis E. 02/09/63   02/10/63
Mallen, Susanna (Mrs.) died 12/26/65   12/28/65
Maller, James N. married Carr, Helen 05/19/64   05/25/64
Mallilieu, Edward married Snead, Sarah E. 05/05/63   05/07/63
Mallon, Minnie died 01/15/64   01/19/64
Mallon, Sarah A. died 11/09/64   11/10/64
Mallon, Sarah A. (Mrs.) died 11/09/64   11/11/64
Mallonee, Cornilla E. died 09/13/64   09/14/64
Mallonee, Mary Ann died 01/16/61   01/22/61
Mallonee, Racael died 11/24/62   11/25/62
Mallonee, Rachel died 11/24/62   11/26/62
Mallonee, Rachel L. (Mrs.) died 08/25/63   08/26/63
Mallonee, Sarah E. married Spangler, J. N. (Rev.) 04/03/62   04/07/62
Mallonnee, William H. married Johnson, Martha Ann 09/25/62   09/30/62
Mallony, Mary Ann died 01/16/61   01/17/61
Malone, Elizabeth married Whayland, Wesley A. 12/24/61   01/07/62
Malone, Hester married Perkins, Charles 12/26/65   12/28/65
Malone, John married Grossman, Mary Ann 12/31/62   01/09/63
Malone, Margaret married Steaveson, William 01/01/62   01/04/62
Malone, Susannah died 10/02/61   10/10/61
Maloney, Andrew Jackson died 05/31/63   06/01/63
Maloney, Ann (Mrs.) died 05/22/64   05/23/64
Maloney, Eliza Ann married Foster, Addison 01/03/65   01/07/65
Maloney, James Cromwell died 02/12/63   02/14/63
Maloney, Mary Ellen died 02/29/64   03/02/64
Maloney, Sarah married Fowler, Daniel D. 05/01/64   05/04/64
Maloney, Thomas died 12/05/65   12/07/65
Malory, Gruey married Emory, Jacob 08/10/65   08/11/65
Malowney, Michael died 02/24/63   02/26/63
Malsburry, Harriet married Buckannan, John 04/06/65   04/08/65
Malseed, Mary died 04/02/64   04/04/64
Maltby, L. U. married Foster, Mattie 02/10/64   02/11/64
Malyn, (Miss) married Minnick, F. M. 09/24/61   09/26/61
```

Manaca, Ida Virginia died 04/08/65   04/12/65
Manahan, Michael died 11/23/62   11/24/62
Manahan, Sarah Elizabeth died 06/22/64   06/24/64
Mangum, Richard married Baldwin, Olivia 01/31/64   02/02/64
Manicot, Charles Edward died 04/28/64   04/29/64
Maning, Henry died 06/17/64   06/18/64
Manion, (Mrs.) died 12/29/61   12/31/61
Manion, Catherine died 06/30/64   07/01/64
Manion, Michael died 09/03/63   09/04/63
Mankin, Isaiah died 04/19/64   04/20/64
Mankin, Virginia E. married Roach, Thomas B. 02/07/61   02/09/61
Mankins, George Washington died 08/17/62   08/22/62
Manley, Elizabeth married Benhardt, Andrew 03/13/64   03/15/64
Manley, Elizabeth A. died 02/16/64   02/18/64
Manly, John died 12/26/63   12/29/63
Manly, John S. married Connor, Mary A. 04/23/63   04/24/63
Manly, Martha Jane died 08/28/63   08/29/63
Mann, Amelia died 02/05/62   02/06/62
Mann, Ann T. (Mrs.) died 07/05/64   07/06/64
Mann, Annie F. (Mrs.) died 07/05/64   07/07/64
Mann, B. N. married Everhart, Louisa H. 03/20/62   03/24/62
Mann, Benjamin F. married Gilmore, Lina 05/17/64   05/19/64
Mann, Cecilia died 04/16/62   04/18/62
Mann, George died 06/21/62   06/23/62
Mann, Jacob died 04/21/65   04/22/65
Mann, John died 04/29/62   05/01/62
Mann, John died 04/29/62   05/06/62
Mann, Joseph died 07/08/63   07/09/63
Mann, Mary Estelle died 09/08/63   09/10/63
Mann, Samuel B. married Sullivan, Emma 01/03/65   01/19/65
Mann, Samuel B. married Sullivan, Emma 01/03/65   01/21/65
Mann, Samuel S. (Lt.) married Greenwood, Harriet A. 10/16/65   10/18/65
Mann, Sarah married Camp, James L. 04/06/65   04/10/65
Mannakee, Phillip died 01/11/64   01/13/64
Manner, Claiborne H. married Flack, Isabella 02/22/61   09/03/61
Manning, Annie married Smith, Thomas H. 05/01/64   05/03/64
Manning, James died 08/01/61   08/02/61
Manning, Patrick died 04/15/62   04/16/62
Mannion, Kate married Swiiny, Cornelius 04/19/63   04/21/63
Manns, Fannie married Fleeharty, Thomas J. 01/10/61   01/12/61
Manns, Fannie married Fluharty, Thomas J. 01/10/61   01/15/61
Manns, Henry C. died 10/28/63   12/03/63
Manoka, Sarah J. married Garreet, Hezekiah 04/22/62   04/23/62
Mansfield, R. W. married Reid, Elizabeth 04/28/64   05/02/64
Mansfield, Sarah died 10/23/62   10/24/62
Manson, John G. married Guy, Indiana F. 12/30/62   12/31/62
Manson, William H. died 04/20/61   05/06/61
Mantle, William married Jones, Josephine 01/17/61   01/18/61
Mantz, Laura Virginia married Myer, James, Jr. 05/10/64   05/25/64
Mantz, William H. married Hoffna, Martha A. 02/28/65   03/02/65
Manuel, Margaret Bangs died 08/19/63   08/22/63
Marbury, Edward died 07/10/64   07/11/64
March, Annie L. married Kilmer, Harry C. 05/12/63   05/14/63
March, Emma married Gilbert, Isaac Wilson 11/19/63   11/21/63
March, Josephine S. married Hannal, Alfred M. (Capt.) 01/14/64   01/15

```
March, Kate died 03/28/63    03/30/63
March, Lilly died 02/01/62    02/03/62
March, Louisa died 01/03/62    01/04/62
March, Washington died 06/30/65    07/03/65
March, William G. married McLachlan, Nettie B. 08/04/63    08/18/63
March, Willie died 10/08/62    10/09/62
Marck, Josephine S. married Channel, Alfred M. 01/07/64    01/19/64
Marcy, Cameia married Pendleton, Edmund H. 04/28/64    05/03/64
Marden, Jesse, Jr. married Brice, Annie M. M. 11/10/64    11/11/64
Marden, Rosana married Eichman, J. C. 05/29/62    05/31/62
Mardens, William died 10/23/63    11/03/63
Marfield, Catherine died 09/16/62    09/17/62
Marfield, Catherine died 09/16/62    09/18/62
Marfield, John S. W. died 01/08/61    01/09/61
Marfield, John S. W. died 01/08/61    01/14/61
Marfield, William died 08/16/61    11/08/61
Mariene, Mary L. married Owings, Elisha 11/17/64    11/19/64
Marin, George W. married Kingston, Catharine 02/19/64    02/24/64
Marine, Fletcher C. died 03/06/64    03/08/64
Marine, William married Cooper, Mary Catherine 11/21/61    11/22/61
Marines, Suzannah E. married Drury, William A. 01/01/65    01/03/65
Marion, Virginia married White, Richard Fabius 01/21/62    01/23/62
Marion, Virginia married White, Richard Fabius 01/21/62    01/24/62
Mariott, Mary J. married Tuttle, Joseph W. (Sgt.) 01/14/63    01/20/63
Mark, Martha died 01/15/65    01/17/65
Mark, Mary married East, Henry 06/16/64    06/18/64
Mark, Mary A. died 10/25/65    10/28/65
Markham, Maralla (Mrs.) died 07/26/64    07/27/64
Markland, Alice E. married Penning, Sylvester E. 06/02/63    06/11/63
Markland, Arabella died 12/17/65    12/19/65
Markland, James H. married Henkle, Georgeiana 01/15/63    01/24/63
Markley, Barbara E. married Hartman, Bernard A. 10/11/64    10/29/64
Markley, Fanny M. died 10/18/65    10/19/65
Markley, Samuel married Christopher, Grace Anne 10/31/65    11/01/65
Marks, Henry married Bennett, Margaret 11/06/63    11/28/63
Marlay, Ellinor (Mrs.) died 03/04/64    03/07/64
Marley, James R. married McIlhaney, Nancy 11/22/65    12/16/65
Marlut, Annie married Allnut, John F. 11/05/63    11/12/63
Marlow, S. D. married Harryman, S. E. 11/23/64    11/28/64
Marlow, Sarah E. (Mrs.) died 05/01/65    05/02/65
Maron, Amanda J. married Smith, George 04/12/64    04/15/64
Marquett, Ida Cedelia died 11/12/65    11/13/65
Marquette, John N. married Leonard, Augusta C. 01/03/61    01/14/61
Marr, John G. married Peterson, Caroline M. 04/20/62    05/12/62
Marriot, Edith died 02/29/64    03/03/64
Marriott, Bushrod died 07/15/64    07/19/64
Marriott, John S. married Barnett, Julia C. 10/17/62    10/28/62
Marriott, Joseph G. W. died 11/07/65    11/08/65
Marriott, Mary married Tuttle, Joseph H. 01/14/63    01/23/63
Marriott, Robert Boyd died 06/23/65    06/24/65
Marriott, Thomas married German, Mary E. 12/26/65    12/29/65
Marriso, Charles married Minzel, Margaret 12/29/62    10/29/63
Marry, Sarah married Sands, Richard H. 02/27/65    04/01/65
Marryman, Dorcass married Forrester, Charles 01/05/64    01/09/64
Marryman, Eleanor J. married Turner, George W. 10/27/64    10/31/64
```

Marsden, Charles T. (Sgt.) died 09/17/62   10/13/62
Marsden, Sophia Verener died 01/13/63   01/15/63
Marsh, C. H. married Creamer, Sallie E. 11/24/63   11/28/63
Marsh, Chester S. married Standiford, Matilda C. 06/28/65   06/30/65
Marsh, Eliza married Strahan, E., Jr. 02/14/61   02/18/61
Marsh, Eliza (Mrs.) died 01/17/64   01/18/64
Marsh, George H. died 02/29/64   03/09/64
Marsh, Mary E. (Mrs.) died 03/16/64   03/18/64
Marsh, Minerva died 04/25/61   04/27/61
Marsh, Richard died 12/27/63   12/28/63
Marsh, Sarah E. (Mrs.) died 03/16/64   03/17/64
Marshael, Reuben married Billmyer, Catherine (Mrs.) 01/25/63   01/29/63
Marshal, Anne Elizabeth died 04/05/63   04/06/63
Marshall, Anna Maria (Mrs.) died 02/08/65   02/09/65
Marshall, Charles E. married McDonnell, Jane 05/23/61   06/14/62
Marshall, Charles H. died 12/06/63   12/08/63
Marshall, Daniel died 12/03/62   12/04/62
Marshall, Florence died 11/04/61   11/08/61
Marshall, Francis E. died 02/13/65   02/24/65
Marshall, H. married Osborn, Matilda U. 06/16/64   06/18/64
Marshall, Hester married Gidley, David 09/12/61   09/14/61
Marshall, Jamel died 08/13/63   08/18/63
Marshall, John married Schuhoff, Williamina 06/16/62   06/17/62
Marshall, John married Schuhoff, Williamina 06/16/62   06/19/62
Marshall, John married Schuhoff, Williamina 06/16/62   06/20/62
Marshall, Joseph M. married Parkes, Mary A. 02/28/65   03/14/65
Marshall, Levin (Cpt.) died 09/16/62   09/17/62
Marshall, M. Jane married Lannay, Louis F. 04/03/62   04/04/62
Marshall, Mahaley (Mrs.) died 02/03/64   02/04/64
Marshall, Margaret A. died 02/29/64   03/02/64
Marshall, Maria died 12/06/63   12/08/63
Marshall, Maria (Mrs.) died 05/13/63   05/15/63
Marshall, Mary H. died 06/03/64   06/06/64
Marshall, Mary Rebecca married Shaffer, John Henry 01/14/63   02/12/63
Marshall, Sarah (Mrs.) died 09/12/63   09/14/63
Marshall, Sarah Eliza died 08/16/62   08/18/62
Marshall, Sarah Eliza died 10/30/62   11/11/62
Marshall, Sarah Eliza died 10/30/62   11/12/62
Marshall, Thomas died 09/06/64   09/07/64
Marshall, Treacy died 02/10/61   02/12/61
Marshall, William married Goodman, Florence no date   04/22/64
Marshall, William married Ruark, Sarah E. 10/01/65   11/03/65
Marshall, William E. Bruce married Gibbs, Josephine 11/24/63   12/05/63
Marshall, William G., Jr. married Linthicum, Gussie 04/11/61   04/16/61
Marshall, William H. married Broadbent, Isabella 12/17/62   12/30/62
Marshall, William M. L. died 05/08/63   06/27/63
Marshall, William T. died 06/30/62   07/01/62
Marsters, Eliza J. (Mrs.) died 04/26/63   05/04/63
Marston, Mary died 05/22/61   05/23/61
Mart, Mary married Clark, George T. 01/21/64   05/06/64
Martenet, Annie Parmelia died 10/31/63   11/11/63
Martenet, Jefferson married Wiegel, Rosie Louise 03/28/64   04/30/64
Marter, David A. (Cpt.) married Thompson, Sarah June 08/09/62   10/16/
Marthlas, Freddie married Brotzel, Jacob 12/24/61   01/01/62
Martien, Joseph married Clark, Isabella 03/24/64   03/25/64

Martien, Joseph G. died 06/10/63 06/11/63
Martien, Leah (Mrs.) died 07/28/65 07/29/65
Martill, Peter died 09/25/62 09/26/62
Martin, A. R. married Krantz, A. A. 05/21/63 02/05/64
Martin, Ann (Mrs.) died 08/21/63 08/22/63
Martin, Ann D. (Mrs.) died 04/22/64 04/27/64
Martin, Annie E. married Cook, William V. 11/20/65 12/05/65
Martin, Caroline (Mrs.) died 08/30/63 09/01/63
Martin, Catharine (Mrs.) died 06/19/64 06/20/64
Martin, Charles died 02/19/61 02/20/61
Martin, Charles Henry died 04/24/62 04/29/62
Martin, Edward married Dentry, Mary A. 09/25/62 09/29/62
Martin, Edward married Orr, Acey 07/08/62 01/07/63
Martin, Eleanor died 09/10/62 09/15/62
Martin, Elizabeth A. (Mrs.) died 05/07/63 05/09/63
Martin, Elizabeth D. died 06/27/62 06/28/62
Martin, Elizabeth L. died 12/19/62 12/20/62
Martin, Ella died 09/27/65 09/29/65
Martin, Ellen (Mrs.) died 05/02/64 05/03/64
Martin, Fannie A. married Courtney, George 09/28/65 10/30/65
Martin, Francis De Sales died 01/04/63 01/15/63
Martin, George A. died 06/22/61 06/25/61
Martin, Grace Genevieve died 06/12/65 06/17/65
Martin, H. W. married Huffington, Amanda 08/31/64 09/12/64
Martin, Harry died 01/10/65 01/13/65
Martin, Hattie R. married Perry, William J. 02/21/61 02/22/61
Martin, Helen married Reip, J. Henry 01/15/61 01/18/61
Martin, Henry married Monroe, Hattie L. 03/26/62 04/01/62
Martin, James died 11/08/64 11/09/64
Martin, James A. (Cpt.) died no date 10/17/62
Martin, James K. D. died 08/01/65 08/03/65
Martin, John died 03/19/62 03/18/62
Martin, John married Hurst, Catherine (Mrs.) 03/17/63 03/23/63
Martin, John married Leace, Mary Jane 09/07/65 09/08/65
Martin, John W. married Homsher, Rebecca 12/29/64 12/30/64
Martin, Johnnie died 01/28/62 01/30/62
Martin, Joseph F. married Clemmens, Elizabeth A. 05/08/64 05/10/64
Martin, Joseph Shipley died 08/29/61 09/03/61
Martin, Josephine married Scott, John Thomas 04/07/63 04/08/63
Martin, Josie died 03/08/63 03/10/63
Martin, Kate A. married Hutchins, Robert H. 09/28/62 10/01/62
Martin, Katy died 08/28/63 08/29/63
Martin, Keziah married Smith, J. Albert 10/30/65 11/02/65
Martin, Lizzie J. married Shipley, C. W. 09/12/65 09/18/65
Martin, Maggie Susannah died 04/26/65 04/27/65
Martin, Mary died 07/26/64 07/27/64
Martin, Mary married Hughes, Peter 01/07/64 01/16/64
Martin, Mary A. died 12/11/63 12/12/63
Martin, Mary A. married Dempsey, John F. 02/12/63 02/14/63
Martin, Mary E. married Pottee, George 08/20/65 09/16/65
Martin, Mary E. (Mrs.) married Cooper, James 11/28/61 11/30/61
Martin, Mary Eliza (Mrs.) died 09/20/63 09/24/63
Martin, Mary Elizabeth died 10/18/63 10/23/63
Martin, Nancy Ann died 02/11/64 02/12/64
Martin, Oliver married Jamison, Lucinda 07/30/61 08/01/61

Martin, Owen died 08/27/63 08/28/63
Martin, Rebecca Jane married More, Harrison 03/21/64 05/17/64
Martin, Rosa F. died 12/14/62 12/16/62
Martin, S. Henson married Ferguson, Maggie J. 08/30/64 09/03/64
Martin, Sally married Christon, James 01/21/64 01/23/64
Martin, Sarah Sophia married Jones, Henry 12/05/64 02/07/65
Martin, Sophia died 04/22/62 04/24/62
Martin, Susan died 04/27/62 04/30/62
Martin, Virginia F. died 07/21/62 07/26/62
Martin, W. H. married Topley, Permelia A. 10/21/63 10/26/63
Martin, W. J. married Spicer, Alice 04/27/65 05/04/65
Martin, Walter Ricaud died 02/17/62 02/28/62
Martin, William died 01/09/62 01/11/62
Martin, William died 12/23/63 12/24/63
Martin, William H. died 06/14/63 08/14/63
Martin, William Melvin died 05/22/63 05/25/63
Martin, William R. married Hutson, Callie C. 12/17/63 12/29/63
Mary, Simmons died 01/28/62 01/29/62
Maseke, Mary (Mrs.) died 01/10/64 01/12/64
Masen, Susan Ann died 04/20/62 04/22/62
Masi, Albert Vincent died 06/22/62 07/03/62
Mask, Catherine died 03/08/61 03/09/61
Mask, John Q. A. married Herring, Emogine E. 11/14/64 11/15/64
Maskell, John Wesley died 03/09/62 03/11/62
Maskimon, Mary Virginia died 12/11/61 12/12/61
Mason, Annie E. married Jones, Owen D. 06/20/65 06/23/65
Mason, Caspar P. married McClellan, Mary A. 04/14/64 08/02/64
Mason, Charles married Biggs, Anna 07/18/65 07/20/65
Mason, Eilback died 06/28/62 08/01/62
Mason, Emeline J. married Henderson, John 06/10/62 06/11/62
Mason, Fannie J. married Scott, James R. 06/01/65 06/13/65
Mason, Garville S. married Fisher, Mary E. 11/24/63 12/22/63
Mason, George died 08/05/63 08/06/63
Mason, George E. married Bitzel, Hennie L. 12/06/64 12/21/64
Mason, George Russell died no date 08/11/62
Mason, Helen F. married Patterson, Frank W. 06/28/65 07/08/65
Mason, Henry G. died 06/16/64 06/17/64
Mason, Ida died 08/16/61 08/19/61
Mason, Ida Belle died 10/23/65 10/25/65
Mason, James A. married Myers, Rebecca 12/06/65 12/23/65
Mason, Joseph T. married Fischer, Catherine A. 03/29/64 03/30/64
Mason, Laura married Robert, Benjamin 09/03/62 09/16/62
Mason, Louis Dungan died 07/12/65 07/14/65
Mason, Maria married Hays, Patrick 01/18/63 01/20/63
Mason, Mary married Tormey, J. Edward 11/05/63 11/06/63
Mason, Mary A. died 10/19/64 10/24/64
Mason, Mary Jane (Mrs.) died 01/01/64 01/02/64
Mason, Moses died 06/13/63 06/15/63
Mason, Philip H. married Harvey, Mary C. 10/03/65 10/11/65
Mason, Rebecca married Butler, Leonard 10/06/63 10/08/63
Mason, Thomas M. died 12/16/61 12/18/61
Mason, William married Griffin, Sarah 05/15/62 05/17/62
Mason, William E. married Burke, M. Cornelia 09/29/64 10/20/64
Mason, William G. married Handley, Catharine 10/26/65 10/28/65
Mason, William, Jr. married Brinson, Mary J. 02/21/61 03/18/61

```
Masor, Susan Perry died 05/11/65   05/12/65
Mass, Ellen M. married Gar, William H. E. (USN) 04/08/64   04/27/64
Mass, Sarah Jennings married Burton, Stephen J. 05/29/65   06/17/65
Mass, Susannah L. (Mrs.) died 01/01/62   01/03/62
Massey, Aquila died 09/05/64   09/06/64
Massey, Caroline married Pindell, Isaiah 10/30/62   11/04/62
Massey, Mary (Mrs.) died 02/02/63   02/10/63
Massey, Rebecca G. (Mrs.) married Thomas, Perry M. 06/15/64   06/17/64
Massicot, E. Hortense died 12/20/64   12/21/64
Massicot, Edward Peter died 09/07/64   09/08/64
Massicot, Edward Peter died 09/07/64   09/09/64
Massicot, P. R. married McGruvy, Hannah 04/25/61   04/30/61
Massicot, William died 11/30/63   12/02/63
Masson, Mary Ann (Mrs.) died 09/02/64   09/03/64
Masson, William (Capt.) died 03/02/65   04/13/65
Mastbaum, Julia G. married Kerngood, Tobias 06/24/63   06/29/63
Masterman, Charles S. married Diffenderfer, Emma G. 04/28/64   05/02/64
Mastermann, Josephine C. married Albridge, Frederick A. 12/24/65
   12/27/65
Masters, Mary Amanda married Greener, Henry 03/21/61   03/25/61
Maston, Alice S. died 06/01/65   06/02/65
Mates, William Robert died 12/28/65   12/29/65
Mathai, Elizabeth (Mrs.) died 07/06/65   07/07/65
Mathaney, Resin B. died 09/29/61   11/30/61
Mathaney, Virginia E. married Dickerson, Isaac W. 02/18/64   02/20/64
Mather, Eliza Ann died 02/04/61   02/08/61
Mather, John died 12/17/64   12/26/64
Mather, Maggie A. married Trimble, R. M. 11/17/63   11/21/63
Mathewes, Charles H. married Bailey, Ann Maria 08/13/63   08/15/63
Mathews, Ann P. died 11/26/65   12/16/65
Mathews, Eliza Jane died 10/13/62   10/15/62
Mathews, John E. married Hann, Margaret Barbara 10/09/64   10/12/64
Mathias, A. Shorb died 01/04/65   01/06/65
Mathoit, Augustus G. married Tucker, Rachel Ann 11/28/65   12/01/65
Matilda, Mary married Place, George 03/06/62   03/08/62
Mattack, Prudena G. died 06/28/62   06/30/62
Matthaei, Anna Veronica died 07/27/62   07/28/62
Matthai, John Nicholas died 06/07/65   06/08/65
Matthes, Chloe A. died 03/18/64   03/19/64
Matthews, Abraham M. married Mumma, Margaret 09/22/64   09/23/64
Matthews, Ann died 11/14/62   11/17/62
Matthews, Benjamin died 12/11/61   12/14/61
Matthews, Benjamin F. married De Moss, Emma 06/22/65   07/07/65
Matthews, Clarry died 08/06/65   08/07/65
Matthews, Daniel Boston died 06/13/65   06/14/65
Matthews, Edwin died 12/04/61   12/05/61
Matthews, Eliza died 02/26/65   02/28/65
Matthews, Elizabeth Ann married Westlake, John A. 12/24/63   01/07/65
Matthews, Emily France married Darly, Rufus T. 04/10/62   04/11/62
Matthews, Emily H. married Hudson, John L. 09/05/61   09/07/61
Matthews, Georgeanne married Demott, William 02/04/64   02/10/64
Matthews, Herbert Thomas died 06/16/61   07/05/61
Matthews, Isaac H. married Deal, Mary R. (Mrs.) 11/28/65   12/05/65
Matthews, Isabella married Toulman, Alfred F. 10/23/61   10/25/61
Matthews, John H. (Cpt.) died 07/23/65   07/27/65
```

```
Matthews, John J. married Laib, Amelia 07/09/61  07/10/61
Matthews, Julia married Gaierty, Patrick 02/11/61  06/08/61
Matthews, Lewis married Grason, Mary Rebecca 06/04/63  06/06/63
Matthews, Mary died 11/25/62  12/01/62
Matthews, Mary Ann died 09/17/61  09/19/61
Matthews, Oliver married Anderson, Mary C. 02/25/64  03/05/64
Matthews, Richard died 11/05/62  11/06/62
Matthews, Richard died 11/05/62  11/07/62
Matthews, Richard J. married Scott, Sallie C. 05/21/62  05/23/62
Matthews, Samuel died 07/17/65  07/18/65
Matthews, Samuel J. died 07/20/63  07/21/63
Matthews, Thomas died 11/28/62  12/10/62
Matthews, Thomas died 10/01/64  10/03/64
Matthews, Thomas R. died 03/29/65  03/31/65
Matthews, William J. married Knorr, Lizzie 02/22/64  03/21/64
Matthews, William N. married Rhodes, Sophia A. 12/01/64  12/07/64
Matthews, Willie T. died 06/13/65  06/17/65
Matthews, Willie Taylor died 07/19/62  07/25/62
Mattier, Jane Inglis died 06/20/62  06/23/62
Mattingly, J. F. died 08/15/65  08/16/65
Mattingly, John died 03/13/61  03/14/61
Mattingly, John H. married Boury, Mollie F. 01/08/61  01/09/61
Mattingly, John Thomas died 09/13/62  09/15/62
Mattingly, Lizzie married Trust, Edwin H. 03/21/65  03/24/65
Mattingly, Mary C. (Mrs.) died 12/21/64  12/22/64
Mauck, Sallie A. married Nicholson, Charles L. 12/22/63  12/24/63
Maud, Margie died 08/22/62  08/26/62
Maul, Elizabeth Elenora Witz died 07/02/64  07/06/64
Maulden, Bettie died 09/24/62  10/08/62
Mauldin, Ellen Louisa died 01/17/64  01/19/64
Maulsby, Aggie Steuart married O'Laughlin, S. Williams 01/06/63
  01/09/63
Maund, Frederick N. (Dr.) died 07/30/62  08/01/62
Maupin, Amanda died 10/27/61  11/06/61
Maurer, C. M. married Berger, M. E. 03/19/65  06/01/65
Maurer, Henry Adolph died 04/09/65  04/15/65
Maurer, Henry Adolph died 04/09/65  04/18/65
Maus, John Henry died 07/19/65  07/20/65
Mauser, Mary Catherine died 07/29/63  07/30/63
Max, Jacob married Bines, Mary B. 09/05/65  12/23/65
Maxfield, William married Stansbury, Rebecca P. 05/04/65  05/20/65
Maxwell, Amelia died 01/13/63  01/14/63
Maxwell, Annie C. married Johnson, Joseph G. 05/18/63  05/26/63
Maxwell, Frances Margaret died 04/28/63  05/02/63
Maxwell, George Russell died 07/27/64  07/28/64
Maxwell, Hannah died 07/30/64  08/01/64
Maxwell, Jennie married Taylor, William J. 10/29/63  10/31/63
Maxwell, John W., Sr. died 08/09/62  08/11/62
Maxwell, Maggie J. married Brooks, George D. 07/01/62  07/11/62
May, John died 09/28/64  12/08/64
May, Mary Ann (Mrs.) died 04/15/65  04/18/65
May, Mary Mahala died 04/04/64  04/06/64
May, William (Cdr.) died 10/10/61  10/12/61
Mayberry, Fannie L. married Knighton, Francis 08/09/65  08/28/65
Mayberry, Mary married Dotter, Joseph 04/13/63  04/20/63
```

Maybury, Thomas H. married Wilson, Amelia J. 11/05/63   11/14/63
Maydwell, Sarah M. died 11/21/62   11/22/62
Maydwell, Sarah M. (Mrs.) died 10/21/62   02/11/63
Maydwell, William H. died 04/25/63   04/27/63
Mayer, Anna M. married Roszel, S. George 12/21/65   12/28/65
Mayer, Dora married Albert, J. Taylor 01/07/64   01/09/64
Mayer, William H. died 04/01/61   04/02/61
Mayer, William H. died 04/01/61   04/03/61
Mayes, Joseph married Giles, Harriet 10/03/63   10/06/63
Mayfield, John Joshua died 05/10/62   05/12/62
Mayfield, William F. married Hudson, S. E. 12/08/64   12/23/64
Mayhew, William E. died 08/30/65   09/02/65
Mayhew, William Green died 04/03/63   04/06/63
Mayn, Annie M. married Firor, John E. 02/10/64   02/15/64
Maynard, Camilla F. married Jesse, George R. 06/14/64   07/20/64
Maynard, Edward Hoffman died 12/26/63   12/31/63
Maynard, Elenor married Wyeth, William N. 02/24/63   02/27/63
Maynard, George W. married Crawford, Josie 12/25/62   12/27/62
Maynard, Henrietta died 07/16/62   07/22/62
Maynard, James (Dr.) died 06/08/61   06/10/61
Maynard, James F. married Keyser, Mary Catharine 12/10/62   12/12/62
Maynard, Julia S. married Thomson, Ignatius Davis (Dr.) 12/19/65   12/21/65
Maynard, Mary died 07/24/61   07/26/61
Maynard, Thomas married Stevenson, Susan 12/19/65   12/20/65
Maynard, Warren married Pyfer, Rachel E. 10/08/63   10/09/63
Mayo, Isaac died 05/18/61   05/31/61
Mayo, James died 11/01/62   11/11/62
Mayo, John died 07/30/63   08/04/63
Mayo, Virginia G. O. M. married Deal, John H. 07/14/63   07/16/63
Mays, John E. died 09/14/62   09/15/62
McAbee, Jemima (Mrs.) died 06/20/65   07/24/65
McAdam, Marianna married McCarroll, Patrick 03/13/65   03/18/65
McAdam, Sarah died 08/31/62   09/01/62
McAdams, James died 04/03/65   04/07/65
McAdams, Matilda died 04/17/65   04/18/65
McAdams, Matilda died 04/17/65   04/19/65
McAdams, Peter died 09/29/65   09/30/65
McAdams, Rose E. married Bohager, Samuel F. 03/27/64   03/31/64
McAdow, Sarah Jane married Little, Thomas Allen 02/05/63   03/07/63
McAfee, James F. married Sinclair, A. E. 05/12/63   05/15/63
McAfee, Martha J. married Clive, Daniel H. 12/08/63   12/10/63
McAfee, Sallie married Hand, Charles C. 07/23/61   07/29/61
MCain, Edward married Knox, Margaret 09/22/58   03/27/61
McAleer, Mary died 02/25/61   02/26/61
McAleese, Mary Jane married Hall, Ben Howard 02/04/62   02/07/62
McAlister, Mary Catherine died 01/22/63   01/31/63
McAllister, Alexander died 08/14/64   08/15/64
McAllister, Annie married Bannon, Patrick 11/26/65   12/05/65
McAllister, Archibald died 07/05/63   07/07/63
McAllister, Emma married Munnis, John 10/17/64   10/20/64
McAllister, Susannah (Mrs.) died 03/15/64   03/23/64
McAllister, William died 04/30/63   05/02/63
McAllister, William married Tanguey, Filis A. 05/03/64   05/06/64
McAllister-Beam, Robert died 01/12/64   01/13/64

McAtee, John H. married Craumer, George E. 12/12/65 12/15/65
Mcauley, Charlotte married Day, William 04/25/64 05/02/64
McAvoy, H. Louis died 03/06/63 03/07/63
McAvoy, John married McKendry, Bridget 03/04/61 04/05/61
McBee, Charles E. married Millen, Maggie 10/02/62 01/23/63
McBee, Emily F. married Pearl, William L. 08/10/65 08/14/65
McBee, Rebecca (Mrs.) died 05/18/63 05/25/63
McBerney, Cleland died 10/08/65 10/09/65
McBlair, Michael died 12/15/61 12/16/61
McBready, Elizabeth A. (Mrs.) died 04/30/64 05/02/64
McBreity, Louisa V. died 10/09/65 10/11/65
McBride, Elizabeth married Scottie, John L. 10/07/63 10/10/63
McBride, Howard died 10/04/64 10/07/64
McBride, Mattie W. married House, Charles H. 12/12/61 12/14/61
McBride, Sarah (Mrs.) died 10/03/64 10/07/64
McBride, Willie Beauregard died 07/22/64 10/07/64
McBriety, Louisa V. died 10/09/65 10/10/65
McBriety, Louisa V. died 10/09/65 11/15/65
McBurney, Louis married Deal, Anna M. 10/16/64 10/17/64
McCabe, Alice died 01/30/61 02/01/61
McCabe, Frances Ann married Jordan, James H. 12/01/64 12/03/64
McCabe, George W. E. died 01/15/63 01/19/63
McCabe, George W. E. died 01/15/63 01/29/63
McCabe, Helen May died 04/19/64 04/20/64
McCabe, Henry H. died 08/12/63 08/13/63
McCabe, James married Ryan, Mary 04/21/61 04/23/61
McCabe, James married Welch, Catherine 02/03/61 02/04/61
McCabe, Jennie T. married Richard, V. P. (M.D.) 10/01/61 10/07/61
McCabe, Kate died 03/29/63 03/30/63
McCabe, Kate A. married Cunningham, Joseph S. 05/28/63 10/29/63
McCabe, Louisa R. (Mrs.) died 08/18/63 08/19/63
McCabe, Margaret married Griffith, John K. 09/17/60 01/18/61
McCabe, Mary Catherine died 08/03/63 08/04/63
McCabe, Michael died 08/08/65 08/11/65
McCabe, Thomas A. married Polton, Annie Jane 10/26/65 12/14/65
McCabe, William H. married Adams, Frank A. 03/16/65 03/24/65
McCadden, Francis died 11/30/65 12/02/65
McCadden, James A. (Lt.) married Moody, Caroline 04/28/64 04/29/64
McCadden, Lizzie R. married Vogeley, George B. 11/16/65 11/27/65
McCaddin, Daniel died 09/23/61 09/24/61
McCaddin, Daniel died 09/23/61 09/25/61
McCaddin, Daniel died no date 06/25/64
McCaddin, Mary died 02/05/62 02/06/62
McCaddin, Mary died 02/05/62 02/07/62
McCafferty, Annie E. married Reather, Charles F. 05/05/63 05/07/63
McCafferty, Mary Ella M. died 02/21/64 02/22/64
McCafferty, Susannah M. married Dadisman, Jacob 04/26/64 04/28/64
McCafferty, William H. died 08/02/65 08/03/65
McCahan, D. L. married Rutledge, Fanny R. 05/21/63 05/23/63
McCahan, E. Luther married Talbot, Elizabeth A. 02/11/64 02/16/64
McCahan, George L. married Crangle, Mary L. 04/30/61 05/04/61
McCahan, Harry married Green, Mary V. 02/09/64 02/10/64
McCahan, Mary Euphemia died 05/03/65 05/04/65
McCahan, Mollie C. married Johnson, Gershom 06/29/64 07/06/64
McCahan, Willie died 04/06/62 04/07/62

McCahen, Mary Louisa died 10/04/65 10/06/65
McCahen, Mary V. died 09/29/65 09/30/65
McCail, Martin died 09/26/64 09/27/64
McCain, Edward married Knox, Margaret 09/22/58 03/27/61
McCain, Mary E. died 05/02/63 05/08/63
McCall, Hugh married Perkins, Mary 11/05/65 11/11/65
McCall, Julia died 09/18/65 09/19/65
McCall, Margaret died 11/19/61 11/20/61
McCall, Margaret died 11/19/61 11/21/61
McCall, Martha Ann died 12/30/64 12/31/64
McCall, Mary died 04/17/61 04/19/61
McCall, Mary married Link, Terrence 04/17/65 04/22/65
McCall, Mary married Link, Terrence 04/17/65 04/24/65
McCall, Mary Mathew died 02/10/61 02/12/61
McCall, Patrick died 06/08/63 06/09/63
McCall, Rose (Mrs.) died 05/04/65 05/05/65
McCallister, Archibald married Kidd, Sarah E. 05/04/65 05/08/65
McCallister, William J. married Carroll, Jane 02/09/63 04/08/63
McCaman, Jane Wilson died 02/28/63 03/02/63
McCambridge, Ann Jane married Coakley, Daniel 02/12/61 02/16/61
McCambridge, Ann Jane married Coakley, Daniel 02/12/61 02/15/61
McCambridge, Ann Jane married Coakley, Daniel 02/12/61 02/14/61
McCambridge, Mary Verona died 03/24/63 03/25/63
McCambridge, Rosetta died 06/11/62 06/12/62
McCan, Thomas died 07/09/62 07/15/62
McCandless, George S. died 12/01/61 12/03/61
McCann, Alexander died 08/10/64 08/12/64
McCann, Anne T. married Toner, James J. 04/06/64 04/08/64
McCann, Charles died 04/01/63 04/25/63
McCann, Jane Stewart married Garvey, James, Jr. 01/20/63 03/16/63
McCann, Joseph married Smith, Laura A. 01/25/61 02/01/61
McCann, Kate Lee died 03/14/63 03/18/63
McCann, Margaret Mary died 08/13/61 08/16/61
McCann, Mary Ann died 06/27/62 06/23/62
McCann, Mary Harvey died 04/24/61 05/09/61
McCann, Mary R. married Owen, Joseph W. (Cpt.) 10/13/64 11/15/64
McCann, Sarah F. married Mitchell, John W. 07/17/61 08/26/61
McCann, Terrence married Dillon, Mary Ann 05/02/64 05/24/64
McCann, William P. died 03/06/62 03/07/62
McCardell, William H. married McNeill, Mollie C. 11/24/63 11/25/63
McCardy, William married Smith, Mary 05/01/63 11/03/63
McCarraher, Mary L. married Bell, Thaddeus 11/17/64 11/28/64
McCarriar, James married Beach, Bertha J. 06/11/61 06/15/61
McCarrick, James died no date 08/14/63
McCarrier, Mary (Mrs.) died 04/21/65 04/22/65
McCarroll, Patrick married McAdam, Marianna 03/13/65 03/18/65
McCart, Bridget Ann died 03/01/64 03/02/64
McCart, James married Clark, Mary A. 01/12/62 06/13/62
McCarthey, Charles married Clemancs, Annie E. 12/25/64 01/10/65
McCarthy, Catherine died 09/19/64 09/22/64
McCarthy, Charles died 04/03/62 04/05/62
McCarthy, Francis Joseph died 12/30/62 01/01/63
McCarthy, John married Jones, Virginia A. 05/23/64 06/01/64
McCarthy, Mary E. died 03/14/62 03/15/62
McCarthy, Mary Ellen died 09/15/64 09/22/64

McCarthy, Susan (Mrs.) died 09/20/64 09/22/64
McCarthy, Thomas died 04/06/62 04/07/62
McCartney, J. Y. (Rev.) died no date 05/15/65
McCartney, Jane died 07/15/62 07/17/62
McCartney, Mary (Mrs.) died 12/13/63 12/14/63
McCarty, Elizabeth died 01/25/65 01/27/65
McCarty, Ellen T. married Farrell, John 02/16/63 02/20/63
McCarty, Mary married McCleary, Robert 01/02/65 01/03/65
McCarty, Michael died 08/23/61 08/27/61
McCarty, Peyton L. married Walker, Sarah Lavinia 03/25/63 03/28/63
McCarty, Roberta Lee died 04/10/65 04/12/65
McCauley, Alexander S. died 08/27/64 09/20/64
McCauley, Alexander T. married Buckingham, H. Virginia 10/21/63 10/24/63
McCauley, Bernard J. married Woodall, Ella 01/07/64 01/21/64
McCauley, C. L. married Wells, Annie E. 01/05/65 01/21/65
McCauley, Charles A. died 02/18/64 02/19/64
McCauley, Clifford Eugene died 10/26/64 10/29/64
McCauley, George E. married Lloyd, Fannie 09/26/65 09/27/65
McCauley, George W. died 07/11/64 07/16/64
McCauley, James married Ruff, Catharine 12/04/64 12/13/64
McCauley, Joseph C. married Watts, Susie 01/06/64 01/13/64
McCauley, Julia A. married Biddison, Thomas C. 09/10/62 09/13/62
McCauley, Laura E. died 11/13/65 11/14/65
McCauley, Laura E. died 11/13/65 11/15/65
McCauley, Laura Jessie died 04/18/64 05/31/64
McCauley, Martha W. married Holtz, David 10/20/64 10/22/64
McCauley, Mary E. died 11/04/64 11/05/64
McCauley, Sarah Rebecca married Poplan, William 04/13/64 04/16/64
McCausland, John J. died 08/17/61 08/20/61
McCausland, Maria married Hopkins, Joseph R. 01/05/65 01/06/65
McCausland, Sarah died 05/05/62 05/10/62
McCay, Ann Elma died 02/07/63 02/17/63
McCeney, Henry C. died 01/22/64 01/28/64
McClain, Samuel B. died 08/22/64 08/30/64
McClaley, John W. married Plumer, Louisa 12/23/62 01/01/63
McClaley, Thomas J. died 11/29/63 11/30/63
McClanahan, Robert J. died 03/19/63 03/23/63
McClane, Stephen J. died 12/02/63 12/04/63
McClaskey, Alfred J. died 11/08/63 11/10/63
McClaskey, Hetty married Hubbel, Augustus 01/05/62 06/30/62
McClatchy, Robert died 04/19/65 04/21/65
McClaughlin, Agnes Cecelia died 07/04/64 07/06/64
McClausand, Elizabeth died 04/22/62 04/26/62
McClausand, James Albert died 01/22/63 02/04/63
McCleary, Jimmy C. died 10/11/62 10/16/62
McCleary, Mary A. (Mrs.) died 11/01/65 11/03/65
McCleary, Mattie A. married Crosly, Samuel (Capt.) 02/07/65 02/21/65
McCleary, Robert married McCarty, Mary 01/02/65 01/03/65
McCleary, William J. married Coleman, Anna R. 02/02/65 11/07/65
McClees, Ellis B. died 03/19/65 05/06/65
McClelen, Joseph died 03/21/64 03/23/64
McClellan, Almira M. died 10/13/63 10/17/63
McClellan, Andrew died 02/20/63 02/21/63
McClellan, George F. married Appold, Levina 01/24/64 01/30/64

McClellan, George F. married Scarf, Emma J. 04/03/65 05/06/65
McClellan, George F. married Scarf, Emma J. 04/03/65 05/08/65
McClellan, Johnny B. died 11/09/63 11/14/63
McClellan, Mary A. married Mason, Caspar P. 04/14/64 08/02/64
McClellan, William A. died 10/19/63 10/22/63
McClelland, Isabella died 03/26/63 03/28/63
McClelland, Robert George died 05/29/63 05/30/63
McClellend, Mary died 12/24/63 12/26/63
McClenaghan, Johnny died 07/28/64 07/29/64
McClenahan, Elizabeth died 05/16/61 05/21/61
McClenahan, Kate died 02/11/63 02/13/63
McClenahan, Mary died 02/24/63 02/25/63
McClenahan, Robert died 04/14/61 04/15/61
McClennahan, Susie A. married Gerlach, George C. 11/10/65 11/15/65
McClennon, George died 03/23/64 03/25/64
McClennon, Levin died 03/19/64 03/25/64
McClernan, John H. died 01/16/64 02/12/64
McClester, Elizabeth died 01/22/64 01/23/64
McClintock, C. W. married Blair, Kate A. B. 08/11/64 08/26/64
McClintock, Eliza died 01/18/61 01/21/61
McClintock, John M., Jr. married Fennelly, M. E. 01/02/61 01/03/61
McClintock, Lizzie married Ramsey, William R. 05/04/65 05/12/65
McClintock, Winfield married McMahon, Mary C. 12/25/60 01/07/61
McCluney, Maggie J. married Saulsbury, Andrew J. 07/02/63 07/07/63
McClure, Charles S. died 10/08/65 10/09/65
McClure, Emmelise Howard died 04/22/62 04/23/62
McCluskling, James married Cooper, Ellen Jane 08/04/64 08/13/64
McCluskling, James married Cooper, Ellen Jane 08/04/64 08/15/64
McClymont, Elizabeth (Mrs.) died 06/10/65 06/12/65
McClymont, Helen E. died 01/14/62 01/15/62
McClymont, William, Sr. died 11/14/62 11/17/62
McCob, William died 09/02/63 09/03/63
McColagan, Michael died 09/17/61 09/18/61
McColgan, Bernard died 04/16/62 04/17/62
McColgan, James married Keenan, Margaret 08/27/65 09/13/65
McColgan, Joanna married Dawson, Hugh 01/23/64 01/28/64
McColgan, Kate (Mrs.) died 07/02/64 07/04/64
McColgan, Mary died 08/18/61 08/19/61
McColgan, Mary died 08/18/61 08/23/61
McCollam, Margaretta died 11/11/62 11/12/62
McCollam, Sarah died 12/13/61 12/14/61
McCollom, Ephraim died 09/28/65 09/29/65
McCollum, John died 11/17/64 11/19/64
McCollum, Nancy married Campbell, John 04/06/63 04/08/63
McColm, Elizabeth A. died 03/16/65 03/17/65
McCom, Charles Bernard died 08/22/62 08/27/62
McComas, Caroline married McKinless, Charles A. 10/08/61 10/12/61
McComas, Francis Everett died 12/28/62 12/29/62
McComas, Harry Lee died 08/26/61 08/30/61
McComas, John S. married Golden, Mary T. J. 03/01/64 03/04/64
McComas, Laura Levering died 12/21/65 12/23/65
McComas, Lizzie married Mitchell, H. Mozart 11/28/61 11/30/61
McComas, Mary E. married Frey, John W. 12/22/64 12/26/64
McComas, Mary H. died 06/28/64 06/30/64
McComas, Mollie H. died 07/28/64 07/09/64

McComas, Olevia J. married Kirby, Richard H. 07/05/64   07/06/64
McCombs, William died 06/19/64   06/20/64
McConica, Mary Ann died 03/18/62   03/19/62
McConkey, Hettie C. married Merryman, Oliver P. 04/18/65   04/24/65
McConkey, James K. P. died 10/10/61   10/15/61
McConkin, John Vincent died 07/30/62   07/31/62
McConnell, John died 11/15/63   11/16/63
McConnell, John died 08/01/64   08/02/64
McConnell, Rachel married Reynolds, William 10/02/60   03/11/61
McConnoughy, Alexander died 02/11/62   02/13/62
McCord, William D. married Tarr, Julia D. 05/16/61   05/23/61
McCorkell, George Foster died 11/14/65   12/01/65
McCormac, Mary died 03/12/62   03/13/62
McCormack, Archibald married Hughes, Ellen 02/19/63   02/21/63
McCormick, Alexander married Councilman, Martha Ann 12/31/63   01/12/64
McCormick, Annie married Lalor, Laurence 06/15/62   06/16/62
McCormick, Archibald died 08/12/63   08/13/63
McCormick, Bertha Scorse died 06/27/64   06/30/64
McCormick, Bridget died 10/12/62   10/14/62
McCormick, Carrie (Mrs.) married McKelvy, James 07/23/65   08/10/65
McCormick, Ella G. married Claypoole, James V. 09/13/64   09/15/64
McCormick, Francis died 05/23/62   05/24/62
McCormick, Harry C. married James, Fanny C. 08/09/64   11/01/64
McCormick, James died 08/07/61   08/08/61
McCormick, John H. married Gorsuch, Julia Anne 04/29/62   05/01/62
McCormick, John Pleasants died 03/25/62   03/27/62
McCormick, John Pleasants died 03/25/62   03/28/62
McCormick, Margaret died 11/07/61   11/09/61
McCormick, Nevin W. died 11/16/61   11/20/61
McCormick, Rosanna died 11/04/63   11/05/63
McCormick, Rose died 06/01/62   06/03/62
McCormick, Samuel died 04/27/63   04/28/63
McCormick, Susan died 08/10/64   08/11/64
McCormick, Tabitha died 11/27/61   11/28/61
McCormick, William J. married Webster, Emma 01/18/63   01/21/63
McCormmick, James Dennis died 07/09/62   07/10/62
McCoskar, Mary Ann married Whiteford, George W. 10/26/62   11/05/62
McCoubray, John Dixon died 01/21/64   01/22/64
McCoulough, John married Galway, Honoria 04/19/61   04/24/61
McCourt, Ann married Kane, James 04/07/61   04/09/61
McCourt, Bridget died 10/31/64   11/01/64
McCourt, Elizabeth (Mrs.) died 10/26/64   10/28/64
McCourt, James K. married Smith, Ann Cecilia 12/27/60   12/10/61
McCourt, John died 06/11/64   06/13/64
McCourt, Peter died 02/19/62   02/20/62
McCoy, Caroline (Mrs.) died 06/11/63   06/17/63
McCoy, David died 03/30/64   04/15/64
McCoy, David married Blair, Agnes 02/28/65   03/04/65
McCoy, Edmunds married Jones, Margaretta 01/14/62   01/17/62
McCoy, Elizabeth married Murry, Thomas 08/29/61   09/25/61
McCoy, Ellen (Mrs.) died 10/17/64   10/19/64
McCoy, Hugh married Williams, Mary E. 08/03/64   09/10/64
McCoy, John J. married McDevitt, Mary 06/22/63   06/29/63
McCoy, Margaret married Dunlap, John 02/28/65   04/14/65
McCoy, Mary died 08/05/61   08/07/61

McCracken, James died 02/01/61   02/02/61
McCrea, George Oliver died 08/14/61   08/15/61
McCready, John O. died 04/27/62   05/01/62
McCreight, Thomas Henry died 10/11/62   11/11/62
McCrieght, Sarah married Owens, Charles H. 11/08/64   11/10/64
McCroden, James died 10/31/65   11/04/65
McCubbin, Elenor died 12/18/63   12/19/63
McCubbin, Emma E. married Quinn, Ambrose 12/23/61   01/08/62
McCubbin, Joseph married Wiger, Claserine M. 04/30/62   05/31/62
McCubbin, Joseph married Wiger, Cezerine M. 04/30/62   06/02/62
McCubbin, Moses married Addeby, Phebia 08/27/63   08/29/63
McCubbin, William F. married Hunt, Mollie 11/05/63   11/07/63
McCuen, John married Shaw, Ellen 02/14/61   02/16/61
McCulley, Willy died 08/03/62   08/04/62
McCullin, S. (Rev.) died 11/20/63   12/10/63
McCullogh, J. Haines, (M.D.) married Tubman, Maria A. 06/03/62   06/04/62
McCullogh, John died 08/29/62   09/02/62
McCullogh, John died 06/06/63   06/10/63
McCulloh, John K. (Dr.) married Watson, Ella 09/29/63   10/06/63
McCullouch, H. D. (Dr.) died 05/09/63   05/20/63
McCullough, George married Alden, Luna T. 01/01/63   01/02/63
McCullough, George S. married Proctor, Mary 06/13/65   06/14/65
McCullough, Mary married Bull, Thomas Nelson 03/09/62   03/12/62
McCullough, Mary (Mrs.) died 05/07/64   05/12/64
McCully, Clinton, E. died 11/27/63   11/28/63
McCurdy, Evaline Louisa died 01/03/64   01/04/64
McCurdy, John A. died 10/16/61   10/17/61
McCurdy, Mary (Mrs.) died 04/18/65   04/19/65
McCurdy, Mary (Mrs.) died 04/18/65   04/20/65
McCurley, Annie married Seymour, Henry C. 06/23/62   02/04/64
McCurley, Edward married Bell, Clara A. 01/14/62   01/20/62
McCurley, Emma married McIlhaney, John 01/15/61   01/23/61
McCuskar, Sarah P. died 05/09/65   05/10/65
McCusker, Jane married Collins, Hugh J. 09/17/65   10/07/65
McDade, Henry died 11/12/64   11/14/64
McDaniel, Laura A. married Casselman, W. C. no date   09/19/61
McDaniel, M. Louisa married James, John T. 01/02/62   01/08/62
McDaniel, Margaret Jackson died 03/18/63   03/20/63
McDaniel, Mary Virginia married Sprenkle, Charles H. 01/31/65   02/11/65
McDaniel, Samuel P. died 02/27/61   02/28/61
McDearmott, Mary married Butler, Peter 06/19/64   06/25/64
McDecitt, Mory died 09/08/62   09/10/62
McDermott, Annie M. married Diggs, William B. 07/03/63   07/27/63
McDermott, Annie M. J. died 03/11/63   03/12/63
McDermott, Annie M. J. died 03/11/63   04/28/63
McDermott, Bernard died 02/15/64   02/18/64
McDermott, Ellen died 11/17/65   11/18/65
McDermott, James W. died 03/10/63   03/12/63
McDermott, Jane (Mrs.) died 07/16/65   07/17/65
McDermott, Kate R. married Daiger, Francis 01/14/64   01/15/64
McDermott, Letitia died 06/16/62   06/20/62
McDermott, Maggie married Smith, Thomas J. 06/30/63   07/07/63
McDermott, Mary married Egan, Michael 04/05/63   04/08/63
McDermott, Mary E. married Hamilton, Orman 11/24/63   11/28/63
McDermott, Mary Hellen married Rainy, Edward J. 04/05/63   04/07/63

```
McDermott, Thomas died 01/24/65  01/25/65
McDevitt, Cornelius married Riley, Bridget 11/17/63  11/19/63
McDevitt, Mary married McCoy, John J. 06/22/63  06/29/63
McDevitt, Susan died 08/01/62  08/02/62
McDonald, Ann (Mrs.) died 09/15/63  09/17/63
McDonald, Anne died 01/16/62  01/17/62
McDonald, Annie M. died 02/19/63  02/23/63
McDonald, Artcher married McDonell, Rose Feletia 02/24/65  02/27/65
McDonald, Catherine died 03/13/61  03/14/61
McDonald, Charles died 04/06/64  04/08/64
McDonald, Charles died 07/07/64  07/09/64
Mcdonald, David H. married Wellmore, Grace R. 04/07/64  04/18/64
McDonald, Elizabeth J. married Curran, Nicholas F. 02/16/65  02/21/65
McDonald, Ellen F. married Waterworth, Thomas J. 11/26/61  12/03/61
McDonald, F. T. (Lt.) married Lloyd, Eugenia (Mrs.) 11/10/64  11/18/64
McDonald, Frances Olevia died 10/11/63  10/12/63
McDonald, Grace (Mrs.) died 09/26/65  09/28/65
McDonald, H. J. married Michael, Martha 02/22/64  03/22/64
McDonald, Horace S. married Michael, Martha 02/22/64  03/29/64
McDonald, Howard died 11/21/63  11/24/63
McDonald, John died 05/28/65  05/29/65
McDonald, John (Lt.) married Benton, Mary 05/07/63  05/11/63
McDonald, Kate died 08/15/61  08/16/61
McDonald, Levinia (Mrs.) died 08/11/64  08/12/64
McDonald, Lilley Ann died no date  09/25/65
McDonald, Margaret E. died 10/26/62  10/28/62
McDonald, Martha (Mrs.) died 09/21/63  09/22/63
McDonald, Mary married Ward, James 12/29/61  01/03/62
McDonald, Mary married Bayne, William C. 12/21/64  01/02/65
McDonald, Mary H. married Bobb, John D., Jr. (Lt.) 09/19/64  10/03/64
McDonald, Mary Isabella died 02/28/63  03/02/63
McDonald, Mary J. died 07/27/64  08/06/64
McDonald, Mattie (Mrs.) died 09/18/64  09/19/64
McDonald, Mattie (Mrs.) died 09/18/64  09/20/64
McDonald, Michael died 11/24/65  11/25/65
McDonald, Patrick died 06/18/63  06/20/63
McDonald, Richard died 12/25/61  12/27/61
McDonald, Russel died 12/26/64  01/14/65
McDonald, Thomas died 09/18/63  09/19/63
McDonald, William died 03/08/61  03/09/61
McDonald, William died 09/05/64  09/09/64
McDonald, William died 08/03/65  08/05/65
McDonell, James married Lany, Mary Jane 08/01/65  09/11/65
McDonell, Rose Feletia married McDonald, Artcher 02/24/65  02/27/65
McDonnal, John J. married Smuck, Sarah E. 05/28/63  06/01/63
McDonnel, Mary died 03/30/65  04/01/65
McDonnell, Eugene married De Loughery, M. Edwardina 09/01/63  09/02/6
McDonnell, James (U.S.N.) married Ryan, Kate 10/01/62  10/03/62
McDonnell, Jane married Marshall, Charles E. 05/23/61  06/14/62
McDonnell, Michael died 07/13/65  07/14/65
McDonnell, Susan Jane married Ellis, James N. 05/06/62  05/21/62
McDonough, Lizzie married Cream, Maurice 10/15/62  11/01/62
McDonough, Mary married Finley, John F. 04/16/63  04/22/63
McDonough, Michael died 03/16/63  03/17/63
McDonough, Susie married Kennedy, William W. 05/27/62  05/29/62
```

McDougall, Elizabeth A. died 06/15/65 06/17/65
McDougall, James T. died 04/24/65 04/25/65
McDowell, Belle married Barry, James B. 06/09/64 06/22/64
McDowell, Elizabeth married Williams, Benjamin S. 04/05/63 04/07/63
McDowell, G. B. married Cheshire, Eugenia 09/18/65 09/19/65
McDowell, Mary Virginia married Smith, Peter B. 06/14/65 06/17/65
McDowell, Robert died 07/15/64 08/09/64
McDowell, Susan G. died 03/08/61 03/09/61
McDowell, Tillie married Miller, T. A. 10/10/61 10/14/61
McDowell, William Ellsworth died 08/13/63 08/15/63
McDowney, Ellen married Patterson, William 07/02/61 07/04/61
McElderry, Annie married Donn, John W. 10/26/65 10/28/65
McElderry, P. Mathews died 01/15/63 01/17/63
McEldowney, Bessie married Hughes, Thomas 03/24/64 03/25/64
McEldowney, John married Scott, Matilda 12/03/61 12/04/61
McEldowney, Robert died 07/01/61 07/02/61
McElfresh, Elizabeth P. died 05/21/64 07/01/64
McElhaney, Kate married Butler, William T. 02/16/63 02/20/63
McElhenny, Ann died 11/01/61 11/02/61
McElmoyle, Archibald married Russell, Amelia 05/02/61 05/06/61
McElmozle, Archibald married Russell, Amelia 05/02/61 05/04/61
McElroy, Andrew married McElroy, Sarah 04/08/61 04/09/61
McElroy, Annie A. married Gentry, Haden 01/03/65 01/18/65
McElroy, Catherine married Bolgiano, Edward 05/14/61 05/16/61
McElroy, Elizabeth died 10/18/65 10/19/65
McElroy, John died 10/29/63 10/30/63
McElroy, John Henry died 01/03/61 01/04/61
McElroy, John W. died 04/21/64 04/23/64
McElroy, Joseph married McFarland, Lizzie 10/25/63 12/11/63
McElroy, Martha married O'Neill, John H. 05/12/63 05/19/63
McElroy, Mary Ann died 08/23/64 09/01/64
McElroy, Mary J. married Waldschmith, Lewis no date 12/28/63
McElroy, Mary Jane married Mittnacht, Benjamin 08/17/65 08/25/65
McElroy, Matthew died 04/24/63 04/27/63
McElroy, Robert died 10/29/62 10/30/62
McElroy, Sarah married McElroy, Andrew 04/08/61 04/09/61
McElroy, Sarah Jane died 07/25/65 07/26/65
McElroy, Tillie Lanahan died 03/04/65 03/06/65
McElroy, William died 01/09/64 01/12/64
McElroy, William D. married Weyraugh, Elizabeth 06/06/65 06/08/65
McElvaney, Mary E. married King, Joseph A. 12/20/63 12/24/63
McElwee, Elizabeth Elliott died 08/09/62 08/14/62
McElwee, Samuel, Sr. died 03/10/65 03/15/65
McElwee, William died 12/13/65 12/15/65
McElwee, William H. married Shirner, Catherine M. 12/03/61 12/03/61
McEnaney, Amey died 08/18/61 08/19/61
McEnheimer, Elizabeth died 12/06/61 12/12/61
McEnnis, John F. died 05/05/65 05/11/65
McEver, Ursula died 05/11/62 04/19/62
McEvers, Anna married Lovey, Henry D. 04/26/64 04/28/64
McEwan, Hugh married Dun, Ellen 10/00/00 01/17/61
McFadden, Cornelius died 12/09/62 12/11/62
McFadden, Francis married McNeil, Sarah 11/01/64 11/03/64
McFadden, George W. married Lambright, Laura V. 07/24/62 08/19/62
McFadden, Lillie Lee died 09/25/65 09/27/65

McFadden, Maggie A. married Stewart, William N. 08/19/63   09/08/63
McFadden, Martha married Dorsey, Richard H., Jr. 02/01/63   02/17/63
McFadden, Sallie Lee died 09/25/65   09/26/65
McFadden, Sarah married Jones, William 08/19/62   09/04/62
McFadden, Sarah (Mrs.) died 12/19/64   12/20/64
McFadden, William died 11/23/65   11/24/65
McFall, Mary died 04/17/61   04/18/61
McFall, Rose married Cook, William H. 03/03/64   03/15/64
McFarland, C. Dodd married Chubb, Emily 11/02/65   11/04/65
McFarland, John died 08/04/62   08/11/62
McFarland, Lizzie married McElroy, Joseph 10/25/63   12/11/63
McFarlane, James married Randall, Sallie A. 03/10/63   03/13/63
McFarlane, Robert died 03/29/61   03/30/61
McFaud, Mary V. married James, Richard J. 11/22/63   11/24/63
McFaul, Charles A. died 04/07/64   04/08/64
McFaul, Daniel died 12/04/63   12/08/63
McFaul, M. Anna (Mrs.) died 01/10/64   01/12/64
McFee, Barbara Ann died 11/17/64   11/23/64
McFee, Thomas Sutherland died 02/03/62   02/05/62
McFern, Edward married Crockard, Sarah A. 11/03/64   11/14/64
McFern, John died 03/26/65   03/27/65
McFrederick, Kate R. married Campbell, Thomas 08/07/62   09/02/62
McGahan, John J. married Kaiser, Lizzie 05/01/65   05/06/65
McGahan, John J. married Kaiser, Lizzie 05/01/65   05/08/65
McGahan, Rozine married Graham, John 10/22/61   10/24/61
McGaity, Francis died 05/19/62   05/20/62
McGall, Mary L. married Hughes, William 04/30/63   05/02/63
McGann, Andrew J. died 11/03/62   11/05/62
McGann, John died 04/21/61   04/22/61
McGarigley, John married Scott, Cecilia 12/19/61   12/25/61
McGarity, Mary Jane died 03/14/65   03/16/65
McGarity, Mary Marcelena died 09/01/63   09/02/63
McGarvey, Mary Jane died 05/27/62   05/29/62
McGaw, Patrick died 03/01/64   03/02/64
McGee, Andrew J. died 08/02/65   08/03/65
McGee, Ann (Mrs.) died 08/28/63   08/29/63
McGee, Anne Teresa died 06/15/64   06/16/64
McGee, Ellen Cecelia died 07/04/63   07/07/63
McGee, Francis Jane died 09/19/61   09/20/61
McGee, George R. married Bayley, Beckie 12/08/63   12/23/63
McGee, James Fletcher died 03/10/63   04/03/63
McGee, Joseph William died 03/12/62   03/13/62
McGee, Mary C. married Miles, William 04/03/61   10/17/61
McGee, Mary Ellen died 06/13/65   06/14/65
McGee, Mary Levinia died 11/26/61   11/27/61
McGee, Robert married Haslup, Susanna 02/07/61   02/12/61
McGee, Rosanna married Feeney, James 05/04/65   05/10/65
McGee, Rose married McQuaid, Charles J. 04/09/63   04/11/63
McGee, William H. married Robinson, Sallie M. 12/24/62   12/29/62
McGee, William Vincent died 06/13/63   06/16/63
McGeehan, Edward J. married Cook, Annie M. 05/23/65   05/25/65
McGeehan, Rachel (Mrs.) died 01/09/63   01/10/63
McGeeney, Owen died 02/29/64   03/02/64
McGehan, Patrick died 03/01/64   03/04/64
McGill, Edward M. married Perry, Ellen Mar 06/10/63   06/11/63

McGill, Patrick died 09/07/64   09/10/64
McGilton, Margaret C. G. married Evans, F. S. (Rev.) 10/22/61   10/23/61
McGinn, Bernard married Coogan, Anastasia E. 04/17/65   04/27/65
McGinn, John married Henry, Margaret 07/24/63   08/11/63
McGinn, Lizzie died 05/13/61   05/25/61
McGinty, Felix died 01/10/62   01/11/62
McGivney, John died 07/14/64   07/15/64
McGlade, Mary Jane died 12/06/62   12/09/62
McGlagihan, Mary Ann died 07/08/64   07/09/64
McGlanan, Thomas married Wright, Caroline 05/14/65   05/18/65
McGlauathlin, Madge died 07/25/61   07/27/61
McGlenan, Charles Boromes died 08/16/62   08/19/62
McGlennan, Mary married Smith, Henry 04/14/64   04/16/64
McGlocklin, Sarah married Cornish, Joseph 05/19/64   05/21/64
McGlone, Barbara (Mrs.) died 10/18/63   10/19/63
McGlothlan, Elizabeth married King, George W. 08/26/64   08/31/64
McGonigal, Catherine died 07/30/62   08/01/62
McGough, James B. died 06/09/63   06/10/63
McGovern, Joseph died 10/20/65   10/21/65
McGovern, Margaret Anne died 11/24/63   11/25/63
McGovern, Thomas died 06/15/62   06/16/62
McGowan, (Mrs.) died 01/31/63   02/02/63
McGowan, Addie V. married Dorrell, W. B. (Lt. Col.) 01/21/64   02/15/64
McGowan, John died 01/26/64   01/27/64
McGowan, Martha died 11/09/61   11/20/61
McGowan, Susan married Denney, John 01/01/63   06/09/63
McGowan, Thomas married Hartin, Agnes 10/17/64   10/20/64
McGrath, Catherine died 04/16/62   04/18/62
McGrath, James A. died 02/05/64   02/06/64
Mcgrath, Margaret died 11/19/64   11/22/64
McGraw, Elizabeth A. married Norris, Thomas 05/16/61   05/31/61
McGraw, William Henry died 05/08/64   05/09/64
McGreevey, Hannah (Mrs.) died 11/05/64   11/07/64
McGreevy, Caroline died 11/18/62   11/19/62
McGrowling, Margaret M. married Otis, George 06/01/64   06/04/64
McGruvy, Hannah married Massicot, P. R. 04/25/61   04/30/61
McGuigan, James died 07/11/65   07/12/65
McGuiggen, James S. M. married Jurnia, Mary E. 09/25/64   09/27/64
McGuiness, James Owen died 04/14/63   04/16/63
McGuire, Ann died 11/20/61   11/22/61
McGuire, Eliza Jane (Mrs.) died 07/07/65   07/08/65
McGuire, John E. married Hubbard, Henrietta no date   07/06/64
McGuire, Patrick married Armstrong, Ann 07/14/65   07/17/65
McGuire, Patrick married Armstrong, Ann 07/14/65   07/18/65
McGuire, Thomas died 10/19/65   10/21/65
McGuire, Thomas C. married Solomon, Matilda A. 09/20/64   09/26/64
McGuirk, Bernard married Fitzpatrick, Catherine 05/07/63   05/12/63
McGuirk, Mary E. married Guynn, Thomas A. 03/01/65   03/04/65
McGuirk, Patrick married Doyle, Catharine 01/02/65   08/02/65
McGunnegle, Isa Ray died 07/21/65   08/07/65
McGurk, Thomas died 08/05/61   08/06/61
McHarry, Margaret Jane married Purcell, Thomas 08/17/62   10/01/62
McHarry, Robert married Carter, Ellen 11/30/65   12/05/65
McHenna, Honora (Mrs.) died 04/17/64   04/18/64
McHenry, Robert W. died 10/12/61   10/15/61

McHugh, Margaret died 07/15/63   07/16/63
McHugh, Michael died 12/27/64   12/28/64
McIlhaney, John married McCurley, Emma 01/15/61   01/23/61
McIlhaney, Nancy married Marley, James R. 11/22/65   12/16/65
McIlhaney, Robert died 08/18/62   08/20/62
McIlhenny, Edward Spedden died 03/29/65   05/12/65
McIlhenny, Jane married Finney, Alex 04/18/61   04/20/61
McIlhenny, John died 01/22/62   01/23/62
McIlvain, Elizabeth married Jones, Edward D. 06/06/62   07/19/62
McIlvain, Laura married Thompson, Columbus E. 09/07/62   09/18/62
McIlvain, Lavinia married Whitehurst, J. Harrison 06/09/64   06/21/64
McIlvaney, Richard married Carse, Margaret 09/22/62   09/25/62
McInerney, Mary (Mrs.) died 11/05/63   11/07/63
McIntire, Philip married Mulligan, Rose 01/17/64   09/02/64
McIntosh, Daniel married Miller, Catharine 02/19/63   02/21/63
McIntosh, Elizabeth A. married Blankford, Jacob 10/31/61   11/02/61
McIntosh, Fleming Charles died 07/12/63   07/14/63
McIntosh, George died 04/14/63   04/18/63
McIntosh, Mary married Beckham, Charles 09/25/62   09/27/62
McIntyre, Alice (Mrs.) died 03/06/65   03/07/65
McIntyre, Harry M. married McKeenan, Cecelia C. 06/05/64   06/23/64
McIntyre, Jennie A. died 11/23/65   11/24/65
McIntyre, John Thomas died 09/17/63   09/18/63
McIntyre, Joseph Francis died 10/23/61   10/24/61
McIntyre, Margaret E. married Lucas, William V. 12/12/65   12/13/65
McIntyre, Mary Catherine died 09/24/64   09/26/64
McIntyre, Patrick died 11/20/61   11/21/61
McJilton, Sarah died 11/07/61   11/08/61
McJilton, Sarah (Mrs.) died 11/06/61   11/07/61
McJilton, Sarah Ann (Mrs.) died 10/20/65   10/24/65
McJilton, William D. married Francis, Helen 03/23/65   03/24/65
McKaig, Irene Myrtle died 06/30/65   07/04/65
McKaig, John Robert died 07/02/64   07/06/64
McKaig, William H. married Hughes, Laura 10/25/65   11/01/65
McKana, Kitty died 07/17/63   07/18/63
McKanna, Thomas married Kerwin, Mary E. 07/02/65   07/07/65
McKay, Elizabeth Ann died 04/06/62   04/07/62
McKay, Elsie (Mrs.) died 07/25/63   07/27/63
McKay, Emma Catherine died 08/10/62   08/11/62
McKay, George Washington died 03/14/61   03/16/61
McKay, John Henry died 07/18/61   07/19/61
McKay, Maggie died 01/20/63   02/07/63
McKean, E. R. (Cpt.) married Powell, Hattie 04/23/63   04/24/63
McKean, Thomas died 08/03/64   08/04/64
McKee, Annie married Henry, Morton P. 12/14/65   12/16/65
McKee, Francis Zavier died 05/02/61   05/06/61
McKee, Joseph Oliver died 03/01/63   03/11/63
McKee, Joseph Oliver died 03/01/63   03/12/63
McKee, Josephine C. died 02/26/63   03/11/63
McKee, Margaret died 12/09/61   12/10/61
McKee, Sophia C. died 02/26/63   03/12/63
McKee, William died 10/18/65   10/19/65
McKeel, Margaret died 08/10/64   11/17/64
McKeel, Matilda died 03/26/62   03/27/62
McKeenan, Cecelia C. married McIntyre, Harry M. 06/05/64   06/23/64

McKeever, James died no date 10/23/63
McKeever, Joseph E. married Keyworth, Isabella A. 02/11/62 02/12/62
McKeever, Sarah A. (Mrs.) died 05/17/63 05/18/63
McKeever, William T. married Gerbrich, Maddue Morselle 01/19/65
    01/23/65
McKeeves, James B. married Storms, Sarah J. 09/09/63 09/12/63
McKeldin, Edward H. died 07/09/64 07/23/64
McKeldin, Ella Caroline died 09/02/62 09/04/62
McKeldin, William died 04/15/64 04/16/64
McKelvy, James married McCormick, Carrie (Mrs.) 07/23/65 08/10/65
McKelvy, Sarah Jane married Pilcher, Joseph H. 01/03/65 01/18/65
McKendry, Bridget married McAvoy, John 03/04/61 04/05/61
McKenna, Catherine died 06/13/65 06/14/65
McKenna, John married Todd, Mary Ann (Mrs.) 02/11/62 02/13/62
McKenna, Mary Ann died 09/12/61 09/13/61
McKenna, Michael married Quigley, Honora 04/19/63 04/23/63
McKenna, Patrick John died 08/01/64 11/07/64
McKenna, Rosa R. married Smith, Charles T. 11/24/64 01/09/65
McKenna, Rosina married Toner, John 10/26/62 11/05/62
McKenna, Susan died 11/07/64 11/08/64
McKenney, William N. (Dr.) died 05/24/63 06/06/63
McKensie, Charles D. died 02/14/65 05/05/65
McKenzia, Aaron L. married Sindall, Hannah E. 12/05/60 12/10/61
McKenzie, James S. (Dr.) married Wilson, Ellen Savage 11/14/65 11/15/65
McKenzie, John P. (Dr.) died 01/14/63 01/15/64
McKeown, Bernard died 08/02/63 08/03/63
McKernin, Alice died 04/13/64 04/14/64
McKever, John William died 11/29/63 12/01/63
McKew, Ann died 08/08/65 08/09/65
McKew, Eddie (female infant) died 12/25/61 12/30/61
McKew, Edward J. died 12/12/62 12/13/62
McKew, Harry died 03/03/62 03/05/62
McKew, Hunter died 05/24/61 05/27/61
McKewen, Anne married Lollas, Patrick 09/07/63 09/11/63
McKewen, Annie C. died 09/16/65 09/19/65
McKewen, John died 02/16/61 02/20/61
McKim, Agnes Jane (Mrs.) died 04/30/64 05/17/64
McKim, Anthony Moore died 07/03/65 07/04/65
McKim, John S. died 01/11/65 01/13/65
McKim, John S. died 01/11/65 01/14/65
McKim, Mary Elizabeth died 01/03/64 01/04/64
McKim, R. married Holter, Agnes Jane 02/25/64 05/17/64
McKinless, Charles A. married McComas, Caroline 10/08/61 10/12/61
McKinless, Charles A. died 06/27/65 06/28/65
McKinley, Maria (Mrs.) died 09/22/64 09/23/64
McKinley, Mary married Asher, John E. 11/02/65 11/11/65
McKinley, Mary Frances married League, John Wesley 06/22/65 06/24/65
McKinley, Nancy died 11/29/61 11/30/61
McKinley, William J. died 01/25/63 01/27/63
McKinly, Hester Ann Maria died 02/10/63 02/14/63
McKinney, James married Kennard, Anne 08/23/65 08/25/65
McKinstry, Calista died 12/21/64 12/31/64
McKinstry, John married Michael, Alice C. 03/28/65 03/30/65
McKinstry, William M. died 12/09/64 12/31/64
McKitrick, Alice died 03/27/64 03/28/64

McKitrick, James married Carr, Theresa 12/18/65   12/23/65
McKitrick, Mary married Finigan, Owen 10/23/64   10/25/64
McKittrick, Philip J. died 03/05/61   03/06/61
McKlee, Curtis married Jacobs, Alverdo A. 01/06/63   01/07/63
McKnew, Annie married Hyatt, Robert V. 08/11/64   08/13/64
McKnew, Elmer Elsworth died 07/25/65   07/27/65
McKnew, Virginia G. died 06/05/64   06/08/64
McKnezie, Francis married Harrick, Kate 01/07/64   01/09/64
McKnight, Alverda M. died 09/30/62   10/01/62
McKnight, Alverdie Melisse died 10/01/62   10/02/62
McKnight, Charles M. died 09/17/62   09/18/62
McKnight, George married Sloan, Matilda 09/13/63   09/15/63
McKnight, Mary Jane died 07/03/64   07/07/64
McKniless, William Francis died 03/20/64   03/22/64
McKoskrey, Peter died 07/30/61   07/31/61
McLachlan, James died 03/04/61   03/06/61
McLachlan, Nettie B. married March, William G. 08/04/63   08/18/63
McLain, John married Leary, Margaret E. 10/27/63   10/28/63
McLain, Sarah E. married Peck, David A. J. 08/23/65   08/26/65
McLaine, William, Jr. married Wolfe, Olevia 05/23/65   05/25/65
McLanahan, George Kennedy died 12/19/65   12/27/65
McLanahan, Isabella B. died 01/16/63   01/17/63
McLanahan, Mary E. died 10/11/65   10/17/65
McLane, Charles S. married Lambdin, (Mrs. E. O.) 01/16/65   01/19/65
Mclane, James died 03/18/62   03/19/62
McLane, Mary died 06/16/61   06/17/61
McLane, Samuel married Moffit, Ann 05/28/61   06/03/61
McLaughlin, Agnes Cecelia died 05/08/62   05/09/62
McLaughlin, Andrew died 01/29/63   01/30/63
McLaughlin, Ann died 01/23/62   01/25/62
McLaughlin, Charles A. B. died 10/13/62   10/14/62
McLaughlin, David married Naler, Hester A. 10/18/63   10/20/63
McLaughlin, Elizabeth died 06/25/65   06/26/65
McLaughlin, Fannie married Wall, Charles A. 11/05/65   11/15/65
McLaughlin, George married Nicholls, Henrietta 06/22/65   06/24/65
McLaughlin, Hattie E. married Diggs, Edward G. 01/28/62   01/19/62
McLaughlin, Henry married Birdsal, Marinda 09/13/64   10/31/64
McLaughlin, Irwin died 05/08/65   05/09/65
McLaughlin, James died 09/30/62   10/01/62
McLaughlin, James Thomas died 10/25/63   10/26/63
McLaughlin, James Will died 08/17/63   08/18/63
McLaughlin, Jane died 09/18/64   09/19/64
McLaughlin, Jane (Mrs.) died 04/12/64   04/14/64
McLaughlin, John died 12/17/64   12/19/64
McLaughlin, Julia died 02/23/62   02/28/62
McLaughlin, Lucie A. died 01/22/64   01/25/64
McLaughlin, Margaret married McLauhlin, G. 09/27/61   10/01/61
McLaughlin, Marinda (Mrs.) died 07/23/65   07/24/65
McLaughlin, Marinda Godfrey died 07/28/65   07/31/65
McLaughlin, Mary Ellen married Cassidy, William 01/01/63   03/03/63
McLaughlin, Mary Josephine died 04/30/64   05/04/64
McLaughlin, Michael died 04/18/64   04/19/64
McLaughlin, P. married Miles, Emma L. 11/22/64   11/28/64
McLaughlin, William married Kerney, Mary A. 12/28/62   01/19/63
McLaughlin, Willie died 01/04/62   01/06/62

McLauhlin, G. married McLaughlin, Margaret 09/27/61 10/01/61
McLaurin, A. died 03/30/64 03/31/64
McLean, Charles H. married Miller, Isabella P. 11/29/61 12/10/61
McLean, Cornelius died 06/16/61 06/18/61
McLean, Edward died 05/31/65 06/01/65
McLean, J. C. J. died 06/11/65 06/13/65
McLean, John died 10/08/63 10/10/63
McLean, Lela Eudora died 08/01/63 08/05/63
McLean, Mary E. married Edwards, Richard G. 11/07/61 11/13/61
McLean, Mary G. married Boshamer, John C. 12/07/63 12/15/63
McLean, Mary G. married Boshammer, John C. 12/07/63 12/24/63
McLean, Sarah Osbourn died 07/05/65 07/12/65
McLeary, Mary Ellen died 05/09/64 05/10/64
McLeary, Sallie married Staylor, Mark J. 07/28/63 08/20/63
McLeish, Ann Catherine died 06/23/61 06/25/61
McLeish, Catherine died 10/06/61 10/07/61
McLure, Sarah died 02/24/65 03/04/65
McMagh, Julia Catherine died 08/13/65 08/15/65
McMahan, Mary died 04/01/64 04/02/64
McMahan, Thomas died 10/08/61 10/09/61
McMahon, Annie married Whalen, James 08/10/63 08/13/63
McMahon, Catherine died 03/16/65 03/17/65
McMahon, James died 03/08/62 03/10/62
McMahon, James died 03/25/64 03/26/64
McMahon, James died 01/14/65 01/16/65
McMahon, James married Loftus, Eliza J. 12/31/63 01/09/64
McMahon, Jan died 01/09/62 01/10/62
McMahon, John died 09/24/63 09/26/63
McMahon, John J. died 06/17/65 07/11/65
McMahon, John T. died 07/28/62 07/30/62
McMahon, Mary (Mrs.) died 08/05/63 08/06/63
McMahon, Mary (Mrs.) married Black, John 07/12/63 07/15/63
McMahon, Mary C. married McClintock, Winfield 12/25/60 01/07/61
McMahon, Mary Cecelia died 01/02/63 01/03/63
McMahon, Mary Ellen died 12/01/64 12/03/64
McMahon, Matthew Patrick died 12/25/62 12/27/62
McMahon, Michael married Gallagher, Susan 06/26/64 03/07/65
McMahon, Michael J. married Collison, Mary E. 12/02/62 12/20/62
McMahon, Patrick died 05/19/62 05/20/62
McMahon, Patrick died 02/04/64 02/05/64
McMahon, Patrick married Rahbine, Annie C. 11/15/64 11/18/64
McMahon, Peter married Coughlin, Ellen 11/22/64 11/30/64
McMahon, William Monahan married Diffley, Kate V. no date 07/07/63
McMaines, John A. died 09/02/63 09/03/63
McMaines, Sarah married Dew, Theodore W. 07/03/65 07/11/65
McMakin, Edith S. A. died 04/21/64 04/22/64
McMallen, Elizabeth died 12/14/62 12/16/62
McMann, Thomas Clinton died 02/13/61 02/14/61
McManus, Alexander died 09/04/64 09/05/64
McManus, Ann died 07/25/61 07/26/61
McManus, Elizabeth died 04/17/62 04/18/62
McManus, Elizabeth Catherine died 03/13/62 03/14/62
McManus, Elizabeth Catherine died 03/13/62 03/15/62
McManus, Ellen M. died 12/07/65 12/09/65
McManus, F. R. married Nicholson, Ellen M. 12/02/62 12/05/62

McManus, John married Rainey, Sarah A. 05/10/63   05/18/63
McManus, John married Feltz, Elizabeth 10/06/63   11/09/63
McManus, John married Sloan, Mary (Mrs.) 07/11/65   09/02/65
McManus, Margaret J. married Richardson, James K. 05/07/61   05/08/61
McManus, Rose died 07/26/64   07/28/64
McMechen, Alice died 06/14/61   06/18/61
McMechen, Charles Glenn died 11/16/63   11/20/63
McMechen, Mary Jane (Mrs.) died 08/23/63   08/25/63
McMillan, Emma C. married Daffy, Edward 12/05/61   12/09/61
McMillan, John died 05/18/65   05/23/65
McMillan, Mary R. died 03/28/62   03/29/62
McMillan, William D. married Aitchison, Laura H. 11/12/63   11/13/63
McMillian, Mary A. married Frederick, Henry C. 05/18/65   08/17/65
McMillin, Margaret Jane Grundy married Cook, John K. 07/04/61   07/18/6
McMinn, Matilda H. died 04/02/62   04/04/62
McMullan, Mary Virginia married Brooks, Charles E. 07/03/65   07/24/65
McMullan, Virginia married Brooks, Robert 07/03/65   07/06/65
McMullen, John died 06/03/63   06/04/63
McMullen, John died 06/03/63   06/05/63
McMullen, Mary Ann married Darbaugh, Daniel 01/14/64   01/19/64
McMurphy, Emma married Ewing, E. E. 07/13/65   07/15/65
McMurray, Elizabeth died 05/04/64   05/06/64
McMurray, Mary C. (Mrs.) died 04/07/65   04/08/65
McNabb, John Dean died 05/12/63   05/14/63
McNalley, Patrick married Todd, Mary 04/05/63   04/08/63
McNally, Bridget died 10/21/61   10/23/61
McNally, Catherine died 02/14/61   02/15/61
McNally, Felix died 08/18/62   08/19/62
McNally, Henry died 06/10/64   06/14/64
McNally, Henry R. married Ducatel, Louise 01/14/63   01/16/63
McNally, Mary (Mrs.) died 02/12/64   02/13/64
McNally, Olevia W. died 08/19/64   08/20/64
McNally, Sara Rebecca died 01/07/65   01/09/65
McNally, Thomas died 01/08/61   01/15/61
McNamara, Emma Agnes died 01/10/64   01/12/64
McNamara, Hugh Charles died 08/27/61   08/28/61
McNamara, Jerome D. married Mister, Cornelia 10/12/65   10/14/65
McNamara, Mary Ann married Crowe, Malachi 05/11/62   05/14/62
McNamara, Simon married McNulty, Julia Ann 01/19/62   01/21/62
McNamara, Timothy died 05/07/62   05/09/62
McNamee, Bridget (Mrs.) died 04/14/65   04/15/65
McNamee, Stephen N. died 12/25/62   12/27/62
McNamer, John C. married Wilson, Arrie E. 01/26/64   01/28/64
McNaughton, Bridget died 06/08/65   06/09/65
McNeal, George married Collins, Susannah (Mrs.) 11/07/65   11/18/65
McNeal, Georgeanna married Whalen, Stephen 02/24/63   03/04/63
McNeal, Henry died 12/01/64   12/05/64
McNeal, James H. married Flaherty, Sarah A. 12/30/61   01/23/62
McNeal, James Thomas died 03/19/65   03/20/65
McNeal, Lewis died 11/12/63   11/13/63
McNeal, Lloyd died 07/09/65   07/10/65
McNeal, Lloyd died 07/09/65   07/11/65
McNeal, Margaret Ann married Miller, John 01/10/65   01/12/65
McNeal, Martha A. died 06/01/61   06/04/61
McNeal, Mary Elizabeth died 07/15/63   07/18/63

McNeal, Matthew died 10/02/62   10/03/62
McNeal, Sarah Jane died no date   12/11/62
McNeal, William died 02/25/61   02/27/61
McNeal, William married Lloyd, Rebecca T. 06/06/63   06/25/63
McNeale, William married Burger, Marie M. 12/25/61   12/30/61
McNear, Frank B. married Haslett, Deborah V. 12/24/64   01/12/65
McNeil, Letitia died 03/08/61   03/09/61
McNeil, Sarah married McFadden, Francis 11/01/64   11/03/64
McNeill, John Franklin died 09/10/64   09/13/64
McNeill, Mary Jane died 02/18/64   02/19/64
McNeill, Maryan died 03/08/63   03/10/63
McNeill, Mollie C. married McCardell, William H. 11/24/63   11/25/63
McNeir, Alice Amelia married Moran, Richard T. 08/18/63   08/25/63
McNeir, Emily M. died 03/09/62   03/10/62
McNeir, William J. married Morrison, Nellie 03/23/64   04/12/64
McNeive, Martin died 08/04/62   09/05/62
McNett, Lucinda died 01/24/61   01/26/61
McNeuny, Sarah Jane died 01/15/65   01/17/65
McNew, Alverda married Selby, James W. 02/22/65   02/25/65
McNew, Eliza Ellen married Virtue, Sackwood D. 08/14/64   09/17/64
McNew, Elizabeth Bell died 01/08/61   01/12/61
McNew, Mary Ann (Mrs.) died 03/07/63   03/09/63
McNew, Susan married Cole, J. Columbus 02/19/62   02/27/62
McNinch, Thomas married Peddicord, Elizabeth A. 03/28/61   04/02/61
McNiven, Mark died 06/07/63   06/08/63
McNulty, Ellen married Harryman, Benjamin B. 03/13/64   03/25/64
McNulty, John A. married Nixon, Laura Virginia 08/02/63   09/16/63
McNulty, Julia Ann married McNamara, Simon 01/19/62   01/21/62
McNulty, Kate married Conway, Michael 02/23/62   02/27/62
McNulty, Kate married Nohe, Charles 06/19/65   07/15/65
McNulty, Margaret (Mrs.) died 01/21/63   01/23/63
McNulty, Rosy married Jones, Henry O. 06/08/63   06/12/63
McNulty, William Edgar died 09/14/63   09/18/63
MCollum, Emma Elizabeth died 08/17/65   08/18/65
McParland, Thomas died 10/19/64   10/20/64
McParlin, Cassandra H. (Mrs.) died 03/12/65   03/14/65
McPhail, Elizabeth Ann died 02/23/64   02/24/64
McPherson, David died 02/05/65   02/07/65
McPherson, Fannie married Dennis, George R. 06/09/64   06/11/64
McPherson, James Washington died 06/11/63   06/12/63
McPherson, John died 01/24/64   01/26/64
McPherson, Joseph V. married Wilhelm, Charlotte 11/12/63   12/03/63
McPherson, William Bruce died 08/02/65   08/03/65
McPhillips, Catherine Dovia died 08/02/63   08/03/63
McPhillips, James died 12/26/64   12/28/64
McPolen, Susan died 12/12/63   12/14/63
McQuade, Elizabeth married Buckles, Henry S. 05/06/65   05/09/65
McQuaid, Charles J. married McGee, Rose 04/09/63   04/11/63
McQuilliams, Rose married Knott, Charles 05/19/64   05/28/64
McQuinn, John S. married Boyer, Margaret 04/21/64   05/05/64
McRea, Elizabeth Wise died 06/09/65   06/16/65
McRoberts, Mary died 11/18/61   12/16/61
McShane, Charles died 12/30/60   01/04/61
McShane, Charles died 01/03/61   01/05/61
McShane, Henry died 03/30/62   03/31/62

McShene, Margaret died 05/20/63   05/21/63
McShene, Margaret died 05/20/63   05/22/63
McSherry, Mary Helena died 01/21/63   01/22/63
McSherry, Mary Helena died 01/21/63   01/23/63
McSorley, James died 10/28/64   10/29/64
McSweeney, Edward died 04/08/63   04/09/63
McSweeney, Edward P. died 09/25/62   09/29/62
McSwiney, Denis died 09/27/61   09/28/61
McTaggart, James died 04/28/63   05/12/63
McVee, Mary Osborn died 02/07/63   02/11/63
McWhister, Agness died 03/27/63   03/28/63
McWilliams, (male infant) died 07/11/61   08/12/61
McWilliams, Clara (Mrs.) died 03/10/64   03/18/64
McWilliams, Kate married Clark, Matthew 05/09/61   05/13/61
McWilliams, Manie married Hooper, James E. 01/07/62   01/14/62
McWilliams, Robert died 08/01/61   08/02/61
McWilliams, Rose died 03/15/61   03/16/61
McWilliams, William died 03/16/64   03/17/64
Meachen, Thomas G. married Jordan, Rachel A. 11/15/64   12/14/64
Mead, Elizabeth Ann died 08/10/63   08/12/63
Mead, Lizzie married Ringgold, Edward H. 11/01/65   11/08/65
Mead, Louisa Cecelia (Mrs.) died 01/10/63   01/20/63
Mead, Rachel M. married Krebs, Jacob Emory 09/15/63   09/17/63
Meade, Mary C. married Eagleston, Abraim 01/01/61   01/03/61
Meade, Mary Elizabeth died 09/03/65   09/06/65
Meade, W. H. died 01/15/62   01/17/62
Meads, Catherine L. married Heird, Samuel C. 04/20/63   04/23/63
Meads, Charlie died 08/09/61   09/17/61
Meads, James T. married Hughes, Emily J. 01/08/63   01/13/63
Meads, Mary Agnes died 09/26/65   10/07/65
Meads, Mary J. married Kauffman, Marion W. 09/14/62   09/16/62
Meads, Nora Bell died 04/05/64   04/09/64
Meads, Sarah Ellen married Kurtz, Martin 05/07/63   05/08/63
Meads, William H. married White, Susan A. 02/25/64   02/27/64
Meads, William Wallace died 12/06/61   12/07/61
Meairs, Rebecca J. died 12/25/62   12/27/62
Meakin, J. W. married Hank, Sally V. 03/17/63   03/23/63
Meakin, Joshua W. married Henck, Sallie V. 03/17/63   03/24/63
Meakin, Nathaniel married Keen, Sallie J. 01/22/63   01/26/63
Meakin, Samuel died 02/10/65   02/13/65
Meakin, Samuel died 02/10/65   02/14/65
Mealy, James R. died 02/20/63   02/21/63
Meaney, Charles F. married Mackey, Mary L. 08/01/65   08/03/65
Meany, Charles F. married Mackey, Mannie L. 08/01/65   08/02/65
Mears, Emma W. married Schiers, J. Henry 10/13/63   10/24/63
Mears, John F. married Calahan, Tabitha E. 11/12/61   11/16/61
Mears, Louisa married Reese, Henry D. 03/05/61   06/01/61
Meath, Mary E. married Norris, Richard V. 07/03/64   10/10/64
Mecaslin, Alverta (Mrs.) died 09/13/63   09/15/63
Mecaslin, Maggie Maria died 08/30/62   01/21/63
Mecaslin, Thomas R. died 04/02/63   04/08/63
Mecham, Ann (Mrs.) died 09/08/64   09/09/64
Mechem, George Washington died 12/19/63   12/21/63
Medairy, Abner Angell died 07/03/63   07/07/63
Medairy, Bell married Welch, B. Frank 04/09/63   04/13/63

Medairy, M. Kate married Angell, A. H. 02/12/63 02/14/63
Medairy, Norman R. died 04/25/61 04/27/61
Medairy, Rachel (Mrs.) died 09/06/64 09/08/64
Medcalf, Francis married Owings, Isabella 06/06/65 06/15/65
Medcalfe, Addison died 03/07/62 03/10/62
Medcalfe, Sarah Ann died 09/08/62 09/09/62
Medcalfe, William M. died 02/11/62 02/12/62
Meddinger, George died 07/31/61 08/01/61
Medford, Charles E. died 06/05/64 06/07/64
Medinger, Charles William died 07/10/62 07/12/62
Medinger, George A. married Slater, Margaret A. 09/27/65 12/04/65
Medinger, Georgeanna died 01/14/63 01/22/63
Medley, Harriet E. married Luhn, Gustave J. 01/08/63 01/16/63
Medtart, Elizabeth died 12/08/65 12/09/65
Medtart, Mary E. married Street, David 03/25/62 03/29/62
Meede, Elizabeth C. died 02/11/64 02/15/64
Meeds, Amanda Priscilla H. died 04/03/61 04/20/61
Meeds, Amanda Priscilla H. died 04/03/61 04/22/61
Meeds, Charles married Smith, Maggy 12/30/62 01/03/63
Meeds, Elizabeth (Mrs.) died 01/02/65 01/03/65
Meeds, William died 08/03/64 08/04/64
Meehan, Ann (Mrs.) died 09/09/64 09/10/64
Meek, Emma D. (Mrs.) died 06/30/63 08/05/63
Meek, James married Ford, Mary 10/30/62 11/01/62
Meek, John Henry died 08/11/64 08/12/64
Meek, Martha Eliza married Johnson, Robert (Cpt.) 11/03/64 11/05/64
Meekins, Charles E. died 01/18/65 01/19/65
Meekins, James T. E. died 04/13/61 04/15/61
Meekins, Joseph Augustus married Owens, Martha Davis 11/05/62 11/06/62
Meekins, Marcella married Cooksey, Thomas H. 10/22/63 10/26/63
Meekins, Mary E. married Hooper, Benjamin T. 10/22/63 10/28/63
Meekins, Nancy died 01/04/62 01/07/62
Meekins, Robert J. married Tall, Henrietta 04/23/63 06/10/63
Meekins, Susannah C. (Mrs.) died 08/08/64 08/09/64
Meekins, Thomas married Cowan, Sophie 09/17/61 10/30/61
Meekins, Thomas died 12/04/63 12/05/63
Meeks, William died 02/09/63 02/11/63
Meeks, William H. married Wilson, Eliza R. 10/20/62 05/14/63
Meeler, Wilhelmine E. (Mrs.) died 07/18/63 07/20/63
Meers, Michael Joseph died 06/25/64 06/27/64
Meeteer, Susan died 03/22/62 03/26/62
Meeter, Mary E. married Sherman, John 10/02/65 10/09/65
Megarry, Ellen died 07/19/61 07/20/61
Megary, James Washington died 06/10/63 06/18/63
Megary, Jane married Denison, John R. 12/23/60 01/05/61
Megee, Alverda died 12/29/63 12/31/63
Megenhardt, Louise died 04/03/61 04/04/61
Megenhardt, Richard died 12/26/63 12/29/63
Megillay, Sarah Alice died 11/23/63 11/24/63
Meginniss, C. G. married Applegarth, Mollie E. 03/28/65 04/04/65
Megraw, John married Benham, Annie 11/08/64 11/10/64
Mehaffy, Elizabeth (Mrs.) died 08/25/63 08/28/63
Meinkranz, Catharine married Pfrom, Adam 10/18/63 10/30/63
Meinkranz, Theodore married Clemmons, Annie B. 02/28/64 03/05/64
Meixel, William Hamilton died 06/03/65 06/07/65

```
Meixsel, Joseph H. married Lerew, Matilda J. 06/28/64  06/29/64
Meixsel, Mary A. (Mrs.) died 01/12/63  01/13/63
Melcher, George W. married James, Elizabeth 11/07/65  11/23/65
Melchior, Francis P. married Shale, Elizabeth 05/26/64  05/27/64
Melchior, Louis married Englebach, Annie 08/04/64  08/08/64
Melchior, Louisa H. married Stewart, James F. 12/20/64  12/24/64
Mellon, Mary died 01/30/61  01/31/61
Mellon, William died 07/10/64  07/12/64
Mellor, James B. married Jones, Julia M. 06/01/63  07/03/63
Mellor, John B. married Larrabee, Maggie 11/05/63  11/07/63
Melony, John Primrose died 02/17/63  02/19/63
Melville, Sarah A. (Mrs.) died 07/20/64  07/21/64
Melville, Sarah U. died 05/06/61  05/07/61
Melvin, Joseph died 12/07/62  12/09/62
Menger, William died 05/19/64  05/21/64
Mennig, Christiana married Shunck, Robert 04/07/64  04/12/64
Menslage, William died 09/27/65  09/28/65
Mentzel, George R. died 11/19/62  11/21/62
Mentzel, Rachel (Mrs.) died 02/14/65  02/16/65
Mentzell, Frederick died 07/22/62  07/23/62
Mentzell, Sophia died 07/22/62  07/23/62
Menzman, Victor S. died 08/19/64  08/20/64
Mercer, Annie died no date  02/27/65
Mercer, C. married Reich, Annie R. 05/17/65  05/20/65
Mercer, Eleanor married Bryan, Charles H. 10/23/64  10/25/64
Mercer, Leanna married Wall, John 10/19/65  10/23/65
Mercer, Mary S. (Mrs.) died 04/17/64  04/19/64
Mercer, Thomas Lindley died 08/03/64  08/04/64
Mercer, Thomas V. married Woods, Ellen A. 01/31/61  02/02/61
Merceret, Francis Margaret died 11/02/65  11/11/65
Merceret, John Henry died 07/09/65  07/12/65
Merceret, Jules died 03/11/65  04/01/65
Merceret, Mary Natalie (Mrs.) died 08/31/65  09/01/65
Merchant, Rosetta married Whitney, George W. 12/02/62  12/08/62
Merchant, Sarah Ann died 12/16/62  12/17/62
Merchant, Sarah Ann died 12/16/62  12/18/62
Meredith, B. R. died 08/11/61  08/12/61
Meredith, Charles Frederick died 11/10/61  11/12/61
Meredith, Elizabeth G. (Mrs.) died 04/26/64  05/07/64
Meredith, Emma F. married Kirby, James S. 03/03/63  03/10/63
Meredith, James died 02/03/61  02/05/61
Meredith, Josephine died 02/14/65  02/15/65
Meredith, Margaret died 10/01/65  10/02/65
Meredith, Margaret Ann (Mrs.) died 09/13/65  09/15/65
Meredith, Mary Virginia married Stivers, Charles Henry 10/28/63
     11/02/63
Merideth, Alexander L. died 06/27/63  12/15/63
Merker, George O. died 02/22/65  02/23/65
Merriam, G. F. (Maj.) married Scott, Nina 09/29/63  10/03/63
Merrifield, Charles E. married Robins, Sallie J. 01/19/65  01/20/65
Merriken, Alphonza Elizabeth married Wood, William A. 04/10/62  04/15/
Merriken, David died 03/19/62  03/20/62
Merriken, Elizabeth A. died 03/24/61  03/26/61
Merriken, Ella Virginia died 07/07/65  07/08/65
Merriken, Francis Marion died 11/14/61  11/15/61
```

Merriken, Franklin (Esq.) married Boone, Mary E. 12/29/63 01/01/64
Merriken, James, Sr. died 04/26/61 04/27/61
Merriken, John D. died no date 11/05/64
Merriken, Lizzie died 09/05/65 09/06/65
Merriken, Lou married Cummings, S. H. (Rev.) 12/22/63 12/24/63
Merriken, Mary Eugenia died 10/30/62 11/01/62
Merriken, William married Livingston, Mary J. 11/19/63 11/16/63
Merrill, James A. (USN) married Knode, Annie V. 12/08/63 12/11/63
Merrill, Richard S. married Lewis, Sarah R. 10/24/65 10/28/65
Merrit, Maggie R. married Rider, Abraham 02/23/65 02/27/65
Merritt, Alfred Clifton died 02/24/63 02/25/63
Merritt, Clara Theresa died 02/04/62 02/07/62
Merritt, James married Nicholson, Lottie 09/21/64 02/16/65
Merritt, John died 12/19/63 12/25/63
Merritt, John died 09/30/64 10/03/64
Merritt, John G. married Hoddinott, Mary A. 03/14/63 03/14/63
Merritt, Martin died 06/13/63 06/16/63
Merritt, Susannah died 12/03/65 12/05/65
Merritt, William H. married Jacobs, Martha 01/19/64 01/23/64
Merryman, Charles died 11/10/65 11/11/65
Merryman, Ella E. died 07/02/64 07/06/64
Merryman, George J. married Powell, Fannie A. 02/09/65 02/14/65
Merryman, Jemima died 12/16/62 12/17/62
Merryman, John B. died 06/11/61 06/15/61
Merryman, Joseph P. married Lucas, Ellie J. 11/17/63 11/20/63
Merryman, Mary Ann B. (Mrs.) died 01/05/64 01/06/64
Merryman, Mary Lizzie married Fennimore, William 05/06/63 05/07/63
Merryman, Oliver P. married McConkey, Hettie C. 04/18/65 04/24/65
Merryman, Willie Long died 05/12/62 05/12/62
Merson, Charles E. married Beauchamp, Annie E. 02/11/61 02/20/61
Merson, James E. died 03/23/62 04/05/62
Merson, Jane R. married Leonard, William H. 04/08/61 04/18/61
Merson, Sarah Ann died 03/16/62 04/05/62
Merson, William died 11/24/63 12/04/63
Mesner, Virginia married Negengerd, Frederick A. 06/23/63 06/25/63
Messer, Annie Margaret married Boller, William 04/14/63 04/15/63
Messer, Henry died 06/25/64 06/27/64
Messersmith, Catharine (Mrs.) died 03/17/64 03/18/64
Messersmith, Emmanuel died 03/18/64 03/19/64
Metcalf, Mary E. married Church, W. C. 04/02/63 04/03/63
Methany, Ida Virginia died 05/17/61 05/21/61
Mettam, Rebecca R. married Davis, Michael 10/08/63 10/14/63
Mettee, August married Reed, Charlotte M. 12/04/65 12/15/65
Mettee, Leonard married Wilson, Mary W. 04/11/65 04/18/65
Mettee, Leonard, C. died 08/14/65 08/16/65
Mettee, Lewis A. died 08/08/61 08/09/61
Mettee, Lisabel Watkins died 03/02/63 03/03/63
Mettee, Mary E. married Hall, William A. 10/29/63 11/03/63
Mettee, Neanie J. married Tally, William Wallace 08/21/61 08/26/61
Mettee, Susannah G. died 02/20/62 03/06/62
Mettee, William H. married Chamberlin, Emma 08/19/62 08/21/62
Mettle, Ann Jane died 05/27/62 05/29/62
Mety, Annie M. married Edwards, Charles R. 03/10/63 03/12/63
Metz, Anna Bell died 01/02/65 01/04/65
Metz, Charlotte died 02/09/63 02/10/63

Metzger, Mary died 11/18/62 11/19/62
Metzger, Mary E. married Yingling, William 09/15/64 09/27/64
Meushaw, George W. died 08/25/63 08/26/63
Mewburn, Joseph P. married Campbell, Lucie J. 01/27/64 02/02/64
Mewshaw, Louisa married Lineberger, Francis M. 04/26/63 04/30/63
Mewshaw, Rachel married Gaither, Denis 05/29/62 05/31/62
Meyer, Amelia married Welch, J. G. 11/05/63 11/20/63
Meyer, Amelia married Vansant, J. Wehrly 05/14/65 05/24/65
Meyer, Ann died 07/26/62 08/01/62
Meyer, Burchard died 07/17/61 07/18/61
Meyer, Frederick A. died 11/05/61 11/06/61
Meyer, Frederick G. died 10/07/65 10/09/65
Meyer, George married Kine, Rosina 01/17/62 01/24/62
Meyer, Georgie married Kine, Rosina 01/17/62 01/23/62
Meyer, Johan Garhard died 12/20/65 12/22/65
Meyer, John G. died 09/19/61 09/20/61
Meyer, John Henry died 02/27/64 02/29/64
Meyer, Mary Eliza died 09/26/63 09/29/63
Meyer, Mary Williamina married Boeschi, Henry William 11/30/62 12/10/
Meyers, Charles H. died 01/15/63 01/16/64
Meyers, Emily J. died 02/02/62 02/04/62
Meyers, George Albert died 03/28/64 03/31/64
Meyers, Georgeanna died 10/27/62 10/29/62
Meyers, Harriet Ann married Crawford, William Henry 12/18/62 12/20/62
Meyers, J. D. died 09/13/65 09/20/65
Meyers, Jacob, Jr. married Proctor, Rebecca H. 07/21/62 09/25/62
Meyers, Louise married Long, Upton T. 09/17/63 10/10/63
Meyers, Nelson B. married Boyd, Elizabeth A. 10/19/65 10/24/65
Meyler, John James died 05/08/64 05/09/64
Mezick, Baptist (Capt.) died 03/15/63 03/17/63
Mezick, Baptist (Capt.) died 03/15/63 03/18/63
Mezick, Charlotte (Mrs.) died 04/29/65 05/01/65
Mezick, James W. died 03/16/65 03/23/65
Mezick, Mary died 08/25/62 08/26/62
Mezick, Sarah Burn died 04/30/63 05/02/63
Mezies, James died 12/13/63 12/15/63
Michael, Alice C. married McKinstry, John 03/28/65 03/30/65
Michael, Anna M. (Mrs.) died 02/24/63 02/25/63
Michael, Christina C. died 06/27/62 07/01/62
Michael, Ella married Griffith, G. S. 06/14/64 06/22/64
Michael, Helen Elizabeth died 05/09/62 05/12/62
Michael, Henry E. died 01/03/65 01/14/65
Michael, Jacob married Hand, Susan (Mrs.) 05/11/63 05/18/63
Michael, Jacob married Hann, Susan 05/11/63 05/19/63
Michael, Jacob D. married Wallace, Mollie A. 06/14/64 06/15/64
Michael, James H. married Keen, Lizzie 02/12/63 02/13/63
Michael, Laura E. married Price, Edward Rutledge 01/19/65 01/21/65
Michael, Louis D. married Hollis, Ella A. 01/12/64 01/30/64
Michael, Martha married McDonald, H. S. 02/22/64 03/22/64
Michael, Martha married McDonald, Horace C. 02/22/64 03/29/64
Michael, Martha Elizabeth died 04/27/62 04/28/62
Michael, Mary A. died 11/06/65 11/08/65
Michael, Mary Emma died 04/21/65 04/24/65
Michael, Mary M. married Cromwell, Jacob G. 05/17/65 05/19/65
Michael, S. Jane married League, William H. 02/28/65 06/15/65

Michael, Susie L. married Sutherland, John M. 07/14/63   07/17/63
Michael, William B. married Taylor, Rachel E. 12/23/63   12/24/63
Michael, William Frederick died 01/06/62   01/06/62
Micheals, Clementine C. married Ireland, John B. 06/23/63   06/26/63
Micheau, Charles died 07/02/63   07/07/63
Michel, Martin died 05/29/65   05/31/65
Mickel, Elizabeth married Block, Henry 01/18/61   01/21/61
Mickle, Edward died 09/25/65   11/14/65
Mickle, Robert, Jr. died 10/31/61   11/02/61
Middelkauf, Mary Margaret died 03/28/62   03/31/62
Middlekauf, Amanda Grace died 04/03/65   04/06/65
Middleton, Ann Elizabeth died 10/15/65   10/19/65
Middleton, Annie E. married Hanson, A. B. 12/01/64   12/02/64
Middleton, David died 10/15/63   10/21/63
Middleton, Elizabeth C. (Mrs.) died 02/18/64   02/20/64
Middleton, Frances Augusta married Reigart, John M. 05/02/65   05/10/65
Middleton, Henry married Nail, Mary A. 11/30/64   12/01/64
Middleton, Isadore A. married Farless, Benjamin 06/29/65   07/07/65
Middleton, James P. died no date   08/22/62
Middleton, Richard H. died 03/29/64   03/30/64
Middleton, Sarah R. (Mrs.) died 01/25/65   01/27/65
Middleton, Susan D. died 03/12/61   03/14/61
Middleton, William Thomas died 08/19/65   07/20/65
Milan, Emily (Mrs.) died 09/06/63   09/10/63
Milbourne, Mary Ann (Mrs.) died 11/06/64   11/07/64
Milburn, Clara M. married Brown, Felix E. (Dr.) 10/26/65   11/02/65
Milburn, James O. P. died 01/16/64   01/18/64
Milburn, John Henry died 06/16/63   06/17/63
Milburn, Robert N. died 08/14/61   08/15/61
Milburn, T. H. married Price, Amanda V. 05/22/62   06/10/62
Milburn, Thurya died 10/07/62   10/18/62
Miles, Ann Rebecca married Lewis, John 11/27/61   11/30/61
Miles, B. F. (Rev.) married Bull, Virginia 12/26/61   01/08/62
Miles, Charles M. married Entz, Williamina T. 06/05/62   06/11/62
Miles, Clara Ann died 09/05/64   09/06/64
Miles, Clara Ann died 09/05/64   09/08/64
Miles, Emma L. married McLaughlin, P. 11/22/64   11/28/64
Miles, Emma V. married Goss, William R. 05/14/62   05/16/62
Miles, George Henry died 01/18/63   01/19/63
Miles, John died 03/14/65   03/16/65
Miles, Lottie A. married Sentenn, Walter J. 11/03/63   11/05/63
Miles, Lydia Ann died 07/13/62   07/14/62
Miles, Mary Ann married Howard, Jeremiah 05/01/62   05/03/62
Miles, Mollie A. married Smith, Daniel A. 02/09/64   02/10/64
Miles, Philip Thomas died 07/17/63   07/18/63
Miles, Richard D. died 08/14/65   08/15/65
Miles, Richard D. died 08/14/65   08/16/65
Miles, Susan W. married Anderson, R. N. 02/26/61   03/08/61
Miles, Uriah died 01/09/63   01/10/63
Miles, William married McGee, Mary C. 04/03/61   10/17/61
Miles, William E. married Orem, Mary E. no date   07/12/64
Milholland, E. F. (Dr.) married Saunders, Mary C. 10/25/64   10/31/64
Milk, James Goldsmith died 04/20/64   04/23/64
Millan, John G. married Carman, Mary J. 05/24/63   05/27/63
Millan, Mary A. died 02/22/61   02/26/61

```
Millan, N. M. married Caruthers, Virginia 02/21/65  02/27/65
Millar, Alexander died 05/13/63  05/15/63
Millar, Ellen died 06/20/61  06/21/61
Millar, Fannie died 06/20/61  07/03/61
Millar, John died 09/19/61  09/20/61
Millar, Nellie died 06/20/61  07/03/61
Millar, Wesley D. died 10/25/61  11/01/61
Millburn, Catherine M. married Bruscup, George R. 10/16/62  10/18/62
Millemun, George died 10/29/61  10/30/61
Millemun, John D. died 12/19/62  12/20/62
Millen, Maggie married McBee, Charles E. 10/02/62  01/23/63
Millen, Mary Jane died 07/17/61  01/30/62
Miller, A. Berkley married Baldwin, Mary E. 10/21/62  10/29/62
Miller, Amelia J. married Keller, Andrew J. 03/08/63  04/30/63
Miller, Annie married Thayer, Henry C. 05/13/63  05/15/63
Miller, Annie married Reid, Thomas B. 06/20/64  07/08/64
Miller, Ava married Riffle, Thomas 02/23/64  02/25/64
Miller, B. F. married Quigley, Maggie 02/26/63  03/03/63
Miller, Benjamin married Benjamin, Hester 01/21/64  01/25/64
Miller, Catharine married McIntosh, Daniel 02/19/63  02/21/63
Miller, Catharine died 03/28/65  03/30/65
Miller, Catherine (Mrs.) died 07/05/65  07/06/65
Miller, Chanlur married Clark, Susan S. 01/22/62  01/28/62
Miller, Charles F. died 11/23/61  11/26/61
Miller, Charles H. married Biscoe, Isabella 03/21/64  03/28/64
Miller, Columbus died 01/12/62  01/13/62
Miller, Daniel died 05/14/65  05/16/65
Miller, Edward G. married Church, Mary F. 07/07/64  08/01/64
Miller, Edward N. married Southard, Mary Eliz. (Mrs.) 04/18/65  06/03/
Miller, Elanor married Spurrier, Edward 11/13/63  11/16/63
Miller, Elizabeth died 10/20/64  10/21/64
Miller, Elizabeth married Arnold, Alexander 07/28/62  04/30/63
Miller, Emma V. married Elliott, A. James 10/27/64  11/01/64
Miller, Emojean died 09/28/61  10/01/61
Miller, Florence died 10/31/63  11/03/63
Miller, Frances Ann died 12/01/62  12/16/62
Miller, Frances Jane married Benson, William H. 10/13/63  10/24/63
Miller, Franklin A. married Haynes, Emma 05/23/65  06/01/65
Miller, Genyra C. married Dennis, James M. 08/24/62  08/26/62
Miller, George Alexandria married Dorsey, Sarah Rebecca 11/22/63
    12/01/63
Miller, George C. died 05/24/65  05/25/65
Miller, George H. married Fagen, Mary Ann 11/24/62  12/01/62
Miller, George P. died 07/05/65  07/06/65
Miller, George W. married Brown, Mary 07/07/64  07/11/64
Miller, George W. married Zeitler, Augusta 06/05/64  06/06/64
Miller, Henrietta married Conyers, Walter 05/11/61  09/05/61
Miller, Henry died 08/18/62  08/25/62
Miller, Henry married Robinson, Sarah A. 07/07/92  03/06/63
Miller, Henry married Weiss, Elizabeth 01/14/64  01/22/64
Miller, Howard B. died 12/07/64  12/09/64
Miller, Isaac died 08/31/64  09/01/64
Miller, Isaac S. died 10/10/62  10/13/62
Miller, Isabella P. married McLean, Charles H. 11/29/61  12/10/61
Miller, J. Poulson married Byers, Irene S. 11/05/63  11/07/63
```

Miller, Jacob died 07/21/61 07/23/61
Miller, Jacob H. married Dulany, Eliza V. 02/12/63 02/17/63
Miller, James (Cpt.) married Roberts, Ellen Jane 11/03/63 11/06/63
Miller, James D. married Norfolk, Mollie K. 05/30/65 07/31/65
Miller, Jeremiah married Hughes, Georgeanna 12/02/62 12/05/62
Miller, Jeremiah died 12/18/63 12/28/63
Miller, Jerome N. died 04/30/63 05/02/63
Miller, John died 09/03/63 09/04/63
Miller, John married McNeal, Margaret Ann 01/10/65 01/12/65
Miller, John C. died 01/22/65 02/07/65
Miller, John H. married Rothrell, Sarah Jane 11/28/61 01/18/62
Miller, John H. married Brown, Elizabeth 05/21/63 05/23/63
Miller, John Thomas died 02/25/63 03/03/63
Miller, Jonathan married Lemmon, Sarah Ellen 11/12/61 11/14/61
Miller, Joseph married Werling, Maggie 03/12/63 03/13/63
Miller, Joseph W. married Johnson, Sarah C. 08/17/65 08/22/65
Miller, Josephine married Gontrum, William N. 10/30/65 11/04/65
Miller, Kate married Ningardt, Frederick W. 01/13/62 01/28/62
Miller, Kate A. married Winn, James P. 07/28/64 08/03/64
Miller, Laura E. died 02/17/62 02/19/62
Miller, Leonard D. married Dickinson, Ann Maria 04/19/64 04/30/64
Miller, Lewis H. married Zachary, Sarah L. 10/22/62 03/23/63
Miller, Lizzie A. married Sanders, George W. 10/14/62 10/18/62
Miller, Louisa (Mrs.) died 02/01/64 02/03/64
Miller, Louisa E. married Beohm, John 06/22/64 06/24/64
Miller, M. A. married Hess, J., Jr. 10/23/65 10/25/65
Miller, M. M. married Holloway, James H. 11/02/65 12/07/65
Miller, Maggie A. died 12/20/64 12/24/64
Miller, Maggie A. married Comfort, H. J. (Rev.) 10/06/64 10/22/64
Miller, Margaret died 11/12/61 11/13/61
Miller, Margaret married 11/12/61 11/14/61
Miller, Margaret died 11/30/62 12/30/62
Miller, Maria C. married Hearn, Samuel C. 12/13/64 12/16/64
Miller, Mary Amma died 11/15/61 11/19/61
Miller, Mary E. married Smith, John H. 04/16/63 04/20/63
Miller, Mary Emeline died 05/31/61 06/01/61
Miller, Mary F. married Cooper, George C. 05/11/63 05/13/63
Miller, Mary L. died 05/07/64 05/10/64
Miller, Olevia S. died 05/10/63 05/11/63
Miller, Rebecca died 05/05/65 05/08/65
Miller, Ridie married Hearn, Samuel C. 12/13/64 12/15/64
Miller, Sarah Ellen died 07/06/64 07/07/64
Miller, Sarah Jane died 07/25/61 07/27/61
Miller, Sophia married Tindall, William 07/27/63 08/10/63
Miller, Sue L. married Hough, William T. 04/13/64 04/14/64
Miller, T. A. married McDowell, Tillie 10/10/61 10/14/61
Miller, Thomas C. died 05/11/61 05/13/61
Miller, Thomas Daniel died 06/19/65 06/20/65
Miller, Thomas H. married Barbour, Emma 06/04/63 06/27/63
Miller, Thomas Jefferson died 08/13/61 08/14/61
Miller, Virginia married Carrick, William J. 11/01/64 11/02/64
Miller, Walter T. H. married Taylor, Helen M. 12/10/63 12/12/63
Miller, Wiliam C. died 04/16/61 04/17/61
Miller, William died 03/21/64 03/23/64
Miller, William E. married Fawcus, Mary Ann 07/17/65 09/26/65

Miller, William Edward died 11/11/62   11/14/62
Miller, William Watkins died 01/18/63   01/20/63
Milles, Rebecca died 05/05/65   05/06/65
Milligan, Mary Howell died 01/17/61   01/21/61
Milligan, Susan H. married Carroll, C. T. 12/08/63   12/09/63
Milliken, Willie Nichols died 10/31/62   11/01/62
Mills, Amelia married Dell, Thomas E. 03/31/63   04/08/63
Mills, Benjamin F. married Webb, Emma 11/24/64   11/26/64
Mills, Edward died 12/16/63   01/30/64
Mills, Elizabeth (Mrs.) died 09/03/64   09/05/64
Mills, Franklin L. married Kraft, Susannah E. K. 12/12/65   12/14/65
Mills, George died 05/16/65   05/17/65
Mills, James F. married Rous, Mollie E. 10/05/65   10/16/65
Mills, Kate C. died 11/14/65   11/15/65
Mills, Leah Ellen died 10/15/63   10/17/63
Mills, Margret married Forrester, John J. 10/01/63   10/03/63
Mills, Mary Jane (Mrs.) died 01/22/63   01/24/63
Mills, Richard B. married Hall, Margaret H. 12/30/61   01/10/62
Mills, Rufus married Hut, Rebecca 02/04/64   02/06/64
Mills, S. S., Jr. married Webb, Ella 01/12/65   06/27/65
Mills, Sally Holtze died 08/05/63   08/08/63
Mills, Sarah Rebecca died 04/21/63   04/22/63
Mills, Susie died 11/27/61   12/02/61
Mills, Theodore J. died 07/18/64   07/20/64
Mills, Thomas married Moore, Sarah 05/17/64   05/21/64
Mills, Thomas A. (1st Lt.) died 08/24/64   08/27/64
Mills, Thomas P. died 04/29/63   05/09/63
Mills, William E. died 08/08/63   08/21/63
Milnor, Josephine A. married Walmsley, Morris 04/09/63   04/11/63
Milroy, Alexander married Cragg, Annie 10/22/61   11/04/61
Milstead, Annie married Bennett, John A. 01/26/64   02/01/64
Minch, Lewis married Murray, Cecilia 12/25/60   01/16/61
Mincher, Elizabeth died 08/12/65   08/16/65
Mincher, John died 10/14/62   10/16/62
Mincher, Lillian R. died 10/01/63   10/03/63
Minehan, Daniel married Roach, Joanna 04/16/65   04/18/65
Miner, Catharine (Mrs.) died 06/02/63   06/04/63
Minevaden, Josephine died 03/10/63   03/11/63
Minifie, Annie Maude died 12/06/61   12/09/61
Minifie, J. Woodfin married Southgate, Maggie A. 05/15/65   05/16/65
Minifie, Jane S. married Sheckells, Charles R. 01/10/61   01/21/61
Minker, Sarah died 08/25/65   09/05/65
Minkle, Edward died 09/25/65   10/05/65
Minner, Frances Augusta died 03/04/62   03/06/62
Minner, William Edwin died 02/01/62   02/05/62
Minnick, Conrad married Reynolds, Loumonia L. 12/27/61   01/16/62
Minnick, David Maxwell died 12/28/63   12/31/63
Minnick, F. M. married Malyn, (Miss) 09/24/61   09/26/61
Minnick, Francis Saville died 04/26/64   04/27/64
Minnick, George W. died 06/04/62   06/06/62
Minnick, J. M. E. married Hardesty, Marietta 08/05/61   08/10/61
Minnick, Jesse died 01/12/61   01/18/61
Minnick, John Joseph died no date   08/13/63
Minnick, Mary Ann died 12/25/65   12/27/65
Minnick, Robert Edmund Lee died 02/01/65   02/08/65

Minnick, Robert Edmund Lee died 02/01/65 02/09/65
Minnis, Annie died 03/06/65 03/08/65
Minor, Alfronsso died 12/28/62 01/01/63
Minter, Stephen S. died 05/06/65 05/10/65
Minzel, Margaret married Marriso, Charles 12/29/62 10/29/63
Miskell, Ann (Mrs.) married Fowler, William W. 03/15/63 03/18/63
Miskelly, Eliza (Mrs.) died 05/24/63 05/26/63
Miskelly, Elizabeth Gorley married Yent, Charles Augustus 09/14/65 10/31/65
Miskelly, Joseph married Barton, Caroline 12/31/63 02/17/64
Miskimon, Mary E. married Arthur, John T. 02/11/64 02/15/64
Miskimon, Phillip married Casby, Mary 01/11/64 01/16/64
Miskmon, Clara Frances died 11/03/62 11/05/62
Mister, Abraham died 08/31/65 09/01/65
Mister, Abraham died 08/31/65 09/02/65
Mister, Cornelia married McNamara, Jerome D. 10/12/65 10/14/65
Mister, George W. died 06/12/65 06/13/65
Mister, Thomas R. married Foster, Janette 01/04/63 01/07/63
Mitchel, John Francis married Staylor, Maria Theresa 01/19/63 02/03/63
Mitchel, Sarah Jane married Goldsmith, John B. 06/16/63 08/01/63
Mitchell, Alexander died 10/19/65 10/21/65
Mitchell, Alice died 03/20/62 03/21/62
Mitchell, Alice Florence died 08/21/64 09/03/64
Mitchell, Ann Maria died 09/08/62 09/09/62
Mitchell, Ann Maria died 04/18/65 04/19/65
Mitchell, Anna M. married Waerham, John N. 11/10/61 11/19/61
Mitchell, Bridget died 03/01/61 03/02/61
Mitchell, Carrie A. married Smith, William H. 10/27/63 11/02/63
Mitchell, Charles E. married Benezet, Annie M. 11/02/64 11/04/64
Mitchell, Charles E. married Benezet, Annie M. 11/01/64 11/03/64
Mitchell, Cornelia J. married Bell, Josiah V. 11/30/65 12/04/65
Mitchell, Edward died 11/08/63 11/10/63
Mitchell, Edward C. died 03/01/64 03/02/64
Mitchell, Elisha married Waerham, John 11/10/61 11/23/61
Mitchell, Eliza E. married Raymond, Sidney D. 05/05/62 05/07/62
Mitchell, Elizabeth L. married Posliff, Edward 10/17/63 10/21/63
Mitchell, Emma Susannah died 06/11/63 06/12/63
Mitchell, Emma Virginia died 06/23/65 06/24/65
Mitchell, Emory G. married Randall, Mary Susana 11/04/63 11/07/63
Mitchell, F. J. married Stansbury, Arabella 12/06/63 01/11/64
Mitchell, Florence V. died 12/15/64 12/16/64
Mitchell, Francis married Taylor, Esther 02/26/61 02/28/61
Mitchell, Frederick John died 10/30/65 11/01/65
Mitchell, George married Crook, Matilda 03/28/61 03/30/61
Mitchell, George died 07/21/64 09/16/64
Mitchell, George Franklin died 06/09/63 06/10/63
Mitchell, George H. died 06/26/62 07/02/62
Mitchell, George W. married Stewart, Annie 11/13/64 11/15/64
Mitchell, George W. (Cpt.) married Bowlings, Susia 12/16/63 12/19/63
Mitchell, George Washington died 12/16/63 12/18/63
Mitchell, Georgeanna married Comegys, John P. 12/30/62 01/03/63
Mitchell, H. Mozart married McComas, Lizzie 11/28/61 11/30/61
Mitchell, Harrie McComas died 07/14/63 07/15/63
Mitchell, Henrietta L. married Gibbons, Robert A. 04/05/64 04/13/64
Mitchell, James B. married Sullivan, Emma J. 08/22/65 08/24/65

```
Mitchell, James H. died 03/13/64   08/13/64
Mitchell, James T. married Simonson, Sue 11/08/65   11/11/65
Mitchell, Jarrett, T. married Joyce, Mollie E. 04/03/64   04/23/64
Mitchell, Jeremiah Osborn married Murphy, Mary Ann 04/25/61   04/27/61
Mitchell, John H. W. married Shipley, Elizabeth 06/29/62   07/02/62
Mitchell, John R. married Morse, Lizzie 10/04/64   10/10/64
Mitchell, John Thomas married Slicer, Lowllen 02/27/61   02/28/61
Mitchell, John W. married Morgan, Louisa B. 01/10/61   01/12/61
Mitchell, John W. married McCann, Sarah F. 07/17/61   08/26/61
Mitchell, John W. married Broom, Fannie 08/06/63   09/17/63
Mitchell, John W. (Cpt.) married Askey, Lizzie E. 05/11/63   05/14/63
Mitchell, Josephine married Johnson, Stephen 12/25/63   01/02/64
Mitchell, Kate married Wright, Charles Albert 04/19/63   04/23/63
Mitchell, Laura Belle died 08/05/65   08/07/65
Mitchell, Laura Elizabeth died no date   07/15/64
Mitchell, Laura P. married Payne, George C. 06/17/63   06/19/63
Mitchell, Louisa B. died 04/24/65   04/25/65
Mitchell, Lucy Compton died 06/12/65   06/13/65
Mitchell, M. E. married Walker, R. H. 07/05/60   02/05/61
Mitchell, Maggie E. married Wooten, John H. 05/04/65   05/05/65
Mitchell, Marcellus Aaron died 09/18/65   09/19/65
Mitchell, Margaret J. married Fisher, John H. 09/07/64   09/10/64
Mitchell, Margaret Jeanette married Feinour, Edward 10/14/62   10/16/62
Mitchell, Marion Woodward died 06/26/61   06/28/61
Mitchell, Mary A. died 06/30/61   07/02/61
Mitchell, Mary Ann married Kalbus, Louis 04/12/62   04/14/62
Mitchell, Mary Ann died 09/06/63   09/07/63
Mitchell, Mary Caroline died 01/27/62   01/31/62
Mitchell, Mary E. married Diggs, J. Wesley S. 11/29/65   12/01/65
Mitchell, Mary E. married Diggs, J. Wesley S. 11/29/65   12/02/65
Mitchell, Mary Susanna died 01/20/64   01/23/64
Mitchell, Rebecca married Johnson, Marion 10/26/65   10/31/65
Mitchell, Robert D. S. died 05/14/65   05/20/65
Mitchell, Rose Anna married Dixon, Patrick 02/07/61   02/13/61
Mitchell, Sadie C. married Abbott, David M. 08/03/65   08/09/65
Mitchell, Sarah E. married Keen, William 05/24/64   06/03/64
Mitchell, Sedalia Ellisworth died 05/01/65   05/08/65
Mitchell, Thomas (Cpt.) married Wolfe, Isabelle 01/13/63   01/15/63
Mitchell, Thomas J. married Cookseu, Helen M. 12/10/61   12/11/61
Mitchell, Uriah died 03/13/64   03/15/64
Mitchell, Walter Farnandis died 12/18/62   12/19/62
Mitchell, William (Capt.) married Hay, Lizzie J. 01/15/62   01/18/62
Mitchell, William (Capt.) married Hay, Lizzie J. 01/15/62   01/20/62
Mitchell, William Hervey died 06/18/65   06/20/65
Mitchell, William T. married Turner, Mary A. 03/28/65   04/04/65
Mitchem, Lydia A. married Witherill, Joseph R. 06/13/61   06/14/61
Mittnacht, Benjamin married McElroy, Mary Jane 08/17/65   08/25/65
Mittnacht, Jean married Atkinson, William C. 03/04/62   03/06/62
Moale, Ann G. (Mrs.) died 03/13/65   03/14/65
Moale, Edward (USA) married Wilson, Jeannie 08/24/63   08/25/63
Moale, Fred L. married Fitzgerald, Maria K. 07/09/61   07/10/61
Moale, George N. married Wright, Millie C. 04/14/62   04/16/62
Moale, Henry married Elder, Margaretta M. 10/28/62   11/01/62
Moale, Susan P. married Belt, S. Sprigg 06/05/62   06/07/62
Moan, Terrance died 11/13/63   11/14/63
```

Mobberly, Louisa married Yong, McLintock 06/19/62   06/28/62
Mobley, Lydia married Allard, William H. 05/27/63   05/29/63
Mockhoff, Catherine married Esenhart, John August 03/09/63   03/16/63
Moelich, Bertha F. married Keferstein, Emile J. 03/26/63   03/31/63
Moffet, Ann died 02/19/61   02/22/61
Moffet, George W. married Wren, Mary Jane 05/01/64   05/16/64
Moffett, David B. died 09/08/65   09/11/65
Moffett, Sallie J. H. died 05/06/65   05/08/65
Moffit, Ann married McLane, Samuel 05/28/61   06/03/61
Moffit, Samuel S. died 09/16/62   09/18/62
Moffitt, Elizabeth married Dehn, August 06/04/63   06/06/63
Moffitt, Ellenor married Roberts, Charles H. 09/25/64   10/03/64
Moffitt, Samuel S. married Dew, Ellen S. 03/31/62   04/07/62
Mohe, Mahlon K. died 02/19/62   02/21/62
Mohler, Rosie A. married Norman, Prince 04/28/63   04/29/63
Mohun, Richard B. married Dorsey, Anna Clare 05/05/63   05/07/63
Moir, James died 02/12/65   02/13/65
Moke, Emma died 12/25/65   12/27/65
Moke, John died 08/28/64   09/21/64
Molans, Patrick died 08/10/64   08/11/64
Mollinger, Jacob died 08/15/62   08/18/62
Mollman, Elizabeth married Pfifer, William 12/22/63   12/24/63
Mollowry, Ann married Berry, John 10/11/63   11/09/63
Molowney, William died 04/18/61   04/20/61
Molsed, Eliza died 09/11/62   09/13/62
Molty, Jacob C. died 09/27/63   10/03/63
Moltz, Catherine died 12/24/65   12/30/65
Monaghan, Daniel died 04/05/63   04/08/63
Monaghan, James died 05/03/64   05/04/64
Monaghan, Mary (Mrs.) died 02/04/63   02/05/63
Monaghan, Mary (Mrs.) died 02/04/63   02/06/63
Monahan, J. Fry died 05/10/65   05/12/65
Monbar, Anatob H. Mion married Thomas, Mattie R. 02/20/65   10/17/65
Mondowny, Mary Ellen married Brown, George W. 11/17/63   11/19/63
Monk, Rebecca died 02/04/64   02/05/64
Monk, Samuel died 02/29/64   03/02/64
Monroe, (Mrs. C. E.) died 02/27/62   03/01/62
Monroe, Aloysius died 10/11/65   10/12/65
Monroe, Catherine E. died 02/27/62   03/12/62
Monroe, H. Daniel died 10/09/64   10/12/64
Monroe, Hattie L. married Martin, Henry 03/26/62   04/01/62
Monroe, Laura C. married Ward, Philip G. W. 11/08/64   11/09/64
Monroe, Mary Amelia died 08/17/64   08/19/64
Monroe, Thomas H. W. (Rev.) died 07/28/64   07/30/64
Monsarrat, Ellen died 05/22/62   05/23/62
Monsarrat, Ellen died 05/22/62   05/24/62
Montague, Charley Edward died 08/03/61   08/15/61
Montague, Emma Virginia married Taylor, William no date   12/20/61
Montell, Eliza F. married Rogers, Nathan 12/19/61   02/06/62
Montell, Laura M. married Taylor, James M. 06/02/64   07/13/64
Montgomery, Annie T. married Bosley, John C. 05/01/62   05/08/62
Montgomery, Caroline A. died 11/27/65   11/28/65
Montgomery, Eliza Jane married Richmond, Samuel 11/13/65   11/28/65
Montgomery, Eliza Jane married Richmond, Samuel 11/13/65   11/29/65
Montgomery, George died 12/19/64   12/20/64

Montgomery, James married Von Santen, Johanna 06/24/65   06/30/65
Montgomery, John H. died 04/09/65   04/10/65
Montgomery, Martha married Simonds, L. Warren 09/01/64   09/07/64
Montgomery, Philis died 07/13/62   07/17/62
Montgomery, Rose P. (Mrs.) died 09/17/63   09/18/63
Montgomery, Rosetta died 02/26/64   02/27/64
Montgomery, Sarah A. married Cooper, George F. 10/26/65   10/27/65
Montressor, Maria Estella died 12/15/60   01/07/61
Moodine, Henry J. died 09/15/64   09/23/64
Moody, Caroline married McCadden, James A. (Lt.) 04/28/64   04/29/64
Moody, John B. died 08/24/61   08/26/61
Moody, Joseph T. died no date   12/20/62
Moody, Mary Ann (Mrs.) died 03/25/65   03/27/65
Mooers, Sarah E. married Morris, Charles 07/14/63   10/29/63
Moon, Hester died 01/30/64   02/01/64
Moon, Margaret died 01/25/63   01/27/63
Moon, Mary Ann died 04/15/64   04/16/64
Moon, Mary Caroline died 01/15/63   01/16/63
Moon, Mary Caroline died 01/15/63   01/17/63
Moon, Richard N. married Thomas, Laura S. 01/03/65   01/07/65
Moon, Sarah E. died 11/27/65   11/29/65
Moon, Virginia C. died 10/31/62   11/01/62
Mooner, William died 09/18/64   09/19/64
Mooney, Alice married Tomlinson, Perry 09/23/63   09/29/63
Mooney, Elizabeth Joanna died 07/08/64   07/13/64
Mooney, Hannah (Mrs.) died 05/06/63   05/07/63
Mooney, Hannah (Mrs.) died 05/06/63   05/08/63
Mooney, James died 08/08/62   08/11/62
Mooney, James Patrick died 07/14/64   07/15/64
Mooney, Laurence married Quinn, Julia 05/08/64   05/14/64
Mooney, Mary died 07/17/63   07/20/63
Mooney, Mary (Mrs.) died 01/26/65   01/27/65
Mooney, Mary Ann died 12/12/61   12/14/61
Mooney, Richard married Boland, Mary 09/03/63   09/07/63
Mooney, Richard died 02/06/65   02/07/65
Mooney, Richard died 02/06/65   02/08/65
Moonyer, William M. married Lecount, Rachel A. 08/31/62   09/04/62
Moor, Daniel married Leescey, Julia 06/11/63   06/15/63
Moor, Gustavus married Hasson, Isabella 02/28/65   03/03/65
Moor, Robert died 08/14/65   08/16/65
Moor, William T. died 03/01/62   03/05/62
Moore, Alice died 06/01/65   06/03/65
Moore, Ann L. (Mrs.) died 03/22/63   03/27/63
Moore, Anna Hedges died 12/23/63   12/24/63
Moore, Annie died 02/03/61   02/08/61
Moore, Catherine (Mrs.) died 02/24/65   02/25/65
Moore, Catherine S. died 09/08/65   09/09/65
Moore, Cecelia E. died 11/25/62   11/26/62
Moore, Crawford married Williams, Rebecca F. 12/25/60   02/08/61
Moore, Crawford married Williams, Rebecca F. 12/25/60   02/09/61
Moore, David married Briscoe, Mary 10/23/62   10/25/62
Moore, David married Briscoe, Mary 10/23/62   10/27/62
Moore, Elizabeth married Boyce, James 09/27/61   10/01/61
Moore, Ellen Elizabeth (Mrs.) died 01/15/65   01/17/65
Moore, Fanny died 04/29/63   05/04/63

Moore, Frances married Smallwood, Nicholson 04/14/63   04/17/63
Moore, Francis J. died 11/19/62   11/24/62
Moore, George married Rieman, Harriett 03/13/61   03/15/61
Moore, George died 08/23/63   08/27/63
Moore, George Roberts died 11/14/62   11/21/62
Moore, George W. died 09/22/62   09/24/62
Moore, H. P. (Cpt.) married Daley, Amanda J. 09/29/64   10/05/64
Moore, Hannah (Mrs.) married Weaver, William H. H. 12/06/64   12/08/64
Moore, Helena S. married Dillehunt, George R. 02/15/65   02/17/65
Moore, Henrietta married Cundiff, A. T. (Cpt.) 05/13/63   05/23/63
Moore, Henry D. married Jones, Alice 08/30/64   08/31/64
Moore, J. G. married Sadler, C. A. 02/07/65   02/22/65
Moore, J. T. (Capt.) died no date   11/16/65
Moore, James married Myers, Louisa 06/22/61   08/07/61
Moore, James (Rev.) married Ninde, Theresa C. 10/18/64   10/22/64
Moore, Jesse B. married Morrison, Lizzie 12/29/63   01/21/64
Moore, John A. married Shorb, Ella 05/15/65   05/31/65
Moore, John F. died 08/16/63   08/17/63
Moore, John R. died 04/03/64   04/04/64
Moore, John T. married Hopkins, Mary M. 12/02/62   12/03/62
Moore, John W. married Cromwell, Mary C. 12/23/63   01/14/64
Moore, Joseph B. died 08/11/63   08/12/63
Moore, Josephine died 08/09/62   08/12/62
Moore, Kate E. died 09/28/62   09/29/62
Moore, Laura M. died 12/14/64   12/16/64
Moore, Leonard married Smith, Martha E. 09/01/64   09/03/64
Moore, Lizzie died 08/05/61   08/06/61
Moore, Lorinda H. (Mrs.) died 04/23/63   04/24/63
Moore, Lorinda H. (Mrs.) died 04/23/63   04/25/63
Moore, Louisa E. died 11/30/62   12/02/62
Moore, Lydia Cook died 08/30/61   09/02/61
Moore, Maggie A. married Leslie, H. Clay (U.S.N.) 08/08/65   08/11/65
Moore, Margaret died 02/11/61   02/12/61
Moore, Margaret died 12/18/61   12/20/61
Moore, Margaret (Mrs.) died 06/12/64   06/14/64
Moore, Margaret Ann died 03/30/61   04/01/61
Moore, Margaret Eugenia died 10/18/61   10/19/61
Moore, Martha Jane died 11/08/63   11/16/63
Moore, Martha Virginia Elder died 08/23/62   08/25/62
Moore, Mary married Wilderman, William C. 10/01/63   10/31/63
Moore, Mary (Mrs.) died 08/09/63   08/10/63
Moore, Mary C. married Clautice, Francis 11/24/63   11/28/63
Moore, Mary Jane married Hunt, Charles (Cpt.) 10/12/64   10/15/64
Moore, Matthew married Barnes, Josephine 01/19/62   01/21/62
Moore, Missouri married Loker, John W. 11/28/62   12/01/62
Moore, Molly B. died 03/21/63   03/23/63
Moore, P. M. (Sgt.) died 07/10/63   11/20/63
Moore, Pamela died 10/10/64   10/12/64
Moore, Permelia married Parkhurst, Pardon C. 07/02/64   07/08/64
Moore, Priscilla (Mrs.) died 02/13/63   02/14/63
Moore, Rosetta married Waters, John 06/11/63   06/13/63
Moore, Rosetta (Mrs.) married Grasson, Samuel 08/30/64   09/01/64
Moore, Samuel married Gray, Lucinda 03/06/61   03/07/61
Moore, Samuel died 09/02/63   09/19/63
Moore, Sarah married Mills, Thomas 05/17/64   05/21/64

Moore, Sarah E. died 04/21/64 04/22/64
Moore, Sarah E. died 04/21/64 04/23/64
Moore, Thomas married Hawkins, Gertrude Virginia 07/21/64 07/26/64
Moore, Thomas P. died 12/09/62 12/10/62
Moore, Thomas Shipley died 11/04/63 11/05/63
Moore, Virginia C. married Craig, Seldon (Cpt.) 04/19/64 04/28/64
Moore, William died 02/24/65 02/25/65
Moore, William A. died 01/12/64 01/19/64
Moore, William R. died 09/09/64 09/13/64
Moore, William T. married Tarr, Charlotte E. 08/21/65 08/23/65
Moore, William W. married Forsyth, Maggie 03/29/63 04/10/63
Moore, William Welling died 11/18/62 11/21/62
Moorehead, Howard died 03/25/63 03/27/63
Moorehead, Samuel died 06/19/65 06/20/65
Moorehead, Samuel died 06/19/65 06/21/65
Moores, Marie Louisa died 01/26/63 01/27/63
Moores, Rachel Elizabeth died 02/19/64 02/23/64
Moors, Charles H. died 08/31/61 09/03/61
Moorsbury, Mary Jane married Grays, Alexander 01/10/61 01/12/61
Mopps, James S. died 10/31/64 12/16/64
Mopps, James Sommerfield died 10/31/64 11/02/64
Mopps, Martha A. married Spicer, Franklin A. 07/14/64 07/18/64
Moran, Bridget died 09/22/62 09/23/62
Moran, Bridget died 09/22/62 09/24/62
Moran, Charles married Killard, Alicia 06/18/65 06/20/65
Moran, George W. married Cadwell, Mary E. 10/17/65 10/21/65
Moran, John Edward died 02/25/62 02/27/62
Moran, John P. died 08/27/64 08/29/64
Moran, Mary died no date 07/07/62
Moran, Mary married Russell, Patrick 09/20/64 09/21/64
Moran, Mary Bell died 02/25/62 02/26/62
Moran, Richard T. married McNeir, Alice Amelia 08/18/63 08/25/63
Moran, Sarah V. married Dorsey, Thomas E. 06/18/63 06/20/63
Mordrow, Isabella died 06/28/64 01/19/65
More, Harrison married Martin, Rebecca Jane 03/21/64 05/17/64
More, Rebecca Jane married Traviss, Peter Henry 11/19/61 11/27/61
More, Susan married Pinket, Joseph 12/24/64 12/26/64
Moree, Eliza Ann died 01/21/61 01/23/61
Moree, Mary Amanda died 01/27/61 01/28/61
Moree, William Anderson died 01/22/61 01/23/61
Moreland, David died 03/23/62 03/24/62
Moreland, George W. died 07/18/65 07/19/65
Moreland, George W. died 07/18/65 07/28/65
Morell, Hannah died 12/31/63 01/02/64
Moreton, Sarah C. died 08/15/61 08/16/61
Morey, George F. married Chenowith, Mary E. 04/16/65 05/06/65
Morfit, Henry Mason died 12/01/65 12/07/65
Morford, Ann E. married Tracey, William 11/21/61 11/23/61
Morgan, (Mrs.) died 09/01/63 09/02/63
Morgan, (Mrs.) died 09/01/63 09/03/63
Morgan, Alice married Deegan, William P. 01/24/61 01/28/61
Morgan, Alverda F. died 04/03/63 04/04/63
Morgan, Anna W. died no date 08/20/62
Morgan, Annie (Mrs.) died 01/20/65 01/23/65
Morgan, Catherine Ann (Mrs.) died 02/18/63 02/19/63

Morgan, Catherine Ann (Mrs.) died 02/18/63 02/20/63
Morgan, Charles C. married Jones, S. Virginia 06/08/63 06/10/63
Morgan, Charlton H. married Howard, Ellen Key 12/07/65 12/11/65
Morgan, Charlton H. married Howard, Ellen Key 12/07/65 12/12/65
Morgan, DeWitt C. married Hurst, Sarah B. 05/11/65 05/13/65
Morgan, Edward died 01/28/62 01/30/62
Morgan, Edward married Chipley, Emily O. 09/20/64 10/01/64
Morgan, Egbert W. C. died 11/20/61 11/21/61
Morgan, Eleanor (Mrs.) died 01/03/64 01/22/64
Morgan, Eliza B. married Bergers, William 04/06/64 04/07/64
Morgan, Eliza J. married Franklin, Charles C. 06/11/61 06/15/61
Morgan, Elizabeth died 04/12/64 04/14/64
Morgan, Geoffrey S. R. died 02/10/64 02/13/64
Morgan, George married Elbert, Margaret 10/23/62 10/25/62
Morgan, George H. married Denmeade, Mary J. 02/16/65 02/22/65
Morgan, J. Asbury (Professor) married Sellers, Susan J. 08/01/65 08/16/65
Morgan, J. F. (M.D.) married Gough, M. E. 04/22/62 04/23/62
Morgan, James died 03/08/64 03/11/64
Morgan, James A. died 03/11/61 03/13/61
Morgan, Jennie married Wilkinson, Walter S. 08/13/61 08/16/61
Morgan, John Louis died 05/06/63 05/07/63
Morgan, John T. married Fife, Helen E. 11/01/61 04/19/62
Morgan, Louisa B. married Mitchell, John W. 01/10/61 01/12/61
Morgan, Mary E. died 08/19/62 08/20/62
Morgan, Mary F. V. married Saunders, Thomas B. 09/12/63 10/15/63
Morgan, Mary Jane married Thorpe, Thomas G. 08/07/64 08/09/64
Morgan, Mary Regina died 03/10/64 03/11/64
Morgan, Nelly married Crain, Robert (Dr.) 06/01/64 06/04/64
Morgan, Sarah E. married Hickman, George W. 08/03/65 08/05/65
Morgan, Sarah Ellen died 04/26/65 04/27/65
Morgan, Sophia L. married Shehan, George E. 03/05/63 03/25/63
Morgan, Susannah (Mrs.) died 04/30/63 05/02/63
Morgan, Thomas died no date 11/07/63
Morgan, Thomas Jr. died 09/11/63 09/12/63
Morgan, Walter T. married Benson, Agnes A. 01/26/64 01/28/64
Morgan, William married Smith, Catharine 08/16/62 08/29/62
Morgan, William F. married Hussey, Sophia W. 11/09/62 11/26/62
Morgan, William H. died 10/13/64 10/19/64
Morgan, William Henry died 02/04/61 02/06/61
Morhiser, Sarah Ann died 05/26/61 04/29/61
Morine, Amanda Virginia married Cruse, Andrew J. 02/07/61 04/11/61
Morison, Frank married Fiske, Lucy A. 10/10/65 10/16/65
Morison, James W. married Toscum, Sarah Jane 05/24/64 05/28/64
Morling, Pattie C. married Singleton, H. L. (Rev.) 10/20/63 10/24/63
Morningstar, Nancy Jane (Mrs.) died 04/26/63 05/02/63
Morran, Michael died 09/13/64 09/14/64
Morrell, Seaman V. married Lowry, Mary J. 12/17/65 12/19/65
Morrill, Mary A. died 09/09/64 09/20/64
Morrill, William Edward died no date 08/03/65
Morrin, William C. died 12/09/65 12/11/65
Morris, Adeline R. married Wallace, William T. 08/03/63 08/05/63
Morris, Annette died 02/16/65 02/17/65
Morris, Arabelle married Clark, Leonard 10/14/63 10/23/63
Morris, Barney died 05/11/64 05/13/64

Morris, Catherine died 05/26/62 05/27/62
Morris, Charles married Mooers, Sarah E. 07/14/63 10/29/63
Morris, Charlotte married Spence, William W. 11/10/64 11/12/64
Morris, Elizabeth died 10/01/62 10/02/62
Morris, Emily died 02/13/61 02/14/61
Morris, Emma L. married Wilhelm, Charles S. 06/07/61 11/30/61
Morris, George married Richard, Mary 05/24/63 07/28/63
Morris, George W. married Sprague, Margaret Treese 05/05/62 05/06/62
Morris, Jacob died 12/01/65 12/02/65
Morris, James married Norman, Sophia 03/28/61 04/02/61
Morris, James died 06/08/65 06/09/65
Morris, James H. married Neal, Letitia 07/03/62 07/16/62
Morris, John H. married Wheeder, Minnie E. 12/26/61 02/17/62
Morris, John T. married Rouselot, Susan 08/29/64 09/05/64
Morris, John Wesley died 06/02/64 06/04/64
Morris, Joseph died 06/25/64 06/27/64
Morris, Josephine S. married Barron, P. D. 06/02/63 06/17/63
Morris, Kate J. died 06/13/61 06/21/61
Morris, Maggie died 08/18/63 08/20/63
Morris, Mary (Mrs.) died 02/20/63 02/21/63
Morris, Mary (Mrs.) died 11/22/63 11/23/63
Morris, Mary Ann died 08/11/61 08/13/61
Morris, Robert died 03/29/64 03/30/64
Morris, Rosetta died 12/04/61 12/06/61
Morris, Samuel C. died 04/07/62 04/08/62
Morris, Sophia died 02/13/65 02/15/65
Morris, Stephen died 12/31/60 01/02/61
Morris, Theresa died 07/03/64 07/04/64
Morris, Thomas C. died 03/28/62 03/29/62
Morrison, Anna Elizabeth died 12/12/62 12/24/62
Morrison, Bettie J. died 10/29/64 11/05/64
Morrison, Caroline M. died 09/18/62 09/20/62
Morrison, Edward died 08/23/62 08/25/62
Morrison, Ella B. died 05/24/61 05/25/61
Morrison, Emilie H. married Trail, R. H. 12/23/65 12/23/65
Morrison, Ezekial died 03/26/62 03/27/62
Morrison, F. D. married Patrick, M. A. 07/31/65 08/11/65
Morrison, James A. married Norfolk, Julia A. 03/24/63 07/20/63
Morrison, Juliana (Mrs.) died 07/05/64 07/06/64
Morrison, Lizzie married Moore, Jesse B. 12/29/63 01/21/64
Morrison, Maggie E. married Hanna, Robert M. (Cpt.) 01/03/63 01/06/63
Morrison, Margaret E. married Hanna, Robert M. (Cpt.) 01/03/63 01/05/
Morrison, Mary (Mrs.) died 03/24/64 03/25/64
Morrison, Nellie married McNeir, William J. 03/23/64 04/12/64
Morrison, Parker married Eckles, Elizabeth (Mrs.) 10/23/64 10/26/64
Morrison, Rhodie M. married Robinson, James H. 12/07/63 02/27/64
Morrison, Sarah died 01/22/61 01/29/61
Morrison, Wilbur H. (Dr., CSA) died 07/03/63 07/20/63
Morrison, William died 01/22/63 01/23/63
Morrison, William died 01/31/65 02/02/65
Morrison, William died 11/01/65 11/08/65
Morrison, William Ebenezer married Tippett, Margaret (Mrs.) 12/25/64 12/28/64
Morrisroe, Andrew married Finegan, Hanora 01/20/62 09/04/62
Morriss, Estelle died 02/08/61 02/09/61

Morroe, William died 07/30/63 07/31/63
Morrow, Agnes died 04/12/62 04/14/62
Morrow, Cora May died 05/11/64 05/12/64
Morrow, Deborah E. (Mrs.) died 03/31/63 04/07/63
Morrow, Eliza J. died 10/12/62 10/14/62
Morrow, Ellen C. married Runkle, Brice 01/30/61 02/15/61
Morrow, Harry E. died 12/02/63 12/03/63
Morrow, Isabella (Mrs.) died 01/19/63 01/22/63
Morrow, Jennie A. married Pitcher, Thomas J. 09/24/63 09/30/63
Morrow, Lizzie C. married Perine, Thomson P. 09/21/63 09/23/63
Morrow, Robert died 08/10/63 08/13/63
Morrow, Robert died 11/09/63 11/11/63
Morrow, Silas married Gardner, Martha R. 04/09/62 04/10/62
Morrow, Thomas G. married Bradford, Rosa 09/08/63 09/12/63
Morry, Henry died 03/23/61 03/25/61
Morse, Charlie H. N. died 04/09/62 04/11/62
Morse, Lizzie married Mitchell, John R. 10/04/64 10/10/64
Morse, Louisa died 06/21/61 06/22/61
Morse, Robert Hays died 05/25/63 05/27/63
Morse, Robert Hays died 05/25/63 05/26/63
Morsel, Z. J. married Anderson, Louisa J. 01/20/63 01/23/63
Morsell, Bettie died 05/13/62 06/05/62
Morsell, Lou married Lamdin, J. F. (USN) 09/09/61 09/11/61
Morsell, Rosanna married Franklin, George 07/26/65 08/09/65
Morsell, William married Buckley, Josephine 07/27/65 08/01/65
Mortimer, Henry W. married MacLaskey, Mary 08/07/65 08/12/65
Mortimer, John H. married York, Amelia C. 08/31/63 09/02/63
Mortimer, John, Sr. died 06/14/61 06/15/61
Mortimer, Mary W. married Easter, James H. 06/12/62 06/13/62
Mortimer, May E. married Blaumont, Charles E. 08/27/62 09/04/62
Mortimer, Rebekah died 03/30/62 04/01/62
Mortimer, Thomazine L. married Carroll, P. H. 03/26/65 05/18/65
Morton, Alice married Lawson, S. Allen 11/22/65 11/23/65
Morton, Frederick A. died 04/02/63 04/04/63
Morton, James Owen died 02/07/64 02/09/64
Morton, Jennie married Strahan, Charles 06/25/63 10/14/63
Morton, John died 06/22/64 06/23/64
Morton, Margaret died 03/04/65 03/07/65
Morton, Margaret (Mrs.) died 03/04/65 03/06/65
Morton, Maria Antonette (Mrs.) died 03/03/64 03/09/64
Morton, Michael died 01/08/62 01/09/62
Morton, Robert died 03/20/65 03/22/65
Moser, Max died 05/25/63 05/26/63
Mosher, Ann (Mrs.) died 03/04/63 03/10/63
Mosher, Janie C. died 07/08/64 07/09/64
Mosher, Lizzie W. married Gafford, Samuel L. 10/22/61 10/24/61
Moss, Emma J. married Bennett, George H. M. 05/29/65 05/30/65
Mossinger, Gustavus (Dr.) married Ferciot, Maria Louisa 05/05/64 05/09/64
Most, Mary A. married Stoner, D. W. (USN) 12/05/62 01/27/63
Most, Mary Margaret died 09/05/63 09/07/63
Mott, Henry B. married Proctor, Caroline M. 07/23/63 07/25/63
Mott, Mary (Mrs.) died 02/28/65 03/01/65
Mott, Rachel M. died 12/20/63 12/21/63
Mott, William died 12/08/61 12/09/61

Motter, J. Taylor married Galt, Margaret E. 11/28/65   11/30/65
Mottu, Alfred George died 09/16/63   09/17/63
Mottu, Theodore married George, Maggie 08/20/61   08/21/61
Moudy, William (USN) married Brown, Mary A. 10/16/65   11/28/65
Moughan, Sarah Agnes died 08/30/63   08/31/63
Mouland, John H. married Ijams, Josephine 04/23/61   05/04/61
Moulden, Sarah Jane married Thomas, Joseph 04/24/62   05/03/62
Moult, Thomas H. married Willis, Cordelia A. 01/21/61   01/23/61
Moulton, James F., Jr. married DuHamel, Mary E. 08/06/63   08/12/63
Moulton, M. Annie married Uniack, Edward M. 01/12/63   01/15/63
Moulton, Minnie M. married Uniack, John J. 04/24/61   04/26/61
Moulton, Willie Du Hamel died 11/21/64   11/22/64
Mount, Matthew died 07/11/62   07/12/62
Mountgarety, William Thomas married Walker, Elizabeth H. 09/08/63   09/28/63
Mouton, John D. married Owens, Maggie A. 01/19/64   01/23/64
Move, Charles J. died 01/11/62   01/21/62
Mowbray, G. W. Russell died 06/25/65   06/26/65
Mowbray, Martin L. married Walker, Sarah Catherine 02/16/64   02/19/64
Mowbray, Washington F. died 06/22/62   06/24/62
Mowell, Joseph married Helmlin, Emma 08/21/62   12/08/62
Mowton, Hannah died 09/01/63   09/02/63
Moxley, Kennedy died 11/09/63   11/11/63
Moxley, Moses married Pearce, Mary A. 12/22/64   12/24/64
Moxley, Permelia Frances died 02/18/61   02/21/61
Moxley, Robert Henry died 10/15/63   10/23/63
Moylan, Dennis died 07/19/63   07/20/63
Mozingo, Alford S. died 02/15/65   02/17/65
Muckelroy, John died 03/29/64   03/30/64
Muckelroy, John died 03/29/64   03/31/64
Mudd, Margaret (Mrs.) died 12/22/64   12/23/64
Mudd, Virginia married Banghart, Perry 10/27/65   11/04/65
Muer, Agnes married White, Alexander 03/17/64   03/18/64
Muffitt, Louisa married Harrington, William S. 03/31/61   04/30/61
Muhlhofer, William F. married Peppler, Mary 02/05/61   02/12/61
Muir, Charles died 07/05/63   07/07/63
Muir, Henry married Wilson, Anna 05/15/65   07/22/65
Muir, James (USN) died 10/09/64   10/11/64
Muir, Virginia married Flaherty, Andrew J. 06/01/64   06/17/64
Muirhead, Eliza Ellen died 01/13/64   01/28/64
Muirs, William E. married Kurzmaul, Elizabeth H. 08/18/64   08/22/64
Mulen, Isabelle G. W. married Chason, Joseph L. 06/12/61   06/19/61
Mules, Margaret A. married Sheckells, Otis B. 02/25/63   03/17/63
Mules, Rosa Greaner died 07/25/64   08/30/64
Mules, Rose Greaner died 07/25/64   07/26/64
Mules, Rosina (Mrs.) died 07/14/65   07/15/65
Mules, Wilmima A. married Gennett, John A. 04/20/65   04/21/65
Mulgrew, Ellen (Mrs.) died 01/12/63   01/13/63
Mulhare, John M. married O'Brien, Nora A. 05/30/64   06/04/64
Mulhare, Sarah E. died 07/26/64   07/27/64
Mulheir, Sarah died 11/22/62   11/24/62
Mulkern, Bridget (Mrs.) died 01/10/65   01/11/65
Mullan, Edward B. married Lieutaud, Rosalie A. 01/01/63   01/05/63
Mullan, Elizabeth (Mrs.) died 11/30/64   12/02/64
Mullan, James (Cpt.) died 07/31/64   08/02/64

Mullan, Jane died 06/27/64   06/28/64
Mullan, John married Williamson, Rebecca 04/28/63   05/05/63
Mullan, Louis A. married Seaman, Ada 02/22/63   04/29/63
Mullan, Mary Perdue died 05/02/64   05/03/64
Mullan, Samuel E. married Hammer, Mary A. M. 10/05/63   10/07/63
Mullan, William died 08/02/61   08/07/61
Mullan, William H. married Jordan, Martha 12/13/64   12/19/64
Mullane, Hannah M. (Mrs.) died 05/25/63   05/26/63
Mullane, John M. married Murphy, Hannah M. 12/15/61   12/27/61
Mullane, Mary Catherine died 07/21/63   07/22/63
Mullaney, Mary Ann died 03/05/62   03/07/62
Mullen, Bernard died 08/11/62   08/12/62
Mullen, Catherine Maria (Mrs.) died 02/23/64   02/24/64
Mullen, Elizabeth died 04/13/62   04/15/62
Mullen, Ellen died 07/05/61   07/10/61
Mullen, Ellen married Gallagher, Joseph 05/14/63   05/23/63
Mullen, James died 12/28/61   12/30/61
Mullen, Kate died 08/02/61   08/03/61
Mullen, Mary died 12/06/61   12/07/61
Mullen, Sarah married Howit, George H. 01/06/62   01/14/62
Mullen, Sarah died 04/20/65   04/21/65
Mullen, Sarah died 12/17/65   12/18/65
Mullen, Sarah died 12/17/65   12/19/65
Mullen, Timothy married Brady, Margaret 04/27/62   04/29/62
Mulleneux, John H. married Mullineux, Ann R. 07/04/65   07/07/65
Muller, Angeline married Purnell, C. (Cpt.) 08/31/65   09/02/65
Muller, Eudocia married Armstrong, Robert W. 11/28/65   12/04/65
Muller, Helen died 02/16/65   02/17/65
Muller, Helen died 02/16/65   02/18/65
Muller, James died 07/12/63   07/13/63
Muller, John died 08/12/61   08/15/61
Muller, Kate married Jacobson, Charles 10/02/63   10/10/63
Muller, William died 06/02/61   06/03/61
Mulligan, Mary married Joyce, John 05/13/63   05/19/63
Mulligan, Mary Ann died 09/06/63   09/07/63
Mulligan, Rebecca died 04/12/65   04/13/65
Mulligan, Rose married McIntire, Philip 01/17/64   09/02/64
Mulligan, Sarah died 01/07/61   01/08/61
Mullikin, Ann D. married Hall, B. D. 06/30/63   07/07/63
Mullikin, Beale D. married Hamilton, Tobitha W. 12/12/65   12/16/65
Mullikin, Olivia married King, William H. 10/26/65   10/30/65
Mullikin, Osborn W. died 12/21/60   01/07/61
Mullikin, Samuel Emory died 05/05/64   05/06/64
Mullikin, Talitha (Mrs.) died 01/19/64   02/08/64
Mullin, Elizabeth married Owens, Peter 10/15/61   10/16/61
Mullin, Jane died 05/26/64   05/27/64
Mullineux, Ann R. married Mulleneux, John H. 07/04/65   07/07/65
Mullinfaux, Basil R. married Parren, Margaret Ann 11/27/62   12/01/62
Mullinix, Maggie married Scottie, John W. 05/13/63   05/22/63
Mullon, Mary died 09/23/62   09/24/62
Mullowney, Bridget (Mrs.) died 02/18/63   02/19/63
Multz, Annie M. married Buckingham, Alfred 06/09/64   07/16/64
Mulvilhill, Rose married Sirens, Michael 05/25/61   06/28/61
Mulville, Honora died 12/16/65   12/18/65
Mumma, Ann died 11/09/62   11/10/62

Mumma, David died 09/21/64   09/22/64
Mumma, George died 11/29/63   11/30/63
Mumma, Georgeanna married Cromwell, Louis 12/14/65   12/21/65
Mumma, Margaret married Matthews, Abraham M. 09/22/64   09/23/64
Munder, Lewis F. died no date   12/19/63
Munder, Mary E. (Mrs.) died 12/22/64   12/24/64
Mundorff, Catharine (Mrs.) died 06/22/63   06/25/63
Mundorff, Mary E. married Wood, John M. 10/30/64   11/04/64
Munnikhuysen, Mittie married Bond, Howard B. 01/15/61   01/18/61
Munnis, John married McAllister, Emma 10/17/64   10/20/64
Munroe, Anne (Mrs.) died 07/26/63   07/27/63
Munroe, Harry J. died 11/30/63   12/07/63
Munroe, Nathaniel died 05/08/61   05/09/61
Muray, Mary A. (Mrs.) died 04/24/64   04/26/64
Murdoch, Catherine died 12/16/61   12/25/61
Murdoch, Helen married Simonton, A. G. (Rev.) 03/19/63   03/23/63
Murdoch, Henry Turnbull died 12/06/65   12/07/65
Murdoch, Lousia C. married Jamieson, Andrew 05/24/65   05/27/65
Murdoch, Margaret married Lind, Edmond G. 04/28/63   05/02/63
Murdoch, Mary married Chase, Samuel 01/29/63   01/31/63
Murdoch, Matilda (Mrs.) married Route, James 03/24/63   03/27/63
Murdock, Charles died 10/04/63   10/05/63
Murdock, Charles died 10/04/63   10/06/63
Murdock, Fidelia R. (Mrs.) died 11/30/63   12/01/63
Murguiondo, Charles S. died 10/25/64   10/26/64
Murkelroy, John J. married Griffin, Georgeanna 04/21/63   07/25/63
Murphy, Annie married Campbell, Benjamin F. 04/18/65   04/19/65
Murphy, Annie Roe died 12/03/62   12/10/62
Murphy, Bartholomew died 03/14/65   03/15/65
Murphy, Catherine married Wand, Bernard E. 08/22/63   09/01/63
Murphy, Charles died 12/29/63   12/30/63
Murphy, Dorothy (Mrs.) died 09/05/64   09/08/64
Murphy, Edward died 06/24/64   06/25/64
Murphy, Eliza married Cosgrove, James H. 02/24/62   03/11/62
Murphy, Elizabeth Eichberger died 09/11/64   09/16/64
Murphy, Ellen died 10/20/62   10/21/62
Murphy, Fannie married Castle, P. A. (Lt.) 10/19/64   10/20/64
Murphy, Hannah M. married Mullane, John M. 12/15/61   12/27/61
Murphy, Harriet Amanda died 02/16/61   02/21/61
Murphy, Hettie V. married Young, Thomas J. 06/15/63   06/19/63
Murphy, James died 03/04/62   03/05/62
Murphy, James married Hoofnagel, Lydia Maria 03/19/65   07/06/65
Murphy, Jesse Irvin died 10/17/65   10/21/65
Murphy, John married Trumbo, Maria 07/17/61   07/20/61
Murphy, John died 08/31/65   11/29/65
Murphy, John died 08/31/65   11/30/65
Murphy, John F. married Caldwell, Jane 05/23/65   06/03/65
Murphy, John P. married Caldwell, Jane 05/25/65   05/25/65
Murphy, John T. married Cramblitt, Jennie 07/09/62   08/27/62
Murphy, Joseph W. married Dorman, Adaline 09/27/65   09/29/65
Murphy, Margaret died 08/27/65   08/28/65
Murphy, Margaret married Donnelly, John 02/07/64   02/11/64
Murphy, Mary died 03/12/65   03/14/65
Murphy, Mary (Mrs.) died 03/12/65   03/13/65
Murphy, Mary Ann married Mitchell, Jeremiah Osborn 04/25/61   04/27/61

Murphy, Mary Ann died 12/02/62   12/04/62
Murphy, Mary Ellen died 09/08/62   09/09/62
Murphy, Matthias died 11/12/63   11/13/63
Murphy, Michael died 06/26/61   07/01/61
Murphy, Mollie married Keen, George B. 10/03/61   10/04/61
Murphy, Owen died 10/05/63   10/06/63
Murphy, Patrick died 01/14/61   01/15/61
Murphy, Peter died 04/19/65   04/21/65
Murphy, Sallie E. married Davis, Thomas R. 07/07/63   07/28/63
Murphy, Teresa J. married Swegler, Joseph P. 01/05/64   01/07/64
Murphy, Thomas L. died 03/16/61   03/18/61
Murphy, Thomas M. died 10/02/65   10/03/65
Murphy, Thomas S. (Mrs.) died 04/28/64   04/30/64
Murphy, William married Block, Henrietta 10/07/61   10/12/61
Murphy, William Albert died 04/08/62   04/16/62
Murphy, William Jackson died 02/09/63   02/12/63
Murphy, William S. married Richards, Annie E. 06/12/65   06/16/65
Murphy, William [retract] married Block, Henrietta [retract] no date
    10/15/61
Murphy, Willie died 06/21/61   06/24/61
Murphy, Winnefred married Crangle, Michael 07/24/65   07/26/65
Murr, Henry married Weber, Catherine (Mrs.) 11/26/65   12/02/65
Murray, Albert A. married Holliday, Mary E. 10/17/65   10/19/65
Murray, Alice A. married Hammond, Thomas W. 10/19/65   10/23/65
Murray, Andrew V. died 01/12/63   01/13/63
Murray, Ann (Mrs.) died 12/31/61   01/04/62
Murray, Calvert died 10/23/61   10/25/61
Murray, Catharine B. (Mrs.) died 07/16/64   07/30/64
Murray, Catherine (Mrs.) died 08/12/64   08/13/64
Murray, Catherine Vincent died 09/29/62   09/30/62
Murray, Cecilia married Minch, Lewis 12/25/60   01/16/61
Murray, Charles died 08/11/63   08/13/63
Murray, Edwardina died 01/07/61   01/08/61
Murray, Eleanor died no date   12/10/62
Murray, Eliza (Mrs.) died 10/29/63   12/10/63
Murray, Elizabeth (Mrs.) died 02/21/64   02/24/64
Murray, Elizabeth A. (Mrs.) died 11/06/63   11/17/63
Murray, Elizabeth Flitchen died 12/19/65   12/21/65
Murray, Ellen C. died 05/28/65   05/29/65
Murray, Ellen C. died 05/28/65   05/30/65
Murray, Emma Virginia died 07/10/64   07/11/64
Murray, Florence Gertrude died 10/16/61   10/17/61
Murray, Frederick F. married Fresch, Christina 02/27/65   03/02/65
Murray, George died 07/06/62   07/07/62
Murray, George died 07/06/62   07/08/62
Murray, Indiana married Jacob, Richard Isaac 09/04/62   09/06/62
Murray, J. Thomas (Rev.) married Emory, Mary A. W. 06/14/64   06/21/64
Murray, James died 07/22/61   08/03/61
Murray, James died 01/02/63   01/03/63
Murray, James died 05/29/63   05/30/63
Murray, James married Barnes, Sallie 12/22/64   12/26/64
Murray, James D. married Spencer, Elizabeth M. 05/25/64   06/04/64
Murray, James E. died 06/01/63   06/02/63
Murray, John died 10/03/62   10/04/62
Murray, John D. married MacNeal, Ella A. 04/06/64   04/08/64

Murray, John Roger died 04/30/61   05/07/61
Murray, Judith died 05/22/62   05/23/62
Murray, M. Alice married Broadbent, Stephen 10/25/64   10/26/64
Murray, Maggie died 08/07/61   08/08/61
Murray, Maggie married Dodge, A. W. (Dr.) 09/29/63   10/10/63
Murray, Maggie married Heard, William F. 09/12/65   09/16/65
Murray, Margaret (Mrs.) died 06/02/64   06/03/64
Murray, Margaret Catherine died 09/14/62   09/15/62
Murray, Mary Ann died 05/15/61   05/16/61
Murray, Mary Elizabeth died 04/07/61   04/09/61
Murray, Mary Francis died 08/13/62   08/14/62
Murray, Michael died 10/14/64   12/05/64
Murray, Milton Roger died 08/12/64   08/18/64
Murray, Oliver P. married Cannon, Mary E. 10/27/61   10/29/61
Murray, Orlando T. married Purkey, Georgia A. 04/03/65   04/17/65
Murray, Patrick died 12/16/64   12/17/64
Murray, R. C. (Mrs.) died 05/28/65   05/30/65
Murray, Rebecca married Richards, Solomon 12/03/63   12/10/63
Murray, Sarah married O'Nail, Edward 02/04/64   02/17/64
Murray, Stanley married Wilson, Hester 10/17/61   10/19/61
Murray, Thomas died 11/16/61   11/18/61
Murray, Thomas Exavin died 09/28/65   10/07/65
Murray, Thomas H. D. died 08/15/65   08/21/65
Murray, Thomas S. married Blanche, Ada 11/21/65   11/24/65
Murray, William died 04/10/65   04/12/65
Murray, William E. died 04/01/65   04/03/65
Murray, William Owen died 11/03/63   11/05/63
Murray, William Thomas died 07/19/64   07/21/64
Murry, Albert died 04/17/64   04/19/64
Murry, Belle married Goodacre, Daniel M. 09/25/64   10/03/64
Murry, Hubart married Buckley, Annie 01/08/61   01/11/61
Murry, Thomas married McCoy, Elizabeth 08/29/61   09/25/61
Murtaugh, John married Clarke, Mary 05/03/63   05/07/63
Murtugh, Catherine married Gallagher, Hugh no date   05/29/62
Murty, Mary (Mrs.) died 07/15/64   07/16/64
Musette, George Michael died 10/14/62   10/20/62
Musgrave, Andrew J. died 02/02/65   02/24/65
Musgrave, James Henry died 08/17/63   08/20/63
Musgrave, Mary Ann died 10/08/62   10/09/62
Musgrove, Mary E. died 11/02/62   11/07/62
Musik, Lydia Ida married Youse, Henry W. 05/15/62   05/17/62
Mussetter, Sarah A. married Howser, Frank T. 04/30/62   05/02/62
Mussleman, Howard J. died 03/14/62   03/18/62
Mussman, John S. died 05/20/65   05/22/65
Musten, Mary died 06/24/62   06/30/62
Muth, Edward Sylvester died 01/16/64   01/18/64
Muth, John Henry died 10/02/62   10/04/62
Muth, M. Joseph married Katzenberger, Josephine 01/19/64   01/21/64
Mycroft, Ann Bellemy died 09/16/65   09/21/65
Myder, Roseanna died no date   04/30/62
Myer, Abraham died 07/05/61   07/06/61
Myer, Hannah (Mrs.) married Greensfelder, B. 12/29/63   12/31/63
Myer, Ida Lavenia died 05/05/64   05/07/64
Myer, James, Jr. married Mantz, Laura Virginia 05/10/64   05/25/64
Myer, Maggie married Evans, Thomas B. 10/16/61   10/18/61

Myerly, Clementine married Blizzard, Joel 11/02/65 11/03/65
Myers, Alice married Wagner, B. Lansing 10/13/63 10/21/63
Myers, Andrew C. married Henderson, Emma G. 08/08/65 08/21/65
Myers, Annie married Goodman, William V. (Cpt.) 05/15/62 05/17/62
Myers, Annie Heiniken married Hedian, Thomas no date 04/25/62
Myers, Caroline married Cohen, Edward 12/06/65 12/09/65
Myers, Charles died 06/04/62 06/05/62
Myers, Charles H. died 09/17/64 09/19/64
Myers, Charles H. married Timmons, Cecelia A. 12/28/64 12/29/64
Myers, Daniel died 06/30/65 07/01/65
Myers, Diederich H. died 05/05/62 05/06/62
Myers, Edward William died 04/20/65 04/22/65
Myers, Elizabeth married Waxter, Charles P. 05/19/61 05/21/61
Myers, Ellie M. married Cochran, Harry W. 02/16/64 02/24/64
Myers, Henry L. married Jenkins, Georgiana 08/30/64 09/01/64
Myers, Jacob died 03/27/63 03/30/63
Myers, James A. married Burke, Johanna T. 10/18/65 10/24/65
Myers, Jane R. married Wilson, James 12/14/65 12/15/65
Myers, Jennie married Gittinger, Louis C. 12/10/63 12/17/63
Myers, John married Reinick, Hannah E. 05/25/65 05/31/65
Myers, John married Taylor, Mary R. 12/28/65 12/30/65
Myers, John Henry died 03/17/65 03/20/65
Myers, Joshua married Wheeler, Charlotte A. 05/29/64 05/31/64
Myers, Kate M. died 10/14/63 10/16/63
Myers, Lewis married Brenner, Sarah 09/21/64 09/22/64
Myers, Lewis married Brenner, Sarah 09/21/64 09/23/64
Myers, Louisa married Moore, James 06/22/61 08/07/61
Myers, Lucretia A. married Carrick, George W. 11/01/65 11/23/65
Myers, Maria F. married Stokes, John R. 12/26/65 12/28/65
Myers, Mary died 12/13/61 12/14/61
Myers, Mary died 12/17/62 12/19/62
Myers, Mary married Jenks, John N. 02/14/64 02/15/64
Myers, Mary (Mrs.) died 02/24/64 02/25/64
Myers, Mary E. married Speed, Christopher C. 12/15/64 12/22/64
Myers, Mary Jane died 06/04/65 06/07/65
Myers, Matilda died 01/28/62 01/30/62
Myers, O. A. married Kemp, Catherine Ann 09/10/61 09/11/61
Myers, Philip died 07/20/65 07/21/65
Myers, Randolph died 06/12/65 06/13/65
Myers, Rebecca married Mason, James A. 12/06/65 12/23/65
Myers, Rebecca (Mrs.) died 09/15/65 09/16/65
Myers, Sarah died 02/17/61 02/18/61
Myers, Sarah Agnes (Mrs.) died 12/13/63 12/16/63
Myers, Sue died 08/04/62 08/05/62
Myers, Thomas A. married Abbott, Clara E. 10/09/62 10/11/62
Myers, William married Gibson, Maria (Mrs.) 01/15/65 01/18/65
Myers, William Edward died 05/09/64 05/11/64
Myers, William H. married Riggs, Amelia 12/19/60 01/03/61
Myers, William H. married Jackson, Lucy 12/26/65 12/28/65
Myers, William Maxwell died 06/22/62 06/27/62
Myers, Willie H. died 01/13/65 01/14/65
Myrick, Joseph (Cpt.) died 11/05/63 11/13/63
Nace, William Henry Murray died 02/28/63 03/02/63
Nace, William L. married Burnham, Louise 04/08/63 04/14/63
Nachman, Adolph married Cohen, Fanny 03/09/64 03/12/64

Nachman, Matilda died 07/08/64 07/09/64
Nachman, Solomon died 06/09/64 06/11/64
Nachman, Theresa died 09/03/63 09/04/63
Nagel, Mary C. Bopp married Kreis, George J. 02/21/65 02/23/65
Nagel, Peter died 11/02/61 11/04/61
Nagle, John G. married Sheckells, Anna E. 12/06/65 12/11/65
Nagle, John H. married Spalding, Mary A. 10/10/65 11/04/65
Nagle, Joseph H. married Pennington, Elizabeth A. 10/12/65 10/14/65
Nagle, Sarah died 09/08/64 09/09/64
Nail, Mary A. married Middleton, Henry 11/30/64 12/01/64
Naill, H. Clay married Angel, Maggie 01/15/63 01/16/63
Nairn, John C. (Dr.) died 12/08/65 12/11/65
Naler, Hester A. married McLaughlin, David 10/18/63 10/20/63
Nalk, Margaret Lilly died 04/09/64 04/11/64
Nalls, Emma D. married Dowell, George E. 10/12/65 10/23/65
Nalls, Mary Susanna died 04/12/64 04/13/64
Nalls, Thomas F. (Sgt.) married Wilcox, Ethel Dera A. 11/02/65 11/07/
Nally, Martha E. married Dillow, John R. 06/06/65 06/07/65
Nance, Ella W. died 08/17/65 08/28/65
Nants, Effie died 11/28/61 11/30/61
Nanz, Thomas married Radcliffe, Cornelia A. 12/08/64 12/10/64
Nash, James (CSA) died 07/16/63 08/22/63
Nash, John Thomas died 04/14/65 04/15/65
Nash, Rebecca married Smith, James 06/22/62 07/01/62
Nash, Thomas died 08/02/63 08/03/63
Nason, Mary E. married Gover, E. L. no date 07/29/64
Nason, Mary E. married Gover, Edward L. 07/20/64 07/30/64
Nathan, Adam married Howard, Louisa 08/17/65 08/19/65
Nathan, Justina married Cohen, Medes 10/18/65 10/26/65
Nathans, Phoebe Ann died 01/24/62 01/25/62
Naudain, T. M. married Perkins, S. H. 03/06/65 03/15/65
Navey, Lilian Cobb died 12/23/64 12/28/64
Navin, William died 09/02/62 09/04/62
Navy, George Washington died 04/19/63 04/23/63
Navy, Loretta Estelle died 06/02/65 06/03/65
Navy, Virginia married Aderon, H. Clay 02/09/61 02/15/61
Naylor, Alfred Barteen died 03/03/63 03/09/63
NcGibty, Felix died 01/01/64 01/02/64
Neal, Francis William died 11/29/65 12/14/65
Neal, John died 06/13/62 06/16/62
Neal, Letitia married Morris, James H. 07/03/62 07/16/62
Neal, Martha Ann married Snowden, James T. 02/04/64 02/06/64
Neal, Mattie married Gore, A. Washington 01/05/65 01/10/65
Neal, Sarah married Smith, Charles 04/17/64 04/25/64
Neale, Demmie married Quincy, John D. 11/18/63 11/20/63
Neale, Susannah Evelina married Bowling, John J. 10/22/65 10/27/65
Neale, William Marshall married Burger, Marie M. 12/25/61 12/31/61
Neale, Willy M. N. died 03/04/64 03/05/64
Neblett, Mary A. married Gittings, Martin V. 05/15/62 05/20/62
Needhammer, William married Bailey, Harriet Lydia 11/12/63 04/18/64
Needhaven, Josephine married Khue, Baszal M. 07/29/63 08/04/63
Neel, Mary married Waters, William A. (Dr.) 01/27/63 02/02/63
Neely, Eliza married Neely, Robert (Lt.) 03/15/64 03/17/64
Neely, Joseph married Coggins, Emma 11/09/65 11/11/65
Neely, Maggie married Ehlies, J. Henry 06/25/61 07/10/61

Neely, Maggie married Ehlies, W. Henry 06/25/61   07/11/61
Neely, Robert (Lt.) married Neely, Eliza 03/15/64   03/17/64
Neely, William John died 02/13/62   02/14/62
Neepier, George M. died 03/11/64   03/12/64
Negengerd, Frederick A. married Mesner, Virginia 06/23/63   06/25/63
Negengerd, Virginia (Mrs.) died 02/27/64   02/29/64
Neibergall, John W. died 04/20/63   04/21/63
Neider, Mary Josephine married Ramsay, Albert R. 12/22/63   12/28/63
Neidhamer, Emma Gertrude died 01/03/63   01/06/63
Neidhamer, John died 02/07/64   02/08/64
Neighoff, Samuel F. died 10/06/63   10/07/63
Neihoff, Martha married Crisp, Edward T. 10/27/64   11/04/64
Neilson, Cynthia J. married Adams, Charles W. 05/10/65   05/18/65
Neilson, Emily married Byrd, Thomas T. 05/20/61   04/23/61
Neilson, Harry Winfield died 07/21/63   07/22/63
Neilson, Joseph E. married Maccubbin, Maggie E. 04/04/64   04/07/64
Neilson, Lizzie married Stevens, Charles P. 04/25/61   04/26/61
Neilson, Mary P. married Young, Arthur M. 09/21/64   09/26/64
Neilson, Sarah Rebecca died 09/02/62   09/03/62
Neily, J. Wilson married Hands, Haddie W. 02/22/65   02/24/65
Neimeyer, Hermann died 07/17/65   07/29/65
Neimyer, Robert Noble died 01/17/65   01/20/65
Nelker, Henrietta married Klopfenstein, Philip 08/30/65   09/08/65
Nelker, J. F. married Frey, Louisa C. 11/15/64   11/26/64
Nelligan, Maurice married Doyle, Eliza 05/22/64   05/28/64
Nelson, Daniel McPhail died 07/17/65   07/19/65
Nelson, George A. married Gallup, Lizzie A. 01/03/61   01/10/61
Nelson, Henry died 06/26/65   06/28/65
Nelson, Horace B. married Goodman, Harriet Ann 12/13/64   12/15/64
Nelson, Johanna (Mrs.) died 01/04/64   01/05/64
Nelson, John married Calhoun, Mary 10/20/63   10/22/63
Nelson, Lawrence died 02/19/64   02/22/64
Nelson, Lizzie married DeLeue, Albert 06/08/65   07/03/65
Nelson, Louisa married Rayne, William 01/20/64   01/25/64
Nelson, Marshall died 06/28/63   07/17/63
Nelson, Mary died 05/25/65   05/26/65
Nelson, Matilda died 02/02/62   02/04/62
Nelson, Nancy married Ward, Lewis 02/05/62   03/03/62
Nelson, Robert died 03/17/63   03/18/63
Nelson, Thomas died 10/07/65   10/09/65
Nelson, Thomas F. (USN) married Ames, Annie Janette 06/14/65   06/17/65
Nesbitt, Mary married Green, James H. 01/05/64   02/17/64
Ness, George B. died 01/17/61   01/21/61
Ness, William H. (Cpl.) died 10/10/64   10/17/64
Nestor, John died 01/14/63   01/15/63
Neter, Elizabeth Billifelt died no date   08/12/62
Netre, Ferdinand died 02/06/64   02/08/64
Netsel, Annie married Bartlett, James F., Jr. 02/14/64   02/26/64
Neuberth, Mary C. married Hennick, Francis Marion 04/21/63   04/23/63
Neuwieler, John C. married Brown, Emma Marion 09/29/64   10/05/64
Neville, John died 09/26/61   10/03/61
Neville, Martha E. married Cole, William 03/26/61   03/29/61
Nevin, Thomas married Ennis, Matilda E. 09/26/61   12/28/61
Nevins, Ellen died 01/25/62   02/08/62
Nevitt, Henry C. married Nevitt, Mary A. Marcella 06/25/61   06/26/61

Nevitt, J. Edward died 09/06/64   09/10/64
Nevitt, Mary A. Marcella married Nevitt, Henry C. 06/25/61   06/26/61
Nevitt, Rebecca married Richardson, John 10/15/63   10/17/63
New, John married Robinson, Fannie 03/24/64   05/28/64
Newberger, G. married Burgunder, Rebecca 03/10/61   03/13/61
Newberth, John M. married Gombert, Anne G. (Mrs.) 10/04/64   10/08/64
Newcomb, Clara S. died 12/31/60   01/02/61
Newcomer, Emma A. married Chritzman, H. G. (Dr.) 12/24/63   12/25/63
Newcomer, Jessie married Lowther, Maggie L. 08/01/65   08/04/65
Newell, George R. married Stewart, Louisa 08/31/64   09/10/64
Newell, John Henry died 08/03/63   08/04/63
Newell, Maria died 02/23/62   02/25/62
Newell, Maria died 02/23/62   02/26/62
Newell, Matilda C. (Mrs.) married Floyd, Robert L. (Rev.) 10/15/61
   10/22/61
Newgent, Walter H. married Gordon, Sarah E. 01/01/61   01/02/61
Newhouse, Jacob died 04/14/61   05/11/61
Newhouse, Jacob died 04/14/61   05/14/61
Newkirk, Alice Virginia died 03/25/61   03/27/61
Newkirk, Edward V. married Kirby, Amanda 09/08/63   09/17/63
Newkirk, Emma married Watson, George W. 07/02/65   09/08/65
Newman, Ann Elizabeth (Mrs.) died 10/03/64   10/05/64
Newman, Ann Matilda married Leonard, Jonathan H. 04/22/63   04/28/63
Newman, Annie E. died 09/28/61   09/30/61
Newman, Benjamin married Selegee, Caroline 08/13/65   08/14/65
Newman, Clara, A. J. married Wilson, Allen N. 12/29/64   01/02/65
Newman, Edward Laws died 09/01/65   09/02/65
Newman, Edward Peyton died 05/24/62   05/26/62
Newman, Elizabeth A. married Engler, Augustus C. 02/14/61   02/19/61
Newman, Harry Lawson died 11/25/62   11/26/62
Newman, Henrietta married Bailey, Henry 05/15/64   05/21/64
Newman, Lydia Cecilia died 10/11/65   10/17/65
Newman, Mary E. died 02/20/65   04/18/65
Newman, Mary Elizabeth married Dickerson, Josiah F. 06/25/65   06/27/65
Newman, Mary Elizabeth (Mrs.) died 02/20/65   02/22/65
Newman, Richard B. died 12/14/63   01/30/64
Newman, Robert H. married Spauldin, Henrietta 05/02/61   05/06/61
Newman, Sidney C. married Price, Virginia E. 09/03/61   09/14/61
Newmeyer, Charles A. died 04/10/65   04/12/65
Newmyer, Mary J. married Englert, Philip 11/12/65   11/16/65
Newton, Ann J. (Mrs.) died 06/25/64   06/29/64
Newton, J. W. (Capt.) married Eskridge, M. W. 02/14/61   02/19/61
Newton, Mary E. married Weidner, Frederick 01/21/64   02/17/64
Nibbleit, Nancy died 02/08/61   02/09/61
Nice, Robert Vinton died 04/09/63   04/11/63
Nicelson, Eliza A. Becker married Frazer, James 05/16/64   05/18/64
Nicely, Henry Shryock died 02/08/65   02/09/65
Nicely, Thomas Sewell died 10/21/63   10/24/63
Nichol, David died 10/14/64   10/15/64
Nichol, Matilda married Appleby, William H. 01/27/61   02/11/61
Nicholas, Elizabeth married Sampson, Kevener K. 07/07/64   07/09/64
Nicholas, George died 08/29/62   09/25/62
Nicholas, J. S. (Cpt., U.S.N.) died 07/18/65   07/20/65
Nicholas, Jane Hollins died 05/24/65   05/26/65
Nicholas, Matilda married Lewis, Francis 11/21/61   11/22/61

Nicholas, Spear (Sgt.) died 09/21/62   10/11/62
Nicholls, Henrietta married McLaughlin, George 06/22/65   06/24/65
Nicholls, Reuben H. died 02/08/62   02/11/62
Nicholls, Samuel T. died 03/17/63   03/19/63
Nichols, Adele married Hubbell, Clark 11/08/63   11/10/63
Nichols, Caroline (Mrs.) died 03/15/65   03/16/65
Nichols, Dianna died 10/01/63   10/03/63
Nichols, John Henry Rhea died 04/11/62   04/12/62
Nichols, Margaret Ann married Simms, Alexander 02/21/65   02/24/65
Nichols, Mariah died 12/15/63   12/16/63
Nichols, Rebecca M. married Chenoweth, Robert 01/20/63   01/29/63
Nichols, Sinclair died 03/28/62   03/31/62
Nichols, Warren died 01/28/61   02/15/61
Nichols, Zachariah married Bond, Ellen L.(Mrs.) 10/09/64   10/11/64
Nicholson, Ann Sophia died 11/02/61   11/04/61
Nicholson, Beverly Howard died 12/27/65   12/28/65
Nicholson, Charles G. married Goldsborough, Emilie J. 06/04/61   06/11/61
Nicholson, Charles L. married Mauck, Sallie A. 12/22/63   12/24/63
Nicholson, Colombus J. died 02/04/64   02/05/64
Nicholson, Drew J. married Dunkell, Rebecca T. 09/21/65   09/23/65
Nicholson, Ellen M. married McManus, F. R. 12/02/62   12/05/62
Nicholson, Emily Erving married Magruder, John Meade 06/29/65   07/03/65
Nicholson, Emma Barrow died 02/08/63   02/10/63
Nicholson, Emma F. married House, Edwin 07/23/61   07/26/61
Nicholson, George T. L. married Fulton, Emma W. 11/17/63   11/19/63
Nicholson, George W. died 03/11/64   03/12/64
Nicholson, Georgeanna married Temple, John H. 02/02/64   02/20/64
Nicholson, Georgiana married Ilgenfritz, Jackson 03/31/61   04/03/61
Nicholson, Isaac married Bias, Caroline (Mrs.) 11/28/61   12/03/61
Nicholson, Jenette Barker died 11/01/63   11/02/63
Nicholson, Joseph died 09/17/63   09/19/63
Nicholson, Joseph J. died 06/16/64   06/20/64
Nicholson, Joshua W. married Hurdle, Georgeanna 06/13/65   06/27/65
Nicholson, Lambert married Ringgold, Susanna 04/02/63   04/18/63
Nicholson, Lottie married Merritt, James 09/21/64   02/16/65
Nicholson, Louisa died 04/28/63   05/02/63
Nicholson, Maggie E. married Farquar, William P. 03/17/65   03/21/65
Nicholson, Mary E. married Smith, Frank M. (Cpt.) 10/04/65   10/24/65
Nicholson, Mary Emma died 04/26/63   04/28/63
Nicholson, Mary F. married Baker, John W. 12/22/64   12/30/64
Nicholson, Mary Jane married Betton, Alfred J. 10/14/62   10/23/62
Nicholson, Mary Susan died 06/18/61   06/20/61
Nicholson, Nickson married Williams, Lydia Ann 12/08/61   12/16/61
Nicholson, Thomas died 02/26/65   02/27/65
Nicholson, Thomas died 02/26/65   02/28/65
Nicholson, William died 05/06/62   05/06/62
Nickerson, George B. married Harding, Eliza 06/11/65   06/30/65
Nicklas, George married Zell, Emma E. 04/20/65   04/21/65
Nickol, Janett F. married Little, Stephen 10/15/60   05/30/61
Nickum, Samuel died 07/15/63   07/18/63
Nicodemus, Mary A. married Colladay, Charles R. 11/26/62   12/02/62
Nicodemus, Willie E. died 11/12/62   11/13/62
Nicol, Lottie E. married Witters, Thomas D. 01/26/64   10/04/64
Nicolassen, George A. died 09/01/65   09/02/65
Nicolassen, Thomas C. died 09/30/65   10/02/65

```
Nicoll, Ida Euhamma died 08/05/65   08/09/65
Nicoll, Mary died 03/15/62   03/17/62
Nicoll, Robert D. died 03/22/64   03/24/64
Nicoll, William married Costello, Elizabeth 10/12/62   10/14/62
Nicols, Peary E. Noel died 06/12/65   06/13/65
Nicolson, Lucretia married Wilson, Henry 12/28/65   12/29/65
Nicolsson, William H. died 09/26/61   09/28/61
Niedheimer, Lydia Lucia died 05/17/65   05/18/65
Nield, Mary A. married Child, T. C. 09/29/64   11/11/64
Nielson, Agnes Maria F. died 06/18/63   06/19/63
Nielson, Lydia M. (Mrs.) died 03/14/65   03/15/65
Nielson, Lydia M. (Mrs.) died 03/14/65   03/16/65
Nielson, William died 08/10/62   08/13/62
Niles, Mary Ann married Stuart, James 10/09/62   10/11/62
Niles, Sarah Jane married Gilbert, Pacca Thomas 04/16/63   04/18/63
Nily, A., Jr. married Lemmon, Elizabeth Ellen 04/23/63   04/25/63
Nily, Magaretha married Ruths, George (Lt.) 05/05/62   05/08/62
Nimmo, Charlie died 09/12/62   09/18/62
Nimmo, Joseph C. C. died 03/09/65   03/14/65
Nimmo, Rebecca Jane died 04/28/62   04/30/62
Nimmo, William T. married Bickham, Sarah E. 04/06/64   05/16/64
Nimno, Rush J. died 07/29/64   08/01/64
Ninde, Theresa C. married Moore, James (Rev.) 10/18/64   10/22/64
Ningardt, Frederick W. married Miller, Kate 01/13/62   01/28/62
Niser, Elizabeth married Jordan, Alexander 11/20/64   11/22/64
Nittnacht, Jean married Atkinson, William C. 03/04/62   03/05/62
Nitzel, Michael died 05/09/63   05/11/63
Nixdorff, Harrison died 08/10/64   08/12/64
Nixdorff, T. S. married Everhart, Sue 11/15/64   11/22/64
Nixdorff, Tobias died 09/09/62   09/11/62
Nixon, Alfred (Dr.) married Patterson, Ellen B. 04/30/63   05/02/63
Nixon, Laura Virginia married McNulty, John A. 08/02/63   09/16/63
Nixon, Patrick married Landers, Annie 01/14/64   01/22/64
Nizer, Mary (Mrs.) died 09/10/63   09/12/63
Nizer, Rachel Olivia married Reeder, Samuel T. 01/25/63   01/28/63
Noble, John A. married Stewart, Mary R. 03/30/65   04/07/65
Noble, Roswell died no date   02/18/64
Noblet, John married James, Margaret (Mrs.) 01/16/65   01/25/65
Noblet, Sarah died 02/10/61   02/13/61
Noblett, John died 02/02/65   02/02/65
Noel, John Rothrock died 12/16/62   12/17/62
Noel, W. A. (Lt.) married Rothrock, Sarah E. 02/05/62   02/08/62
Nohe, Charles married McNulty, Kate 06/19/65   07/15/65
Nolan, Deliah died 06/29/64   06/30/64
Nolan, Jane married Joyce, S. H. 12/07/65   12/18/65
Nolan, John died 02/13/63   02/14/63
Nolan, Julia A. died 10/08/65   10/10/65
Nolan, Mary Ellen died 06/13/63   06/16/63
Nolan, Rosanna died 09/09/64   09/10/64
Nolen, J. D. Readel died 05/25/62   05/26/62
Nolen, Sarah Jane died 05/30/64   06/01/64
Noll, John died 04/02/61   04/04/61
Noll, Katee married Kemp, Oliver 11/14/65   11/17/65
Nomen, William E. married Ward, Sallie E. 07/28/63   08/03/63
Nonamaker, Celia married Selby, Edwin D. 08/20/63   08/21/63
```

Nones, Henry S. married Deal, Mary D. 07/14/62   07/25/62
Noonan, Cornelius died 03/22/63   03/23/63
Noonan, James A. died 10/29/62   10/30/62
Noonan, Margaret died 09/27/61   09/28/61
Noonan, Thomas died 08/12/64   08/20/64
Norfolk, Celia J. married Bird, Samuel R. 06/17/62   06/18/62
Norfolk, James Richard died 03/01/61   03/02/61
Norfolk, John (Pvt.) died 08/00/00   09/17/64
Norfolk, John H. died 09/30/63   10/01/63
Norfolk, Joseph S. married Foley, Julia S. 06/14/65   06/16/65
Norfolk, Julia A. married Morrison, James A. 03/24/63   07/20/63
Norfolk, Mary A. married Earle, Henry 01/03/65   01/05/65
Norfolk, Mollie K. married Miller, James D. 05/30/65   07/31/65
Norfolk, Richard H. T. married Staum, Elizabeth B. 07/22/62   07/23/62
Norfolk, William H. married Tucker, Fannie M. no date   10/22/62
Norfolk, William W. H. died 09/20/61   10/08/61
Norgan, Arthur Merriman died 07/03/63   07/07/63
Norman, Caroline (Mrs.) died 01/22/63   01/23/63
Norman, Charlotte Grace died 10/13/64   10/14/64
Norman, Elizabeth A. A. died 11/12/64   11/14/64
Norman, Joseph married Doggett, Annie R. 01/22/63   01/24/63
Norman, Louisiana E. married Tanner, Cornelius S. 12/14/65   12/15/65
Norman, Prince married Mohler, Rosie A. 04/28/63   04/29/63
Norman, Rosetia L. married Weems, Edwin D. (USN) 09/22/64   09/24/64
Norman, Sophia married Morris, James 03/28/61   04/02/61
Norries, Esrom married Harper, Mary E. 08/08/65   09/06/65
Norris, Annie Howard died 03/18/63   03/20/63
Norris, Caroline Elizabeth died 08/04/62   08/05/62
Norris, Caroline Elizabeth died 08/04/62   08/06/62
Norris, Cassandra died 06/18/65   06/21/65
Norris, Cassandra died 06/18/65   06/22/65
Norris, Charles died 10/04/61   10/08/61
Norris, Charles died 11/04/62   11/06/62
Norris, Charles Thomas died 12/26/61   12/30/61
Norris, Cornelia married Scott, Daniel 11/18/63   12/12/63
Norris, Edward Vernon died 05/30/62   06/12/62
Norris, F. William Pinckney died 02/15/61   02/21/61
Norris, Fannie married Owings, U. G. 08/14/62   08/20/62
Norris, Frances A. died 06/15/61   06/17/61
Norris, Frank Morgan died 06/11/64   06/13/64
Norris, Hannah Eliza died 06/23/65   06/24/65
Norris, Hannah R. married Smith, A. J. 02/23/64   02/24/64
Norris, Harry Godey died 08/26/64   08/27/64
Norris, Henry Johns died 07/01/62   07/08/62
Norris, Isaac died 08/23/62   08/26/62
Norris, J. Alexander married Hyde, Cornelia 11/16/65   11/27/65
Norris, J. Charles died 09/08/65   09/20/65
Norris, John died 08/07/64   09/09/64
Norris, Joseph A. married Hyde, Cornelia 11/16/65   11/29/65
Norris, Joseph T. married Calder, Jane 07/06/65   07/20/65
Norris, Lydia C. died 04/08/64   04/11/64
Norris, M. Lizzie married Buckey, D. 11/19/61   11/21/61
Norris, Mary died 12/07/61   12/11/61
Norris, Mary (Mrs.) died 02/16/63   02/19/63
Norris, Mary A. died 05/11/62   05/13/62

Norris, Mary E. married Cornor, William E. 07/08/62   07/16/62
Norris, Mary F. married Culley, Robert J. 04/26/64   05/09/64
Norris, Mary Jane married Gorsuch, Washington 05/17/64   05/20/64
Norris, Minneolia died 02/19/62   02/24/62
Norris, Rachel S. married Corse, Robert S. 02/24/64   02/29/64
Norris, Rachel Ann married Richfield, George W. 11/26/65   12/18/65
Norris, Richard (Rev.) married Baker, Sadie A. W. 01/01/61   01/02/61
Norris, Richard V. married Meath, Mary E. 07/03/64   10/10/64
Norris, Robert Thaddeus died 05/15/64   01/12/65
Norris, Sadie Virginia Lee died 10/31/64   11/01/64
Norris, Sarah H. died 12/09/62   12/13/62
Norris, Susan M. died 01/19/65   01/21/65
Norris, Susannah married Blades, Thomas W. 10/01/62   10/04/62
Norris, Sydney C. died 01/07/64   01/08/64
Norris, Thomas married McGraw, Elizabeth A. 05/16/61   05/31/61
Norris, Thomas S. A. died 03/28/65   03/30/65
Norris, William married Magers, Elizabeth 04/22/62   04/23/62
Norris, William B., Jr. married Rice, Addis 12/22/64   12/31/64
Norris, William E. died 05/31/63   06/01/63
Norris, William E. died 05/31/63   06/02/63
Norris, William H. (Dr.) married Suter, Mollie E. 06/09/63   06/12/63
North, Clara Jane died 02/11/63   02/12/63
North, Elizabeth (Mrs.) died 10/09/63   10/10/63
North, Emily married Applegate, Arthur W. 11/26/61   12/10/61
North, Harry C. died 09/28/62   09/30/62
North, James H. died 09/06/61   09/07/61
North, John Wesley died 02/02/63   02/04/63
North, Laura Virginia died 10/28/63   10/29/63
North, Maggie died 01/26/61   01/28/61
North, William C. married Sanders, Mary E. 12/15/63   12/18/63
North, William Edward died 02/24/62   02/28/62
Northcraft, Francis married Leishear, Catherine 04/22/63   04/28/63
Northup, D. D. Frank married Tucker, Annie D. 02/15/64   02/19/64
Norton, James M. (Sgt. CSA) died 10/03/62   02/14/63
Norton, Kate married Williard, E. H. 01/01/64   01/02/64
Norville, Sarah A. married Baker, William J. 12/14/65   12/18/65
Norwood, B. R. married Valentine, Susan A. 02/01/63   02/05/63
Norwood, Charles H. died 10/26/65   10/28/65
Norwood, Charles Milton died 10/01/61   10/04/61
Norwood, Delos M. married Anschutz, Kate 11/27/63   12/07/63
Norwood, Ebenezer married Gosnell, Maria 09/18/64   09/30/64
Norwood, George W. died 12/23/63   12/24/63
Norwood, Hattie R. married Rutter, Edward J. 10/24/65   10/26/65
Norwood, Jennie married Coursley, George 10/21/62   10/24/62
Norwood, John died 01/09/63   01/12/63
Norwood, John M. died 04/05/64   04/07/64
Norwood, Kate died 07/10/62   07/11/62
Norwood, Margaret died 02/24/61   02/25/61
Norwood, Mary Ann died 05/30/65   05/31/65
Norwood, Susan died 02/01/61   02/02/61
Notherman, Isabella died 06/23/65   06/27/65
Nowlan, Thomas died 10/04/61   10/05/61
Noyes, Edward C. married Abbett, V. Eudora 11/09/64   11/10/64
Noyes, Enoch (Dr.) died 03/23/62   03/25/62

```
Noyes, Henry married Ely, Mary Jane 11/19/61   11/21/61
Nugent, A. Jane married Kilmer, John W. 10/07/62   10/10/62
Nugent, Agnes married Johnson, Richard 10/02/64   10/04/64
Nugent, Bernard died 07/08/62   07/09/62
Nugent, Catherine died 07/10/65   07/11/65
Nugent, John P. died 07/20/64   07/21/64
Nugent, Lizzie married Keller, George 07/06/64   12/03/64
Nugent, Mary A. married Cooney, Thomas J. 02/08/64   02/16/64
Nugent, Mary Virginia died 11/17/63   11/19/63
Numsen, Lizzie Gertrude died 02/09/63   02/10/63
Numsen, Mary Catherine died 02/18/61   02/20/61
Nunan, Denis died 10/13/61   10/14/61
Nunan, George F. died 01/26/64   01/28/64
Nunn, Stephen E. married King, Louisa A. 07/06/62   07/24/62
Nunn, Stephen E. married Krug, Louisa A. 07/06/62   07/25/62
Nurnburger, E. A. married Schumacher, H. J. 10/09/65   10/11/65
Nusz, Luther Oliver died 12/02/63   12/09/63
Nusz, Sophia died 08/08/62   08/09/62
Nute, Catharine died 02/24/65   02/25/65
Nuthall, Martha Roberta died 12/03/61   12/05/61
Nuther, Edward M. died 10/21/63   10/22/63
Nuttall, John H. married Humphrys, Elizabeth 12/17/65   12/19/65
Nutwell, Ellen Hazard (Mrs.) died 12/09/62   02/14/63
Nutwell, George married Reynolds, Mollie L. 06/13/65   06/14/65
Nutwell, James E. married Owens, Martha E. 04/09/61   04/16/61
Nyrsinger, Eliza Jane died 08/11/62   08/12/62
O'Boile, Michael died 03/19/65   03/21/65
O'Brien, Ally died 07/01/63   07/02/63
O'Brien, Anne died 04/22/64   04/23/64
O'Brien, Bridget married Gault, Richard 08/08/58   01/11/65
O'Brien, Bridget married Gault, Richard 08/08/58   01/12/65
O'Brien, Bridget married Gault, Richard 08/08/58   01/13/65
O'Brien, Charles E. died 10/23/65   11/04/65
O'Brien, Daniel died 05/22/62   05/24/62
O'Brien, Della married Whittle, Thomas Xavier 05/04/63   05/27/63
O'Brien, Emily Kate died 07/03/64   07/04/64
O'Brien, Frank died 11/24/62   11/25/62
O'Brien, Giles J. married Sandler, Emma Augusta 12/10/65   12/25/65
O'Brien, Henry died 10/08/62   10/09/62
O'Brien, James L. married Hopkins, Mary Anne 08/15/63   08/24/63
O'Brien, Jane married Gallagher, Francis 01/01/62   04/26/62
O'Brien, John C. died 07/15/65   07/18/65
O'Brien, Margaret Ann died 02/13/64   02/17/64
O'Brien, Mary died 08/13/64   08/15/64
O'Brien, Mary married Lynn, Michael 02/19/65   02/25/65
O'Brien, Mary (Mrs.) died 08/01/64   08/11/64
O'Brien, Mary A. died 07/22/61   07/23/61
O'Brien, Michael J. died 03/17/63   03/18/63
O'Brien, Nora A. married Mulhare, John M. 05/30/64   06/04/64
O'Brien, Richard died 10/27/64   10/28/64
O'Bryon, Sarah C. died 07/10/62   07/12/62
O'Buckingham, Sally married Poinst, Charles Dominick 06/06/63   01/06/64
O'Callaghan, Timothy died 12/10/62   12/12/62
O'Conell, Ellen (Mrs.) died 09/11/64   09/13/64
O'Connell, Annie married Barrett, James E. 02/28/65   03/08/65
```

O'Connell, Daniel died 09/07/65   09/08/65
O'Connell, Ellen died 10/19/63   10/20/63
O'Connell, Ellen (Mrs.) died 09/11/64   09/12/64
O'Connell, Nellie married Carey, David F. 11/24/63   12/01/63
O'Connell, Patrick died 04/03/62   04/04/62
O'Connell, Timothy died 03/17/61   03/19/61
O'Connell, William Eugene died 09/28/63   10/01/63
O'Connnor, Francis died 04/13/61   04/19/61
O'Connor, Andrew P. died 09/21/64   09/23/64
O'Connor, Anna (Mrs.) died 03/15/64   03/17/64
O'Connor, Catherine died 02/28/64   02/29/64
O'Connor, Catherine (Mrs.) died 05/10/63   05/11/63
O'Connor, Elizabeth died 01/24/61   01/26/61
O'Connor, Emily Louisa (Mrs.) died 09/05/63   09/07/63
O'Connor, James died 10/22/62   10/23/62
O'Connor, James died 04/19/63   04/21/63
O'Connor, John Thomas died 10/09/65   10/10/65
O'Connor, John Thomas died 10/09/65   10/11/65
O'Connor, John William died 06/01/63   06/02/63
O'Connor, Mary E. died 05/03/63   05/04/63
O'Connor, Thomas died 04/17/64   04/18/64
O'Connors, Thomas died 11/14/65   11/15/65
O'Dell, Alexina married Brewer, D. R. (Dr.) 12/26/65   12/30/65
O'Dell, Walter J. died 03/19/63   03/24/63
O'Denahal, Rosalie A. Bobee died 10/06/61   10/08/61
O'Donahue, Ann died 08/24/61   08/26/61
O'Donahue, Kate married Taylor, James B. 07/13/65   07/26/65
O'Donald, Michael died 01/17/63   01/19/63
O'Donald, Samuel Edward died 02/28/64   02/29/64
O'Donnell, Augustus P. died 11/26/63   11/30/63
O'Donnell, C. Oliver (Mrs.) died no date   08/18/65
O'Donnell, Columbus, Jr. died 04/25/64   04/26/64
O'Donnell, Columbus, Jr. died 04/25/64   04/27/64
O'Donnell, E. Lewis married Johnson, Caroline 12/20/65   12/22/65
O'Donnell, James S. married Bilson, Louisa 08/02/63   11/09/63
O'Donnell, John died 03/12/65   03/13/65
O'Donnell, Joseph F. died 06/21/61   06/22/61
O'Donnell, Mary J. (Mrs.) died 04/29/64   04/30/64
O'Donnell, Mary J. (Mrs.) died 04/29/64   05/02/64
O'Donnell, Sodre (Dr.) died 07/23/65   08/08/65
O'Donoghue, Eleanor married Clements, W. Diles 10/06/64   10/21/64
O'Donovan, Michael died 11/28/63   11/30/63
O'Doud, Thomas Patrick died 09/28/65   09/29/65
O'Farrell, Michael died 10/03/64   10/04/64
O'Ferrall, John married Stapleton, Maggie 05/04/63   05/11/63
O'Grady, Johanna died 02/20/65   02/21/65
O'Hara, John married Dail(e)y, Susie 04/28/65   05/04/65
O'Keefe, Bridget died 01/12/62   01/14/62
O'Keefe, Edward J. died 01/20/62   01/21/62
O'Keefe, Kate A. married Hogan, John J. 07/14/61   08/01/61
O'Keefe, Thomas died 04/23/62   04/24/62
O'Keeffe, Daniel died 06/30/63   07/01/63
O'Laughlin, Elizabeth C. died 08/10/62   08/11/62
O'Laughlin, Ellen F. (Mrs.) died 10/21/63   10/23/63
O'Laughlin, S. Williams married Maulsby, Aggie Steuart 01/06/63

```
                                                       01/09/63
O'Laughlin, Stacia M. married Homer, Robert H.  02/24/64   02/29/64
O'Leary, Annie died 04/19/64   04/20/64
O'Leary, Augustus M. died 10/04/64   10/06/64
O'Leary, Augustus M. died 10/04/64   10/10/64
O'Leary, Elizabeth (Mrs.) died 03/10/65   03/11/65
O'Leary, James died 05/03/61   05/04/61
O'Leary, Richard died 06/19/65   06/30/65
O'Leary, William F. married Lacy, Mary A.  10/13/61   10/15/61
O'Malley, George married Riordan, Mary A.  03/31/64   04/04/64
O'Nail, Edward married Murray, Sarah 02/04/64   02/17/64
O'Neal, Alonza died 09/01/63   09/08/63
O'Neal, Annie Elizabeth died 07/14/62   07/15/62
O'Neal, Frances died 11/16/61   11/18/61
O'Neal, James P. married Jewel, Arkansas A.  06/27/61   06/29/61
O'Neal, Oliver B. died 10/13/63   10/17/63
O'Neal, Rody died 03/06/62   03/12/62
O'Neil, Arkansas died 07/01/64   07/02/64
O'Neil, Charles C. died 04/18/64   04/21/64
O'Neil, Charles Z. (Capt.) died 05/08/64   11/10/65
O'Neil, Cornelius died 07/20/63   07/22/63
O'Neil, Honora died 10/29/62   10/30/62
O'Neil, Lewis C. died 06/03/64   06/09/64
O'Neil, Mary died 06/15/64   06/17/64
O'Neil, Patrick died 10/31/64   11/01/64
O'Neil, Terrence died 04/19/61   04/20/61
O'Neill, Alicia (Mrs.) died 07/18/64   07/21/64
O'Neill, Alicia (Mrs.) died 07/18/64   07/22/64
O'Neill, Catherine Ann died 09/10/61   09/11/61
O'Neill, Daniel died 06/22/62   06/23/62
O'Neill, Daniel died 09/18/64   09/19/64
O'Neill, Edward died 05/09/64   05/10/64
O'Neill, Eliza Jane died 05/16/65   05/18/65
O'Neill, Ellen (Mrs.) died 05/23/63   05/25/63
O'Neill, H. E. (Sgt.) married Kirby, Frances 11/12/63   12/29/63
O'Neill, Howard D. died 08/27/61   08/29/61
O'Neill, James died 06/08/64   06/09/64
O'Neill, James H. married Smyth, Mary A.  11/01/64   11/05/64
O'Neill, John died 04/06/63   04/25/63
O'Neill, John died 07/03/64   07/08/64
O'Neill, John F. married Gallagher, Mary Lavinia 06/27/65   06/30/65
O'Neill, John H. married McElroy, Martha 05/12/63   05/19/63
O'Neill, Julia died 08/15/63   08/17/63
O'Neill, Lewis N. died 07/21/64   07/23/64
O'Neill, Lucinda died 09/12/63   09/15/63
O'Neill, Margaret died 09/20/62   09/22/62
O'Neill, Margaret died 12/20/64   12/21/64
O'Neill, Margaret A. married Mahrer, Henry 01/12/64   03/11/64
O'Neill, Mary died 12/27/65   12/28/65
O'Neill, Mary died 12/27/65   12/29/65
O'Neill, Mary Ann (Mrs.) died 07/24/64   07/25/64
O'Neill, Patrick died 04/11/65   04/13/65
O'Neill, Patrick Henry died 04/28/62   04/29/62
O'Neill, Robert died 05/12/62   05/14/62
O'Niel, Ellen married Solan, Michael 01/27/61   02/05/61
```

O'Niel, Mary Ann died 12/21/61   12/23/61
O'Niell, Lottie died no date   10/31/65
O'Reilly, Bessie married Loveaire, H. F. 06/16/64   06/17/64
O'Reilly, Bessie married Loveaire, Harry F. 06/16/64   06/18/64
O'Reilly, Bessie married Loveaire, Harry F. 06/16/64   06/20/64
O'Reilly, Catherine Ann died 09/18/62   09/19/62
O'Roke, John married Gahagan, Annie 09/19/65   09/21/65
O'Rourke, Mary died 10/18/63   10/19/63
O'Rourke, William married Fletcher, Kate F. 10/09/64   10/13/64
O'Shea, Abby died 03/14/65   03/15/65
Oakes, James died 11/24/63   11/25/63
Oakes, Mollie C. married Griard, A. B. 11/09/65   11/10/65
Ochemey, Adeline died 12/05/65   12/07/65
Ockerme, Mary A. married Brown, Milton no date   08/05/63
Ockmay, Sarah Ann married Carroll, Henry 03/21/61   03/25/61
Ocstate, Nicholas died 05/17/64   05/18/64
Odell, Greenleaf N. married Clark, Mary C. 04/21/64   04/25/64
Odend'Hal, Kate Estelle married James, R. F. 01/14/61   01/15/61
Odend'Hal, Mary M. married Ferrat, John B. 01/14/61   01/15/61
Odenheimer, M. (Mrs.) died 07/23/65   07/24/65
Ody, Sarah Eliza died 12/10/62   12/12/62
Oehm, Francis F. married Bond, Anna Helena 12/15/64   12/17/64
Oelegrath, Louisa married Harmon, George 01/20/63   01/27/63
Oersler, Susan died 05/21/62   05/23/62
Oetter, Margaret Sophia married Boesche, William Henry 01/08/65   01/10/65
Oewns, Norvel W. married Reese, Emma S. 11/30/65   12/01/65
Offutt, Annie L. L. died 06/22/65   06/23/65
Offutt, James Columbus died 07/25/61   07/26/61
Offutt, William Albert died 05/21/63   05/22/63
Ogborn, Caleb died 02/13/63   03/19/63
Ogden, Virginia C. married Reynolds, Thomas 02/12/63   02/13/63
Oge, Phoebe died 06/27/64   06/28/64
Ogier, Warren N. died 05/14/65   05/16/65
Ogle, Elizabeth A. died 09/02/64   09/03/64
Ogle, James M. married Gardner, Mary E. 12/26/61   12/30/61
Ogle, Lillian died 11/22/63   11/23/63
Ogle, Mary E. married Holmes, Samuel 10/28/63   11/04/63
Ogle, Mary Elizabeth Virginia died 08/25/62   08/26/62
Ogle, Robert died 05/14/64   05/16/64
Ogle, Sarah Ann married Scott, Philip (Rev.) 10/17/65   10/19/65
Ogle, Victoria married Hayden, John Frances 10/10/65   10/14/65
Ohem, Kisziah M. (Mrs.) died 06/05/65   06/06/65
Ohlendorf, Johanna married Fahlen, Charles 06/11/61   06/12/61
Ohlendorf, Joseph C. married Eschbach, Mary Thresia 09/24/61   09/25/61
Ohlendorf, William G. married Eschbach, Margaret V. 10/11/65   10/12/65
Ohrenschall, Mary A. married Ziegler, Charles 03/13/65   03/14/65
Old, Mary J. (Mrs.) married Guthridge, John F. 05/02/65   05/03/65
Olden, Mary died 05/03/61   05/04/61
Oldham, Olivia R. married Holtz, John C. 04/30/65   05/03/65
Olds, Isaac (Cpt.) married Trigg, Kate 03/03/63   03/07/63
Oler, Henry married Holson, Harriet 07/31/65   08/02/65
Oler, Johnsey William died 01/29/63   01/31/63
Olive, John died 11/05/63   11/06/63
Oliver, Allen died 08/31/63   09/01/63

Oliver, Ann (Mrs.) died 07/09/63 07/10/63
Oliver, Annie M. F. married Barton, Philip A. 01/31/65 02/06/65
Oliver, Dolphus married Dorsey, Amanda 11/15/64 11/17/64
Oliver, Edward Eugene died 09/19/62 09/20/62
Oliver, Francis married Gebb, Mary A. 11/18/63 11/20/63
Oliver, Frank died 08/08/65 08/17/65
Oliver, Joseph L. died 01/02/65 01/04/65
Oliver, Nathan E. married Hughes, T. A. Augusta 02/25/63 06/20/63
Oliver, Rebecca E. (Mrs.) died 01/26/64 01/27/64
Oliver, Richard died 11/10/63 11/11/63
Oliver, Sarah Elizabeth married Hitchins, August 02/07/61 02/09/61
Oliver, Susan Emily died 09/23/63 09/24/63
Oliver, Susan Emily died 09/23/63 09/25/63
Oliver, William died 08/20/62 08/21/62
Oliver, William George died 08/30/65 09/02/65
Oliver, William James died 05/13/64 05/17/64
Oltmans, Maria married Zollinhafer, George 10/25/64 11/22/64
Omelea, Eliza married Doyle, Michael H. 03/30/65 05/22/65
Onderdonk, Harriette S. (Mrs.) died 08/22/61 08/23/61
Onion, E. Healy died 03/31/62 04/01/62
Onion, James B. J. died 09/21/64 09/22/64
Onion, James H. married Brooks, Celia C. 10/20/64 10/21/64
Onion, Sarah Ann died 09/12/61 09/13/61
Onion, W. F. H. died 12/02/64 12/05/64
Onion, William Rouse died 07/06/63 07/08/63
Onthank, Joseph died 05/02/64 05/03/64
Onthank, Joseph died 05/02/64 05/04/64
Onthank, Margaret (Mrs.) died 05/13/64 05/14/64
Onthank, Mary (Mrs.) died 02/14/63 02/16/63
Opel, John T. married Brooks, Mary C. 09/29/63 10/01/63
Opitz, George died 02/20/64 02/23/64
Opitz, John married Rentz, Elizabeth M. 09/06/63 09/22/63
Oppenheimer, D. S. married Leoplod, Jenny 11/06/64 11/09/64
Oppenheimer, David died 02/22/64 02/25/64
Oppenmyer, Anna Louise died 06/03/61 06/05/61
Opperhein, Hannah married Louis, Julius 01/05/65 02/08/65
Oram, James D. married Dawson, Emma J. 12/24/63 01/04/64
Oram, John H. died 09/03/61 09/11/61
Orchard, George W. died 02/08/65 02/11/65
Orem, Ann Rebecca married Long, William Lewis 08/29/61 09/05/61
Orem, Carrie Virginia died 08/04/63 08/05/63
Orem, Catherine married Kirk, George 06/05/63 06/16/63
Orem, Charles Albert died 08/19/63 08/20/63
Orem, Elizabeth A. died 09/27/63 09/29/63
Orem, Frank D. died 06/09/61 06/10/61
Orem, Hugh S. died 02/01/65 02/02/65
Orem, Hugh S. died 02/01/65 02/03/65
Orem, James H. died 01/29/64 02/04/64
Orem, Josephine V. married Lee, William 06/30/64 07/07/64
Orem, Joshua married Howard, Eliza 09/20/64 10/06/64
Orem, Joshua married Howard, Elizabeth S. 09/20/64 09/27/64
Orem, Mary E. married Miles, William E. no date 07/12/64
Orem, Rachel (Mrs.) died 03/07/64 03/08/64
Orem, Sarah Ann married Goodman, William 06/28/65 06/30/65
Orem, Sarah Ella died 01/26/62 01/28/62

Orem, Sarah Ella died 01/26/62 01/29/62
Orem, William Morris married West, Helen E. 02/14/61 02/16/61
Orendorff, Kate married Howard, B. W. 06/21/64 06/23/64
Orme, Octavia married Russum, George M. 11/03/62 11/04/62
Orndorf, Robert Lee died 09/06/65 09/07/65
Orndorf, Wilson H. died 10/26/65 10/28/65
Orndorff, Howard Harvey died 09/15/64 09/16/64
Orndorff, John T. died 01/12/62 01/13/62
Orndorff, Kate Oliver died 01/31/65 02/02/65
Orndorff, Mary Ridgely died 01/22/62 01/24/62
Orr, Acey married Martin, Edward 07/08/62 01/07/63
Orr, Ellen C. married Russell, Willie H. 05/07/62 05/19/62
Orrell, Edward N. married Giles, Elvira G. 03/13/62 03/15/62
Orrick, John C. (Dr.) died 12/29/63 12/30/63
Orrick, Mollie A. married Entz, Andrew 11/22/65 11/24/65
Osborn, Alethia W. died 04/13/62 04/16/62
Osborn, America married Walling, Jacob 01/02/65 01/05/65
Osborn, Charles died 12/07/62 12/08/62
Osborn, George A. married Ambrose, Sallie A. 08/28/64 09/05/64
Osborn, Harriet died 02/11/65 02/16/65
Osborn, John died 04/04/65 05/02/65
Osborn, Louis Schley died 02/26/65 02/28/65
Osborn, Matilda U. married Marshall, H. 06/16/64 06/18/64
Osborn, Thomas died 06/04/63 06/12/63
Osborn, W. H. (Dr.) married Zell, Louisa M. 01/06/63 01/12/63
Osborne, Henry married Leonard, Angelina (Mrs.) 09/30/64 10/03/64
Osbourn, Sobina married Rohner, Louis P. 02/02/64 02/09/64
Osburn, Emory W. married Brown, Mary H. 10/25/64 11/03/64
Osburn, Hannah died 01/19/61 01/25/61
Osgodby, Mary died 12/22/61 12/24/61
Osing, George Henry died 11/24/65 11/25/65
Osing, H. Francis died 12/24/61 12/25/61
Osmonde, Julian married Fisher, Alcester A. 12/24/63 12/31/63
Ostendorf, Henry married Debring, Mary 05/13/62 05/15/62
Ostendorf, J. A. married Getty, Virginia A. 07/02/62 07/04/62
Ostendorf, Theodore died 03/12/64 03/15/64
Oster, Kate married Fulton, James 01/19/64 02/09/64
Ostlip, Samuel W. married Carter, Hannah J. 11/08/64 11/14/64
Oswald, Ann (Mrs.) died 07/18/62 05/05/64
Oswinkle, Joseph married Hammon, Susana 02/08/64 02/10/64
Otis, George married McGrowling, Margaret M. 06/01/64 06/04/64
Ott, George F. married Elsroad, Lennie 01/31/61 04/05/61
Ott, Kate E. married Pedrick, George G. 04/30/62 05/03/62
Ott, Kate E. married Pedrick, George G. 04/30/62 05/05/62
Ottenburger, Joseph died 02/17/64 02/23/64
Otter, S. Virginia married Warburton, Fred J. 04/11/65 04/12/65
Otterson, James died 08/27/62 08/28/62
Otterson, Jane S. died 10/20/62 10/21/62
Ould, Charles E. E. died 11/17/63 12/29/63
Ould, Henry E. died 01/29/61 01/30/61
Ould, Perry N. died 08/18/63 08/19/63
Oursien, Matilda P. married Bortle, Lysander 12/15/64 12/17/64
Oursler, Annie M. died 06/20/64 06/29/64
Oursler, Charles W. died 11/18/63 11/19/63
Oursler, John E. married Holton, Jane A. 04/25/64 09/27/64

Oursler, Maggie married Kendell, Charles 07/30/62   09/22/62
Over, Alexander died 11/16/64   11/17/64
Over, John H. died 10/01/64   10/03/64
Overacre, John W. married Day, Juliet S. 12/25/65   12/30/65
Overbeck, Bertha died 02/26/61   02/28/61
Owen, Edith died 02/01/65   02/02/65
Owen, Jane died 04/12/65   04/13/65
Owen, Jane died 04/12/65   04/14/65
Owen, Joseph W. (Cpt.) married McCann, Mary R. 10/13/64   11/15/64
Owen, Laura A. married Hobbs, William H. H. 12/18/62   12/24/62
Owen, Lizzie J. married Jones, Henry C. 01/29/63   02/07/63
Owen, Mary E. married Barnsley, J. D. 05/24/64   05/27/64
Owen, Thomas married Williams, Mary A. 03/09/65   03/11/65
Owen, Thomas G. died 12/02/64   12/03/64
Owen, William H. married Russell, Harriet H. 12/18/62   12/23/62
Owens, (Mrs. Owen G.) died 06/04/63   06/06/63
Owens, Ann married Donahue, B. O. 04/19/61   05/28/61
Owens, Augustus G. W. (Dr.) died 06/25/65   06/29/65
Owens, Basil married Askins, Eleanora 10/18/64   10/20/64
Owens, Baziel married Bayly, Henrietta (Mrs.) 12/17/62   12/17/62
Owens, Betsy married Reilly, John 11/26/63   12/15/63
Owens, Bettie A. married Byrd, F. Marion 01/21/64   01/29/64
Owens, Charles H. married McCrieght, Sarah 11/08/64   11/10/64
Owens, Elizabeth A. married Longley, Joshua 09/09/63   09/11/63
Owens, Fobert (Cpt.) died 07/22/65   07/24/65
Owens, Francis died 11/07/61   11/11/61
Owens, Francis died 01/01/65   01/02/65
Owens, George died 11/03/63   11/04/63
Owens, James died 07/06/62   07/07/62
Owens, James E. died 10/22/63   10/27/63
Owens, Jane (Mrs.) died 06/24/64   06/25/64
Owens, John married Johnson, Ann Maria 12/18/62   12/19/62
Owens, Joseph R. (Dr.) married Zimmerman, Roberto V. 11/24/63   11/26/63
Owens, Maggie A. married Mouton, John D. 01/19/64   01/23/64
Owens, Margaret died 10/10/61   10/11/61
Owens, Martha Davis married Meekins, Joseph Augustus 11/05/62   11/06/62
Owens, Martha E. married Nutwell, James E. 04/09/61   04/16/61
Owens, Mary died 11/12/65   11/13/65
Owens, Mary Ann married Thompson, Thomas H. 07/16/65   07/19/65
Owens, Peter married Mullin, Elizabeth 10/15/61   10/16/61
Owens, Philip married Kepler, Elizabeth Ann 05/08/64   07/23/64
Owens, Robert Dawson died 01/17/65   01/28/65
Owens, Roberto V. (Mrs.) died 09/07/64   09/10/64
Owens, Sabina married Pollard, David M. 10/29/63   11/03/63
Owens, Sallie married Jamison, Daniel 07/23/65   07/27/65
Owens, Sallie M. died 08/28/63   08/29/63
Owens, Thomas A. married Dodson, Maggie A. 02/05/63   02/10/63
Owens, William (Capt.) died 07/20/63   07/21/63
Owens, Willie A. died 12/21/63   12/22/63
Owings, Basal married Baily, Ann Rebecca (Mrs.) 12/11/62   01/05/63
Owings, Caroline died 01/03/64   01/04/64
Owings, Catherine (Mrs.) died 03/19/63   03/21/63
Owings, Clementina died 10/17/62   10/22/62
Owings, Elisha married Mariene, Mary L. 11/17/64   11/19/64
Owings, Eliza H. died 03/05/61   03/07/61

Owings, Ettie May died 12/12/61   12/20/61
Owings, Henry W. married Sunderland, Rachel A. 11/27/61   11/28/61
Owings, Isabella married Medcalf, Francis 06/06/65   06/15/65
Owings, James E. died 10/22/63   10/23/63
Owings, Jane married Hutchings, J. T. 10/11/64   10/12/64
Owings, John married Harp, Sarah J. 02/28/64   03/01/64
Owings, Laura married Mackenzie, Thomas G. (Dr.) 02/17/63   02/28/63
Owings, Laura married Mackenzie, Thomas G. (Dr.) 02/17/63   03/03/63
Owings, Mary C. married Busch, William H. 04/08/61   04/13/61
Owings, Matilda Dye died 04/01/63   04/03/63
Owings, Matilda Dye died 04/01/63   04/04/63
Owings, Richard married Simms, Mary J. 11/19/63   03/01/64
Owings, Ruth died 05/08/65   05/13/65
Owings, Samuel Jene died 07/27/62   07/29/62
Owings, Sophia R. married Conn, Silas W. 01/15/63   01/22/63
Owings, Thomas died 02/19/63   03/07/63
Owings, U. G. married Norris, Fannie 08/14/62   08/20/62
Oyeman, Anna C. M. (Mrs.) died 01/15/65   01/17/65
Ozmon, Mary M. married Johnson, Henry Clay 02/13/62   02/14/62
Pabst, A. married Horn, Annie E. 01/16/62   01/28/62
Paca, Harriet died 12/03/61   12/05/61
Packie, Alexander, Jr. married Hubbard, Mary A. 07/14/65   08/15/65
Paddington, Edward died 04/17/62   04/19/62
Paddington, Isabella married Gigg, William D. 02/08/64   02/09/64
Paddington, Martha married Reynolds, John R. 09/13/64   11/19/64
Padgette, Mary Elizabeth died 09/25/63   09/26/63
Page, Carrie Virginia died 08/19/63   08/20/63
Page, Sophia died 08/14/65   08/15/65
Page, Thomas Taylor married Whitlock, Maria Bacon 11/02/63   11/04/63
Pagels, Rosina died 03/31/62   04/01/62
Paine, Allen Trust died 06/23/64   06/25/64
Paine, James R. died 08/25/63   08/27/63
Paine, Mary Virginia died 07/27/63   07/28/63
Paine, William Henry died 02/01/61   02/08/61
Pairo, Jane Duncan died 04/12/61   04/17/61
Pairo, Jane Duncan died 04/12/61   04/16/61
Paisal, Minnie died 02/12/62   02/22/62
Paiste, Eliza died 04/17/61   04/19/61
Pakie, William died 07/26/64   07/27/64
Palagano, D. married Green, Sarah G. 11/24/63   11/28/63
Palmer, Ann (Mrs.) died 11/19/63   11/28/63
Palmer, Catherine died 11/21/63   11/23/63
Palmer, Charley Smith died 11/17/63   11/20/63
Palmer, Edward died 02/25/64   02/27/64
Palmer, Edward T. died 02/14/62   02/15/62
Palmer, Elizabeth B. married Fowler, John B. 12/17/63   12/19/63
Palmer, Fanny D. married Wilson, William H. 07/02/65   07/12/65
Palmer, Harriet (Mrs.) died 05/31/65   06/05/65
Palmer, Harriet B. married Pollett, Edward D. 07/20/65   07/22/65
Palmer, Mary (Mrs.) died 12/11/64   12/14/64
Palmer, Mary C. died 03/30/63   04/01/63
Palmer, Mary C. died 03/30/63   04/02/63
Palmer, Mary Virginia died 08/15/62   08/16/62
Palmer, Moses died 09/27/64   10/03/64
Palmer, Nellie Lee died 06/09/64   06/10/64

Palmer, Sarah H. died 04/19/64 05/04/64
Palmer, William C. married Davis, M. R. 03/07/61 03/13/61
Palmer, William C. died 07/07/65 07/08/65
Pamphellion, William H. married Deford, Mary E. 08/06/65 08/10/65
Pamphilion, Margaret married Lawton, Richard 05/19/61 05/22/61
Pancoast, Martha died 07/27/64 07/28/64
Pancoast, N. F. married Hoff, Mary E. 02/21/61 02/25/61
Pancoast, Sallie W. married Richardson, Samuel T. 11/25/63 11/28/63
Pannell, Isabell W. married Strausbaugh, A. Henry 10/30/62 11/03/62
Pannell, Susan (Mrs.) died 04/30/62 05/08/62
Paraway, Amanda E. married Wolford, Thomas L. 07/06/64 07/08/64
Paraway, Oliver, died 08/28/61 08/30/61
Pardee, John A. died 09/19/62 09/20/62
Pardoe, Robert A. married Henderson, Catherine A. 03/21/65 03/28/65
Pardoe, William married Grainger, Mary Frances 07/21/64 07/23/64
Parish, William married Whiteley, Sarah E. 10/12/64 10/15/64
Parish, William Howard married 11/09/63 11/11/63
Parker, Ann Mary died 09/09/61 09/11/61
Parker, Anna E. died 05/21/61 05/27/61
Parker, Clara died 04/24/64 04/27/64
Parker, Edward M. died 06/27/61 08/22/61
Parker, Elias married Shutler, Mary Elizabeth 11/24/63 11/28/63
Parker, Elizabeth married Brown, Zachariah 03/17/63 03/21/63
Parker, Foxhall A. (USN) married Donaldson, Caroline 10/20/63 10/22/63
Parker, George W. married Springman, Hannah R. 08/16/65 08/19/65
Parker, Harriet married Lewis, Samuel D. 01/02/62 01/08/62
Parker, Henry died 03/21/61 03/22/61
Parker, James H. married Lee, Alice 06/25/61 06/26/61
Parker, Jane (Mrs.) died 04/17/63 04/18/63
Parker, John died 09/19/64 09/27/64
Parker, John C. died 12/05/63 12/07/63
Parker, John W. died 11/05/63 11/06/63
Parker, John Wesley died 08/06/65 08/07/65
Parker, Josephine V. married Jones, Alfred T. 09/27/65 09/29/65
Parker, Julia F. married Danna, John 03/07/65 04/15/65
Parker, Richard died 07/11/65 07/12/65
Parker, Selena married Jackson, Hezekiah 11/19/63 11/21/63
Parker, Susanna died 10/03/62 10/04/62
Parker, Thomas Yearly died 08/20/61 08/22/61
Parker, William E. died 12/23/63 12/30/63
Parker, William H. died 11/08/62 11/10/62
Parker, William H. died 03/13/64 03/15/64
Parkes, Catharine (Mrs.) died 04/30/63 05/02/63
Parkes, Mary A. married Marshall, Joseph M. 02/28/65 03/14/65
Parkhill, Julius B. died 07/02/65 07/03/65
Parkhill, Robert died 08/02/64 08/03/64
Parkhill, Robert died 08/02/64 08/04/64
Parkhill, Robert married Carr, Matilda 10/25/65 10/26/65
Parkhill, William H. died 03/28/64 03/29/64
Parkhurst, Ellen Gilman died 11/22/63 11/23/63
Parkhurst, Pardon C. married Moore, Permelia 07/02/64 07/08/64
Parkhurst, Willie Andy died 08/13/65 08/15/65
Parkill, Annie M. died 11/04/61 11/05/61
Parkinson, Dora died 07/07/65 07/08/65
Parkinson, Henrietta (Mrs.) died 08/24/63 08/26/63

Parkinson, James died 03/25/64 03/26/64
Parks, David died 10/19/62 10/20/62
Parks, Edward Furlong died 03/21/64 03/22/64
Parks, Florence Amanda died 08/03/63 08/04/63
Parks, Francis Marion died 06/02/62 06/05/62
Parks, Francis S. married Lambert, Margaret A. 09/11/61 09/13/61
Parks, Henrietta married Piper, Richard M. 09/25/61 09/28/61
Parks, Ida married Woolsey, Carey 10/19/65 11/07/65
Parks, Matilda married Schaeffer, W. C. 10/09/65 10/17/65
Parks, Samuel James died 09/21/64 09/23/64
Parks, William B. died 11/12/64 11/18/64
Parks, William H. H. married Smith, Celia 09/27/63 09/28/63
Parks, William H. H. married Smith, Cecelia 10/19/63 04/07/64
Parlet, Henry J. married Kenny, Mary 05/28/62 06/04/62
Parlett, Benjamin J. married Stewart, Emma J. 07/03/63 07/06/63
Parlett, Benjamin J. married Stewart, Emma J. 07/03/63 07/07/63
Parlett, Elizabeth died 11/07/62 11/08/62
Parlett, Elizabeth (Mrs.) died 11/09/63 11/10/63
Parlett, Elizabeth A. married Cook, Lewis E. 07/02/63 07/31/63
Parlett, Lavinia died 10/27/63 10/29/63
Parlett, Lavinia (Mrs.) died 09/11/63 09/12/63
Parlett, Moses married Welsh, Matilda E. H. 05/19/64 05/20/64
Parlett, William J. married Amoss, Anna R. 12/21/65 12/22/65
Parnell, William H. died 12/03/62 12/05/62
Parr, Elizabeth died 02/09/61 02/13/61
Parr, Jane A. (Mrs.) died 09/04/63 09/05/63
Parr, John Newton died 12/28/63 12/29/63
Parr, Margaret (Mrs.) died 01/04/63 01/06/63
Parr, Rachel married Dean, John 03/01/64 03/07/64
Parren, Margaret Ann married Mullinfaux, Basil R. 11/27/62 12/01/62
Parris, Dennis married Freemon, Minty (Mrs.) 04/12/63 04/18/63
Parrish, Edward married Woodfield, Kate 12/16/62 12/23/62
Parrish, John married Ware, Mary C. 01/15/63 01/21/63
Parrish, Mordecai died 11/30/64 12/01/64
Parrott, Frank married Fisher, Mary Anna 06/03/62 06/06/62
Parrott, George W. (Cpt.) died no date 08/15/64
Parrott, Joseph J. married Read, Sarah Osgood 08/29/61 08/30/61
Parrott, William Stuart died 09/06/63 09/15/63
Parry, James O. D. married West, Amelia 08/10/62 09/02/62
Parry, William Davidson died 08/19/63 08/21/63
Parsley, Mary Sophia married Shipley, William B. 04/28/63 04/30/63
Parson, Fannie May died 05/28/64 05/31/64
Parsons, Almira G. married Hardester, William B. 09/02/61 09/04/61
Parsons, Charles Helen died 09/11/64 09/12/64
Parsons, Elizabeth died 03/08/62 03/13/62
Parsons, Harriett died 08/25/65 08/28/65
Parsons, James died 11/13/63 11/14/63
Parsons, Joseph died 10/31/65 11/01/65
Parsons, L. married Vickers, Mary A. 12/13/64 12/15/64
Parsons, Mary Belle died 09/13/62 09/16/62
Parsons, Nellie W. married Knapp, F. H. (Capt.) 03/04/65 05/04/65
Parsons, Sarah Ann died 10/17/62 10/23/62
Parsons, Thomas C. died 04/12/64 04/13/64
Parsons, William married Gosnell, Mary Emma 09/04/64 09/10/64
Parsons, William married Black, Ezelia 10/24/65 10/26/65

Partington, Richard M. married Grimes, Barbara E. 06/30/64   07/02/64
Parton, John W. married Johnson, Sidney 07/04/61   07/06/61
Partridge, Jennie E. married Billings, Henry J. 04/03/63   04/09/63
Partridge, John died 04/04/64   04/05/64
Partridge, N. C. married Groves, M. A. 07/09/63   07/22/63
Pascal, Addie A. married Jefferson, John B. H. 04/05/65   04/08/65
Pascal, David died 12/16/63   12/17/63
Pascal, James, L. P. (Capt.) died 07/03/65   07/04/65
Pascal, Peter Alexander died 02/18/63   02/19/63
Paschal, Mary Ann died 06/17/62   06/20/62
Paschal, Mary Ann died 06/17/62   06/27/62
Pascoe, Elizabeth married Harrop, Charles 12/15/64   12/16/64
Pasquay, Fredericka died 08/13/62   08/15/62
Pasquay, Jacob died 03/28/63   03/30/63
Passano, Alexander died 07/08/63   07/09/63
Passano, Joseph married Crawford, Parthenia S. 04/07/63   04/10/63
Passano, Joseph died 05/26/65   05/27/65
Passano, Joseph J. died 03/13/65   03/15/65
Pasterfield, Martha A. married Coombes, Richard J. 09/18/64   09/20/64
Pasterfield, Martha A. married Debow, Christian 12/13/65   12/23/65
Pasterfield, Sally W. married Thomas, Edwin 10/23/64   11/05/64
Pasters, Francis died 12/16/64   12/19/64
Pate, Mary Jane Geneva died 09/24/64   09/28/64
Paterson, Margaret M. married Cummins, Robert Keys 06/02/64   06/13/64
Patien, W., Jr. died 10/27/65   10/30/65
Patrick, George C. married Ford, Ann 07/16/65   08/05/65
Patrick, M. A. married Morrison, F. D. 07/31/65   08/11/65
Patrick, Thomas L. (Dr.) married Brokel, Mary 06/21/64   06/28/64
Patterson, Agnes Reed died 09/14/64   10/08/64
Patterson, Agnes Reid died 09/14/64   09/16/64
Patterson, Alice M. married Barry, H. A. 10/12/65   10/24/65
Patterson, Amelia married Brown, Augustus 04/06/64   04/07/64
Patterson, Benjamin George died 11/04/61   11/08/61
Patterson, Binnie G. married Kemp, Thomas E. 11/21/65   11/25/65
Patterson, Edward died 09/24/65   09/26/65
Patterson, Ellen B. married Nixon, Alfred (Dr.) 04/30/63   05/02/63
Patterson, Fannie Woodward married Beard, Henry Clay 09/24/62   09/27/62
Patterson, Frank W. married Mason, Helen F. 06/28/65   07/08/65
Patterson, Isaac M. married Linton, Fanny G. 09/17/63   09/18/63
Patterson, Jacob died 08/30/65   08/31/65
Patterson, James died 04/02/65   04/03/65
Patterson, James died 04/02/65   04/04/65
Patterson, James B. died 08/29/63   08/31/63
Patterson, Jane died 12/11/65   12/13/65
Patterson, John died 06/11/64   06/13/64
Patterson, John Allen died 03/04/65   03/06/65
Patterson, John Allen died 03/04/65   03/07/65
Patterson, John Burris died 08/16/63   11/03/63
Patterson, Kate married Mahon, John 05/28/65   06/01/65
Patterson, Laura J. married Working, William M. 09/10/61   09/17/61
Patterson, Laura V. married Paxton, John W. 04/06/65   04/13/65
Patterson, Martha married Edds, Isaac 10/18/63   10/20/63
Patterson, Mary Hawkins died 12/25/62   12/27/62
Patterson, Rebecca M. married Fallon, Daniel J. 10/10/65   10/17/65
Patterson, Robert married Devinney, Mary Ann 01/15/63   01/17/63

Patterson, Robert married Hackett, Louisa C. 07/21/64 07/22/64
Patterson, Sophia died 05/31/61 06/01/61
Patterson, William married McDowney, Ellen 07/02/61 07/04/61
Patterson, William died 10/14/61 10/16/61
Patterson, William died 07/18/64 07/19/64
Patterson, William died 07/18/64 07/20/64
Patterson, William died 08/25/64 02/21/65
Patterson, William A. died 01/13/63 01/15/64
Patterson, William P. died 11/16/65 11/18/65
Pattison, A. Augustus married Byus, Laura Estelle 12/02/63 12/04/63
Pattison, John R. married Devalis, Emily 12/21/65 12/29/65
Pattison, Mary E. married Brashear, William G. 03/02/65 03/06/65
Pattison, Sarah A. (Mrs.) married Strahler, John W. 01/08/65 01/28/65
Patton, Agnes married Aitken, Robert 10/20/63 10/22/63
Patton, Elizabeth (Mrs.) died 11/05/63 11/06/63
Patton, Elizabeth (Mrs.) died 11/05/63 11/07/63
Patton, Robert J. (Dr.) married Taylor, Kate Elvira 01/24/61 01/25/61
Patton, Sarah Elizabeth married Wittbecker, John 11/18/62 11/26/62
Patton, William G. died 09/05/61 09/06/61
Paul, Agnes Ann Carter died 04/15/64 04/19/64
Paul, Conrad L. died 04/17/64 04/18/64
Paul, Conrad L. died 04/17/64 04/19/64
Paul, Eliza Ann (Mrs.) died 08/04/63 08/05/63
Paul, Emily died 12/10/61 12/14/61
Paul, James died 02/27/63 03/16/63
Paul, John married Imhoff, Margaret 04/09/65 04/12/65
Paul, Nicholas Forester died 03/07/63 03/10/63
Paul, Paulina married Rosello, Antonio 02/23/65 02/27/65
Pawley, Victoria A. married Shipley, Lovelace no date 02/27/64
Pawlrey, Alfred David died 07/22/65 07/24/65
Paxton, John W. married Patterson, Laura V. 04/06/65 04/13/65
Paxton, Laura V. (Mrs.) died 07/09/65 07/15/65
Paxton, Lewis Demonia died 03/06/61 03/28/61
Paxton, Zelia E. married Bowersox, David M. 08/17/62 08/29/62
Payne, George C. married Mitchell, Laura P. 06/17/63 06/19/63
Payne, Marion married Callender, George W. 11/20/62 12/12/62
Payne, Mary Ann married Wiley, James A. 01/20/63 01/27/63
Payne, Mary Catherine married Childs, Zachariah W. 05/05/63 05/08/63
Payne, William T. married Bateman, Sydney A. 11/24/64 11/29/64
Peaco, Mary Jane died 06/07/64 09/06/64
Peacock, Ellen E. died 12/07/61 12/12/61
Peacock, Emma Jane died 07/22/61 07/23/61
Peacock, Nellie Moore died 08/30/64 09/12/64
Peacock, Samuel died 04/03/62 04/04/62
Peale, Martha died 05/13/62 05/14/62
Pearce, Charles married Phillips, Sarah E. 08/18/64 08/22/64
Pearce, Elizabeth died 07/24/62 07/25/62
Pearce, George Wayson died 05/12/61 05/15/61
Pearce, Jacob M. married Holmes, Laura J. 04/10/61 04/11/61
Pearce, James Henry married Burly, Charlotte G. 09/26/61 10/01/61
Pearce, John F. married Wheeler, Annie E. 01/16/65 02/20/65
Pearce, John P. died 05/30/64 06/02/64
Pearce, Joseph S. died 11/07/62 11/10/62
Pearce, Lydia (Mrs.) died 07/01/64 07/02/64
Pearce, Mary A. died 01/16/62 01/18/62

Pearce, Mary A. married Moxley, Moses 12/22/64   12/24/64
Pearce, Mary Ann married Watts, Allen 09/09/62   09/10/62
Pearce, Mary Ann Emery died 09/14/63   09/15/63
Pearce, Mary Virginia (Mrs.) died 05/26/64   05/27/64
Pearce, Walter Augustus died 06/03/63   06/11/63
Pearce, William C. died 12/31/63   01/01/64
Pearl, William L. married McBee, Emily F. 08/10/65   08/14/65
Pearson, Amy died 02/05/63   02/06/63
Pearson, Charles B. married Seebol, M. Lizzie 10/06/63   10/29/63
Pearson, George S. died 05/07/64   05/09/64
Pearson, Harry C. died 05/25/64   05/26/64
Pearson, Henry married Peters, Mary A. 09/04/61   09/09/61
Pearson, James H. married Hardy, Mary E. 12/21/65   12/23/65
Pearson, Levi, Jr. married Thompson, Mahala J. 12/05/65   12/19/65
Pearson, Robert W. married Smith, Julia A. 06/02/62   06/12/62
Pearson, Sarah E. married Hudson, Edward 09/21/64   09/27/64
Pearson, William married Boyle, Susan 04/18/64   04/21/64
Peary, S. Elizabeth married Baker, Nelson R. 09/11/61   09/13/61
Pease, Mary F. married Wheeler, Edward 02/08/65   06/01/65
Pease, Sarah Anna died 10/20/63   11/06/63
Peaster, Louisa M. married Smith, Thomas J. 02/10/63   02/11/63
Peat, William married Peterson, Mary V. 02/16/64   02/22/64
Peck, Daniel Coker married Amos, Sarah Jane 06/25/63   06/27/63
Peck, David A. J. married McLain, Sarah E. 08/23/65   08/26/65
Peck, Henry died 02/13/65   02/14/65
Peck, John D. married Kennard, Marion A. 10/25/63   10/28/63
Peck, John D. died 01/21/65   01/23/65
Peck, John D. died 01/21/65   01/24/65
Peckocheck, John M. died 06/09/65   06/13/65
Pecor, Mary Alice died 09/22/62   09/23/62
Peddicord, Elizabeth A. married McNinch, Thomas 03/28/61   04/02/61
Pedicord, Theodore died 08/26/65   08/28/65
Pedrich, Kate Estella died 12/03/62   12/17/62
Pedrick, George G. married Ott, Kate E. 04/30/62   05/03/62
Pedrick, George G. married Ott, Kate E. 04/30/62   05/05/62
Pedro, Joseph died 11/14/61   11/16/61
Peduezzi, Florence Ella died 03/18/64   03/19/64
Peduzzi, Catharine (Mrs.) died 01/26/65   01/27/65
Peduzzi, Emma Virginia died 11/24/65   11/25/65
Peerce, Robert C. married Rowen, S. Elizabeth 08/05/65   08/08/65
Peirce, Letitia (Mrs.) died 08/09/64   08/10/64
Peirce, Letitia (Mrs.) died 08/09/64   08/11/64
Peirce, Mary Lee died 09/07/63   09/09/63
Peircy, Samuel Coe died 11/12/64   11/18/64
Peirsol, Mary died 12/02/65   12/06/65
Pell, Theresa C. married King, Benjamin B. 04/18/61   07/31/61
Pelton, Sarah A. died 02/17/65   02/18/65
Pembroke, Sallie married Schofield, Joseph 04/10/64   04/14/64
Pendergast, James F. married Wilson, Minnie 11/03/64   11/05/64
Pendergast, John died 03/25/64   03/26/64
Pendergast, Margaret died 09/05/62   09/06/62
Pendexter, Henry, Jr. died 03/17/65   03/18/65
Pendleton, Bettie (Mrs.) died 03/24/63   03/28/63
Pendleton, David E. married Slater, Laura C. 03/14/64   04/21/64
Pendleton, Edmund H. married Marcy, Cameia 04/28/64   05/03/64

Pendleton, Nathaniel Greene died 06/15/61 06/17/61
Pendleton, Philip died 09/06/65 09/07/65
Pendleton, Philip died 09/06/65 09/08/65
Pendleton, Robert W. died 04/17/61 04/19/61
Pendleton, Virenda A. married Sappington, George W. 10/24/65 10/25/65
Pendlton, Sally Boyd married Van Rensselaer, Eugene 04/26/65 04/28/65
Penington, Andrew John died 08/05/64 08/08/64
Penington, Howard died 08/03/64 08/04/64
Penn, Elizabeth died 08/17/62 08/18/62
Penn, George W. married Zeigler, Sarah Lizzie 03/15/63 03/26/63
Penn, Jacob, Jr. married Leddon, Anna R. 11/26/63 12/07/63
Penn, Jacob, Sr. married Justice, Emma C. 10/19/65 10/21/65
Penn, John W. married Swigent, Annie G. S. 10/06/63 10/14/63
Penn, Lucy Elizabeth married Leach, J. Holland (Sgt.) 12/01/63 12/08/
Penn, Mary Eliza died 07/23/65 07/25/65
Penn, Matthew J. A. married Curry, Parmilia F. 10/06/63 10/09/63
Penniman, Henrietta died 03/07/64 03/08/64
Penning, Sylvester E. married Markland, Alice E. 06/02/63 06/11/63
Pennington, Ann (Mrs.) died 09/24/63 09/26/63
Pennington, Charles P. died 10/30/65 11/04/65
Pennington, Cora Virginia died 01/20/62 01/23/62
Pennington, Elizabeth A. married Nagle, Joseph H. 10/12/65 10/14/65
Pennington, Eugene Whitely died 02/17/65 02/18/65
Pennington, John F. died 09/18/63 09/26/63
Pennington, Mary Ann (Mrs.) died 12/27/63 12/28/63
Penny, Susan Emeline died 04/03/64 04/13/64
Pentland, Ann died 10/11/63 10/13/63
Pentland, Roseanna died 07/08/62 07/10/62
Penty, Agnes Steward died 12/08/62 12/09/62
Pentz, (female infant) died 07/27/61 07/29/61
Pentz, Catherine died 06/09/65 06/12/65
Pentz, Jacob H. died 09/01/65 09/02/65
Pentz, John died 08/02/62 08/05/62
Pentz, Laura L. married Dodge, Asaph 10/03/65 10/07/65
Pentz, Lily V. died 05/15/64 05/17/64
Pentz, Maggie A. married Knighton, John F. 11/17/64 11/18/64
Pentz, Martha A. married Holden, Daniel L. 09/12/65 09/14/65
Pentz, P. Henry died 02/15/64 02/16/64
Pentz, Rachel D. died 09/22/65 09/23/65
Pentz, Samuel Jennings died 08/01/62 08/02/62
Peppler, Elizabeth C. died 08/14/65 08/16/65
Peppler, Elizabeth C. died 08/14/65 08/17/65
Peppler, Elizabeth C. (Mrs.) died 08/14/65 08/15/65
Peppler, Mary married Muhlhofer, William F. 02/05/61 02/12/61
Percon, Ellen married Davis, John 06/16/62 06/19/62
Perdue, Mary E. married Quinlin, Charles H. 05/25/65 05/26/65
Perdue, Rachel (Mrs.) died 07/18/63 08/05/63
Perdue, Sarah J. died 03/04/62 06/25/62
Peregoy, (Miss) married Ahler, George E. 02/19/64 02/23/64
Peregoy, Althea died 05/07/65 05/08/65
Peregoy, Calvin T. died 04/04/64 04/05/64
Peregoy, David B. died 12/18/65 12/21/65
Peregoy, Elizabeth C. died 11/17/65 11/18/65
Peregoy, Emma Ophelia died 01/31/63 02/02/63
Peregoy, Henrietta (Mrs.) married Davidson, Edward 06/09/64 09/19/64

Peregoy, John H. married Blunt, Sarah 12/28/62 12/30/62
Peregoy, Joseph died 02/25/61 02/26/61
Peregoy, Laura Virginia died 07/19/64 07/20/64
Peregoy, Nathan W. died 09/10/62 09/12/62
Peregoy, Robert H. died 09/02/63 09/03/63
Peregoy, Sarah T. died 02/09/65 02/10/65
Peregoy, William E. married Van Newkirk, Mary E. no date 03/10/63
Perigoy, A. J. married Kelley, Oliver J. 12/24/61 12/25/61
Perin, Charles B. died 01/20/64 01/21/64
Perin, Ida Brooks died 07/19/64 07/21/64
Perin, Olevia died 11/29/61 11/30/61
Perine, Benjamin Bond died 10/23/62 10/24/62
Perine, E. Glenn married Washington, Eliza 04/25/65 04/26/65
Perine, Eliza (Mrs.) died 11/10/65 11/11/65
Perine, Mary died 09/29/61 10/01/61
Perine, Mary died 09/29/61 10/02/61
Perine, Maulden died 05/30/65 05/31/65
Perine, Maulden died 05/30/65 06/01/65
Perine, Michaemma died 10/03/62 10/06/62
Perine, Sarah Jane married Bates, Martin 08/23/63 09/12/63
Perine, Thomas Harwood (Rev.) died 05/06/61 05/10/61
Perine, Thomson P. married Morrow, Lizzie C. 09/21/63 09/23/63
Perine, William B. died 05/08/63 05/11/63
Perine, William P. married Lee, Bessie 12/26/61 12/28/61
Perkens, Margaret Ann married Williams, James H. 01/29/63 01/31/63
Perkins, B. W. (Cpt.) died 10/29/62 11/01/62
Perkins, Charles married Malone, Hester 12/26/65 12/28/65
Perkins, E. married Tapp, George (Lt.) 05/07/64 09/09/64
Perkins, Elenor (Mrs.) died 08/05/63 08/06/63
Perkins, Elenor (Mrs.) died 08/05/63 08/08/63
Perkins, Elizabeth died 07/22/62 07/23/62
Perkins, Eugene T. married Wheatley, Elizabeth 06/17/62 06/23/62
Perkins, Henry C. married Work, Virlinda 08/10/65 08/12/65
Perkins, Laura E. died 03/01/64 03/05/64
Perkins, Mary married McCall, Hugh 11/05/65 11/11/65
Perkins, Mary E. married Wiley, William 01/01/62 03/17/65
Perkins, S. H. married Naudain, T. M. 03/06/65 03/15/65
Perkins, Sallie married Schmenner, J. Henry 12/04/60 05/02/61
Perkins, William married Hogister, Mary 06/02/62 06/06/62
Perks, John married Harvey, Hester Ann 02/05/64 03/25/64
Perl, Mary E. died 05/22/65 05/24/65
Perram, Charlotte H. married Smith, James 03/21/61 06/18/61
Perrin, Alice died 11/15/63 11/16/63
Perry, Albert died 09/16/61 09/17/61
Perry, Ancel F. C. married Love, Amelia H. 07/11/64 07/13/64
Perry, Anna S. married Schafer, John F. 10/19/64 05/16/65
Perry, Charles Dickerson died 08/07/65 08/08/65
Perry, Edward married Anderson, Henrietta 08/23/63 08/26/63
Perry, Ella Lee died 06/29/64 07/06/64
Perry, Ellen Mar married McGill, Edward M. 06/10/63 06/11/63
Perry, John died 12/02/64 12/03/64
Perry, Margaret married Diggs, Cyrus M. 03/22/64 03/23/64
Perry, Mary E. married Rosensteel, Theodore 05/02/61 05/04/61
Perry, Mary Frances died 08/06/64 08/08/64
Perry, Mary Francis married Ford, Robert 01/21/64 01/26/64

Perry, Mary Jane died 11/28/63 12/02/63
Perry, Susan E. L. (Mrs.) died 04/23/63 04/24/63
Perry, Susie Emma died 11/08/63 11/09/63
Perry, Thomas (Hon.) married Loney, E. Catherine 12/04/61 12/07/61
Perry, William J. married Martin, Hattie R. 02/21/61 02/22/61
Perryman, Isabella died 12/19/64 02/02/65
Personette, A. M. Rachel died 08/01/64 08/04/64
Personette, Georgeanna married Chambers, William W. 01/01/62 01/03/62
Perveil, Amelia died 05/29/63 05/30/63
Pery, Sue H. married Wilcox, William L., Jr. 06/25/63 06/29/63
Pescud, Edward (Capt.) died 04/06/64 04/07/64
Peter, P. Orange married Fizpatrick, Mary W. (Mrs.) 05/20/62 09/11/62
Peter, Park Custis died 04/23/61 04/27/61
Peters, C. George (Lt.) married Keen, Millicent L. 11/24/64 12/07/64
Peters, Eliza died 03/19/61 03/21/61
Peters, Elizabeth married Stanton, Samuel 03/30/64 04/05/64
Peters, Elizabeth (Mrs.) died 05/19/64 05/20/64
Peters, F. Amilia died 07/30/64 08/01/64
Peters, George died 03/16/63 03/18/63
Peters, George (Col.) died 08/29/65 09/01/65
Peters, John R. married Mahorney, Maria 07/26/63 08/08/63
Peters, John Richard died 09/09/64 09/10/64
Peters, Mary A. married Pearson, Henry 09/04/61 09/09/61
Peters, Rosina died 06/27/63 06/29/63
Peters, Sally died 06/15/61 06/19/61
Peters, Wilhelmina married Spindler, Henry 09/10/65 09/15/65
Peters, William died 12/16/62 12/18/62
Peters, William died 10/27/63 10/28/63
Peters, William died 11/21/63 11/23/63
Peters, William died 11/21/63 11/24/63
Peters, William Henry died 11/05/63 11/06/63
Peters, William Henry died 11/05/63 11/07/63
Peterson, Caroline M. married Marr, John G. 04/20/62 05/12/62
Peterson, Carrie married Dorman, J. Franklin 04/04/61 05/28/61
Peterson, Elizabeth died 11/08/62 11/10/62
Peterson, Estelle W. died 12/13/63 12/15/63
Peterson, Francis died 05/29/65 05/30/65
Peterson, Joseph died 01/24/65 02/09/65
Peterson, Martin died 04/27/63 04/28/63
Peterson, Mary V. married Peat, William 02/16/64 02/22/64
Peterson, Peter married Harrington, Catherine 08/13/65 08/15/65
Peterson, Thomas married Wilmer, Emily A. 04/19/64 04/21/64
Petherbridge, Benjamin F. died 06/13/64 06/16/64
Petherbridge, Emma J. married Dougherty, William C. 05/18/65 05/20/65
Petherbridge, Henry C. died 08/21/65 08/26/65
Petherbridge, William O. married Selvage, Maggie A. 11/25/61 11/30/61
Petinger, Joseph died no date 01/13/63
Petrie, Carrie A. married Sheppard, N. 02/26/64 03/19/64
Pettebone, Ella died 12/24/65 12/27/65
Pettebone, J., Jr. married Joyce, Josephine A. 03/28/61 04/12/61
Pettecord, Mary C. died 11/25/62 11/27/62
Petticord, Adeline married Taylor, John E. 11/27/64 11/29/64
Petticord, Catharine died 11/21/63 11/23/63
Petticord, Catharine married King, John C. 09/25/65 10/03/65
Petticord, Eliza J. died 11/14/63 11/16/63

Petticord, Elridge Fell died 01/07/61   01/10/61
Petticord, George W. married Bryan, Catherine 03/12/61   03/29/61
Petticord, John Morriss died 08/31/61   09/14/61
Petticord, Ruth (Mrs.) married Holmes, James 01/19/65   01/23/65
Pettigrew, Maria Looclace married Luber, Eugene N. 05/09/61   05/22/61
Pettinos, J. W. (Dr.) married Duval, Rena R. 03/08/63   03/26/63
Pettit, Isaac died 04/17/61   04/18/61
Petty, John S. married Hunt, Sallie A. 12/21/65   12/22/65
Petty, Robert died 03/13/62   03/15/62
Peyton, William died 03/24/64   03/25/64
Pfeiffer, Kate Rosenthal died 03/22/63   03/23/63
Pfifer, William married Mollman, Elizabeth 12/22/63   12/24/63
Pfleig, Lizzie married Rockaway, Henry 04/23/61   04/26/61
Pflounbacher, Mina married Degen, Solomon 03/13/61   03/14/61
Pfrom, Adam married Meinkranz, Catharine 10/18/63   10/30/63
Pfrom, Adam died 02/05/65   02/07/65
Phalan, Joseph married Fleming, Mary Anne 03/09/64   03/02/65
Phalin, Joseph married Fleming, Mary Anne 03/09/64   03/04/65
Phebus, Rosannna B. died 02/03/63   02/04/63
Phelan, Daniel L. married Cornor, Anna Maria 02/21/65   02/28/65
Phelan, Daniel L. married Corner, Anna Maria 02/21/65   03/01/65
Phelan, Lizzie T. married Franck, Martin V. B. 11/23/63   12/02/63
Phelan, Thomas Jefferson died 03/17/63   03/18/63
Phellen, Ellen married Been, Thomas C. 02/10/61   02/26/61
Phelps, Ann S. married Clarke, William P. 11/29/64   12/01/64
Phelps, Celia E. married Jean, William F. D. 09/17/63   09/19/63
Phelps, Elizabeth (Mrs.) died 11/20/63   11/24/63
Phelps, Emma D. died 01/10/62   01/13/62
Phelps, Isabel C. married Cromwell, Frank T. 02/06/62   02/08/62
Phelps, Joseph married Sisselberger, Averilla V. 04/22/62   05/01/62
Phelps, Joseph R. married Carroll, Eliza A. (Mrs.) 04/20/65   04/22/65
Phelps, Mary Ayres married Robbins, Horace W., Jr. 09/27/65   10/12/65
Phelps, William died 03/10/65   03/15/65
Phenix, B. C. Howard died 12/02/65   12/16/65
Phester, Kate married Henry, Joseph M. 11/15/65   11/17/65
Philes, Mary L. married Weitzel, Jacob 01/05/62   06/21/62
Philip, Louisa Adaline died 02/00/00   10/06/62
Philips, Hattie married Young, Charles Lewis 06/05/62   06/09/62
Philips, John L. married Williams, Melvina 06/24/65   07/27/65
Philips, Laura Virginia died 07/09/61   07/10/61
Phillips, B. F. married Barnes, Jennie 01/03/61   01/08/61
Phillips, Blanch died 12/13/63   12/15/63
Phillips, Catharine (Mrs.) died 12/23/63   12/24/63
Phillips, Charles C. married Thomas, Amanda A. 07/31/65   08/25/65
Phillips, Charles Henry died 10/13/65   10/14/65
Phillips, E. J. married Roberts, W. C. 12/22/63   02/05/64
Phillips, Elizabeth married Allen, William H. 11/16/62   12/02/62
Phillips, Emma (Mrs.) married Rupp, William 03/16/65   03/21/65
Phillips, Harriet E. married Day, Charles S. 07/06/65   07/08/65
Phillips, Henry M. married Kirkpatrick, Emma V. 03/23/63   12/28/63
Phillips, Howard Lee died 03/06/65   03/07/65
Phillips, Israel B. died 07/12/62   07/14/62
Phillips, J. A. married Lewis, Sarah F. 06/14/63   08/21/63
Phillips, James Henry died 03/20/63   03/21/63
Phillips, Jane H. died 09/27/65   09/28/65

Phillips, Jemima died 11/19/61   12/12/61
Phillips, Jennie married Bowen, John L. 04/02/63   05/20/63
Phillips, John died 02/27/63   03/05/63
Phillips, John (Cpt.) died 10/22/63   10/27/63
Phillips, John E. married Dailey, Sarah A. 08/26/64   11/01/64
Phillips, John W. married Huffington, Isabel S. 03/17/63   03/24/63
Phillips, Kate married Waiiz, Henry F. 10/12/62   10/30/62
Phillips, Lizzie married Harrison, George W. 12/06/60   02/12/61
Phillips, Llewellyn died 03/19/65   03/21/65
Phillips, Margaret died 01/27/63   01/29/63
Phillips, Margaret A. S. married Skinner, Willbur F. 06/29/62   07/04/62
Phillips, Margaret P. (Mrs.) died 03/30/64   04/05/64
Phillips, Mary E. married Stevenson, Henry S. 07/13/64   07/16/64
Phillips, Mary Ellen died 01/23/61   01/24/61
Phillips, Mary N. married Roberts, Edward T. 02/12/61   02/13/61
Phillips, Richard married Bolton, Anna L. 05/09/65   05/15/65
Phillips, Sarah (Mrs.) died 11/20/63   11/21/63
Phillips, Sarah E. married Pearce, Charles 08/18/64   08/22/64
Phillips, Wellsetta died 10/14/65   10/16/65
Phillips, William C. died 12/09/63   12/10/63
Phillips, William F., Sr. died 08/06/62   08/12/62
Phillips, William H. (USA) married Haupt, Mary E. 10/14/63   10/16/63
Phillips, William R. married Potter, Kate 11/03/63   11/07/63
Phillips, William S. died 06/04/62   06/06/62
Phipps, Bettie married Rodgers, Joseph W. 04/23/63   05/06/63
Phipps, Martha Ann married Ford, Samuel 09/22/63   09/26/63
Phipps, Richard H. married Starr, Martha F. 06/20/65   06/21/65
Phipps, William married Aisquith, Mary Elizabeth 09/27/61   10/08/61
Phipps, William died 02/26/64   02/27/64
Phoebus, Edwin died 05/28/61   05/30/61
Pic, Mary married Davey, Henry 01/17/61   01/23/61
Piccioli, Adelaide C. died 12/08/63   12/09/63
Piccioli, Joshua died 06/29/65   08/15/65
Pickering, Amanda E. married Farquhar, John C. 07/23/63   08/22/63
Pickering, John, Jr. died 05/15/63   05/26/63
Pickering, M. Cecelia married Jackson, J. Stewart 01/03/64   05/25/64
Pickering, William J. married Beam, Sarah E. 03/07/64   10/03/64
Pickett, John Franklin died 09/11/64   09/13/64
Pickett, Lucy E. married Firoved, Anderson H. 07/07/63   07/13/63
Pickett, Richard died 08/15/62   10/03/62
Pickett, Susie married Dotterweih, Frederick 06/08/65   06/12/65
Pickrell, John Franklin died 09/11/64   09/14/64
Piepe, Anna E. died 08/27/65   08/28/65
Pierce, Andrew J. died 03/05/61   03/06/61
Pierce, Daniel S. died 05/25/64   05/26/64
Pierce, George W. married Arnold, Madora W. 09/26/61   09/30/61
Pierce, George W. died 02/26/65   02/27/65
Pierce, George W. died 02/26/65   02/28/65
Pierce, H. Lindsley (M.D.) married Purington, Kate E. 03/24/62   04/15/
Pierce, James Robert died 06/01/61   06/07/61
Pierce, John married Davage, Belinda 05/09/61   05/11/61
Pierce, Louisa died 11/03/65   11/06/65
Pierce, Margaret A. married Gohegan, Phi'n 12/19/64   01/09/65
Pierce, Sarah A. married Riddle, Charles 05/13/63   05/15/63
Pierce, Villety (Mrs.) died 05/29/64   06/14/64

Piercey, Agnes Gertrude died 06/24/64   07/01/64
Piercy, Corp. George W. died 02/21/63   02/24/63
Piercy, Hannah E. died 03/30/61   04/03/61
Piercy, Samuel C. died 11/12/64   11/14/64
Pierol, Willie Thomas died 09/05/62   09/06/62
Pierpont, Emma Jane died 03/01/64   03/02/64
Pierpont, Isabela died 08/16/63   08/21/63
Pierpont, James Wesley died 09/02/65   09/05/65
Pierpont, Jane (Mrs.) married Royer, J. B. 10/20/65   11/04/65
Pierpont, Sarah E. married Lawrence, John W. no date   10/16/62
Pierpont, Thomas B. S. married Shinnick, Annie 02/21/61   12/02/61
Pierpont, Thomas B. S. married Shinnick, Annie 11/28/61   02/25/62
Pierpont, Thomas B. S. died 07/06/65   07/07/65
Pierson, John William Zebedee died 07/22/64   07/23/64
Pietsch, Christine A. died 10/25/61   10/26/61
Pifer, Adeline D. married Greene, Charles H. 09/10/62   09/12/62
Piggot, Lydia McDonough died 09/30/65   10/02/65
Piggott, Rebecca Snowden died 11/16/65   11/17/65
Pigman, Anna B. married Fisher, Robert A. 01/16/65   01/18/65
Pigott, Kate (Mrs.) died 08/02/63   08/03/63
Pike, Mary died 03/14/61   03/18/61
Pilcher, Joseph H. H. married McKelvy, Sarah Jane 01/03/65   01/18/65
Pilkerton, Elizabeth (Mrs.) died 10/27/65   10/28/65
Pillman, Edward died 09/02/65   09/04/65
Pilsbury, Mary H. died 03/24/63   03/26/63
Pilson, John T. married Chaney, Emma 04/13/65   05/13/65
Pinckney, Rebecca died 09/21/63   09/22/63
Pinckney, William died 08/04/61   08/06/61
Pindar, John H. C. married Wells, Isabella 04/29/62   05/01/62
Pindel, M. A. (Mrs.) married Shipley, A. P. 11/23/65   12/07/65
Pindell, Edward H. died 07/11/64   07/13/64
Pindell, Isaiah married Massey, Caroline 10/30/62   11/04/62
Pindell, M. Alice married Maclin, J. J. 01/10/65   02/07/65
Pindell, Philip (CSA) died 08/21/63   08/24/63
Pindell, Philip M. married Cooper, Sarah Catherine 04/04/64   04/07/64
Pindell, R. M. married Drury, Fanny 09/10/63   09/15/63
Pindell, Sarah died 09/05/62   09/12/62
Pindill, Philip McHarvey died 07/30/64   08/22/64
Pindle, Rosetta married Scott, John 12/23/61   12/25/61
Pineo, Mary D. died 05/04/64   05/05/64
Pinket, Joseph married More, Susan 12/24/64   12/26/64
Pinkney, Ann married Boone, Denis 09/17/65   09/23/65
Pinkney, Emily M. married Hanan, John S. 11/17/63   11/19/63
Pinkny, Frances married Brundon, Samuel 06/02/61   06/05/61
Pinkny, Francis married Brundon, Samuel 05/12/61   06/04/61
Pinney, William died 07/04/64   10/04/64
Piper, Charles Thomas died 05/26/63   05/27/63
Piper, Richard M. married Parks, Henrietta 09/25/61   09/28/61
Piper, Robert H. married Bayley, Eliza Jane 07/07/63   07/11/63
Piper, William T. married Coggins, Sarah C. 07/07/64   07/13/64
Pippin, Solomon married Vinton, Harriet A. 12/19/65   12/27/65
Piquett, Catharine Cecelia died 07/28/61   07/31/61
Piquett, Edgar Jackson died 08/14/64   08/16/64
Piquett, Edmond died 02/21/64   02/22/64
Piquett, Frank Ashby died 07/16/64   07/18/64

Piquett, Frank Ashby died 07/16/64 08/16/64
Pirres, Sarah E. married Brown, Isaiah 05/05/62 05/07/62
Pissen, Edward Leigh died 08/17/61 08/20/61
Pitcher, Kate (Mrs.) died 02/13/63 02/16/63
Pitcher, Thomas J. married Morrow, Jennie A. 09/24/63 09/30/63
Pitcher, Willie died 03/26/64 03/28/64
Pitt, Lewis T. died 03/27/63 03/28/63
Pitt, Mary J. married Yingling, Henry 10/05/65 10/06/65
Pittenger, John Theodore died 06/23/62 06/26/62
Pittenger, Joseph died 12/30/62 12/31/62
Pittenger, William B. died 01/04/61 01/05/61
Pittinger, Alice J. married Ricketts, Granville C. no date 12/19/64
Pittinger, Victoria married Rooney, James 04/14/61 04/16/61
Pittman, Mary Hattie died 07/07/63 07/10/63
Pitts, Charles H. died 08/14/64 08/15/64
Place, George married Matilda, Mary 03/06/62 03/08/62
Placide, Henry F. died 08/05/61 08/06/61
Placide, W. H. married Hardesty, Margaret H. 01/13/63 01/16/63
Placide, W. William H. married Hardesty, Margaret H. 01/15/63 01/23/6
Plant, Charles Marks died 06/21/61 06/22/61
Platt, Mary Ann died 04/20/61 04/22/61
Platt, Thomas Mitchell married Canavan, Jamine H. 01/13/62 01/18/62
Platte, Priscilla died 07/14/61 07/16/61
Pleasants, Charles married Denvir, Rose M. 12/08/64 01/04/65
Pleasants, James Snowden died 10/14/63 10/26/63
Pleasants, Richard Poultney died 11/24/63 11/28/63
Plitt, Margaret Emma died 06/16/64 06/18/64
Plowman, H. Nannie married Baily, Edwin L. 12/04/62 12/06/62
Plowman, Harry J. Ellsworth died 11/28/64 11/30/64
Plowman, Jacob H. married Smith, Elizaeth V. 12/27/60 01/07/61
Plowman, James L. died 01/26/63 01/27/63
Plowman, James T. died 01/26/63 01/28/63
Plowman, James T. married Huleit, Caroline 07/16/65 08/24/65
Plowman, Louie Milton died 07/22/63 07/24/63
Plowman, Margaret died 12/14/64 12/15/64
Plowman, Mary Elizabeth died 11/09/61 11/15/61
Plowman, Tillie died 11/14/61 11/15/61
Plumer, Louisa married McClaley, John W. 12/23/62 01/01/63
Plumer, Mary Frances died 06/09/61 06/11/61
Plumley, Ira married Robinson, Elvencedore 12/31/63 01/02/64
Plummer, Caroline (Mrs.) died 11/11/64 11/12/64
Plummer, Edward died 02/21/63 02/23/63
Plummer, Henrietta died 12/19/62 12/20/62
Plummer, J. M. married Bull, Francis 11/05/63 12/08/63
Plummer, John B. married Smith, Susan (Mrs.) 01/01/63 03/24/63
Plummer, John William married Trigg, Lizzie J. 08/11/63 08/20/63
Plummer, Margaret A. died 08/16/62 08/18/62
Plummer, Margaret A. died 08/16/62 08/19/62
Plummer, Martha died 05/08/63 05/14/63
Plummer, Mary V. married Watt, George L. 04/24/62 07/17/62
Plummer, Rebecca married Uncles, Isaac 11/14/61 12/14/61
Plummer, Sarah Jane married Gorsuch, James 12/16/62 12/20/62
Plummer, Susanna died 01/02/61 01/07/61
Plunket, Mary married Hussey, Martin 07/24/62 07/26/62
Plunkett, Mary J. died 06/07/62 06/09/62

Pochon, Marie Therese died 06/30/64   07/02/64
Pocock, Deliah died 01/22/61   01/23/61
Poe, Fannie Elliott married Gilpen, Albert G. 06/01/65   06/08/65
Poe, George died 07/21/64   07/23/64
Poe, John Prentiss married Johnson, Anne 03/02/63   03/05/63
Poe, Sallie C. died 05/24/61   07/11/61
Pogue, Lucinda E. died 12/23/65   12/25/65
Poinst, Charles Dominick married O'Buckingham, Sally 06/06/63   01/06/64
Poisal, Francis A. (Lt.) married Hoffman, Maranda A. 10/01/63   10/05/63
Poisal, John R. died 11/00/00   12/20/62
Poist, Lilly Bartlett died 09/25/64   09/26/64
Polack, Elizabeth married Rosenstock, Joseph 02/24/64   03/02/64
Pole, Charles H. married Hobbs, Columbia E. 10/11/63   10/16/63
Pole, Margaret E. married Landon, Joseph W. 10/31/65   11/01/65
Polk, Anna Elizabeth married Thompson, Jacob 02/10/65   02/13/65
Polk, E. O. (Mrs.) died 10/05/61   10/08/61
Polk, Lizzie married Pomeroy, Eugene H. 11/21/65   11/23/65
Polk, Lizzie married Pomeroy, Eugene H. 11/21/65   11/24/65
Polk, Nellie Maury married Leidy, Philip 02/15/65   02/17/65
Polk, William J. died 10/13/63   10/15/63
Pollack, Lewis married Goldsmith, Sarah Virginia 08/15/61   08/16/61
Pollard, David M. married Owens, Sabina 10/29/63   11/03/63
Pollard, Helen married Keagle, George P. 10/10/64   10/22/64
Pollett, Edward D. married Palmer, Harriet B. 07/20/65   07/22/65
Polley, Richard G. married Randall, Sarah J. 06/17/62   08/30/62
Pollock, Ella married Wilson, Thomas J. 12/17/61   12/24/61
Pollock, William John died 07/24/64   07/28/64
Polmyer, Caroline (Mrs.) died 08/06/63   08/08/63
Polton, Annie Jane married McCabe, Thomas A. 10/26/65   12/14/65
Polton, Elizabeth (Mrs.) died 09/26/64   09/28/64
Polton, George H. married Ingals, Sarah 02/28/62   03/04/62
Pomeroy, Eugene H. married Polk, Lizzie 11/21/65   11/23/65
Pomeroy, Eugene H. married Polk, Lizzie 11/21/65   11/24/65
Pomplitz, Frederick August died no date   02/27/63
Ponn, David died 12/31/61   01/02/62
Pontier, Edward died 04/26/64   04/28/64
Pontier, Thomas A. died 10/13/65   10/16/65
Pool, Cornelius died 05/25/63   05/27/63
Pool, Matilda married Keller, George J. 05/31/64   06/07/64
Pool, Ruth A. died 06/15/61   06/20/61
Pool, Thomas died 11/26/63   11/28/63
Poole, Esther died 04/03/64   04/07/64
Poole, George R. died 04/14/65   04/15/65
Poole, George R. married Scott, Elizabeth 03/29/65   04/15/65
Poole, Maggie married Richardson, E. 04/13/65   04/15/65
Poole, Margaret M. died 12/27/61   12/30/61
Poole, Mary A. (Mrs.) died 12/17/65   12/19/65
Poole, Mary A. (Mrs.) died 12/17/65   12/20/65
Poole, Nancy married Brown, Shadrick 01/28/64   01/30/64
Poole, Sarah E. married Reese, Thomas Sargant 05/24/64   06/07/64
Poole, Susan C. married Beardsley, John D. (Maj.) no date   09/13/65
Poole, Thomas married Wright, Isabella 02/19/62   02/26/62
Popalus, Joseph married Johnson, H. L. (Mrs.) 05/15/63   05/19/63
Pope, Catherine M. married Waltz, Jacob 04/06/64   04/08/64
Pope, Christian died 06/20/62   06/23/62

Pope, George H. died 01/09/63 01/10/63
Poplan, William married McCauley, Sarah Rebecca 04/13/64 04/16/64
Popp, Mary Virginia died 03/20/63 03/24/63
Popp, Rosanna (Mrs.) died 08/08/63 08/14/63
Popplien, Andrew married Huggins, Jessie 04/24/65 04/28/65
Porter, A. E. married Hatter, Charles William 05/10/64 05/11/64
Porter, Amanda M. (Mrs.) died 05/03/65 05/05/65
Porter, Cassandra died 04/17/61 04/18/61
Porter, Charles died 05/10/65 05/11/65
Porter, Edward O. died 05/08/64 05/09/64
Porter, Elizabeth F. died 10/25/61 10/26/61
Porter, Ellenora married Bruff, William W. 01/24/61 01/25/61
Porter, F. E. married Jeffries, Ettie J. 06/27/65 06/30/65
Porter, George A. died 12/31/64 01/02/65
Porter, Grant V. died 06/22/64 06/25/64
Porter, Henrietta (Mrs.) married Evans, James 10/01/65 10/05/65
Porter, Henry died 01/31/63 02/02/63
Porter, Henry died 01/31/63 02/03/63
Porter, Isabella died 01/31/65 02/01/65
Porter, Joseph married Hyde, Elizabeth 08/15/65 08/18/65
Porter, Joseph T. married Hyde, Elizabeth 08/15/65 08/24/65
Porter, Julia Ann died 07/19/63 07/20/63
Porter, Lucius P. married Harrington, Emily T. 10/22/62 10/28/62
Porter, Lucretia D. married Gaither, Thomas B. 04/25/65 04/29/65
Porter, Margaret married Woodside, Edmund L. 04/17/62 04/21/62
Porter, Mary died 03/23/64 03/24/64
Porter, Mary (Mrs.) died 07/31/65 08/01/65
Porter, Mary Jane died 08/07/62 08/19/62
Porter, Robert Buck died 08/10/64 08/11/64
Porter, Robert L. died 04/09/61 04/10/61
Porter, Sarah E. married Knight, Charles D. 12/29/63 01/06/64
Porter, Susan (Mrs.) died 08/31/63 09/01/63
Porter, Thomas died 02/06/63 02/07/63
Porter-Wood, Mary married Beale, A. M. no date 01/14/64
Porteus, Robert L. married Zachary, Annie 02/25/63 03/06/63
Ports, Alfred married Thomas, Sarah W. 04/28/64 05/04/64
Ports, C. J. married Long, C. A. (Mrs.) 12/01/64 12/20/64
Ports, J. William married Bilson, Sallie 02/16/65 02/18/65
Posern, Theodore married Yenrick, Mary E. 01/04/64 01/12/64
Posey, Chloe M. married Jones, Stephen 03/27/65 03/30/65
Posey, Margaret Ellen (Mrs.) died 04/13/64 04/22/64
Posliff, Edward married Mitchell, Elizabeth L. 10/17/63 10/21/63
Post, Lutie M. died 08/18/65 08/22/65
Post, Sallie L. married Barrett, F. Oliver 11/12/63 11/13/63
Posterfield, Martha Ann married Green, James P. 12/19/61 12/24/61
Posterly, Mortimer married Ayres, Sallie E. 11/09/64 11/10/64
Postlethwaite, Charlotte C. married Doyle, Thomas G. 07/25/65 08/02/6
Poston, Daniel T. married Frederick, Mary A. 12/25/64 01/02/65
Poston, John H. married Wise, Maggie C. 11/13/65 12/16/65
Potee, Elizabeth died 01/12/65 01/13/65
Potee, Elizabeth died 01/12/65 01/14/65
Potee, Lizzie A. married Smoot, Hiram H. 03/22/64 04/02/64
Potee, Mary married Reitlring, Lewis 02/05/65 02/07/65
Poteet, William W. died 02/04/65 02/08/65
Pottee, George married Martin, Mary E. 08/20/65 09/16/65

```
Potteet, Martha Ann died 12/28/64   12/29/64
Pottenger, Sarah W. (Mrs.) died 03/12/63   03/24/63
Pottenger, Thomas B. died 04/01/63   04/02/63
Potter, Abraham S. married Jones, Madossa 07/16/62   07/22/62
Potter, B. F. married Connolly, Mary A. 09/14/65   09/19/65
Potter, Charlotte (Mrs.) died 11/11/63   11/12/63
Potter, Flavius (USA) married Green, Mary E. 07/14/63   07/16/63
Potter, J. H. (Rev.) married Stevens, Sybyl A. 01/24/61   02/04/61
Potter, Jane A. married Reipe, Joseph H. 04/29/61   10/11/61
Potter, John T. died 10/31/61   11/01/61
Potter, Kate married Phillips, William R. 11/03/63   11/07/63
Potter, Malissa M. C. married Warner, Robert N. 10/01/63   10/03/63
Potter, Martin married Pritchett, Martha J. 03/02/65   03/06/65
Potter, Mary Emma (Mrs.) died 05/28/65   06/02/65
Potter, Sarah married Tenant, George 01/15/61   01/17/61
Potter, Susan married Shirlkel, William C. 07/22/63   07/25/63
Potter, Susan married Thirlkel, William C. 07/22/63   07/27/63
Potts, Amanda married Stoddard, Henry C. 12/24/62   12/30/62
Potts, Charles Filmore died 04/07/65   04/08/65
Potts, Richard C. married Kimberly, Cornelia R. 04/11/61   04/13/61
Pouder, Edward died 01/05/64   01/09/64
Pouder, Julia C. married Edmonds, Samuel 10/15/63   10/21/63
Poulson, Clara married Conradt, George B. 04/02/63   04/03/63
Poulson, Isabella married Shepherd, Stephen 10/22/63   10/24/63
Poultman, Mary E. died 06/03/65   06/07/65
Poultney, Georgianna died 08/12/65   08/14/65
Poultney, Jane died 09/11/61   09/13/61
Poultney, Maria married Handy, Thomas P. 10/31/65   11/02/65
Poultney, Nannie T. married Falconar, A. Smith 11/12/63   11/16/63
Poultney, Samuel died 08/27/64   08/30/64
Poulton, Alexander died 12/26/61   12/30/61
Poulton, Charles married Rea, Irene 08/11/65   08/16/65
Poulton, George C. married South, Rachel Ann 09/27/64   09/28/64
Poulton, William E. married Travers, Susie E. 12/03/63   12/10/63
Poumairot, Charles Henry died 05/02/63   05/04/63
Powel, Margaret died 06/04/61   06/05/61
Powell, Ann E. married Johnson, Thomas 02/10/64   02/13/64
Powell, Ann Elizabeth died 04/18/62   04/19/62
Powell, Fannie A. married Merryman, George J. 02/09/65   02/14/65
Powell, Grafton died 09/11/65   09/13/65
Powell, Harriett E. married Hutchins, Sheadrick V. 06/22/65   06/29/65
Powell, Hattie married McKean, E. R. (Cpt.) 04/23/63   04/24/63
Powell, Henrietta married Jones, Jason A. 05/24/63   06/10/63
Powell, James H. married Kindig, Susan J. 10/20/63   10/27/63
Powell, John died 12/21/64   12/22/64
Powell, Mary died 11/19/65   11/20/65
Powell, Mary (Mrs.) died 11/19/65   11/21/65
Powell, Mary Ann died 12/10/61   12/11/61
Powell, Samuel married Williams, Mary 10/31/65   11/02/65
Powell, Samuel S. married Inloes, Elizabeth 01/06/64   01/08/64
Powell, William H. died 06/24/64   06/25/64
Powell, William N. died 04/13/63   04/14/63
Powell, William T. married Low, Pauline E. 09/24/65   11/08/65
Power, Albert Joseph Ignatius died 07/21/61   07/27/61
Power, William T. died 07/29/64   08/01/64
```

Powers, Helen died 12/13/62 12/16/62
Powers, Mary married Foster, Uriah L. P. 10/24/65 12/12/65
Powers, Peter died 09/23/63 09/26/63
Powers, Peter died 09/23/63 09/29/63
Pracht, George R. B. died 06/12/62 06/17/62
Pracht, Willie C. died 01/16/62 01/18/62
Prag, Ellen (Mrs.) died 10/22/65 10/24/65
Prather, Emma H. married Farson, George W. 12/29/63 01/01/64
Pratt, Benjamin married Wallace, Mary 05/24/63 05/26/63
Pratt, Elizabeth died 02/05/65 03/15/65
Pratt, Frank E. died 04/29/62 04/30/62
Pratt, Jabey D. died 03/03/65 03/04/65
Pratt, John G. died 06/29/63 07/01/63
Pratt, Joseph G. married Wiche, Elizabeth 02/10/65 03/08/65
Pratt, Rebecca married Brice, Abraham 02/07/65 02/11/65
Pratt, Sarah Elizabeth married Calhoun, James 05/15/62 05/17/62
Pratt, Susan married Roberts, William 06/01/65 06/03/65
Preadasell, Caroline Elizabeth married Favre, Francois H. 09/06/65 09/07/65
Preice, Mary L. married Price, Washington L. 10/20/64 10/24/64
Preiter, Louisa M. married Brass, James H. 03/28/65 04/05/65
Prenier, Henry L. E. married Hamill, Mary A. 05/18/65 05/31/65
Prentiss, Elizabeth V died 05/13/61 05/17/61
Presbury, George G. died 08/09/63 08/11/63
Preston, Ann L. married Brown, Richard 08/01/64 08/03/64
Preston, Anna Nora married Killmon, Thomas T. 08/19/60 10/07/62
Preston, Caroline died 09/23/61 09/28/61
Preston, Henry married Grenage, Emeline 07/31/64 08/03/64
Preston, Hosea F. died 09/05/64 10/12/64
Preston, Josephine died 08/08/64 08/09/64
Preston, Sarah Ann married Collins, William E. 02/16/64 02/18/64
Preston, Susan R. married Grace, Thomas E. 05/19/64 05/23/64
Preston, Timothy died 01/06/65 01/07/65
Preston, William died 12/16/61 12/17/61
Preston, William died 10/24/63 10/26/63
Preston, William died 09/12/65 09/13/65
Preston, William McKim died 06/17/64 07/30/64
Presun, Charles H. died no date 06/07/65
Prettyman, Eliza Barratt died 02/26/61 02/27/61
Prettyman, Eliza Barratt died 02/26/61 02/28/61
Prettyman, Emma A. died 12/13/65 12/19/65
Prettyman, Emma A. died 12/13/65 12/20/65
Prettyman, William E. married Macubbin, Augusta M. 04/19/64 05/02/64
Prevost, Gustave died 01/07/61 01/09/61
Prevost, Marie Clara S. died 10/22/64 10/27/64
Price, Alfred A. died 06/04/63 06/05/63
Price, Alfred Lee married Hodges, Annie R. 11/25/64 12/05/64
Price, Allen married Adams, Hattie 05/21/63 05/23/63
Price, Amanda V. married Milburn, T. H. 05/22/62 06/10/62
Price, Ann (Mrs.) died 08/05/63 08/15/63
Price, Anna Corilla married Etchison, Lysander 02/12/61 02/18/61
Price, Annie S. married Audoun, Lewis W. 06/30/64 08/09/64
Price, Annor died 12/11/63 12/14/63
Price, Capt. Alfred C. died 07/07/62 01/17/63
Price, Carrie Dunbar died 10/11/65 10/12/65

Price, Catharine Ann married Sykes, Columbus W. 12/20/59 07/30/64
Price, Catherine died 02/18/61 02/23/61
Price, Charles Adolphus died 07/17/64 07/19/64
Price, Charley died 01/18/63 01/19/63
Price, Charlotte Eugenia died 03/23/63 03/25/63
Price, David F. died 07/29/61 07/30/61
Price, David, Sr. died 06/02/61 06/03/61
Price, Edward Rutledge married Michael, Laura E. 01/19/65 01/21/65
Price, Emma G. (Mrs.) died 07/06/63 07/07/63
Price, Fannie married Leeds, Edward W. 08/22/65 09/08/65
Price, G. W. (Cpt.) married Webb, Aphia M. 11/20/65 11/27/65
Price, Geoffrey W. married Williams, Mattie E. 03/24/64 03/29/64
Price, George F. F. died 07/11/63 07/13/63
Price, George W. (Cpl.) died 10/29/64 11/18/64
Price, George W. (Cpl.) died 10/29/64 11/19/64
Price, Henry (Rev.) died 02/20/63 02/24/63
Price, Ida Virginia died 05/10/62 05/14/62
Price, J. T. married Butler, Ella M. 10/24/65 10/28/65
Price, James H. G. died 10/09/64 10/11/64
Price, Jessie married Gore, Jennie 09/19/61 09/25/61
Price, John died 04/29/61 04/30/61
Price, John Basil married Taylor, Catherine 11/07/61 11/09/61
Price, John F. died 04/11/65 05/03/65
Price, John F. died 04/11/65 05/10/65
Price, John W. married Woodward, Annie L. 01/06/63 01/14/63
Price, Joseph died 05/26/63 05/27/63
Price, Joshua C. died 10/26/64 10/27/64
Price, Joshua C. died 10/26/64 10/28/64
Price, Keturah died 03/28/65 04/04/65
Price, Levi married Elfresh, Laura V. 02/19/63 02/21/63
Price, Louis married Cobey, Jane 11/12/61 11/16/61
Price, M. Evlean married Grice, Joseph T. P. 09/07/65 09/08/65
Price, Martha (Mrs.) died 01/03/64 01/04/64
Price, Mary A. married Mac, Thomas A. 01/05/62 01/07/62
Price, Mary A. married Kinsey, Johnm 11/22/62 11/27/62
Price, Mary Ann married Arminger, B. Franklin 12/06/60 07/19/61
Price, Mary Isabel died 08/15/62 08/28/62
Price, Mary Louise died 08/15/63 08/21/63
Price, Mernivia A. died 07/15/63 08/15/63
Price, Mollie E. married Clarke, George C. 12/14/65 12/21/65
Price, Nathan died 06/29/65 06/30/65
Price, Richard E. married Littleton, Elizabeth V. 03/20/62 03/21/62
Price, Richard G. died 03/21/62 03/28/62
Price, Ruth Ann married Curry, Robert F. 07/01/63 07/03/63
Price, Sallie E. married Shorb, James E. 06/23/63 06/29/63
Price, Samuel D. died 10/08/63 10/10/63
Price, Samuel S. died 04/26/62 04/28/62
Price, Sarah J. married Hanson, James H. 07/27/65 09/19/65
Price, Sarah John died 07/31/61 08/01/61
Price, Thomas married Brooks, Annie 12/24/61 12/27/61
Price, Vinie married Robertson, J. E. (Dr.) 03/28/65 04/06/65
Price, Virginia E. married Newman, Sidney C. 09/03/61 09/14/61
Price, Washington L. married Preice, Mary L. 10/20/64 10/24/64
Price, William died 04/14/64 05/10/64
Price, William Denwood died 12/06/64 12/08/64

Prichard, Mary Jane married Wilson, David A. 01/29/63 01/31/63
Prichard, William H. died 10/30/64 10/31/64
Pridgeon, John married Underhill, Esther A. 11/07/65 11/09/65
Pridham, W. F. (Cpt.) married Davies, Catharine Jane 12/05/64 12/08/6
Prime, Harriet E. (Mrs.) died 02/28/64 02/29/64
Prime, William T. married Dove, Sarah A. 05/17/65 05/19/65
Primrose, Breenbury married Ringgold, Sally 11/30/62 12/02/62
Primrose, James W. married Townsend, Mary Frances 07/27/65 08/01/65
Primrose, John Francis died 06/24/64 06/28/64
Primrose, Samuel F. married Lutts, Josephine 04/15/61 07/10/61
Primrose, Samuel F. married Luits, Josephine 04/15/61 07/06/61
Primrose, Samuel F. married Lutts, Josephine 04/15/61 07/11/61
Primrose, Samuel F. died 07/05/63 07/06/63
Primrose, William died 05/02/62 05/03/62
Prince, Hattie E. died 07/07/64 07/08/64
Prince, Hattie E. died 07/07/64 07/09/64
Prince, Ida Sidney died 11/09/63 11/10/63
Prince, L. Thomas died 03/29/65 03/30/65
Prince, Lemuele S. died 10/09/62 10/10/62
Prince, Mary Elizabeth died 10/30/63 10/31/63
Prince, Sarah E. married Dougherty, William H. 12/23/60 02/19/61
Prior, Ida May died 01/10/61 01/16/61
Pritchard, Irvin S. married Gouley, Julie E. C. 07/12/65 07/19/65
Pritchard, Williamine Webster died 09/22/63 09/23/63
Pritchett, Louisa E. married Benner, Ferdinand C. 02/19/63 02/24/63
Pritchett, Martha J. married Potter, Martin 03/02/65 03/06/65
Pritchett, Samuel married Andrews, Miranda 08/18/64 08/27/64
Pritchett, William died 12/01/61 12/02/61
Pritchett, William died 12/01/61 12/03/61
Privy, Emma married Schlarb, Henry 09/01/64 09/03/64
Proctor, Caroline M. married Mott, Henry B. 07/23/63 07/25/63
Proctor, J. T. A. married Conley, Calinda (Mrs.) 08/04/64 12/24/64
Proctor, Mary married McCullough, George S. 06/13/65 06/14/65
Proctor, Rebecca died 08/07/63 08/08/63
Proctor, Rebecca H. married Meyers, Jacob, Jr. 07/21/62 09/25/62
Proctor, William married Benard, Caroline 11/26/63 12/10/63
Proctor, Willie died 08/13/61 08/14/61
Protchard, Joseph R. died 01/23/65 01/26/65
Protopapes, Kate Rebecca died 11/25/63 11/28/63
Proud, John G. died 07/12/65 07/13/65
Proud, John G. died 07/12/65 07/14/65
Proudfoot, George W. died 01/14/65 01/16/65
Prout, Henry W. died 04/30/65 04/29/65
Prout, John married Webb, C. 12/06/65 12/23/65
Prout, John W. married Kolb, Mary 11/13/64 11/16/64
Prout, Joseph R. married Chase, Sue V. 12/15/64 12/17/64
Prout, Sarah died 04/02/62 04/12/62
Pruett, Amanda M. married Lamb, John H. 03/02/62 03/18/62
Pruett, Annie married Reynolds, John H. 11/22/63 11/26/63
Pruett, Elizabeth died 02/21/63 02/23/63
Pruett, Elizabeth died 02/21/63 02/24/63
Pruett, James A. married Burrier, Lizze S. 11/09/65 11/15/65
Prunty, Mary E. (Mrs.) died 01/08/65 01/10/65
Pryer, Edward married Cowan, Almira V. 02/19/61 06/03/61
Pryor, Agnes M. married Wicks, James S. 10/19/63 12/25/63

Pryor, Anna S. married Harrison, James T. 05/12/64   05/16/64
Pryor, Anna S. (Mrs.) married Harrison, James S. 05/12/64   05/14/64
Pryor, Charles died 05/02/65   05/10/65
Pryor, Clara Josephine died 06/14/63   06/15/63
Pryor, James E. died 09/01/62   09/02/62
Pryor, John died 04/03/61   04/05/61
Pryor, Laura E. married Favier, Peter A. 04/02/65   06/27/65
Pryor, Mark Francis died 06/10/63   06/12/63
Pryor, Richard W. married Farrenger, M. A. 08/06/65   08/08/65
Puckett, Rebecca J. married Rice, John R. 04/01/64   01/14/65
Pue, Priscilla H. died 09/03/63   09/04/63
Pue, Rebecca D. married Craigen, William J. (Dr.) 10/13/64   10/19/64
Pugh, Ann P. died 10/10/65   10/11/65
Pugh, Julia P. died 05/31/61   06/05/61
Puhl, George died 11/21/62   11/22/62
Puhl, Mary Elizabeth married Hooper, William 02/15/63   02/17/63
Pulley, Ida Grace died 01/27/62   01/28/62
Pulley, James W. (Cpt.) died 12/11/64   12/14/64
Pullman, William died 11/26/64   01/17/65
Pully, James married Freeman, Ellenora 09/02/62   09/06/62
Pump, Charles H. married Therrough, Sallie D. 08/06/63   08/08/63
Pumphery, Thomas J. married Anderson, G. E. 11/29/64   12/08/64
Pumphrey, Adeline R. married Warfield, John L. 12/30/62   01/30/63
Pumphrey, Josephine L. married Fairbank, Joshua M. 05/12/64   05/14/64
Pumphrey, Maggie E. married Tickner, William J. 05/31/65   06/07/65
Pumphrey, Margaret died 12/27/65   12/28/65
Pumphrey, Mary C. married Fairbank, William J. 10/15/61   10/17/61
Pumphrey, Richard G. died 10/14/64   10/15/64
Pumphrey, Solon died 07/15/61   07/17/61
Pumphrey, Walter died 07/26/64   07/28/64
Pund, Mary E. died 09/20/65   09/22/65
Pund, Mary E. died 09/20/65   09/23/65
Purcell, Alice died 03/28/64   03/29/64
Purcell, James died 04/02/65   04/05/65
Purcell, Margaret Jane (Mrs.) died 06/12/63   06/13/63
Purcell, Thomas married McHarry, Margaret Jane 08/17/62   10/01/62
Purder, Susannah died 02/07/62   02/10/62
Purdy, Margaret Elizabeth died 05/23/61   05/27/61
Purdy, Warren G. married Colby, Acca L. 03/13/65   03/17/65
Purington, Kate E. married Pierce, H. Lindsley (M.D.) 03/24/62   04/15/62
Purkey, Georgia A. married Murray, Orlando T. 04/03/65   04/17/65
Purnel, Charles F. married Weaver, Rocksey Ann 11/14/61   11/16/61
Purnell, Ann Eliza (Mrs.) died 09/11/63   09/15/63
Purnell, C. (Cpt.) married Muller, Angeline 08/31/65   09/02/65
Purnell, Charles I. married Roby, Marcelline V. 09/30/63   10/05/63
Purnell, L. B. married Hurst, Mary E. B. 12/14/65   12/18/65
Purnell, Lemuel H. died 01/10/61   01/11/61
Purnell, Moses T. died 02/09/64   02/22/64
Purnell, Rebecca (Mrs.) died 12/13/63   12/15/63
Purvis, Ann E. married Wright, Mathew U. 04/14/64   04/16/64
Purvis, Isaac F. married Fiske, Phebe P. 01/20/63   01/30/63
Purvis, Phoebe P. (Mrs.) died 10/21/64   10/24/64
Pusen, Theodore married Tenrick, Mary E. 01/04/64   01/08/64
Pusey, Nathan died 05/25/65   05/26/65
Putts, Mary M. married Bready, G. C. 11/03/62   11/06/62

Putts, Rebecca married Smith, William J. 02/17/63   03/10/63
Puzenett, Emily (Mrs.) died 04/30/64   05/24/64
Pyatt, Mrs. Elizabeth A. died 01/17/65   01/19/65
Pyfer, Rachel E. married Maynard, Warren 10/08/63   10/09/63
Pyfer, William H. died 11/08/63   11/26/63
Pyle, Elizabeth died 01/05/61   03/21/61
Pyne, James F. married Carlisle, Sarah 10/19/65   10/23/65
Pyne, William H. married Magness, Sarah Jane 01/30/62   02/03/62
Qeeney, Anna died 06/27/61   06/28/61
Qiugley, Edward died 10/18/63   10/19/63
Quackenboss, L. J. married Shelton, Annie C. 07/02/65   07/11/65
Quail, George K. died 03/27/64   03/28/64
Quallion, Mordica married Lockerman, Keziah 05/22/61   05/25/61
Quanz, Henry Antone died 05/03/62   05/04/62
Quark, John Charles died 09/10/62   09/11/62
Quarles, Charlotte died 02/01/62   02/05/62
Quarles, Charlotte died 02/01/62   02/06/62
Quarles, Edward died 08/16/62   08/28/62
Quarles, Merriwether S. married Watts, Jennie 11/30/65   12/02/65
Quarles, Virginia married Thomas, David E., Jr. 09/02/65   09/05/65
Quarz, Freddy died 09/05/62   09/16/62
Quarz, John Jacob died 09/14/62   09/16/62
Quebec, James H. married Johnson, Eliza J. 07/31/62   08/27/62
Queeny, Mary died 02/16/62   02/17/62
Quell, Helen Magdalen died 09/10/65   09/13/65
Quell, William F. married Kaufman, Rettie H. 09/12/64   09/14/64
Quick, George married Shone, Annie 07/06/62   07/19/62
Quickley, Sarah A. died 04/25/61   04/26/61
Quickley, Zachariah Harvey died 11/21/65   11/23/65
Quigley, Ann died 02/21/65   02/22/65
Quigley, Ellen died 02/28/65   03/02/65
Quigley, Honora married McKenna, Michael 04/19/63   04/23/63
Quigley, Jane married Flanagin, Patrick 07/24/64   07/30/64
Quigley, Joseph Edward died 07/23/64   07/25/64
Quigley, Maggie married Miller, B. F. 02/26/63   03/03/63
Quigley, Mary (Mrs.) died 03/09/63   03/10/63
Quigley, Mary Ellen (Mrs.) married Saunders, Willie Russell 12/19/64   02/04/65
Quigley, Willy died 12/22/62   12/23/62
Quin, Hugh died 06/23/61   06/24/61
Quinan, Margaret A. died 12/02/61   12/03/61
Quincy, John D. married Neale, Demmie 11/18/63   11/20/63
Quinlan, Elizabeth died 10/18/65   10/19/65
Quinlan, Ella died 05/25/63   05/26/63
Quinlan, Jane F. died 05/27/61   05/29/61
Quinlan, John F. died 07/04/65   07/06/65
Quinlan, Martha (Mrs.) died 09/22/64   09/23/64
Quinlin, Charles H. married Perdue, Mary E. 05/25/65   05/26/65
Quinn, Ambrose married McCubbin, Emma E. 12/23/61   01/08/62
Quinn, Ann died 04/15/61   04/16/61
Quinn, Annie Davis died 06/20/64   06/21/64
Quinn, Bridget died 04/08/61   04/09/61
Quinn, Bridget (Mrs.) died 06/01/63   06/02/63
Quinn, Edward died 07/17/65   07/18/65
Quinn, Francis Jerome died 10/24/64   10/26/64

Quinn, Isabella died 04/10/62 04/12/62
Quinn, James Lyman died 01/17/61 01/19/61
Quinn, John died 04/11/65 04/12/65
Quinn, John Bernard died 04/29/64 04/30/64
Quinn, John W. died 05/02/63 05/05/63
Quinn, Julia married Mooney, Laurence 05/08/64 05/14/64
Quinn, Martin married Shehan, Ellen 04/23/65 05/10/65
Quinn, Mary married Donally, Cornelius 02/27/62 03/15/62
Quinn, Mary Ellen died 10/04/64 10/05/64
Quinn, Mathew E. married Kennedy, Kate 08/14/64 08/22/64
Quinn, Michael T. died 11/01/62 11/03/62
Quinn, Peter died 12/21/61 12/23/61
Quinn, Sarah A. married Wallace, James E. 04/23/62 01/19/63
Quinn, Winfred (Mrs.) died 09/20/63 09/23/63
Quirk, John died 03/31/61 04/01/61
Rabbitt, Margaret married Daily, Bartholomew 02/17/63 02/20/63
Rabe, John F. married Stein, Catharine A. E. 09/24/63 09/29/63
Raborg, Christopher died 01/19/62 01/21/62
Raborg, Henrietta S. married Bourke, John W. 11/14/61 11/16/61
Raborg, Mary married Woodward, Rignal T. 01/26/64 01/28/64
Rachels, Sallie Augusta died 02/06/64 02/09/64
Radcliffe, Cornelia A. married Nanz, Thomas 12/08/64 12/10/64
Radcliffe, Everett Harrison died 08/12/61 08/14/61
Radcliffe, Martin V. B. died 02/03/61 02/05/61
Rae, Annie V. married Coulter, Robert A. 04/21/62 04/26/62
Rae, Robert married Forster, Mary C. 04/07/64 11/28/64
Rafferty, Hugh married Hiestand, Sarah M. 11/14/65 11/28/65
Rafferty, Kate (Mrs.) died 09/13/64 09/15/64
Ragan, Mary died 10/02/65 10/03/65
Ragan, Richard married Howell, Margaretta 11/18/61 11/22/61
Rahbine, Annie C. married McMahon, Patrick 11/15/64 11/18/64
Raiff, William H. died 05/07/62 05/08/62
Rain, Charles H. B. married Kraber, Mary Ann 01/02/61 01/04/61
Raine, Albert married Rash, Mina 01/07/64 01/21/64
Raine, Sophia married Hanck, Frederick 10/19/62 10/21/62
Raine, Sophia married Houck, Frederick 10/19/62 10/22/62
Rainer, Anne Cecelia died 08/25/65 08/29/65
Rainer, Eliza married Jones, John 07/01/61 07/11/61
Rainer, Joseph D. married Wimpsett, Martha V. 05/19/63 05/21/63
Rainey, Sarah A. married McManus, John 05/10/63 05/18/63
Rainier, Caroline married Jobes, Edwin S. 01/02/65 01/07/65
Rainy, Edward J. married McDermott, Mary Hellen 04/05/63 04/07/63
Raite, Lizzie E. married Ege, A. G. 10/29/63 10/30/63
Ramey, Carrie Mahalae died 02/17/65 02/20/65
Ramey, Charles Patterson died 08/22/64 08/24/64
Ramsay, Agnes died 07/23/61 07/24/61
Ramsay, Albert R. married Neider, Mary Josephine 12/22/63 12/28/63
Ramsay, David F. died 10/13/65 10/17/65
Ramsay, Isaac (Capt.) died 11/12/65 11/13/65
Ramsay, James Judson died 10/22/65 10/23/65
Ramsay, Richard H. (Dr.) died 08/09/62 08/14/62
Ramsay, Robert E. H. died 07/28/64 07/29/64
Ramsay, Willie Wallis died 08/31/61 09/04/61
Ramsburg, Amanda H. (Mrs.) died 03/07/64 03/09/64
Ramsburg, Israel died no date 01/22/63

Ramsey, Isaac T. (Capt.) died 11/12/65 11/14/65
Ramsey, Jane died 02/27/64 02/29/64
Ramsey, Jane died 02/27/64 03/01/64
Ramsey, Maria Louisa died 07/25/62 07/26/62
Ramsey, William R. married McClintock, Lizzie 05/04/65 05/12/65
Ramsy, Carrie Mahalae died 02/17/65 02/18/65
Randall, Addison T. married Watson, Monterey 01/24/65 01/25/65
Randall, Caroline died 05/12/61 05/14/61
Randall, Christopher died 08/06/62 09/15/62
Randall, Daniel died 03/04/62 03/06/62
Randall, Elisha died 01/25/61 01/26/61
Randall, Enoch died 08/21/61 08/21/61
Randall, Enoch died no date 08/22/61
Randall, John W. married Hood, Elizabeth A. 01/05/64 01/15/64
Randall, Mary Susana married Mitchell, Emory G. 11/04/63 11/07/63
Randall, Sallie A. married McFarlane, James 03/10/63 03/13/63
Randall, Samuel O. died 05/22/63 05/23/63
Randall, Sarah J. married Polley, Richard G. 06/17/62 08/30/62
Randall, Soloman married Facts, Rebecca 05/16/61 05/18/61
Randanne, J. B. (Rev.) died 08/11/64 08/13/64
Randle, Rachel Anne died 11/06/61 11/08/61
Randolph, Eugenia M. died 09/09/61 09/10/61
Randolph, J. Corrigan died 12/23/61 12/24/61
Randolph, Mary F. married Trotton, Ferdinand 11/07/61 11/09/61
Randolph, Peyton T. died 10/02/63 10/03/63
Randolph, William Augustus died 02/26/64 02/27/64
Ranft, Caroline Regina died 10/07/65 10/09/65
Rankin, John died 08/18/63 09/08/63
Rankin, Robert died 08/29/63 08/31/63
Rankin, William married Ferguson, Kate 09/14/65 09/29/65
Rankle, William married Reirig, Maggie 08/29/65 09/13/65
Rannelbarger, Sallie E. married Bowie, David H. 07/07/64 07/09/64
Ransford, Norton C. married Skinner, Hattie 01/23/62 02/06/62
Raphael, Henry M. (Dr.) died 08/22/65 08/07/65
Raphel, S. Amedee married White, Louise H. 04/29/63 05/02/63
Rarrick, Charles H., Jr. married Douglass, Elizabeth A. 04/19/64 04/21/64
Rash, Mina married Raine, Albert 01/07/64 01/21/64
Rasher, Isaac married Sylvester, Temperance Ann 12/29/63 01/06/64
Rasin, J. Freemay married Claypoole, Julia A. 03/04/62 03/11/62
Rasin, Lileone Regina died 04/24/64 04/27/64
Rasin, Martha Annie died 09/28/65 09/29/65
Raszell, Henry died 10/10/62 11/06/62
Ratchford, Margaret (Mrs.) died 02/02/63 02/04/63
Ratcliffe, Charles Larew died 03/16/65 03/16/65
Ratcliffe, Josephine died 04/11/65 04/12/65
Ratcliffe, Mary C. married Hamill, Robert J. B. 02/09/63 02/12/63
Ratty, Catherine (Mrs.) died 12/29/64 12/30/64
Ratty, Catherine (Mrs.) died 12/29/64 12/31/64
Ratty, Christopher died 01/24/65 01/25/65
Ratty, Henry died 03/25/63 03/26/63
Rau, Elizabeth (Mrs.) died 11/20/65 11/21/65
Rau, Elizabeth (Mrs.) died 11/20/65 11/22/65
Rau, John C. died 05/01/64 05/02/64
Rauch, Nicholas died 06/05/65 06/06/65

Rausch, Christiana A. married Sterling, Thomas J. 09/08/64 09/08/64
Rausch, John died 12/02/63 12/03/63
Rausch, John died 12/02/63 12/04/63
Rausch, John H. married Lemcke, Sophia 09/15/64 09/17/64
Raves, Emma married Bowen, Edward 12/25/62 12/29/62
Rawlings, Ada E. married Carroll, William P. 09/05/65 09/23/65
Rawlings, J. Soule married Snyder, Maggie D. 06/21/65 06/24/65
Rawlings, Lilian May died 10/24/63 10/29/63
Rawlings, Mary E. married Watters, John 10/10/65 10/12/65
Rawlings, Mary Zora married Garner, Benjamin R. 02/09/64 03/04/64
Rawlings, Sarah C. married Cruett, John W. 12/03/63 12/07/63
Ray, B. M. married Wolf, Josie C. 06/23/65 10/05/65
Ray, Benjamin died 03/11/63 03/13/63
Ray, Eliza (Mrs.) died 07/03/63 07/04/63
Ray, Emma married Spangler, James D. (Lt.) 12/17/61 12/20/61
Ray, Emma Rebecca died 07/28/64 07/29/64
Ray, Francis married Bervard, Mary 01/09/62 01/13/62
Ray, Hollis F. married Deford, Julia A. 11/21/65 11/23/65
Ray, John died 05/07/63 05/08/63
Ray, John died 09/26/65 09/27/65
Ray, John H. married Magruder, Sarah 03/31/64 04/02/64
Ray, Joseph married Wilson, Willia Ann (Mrs.) 04/23/63 04/25/63
Ray, Mary M. died 09/14/61 09/16/61
Ray, Stella died 06/04/65 06/06/65
Ray, Thomas died 09/17/61 09/19/61
Ray, William married Hinder, Sarah 05/22/62 05/24/62
Ray, William G. married Cross, Sophie 01/27/63 01/31/63
Rayhice, M. Cecelia married Scott, Edward M. 01/08/63 01/12/63
Raymo, Anna Louisa died 02/28/62 03/01/62
Raymo, Francis married Weyrough, Louisa 08/07/61 09/25/61
Raymond, Catharine Celia married Faid, John 11/10/65 12/19/65
Raymond, Mary Christiana died 07/14/64 07/16/64
Raymond, Sidney D. married Mitchell, Eliza E. 05/05/62 05/07/62
Rayne, Jannet McKinlay died 11/06/62 11/07/62
Rayne, William married Nelson, Louisa 01/20/64 01/25/64
Raynolds, Annie Roberts (Mrs.) died 10/31/64 11/04/64
Raynolds, Stephen P. married Cadwallader, Emma L. 04/28/64 05/03/64
Raynor, John married Harvey, Susan 01/02/65 01/05/65
Raynor, Willie died 05/12/62 05/13/62
Raysinger, Emma died 12/10/65 12/11/65
Rea, (Mrs. James) died 12/13/61 12/14/61
Rea, E. J. married Davis, Reverdy P. 07/16/63 04/26/64
Rea, Irene married Poulton, Charles 08/11/65 08/16/65
Rea, Joseph B. married Arnold, Martha Jane 12/13/64 12/20/64
Read, Howard Cornwell died 10/17/62 10/18/62
Read, Jinnie died 07/09/63 07/10/63
Read, Laura Revere died 07/30/64 08/02/64
Read, Martha married Tomlinson, R. Burns 05/28/63 06/01/63
Read, Nelson S. died 03/11/64 03/19/64
Read, Robert died 06/15/64 06/20/64
Read, Samuel E. died 10/30/61 11/22/61
Read, Sarah Elizabeth died 10/05/63 10/06/63
Read, Sarah Osgood married Parrott, Joseph J. 08/29/61 08/30/61
Read, William J. married Shipley, Medora M. 10/04/65 10/11/65
Readasel, Jacob F. died no date 11/18/64

Readel, Martha (Mrs.) died 03/03/63   03/05/63
Readsel, Jacob Franklin died 08/18/64   09/10/64
Reagan, Arsceanas married Thomas, Louisa 05/10/64   05/17/64
Realy, Laura J. married Wilson, Ezekial 04/14/64   04/15/64
Reaney, Alexander J. married Forsyth, Virginia 02/20/61   03/20/62
Reaney, Alexander J. married Forsyth, Jennia S. 02/20/61   03/21/62
Rearden, William H. married Kelly, Mary A. 02/02/64   02/08/64
Reardon, Daniel died 11/01/64   11/02/64
Reason, Ann Rebecca married Bond, George W. 12/21/62   12/23/62
Reather, Charles F. married McCafferty, Annie E. 05/05/63   05/07/63
Reather, Jennie married Hughes, William H. 03/10/61   03/11/61
Reay, David, Sr. died 12/07/61   12/09/61
Reckerd, Sarah J. married Diven, George E. 10/01/63   10/21/63
Reckert, Charles A. married Almack, Hester A. 05/05/63   05/11/63
Reckert, John C. died 05/09/64   05/10/64
Reckert, Matilda (Mrs.) died 12/30/64   12/31/64
Reckert, Sarah Rebecca married Dueur, Orlando 02/04/64   02/08/64
Reckitt, Matilda C. married Sloan, Casper B. 07/14/64   07/15/64
Reckitts, Lawrence Malcom died 12/02/61   12/06/61
Record, Elmira died 09/15/64   09/22/64
Reddall, Eliza Jane died 08/21/63   08/24/63
Redding, Mary died 06/09/63   06/10/63
Reddish, Holton died 12/19/64   12/20/64
Reddish, Sarah died 01/16/65   01/18/65
Reddish, William died 01/15/63   01/17/63
Reddish, William Higgins died 11/22/62   11/24/62
Reddish, William K. (Capt.) died 03/15/62   03/17/62
Redgrave, Georgie Washington died 08/31/64   09/02/64
Redifer, John Smith died 04/09/61   04/10/61
Redifer, Mary Ann (Mrs.) died 01/03/65   01/21/65
Reding, George married Gatch, Elmira V. 05/02/62   05/03/62
Redish, Annie E. married Sutch, Daniel B. 08/21/64   09/10/64
Redish, Martha (Mrs.) died 03/20/63   04/18/63
Redman, Adolphus married Walters, Anna M. 12/24/61   12/31/61
Redman, Elizabeth died 01/14/63   01/16/63
Redman, Mary A. died 05/18/61   07/01/61
Redman, Thomas V. married Horney, Sallie E. 12/25/65   12/30/65
Redmond, Charlotte E. married Gale, Charles H. 11/20/65   12/16/65
Redmond, Charlotte Hamilton died 11/30/65   12/05/65
Redmond, Helen R. married Harrisk, John E. 03/04/62   03/10/62
Redmond, Hugh died 05/12/65   05/13/65
Redmond, Josephine M. married Jones, Charles H. 07/11/61   07/26/61
Redmond, Milley died 06/29/62   07/01/62
Redmond, Sarah J. married Rodgers, John C. 09/17/61   10/02/61
Redue, Isabel (Mrs.) died 11/02/65   11/22/65
Reece, Joshua died 07/09/64   07/11/64
Reed, Alexandra died 04/07/65   04/08/65
Reed, Amelia married Jones, Thomas D. 10/26/64   10/29/64
Reed, Ann V. married Kernan, James 10/26/65   10/28/65
Reed, Ann V. married Kernan, James 10/26/65   10/30/65
Reed, Ann West died 06/05/62   06/14/62
Reed, Anne married King, Alexander K. 07/02/62   07/12/62
Reed, Anne married Cromey, John H. 06/09/63   06/12/63
Reed, Annie married Fales, Lawrence H. 02/20/62   03/18/62
Reed, Caroline M. married Chase, Samuel W., Jr. 03/12/63   04/07/63

Reed, Catherine died 08/17/65   08/19/65
Reed, Charlotte M. married Mettee, August 12/04/65   12/15/65
Reed, Eliza died 08/21/62   08/22/62
Reed, Emma Jane died 07/29/64   08/02/64
Reed, George B. W. married Bowen, Emma A. 09/09/62   09/25/62
Reed, Harris Corner died 03/13/65   03/15/65
Reed, J. Harris married Corner, Mary S. 02/20/61   02/25/61
Reed, J. L. married Kirby, M. E. 04/25/65   05/29/65
Reed, Jennie Nelson married Zimmerman, William Henry 06/04/63   06/13/63
Reed, John H. died 10/22/62   10/30/62
Reed, John H. died 08/12/63   08/13/63
Reed, John H. died 07/29/64   07/30/64
Reed, Martha J. married Carr, William H. 12/24/62   12/27/62
Reed, Mary Leonora died 06/23/61   06/25/61
Reed, Michael J. died 07/29/64   07/30/64
Reed, Noah R. married Chambers, Mary Ann 11/24/63   12/05/63
Reed, Patsey married Bommen, Clemen 09/10/63   09/12/63
Reed, Rebecca married Carroll, Henry 07/16/63   07/18/63
Reed, Rebecca E. married Holtzman, Israel 04/13/62   04/16/62
Reed, Richard married Jones, Achias Anna A. 12/22/64   12/24/64
Reed, Samuel Pattison died 10/05/61   11/25/61
Reed, Sylvester H. died 11/17/61   11/18/61
Reed, Thomas died 11/11/65   11/15/65
Reed, W. H. W. married Seymour, Lizzie 12/07/65   12/14/65
Reed, William died 11/18/61   11/19/61
Reed, Willie married Richards, Julia 09/25/65   09/30/65
Reeder, Bertha died 02/01/65   02/02/65
Reeder, Samuel T. married Nizer, Rachel Olivia 01/25/63   01/28/63
Reekert, Mary Elenora died 08/31/63   09/02/63
Rees, Bernard died 01/02/64   01/25/64
Reese, Annie O. married Sewell, James M. 10/12/65   10/16/65
Reese, August married Arnold, Laura 10/22/65   10/24/65
Reese, Catherine died 09/26/65   09/28/65
Reese, Charles married Copeland, Mary Ann 04/09/63   04/11/63
Reese, Clara Virginia died 01/19/65   02/06/65
Reese, E. E. married Henderson, Samuel A. 06/01/63   06/03/63
Reese, E. Yeates (Rev.) died 09/14/61   09/16/61
Reese, Emma S. married Oewns, Norvel W. 11/30/65   12/01/65
Reese, Franklin died 04/16/65   04/18/65
Reese, George S. married Foote, Josephine C. 09/11/61   09/13/61
Reese, Harry died 07/07/62   07/08/62
Reese, Henry died 02/11/64   02/12/64
Reese, Henry D. married Mears, Louisa 03/05/61   06/01/61
Reese, Howard Renfrhew died 02/01/63   02/05/63
Reese, M. F. married Dryden, Mary A. R. 06/16/62   06/17/62
Reese, Mamie Young died 05/08/61   05/09/61
Reese, Martha Ann married Ford, William H. 09/20/65   09/25/65
Reese, Mary A. R. (Mrs.) married Kensett, Thomas H. 10/19/65   10/20/65
Reese, Mary C. married Blessing, John 07/16/63   07/18/65
Reese, Matthias Forney died 02/09/63   02/10/63
Reese, Matthias Forney died 02/09/63   02/11/63
Reese, Mattie T. married Banty, P. S. 11/03/64   11/12/64
Reese, Sue R. married Addison, Frank R. 07/09/63   09/15/63
Reese, Thomas H. married Haney, Novella 08/28/64   09/07/64
Reese, Thomas Sargant married Poole, Sarah E. 05/24/64   06/07/64

Reese, William E. married Torby, Mary 08/19/62   08/25/62
Reese, William Thomas died 07/02/62   07/04/62
Reeside, Catharine A. (Mrs.) died 04/21/64   04/23/64
Reesides, Annie married Higdan, Robert 02/28/65   03/11/65
Reever, Mary Ann (Mrs.) died 10/15/63   10/17/63
Reeves, Aaron T. married Johnson, Mary E. 03/14/61   03/16/61
Reeves, Emma H. married Simms, J. T. 03/28/63   05/16/63
Reeves, G. Washington married Sapp, Jemima (Mrs.) 11/30/64   12/20/64
Reeves, William, Jr. married Belt, Lucretia A. 11/23/64   11/26/64
Regan, Catherine A. married Jenkins, Thomas 01/11/63   02/03/63
Regelein, Rose A. married Hoover, William H. 04/20/65   04/28/65
Reges, R. Wilson (Lt.) died 07/30/64   08/04/64
Regester, Lizzie died 01/22/63   01/24/63
Regester, Mary F. died 04/09/61   04/13/61
Regester, Samuel W. married Church, Clara 10/04/64   10/06/64
Reich, Annie R. married Mercer, C. 05/17/65   05/20/65
Reichenberger, Dinah married Wallenstein, Solomon 03/23/62   03/25/62
Reid, Archibald died 10/12/62   10/13/62
Reid, Eliza Jane died 02/21/61   02/22/61
Reid, Elizabeth married Mansfield, R. W. 04/28/64   05/02/64
Reid, Elizabeth (Mrs.) died 01/27/63   01/29/63
Reid, Ellen E. (Mrs.) married Brewer, Vincent 02/19/63   02/25/63
Reid, Fannie E. married Root, Daniel E. 10/01/65   10/31/65
Reid, James married Watson, Elizabeth A. 12/03/63   12/29/63
Reid, Lizzie K. married Riley, William R. 12/08/63   12/11/63
Reid, Margaret Durbin died 07/27/63   07/29/63
Reid, Mary Ann died 11/27/63   11/28/63
Reid, Sallie married Flynn, Lewis 03/07/65   03/28/65
Reid, Thomas B. married Miller, Annie 06/20/64   07/08/64
Reid, William died 06/08/65   06/09/65
Reid, William D. M. died 10/26/65   10/27/65
Reid, William H. died 11/29/64   11/30/64
Reid, William James died 05/01/61   05/02/61
Reifsnider, John L. married Billingslea, Lizzie H. 12/10/61   12/11/61
Reifsnider, William died 12/05/62   12/09/62
Reifsnider, William E. married Sheets, Hattie V. 10/18/65   10/23/65
Reifsnider, William E. married Sheets, Hattie V. 10/18/65   10/25/65
Reigart, John M. married Briscoe, Lewis J. 05/02/65   05/11/65
Reigart, John M. married Middleton, Frances Augusta 05/02/65   05/10/65
Reigart, Milton J. died 05/21/62   06/21/62
Reigelien, Drusilla E. died 03/24/62   03/26/62
Reil, Caroline died 01/08/65   01/10/65
Reiley, Susan J. G. died 12/18/64   12/19/64
Reilley, Peter married Butler, Mary A. (Mrs.) 10/14/61   10/19/61
Reilley, Rose A. married Kelly, James 04/20/65   04/28/65
Reilly, Alice died 04/23/62   04/25/62
Reilly, Alice died 01/20/64   01/21/64
Reilly, Catherine died 10/17/65   10/19/65
Reilly, Catherine Ann died 08/30/62   09/01/62
Reilly, Edward E. married Madigan, Mary 12/02/62   12/05/62
Reilly, Frances Virginia died 04/05/62   04/07/62
Reilly, George Edward died 10/18/63   10/19/63
Reilly, Henrietta died 08/23/62   08/26/62
Reilly, James died 11/19/62   11/26/62
Reilly, Jane married Brown, Archibald 02/07/61   03/25/61

Reilly, John married Owens, Betsy 11/26/63 12/15/63
Reilly, Josephine married Dean, William H. 03/28/64 03/30/64
Reilly, Mary (Mrs.) died 08/10/64 08/13/64
Reilly, Rose Anna married Cursey, William 12/09/62 12/12/62
Reilly, Rosetta Virginia married Kirby, Thomas Edward 09/27/64 10/01/64
Reilly, Sarah A. married Stone, William L. 06/25/65 07/07/65
Reilly, William John died 03/30/64 04/01/64
Reily, Charles married Legburn, Minice 02/26/62 03/01/62
Reily, Thomas died 08/06/62 08/07/62
Reinhardt, Amelia married Greene, Samuel S. 10/26/63 11/07/63
Reinhardt, Charles married Colter, Virginia 02/03/65 02/22/65
Reinhart, George P. married Bayley, Mary A. E. 09/18/64 09/21/64
Reinholt, Charles C. died 02/20/64 02/22/64
Reinick, Hannah E. married Myers, John 05/25/65 05/31/65
Reinicker, Charles R.C. (Cpt.) died 05/06/64 06/11/64
Reinicker, Morrison Harris died 10/24/63 10/26/63
Reip, J. Henry married Martin, Helen 01/15/61 01/18/61
Reip, Lavinia C. married Smith, J. Stewart 06/14/64 06/18/64
Reip, Lawrence J. died 04/02/65 04/04/65
Reipe, Joseph H. married Potter, Jane A. 04/29/61 10/11/61
Reirig, Maggie married Rankle, William 08/29/65 09/13/65
Reisdorph, S. A. married Dutton, Fannie G. 09/27/64 10/03/64
Reisinger, Amelia married Gettiet, William H. 10/18/64 10/29/64
Reisinger, Marian Virginia died 12/23/64 12/24/64
Reisner, Albert W. married Hagner, Mattie 02/14/65 02/21/65
Reister, Annie R. died 11/07/63 11/09/63
Reister, Elias died 09/10/63 09/11/63
Reister, John G. died 04/09/62 04/11/62
Reister, Jonathan D. married Canox, Carie 08/23/65 08/25/65
Reister, Mary E. P. married Rogers, Charles M. 09/22/63 09/24/63
Reister, Peter P. married Broharn, Sarah J. (Mrs.) 11/08/65 11/10/65
Reiter, Andrew J. died 09/27/64 09/29/64
Reiter, Georgie Woodbourn died 03/07/64 03/08/64
Reiter, Peter A. died 11/15/64 11/16/64
Reitlring, Lewis married Potee, Mary 02/05/65 02/07/65
Reitz, Mary C. died 11/29/62 12/01/62
Reitz, Mary C. died 11/29/62 12/03/62
Reitz, William H. L. married Roszel, Mary S. 05/22/61 06/04/61
Remick, John H. married Lewis, Annie E. 09/25/64 09/27/64
Remick, Robert Canfield died 07/28/63 07/29/63
Remley, Isabella married Depass, John 03/09/65 03/13/65
Remmell, John H. married Lewis, Mary E. 11/17/64 11/18/64
Renhoe, E. M. married Magill, C. J. 04/02/64 04/28/64
Renick, Isabel Hamilton died 08/03/64 08/30/64
Renner, Elizabeth married Turner, George W. 04/10/61 04/13/61
Rennie, David P. married Hipsley, Sallie E. 10/18/65 10/26/65
Rennous, John A. died 10/19/61 10/22/61
Renoff, George W. married Holton, Annie H. 06/13/64 10/04/64
Renoff, Mary E. married String, John F. 07/31/61 12/09/61
Renshaw, Emma Kate died 08/07/63 08/08/63
Renshaw, John died 06/13/61 06/15/61
Renshaw, John Franklin married Wolf, Henrietta Feby Ann 04/28/63
    05/05/63
Renshaw, Loretto died 07/30/63 08/01/63
Renshaw, Lucy Carter died 09/15/65 09/18/65

Renshaw, Margaret C. died 10/18/65 10/30/65
Renshaw, Sarah died 04/27/64 04/28/64
Renshaw, Sarah (Mrs.) died 10/30/65 11/02/65
Renshaw, William Samuel died 11/09/63 11/16/63
Renter, William Oscar died 01/31/64 02/01/64
Rentz, Elizabeth M. married Opitz, John 09/06/63 09/22/63
Rentz, George F. married Ely, Caroline 11/30/65 12/04/65
Reppard, (infant daughter) died 08/12/61 08/13/61
Reppert, Hannah died 10/16/65 10/18/65
Reppert, Lewis F. died 07/17/62 07/19/62
Resch, Vallentine died 10/20/65 10/21/65
Resham, Henrietta married Weber, Theodore 12/09/64 12/13/64
Resor, Maggie married Cassard, George Carleton 11/30/65 12/16/65
Resse, Sophia died 11/04/62 11/06/62
Reuppersberger, Gustave W. married Schaeffer, Mary C. 09/07/65 09/18/6
Reuter, Fredericke married Sehl, Justus 09/01/63 09/05/63
Reuter, Sophia H. married Knox, Julius W. 07/21/61 07/24/61
Revans, Emily Sumner (Mrs.) died 02/13/64 02/25/64
Revels, James married Downs, Elizabeth 04/09/62 04/11/62
Revere, Willie B. died 07/21/65 07/29/65
Revill, Mary died 06/26/64 06/27/64
Rew, Anna S. married Crane, George H. 11/30/64 12/02/64
Rex, Virginia Hooper died 06/24/62 07/01/62
Reynolds, Alfred D. married Aler, Rox A. V. 04/21/64 05/19/64
Reynolds, Alfred D. (Lt.) died 08/18/64 08/31/64
Reynolds, Barney died 09/18/65 09/19/65
Reynolds, Bazzari R. died 04/14/64 04/15/64
Reynolds, Charles Albert J. died 10/25/63 10/29/63
Reynolds, Chauncey A. married Hullings, Elizabeth 06/09/64 06/11/64
Reynolds, Dennis died 05/23/65 05/25/65
Reynolds, Edward died 04/15/62 04/18/62
Reynolds, Edward T. died 08/16/65 08/18/65
Reynolds, Elizabeth married Shade, David 12/10/65 12/23/65
Reynolds, George W. married Greener, Caroline 10/15/63 10/20/63
Reynolds, Georgie B.M. died 07/29/63 07/30/63
Reynolds, Jenette died 05/18/64 05/20/64
Reynolds, John married Brown, Annie 06/11/61 07/27/61
Reynolds, John H. married Pruett, Annie 11/22/63 11/26/63
Reynolds, John R. married Paddington, Martha 09/13/64 11/19/64
Reynolds, Joseph P. married Supplee, Amanda L. 08/17/63 08/27/64
Reynolds, Loumonia L. married Minnick, Conrad 12/27/61 01/16/62
Reynolds, Mary died 02/22/61 02/25/61
Reynolds, Mary E. (Mrs.) married Biggs, Zacharia K. 01/10/65 01/16/65
Reynolds, Michael died 02/11/65 02/13/65
Reynolds, Mollie L. married Nutwell, George 06/13/65 06/14/65
Reynolds, O. B. married Cropp, Jennie F. 03/18/63 04/08/63
Reynolds, Oliver Benson died 08/26/63 08/27/63
Reynolds, Sallie married Hinton, Theodore 02/09/64 02/19/64
Reynolds, Sarah A. married Wilson, Edward H. 09/01/64 09/09/64
Reynolds, Thomas married Ogden, Virginia C. 02/12/63 02/13/63
Reynolds, Virginia married Cable, George S. 10/29/63 10/31/63
Reynolds, Willard Israel died 12/07/62 12/09/62
Reynolds, William married McConnell, Rachel 10/02/60 03/11/61
Reynolds, William H. married Underwood, M. S. 11/08/65 11/16/65
Reynols, J. R. married Cropp, Jennie F. 03/18/63 06/16/63

Rhea, Frank Miller died 03/31/62   03/01/62
Rhea, John L. married Shaver, Lucy C. 04/20/65   05/11/65
Rheim, William Henry died 09/15/64   09/16/64
Rhein, Josephine (Mrs.) died 12/14/64   12/16/64
Rhein, Philip died 03/30/65   03/31/65
Rhine, John W. married Fisher, Catherine L. 03/24/63   03/25/63
Rhinehart, Lizzie E. married Smallwood, Charles 03/06/64   03/21/64
Rhinehart, Mary C. married Hooper, Samuel T. 05/14/62   05/16/62
Rhlers, Annie Eliza died 07/08/65   07/14/65
Rhoads, Abraham died 08/17/63   08/19/63
Rhoads, Annie J. married Maddocks, John B. 01/04/63   03/10/63
Rhoads, Myra E. died 07/31/61   08/01/61
Rhoads, Willard died 08/28/63   08/29/63
Rhoder, Barbara (Mrs.) died 03/08/64   03/11/64
Rhoderick, Susie married Kinkade, J. Nixon (Lt.) 11/19/63   11/30/63
Rhodes, Benjamin C. died 06/24/62   06/24/62
Rhodes, Helen Vans died 01/24/64   02/04/64
Rhodes, John H. died 01/01/64   01/02/64
Rhodes, John Richardson died 09/01/63   09/02/63
Rhodes, Margaret (Mrs.) died 10/18/63   10/19/63
Rhodes, Marion Greeves died 06/01/64   06/02/64
Rhodes, Sophia A. married Matthews, William N. 12/01/64   12/07/64
Rhule, Martha married Charles, Benjamin 12/06/65   12/09/65
Rhunamond, Henry died 09/04/65   09/05/65
Rial, James Alexious died 01/05/64   01/06/64
Riall, Margie A. married Grumbine, Emanuel 10/31/65   11/09/65
Riall, Mary died 12/16/62   12/20/62
Riall, Morgiana K. married Crumbine, Emanuel 10/31/65   11/04/65
Rians, Marcella M. married Skinner, Francis 06/19/64   06/21/64
Rice, Addis married Norris, William B., Jr. 12/22/64   12/31/64
Rice, Catherine L. (Mrs.) died 02/25/64   02/27/64
Rice, Charles married Startt, Emma J. 07/28/62   10/28/62
Rice, Charles died 08/08/63   08/10/63
Rice, Charles Thomas died 03/26/62   03/27/62
Rice, Edward Carroll died 07/21/62   07/23/62
Rice, John L. married Rogers, Mary H. 07/27/65   07/31/65
Rice, John R. married Puckett, Rebecca J. 04/01/64   01/14/65
Rice, Lewis married Housnick, Francis 09/05/64   09/08/64
Rice, Mary Adelaide died 08/13/62   08/14/62
Rice, Mary Adelaide died 08/13/62   09/24/62
Rice, Mary Ellen died 05/01/65   05/02/65
Rice, Peter married Freeze, Mary J. 04/10/64   05/30/64
Rice, Robert married Claney, Catherine 02/09/64   02/16/64
Rice, Rose married Simon, Mark 11/29/65   12/14/65
Rice, Stephen married Freeze, Margaret 01/06/61   01/22/61
Rice, Stephen died 09/19/64   09/20/64
Rich, Anton married Springer, Elizabeth 05/03/63   05/11/63
Rich, Mary Rebecca died 09/07/61   09/10/61
Rich, Samuel A. died 06/20/64   06/21/64
Richard, Mary married Morris, George 05/24/63   07/28/63
Richard, Mary Elizabeth married Smith, Sebastian 11/16/65   11/18/65
Richard, Nila Warner died 12/21/65   12/22/65
Richard, V. P. (M.D.) married McCabe, Jennie T. 10/01/61   10/07/61
Richards, Annie E. married Murphy, William S. 06/12/65   06/16/65
Richards, Cecelia (Mrs.) died 05/23/63   05/25/63

Richards, Charlotte L. married Sparks, Walter J. 03/06/61   03/08/61
Richards, Cora J. married Weishampel, Benjamin F. 03/07/65   03/09/65
Richards, George Smith died 12/03/64   12/06/64
Richards, Harriet (Mrs.) died 01/21/63   01/23/63
Richards, Henry H. married Slaughter, Alice T. 09/15/62   09/17/62
Richards, Hester A. married Boone, Joshua 11/17/61   11/19/61
Richards, Johannah married Strader, A. M. 03/05/65   05/15/65
Richards, John M. married Locke, Sarah M. 06/24/65   06/28/65
Richards, John T. married Waer, Elizabeth 03/05/61   03/07/61
Richards, Joshua married Fields, Catharine 01/26/65   01/28/65
Richards, Julia married Reed, Willie 09/25/65   09/30/65
Richards, Mary A. married Byers, James F. 02/04/64   02/05/64
Richards, Mary F. married Downes, William H. (Dr.) 04/30/65   05/04/65
Richards, Mary Jane died 10/23/61   10/31/61
Richards, Matilda died 04/09/62   04/11/62
Richards, Sarah Frances died 06/27/64   06/28/64
Richards, Solomon married Murray, Rebecca 12/03/63   12/10/63
Richards, William D. died 09/15/64   09/17/64
Richards, William Edward died 12/31/63   01/02/64
Richardson, A. M. Marilla died 02/03/62   02/04/62
Richardson, Anna M. (Mrs.) died 09/22/63   09/24/63
Richardson, Catharine J. died 01/01/62   01/02/62
Richardson, Cecelia (Mrs.) died 03/22/65   03/24/65
Richardson, Charlotte died 08/15/62   08/16/62
Richardson, E. married Poole, Maggie 04/13/65   04/15/65
Richardson, Ennis Ford died 06/11/64   06/13/64
Richardson, Florence married Kelso, J. Russell 11/07/61   11/08/61
Richardson, Francis A. married Howard, Margaret 01/15/61   01/16/61
Richardson, Geoffrey I. married Bowly, Mary 03/08/64   03/10/64
Richardson, George (Cpt.) died 12/12/62   01/26/63
Richardson, Henry married Hubbard, Eliza 11/12/63   11/14/63
Richardson, Howard, Jr. married Holcombe, Kitta 10/04/65   10/17/65
Richardson, Isabella W. married Bowie, Charles 01/29/61   01/31/61
Richardson, James K. married McManus, Margaret J. 05/07/61   05/08/61
Richardson, John married Nevitt, Rebecca 10/15/63   10/17/63
Richardson, John S. died 07/30/63   08/03/63
Richardson, Julia Ann married Welsh, Samuel P. 07/05/63   07/10/63
Richardson, Margaret died 03/11/62   03/12/62
Richardson, Margaret died 03/11/62   03/13/62
Richardson, Matilda B. died 03/16/64   03/26/64
Richardson, Morris died 12/15/62   12/18/62
Richardson, Rachel (Mrs.) died 06/10/63   06/11/63
Richardson, Robert died 05/18/63   05/19/63
Richardson, Sadie M. married Brenaman, Charles H. 11/21/63   12/01/63
Richardson, Sallie R. married Tompkins, Judge 01/06/63   01/26/63
Richardson, Samuel married Begg, Sarah 02/04/64   02/13/64
Richardson, Samuel T. married Pancoast, Sallie W. 11/25/63   11/28/63
Richardson, Samuel, Sr. died 06/25/61   06/28/61
Richardson, Skelton S. died 11/03/61   11/05/61
Richardson, Summerfield died 03/26/65   11/09/65
Richardson, Thomas C. married Wirth, Christina 12/08/61   12/30/61
Richardson, Tillie B. married Bowen, A. Evan 08/02/62   04/04/63
Richardson, William H., Jr. died 10/13/61   10/14/61
Richfield, George W. married Norris, Rachel Ann 11/26/65   12/18/65
Richmond, Anna Catherine died 07/30/61   07/31/61

```
Richmond, Josephine died 11/30/64   12/03/64
Richmond, Lavinia H. (Mrs.) died 04/08/65   04/10/65
Richmond, May Teresa died 01/08/64   01/09/64
Richmond, Samuel married Montgomery, Eliza Jane 11/13/65   11/28/65
Richmond, Samuel married Montgomery, Eliza Jane 11/13/65   11/29/65
Richmond, Sarah E. married Johnson, James W. 01/28/64   02/22/64
Richmond, William H. died 12/30/61   01/01/62
Richse, Gesina died 09/17/65   09/18/65
Richstein, Elenora (Mrs.) married Thompson, Salem H. 09/10/62   09/19/62
Richstein, Retta J. married Bird, Frank L. 09/12/65   09/15/65
Richstein, William F. married Lester, Jemima R. 03/19/62   03/20/62
Richter, Charles A. married Cooper, Susan A. H. 08/10/61   08/19/61
Richter, G. H. married Woods, Catherine A. 09/26/65   10/10/65
Richter, Mary C. married Guard, Charles H. 06/26/62   06/30/62
Rickers, Henry N. married Schiers, Lizzie 04/28/63   05/05/63
Ricketts, David married Rountree, Adelaide Virginia 03/03/65   05/11/65
Ricketts, Granville C. married Pittinger, Alice J. no date   12/19/64
Ricketts, Margaret Ann died 08/26/62   08/27/62
Ricketts, Thomas M. died 05/06/65   05/09/65
Ricktor, Frederick died 03/21/64   03/22/64
Ricktor, Samuel married King, Sarah C. 04/09/65   06/05/65
Riddle, A. P. married Hyatt, Sarah Elizabeth (Mrs.) 04/21/63   04/25/63
Riddle, Ariana Rebecca married Yoe, Benjamin Rush 05/16/61   05/30/61
Riddle, Charles married Pierce, Sarah A. 05/13/63   05/15/63
Riddle, George W. married Beckett, Ann R. 01/10/61   01/17/61
Riddle, Rebecca M. died 08/12/62   08/19/62
Riddle, Sarah Ann died 06/23/65   06/24/65
Riddle, Sarah Jane died 09/11/63   09/12/63
Ridenmayer, Edwin died 03/09/64   03/10/64
Rider, Abraham married Merrit, Maggie R. 02/23/65   02/27/65
Rider, David A. died 02/13/64   02/15/64
Rider, Emanuel died 04/14/61   04/15/61
Rider, Emma Z. married Christie, Jas. J. 01/03/65   01/06/65
Rider, Henry died 02/03/64   02/05/64
Rider, Sarah died 11/17/62   12/08/62
Rider, Surfeener married Freedy, Alfred 03/16/61   05/22/61
Rideway, Thomas married Dashiell, Monteray H. 10/16/61   11/01/61
Ridgaway, A. C. married Macher, J. S. 12/15/64   12/24/64
Ridgaway, Jeanette died 09/13/63   09/14/63
Ridgaway, John E. died 08/23/61   08/24/61
Ridgaway, Kate died 02/22/64   02/24/64
Ridgaway, Robert O. died 04/27/61   04/29/61
Ridgaway, Thomas A. died 10/23/63   10/28/63
Ridgaway, Thomas S. married Bennett, Georgie A. 06/03/63   06/09/63
Ridge, Andrew Jackson died 12/03/65   12/04/65
Ridge, Ann (Mrs.) died 03/28/63   03/30/63
Ridge, Mary Ellen married Green, James Morris 02/04/64   02/11/64
Ridgeley, Elizabeth died 08/28/62   08/29/62
Ridgeley, Lydia died 06/10/61   06/12/61
Ridgeley, Mary E. married Smothers, George H. 11/30/63   12/08/63
Ridgely, Bruneston died 01/22/61   01/24/61
Ridgely, Edgar died 08/13/64   08/20/64
Ridgely, Eliza married Uhler, John R. 04/19/64   04/21/64
Ridgely, Elizabeth Herring died 01/23/63   01/24/63
Ridgely, Emily died 03/10/61   03/12/61
```

Ridgely, Emily L. died 03/10/61   04/06/61
Ridgely, Gustavus W. married Hammond, Camille 11/11/63   11/12/63
Ridgely, Isabella (Mrs.) died 09/06/65   09/09/65
Ridgely, Mary Louisa (Mrs.) died 11/08/63   11/10/63
Ridgely, Mary Machall died 06/05/64   06/06/64
Ridgely, Mary S. died 07/21/62   07/25/62
Ridgely, N. G. (Dr.) married Deshon, Ida C. 09/06/64   09/08/64
Ridgely, Octavia married Stewart, Joseph B. 09/02/61   09/04/61
Ridgeway, Georgie married Caldwell, Reuben T. 01/13/64   01/19/64
Ridgeway, William H. married Borderly, Margaret A. 02/04/64   02/05/64
Ridgley, William married Denisson, Mary Eliza 05/28/63   05/30/63
Ridgly, Fannie married Lucas, George 04/07/64   04/15/64
Riefle, Henry died 05/06/62   05/07/62
Rieger, Joseph died 11/23/65   12/05/65
Riel, Jane died 10/28/65   10/30/65
Rielly, John died 11/29/63   12/01/63
Rielly, Rose A. married Way, John H. 10/06/64   10/18/64
Riely, John James died 11/09/65   11/11/65
Rieman, George Henry died 02/19/65   02/20/65
Rieman, Harriett married Moore, George 03/13/61   03/15/61
Rieman, Henriette W. L. E. died 08/18/64   08/19/64
Rieman, Henry died 04/27/65   04/29/65
Rieman, Joseph M. married Lowe, Annie 10/03/61   10/08/61
Rieman, Martha G. married Early, John D., Jr. 04/27/65   04/29/65
Rieman, Mathilde died 02/17/65   02/18/65
Riepe, Joseph Eugene died 09/17/65   09/23/65
Rier, Carrie E. died no date   08/21/61
Riffle, Thomas married Miller, Ava 02/23/64   02/25/64
Rigby, Charles died 01/14/62   01/15/62
Rigby, William Rusk died 06/05/64   08/06/64
Rigger, Willie died 06/16/64   06/17/64
Riggin, Alice married Busch, Abram V. 12/25/62   02/10/63
Riggin, Emily (Mrs.) died 04/22/65   04/24/65
Riggin, Israel died 05/27/62   05/29/62
Riggin, Mary Jane died 02/24/64   02/29/64
Riggins, Charles married Crouch, Martha 08/16/64   09/07/64
Riggs, Amelia married Myers, William H. 12/19/60   01/03/61
Riggs, Carrie Field died 09/07/61   09/09/61
Riggs, Elizabeth Swan (Mrs.) died 11/24/63   11/26/63
Riggs, George W. died 08/27/64   08/29/64
Riggs, John died 07/29/63   08/03/63
Riggs, John died 07/22/64   07/23/64
Riggs, Mary (Mrs.) died 09/13/63   09/14/63
Rigley, Samuel married Johnson, Frances Jane 10/06/64   10/08/64
Rigney, George married Shane, Catherine 08/31/64   09/03/64
Rigney, James married Burns, Kate 09/17/61   10/07/61
Rigney, John C. married Connor, Elizabeth C. 12/25/64   01/02/65
Rigney, Sarah Sophia died 08/15/63   08/19/63
Rilby, Patrick F. married Hagner, Rebecca Jane 12/20/63   02/05/64
Riley, Bridget married McDevitt, Cornelius 11/17/63   11/19/63
Riley, Catharine died 07/17/63   07/20/63
Riley, E. S., Sr. married Barbour, Lillie A. M. 08/11/64   08/16/64
Riley, Elizabeth died 06/16/65   06/17/65
Riley, Ellen married Sullivan, John 01/23/62   01/24/62
Riley, Emanuel married Bentley, Jane 01/08/63   01/17/63

Riley, George died 09/09/63 09/10/63
Riley, Harry E. married Fay, Virginia 06/02/64 06/13/64
Riley, Margaret married Toben, Clarence 02/11/62 02/15/62
Riley, Mary (Mrs.) died 06/30/63 07/07/63
Riley, Mary Jane died 10/30/62 11/01/62
Riley, Mary Jane married Roberts, Valentine 07/14/64 07/20/64
Riley, Thomas died 07/22/63 07/23/63
Riley, William E. (USA) died 11/24/63 12/03/63
Riley, William R. married Reid, Lizzie K. 12/08/63 12/11/63
Rimby, Jacob (Lt.) died 08/31/64 09/02/64
Rimby, Jacob Gregory died 08/31/64 09/02/64
Rind, Samuel Seabrook died 06/02/62 08/27/62
Rind, William Alexander died 03/04/63 03/05/63
Rineck, Jacob Jefferson died 12/04/65 12/05/65
Rineck, Jacob Jefferson died 12/04/65 12/06/65
Rinehart, Louis married Bunting, E. 01/27/65 09/02/65
Rinehart, Sarah (Mrs.) died 06/09/65 06/10/65
Rinehart, Susan married Davis, Miles 12/20/64 01/04/65
Rineman, George Mabary died 06/26/64 06/28/64
Rineman, John married Coltrider, Amanda 01/28/63 02/07/63
Rinerman, C. Miranda married Chandler, Robert J. 08/29/65 09/12/65
Ringgold, Edward H. married Mead, Lizzie 11/01/65 11/08/65
Ringgold, Hezekiah died 03/19/64 03/21/64
Ringgold, John died 01/18/65 01/18/65
Ringgold, Joseph died 12/01/63 12/04/63
Ringgold, Mary Clare died 01/22/61 01/24/61
Ringgold, Richard died 09/11/62 09/12/62
Ringgold, Sally married Primrose, Breenbury 11/30/62 12/02/62
Ringgold, Susanna married Nicholson, Lambert 04/02/63 04/18/63
Ringgold, W. H. married Smith, Ann Frances 12/29/64 12/30/64
Ringll, Lenard married Lutin, Sarah 06/13/61 06/14/61
Ringloes, Rachael Mereaner died 01/27/62 01/30/62
Ringold, Ann Maria married Wesley, William 04/14/61 04/16/61
Ringold, Daniel Thomas married Carr, Mary Ellen 11/07/61 11/11/61
Ringold, Eliza died 11/02/62 11/03/62
Ringold, Jacob died 11/08/64 11/10/64
Ringold, P. died 08/29/65 08/31/65
Ringrose, James died 01/26/61 01/28/61
Ringrose, Mary Bell married Garash, John Benjamin 03/29/63 04/09/63
Ringrose, Olivia married Carter, William James M. 11/30/62 12/05/62
Ringrose, Robert married Shea, Frances 06/26/61 07/03/61
Ringrose, Robert died 08/14/61 08/17/61
Ringrose, Sarah (Mrs.) died 10/01/64 10/03/64
Ringrose, Susanna died 03/10/64 03/11/64
Ringrose, William Walter died 06/22/61 06/24/61
Rinker, George E. married Chalmers, Maggie A. 10/10/65 10/18/65
Rinn, Francis died 03/25/63 04/21/63
Rinn, Francis died 03/25/63 04/22/63
Rion, Thomas married Garner, Emily 11/26/63 11/28/63
Riordan, Mary A. married O'Malley, George 03/31/64 04/04/64
Riordan, Michael married Courtney, Mary 02/08/63 02/17/63
Riordoun, James M. died 07/02/65 07/03/65
Ripley, Martha J. died 01/03/63 01/07/63
Ripley, William W. married Hudgins, Mary E. 04/02/63 04/07/63
Rippard, (infant daughter) died 08/12/61 08/15/61

Rippard, Anne (Mrs.) died 01/05/63   01/07/63
Risteau, Kate V. married Kepler, Samuel, Jr. (Dr.) 05/02/61   05/04/61
Risteau, Mary O. married Wilson, J. Oliver (Rev.) 08/11/63   08/12/63
Riston, Emily A. married White, John E. 02/05/62   02/07/62
Ritchie, C. M. (Mrs.) died 10/20/65   10/21/65
Ritchie, Emma died 08/29/64   08/31/64
Rites, Arey died 03/13/62   03/21/62
Ritteau, Margaret married Harrison, Robert V. 09/04/64   09/20/64
Ritter, Addie married Deems, George 11/02/65   11/08/65
Ritter, Dorothy Catherine died 04/24/61   04/25/61
Ritter, Edward B. died 12/31/62   01/01/63
Ritter, G. M. married Huzza, Anna C. 11/11/61   12/05/61
Ritter, George M. died 04/17/64   04/21/64
Ritter, Helen Mar married Lloyd, William J. 01/03/65   01/04/65
Ritter, J. Rebecca married Tucker, John L. 06/21/65   06/27/65
Ritter, Margaret E. married Clarke, Charles H. 10/05/65   10/09/65
Ritter, Mary E. died 08/03/64   08/04/64
Ritter, Richard A. died 06/09/63   06/10/63
Ritter, Sarah died 02/28/62   03/01/62
Ritter, Sarah Ann died 01/09/62   01/11/62
Ritter, Willie Apolphus died 11/23/65   11/25/65
Rivers, C. M. (Mrs.) died 04/18/64   04/19/64
Rives, Maria married Horwitz, Orville 11/07/61   11/13/61
Roach, Bridget died 11/30/61   12/05/61
Roach, Charles E. married Rowland, Alice V. 06/19/64   06/23/64
Roach, Elizabeth S. (Mrs.) died 10/08/63   10/10/63
Roach, Eugene died 10/17/62   10/18/62
Roach, Fanny (Mrs.) died 06/24/63   06/25/63
Roach, Joanna married Minehan, Daniel 04/16/65   04/18/65
Roach, John W. died 05/24/64   05/25/64
Roach, Mary died 01/15/61   01/17/61
Roach, Mary died 08/20/63   08/21/63
Roach, Mary died 06/22/65   06/23/65
Roach, Mary Agnes died 08/15/61   08/16/61
Roach, Thomas B. married Mankin, Virginia E. 02/07/61   02/09/61
Roach, William Edward died 07/15/64   07/16/64
Roach, William Edward died 07/15/64   08/12/64
Roane, Addie died 03/27/65   03/29/65
Roane, Henry W. married Trego, Estelle 06/09/63   06/12/63
Robb, James A. died 07/15/65   07/17/65
Robb, John married Billingslea, Ethlin 02/05/61   02/06/61
Robb, Leander A. married Hodge, Annie E. 09/08/64   09/20/64
Robb, Rosannia married Wales, Wesley 03/26/65   03/30/65
Robbins, David B. married Absolam, Annie 03/09/64   03/22/64
Robbins, Horace W., Jr. married Phelps, Mary Ayres 09/27/65   10/12/65
Robbins, K. R. (Lt.) married Green, Alice B. 10/19/65   10/31/65
Robbins, Mary (Mrs.) died 04/17/63   05/09/63
Robbins, Milbe married Long, Elizabeth (Mrs.) 01/01/63   01/05/63
Robbins, Moses S. married Williams, Mary A. 09/06/64   09/08/64
Robbins, Orlando married Wilkins, Georgeanna 06/19/62   06/24/62
Robbins, Rowland, F. W. died 06/04/64   06/06/64
Roberson, Benjamin married Sollers, Jane R. 07/24/62   07/26/62
Roberson, Emeline married Barney, James Henry 12/11/62   12/13/62
Robert, Benjamin married Mason, Laura 09/03/62   09/16/62
Robert, Charles died 08/17/64   08/18/64

Roberts, Ann Rebecca (Mrs.) died 01/29/63   01/30/63
Roberts, Benjamin G. died 12/01/63   02/18/64
Roberts, Cecelia C. M. married Jenkins, Henry 09/13/64   01/11/65
Roberts, Charles H. married Moffitt, Ellenor 09/25/64   10/03/64
Roberts, Clayton died 06/07/65   06/08/65
Roberts, Edward T. married Phillips, Mary N. 02/12/61   02/13/61
Roberts, Edward Warwick died 09/27/63   09/29/63
Roberts, Eliza (Mrs.) died 02/04/64   02/08/64
Roberts, Eliza Jane died 08/14/64   08/16/64
Roberts, Eliza N. (Mrs.) died 12/16/65   12/18/65
Roberts, Ellen Jane married Miller, James (Cpt.) 11/03/63   11/06/63
Roberts, Emily Virginia died 06/26/64   06/27/64
Roberts, George Alexander died 09/25/65   09/26/65
Roberts, George S. married Carmack, Laura A. 04/17/62   04/19/62
Roberts, Gussie died 09/11/64   09/13/64
Roberts, Harry T. married Keating, Martha J. 02/16/63   02/19/63
Roberts, Henry married Wright, Mary 02/21/63   02/24/63
Roberts, J. Harvey married Lawrenson, Fida S. 12/22/64   12/24/64
Roberts, John died 03/28/65   04/03/65
Roberts, John B. married Burns, Mary A. 04/07/64   04/11/64
Roberts, John M. (Dr.) died 09/11/65   09/16/65
Roberts, Joseph married Hutton, Caroline 02/26/61   02/27/61
Roberts, Joshua Thomas married Taylor, Sarah Linda 05/04/62   05/13/62
Roberts, Julie married Bausmith, Charles 10/25/64   11/04/64
Roberts, Justina married Davis, John 02/22/65   03/07/65
Roberts, Laura (Mrs.) died 07/11/64   07/16/64
Roberts, Laura A. died 09/25/65   09/26/65
Roberts, Laura A. died 09/25/65   09/27/65
Roberts, Lewis married Ady, Mary 03/18/65   04/03/65
Roberts, Margaret died 10/02/65   10/03/65
Roberts, Margaret S. married Johson, William 10/06/65   10/10/65
Roberts, Margret Ann married Ford, John 01/04/63   01/06/63
Roberts, Maria Jane (Mrs.) died 12/23/63   01/20/64
Roberts, Mary married Tyson, John S. 02/02/65   02/07/65
Roberts, Mary Alice married Bell, George H. 01/27/63   02/02/63
Roberts, Nelson died 01/20/63   01/22/63
Roberts, Owen James died 03/31/63   04/01/63
Roberts, Richard married Russell, Ann R. 07/03/61   07/29/61
Roberts, Sarah B. married Bowman, Henry C. 05/18/65   05/26/65
Roberts, Thomas Chaplain died 10/04/63   10/05/63
Roberts, Valentine married Riley, Mary Jane 07/14/64   07/20/64
Roberts, W. C. married Phillips, E. J. 12/22/63   02/05/64
Roberts, William married Pratt, Susan 06/01/65   06/03/65
Roberts, William, Jr. married Greble, Mary S. 10/31/64   11/02/64
Roberts, William, Jr. married Greble, Mary S. 10/31/64   11/03/64
Robertson, Adelia Ellsworth died 04/13/64   04/16/64
Robertson, Anna M. married Ford, John H. 07/11/65   07/15/65
Robertson, Henry W. married Walters, Emma E. 09/05/65   09/08/65
Robertson, J. E. (Dr.) married Price, Vinie 03/28/65   04/06/65
Robertson, John T., Sr. died 04/01/61   04/02/61
Robertson, Julia (Mrs.) married Harris, Stephen 12/14/65   12/16/65
Robertson, Nathaniel Lee died 06/26/64   06/27/64
Robertson, Sallie M. married Maihl, Thomas 10/24/65   10/27/65
Robertson, Sarah (Mrs.) died 03/22/65   03/25/65
Robier, Benjamin F. died 02/03/65   02/06/65

Robier, Benjamin F. died 02/03/65   02/07/65
Robins, Jesse Bowen died 09/30/64   10/01/64
Robins, Sallie J. married Merrifield, Charles E. 01/19/65   01/20/65
Robinson, Alexander married Jackson, Catharine 06/26/62   06/28/62
Robinson, Alexander died 05/03/64   05/04/64
Robinson, Alphias Francis died 03/27/64   03/28/64
Robinson, Alphonso married Lowrey, Sarah C. 09/24/63   09/28/63
Robinson, Alvinder married Thompson, John H. 02/05/63   02/07/63
Robinson, Andrew married White, Isabella 02/01/61   03/05/61
Robinson, Andrew married White, Isabella 02/01/61   03/04/61
Robinson, Ann R. married Bankert, Jacob 06/20/65   06/23/65
Robinson, Anna married Lewis, A. J. (Lt.) 03/02/65   05/12/65
Robinson, Arthur died 12/23/63   02/10/64
Robinson, Benjamin married Williams, Maria 12/19/65   12/23/65
Robinson, Benjamin N. married Cracroft, Mary C. 02/02/64   03/04/64
Robinson, Caleb married Thomas, Martha 04/09/63   04/11/63
Robinson, Caroline married Schonnofull, John 10/09/65   10/13/65
Robinson, Caroline married Schonnofull, John 10/09/65   10/16/65
Robinson, Caroline L. died 06/21/62   07/15/62
Robinson, Carrie Virginia died 12/11/64   12/12/64
Robinson, D. Jane married Lewin, John C. 12/12/61   12/18/61
Robinson, Daniel died 10/09/63   11/03/63
Robinson, Delia died 06/14/65   06/20/65
Robinson, Dennis F. died 11/17/64   11/19/64
Robinson, Dorsey married Downs, Mary A. 06/23/64   06/30/64
Robinson, Edwina Jane died 04/17/62   04/19/62
Robinson, Eliza (Mrs.) died 05/06/64   05/07/64
Robinson, Elizabeth (Mrs.) died 07/27/63   08/03/63
Robinson, Ellen J. married Brown, George H. 06/26/62   06/28/62
Robinson, Elvencedore married Plumley, Ira 12/31/63   01/02/64
Robinson, Emily M. died 05/09/65   05/10/65
Robinson, Emma Elizabeth married Aspril, James L. 09/22/63   10/07/63
Robinson, Fannie married New, John 03/24/64   05/28/64
Robinson, Francis J. married Robinson, Sarah L. 01/01/62   06/19/62
Robinson, George married Bishop, Laura Virginia 12/18/62   12/23/62
Robinson, George Columbus died 01/15/61   01/19/61
Robinson, George F. (USA) married Cline, Mary E. (Mrs.) 03/17/63   03/26/63
Robinson, George R. married Tillery, Jane 03/11/61   03/13/61
Robinson, George W. married Rorick, Eliza F. R. 01/11/64   01/13/64
Robinson, George W., Jr. married Bryant, Recharda S. 10/08/63   10/09/6
Robinson, Grace died 11/26/61   11/27/61
Robinson, Hannah married Henderson, John M. 04/06/65   04/08/65
Robinson, Harriet died 09/09/63   09/10/63
Robinson, Helen died 07/02/62   07/16/62
Robinson, Henry S. married Lowe, Kate (Mrs.) 09/07/64   11/14/64
Robinson, Henry Slicer died 12/10/61   12/11/61
Robinson, J. B. (Dr.) married Claude, Adele 10/26/65   11/07/65
Robinson, James died 10/24/62   10/29/62
Robinson, James C. married Beeman, Susan J. 10/06/63   10/08/63
Robinson, James H. died 02/25/64   02/26/64
Robinson, James H. died 02/25/64   02/27/64
Robinson, James H. married Morrison, Rhodie M. 12/07/63   02/27/64
Robinson, James M. married Hayes, Mary J. 06/22/65   06/27/65
Robinson, James W. married Hayes, Mary J. 06/22/65   06/26/65

Robinson, Janet (Mrs.) died 04/07/63 04/09/63
Robinson, Jeanette B. married White, Samuel J. 01/19/65 01/23/65
Robinson, John A. married Wood, Sarah E. 12/05/61 03/14/62
Robinson, John W. married Bordley, Maggie V. 06/11/65 06/14/65
Robinson, Joseph died 03/17/63 03/18/63
Robinson, Joseph (Gen.) died 03/17/63 03/19/63
Robinson, Joseph W. S. died 02/27/61 02/28/61
Robinson, Lewis H., Jr. married Rust, Mary Althea 10/10/65 10/14/65
Robinson, Louis H. married Rust, Mary Althea 10/10/65 10/13/65
Robinson, Louisa married Curtain, Henry G. 02/18/63 02/25/63
Robinson, M. Caleb died 09/12/64 09/14/64
Robinson, Mahaly died 11/14/61 11/15/61
Robinson, Margarette died 04/21/61 04/23/61
Robinson, Maria H. married Server, William H., Jr. 12/20/63 01/01/64
Robinson, Mary died 04/06/62 04/11/62
Robinson, Mary E. married Mahtison, Alexander 10/30/64 11/01/64
Robinson, Matilda E. married Edwards, Thomas B. 07/02/63 07/07/63
Robinson, Mollie R. married Jordan, James A. 12/18/61 12/20/61
Robinson, Richard B. married Howard, Lizzie 12/24/64 01/19/65
Robinson, Ruth married Cunningham, James M. 09/03/61 03/08/62
Robinson, Sallie M. married McGee, William H. 12/24/62 12/29/62
Robinson, Samuel James died 09/29/63 09/30/63
Robinson, Sarah died 03/13/61 03/14/61
Robinson, Sarah died 10/23/64 10/31/64
Robinson, Sarah A. married Miller, Henry 07/07/92 03/06/63
Robinson, Sarah L. married Robinson, Francis J. 01/01/62 06/19/62
Robinson, Sarah Lavinia (Mrs.) died 05/24/64 05/26/64
Robinson, Susan died 01/31/61 02/01/61
Robinson, Susan died 05/12/61 05/13/61
Robinson, Thomas died 11/12/61 11/14/61
Robinson, Thomas died 01/10/62 01/14/62
Robinson, William died 08/10/62 08/11/62
Robinson, William died 08/03/65 08/04/65
Robinson, William H. died 09/19/63 09/21/63
Robinson, William H. died 12/04/63 12/05/63
Robinson, William H. married Hollingsworth, Louisa 02/14/65 02/15/65
Roborg, William L. died 08/03/63 08/10/63
Roby, Marcelline V. married Purnell, Charles I. 09/30/63 10/05/63
Roby, Washington (Rev.) died 07/31/62 08/02/62
Roby, Willie F. married Gerbrick, Mattie A. 10/09/64 10/13/64
Roche, James died 07/12/62 07/14/62
Roche, James V. died 08/20/61 08/23/61
Roche, John died 12/24/63 12/25/63
Roche, Lilly died 07/13/65 07/14/65
Roche, Maria (Mrs.) died 03/13/63 03/14/63
Roche, Patrick died 12/12/63 12/14/63
Rochester, Eliza (Mrs.) died 01/17/63 01/20/63
Rochester, Matthew died 08/09/63 08/10/63
Rock, Elizabeth married Francis, John A. 04/24/62 04/29/62
Rockaway, Henry married Pfleig, Lizzie 04/23/61 04/26/61
Rockhold, Fannie E. died 03/01/61 03/02/61
Rockhold, Sarah Ann died 07/10/62 07/11/62
Rocks, Patrick married Goodwin, Mary 04/20/62 04/26/62
Roddy, Sarah (Mrs.) married Holloran, Michael 06/14/64 06/17/64
Roden, Jane married Scott, Charles M. 12/26/65 12/30/65

Rodenhi, Mary Elizabeth (Mrs.) died 01/27/63 01/28/63
Rodenhi, Mary Elizabeth (Mrs.) died 01/27/63 01/29/63
Rodenhi, Thomas S. married Keifal, Martha L. 04/23/64 07/18/64
Rodenmayer, Rebecca (Mrs.) died 10/07/63 10/08/63
Rodenmayer, Rebecca (Mrs.) died 10/07/63 10/09/63
Roder, John E. married Hopps, Rebecca 09/12/65 09/14/65
Roder, Mathilde Regine married Griffith, Louis P. 04/26/64 04/28/64
Roderick, William H. married Sullivan, Elvira E. 09/25/65 10/10/65
Rodgers, Angeline died 05/11/61 05/13/61
Rodgers, Annie Lee died 02/21/65 02/21/65
Rodgers, Annie Lee died 02/20/65 02/22/65
Rodgers, Annie M. married Holt, Albert A. no date 12/29/64
Rodgers, Elizabeth died 02/14/61 02/15/61
Rodgers, Henry J. (Maj.) married Bayne, Lucia 10/12/65 10/16/65
Rodgers, Hester E. (Mrs.) married Atwell, George M. 11/28/65 12/06/65
Rodgers, John died 11/23/61 11/25/61
Rodgers, John C. married Redmond, Sarah J. 09/17/61 10/02/61
Rodgers, Joseph married Bowen, Mary E. 09/19/61 09/21/61
Rodgers, Joseph W. married Phipps, Bettie 04/23/63 05/06/63
Rodgers, Kate married Leapin, Francis 11/03/61 12/09/61
Rodgers, Madora Ellsworth died 05/30/64 05/31/64
Rodgers, Samuel married Gilkenson, Martha E. 03/21/65 08/08/65
Rodgers, Stephen died 09/16/64 10/12/64
Rodgers, W. Edward died 07/15/64 08/20/64
Rodier, Albert married Flynn, Alice 04/20/63 04/22/63
Rodney, John M. married Scott, Mary Agnes 12/19/61 12/23/61
Roeck, Thomas died 10/15/63 10/17/63
Roelhey, Henry died 01/29/65 02/07/65
Roemer, Charles George died 08/04/64 08/06/64
Roff, Julia died 07/24/64 07/25/64
Rogers, Albert Perry died 10/31/63 11/03/63
Rogers, Carrie R. married Wix, Henry A. 05/08/62 05/12/62
Rogers, Charles Alexander died 08/27/63 09/02/63
Rogers, Charles M. married Reister, Mary E. P. 09/22/63 09/24/63
Rogers, Charles R. died 04/24/63 04/25/63
Rogers, Elizabeth died 07/03/63 07/27/63
Rogers, Elizabeth (Mrs.) died 04/08/65 04/10/65
Rogers, Emily B. married Williams, James W. 09/01/63 09/07/63
Rogers, Eunice F. married Bayly, Marcus Buck 10/22/64 10/29/64
Rogers, George William Brown died 09/04/62 09/05/62
Rogers, Isaac died 11/12/65 11/14/65
Rogers, James S. married Leef, Fannie 01/14/64 01/26/64
Rogers, Maggie B. died 10/03/64 10/06/64
Rogers, Margaret died 08/26/64 08/27/64
Rogers, Margaret Ann married Ruckle, Oliver P. 08/27/63 09/08/63
Rogers, Mary died 04/30/62 05/01/62
Rogers, Mary married Schwartz, Andrew 12/07/65 12/16/65
Rogers, Mary (Mrs.) died 03/13/65 03/14/65
Rogers, Mary A. (Mrs.) died 11/20/64 12/10/64
Rogers, Mary Ade died 02/24/63 02/25/63
Rogers, Mary H. married Rice, John L. 07/27/65 07/31/65
Rogers, Mary Woodward died 06/29/63 07/27/63
Rogers, Mary Yeates died 09/18/65 09/19/65
Rogers, Murty died 04/03/64 04/04/64
Rogers, Nathan married Montell, Eliza F. 12/19/61 02/06/62

Rogers, Nathaniel died 01/05/62 01/06/62
Rogers, R. J. married Hewitt, Elizzie 08/27/63 08/31/63
Rogers, Samuel B. died 07/29/64 08/24/64
Rogers, Sarah E. married Cox, Joal S. 04/17/63 05/05/63
Rogers, Seth S. died 04/05/65 04/06/65
Rogers, Sophia Gough died 07/10/63 07/27/63
Rogers, T. Bertha died 12/20/63 12/21/63
Rogers, Virginia died 06/13/61 06/19/61
Rogers, William died 10/03/62 10/04/62
Rogers, William married Hall, Emma J. 08/24/65 08/26/65
Rogers, William F. married Holloway, Emma A. 01/01/61 01/02/61
Rogers, William P. (Capt.) died 04/19/62 04/24/62
Rogers, Willie died 09/10/65 09/11/65
Rogers, Willie Norris died 09/10/65 09/19/65
Rogesen, Ann married Dupre, Frank 05/12/62 05/14/62
Rohan, Elizabeth (Mrs.) married Jordan, M. W. 06/19/64 06/22/64
Rohner, Louis P. married Osbourn, Sobina 02/02/64 02/09/64
Rokess, John M. died 07/23/63 07/24/63
Roland, Thomas, Jr. married Donnolly, Teresia M. 04/13/64 04/18/64
Rolfe, Chester E. married Cranmer, Mary E. 02/11/64 02/12/64
Rollins, Edward, Jr. died 05/23/64 05/25/64
Rollins, Emma A. married Collins, William H. H. 03/23/62 04/29/62
Rollins, Isaac died 10/21/64 10/26/64
Rollins, Joseph Frank died 04/24/62 04/28/62
Rollins, Willie died 08/16/63 08/18/63
Roloson, William L. died 10/23/64 10/26/64
Rolston, Annie M. W. married Boyd, Joseph E. 06/16/63 06/17/63
Roluson, Lucy S. died 01/22/62 01/27/62
Romaine, A. L. married Wilson, Sallie N. 09/04/65 09/07/65
Romney, Jane (Mrs.) died 01/16/64 01/18/64
Romoser, Jacob Frederick died 12/03/64 12/05/64
Romoser, John M. died 12/21/65 12/25/65
Romoser, Louisa (Mrs.) died 12/12/65 12/14/65
Rondo, Bartholomew died 12/30/64 12/31/64
Roney, Anna Elizabeth died 11/14/64 11/16/64
Roney, Edward P. married Thomson, Cordelia M. 08/13/63 08/14/63
Roney, John died 02/19/65 04/08/65
Roney, Louisa married Dougherty, Charles H. 10/22/64 10/29/64
Ronsaville, Dayton died no date 08/03/65
Ronsaville, Dayton died 07/27/65 08/04/65
Ronsaville, William died 07/27/65 08/04/65
Ronsaville, Willie died no date 08/03/65
Rooher, Mary A. (Mrs.) died 02/21/65 04/08/65
Rooke, Teresa W. married Jenkins, Thomas W. 02/02/65 02/09/65
Rooker, Rebecca died 12/22/62 12/23/62
Rooker, Sydney Virginia married Yates, Francis 06/25/63 08/13/63
Roome, Theodore E. married Dopman, Mary M. 12/09/62 02/14/63
Rooney, Amey died 12/18/63 12/19/63
Rooney, Ann married Maguire, Patrick 05/02/61 05/14/61
Rooney, Catherine (Mrs.) died 01/31/63 02/02/63
Rooney, Ellen died 12/14/62 12/16/62
Rooney, Ellen (Mrs.) died 05/05/65 05/06/65
Rooney, James married Pittinger, Victoria 04/14/61 04/16/61
Rooney, James died 02/23/64 02/24/64
Rooney, James H. died 11/17/65 11/20/65

Rooney, Joseph Michael died 11/06/61 11/07/61
Rooney, Mary died 02/16/62 02/17/62
Rooney, Michael D. died 11/11/63 11/12/63
Rooney, Michael D. died 11/11/63 11/13/63
Root, (Mrs. C. S.) died 12/07/65 12/09/65
Root, Daniel died 05/10/61 07/30/61
Root, Daniel E. married Reid, Fannie E. 10/01/65 10/31/65
Root, Fanny died 06/26/62 06/28/62
Root, G. Denison married Forbes, Allie 06/25/63 07/01/63
Root, Lewis Emmett died 07/03/64 07/04/64
Roppelt, Benjamin Franklin died 10/28/63 11/03/63
Roque, Delia Eliza died 11/06/65 11/07/65
Rorick, Eliza F. R. married Robinson, George W. 01/11/64 01/13/64
Rork, Sara R. married Clark, John W. 01/19/65 01/24/65
Rosan, C. J. married Burke, Henrietta B. 01/27/63 01/30/63
Rosan, C. J. died 12/05/64 12/06/64
Rosan, Elizabeth A. died 01/15/61 01/16/61
Rose, Alpheus Wilson died 12/08/63 12/11/63
Rose, Amelia died 04/11/64 04/18/64
Rose, Anne Jane (Mrs.) died 03/03/65 03/04/65
Rose, Annie E. married Wright, J. L., Jr. 03/26/63 03/31/63
Rose, Annie Jenette died 09/23/63 09/24/63
Rose, Doretha married Santenberger, William no date 05/26/63
Rose, E. Sophia married Eareckson, R. A. (Dr.) 11/21/61 11/28/61
Rose, Fanny married Almer, John 07/29/65 08/01/65
Rose, Henny married Hammerslaugh, Julius 08/24/62 08/30/62
Rose, Israel L. died 11/30/62 12/01/62
Rose, Jacob J. died 09/03/65 09/04/65
Rose, John died 10/09/64 10/10/64
Rose, John married Stockman, Elvie Ann 12/18/65 12/21/65
Rose, John Henry died 11/26/64 11/28/64
Rose, Joseph Bernard died 07/20/64 07/21/64
Rose, Joseph Franklin died 08/11/63 08/13/63
Rose, Mary Elizabeth died 09/28/61 10/03/61
Rose, Mary J. M. married Torney, John H. 03/03/62 03/10/62
Rose, Mary Susan (Mrs.) died 01/05/65 01/06/65
Rose, Walter Purnell died 05/09/64 05/10/64
Rose, William Hooper died 12/09/63 12/10/63
Rosecrans, William Starke died 08/19/64 08/23/64
Rosello, Antonio married Paul, Paulina 02/23/65 02/27/65
Rosenberry, Barbara died 04/01/62 04/02/62
Rosenberry, Cassie A. married Tisling, Frederick 07/21/63 07/09/63
Rosenberry, Ida Virginia died 09/13/61 09/17/61
Rosenberry, Mary Elizabeth died 02/14/62 02/22/62
Rosenfeld, Adaline married Harsh, Moses 10/16/65 10/21/65
Rosenfeld, Pauline married Swope, Joel 06/22/64 06/30/64
Rosenfeld, Rachel married Hohenthal, Herman 10/15/65 10/21/65
Rosenfield, Moses died 04/15/65 04/19/65
Rosensteel, Joseph died 04/29/63 04/30/63
Rosensteel, Joseph G. W. died 07/07/62 07/08/62
Rosensteel, Theodore married Perry, Mary E. 05/02/61 05/04/61
Rosensteel, Victoria (Mrs.) died 03/13/64 03/14/64
Rosenstein, Simon married Lebon, Marcellina M. L. 11/08/62 01/01/63
Rosenstock, Joseph married Polack, Elizabeth 02/24/64 03/02/64
Rosenstock, S. married Frank, Hannah 01/20/64 02/25/64

Rosenteel, John L. married Cassidy, Maggie 12/03/61   12/05/61
Rosenteel, John L. [retract] married Cassidy, Maggie [retract] no date
    12/06/61
Rosenthal, William married Wittig, Kate 03/28/64   04/02/64
Rosewag, Charles F. died 12/29/65   12/30/65
Rosewald, Simon married Stoll, Esther 10/25/63   10/26/63
Roshen, Thomas Throft died 07/23/62   07/28/62
Rosier, Harriet died 01/28/65   01/31/65
Rosmoser, Mary E. married Wain, William L. 11/07/61   11/13/61
Ross, Agnes Jane died 08/09/63   08/10/63
Ross, Albert died 02/09/61   02/20/61
Ross, Ann Maria died 09/27/64   09/28/64
Ross, Anthony P. married Woodland, Laura A. 02/16/63   02/17/63
Ross, Bridget died 05/05/63   05/08/63
Ross, Caroline married Stanley, Josiah 11/02/65   11/03/65
Ross, Charles Hiram died 01/20/61   01/21/61
Ross, Charles Hiram died 01/20/61   01/22/61
Ross, Christopher married Hurtt, Mattie J. 02/18/64   02/27/64
Ross, Daniel died 08/16/63   08/17/63
Ross, Elizabeth married Jackson, George 03/02/65   03/25/65
Ross, George B. died 01/08/64   01/11/64
Ross, Jacob died 01/17/64   01/18/64
Ross, James married Bowen, Emily 12/20/61   12/31/61
Ross, James D. died 12/26/64   12/29/64
Ross, James E. died 05/20/64   05/23/64
Ross, Kate married Barnes, John A. 04/28/64   04/30/64
Ross, Maggie A. died 11/15/64   11/22/64
Ross, Maria died 07/31/65   08/02/65
Ross, Mary died 03/29/62   04/05/62
Ross, Mary Anna married Tress, Nelson 09/27/64   10/03/64
Ross, Mary E. died 10/17/65   10/18/65
Ross, Mary E. (Mrs.) died 03/07/64   03/08/64
Ross, Robert Irvin married Dunn, Susan H. 10/24/61   11/18/61
Ross, William married Kirby, Alice C. 04/15/62   05/15/62
Rosseau, Rachel died 05/25/61   05/30/61
Rossie, James B. died 09/12/61   09/13/61
Rosston, Laura Adelaide died 05/11/63   05/13/63
Roswald, Blemma married Hecht, Isaac 07/06/62   07/08/62
Roszel, Mary S. married Reitz, William H. L. 05/22/61   06/04/61
Roszel, S. Calvert died 09/16/65   09/22/65
Roszel, S. Calvert died 09/16/65   09/23/65
Roszel, S. G. died 01/20/61   01/22/61
Roszel, S. George married Mayer, Anna M. 12/21/65   12/28/65
Roszell, Ennalls died 06/01/61   06/07/61
Rote, Rosetta married Baxter, W. H. 02/21/61   02/22/61
Roth, Albert died 01/22/63   01/24/63
Roth, Mary C. married Wild, John F. 11/30/65   12/11/65
Rothel, Charles Albert died 03/21/64   03/26/64
Rothel, Thomas Everet died 04/06/64   04/09/64
Rothell, Agnes Krebs died 12/17/63   12/18/63
Rothert, Mary died 03/17/64   03/18/64
Rothrell, Sarah Jane married Miller, John H. 11/28/61   01/18/62
Rothrock, Catherine R. died 08/01/61   08/02/61
Rothrock, George W. died 12/09/65   12/14/65
Rothrock, Sarah E. married Noel, W. A. (Lt.) 02/05/62   02/08/62

Rothrock, Thomas married Brant, Martha A. 12/10/61 02/07/62
Rouark, Thomas H. died 10/06/64 10/22/64
Rouch, Elizabeth married Kelley, Charles D. 04/19/63 04/21/63
Rountree, Adelaide Virginia married Ricketts, David 03/03/65 05/11/65
Rountree, Mary E. (Mrs.) died 02/25/64 02/27/64
Rountree, William (Cpt.) died 10/30/64 10/31/64
Rourk, Sarah Elizabeth died 11/15/61 11/19/61
Rourke, Mary Agnes died 11/01/61 11/02/61
Rourke, Mary Ann married Lear, Wiliam L. 08/18/64 10/08/64
Rourke, Michael died 06/18/65 08/31/65
Rous, Lucy Chase married Cassard, John 10/08/63 10/13/63
Rous, Mollie E. married Mills, James F. 10/05/65 10/16/65
Rouse, Benjamin died 08/23/63 08/24/63
Rouse, Catharine (Mrs.) died 12/25/64 12/28/64
Rouse, Catharine (Mrs.) died 12/25/64 12/30/64
Rouse, William married Hillman, Mary Ann 11/24/64 11/28/64
Rouselot, Susan married Morris, John T. 08/29/64 09/05/64
Roussell, Emma died 02/24/65 02/27/65
Rousselot, Charles A. died 10/22/65 10/28/65
Route, James married Murdoch, Matilda (Mrs.) 03/24/63 03/27/63
Rouvenac, C. married Weilant, Emma 02/25/63 03/03/63
Rowbothan, Hannah died 08/14/62 08/16/62
Rowe, F. A. died 01/06/63 01/13/63
Rowe, Gloria Ann died 05/29/62 05/31/62
Rowe, H. Lizzie married Bixler, William H. H. 04/06/65 04/08/65
Rowe, J. A. married Curry, Eliza J. 03/21/61 04/02/61
Rowe, James McCain died 05/09/64 05/10/64
Rowe, Margaret Ann married Ward, William George 12/12/65 12/14/65
Rowe, Ruth died 01/04/61 01/05/61
Rowe, Sarah E. died 12/16/64 12/26/64
Rowe, Thomas N. married Knauff, Sarah E. 02/10/63 04/27/63
Rowen, S. Elizabeth married Peerce, Robert C. 08/05/65 08/08/65
Rowland, Alice V. married Roach, Charles E. 06/19/64 06/23/64
Rowland, Rachel Ann died 07/12/61 07/16/61
Rowles, Eliza Ann married Floyd, George M. 08/29/61 09/03/61
Rowles, Laura Virginia died 12/15/62 12/17/62
Rowley, Thomas Waddy died 04/12/63 04/15/63
Roy, Lydia Mary died 11/15/65 11/27/65
Roycroft, Sarah E. married Andrews, Charles H. 04/04/61 04/06/61
Royer, J. B. married Pierpont, Jane (Mrs.) 10/20/65 11/04/65
Royer, W. Harry married Clemm, Laura J. M. 10/04/64 10/07/64
Royster, E. Augusta married Crook, F. M. 02/20/65 02/24/65
Royston, Ciscelia married Carter, D. J. 11/16/65 12/02/65
Royston, Clara H. died 10/15/61 10/15/62
Royston, John Henry B. married Cole, Mary Watts 02/19/63 02/20/63
Royston, Mary W. (Mrs.) died 08/01/63 08/03/63
Royston, Robert died 01/15/62 01/16/62
Royston, Willie Lamdin died 01/20/64 01/21/64
Rozell, Howard died 03/21/61 03/23/61
Rozell, Louisa H. D. died 03/08/65 04/07/65
Ruane, Thomas died 08/01/64 08/02/64
Ruark, Edward died 12/11/65 12/13/65
Ruark, Emanual W. married Diggs, Elizabeth S. 01/30/61 01/31/61
Ruark, John married Lambert, Joanna 12/24/65 12/27/65
Ruark, Peter M. married Goss, Annie C. 11/23/65 11/25/65

Ruark, Sarah married Williams, Thomas 07/11/65   08/03/65
Ruark, Sarah E. married Marshall, William 10/01/65   11/03/65
Rubens, Charles married Walter, Clara 09/11/65   09/12/65
Rubens, Mary (Mrs.) died 03/25/64   03/29/64
Ruberg, William. married Brackenridge, Susan 08/19/63   09/08/63
Rubu, William H. married Whitter, Annie E. 05/14/65   06/03/65
Ruckle, Oliver P. married Rogers, Margaret Ann 08/27/63   09/08/63
Ruddach, Rebecca Stillwagen died 05/28/64   05/30/64
Rueckert, John L. married Toberer, Louisa 08/29/65   08/30/65
Rueckert, John Philip died 07/29/62   07/31/62
Rueckert, P. L. married Traband, A. C. 11/01/63   11/11/63
Ruff, Catharine married McCauley, James 12/04/64   12/13/64
Ruff, Elizabeth died 10/14/64   10/15/64
Ruff, John died 11/21/65   11/22/65
Ruff, Mary J. married White, David 11/04/62   11/06/62
Ruff, William Henry married Brown, Mary 02/02/62   02/04/62
Ruffin, Sallie Blunt died 12/05/63   12/19/63
Ruffin, Thomas (Col.) died 10/14/63   12/19/63
Ruhl, Edgar Monroe (Cpt.) died 10/19/64   11/24/64
Ruley, Samuel W. died 10/27/63   10/29/63
Ruley, Samuel W. died 10/27/63   10/30/63
Ruley, Zenetter married Hartlove, William H. 12/15/63   01/28/64
Rullman, Geoffrey died 04/03/64   04/04/64
Rummel, Charles V. (USN) married Bonday, Mary A. 10/26/65   10/30/65
Rummel, John W. died 11/21/65   11/22/65
Rumney, Ada May died 09/19/63   09/24/63
Rumney, Emily J. married Wain, George H. (USA) 11/26/63   11/28/63
Rumstine, Ellen married Byrely, James T. 05/07/63   05/23/63
Rumstine, Mary A. married Appleby, James H. 05/18/63   05/23/63
Rundle, George Edward died 07/09/61   07/10/61
Runkle, Brice married Morrow, Ellen C. 01/30/61   02/15/61
Rupley, A. (Admiral) died 04/25/61   04/27/61
Rupley, Charles P. married Huster, Maggie V. 12/11/62   12/15/62
Rupp, Ann Eliza (Mrs.) died 03/23/63   03/25/63
Rupp, Elizabeth died 09/16/65   09/18/65
Rupp, Emma V. died 10/04/65   10/05/65
Rupp, Hezekiah died 02/24/64   02/25/64
Rupp, Jacob died 09/23/63   09/25/63
Rupp, Maurice C. died 03/30/62   03/31/62
Rupp, William married Phillips, Emma (Mrs.) 03/16/65   03/21/65
Rupp, William Harris died 07/03/65   07/12/65
Ruppert, Ann (Mrs.) died 12/11/63   12/23/63
Ruppert, Martin died 01/06/64   01/07/64
Rush, Barbara died 11/28/64   11/29/64
Rush, Charles Oliver died 10/09/63   10/10/63
Rush, D. G. married Davis, Lyle J. (Mrs.) 12/27/64   01/10/65
Rusk, Abraham K. died 12/22/62   12/23/62
Rusk, Abraham K. died 12/22/62   12/24/62
Rusk, Abraham K. died 12/22/62   12/25/62
Rusk, Belina Marion died 01/11/61   01/12/61
Rusk, Ella S. died 12/24/63   12/25/63
Rusk, Hester A. married Keizer, Lewis R. 12/26/65   12/29/65
Rusk, Hester H. married Keizer, Lewis R. 12/26/65   12/28/65
Rusk, John G. married Blunt, Mary A. 11/22/63   11/24/63
Rusk, William married Carter, Josephine 01/05/64   01/14/64

Rusk, William Beauregard died 02/03/62 02/05/62
Rusk, Willie Lawrence died 12/30/62 12/31/62
Rusk, Willie Lawrence died 12/30/62 01/01/63
Rusling, S. C. married Clendenin, Martha E. 05/04/64 05/12/64
Russel, Elizabeth Margaret died 02/23/65 02/25/65
Russel, James married Hall, Mary L. 01/19/65 01/21/65
Russel, Robert died 06/07/62 06/09/62
Russell, Michael died 07/05/65 07/06/65
Russell, Aaron died 10/13/62 10/14/62
Russell, Agness Elizabeth died 05/20/61 05/22/61
Russell, Alexander Jr. died 03/20/65 03/24/65
Russell, Amelia married McElmoyle, Archibald 05/02/61 05/06/61
Russell, Amelia married McElmozle, Archibald 05/02/61 05/04/61
Russell, Ann R. married Roberts, Richard 07/03/61 07/29/61
Russell, Anna M. died 12/21/64 12/23/64
Russell, Annie died 04/10/65 04/12/65
Russell, Barbara (Mrs.) died 01/18/64 01/27/64
Russell, Bella Rose died 10/06/64 10/07/64
Russell, Clem died 03/06/63 03/07/63
Russell, Esther Ann died 10/19/62 10/21/62
Russell, Frances died 05/31/61 06/01/61
Russell, Francis married Wesley, Gabriel 06/14/63 06/20/63
Russell, George W. married Wain, Elizabeth A. 12/19/65 12/21/65
Russell, Harriet H. married Owen, William H. 12/18/62 12/23/62
Russell, Isabel R. married Flemming, Charles H. 04/07/64 05/17/64
Russell, J. L. married Denison, Mary L. 12/08/64 12/17/64
Russell, James married Angel, Mary Ann 04/04/61 06/03/61
Russell, James died 07/10/65 07/11/65
Russell, James Henry died 04/06/64 04/08/64
Russell, James, Jr. married Wilkins, Maria D. 12/20/65 12/27/65
Russell, John married Henson, Mary 12/01/63 12/02/63
Russell, John died 11/06/65 11/08/65
Russell, John married Grant, Minia 08/13/64 09/03/64
Russell, John L. married Sherwood, E. A. 01/01/62 01/03/62
Russell, John S. married Bump, Mary E. 08/02/65 08/11/65
Russell, Louisa married Dorsey, William 02/09/64 02/10/64
Russell, Mary (Mrs.) died 05/09/64 05/10/64
Russell, Mary E. married Wooden, Enos W. 05/03/64 05/06/64
Russell, Patrick died 03/06/64 03/07/64
Russell, Patrick married Moran, Mary 09/20/64 09/21/64
Russell, Rachel died 03/13/62 03/14/62
Russell, Richard B. married Sulaven, Maria H. 01/28/64 01/30/64
Russell, Robert died 06/07/62 06/10/62
Russell, S. B. married Levis, Amelia 10/23/61 11/01/61
Russell, S. B. married Lewis, Amelia 10/23/61 10/30/61
Russell, Samuel died 09/30/63 10/02/63
Russell, Susanna (Mrs.) died 12/04/64 12/05/64
Russell, Virginia married Hoopes, William 11/20/61 12/07/61
Russell, Virginia Lee died 10/25/63 10/26/63
Russell, W. L. married Hall, Cecelia 07/10/62 07/16/62
Russell, William died 12/05/61 12/06/61
Russell, William Henry married Jones, Johannah 09/06/64 09/07/64
Russell, Willie H. married Orr, Ellen C. 05/07/62 05/19/62
Russum, George M. married Orme, Octavia 11/03/62 11/04/62
Rust, Charles died 11/26/60 01/17/61

Rust, Mary Althea married Robinson, Louis H. 10/10/65 10/13/65
Rust, Mary Althea married Robinson, Lewis H., Jr. 10/10/65 10/14/65
Rust, Samuel died 02/22/64 02/24/64
Ruth, James M. died 08/06/64 08/26/64
Ruth, John S. died 03/26/61 03/27/61
Rutherford, John William died 06/09/64 06/11/64
Rutherford, Nancey died 03/21/63 03/23/63
Ruths, George (Lt.) married Nily, Magaretha 05/05/62 05/08/62
Rutledge, Elizabeth died 10/28/65 10/30/65
Rutledge, Fanny R. married McCahan, D. L. 05/21/63 05/23/63
Rutledge, Mary Ann died 09/19/61 09/20/61
Rutledge, Mary Jane died 07/21/65 07/22/65
Rutledge, Mary Jane died 07/21/65 07/26/65
Rutter, Andrew C. married Dull, Emma S. 11/05/63 11/17/63
Rutter, Edward J. married Norwood, Hattie R. 10/24/65 10/26/65
Rutter, Frances (Mrs.) died 12/16/64 12/28/64
Rutter, George H. died 12/14/64 12/16/64
Rutter, George W. died 06/17/64 06/27/64
Rutter, George W. died 06/17/64 11/22/64
Rutter, Hanson Pettington died 02/26/64 02/27/64
Rutter, Harrie Johnson died 01/23/63 01/26/63
Rutter, Harry T. B. died 12/01/64 12/02/64
Rutter, Mary Ellen died 03/21/63 03/25/63
Rutter, P. E. died 03/19/65 03/21/65
Rutter, Philip died 12/18/62 12/22/62
Rutter, Susanna (Mrs.) married Lyles, Henry 10/04/64 10/19/64
Rutter, Thomas C. died 09/10/65 09/11/65
Rutter, Virginia died 06/01/61 06/15/61
Ruudles, Amanda M. (Mrs.) died 01/01/63 01/03/63
Ryan, Catherine married Farrell, Martin 11/24/61 11/26/61
Ryan, Edward Pierce died 04/22/64 04/23/64
Ryan, George K. died 01/30/63 02/05/63
Ryan, Honora died 02/19/63 02/20/63
Ryan, Honora died 02/19/63 02/21/63
Ryan, James A. married Ford, Elizabeth A. 11/19/65 11/22/65
Ryan, John died 12/25/64 12/28/64
Ryan, John F. married Whitely, Elizabeth 03/20/64 03/22/64
Ryan, John Thomas died 04/24/61 04/25/61
Ryan, Kate married McDonnell, James (U.S.N.) 10/01/62 10/03/62
Ryan, Kate Agness died 02/17/63 02/20/63
Ryan, Maggie W. married Salmon, Anthony 05/23/65 05/25/65
Ryan, Margaret died 02/11/62 02/12/62
Ryan, Mary married McCabe, James 04/21/61 04/23/61
Ryan, Mary died 08/23/61 08/24/61
Ryan, Mary A. married Carroll, Robert 04/29/65 05/02/65
Ryan, Mary E. married Keenan, William 05/02/62 05/05/62
Ryan, Mary Jane died 11/20/63 11/21/63
Ryan, Michael died 08/04/61 08/05/61
Ryan, Samuel married Baxter, Mary C. 10/20/63 12/05/63
Ryan, Thomas died 11/04/62 11/05/62
Ryan, William H. married Jackson, Virginia A. 07/23/63 07/30/63
Ryans, Mary E. died 03/06/62 03/07/62
Ryland, S. S. married Smith, Lydia (Mrs.) 02/23/65 02/27/65
Rynehart, Sarah Jane married Johns, Kensey 05/22/65 05/25/65
Rynehart, William H. married Dillen, Sallie M. 02/23/64 02/25/64

Ryrie, Johanna married Lowrey, Benjamin F. 03/15/64 03/18/64
Saale, Kenly Elsworth died 07/29/63 07/31/63
Sable, Annie R. married Donnelly, James 02/04/61 02/05/61
Sache, Justin married Berger, Mary 12/25/61 12/27/61
Sadler, C. A. married Moore, J. G. 02/07/65 02/22/65
Sadler, George died 01/19/64 01/20/64
Sadler, Henry died 12/14/63 12/16/63
Sadler, John died 01/09/63 01/12/63
Sadler, John C. married Thompson, Amanda 01/21/64 01/26/64
Sadler, Mary died 04/21/61 04/23/61
Sadtler, Charles H. married Webster, R. Priscilla 11/05/63 11/09/63
Sadtler, Sarah T. died 02/16/65 02/17/65
Saffell, Celsus L. married Gorton, Marie Louise 11/16/64 11/22/64
Sagaser, Catharine (Mrs.) died 11/07/63 11/09/63
Sage, George D. married Fishach, Kate 04/25/63 04/28/63
Sahm, George died 01/30/61 01/31/61
Sahm, Julius G. died 11/30/63 12/01/63
Sailesbury, Isabella V. died 12/26/65 12/27/65
Sakers, John S. married Bostick, Sarah F. 09/29/64 10/11/64
Sales, Henry died 03/09/65 03/11/65
Salgee, Sarah A. married Lane, George A. 05/09/65 05/12/65
Salinas, Carlos Hernandes died 12/02/64 12/07/64
Salisbury, Augusta J. married Chrismer, Alexander D. 07/17/65 07/22/6
Salisbury, Mary E. died 10/07/65 10/09/65
Salmon, Anthony married Ryan, Maggie W. 05/23/65 05/25/65
Salmon, Kate married Armstrong, John, Jr. 07/02/63 08/08/63
Salmon, Warren L. died 02/03/63 02/05/63
Salom, Francis died 05/27/63 05/28/63
Salze, Caroline married Yeamans, Joseph N. 02/18/64 02/27/64
Sample, Margaret married Bevans, William 05/14/63 05/16/63
Sampson, James died 03/31/61 04/02/61
Sampson, Julia married Hilliard, Robert 12/16/62 01/06/63
Sampson, Kevener K. married Nicholas, Elizabeth 07/07/64 07/09/64
Sampson, Lilley died 01/24/65 01/25/65
Samson, Serina married Handy, John 04/17/61 04/20/61
Sanborn, D. M. (Dr.) married Jester, Amanda 04/30/63 05/04/63
Sandears, Moses died 12/02/62 12/04/62
Sander, Annette died 08/11/65 08/16/65
Sander, Clemens died 12/23/65 12/27/65
Sander, George P. H. died 09/13/61 09/14/61
Sanders, Charles L. married Chestnut, Maggie J. 10/10/65 10/11/65
Sanders, Edward Jerome died 03/12/61 03/13/61
Sanders, Edward Jerome died 03/12/61 03/23/61
Sanders, Eliza married Jacobs, Mathias 05/02/65 05/05/65
Sanders, Ella Rebecca died 10/21/63 10/23/63
Sanders, Emma P. married Shriver, A. K. 11/21/65 11/24/65
Sanders, Frederick died 01/19/63 03/20/63
Sanders, George E. married Frazier, Lizzie A. 12/23/62 12/27/62
Sanders, George Paxton died 10/29/65 10/30/65
Sanders, George W. married Miller, Lizzie A. 10/14/62 10/18/62
Sanders, George W. married Bull, Kate D. 10/27/63 10/29/63
Sanders, Joseph Thomas died 06/19/65 07/31/65
Sanders, Leonidas A. died 10/27/65 11/01/65
Sanders, Mary E. married North, William C. 12/15/63 12/18/63
Sanders, Mary E. (Mrs.) died 10/23/64 10/25/64

Sanders, Moses died no date 12/18/62
Sanders, Nettie married Stuart, Edward V. 11/24/63 12/01/63
Sanders, Obediah died 01/16/65 01/18/65
Sanders, Oliver Asbury died 01/18/64 01/20/64
Sanders, Sarah E. married Coleman, William H. 11/04/62 11/06/62
Sanders, William Albert M. died 12/06/63 12/08/63
Sanderson, Edward Dyer (Hon.) died 04/20/61 05/31/61
Sanderson, Ellen married Egerton, William A. 02/10/61 02/18/61
Sanderson, Emily P. married Fleicher, Samuel 01/22/61 02/02/61
Sanderson, Frank H. died 07/04/63 07/13/63
Sanderson, Henry S. married Wilson, Margie E. 09/07/65 09/12/65
Sanderson, Rachel E. married Elliot, William T. 02/21/61 03/23/61
Sanderson, Sallie married Sanderson, William 01/10/61 01/21/61
Sanderson, William married Sanderson, Sallie 01/10/61 01/21/61
Sandler, Emma Augusta married O'Brien, Giles J. 12/10/65 12/25/65
Sands, Augustus married Geiger, Sophie 01/22/65 04/01/65
Sands, Bridget died 08/09/62 08/11/62
Sands, Ellen died 03/16/62 03/18/62
Sands, Emelia married Smallwood, James B. 05/28/63 06/02/63
Sands, John died 09/06/65 09/06/65
Sands, Margaret died 10/27/61 10/28/61
Sands, Mary married Turner, Richard M. 10/28/64 11/01/64
Sands, Richard H. married Marry, Sarah 02/27/65 04/01/65
Sands, Sallie S. married Creager, George U. 03/19/61 03/27/61
Sands, Sarah Ann died 09/08/61 09/09/61
Sandy, Emelie married Smallwood, James B. 05/28/63 06/01/63
Sandys, George Walter died 07/21/63 07/22/63
Sangforce, Eliza Jane died 03/01/62 03/03/62
Sangston, B. Whitely married Henrix, Ridie H. 07/08/63 07/10/63
Sangston, Catherine M. (Mrs.) died 03/09/63 03/13/63
Sangston, Charlotte Jane married Beatty, William J. A. 04/22/62
    04/24/62
Sangston, Edwin died 11/22/62 11/26/62
Sangston, George E. married Duvall, Mary E. 01/20/63 01/28/63
Sangston, Hannah Mary died 07/01/61 07/03/61
Sangston, Jennie R. married Bacon, Samuel H. 06/22/65 06/26/65
Sangston, John Elmer died 09/20/63 09/23/63
Sangston, Rebecca died 06/14/61 06/15/61
Sanks, Elizabeth married Leonard, John Henry 01/01/62 01/03/62
Sanks, Laura A. died 08/17/64 08/18/64
Sanner, Alice A. Dashiell died 03/06/64 03/07/64
Sanner, Emma J. married Lynch, Joseph S. 06/14/65 07/19/65
Sanner, George W. died 11/17/65 11/21/65
Sanner, Louis died 08/09/62 08/11/62
Sanner, Maria D. married Shermantine, John A. B. 11/29/64 12/01/64
Sanners, Johachan B. married Garthwaite, Elizabeth 11/09/63 11/19/63
Santenberger, William married Rose, Doretha no date 05/26/63
Sap, Mary Elizabeth died 06/25/62 06/26/62
Sap, Sophia married Shreck, Jacob E. 01/14/64 01/20/64
Sapp, Elizabeth Ann (Mrs.) died 08/22/63 08/24/63
Sapp, Hanson H. died 06/18/62 06/28/62
Sapp, Henry R. married Smith, Ann E. 08/20/62 09/25/62
Sapp, Jemima (Mrs.) married Reeves, G. Washington 11/30/64 12/20/64
Sapp, John died 01/20/61 01/24/61
Sapp, John married Wheatley, Lizzie J. 08/24/62 08/26/62

Sapp, John Hack Warner died 03/14/62 03/19/62
Sapp, Joseph married Walstrum, Rosalia E. 10/25/64 11/01/64
Sapp, Joshua F. B. died 03/25/64 03/26/64
Sapp, Lydia A. died 09/10/61 09/11/61
Sapp, Martha married Bootman, John W. 02/23/65 02/25/65
Sapp, Walter Lee died 11/06/65 11/08/65
Sappington, George W. married Pendleton, Virenda A. 10/24/65 10/25/65
Sappington, Nicholas J. married Birkey, Maria E. 01/15/61 01/17/61
Sarbaugh, Jacob (Cpt.) died 08/14/62 10/11/62
Sargeant, Samuel R. died 11/11/64 11/12/64
Sargent, Gough Carroll died 02/10/65 02/13/65
Sargent, Oliver B. married Cox, Maria 11/13/65 11/18/65
Sargent, Sophia Carroll married Snowden, Harry W. 09/07/65 09/09/65
Sarsfied, Margaret died 04/27/62 05/05/62
Sarsfield, Stephen, Sr. died 03/20/63 03/24/63
Sasscer, Henrietta M. married Jenkins, Richard L. 10/23/62 10/24/62
Saterfield, Anna E. married Lee, George W. 11/01/61 12/05/61
Satterfield, Hannah Maria died 11/29/61 11/30/61
Sauerbrey, Ernst A. (Lt.) married Fredricks, Agnes Eugenia 02/02/63
    02/04/63
Sauers, Mary (Mrs.) died 05/03/64 05/04/64
Sauers, Mary (Mrs.) died 05/03/64 05/05/64
Sauerwein, Eugene died 08/05/62 08/08/62
Sauerwein, George died 10/03/64 10/04/64
Sauerwein, George died no date 11/24/64
Saulsbury, Alfred G. married Sinz, Lena 04/04/61 04/08/61
Saulsbury, Alverta V. died 08/23/63 08/25/63
Saulsbury, Andrew J. married McCluney, Maggie J. 07/02/63 07/07/63
Saulsbury, Julia A. died 08/07/61 08/08/61
Saum, George died 01/30/61 02/01/61
Saumenig, F. E. married Wilson, Mary J. 01/13/63 01/16/63
Saumenig, Marion died 08/27/63 09/02/63
Saumenig, Mary Florence died 09/28/65 10/03/65
Saumenig, William A. married Basil, Henrietta 05/15/61 05/24/61
Saums, Louisa (Mrs.) died 04/28/64 04/29/64
Saunders, Elizabeth died 03/03/62 03/04/62
Saunders, Elizabeth died 03/03/62 03/05/62
Saunders, George married Jones, Anna M. 09/04/64 09/06/64
Saunders, Mary A. married Chase, Delos 01/09/65 01/11/65
Saunders, Mary C. married Milholland, E. F. (Dr.) 10/25/64 10/31/64
Saunders, Rachel Ann married Fenton, Harrison 06/30/64 07/02/64
Saunders, Sarah E. married Cropper, Samuel J. 12/19/61 12/23/61
Saunders, Thomas B. married Morgan, Mary F. V. 09/12/63 10/15/63
Saunders, William died 01/24/65 01/25/65
Saunders, Willie Russell married Quigley, Mary Ellen (Mrs.) 12/19/64
    02/04/65
Saurwein, Kates S. married Boehm, Charles T. 10/10/61 10/11/61
Sauter, Barbay died 12/14/62 12/15/62
Sauter, Charles died 10/27/63 10/28/63
Savage, George T. died 12/12/65 12/13/65
Savage, George T. died 12/12/65 12/14/65
Savage, Isabel married Heilner, Samuel 07/23/65 08/16/65
Savage, Sarah (Mrs.) died 01/24/63 01/27/63
Savier, Joseph B. died 01/29/65 06/07/65
Savill, Francis William died 09/07/62 09/08/62

Saville, Alexander married Dorsey, Mary C. 04/08/62 04/09/62
Saville, William N. married Watlington, Kate 12/14/63 12/16/63
Saville, William N. S. died 12/21/64 12/22/64
Savin, Annie E. died 04/12/61 04/13/61
Savin, F. W. died 02/22/65 02/23/65
Savin, Harrey Archer died 07/07/61 07/08/61
Savin, Marcus D. married Lytle, Jennie Olive 04/23/63 04/27/63
Savin, R. T. married Aitken, J. A. M. 07/10/61 07/13/61
Savington, John H. married Small, Mary Virginia 06/13/61 07/01/61
Savournin, William H. married Cook, Henrietta 02/04/62 02/06/62
Savoy, Barson died 06/27/65 06/28/65
Sawin, Thomas Henry died 12/13/65 12/15/65
Sawkins, Sebella S. (Mrs.) died 01/01/65 01/02/65
Sawyer, William married Judik, C. Josephine 11/21/65 11/23/65
Saxon, John died 01/21/62 01/22/62
Saxton, A. H. (Dr.) married White, Mary Rosa 06/09/64 06/10/64
Say, Henry (Pvt.) died 09/06/64 09/08/64
Saylor, Mary E. married Williams, James 09/12/61 09/19/61
Sayre, William H. married Hamilton, Sarah Elizabeth 01/02/62 01/08/62
Scanlan, Maggie A. married Hamilton, James A. 05/08/62 06/04/62
Scanlon, Margaret (Mrs.) died 12/09/64 12/10/64
Scantland, James died 11/24/65 11/25/65
Scarborough, Amos W. died 01/01/62 01/03/62
Scarborough, George Willis died 09/15/63 09/17/63
Scarborough, John M. died 06/17/65 06/19/65
Scarborough, John M. died 06/17/65 06/21/65
Scarborough, John T. died 09/11/65 09/12/65
Scarborough, Susannah married Hadley, John W. 10/05/65 10/09/65
Scarborough, Wilson married Shipley, Caroline M. 04/30/63 05/12/63
Scarbourough, John died 01/07/64 01/09/64
Scarf, Emma J. married McClellan, George F. 04/03/65 05/06/65
Scarf, Emma J. married McClellan, George F. 04/03/65 05/08/65
Scarff, Amanda married Ayres, James E. 07/03/64 07/12/64
Scarff, E. Norriss married Winingder, Martha P. 01/14/64 01/18/64
Scarlett, George H. U. died 02/21/65 02/23/65
Schaaf, Elizabeth A. died 02/09/62 02/10/62
Schaefer, Alice died 07/21/64 07/22/64
Schaefer, Anna Martha died 09/03/64 09/07/64
Schaefer, Christian A. died 04/14/64 04/16/64
Schaefer, Eliza A. V. married Hood, Thomas 05/02/65 05/25/65
Schaefer, Elizabeth married Boyd, Benjamin F. 06/26/65 07/04/65
Schaefer, Harry Clay died 11/30/62 12/02/62
Schaefer, John died 07/14/64 07/23/64
Schaefer, John F. married Curley, Sallie E. V. 11/15/65 11/29/65
Schaefer, John W. died 11/23/63 11/25/63
Schaefer, Mary A. (Mrs.) died 11/10/63 11/12/63
Schaefer, Richard Fuller died 07/06/64 07/09/64
Schaeffer, John C. married Feistel, Pelena A. 09/07/65 09/18/65
Schaeffer, Mary C. married Reuppersberger, Gustave W. 09/07/65 09/18/65
Schaeffer, W. C. married Parks, Matilda 10/09/65 10/17/65
Schaer, Theodore C. died 08/15/64 08/16/64
Schafer, Daniel R. married Kelly, Priscilla 10/06/63 10/07/63
Schafer, John F. married Perry, Anna S. 10/19/64 05/16/65
Schafer, William died 03/04/64 03/22/64
Schaffer, Blanch S. (Mrs.) died 01/16/65 01/19/65

Scharf, Adelaide Yost married Kremer, William V. 07/14/64   07/16/64
Scharf, Laura V. married Keefe, John 10/02/64   10/04/64
Scharf, Mary C. married Spicer, H. Louis 03/28/64   03/31/64
Scharf, Sallie H. married Cooke, Warren E. 07/14/64   07/16/64
Scharf, Secelia died 05/27/64   05/28/64
Scharf, Susa died 09/19/64   09/23/64
Scharff, Samuel R. married Young, Fanny G. 08/17/64   08/27/64
Scheckells, Anastasia (Mrs.) died 07/09/63   07/11/63
Scheese, Mary Louisa married Kurzmaul, William F. 12/15/63   12/19/63
Scheffer, Frederica Louisa died 08/29/63   08/31/63
Scheibler, Andrew K. married Shipley, Mary E. 02/12/63   02/14/63
Schelb, Helena Catharine died 11/14/65   11/16/65
Scheldt, Harry Julius died 12/23/62   12/24/62
Scheler, J. Frederick died 08/14/61   08/17/61
Schell, Mary Virginia died 11/24/65   11/27/65
Schelley, J. F. married Little, A. M. 01/17/61   12/19/61
Schenck, Roelof died 03/13/61   03/14/61
Schenkel, Adam died 11/25/64   11/26/64
Schenkel, Emelia died 04/06/63   04/07/63
Schenkel, Jacob Wesley died 05/07/64   05/09/64
Schenkel, Philip Jerome Peter died 03/24/65   03/25/65
Schenner, Ernestine married Gill, John G. 04/25/65   04/27/65
Scherer, Frederick H. married Bregel, Elizabeth 12/25/62   12/30/62
Scherer, Leonard married Wagner, Kate 01/18/63   01/21/63
Scherf, Bertha married Sheets, Philip 04/12/64   04/16/64
Scheuhts, Louisiana Frances married Sewell, James B. F. 10/02/62
    10/21/62
Schiebler, Christian died 05/02/65   05/19/65
Schiers, J. Henry married Mears, Emma W. 10/13/63   10/24/63
Schiers, Lizzie married Rickers, Henry N. 04/28/63   05/05/63
Schillinger, Fredericka died 09/03/63   09/05/63
Schimmel, Margaret Jane died 11/25/63   11/26/63
Schimp, Martin P. married Hollitt, Emma 07/24/65   07/26/65
Schlarb, Henry married Privy, Emma 09/01/64   09/03/64
Schleich, William married Smith, Harriet (Mrs.) 08/30/64   08/31/64
Schleigh, Emma Jane died 11/05/62   11/06/62
Schleigh, Millie married Street, M. L. 10/21/62   10/30/62
Schley, Elizabeth (Mrs.) married Cannon, James 10/07/64   10/17/64
Schley, Ellen E. married Gambrill, H. D. 11/25/62   11/27/62
Schley, Linda S. died 01/08/64   01/11/64
Schley, Nettie married Fisher, Parks 06/08/65   06/10/65
Schley, Sallie A. died 12/16/65   12/19/65
Schley, Winfield Scott (USN) married Franklin, Anne R. 09/10/63
    09/11/63
Schlosser, Harry died 09/14/65   09/15/65
Schmenner, J. Henry married Perkins, Sallie 12/04/60   05/02/61
Schmidt, Emma Virginia died 07/23/64   07/25/64
Schmidt, Francis C. died 04/14/64   04/15/64
Schmidt, Gotthilf Simon died 03/27/65   03/29/65
Schmidt, Henry D. married Bobeth, Matilda H. 03/27/62   04/04/62
Schmidt, Napier Merchant died 01/18/61   01/19/61
Schneades, Anna Margaret married Dibb, James 06/09/64   06/11/64
Schneider, Charlotte married Campen, John 03/02/62   03/04/62
Schneider, Eliza Ann (Mrs.) died 01/24/65   01/25/65
Schneider, Elizabeth died 11/02/62   11/03/62

Schneider, Elizabeth died 11/02/62 11/04/62
Schneider, Helen died 03/01/61 03/02/61
Schneider, Henry married Becker, Louisa Jane 04/07/63 04/11/63
Schnibbe, James died 08/05/63 08/10/63
Schock, Wilton G. married Henderson, Mary E. 09/24/64 09/27/64
Schoemaker, William Thomas died 05/05/62 05/05/62
Schoenthaler, F. C. married Thorman, Dora 12/12/65 12/13/65
Schofield, Ellen (Mrs.) died 01/01/62 01/02/62
Schofield, Hannah E. married Sitler, Morris, Jr. 12/12/61 12/14/61
Schofield, Joseph married Pembroke, Sallie 04/10/64 04/14/64
Schofield, Mary A. died 10/12/63 10/13/63
Schofield, Sarah A. married Wise, Thomas M. 02/26/63 02/28/63
Schofield, Victoria Alice died 08/27/63 08/28/63
Scholl, George H. died 06/17/64 06/24/64
Scholl, Mary died 07/04/62 07/18/62
Schone, John Harman died 07/18/61 07/20/61
Schonnofull, John married Robinson, Caroline 10/09/65 10/13/65
Schonnofull, John married Robinson, Caroline 10/09/65 10/16/65
Schoreck, Elizabeth Ann married Summers, Henry 07/12/64 07/14/64
Schott, Dorothea married Doenges, George 06/05/65 06/08/65
Schotta, C. married Thomas, M. 11/24/61 11/26/61
Schraeder, Willie Oliver L. died 04/26/62 04/29/62
Schreiner, Albert married Stoll, Mary Catherine 02/12/65 02/27/65
Schriner, John G. married Wilt, Sophia E. 02/27/62 03/01/62
Schriner, John G. married Wilt, Sophia E. 02/27/62 03/03/62
Schritz, John A. married Shannon, Katie A. 02/28/65 04/14/65
Schrivner, Margaret married Hoenes, Albert Frederick 01/08/61 02/09/61
Schroedel, Sabrina died 01/25/64 01/26/64
Schroeder, Henrietta E. married Inks, John E. 10/09/65 10/11/65
Schroeder, Henrietta M. married Hobson, George Withington 04/03/61 04/08/61
Schroeder, Jacob died 12/14/61 12/16/61
Schrote, James Henry died 06/28/65 06/29/65
Schueler, Lewis married Baryer, Catherine 12/01/63 12/02/63
Schuhoff, Williamina married Marshall, John 06/16/62 06/17/62
Schuhoff, Williamina married Marshall, John 06/16/62 06/19/62
Schuhoff, Williamina married Marshall, John 06/16/62 06/20/62
Schuking, Kathinka married Sutro, Emil 10/22/61 10/24/61
Schukle, Mary C. married Altpeter, George 01/18/63 01/21/63
Schulte, Mary I. died 10/23/65 10/25/65
Schultz, George T. married Swain, Eliza W. 10/10/65 10/16/65
Schultz, James L. died 10/29/65 10/30/65
Schultz, Lillie died 09/18/63 09/19/63
Schulze, Barbara (Mrs.) died 03/31/65 04/05/65
Schulze, Jonathan Thorpe died 06/25/64 06/30/64
Schumacher, Frederick, Jr. died 11/29/61 12/06/64
Schumacher, H. J. married Nurnburger, E. A. 10/09/65 10/11/65
Schumacher, Mary died 01/16/64 01/18/64
Schumacher, Mary R. married Huntemuller, H. William 07/01/62 07/03/62
Schumacher, William A. died 04/16/63 04/17/63
Schumacher, Willie died 03/30/64 03/31/64
Schumaker, Mary Louisa died 05/03/62 06/20/62
Schunck, Joseph died 07/19/65 10/12/65
Schunk, Mary Virginia died 03/13/64 03/15/64
Schurmann, Annette married Wittig, C. 08/11/64 08/15/64

Schutze, John Augustus died 04/22/65 04/25/65
Schwab, Henry married Straus, Henrietta 08/16/63 08/18/63
Schwab, Morris married Coblens, Hannah 10/22/65 10/23/65
Schwab, Morris married Coblens, Hannah 10/22/65 10/25/65
Schwartz, Andrew married Rogers, Mary 12/07/65 12/16/65
Schwartz, John Stalfort died 03/13/63 03/16/63
Schwartz, Louisa Virginia died 07/16/63 07/18/63
Schwartze, Augustus F. died 06/12/64 06/16/64
Schwearer, Christina died 01/06/61 01/08/61
Schwearer, Christina W. died 01/06/61 01/07/61
Schwearer, George P. died 06/26/63 06/29/63
Schwearer, Mary R. C. died 04/03/61 04/05/61
Schweikert, Elizabeth (Mrs.) married Winkler, Peter 09/17/65 10/05/65
Schweikert, Robert James died 05/28/61 05/30/61
Schweitzer, Mary Jane (Mrs.) died 12/29/63 12/30/63
Schweitzer, Mary Jane (Mrs.) died 12/29/63 12/31/63
Schwrar, George died 02/25/62 03/04/62
Scobell, J. H. H. died 01/02/64 01/05/64
Scoggins, Annie Rebecca died 06/22/64 06/23/64
Scoggins, Milton married Williams, Elizabeth 05/08/62 06/02/62
Scoggins, Susan Charlotte died 08/26/63 08/27/63
Scoggins, William Frances died 09/07/65 09/08/65
Scoley, Ann died 07/23/65 07/25/65
Scollens, James died 08/23/65 08/28/65
Score, Martha married Cook, Francis 03/07/61 03/11/61
Scott, Alcinda E. (Mrs.) died 05/17/63 05/19/63
Scott, Cassandra (Mrs.) died no date 03/24/64
Scott, Cecilia married McGarigley, John 12/19/61 12/25/61
Scott, Charles M. married Roden, Jane 12/26/65 12/30/65
Scott, Daniel married Norris, Cornelia 11/18/63 12/12/63
Scott, Edward M. married Rayhice, M. Cecelia 01/08/63 01/12/63
Scott, Edwin Ellsworth died 05/24/64 05/26/64
Scott, Eliza Jane married Gill, William E. 10/14/62 10/20/62
Scott, Eliza Jane married Gill, William Ensor 10/14/62 10/23/62
Scott, Elizabeth married Poole, George R. 03/29/65 04/15/65
Scott, F. H. died 01/04/65 01/05/65
Scott, Ferdinand died 01/18/61 01/19/61
Scott, George married Heigle, Anna R. 01/18/63 01/24/63
Scott, George F. died 11/27/63 01/01/64
Scott, Georgeanna married Graham, John 02/09/63 03/10/63
Scott, James married Sorrell, Sarah E. 03/24/65 04/26/65
Scott, James A. married Cole, Mary A. 04/05/65 04/08/65
Scott, James M. married Freeland, Helen Augusta 02/08/65 02/28/65
Scott, James R. married Mason, Fannie J. 06/01/65 06/13/65
Scott, John married Pindle, Rosetta 12/23/61 12/25/61
Scott, John B. married Wells, Lucy E. 11/25/63 12/21/63
Scott, John Thomas married Martin, Josephine 04/07/63 04/08/63
Scott, John W. married Lane, Rachel A. R. 12/17/63 12/19/63
Scott, Jonathan W. married Swatrz, Rose A. 06/19/65 06/22/65
Scott, Josephine R. married Johnson, Elizabeth H. 04/14/63 11/11/63
Scott, Lizzie married Keller, Jacob J. 12/29/64 01/14/65
Scott, Maggie A. married Sparks, Josiah 05/14/63 06/24/63
Scott, Margaret died 12/04/65 12/05/65
Scott, Martha E. married Hartley, Charles L. 03/22/64 03/29/64
Scott, Mary married Cutaiar, Francis 09/14/65 09/18/65

```
Scott, Mary A. died 12/17/65   12/18/65
Scott, Mary Agnes married Rodney, John M. 12/19/61   12/23/61
Scott, Mary Ann (Mrs.) died 07/02/64   07/07/64
Scott, Mary Ellen married Gough, James 02/15/63   03/07/63
Scott, Mary J. married Cutaiar, Francis 09/14/65   09/16/65
Scott, Matilda married McEldowney, John 12/03/61   12/04/61
Scott, Nina married Merriam, G. F. (Maj.) 09/29/63   10/03/63
Scott, Otho died 03/09/64   03/10/64
Scott, Philip died 07/07/64   07/09/64
Scott, Philip (Rev.) married Ogle, Sarah Ann 10/17/65   10/19/65
Scott, R. V. married Kennard, Lewis E. 01/26/65   01/31/65
Scott, R. V. married Kennard, Lewis E. (Lt.) 01/26/65   02/01/65
Scott, Rachel (Mrs.) died 02/05/64   02/12/64
Scott, Robert died 11/09/62   11/10/62
Scott, Robert married Ermy, Sermena 08/09/64   08/11/64
Scott, Sallie C. married Matthews, Richard J. 05/21/62   05/23/62
Scott, Susan married Hemlick, Jacob 02/05/64   09/19/64
Scott, Susan Ann Elizabeth died 02/24/61   02/26/61
Scott, Susan Jane married Lyles, Thomas 09/30/62   10/07/62
Scott, Thomas R. died 08/23/65   09/11/65
Scott, William F. L. died 08/24/64   08/27/64
Scott, William Henry died 06/29/63   07/03/63
Scott, William R. died 09/18/65   09/19/65
Scott, Willie died 06/01/64   06/02/64
Scotti, Charles Ferdinand died 07/21/63   07/23/63
Scottie, John L. married McBride, Elizabeth 10/07/63   10/10/63
Scottie, John W. married Mullinix, Maggie 05/13/63   05/22/63
Scriven, George W. died 10/31/65   11/01/65
Scriven, George W. died 10/31/65   11/02/65
Scrivener, John H. died 01/15/63   01/20/63
Scrivener, Rosie M. married Burgy, William Corwin 06/14/64   06/16/64
Scrivner, Mary F. died 06/22/62   07/04/62
Scully, Edward died 07/07/64   07/08/64
Seabold, Ida Sophia died 01/10/64   01/12/64
Seabright, Elizabeth died 06/12/61   06/13/61
Seaman, Ada married Mullan, Louis A. 02/22/63   04/29/63
Seamon, Laura died 01/22/61   02/02/61
Searly, Elizabeth (Mrs.) died 06/17/63   06/18/63
Sears, Charles C. married Skinner, Jennie 04/17/62   04/21/62
Sears, Jason S. married Cochran, Ella V. 11/26/63   03/15/64
Sears, Julia M. died 11/02/61   11/04/61
Sears, Thomas died 02/27/63   02/28/63
Sears, Thomas died 10/09/65   10/10/65
Sedden, Jacob died 06/24/63   06/25/63
Sedicom, William Gilmour died 08/15/65   08/21/65
Sedwick, John C. married Williams, Sarah F. 12/22/64   12/23/64
Seebode, Albert W. married Klessell, Augusta E. 06/08/65   06/17/65
Seebode, Louis married Stockett, Mary E. 09/17/62   09/19/62
Seebol, M. Lizzie married Pearson, Charles B. 10/06/63   10/29/63
Seebold, Philip D. married Eagleston, Marion Virginia 01/05/63   01/20/63
Seeger, Sophie died 01/07/63   01/09/63
Seeman, Laura Julia Hermine died 01/22/61   01/25/61
Seevers, Jesse died 02/04/63   02/05/63
Sefton, John W. married Foutz, Debbie 11/13/61   11/15/61
Sefton, Sevilla married Bennett, Harry 03/12/63   03/14/63
```

Segerman, Eliza (Mrs.) died 12/18/63   12/19/63
Segerman, Henry H. (Capt.) died 02/16/64   02/17/64
Segerman, Jane (Mrs.) died 03/19/63   03/20/63
Segerman, William H. married Divine, Agnes 01/28/64   02/05/64
Segers, Francis died 04/05/63   04/06/63
Seguin, Georgian B. died 11/06/65   11/08/65
Sehl, Justus married Reuter, Fredericke 09/01/63   09/05/63
Seibel, Gertrude E. married Brandenburg, Frederick William 06/07/64
    06/10/64
Seibel, Mary Virginia died 09/12/62   09/13/62
Seibert, Edward married Fossett, Jennie 11/27/62   12/04/62
Seibert, Fannie died 07/28/65   07/29/65
Seibert, Margaret R. died 03/03/64   03/05/64
Seibert, Newton W. married Dunn, Josephine A. 07/07/65   07/15/65
Seibold, George W. married Gordon, Louisa 03/21/61   07/25/61
Seibold, Lewis P. married Dawson, Josephine B. 10/02/61   02/13/62
Seidenstricker, Henry A. married Bullymore, Frank C. 11/19/63   11/28/63
Seidenstricker, Ruth (Mrs.) died 03/13/64   03/15/64
Seidenstricker, Virginia Davis died 03/30/63   04/14/63
Seiderstricker, William D. married Litsinger, Elizabeth 06/30/64
    07/15/64
Seip, William died 11/05/65   11/07/65
Seipp, Adolf died 08/14/62   08/15/62
Seipp, Adolphus died 02/27/63   02/28/63
Seipp, Christopher died 02/09/63   02/10/63
Seipp, Frederick married Lantz, Elizabeth 08/27/63   09/23/63
Seipp, Laura Virginia died 07/09/65   07/11/65
Selby, Edwin D. married Nonamaker, Celia 08/20/63   08/21/63
Selby, Fannie R. married Zell, Oliver C. 10/23/62   10/24/62
Selby, James H. married Jones, Rachel 04/12/64   04/15/64
Selby, James W. married McNew, Alverda 02/22/65   02/25/65
Selby, Joseph E. (Sgt.) married Ayres, Maggie A. 04/07/64   04/13/64
Selby, Nicholas A. married Cross, Eugenia 11/22/64   11/29/64
Seldon, George L. (Cmdr.) died 02/14/64   02/17/64
Selecman, Maggie A. married Gill, George H. 08/02/63   08/19/63
Selegee, Caroline married Newman, Benjamin 08/13/65   08/14/65
Self, Mahala died 11/04/61   11/06/61
Seligman, Adolph married Blondheim, Kate 07/25/64   07/28/64
Seligman, Ike J. married Getz, Belle 08/26/63   08/27/63
Selinger, Philipina married Weglein, Louis 06/17/63   06/18/63
Sellers, J. Henry died 03/19/65   03/20/65
Sellers, J. Henry died 03/19/65   03/21/65
Sellers, Susan J. married Morgan, J. Asbury (Professor) 08/01/65
    08/16/65
Sellman, James T. married Holland, Maggie A. 04/10/62   05/06/62
Sellman, John F. married Tucker, Fannie E. 05/25/61   05/29/61
Seltz, William Frederick died 06/13/64   06/15/64
Seltzer, Elizabeth (Mrs.) died 01/22/64   01/23/64
Seltzer, John Joseph died 10/14/62   10/18/62
Seltzer, Mary (Mrs.) died 09/17/63   09/18/63
Selvage, Maggie A. married Petherbridge, William O. 11/25/61   11/30/61
Selvage, William B. died 02/22/65   02/23/65
Semmes, A. A. married Dorsey, Mary M. 02/09/64   02/10/64
Semmes, Kate Middleton married Gibson, Frederick (Rev.) 12/26/65
    12/28/65

Semmes, Rebecca died 01/01/65 02/02/65
Semmes, Robert D. married Egerton, Julia C. 02/21/61 02/23/61
Semon, Benjamin died 11/17/65 11/23/65
Semore, Margaret C. married Stalings, John 08/05/60 01/30/61
Semore, Margaret C. married Stalings, John 01/05/61 01/29/61
Senderling, John died 12/28/65 12/29/65
Senderling, Sarah A. married Atkins, Edward 06/05/64 06/07/64
Senderling, Sarah Ann (Mrs.) died 04/08/65 04/10/65
Senft, Henry died 04/15/62 04/16/62
Sentenn, Walter J. married Miles, Lottie A. 11/03/63 11/05/63
Sephus, Elizabeth died 03/16/65 03/18/65
Sergeant, Kate married Bevan, Thomas W. 05/31/64 06/01/64
Sermon, Mary Virginia died 09/27/63 09/29/63
Sermons, Mary Ann died 12/18/62 12/19/62
Server, William H., Jr. married Robinson, Maria H. 12/20/63 01/01/64
Sesions, John W. Webster died 04/13/65 04/14/65
Sessford, John Herbert S. died 08/25/63 08/26/63
Sessford, John Herbert S. died 08/25/63 08/27/63
Sessions, Charles Edwin died 02/07/64 02/08/64
Sessions, Mary C. married White, William W. 11/30/65 12/04/65
Setchel, (Prof.) married Lindsey, Laura A. 12/15/63 12/22/63
Seth, Charles died 09/07/65 09/09/65
Seth, Mollie M. married Benson, P. V. (M.D.) 12/04/62 12/09/62
Seth, Robert L. died 11/02/65 11/03/65
Seth, William G. died 02/25/64 02/27/64
Setten, Roseanna married Wagner, Charles Henry 10/10/62 10/16/62
Setten, Roseanna married Waggner, Charles Henry 10/10/62 10/17/62
Seusner, Catherine (Mrs.) died 09/24/64 09/26/64
Sevestre, Catherine died 03/14/62 03/15/62
Sevier, Charles E. married Keefer, Annie C. 12/27/60 01/18/62
Sevier, Charles H. married Stewart, Virginia 07/20/65 07/21/65
Sevier, Henry Randolph died 09/23/65 09/27/65
Seward, Barbara (Mrs.) died 08/14/63 08/15/63
Seward, Charles Napoleon died 06/03/61 06/04/61
Seward, Charlotte married Kenny, William 10/08/61 11/06/61
Seward, George B. McClellan died 02/29/64 03/02/64
Seward, James H., Jr. died 10/24/65 10/25/65
Seward, Levi died 09/18/63 09/19/63
Sewell, Charles A. died 02/15/65 02/17/65
Sewell, Charles Alexander married Whitney, Lizzie J. 03/12/61 03/14/61
Sewell, Elizabeth died 10/12/65 10/13/65
Sewell, Elizabeth Wrightson died 01/13/63 01/15/63
Sewell, Ellen R. married Brown, Absalom 07/06/62 07/14/62
Sewell, Henry died 03/07/64 03/10/64
Sewell, James B. F. married Scheuhts, Louisiana Frances 10/02/62
    10/21/62
Sewell, James M. married Reese, Annie O. 10/12/65 10/16/65
Sewell, Joseph married Freburger, Mary E. 11/14/65 11/16/65
Sewell, Laura V. married Fuller, Charles W. 07/29/63 07/31/63
Sewell, M. Augusta married Weech, William T. L. (Rev.) 11/28/61
    12/09/61
Sewell, Maggie M. married Lowry, William Palmer 06/18/65 06/10/65
Sewell, Margaret A. died 08/12/62 08/13/62
Sewell, Mary Ann Elizabeth died 04/28/62 05/01/62
Sewell, Mary Eliza died 08/22/64 08/24/64

Sewell, Richard died 01/07/63   01/08/63
Sewell, Willeller Warren died 02/23/64   02/24/64
Sewell, William H. C. married Howard, Mary Amelia 03/31/62   04/30/62
Sewell, William H. C. died 07/04/63   07/06/63
Sewell, William H. C. (Cpt.) died 07/04/63   07/18/63
Sexton, Rachel died 11/20/65   11/22/65
Seymour, Ann E. died 01/02/61   01/04/61
Seymour, Daniel H. died 10/29/63   11/04/63
Seymour, H. O. married Anzmann, A. 07/21/64   04/22/65
Seymour, Henry C. married McCurley, Annie 06/23/62   02/04/64
Seymour, Isabella died 01/21/65   01/24/65
Seymour, John W. died 04/11/63   04/13/63
Seymour, John Wesley died 07/29/61   07/31/61
Seymour, Lizzie married Reed, W. H. W. 12/07/65   12/14/65
Seymour, S. K. married Street, J. 11/26/65   11/03/65
Seymour, S. Kate married Street, R. J. 11/26/65   11/06/65
Seymour, Sarah E. married Baynes, William W. 07/27/65   07/29/65
Seymour, William S. married Hobbs, Laura A. 10/26/64   10/27/64
Shaab, Mary Annie died 01/05/65   01/06/65
Shaab, Mary Virginia died 08/12/61   08/13/61
Shade, Chilla died 06/01/62   06/03/62
Shade, David married Reynolds, Elizabeth 12/10/65   12/23/65
Shadrick, William R. married French, Ellen A. 12/28/62   02/24/63
Shaefer, Christian A. died 04/14/64   04/15/64
Shaeffer, Kate L. died 06/24/64   06/25/64
Shaffer, Elly Charles died 03/11/63   03/12/63
Shaffer, Fannie A. married Bailey, Thomas 01/07/64   01/09/64
Shaffer, George G. died 03/28/62   03/31/62
Shaffer, George T. died 12/04/63   12/05/63
Shaffer, John Henry married Marshall, Mary Rebecca 01/14/63   02/12/63
Shaffer, Katie died 08/09/64   08/10/64
Shaffner, Jacob died 02/12/61   02/13/61
Shaffner, Jacob died 02/12/61   02/14/61
Shaffner, Phoebe died 09/17/65   09/18/65
Shaffner, Phoebe died 09/17/65   09/19/65
Shafler, Virginia S. married Hauptmann, Garrett 11/24/64   11/26/64
Shakelford, Louisa died 10/06/65   10/07/65
Shakespear, Stephen died 07/23/61   07/24/61
Shale, Elizabeth married Melchior, Francis P. 05/26/64   05/27/64
Shaler, Victorine died 10/24/65   10/25/65
Shallus, Sarah Belle died 07/26/65   07/31/65
Shamburg, Josh married Cross, Elizabeth 02/18/64   02/19/64
Shamer, Theodore married Crow, Mary Jane 11/29/64   12/07/64
Shanahan, John died 10/07/64   10/08/64
Shanahan, Martin married Enright, Mary 09/24/63   09/26/63
Shanaman, Edward Duffield died 03/01/64   03/02/64
Shanaman, Harriet (Mrs.) died 12/12/63   12/16/63
Shanaman, Zadoc Henry died 08/17/62   08/18/62
Shanck, Ellen died 03/15/62   03/17/62
Shane, Catherine married Rigney, George 08/31/64   09/03/64
Shane, Edward M. died 11/11/62   11/13/62
Shane, John H. (Lt) married Evans, Virginia R. 03/11/64   03/22/64
Shank, Barbara (Mrs.) died 12/25/65   12/30/65
Shank, Mary A. married Lancaster, John Henry 05/31/61   06/03/61
Shank, S. N. married Stansbury, G. W. 07/27/61   08/10/61

Shanklin, Elizabeth married Stuart, William H. 03/12/63   03/13/63
Shanklin, J. W. married Cromwell, Maggie E. 09/21/64   09/26/64
Shanklin, Ruth W. died 11/11/61   11/12/61
Shanley, William died 08/07/63   08/08/63
Shannan, William married Cromer, Hermie E. 03/09/65   03/13/65
Shannon, Dennis died 02/18/61   02/20/61
Shannon, Katie A. married Schritz, John A. 02/28/65   04/14/65
Shannon, M. Lizzie died 02/11/65   02/13/65
Shannon, Margaret Agnes died 04/26/63   04/28/63
Shannon, Margaret Agnes died 04/26/65   05/10/65
Shannon, Richard B. died 01/31/65   02/17/65
Shanon, Ann died 06/17/62   06/18/62
Sharar, Ann F. (Mrs.) died 09/13/63   09/14/63
Sharar, Ann F. (Mrs.) died 09/13/63   09/15/63
Share, Jane Isabella died 06/11/61   06/12/61
Share, Joseph R. died 06/30/62   07/01/62
Sharkey, Edward died 09/26/63   09/28/63
Sharkey, Margaret died 02/06/61   02/07/61
Sharkey, Patrick died 02/01/65   02/03/65
Sharkley, Ann (Mrs.) died 01/09/64   01/11/64
Sharp, Mary H. G. married Hollingsworth, T. H. Benton 11/13/62   12/01/62
Sharpe, Mary A. married Johnson, John Henry 01/20/65   01/23/65
Sharpe, Mary Elizabeth married Johnson, Thomas C. 04/21/62   04/23/62
Sharpley, John died 08/04/62   08/05/62
Shaugnessy, Isabella Ellen died 06/05/64   06/06/64
Shaver, Lucy C. married Rhea, John L. 04/20/65   05/11/65
Shaw, Alexander J. (Cpt.) married Hughes, Margaretta H. 05/07/63
     05/09/63
Shaw, Ann Elizabeth died 11/05/64   11/07/64
Shaw, Arthur died 10/02/65   10/03/65
Shaw, Bell S. married Kemp, Richard 10/03/65   10/05/65
Shaw, Catherine G. died no date   08/14/65
Shaw, Daniel W. married Hayman, Mary 09/07/62   09/13/62
Shaw, Ellen married McCuen, John 02/14/61   02/16/61
Shaw, Ellenora died 11/01/62   11/03/62
Shaw, Eugenia Maria died 11/30/65   12/01/65
Shaw, Henry Fulton died 09/04/65   09/05/65
Shaw, Hugh died 05/23/65   05/24/65
Shaw, James F. died 10/28/63   10/29/63
Shaw, Jane (Mrs.) died 04/03/63   04/04/63
Shaw, Julia Francis died 03/25/65   03/27/65
Shaw, Laura married Emmert, A. D. 02/10/64   02/16/64
Shaw, Leila E. married Boteler, Charles J. 07/01/62   07/07/62
Shaw, Little Lalla died 11/23/62   11/24/62
Shaw, Lucretia M. married Darby, Harrison D. 11/22/64   01/14/65
Shaw, Margaret (Mrs.) died 04/22/64   04/23/64
Shaw, Mary Agnes died 11/15/64   11/16/64
Shaw, Mary E. married Stearns, Charles W. 07/02/62   07/04/62
Shaw, William D. married Wilson, Catharine A. 01/18/63   01/24/63
Shaws, William B. married Legg, Susan A. 11/10/64   11/12/64
Shays, Robert G. married Weems, Lizzie K. 09/22/63   09/23/63
Shea, Daniel married Finn, Mary 07/20/64   09/23/64
Shea, Ellen (Mrs.) died 11/14/63   11/16/63
Shea, Frances married Ringrose, Robert 06/26/61   07/03/61
Shea, George married Fosler, Mary S. 12/08/64   12/20/64

Shea, Margaretta died 08/20/62 08/21/62
Sheaf, Catherine A. married Bailey, John 06/20/61 06/22/61
Sheafer, Annie E. married Thompson, John 03/07/65 04/27/65
Sheaff, Joseph married Bulett, Elizabeth 03/18/61 03/25/61
Sheaff, Joseph died 11/19/65 11/20/65
Sheahan, John P. died 02/14/61 02/28/61
Sheares, Harman F. married Cole, Anna Maria 11/07/65 11/16/65
Shearlock, Augustus died 06/17/62 06/19/62
Shearlock, Rebecca Caroline died 04/07/63 04/09/63
Shears, Susan A. (Mrs.) died 03/31/64 04/02/64
Sheckells, Albert Dorsey died 05/31/64 06/01/64
Sheckells, Anna E. married Nagle, John G. 12/06/65 12/11/65
Sheckells, Catharine married Duyer, Cyrus 05/02/64 05/04/64
Sheckells, Charles R. married Minifie, Jane S. 01/10/61 01/21/61
Sheckells, Mrs Ann died 10/20/63 10/23/63
Sheckells, Otis B. married Mules, Margaret A. 02/25/63 03/17/63
Sheckels, John married Huber, Lavina 03/14/64 03/17/64
Shedrick, Amelia Jane died 01/24/62 02/06/62
Shedrick, Anna Catherine died 01/27/62 02/06/62
Sheeler, Anthony married Gibson, John 08/15/60 02/06/61
Sheeler, Cordelia A. married Elliott, William H. N. 10/26/65 11/01/65
Sheeler, Samuel Ripple died 06/14/64 06/16/64
Sheeman, Hannah L. married Burrows, William 01/18/64 02/27/64
Sheesley, Daniel married Tumey, Mary 01/23/61 01/25/61
Sheets, Hattie V. married Reifsnider, William T. 10/18/65 10/23/65
Sheets, Hattie V. married Reifsnider, William E. 10/18/65 10/25/65
Sheets, Philip married Scherf, Bertha 04/12/64 04/16/64
Sheey, Ada died 10/19/65 10/20/65
Sheffer, Daniel H. died 07/23/62 07/24/62
Sheffer, Jesse married Keifel, Isabel 12/10/61 12/12/61
Sheffer, John W. died 12/13/65 12/14/65
Sheffield, George W. died 07/08/65 07/10/65
Sheffield, Mary Ann died 10/25/62 10/29/62
Shehan, Ellen married Quinn, Martin 04/23/65 05/10/65
Shehan, George Alexandre died 08/17/61 08/19/61
Shehan, George E. married Morgan, Sophia L. 03/05/63 03/25/63
Shehan, Mary died 08/04/63 08/06/63
Sheiblein, Sarah Virginia died 12/21/65 12/22/65
Sheibler, Elizabeth married Ament, George Louis 06/16/63 06/18/63
Shekell, Annie W. married Bradford, H. Harrison 06/22/65 06/27/65
Shekells, Annie married Baker, H. B. (Cpt.) 05/09/64 05/11/64
Sheldon, Georgie Ellen (Mrs.) died 09/29/64 10/01/64
Sheldon, John B. married Tarr, Melissa 10/08/63 10/13/63
Shell, Annie married Dougherty, Thomas B. 12/28/61 01/11/62
Shelley, Eugenia died 11/04/65 11/15/65
Shelley, George K. married Brown, Mary 01/16/63 01/22/63
Shelly, Annie C. married Everhart, O. T. (Dr.) 10/18/64 10/19/64
Shelton, Annie C. married Quackenboss, L. J. 07/02/65 07/11/65
Shenck, Lilly married Bowser, Samuel B. 03/05/63 03/12/63
Shenckel, Rosalie married Geoghegan, James A. 05/03/63 05/07/63
Shepard, Jacob S. married Harris, Caroline 12/29/64 12/30/64
Shepard, James W. married Douglas, Caroline 12/31/60 11/09/61
Shepard, John married Smith, Fredericka 01/18/61 01/23/61
Shepard, Mary Ann (Mrs.) died 01/07/65 01/09/65
Sheperd, R. D. died 11/10/65 11/20/65

Shepherd, Stephen married Poulson, Isabella 10/22/63   10/24/63
Sheppard, Charles F. married Dashiell, Mary Emma 11/11/63   11/14/63
Sheppard, George W. died 09/20/64   09/22/64
Sheppard, Harriet Ann died 06/11/62   06/12/62
Sheppard, Jennie (Mrs.) died 01/24/64   01/27/64
Sheppard, Josephine B. married Waltemeyer, Jacob 02/19/63   02/21/63
Sheppard, Mary died 08/12/61   08/27/61
Sheppard, Mary Ann C. died no date   04/13/61
Sheppard, Mary Jane died 07/27/65   07/31/65
Sheppard, N. married Petrie, Carrie A. 02/26/64   03/19/64
Sheppard, Thomas died 07/21/65   07/26/65
Sheppard, Thomas D. married Hamilton, Carrie 07/05/64   07/07/64
Sheppard, William James died 03/17/64   03/22/64
Sherbert, Annie married Akers, Joseph 08/08/61   08/10/61
Sherbett, Daniel M. (USA) died 07/05/63   07/28/63
Sheridan, Jennie married Appleby, George 06/22/65   06/27/65
Sheridan, Lizzie married Kirk, Elijah 02/21/65   03/04/65
Sheridan, Michael married Grady, Mary 03/23/63   03/23/63
Sheriff, James Morris died 12/26/65   12/30/65
Sherlock, Sallie Jane married Way, George 11/16/64   11/17/64
Sherlock, William married Crawford, Anna 12/09/61   12/12/61
Sherman, Jennive Blanche died 08/23/64   08/24/64
Sherman, John married Barenger, Catherine 08/10/63   08/15/63
Sherman, John married Barrenger, Sarah C. 08/10/63   08/20/63
Sherman, John married Meeter, Mary E. 10/02/65   10/09/65
Shermantine, John A. B. married Sanner, Maria D. 11/29/64   12/01/64
Sherrard, Fannie Bell died 08/15/61   08/20/61
Sherrard, Frances Bell died 08/15/61   08/19/61
Sherrard, Robert W. died 07/06/62   07/07/62
Sherrer, Barbara married Broadbeck, William 08/21/61   08/23/61
Sherrer, Barbara married Broadbeck, William 08/21/61   08/24/61
Sherry, P. married Binnix, Maggie 03/29/64   03/31/64
Sherry, Thomas Patrick died 10/15/61   10/16/61
Sherwood, Charles W. died 12/30/62   01/02/63
Sherwood, E. A. married Russell, John L. 01/01/62   01/03/62
Sherwood, Elizabeth H. died 05/22/63   05/23/63
Sherwood, Henry A. died 12/26/63   11/28/63
Sherwood, John Johns died 03/15/64   03/17/64
Sherwood, Joseph died 02/21/65   02/22/65
Sherwood, Joseph died 02/21/65   02/23/65
Sherwood, Kate R. married Welch, Benjamin P. 12/13/64   12/15/64
Sherwood, Kate R. married Welch, Benjamin T. 12/13/64   12/16/64
Sherwood, Philip Francis died 07/30/64   08/01/64
Sherwood, Willliam H. married Wimpsett, Sarah S. 05/19/64   05/24/64
Shesgreen, Charles died 02/02/64   02/04/64
Shetter, John George died 11/21/64   11/23/64
Shew, Harry married Vinson, Annie 07/30/62   09/10/62
Shia, Emeline married Gethins, Thomas 01/22/63   01/23/63
Shiel, Annie (Mrs.) died 08/21/63   08/22/63
Shield, John J. married Hyatt, Mary E. 03/16/63   03/19/63
Shield, Sarah B. died 03/12/63   03/14/63
Shields, Agnes died 01/26/61   01/31/61
Shields, Charles A. died 12/27/65   12/28/65
Shields, James married Brady, Margaret 06/22/62   06/24/62
Shields, John William married Jones, Mary E. 02/11/61   03/20/61

Shields, Maggie A. married Hanes, Frank M. 12/01/63 12/08/63
Shields, Mary Elizabeth (Mrs.) died 01/02/64 01/04/64
Shields, Sarah married Hynes, Thomas 05/18/65 05/20/65
Shilling, John Charles married Keyser, Margaret 11/25/63 11/28/63
Shilling, Sarah died 11/25/62 11/27/62
Shillinger, Amelia S. married Stockley, Albert A. 06/22/65 07/01/65
Shillinger, Philip died 12/22/62 12/31/62
Shillington, Mary died 10/28/61 10/29/61
Shinnick, Annie married Pierpont, Thomas B. S. 02/21/61 12/02/61
Shinnick, Annie married Pierpont, Thomas B. S. 11/28/61 02/25/62
Shinnick, Georgia A. married Dawson, Thomas L. 08/04/63 08/19/63
Shinnick, John Thomas died 07/21/64 07/23/64
Shinton, Annie E. married Jones, Thomas 06/16/64 06/18/64
Shipley, A. P. married Pindel, M. A. (Mrs.) 11/23/65 12/07/65
Shipley, Andrew Wesley died 02/27/63 02/28/63
Shipley, Ann died 01/16/64 01/18/64
Shipley, Bradley J. married Ford, Mary V. 01/07/62 01/09/62
Shipley, C. W. married Martin, Lizzie J. 09/12/65 09/18/65
Shipley, Caroline married Hisey, John A. 01/10/65 01/12/65
Shipley, Caroline M. married Scarborough, Wilson 04/30/63 05/12/63
Shipley, Catherine Sellman died 04/01/63 04/02/63
Shipley, Christopher C. married Brown, Elizabeth A. 12/24/62 01/01/63
Shipley, Christopher C. died 05/04/64 05/05/64
Shipley, Clara Belle died 05/30/64 05/31/64
Shipley, Cornelius died 02/03/62 02/05/62
Shipley, Edwin G. died 11/06/65 11/07/65
Shipley, Eliza E. married Shipley, John T. 10/19/65 11/04/65
Shipley, Eliza Jane died 01/30/62 02/01/62
Shipley, Elizabeth married Mitchell, John H. W. 06/29/62 07/02/62
Shipley, Elizabeth died 02/05/65 02/07/65
Shipley, Enos died 06/09/65 06/13/65
Shipley, George died 01/19/62 01/21/62
Shipley, Haddie died 07/30/63 08/04/63
Shipley, Harry died 04/19/62 04/22/62
Shipley, Henry Clay died 01/06/64 01/07/64
Shipley, J. Lester (Rev.) married Gere, E. Gussie 10/26/65 10/27/65
Shipley, John died 12/18/65 12/29/65
Shipley, John T. died 09/21/61 09/23/61
Shipley, John T. married Shipley, Eliza E. 10/19/65 11/04/65
Shipley, John Wesley died 10/08/63 10/09/63
Shipley, Joseph married Husband, Mary L. 08/11/63 08/22/63
Shipley, Joseph H. died 08/14/65 08/18/65
Shipley, Julia E. married Heald, Samuel W. 11/03/62 12/05/62
Shipley, Laura H. died 07/29/63 08/04/63
Shipley, Lizzie died 07/30/65 08/01/65
Shipley, Lovelace married Pawley, Victoria A. no date 02/27/64
Shipley, Lydia Goar died 09/25/63 09/26/63
Shipley, Mary died 07/21/62 07/23/62
Shipley, Mary Almeda died 09/17/63 09/19/63
Shipley, Mary E. married Scheibler, Andrew K. 02/12/63 02/14/63
Shipley, Medora M. married Read, William J. 10/04/65 10/11/65
Shipley, Nancy (Mrs.) died 01/27/63 01/29/63
Shipley, Nannie died 03/28/63 03/31/63
Shipley, Owen died 03/08/65 03/14/65
Shipley, Peter A. married Chenoweth, Sarah J. 05/21/63 05/28/63

Shipley, Rhoda Camilla died 02/27/64 03/11/64
Shipley, Richard married Bordley, Hester 10/21/62 10/22/62
Shipley, Richard Jefferson died 08/06/63 08/12/63
Shipley, Robert Q. died 07/28/63 08/04/63
Shipley, Samuel (Sgt.) married Hanes, Mary E. 02/18/63 02/25/63
Shipley, Sarah Virginia died 03/31/63 04/01/63
Shipley, Thomas died 03/05/64 03/11/64
Shipley, Thomas Benton died 12/20/65 12/21/65
Shipley, Washington died 10/19/61 10/26/61
Shipley, William B. married Parsley, Mary Sophia 04/28/63 04/30/63
Shipley, William Henry died 09/02/61 09/03/61
Shipley, William Kemp died 10/26/64 12/22/64
Shirden, James married Greenwood, Angeline A. 02/18/64 02/24/64
Shirdy, Martha (Mrs.) died 11/22/63 11/24/63
Shirley, Cephas died 10/02/63 10/03/63
Shirley, Eliza Ann died 08/13/61 08/15/61
Shirley, William Henry married Everheart, Christina 05/04/62 05/06/62
Shirlkel, William C. married Potter, Susan 07/22/63 07/25/63
Shirner, Catherine M. married McElwee, William H. 12/03/61 12/03/61
Shitele, Charles W. married Boone, Maggie S. 11/08/64 11/12/64
Shlens, G. A. married Wilkens, Henriette 02/25/64 02/26/64
Shoaff, Laura Virginia died 06/01/64 06/02/64
Shock, Dewitt Clinton married Wonderly, Mary A. 06/21/65 06/23/65
Shock, Thomas Holiday Hicks died 12/27/64 01/03/65
Shock, William W. married Spalding, Sarah F. 07/11/65 07/13/65
Shoemaker, Frederick S. died 01/24/63 03/18/63
Shone, Annie married Quick, George 07/06/62 07/19/62
Shope, Mary Bedford died 01/13/63 01/14/63
Shorb, Charles A. died 02/08/63 02/13/63
Shorb, Ella married Moore, John A. 05/15/65 05/31/65
Shorb, James E. married Price, Sallie E. 06/23/63 06/29/63
Shorey, Martha A. (Mrs.) died 09/09/63 09/11/63
Short, Ann G. married Killman, William T. 07/14/64 07/15/64
Short, John Hicks died 07/20/62 07/21/62
Short, Joseph A. married James, Rebecca A. 05/04/65 05/08/65
Short, Mary Augusta died 01/01/61 01/03/61
Short, Nellie C. married Burlin, Robert L. 04/21/64 05/23/64
Short, Perry married Gadd, Dally 06/25/62 07/07/62
Short, William Hudson died 07/22/63 07/23/63
Short, William Hudson died 07/22/63 08/24/63
Shorter, Jane (Mrs.) died 06/02/63 06/04/63
Shorter, Mary E. (Mrs.) died 06/02/63 06/04/63
Shorter, Mary Josephine died 09/28/64 09/30/64
Shorter, Sylvester died 12/30/61 12/31/61
Shortt, Harriet Josephine died 01/16/64 01/18/64
Shotts, Lewis J. died 10/25/63 10/27/63
Shoughnessy, Catherine died 12/30/62 12/31/62
Showacre, Michael S. married Little, Annie R. 10/20/62 10/25/62
Showalter, Elizabeth C. (Mrs.) died 03/18/63 03/20/63
Showalter, Harry married Hanes, Lida A. 12/14/65 12/21/65
Shower, Eleanora died 07/25/61 07/30/61
Shower, Theodore A. married Gomber, Sarah A. 06/04/61 06/19/61
Shreck, Addie E. married Davidson, A. E. 09/26/65 09/27/65
Shreck, Jacob E. married Sap, Sophia 01/14/64 01/20/64
Shreeve, J. (Rev.) married Taylor, Emily C. 01/16/62 01/17/62

Shreeve, Joshua B. died 05/03/63   05/05/63
Shreeves, Charles Franklin died 01/17/63   01/19/63
Shreeves, Joshua P. died 09/07/62   09/09/62
Shreeves, Mary Ann died 09/07/61   09/09/61
Shreeves, S. J. (USA) married Greer, Ella 11/02/63   11/05/63
Shriner, Basil died 05/11/63   05/14/63
Shriver, A. K. married Sanders, Emma P. 11/21/65   11/24/65
Shriver, Alexander died 02/08/64   02/10/64
Shriver, Ephraim Henry died 05/21/64   05/24/64
Shriver, John A. died 05/09/65   05/10/65
Shriver, John L. married Cassin, Roberta E. 10/19/65   11/01/65
Shriver, Mary married Johnson, Madison 10/20/64   10/22/64
Shriver, William H. married Winckelman, Susan L. 10/15/61   10/19/61
Shroat, Catharine died 12/19/61   12/20/61
Shroeder, Cecelia Ghequire died 07/06/63   08/08/63
Shroff, John Washington died 10/14/65   10/21/65
Shrote, John E. married Jones, Mary A. 02/22/65   03/29/65
Shrote, Sarah Elizabeth married Joyce, James A. A. 01/15/63   01/24/63
Shugars, Mary G. married Gettier, J. M. 03/10/64   03/16/64
Shuler, Lizzie died 07/22/65   08/01/65
Shultz, Bernhard married Alterhoff, (Miss) 07/02/63   09/24/63
Shultz, Robert Adams died 03/13/63   03/14/63
Shultz, William F. married Symonds, Susannah 02/19/62   02/22/62
Shumaker, George Washington died 02/02/63   02/03/63
Shunck, Jacob married Wells, Laura Virginia 12/24/61   01/03/62
Shunck, Robert married Mennig, Christiana 04/07/64   04/12/64
Shurles, Laura V. married Blocher, Henry W. 11/21/65   11/29/65
Shurles, Margaret A. (Mrs.) died 04/27/64   04/28/64
Shurley, James died 09/13/63   09/14/63
Shurman, August died 12/01/63   12/05/63
Shurmann, Lilli died 09/05/61   09/07/61
Shurter, Mary Mandy died 10/30/65   10/31/65
Shurtter, George married Elliott, Eliza 01/23/63   11/20/63
Shurtz, Ella died 08/18/63   08/19/63
Shutler, Mary Elizabeth married Parker, Elias 11/24/63   11/28/63
Shuts, Henry married Linzie, Mary 08/02/64   08/04/64
Shutt, John W. married Hubbard, Maggie M. 03/09/63   03/12/63
Shutt, Mary Ann died 09/09/61   09/10/61
Shutze, John Augustus died 04/22/65   04/24/65
Siar, Sallie (Mrs.) died 03/31/63   04/02/63
Sickel, Edward married Halbert, Sarah R. 06/26/61   06/28/61
Sickell, Sarah Rebecca died 08/04/65   08/05/65
Side, James R. died 12/14/64   12/31/64
Siegle, Frances S. married Golderman, Jacob 01/31/64   02/04/64
Siegmann, Johanna Henriette died 10/04/61   10/05/61
Sigler, Emma A. married Brown, J. Henry 03/03/63   03/06/63
Sikes, Columbus H. married Hahn, Joanna D. 04/06/65   04/14/65
Sikken, Charles M. died 11/07/63   11/09/63
Silence, Harry C. died 10/12/62   10/17/62
Siller, Sallie A. married Hughes, Thomas S. 06/08/65   06/12/65
Sillery, Bridget Catherine died 01/02/63   01/12/63
Sillman, William Harrison died 03/31/64   04/02/64
Silver, Mary E. married Booz, Henry P. 09/24/65   09/27/65
Silverwood, Lucy died 06/16/64   06/18/64
Silvey, Nancy (Mrs.) died 06/12/65   06/13/65

```
Silwright, James died 12/11/64   12/12/64
Simes, Elizabeth married Johnson, Rudolph 12/08/62   12/29/62
Simes, William D. married Hogg, Clara 11/03/63   11/06/63
Simmering, Delphine married Emmart, John 03/12/63   04/28/63
Simmes, Christiana (Mrs.) died 03/01/63   03/04/63
Simmonds, Rachel married Blufford, William H. 07/27/65   07/29/65
Simmonds, Sarah J. married Bond, Benjamin 12/24/61   12/25/61
Simmons, Anna married Hale, Jonathan H. 06/27/65   06/29/65
Simmons, Hester Ann died 12/26/61   12/30/61
Simmons, Isaac G. married Linsay, Emilia 04/11/64   04/13/64
Simmons, James Robert died 12/20/61   12/24/61
Simmons, John died 07/07/64   07/09/64
Simmons, Margaret married Gosnell, Mordicae 05/05/61   05/18/61
Simmons, Mary died 01/28/62   01/30/62
Simmons, Thomas E. married Evans, Henrietta 08/13/62   08/15/62
Simmons, William Henry died 12/22/61   12/24/61
Simmont, Jesse Lee died 01/15/64   01/18/64
Simmont, M. Amelia married Burnett, William T. 06/20/64   06/24/64
Simms, Alexander married Nichols, Margaret Ann 02/21/65   02/24/65
Simms, Eddie married Warren, William J. 01/29/61   01/31/61
Simms, Eliza died 04/07/65   04/08/65
Simms, Emma died 02/17/63   02/24/63
Simms, J. T. married Reeves, Emma H. 03/28/63   05/16/63
Simms, John C. died 12/09/61   12/11/61
Simms, Joseph Lucas died 07/14/62   07/23/62
Simms, Margaret E. died 11/04/63   11/09/63
Simms, Mary J. married Owings, Richard 11/19/63   03/01/64
Simms, Mary J. married Conrad, J. M. M. 12/12/65   12/14/65
Simms, Matilda A. married Tyson, James E. 12/06/64   12/08/64
Simms, Peter married Wilson, Sarah E. 01/08/63   01/10/63
Simon, Amelia Johanna died 05/21/65   05/23/65
Simon, Lewis died 12/08/61   12/18/61
Simon, Louisa married Wehrhane, Charles 05/31/65   06/01/65
Simon, Mark married Rice, Rose 11/29/65   12/14/65
Simon, Nattie died 07/17/64   07/18/64
Simonds, Atala died 06/04/61   06/06/61
Simonds, L. Warren married Montgomery, Martha 09/01/64   09/07/64
Simonson, John died 02/09/63   02/10/63
Simonson, Sue married Mitchell, James T. 11/08/65   11/11/65
Simonton, A. G. (Rev.) married Murdoch, Helen 03/19/63   03/23/63
Simonton, Helen Murdoch (Mrs.) died 06/27/64   08/15/64
Simpson, Alice Ann died 09/25/63   09/26/63
Simpson, Alice Richannah died 07/09/64   07/11/64
Simpson, Ann died 04/21/62   04/24/62
Simpson, Annetta E. died 12/25/64   12/28/64
Simpson, Barbara R. married Lewis, Jacob S. 06/22/65   06/28/65
Simpson, Charles H. married Bishop, Henrietta S. 12/24/61   01/15/62
Simpson, Emma D. died 07/05/63   07/06/63
Simpson, George W. married Taylor, Mary O. 08/14/62   09/15/62
Simpson, Henry C. married Bunting, Anna M. 11/17/64   11/22/64
Simpson, Horace Newton died no date   09/14/61
Simpson, Ida Cora died 04/17/61   04/18/61
Simpson, James Fenn died 06/23/65   06/24/65
Simpson, Jerome died 11/09/64   11/11/64
Simpson, John R. died 10/29/64   10/31/64
```

```
Simpson, John S. married Stanley, Amelia 02/28/61   03/02/61
Simpson, Lizabell died 10/25/65   10/26/65
Simpson, Marshal died 06/27/61   06/28/61
Simpson, Mary (Mrs.) died 02/17/63   02/19/63
Simpson, Mary (Mrs.) died 02/17/63   02/20/63
Simpson, Mary Ann died 01/15/62   01/17/62
Simpson, Mary Ann died 04/11/62   04/12/62
Simpson, Mary C. married Kent, William Jessie 05/10/65   05/16/65
Simpson, Mary Jane died 06/10/61   06/11/61
Simpson, Mina died 11/29/65   11/30/65
Simpson, Richard F. died 08/23/63   08/24/63
Simpson, Richard F. married Little, Ellen P. 02/11/63   02/26/63
Simpson, Sarah Elizabeth died 08/07/62   08/08/62
Simpson, Thomas Albert died 01/08/65   01/09/65
Simpson, William died 01/12/62   01/14/62
Simpson, Willie died 11/14/63   11/16/63
Sims, Agnes C. married Hess, George H. 07/24/62   07/26/62
Sims, Mary E. married Beach, William J. 06/17/65   06/20/65
Simund, Andrew H. died 09/22/61   09/23/61
Sinclair, A. E. married McAfee, James F. 05/12/63   05/15/63
Sinclair, Ellen died 02/08/65   02/09/65
Sinclair, J. E. married Jenkins, Sarah C. 12/10/61   12/18/61
Sinclair, James Alexander died 01/26/63   01/27/63
Sinclair, John married Giddings, Eliza 12/05/64   05/08/65
Sinclair, Laura F. married Volkman, Henry C. 04/02/61   04/05/61
Sinclair, Mary Windsor died 08/01/64   08/02/64
Sinclair, William married Johnston, Elizabeth 07/03/63   07/29/63
Sinclair, William B. died 06/16/63   06/18/63
Sinclair, William Fletcher married Smith, Mary E. C. 03/17/63   03/24/6
Sindall, Charles A. married Ferry, Mollie E. 11/28/65   12/02/65
Sindall, Hannah E. married McKenzia, Aaron L. 12/05/60   12/10/61
Sindall, Mary E. married Harrison, William Henry 08/09/65   08/12/65
Sinex, Susan C. (Mrs.) died 07/28/64   07/29/64
Singewald, Hannah Sophia died 07/17/62   07/18/62
Singewald, Johanna Sophia died 07/31/62   08/02/62
Singleton, H. L. (Rev.) married Morling, Pattie C. 10/20/63   10/24/63
Singleton, Mary died 08/22/65   08/23/65
Singleton, Mary Ann married Washington, George 06/08/62   06/12/62
Sinkskey, John E. married Hartlove, Elizabeth Ann 06/04/61   01/03/62
Sinkskey, John Henry died 03/21/62   03/22/62
Sinn, Arther Greaner died 03/29/63   03/31/63
Sinn, Arthur Greaner died 03/29/63   03/30/63
Sinn, Haddie Bonn died 03/30/63   03/31/63
Sinn, John H. married Fackler, Mary 06/23/63   06/24/63
Sinsey, Nicholas died 02/03/65   02/04/65
Sinz, George Philip died 06/10/63   06/11/63
Sinz, Henreeta married Carr, Edward 03/25/63   04/02/63
Sinz, Lena married Saulsbury, Alfred G. 04/04/61   04/08/61
Sipple, Margaret A. married Trittle, Jeremiah W. 04/14/62   07/04/62
Sipple, William S. died 06/30/63   08/01/63
Sirens, Michael married Mulvilhill, Rose 05/25/61   06/28/61
Sisco, Charles died 10/02/63   10/03/63
Sisco, J. Edward married Frey, Lizzie S. 12/17/61   12/18/61
Sisco, Laura J. married Bunting, Eben B. 06/03/61   06/10/61
Sisco, Laura J. married Hunting, Eben B. 06/03/61   06/11/61
```

```
Sisselberger, Averilla V. married Phelps, Joseph 04/22/62   05/01/62
Sisson, William died 06/27/64   06/28/64
Sitler, Bettie married Coskery, Henry J. 12/09/65   12/12/65
Sitler, Morris, Jr. married Schofield, Hannah E. 12/12/61   12/14/61
Sitler, Susie married Grimes, Charles E. 11/23/65   11/28/65
Size, Elizabeth married Langley, John W. 03/05/65   06/01/65
Skepwith, Charles died 09/04/62   09/22/62
Skiffington, Patrick died 09/16/63   09/18/63
Skillen, Mary married Cannon, Alfred D. 11/10/61   11/28/61
Skillman, Charles married Skillman, Laura V. 10/12/65   10/14/65
Skillman, George died 03/30/64   04/04/64
Skillman, Laura V. married Lurty, Thomas W. 06/16/61   06/28/61
Skillman, Laura V. married Skillman, Charles 10/12/65   10/14/65
Skillman, Rebecca (Mrs.) married Hedley, William F. 06/11/63   06/13/63
Skillman, William Pierce died 06/19/64   06/20/64
Skinner, Alice married Bartheson, Alonzo D. 04/20/65   04/26/65
Skinner, Alice married Bartheson, Alonzo D. 04/20/65   04/27/65
Skinner, Ann died 05/19/61   05/22/61
Skinner, Ann died no date   05/24/61
Skinner, Ella V. married Didier, Henry D. 04/26/65   04/29/65
Skinner, Emily married Johns, George W. 08/02/65   08/04/65
Skinner, Fannie married Culpepper, D. W. 09/23/65   09/26/65
Skinner, Francis married Rians, Marcella M. 06/19/64   06/21/64
Skinner, Hattie married Ransford, Norton C. 01/23/62   02/06/62
Skinner, J. Bucey died 08/16/63   08/22/63
Skinner, Jennie married Sears, Charles C. 04/17/62   04/21/62
Skinner, Jeremiah P. died 12/10/61   12/12/61
Skinner, John B. married Disney, Lucy A. 04/28/64   05/11/64
Skinner, John W. died 03/14/65   03/16/65
Skinner, Julia A. married Johnson, Richard A. 02/11/64   02/16/64
Skinner, Lewis Oscar died 10/18/64   10/19/64
Skinner, Martha Cornelia died 05/04/61   05/06/61
Skinner, Martha Cornelia died 05/04/61   06/05/61
Skinner, Rachel A. married Skinner, Richard D. 10/19/61   10/21/61
Skinner, Richard married Whittington, Anna 01/25/64   01/27/64
Skinner, Richard D. married Skinner, Rachel A. 10/19/61   10/21/61
Skinner, Truman married Constable, Isabel S. 11/12/63   11/14/63
Skinner, Willbur F. married Phillips, Margaret A. S. 06/29/62   07/04/62
Skinner, William J. married Jones, Mary V. 10/26/63   11/11/63
Skipper, Eathy A. died 10/24/64   10/28/64
Skipper, James D. died 08/15/64   08/16/64
Skipper, Mary Catherine died 10/21/64   10/28/64
Skipper, William Thomas died 09/12/64   10/28/64
Slack, Charlotte died 03/31/63   04/02/63
Slack, Emily Marion died 06/22/61   06/25/61
Slack, Fanny Estelle died 07/08/64   07/19/64
Slack, Francinia M. died 08/16/63   08/17/63
Slack, George A. married Achey, Mary L. 11/10/63   11/11/63
Slack, George S. married Davis, Eliza J. 10/05/63   10/15/63
Slack, Mary E. married Iglehart, Rufus 11/02/65   11/05/65
Slack, Thomas H. died 08/09/63   08/17/63
Slack, William B. died 12/18/62   12/19/62
Slack, William T. died 12/25/61   12/27/61
Slack, William T. died 12/25/61   01/02/62
Slacum, George W. died 03/09/61   03/19/61
```

Slade, Belinda T. married Slade, William A. 04/25/61 04/26/61
Slade, Fenner P. died 10/02/62 10/15/62
Slade, Lewis died 08/12/62 08/16/62
Slade, Nancy (Mrs.) died 04/22/63 04/27/63
Slade, William A. married Slade, Belinda T. 04/25/61 04/26/61
Slater, Barbary (Mrs.) died 05/09/64 05/14/64
Slater, Charles Henry died 08/10/61 08/12/61
Slater, George died 05/24/65 06/14/65
Slater, Hamilton married Burley, Julia A. 12/30/62 01/01/63
Slater, Henry died 11/28/64 11/30/64
Slater, John T. married Wheeler, Prudence A. 11/20/64 10/21/64
Slater, Laura C. married Pendleton, David E. 03/14/64 04/21/64
Slater, Margaret A. married Medinger, George A. 09/27/65 12/04/65
Slater, Mary Catharine died 09/22/64 09/26/64
Slater, William died 10/31/62 11/04/62
Slater, William died 10/03/65 10/05/65
Slater, William died 10/03/65 10/06/65
Slatford, Geoffrey W. died 03/17/64 03/23/64
Slattery, Catherine died 03/24/61 03/25/61
Slattery, Ellen married Smith, Cornelius W. 10/10/65 10/25/65
Slaughter, Alice T. married Richards, Henry H. 09/15/62 09/17/62
Slaughter, Ann C. died 06/16/64 06/18/64
Slaughter, Ann Frances (Mrs.) died 03/20/65 04/06/65
Slaughter, Anna Elizabeth died 09/15/61 09/16/61
Slaughter, Anna Virginia married Wiley, John H. 01/21/63 01/24/63
Slaughter, Emma V. died 04/28/65 04/29/65
Slaughter, Francis H. died 09/09/65 09/11/65
Slaughter, Hannah Cromwell died 05/06/62 05/08/62
Slaughter, Henry B. died 10/26/65 10/27/65
Slaughter, James Cromwell died no date 12/01/63
Slaughter, Joel C. married Warren, Mary 12/14/65 12/23/65
Slaughter, Madison died 01/05/61 01/10/61
Slaven, Patrick died 11/21/64 11/22/64
Slavin, Michael died 02/22/63 02/24/63
Slee, Eliza died 12/20/64 02/03/65
Slee, Joseph married Edwards, Sarah C. 03/06/64 03/09/64
Slee, Sarah R. married Constance, Joseph 12/18/62 01/28/63
Sleeger, George S. V. died 03/13/65 03/16/65
Slemaker, Eliza married Hubbard, James F. 12/07/65 12/13/65
Slemmer, South Carrie Lee died 11/11/63 11/12/63
Slert, Kate (Mrs.) died 02/10/63 02/11/63
Slicer, Andrew (Col.) died 06/20/65 06/21/65
Slicer, Henry died 12/10/61 12/11/61
Slicer, Lowllen married Mitchell, John Thomas 02/27/61 02/28/61
Slicer, Mary A. married Gees, B. Franklin 12/01/63 12/02/63
Slimmar, John Wesley died 03/12/61 03/13/61
Slingluff, C. Bohn married de Dorsner, Albine Valerie 09/29/64 11/11/
Sloan, Casper B. married Reckitt, Matilda C. 07/14/64 07/15/64
Sloan, Harriet died 05/20/61 05/24/61
Sloan, Mary (Mrs.) married McManus, John 07/11/65 09/02/65
Sloan, Matilda married McKnight, George 09/13/63 09/15/63
Sloan, Neal died 07/11/63 07/13/63
Sloan, Pemperton married Wormsley, Lucretia 08/01/65 08/03/65
Sloane, Emma (Mrs.) died 03/05/64 03/07/64
Sloane, G. F. W. died 08/13/63 08/14/63

Sloane, John Joseph married Gott, Annie 09/11/62   09/23/62
Slorp, Dorothy died 04/07/64   04/08/64
Slorp, Eliza J. married Conley, Dominick C. 08/09/65   08/25/65
Smaizel, Charles Henry died 08/06/65   08/08/65
Small, Charlie Kennard died 05/03/65   05/04/65
Small, Edward C. married Hepburn, Janette S. 05/03/64   05/09/64
Small, Ellen died 01/30/63   01/31/63
Small, Isabella married White, William H. 04/16/63   04/17/63
Small, Mary died 10/26/62   10/27/62
Small, Mary Virginia married Savington, John H. 06/13/61   07/01/61
Small, Sallie married Wagner, Henry C. 07/08/65   07/11/65
Small, Thomas B. died 03/17/61   03/18/61
Smallwood, Annette Morrow died 08/04/61   08/07/61
Smallwood, Charles married Rhinehart, Lizzie E. 03/06/64   03/21/64
Smallwood, Eliza Janet died 03/11/61   03/13/61
Smallwood, George J. died 02/28/65   03/01/65
Smallwood, Harriet married Tucker, William C. 10/03/64   10/04/64
Smallwood, James B. married Sandy, Emelie 05/28/63   06/01/63
Smallwood, James B. married Sands, Emelie 05/28/63   06/02/63
Smallwood, John died 03/05/62   03/06/62
Smallwood, Mary M. died 10/01/65   10/03/65
Smallwood, Nicholson married Moore, Frances 04/14/63   04/17/63
Smart, Isma died 03/03/64   03/04/64
Smead, E. S. married Ayler, Mahala F. 10/24/65   10/26/65
Smead, James B. married Ayler, Ann E. 09/10/63   09/22/63
Smeck, Henry died 03/18/63   04/27/63
Smiley, Eliza Virginia died 12/31/63   01/04/64
Smiley, James married Lawrenson, Emma V. 08/26/62   09/02/62
Smiley, John (Lt.) married Greason, Maggie J. 01/08/63   01/12/63
Smiley, Joseph married Holden, Laura V. 11/25/63   11/30/63
Smiser, Harry Milton Banard died 01/04/63   01/09/63
Smith, A. C. married Kauffman, Amelia 11/15/64   11/18/64
Smith, A. J. married Norris, Hannah R. 02/23/64   02/24/64
Smith, Adel married Wilson, Charles H. 01/22/61   01/23/61
Smith, Adelia M. married Hall, George W. S. 04/30/61   05/04/61
Smith, Aimee Maria Searl died 03/04/62   03/05/62
Smith, Alan P. married James, Emelie A. 10/15/62   10/17/62
Smith, Albena C. married Thomas, Benjamin F. 11/02/65   12/21/65
Smith, Albert Colburn married Duffey, Julia Ann 01/27/64   01/29/64
Smith, Alice Gertrude died 09/12/64   09/20/64
Smith, Alverty died 04/01/65   04/04/65
Smith, Amelia died 11/11/65   11/13/65
Smith, Amelia Frances died 08/18/63   08/19/63
Smith, Andrew died 08/31/61   09/02/61
Smith, Ann Cecilia married McCourt, James K. 12/27/60   12/10/61
Smith, Ann E. married Sapp, Henry R. 08/20/62   09/25/62
Smith, Ann Frances married Ringgold, W. H. 12/29/64   12/30/64
Smith, Ann Rebecca married Thompson, Charles Wesley 01/08/63   01/10/63
Smith, Ann W. (Mrs.) died 10/27/63   10/30/63
Smith, Anna Leonora died 11/29/65   12/16/65
Smith, Anna M. married Daiger, James V. 10/17/65   10/20/65
Smith, Anna Maria married Wagner, John 04/28/64   05/04/64
Smith, Anne M. W. married Waller, William N. (Dr.) 05/28/63   06/16/63
Smith, Annie died 03/15/62   03/17/62
Smith, Annie E. married Jones, Thomas M. 10/31/64   11/02/64

Smith, Annie L. married Gleim, Henry 09/01/64 10/11/64
Smith, Annie M. died 08/19/65 08/21/65
Smith, Anthony died 08/21/63 08/22/63
Smith, Arthur R. (Dr.) died 09/13/65 09/16/65
Smith, Arthur Sedgely died 06/30/61 07/22/61
Smith, B. E. married Dobbs, Ann Elizabeth 05/08/62 05/20/62
Smith, Barbara married Watts, R. W. 09/27/65 12/01/65
Smith, Benjamin died 07/10/65 07/10/65
Smith, Benjamin B. died 06/15/65 07/20/65
Smith, Benjamin Brown died 06/25/65 06/27/65
Smith, Benjamin Franklin died 09/23/65 09/25/65
Smith, Bridget died 07/11/65 07/12/65
Smith, Catharine married Morgan, William 08/16/62 08/29/62
Smith, Catharine (Mrs.) died 02/03/64 02/06/64
Smith, Catherine married Smith, James 12/19/61 12/25/61
Smith, Catherine (Mrs.) died 01/09/64 01/11/64
Smith, Catherine (Mrs.) died 02/03/64 02/05/64
Smith, Cecelia died 05/14/65 05/16/65
Smith, Cecelia married Parks, William H. H. 10/19/63 04/07/64
Smith, Celia married Parks, William H. H. 09/27/63 09/28/63
Smith, Charles married Neal, Sarah 04/17/64 04/25/64
Smith, Charles E. died 03/09/65 03/18/65
Smith, Charles Ellis died 01/02/63 01/07/63
Smith, Charles F. married Krebs, Hester G. 11/14/61 11/16/61
Smith, Charles H. died 04/06/65 04/17/65
Smith, Charles R. died 07/22/64 07/28/64
Smith, Charles T. married McKenna, Rosa R. 11/24/64 01/09/65
Smith, Charles W. died 11/01/63 11/02/63
Smith, Chase Orem died 01/16/63 01/17/63
Smith, Clara Augusta married Jones, Isaiah 06/01/65 06/03/65
Smith, Clementus R. married Head, Mary W. 04/04/65 04/11/65
Smith, Cordelia J. married Holms, George L. 12/12/64 12/14/64
Smith, Cornelia married Ewing, William 01/14/62 01/17/62
Smith, Cornelius W. married Slattery, Ellen 10/10/65 10/25/65
Smith, D. J. (Lt.) married Smith, Susie 12/28/63 01/01/64
Smith, Daniel A. married Miles, Mollie A. 02/09/64 02/10/64
Smith, Daniel H. died 05/30/64 06/01/64
Smith, David C. died 12/29/62 12/30/62
Smith, David C. died 12/29/62 12/31/62
Smith, David Clifford Grason died 11/02/63 11/05/63
Smith, E. Jenny married Thomas, George C. 12/01/63 12/03/63
Smith, Edmund died 05/28/63 05/29/63
Smith, Edward married Edwards, Sarah Ann 12/11/62 12/13/62
Smith, Edward died 04/14/65 04/15/65
Smith, Eleanor DeF. married Boteler, Andrew K. 01/04/65 01/06/65
Smith, Eli married England, Mary E. 12/08/64 12/14/64
Smith, Elijah died 11/01/63 11/02/63
Smith, Eliza died 01/24/64 01/26/64
Smith, Eliza A. married Wright, Charles W. 11/22/63 12/05/63
Smith, Elizabeth died 03/05/62 03/06/62
Smith, Elizabeth married Bowers, William 06/16/64 07/11/64
Smith, Elizabeth married Gipson, John Henry 01/15/65 01/17/65
Smith, Elizabeth (Mrs.) died 04/07/63 04/09/63
Smith, Elizabeth A. (Mrs.) died 05/24/64 05/26/64
Smith, Elizabeth C. married Deacker, Lewis 08/23/64 09/01/64

Smith, Elizabeth C. (Mrs.) married Decker, Louis N. 08/23/64 09/23/64
Smith, Elizabeth Mosley died 05/01/64 05/07/64
Smith, Elizabeth V. married Plowman, Jacob H. 12/27/60 01/07/61
Smith, Ella May died 11/16/65 11/18/65
Smith, Ella Virginia died 08/09/65 08/21/65
Smith, Ellen married Valintine, John Henry 09/17/61 09/18/61
Smith, Ellen died 10/04/63 10/05/63
Smith, Elliah P. married Turner, Helen V. 01/12/64 01/14/64
Smith, Emily (Mrs.) died 11/19/64 11/21/64
Smith, Emily J. married Campher, George W. 07/04/65 07/06/65
Smith, Emma Amelia married Hohn, Edward A. 08/23/64 08/25/64
Smith, Emma R. married Cain, A. J. 05/25/61 08/12/61
Smith, Etta M. married Wightman, A. C. 06/30/64 07/07/64
Smith, Eugene married Witte, Emma E. 08/10/65 08/12/65
Smith, Ezra Morgan died 11/20/63 11/21/63
Smith, F. Gist (Mrs.) married Brannan, Thomas 01/01/65 02/28/65
Smith, Ferdinand, Sr. died 07/11/63 07/13/63
Smith, Foxhall Parker (USN) died 01/19/63 01/28/63
Smith, Francis Pius died 03/02/63 03/04/63
Smith, Frank M. (Cpt.) married Nicholson, Mary E. 10/04/65 10/24/65
Smith, Franklin died 01/21/61 01/23/61
Smith, Franklin died 03/09/62 03/11/62
Smith, Frederick C. died 02/21/65 02/22/65
Smith, Fredericka married Shepard, John 01/18/61 01/23/61
Smith, G. R. married Conner, Mary E. 06/27/65 06/29/65
Smith, G. W. married Kemp, Mary E. 10/31/65 11/07/65
Smith, George died 11/11/63 11/16/63
Smith, George married Maron, Amanda J. 04/12/64 04/15/64
Smith, George E. married Cacy, Eliza A. 09/14/65 09/15/65
Smith, George Joseph Samuel died 05/25/64 05/26/64
Smith, George R. married Sutton, Mary E. 07/01/61 07/03/61
Smith, George W. married Howard, Margaret A. 09/09/62 09/17/62
Smith, George W. died 02/11/63 03/18/63
Smith, Georgeanna married Young, George Washington 12/30/62 01/01/63
Smith, Harriet (Mrs.) married Schleich, William 08/30/64 08/31/64
Smith, Harriet Ann Elizabeth died 08/27/63 08/28/63
Smith, Harriet Ann Ophelia married Callwell, John 04/10/60 03/26/61
Smith, Helena married Bloodgood, Harry 09/08/64 09/14/64
Smith, Hennie married Horsy, George W. 06/23/63 06/25/63
Smith, Henry died 02/07/62 02/11/62
Smith, Henry died 11/04/62 11/05/62
Smith, Henry died 12/08/62 12/10/62
Smith, Henry died 11/08/64 11/10/64
Smith, Henry died 12/08/64 12/10/64
Smith, Henry married Kline, Mary 08/10/64 08/11/64
Smith, Henry married McGlennan, Mary 04/14/64 04/16/64
Smith, Henry married Brady, Anna 09/13/65 09/18/65
Smith, Henry Albert died 12/14/61 12/16/61
Smith, Hester married Francis, Noah 12/24/65 12/28/65
Smith, Hettie married Gains, Mason 02/22/64 02/26/64
Smith, Ida Bell died 06/05/62 06/07/62
Smith, Ida Florence died 07/05/64 07/06/64
Smith, J. Albert married Martin, Keziah 10/30/65 11/02/65
Smith, J. Bowen, Esq. died 11/10/62 11/11/62
Smith, J. Christian died 01/12/63 01/14/63

Smith, J. J. died 08/27/65 08/28/65
Smith, J. Stewart married Reip, Lavinia C. 06/14/64 06/18/64
Smith, Jacob died 03/16/62 03/17/62
Smith, Jacob married Blue, Alice 01/04/65 01/07/65
Smith, Jacob A. married Baker, Susan F. 10/22/64 10/29/64
Smith, Jacob Henry married Hapner, Ann Rebecca 09/22/63 09/24/63
Smith, James married Perram, Charlotte H. 03/21/61 06/18/61
Smith, James married Smith, Catherine 12/19/61 12/25/61
Smith, James married Blundan, Jane 01/16/62 01/18/62
Smith, James married Coulter, Margaret 06/04/62 06/20/62
Smith, James married Nash, Rebecca 06/22/62 07/01/62
Smith, James married Hill, Julian 03/19/63 03/20/63
Smith, James died 05/05/65 05/06/65
Smith, James died 08/10/65 08/11/65
Smith, James married Coal, Mary 06/02/64 06/07/64
Smith, James Asbury died 06/20/61 06/27/61
Smith, James Davis died 12/06/63 12/07/63
Smith, James Davis died 05/27/64 05/31/64
Smith, James E. died 10/13/64 11/07/64
Smith, James F. married Fay, Sarah J. 10/25/65 11/09/65
Smith, James H. married Kemp, Mary V. 03/03/64 04/12/64
Smith, James Pius died 03/02/63 03/03/63
Smith, James R. died 08/03/65 08/09/65
Smith, James R. married Hopkins, Priscilla 04/28/64 04/30/64
Smith, James S. died 02/11/65 03/27/65
Smith, Jane Rebecca died 11/22/61 11/25/61
Smith, Jesse died 07/28/62 07/30/62
Smith, John died 01/12/62 01/14/62
Smith, John married Harman, Susan 11/26/63 11/28/63
Smith, John H. married Eaton, Maggie E. 02/11/63 04/04/63
Smith, John H. married Miller, Mary E. 04/16/63 04/20/63
Smith, John H. married De Moss, Mary J. 07/04/65 07/10/65
Smith, John Henry married Burwick, Johanna 05/17/65 05/24/65
Smith, John J. died 11/20/63 11/23/63
Smith, John J. died 11/20/63 11/24/63
Smith, John S. married Winingder, Maggie A. 11/13/63 11/17/63
Smith, John Sullivan died 12/24/62 12/29/62
Smith, John Summerfield married Fletcher, Annie Augusta 02/18/64 02/19/64
Smith, John Thomas married Trayer, Susan Emma 12/18/62 12/19/62
Smith, John Thomas died 08/18/63 08/19/63
Smith, Jonathan died 01/07/62 01/09/62
Smith, Joseph died 07/19/64 07/20/64
Smith, Joseph married Carney, Kate 01/06/64 01/09/64
Smith, Joseph S. died 01/20/64 01/21/64
Smith, Joseph S. died 01/20/64 01/22/64
Smith, Judson McClellan died 03/31/63 04/01/63
Smith, Julia A. married Pearson, Robert W. 06/02/62 06/12/62
Smith, Julia A. married Gelbach, George 10/03/65 10/07/65
Smith, Julia Ann married Coursey, William H. 03/24/64 03/30/64
Smith, Julia C. A. (Mrs.) died 04/16/63 04/18/63
Smith, Kate married Warnick, William B. 05/19/64 05/31/64
Smith, Kate D. married Bates, James 06/09/63 06/15/63
Smith, Laura A. married McCann, Joseph 01/25/61 02/01/61
Smith, Laura V. married Fowler, David Q. 01/23/61 01/26/61

Smith, Laurence R. married Taylor, Sarah J. (Mrs.) 08/13/63   09/02/63
Smith, Lelia Emilia died 06/23/64   06/24/64
Smith, Leonidas L. died 11/01/65   11/03/65
Smith, Levin Winder died 06/15/62   06/16/62
Smith, Logan D. married Smith, Mollie E. 07/12/64   07/21/64
Smith, Lola died 08/12/62   08/15/62
Smith, Luther Marin died 08/13/63   08/14/63
Smith, Lydia (Mrs.) married Ryland, S. S. 02/23/65   02/27/65
Smith, Maggie died 02/24/64   02/29/64
Smith, Maggie married Heath, S. P. (Cpt.) 04/23/63   04/29/63
Smith, Maggy married Meeds, Charles 12/30/62   01/03/63
Smith, Margaret (Mrs.) died 04/17/63   04/18/63
Smith, Margaret A. married Doyle, James E. 04/11/61   04/16/61
Smith, Margaret C. married Carmichael, J. E. 11/26/62   12/13/62
Smith, Margaretta died 02/08/62   02/10/62
Smith, Maria married Burns, John H. 12/14/62   12/16/62
Smith, Marianne married Brune, William F. 06/05/62   06/11/62
Smith, Martha (Mrs.) died 12/21/64   12/22/64
Smith, Martha Ann died 11/10/62   11/12/62
Smith, Martha E. married Moore, Leonard 09/01/64   09/03/64
Smith, Martha M. died 02/12/65   02/15/65
Smith, Martha Shearer (Mrs.) died 12/29/64   01/31/65
Smith, Mary married Alt, Peter 11/18/62   01/07/63
Smith, Mary married McCardy, William 05/01/63   11/03/63
Smith, Mary Ann died 11/07/65   11/08/65
Smith, Mary Catherine died 07/18/62   07/19/62
Smith, Mary Cecelia died 09/27/63   09/28/63
Smith, Mary E. married Hughes, William H. 08/09/64   08/12/64
Smith, Mary E. married Bramble, Grason 07/05/65   07/15/65
Smith, Mary E. C. married Sinclair, William Fletcher 03/17/63   03/24/63
Smith, Mary Eliza died 01/20/64   01/21/64
Smith, Mary Eliza died 01/20/64   01/30/64
Smith, Mary J. married Britton, Richard N. 09/05/64   09/13/64
Smith, Matthew died 07/11/65   07/12/65
Smith, Matthew died 07/11/65   07/13/65
Smith, Matthew N. married Brooks, Margaretta 02/25/64   02/27/64
Smith, Michael died 09/28/64   09/29/64
Smith, Milton W. died 01/27/65   01/30/65
Smith, Mollie E. married Smith, Logan D. 07/12/64   07/21/64
Smith, Mollie L. married Bandel, George W. 02/15/65   02/20/65
Smith, Molly (Mrs.) died 06/25/65   06/26/65
Smith, Nicholas died 09/10/64   09/12/64
Smith, Nicholas M. married King, Mary E. 04/23/63   04/27/63
Smith, Nisia Agnes died 05/20/61   05/21/61
Smith, Oliver N. married Albright, Tresay A. 07/16/61   07/17/61
Smith, Patrick died 09/04/62   09/05/62
Smith, Patrick died 09/04/62   09/06/62
Smith, Patrick died 11/06/62   11/07/62
Smith, Peter died 12/01/62   12/29/62
Smith, Peter B. married McDowell, Mary Virginia 06/14/65   06/17/65
Smith, Peter M. died 08/20/62   08/22/62
Smith, Pius Edward died 10/30/64   10/31/64
Smith, Pony (Mrs.) died 08/27/65   08/28/65
Smith, R. Stump married Brannan, Laura 12/16/62   12/18/62
Smith, Rachael A. married Weaver, Benjamin 08/11/61   08/14/61

Smith, Rachel died 05/16/61   05/17/61
Smith, Rachel (Mrs.) died 03/17/63   03/18/63
Smith, Richard A. married Littleton, Marion 09/24/62   10/15/62
Smith, Richard G. married Dashiell, Ellen J. 12/05/64   12/23/64
Smith, Robert married Button, Martha 01/12/65   01/18/65
Smith, Robert F. married Bertier, Mary Ann 06/13/65   06/28/65
Smith, Robert H. married Willson, Laura 08/08/65   08/16/65
Smith, Robert W. died 02/01/64   02/10/64
Smith, Rose married Cookesey, Thomas Neilson 08/13/65   08/16/65
Smith, S. A. married Emerson, W. L. 06/21/63   06/26/63
Smith, Samuel died 07/18/61   07/19/61
Smith, Samuel E. died 04/25/62   04/26/62
Smith, Samuel E. married Goodwin, Mary R. 10/07/61   03/06/62
Smith, Samuel E. married Dillihunt, Mary Elizabeth 01/01/63   01/13/63
Smith, Samuel R. married Armstrong, Mary A. 06/30/64   07/21/64
Smith, Samuel, Jr. died 09/30/64   10/01/64
Smith, Sarah died 04/06/61   04/08/61
Smith, Sarah died 12/27/62   12/29/62
Smith, Sarah married Hall, Benjamin 09/25/64   09/20/64
Smith, Sarah married Howard, Jacob 06/05/65   06/08/65
Smith, Sarah (Mrs.) died 11/26/65   11/29/65
Smith, Sarah (Mrs.) married Hyde, Nathaniel 06/28/63   03/29/65
Smith, Sarah (Mrs.) married Hyde, Nathaniel S. 06/28/63   03/30/65
Smith, Sarah (Mrs.) married Hyde, Nathaniel S. 03/28/65   03/31/65
Smith, Sarah Ann (Mrs.) died 05/31/64   06/02/64
Smith, Sarah Ann Elizabeth died 12/31/61   01/01/62
Smith, Sarah K. died 03/24/62   04/01/62
Smith, Sebastian married Richard, Mary Elizabeth 11/16/65   11/18/65
Smith, Smith H. died 12/25/65   12/27/65
Smith, Socrates A. died 05/12/63   05/13/63
Smith, Sue Melissa married Barnett, Richard M. 12/29/64   01/02/65
Smith, Susan (Mrs.) married Plummer, John B. 01/01/63   03/24/63
Smith, Susan J. married Green, Joshua J. 04/21/64   05/06/64
Smith, Susanna died 08/02/62   08/05/62
Smith, Susie married Smith, D. J. (Lt.) 12/28/63   01/01/64
Smith, Susie R. married Collins, Charles E. 07/12/65   07/21/65
Smith, Sylvester V. B. died 11/27/64   11/07/64
Smith, Sylvester V. B. died 10/27/64   11/08/64
Smith, Thomas died 10/01/61   10/29/61
Smith, Thomas died 07/14/62   07/16/62
Smith, Thomas A. married Lewis, Elizabeth A. 10/08/63   10/10/63
Smith, Thomas H. married Button, Sarah Jane 12/17/61   12/18/61
Smith, Thomas H. married Barton, Lizzie J. 07/02/61   07/08/61
Smith, Thomas H. married Manning, Annie 05/01/64   05/03/64
Smith, Thomas J. died 08/28/63   08/25/63
Smith, Thomas J. married Peaster, Louisa M. 02/10/63   02/11/63
Smith, Thomas J. married McDermott, Maggie 06/30/63   07/07/63
Smith, Thomas N. (Sgt.) married Hook, Mary E. 05/26/63   06/02/63
Smith, Thomas W. died 10/08/62   10/17/62
Smith, Thomas William died 03/28/64   03/29/64
Smith, W. D. married Leef, Emily J. 12/24/62   01/19/63
Smith, Walter D. married Lusk, Mary M. 11/26/63   11/30/63
Smith, Walter P. (Dr.) died 07/10/63   07/20/63
Smith, Walter Way died 09/10/61   09/11/61
Smith, Washington A. married Travers, Martha E. 12/06/64   12/07/64

Smith, William married Dunn, Susanna 03/30/61   04/01/61
Smith, William died no date   04/13/61
Smith, William died 12/22/62   12/25/62
Smith, William died 02/02/63   02/07/63
Smith, William died 08/31/64   09/01/64
Smith, William died 12/07/65   12/09/65
Smith, William married Towson, Sarah J. 12/15/64   01/23/65
Smith, William Christiana died 03/29/65   03/30/65
Smith, William F. died 11/11/63   11/13/63
Smith, William H. married Dorsey, Rachael Ann 01/30/62   02/01/62
Smith, William H. married Kirk, Margaret A. 06/02/63   06/03/63
Smith, William H. married Mitchell, Carrie A. 10/27/63   11/02/63
Smith, William H. died 02/15/65   02/16/65
Smith, William H. married Day, Margaret 08/06/65   08/08/65
Smith, William H. V. married Judik, Lidie 04/18/64   04/20/64
Smith, William Hamilton died 03/21/63   03/26/63
Smith, William Hamilton died no date   03/27/63
Smith, William Henry married League, Alice Virginia 12/17/62   12/19/62
Smith, William J. married Putts, Rebecca 02/17/63   03/10/63
Smith, William M. died 06/25/64   06/27/64
Smith, William Purnell (Col.) married Treichel, Belle N. 09/26/61   12/30/61
Smith, William Purnell (Col.) married Treichel, Belle N. 09/26/61   12/28/61
Smith, Winchester Bishop died 04/26/64   04/28/64
Smithson, Gabriel died 01/25/64   01/27/64
Smithson, George W. died 03/31/61   04/01/61
Smithson, Thomas died no date   08/10/65
Smithson, William married Welch, Julia A. 02/24/63   02/26/63
Smoot, George W. married Welsh, Mary E. 01/20/63   01/23/63
Smoot, Hiram H. married Potee, Lizzie A. 03/22/64   04/02/64
Smoot, John B. married Woolford, Emily E. 11/14/65   11/17/65
Smoot, Joseph F. died 06/12/65   06/13/65
Smoot, Sallie E. married Yeager, Jessie H. 10/23/64   06/01/65
Smoots, William H. married Genals, Louisa 11/14/61   11/16/61
Smothers, George H. married Ridgeley, Mary E. 11/30/63   12/08/63
Smuck, J. Summerfield married Helfrich, Mary T. 11/09/65   11/11/65
Smuck, Sarah E. married McDonnal, John J. 05/28/63   06/01/63
Smull, Annie E. (Mrs.) died 07/23/64   07/27/64
Smute, Kata A. married Lewin, W. H. 01/28/64   02/02/64
Smuthers, Anna married Hill, Henry 10/30/64   11/01/64
Smyrk, Shayler died 02/07/62   04/18/62
Smyser, Emanuel D. married Twilly, Mary Elizabeth 06/04/61   06/07/61
Smyser, Walter Adam died 12/15/62   12/20/62
Smyser, William H. married Foekemmer, Mary A. 07/05/64   07/07/64
Smyth, Hill C. died 03/18/65   04/06/65
Smyth, James W. died 02/10/63   02/11/63
Smyth, Mary A. married O'Neill, James H. 11/01/64   11/05/64
Smyth, Mary Jane died 09/10/62   09/11/62
Snapp, Levi married Stewart, Eliza J. 03/22/63   03/25/63
Snavely, Kate died 04/05/64   04/07/64
Snavely, Winfield Scott died 05/16/64   05/17/64
Snead, Etta Herbert died 06/06/64   06/08/64
Snead, John E. married Buck, Minnie W. 01/31/61   02/04/61
Snead, Lizzie Lee died 02/21/64   02/22/64

Snead, Sarah E. married Mallilieu, Edward 05/05/63   05/07/63
Sneath, W. A. married Spicer, M. Louisa 01/27/63   02/03/63
Snee, John Thomas died 08/31/61   09/02/61
Snee, Winna died 12/18/64   12/20/64
Sneed, John died 03/25/63   03/30/63
Snider, Margaretta (Mrs.) died 07/20/65   07/27/65
Sniper, Zachariah L. died 02/07/64   02/08/64
Snively, Elizabeth Jane died 03/10/64   03/12/64
Snow, Charles Goodrich died 06/08/62   06/10/62
Snow, Edgar Wight died 10/04/61   10/05/61
Snow, Walter P. died 02/01/64   02/12/64
Snow, Walter Scott died 03/24/62   03/25/62
Snowden, Harry died 12/06/65   12/11/65
Snowden, Harry W. married Sargent, Sophia Carroll 09/07/65   09/09/65
Snowden, James T. married Neal, Martha Ann 02/04/64   02/06/64
Snowden, Marie Jane married Greenleaf, Albert C. 01/30/62   02/05/62
Snowden, Rezin married Dixon, Alverdi 05/25/62   05/27/62
Snowden, Robert died 11/11/62   11/12/62
Snowden, Samuel married Hoff, S. Emma 05/14/63   05/18/63
Snyder, A. married Adams, Mary J. 03/15/65   03/16/65
Snyder, Amanda married Griffith, Thomas 10/31/61   11/02/61
Snyder, Anna E. married Byers, John T. 12/21/63   12/21/63
Snyder, C. Ann married Wilkins, John C. 02/05/64   02/08/64
Snyder, Eliza married Clagett, Samuel A. 04/25/65   04/27/65
Snyder, Henry married Kerr, Agnes E. 10/09/61   10/12/61
Snyder, Henry died 04/12/64   04/14/64
Snyder, John C. died 02/06/65   02/07/65
Snyder, John Henry married Dungan, Susana 06/25/61   06/26/61
Snyder, Leah Isabell died 02/01/64   02/02/64
Snyder, Lydia died 02/10/65   02/11/65
Snyder, Lydia Ann married Temple, John J. 08/03/65   08/07/65
Snyder, Maggie D. married Rawlings, J. Soule 06/21/65   06/24/65
Snyder, Mary married Fisher, Henry W. 12/18/61   12/30/61
Snyder, Mary Ellen died 01/12/63   01/13/63
Snyder, Mary Ellis (Mrs.) died 03/04/64   03/19/64
Snyder, Mary R. (Mrs.) died 05/27/63   06/02/63
Snyder, Rachel died 08/12/64   08/15/64
Snyder, Robert R. died 10/06/64   10/10/64
Snyder, Walter married Clagett, Priscilla J. 06/13/65   06/15/65
Snyder, William married Davidson, Frances Ann 01/13/63   01/15/63
Snyder, William Wallace died 11/10/65   11/15/65
Soden, Georgeanna married Dilehay, Thomas T. 04/16/63   04/25/63
Soffell, Martha M. married Hodgson, Joseph 06/19/64   06/24/64
Sohl, George died 08/20/62   08/22/62
Sohupp, Henry died 08/06/65   08/07/65
Soiecki, Elizabeth died 12/10/61   12/13/61
Solan, Michael married O'Niel, Ellen 01/27/61   02/05/61
Sollers, James H. (Lt.) died 03/14/64   04/04/64
Sollers, Jane R. married Roberson, Benjamin 07/24/62   07/26/62
Sollers, Susanna died 08/27/61   08/31/61
Sollers, T. Everist married Bennette, Mary A. 04/12/64   04/13/64
Solomom, Sarah (Mrs.) died 01/03/63   01/12/63
Solomom, William died 09/04/63   09/05/63
Solomon, Benjamin D. married Hamilton, Ruth 09/28/65   10/16/65
Solomon, Eliza (Mrs.) died 05/29/64   06/01/64

```
Solomon, John William died 04/01/61   04/05/61
Solomon, Letitia E. died 04/16/62   04/17/62
Solomon, Matilda A. married McGuire, Thomas C. 09/20/64   09/26/64
Solter, George L. married Calvert, Mary C. 09/19/61   10/12/61
Solter, George L. married Colbert, Mary C. 09/19/61   10/14/61
Solter, Magdolena Madora died 01/19/65   01/20/65
Solter, Robert L. died 03/18/65   03/20/65
Somer, Diana died 06/15/61   06/17/61
Somerlott, Frederick married Waltenmeyer, Rachel R. 04/15/63   05/02/63
Somervill, Mary E. married Wilson, N. D. 06/13/61   07/02/61
Somerville, M. married League, E. L. 08/25/64   08/30/64
Somerville, Rachel died 03/07/63   03/09/63
Somerville, Rebecca (Mrs.) died 05/08/63   05/11/63
Sommer, Anna A. married Stevens, Joseph 12/22/63   12/25/63
Sommer, Maggie O. died 10/06/63   10/07/63
Sommer, Molly M. died 04/11/62   04/12/62
Sommerkamp, Edward F. died 04/22/64   05/03/64
Sommerkamp, Edward F. died 04/22/64   05/04/64
Sommers, James M. married Armstrong, Mary G. 12/07/65   12/13/65
Sommers, Rosina Carthina died 01/09/62   01/10/62
Sommerville, M. married League, E. L. 08/25/64   08/31/64
Sommerville, Margaret E. died 11/14/65   11/16/65
Sonnehill, Julie died 03/20/64   03/22/64
Soper, Ella Blanche died 03/13/62   03/14/62
Soper, Samuel J. married Hiss, Sallie A. 10/16/61   10/17/61
Soran, Ellen C. died 09/24/61   09/28/61
Soran, Emmeline F. (Mrs.) died 03/28/64   03/31/64
Sorrell, Emily Jane married Johnson, William 08/26/64   08/31/64
Sorrell, Sarah E. married Scott, James 03/24/65   04/26/65
Sorrell, William Franklin married Franklin, Mary J. 10/06/64   10/07/64
Sorter, John died 07/03/65   07/04/65
Sothoron, J. B. F. married Williams, Ann Rebecca 06/09/64   06/13/64
Sothoron, Levin J. married Canter, Lydia R. 12/08/63   12/11/63
Souder, C. S. married Barth, Helen 10/05/65   10/09/65
Souder, Elizabeth died 01/31/64   02/02/64
Souder, Mary Ann (Mrs.) died 03/30/63   04/01/63
Soule, Lucy D. married Hack, Henry C. (Lt.) 06/14/61   05/19/62
Soule, Lucy D. married Hack, Henry C. (Lt.) 06/14/61   05/20/62
South, Rachel Ann married Poulton, George C. 09/27/64   09/28/64
Southard, James died 01/22/62   01/28/62
Southard, Mary Eliz. (Mrs.) married Miller, Edward N. 04/18/65   06/03/65
Southcomb, Margaret died 06/04/61   06/05/61
Southcombe, Alexander E. died 02/10/64   02/11/64
Southgate, John died 06/15/61   07/06/61
Southgate, Maggie A. married Minifie, J. Woodfin 05/15/65   05/16/65
Southworth, Mary Brown died 02/15/62   02/17/62
Sowders, Harman B. married Kirby, Emma R. 03/25/63   03/28/63
Sowers, Ann married Wright, John 05/24/63   05/26/63
Spafford, Ann (Mrs.) died 04/25/63   04/27/63
Spalding, Basil died 07/19/62   09/22/62
Spalding, Basil R. died 12/07/62   12/09/62
Spalding, Benjamin P. Power died 05/21/62   05/24/62
Spalding, Ella M. married Carroll, John 04/09/63   04/13/63
Spalding, Mary A. married Nagle, John H. 10/10/65   11/04/65
Spalding, Sarah F. married Shock, William W. 07/11/65   07/13/65
```

Spamer, Edith Julia died 01/24/61   01/26/61
Spangler, Augustus R. died 12/08/62   12/09/62
Spangler, Clara Rebecca died 04/14/64   04/16/64
Spangler, J. N. (Rev.) married Mallonee, Sarah E. 04/03/62   04/07/62
Spangler, Jacob H. died 01/05/61   01/07/61
Spangler, James Allen died 08/23/61   08/24/61
Spangler, James D. (Lt.) married Ray, Emma 12/17/61   12/20/61
Spangler, Mary (Mrs.) died 07/24/64   07/25/64
Spangler, William H. died 05/10/65   05/11/65
Sparklin, Ida Rebecca died 06/21/64   06/27/64
Sparklin, Mary Rebecca died 01/23/65   01/24/65
Sparks, Edward died 12/04/63   12/09/63
Sparks, Harry F. died 03/22/65   04/11/65
Sparks, Josiah married Scott, Maggie A. 05/14/63   06/24/63
Sparks, Marceline died 09/04/63   09/10/63
Sparks, Samuel Edward died 02/11/63   02/13/63
Sparks, Walter J. married Richards, Charlotte L. 03/06/61   03/08/61
Sparks, William Clinton died 08/18/63   08/22/63
Sparrow, Anne (Mrs.) died 10/15/63   10/20/63
Sparrow, H. C. died 04/07/63   04/14/63
Sparrow, Lewis G. married Gant, Emily W. 02/12/61   02/13/61
Sparrow, Priscilla (Mrs.) married White, Cary 04/02/63   04/04/63
Sparrow, Tillie died 08/14/63   08/15/63
Spates, Fannie (Mrs.) married Spedden, O. W. 03/03/62   03/24/62
Spauldin, Henrietta married Newman, Robert H. 05/02/61   05/06/61
Spaulding, Alva E. married King, Mary L. 06/22/65   06/27/65
Spaulding, James A. died 07/29/62   07/30/62
Spaulding, James C. married Johnston, Carrie V. 06/05/65   06/09/65
Spavin, James Walter died 05/02/63   05/05/63
Spear, Alice (Mrs.) died 03/11/64   03/14/64
Spear, Alice Tombs died 05/28/64   05/31/64
Spear, Alva G. died 08/30/65   09/21/65
Spear, Amanda J. (Mrs.) died 12/22/63   12/23/63
Spear, Emma died 12/19/63   12/21/63
Spear, John Edgar died 04/05/62   04/08/62
Spear, P. Forney married Heagy, Annie V. 10/22/63   10/23/63
Spear, Rebecca married Wooden, Jarrett 11/29/63   12/30/63
Spears, Franklin P. died 02/11/62   02/13/62
Spedden, Daniel married Wilkins, Laura V. 10/05/65   10/12/65
Spedden, Ellennora married Steiner, Otto 04/02/61   04/04/61
Spedden, Emily married Gambrill, George 04/14/64   04/16/64
Spedden, Levin married Greenwell, Mary A. 12/22/62   12/30/62
Spedden, Maggie Eliza died 01/09/65   01/10/65
Spedden, Mary M. died 05/17/63   05/18/63
Spedden, May M. died 05/17/63   05/22/63
Spedden, O. W. married Spates, Fannie (Mrs.) 03/03/62   03/24/62
Spedden, William Henry died 09/06/64   09/07/64
Spedder, Emma Belle died 08/10/64   08/13/64
Speed, Christopher C. married Myers, Mary E. 12/15/64   12/22/64
Speiden, William died no date   12/19/61
Speights, Charles H. died 03/10/61   05/14/61
Speights, Maria T. died 03/21/61   06/11/61
Spellman, Almira married Gimper, William F. 08/25/65   08/26/65
Spelman, Annie R. married Cruse, Joseph A. 08/13/61   08/20/61
Spence, Agnes C. died no date   08/04/64

Spence, Jane married Trainor, James 12/03/63 12/19/63
Spence, John married Harmon, Henrietta (Mrs.) 10/25/64 10/29/64
Spence, John E. married Conway, Mary E. 02/06/62 02/28/62
Spence, Margaret Theresa died 08/02/65 08/03/65
Spence, Thomas B. married Gamble, Elizabeth L. 09/29/65 10/24/65
Spence, William W. married Morris, Charlotte 11/10/64 11/12/64
Spencer, David J. married Bevans, Maria 02/07/65 02/11/65
Spencer, Edward married Harrison, A. C. Braddie 11/25/61 11/28/61
Spencer, Edward N. married Brooks, Cecilia (Mrs.) 11/07/60 07/13/61
Spencer, Elizabeth M. married Murray, James D. 05/25/64 06/04/64
Spencer, J. E. married Hall, R. G. 11/09/65 11/15/65
Spencer, John died 01/06/62 01/07/62
Spencer, John married Tootill, Mary Ann 02/14/64 02/17/64
Spencer, John Beauregard died 07/27/63 07/29/63
Spencer, Lottie married Withered, John L. 01/14/62 02/03/62
Spencer, Margaret Ruth died 06/17/61 06/18/61
Spencer, Maria Victoria married Henderson, John 06/16/63 06/18/63
Spencer, Mary S. married Atwell, George A. 12/15/65 12/18/65
Spencer, Nannie C. married Sutton, John C. 11/12/63 11/24/63
Spencer, Phoebe A. died 08/04/61 08/06/61
Spencer, Sallie E. married Blake, Frank (Lt., U.S.N.) 05/25/61 05/28/61
Spencer, Susan (Mrs.) died 10/21/64 10/22/64
Spencer, W. A. R. married Bowen, Mary 08/11/64 06/09/65
Spences, Agnes C. died 04/30/64 05/23/64
Sperry, Cornelia M. (Mrs.) died 02/19/63 02/20/63
Sperry, Kate E. married Winfreerud, C. (Dr., CSA) 11/24/62 01/06/63
Sperver, John married Forewood, Hannah J. 11/22/64 11/23/64
Spicer, Alice married Martin, W. J. 04/27/65 05/04/65
Spicer, E. J. (Mrs.) died 05/20/61 05/21/61
Spicer, Elizabeth E. married Dawson, Thomas E. 12/03/63 12/08/63
Spicer, Elizabeth L. married Dawson, Thomas E. 12/03/63 12/05/63
Spicer, Frank died 08/26/65 09/18/65
Spicer, Franklin A. married Mopps, Martha A. 07/14/64 07/18/64
Spicer, H. Louis married Scharf, Mary C. 03/28/64 03/31/64
Spicer, John W. married Kroh, Mary E. 10/24/64 10/27/64
Spicer, M. Louisa married Sneath, W. A. 01/27/63 02/03/63
Spicer, Thomas died 03/12/64 03/14/64
Spidel, George died 05/06/64 05/07/64
Spieker, Herman Henry died 08/30/61 08/31/61
Spier, Jane died 02/09/62 02/14/62
Spier, T. Hamilton married Clephane, Mary A. 05/22/61 05/25/61
Spies, Susanna died 09/16/65 09/20/65
Spies, Victoria Sophia died 07/24/61 07/27/61
Spillane, James married Deacey, Catharine 06/14/64 06/17/64
Spiller, Henrietta Louise died 07/31/63 08/01/63
Spilman, Adaline died 08/28/65 09/04/65
Spindle, Dandridge married Johnston, Rachel 02/25/64 03/01/64
Spindler, Henry married Peters, Wilhelmina 09/10/65 09/15/65
Spradling, John W. married Kelly, Catherine 10/03/61 10/09/61
Sprague, Alida M. (Mrs.) died 05/04/64 05/06/64
Sprague, George (Capt.) died 03/14/65 03/16/65
Sprague, Margaret Treese married Morris, George W. 05/05/62 05/06/62
Sprague, Mary Agnes died 12/11/61 12/12/61
Spreight, Catherine died 11/14/65 11/18/65
Sprenkle, Charles died 03/10/63 03/11/63

Sprenkle, Charles H. married McDaniel, Mary Virginia 01/31/65 02/11/6
Sprigg, Jane E. married Davis, Benjamin M. 05/26/64 05/28/64
Sprigg, M. Louisa married Carr, William T. 11/07/65 11/09/65
Sprigg, Violetta L. (Mrs.) died 04/13/65 04/15/65
Spriggs, Mary Ann C. died 11/27/64 11/29/64
Spriggs, Prince Albert died 02/19/61 02/21/61
Spring, Elizabeth married Hamlin, George P. 11/01/61 01/14/62
Springer, Elizabeth married Rich, Anton 05/03/63 05/11/63
Springer, George died 05/31/61 06/01/61
Springer, Mary E. married Lott, William 07/16/65 08/05/65
Springman, Hannah R. married Parker, George W. 08/16/65 08/19/65
Springsteen, Benjamin died 04/03/65 04/04/65
Springsteen, Benjamin died 04/03/65 04/06/65
Sprole, Sarah Jane married Busch, George E. 02/20/65 02/24/65
Sproston, Jane G. (Mrs.) died 09/03/65 09/04/65
Sproston, Jane G. (Mrs.) died 09/03/65 09/05/65
Sprows, William Henry married Jones, Emmer Jane 04/02/63 04/04/63
Spurrier, Edward married Miller, Elanor 11/13/63 11/16/63
Spurrier, John Alfred died 01/07/65 01/09/65
Spurrier, Windham died 04/11/62 04/15/62
Squirer, George W. died 07/27/61 08/03/61
Squires, Adealia died 09/15/63 09/16/63
Squires, John H. married Hennicks, Amanda J. 09/26/64 09/28/64
Squirrell, John Wesley died 06/09/65 06/10/65
Sroud, Elizabeth Ann married Cole, John W. 01/10/65 01/14/65
Sroud, John died 11/02/63 11/04/63
St. Germain, Isaac married Collopy, Anne M. 01/21/62 01/27/62
St. John, Ann Rebecca died 01/23/62 01/24/62
St. John, Frederick married Turner, Laura Jane 05/14/65 05/23/65
St. John, Rebecca died 01/23/62 02/03/62
St. John, Roberta died 03/04/62 03/05/62
St.John, Clara died 07/22/64 07/23/64
Stabler, James died 05/28/64 05/30/64
Stabler, Mary (Mrs.) died 12/03/63 01/25/64
Stafford, Catherine married Kelly, William O. 12/30/60 01/03/61
Stafford, James died 07/31/64 08/18/64
Stafford, James Lawrence died 09/24/64 09/26/64
Stafford, John P. Milton died 06/26/64 06/30/64
Stafford, Moses died 01/14/61 01/15/61
Stahl, Harriet died 04/01/62 04/03/62
Stahl, Jacob married Bargan, Julia 11/05/63 11/10/63
Stahl, Kate married Strickland, William 09/28/65 10/10/65
Staley, Catherine died 08/23/61 08/28/61
Stalings, John married Semore, Margaret C. 08/05/60 01/30/61
Stalings, John married Semore, Margaret C. 01/05/61 01/29/61
Stall, Addie E. married Long, Leonard A. 12/14/63 12/16/63
Stall, Lizzie A. married Bodensick, William T. 01/19/64 02/01/64
Stall, Sydenham C. died 05/12/65 05/16/65
Stallings, Aletha married Stinchcomb, William V. 11/15/64 11/16/64
Stallings, Elizabeth L. died 12/18/62 12/25/62
Stallings, Hester Ann married Collinson, William J. 07/06/65 07/10/65
Stallings, Maggie married Kemper, John 09/18/64 09/20/64
Stallings, Mary Julia died 12/24/61 12/25/61
Stallings, Samuel died 08/28/61 08/29/61
Stambaugh, Henry married Ebaugh, Mary 03/27/62 04/01/62

Stambaugh, John P. married Broadbent, Celia E. 09/20/64   09/22/64
Stampe, Jacob J. married Thiernauch, Mary M. 01/23/62   01/24/62
Standclif, John David married Gardner, Elizabeth 12/06/63   12/09/63
Standeford, Jacob died 07/04/63   07/06/63
Standiford, Amanda E. married Callan, Owen T. 05/21/62   05/23/62
Standiford, Cordelia died 09/23/61   09/24/61
Standiford, Edward Randolph died 06/13/64   06/15/64
Standiford, Hannah (Mrs.) died 09/30/64   10/01/64
Standiford, Lydia Jane died 12/18/64   12/20/64
Standiford, Mary Louisa (Mrs.) died 11/30/63   12/03/63
Standiford, Matilda C. married Marsh, Chester S. 06/28/65   06/30/65
Stanford, Emily Kate married Cooke, Thomas 04/06/65   04/11/65
Stanford, Maggie J. married Varnum, John A. M. 08/31/65   09/06/65
Stanford, R. A. (Mrs.) died 11/22/63   11/24/63
Stanhagen, Margaret (Mrs.) died 06/16/64   06/24/64
Stanley, Amelia married Simpson, John S. 02/28/61   03/02/61
Stanley, Charles A. married Duer, Laura A. 11/15/64   11/18/64
Stanley, Edward Elmer died 10/04/63   10/06/63
Stanley, Harriet (Mrs.) died 01/26/64   01/28/64
Stanley, Josiah married Ross, Caroline 11/02/65   11/03/65
Stanley, Medora married Franklin, George B. 03/31/64   04/04/64
Stanley, William D. died 10/04/63   10/06/63
Stanly, Lizzie Virginia died 08/10/64   08/11/64
Stanly, Moses married Henson, Eliza 05/18/65   05/20/65
Stansbury, (Mrs. Albert) died 01/21/63   01/30/63
Stansbury, Anna J. L. died 03/08/63   05/09/63
Stansbury, Arabella married Mitchell, F. J. 12/06/63   01/11/64
Stansbury, Ataway died 12/16/65   12/18/65
Stansbury, Belle died 09/09/61   09/19/61
Stansbury, Carville S. died 04/02/65   04/03/65
Stansbury, Charles Franklin died 01/24/65   01/25/65
Stansbury, Charles Gardner died 06/07/65   06/08/65
Stansbury, Daniel L. married Bailey, Rebecca A. 06/25/61   06/27/61
Stansbury, Edward O. N. died 04/16/63   05/06/63
Stansbury, Eliza married Jones, J. H. 01/17/62   01/18/62
Stansbury, Eliza married Jones, J. W. 01/17/62   01/20/62
Stansbury, Ella Virginia died 08/18/64   08/23/64
Stansbury, Eloise married Lynch, Charles E. 04/23/63   05/02/63
Stansbury, Emma C. married Arnold, John W. 11/17/63   11/19/63
Stansbury, G. W. married Shank, S. N. 07/27/61   08/10/61
Stansbury, George H. married Follen, Martha R. 02/29/64   03/04/64
Stansbury, Gertrude R. died 11/12/64   11/14/64
Stansbury, Grafton Johnson died 10/28/64   10/29/64
Stansbury, Isaac (Col.) died 02/12/65   02/21/65
Stansbury, J. N. (Rev.) married Wolbert, Emma 06/03/61   06/11/61
Stansbury, J. N. (Rev.) married Wolbert, Emma 06/03/61   06/10/61
Stansbury, Jacob died 04/10/62   02/23/63
Stansbury, Jane C. (Mrs.) died 07/29/65   08/01/65
Stansbury, Jarred died 11/20/61   11/22/61
Stansbury, John died 01/11/61   02/13/61
Stansbury, John died 11/26/64   11/28/64
Stansbury, John Graff died 01/03/61   01/04/61
Stansbury, Julia A. married Johnson, Finley 09/21/63   09/26/63
Stansbury, Lucinda married Crouse, Jesse B. 09/10/63   09/14/63
Stansbury, Mary Catherine died 04/16/61   04/25/61

Stansbury, Mary Elizabeth died 08/06/62   08/27/62
Stansbury, Mary V. (Mrs.) married Taylor, Charles A. 10/07/64   10/12/64
Stansbury, Rebecca P. married Maxfield, William 05/04/65   05/20/65
Stansbury, Sarah married Wilson, Arthur 06/11/65   06/13/65
Stansbury, Sarah Ann died 12/16/65   12/18/65
Stansbury, William (Col.) died 02/08/64   02/10/64
Stanton, Benjamin F. died 04/21/62   04/22/62
Stanton, D. L. (Lt. Col.) married Hodson, Lizzie H. 02/09/65   02/24/65
Stanton, Patrick died 03/15/65   03/16/65
Stanton, Samuel married Peters, Elizabeth 03/30/64   04/05/64
Stanton, Thomas died 06/10/64   06/11/64
Stanton, Thomas Edwin died 10/18/62   10/20/62
Stanton, Thomas Hervey died 08/26/64   08/27/64
Stapleton, Edward married Turner, Margaret Christiana 05/04/63   05/07/6
Stapleton, Maggie married O'Ferrall, John 05/04/63   05/11/63
Stapleton, Mollie E. married Maguire, John F. 06/02/64   06/09/64
Stark, Catherine died 04/17/64   04/18/64
Stark, Charles Henry died 05/06/62   05/07/62
Starkey, Catherine died 05/10/62   05/12/62
Starkey, Catherine died 05/10/62   05/14/62
Starkey, Emma Arcelia died 02/09/61   02/13/61
Starkey, Emma Arcelia died 02/09/61   02/12/61
Starkey, Martha Elizabeth died 01/07/63   01/10/63
Starkey, Martha Elizabeth died 01/01/63   01/12/63
Starkey, William Mortimer died 03/17/65   03/18/65
Starkweather, Laura A. married Whitney, E. Eugene 01/16/63   01/19/63
Starr, Anna J. married Hardesty, Thomas H. 11/07/61   12/09/61
Starr, John married Fleming, Eliza 02/01/65   02/23/65
Starr, Joseph Howard died 08/22/63   08/24/63
Starr, Joseph T. died 11/19/62   11/22/62
Starr, Martha F. married Phipps, Richard H. 06/20/65   06/21/65
Starr, Peter died 10/03/63   10/24/63
Starr, Phillipa Y. (Mrs.) died 01/21/65   01/21/65
Starr, Phillipa Y. (Mrs.) died 01/21/65   01/24/65
Starr, Robert died 04/23/62   04/25/62
Starr, Sydney A. married Kirk, R. Edwin 06/19/62   06/24/62
Starr, William Henry died 11/03/62   11/04/62
Start, Katherine married Lavery, Joseph 05/20/61   05/22/61
Start, Sarah (Mrs.) died 01/09/63   01/10/63
Start, Solomon R. married Williams, Clara V. 10/25/60   01/04/61
Startt, Emma J. married Rice, Charles 07/28/62   10/28/62
Startzman, John William died 07/25/65   07/26/65
Startzman, Maggie R. died 01/18/65   01/20/65
Staub, Bettie P. died 04/21/61   04/26/61
Staub, Henry died 09/29/64   10/10/64
Stauf, Charles died 10/30/61   10/31/61
Stauffer, Daniel P. died 02/20/64   02/22/64
Stauffer, George W. married Cornthwait, Henrietta C. 05/01/61   05/06/6
Stauffer, John F. died 06/27/65   11/16/65
Stauffer, Willie Albert died 07/17/64   07/18/64
Staum, Christian died 11/25/65   11/27/65
Staum, Elizabeth B. married Norfolk, Richard H. T. 07/22/62   07/23/62
Staum, M. F. married Brummel, A. O. (Lt., C.S.A.) 02/10/62   02/20/62
Staum, Mary Frances married Brumwell, C. O. (Lt., C.S.A.) 02/04/62
    02/07/62

Stayle, Catharine H. (Mrs.) died 09/29/63   11/03/63
Staylor, Emily Rebecca died 01/29/61   01/31/61
Staylor, Henry, Sr. died 01/02/63   01/03/63
Staylor, John died 04/26/62   04/28/62
Staylor, Maria Theresa married Mitchel, John Francis 01/19/63   02/03/63
Staylor, Mark J. married McLeary, Sallie 07/28/63   08/20/63
Staylor, Mary C. married Carlin, James S. (Dr.) 06/02/64   06/06/64
Staylor, Samuel Wylie died 11/19/63   11/20/63
Staylor, Thomas J. married Summerson, Fannie 01/23/62   01/27/62
Stayman, Ada married Hodges, J. Wilson 10/12/65   10/14/65
Stayman, Eliza L. (Mrs.) died 01/08/63   01/09/63
Steadman, H. B. married Collimore, E. V. 11/28/61   02/12/62
Stearns, Charles W. married Shaw, Mary E. 07/02/62   07/04/62
Stearns, Ellen R. died 10/03/62   11/12/62
Stearns, Henry A. died 05/29/63   06/01/63
Stearns, John (Dr.) married Long, Mariana 04/04/65   04/06/65
Steaveson, William married Malone, Margaret 01/01/62   01/04/62
Stebbing, Jesse married Macartney, Kerana E. 04/28/64   05/07/64
Steck, Christianna S. (Mrs.) died 02/24/63   03/04/63
Steed, William Myles died 06/30/64   07/01/64
Steel, Samuel married Hays, Kate 05/26/61   06/08/61
Steele, Annie Key married Bartow, J. F. 01/06/64   01/09/64
Steele, Catherine A. (Mrs.) died 04/11/65   04/13/65
Steele, Henry died 03/09/65   03/11/65
Steele, Henry M. died 03/29/63   04/02/63
Steen, Lavinia died 05/04/61   05/07/61
Steer, George Adams died 06/14/64   06/15/64
Steer, Rachel T. (Mrs.) died 10/16/64   10/17/64
Steever, George Edwin died 11/12/61   11/13/61
Steever, George Edwin died 11/12/61   12/18/61
Steffe, Louis died 10/09/65   10/10/65
Stegman, Frederick William died 07/19/61   07/29/61
Steibel, Augustus married Streit, Helene 09/01/63   09/02/63
Steibel, Helena died 06/20/65   06/22/65
Steiff, Charles M. died 01/01/62   01/03/62
Steiff, Idia Florence died 07/31/61   08/05/61
Steigelman, Abraham died 10/21/64   10/22/64
Steigelman, Edwin Duvall died 12/03/64   12/05/64
Steiger, Joseph died 01/24/61   01/26/61
Steigerwald, Betty married Leisburger, Marks 03/26/65   03/27/65
Stein, Bertha married Fleishman, Israel 11/05/65   11/07/65
Stein, Carrie died 09/29/65   10/03/65
Stein, Catharine A. E. married Rabe, John F. 09/24/63   09/29/63
Stein, Elizabeth married Hart, Francis 01/07/63   01/19/63
Stein, Lizzie (Mrs.) died 04/13/63   04/15/63
Stein, Sophia died 07/31/64   08/03/64
Stein, Sophia (Mrs.) died 07/31/64   08/02/64
Stein, Sophia C. married Codori, John A. 12/17/61   12/19/61
Steinbach, Charles Justis died 06/22/61   06/24/61
Steinbach, George Edwin died 09/09/64   09/10/64
Steiner, Bettie married Yohe, Charles A. 12/30/62   12/31/62
Steiner, Otto married Spedden, Ellennora 04/02/61   04/04/61
Steinfeld, Jacob married Stern, Caroline 08/06/65   08/09/65
Stellmann, Ernestine Helene died 07/10/65   07/11/65
Stembler, Edwin Eggleston died 03/08/61   03/13/61

Stembler, Harriet A. died 08/17/63   08/18/63
Stembler, Harry M. died 05/31/64   06/01/64
Stembler, John Archibald died 12/11/62   12/13/62
Stembler, John Valentine died 06/02/63   06/04/63
Stembler, Mary H. E. died 09/30/62   10/01/62
Stembler, Nicholas died 10/12/63   10/14/63
Stent, Joseph W. died 06/15/64   06/16/64
Stephens, Alexander, Sr. died 05/12/63   05/14/63
Stephens, Amanda M. died 08/08/62   08/09/62
Stephens, Anna S. married Hurlock, Alfred S. 12/02/62   12/03/62
Stephens, Anna S. married Hurlock, Fred S. 12/02/62   12/04/62
Stephens, Bridget died 02/16/65   02/18/65
Stephens, Charlotte Rebecca married Allen, James 01/11/65   01/14/65
Stephens, George R. married Beacham, Mary E. 05/26/64   06/07/64
Stephens, John died 12/05/62   12/06/62
Stephens, John G. died 06/18/63   09/24/63
Stephens, Sarah R. (Mrs.) died 12/31/63   01/02/64
Stephens, Thomas M. died 04/03/65   04/04/65
Stephens, Thomas M. died 04/03/65   04/05/65
Stephenson, Anna married Davies, James 03/13/64   03/15/64
Stephenson, Deborah died 12/11/64   12/13/64
Stephenson, Ellen (Mrs.) died 02/20/64   02/22/64
Stephenson, James married Bateman, Sarah Ann 08/23/64   08/25/64
Stephenson, John R. married Key, Josephine 05/01/65   05/05/65
Stephenson, Joseph B. married Burke, Catharine (Mrs.) 09/08/64   09/12/
Stephenson, Sallie E. married Baversack, John W. 01/06/64   01/23/64
Stepney, William married Edwards, Charlotte 10/08/63   10/10/63
Sterett, J. Sears (Commodore) died 09/03/64   09/17/64
Sterling, Christopher C. married Kremer, Mary E. 12/27/64   01/02/65
Sterling, Thomas J. married Rausch, Christiana A. 09/08/64   09/08/64
Sterm, C. Albert married Webb, Rachel 03/08/64   03/12/64
Stern, Caroline married Steinfeld, Jacob 08/06/65   08/09/65
Stern, Hannah married Adler, Henry 02/24/61   02/26/61
Stern, Hannah married Stern, Samuel 10/22/65   10/25/65
Stern, Lena died 02/23/63   02/24/63
Stern, Rosa married Kaufman, Joseph 12/01/61   12/02/61
Stern, Rosa married Whitehill, John 04/13/64   05/07/64
Stern, Samuel married Stern, Hannah 10/22/65   10/25/65
Sterns, Walter died 01/26/64   01/28/64
Sterrett, Norman B. married Jones, Susan A. 04/05/64   04/15/64
Sterrett, Rachel A. died 01/11/63   01/12/63
Stetten, Robert A. married Boyd, Margaret A. 07/16/63   07/21/63
Stetyenbach, Louisa P. married Haupt, John C. 02/21/64   02/24/64
Steuart, Annie R. died 11/06/64   11/08/64
Steuart, Annie R. died 11/06/64   11/09/64
Steuart, Elmira A. died 05/19/62   05/20/62
Steuart, H. R. died 12/02/63   12/04/63
Steuart, Mary Elizabeth died 02/21/61   02/23/61
Steuart, Richard S., Jr. died 10/07/61   10/10/61
Steuart, Thomas E. married Edmondson, Mary 10/15/64   11/05/64
Steuart, Thomas Edmondson died 02/16/65   02/17/65
Steuart, Virginia died 08/18/61   08/24/61
Steuart, William L. (Lt., CSA) died 05/21/64   06/16/64
Steuyvesant, Margaret died 08/01/62   08/02/62
Stevens, Alexander married Taylor, Emily 04/14/63   04/16/63

Stevens, Ann M. (Mrs.) died 12/15/65   12/16/65
Stevens, Annie married Kirkpatrick, A. S. 04/14/62   04/15/62
Stevens, Annie M. married Fleehearty, John T. 07/20/60   04/09/61
Stevens, Barbara died 12/08/61   12/10/61
Stevens, Charles P. married Neilson, Lizzie 04/25/61   04/26/61
Stevens, Charlotte Amanda died 02/24/64   03/17/64
Stevens, Daniel G. married Ford, Kate B. 09/30/63   10/01/63
Stevens, Edward died 03/08/62   03/17/62
Stevens, Edward Maurice died 06/21/64   06/22/64
Stevens, Elizabeth died 02/07/61   02/08/61
Stevens, Emma Octavia died 07/30/62   08/29/62
Stevens, F. P. married Bouldin, Alexina 09/27/64   09/30/64
Stevens, Fanney died 03/13/63   03/16/63
Stevens, Fannie Virginia Mead died 07/15/64   07/18/64
Stevens, Georgeanna died 11/07/63   11/20/63
Stevens, Granger F. married Hardesty, Sophia A. 04/24/62   04/29/62
Stevens, Helen M. married Hill, George C. 10/15/63   10/16/63
Stevens, James W. died 12/14/65   12/16/65
Stevens, Jane Albion died 02/07/62   02/08/62
Stevens, John G. died 09/15/62   09/16/62
Stevens, John G. died 09/15/62   09/17/62
Stevens, John H. (Dr.) died 06/14/63   06/17/63
Stevens, Joseph married Sommer, Anna A. 12/22/63   12/25/63
Stevens, Joseph died 03/12/65   03/14/65
Stevens, Lottie C. married Ford, Richard C. 09/17/61   12/04/61
Stevens, Margaret E. died 05/02/65   05/06/65
Stevens, Mary died 05/26/65   05/27/65
Stevens, Mary Susan married Lane, James Wesley 09/06/65   09/09/65
Stevens, Pamelia H. (Mrs.) died 06/20/64   06/22/64
Stevens, Rachel Ann married Lee, John Henry 05/23/61   05/25/61
Stevens, Sarah (Mrs.) died 11/10/63   11/11/63
Stevens, Sarah E. married Wood, Robert F. 02/17/64   02/19/64
Stevens, Susan married Wilson, George 07/06/65   07/07/65
Stevens, Susan married Wilson, George 07/06/65   07/08/65
Stevens, Sybyl A. married Potter, J. H. (Rev.) 01/24/61   02/04/61
Stevens, Timothy died 08/13/64   08/19/64
Stevens, William died 12/09/62   12/11/62
Stevenson, Annie T. died 03/24/62   03/27/62
Stevenson, Annie T. died 11/17/64   11/18/64
Stevenson, Elizabeth died 05/19/61   05/22/61
Stevenson, Elizabeth Jane died 08/11/64   08/12/64
Stevenson, Frances died 01/10/62   01/15/62
Stevenson, George died 01/19/64   01/21/64
Stevenson, George Fletcher died 07/14/63   07/15/63
Stevenson, Henry S. married Phillips, Mary E. 07/13/64   07/16/64
Stevenson, Ivanora died 11/04/64   11/10/64
Stevenson, James married Thompson, Mary 08/09/63   08/18/63
Stevenson, James married Kirk, Julia 08/09/65   08/12/65
Stevenson, John H. married Fletcher, Margaretta J. 10/06/63   10/12/63
Stevenson, Lizzie A. married Thompson, Elias J. 02/21/62   02/07/62
Stevenson, M. A. (Mrs.) married Berg, Adolph (Maj.) 09/14/65   09/15/65
Stevenson, M. A. (Mrs.) married Bery, Adolph (Maj.) 09/14/65   09/27/65
Stevenson, Margaret Ann Waters died 06/28/62   06/30/62
Stevenson, Mary Ann died 01/26/63   01/27/63
Stevenson, Mary Jane (Mrs.) married Harris, George 11/05/63   11/07/63

Stevenson, Mary W. (Mrs.) died 02/06/64   02/08/64
Stevenson, Sidney Maria married Thompson, William 12/11/61   12/12/61
Stevenson, Susan married Maynard, Thomas 12/19/65   12/20/65
Stevenson, Walter B. died 08/25/63   08/26/63
Stevenson, Washington married Gatch, Anna W. 06/02/63   06/04/63
Stevenson, William J. (Rev.) married Baer, Hattie S. 12/15/64   12/19/64
Stevenson, William W. married High, Anne M. 01/14/63   01/29/63
Stevers, Joseph married Campbell, Mary 12/10/61   12/18/61
Steverson, Margaret M. married Lishear, Albert F. 10/27/65   11/29/65
Stew, Charles R. died 10/14/63   10/15/63
Steward, Annie L. married Lane, Sylvester C. 08/16/64   08/18/64
Steward, Charles Lorenzo died 08/08/61   08/12/61
Steward, William L. married Chew, Isabella E. 05/15/62   05/19/62
Stewart, Adelaide Morton died 11/26/63   11/28/63
Stewart, Andrew married Houck, Amanda (Mrs.) 04/21/64   04/23/64
Stewart, Annie married Mitchell, George W. 11/13/64   11/15/64
Stewart, Belle married Todd, John T. 01/14/64   01/18/64
Stewart, C. D. married Crogan, A. E. 12/29/64   12/30/64
Stewart, C. Wesley married Sticher, Maggie 01/17/61   01/19/61
Stewart, Catherine died 11/08/62   11/11/62
Stewart, Cecilia died 12/20/62   12/22/62
Stewart, Charles J. married Jackson, Eliza Ann 04/06/63   04/08/63
Stewart, Charles M. married Hamill, Elizabeth 03/19/61   03/21/61
Stewart, Charles McClellan died 03/28/63   03/30/63
Stewart, Clara L. (Mrs.) married Udderzook, William E. 10/17/65   10/18/65
Stewart, Delmer Hamill died 08/26/63   08/28/63
Stewart, Donald died 05/23/64   05/24/64
Stewart, Eliza J. married Snapp, Levi 03/22/63   03/25/63
Stewart, Eliza W. married Goss, Winfield S. 11/26/63   12/01/63
Stewart, Elizabeth died 12/22/64   12/24/64
Stewart, Elizabeth (Mrs.) died 02/12/63   02/14/63
Stewart, Elizabeth A. married Boyd, John E. 02/17/61   02/20/61
Stewart, Elizabeth A. married Dentry, Henry H. 02/03/63   02/05/63
Stewart, Ella R. married Fuller, F. 01/14/64   01/15/64
Stewart, Ellen (Mrs.) died 10/14/64   10/15/64
Stewart, Emma married Johnson, William A. 03/16/65   03/18/65
Stewart, Emma J. married Parlett, Benjamin J. 07/03/63   07/06/63
Stewart, Emma J. married Parlett, Benjamin J. 07/03/63   07/07/63
Stewart, Fannie Bell died 10/27/65   11/02/65
Stewart, Fanny Bell died 10/27/65   11/03/65
Stewart, Fielder Thomas died 09/14/63   09/15/63
Stewart, George A. died 01/13/61   01/15/61
Stewart, George Clarence died 08/14/63   08/17/63
Stewart, George F. married Turner, Mollie F. 05/12/63   05/15/63
Stewart, George Vincent died 07/23/61   07/24/61
Stewart, Henry A. died no date   05/13/62
Stewart, Hugh died 03/29/63   03/30/63
Stewart, Isabella married Kennedy, Levi 04/19/63   04/21/63
Stewart, Isabella married Durr, Charles L. 08/10/63   08/18/63
Stewart, James F. married Melchior, Louisa H. 12/20/64   12/24/64
Stewart, James Hall died 10/22/62   10/24/62
Stewart, James William died 07/14/62   07/17/62
Stewart, John died 04/09/65   04/10/65
Stewart, John died 04/09/65   04/11/65

Stewart, John Francis died 12/02/64 12/05/64
Stewart, John N. married Watkins, Laura A. 01/06/62 01/07/62
Stewart, Joseph B. married Ridgely, Octavia 09/02/61 09/04/61
Stewart, Kate married Magilley, William 10/05/62 10/22/62
Stewart, Leo P. died 01/14/61 01/23/61
Stewart, Louie Harrison married Cowan, Charles H. 07/02/61 07/09/61
Stewart, Louisa married Newell, George R. 08/31/64 09/10/64
Stewart, Maggie E. died 06/09/64 06/10/64
Stewart, Maggie M. married Hill, John 11/07/65 11/09/65
Stewart, Mary died 09/02/63 09/18/63
Stewart, Mary A. died 10/28/62 10/30/62
Stewart, Mary Ann died 05/22/63 05/23/63
Stewart, Mary E. died no date 01/30/61
Stewart, Mary E. (Mrs.) died 08/28/64 08/29/64
Stewart, Mary R. married Noble, John A. 03/30/65 04/07/65
Stewart, Matilda A. died 02/21/61 02/22/61
Stewart, Matilda A. died 02/21/61 02/23/61
Stewart, Michael Albah died 09/06/63 09/18/63
Stewart, Rebecca B. married Barter, Richard H. 04/23/61 05/01/61
Stewart, Rebecca E. died 05/18/62 05/19/62
Stewart, Rhoda (Mrs.) died 03/01/65 03/03/65
Stewart, Robert died 12/16/63 12/18/63
Stewart, Sallie Maria died 07/12/62 07/17/62
Stewart, Sarah married Tall, Bruff W. (Lieut.) 01/07/62 01/11/62
Stewart, Sarah (Mrs.) died 06/18/63 06/19/63
Stewart, Sarah A. died 10/01/61 10/03/61
Stewart, Virginia married Sevier, Charles H. 07/20/65 07/21/65
Stewart, Walter H. married Lombard, Isabella 12/24/65 12/29/65
Stewart, William F. died 08/05/65 09/08/65
Stewart, William N. married McFadden, Maggie A. 08/19/63 09/08/63
Stewart, William P. died 12/20/63 12/22/63
Stewart, William Thomas died 06/20/61 06/21/61
Sticher, Maggie married Stewart, C. Wesley 01/17/61 01/19/61
Stickney, Henry died 05/01/62 06/27/62
Stidham, J. F. (Rev,) married Dutton, Nannie J. 06/28/64 06/30/64
Stidham, James D. married Willard, Eleanora 04/04/65 05/13/65
Stidham, Jonas died 04/24/65 04/26/65
Stiefel, Caroline Marie died 09/26/61 09/30/61
Stieff, Charles M. died 01/01/62 01/02/62
Stier, Alice Virginia died 12/13/63 12/22/63
Stier, Anna M. (Mrs.) married Bauerfeind, Christoph 04/24/64 04/26/64
Stier, Charles Albert died 11/27/63 12/22/63
Stier, George Francis died 01/08/64 01/20/64
Stier, Hannah C. died 08/26/65 09/06/65
Stier, Jane died 02/12/62 02/15/62
Stier, John G. died 03/09/63 03/10/63
Stier, Mary Florence died 12/07/63 12/22/63
Stier, Sarah D. B. married Wilson, Charles W. 06/13/64 06/18/64
Stier, Sarah F. B. married Williams, Charles W. 06/13/64 06/17/64
Stiffler, John N. married Hanson, Mary E. 12/07/65 12/16/65
Stigers, Ann (Mrs.) died 11/16/63 11/28/63
Stiles, Mary B. died 09/10/65 10/28/65
Stilley, Harvey Crittenden died 09/19/63 09/21/63
Stimbler, Nicholas died 10/12/63 10/13/63
Stime, Joseph C. married Douglass, Mary 05/17/63 05/20/63

Stinchcomb, Annie Brown died 05/06/64 05/14/64
Stinchcomb, Joshua died 07/06/64 07/07/64
Stinchcomb, Nelson P. married Fowler, Rachel 11/30/62 12/02/62
Stinchcomb, Sarah E. married Jones, Alfred I. 07/14/62 07/22/62
Stinchcomb, Teresa (Mrs.) died 09/20/63 09/21/63
Stinchcomb, Teresa (Mrs.) died 09/20/63 09/22/63
Stinchcomb, Thomas Wesley died 04/30/64 05/02/64
Stinchcomb, William V. married Stallings, Aletha 11/15/64 11/16/64
Stinchcomb, William W. married Turner, Belle 12/12/65 12/18/65
Stine, Addie E. died 04/01/64 04/02/64
Stine, Albert died 12/13/61 12/14/61
Stine, Joseph C. married Douglass, Sarah 05/17/63 05/22/63
Stine, Sallie J. married Hammer, James V. 03/08/64 03/10/64
Stine, Sarah Ann (Mrs.) died 04/11/64 04/13/64
Stine, Willie Franklin died 06/06/63 06/08/63
Stinemier, Johana Henrietta V. died 01/21/65 01/23/65
Stinhagen, Sarah Elizabeth died 08/25/63 08/28/63
Stinnecke, Henry A. died 09/22/65 09/23/65
Stinner, Benjamin F. married Hutchins, Sarah A. 10/15/65 11/27/65
Stinson, Charles R. died 10/12/64 10/15/64
Stinson, William F. died 07/30/63 07/31/63
Stinson, William H. (Dr.) died 12/19/64 12/20/64
Stipes, William died 10/07/62 10/09/62
Stirling, Cornelia H. (Mrs.) died 03/18/64 03/19/64
Stirling, James Edward died 06/03/64 06/04/64
Stirling, John H. (Cpt.) died 10/28/62 10/31/62
Stirling, Margaret died 08/02/65 08/04/65
Stirn, Louis died 12/29/61 12/30/61
Stirrat, David died 02/13/62 02/14/62
Stirrat, David died 02/13/62 02/15/62
Stirrat, James died 11/01/64 11/03/64
Stirrat, James died 11/01/64 11/04/64
Stitcher, Ellen died 05/09/63 05/11/63
Stitcher, Henry A. Anthony died 05/11/64 05/12/64
Stites, Elizabeth O.(Mrs.) died 09/04/64 09/06/64
Stites, James married Hewitt, Frances F. 11/01/64 11/04/64
Stites, John A. died 07/23/63 07/30/63
Stites, John A. married Greenawalt, Cinderubed 07/23/63 07/30/63
Stites, William H. died 12/30/62 12/31/62
Stiver, Bridget M. (Mrs.) married Brady, Samuel 08/31/64 09/03/64
Stivers, Charles Henry married Meredith, Mary Virginia 10/28/63 11/02/63
Stockdail, Robert Emory died 07/01/64 07/02/64
Stockdale, Abarilla died 04/05/61 04/06/61
Stockdale, Benjamin C. died 01/09/65 01/10/65
Stockdale, Julia married Dorsey, Jonathan M. 02/10/63 02/18/63
Stockett, Annie Lavinia died 09/27/63 09/29/63
Stockett, Carrie married Davis, James H. 11/16/65 11/28/65
Stockett, George Franklin died 10/20/62 10/24/62
Stockett, Mary E. married Seebode, Louis 09/17/62 09/19/62
Stockham, John Q. married Baoyer, Mary C. 06/15/64 06/20/64
Stockley, Albert A. married Shillinger, Amelia S. 06/22/65 07/01/65
Stockman, Elvie Ann married Rose, John 12/18/65 12/21/65
Stocksdale, E. C. married Bower, Elizabeth 01/17/65 01/18/65
Stocksdale, Elias M. died 10/25/65 10/27/65

Stocksdale, Elias M. died 10/25/65   11/10/65
Stocksdale, Nelson R. died 01/01/62   01/02/62
Stocksdale, Solomom died 11/17/64   11/24/64
Stocksdale, William J. died 04/28/63   05/15/63
Stockton, Mary E. A. married Cole, Charles B. 05/02/65   05/04/65
Stockton, Richard D. married Grant, Harriet Chesnut 07/10/65   08/10/65
Stoddard, Frederick S. married Harris, Mary Leslie 12/21/64   12/29/64
Stoddard, Henry C. married Potts, Amanda 12/24/62   12/30/62
Stoddard, Kate B. died 10/22/65   11/17/65
Stoddard, Lee died 05/24/65   05/31/65
Stoddart, Albert died 02/07/62   02/08/62
Stokes, Clarence H. died 02/24/65   02/25/65
Stokes, Darius died 02/03/62   06/30/62
Stokes, Dianah died 01/22/65   01/24/65
Stokes, George W. married Clapsaddle, Ella 11/27/64   11/29/64
Stokes, Henrietta M. C. died 07/11/62   07/12/62
Stokes, Henry married Jackson, Ann Maria 02/05/63   02/07/63
Stokes, John married Bond, Mary S. 10/28/65   11/04/65
Stokes, John R. married Myers, Maria F. 12/26/65   12/28/65
Stokes, Louis N. married Thomas, Etta E. 12/10/63   12/12/63
Stokes, Margaret Luisa died 01/07/65   01/09/65
Stokes, Sarah died 04/23/65   04/24/65
Stokes, Sarah died 04/23/65   04/25/65
Stokes, Sarah A. (Mrs.) died 11/25/63   11/26/63
Stokes, William B. (M.D.) died 08/15/61   08/16/61
Stoll, Elenora married Brinkman, C. Henry 10/10/65   10/13/65
Stoll, Esther married Rosewald, Simon 10/25/63   10/26/63
Stoll, Mary Catherine married Schreiner, Albert 02/12/65   02/27/65
Stone, A. A. died 10/01/61   11/13/61
Stone, Almeda married Johnson, George W. 06/08/65   06/10/65
Stone, Eben Asley died 11/07/64   11/09/64
Stone, Elizabeth A. died 03/05/65   03/06/65
Stone, J. H. married Brown, Sarah A. 03/06/61   03/07/61
Stone, James H. died 08/21/63   09/18/63
Stone, Jane E. (Mrs.) died 06/26/64   06/27/64
Stone, Johanna Frederica died 11/30/61   12/02/61
Stone, Mary D. married Buckingham, George L. 06/16/64   06/25/64
Stone, Sarah E. married Gould, W. H. H. 08/21/62   08/29/62
Stone, William E. married Elliott, Julia A. 06/13/65   06/15/65
Stone, William J. died 01/18/61   01/19/61
Stone, William L. married Reilly, Sarah A. 06/25/65   07/07/65
Stonebraker, Mary Jane married Foster, John Tucker 03/01/64   03/02/64
Stoner, D. W. (USN) married Most, Mary A. 12/05/62   01/27/63
Stonsifer, Amos died 08/05/65   09/05/65
Stonsinbury, George W. died 06/02/62   06/06/62
Stoops, Josephine married Henderson, Samuel S. 02/01/64   02/06/64
Stork, R. B. died 05/05/64   05/10/64
Stork, William L. married Warner, Clintonia W. 11/01/65   11/06/65
Storks, Bernard Ellsworth died 07/01/64   07/02/64
Storksdale, Jesse died 05/25/62   05/27/62
Storms, Mary died 03/16/64   03/18/64
Storms, Sarah J. married McKeeves, James B. 09/09/63   09/12/63
Storrey, William J. married Heursch, Emma V. 08/21/65   08/23/65
Stoss, Elizabeth married Kunkel, Charles 07/30/65   08/03/65
Stoss, John married Traughtman, Catherine 08/06/65   08/08/65

Stouffer, Ann died 02/22/62 02/24/62
Stouffer, Ann Clair (Mrs.) died 11/09/64 11/11/64
Stoutsburger, John died 08/23/63 08/24/63
Stove, Harriet Amanda died 12/27/64 11/28/64
Stow, Louis married Gazam, Marguerite De Loche 10/19/65 10/21/65
Stowman, Hannah V. married Watts, George H. 05/25/65 05/27/65
Strader, A. M. married Richards, Johannah 03/05/65 05/15/65
Straesburgh, Harry married Deets, Mary 12/25/62 01/16/63
Strahan, Charles married Morton, Jennie 06/25/63 10/14/63
Strahan, Charles Grafton died 06/29/64 07/02/64
Strahan, E., Jr. married Marsh, Eliza 02/14/61 02/18/61
Strahan, Ebeneezer, Sr. died 06/12/65 06/14/65
Strahler, John W. married Pattison, Sarah A. (Mrs.) 01/08/65 01/28/65
Strandley, Albina D. married Brewer, Marbury 04/30/62 05/03/62
Straney, Agnes (Mrs.) died 12/18/65 12/22/65
Straney, Ann died 03/25/65 03/29/65
Strang, Edgar G. married Isaacs, Sarah Jane 01/24/65 02/02/65
Stranley, Harry Revere died 08/15/64 08/22/64
Strasbaugh, Susan married Fraley, Harry 12/21/65 11/28/65
Strasser, Mathias died 03/25/64 04/08/64
Straton, Benjamin Alfred died 09/11/64 09/12/64
Stratton, Thomas H. married Carroll, Janey 07/21/63 09/02/63
Stratton, Thomas H. died 01/22/64 01/23/64
Straughan, Harry died 06/13/64 06/15/64
Straus, Henrietta married Schwab, Henry 08/16/63 08/18/63
Strausbaugh, A. Henry married Pannell, Isabell W. 10/30/62 11/03/62
Strausberger, Ellen died 03/11/62 03/12/62
Strauss, Anne Fredericka died 03/23/63 03/24/63
Strauss, Sophia married Goldsmith, Solomon 08/27/65 09/02/65
Strayler, Andrew died 07/24/64 10/29/64
Streb, Louisa M. died 09/28/64 09/30/64
Strebeck, Charles L. married Watson, Anna V. 12/19/65 12/21/65
Street, David married Medtart, Mary E. 03/25/62 03/29/62
Street, E. F. married Bennett, Maria S. 03/07/64 03/10/64
Street, Elizabeth died 07/31/62 08/01/62
Street, J. married Seymour, S. K. 11/26/65 11/03/65
Street, M. L. married Schleigh, Millie 10/21/62 10/30/62
Street, Mollie died 04/04/65 04/07/65
Street, R. J. married Seymour, S. Kate 11/26/65 11/06/65
Street, St. Clair (Dr.) died 09/16/64 11/26/64
Street, Thomas died 06/30/61 07/01/61
Streets, Mary Jane (Mrs.) died 01/05/65 01/07/65
Streets, Samuel W. died 05/23/62 05/24/62
Streets, Thomas died 05/19/61 05/21/61
Streett, Isabell A. married Jarrett, A. Bond 06/27/61 06/28/61
Streett, Mary died 12/09/63 12/10/63
Streett, Susan died no date 02/16/61
Strein, Mary E. married Vickers, Hamilton R. 01/20/63 01/23/63
Streit, Helene married Steibel, Augustus 09/01/63 09/02/63
Streper, Peter Mowell died 05/12/63 05/14/63
Streper, Sarah (Mrs.) died 04/24/63 04/25/63
Strett, Maria (Mrs.) died 02/24/64 03/15/64
Strett, Shadrach married Wright, Julia A. 01/02/63 01/03/63
Strible, George M. died 02/13/64 02/16/64
Strickland, William married Stahl, Kate 09/28/65 10/10/65

Strider, Charlotte (Mrs.) died 08/08/63 08/11/63
String, John F. married Renoff, Mary E. 07/31/61 12/09/61
Strobel, Albert died 02/12/64 02/13/64
Strocke, Catherine (Mrs.) died 02/17/63 02/18/63
Strodtman, J. H. married Kleibacker, Mary C. 12/05/65 12/12/65
Strohler, Catharine H. (Mrs.) died 10/29/63 10/30/63
Strohm, J. F. died 09/21/63 09/23/63
Stromberger, Christian died 12/20/63 12/24/63
Stromenger, John died 11/08/62 11/10/62
Strong, Augustus R. married Wallace, Sarah E. 01/25/61 01/31/61
Strong, Henry (Lt.) married Hamill, Kate 07/16/65 07/27/65
Strong, Joseph (Col.) died 03/15/61 03/18/61
Strong, Samuel S. married Werner, Margaret 12/25/62 12/27/62
Strott, Katherine married Christ, Henry 05/14/65 05/19/65
Stroud, Rebecca (Mrs.) died 02/17/63 02/18/63
Strovall, Samuel Frinklin died 04/05/63 04/14/63
Struthoff, Elizabeth died 03/17/61 03/18/61
Stuart, C. P. married Wilson, M. E. 10/16/65 12/04/65
Stuart, Edward V. married Sanders, Nettie 11/24/63 12/01/63
Stuart, Elizabeth J. died 09/04/65 09/07/65
Stuart, Eugene married Van Ness, Laura M. 01/01/63 01/27/63
Stuart, George died 01/15/63 02/27/63
Stuart, Harry C. married Hall, Elizabeth C. (Mrs.) 05/05/64 05/12/64
Stuart, James married Niles, Mary Ann 10/09/62 10/11/62
Stuart, James died 10/21/63 10/22/63
Stuart, John A. married Dorsey, Mary J. 01/01/61 01/03/61
Stuart, Lemuel died 01/27/63 01/30/63
Stuart, Lizzie married Denny, R. Augustus 04/26/65 04/28/65
Stuart, Mary died 07/26/62 07/30/62
Stuart, William H. married Shanklin, Elizabeth 03/12/63 03/13/63
Stuart, William Henry died 12/30/64 01/02/65
Stuart, William Keating (M.D.) died 06/03/65 06/05/65
Stubbins, Thomas G. married Jones, Amelia A. 10/20/62 10/22/62
Stubbs, Harriet Tully died 02/20/65 02/22/65
Stubbs, Joseph S. married Beard, Emma F. 04/07/62 04/08/62
Stubbs, Kate Virginia died 07/04/63 07/10/63
Stubbs, Mamie E. died 01/18/65 01/20/65
Stubbs, Richard P. married Coulbourn, Elizabeth A. 03/10/64 03/14/64
Stubbs, Sallie C. died 02/16/65 02/18/65
Stuchell, James married Leckie, Levinia M. 03/16/63 03/21/63
Stuchell, Thompson Martin died 06/15/65 06/21/65
Stuchfield, Ida R. died 04/20/64 04/21/64
Stuck, Jane married Claflin, Ira W. (Cpt.) 04/21/63 04/25/63
Stuck, Rebecca died 07/29/64 08/01/64
Stump, John Kelly died 02/09/62 02/27/62
Stump, John W. died 10/21/62 10/23/62
Stump, Maggie married White, Robert W. 05/03/65 05/11/65
Stump, Priscilla died 07/16/65 07/18/65
Stump, William died 08/15/62 08/19/62
Stumptner, Margaret married Tenweeges, August 11/25/62 11/26/62
Stup, Joseph C. married Kaufman, Alice V. 03/36/65 03/28/65
Sturgeon, Catherine Elizabeth died 07/31/64 08/02/64
Sturgeon, Thomas M. died 09/26/64 10/01/64
Sturges, Nancy died 11/09/65 11/21/65
Sturgis, Nancy died 11/09/65 11/22/65

Sturley, Mary married Cullington, Daniel 09/13/64   09/19/64
Sturm, Caroline died 08/23/63   08/25/63
Sugden, George married Vigans, Maria Theresa 06/03/62   06/06/62
Suggicks, Raisin married Bell, Eliza 02/11/64   02/13/64
Sulaven, Maria H. married Russell, Richard B. 01/28/64   01/30/64
Sullavin, Eugene Owen died 10/17/61   10/18/61
Sullivan, Catharine died 03/15/62   03/17/62
Sullivan, Dennis died 04/10/65   04/11/65
Sullivan, Edward married Gibson, Elizabeth A. 01/18/63   01/19/63
Sullivan, Elvira E. married Roderick, William H. 09/25/65   10/10/65
Sullivan, Emma married Mann, Samuel B. 01/03/65   01/19/65
Sullivan, Emma married Mann, Samuel B. 01/03/65   01/21/65
Sullivan, Emma J. married Mitchell, James B. 08/22/65   08/24/65
Sullivan, Honorah F. married Kell, Peter 01/14/62   04/23/62
Sullivan, James died 01/06/63   01/21/63
Sullivan, James died 08/31/64   09/01/64
Sullivan, Jane died 07/09/63   07/11/63
Sullivan, Jeremiah Steven died 05/19/62   05/21/62
Sullivan, John married Riley, Ellen 01/23/62   01/24/62
Sullivan, John married Wilson, Ruth 09/19/62   09/30/62
Sullivan, John died 10/28/65   12/09/65
Sullivan, John married Sullivan, Mary 10/24/65   11/02/65
Sullivan, Joseph died 04/05/63   04/06/63
Sullivan, Joseph died 09/01/63   09/02/63
Sullivan, Julia M. married Brewer, G.G. 04/10/61   04/17/61
Sullivan, Margaret A. (Mrs.) died 04/04/63   04/06/63
Sullivan, Mary married Sullivan, John 10/24/65   11/02/65
Sullivan, Mary Ann died 03/03/63   03/04/63
Sullivan, Mary E. married House, Samuel A. 10/10/61   10/16/61
Sullivan, Mary E. married Crey, Henry 01/15/65   01/18/65
Sullivan, Owen died 04/13/63   04/14/63
Sullivan, Owen died 04/13/63   04/15/63
Sullivan, Philip T. married Dorsey, Medora A. 06/02/64   06/07/64
Sullivan, Sue E. married Hamilton, John 02/09/64   02/11/64
Sullivan, Thomas E. married Dunlevy, M. Raphie 07/02/61   07/04/61
Sullivan, William died 12/23/62   12/25/62
Sullivan, William W. died 04/07/65   04/08/65
Sulliven, John died 11/11/63   11/12/63
Summerfield, John died 07/11/62   07/12/62
Summerfield, Wesley died 03/21/61   03/25/61
Summers, Albert died 12/07/62   12/08/62
Summers, Frank died 11/09/65   11/10/65
Summers, Helen died 05/20/61   05/21/61
Summers, Henry married Schoreck, Elizabeth Ann 07/12/64   07/14/64
Summers, Norah died 04/21/63   04/22/63
Summers, Sarah married Lester, Thomas 01/13/62   01/16/62
Summerson, Fannie married Staylor, Thomas J. 01/23/62   01/27/62
Summerville, Emily Eugenia died 08/03/65   08/04/65
Sumpter, Marion died 01/12/62   01/15/62
Sumstrom, Lizzie married Hollingshead, James 06/15/65   06/17/65
Sumwalt, Albert W. W. died 01/08/61   01/09/61
Sumwalt, Alice died 12/11/62   12/16/62
Sumwalt, Alice A. died 01/23/64   01/27/64
Sumwalt, Charles L. K. (Col.) married Horner, Emma J. 01/29/63   02/10/
Sumwalt, John Albert died 11/01/61   11/04/61

Sumwalt, John James died 09/19/64 09/20/64
Sumwalt, Maggie died 10/01/62 10/03/62
Sumwalt, Margaret (Mrs.) died 01/28/63 01/30/63
Sumwalt, Margaret A. married Eppley, Julius A. 01/28/61 02/02/61
Sunderland, Elizabeth (Mrs.) died 12/14/64 12/15/64
Sunderland, Elizabeth (Mrs.) died 12/14/64 12/16/64
Sunderland, James died 09/02/64 12/12/64
Sunderland, Joseph Augustus died 07/03/64 07/07/64
Sunderland, Margaret M. (Mrs.) died 11/01/64 11/16/64
Sunderland, Rachel A. married Owings, Henry W. 11/27/61 11/28/61
Sunstrom, Rachel married Kennedy, William T. H. 11/25/62 02/25/63
Sunstrom, William died 10/23/61 10/25/61
Sunstroum, Mary E. married Tall, Levin Y. 07/20/62 07/23/62
Supple, Martha (Mrs.) died 03/27/65 03/29/65
Supplee, Amanda L. married Reynolds, Joseph P. 08/17/63 08/27/64
Surdall, Charles A. married Ferry, Mollie E. 11/28/65 12/01/65
Surudy, Hamilton married Johnson, Rachel Ann 10/10/61 10/12/61
Survoy, J. S. married Wilson, Rebecca 03/03/64 03/08/64
Sutch, Daniel B. married Redish, Annie E. 08/21/64 09/10/64
Suter, Ann Maria (Mrs.) died 08/07/64 08/08/64
Suter, Charles Henry died 07/28/64 07/29/64
Suter, Daniel Edward died 08/12/61 08/15/61
Suter, Frederick married Hamilton, Josie 10/22/63 10/24/63
Suter, George A. married Kelly, Cicelia 12/26/64 12/31/64
Suter, Laura married Guyton, Elisha J. 03/01/64 03/04/64
Suter, Mollie E. married Norris, William H. (Dr.) 06/09/63 06/12/63
Sutherland, John M. married Michael, Susie L. 07/14/63 07/17/63
Sutherland, Martha Jane died 01/10/61 01/12/61
Suthkopff, Charles E. died 03/13/63 03/14/63
Suton, Ann (Mrs.) married Fetters, John F. 06/07/64 06/09/64
Sutro, Emil married Schuking, Kathinka 10/22/61 10/24/61
Sutter, Josephine married Brown, Joseph M. 10/16/62 10/23/62
Sutton, Anna married Lippincott, Ezra 06/17/62 06/24/62
Sutton, Cornelia A. B. married Fesler, Edward A. 03/12/63 03/17/63
Sutton, Frank G. married Sutton, Mary F. 05/26/63 06/19/63
Sutton, George H. (Sgt.) died 09/06/64 09/09/64
Sutton, James N. died 11/02/62 11/06/62
Sutton, John married Lee, Caroline 06/05/62 06/07/62
Sutton, John C. married Spencer, Nannie C. 11/12/63 11/24/63
Sutton, Martha W. died 10/10/65 10/11/65
Sutton, Mary E. married Smith, George R. 07/01/61 07/03/61
Sutton, Mary F. married Sutton, Frank G. 05/26/63 06/19/63
Sutton, Mary R. died 04/24/61 05/02/61
Sutton, Mordecai died 10/02/65 10/03/65
Sutton, Nannie married Berry, A. M. 11/07/65 11/11/65
Sutton, Rebecca (Mrs.) died 10/30/65 11/01/65
Sutton, Samuel died 08/20/62 08/26/62
Sutton, Samuel married Brandt, Barbara E. 06/08/63 06/09/63
Sutton, Samuel V. married Lacey, Emma L. 02/25/62 03/05/62
Sutton, Sarah married Brook, Elias 04/02/62 04/04/62
Sutton, Thomas Benton married Thompson, Maria Virginia 07/21/62 07/23/62
Swadaner, Henrietta married Harry, William O. 05/21/61 05/23/61
Swain, Albert Irvin died 12/19/61 12/21/61
Swain, Annie Matilda died 08/09/62 08/11/62

Swain, Charles died 05/14/61   05/17/61
Swain, Eliza W. married Schultz, George T. 10/10/65   10/16/65
Swain, Helen M. died 03/28/61   04/03/61
Swain, Irvinia died 10/03/61   10/04/61
Swain, J. Francis married Callow, Katie P. 07/03/65   07/17/65
Swain, James W. married Connor, Lucinda J. 06/20/65   06/24/65
Swain, Mary Louisa married Browning, Edward 10/22/63   12/09/63
Swain, William died 01/06/64   01/08/64
Swain, William Emmet died 06/18/62   06/19/62
Swainscott, Emaline married Hughes, Joseph no date   01/28/61
Swan, Eliza Olivia died 08/28/64   11/21/64
Swan, Ludia (Mrs.) died 12/28/63   01/20/64
Swan, Richard Elsworth died 11/19/64   11/21/64
Swann, Bettie A. married Anderson, John W. 04/30/61   05/03/61
Swann, Eliza Elevia died 08/27/64   08/29/64
Swann, Emma Isabel died 07/19/62   07/23/62
Swann, Florence Clifton died 08/25/64   08/26/64
Swann, Louisa married Latrobe, Ferdinand C. 12/26/61   12/28/61
Swartz, Mary A. died 03/08/65   04/24/65
Swatrz, Rose A. married Scott, Jonathan W. 06/19/65   06/22/65
Swaurtze, Mary (Mrs.) died 12/14/62   01/08/63
Swearer, Charles married Tomlinson, Cornelia O. 12/04/62   12/09/62
Swearer, John Joseph died 04/19/64   04/22/64
Sweeney, Elizabeth died 03/31/65   04/01/65
Sweeney, John W. married Johnson, Sarah C. 05/18/61   05/21/61
Sweeney, Margaret (Mrs.) died 06/30/64   07/01/64
Sweeney, Margaret (Mrs.) died 06/30/64   07/02/64
Sweeney, Willie H. died 02/05/65   02/09/65
Sweeny, Addah died 11/23/63   11/26/63
Sweeny, Ellen Fraser died 05/21/61   05/23/61
Sweeny, Mary R. died 06/08/61   07/13/61
Sweeny, Susan died 10/26/63   10/31/63
Sweeting, Mary A. married Lambright, William 02/27/65   03/02/65
Sweeting, Rebecca A. (Mrs.) died 11/08/65   11/13/65
Sweeting, William Edward married Wright, Eugenia H. 05/30/61   06/05/61
Sweeting, William H. R. died 09/25/63   10/03/63
Swegler, Joseph P. married Murphy, Teresa J. 01/05/64   01/07/64
Swift, Chaney H. married Fuller, Maria Elizabeth 03/26/63   04/03/63
Swift, John married Hurtt, Tilly 12/13/65   12/15/65
Swift, Walton Julian died 11/10/64   12/24/64
Swigent, Annie G. S. married Penn, John W. 10/06/63   10/14/63
Swigert, Augustus died 02/12/65   02/13/65
Swigert, D. Amos married Fisher, E. Jane 12/25/62   12/27/62
Swigert, Mary Elizabeth died 05/01/65   05/03/65
Swiiny, Cornelius married Mannion, Kate 04/19/63   04/21/63
Swindell, Mary (Mrs.) died 12/10/64   12/12/64
Switser, Almira died 08/31/65   09/09/65
Switser, John W. married Burke, Mary M. 06/23/64   06/30/64
Switzer, Betsy married Delevie, Isaac S. 01/18/63   01/20/63
Switzer, Elizabeth Ann died 05/15/65   05/16/65
Switzer, Emily married Allard, Edward C. 03/29/64   04/05/64
Switzer, Emory died 12/27/61   01/02/62
Switzer, Sarah Elizabeth died 11/11/61   11/13/61
Switzer, Susannah married Underwood, George W. 11/18/64   11/22/64
Switzer, William died 08/24/62   09/13/62

Switzer, William married Hartzell, Mary Alexine 12/31/61 01/03/62
Swope, Jacob died 03/15/63 03/18/63
Swope, Jacob died 03/15/63 03/19/63
Swope, Joel married Rosenfeld, Pauline 06/22/64 06/30/64
Sword, William Henry died 08/04/61 08/16/61
Swormstedt, Richard married Creager, Barbara C. 06/19/64 06/21/64
Swyrp, Cornelia A. (Mrs.) married Lusby, Charles A. 02/26/63 04/02/63
Syayne, M. E. N. married Beall, George W. 03/05/61 03/09/61
Sybry, Bassesto married Cotman, Catherine 02/08/64 02/10/64
Sye, Charles married Williams, Mary Rebecca 04/16/63 04/18/63
Sykes, Columbus W. married Price, Catharine Ann 12/20/59 07/30/64
Sykes, Frank Goldsborough died 01/05/65 01/06/65
Sykes, Frank Goldsborough died 01/05/65 01/07/65
Sykes, William married Campbell, Sarah 07/24/62 07/26/62
Sylvester, Mary died 03/26/63 03/27/63
Sylvester, Solion died 10/24/62 10/31/62
Sylvester, Solion died 10/24/62 11/01/62
Sylvester, Temperance Ann married Rasher, Isaac 12/29/63 01/06/64
Symonds, Sarah A. married Thornton, Elijah A. 03/19/63 04/01/63
Symonds, Susannah married Shultz, William F. 02/19/62 02/22/62
Synder, George Washington died 12/31/62 01/05/63
Szezutkouski, George Michael died 12/12/62 12/13/62
Tabb, Francis Philip died 12/26/63 12/28/62
Tabb, Lee Marrin died 01/22/64 01/25/64
Tabbs, George married Johnson, Rebecca 11/03/64 11/30/64
Tadgenhorst, Frederick William married Bregel, Mary Rebecca 08/14/64 08/17/64
Tagart, Samuel married Gardner, Annie J. 07/21/64 07/22/64
Taggart, Elizabeth Fairgrieve died 10/11/65 10/13/65
Talbot, Alice married Filton, John 10/20/62 10/21/62
Talbot, Aquila died 02/24/65 02/25/65
Talbot, Elizabeth A. married McCahan, E. Luther 02/11/64 02/16/64
Talbot, George W. (Cpt.) died 08/12/64 08/27/64
Talbot, H. Oden married Claggett, Sarah E. 02/05/63 02/10/63
Talbot, Thomas Roberts died 10/09/64 10/11/64
Talbott, Ann Maria (Mrs.) married Talbott, James 10/31/64 11/02/64
Talbott, George T. died 10/25/63 11/11/63
Talbott, George W. (Cpt.) died 08/12/64 08/30/64
Talbott, James married Talbott, Ann Maria (Mrs.) 10/31/64 11/02/64
Talbott, Jesse died 01/02/64 01/04/64
Talbott, Lizzie married Kelley, Elisha F. 10/31/61 11/06/61
Talbott, Maggie married Hardesty, Richard 07/05/62 07/07/62
Talbott, Mary Laura died 03/05/61 03/06/61
Talbott, R. Amanda died 07/26/62 08/15/62
Taliaferro, Charles S. died 10/19/62 10/20/62
Taliaferro, Susie P. married Boswell, Milton A. 03/29/64 04/05/64
Talkfuths, Mary E. married Thomsouth, Thomas 08/04/61 08/08/61
Tall, Anthony died 09/15/64 09/16/64
Tall, Anthony married Tunis, Georgie 08/02/64 08/03/64
Tall, Bruff W. (Lieut.) married Stewart, Sarah 01/07/62 01/11/62
Tall, Henrietta married Meekins, Robert J. 04/23/63 06/10/63
Tall, Isabella married Crew, George T. 06/19/65 06/24/65
Tall, Levin Y. married Sunstroum, Mary E. 07/20/62 07/23/62
Tallent, James Henry died 09/21/62 09/22/62
Tallent, Robert L. died 07/12/62 11/06/62

Talley, Neanie J. (Mrs.) died 07/25/63   08/04/63
Tallmadge, Mary died 06/29/61   07/01/61
Tally, William Wallace married Mettee, Neanie J. 08/21/61   08/26/61
Taman, Mary married Toner, William H. 08/24/65   09/28/65
Tamison, Catherine (Mrs.) died 01/10/63   01/12/63
Tammey, Ann Eliza (Mrs.) died 07/13/64   07/15/64
Taney, Martha died 05/30/62   06/13/62
Taneyhill, Sophia W. married White, J. Wesley 03/19/63   03/24/63
Tangney, Kate married Fitzpatrick, Patrick 04/20/62   05/01/62
Tanguey, Filis A. married McAllister, William 05/03/64   05/06/64
Tanner, Cornelius S. married Norman, Louisiana E. 12/14/65   12/15/65
Tanner, Elizabeth married Armiger, Joseph 04/10/65   04/27/65
Tansey, Anne married Flanigan, Thomas 01/05/64   01/09/64
Tanzey, Ann Jane married Cullison, Jesse M. 11/19/61   11/30/61
Tapp, George (Lt.) married Perkins, E. 05/07/64   09/09/64
Tapscott, William T. died 06/23/63   07/29/63
Tarleton, Ann died 10/17/61   10/18/61
Tarleton, Mary E. married Lowrey, John H. 09/11/64   09/27/64
Tarr, Annie W. died 11/03/65   11/04/65
Tarr, Augustus DeKalb died 06/01/62   06/04/62
Tarr, Charlotte E. married Moore, William T. 08/21/65   08/23/65
Tarr, Frances Elizabeth married Tows, Charles 08/20/63   08/28/63
Tarr, Grilcildia (Mrs.) died 11/05/64   11/07/64
Tarr, Howard died 08/21/62   08/23/62
Tarr, Joseph B. (Cpt.) died 10/11/61   11/12/61
Tarr, Julia D. married McCord, William D. 05/16/61   05/23/61
Tarr, Melissa married Sheldon, John B. 10/08/63   10/13/63
Tarr, Wesley B. died 09/08/63   09/09/63
Tarring, Elizabeth D. died 05/12/61   05/15/61
Tasco, Maria married Johnson, George 09/03/63   09/25/63
Tash, Nancy (Mrs.) died 02/29/64   03/01/64
Tate, Robert died 09/15/64   09/16/64
Tate, William P. died 07/08/64   07/09/64
Tatem, Joseph died 05/09/61   05/10/61
Tatem, Mary Jane died 02/12/63   02/14/63
Tatman, Mary Elizabeth married Bristow, Columbus W. 03/08/64   03/09/64
Tatman, Sarah Jane married Bristow, Richard 12/08/61   12/24/61
Tavenner, George married Williams, Josephine 12/26/65   12/28/65
Tayler, William A. married Gladfelter, Jane R. 07/15/62   07/19/62
Tayleure, Clifton William died 08/06/63   08/08/63
Taylor, (Mrs. Joseph) died 09/29/63   09/30/63
Taylor, Adelaide Gertrude died 08/11/62   08/12/62
Taylor, Amanda A. married Tyler, George T. 04/27/65   05/01/65
Taylor, Anna Jane married Vellines, Benton H. 01/01/61   02/19/61
Taylor, Belle married Clarke, H. F. (Maj. U.S.A.) 09/24/61   10/11/61
Taylor, Benjamin married Burly, Louisa 03/07/61   03/08/61
Taylor, Carrie A. married Gibson, William H. 10/20/64   10/21/64
Taylor, Catherine married Price, John Basil 11/07/61   11/09/61
Taylor, Charles A. married Stansbury, Mary V. (Mrs.) 10/07/64   10/12/6
Taylor, Charles E. died 02/22/65   02/24/65
Taylor, Elizabeth died 11/17/64   11/19/64
Taylor, Elizabeth R. died 08/24/63   08/25/63
Taylor, Elizabeth Tippett died 09/15/63   07/22/64
Taylor, Ellen J. married Coulter, A. W. 03/09/64   03/14/64
Taylor, Emily married Stevens, Alexander 04/14/63   04/16/63

Taylor, Emily C. married Shreeve, J. (Rev.) 01/16/62 01/17/62
Taylor, Emily Rebecca married Warfield, Columbus 12/22/63 12/24/63
Taylor, Esther married Mitchell, Francis 02/26/61 02/28/61
Taylor, Ezekiel died 07/26/63 07/29/63
Taylor, Florence married Van Rensalaer, John J. 10/20/64 10/21/64
Taylor, George M., Jr. married Irving, Alice 09/05/65 09/07/65
Taylor, George W. died 01/22/64 01/23/64
Taylor, Helen M. married Miller, Walter T. H. 12/10/63 12/12/63
Taylor, Henry died 04/06/61 04/08/61
Taylor, Henry T. married Bartlett, Susan 11/20/65 12/04/65
Taylor, Henry W. died 12/09/63 12/12/63
Taylor, Isabella (Mrs.) died 11/25/63 11/26/63
Taylor, Jacob married Fitzchew, Elizabeth 12/17/63 12/19/63
Taylor, James died 06/27/64 06/28/64
Taylor, James B. married O'Donahue, Kate 07/13/65 07/26/65
Taylor, James Edward died 05/04/63 05/05/63
Taylor, James M. married Montell, Laura M. 06/02/64 07/13/64
Taylor, James Rhesa died 06/16/62 07/03/62
Taylor, Jane married Whitton, William 05/30/63 06/03/63
Taylor, Jesse C. married Thompson, Mary 06/03/63 06/05/63
Taylor, John married Ing, Sarah C. 02/18/64 02/19/64
Taylor, John E. married Petticord, Adeline 11/27/64 11/29/64
Taylor, John Edward Cooper died 07/19/64 07/22/64
Taylor, John H. H. married Green, Martha A. 06/11/63 06/13/63
Taylor, John H. H. married Green, Martha A. 06/11/63 06/18/63
Taylor, John S. married Kessler, Maggie 05/14/63 05/16/63
Taylor, Joseph died 10/22/63 10/24/63
Taylor, Joseph died 06/27/64 06/29/64
Taylor, Judge died 12/28/64 12/29/64
Taylor, Judge died 12/28/64 12/30/64
Taylor, Julia married Brown, Geoffrey J. 01/31/64 02/02/64
Taylor, Kate married Banks, William H. S. 07/25/61 12/18/61
Taylor, Kate Elvira married Patton, Robert J. (Dr.) 01/24/61 01/25/61
Taylor, Kate Walter died 07/22/64 07/23/64
Taylor, Katie Bell died 08/27/65 08/28/65
Taylor, Lavinia C. married Lewis, John W. 04/14/64 04/16/64
Taylor, Levi Reese died 08/29/62 08/30/62
Taylor, Lizzie died 07/18/65 07/20/65
Taylor, Lizzie A. married Atwell, James R. 02/15/63 03/04/63
Taylor, Lizzie A. married Yearsly, Albin 06/22/65 06/28/65
Taylor, Lizzie C. married Haussdoerffer, John 12/01/60 01/28/61
Taylor, Lizzie C. married Haussdoerffer, John 12/01/60 01/29/61
Taylor, Lydia died 04/21/61 04/22/61
Taylor, M. S. (Dr.) married Hamer, Lizzie A. 01/15/61 01/18/61
Taylor, Maggie W. died 10/11/61 11/08/61
Taylor, Mary Ann died 05/28/61 05/29/61
Taylor, Mary B. (Mrs.) died 09/02/63 09/05/63
Taylor, Mary E. married Caston, Alfred H. 04/18/61 04/23/61
Taylor, Mary E. married Andrews, Matthew 10/12/65 10/14/65
Taylor, Mary Elizabeth died 12/03/62 12/04/62
Taylor, Mary J. married Lilly, Charles R. 10/20/64 11/09/64
Taylor, Mary Jane married Daugherty, Thomas 12/02/60 01/23/61
Taylor, Mary L. (Mrs.) died 03/13/63 03/16/63
Taylor, Mary O. married Simpson, George W. 08/14/62 09/15/62
Taylor, Mary R. married Myers, John 12/28/65 12/30/65

Taylor, Mary V. married Bolton, John H. 05/07/63 05/11/63
Taylor, Matthew died 01/25/64 01/27/64
Taylor, Mollie E. married Veader, Daniel H. 05/16/65 05/18/65
Taylor, Mortimer married Crowl, Isabel 06/29/65 07/06/65
Taylor, Nancy (Mrs.) died 12/27/63 12/29/63
Taylor, Rachal A. married Magaw, Samuel J. 01/10/61 01/21/61
Taylor, Rachel died 11/11/65 11/18/65
Taylor, Rachel E. married Michael, William B. 12/23/63 12/24/63
Taylor, Rebecca L. married Benjamin, James W. 02/12/63 03/04/63
Taylor, Robert A. died 10/15/63 10/16/63
Taylor, Robert A. died 10/15/63 10/17/63
Taylor, Robert T. married Barman, Cecelia M. 10/07/62 10/10/62
Taylor, Sallie married Hubard, James R. (Rev.) 06/01/64 06/13/64
Taylor, Sarah A. married Adams, George L. 12/30/64 01/02/65
Taylor, Sarah Elizabeth died 03/06/65 03/07/65
Taylor, Sarah J. died 10/31/62 11/04/62
Taylor, Sarah J. (Mrs.) married Smith, Laurence R. 08/13/63 09/02/63
Taylor, Sarah Linda married Roberts, Joshua Thomas 05/04/62 05/13/62
Taylor, Sidney T. married Baxter, Annie Olivia 05/05/61 05/11/61
Taylor, Susan died 01/20/65 01/21/65
Taylor, Talbott Jones died 10/27/61 10/29/61
Taylor, Thomas married Halfpenny, Matilda 09/28/61 10/07/61
Taylor, Thurston M. died 02/28/64 03/03/64
Taylor, Virginia P. married Guest, Richard S. 04/15/62 04/17/62
Taylor, W. J. married Brown, M. A. 11/10/65 11/11/65
Taylor, William married Montague, Emma Virginia no date 12/20/61
Taylor, William died 08/12/65 08/16/65
Taylor, William Albert died 09/17/63 09/21/63
Taylor, William H. married Cornell, Mary 05/02/61 05/04/61
Taylor, William H. married Giddings, Mary M. 06/19/62 06/21/62
Taylor, William Henry died 06/06/65 06/07/65
Taylor, William J. married Maxwell, Jennie 10/29/63 10/31/63
Tayman, James William died 01/13/63 01/14/63
Tayman, Margaret Alice died 01/17/63 01/19/63
Tayman, Mollie J. married Fowler, William R. 05/10/64 05/12/64
Tazewell, Samuel Oliver died 01/10/61 01/11/61
Teackle, Emma Jane died 12/19/61 12/20/61
Teackle, Thomas U. died 09/13/63 09/15/63
Teal, Elizabeth (Mrs.) died 05/10/64 05/11/64
Tear, Alice R. married Curtiss, F. (Sgt.) 03/12/64 04/20/64
Tear, Benjamin F. died 05/30/62 05/31/62
Tear, Joseph R. died 10/13/62 10/14/62
Tear, Joseph R. died 10/13/62 10/15/62
Tear, Sarah E. (Mrs.) died 08/27/63 09/08/63
Teas, Elizabeth died 05/13/61 05/15/61
Tebelmann, John George died 06/13/63 06/17/63
Tedds, Lillian died 08/11/64 09/13/64
Teemyer, E. Florence died 02/01/63 02/02/63
Teepe, Mary C. died 05/06/62 05/07/62
Temple, John H. married Nicholson, Georgeanna 02/02/64 02/20/64
Temple, John J. married Snyder, Lydia Ann 08/03/65 08/07/65
Temple, Matthew died 11/18/64 11/26/64
Templeman, Hensie died 06/17/65 06/20/65
Templeman, James Gerald died 08/02/61 08/06/61
Templemon, Allen died 09/14/61 09/17/61

Tenant, George married Potter, Sarah 01/15/61   01/17/61
Tenant, George W. died 03/09/65   03/11/65
Tennant, Annie C. married Hahn, C. Otto 03/02/65   03/07/65
Tenrick, Mary E. married Pusen, Theodore 01/04/64   01/08/64
Tensfield, Arnold died 08/08/61   08/09/61
Tensfield, MaryJane married Wise, Stephen Collin 01/05/64   01/06/64
Tenweeges, August married Stumptner, Margaret 11/25/62   11/26/62
Terral, Michael F. (Cpt.) died 09/07/64   10/13/64
Terry, Isaiah died 10/10/61   10/11/61
Tesdorpf, J. H. married Kremelberg, Mathilde 06/24/63   06/27/63
Tevis, C. Welsh (Mrs.) died 10/29/65   11/02/65
Tevis, Josephine A. married Brown, Charles W. 11/10/62   12/05/62
Thackry, William A. married Armstrong, Laura A. 03/31/64   04/02/64
Thamert, Elizabeth married Lewis, John F. 03/16/62   03/22/62
Thatcher, Cassandra died 12/23/63   01/05/64
Thater, Catherine died 11/08/61   11/09/61
Thater, Philip died 03/12/61   03/13/61
Thawley, Annie E. married Fountain, Marcy, Jr. 01/20/63   01/27/63
Thawley, Thomas E. died 11/02/62   11/04/62
Thayer, Georgia E. died 07/18/61   08/01/61
Thayer, Henry C. married Miller, Annie 05/13/63   05/15/63
Thayer, John Laban died 04/07/64   04/09/64
Thearns, Patrick died 12/05/65   12/07/65
Thelin, Rebecca (Mrs.) died 03/19/63   03/20/63
Therrough, Sallie D. married Pump, Charles H. 08/06/63   08/08/63
Thiede, Mary Coraline died 04/02/61   04/03/61
Thiede, Thomas J. J. died 01/26/65   01/28/65
Thiem, John married Kabernagel, Louisa 10/11/64   10/18/64
Thiernauch, Mary M. married Stampe, Jacob J. 01/23/62   01/24/62
Thierrouch, Sallie D. married Jump, Charles H. 08/06/63   08/10/63
Thigne, Annie died 08/17/63   08/18/63
Thilghman, Francis married Chaplin, Isabella 03/17/63   03/21/63
Thirckel, Harriet died 04/09/64   04/13/64
Thirion, Margaret married Wells, Oscar M. 06/18/65   06/20/65
Thirlkel, J. Barney died 11/28/63   12/02/63
Thirlkel, William C. married Potter, Susan 07/22/63   07/27/63
Thom, Ella L. died 01/25/61   01/26/61
Thoma, Ella Virginia Lee died 08/18/64   08/19/64
Thoman, Herman A. died 05/02/64   05/03/64
Thoman, John married Breuning, Annie 11/26/63   11/28/63
Thoman, Mary B. married Busse, L. V. 02/10/63   02/11/63
Thomas, Adam married Johnson, Mary J. 08/20/61   08/24/61
Thomas, Adolf died 06/16/61   06/20/61
Thomas, Amanda A. married Phillips, Charles C. 07/31/65   08/25/65
Thomas, Ann (Mrs.) died 08/28/63   08/31/63
Thomas, Ann (Mrs.) died 06/19/65   06/30/65
Thomas, Ann L. A. died 11/01/65   11/03/65
Thomas, Anna Maria died 09/28/65   09/29/65
Thomas, Annie T. married Lyons, Daniel 11/22/64   11/24/64
Thomas, Asberry Bradford died 11/29/63   12/02/63
Thomas, Benjamin F. married Smith, Albena C. 11/02/65   12/21/65
Thomas, Bertha died 10/18/65   10/19/65
Thomas, Carrena died 06/18/64   06/20/64
Thomas, Charles Jerome died 12/31/62   01/01/63
Thomas, Charles W. married Trusty, Adelia 10/27/63   11/03/63

Thomas, David E. died 10/18/64   10/19/64
Thomas, David E. died no date   10/20/64
Thomas, David E., Jr. married Quarles, Virginia 09/02/65   09/05/65
Thomas, Desdemona married Bowen, John H. 12/16/62   12/23/62
Thomas, Edward Wayne died 10/11/61   10/15/61
Thomas, Edwin married Pasterfield, Sally W. 10/23/64   11/05/64
Thomas, Elizabeth married Thompson, George R. 09/14/62   10/17/62
Thomas, Emma died 05/18/62   05/20/62
Thomas, Emma Florence died 12/16/62   12/17/62
Thomas, Emma Jane died 02/27/62   02/28/62
Thomas, Etta E. married Stokes, Louis N. 12/10/63   12/12/63
Thomas, Evan died 04/25/63   04/28/63
Thomas, Frances married Well, Thomas B. 12/31/63   01/02/64
Thomas, George C. married Smith, E. Jenny 12/01/63   12/03/63
Thomas, Griffith married Dunn, Hannah 03/08/65   03/11/65
Thomas, Hannah died 04/24/61   04/26/61
Thomas, Harriet (Mrs.) died 09/09/63   09/14/63
Thomas, Helen M. married Blair, Henry H. 06/25/63   06/27/63
Thomas, Henry Hammond died 06/25/63   06/26/63
Thomas, Henry P. married Chalfant, Anna M. 12/24/63   12/31/63
Thomas, Henry T. died 03/28/64   04/08/64
Thomas, James T. married White, Elizabeth 05/14/63   05/16/63
Thomas, James Whitall died 09/05/65   09/07/65
Thomas, James Young died 06/13/65   06/15/65
Thomas, Jane died 03/15/65   03/18/65
Thomas, Jane (Mrs.) died no date   05/08/63
Thomas, Jane (Mrs.) died 04/28/64   04/30/64
Thomas, John died 10/27/63   10/29/63
Thomas, John died 12/03/64   12/15/64
Thomas, John A. died 12/22/62   12/23/62
Thomas, John Chew died 08/29/62   08/30/62
Thomas, John H. died 03/30/65   04/01/65
Thomas, John L., Jr. married Hussey, Azalia 01/14/63   01/16/63
Thomas, John Monkur married Walk, Kate 01/05/65   01/05/65
Thomas, John Tyler died 01/02/63   01/03/63
Thomas, Joseph died 08/04/61   08/07/61
Thomas, Joseph married Moulden, Sarah Jane 04/24/62   05/03/62
Thomas, Joseph died 04/24/65   04/26/65
Thomas, Joseph married Brooks, Mary Elizabeth 07/04/65   07/11/65
Thomas, Joseph B. died 09/13/62   09/16/62
Thomas, Joseph E. married Lague, Sarah A. (Mrs.) 08/31/64   09/01/64
Thomas, Josiah married Woodland, Georgeanna 03/01/63   03/03/63
Thomas, Kesiah died 02/24/63   02/26/63
Thomas, Laura Neal died 04/05/61   04/09/61
Thomas, Laura S. married Moon, Richard N. 01/03/65   01/07/65
Thomas, Levin married Buck, Catherine 11/01/63   11/03/63
Thomas, Lizzie C. married Appler, Ferdinand C. 05/24/64   06/01/64
Thomas, Louis Wesley died 10/06/65   10/09/65
Thomas, Louisa married Reagan, Arsceanas 05/10/64   05/17/64
Thomas, M. married Schotta, C. 11/24/61   11/26/61
Thomas, Maggie married Dix, William H. 03/24/61   04/01/61
Thomas, Maggie died 07/10/61   07/11/61
Thomas, Mahlom married Armstrong, James 05/18/63   05/20/63
Thomas, Martha married Robinson, Caleb 04/09/63   04/11/63
Thomas, Mary died 01/29/64   01/30/64

Thomas, Mary married Hudson, James 10/27/63   10/29/63
Thomas, Mary (Mrs.) died 01/12/63   01/13/63
Thomas, Mary Ann (Mrs.) died 03/03/63   03/04/63
Thomas, Mary E. married Jones, Thomas H. 04/08/61   04/10/61
Thomas, Mary E. married Jones, Thomas W. 04/08/61   04/13/61
Thomas, Mary Frances died 09/08/61   09/14/61
Thomas, Mary Goldsborough married Dallam, John Paca 10/09/62   10/13/62
Thomas, Mary Jane married Hill, William 05/03/64   05/05/64
Thomas, Mary Virginia died 02/05/62   02/06/62
Thomas, Mary Virginia Davis died 12/16/63   12/19/63
Thomas, Mattie R. married Monbar, Anatob H. Mion 02/20/65   10/17/65
Thomas, Maylyum married Armstrong, James 05/18/63   05/21/63
Thomas, Minty married Fuller, William H. 05/02/61   05/08/61
Thomas, Nettie died 01/02/61   01/03/61
Thomas, Perry M. married Massey, Rebecca G. (Mrs.) 06/15/64   06/17/64
Thomas, Philip E. died 09/01/61   09/02/61
Thomas, Philip W. died 07/15/61   07/23/61
Thomas, Priscilla died 10/26/64   10/28/64
Thomas, S. Drew married Finley, Martha Elsie 02/25/63   02/27/63
Thomas, Samuel (Cpt.) died 10/17/63   10/24/63
Thomas, Samuel Henry died 06/03/62   06/05/62
Thomas, Samuel K. died 05/23/63   05/25/63
Thomas, Sarah (Mrs.) died 01/17/63   01/19/63
Thomas, Sarah W. married Ports, Alfred 04/28/64   05/04/64
Thomas, Seth died 06/05/65   06/06/65
Thomas, Sterling died 01/11/65   01/12/65
Thomas, Sterling W. married Davidson, Frances J. 11/29/63   01/12/64
Thomas, Warner died 05/30/65   05/31/65
Thomas, Will R. married Lambdin, Mannie J. 06/23/65   07/07/65
Thomas, William died 01/29/63   01/30/63
Thomas, William died 06/24/64   06/25/64
Thomas, William B. died 11/16/62   11/18/62
Thomas, William B. died 11/16/62   11/22/62
Thomas, William Emory died 05/02/61   05/03/61
Thomas, Williamine G. died 05/16/62   05/19/62
Thompsen, Ann L. died 04/26/62   04/28/62
Thompson, Addie died 07/26/63   07/28/63
Thompson, Adela died 03/05/62   03/07/62
Thompson, Alexander died 05/03/65   05/04/65
Thompson, Alexina died 05/16/61   05/18/61
Thompson, Alfred W. died 03/18/65   03/20/65
Thompson, Amanda married Sadler, John C. 01/21/64   01/26/64
Thompson, Amanda M. married Auld, Thomas (Capt.) 05/23/65   05/26/65
Thompson, Andrew J. died 03/15/65   03/16/65
Thompson, Annie E. died 06/04/64   06/08/64
Thompson, Annie R. married Hack, Henry C. 01/17/63   01/21/63
Thompson, Charles married Anderson, Rozena 12/10/63   12/23/63
Thompson, Charles Edward died 10/10/62   10/11/62
Thompson, Charles Groom died 04/27/63   04/29/63
Thompson, Charles P. died 07/29/64   08/04/64
Thompson, Charles Wesley married Smith, Ann Rebecca 01/08/63   01/10/63
Thompson, Columbus E. married McIlvain, Laura 09/07/62   09/18/62
Thompson, David P. married Haislett, Amney E. 02/28/64   04/13/64
Thompson, Edward died 07/16/61   07/18/61
Thompson, Edward died 07/20/65   07/21/65

Thompson, Edward died 07/20/65   07/22/65
Thompson, Edward Thomas died 10/11/63   10/13/63
Thompson, Elias J. married Stevenson, Lizzie A. 02/21/62   02/07/62
Thompson, Eliza C. married Greist, William F. 05/05/64   05/09/64
Thompson, Elizabeth died 08/28/61   08/29/61
Thompson, Elizabeth died 07/03/62   07/04/62
Thompson, Elizabeth married Hodgman, William 11/28/64   01/02/65
Thompson, Elizabeth A. married Tudor, John W. 03/02/65   05/23/65
Thompson, Emma Belle married Dill, George E. A. 11/29/64   12/03/64
Thompson, Forester died 07/27/63   07/28/63
Thompson, Frank J. died 05/12/62   05/13/62
Thompson, Frederick married Johnson, Julia R. 10/06/64   10/14/64
Thompson, George died 02/02/63   02/03/63
Thompson, George A. died 06/26/64   06/28/64
Thompson, George R. married Thomas, Elizabeth 09/14/62   10/17/62
Thompson, Gideon Campbell died 04/06/62   04/08/62
Thompson, Harry died 08/22/64   08/24/64
Thompson, Henry married Hitchens, Mary Eliza 04/20/65   04/22/65
Thompson, Henry Alexander died 01/20/63   01/22/63
Thompson, Isabella B. married Gorsuch, James D. 04/12/64   04/14/64
Thompson, Isabella D. married Brown, Claudius G. 01/10/61   01/15/61
Thompson, J. C. married Brewer, Jennie 12/10/62   01/30/63
Thompson, Jacob married Polk, Anna Elizabeth 02/10/65   02/13/65
Thompson, James married Brooks, Isabella 01/18/65   02/22/65
Thompson, James A. died 06/23/62   06/28/62
Thompson, James C. married Dashiell, Mary B. 11/14/65   11/15/65
Thompson, James H. married Wilson, Catharine 07/14/62   07/16/62
Thompson, John died 01/29/64   01/30/64
Thompson, John died 09/16/64   09/23/64
Thompson, John married Sheafer, Annie E. 03/07/65   04/27/65
Thompson, John Alexander died 12/30/62   01/01/63
Thompson, John C. married Walton, Mary S. 06/22/65   06/23/65
Thompson, John H. married Robinson, Alvinder 02/05/63   02/07/63
Thompson, Joseph married Knapp, Susie E. 12/02/62   12/20/62
Thompson, Julia Ann died 12/18/62   12/19/62
Thompson, Kate married Dunlap, A. H. 12/15/64   12/16/64
Thompson, Keziah died 06/01/61   06/03/61
Thompson, L. S. B. married Carter, Annie 10/29/61   11/22/61
Thompson, Levie Georgia married Kramer, S. R. 03/06/61   03/11/61
Thompson, Louisa married Butler, Elijah 06/30/63   07/02/63
Thompson, M. Virginia married Goldsborough, Louis D. 12/03/63   12/07/6
Thompson, Mahala J. married Pearson, Levi, Jr. 12/05/65   12/19/65
Thompson, Margaret died 08/20/61   08/24/61
Thompson, Margaret died 05/19/63   05/20/63
Thompson, Margaret married Collins, Charles H. 11/06/64   11/08/64
Thompson, Margaret A. married Baker, George 01/27/61   02/07/61
Thompson, Margaret A. died 12/16/63   12/18/63
Thompson, Margaret B. (Mrs.) died 11/01/64   11/03/64
Thompson, Margaret M. married Jordan, Richard J. 03/21/65   03/25/65
Thompson, Maria Virginia married Sutton, Thomas Benton 07/21/62
    07/23/62
Thompson, Martha Jane died 02/15/64   02/16/64
Thompson, Mary died 01/12/61   01/15/61
Thompson, Mary died 08/11/61   08/13/61

Thompson, Mary married Taylor, Jesse C. 06/03/63 06/05/63
Thompson, Mary married Stevenson, James 08/09/63 08/18/63
Thompson, Mary (Mrs.) died 06/15/64 06/16/64
Thompson, Mary A. married Graham, William 11/30/65 12/02/65
Thompson, Mary Anna died 05/26/61 05/28/61
Thompson, Mary E. married Harvey, Charles A. 02/07/61 02/16/61
Thompson, Mary Geneeve married Griffith, Barzillia 04/02/61 04/06/61
Thompson, Mary J. (Mrs.) died 03/03/64 03/04/64
Thompson, Mary Louise married Brown, Robert H. 10/27/64 11/05/64
Thompson, Mary Rebecca died 01/17/62 01/18/62
Thompson, Mary Rosalia married Kegler, John A. 01/10/65 01/20/65
Thompson, Miriam (Mrs.) died 11/30/64 12/01/64
Thompson, Mollie C. married Wright, John R. 02/17/64 02/25/64
Thompson, Rachel died 06/18/63 06/19/63
Thompson, Robert married Allen, Jane 02/15/63 04/08/63
Thompson, Robert died 02/24/65 02/25/65
Thompson, Robert Lee died 04/26/64 04/28/64
Thompson, Rose (Mrs.) died 11/11/64 11/12/64
Thompson, S. C. married Brewer, Jennie 12/10/62 01/31/63
Thompson, Salem H. married Richstein, Elenora (Mrs.) 09/10/62 09/19/62
Thompson, Sallie E. married Lucas, John D. 04/30/62 05/03/62
Thompson, Samuel died 10/20/62 10/21/62
Thompson, Samuel (Sgt. Major) died no date 07/15/63
Thompson, Sarah A. K. died 01/18/63 01/19/63
Thompson, Sarah June married Marter, David A. (Cpt.) 08/09/62 10/16/62
Thompson, Stephen married Fletcher, Julia Ann 02/02/63 03/06/63
Thompson, Thomas died 06/24/62 06/27/62
Thompson, Thomas H. married Owens, Mary Ann 07/16/65 07/19/65
Thompson, W. A. married Dixon, Ellenora 07/13/64 07/18/64
Thompson, William married Stevenson, Sidney Maria 12/11/61 12/12/61
Thompson, William died 07/20/63 07/21/63
Thompson, William C. died 07/23/63 07/25/63
Thompson, William H. married Anderson, Annie 02/17/63 02/27/63
Thompson, William James died 07/08/62 07/10/62
Thompson, William P. married Woods, Sarah 05/14/61 05/16/61
Thompson, Zelina J. died 12/24/61 12/27/61
Thomson, Alexander died 08/20/61 08/22/61
Thomson, Cordelia M. married Roney, Edward P. 08/13/63 08/14/63
Thomson, Henry died 12/18/63 12/19/63
Thomson, Ignatius Davis (Dr.) married Maynard, Julia S. 12/19/65 12/21/65
Thomson, Jane Kerr married Duvall, William W. 03/31/64 04/16/64
Thomson, Julia Ann died 11/30/62 12/02/62
Thomson, Margaretta Ann died 05/16/62 05/20/62
Thomson, Mary (Mrs.) died 04/03/65 04/04/65
Thomson, William married Lang, Mary C. 01/21/61 01/24/61
Thomsouth, Thomas married Talkfuths, Mary E. 08/04/61 08/08/61
Thorington, Fannie Elizabeth died 06/28/62 07/04/62
Thorington, Mary Jane died 03/31/62 04/03/62
Thorman, Dora married Schoenthaler, F. C. 12/12/65 12/13/65
Thorn, Columbus W. married Addison, Sallie R. 05/11/65 05/29/65
Thorne, Caroline Elizabeth married Crossley, Joseph 12/29/64 12/30/64
Thorner, Francis married Holloway, Fanny 06/29/64 07/08/64
Thornley, Mary died 04/22/61 04/29/61
Thornton, Elijah A. married Symonds, Sarah A. 03/19/63 04/01/63

Thornton, Francis A. (U.S.N.) died 02/26/62 03/01/62
Thornton, Frederick married Hart, Catharine 09/10/63 09/12/63
Thornton, James N. died 02/14/63 02/16/63
Thornton, Jessee Melvin died 11/05/65 11/13/65
Thornton, John William died 08/25/61 08/29/61
Thornton, Julia married Breckenridge, Philip 10/23/64 10/26/64
Thornton, Martha (Mrs.) died 03/06/63 03/07/63
Thornton, Thomas H. died 02/22/63 02/24/63
Thornton, Thomas Lockwood died 01/13/63 01/16/63
Thorpe, Mary (Mrs.) died 01/07/63 01/09/63
Thorpe, Thomas G. married Morgan, Mary Jane 08/07/64 08/09/64
Thorton, Eugenia E. married Watkins, F. Bascom 02/07/65 02/10/65
Thrift, John died 03/24/63 03/26/63
Thrifty, Emma married Wernex, George D. 12/22/63 01/13/64
Thronthwaite, Jane (Mrs.) died 01/27/64 01/30/64
Thrush, Nicholas died 04/04/65 04/06/65
Thrush, Rebecca (Mrs.) died 04/16/64 04/18/64
Thurlow, Mary E. married Hokfland, Charles H. 12/25/64 12/28/64
Thurlow, Mary E. married Holyland, Charles 12/25/64 12/29/64
Thursby, Anna Bell died 03/06/65 03/07/65
Thursby, Edward Everett died 02/27/65 03/01/65
Thursby, Harry Martin died 02/26/65 02/27/65
Thursby, Mary Ann (Mrs.) died 02/07/64 03/30/64
Tibbals, John G. married Fields, Maria 11/24/64 12/01/64
Tibbles, Thomas died 10/14/65 10/16/65
Tickner, William J. married Pumphrey, Maggie E. 05/31/65 06/07/65
Tidings, Edwin Randall (Dr.) died 12/06/64 12/07/64
Tiernan, Laura C. married Klingle, J. Pierce 10/17/65 10/20/65
Tiernan, Patrick Hance died 07/31/63 08/01/63
Tiernan, William H. died 03/18/63 03/19/63
Tierney, Ann (Mrs.) died 04/16/64 04/18/64
Tierney, John F. died 07/31/64 08/01/64
Tierney, Mary married Fowley, William 04/07/61 04/10/61
Tierney, Michael Richard died 07/12/65 07/13/65
Tierney, William died 09/17/65 09/19/65
Tierny, Mary Jane died 03/10/63 03/11/63
Tighe, Mary died 06/27/65 06/28/65
Tighlman, Thomas Jefferson died 09/14/64 09/15/64
Tighlman, Thomas Jefferson died 09/14/64 09/16/64
Tilden, Atkinson S. died 01/12/65 01/14/65
Tilden, John R. died 06/25/65 07/01/65
Tilett, George died 06/28/62 07/04/62
Tilghman, Annie Maria died 10/13/62 10/18/62
Tilghman, Catherine (Mrs.) died 02/05/63 02/07/63
Tilghman, Kate married Lowndes, Charles 09/25/62 10/03/62
Tilghman, Richard married Keyes, Hester Ann 09/15/64 09/17/64
Tillery, Jane married Robinson, George R. 03/11/61 03/13/61
Tillery, John A. married Dulaney, Eliza J. 02/19/65 02/24/65
Tilley, Hallie H. married Yates, Edmund L. (Col.) 04/29/61 05/06/61
Tilling, Ella Virginia died 11/04/63 11/05/63
Tillman, William H. married Barton, Elizabeth 01/01/63 01/07/63
Tilly, John B. died 06/09/63 06/15/63
Tilton, Clara married Emory, Campbell Dallas 12/29/64 01/02/65
Tilton, Samuel W. married Wilkinson, Mary E. 08/22/65 08/24/65
Tilyard, Philip T. married Brown, A. Virginia 02/25/62 03/01/62

Timanus, Emma J. died 04/30/62 05/02/62
Timanus, Luther married George, Mary F. 05/29/61 06/01/61
Timanus, Margaret (Mrs.) died 01/21/63 01/22/63
Timbs, Laura H. died 06/24/62 06/25/62
Timbs, William died 01/08/64 01/12/64
Timmins, William died 11/11/62 11/13/62
Timmons, Cecelia A. married Myers, Charles H. 12/28/64 12/29/64
Timmons, Charles died 08/25/63 08/26/63
Timothy, John died 03/24/65 03/25/65
Timpson, Frederick Arthur died 06/08/61 06/11/61
Tindall, William married Miller, Sophia 07/27/63 08/10/63
Tindle, Robert W. died 09/13/62 09/15/62
Tinges, Mary Harvey died 06/29/61 07/03/61
Tingstrom, Charles J. married Anderson, Mary L. 01/02/63 01/22/63
Tipett, Isabell died 02/16/62 02/21/62
Tippett, Margaret married Bosworth, John 07/26/63 07/28/63
Tippett, Margaret (Mrs.) married Morrison, William Ebenezer 12/25/64 12/28/64
Tippett, William C. married Turner, Harriet Rebecca 12/15/64 12/16/64
Tipton, Caroline C. died 03/30/65 04/05/65
Tipton, Ellen M. married Gill, Andrew B. 10/23/62 10/25/62
Tipton, Emma died 11/15/61 11/18/61
Tipton, John H. married Jones, Rebecca 05/11/63 06/16/63
Tipton, Martha A. died 11/12/64 11/14/64
Tiroved, Sarah E. married Barton, William 12/30/61 01/03/62
Tischmeyer, Harriet died 05/07/61 05/08/61
Tisling, Frederick married Rosenberry, Cassie A. 07/21/63 07/09/63
Titting, Mary Catherine died 08/24/63 08/25/63
Tittle, Ammelia died 04/09/62 04/11/62
Toben, Clarence married Riley, Margaret 02/11/62 02/15/62
Toberer, Carrie died 07/28/64 07/29/64
Toberer, Louisa married Rueckert, John L. 08/29/65 08/30/65
Toberer, Mary died 11/16/62 11/18/62
Tobin, Mary married Dixon, David 01/19/64 01/25/64
Tobin, Thomas W. died 04/15/62 04/16/62
Todd, Adelaide Augusta died 12/27/64 12/29/64
Todd, Anna Belle died 04/30/64 05/02/64
Todd, Emma Florence died 05/22/64 05/23/64
Todd, Hanna died 10/11/63 10/12/63
Todd, Henry D. (USN) married Johnson, Flora 09/28/65 10/04/65
Todd, James died 10/03/65 10/05/65
Todd, John T. married Stewart, Belle 01/14/64 01/18/64
Todd, John W. married Elliott, Wilhelmina 12/11/65 12/13/65
Todd, Josiah died 03/11/64 03/16/64
Todd, Kate Isabella died 07/20/65 07/24/65
Todd, Mary married McNalley, Patrick 04/05/63 04/08/63
Todd, Mary Ann (Mrs.) married McKenna, John 02/11/62 02/13/62
Todd, Mary Ann (Mrs.) died 10/16/63 10/17/63
Todd, Mary E. died 02/15/63 02/16/63
Todd, Patience Ann married Duvall, Thomas 06/20/62 07/04/62
Todd, Rosalie died 11/11/64 11/12/64
Todd, Rose (Mrs.) married Cox, Madison 09/09/65 09/12/65
Todd, Sarah Elizabeth died 07/30/62 07/31/62
Todd, Walter Rockwell died 09/07/61 09/09/61
Todd, William A. married Archbold, Beckie 06/11/63 06/25/63

Todd, William J. married Irwin, Honoria A. 09/02/62 09/04/62
Toel, Charles H. married Beam, Sarah C. 10/19/65 10/23/65
Toffling, Ada died 04/14/62 04/15/62
Toft, Ellen died 05/11/64 05/12/64
Toland, Martha died 12/24/63 12/26/63
Toldridge, Augusta A. married Dulaney, William H. (Dr.) 09/07/65 09/11/65
Tolley, Elizabeth (Mrs.) died 08/14/64 08/15/64
Tolley, Jeremiah married Caskey, Mary E. 10/30/65 11/14/65
Tolley, Travers W. (Capt.) died 04/19/63 04/20/63
Tolou, George Lewis died 01/29/64 02/01/64
Tolson, Alice C. married Eichelberger, Frank T. 05/20/64 05/23/64
Tolson, Alice G. C. married Eichelberger, Frank T. 05/20/64 05/24/64
Tolson, H. M. married Cockey, Mary V. 05/19/64 05/27/64
Tolson, Mary Elizabeth E. died 03/08/63 03/09/63
Tolson, Perry married Watts, Mary J. 03/19/63 03/23/63
Tolson, Virginia C. (Mrs.) died 11/21/63 11/23/63
Toman, Mary died 02/26/63 02/27/63
Tomlins, Morton C. married West, Maria E. 09/06/64 09/13/64
Tomlinson, (Tomlison) Kate married Bartscher, John 01/05/65 01/07/65
Tomlinson, B. Price died 02/05/64 02/06/64
Tomlinson, B. Price died no date 07/14/64
Tomlinson, Cornelia O. married Swearer, Charles 12/04/62 12/09/62
Tomlinson, Helen A. married Bradshaw, John J. 01/05/65 01/07/65
Tomlinson, Mallie W. died 09/05/62 09/08/62
Tomlinson, Perry married Mooney, Alice 09/23/63 09/29/63
Tomlinson, R. Burns married Read, Martha 05/28/63 06/01/63
Tompkins, Judge married Richardson, Sallie R. 01/06/63 01/26/63
Toner, Annie E. married Bracken, John F. 05/15/65 05/29/65
Toner, Bridget died 08/17/65 08/18/65
Toner, George died 05/16/64 05/17/64
Toner, George M. died 06/21/64 12/28/64
Toner, George, Jr. died 06/21/65 06/23/65
Toner, James J. married McCann, Anne T. 04/06/64 04/08/64
Toner, John married McKenna, Rosina 10/26/62 11/05/62
Toner, Letitia died no date 07/25/61
Toner, Michael died 08/21/62 08/22/62
Toner, Sarah died 03/28/63 03/30/63
Toner, William H. married Taman, Mary 08/24/65 09/28/65
Tonge, Ann died 12/15/62 12/17/62
Toomey, Emily died 01/28/62 01/29/62
Toomey, Josiah H. G. died 06/24/65 06/26/65
Toomey, William H. died 06/16/62 06/17/62
Toomy, Mary Statia married Gross, John J. 05/26/64 05/30/64
Tootill, Mary Ann married Spencer, John 02/14/64 02/17/64
Topless, William Summerfield died 07/12/61 07/13/61
Topley, Permelia A. married Martin, W. H. 10/21/63 10/26/63
Torborg, George died 05/26/61 05/27/61
Torby, Mary married Reese, William E. 08/19/62 08/25/62
Tormey, F. D. married Flannigan, Sarah 11/17/64 11/18/64
Tormey, J. Edward married Mason, Mary 11/05/63 11/06/63
Tormey, Timothy died 09/18/62 09/19/62
Torney, Albert G. married Wright, Mary Alice 03/03/64 03/29/64
Torney, John H. married Rose, Mary J. M. 03/03/62 03/10/62
Torney, Otto died 07/13/65 07/14/65

Torrence, Mary died 01/24/65   01/28/65
Torrington, John died 06/10/65   06/23/65
Torsch, Mary Louise died 09/05/62   09/06/62
Toscum, Sarah Jane married Morison, James W. 05/24/64   05/28/64
Touell, Samuel died 11/09/64   12/13/64
Tough, John H. died 09/04/61   09/05/61
Tough, William S. married Abernathy, Hattie E. 10/25/65   11/01/65
Toulman, Alfred F. married Matthews, Isabella 10/23/61   10/25/61
Touvel, Caleb died 04/02/62   04/12/62
Towers, Wesley M. died 03/18/64   05/11/64
Towles, Eliza Harwood died 01/29/64   01/30/64
Towles, James Oliver died 11/13/61   11/15/61
Town, Elizabeth Baker died 04/14/65   04/19/65
Towner, T. Harris (Cpt.,C.S.A) died 03/24/62   04/04/62
Towns, Mary Frances died 01/27/65   01/30/65
Townsend, Ann died 09/24/63   09/25/63
Townsend, Ann (Mrs.) died 05/15/63   05/16/63
Townsend, Fillmore died 08/13/64   08/15/64
Townsend, Jeremiah married Frost, Carrie B. 01/27/63   01/30/63
Townsend, Mary Frances married Primrose, James W. 07/27/65   08/01/65
Townsend, William Diffenderfer died 03/01/63   03/03/63
Townsend, William M. died 10/12/63   10/14/63
Townsend, William S. died 08/05/62   08/06/62
Townsley, Henry (Maj., CSA) died 11/10/63   12/08/63
Townsley, Henry Major died 11/10/63   11/08/63
Tows, Charles married Tarr, Frances Elizabeth 08/20/63   08/28/63
Towsen, Elizabeth married Jaiser, Carlis 09/29/63   10/03/63
Towson, Charles Edward died 12/30/63   01/02/64
Towson, Henry C. married Coahly, Martha 01/10/65   01/12/65
Towson, Sarah died 06/20/65   06/21/65
Towson, Sarah died 06/20/65   06/22/65
Towson, Sarah (Mrs.) died 04/05/65   04/06/65
Towson, Sarah J. married Smith, William 12/15/64   01/23/65
Toy, Lydia married Wheeler, John 09/29/64   10/01/64
Toy, Margaret (Mrs.) died 02/25/63   02/27/63
Toy, Richard H. married Freeman, Puella 04/11/61   04/18/61
Toy, Samuel D. died 03/25/65   03/27/65
Toy, Thomas B. married Turner, Susanna H. 05/05/61   01/18/65
Traband, A. C. married Rueckert, P. L. 11/01/63   11/11/63
Traband, George W. married Hines, Susie J. 05/04/65   05/06/65
Traband, M. Virginia married Gettier, John L. 06/29/65   08/01/65
Tracey, Ellen married Connolly, John 09/08/62   09/11/62
Tracey, Fannie A. married Evans, Andrew J. 08/04/64   08/08/64
Tracey, Martin died 06/17/61   06/18/61
Tracey, Susanna married Jones, Elisha 12/03/63   02/17/64
Tracey, Thomas C. died 03/26/63   03/28/63
Tracey, Thomas Edward died 02/19/64   02/20/64
Tracey, William married Morford, Ann E. 11/21/61   11/23/61
Tracey, William died 01/13/63   01/15/63
Tracy, Ann Elizabeth married Fray, William 08/14/62   09/17/62
Tracy, Charles H. died 10/06/62   10/28/62
Tracy, John E. died 05/22/61   05/23/61
Trail, Daisy died 07/19/65   07/20/65
Trail, Eleonora L. married Harrison, John 10/20/61   10/21/61
Trail, Maria L. (Mrs.) died 04/24/63   04/25/63

Trail, R. H. married Morrison, Emilie H. 12/23/65 12/23/65
Traille, Rebecca A. married Warfield, Wallace 09/17/63 09/18/63
Trainer, Louisa Ann died 03/07/63 03/12/63
Trainor, James married Spence, Jane 12/03/63 12/19/63
Trainor, John R. died 06/05/65 06/29/65
Trainor, Peter Francis died 03/28/62 03/29/62
Trainor, Virginia Lee died 07/07/64 07/09/64
Trainor, Washington Irving died 12/26/64 12/28/64
Trainor, William died 10/05/65 10/06/65
Trannear, Patrick Henry married Denney, Kate S. 07/12/63 07/23/63
Traughtman, Catherine married Stoss, John 08/06/65 08/08/65
Trautfelter, Henry married Davis, Margaret Ann 06/09/61 06/11/61
Travers, Ada married Griffith, Edwin L. 02/10/63 02/13/63
Travers, Aronia Dove died 12/11/61 12/13/61
Travers, Charlotte married Chew, Ambrose 08/17/63 08/19/63
Travers, Elizabeth A. died 07/29/61 07/30/61
Travers, Elizabeth O. married Johnson, John L. (Capt.) 12/26/61 12/28/61
Travers, Henry died 07/08/64 07/09/64
Travers, Kate C. married Wilkinson, J. V. 07/14/61 08/08/61
Travers, Martha E. married Smith, Washington A. 12/06/64 12/07/64
Travers, Priscilla Pearce died 12/09/63 12/10/63
Travers, Rose Ann married Jones, Thomas A. 08/15/64 09/06/64
Travers, Samuel died 12/08/64 12/10/64
Travers, Susie E. married Poulton, William E. 12/03/63 12/10/63
Traviss, Peter Henry married More, Rebecca Jane 11/19/61 11/27/61
Trayer, Susan Emma married Smith, John Thomas 12/18/62 12/19/62
Treadwell, Fanny married Jenkins, E. Courtney 11/08/65 11/14/65
Treadwell, Stepensons died 11/14/63 11/24/63
Treager, Charles (Sgt.) died 06/14/63 07/22/63
Treakle, Elizabeth died 01/23/63 02/05/63
Treamen, Emilie E. (Mrs.) died 10/12/62 01/26/63
Treasman, Mary married Howard, William Henry 10/01/63 10/05/63
Tredway, Mary Ann died 10/25/65 11/06/65
Tredwell, William married Wonn, Virginia 01/05/65 01/10/65
Trego, Annie died 04/30/61 05/01/61
Trego, Estelle married Roane, Henry W. 06/09/63 06/12/63
Trego, James D. married Killin, Anne B. 01/23/61 01/26/61
Trego, John D. L. died 08/12/63 01/27/64
Trego, John Thomas died 04/07/65 04/11/65
Trego, Sarah died 10/31/61 12/05/61
Tregoe, George W. married Kinnemon, Rebecca D. 10/15/61 10/18/61
Treichel, Belle N. married Smith, William Purnell (Col.) 09/26/61 12/30/61
Treichel, Belle N. married Smith, William Purnell (Col.) 09/26/61 12/28/61
Trekel, Sarah A. died 01/18/62 01/20/62
Tremmea, Florence married Bishop, D. A. 01/01/65 03/13/65
Trenweth, Ralph T. married Wolfe, Margaret E. 09/08/64 09/09/64
Tress, John married Knox, Christiana 10/01/65 10/14/65
Tress, Nelson married Ross, Mary Anna 09/27/64 10/03/64
Treucsh, Adam died 11/25/61 11/27/61
Treuman, Max married Binswanger, Amelia 09/27/64 09/29/64
Treusch, Adam died 11/25/61 11/28/61
Treusch, Phillipina H. died 04/22/64 04/25/64

Treuxsein, Erwina married Jeanneret, Z. 07/11/63 07/14/63
Tridel, Fanney died 01/31/65 02/08/65
Tridel, Johney died 01/31/65 02/08/65
Trigg, Kate married Olds, Isaac (Cpt.) 03/03/63 03/07/63
Trigg, Lizzie J. married Plummer, John William 08/11/63 08/20/63
Trilley, Anne died 09/26/62 09/27/62
Trim, W. C. married Hinton, Ann E. 07/27/65 08/08/65
Trimble, Elizabeth A. died 04/29/61 05/03/61
Trimble, Elizabeth S. died 12/27/62 12/29/62
Trimble, R. M. married Mather, Maggie A. 11/17/63 11/21/63
Trimble, William P. married Emery, Elizabeth 01/01/61 01/02/61
Trimmer, Abraham married DeBow, Emily E. 12/20/60 01/03/61
Trimmer, Annie L. died 08/14/63 08/22/63
Trine, Sarah married Crosby, George W. 04/21/61 04/29/61
Trine, William H. married Twaddle, Jennie 07/07/64 08/13/64
Triplet, Hannah A. T. married Fingan, Arthur 10/07/64 10/08/64
Trittle, Jeremiah W. married Sipple, Margaret A. 04/14/62 07/04/62
Trives, Rebecca married Trusty, A. H. 12/12/65 12/14/65
Tropnell, Emily G. died 03/11/62 03/13/62
Trott, Ann Amelia died 05/10/63 05/12/63
Trott, Edgar Reed died 01/06/63 01/14/63
Trott, George Alexander died 06/30/63 07/07/63
Trott, George L. died 05/00/00 10/29/62
Trott, Isabell married Gluelett, James 01/12/63 01/20/63
Trott, James married Cowan, Sallie E. 04/22/62 04/24/62
Trott, Kate Eugene died 06/05/63 06/08/63
Trott, Nathaniel J. married Camper, Clara J. 12/02/62 05/13/63
Trott, Richard H. died 09/03/63 09/04/63
Trott, Thomas G. (Cpt.) married Young, Catharine J. 02/13/62 03/14/62
Trott, William A. died 05/29/63 06/02/63
Trotten, John C. married Armstrong, Tillie C. 10/31/65 11/04/65
Trotton, Eliza (Mrs.) died 11/24/64 11/26/64
Trotton, Eugene Randolph died 06/26/64 06/27/64
Trotton, Ferdinand married Randolph, Mary F. 11/07/61 11/09/61
Trotton, Thomas married Diffenderffer, Sarah A. (Mrs.) 11/30/65 12/04/65
Trought, Anna Virginia died 03/10/63 03/12/63
Trought, John T. died 12/17/63 12/18/63
Trout, Adam M. married Anderson, Mary Agnes 11/07/61 12/03/61
Trowbridge, James A. died 06/05/61 06/07/61
Troxell, David M. died 08/30/65 09/05/65
Troxell, John G. married Gosnell, Mary E. 04/04/65 04/10/65
Truitt, Ambrose married Blake, Mary 06/18/63 06/20/63
Truman, Mary died 09/13/64 09/14/64
Trumbo, Emma Virginia died 01/10/62 01/11/62
Trumbo, F. Augustus died 03/05/65 07/31/65
Trumbo, John Hennings died 06/24/65 06/26/65
Trumbo, Maria married Murphy, John 07/17/61 07/20/61
Trumbo, Theodore A. died 06/02/61 06/26/61
Trump, Susan H. died 07/27/62 07/29/62
Trundle, James Otho married Dorsey, Elizabeth 02/18/64 02/22/64
Trundle, Mattie J. married Heffner, John T. 04/08/62 04/11/62
Trunk, Josephine married Bayles, Frederick 05/28/63 06/01/63
Truslow, Julietta died 10/31/65 11/03/65
Trust, Edwin H. married Mattingly, Lizzie 03/21/65 03/24/65

Trusty, A. H. married Trives, Rebecca 12/12/65 12/14/65
Trusty, Adelia married Thomas, Charles W. 10/27/63 11/03/63
Trusty, Charles N. died 12/24/61 12/25/61
Trusty, Henrietta E. married Gordon, George 04/07/63 05/02/63
Trusty, Robert married Johnson, Maria 11/11/63 11/24/63
Trusty, William Henry died 03/31/65 04/01/65
Tubman, Maria A. married McCullogh, J. Haines, (M.D.) 06/03/62 06/04/6
Tubman, Nettie married Waters, R. E. 05/03/64 05/04/64
Tubman, Richard W. died 11/13/63 12/09/63
Tubman, Robert F. (Dr.) died 12/30/64 01/12/65
Tucker, Ann Maria died 12/23/61 12/25/61
Tucker, Anna Maria died 12/23/61 12/24/61
Tucker, Annie D. married Northup, D. D. Frank 02/15/64 02/19/64
Tucker, Benjamin E. died 11/13/63 11/14/63
Tucker, Bessie died 03/03/64 03/04/64
Tucker, Catherine E. died 07/26/62 08/20/62
Tucker, Charles C. married Evans, M. A. (Mrs.) 11/29/64 11/30/64
Tucker, Cora Belle died 02/11/65 02/13/65
Tucker, Fannie E. married Sellman, John F. 05/25/61 05/29/61
Tucker, Fannie M. married Norfolk, William H. no date 10/22/62
Tucker, Florence E. married Duvall, Charles 06/16/63 06/25/63
Tucker, George W. married James, Hester A. 08/13/62 04/21/65
Tucker, Hennie D. died 09/23/61 10/02/61
Tucker, Henry A. married Welsh, Mary E. 05/07/63 05/09/63
Tucker, James Madison died 07/30/64 08/01/64
Tucker, James, Jr. died 06/29/63 07/01/63
Tucker, Jinnie married Wincks, Wesley 12/11/64 12/16/64
Tucker, John married Wheatley, Ann E. 04/27/65 05/05/65
Tucker, John A. married Jeffries, Lizzie L. 05/11/65 05/20/65
Tucker, John L. married Ritter, J. Rebecca 06/21/65 06/27/65
Tucker, John M. married Atwell, Sarah E. 11/06/64 11/08/64
Tucker, Mary (Mrs.) died 03/24/65 03/29/65
Tucker, Mary E. married Hall, Thomas A. 11/24/64 12/01/64
Tucker, Mary J. married Jones, P. T. W. 02/14/61 02/18/61
Tucker, Mary L. married Woodward, Frank M. 10/27/65 11/01/65
Tucker, Mollie G. married Clagett, J. Thomas 11/09/65 11/11/65
Tucker, Rachel Ann married Mathoit, Augustus G. 11/28/65 12/01/65
Tucker, Sarah died 03/12/64 03/14/64
Tucker, Susan R. married Duyer, Albert 01/02/65 01/11/65
Tucker, Susanna G. married Hugg, Benjamin F. 04/12/64 04/15/64
Tucker, Thomas died 07/01/63 07/04/63
Tucker, William died 09/02/64 09/03/64
Tucker, William died 12/07/65 12/12/65
Tucker, William A. died 01/05/63 01/06/63
Tucker, William B. married Greenwell, Alethia 11/28/63 12/03/63
Tucker, William C. married Smallwood, Harriet 10/03/64 10/04/64
Tuckers, Sallie S. married Buck, William H. 03/17/64 03/22/64
Tuckey, Mary L. married Graham, George R. (Cpt.) 10/09/62 10/14/62
Tudor, John W. married Thompson, Elizabeth A. 03/02/65 05/23/65
Tuell, Margaret E. married Wilkinson, Joseph 02/20/62 03/21/62
Tuer, Thomas married Heaps, Annie Rebecca 05/23/65 05/25/65
Tull, Caroline E. W. (Mrs.) died 07/31/63 08/03/63
Tull, J. Emory (Dr.) married Freeman, Lizzie L. 03/02/65 03/04/65
Tull, Richard C. married Works, Mary J. 04/10/65 04/12/65
Tulley, Alexander Jacob died 01/29/65 01/30/65

Tulley, Anney died 07/06/64   07/07/64
Tully, Charles E. married Chester, Sarah E. 05/08/64   06/07/64
Tully, Kate died 09/10/65   09/11/65
Tumbleson, William T. married Clabaugh, Emma 08/30/65   11/02/65
Tumblinson, William died 04/26/63   04/27/63
Tumblinson, William, Sr. died 04/26/63   04/28/63
Tumblison, Samuel Ready died 01/28/63   01/29/63
Tumey, Mary married Sheesley, Daniel 01/23/61   01/25/61
Tumoney, Anne (Mrs.) died 10/30/65   10/31/65
Tunis, Emma M. married Codd, Edward J. 05/31/65   06/30/65
Tunis, Georgie married Tall, Anthony 08/02/64   08/03/64
Tunnay, Julia died 09/04/64   09/05/64
Tupper, Eliza P. died 09/24/65   10/04/65
Tupper, Lewis B. died 05/27/65   06/05/65
Turbett, George W. died 11/08/64   11/09/64
Turfield, Mary died 11/13/62   11/22/62
Turk, Maggie J. married Foy, Isaac William 08/20/63   08/26/63
Turnbull, Duncan M. died 01/27/64   01/28/64
Turnbull, S. Graeme died 03/29/63   04/23/63
Turner, Adda Z. died 09/18/64   09/19/64
Turner, Alice married Little, Robert P. 03/19/63   03/21/63
Turner, Ann (Mrs.) died 01/28/63   01/30/63
Turner, Ann B. died 04/08/64   04/11/64
Turner, Anna M. married Hicks, Samuel 10/20/64   10/21/64
Turner, Belle married Stinchcomb, William W. 12/12/65   12/18/65
Turner, Charles C. died 03/04/61   03/06/61
Turner, Charles Ellsworth died 12/21/62   12/22/62
Turner, Charlotte (Mrs.) died 07/23/63   07/24/63
Turner, Edward Wilder died 08/23/64   09/03/64
Turner, Elizabeth died 04/01/61   04/03/61
Turner, Elizabeth died 11/18/61   11/19/61
Turner, Francis M. died 11/18/65   12/06/65
Turner, George married Bond, Caroline 06/09/61   06/11/61
Turner, George died 12/22/65   12/23/65
Turner, George died 12/22/65   12/25/65
Turner, George W. married Renner, Elizabeth 04/10/61   04/13/61
Turner, George W. married Marryman, Eleanor J. 10/27/64   10/31/64
Turner, Georgeanna died 02/06/61   02/07/61
Turner, Georgeanna died 02/06/61   02/08/61
Turner, Harriet Rebecca married Tippett, William C. 12/15/64   12/16/64
Turner, Helen V. married Smith, Elliah P. 01/12/64   01/14/64
Turner, Humphrey M. married Warfield, Francis E. 03/12/63   03/20/63
Turner, James died 06/02/65   06/03/65
Turner, James (Hon.) died 03/28/61   03/30/61
Turner, James Henry died 01/04/63   01/06/63
Turner, James P. married Bailey, Emeline 05/17/63   05/19/63
Turner, John died 10/03/62   10/04/62
Turner, John D. (Cpt.) died 09/06/64   09/07/64
Turner, John Hanson died 09/20/64   09/22/64
Turner, John O. (Cpt.) died 09/05/64   09/06/64
Turner, Juliet died 01/27/61   01/29/61
Turner, Kate M. married Keenan, Daniel 01/15/65   10/05/65
Turner, Laura Jane married St. John, Frederick 05/14/65   05/23/65
Turner, Lily Ashley died 04/27/63   04/28/63
Turner, Lily Ashley died 04/27/63   04/29/63

Turner, Lucy Virginia died 08/06/61 08/08/61
Turner, Lydia (Mrs.) died 11/13/65 11/16/65
Turner, Margaret (Mrs.) died 09/09/64 09/10/64
Turner, Margaret Christiana married Stapleton, Edward 05/04/63 05/07/6
Turner, Marion married Brown, Edward 10/01/61 11/06/61
Turner, Martha (Mrs.) died 08/06/64 08/08/64
Turner, Mary A. married Mitchell, William T. 03/28/65 04/04/65
Turner, Mary Louisa died 01/11/63 01/13/63
Turner, Mathew H. married Wonn, Susan 04/29/62 05/06/62
Turner, Matilda married Burchall, William 09/02/62 09/29/62
Turner, Matilda died 08/31/65 09/02/65
Turner, Mollie F. married Stewart, George F. 05/12/63 05/15/63
Turner, Rebecca (Mrs.) died 03/15/64 03/16/64
Turner, Rebecca (Mrs.) died 03/15/64 03/17/64
Turner, Richard M. married Sands, Mary 10/28/64 11/01/64
Turner, Rosabelle died 09/09/63 09/12/63
Turner, Samuel George died 08/08/61 08/09/61
Turner, Sarah E. married Davis, Edward 10/22/65 10/27/65
Turner, Susan Rebecca died 10/17/65 10/19/65
Turner, Susanna H. married Toy, Thomas B. 05/05/61 01/18/65
Turner, Susie J. married Klinefelter, Victor H. 12/15/64 12/17/64
Turner, Thomas Shirley died 10/29/65 10/31/65
Turner, Thomas T. married Brown, Harriet S. 10/10/65 10/11/65
Turner, Walter B. married Lowthers, Emma S. 09/15/64 09/16/64
Turner, William married Woodbridge, Eliza 07/09/61 07/19/61
Turner, William J. married Crise, Josie E. 01/19/65 01/20/65
Turpin, Joshua C. died 08/04/65 08/05/65
Tustin, Clara E. married Brecht, Ernest F. 07/06/64 07/09/64
Tustin, Clara E. married Brecht, Ernest F. R. 07/06/64 07/11/64
Tutcheon, Theodore married Goodwin, Emma Jane 11/10/64 11/15/64
Tutell, Richard S. died 01/21/63 01/23/63
Tuttle, Ellie Florence died 04/03/63 04/04/63
Tuttle, Joseph H. married Marriott, Mary 01/14/63 01/23/63
Tuttle, Joseph W. (Sgt.) married Mariott, Mary J. 01/14/63 01/20/63
Tuttle, Marian V. married Cole, William H. 06/19/65 06/20/65
Tuttle, Robert Morris died 06/11/64 06/14/64
Tuttle, Samuel Davidson died 09/23/62 09/26/62
Tuttle, William N. died 06/17/64 06/18/64
Tuxford, Mary A. married Fullum, James 01/15/63 01/23/63
Tuxford, Mary Ann married Fullum, James 01/18/63 01/20/63
Tuxworth, Anna E. married Gaddess, Virginius 12/13/64 12/17/64
Tuxworth, Laura V. married Davenport, Charles E. 06/14/64 06/20/64
Twaddle, Jennie married Trine, William H. 07/07/64 08/13/64
Tweedale, James died 09/06/64 09/07/64
Twiford, Harry Hoffman died 11/07/63 11/09/63
Twiford, Mary D. (Mrs.) died 09/14/63 09/16/63
Twigg, Thomas died 07/27/63 07/29/63
Twilly, Mary Elizabeth married Smyser, Emanuel D. 06/04/61 06/07/61
Twining, D. H. married Baynes, Alice P. 12/14/65 12/16/65
Twynham, Ann (Mrs.) died 09/07/65 09/11/65
Tydings, Hannah Ann married Kirby, Richard Henry 10/10/61 10/29/61
Tydings, Richard died 10/03/65 10/12/65
Tyler, Columbus M. married Waterton, Sarah A. 02/25/64 03/04/64
Tyler, Daniel M. married Brooks, Lizzie Anthony 09/02/62 09/05/62
Tyler, G. B. (Gen.) married Cassard, Emily 11/21/65 11/24/65

Tyler, George G. married Goodenow, Sophia W. 10/18/65 10/21/65
Tyler, George T. married Taylor, Amanda A. 04/27/65 05/01/65
Tyler, Lucy B. married Hoopes, Edwin O. 11/20/62 11/26/62
Tyler, R. Bradley (Dr.) married Brengle, E. Jane 11/15/65 11/30/65
Tyler, Rachel died 02/19/61 02/21/61
Tylor, James W. married Wilhelm, Annie E. 11/01/65 11/08/65
Tyman, Denis died 08/19/62 08/20/62
Tysinger, Margaret Virginia died 01/09/62 01/16/62
Tysinger, William E. died 08/30/62 01/12/63
Tyson, Anne married Kirk, William 06/11/61 06/12/61
Tyson, Henry G. married White, Maggie 04/07/63 04/21/63
Tyson, Isaac died 01/30/64 02/01/64
Tyson, Isaac, Jr. died 11/24/61 11/26/61
Tyson, James E. married Simms, Matilda A. 12/06/64 12/08/64
Tyson, John S. married Roberts, Mary 02/02/65 02/07/65
Tyson, John S., Sr. died 10/03/64 10/04/64
Tyson, Robert married Gambrill, Janie 06/04/63 06/06/63
Tyte, Charles Frederick died 11/29/62 12/01/62
Udderzook, William E. married Stewart, Clara L. (Mrs.) 10/17/65
    10/18/65
Uhel, Kate married Wald, Henry E. 10/19/62 10/22/62
Uhl, Andrew died 06/07/64 06/09/64
Uhl, Catherine died 11/11/61 11/12/61
Uhl, Emma Grace died 12/31/61 01/01/62
Uhl, Francis Edward died 07/15/63 07/16/63
Uhl, Lewis died 05/08/62 05/09/62
Uhler, John R. married Ridgely, Eliza 04/19/64 04/21/64
Uhler, John R. (Dr.) married Hamilton, Eliza R. 04/19/64 04/20/64
Uhler, Sarah A. married Elliott, William H. 12/26/65 12/30/65
Uhlhorn, Eliza Jane (Mrs.) died 10/15/64 10/17/64
Uhlhorn, Francis A. married Jordan, Johnna 12/26/61 12/27/61
Uhlhorn, Francis A. died no date 03/31/65
Uhlhorn, Francis A. died 03/30/65 04/01/65
Ulery, E. G. married Houseman, Laura A. 03/19/61 03/26/61
Ulery, Effie died 07/13/64 07/14/64
Ullrich, Ernest William died 08/10/65 08/11/65
Ulm, Elizabeth married Froakman, William 08/26/64 08/27/64
Ulman, Jacob B. died 04/20/64 04/23/64
Ulman, Jacob B. died 04/20/64 04/25/64
Ulrich, Augusta Cecelia married Hack, William A. 10/08/63 10/13/63
Ulrich, Ferdinand A. A. died 08/10/63 08/11/63
Umbaugh, Elizabeth Ellener died 04/16/61 04/18/61
Umbrage, Annie died 02/25/64 02/26/64
Umbrage, Joseph married Brady, Catharine 04/06/63 04/13/63
Umstattd, Richard S. married Austin, Frances Ellen 01/06/63 01/08/63
Uncles, Ann (Mrs.) died 10/07/65 10/09/65
Uncles, Isaac married Plummer, Rebecca 11/14/61 12/14/61
Underhill, Esther A. married Pridgeon, John 11/07/65 11/09/65
Underwood, Albert died 08/25/64 08/26/64
Underwood, Enoch died 02/19/64 02/26/64
Underwood, George W. married Switzer, Susannah 11/18/64 11/22/64
Underwood, James Bryan died 05/22/63 05/26/63
Underwood, Louisa (Mrs.) died 02/25/63 02/27/63
Underwood, M. S. married Reynolds, William H. 11/08/65 11/16/65
Underwood, Mary Ann died 11/04/65 11/09/65

Underwood, Robert N. died 12/15/64 12/17/64
Underwood, Sallie C. married Downs, William H. 05/12/64 05/16/64
Underwood, Sallie C. married Downs, William H. 05/12/64 05/20/64
Underwood, Sarah F. married Irving, Edward 01/19/65 01/27/65
Underwood, Sarah Virginia died 07/15/64 07/16/64
Unduch, Annie Amelia died 09/11/61 09/12/61
Uniack, Edward M. married Moulton, M. Annie 01/12/63 01/15/63
Uniack, J. D. Moulton died 03/04/65 03/06/65
Uniack, John J. married Moulton, Minnie M. 04/24/61 04/26/61
Uniack, Minnie Moulton died 07/12/65 07/13/65
Unkle, Sallie R. married Wise, James A. 04/09/61 04/23/61
Upperman, John died 09/23/65 09/25/65
Upperman, Laura V. married Leonard, John W. R. 04/08/63 06/08/63
Upperman, Thomas married Bowman, Mary E. 02/18/64 02/23/64
Uptherhither, Louis died 03/29/64 04/01/64
Usher, Sarah died 07/14/63 07/16/63
Uthman, Frederick W. died 01/08/64 10/21/64
Uthman, Gertrude died 01/15/63 01/16/64
Vail, John K. married Johnson, Louisa A. 10/22/65 10/25/65
Vain, George Lawrence died 12/31/60 01/02/61
Vain, Margaret died 01/11/62 01/13/62
Vaine, Caroline Busk died 09/12/63 09/15/63
Valen, Francina T. married Breck, Charles J. 01/03/64 01/08/64
Valentine, John died 10/29/61 10/31/61
Valentine, Susan A. married Norwood, B. R. 02/01/63 02/05/63
Valiant, Charles A. died 06/30/64 07/01/64
Valiant, Henry Nicholas died 06/26/65 06/27/65
Valiant, James B. married Gardner, Mary L. 03/28/64 04/02/64
Valiant, Lavinia Bell married Bayleys, Samuel Smith (Cpt.) 02/16/63 02/20/63
Valintine, John Henry married Smith, Ellen 09/17/61 09/18/61
Vallee, Francis died 09/28/63 09/30/63
Van Bibber, Abraham died 02/12/61 02/15/61
Van Bokkelen, Bertha died 01/25/63 01/26/63
Van Daniker, Joseph married Garvey, Rose E. 06/14/65 07/04/65
Van Daniker, William died 05/16/65 05/20/65
Van Horn, Harrie Cooper died 03/11/65 03/13/65
Van Horn, William Henry died 12/14/65 12/15/65
Van Horn, William Henry died 12/14/65 12/16/65
Van Meter, Sallie E. married Frames, James F. 07/02/61 07/04/61
Van Meter, Thomas Hurley died 02/04/63 02/06/63
Van Ness, Eugene (Lt. Col.) died 05/28/62 05/30/62
Van Ness, Laura M. married Stuart, Eugene 01/01/63 01/27/63
Van Ness, Matilda E. died 11/14/63 11/16/63
Van Newkirk, Mary E. married Peregoy, William E. no date 03/10/63
Van Pelt, James Franklin died 11/13/64 11/28/64
Van Rensalaer, John J. married Taylor, Florence 10/20/64 10/21/64
Van Rensselaer, Eugene married Pendlton, Sally Boyd 04/26/65 04/28/65
Van Seggern, Mary Elizabeth died 09/24/65 09/28/65
Van Tromp, Annie Murray died 03/01/65 03/03/65
Van Tromp, Margaret Ann died 04/24/65 04/25/65
Van Tromp, Willie died 08/05/62 08/06/62
Van Zelst, Lemuel F. died 09/23/65 09/25/65
Vanbill, James Watt died 08/06/61 08/07/61
Vance, George T. died 04/12/64 05/09/64

Vance, Joseph L. married Ball, Sarah L. 07/31/65 08/14/65
Vancourt, Annie Virginia died 12/13/65 12/15/65
Vancourt, John W. married Hatton, Annie M. 01/23/62 02/07/62
Vandaniker, Kate married Little, William B. 05/02/64 05/06/64
Vandaniker, William Ridgeley died 01/25/63 01/26/63
Vandegrift, Benjamin P. died 05/20/64 05/21/64
Vandegrift, Jane died 01/19/65 01/21/65
Vanderford, William H. died 03/15/62 03/18/62
Vanderkieft, Josephine (Mrs.) died 09/24/65 09/26/65
Vanes, Martha died 01/17/62 01/29/62
Vanhorn, Annie married German, Thomas E. A. 08/15/61 08/17/61
Vanhorn, Fanny A. married Billups, John R. 08/23/64 08/30/64
Vanhorn, James Polk died 03/27/63 03/28/63
Vansant, Charles McCullough died 11/06/64 11/07/64
Vansant, Frank Leroy died 01/07/65 01/09/65
Vansant, J. Wehrly married Meyer, Amelia 05/14/65 05/24/65
Vansant, James G. died 06/12/65 06/13/65
Vansant, James H. married Kimball, Mary E. 11/05/63 11/17/63
Vansant, Margaret Virginia died 11/19/64 11/21/64
Vansant, Matilda died 03/22/61 03/23/61
Vansant, Sarah D. married Lewis, John 09/01/64 09/03/64
Vanvorst, William H. married Dally, Rebecca 06/23/63 07/03/63
Varney, Mitchel J. died 10/25/64 12/02/64
Varnum, John A. M. married Stanford, Maggie J. 08/31/65 09/06/65
Vaugh, Michael died 02/28/64 03/01/64
Vaughan, Daniel died 07/05/65 07/06/65
Vaughan, Kate Agnes died 08/15/64 08/17/64
Vaughan, Martin died 10/20/63 10/21/63
Vaughan, Mary died 07/31/63 08/01/63
Vaughan, Thomas died 07/17/65 07/18/65
Vaughen, Catherine died 06/26/61 06/28/61
Vaughen, William P. married Gibbons, Laura S. 07/07/65 08/30/65
Vaughn, James H. died 01/23/65 01/25/65
Vaughn, Jane died 01/18/65 01/19/65
Veader, Daniel H. married Taylor, Mollie E. 05/16/65 05/18/65
Veara, Mary Jane Bokee died 05/06/63 05/08/63
Veazy, Ellen (Mrs.) died 10/08/63 10/10/63
Veazy, Henry C. married Ward, H. Amanda 03/19/62 03/22/62
Veazy, John died 03/23/62 03/24/62
Veirs, Kate married Cumming, William A. 10/28/62 10/31/62
Veitch, E. R. (Dr.) died 01/20/63 02/11/63
Veitch, Florence died 09/06/64 09/12/64
Vellines, Benton H. married Taylor, Anna Jane 01/01/61 02/19/61
Verdi, Ciro S. (Dr.) married Gordon, Fannie 04/28/63 04/29/63
Verlander, Mary Ellen died 12/23/61 12/25/61
Verlanders, Daniel married Elliott, Mary Ellen 01/01/61 01/28/61
Vermillion, John T. married Burton, Martha C. 12/13/64 12/21/64
Vermilya, James H. married Berlin, Sadie A. 11/23/65 11/28/65
Vermilyn, James H. married Berlin, Sadie A. 11/23/65 11/27/65
Vernay, Anna Elizabeth died 09/18/62 09/29/62
Vernetson, Sue married Carroll, William P. 12/04/61 03/04/62
Verney, John J. married Wright, Elizabeth Ann 03/05/62 03/07/62
Vernon, Ella died 09/16/63 09/22/63
Vest, Lucy A. married Chambers, Robert M. 12/07/65 12/23/65
Vezey, Ann (Mrs.) died 03/01/63 03/02/63

Vick, Bushrod Washington died 10/25/64   01/21/65
Vickers, Charles Edwin died 12/21/63   12/22/63
Vickers, Charles Edwin died 12/21/63   12/23/63
Vickers, Clement died 02/15/64   02/25/64
Vickers, Emma married Childs, George W. 10/30/62   10/31/62
Vickers, Emma married Childs, George W. 10/30/62   11/01/62
Vickers, Emma married Childs, George W. 10/30/62   11/03/62
Vickers, Emma Virginia Reece died 05/15/64   05/31/64
Vickers, George Jefferson died 05/01/64   05/03/64
Vickers, Hamilton R. married Strein, Mary E. 01/20/63   01/23/63
Vickers, Henrietta married Baldwin, Charles E. 04/05/64   04/06/64
Vickers, James Albert died 05/04/65   05/06/65
Vickers, James M. died 05/08/62   05/21/62
Vickers, Jenny Louisa died 12/07/61   12/09/61
Vickers, John married Crem, Sarah C. 12/24/62   01/05/63
Vickers, Joseph died 12/10/64   01/03/65
Vickers, Leroy died 10/15/64   10/17/64
Vickers, Margaret E. died 05/12/62   05/21/62
Vickers, Mary A. married Parsons, L. 12/13/64   12/15/64
Vickers, Mary Agnes died 01/24/63   01/26/63
Vickers, Mary Virginia married Bennett, David 01/07/64   01/14/64
Vickers, Thomas W. died 07/30/61   08/16/61
Vickers, William George died 03/20/63   03/21/63
Victoire, Mary married Machrill, William Richardson 03/29/65   03/30/65
Victoria, Catherine married Hill, John Thomas 04/05/64   04/14/64
Viese, John married Ferguson, Catherine Ann 11/16/65   10/21/65
Vigans, Maria Theresa married Sugden, George 06/03/62   06/06/62
Vincent, David Brown died 04/16/61   04/18/61
Vincent, Lucy Ann died 08/06/62   08/08/62
Vincent, Thomas B. married Bennett, Helen 11/03/63   07/07/64
Vincent, William died 09/17/62   09/18/62
Vincent, William Henry died 12/05/61   12/06/61
Vincent, William T. married Willig, S. A. 11/24/63   12/04/63
Vinger, Charlie died 11/09/64   11/11/64
Vinkier, Adaline died 10/16/64   10/17/64
Vinkier, Adaline died 10/16/64   10/18/64
Vinkler, Jane (Mrs.) died 07/29/64   07/30/64
Vinsant, Margaret H. (Mrs.) died 04/30/64   05/02/64
Vinson, Annie married Shew, Harry 07/30/62   09/10/62
Vinson, Catharine died 12/10/64   12/13/64
Vinson, Catharine Ann died 10/27/65   11/01/65
Vinson, Forresta died 06/22/64   06/23/64
Vinson, Samuel J. died 10/11/63   10/12/63
Vinton, Catharine Virginia died 08/14/62   08/16/62
Vinton, Harriet A. married Pippin, Solomon 12/19/65   12/27/65
Virtue, A. M. married Blondel, Emma J. 11/16/62   01/10/63
Virtue, Sackwood D. married McNew, Eliza Ellen 08/14/64   09/17/64
Visher, John died 08/20/65   08/21/65
Voegele, Eva Margaretta died 06/28/61   07/02/61
Voegler, Willie died 04/24/63   04/27/63
Vogelesang, Charles died 07/07/64   07/08/64
Vogeley, George B. married McCadden, Lizzie R. 11/16/65   11/27/65
Vogelgesang, Jacob died 02/14/64   02/15/64
Vogelsang, Jacob died 11/14/65   11/15/65
Vogt, John Henry died 07/09/65   07/12/65

Vogt, Rebecca Dorothea died 04/20/64   04/21/64
Voight, Katharine died 09/09/64   09/10/64
Volk, William John died 07/16/64   07/18/64
Volka, Mary Catherine died 05/22/63   05/23/63
Volker, Elizabeth married Hoffmeister, John 10/20/63   10/22/63
Volker, Elizabeth (Mrs.) died 04/23/64   04/25/64
Volkman, Henry C. married Sinclair, Laura F. 04/02/61   04/05/61
Volkmar, Henry J. died 08/14/65   08/15/65
Vollandt, Christian died no date   10/26/65
Vollow, William H. married Emerson, Sophia Elizabeth 03/29/64   04/07/64
Von Hein, George James died 11/04/64   11/10/64
Von Lingen, George A. married Webb, Alba H. 03/09/65   03/14/65
Von Lombines, D. Carbacies died 10/23/64   10/25/64
Von Santen, Johanna married Montgomery, James 06/24/65   06/30/65
Von Trobler, Henry Graf (Lt.) married Chenowith, Elleanor D. 05/23/65   05/27/65
Vonderhorst, John H. died 08/12/63   08/13/63
Vondersmith, Eliza (Mrs.) died 02/21/64   02/23/64
Vondersmith, Julia W. died 07/29/65   08/04/65
Vondersmith, Julia W. died no date   08/08/65
Vondersmith, Lizzie died 07/16/63   07/18/63
Vondersmith, Samuel Fleming died 01/12/65   01/13/65
Voshell, Gertrude married Kleff, Arnold 01/26/64   01/27/64
Voss, Charles (Lt.) died 05/24/63   09/17/63
Voss, Louisa A. married Brecht, Theodore C. 06/12/62   06/17/62
Vowel, John D. died 11/30/62   12/13/62
Voyce, George W. died 11/12/65   11/13/65
Wachsmuth, Sophia died 02/02/63   02/04/63
Waddell, Isabella married Gibbons, William J. T. 11/18/64   11/19/64
Waddy, Clarissa E. died 09/30/61   10/01/61
Waddy, Mary A. married Gibson, Ishmael H. 11/03/64   11/05/64
Wade, B. L. married Gross, S. L. 03/13/63   09/03/63
Wade, Larkin died 07/04/65   07/06/65
Wade, Laura Jane died 11/10/63   12/02/63
Wade, Laura Jane died 11/10/63   12/03/63
Wade, R. B. (Cpt.) died 06/12/62   09/17/62
Waer, Elizabeth married Richards, John T. 03/05/61   03/07/61
Waerham, John married Mitchell, Elisha 11/10/61   11/23/61
Waerham, John N. married Mitchell, Anna M. 11/10/61   11/19/61
Waesche, Frederick R. died 07/31/64   08/01/64
Wager, Ellen A. (Mrs.) died 09/22/64   09/29/64
Waggner, Charles Henry married Setten, Roseanna 10/10/62   10/17/62
Waggner, George died 09/19/62   09/20/62
Waggner, George W. G. died 10/25/64   10/27/64
Waggner, Mary A. died 12/09/65   12/11/65
Waggner, Mollie died 09/19/64   10/27/64
Wagner, George W. died 12/21/65   12/27/65
Wagner, Amelia S. married Wattenscheidt, Ewald 12/14/65   12/21/65
Wagner, B. Lansing married Myers, Alice 10/13/63   10/21/63
Wagner, Bertha died 06/02/62   06/03/62
Wagner, Catherine died 01/04/65   01/06/65
Wagner, Charles Henry married Setten, Roseanna 10/10/62   10/16/62
Wagner, Ella G. died 12/31/62   01/03/63
Wagner, Emma married Long, John 04/06/63   04/08/63
Wagner, Evelyn died 02/19/65   02/21/65

Wagner, George J. married Green, Lizzie E. 09/11/60 07/15/61
Wagner, George, Jr. died 05/05/63 05/07/63
Wagner, Henry died 03/06/65 03/08/65
Wagner, Henry C. married Small, Sallie 07/08/65 07/11/65
Wagner, J. Dolly died 08/11/65 08/14/65
Wagner, John married Fales, Bettie 07/16/63 08/17/63
Wagner, John married Kienzle, Sophia E. 06/26/64 06/28/64
Wagner, John married Smith, Anna Maria 04/28/64 05/04/64
Wagner, John S. (1st Lt.) died 06/23/64 08/30/64
Wagner, Kate married Scherer, Leonard 01/18/63 01/21/63
Wagner, Maria M. died 10/01/63 10/02/63
Wagner, Mollie A. died 09/19/64 09/21/64
Wagonfield, Frederick married Hamilton, Margaret Jane 05/12/62 05/23/6
Wahl, Annie V. married Benzinger, Joseph C. (Dr.) 09/27/65 09/29/65
Wahl, August died 07/06/62 07/08/62
Waicher, George died 12/13/62 12/15/62
Waicher, George died 12/13/62 12/16/62
Waidner, Catherine A. (Mrs.) died 06/13/64 06/14/64
Waidner, Franklin died 08/20/65 08/22/65
Waidner, John Jacob married Hummer, Cassandra 03/19/61 03/21/61
Waiiz, Henry F. married Phillips, Kate 10/12/62 10/30/62
Wain, Elizabeth A. married Russell, George W. 12/19/65 12/21/65
Wain, George H. died 06/29/65 06/30/65
Wain, George H. died 06/29/65 07/03/65
Wain, George H. (USA) married Rumney, Emily J. 11/26/63 11/28/63
Wain, Sarah Ann died 07/27/64 07/28/64
Wain, William L. married Rosmoser, Mary E. 11/07/61 11/13/61
Wainwright, Elizabeth A. married White, John R. 04/30/63 06/02/63
Wainwright, Martha Virginia died 10/25/63 10/26/63
Wainwright, Thomas K. G. died 08/27/65 08/29/65
Wait, Charles died 09/19/64 09/21/64
Wait, Richard B. died 12/19/64 12/20/64
Waite, Carey H. died 08/13/63 08/18/63
Waite, Lizzie (Mrs.) died 10/24/64 10/26/64
Waite, Louisa Brett O. died 02/08/62 02/10/62
Waite, Richard B. died 10/03/62 10/04/62
Waite, Richard B. died 12/19/64 12/21/64
Waite, Samuel Brett died 10/02/61 10/03/61
Waite, William Henry died 04/07/62 04/08/62
Waits, John Edwin died 02/27/64 02/29/64
Waizl, Henrietta died 10/10/65 10/13/65
Wake, Ella Virginia died 01/16/63 01/20/63
Wakeland, Rebecca A. married Diffenderfer, Joseph T. 01/13/61 01/22/61
Wakely, James died 02/03/63 02/05/63
Walace, Mary F. (Mrs.) died 05/26/64 05/28/64
Walcott, Orville D. married Gardner, Nellie 10/25/64 05/30/65
Wald, Henry E. married Uhel, Kate 10/19/62 10/22/62
Waldanl, Rachel married Baer, Abraham 11/13/64 11/19/64
Walderford, Mary C. died 07/20/65 07/28/65
Waldin, Frederick A. died 09/06/61 09/09/61
Waldman, William H. died 07/04/65 07/06/65
Waldmann, Clara died 02/28/61 03/01/61
Waldron, N. Sheafe died 01/04/64 01/05/64
Waldschmith, Lewis married McElroy, Mary J. no date 12/28/63
Wales, Daphney died 04/16/64 04/18/64

Wales, James Thomas died 02/11/64 04/28/64
Wales, Philip S. died 10/17/62 10/20/62
Wales, Wesley married Robb, Rosannia 03/26/65 03/30/65
Walk, Kate married Thomas, John Monkur 01/05/65 01/05/65
Walker, Alexander died 12/26/64 12/28/64
Walker, Alice married Keyser, William W. 06/13/64 06/14/64
Walker, Amelia Jane married Collins, Robert 02/06/62 02/08/62
Walker, Ann Eliza died 09/26/62 09/27/62
Walker, Annie Beel died 11/24/64 11/29/64
Walker, Catherine died 11/01/65 11/08/65
Walker, Elizabeth died 05/30/63 06/05/63
Walker, Elizabeth H. married Mountgarety, William Thomas 09/08/63 09/28/63
Walker, Ella Lee died 01/24/65 02/16/65
Walker, Emily (Mrs.) died 08/05/65 08/07/65
Walker, Fanny A. married Chairs, William B. 05/06/62 05/15/62
Walker, Francis died 06/27/64 06/29/64
Walker, George F. married Elliott, Laura H. 11/27/62 12/01/62
Walker, Harriet A. married George, William F. 04/28/64 06/21/64
Walker, Helena K. married Armstrong, R. D. 04/30/62 05/02/62
Walker, John F. died 03/29/64 03/30/64
Walker, John Henry died 03/17/61 03/18/61
Walker, John N. died 10/31/64 11/01/64
Walker, John Weley died 12/26/63 12/28/63
Walker, Joseph died 04/30/61 05/02/61
Walker, Joshua died 10/08/64 10/11/64
Walker, Kinsey L. died 11/16/60 02/13/61
Walker, Leonard R. married Cusick, Adolpha E. 01/11/65 01/13/65
Walker, Louisa married Ewalt, John H. 02/16/65 02/20/65
Walker, Lovey (Mrs.) died 09/19/64 09/21/64
Walker, Margaret R. (Mrs.) married Welch, Henry 10/05/65 10/07/65
Walker, Mary died 01/20/63 01/21/63
Walker, Mary A. married Ken, Jason 09/01/64 10/01/64
Walker, Mary Ann died 01/11/64 01/12/64
Walker, Mary Elizabeth died 01/05/62 01/06/62
Walker, Mary Isabella died 02/17/61 02/19/61
Walker, R. H. married Mitchell, M. E. 07/05/60 02/05/61
Walker, Rachel married Brevitt, Joseph W. 12/02/62 12/06/62
Walker, Richard died 08/05/61 08/07/61
Walker, Richard died 01/20/64 01/21/64
Walker, Richard B. died 11/22/62 11/24/62
Walker, S. D. died 07/12/63 07/13/63
Walker, Samuel died 12/03/65 12/04/65
Walker, Samuel died 12/03/65 12/05/65
Walker, Sarah B. died 02/23/61 02/25/61
Walker, Sarah Catherine married Mowbray, Martin L. 02/16/64 02/19/64
Walker, Sarah Lavinia married McCarty, Peyton L. 03/25/63 03/28/63
Walker, Sarah O. married Doud, Oliver B. 05/07/63 05/25/63
Walker, Sarah Olivia married Doud, Oliver B. 05/07/63 05/26/63
Walker, Thomas H. married Brown, Charlotte C. 03/12/62 04/14/62
Walker, Thomas S. married Earhart, Hadie M. 04/21/64 04/22/64
Walker, Thomas W. died 09/30/62 10/27/62
Walker, Virginia married Lomax, William H. 04/26/64 05/19/64
Wall, A. J. married Brunfield, Nathan 11/16/65 11/24/65

Wall, Alice Harrington died 10/05/61 10/09/61
Wall, Charles A. married McLaughlin, Fannie 11/05/65 11/15/65
Wall, Jane O. married Carr, Uriah 11/16/65 11/24/65
Wall, John married Mercer, Leanna 10/19/65 10/23/65
Wall, Jude Kyle married Ford, Sample (Dr.) 10/05/64 10/06/64
Wall, Laura N. died 07/19/65 07/21/65
Wall, Mary (Mrs.) died 07/27/63 07/28/63
Wall, Michael died 01/28/61 01/30/61
Wall, Olin M. married Fairbank, Virginia 06/27/64 06/29/64
Wall, Robert A. died 11/01/61 11/02/61
Wall, Ruth died 01/25/62 02/03/62
Wallace, Amelia Ann married Bias, John W. 06/05/62 06/07/62
Wallace, Andrew J. married Gorden, Harriet A. 10/16/62 10/29/62
Wallace, Charles H. married Grimes, Mary Ann 08/08/64 08/25/64
Wallace, Charles Henry died 08/16/63 08/17/63
Wallace, Daniel married Wilson, Ann 05/29/62 05/30/62
Wallace, David died 05/23/64 05/24/64
Wallace, Elizabeth died 02/03/62 02/05/62
Wallace, Emily died 01/16/61 01/18/61
Wallace, Helen died 01/13/65 02/06/65
Wallace, Helen died 01/13/65 02/06/65
Wallace, Hugh M. married Cross, Sarah M. 05/26/64 06/03/64
Wallace, James died 03/25/63 03/27/63
Wallace, James E. married Quinn, Sarah A. 04/23/62 01/19/63
Wallace, John Murray died 08/31/65 09/04/65
Wallace, Marrion married White, Horace D. 11/16/64 11/22/64
Wallace, Mary married Pratt, Benjamin 05/24/63 05/26/63
Wallace, Mary Elizabeth died 06/19/64 06/20/64
Wallace, Mary Kay (Mrs.) died 01/09/64 01/15/64
Wallace, Mattie Crawford married Wilcox, Lewis E. 04/07/63 04/11/63
Wallace, Mollie A. married Michael, Jacob D. 06/14/64 06/15/64
Wallace, Sarah E. married Strong, Augustus R. 01/25/61 01/31/61
Wallace, Thomas A. died 02/04/65 02/09/65
Wallace, William Frank died 05/31/63 06/01/63
Wallace, William H. married Lake, Mary Francis 04/18/61 05/01/61
Wallace, William T. married Morris, Adeline R. 08/03/63 08/05/63
Wallaes, Willie Thomas died 01/19/63 01/20/63
Wallaes, John V. married Dahl, Louisa 06/15/62 06/19/62
Wallenstein, Solomon married Reichenberger, Dinah 03/23/62 03/25/62
Waller, Annie H. married Evans, George W. (Cpt.) 04/18/64 04/20/64
Waller, William N. (Dr.) married Smith, Anne M. W. 05/28/63 06/16/63
Walling, Jacob married Osborn, America 01/02/65 01/05/65
Wallis, Edward died 01/16/64 01/18/64
Wallis, Edward died 01/16/64 01/19/64
Wallis, John W. died 02/05/65 02/08/65
Wallis, William H. married Cannon, Mary A. 08/13/62 08/27/62
Walmsley, Morris married Milnor, Josephine A. 04/09/63 04/11/63
Wals, Priscilla A. died 08/19/62 08/28/62
Walsh, Catherine died 05/14/63 05/16/63
Walsh, Coza G. married Jenkins, Elizabeth C. 11/03/63 11/07/63
Walsh, Elizabeth (Mrs.) died 03/13/64 03/14/64
Walsh, Ellen (Mrs.) died 05/10/63 05/12/63
Walsh, Harriet T. died 01/25/62 01/28/62
Walsh, Henry E. married Male, Mary E. 10/27/62 11/03/62
Walsh, Henry E. died 08/23/65 08/24/65

```
Walsh, James died 12/04/61   12/17/61
Walsh, James married White, Louisa 07/22/62   07/26/62
Walsh, James Thomas died 10/13/64   10/14/64
Walsh, Kate died 01/03/62   01/04/62
Walsh, Kate died 01/03/62   01/28/62
Walsh, Lawrence died 09/23/61   09/25/61
Walsh, Mary Anne died 08/25/63   08/27/63
Walsh, Patrick Bernard died 08/02/63   08/27/63
Walsh, Thomas Yates died 01/20/65   01/21/65
Walsh, Virginia died 01/16/62   01/18/62
Walsh, Virginia died 01/16/62   01/28/62
Walsh, Washington Grant died 09/09/65   09/11/65
Walsh, William B. died no date   09/14/65
Walsh, William G. died 10/15/61   10/16/61
Walsh, William G. died 10/15/61   10/17/61
Walshum, Rosalia E. died 02/22/65   03/08/65
Walstrom, Charles E. married Hawkins, Mary 12/15/62   01/12/63
Walstrum, Rosalia died 02/22/65   03/09/65
Walstrum, Rosalia E. married Sapp, Joseph 10/25/64   11/01/64
Waltemeyer, Jacob married Sheppard, Josephine B. 02/19/63   02/21/63
Waltemyer, Margaret E. died 07/29/63   07/30/63
Walten, Henry died 07/26/65   07/28/65
Waltenmeyer, John married Williston, Anna E. 03/16/62   10/14/62
Waltenmeyer, Rachel R. married Somerlott, Frederick 04/15/63   05/02/63
Walter, Annie M. married Egan, William J. 04/13/64   04/20/64
Walter, Charles died no date   04/23/62
Walter, Clara married Rubens, Charles 09/11/65   09/12/65
Walter, Frederick Lewis married Dressel, Elizabeth 10/13/63   11/03/63
Walter, Hiram C. died 01/14/63   01/15/63
Walter, Hiram Cochran died 01/14/63   01/19/63
Walter, Jacob died 05/12/65   05/13/65
Walter, Lewis married Jennings, Minnie Ann 05/16/64   05/19/64
Walter, Mary died 08/06/65   08/09/65
Walter, Mary A. married Guire, W. James 12/21/63   12/24/63
Walter, Richard N. died 05/29/64   05/30/64
Walter, Richard N. died 05/29/64   05/31/64
Walter, Sarah E. married Bradley, Wilson 08/30/64   08/31/64
Walter, Thomas married Ashby, Laura A. 04/14/63   04/20/63
Walters, Anna M. married Redman, Adolphus 12/24/61   12/31/61
Walters, Benjamin married Hollifield, Laura R. 02/25/64   03/03/64
Walters, Edward Anderson died 12/14/63   12/16/63
Walters, Ellen died 11/13/62   12/02/62
Walters, Emma E. married Robertson, Henry W. 09/05/65   09/08/65
Walters, George F. died 11/02/65   11/03/65
Walters, J. Blake married Clark, Louisa 06/06/65   06/07/65
Walters, John died 03/13/63   03/20/63
Walters, John W. married Brainard, Virginia E. 01/26/65   01/27/65
Walters, Joseph T. married Galt, Henrietta 09/07/65   09/14/65
Walters, Rebecca Ann died 09/21/65   09/22/65
Walters, Viginia married Brown, Benjamin H. 06/10/62   06/12/62
Walters, William H. (Lieut.) died 12/29/62   12/30/62
Walters, William J. died 01/19/63   01/26/63
Waltham, Maria M. (Mrs.) died 04/23/63   04/24/63
Walther, Georgiana R. died 07/23/63   07/25/63
Waltmeyer, Hester Anne died 05/01/62   05/02/62
```

Walton, Eleanora (Mrs.) died 05/12/64 05/13/64
Walton, Frank married Flanagan, M. J. 06/02/64 06/04/64
Walton, George died 04/09/65 04/10/65
Walton, George W. married Grow, Mary A. 03/29/63 05/02/63
Walton, Mary E. married Bolgiano, Joseph A. 05/28/63 06/01/63
Walton, Mary S. married Thompson, John C. 06/22/65 06/23/65
Walton, T. O. (Dr.) married Hopkins, Kate 01/29/63 02/12/63
Waltz, George died 03/20/64 03/21/64
Waltz, Jacob married Pope, Catharine M. no date 04/08/64
Waltzen, Joseph Francis died 08/30/63 09/02/63
Waltzen, Milton Alonzo died 09/12/64 09/15/64
Walzl, Augustus died 11/13/63 11/18/63
Walzl, John died 08/27/63 09/01/63
Wamsley, Isabella died 03/15/63 06/10/63
Wamsley, Laura J. married Jackson, J. K. P. 06/25/63 07/01/63
Wamsley, Sarah Isabella died 03/15/63 03/17/63
Wamsly, Mary E. died 11/22/65 11/23/65
Wand, Bernard E. married Murphy, Catherine 08/22/63 09/01/63
Wandling, Ellen died 06/16/62 06/21/62
Wands, Alexander Hamilton died 04/14/65 04/20/65
Warburton, Fred J. married Otter, S. Virginia 04/11/65 04/12/65
Ward, Ade Kenly died 12/14/63 12/15/63
Ward, Alexander W. (Cpt.) died 11/18/64 11/22/64
Ward, Anastaztia died 08/01/65 08/02/65
Ward, Ann (Mrs.) died 08/27/63 08/28/63
Ward, Caroline A. M. (Mrs.) died 04/10/63 04/13/63
Ward, Edward married Woddy, Elizabeth 11/10/64 11/12/64
Ward, Edward Hamilton died 11/08/63 11/09/63
Ward, Elizabeth died 08/11/62 08/12/62
Ward, Emily Jane married Derry, James S. 03/06/62 03/08/62
Ward, Emily Josephine died 11/13/61 11/14/61
Ward, Frances Ann married Franklin, Jesse 11/14/61 11/16/61
Ward, H. Amanda married Veazy, Henry C. 03/19/62 03/22/62
Ward, Helena V. married Barker, Joseph H. 04/22/62 04/28/62
Ward, Henry D. died 03/06/64 03/08/64
Ward, Hugh died 07/28/65 08/29/65
Ward, Ida died 11/03/62 11/06/62
Ward, J. Joseph married Weaver, Julia Almira 05/12/63 05/18/63
Ward, James married McDonald, Mary 12/29/61 01/03/62
Ward, James died 01/13/63 01/14/64
Ward, James died 05/02/64 05/03/64
Ward, Jane died 07/21/65 07/22/65
Ward, John died 04/10/62 04/12/62
Ward, John Thomas died 02/09/65 02/11/65
Ward, Joseph Elmer died 02/04/65 02/07/65
Ward, Joseph W. died 11/22/61 11/23/61
Ward, Joshua died 12/07/63 12/19/63
Ward, Kate (Mrs.) died 03/25/65 03/27/65
Ward, Lewis married Nelson, Nancy 02/05/62 03/03/62
Ward, Margaret died 11/07/62 11/08/62
Ward, Margaret (Mrs.) died 12/30/63 12/31/63
Ward, Margaret (Mrs.) married Carmine, Samuel B. 01/25/63 01/27/63
Ward, Margery A. (Mrs.) died 11/09/63 11/14/63
Ward, Maria (Mrs.) died 01/16/63 01/19/63
Ward, Martha married Woodman, John 10/20/63 11/06/63

Ward, Mary (Mrs.) died 11/03/63 11/04/63
Ward, Mary A. married Bennett, G. W. (Lt.) 02/13/62 02/19/62
Ward, Patrick died 02/07/65 02/08/65
Ward, Perry married Clara Henson 10/07/62 10/11/62
Ward, Philip G. W. married Monroe, Laura C. 11/08/64 11/09/64
Ward, Robert F. died 01/10/65 02/23/65
Ward, Ruth died 05/26/65 05/27/65
Ward, Sallie E. married Nomen, William E. 07/28/63 08/03/63
Ward, Sarah (Mrs.) died 02/02/63 08/21/63
Ward, Sarah Louisa died 04/03/64 04/04/64
Ward, Silas Wright died 09/11/63 09/14/63
Ward, Sophia T. married Jones, Samuel George 12/20/64 12/24/64
Ward, Thomas died 11/06/61 11/07/61
Ward, Thomas H. married Fountin, Orpha H. 12/31/61 01/02/62
Ward, Thomas Harold died 08/10/64 08/11/64
Ward, Virginia died 01/20/65 01/24/65
Ward, Virginia I. married Cox, William A. 04/19/64 04/21/64
Ward, William George married Rowe, Margaret Ann 12/12/65 12/14/65
Ward, William H. married Chatard, Kate M. 09/28/63 10/05/63
Wardell, Anne Maria died 12/31/61 01/01/62
Wardell, Catherine Jane (Mrs.) died 01/05/64 01/06/64
Wardell, James Washington died 12/29/61 12/30/61
Wardell, Katie B. died 03/31/65 03/31/65
Wardell, Maggie married Green, Nathan G. B. 01/17/61 01/25/61
Wardell, Maria (Mrs.) died 01/17/63 01/21/63
Wardell, Samuel died 05/02/64 05/03/64
Warden, Jordan died 12/26/64 01/02/65
Warden, Matilda married Weaver, Joseph 10/12/62 10/29/62
Wardenburg, William died 12/19/63 12/21/63
Wardenburg, William died 12/19/63 12/23/63
Ware, Anna M. married Atlee, James 10/27/63 10/29/63
Ware, Caroline C. married Christee, James 12/13/64 02/21/65
Ware, Elias died 11/24/65 11/28/65
Ware, Mary C. married Parrish, John 01/15/63 01/21/63
Wareham, Isaac died 01/22/65 01/23/65
Warfield, Achsah married Disney, G. F. 12/08/63 12/10/63
Warfield, Alexander G. died 06/06/61 06/25/61
Warfield, Ann Eliza married Johnson, Edward 09/03/62 09/06/62
Warfield, Ann M. married Disney, Andrew J. 09/20/63 09/22/63
Warfield, B. G. died 09/04/62 09/10/62
Warfield, Caleb Hersey died 06/20/64 06/21/64
Warfield, Charles A. married Hands, Sarah M. 11/17/64 11/21/64
Warfield, Columbus married Taylor, Emily Rebecca 12/22/63 12/24/63
Warfield, Ellen L. married Haslup, John 11/24/63 12/17/63
Warfield, Francis E. married Turner, Humphrey M. 03/12/63 03/20/63
Warfield, George died 03/24/64 03/25/64
Warfield, John L. married Pumphrey, Adeline R. 12/30/62 01/30/63
Warfield, Joseph died 09/10/63 10/10/63
Warfield, L. A. (Cpt.) died no date 01/16/63
Warfield, L. A. (Cpt.) died no date 01/17/63
Warfield, Lancelot married Baird, Margaret E. 07/05/64 07/12/64
Warfield, Laura E. died 12/15/62 12/18/62
Warfield, Margaret Jane married Jury, Joseph H. 09/15/62 09/17/62
Warfield, Margaret S. married Disney, Wesley 03/26/61 03/30/61
Warfield, Margaretta married Conway, William W. 09/24/65 09/26/65

Warfield, Martha married Currey, James H. (Dr.) 04/23/61 04/26/61
Warfield, Narcissa E. married Wilson, Cornelius 11/21/65 11/24/65
Warfield, Sarah A. died 11/03/62 11/04/62
Warfield, Thomas married Gosnell, Susie 09/27/65 10/14/65
Warfield, Wallace married Traille, Rebecca A. 09/17/63 09/18/63
Waring, Mary died 03/20/61 03/22/61
Waring, Phiania S. died 03/06/62 03/11/62
Waring, Sarah (Mrs.) died 07/01/65 07/03/65
Waring, Sue A. married Gibbond, J. H. S. 10/05/65 10/07/65
Warner, Asa married Hatton, Margaret Ann 02/14/61 02/16/61
Warner, Catherine died 10/23/63 10/24/63
Warner, Clintonia W. married Stork, William L. 11/01/65 11/06/65
Warner, George Cuthbert died 06/30/63 07/02/63
Warner, George K., Jr. died 08/07/64 08/08/64
Warner, George T. died 09/26/64 09/28/64
Warner, Georgeanna died 01/22/63 01/24/63
Warner, Georgie married Woodburn, David E. 11/07/61 11/12/61
Warner, Hellen died 02/27/63 02/28/63
Warner, Ida Evans died 09/27/63 09/28/63
Warner, James H. died 09/29/63 09/30/63
Warner, Joseph P. (Col.) died 09/30/62 10/01/62
Warner, Katey died 09/08/65 09/13/65
Warner, Luther F. married Etchison, Josephine F. 05/29/62 05/31/62
Warner, Maggie V. married King, Samuel R. 10/19/63 11/16/63
Warner, Margaretta died 03/28/64 03/29/64
Warner, Mary R. married Lord, Luther 05/31/65 06/01/65
Warner, Michael, Jr. died 12/04/64 12/06/64
Warner, Michael, Jr. died 12/04/64 12/07/64
Warner, Robert N. married Potter, Malissa M. C. 10/01/63 10/03/63
Warner, William died 05/29/65 05/30/65
Warnick, Caroline M. married Liddel, James E. 03/14/64 05/18/64
Warnick, Jacob T. died 12/29/61 12/30/61
Warnick, William B. married Smith, Kate 05/19/64 05/31/64
Warnken, Henrietta Caroline died 07/04/62 07/15/62
Warnken, Lur died 06/27/65 06/28/65
Warren, David M. died 03/10/61 03/12/61
Warren, Gouverneur K. (USA) married Chase, Emily F. 06/17/63 06/18/63
Warren, Mary married Slaughter, Joel C. 12/14/65 12/23/65
Warren, Mary (Mrs.) died 04/11/63 04/21/63
Warren, Virginia Lester died 07/05/63 07/06/63
Warren, William J. married Simms, Eddie 01/29/61 01/31/61
Warrick, C. (Mrs.) married Bozman, Edward 11/10/64 11/12/64
Warters, I. Dorsey died 09/04/63 09/10/63
Wartman, Edmund W. married Drury, Susan E. (Mrs.) 06/20/61 06/21/61
Wartman, Lawrence died 07/20/64 07/21/64
Wartman, Michael K. died 10/06/65 10/09/65
Warwick, John G. married Lavake, Maria E. 01/05/65 01/06/65
Waseluski, Alfred died 07/03/61 07/12/61
Washborn, Eunice A. married Aler, Sylvanus R. no date 11/06/61
Washburn, Elizabeth T. married Gunnell, Charles E. 07/11/65 07/24/65
Washburn, Elizabeth T. married Grinnell, Charles E. 07/11/65 07/25/65
Washburn, Harry Emerson died 03/18/62 03/19/62
Washington, Eliza married Perine, E. Glenn 04/25/65 04/26/65
Washington, Felix married Hayward, Matilda 01/20/63 01/22/63
Washington, George married Singleton, Mary Ann 06/08/62 06/12/62

Washington, George married Hull, Margaret Jane 11/13/64   11/15/64
Washington, Harriet died 07/22/61   07/24/61
Washington, Isabella married Bishop, George 01/01/63   01/03/63
Washington, James Cunningham died 02/24/65   03/01/65
Washington, James H. died 08/30/65   09/26/65
Washington, Margaret (Mrs.) died 03/15/65   03/17/65
Washington, Martha died 01/23/62   01/25/62
Washington, Mary A. married Keyser, H. Irvine 11/17/64   11/19/64
Washington, Missouri died 07/31/61   08/01/61
Wason, James married Braddock, Laura 02/14/65   02/15/65
Wasson, Wilthia A. married Carter, William J. 04/17/65   08/18/65
Watchman, Ann died 02/22/61   02/23/61
Watchman, George died 04/22/62   04/23/62
Watchman, George died 04/22/62   04/25/62
Watchman, John died 04/11/65   04/12/65
Wate, Elizabeth (Mrs.) died 11/24/64   11/26/64
Waterman, Ann R. died 10/18/61   10/19/61
Waterman, Jane (Mrs.) died 08/27/65   09/05/65
Waters, Andrew G. died 08/08/63   08/10/63
Waters, Andrew G. died 08/08/63   08/11/63
Waters, Benjamin E. married Williams, Elizabeth 05/23/61   05/25/61
Waters, Eliza J. died 07/21/63   07/22/63
Waters, Elizabeth married Chambers, William 06/24/62   06/28/62
Waters, Elizabeth A. married King, George 01/24/64   01/26/64
Waters, Ellen Elvira Kirk died 03/03/64   03/04/64
Waters, George W. died 08/26/63   08/28/63
Waters, Gilbert married Harcum, Ann 03/01/65   03/04/65
Waters, Hattie A. married Cook, Nathan 12/15/63   12/18/63
Waters, Isaac married Maddox, Lucinda 12/11/62   12/23/62
Waters, J. H. (Cpt.) died 12/06/64   12/09/64
Waters, James Neely died 06/13/64   06/15/64
Waters, John married Moore, Rosetta 06/11/63   06/13/63
Waters, John died 10/28/64   11/07/64
Waters, John Summerfield died 07/01/61   07/20/61
Waters, Jonathan (Dr.) died 02/16/63   02/18/63
Waters, Lavenia married Johnson, Charles 07/05/64   07/09/64
Waters, Lizzie J. died 12/11/62   12/12/62
Waters, Mary (Mrs.) died 02/04/65   02/11/65
Waters, Mary (Mrs.) died 02/04/65   02/11/65
Waters, Mary Elizabeth died 07/24/63   07/27/63
Waters, Mary Elverda died 03/15/63   03/18/63
Waters, R. E. married Tubman, Nettie 05/03/64   05/04/64
Waters, Rebecca died 03/19/61   03/22/61
Waters, Richard H. (Rev.) died 12/13/61   12/20/61
Waters, Ruth M. (Mrs.) died 06/09/63   06/10/63
Waters, Sarah R. died 09/10/61   09/18/61
Waters, Susan A. married Cook, William 04/09/61   05/10/61
Waters, Thomas married Dawson, Martha M. 12/06/64   12/30/64
Waters, William died 09/28/64   09/29/64
Waters, William A. (Dr.) married Neel, Mary 01/27/63   02/02/63
Waters, William D. died 10/06/61   10/08/61
Waterton, Sarah A. married Tyler, Columbus M. 02/25/64   03/04/64
Waterworth, Hellen Isabella married Armstrong, Daniel W. 11/16/63
    11/26/63
Waterworth, Thomas J. married McDonald, Ellen F. 11/26/61   12/03/61

Watkins, Ann (Mrs.) died 07/05/65 07/06/65
Watkins, Ann (Mrs.) died 07/05/65 07/07/65
Watkins, Anna Maria died 11/17/64 11/18/64
Watkins, Celinda died 06/23/64 06/24/64
Watkins, Elizabeth Ann (Mrs.) died 02/13/63 02/14/63
Watkins, Ellen E. married Dorsey, J. W. 05/27/62 05/28/62
Watkins, Eugenia E. married Bodine, John W. 12/19/65 12/23/65
Watkins, F. Bascom married Thorton, Eugenia E. 02/07/65 02/10/65
Watkins, Gassaway married Buckmiller, Fannie A. 09/17/63 09/23/63
Watkins, Georgeanna married Wright, George 09/12/61 09/14/61
Watkins, James S. married Gade, Kate T. 12/26/61 12/30/61
Watkins, John died 03/03/64 03/05/64
Watkins, John married Grafton, Eliza no date 10/18/65
Watkins, John H. died 02/04/64 02/06/64
Watkins, Laura A. married Stewart, John N. 01/06/62 01/07/62
Watkins, Nicholas married Wroe, Marion Josephine 12/16/62 12/23/62
Watkins, Nicholas A. married Brainard, Eugenie S. 02/26/65 03/16/65
Watkins, Noble G. died 09/13/62 10/10/62
Watkins, Robert K. died 02/01/64 02/03/64
Watkins, Sally D. died 03/23/63 03/25/63
Watkins, Virgie Ann died 06/21/65 06/24/65
Watkins, William James died 07/19/63 08/22/63
Watkins, William W. died 07/29/62 07/30/62
Watkins, William W. died 06/16/65 06/17/65
Watlington, Kate married Saville, William N. 12/14/63 12/16/63
Watson, Ann died 07/28/64 07/30/64
Watson, Anna V. married Strebeck, Charles L. 12/19/65 12/21/65
Watson, Catharine died 02/18/65 02/20/65
Watson, Charles died 07/09/62 07/10/62
Watson, Charles C. died 02/04/64 02/05/64
Watson, Elizabeth A. married Reid, James 12/03/63 12/29/63
Watson, Ella married McCulloh, John K. (Dr.) 09/29/63 10/06/63
Watson, George W. married Newkirk, Emma 07/02/65 09/08/65
Watson, George Washington died 03/04/62 03/06/62
Watson, John married Clarke, Mary F. 10/27/64 10/31/64
Watson, John S. died 06/22/65 06/26/65
Watson, Margaret died 06/14/62 06/17/62
Watson, Martha A. (Mrs.) married Hill, Jessie 11/13/61 11/15/61
Watson, Monterey married Randall, Addison T. 01/24/65 01/25/65
Watson, Rose B. married Wheeler, Charles N. 10/15/65 11/01/65
Watson, Susan (Mrs.) died 07/07/64 07/11/64
Watson, Thomas died 03/04/64 03/08/64
Watson, Thomas married Galloway, Martha A. 08/10/65 08/17/65
Watson, William H. died 07/10/65 07/11/65
Watt, Caroline married Johnson, Joshua M. 12/10/63 12/23/63
Watt, Elizabeth died 11/27/62 12/01/62
Watt, George died 03/04/64 03/05/64
Watt, George L. married Plummer, Mary V. 04/24/62 07/17/62
Wattenscheidt, Ewald married Wagner, Amelia S. 12/14/65 12/21/65
Watters, Henry G. died 12/21/65 12/28/65
Watters, John married Rawlings, Mary E. 10/10/65 10/12/65
Wattles, Kate A. married Mack, William J. 11/18/63 02/13/64
Watts, Alexander married Lee, Catharine 01/29/65 01/31/65
Watts, Alice married Havez, Jean Constant 10/03/63 10/05/63
Watts, Allen married Pearce, Mary Ann 09/09/62 09/10/62

470

Watts, Benjamin L. died 09/29/62 09/30/62
Watts, Charles William died 10/27/65 10/28/65
Watts, Columbus married Jones, Manie M. 05/18/65 05/20/65
Watts, Ella died 09/04/64 09/12/64
Watts, Emily Milan died 09/06/63 09/08/63
Watts, Francis A. died 02/06/65 02/09/65
Watts, George H. married Stowman, Hannah V. 05/25/65 05/27/65
Watts, George N. died 09/28/62 09/29/62
Watts, George N. died 09/28/62 09/30/62
Watts, Henry R. (Dr., USN) married Goslee, Susie J. 09/21/64 09/23/64
Watts, James died 03/26/62 03/27/62
Watts, Jason Orville died 12/27/61 03/17/62
Watts, Jennie married Brooks, Thomas D. 12/13/64 12/19/64
Watts, Jennie married Quarles, Merriwether S. 11/30/65 12/02/65
Watts, Maria Bell died 03/31/61 04/02/61
Watts, Martha married Derry, Mathias 06/16/61 06/24/61
Watts, Martin died 07/11/62 07/23/62
Watts, Mary J. married Tolson, Perry 03/19/63 03/23/63
Watts, Mary Jane T. died 11/16/63 11/17/63
Watts, Nathaniel S. married Boyle, Cornelia 02/09/64 02/11/64
Watts, Oliver H. married Weller, Sophy 12/30/63 03/22/64
Watts, P. A. married Weitzell, Harriet E. 04/28/62 05/05/62
Watts, R. W. married Smith, Barbara 09/27/65 12/01/65
Watts, Rosella died 10/24/63 10/27/63
Watts, S. E. married Chesley, John W. 08/31/65 11/28/65
Watts, Susie married McCauley, Joseph C. 01/06/64 01/13/64
Watts, Thomas Elhonnon died 08/16/62 08/28/62
Watts, William K. married Booth, Maria E. 11/10/63 11/16/63
Watts, William Thomas died 12/19/62 12/20/62
Watts, William Thomas died 12/19/62 01/19/63
Waugh, Catharine B. died 03/22/65 03/24/65
Waugh, William F. died 05/13/65 05/15/65
Waxter, Charles P. married Myers, Elizabeth 05/19/61 05/21/61
Waxter, James L. died 02/19/64 02/20/64
Way, George married Sherlock, Sallie Jane 11/16/64 11/17/64
Way, John H. married Rielly, Rose A. 10/06/64 10/18/64
Wayman, Bishop married Green, Harriet A. E. 05/17/64 05/23/64
Wayman, John W. died 09/13/64 10/10/64
Wayman, Rachel Jane died 11/12/61 11/13/61
Wayner, George W. died 12/21/65 12/25/65
Ways, Charles Edward married Byer, Lizzie V. 09/09/63 09/10/63
Ways, Leonard Thomas married Hanson, Clara 12/07/63 01/09/64
Ways, Mary Ann died 11/17/62 11/18/62
Wayson, Eliza W. married Howard, William H. (Col.) 01/28/62 01/31/62
Weagley, George F. died 03/05/65 03/07/65
Weagley, Valentine Adams died 06/27/61 06/29/61
Weaters, Mary Remington died 09/23/63 09/24/63
Weatherby, Davis Newton died 06/06/64 06/07/64
Weatherby, Samuel S. married Compton, Rachel K. 03/30/65 04/10/65
Weathers, Jesse Remington died 04/10/61 05/13/61
Weathers, Mary Remington died 09/23/63 09/25/63
Weatherstine, Emily Susanna died 02/16/62 02/18/62
Weatherstine, Hamilton died 06/29/64 06/30/64
Weatherstine, James married Bankert, Barbara Ellen 10/20/61 06/12/62
Weatherstine, William H. died 02/27/62 03/01/62

```
Weaver, A. Ward (Lt. Com.) married Hyatt, Ida 02/13/64  02/19/64
Weaver, Amelia Catherine died no date  10/17/65
Weaver, Amelia Catherine died no date  10/18/65
Weaver, Annie Cora died 08/30/63  09/01/63
Weaver, Annie E. married Willis, Richard 02/06/62  02/10/62
Weaver, Benjamin married Smith, Rachael A. 08/11/61  08/14/61
Weaver, Christena married Burman, Lewis 01/01/63  01/06/63
Weaver, Cloe died 08/25/61  08/26/61
Weaver, David Toole died 10/19/61  10/22/61
Weaver, Frances Sophia died 11/13/61  11/15/61
Weaver, Harry Duherst died 04/15/64  04/22/64
Weaver, James E. married Brown, Josephine 02/16/63  02/17/63
Weaver, John W. died 06/30/64  07/01/64
Weaver, Joseph married Warden, Matilda 10/12/62  10/29/62
Weaver, Julia married Dennis, Josiah 10/12/63  11/06/63
Weaver, Julia Almira married Ward, J. Joseph 05/12/63  05/18/63
Weaver, Kate died 09/14/65  09/15/65
Weaver, Laura J. (Mrs.) died 01/16/65  01/16/65
Weaver, Lewis died 01/18/63  01/23/63
Weaver, Margaret Ann died 08/01/61  08/02/61
Weaver, Margaret Ann died 08/01/61  08/06/61
Weaver, Maria E. died 02/06/61  02/07/61
Weaver, Mary (Mrs.) died 11/14/65  11/16/65
Weaver, Mary (Mrs.) died 11/14/65  11/17/65
Weaver, Mary Elizabeth died 01/26/63  01/28/63
Weaver, Philip L. died 07/27/63  08/11/63
Weaver, Robert Frederick died 01/23/63  01/24/63
Weaver, Rocksey Ann married Purnel, Charles F. 11/14/61  11/16/61
Weaver, Susannah married Lancaster, Andrew J. 01/31/64  02/04/64
Weaver, W. M. married Williams, Mary 01/10/61  01/14/61
Weaver, William H. H. married Moore, Hannah (Mrs.) 12/06/64  12/08/64
Webb, Alanson died 01/31/61  02/15/61
Webb, Alba H. married Von Lingen, George A. 03/09/65  03/14/65
Webb, Aphia M. married Price, G. W. (Cpt.) 11/20/65  11/27/65
Webb, C. married Prout, John 12/06/65  12/23/65
Webb, Carrie married Hewitt, Alexander C. 03/04/61  03/07/61
Webb, Catherine died 03/18/61  03/19/61
Webb, Charles Nathaniel died 03/15/63  03/16/63
Webb, Clara A. died 10/24/62  10/25/62
Webb, Elizabeth C. married Deal, Richard Henry 06/08/64  06/09/64
Webb, Elizabeth W. (Mrs.) died 01/11/63  01/12/63
Webb, Ella married Mills, S. S., Jr. 01/12/65  06/27/65
Webb, Emma married Mills, Benjamin F. 11/24/64  11/26/64
Webb, George H. married Cornelius, Fanny 12/18/62  12/22/62
Webb, Henry A. married Lare, Annie E. 05/19/64  05/20/64
Webb, Howard died 05/27/65  05/29/65
Webb, James married Gayleard, Mary A. 12/10/61  12/25/61
Webb, James Phelan died 08/27/64  08/29/64
Webb, Joanna M. married Weller, Jacob P. 11/23/65  11/24/65
Webb, John died 03/26/65  04/18/65
Webb, John H. died 01/22/63  01/24/63
Webb, Kate T. married Linthicum, George W. 02/14/61  02/25/61
Webb, Levi married Gartrids, Amanda E. 09/03/65  09/05/65
Webb, Lillie died 06/06/64  06/07/64
Webb, Lizzie A. died 06/10/63  06/11/63
```

Webb, Louisa (Mrs.) died 04/23/64   04/25/64
Webb, Maggie died 07/31/64   08/01/64
Webb, Mary C. married Duvall, V. B. 10/10/65   10/14/65
Webb, Mollie died 12/20/64   12/22/64
Webb, Nathan died 11/03/65   11/04/65
Webb, Nathaniel died 02/23/61   02/25/61
Webb, Nathaniel H. married Kennard, S. Louisa 05/19/63   05/20/63
Webb, Nathaniel H. died 07/06/64   07/07/64
Webb, Rachel married Sterm, C. Albert 03/08/64   03/12/64
Webb, Rachel A. married Davis, George W. 12/25/61   12/27/61
Webb, Retty R. died 02/27/63   03/02/63
Webb, Samuel Josephieus died 06/19/65   06/21/65
Webb, Samuel McClellan died 08/31/63   09/02/63
Webb, Sarah (Mrs.) died 10/11/64   10/12/64
Webb, W. A., Jr. married Anderson, Mollie E. 12/26/65   12/30/65
Webber, Benjamin died 02/28/64   03/01/64
Weber, Ann Catherine (Mrs.) died 09/16/63   09/18/63
Weber, Catherine (Mrs.) married Murr, Henry 11/26/65   12/02/65
Weber, George H. married Ely, Mary Elizabeth 05/04/63   05/07/63
Weber, George W. died 10/23/64   10/24/64
Weber, Mary Alvardia died 03/08/65   03/09/65
Weber, Susanna B. died 08/22/64   08/23/64
Weber, Theodore married Resham, Henrietta 12/09/64   12/13/64
Webster, Algernon died 04/09/65   04/11/65
Webster, Cholotta married Young, David F. 12/01/63   12/15/63
Webster, Daniel E. married Collins, Emma 03/15/63   04/07/63
Webster, Elizabeth (Mrs.) died 12/15/63   12/17/63
Webster, Emma married McCormick, William J. 01/18/63   01/21/63
Webster, George died 05/04/62   05/06/62
Webster, George W. married Collins, Elizabeth 11/23/63   11/28/63
Webster, Henry W. died 05/01/63   05/04/63
Webster, Isaac died 09/04/65   09/06/65
Webster, John Lee (Dr.) died 01/22/63   03/03/63
Webster, Lou L. married Finney, George J. 04/26/65   04/27/65
Webster, M. Augusta married Hurst, John J. 05/16/65   05/25/65
Webster, Marcelein Eugene died 04/14/62   04/17/62
Webster, Martin Rizer died 11/20/62   11/22/62
Webster, Mary A. died 05/19/61   05/20/61
Webster, Mary A. died 06/23/62   06/25/62
Webster, Nora died 06/25/63   06/26/63
Webster, Pliny A. died 05/19/61   05/21/61
Webster, R. Priscilla married Sadtler, Charles H. 11/05/63   11/09/63
Webster, Sallie F. married Keating, Thomas J. 06/12/62   06/13/62
Webster, Samuel Dallam died 04/16/64   10/24/64
Webster, Sophia H. died 03/11/62   03/13/62
Webster, Sophie married Hodges, J. Chapman (Cpt.) 11/24/63   11/28/63
Webster, Stephen G. died 05/17/61   05/22/61
Webster, Susie married Lowery, R. B. 08/07/62   08/18/62
Webster, William died 01/13/63   01/14/64
Webster, William Augustus died 10/11/64   10/12/64
Wecker, Catherine E. died 02/04/65   02/09/65
Wederstandt, John C. (Dr.) died 02/09/64   02/10/64
Wedge, Emma A. married Basshor, Thomas C. 11/16/65   11/21/65
Weech, William T. L. (Rev.) married Sewell, M. Augusta 11/28/61
     12/09/61

Weeden, Eliza died 08/12/62   08/25/62
Weedon, John Trove died 06/27/64   06/28/64
Weeks, Elizabeth A. married Gaither, Ellijah 01/05/64   01/15/64
Weeks, Rebecca married Kimble, William 01/24/62   02/04/62
Weeks, Sarah A. V. married Getzendanner, Phineas D. 12/28/65   12/30/65
Weeks, William A. married Gaither, Mary Ann 02/19/61   02/27/61
Weems, Edwin D. (USN) married Norman, Rosetia L. 09/22/64   09/24/64
Weems, Francis M. died 10/06/65   10/11/65
Weems, George died 07/24/62   07/26/62
Weems, George died 07/24/62   07/29/62
Weems, George W. died 10/13/62   10/14/62
Weems, George W. (Cpt.) died 07/20/65   07/21/65
Weems, J. C. (Hon.) died 01/20/62   01/24/62
Weems, Julius B. (Dr.) died 12/19/65   12/20/65
Weems, Lizzie K. married Shays, Robert G. 09/22/63   09/23/63
Weems, Matilda died 09/22/61   09/23/61
Weems, Rebecca Y. married Wilkinson, N. D. 06/01/65   06/17/65
Weems, Sarah Jane died 12/16/65   12/18/65
Weems, Theodore died 02/24/64   02/25/64
Weger, John married Dowling, Elizabeth 10/02/61   11/04/61
Weglein, Louis married Selinger, Philipina 06/17/63   06/18/63
Weglein, Ricka married Hines, Julius 12/30/63   12/31/63
Wehn, Philip L. died 02/27/63   03/03/63
Wehr, Peter died 11/14/64   11/16/64
Wehrhane, Charles married Simon, Louisa 05/31/65   06/01/65
Wehrley, Elizabeth (Mrs.) died 03/19/64   03/21/64
Weibrauch, Mary died 06/27/65   06/28/65
Weidner, Frederick married Newton, Mary E. 01/21/64   02/17/64
Weidner, Maggie A. married Hudson, Henry 06/13/64   06/15/64
Weigant, Frederick Bannanberg died 02/28/63   03/03/63
Weigel, Edwin M. Stanton died 07/16/65   07/17/65
Weigle, William H. (Lt.) married Zachary, Lizzie A. 11/22/61   11/25/61
Weigley, Katherine married Eisenhart, John 12/20/60   01/04/61
Weihbrauch, Louisa died 11/15/65   11/17/65
Weilant, Emma married Rouvenac, C. 02/25/63   03/03/63
Weir, Ann died 07/31/61   08/01/61
Weir, William died 04/14/61   04/15/61
Weiranch, John married Wilson, Georgeanna 04/10/64   04/12/64
Weirauch, George M. married Kyper, Louisa A. 09/07/65   09/18/65
Weirougli, Joseph Beauregard died 04/28/63   04/29/63
Weis, Henrietta married Gable, John 06/11/61   06/15/61
Weise, Barbara died 09/21/65   09/22/65
Weise, Regina married Bayley, George W. 03/08/61   05/08/61
Weishampel, Benjamin F. married Richards, Cora J. 03/07/65   03/09/65
Weishampel, Tillie married Foster, Edward F. 12/13/64   12/19/64
Weisner, Eberhart married Lessner, Rebecca 03/31/61   04/09/61
Weisoff, Martha married Crisp, Edward F. 10/27/64   11/03/64
Weiss, Elizabeth married Miller, Henry 01/14/64   01/22/64
Weity, Harry Ausburn died 01/25/64   02/01/64
Weitzel, Barbara died 12/10/65   12/12/65
Weitzel, George Elmer, E. died 07/09/65   07/11/65
Weitzel, Harry Sigel died 08/15/63   08/17/63
Weitzel, Jacob married Philes, Mary L. 01/05/62   06/21/62
Weitzel, Sarah E. E. died 08/12/64   08/15/64
Weitzell, Harriet E. married Watts, P. A. 04/28/62   05/05/62

```
Welby,  Alfred B. died 07/31/62    08/04/62
Welch,  Annie died 09/24/62    09/25/62
Welch,  B. Frank married Medairy, Bell 04/09/63    04/13/63
Welch,  Benjamin G. married Hancock, Lallie E. 01/11/64    01/16/64
Welch,  Benjamin P. married Sherwood, Kate R. 12/13/64    12/15/64
Welch,  Benjamin T. married Sherwood, Kate R. 12/13/64    12/16/64
Welch,  Catherine married McCabe, James 02/03/61    02/04/61
Welch,  Charles J. died 12/03/62    12/05/62
Welch,  Eliza J. married Wright, Henry V. 08/12/63    08/21/63
Welch,  Eliza J. (Mrs.) married Wright, Henry V. 08/12/63    08/22/63
Welch,  Eliza Jane married Bandel, Grafton J. 01/15/65    02/14/65
Welch,  Elizabeth married Henson, Robert 05/22/62    05/24/62
Welch,  Ferdinand died 09/26/64    09/27/64
Welch,  Frances died 04/24/62    04/25/62
Welch,  Henry married Walker, Margaret R. (Mrs.) 10/05/65    10/07/65
Welch,  J. G. married Meyer, Amelia 11/05/63    11/20/63
Welch,  John married Healy, Josephine N. 03/03/64    03/21/64
Welch,  John C. died 03/02/64    03/03/64
Welch,  Julia A. married Smithson, William 02/24/63    02/26/63
Welch,  Martha E. married Chapman, George R. 05/23/64    06/10/64
Welch,  Michael died 03/29/65    03/30/65
Welch,  Michael died 03/29/65    03/31/65
Welch,  Richard died 12/19/63    12/21/63
Welch,  Sophia (Mrs.) died 10/11/63    10/13/63
Welch,  Thomas Henry died 05/16/64    05/19/64
Welch,  William died 06/19/64    06/22/64
Welch,  William B. married Bennett, Jennie H. 02/04/64    02/06/64
Welde,  Lydia Jane died 10/14/63    10/16/63
Welden, William T. married Arlow, Mollie A. 07/30/65    08/02/65
Welffel, Henry L. married Couchman, Emma J. 03/14/64    03/29/64
Well,   Mary Tarbotten died 01/22/61    01/31/61
Well,   Thomas B. married Thomas, Frances 12/31/63    01/02/64
Wellener, Alice Virginia died 07/20/61    07/22/61
Wellener, Charles Edward died 02/13/62    02/15/62
Wellener, Emma R. W. died 05/29/61    06/03/61
Wellener, Francis Howard died 12/30/64    12/31/64
Weller, Christopher died 10/01/65    10/02/65
Weller, Daniel married Clark, Sarah Elizabeth 07/10/65    07/25/65
Weller, Jacob P. married Webb, Joanna M. 11/23/65    11/24/65
Weller, Liney D. married Bilson, Daniel 12/15/63    03/22/64
Weller, Reuben died 02/01/63    02/03/63
Weller, Sophy married Watts, Oliver H. 12/30/63    03/22/64
Welling, Susan Catharine died 02/04/65    02/08/65
Wellinghoff, Anna died 11/13/62    11/15/62
Wellmore, Edward H. married Maher, Josephine 06/23/64    06/30/64
Wellmore, Grace R. married Mcdonald, David H. 04/07/64    04/18/64
Wellmore, L. M. C. (Mrs.) died 04/12/63    04/13/63
Wells,  Alice died 01/13/62    01/15/62
Wells,  Alice Elizabeth died 10/04/64    10/07/64
Wells,  Alice Elizabeth died 10/04/64    10/20/64
Wells,  Amanda E. married Lane, Lloyd 09/09/60    08/13/61
Wells,  Annie E. married McCauley, C. L. 01/05/65    01/21/65
Wells,  Charles C. died 01/09/62    01/10/62
Wells,  David died 10/27/62    10/31/62
Wells,  Emma E. married Leary, Durias H. 04/08/63    04/11/63
```

Wells, George R. married Lambert, Lizzie A. 06/12/65 06/15/65
Wells, George R. married Lambert, Lizzie A. 06/12/65 06/16/65
Wells, Isabella married Pindar, John H. C. 04/29/62 05/01/62
Wells, James Z. married Duley, Sarah E. 07/20/63 07/29/63
Wells, Jeremiah died 01/05/61 01/10/61
Wells, John married Block, Henrietta 04/19/64 04/25/64
Wells, John Henry died 10/18/64 10/20/64
Wells, John W. died 04/20/65 04/24/65
Wells, Joseph died 08/19/63 08/21/63
Wells, Joseph D. married Hughlett, Mary E. 11/30/65 12/04/65
Wells, Josephine married Bradford, James T. 11/16/65 11/18/65
Wells, Joshua (Rev.) died 01/25/62 01/28/62
Wells, Laura Virginia married Shunck, Jacob 12/24/61 01/03/62
Wells, Lucy E. married Scott, John B. 11/25/63 12/21/63
Wells, Mary Frances married Butler, William H. 02/26/63 02/28/63
Wells, Mary Grace W. died 10/12/64 10/20/64
Wells, Mary Rebecca died 10/10/62 10/11/62
Wells, Oscar M. married Thirion, Margaret 06/18/65 06/20/65
Wells, Peter F. married Layfield, Pricilla A. 05/15/61 05/16/61
Wells, Peter F. married Layfield, Pricilla A. 05/15/61 05/17/61
Wells, Rebecca married Lewis, Charles O. 01/08/61 01/18/61
Wells, Robert H. married Binnie, Mary D. 11/30/65 12/04/65
Wells, Willie died 04/21/65 04/25/65
Welman, William A. married Ayres, Sarah Jane 05/01/64 05/07/64
Welsh, Adelle C. died 10/18/63 10/22/63
Welsh, Catherine died 08/08/61 08/09/61
Welsh, Edward Hobson died 10/31/62 11/01/62
Welsh, Elizabeth died 02/18/63 02/20/63
Welsh, George Henry (Cpt.) died 11/01/62 11/03/62
Welsh, Honora (Mrs.) died 09/02/64 09/03/64
Welsh, Isaac P. died 02/27/65 03/21/65
Welsh, Joseph Merriken died 03/01/64 03/02/64
Welsh, Julia Ann (Mrs.) died 12/28/64 12/30/64
Welsh, Marcilla married Hall, David E. 07/05/63 12/25/63
Welsh, Mary died 09/16/63 09/18/63
Welsh, Mary Catherine died 04/25/62 04/26/62
Welsh, Mary E. married Smoot, George W. 01/20/63 01/23/63
Welsh, Mary E. married Tucker, Henry A. 05/07/63 05/09/63
Welsh, Matilda E. H. married Parlett, Moses 05/19/64 05/20/64
Welsh, Napoleon B. married Kessler, Lizzie 08/09/64 08/10/64
Welsh, Nettie C. married Wickes, Jere L. 02/27/62 03/01/62
Welsh, Patrick E. died 08/07/64 08/08/64
Welsh, Robert E. married Wise, Olivia P. 03/03/65 04/06/65
Welsh, Samuel P. married Richardson, Julia Ann 07/05/63 07/10/63
Welsh, Susan (Mrs.) died no date 12/02/63
Welsh, William Frederick died 05/16/65 05/27/65
Welshoffer, Mary (Mrs.) died 06/19/63 06/20/63
Welslager, George died 02/11/62 02/12/62
Welslager, James T. married Harkin, Henrietta 01/11/64 01/12/64
Wendroth, Adolphus married Kalling, Annie E. 04/03/64 04/04/64
Wenn, James married Whalan, Julia A. 12/14/65 12/18/65
Wentworth, Joseph B. married Lenty, Laura 08/14/64 08/19/64
Wentz, Henry C. married Lutz, Fannie M. 07/21/63 07/27/63
Wentz, Laura died 02/08/65 02/13/65
Werden, Marnix died 05/25/63 05/28/63

```
Werkamp, Louis E. married Beck, Mary C. 10/06/64  10/14/64
Werling, Maggie married Miller, Joseph 03/12/63  03/13/63
Werner, Margaret married Strong, Samuel S. 12/25/62  12/27/62
Wernex, Catharina Adelherd died 12/31/64  01/05/65
Wernex, George D. married Thrifty, Emma 12/22/63  01/13/64
Wernig, Gertrude (Mrs.) died 10/12/63  10/13/63
Wernig, Joseph R. married Wonn, Nelly L. 06/02/64  06/07/64
Wernith, Joseph B. married Baldus, Theresa 02/08/64  02/12/64
Werring, Joseph R. married Wonn, Nelly L. 06/02/64  06/06/64
Wert, William H. H. died 06/03/64  07/26/64
Wertz, John E. died 04/05/63  04/07/63
Wescott, Harry H. died 08/19/65  08/26/65
Wesley, Gabriel married Russell, Francis 06/14/63  06/20/63
Wesley, William married Ringold, Ann Maria 04/14/61  04/16/61
Wessels, Margaret died 03/21/61  03/22/61
Wessels, Margaret died 03/21/61  03/23/61
West, Alexander R. died 11/15/64  11/17/64
West, Amelia married Parry, James O. D. 08/10/62  09/02/62
West, Benjamin R. died 06/08/62  06/09/62
West, Caroline died 07/26/64  07/27/64
West, Charles P. married Bherns, Sarah A. 03/29/64  04/02/64
West, Eliza married Bauerschmidt, John 12/18/64  12/22/64
West, Eliza A. (Mrs.) died 06/03/63  06/04/63
West, Elizabeth died 08/28/61  08/30/61
West, Emma S. died 07/21/65  07/22/65
West, Francis died 08/30/62  09/01/62
West, George F. married Williams, Mollie D. 10/17/65  10/25/65
West, George M. D. died 07/24/63  07/25/63
West, George P. married Burns, Maggie E. 04/23/63  04/27/63
West, George W. married Hopkins, Josephine H. 03/22/64  03/24/64
West, Hannah (Mrs.) died 08/11/63  09/28/63
West, Harriet A. married Broom, George W. 03/08/64  03/10/64
West, Helen E. married Orem, William Morris 02/14/61  02/16/61
West, James Henry died 01/29/61  01/31/61
West, Margaret E. died 09/04/65  09/05/65
West, Margaret E. died 09/04/65  09/06/65
West, Maria E. married Tomlins, Morton C. 09/06/64  09/13/64
West, Robert E. died 06/10/61  06/11/61
West, Salathiel M. married Adams, Emma R. 08/03/63  08/08/63
Westenberger, John R. died 02/21/62  04/09/62
Westervelt, J. Franklin married Brady, Frances M. 01/30/63  02/04/63
Westervelt, Mary A. died 06/28/64  06/29/64
Westervelt, Richard L. died 06/19/64  06/20/64
Westfall, Sallie E. married Greenwahl, L. H. 03/15/64  03/22/64
Westlake, John A. married Matthews, Elizabeth Ann 12/24/63  01/07/64
Westley, Mary (Mrs.) died 04/01/63  04/04/63
Weston, Maria died 03/16/65  03/17/65
Weston, Martha died 04/18/61  04/19/61
Westwood, Mary Lizzie married Cross, James Wesley 04/05/65  05/09/65
Wethered, Elizabeth died 11/30/62  12/02/62
Wethered, George Y. married Irwin, Ann M. 10/01/61  10/03/61
Wethered, Lewin died 04/05/63  04/06/63
Wethered, Mary S. died 07/28/65  07/29/65
Wetmore, Ellen D'Arcy died 04/16/61  04/19/61
Wetter, George R. died 10/30/62  11/05/62
```

Wetzel, Philip married Behrens, Marie 11/23/62   11/26/62
Wetzer, Sarah married Gradwohl, E. C. 02/07/64   02/08/64
Wever, Robert Coates died 09/27/65   10/03/65
Weyfforth, John Jacob died 08/12/65   08/25/65
Weyforth, Elizabeth married Yoe, George A. (USN) 09/07/65   09/09/65
Weyforth, Louisa M. married Berger, P. R. 12/07/65   12/20/65
Weyraugh, Elizabeth married McElroy, William D. 06/06/65   06/08/65
Weyrough, Louisa married Raymo, Francis 08/07/61   09/25/61
Whalan, Julia A. married Wenn, James 12/14/65   12/18/65
Whalen, Bridget died 04/17/62   04/18/62
Whalen, Bridget died 04/17/62   04/19/62
Whalen, James married McMahon, Annie 08/10/63   08/13/63
Whalen, Mary (Mrs.) died 08/29/63   09/04/63
Whalen, Stephen married McNeal, Georgeanna 02/24/63   03/04/63
Whalen, Washington Bright died 06/15/63   06/18/63
Whalen, William died 10/16/64   11/24/64
Whaler, Mary (Mrs.) died 07/14/63   07/15/63
Whaley, Henrietta died 03/21/64   03/23/64
Whalon, Annie R. married Gore, Henry H. 06/28/63   07/03/63
Wharry, Samuel died 07/22/62   07/24/62
Wharton, Mary Jane died 08/03/65   08/05/65
Whayland, Wesley A. married Malone, Elizabeth 12/24/61   01/07/62
Wheat, Alice D. married Foster, G. Nelson 12/10/61   12/19/61
Wheat, Ann Elizabeth married Kuhn, John J. 05/31/63   06/08/63
Wheat, Nathaniel died 07/23/64   07/25/64
Wheatley, Ann E. married Tucker, John 04/27/65   05/05/65
Wheatley, Elizabeth married Perkins, Eugene T. 06/17/62   06/23/62
Wheatley, Levin (Cpt.) died 08/17/64   08/19/64
Wheatley, Levin (Cpt.) died 08/17/64   08/22/64
Wheatley, Lizzie J. married Sapp, John 08/24/62   08/26/62
Wheatley, Mary A. married Dewling, Isiah (Dr.) 08/01/65   08/12/65
Wheatly, Catherine (Mrs.) died 01/26/63   01/28/63
Wheatly, James R. married Johnson, Emily (Mrs.) 08/09/63   08/18/63
Wheeden, James B. married Hall, Mary E. 10/03/65   10/06/65
Wheeden, Mary Rebecca died 11/02/63   11/04/63
Wheeden, Mary Rebecca (Mrs.) died 11/02/63   11/03/63
Wheeden, Thomas J. married Bradyhouse, Arabella 07/22/62   09/05/62
Wheeder, Minnie E. married Morris, John H. 12/26/61   02/17/62
Wheeler, Alfred died 05/29/65   06/01/65
Wheeler, Ann died 09/25/65   09/26/65
Wheeler, Annie married Johnson, William T. (Rev.) 12/25/65   12/29/65
Wheeler, Annie E. married Pearce, John F. 01/16/65   02/20/65
Wheeler, Charles N. married Watson, Rose B. 10/15/65   11/01/65
Wheeler, Charles W. married Hunter, Mary M. 07/31/65   08/09/65
Wheeler, Charlotte A. married Myers, Joshua 05/29/64   05/31/64
Wheeler, Edward married Pease, Mary F. 02/08/65   06/01/65
Wheeler, Elizabeth J. married Justice, J. (Rev.) 01/31/61   02/05/61
Wheeler, Francis Ignatius died 05/04/63   05/08/63
Wheeler, George Edward died 08/06/62   10/01/62
Wheeler, George W. died 07/09/62   07/14/62
Wheeler, Henry (Cpt.) died 06/30/65   07/01/65
Wheeler, James H. married Gipson, Mary A 01/10/65   01/23/65
Wheeler, Jenny died 03/16/65   03/17/65
Wheeler, John married Toy, Lydia 09/29/64   10/01/64
Wheeler, John married Hawkins, Eliza A. 07/03/65   07/06/65

Wheeler, Laura V. married Irwin, James L. 11/03/62 11/05/62
Wheeler, M. A. (Mrs.) married Dorsey, Joseph I. 04/09/61 04/13/61
Wheeler, Maria (Mrs.) died 03/16/63 03/24/63
Wheeler, Mary (Mrs.) died 07/14/63 07/15/63
Wheeler, Mary Adelaide died 05/06/62 05/07/62
Wheeler, Mary Ann (Mrs.) died 03/16/63 03/17/63
Wheeler, Mary Emily married Bennett, Thomas W. (Cpt.) 11/03/63 12/08/63
Wheeler, Mary Hockley died 06/23/64 06/25/64
Wheeler, Mary Jane married Beckworth, Thomas 09/04/61 09/07/61
Wheeler, Prudence A. married Slater, John T. 11/20/64 10/21/64
Wheeler, Richard D. died 01/12/63 01/13/63
Wheeler, Salome H. married Draney, F. M. 03/16/65 04/06/65
Wheeler, Samuel E. died 10/19/63 10/20/63
Wheeler, Sarah married Yundt, Joseph 12/08/64 12/31/64
Wheeler, Sarah (Mrs.) died 01/24/63 01/28/63
Wheeler, Thomas died 02/06/63 02/07/63
Whelan, Ann (Mrs.) died 04/24/63 04/25/63
Whelan, John Thomas died 04/02/62 04/03/62
Whelan, Louis N. died 12/31/62 01/01/63
Whelan, Luke died 08/02/63 08/04/63
Whelan, William died 08/01/61 08/02/61
Wheltle, John Thomas died 07/03/63 07/07/63
Wheltly, Mary Catherine died 08/09/65 08/12/65
Wherrett, Henrietta V. married High, William T. 06/17/62 07/08/62
Wherrett, Sarah died 04/30/62 05/01/62
Wherritt, Emma Virginia died 02/26/63 02/28/63
While, Charles A. died 02/18/64 02/20/64
Whims, Sarah A. married Johnson, Augustus 10/12/63 10/13/63
Whinna, Robert married Evans, Georgie 02/16/64 02/19/64
Whipp, Sarah (Mrs.) died 10/07/65 10/11/65
Whipps, William died 06/01/61 06/07/61
Whisman, Daniel H. married Wiley, Mary V. 08/02/64 08/19/64
Whisman, Laura Virginia died 07/18/65 07/20/65
Whitaer, Susan A. married Fiddis, Benjamin W. 09/25/63 10/06/63
Whitaker, Dorsey H. married Gill, Mary E. 07/04/65 07/20/65
Whitaker, Elizabeth Stansbury died 10/05/63 10/07/63
Whitaker, Joshua died 12/23/61 01/25/62
Whitaker, Matilda died 07/29/64 08/22/64
Whitaker, Willie died 08/06/61 08/07/61
Whitcraft, Hannah married Leis, Thomas no date 07/06/64
White, Aimey died 08/18/64 08/22/64
White, Alexander married Harris, Mary 12/24/63 01/04/64
White, Alexander married Muer, Agnes 03/17/64 03/18/64
White, Alphasis E. married Dix, John T. 11/16/64 11/17/64
White, Amanda M. J. married Grogan, Robert 02/19/65 02/21/65
White, Ann Jane died 05/03/64 05/06/64
White, Anna Elizabeth married Legg, William 05/26/63 05/27/63
White, Annie W. married Bloomer, William F. 08/17/63 08/19/63
White, Carrie died 09/06/65 09/08/65
White, Cary married Sparrow, Priscilla (Mrs.) 04/02/63 04/04/63
White, Catherine Elizabeth died 05/03/63 05/04/63
White, Charles F. died 04/09/61 04/15/61
White, Charles H. married Jones, Sarah Ann 08/21/62 08/25/62
White, Cornelia E. married Caulk, C. J. 12/22/63 01/07/64
White, Cyrus B. married Hobbs, Valary V. 10/28/65 10/31/65

White, Daniel married Elliott, Sarah 06/26/64   06/28/64
White, Daniel H. died 10/21/63   10/23/63
White, David married Ruff, Mary J. 11/04/62   11/06/62
White, Deborah W. married Downs, Thadeus L. 12/19/64   01/09/65
White, Denver Davis died 02/24/61   02/26/61
White, Eliza married Buckler, Thomas H. (Dr.) 11/21/65   11/23/65
White, Elizabeth married Thomas, James T. 05/14/63   05/16/63
White, Elizabeth A. died 09/08/62   09/09/62
White, Elizabeth Ann died 10/13/61   10/14/61
White, Elizabeth Ann (Mrs.) died 09/15/63   09/16/63
White, Elizabeth Catherine died 07/26/65   07/27/65
White, Ellen died 08/13/65   08/14/65
White, Hannah died 02/12/61   03/04/61
White, Harriet M. married Green, Francis A. 06/18/61   06/20/61
White, Henrietta married Goldsborough, Benjamin 12/10/63   12/12/63
White, Henry Sadler died 03/07/63   03/10/63
White, Henson (Cpt.) married Langley, Zilah A. 06/30/63   07/07/63
White, Hester C. married Williams, Richard W. 11/17/63   11/24/63
White, Horace D. married Wallace, Marrion 11/16/64   11/22/64
White, Isabel died 04/27/65   04/28/65
White, Isabella married Robinson, Andrew 02/01/61   03/05/61
White, Isabella married Robinson, Andrew 02/01/61   03/04/61
White, J. Wesley married Taneyhill, Sophia W. 03/19/63   03/24/63
White, Jacob R. died 03/20/65   03/23/65
White, Johanna M. married Hilton, Edward 03/17/63   04/04/63
White, John died 11/15/62   11/17/62
White, John E. married Riston, Emily A. 02/05/62   02/07/62
White, John H. (Capt.) died 08/11/63   08/22/63
White, John R. married Wainwright, Elizabeth A. 04/30/63   06/02/63
White, John, Esq. died 11/15/62   11/21/62
White, Joseph John died 02/21/62   02/22/62
White, Kate Virginia died 03/12/61   03/13/61
White, Lawrence died 02/08/61   02/09/61
White, Lawrence Henry died 08/20/61   08/22/61
White, Letitia married Howard, George Eugene 05/02/65   05/08/65
White, Letitia V. married Howard, George Eugene 05/02/65   05/09/65
White, Lillie died 11/23/65   11/28/65
White, Louisa married Walsh, James 07/22/62   07/26/62
White, Louise H. married Raphel, S. Amedee 04/29/63   05/02/63
White, Lucy E. died 06/25/61   06/27/61
White, Maggie married Tyson, Henry G. 04/07/63   04/21/63
White, Maggie A. married Griffin, Thomas J. 05/21/63   10/13/63
White, Marcellus (Cpt.) married Fowler, Charlotte M. 05/24/63   05/26/63
White, Maria Jane married Ennis, George 04/06/65   04/08/65
White, Martin Parrot died 06/23/61   06/27/61
White, Mary died 05/07/65   05/09/65
White, Mary E. married Knowles, George G. 04/28/64   05/09/64
White, Mary Ellen died 03/23/65   03/24/65
White, Mary Rosa married Saxton, A. H. (Dr.) 06/09/64   06/10/64
White, Priscilla married Benton, Arron T. 03/08/64   03/10/64
White, R. D. (Capt.) died 02/11/64   03/01/64
White, Rachel E. died 06/16/65   06/19/65
White, Rebecca M. married Cox, Sylvester L. 04/28/64   05/05/64
White, Richard Fabius married Marion, Virginia 01/21/62   01/23/62
White, Richard Fabius married Marion, Virginia 01/21/62   01/24/62

White, Robert John married Allison, Janey 12/26/61 12/28/61
White, Robert W. married Stump, Maggie 05/03/65 05/11/65
White, Rosanna (Mrs.) died 02/05/64 02/06/64
White, Rosanna D. (Mrs.) died 02/05/64 02/09/64
White, Rosetta died 04/03/65 04/04/65
White, Samuel died 05/25/61 05/27/61
White, Samuel died 08/08/61 08/09/61
White, Samuel J. married Robinson, Jeanette B. 01/19/65 01/23/65
White, Samuel Joseph died 01/15/63 01/16/63
White, Sarah A. died 03/23/61 03/29/61
White, Sarah A. married Chase, Josiah 12/29/64 01/02/65
White, Sarah F. Hubbard died 08/21/65 08/24/65
White, Susan A. married Meads, William H. 02/25/64 02/27/64
White, Susanna (Mrs.) died 02/12/63 02/16/63
White, Susanna (Mrs.) died 02/12/63 02/17/63
White, Thomas B. married Godmar, Sarah H. 02/18/65 05/02/65
White, Thomas H. married Lucas, Kate B. 05/09/65 05/11/65
White, Thomas P. died 09/01/65 09/02/65
White, Walter W. married Broome, Susanna 05/03/62 06/09/62
White, Wesley F. died 06/10/61 07/22/61
White, William married Hughes, Mary Ann 06/02/61 06/04/61
White, William died 12/26/62 12/27/62
White, William died 05/16/64 05/26/64
White, William H. married Small, Isabella 04/16/63 04/17/63
White, William H. died 10/03/64 11/03/64
White, William H. died 03/03/64 11/09/65
White, William Joseph married Gibbs, Mary Ann 06/18/63 06/20/63
White, William P. died 01/13/63 01/14/64
White, William T. died 05/29/63 05/30/63
White, William W. married Sessions, Mary C. 11/30/65 12/04/65
White, Winfield Scott died 08/16/62 08/22/62
Whitefield, Sophia married Winternity, William 01/11/65 01/06/65
Whiteford, Alfred H. (Dr.) married Dinkel, Mary Elizabeth 12/15/62 01/24/63
Whiteford, Ann (Mrs.) died 12/28/61 12/30/61
Whiteford, David died 06/18/62 06/19/62
Whiteford, Emma Isabella died 11/15/62 11/17/62
Whiteford, George W. married McCoskar, Mary Ann 10/26/62 11/05/62
Whiteford, James died 06/24/63 06/27/63
Whiteford, Mary A. died 11/12/63 11/14/63
Whiteford, Mary Elizabeth died 03/03/63 03/04/63
Whiteford, Robert died 03/27/62 03/29/62
Whiteford, Samuel B. married Horney, Mary Charlotte 03/07/65 03/10/65
Whiteford, Samuel J. died 03/24/62 03/29/62
Whiteford, Sarah Ann M. died 02/22/64 02/24/64
Whitehill, John married Stern, Rosa 04/13/64 05/07/64
Whitehouse, Sarah A. married Andrews, Robert C. 11/25/62 11/27/62
Whitehurst, J. Harrison married McIlvain, Lavinia 06/09/64 06/21/64
Whitehurst, Mary Catharine died 03/04/65 03/07/65
Whiteley, Sarah E. married Parish, William 10/12/64 10/15/64
Whiteley, William H. died 03/20/61 03/22/61
Whiteloch, Ellen H. married Littiston, Thomas 01/14/65 02/02/65
Whiteloch, Margaret married Wilson, Charles H. 03/30/65 04/01/65
Whitelock, Charles died 03/06/63 03/07/63
Whitelock, Emily L. W. died 02/28/61 03/02/61

```
Whitelock, Mary Agnes died 03/10/63   03/12/63
Whitelock, Samuel R. died 01/15/63   01/16/63
Whitely, Elizabeth married Ryan, John F. 03/20/64   03/22/64
Whitemore, Henry died 06/27/63   07/01/63
Whiter, Rachel married Davis, Henry 02/17/61   02/19/61
Whiteside, Eliza J. married Husbeck, Joseph 05/12/64   05/19/64
Whiteside, George died 11/25/63   11/28/63
Whiting, Julia Compton died 07/01/64   07/02/64
Whitington, Emily B. died 08/16/61   08/20/61
Whitlaw, Archibald died 07/07/64   07/09/64
Whitley, Evelyn died 06/24/65   06/26/65
Whitlock, Maria Bacon married Page, Thomas Taylor 11/02/63   11/04/63
Whitlock, William married Crocken, Ann Eliza 10/05/63   10/08/63
Whitmarsh, David died 09/02/65   09/04/65
Whitmarsh, George died 07/20/62   07/29/62
Whitmarsh, John died 02/23/62   02/25/62
Whitmore, Anna Mary married Girvin, James M. 11/10/64   11/12/64
Whitney, Alice Agnes died 08/27/64   08/30/64
Whitney, E. Eugene married Starkweather, Laura A. 01/16/63   01/19/63
Whitney, Eliza died 11/02/65   11/03/65
Whitney, George W. married Merchant, Rosetta 12/02/62   12/08/62
Whitney, Lizzie J. married Sewell, Charles Alexander 03/12/61   03/14/6
Whiton, Henry married Cooper, Mary E. 02/22/65   02/25/65
Whitridge, John A. married Henderson, Ellen 01/06/63   01/08/63
Whitson, Almira (Mrs.) died 09/03/64   09/05/64
Whitson, Almira (Mrs.) died 09/03/64   09/06/64
Whitson, David (Lieut.) died 12/10/61   12/12/61
Whitson, Louise (Mrs.) died 05/22/63   05/23/63
Whittaker, Lewis F. married Blake, Mary A. 08/24/63   08/27/63
Whittemore, Anna M. (Mrs.) died 02/18/63   02/24/63
Whittemore, Hannah M. died 02/21/61   02/22/61
Whittemore, Hannah M. died 02/21/61   02/23/61
Whitter, Annie E. married Rubu, William H. 05/14/65   06/03/65
Whittier, Curtis A. married Davis, Annie A. 11/08/65   11/10/65
Whittimore, Donna A. B. married Irvine, A. Smith 06/27/61   07/08/61
Whittinghan, Mary A. married Wilmer, Charles 11/10/64   11/14/64
Whittington, Anna married Skinner, Richard 01/25/64   01/27/64
Whittington, Charles W. died 03/20/65   03/22/65
Whittington, John died 05/07/61   05/09/61
Whittington, Mary Elizabeth married Dennis, Alfred 05/06/65   05/08/65
Whittington, Matilda D. (Mrs.) died 01/18/65   01/20/65
Whittington, Ulysses Grant died 09/30/65   10/02/65
Whittington, William F. married Crandell, Isabel F. 12/20/64   12/26/64
Whittle, Caroline M. married Hibner, William Frederick 12/25/62
    10/22/63
Whittle, John T. married Carter, Josephine 11/17/64   11/23/64
Whittle, Thomas Xavier married O'Brien, Della 05/04/63   05/27/63
Whitton, William married Taylor, Jane 05/30/63   06/03/63
Whitworth, C. S. (Cpl.) died 10/19/64   11/10/64
Whitworth, Susan (Mrs.) died 01/13/65   01/17/65
Wholey, Joseph died 08/05/63   08/06/63
Whorton, Ida Virginia died 05/23/64   05/25/64
Whorton, James T. married Banks, Elizabeth 04/26/63   05/05/63
Whorton, Mary Jane died no date   08/28/65
Whyett, James died 03/25/64   03/26/64
```

Wible, Robert W. died 04/28/62   04/30/62
Wiche, Elizabeth married Pratt, Joseph G. 02/10/65   03/08/65
Wicken, Anne died 10/28/61   10/29/61
Wicken, Anne died 10/28/61   10/30/61
Wicken, Annie died 08/09/64   08/10/64
Wickens, Annie married Wood, C. Howard 12/11/65   12/30/65
Wicker, William died 04/07/62   04/11/62
Wickersham, Sarah died 02/17/64   02/18/64
Wickert, Samuel C. married Brown, Katie 08/15/65   08/24/65
Wickes, Jere L. married Welsh, Nettie C. 02/27/62   03/01/62
Wickes, Mary died 07/05/62   07/07/62
Wickes, Sophia died 05/22/61   06/01/61
Wickham, John died 01/01/63   01/03/63
Wickham, Mary Ann married Hamilton, William H. 11/16/65   11/25/65
Wicks, Anna Rebecca died 09/08/62   09/19/62
Wicks, James S. married Pryor, Agnes M. 10/19/63   12/25/63
Wicks, Otis Albert died 01/27/61   01/30/61
Widerman, Barbara E. married King, Albert T. 05/31/65   06/07/65
Widerman, Cassandra (Mrs.) died 04/12/63   04/13/63
Widerman, Charles Edward died 08/25/64   08/26/64
Wiegel, Harry Butler S. died 05/29/64   05/30/64
Wiegel, Henry, Sr. died 04/06/65   04/07/65
Wiegel, Rosie Louise married Martenet, Jefferson 03/28/64   04/30/64
Wieker, Mary Catharine died 03/01/64   03/02/64
Wielage, Jon G. died 07/15/63   07/17/63
Wier, Robert died 08/20/61   08/22/61
Wierman, Eva Emma died 05/26/63   05/28/63
Wiese, Lawrence died 03/21/64   03/24/64
Wievel, Joseph A. died 03/19/64   03/21/64
Wigart, Emeline died 09/24/63   09/26/63
Wigart, Sarah Ann died 03/26/62   03/28/62
Wiger, Cezerine M. married McCubbin, Joseph 04/30/62   06/02/62
Wiger, Claserine M. married McCubbin, Joseph 04/30/62   05/31/62
Wiggers, John H. died 03/20/61   03/28/61
Wiggington, George Washington died 08/23/65   08/25/65
Wight, Edward S. died 05/01/63   05/04/63
Wight, Mary Helen died 06/02/62   06/04/62
Wight, Mary Laura died 05/15/62   05/16/62
Wightman, A. C. married Smith, Etta M. 06/30/64   07/07/64
Wightman, Annie Hayden died 05/19/64   07/27/64
Wightman, Harry died 07/12/64   07/27/64
Wightman, William H. died 03/21/62   04/08/62
Wightman, William H. died 07/04/62   07/11/62
Wigley, George married Kelly, Ellen 07/08/63   07/16/63
Wigley, William H. died 08/03/62   09/03/62
Wigley, William Henry died 08/03/62   08/05/62
Wiker, Jacob died 10/16/61   10/26/61
Wiland, Abraham B. died 09/09/63   09/22/63
Wilbur, Samuel Plummer died 03/10/64   03/12/64
Wilburn, Nathaniel J. died 10/24/65   10/25/65
Wilcox, Alice died 02/20/61   02/21/61
Wilcox, Alice Emily died 05/14/63   05/15/63
Wilcox, Annie Virginia died 06/17/65   06/27/65
Wilcox, Cora L. married Eaverson, G. W. 07/25/61   08/17/61
Wilcox, Ethel Dera A. married Nalls, Thomas F. (Sgt.) 11/02/65   11/07/65

Wilcox, Frederick Newton died 05/28/64 05/30/64
Wilcox, George A. died 01/11/63 01/12/63
Wilcox, George M. died 07/17/65 07/18/65
Wilcox, Ida Virginia died 07/20/61 07/22/61
Wilcox, James H. died 06/10/61 06/11/61
Wilcox, John H. married Crozen, Sarah R. (Mrs.) 08/06/65 08/22/65
Wilcox, John R. married Demitz, Mary E. 10/30/64 11/01/64
Wilcox, Lewis E. married Wallace, Mattie Crawford 04/07/63 04/11/63
Wilcox, Lewis Newton died 06/26/65 06/27/65
Wilcox, Martie married Woodside, James S. 11/10/63 11/17/63
Wilcox, Peter died 11/29/61 12/02/61
Wilcox, Sarah M died 12/02/61 12/03/61
Wilcox, William L., Jr. married Pery, Sue H. 06/25/63 06/29/63
Wild, Dorothy died 02/24/62 02/25/62
Wild, John died 05/25/64 05/28/64
Wild, John F. married Roth, Mary C. 11/30/65 12/11/65
Wilderman, Alice M. married Horist, Patrick A. 06/26/62 06/30/62
Wilderman, Mary (Mrs.) died 06/06/64 06/07/64
Wilderman, Robert B. married Doyle, Emma E. 03/18/63 03/21/63
Wilderman, William C. married Moore, Mary 10/01/63 10/31/63
Wildes, Ann died 11/05/62 11/11/62
Wildey, Selenia died 11/17/65 11/18/65
Wilds, John Fillmore died 03/26/61 03/28/61
Wiles, Philip Thomas died 04/19/61 04/20/61
Wiles, Phoebe died 02/03/62 02/12/62
Wiley, David married Wiley, Mary Amanda 01/07/64 01/08/64
Wiley, George R. Wels died 08/03/62 08/05/62
Wiley, Henrietta Eliza died 04/15/65 04/17/65
Wiley, James A. married Payne, Mary Ann 01/20/63 01/27/63
Wiley, James F. (USN) married Brown, Mary E. 07/20/63 07/24/63
Wiley, John H. married Slaughter, Anna Virginia 01/21/63 01/24/63
Wiley, Margaret B. died 08/11/64 08/12/64
Wiley, Mary Amanda married Wiley, David 01/07/64 01/08/64
Wiley, Mary Ann died 04/09/63 04/10/63
Wiley, Mary V. married Whisman, Daniel H. 08/02/64 08/19/64
Wiley, Nellie Nora died 02/23/63 02/25/63
Wiley, Rebecca married Brundige, William 09/25/61 09/28/61
Wiley, Robert R. died 08/19/62 08/25/62
Wiley, Sarah (Mrs.) died 02/09/64 02/11/64
Wiley, William died 03/28/62 03/29/62
Wiley, William married Perkins, Mary E. 01/01/62 03/17/65
Wiley, William Henry died 01/22/65 01/23/65
Wilheim, John F. died 03/27/64 03/28/64
Wilhelm, Susan (Mrs.) died 04/26/63 04/28/63
Wilhelm, Annie E. married Tylor, James W. 11/01/65 11/08/65
Wilhelm, Charles P. died 03/03/65 04/26/65
Wilhelm, Charles S. married Morris, Emma L. 06/07/61 11/30/61
Wilhelm, Charlotte married McPherson, Joseph V. 11/12/63 12/03/63
Wilhelm, Emma L. married Willson, David M. 10/14/63 10/20/63
Wilhelm, James died 08/21/62 08/23/62
Wilhelm, John Frank died 12/12/62 12/13/62
Wilhelm, John H. died 07/17/63 07/18/63
Wilhelm, Mary A. died 08/23/61 08/24/61
Wilhelm, Mollie M. married Lester, J. Thomas 06/13/62 07/01/62
Wilhelm, Sallie E. died 11/02/61 11/04/61

Wilhelm, Sarah A. died 10/01/61   10/03/61
Wilhelm, Susan (Mrs.) died 04/26/63   04/27/63
Wilhelm, Wallace died 07/08/65   07/10/65
Wiliams, Amos A. died 02/03/61   02/04/61
Wiliams, Catharine died 10/29/65   11/06/65
Wilkens, Anna H. married Hashagen, John D. 09/12/61   09/14/61
Wilkens, Henriette married Shlens, G. A. 02/25/64   02/26/64
Wilkerson, Albert F. married Eden, Ella D. G. 01/19/65   01/24/65
Wilkerson, John H. married Genrous, Elizabeth 08/23/64   08/30/64
Wilkie, Robert married Floyd, Mary Ann 12/13/64   12/15/64
Wilkins, Georgeanna married Robbins, Orlando 06/19/62   06/24/62
Wilkins, Georgeanna married Gaines, William R. 12/13/64   12/16/64
Wilkins, Henrietta died 07/11/61   07/19/61
Wilkins, John C. married Snyder, C. Ann 02/05/64   02/08/64
Wilkins, Laura V. married Spedden, Daniel 10/05/65   10/12/65
Wilkins, Margaret Ann died 08/13/61   08/14/61
Wilkins, Maria D. married Russell, James, Jr. 12/20/65   12/27/65
Wilkins, Mary E. married Cottrell, Jeremiah 10/15/64   05/25/65
Wilkins, Rettie M. married Williams, James P. (Cpt.) 09/15/64   09/17/64
Wilkins, William Oliver died 04/29/65   05/01/65
Wilkinson, Charles A. died 06/14/63   06/16/63
Wilkinson, E. H. married Flemming, Kate 08/31/63   09/15/63
Wilkinson, Eliza J. (Mrs.) died 05/09/65   05/11/65
Wilkinson, Fannie Virginia married Abbott, William Martin 07/11/61
    09/11/61
Wilkinson, George W. married Cullison, Eliza 09/04/61   09/05/61
Wilkinson, J. V. married Travers, Kate C. 07/14/61   08/08/61
Wilkinson, James Travers died 12/25/62   12/29/62
Wilkinson, Jesse Gertrude died 02/27/64   02/29/64
Wilkinson, Joseph married Tuell, Margaret E. 02/20/62   03/21/62
Wilkinson, Margaret Ross died 04/10/62   05/20/62
Wilkinson, Mary married Ibbott, Frederick 02/15/61   03/26/61
Wilkinson, Mary Ann (Mrs.) died 05/19/64   05/26/64
Wilkinson, Mary E. died 11/14/62   11/17/62
Wilkinson, Mary E. married Tilton, Samuel W. 08/22/65   08/24/65
Wilkinson, N. D. married Weems, Rebecca Y. 06/01/65   06/17/65
Wilkinson, Nina Ethel died 07/15/65   07/18/65
Wilkinson, Thomas R. died 11/08/62   11/10/62
Wilkinson, Walter S. married Morgan, Jennie 08/13/61   08/16/61
Wilkison, Adaline R. died 12/26/61   12/27/61
Wilks, Mary (Mrs.) died 01/11/63   01/13/63
Willand, Abraham B. died 09/09/63   09/21/63
Willard, Eleanora married Stidham, James D. 04/04/65   05/13/65
Willard, Sarah Ellen died 07/23/65   07/26/65
Willard, Sarah Ellen died 07/23/65   07/27/65
Willcox, George A. died 01/11/63   01/14/63
Willershausen, Josephine died 10/19/65   10/21/65
Willey, Eliza A. married Langville, William T. J. 05/18/65   05/23/65
Willham, Elmira married Cole, Thomas M. 01/29/63   01/31/63
William, Abraham died 05/22/62   05/23/62
William, Rettie M. died 04/27/65   04/29/65
Williams, Alexander died 11/18/61   11/21/61
Williams, Alexander married Bond, Mary 02/13/62   02/15/62
Williams, Alexander McKane died 12/17/65   12/21/65
Williams, Amelia Emma died 09/03/64   09/30/64

```
Williams, Amzi died 01/21/64   01/23/64
Williams, Ann Rebecca married Sothoron, J. B. F. 06/09/64   06/13/64
Williams, Anna married Hayward, Thomas 01/28/61   01/30/61
Williams, Arthur married Badger, Mary Elizabeth 08/08/60   03/09/61
Williams, Asa married Cooper, Mary Jane 04/09/63   04/16/63
Williams, Asa married Falk, Mary 03/14/64   03/24/64
Williams, Benjamin married Cain, Priscilla 01/15/63   01/17/63
Williams, Benjamin died 02/10/64   02/12/64
Williams, Benjamin F. married Black, Susan A. 04/02/63   04/04/63
Williams, Benjamin S. married McDowell, Elizabeth 04/05/63   04/07/63
Williams, Bettie M. died no date   05/10/65
Williams, Charles married Hall, Sophia 06/30/64   07/02/64
Williams, Charles W. married Stier, Sarah F. B. 06/13/64   06/17/64
Williams, Charles Z. died 03/27/61   03/30/61
Williams, Clara died 09/09/64   09/10/64
Williams, Clara V. married Start, Solomon R. 10/25/60   01/04/61
Williams, Daniel V. married Deems, Laura Virginia 05/04/63   05/12/63
Williams, Denny married Holtz, Ann Elizabeth 05/24/63   12/15/63
Williams, Edward married DeGoey, Susan M. 09/15/63   09/16/63
Williams, Edward died 02/04/64   02/05/64
Williams, Edwin died 04/14/65   04/18/65
Williams, Edwin died 04/14/65   04/19/65
Williams, Eliza (Mrs.) died 12/16/64   12/17/64
Williams, Elizabeth married Waters, Benjamin E. 05/23/61   05/25/61
Williams, Elizabeth died 10/28/62   10/30/62
Williams, Elizabeth married Scoggins, Milton 05/08/62   06/02/62
Williams, Elizabeth married Brooks, Harrison 09/18/62   09/20/62
Williams, Elizabeth A. married Keys, Hanson H. 11/25/62   12/01/62
Williams, Ellen married Jackson, Samuel J. 01/02/62   01/14/62
Williams, Ellen Ann married Brooks, John Nelson 08/28/62   08/30/62
Williams, Emma married Evans, Franklin 09/06/60   07/06/61
Williams, Emma Virginia died 08/11/62   08/14/62
Williams, Frances married Gibson, Peary 12/17/63   12/29/63
Williams, Frederick Charles died 05/28/61   06/01/61
Williams, George married Johnson, Mary Letitia 03/12/61   03/14/61
Williams, George died 11/04/61   11/05/61
Williams, George F. married Higgins, Emily T. 12/03/64   12/05/64
Williams, George H. (CSA) died 01/14/63   01/16/63
Williams, George M. married Einhorn, Mary 01/18/64   01/20/64
Williams, George R. married Dix, Ann Elizabeth 10/29/65   11/04/65
Williams, George W. married Elliott, Sarah J. 11/29/63   12/08/63
Williams, Georgennie married Allen, George W. 11/07/65   11/11/65
Williams, Goodwing died 05/17/64   05/18/64
Williams, H. S. married Evans, Ida 01/25/65   02/07/65
Williams, Henrietta married Johnson, Daniel 10/16/62   10/20/62
Williams, Henrietta died 08/18/63   08/19/63
Williams, Henry married Cornel, Elizabeth 06/12/62   06/13/62
Williams, Henry married Wilson, Martha 06/11/63   06/13/63
Williams, Henry married Anderson, Louisa no date   08/31/64
Williams, Henry M. died 04/09/65   04/11/65
Williams, Hester died 02/09/64   02/10/64
Williams, Hester A. R. married Jones, William M. 03/16/64   07/06/64
Williams, Isaac J. married Adams, Jane E. 04/08/62   04/14/62
Williams, James married Saylor, Mary E. 09/12/61   09/19/61
Williams, James H. married Perkens, Margaret Ann 01/29/63   01/31/63
```

Williams, James P. (Cpt.) married Wilkins, Rettie M. 09/15/64   09/17/64
Williams, James St. Julien died 02/12/63   02/13/63
Williams, James T. married Carr, Margaret Virginia 07/04/65   07/07/65
Williams, James W. married Rogers, Emily B. 09/01/63   09/07/63
Williams, James W. married Cross, Birtie 09/21/64   09/26/64
Williams, Jannett R. married Lord, John D. 02/07/61   02/13/61
Williams, Jesse W. married Keck, Emily J. 04/14/64   05/03/64
Williams, John married Bell, Margaret 05/23/63   06/05/63
Williams, John married Brooks, Eliza Jane 02/07/65   02/10/65
Williams, John C. Crafts died 04/03/65   04/18/65
Williams, John D. died no date   05/02/63
Williams, John M. died 02/24/62   02/26/62
Williams, John Thomas died 08/31/63   09/01/63
Williams, Joseph B. died 01/16/64   01/20/64
Williams, Joseph L. married Hawkins, Ellenora 07/06/65   07/12/65
Williams, Josephine married Tavenner, George 12/26/65   12/28/65
Williams, Kate died 01/15/65   01/19/65
Williams, Levi married Branson, Isabella (Mrs.) 05/01/64   05/06/64
Williams, Louisa J. married Kelly, John C. 05/09/64   05/11/64
Williams, Lydia Ann married Nicholson, Nickson 12/08/61   12/16/61
Williams, Madelaine died 10/20/65   10/21/65
Williams, Maggie A. married Young, John 10/22/64   10/24/64
Williams, Margaret married Childs, Henry 05/11/65   05/17/65
Williams, Maria married Robinson, Benjamin 12/19/65   12/23/65
Williams, Maria (Mrs.) died 10/13/63   10/14/63
Williams, Maria (Mrs.) died 11/26/65   11/28/65
Williams, Martha H. married Johnson, William W. 06/01/65   06/05/65
Williams, Mary married Weaver, W. M. 01/10/61   01/14/61
Williams, Mary died 01/29/61   01/30/61
Williams, Mary died 09/30/62   10/02/62
Williams, Mary died 07/03/63   07/09/63
Williams, Mary married Bassett, Richard A. 05/12/64   05/14/64
Williams, Mary married Powell, Samuel 10/31/65   11/02/65
Williams, Mary A. married Robbins, Moses S. 09/06/64   09/08/64
Williams, Mary A. married Owen, Thomas 03/09/65   03/11/65
Williams, Mary Ann died 11/30/62   12/01/62
Williams, Mary E. married Brown, Joseph 06/18/63   06/19/63
Williams, Mary E. married McCoy, Hugh 08/03/64   09/10/64
Williams, Mary Elizabeth married Cane, John 12/06/64   12/08/64
Williams, Mary Ellen died 10/03/64   10/04/64
Williams, Mary Rebecca married Sye, Charles 04/16/63   04/18/63
Williams, Mattie E. married Price, Geoffrey W. 03/24/64   03/29/64
Williams, Maybell B. died 12/24/64   01/02/65
Williams, Melvina married Philips, John L. 06/24/65   07/27/65
Williams, Mollie D. married West, George F. 10/17/65   10/25/65
Williams, Nathaniel died 09/10/64   09/12/64
Williams, Nathaniel F. died 12/25/64   12/26/64
Williams, Phillip died 01/15/65   01/19/65
Williams, Rebecca F. married Moore, Crawford 01/25/61   02/08/61
Williams, Rebecca F. married Moore, Crawford 12/25/60   02/09/61
Williams, Rettie M. (Mrs.) died 04/27/65   04/28/65
Williams, Richard W. married White, Hester C. 11/17/63   11/24/63
Williams, Robert married Hall, Elizabeth Ann 05/25/64   05/27/64
Williams, Robert C. M. married Harrison, Elnorna Virginia 06/02/61   01/02/62

Williams, Rosannah Warfield died 10/25/61 10/28/61
Williams, Rose Whitridge died 01/15/65 01/19/65
Williams, Samuel died 08/03/62 08/08/62
Williams, Samuel died 02/04/63 02/05/63
Williams, Samuel S. died 08/03/61 08/06/61
Williams, Sarah F. married Sedwick, John C. 12/22/64 12/23/64
Williams, Sidney married Banks, Richard 04/06/64 04/09/64
Williams, Solomon married Cromwell, Catharine 11/15/65 11/18/65
Williams, Susan married Hughes, John 02/23/62 02/25/62
Williams, Susan (Mrs.) died 02/20/63 02/21/63
Williams, Tabitha (Mrs.) died 01/19/64 01/20/64
Williams, Thomas married Ruark, Sarah 07/11/65 08/03/65
Williams, Thomas H. married Dove, Emma 03/23/64 03/25/64
Williams, Thomas S., Sr. died 04/02/63 04/04/63
Williams, Virginia Rebecca died 11/02/63 11/04/63
Williams, William Alfred died 12/21/64 12/26/64
Williams, William Gill died 05/11/64 05/21/64
Williams, William J. married Donnelly, Emma P. 03/22/63 03/27/63
Williamson, A. S. (Cpt.) died 08/18/64 10/20/64
Williamson, Abraham died 12/17/62 12/20/62
Williamson, Ann S. (Mrs.) died 09/24/65 09/25/65
Williamson, Annie E. married Jones, Eugene A. 07/25/64 07/27/64
Williamson, Caroline Armstead died 07/29/65 08/02/65
Williamson, Charles H. died 08/01/62 08/19/62
Williamson, Elizabeth A. married Borain, William H. 02/25/64 03/09/64
Williamson, Julia died 12/02/62 12/03/62
Williamson, Maria (Mrs.) died 09/18/65 09/20/65
Williamson, Mary Ann M. (Mrs.) died 09/19/63 09/21/63
Williamson, Rebecca married Mullan, John 04/28/63 05/05/63
Williamson, Riley Seth died 08/22/63 08/26/63
Williamson, Susan died 12/25/61 12/28/61
Williamson, Thomas died 08/06/62 08/07/62
Williard, E. H. married Norton, Kate 01/01/64 01/02/64
Willibough, Elias died 09/18/64 10/07/64
Willig, Mary married Hall, Henry O. (Lt.) 05/06/63 05/07/63
Willig, S. A. married Vincent, William T. 11/24/63 12/04/63
Willing, Christiana married Keys, William W. 06/06/65 06/08/65
Willing, Edward died 12/05/61 12/06/61
Willing, James W. died 08/13/62 08/15/62
Willing, Mary E. died 08/11/61 08/12/61
Willingham, Mary A. married Burket, Frederick 10/01/65 11/14/65
Willinghan, James W. died 02/20/64 02/22/64
Willis, Alexander died 01/12/62 01/16/62
Willis, Charles Henry died 10/18/65 10/19/65
Willis, Charles Henry died 10/18/65 10/20/65
Willis, Cordelia A. married Moult, Thomas H. 01/21/61 01/23/61
Willis, Edward married Dorsey, Charlotte 02/19/63 02/26/63
Willis, Frank died 03/06/61 03/07/61
Willis, George died 07/26/61 07/27/61
Willis, George died 04/08/62 04/09/62
Willis, Georgeanna married Ellis, James A. (Lt.) 11/11/61 02/25/62
Willis, Henry Newton died 03/07/65 03/08/65
Willis, Hollingsworth died 04/27/61 05/01/61
Willis, Lizzie A. married Carr, Benjamin M. 11/06/65 11/14/65
Willis, Lucy M. died 12/02/61 12/03/61

```
Willis, Martin A. died 07/15/64   11/08/64
Willis, Mary F. married Counselman, J. Henry 05/17/65   05/18/65
Willis, Mary L. died no date   04/10/63
Willis, Moreau Lemoine died 10/01/65   10/10/65
Willis, Richard married Weaver, Annie E. 02/06/62   02/10/62
Willis, Thomas died 09/04/64   09/05/64
Willis, Thomas, Sr. died 09/04/64   09/06/64
Willis, William Finlay died 04/13/64   04/16/64
Williston, Anna E. married Waltenmeyer, John 03/16/62   10/14/62
Willman, Mary A. died 01/18/61   01/19/61
Willmore, William married Burk, Mary P. 04/07/65   04/12/65
Wills, Almira married Knight, Columbus 07/02/62   07/07/62
Wills, George R. died 09/14/64   09/20/64
Wills, Harrie died 09/02/65   09/04/65
Wills, John Thomas died 01/18/61   01/21/61
Wills, Walter J. died 10/22/63   10/23/63
Wills, William George died 08/24/65   08/25/65
Willson, Adam died 06/16/63   06/17/63
Willson, Alice died 10/05/65   10/07/65
Willson, Catharine died 07/07/62   07/14/62
Willson, David M. married Wilhelm, Emma L. 10/14/63   10/20/63
Willson, Elizabeth died 10/19/65   10/21/65
Willson, George died 01/18/61   01/21/61
Willson, John W. died 09/28/64   09/30/64
Willson, John W. died 09/28/64   10/01/64
Willson, John W., Sr. died 03/05/63   03/06/63
Willson, Laura married Smith, Robert H. 08/08/65   08/16/65
Willson, Lillie A. died 03/14/63   03/16/63
Willson, William T. married Gramblitt, Virginia G. 04/10/64   04/20/64
Wilmer, Charles married Whittinghan, Mary A. 11/10/64   11/14/64
Wilmer, Emily A. married Peterson, Thomas 04/19/64   04/21/64
Wilmer, Harriet M. died 04/16/62   04/19/62
Wilmer, John W. died 12/15/61   12/17/61
Wilmer, John W. died 12/15/61   12/18/61
Wilmer, Williamson died 01/28/61   01/29/61
Wilmot, John G. died 08/30/64   09/01/64
Wilson, Albert A. married Entwisle, Jennie 06/01/61   05/29/62
Wilson, Allen N. married Newman, Clara, A. J. 12/29/64   01/02/65
Wilson, Alvirdia died 12/26/61   12/28/61
Wilson, Amelia J. married Maybury, Thomas H. 11/05/63   11/14/63
Wilson, Ann married Wallace, Daniel 05/29/62   05/30/62
Wilson, Ann (Mrs.) died 04/10/63   04/11/63
Wilson, Ann (Mrs.) died 03/07/64   03/08/64
Wilson, Ann C. died 07/31/63   08/04/63
Wilson, Ann E. married Davis, Benjamin D. 12/31/60   05/02/61
Wilson, Anna married Muir, Henry 05/15/65   07/22/65
Wilson, Arrie E. married McNamer, John C. 01/26/64   01/28/64
Wilson, Arthur married Stansbury, Sarah 06/11/65   06/13/65
Wilson, Belle, H. married Fontaine, John L. 09/07/64   09/10/64
Wilson, Caroline H. died 06/15/61   06/17/61
Wilson, Carroll Farmer died 03/15/65   03/16/65
Wilson, Catharine married Thompson, James H. 07/14/62   07/16/62
Wilson, Catharine A. married Shaw, William D. 01/18/63   01/24/63
Wilson, Catherine died 10/01/61   10/02/61
Wilson, Charles D. died 03/08/65   03/10/65
```

Wilson, Charles H. married Smith, Adel 01/22/61 01/23/61
Wilson, Charles H. married Whiteloch, Margaret 03/30/65 04/01/65
Wilson, Charles W. married Stier, Sarah D. B. 06/13/64 06/18/64
Wilson, Cooke Luckett died 06/21/65 06/22/65
Wilson, Cornelius married Warfield, Narcissa E. 11/21/65 11/24/65
Wilson, Daniel married Dorsey, Caroline 02/08/65 02/10/65
Wilson, David A. married Prichard, Mary Jane 01/29/63 01/31/63
Wilson, David M. died 12/05/64 12/06/64
Wilson, Edward H. married Reynolds, Sarah A. 09/01/64 09/09/64
Wilson, Eliza died 05/14/61 05/16/61
Wilson, Eliza R. married Meeks, William H. 10/20/62 05/14/63
Wilson, Elizabeth died no date 02/18/62
Wilson, Elizabeth died 08/28/62 08/29/62
Wilson, Elizabeth died 10/06/62 10/11/62
Wilson, Ellen Ann married Butler, John C. 07/10/62 07/12/62
Wilson, Ellen Savage married McKenzie, James S. (Dr.) 11/14/65 11/15/6
Wilson, Elvira Z. married Cox, Isaac 05/17/64 05/20/64
Wilson, Emma Roalla married Bryan, Arthur L. 05/26/64 06/07/64
Wilson, Ezekial married Realy, Laura J. 04/14/64 04/15/64
Wilson, Fannie R. married Griffith, William E. 05/08/62 05/12/62
Wilson, George married Stevens, Susan 07/06/65 07/07/65
Wilson, George married Stevens, Susan 07/06/65 07/08/65
Wilson, George B. married Krebs, Martha 04/21/63 04/23/63
Wilson, George H. married Field, Mary E. 12/25/65 12/27/65
Wilson, George W. married Graham, Carrie E. 10/26/64 11/01/64
Wilson, George Willie died 09/14/63 09/17/63
Wilson, Georgeanna married Weiranch, John 04/10/64 04/12/64
Wilson, Harriet married Hodges, John Fresbey 11/23/65 11/25/65
Wilson, Harriet C. died 09/05/61 09/06/61
Wilson, Henry married Nicolson, Lucretia 12/28/65 12/29/65
Wilson, Hester married Murray, Stanly 10/17/61 10/19/61
Wilson, Hester A. died 05/16/64 05/20/64
Wilson, J. Oliver (Rev.) married Risteau, Mary O. 08/11/63 08/12/63
Wilson, J. Webster married Dickerson, Emma A. 06/29/65 07/01/65
Wilson, Jacob died 01/09/65 01/16/65
Wilson, James died 01/09/63 01/13/63
Wilson, James died 08/23/63 08/25/63
Wilson, James married Myers, Jane R. 12/14/65 12/15/65
Wilson, James (USA) married Brent, Florence C. 07/24/63 07/27/63
Wilson, James H. died no date 10/30/62
Wilson, James S. died 08/21/64 08/22/64
Wilson, James S. died 08/21/64 08/25/64
Wilson, James Walter died 03/01/62 03/03/62
Wilson, Jane died 12/30/62 12/31/62
Wilson, Jane L. died 11/20/65 11/22/65
Wilson, Jeannie married Moale, Edward (USA) 08/24/63 08/25/63
Wilson, Jeremiah married Hudson, Emeline 10/05/62 10/15/62
Wilson, John (Capt.) died 05/27/63 05/30/63
Wilson, John A. married Edwards, Mary Alice 11/23/65 11/24/65
Wilson, John E. married Gilpin, Ella 10/19/65 10/23/65
Wilson, John G. married Foulds, Kate 09/01/63 09/02/63
Wilson, John H. married Cooper, Hester M. 12/22/62 12/24/62
Wilson, John K. died 03/20/62 03/25/62
Wilson, John W. died 09/28/64 09/29/64
Wilson, Joseph died 04/05/65 04/06/65

Wilson, Joshua Inloes Atkinson died 05/28/62   05/29/62
Wilson, Kate married Cronin, Phillip 02/15/64   02/18/64
Wilson, Kate A. (Mrs.) died 05/16/64   05/17/64
Wilson, M. E. married Stuart, C. P. 10/16/65   12/04/65
Wilson, Maggie died 03/06/61   03/07/61
Wilson, Margaret Rebecca died 01/20/63   01/21/63
Wilson, Margie E. married Sanderson, Henry S. 09/07/65   09/12/65
Wilson, Maria married Devries, Christian 01/01/62   01/02/62
Wilson, Martha married Williams, Henry 06/11/63   06/13/63
Wilson, Mary A. married Ermy, Alonzo 02/14/61   02/19/61
Wilson, Mary Alice died 08/25/64   08/26/64
Wilson, Mary E. married Laeth, George W. 05/10/64   05/17/64
Wilson, Mary Eliza died 03/24/64   03/29/64
Wilson, Mary Elizabeth died 03/22/61   03/25/61
Wilson, Mary Ellen married Brown, William 06/05/62   06/07/62
Wilson, Mary F. died 08/12/61   08/14/61
Wilson, Mary Frances died 07/15/64   07/18/64
Wilson, Mary J. married Saumenig, F. E. 01/13/63   01/16/63
Wilson, Mary V. married Knight, Thomas 04/30/63   05/04/63
Wilson, Mary W. married Mettee, Leonard 04/11/65   04/18/65
Wilson, Minnie married Pendergast, James F. 11/03/64   11/05/64
Wilson, N. D. married Somervill, Mary E. 06/13/61   07/02/61
Wilson, Rachel died 12/31/63   01/15/64
Wilson, Rachel Elizabeth died 03/14/63   03/18/63
Wilson, Rebecca married Survoy, J. S. 03/03/64   03/08/64
Wilson, Rebecca (Mrs.) died 07/09/65   07/10/65
Wilson, Richard S. married Irvin, Laura V. 05/19/61   05/21/61
Wilson, Robert died 03/17/62   03/21/62
Wilson, Robert married Aler, Almira 06/09/63   06/15/63
Wilson, Robert died 02/19/65   02/27/65
Wilson, Robert A. died 09/15/63   09/16/63
Wilson, Robert B. died 08/04/65   08/05/65
Wilson, Ruth married Sullivan, John 09/19/62   09/30/62
Wilson, Sallie N. married Romaine, A. L. 09/04/65   09/07/65
Wilson, Samuel F. died 07/17/64   07/22/64
Wilson, Samuel Knox died 08/14/64   08/23/64
Wilson, Sarah (Mrs.) died 09/02/63   09/14/63
Wilson, Sarah A. died 06/30/65   07/01/65
Wilson, Sarah E. married Simms, Peter 01/08/63   01/10/63
Wilson, Susanna (Mrs.) died 07/07/64   07/12/64
Wilson, Susannah married Chandley, John H. 01/01/65   01/19/65
Wilson, Thomas J. married Pollock, Ella 12/17/61   12/24/61
Wilson, W. M. died 04/12/63   04/13/63
Wilson, W. M. died 04/12/63   04/14/63
Wilson, Willia Ann (Mrs.) married Ray, Joseph 04/23/63   04/25/63
Wilson, William died 06/05/61   06/06/61
Wilson, William died 10/15/64   10/19/64
Wilson, William H. died 01/01/62   01/03/62
Wilson, William H. married Palmer, Fanny D. 07/02/65   07/12/65
Wilson, William J. married Lloyd, Maria 04/08/63   04/29/63
Wilson, William J. died 11/03/64   11/05/64
Wilson, William T. married Ammons, Kate 12/24/63   04/13/64
Wilt, John W. married Franklin, Elizabeth Ann 12/29/64   01/02/65
Wilt, Sophia E. married Schriner, John G. 02/27/62   03/01/62
Wilt, Sophia E. married Schriner, John G. 02/27/62   03/03/62

Wimpsett, Martha V. married Rainer, Joseph D. 05/19/63   05/21/63
Wimpsett, Sarah S. married Sherwood, Willliam H. 05/19/64   05/24/64
Wimsatt, Charlotte died 05/23/63   05/25/63
Winand, Sidney (Mrs.) died 04/15/64   04/30/64
Winans, (Mrs. Thomas) died 03/19/61   03/20/61
Winans, (Mrs. Thomas) died 03/19/61   03/21/61
Winans, Ross R. died 06/24/63   06/26/63
Winchester, Alexander died 04/26/61   04/27/61
Winchester, Annie Rebecca died 01/17/64   01/20/64
Winchester, Ella A. married Classen, B. H. 07/14/64   07/15/64
Winchester, H. R. married Beeman, Josephine 06/04/63   06/06/63
Winchester, James E. died 03/24/64   03/25/64
Winchester, Lucy married Fisher, J. Harmanus 10/11/64   10/12/64
Winchester, Margaret married Fisher, Richard D. 11/25/62   11/27/62
Winchester, Perry died 12/01/63   12/10/63
Winchester, William died 01/09/63   01/14/64
Winckelman, Susan L. married Shriver, William H. 10/15/61   10/19/61
Wincks, Wesley married Tucker, Jinnie 12/11/64   12/16/64
Winder, Lucinda married Howard, Isaac 12/22/64   01/04/65
Winder, Mollie H. died 10/10/61   10/14/61
Windham, Eleanor died 06/09/62   06/10/62
Windsor, Glendy S. married Codd, Mary V. 09/26/65   10/04/65
Windsor, Walter Edmund died 11/20/62   11/24/62
Wineberg, Samuel married Lowenstine, Amelia 10/11/63   10/13/63
Winemuller, L. F. married Bowman, Sophie 10/25/63   11/20/63
Winer, W. married Kauffman, A. V. 03/25/63   03/27/63
Winer, William died 04/26/64   04/28/64
Winfield, Samuel died 02/03/63   02/05/63
Winfield, Susanna died 03/10/65   03/13/65
Winfreerud, C. (Dr., CSA) married Sperry, Kate E. 11/24/62   01/06/63
Wingate, Annie M. married Gootee, George S. 11/16/65   11/23/65
Wingate, Matilda died 08/23/61   08/24/61
Wingo, Harriett died 02/03/61   02/07/61
Winifred, Sarah died 01/09/62   01/10/62
Winingdar, Peter G. died 04/15/65   05/31/65
Winingder, Maggie A. married Smith, John S. 11/13/63   11/17/63
Winingder, Martha P. married Scarff, E. Norriss 01/14/64   01/18/64
Winkleman, Susan Elizabeth died 08/16/62   08/20/62
Winkler, Peter married Schweikert, Elizabeth (Mrs.) 09/17/65   10/05/65
Winkley, Mary S. (Mrs.) died 03/22/63   03/23/63
Winks, Sarah A. died 09/08/61   09/10/61
Winks, Walter Millard Fillmore died 02/04/64   02/05/64
Winn, Charlotte (Mrs.) died 01/20/63   02/02/63
Winn, Emma E. married Diffenderfer, Charles F. 09/08/64   09/10/64
Winn, James P. married Miller, Kate A. 07/28/64   08/03/64
Winn, John died 03/31/63   04/02/63
Winsey, Lydia R. died 02/07/65   02/09/65
Winsey, W. H. died 03/13/65   03/14/65
Winter, Gabriel married Davis, Mary J. 02/13/62   02/18/62
Winter, Sarah (Mrs.) died 08/02/63   08/04/63
Winternight, Henry died 01/03/64   01/04/64
Winternity, William married Whitefield, Sophia 01/11/65   01/06/65
Winters, H. A. married Brine, G. W. 07/06/65   07/08/65
Winters, John married Duffy, Elizabeth Ellen 09/24/64   09/26/64
Winters, Willie died 08/14/65   08/15/65

```
Winterson, Gassaway died 12/09/65   12/12/65
Winterson, John G. died 11/26/63   12/03/63
Winthrop, Eliza V. married Hannick, J. C. 06/03/62   06/10/62
Wintling, Jacob died 02/21/61   02/22/61
Wirgman, Rebecca M. died 10/27/62   10/29/62
Wirt, Elizabeth (Mrs.) married Keisle, Robert W. 08/08/65   08/10/65
Wirth, Casalina married Harris, George 05/22/65   06/01/65
Wirth, Christina married Richardson, Thomas C. 12/08/61   12/30/61
Wirth, Henry died 04/30/64   05/04/64
Wirth, Louisa Helen died 06/15/61   06/18/61
Wirty, Elizabeth Elenor died 07/02/64   07/04/64
Wise, Elizabeth (Mrs.) died 04/20/65   04/21/65
Wise, Elizabeth (Mrs.) died 04/20/65   04/22/65
Wise, Ellenora died 04/02/62   05/13/62
Wise, James A. married Unkle, Sallie R. 04/09/61   04/23/61
Wise, John H. married Cole, Mary A. 10/10/61   10/12/61
Wise, Lucinda (Mrs.) died 01/20/65   01/21/65
Wise, Maggie C. married Poston, John H. 11/13/65   12/16/65
Wise, Mary T. married Ensor, Thomas E. 01/01/61   01/08/61
Wise, Olivia P. married Welsh, Robert E. 03/03/65   04/06/65
Wise, Stephen Collin married Tensfield, MaryJane 01/05/64   01/06/64
Wise, Theresa married Josephthal, Moriz 10/11/63   10/20/63
Wise, Thomas M. married Schofield, Sarah A. 02/26/63   02/28/63
Wisner, George died 08/05/63   08/08/63
Wisner, Martha died 08/06/63   08/08/63
Wisog, Thomas died 01/14/62   01/15/62
Wisong, Anne Elizabeth died 07/03/62   07/07/62
Wisong, Kate Elizabeth died 03/20/61   03/21/61
Wisong, Mary Virginia died 07/02/62   07/07/62
Wissman, John H. married Hall, Laura A. 05/06/61   06/08/61
Wissner, Christine married Zink, Philip Frederick 05/24/63   05/30/63
Withered, John L. married Spencer, Lottie 01/14/62   02/03/62
Witherill, Joseph R. married Mitchem, Lydia A. 06/13/61   06/14/61
Withers, Charlotte (Mrs.) died 02/23/65   03/13/65
Withington, Charles died 11/21/64   11/28/64
Wittbecker, John married Patton, Sarah Elizabeth 11/18/62   11/26/62
Witte, Emma E. married Smith, Eugene 08/10/65   08/12/65
Wittel, Benjamin died 11/18/65   11/22/65
Witters, Thomas D. married Nicol, Lottie E. 01/26/64   10/04/64
Wittey, Albert married Bromel, Amanda 11/07/65   11/18/65
Wittig, C. married Schurmann, Annette 08/11/64   08/15/64
Wittig, Frederick W. married Engel, Kate 09/12/65   09/15/65
Wittig, John H. married Elder, Sarah F. 08/23/64   08/26/64
Wittig, Kate married Rosenthal, William 03/28/64   04/02/64
Wittington, Elizabeth married Hammond, Robert 10/10/61   10/12/61
Wittler, Henry F. W. married Heis, Wilhelmine H. L. 06/07/63   06/29/63
Wittler, Rosina married Hoffman, William Henry 05/13/62   05/16/62
Wittman, William W. married Goodhand, Benenia A. 01/10/61   01/14/61
Witts, William married Maguire, Susanna 06/01/65   07/26/65
Witz, Charles Nicholas died 02/21/63   02/23/63
Witz, Francis Emma died 12/31/64   01/03/65
Witz, Mary Kate died 12/28/64   12/31/64
Witz, William married Haul, Elizabeth Elennore 10/01/61   10/05/61
Wivel, Henrietta died 04/13/62   04/14/62
Wix, Henry A. married Rogers, Carrie R. 05/08/62   05/12/62
```

Woddy, Elizabeth married Ward, Edward 11/10/64   11/12/64
Woeltjen, Lizzie died 02/09/62   02/10/62
Wolbert, Emma married Stansbury, J. N. (Rev.) 06/03/61   06/11/61
Wolbert, Emma married Stansbury, J. N. (Rev.) 06/03/61   06/10/61
Wolf, Ada Augusta died 02/13/63   02/16/63
Wolf, Edmond J. (Rev.) married Kemp, Ella 12/13/65   12/14/65
Wolf, Elizabeth M. (Mrs.) died 07/22/64   07/23/64
Wolf, George W. married Browning, Agnes 07/27/65   07/29/65
Wolf, Harry Clinton died 01/09/63   01/10/63
Wolf, Henrietta Feby Ann married Renshaw, John Franklin 04/28/63
    05/05/63
Wolf, Henry C. married Karen, Anna M. 11/29/63   11/04/63
Wolf, John Healy died 08/04/64   08/06/64
Wolf, Josie C. married Ray, B. M. 06/23/65   10/05/65
Wolf, Sallie Olivia died 11/18/63   11/19/63
Wolfe, Caroline A. died 04/18/62   04/25/62
Wolfe, Catharine married Linville, Augustus C. 04/30/63   05/02/63
Wolfe, Florence B. died 07/18/65   07/19/65
Wolfe, Francis Eugene died 01/23/65   01/27/65
Wolfe, George married Colbert, Mary A. 06/04/61   06/20/61
Wolfe, Helen died 02/05/61   02/07/61
Wolfe, Henry Clay died 01/07/63   01/08/63
Wolfe, Isabelle married Mitchell, Thomas (Cpt.) 01/13/63   01/15/63
Wolfe, Margaret E. married Trenweth, Ralph T. 09/08/64   09/09/64
Wolfe, Mary Morris died 04/16/65   04/17/65
Wolfe, Olevia married McLaine, William, Jr. 05/23/65   05/25/65
Wolfe, Thomas died 12/20/61   12/21/61
Wolfenden, Lydia died 10/01/61   10/03/61
Wolfenden, Thomas died 02/24/65   02/27/65
Wolfender, James died 10/29/65   12/02/65
Wolfersberger, John B. married Darley, Mary E. 10/18/64   10/19/64
Wolfersberger, John P. died 05/14/65   05/17/65
Wolfersberger, John P. married Darley, Mary E. 10/18/64   10/20/64
Wolford, Kate L. married Burke, Jacob W. 12/01/64   12/03/64
Wolford, Thomas L. married Paraway, Amanda E. 07/06/64   07/08/64
Wolhelm, Sarah A. died 10/01/61   10/04/61
Wollop, William G. H. married Byrd, Sarah K. 11/14/61   12/14/61
Womb, Amanda C. died 10/14/61   10/17/61
Wonder, Henry married Clark, Mary A. 01/11/63   01/14/63
Wonderly, Jacob died 05/04/62   05/06/62
Wonderly, Joseph D. married Lloyd, Lucy M. 08/30/63   09/01/63
Wonderly, Mary A. married Shock, Dewitt Clinton 06/21/65   06/23/65
Wonderly, Mary Ann died 04/30/62   05/01/62
Wonn, Florence A. married Berry, Benjamin W. 04/13/63   04/21/63
Wonn, James G. married Cottingham, Sarah F. 06/08/64   06/18/64
Wonn, Jefferson Davis died 02/12/62   02/22/62
Wonn, Nelly L. married Werring, Joseph R. 06/02/64   06/06/64
Wonn, Nelly L. married Wernig, Joseph R. 06/02/64   06/07/64
Wonn, Susan married Turner, Mathew H. 04/29/62   05/06/62
Wonn, Virginia married Tredwell, William 01/05/65   01/10/65
Wood, Angelina M. died 11/01/63   11/03/63
Wood, Annie died 08/21/63   08/22/63
Wood, Belle died 11/10/65   11/11/65
Wood, Benjamin F. married Bowen, Elizabeth C. 03/08/64   03/11/64
Wood, C. Howard married Wickens, Annie 12/11/65   12/30/65

Wood, Charles A. died 05/06/62 06/09/62
Wood, Eliza (Mrs.) died 08/03/65 08/05/65
Wood, Emma Kate died 09/29/64 09/30/64
Wood, Fernando died 03/09/61 03/11/61
Wood, Francis M. married Cross, Sarah M. 09/22/63 10/01/63
Wood, George W. died 08/30/62 03/21/63
Wood, Harriet married Brohawn, William 01/16/65 01/24/65
Wood, John died 07/10/61 07/12/61
Wood, John M. married Mundorff, Mary E. 10/30/64 11/04/64
Wood, Joseph W. married Hyde, Lydia A. 12/26/65 12/28/65
Wood, Joshua died 05/30/63 06/01/63
Wood, Lizzie married Lamar, M. T. 10/22/64 10/29/64
Wood, Margaret A. (Mrs.) married Blake, George A. H. (Col.) 12/16/63
    12/18/63
Wood, Margaret E. married Bass, Henry J. 02/05/63 02/13/63
Wood, Mary Jane married Bennett, Conrad F. 08/14/64 10/05/64
Wood, Rachel S. married Hardesty, Richard W. 01/01/61 01/02/61
Wood, Robert F. married Stevens, Sarah E. 02/17/64 02/19/64
Wood, Samuel died 03/19/63 03/21/63
Wood, Sarah A. married Jones, William T. 09/17/65 10/18/65
Wood, Sarah E. married Robinson, John A. 12/05/61 03/14/62
Wood, William A. married Merriken, Alphonza Elizabeth 04/10/62 04/15/62
Wood, William Alexius Krozier died 07/26/62 08/01/62
Woodall, Ann Maria died 09/19/61 10/12/61
Woodall, Charles Eugene died 06/01/63 06/02/63
Woodall, Ella married McCauley, Bernard J. 01/07/64 01/21/64
Woodall, Henry Frederick died 01/15/63 01/16/63
Woodall, Maryetta died 12/15/62 01/16/63
Woodbridge, Eliza married Turner, William 07/09/61 07/19/61
Woodburn, David E. married Warner, Georgie 11/07/61 11/12/61
Woodburn, Ella B. died 10/29/64 09/20/65
Woodburn, Ella B. (Mrs.) died 10/29/64 12/19/64
Woodcock, Harry died 10/10/65 10/12/65
Woodcock, Rebecca married Brown, James M. 02/17/63 03/12/63
Wooden, Enos W. married Russell, Mary E. 05/03/64 05/06/64
Wooden, James M. died 03/07/61 03/08/61
Wooden, Jarrett married Spear, Rebecca 11/29/63 12/30/63
Wooden, John Lee married Bosley, Rebecca E. 04/20/62 04/23/62
Wooden, Rebecca (Mrs.) died 11/25/64 11/28/64
Wooden, Sarah A. (Mrs.) married Ahl, William 11/05/65 11/07/65
Wooders, Mary Jane died 12/14/64 12/20/64
Woodfield, Kate married Parrish, Edward 12/16/62 12/23/62
Woodland, Eliza J. married Hawkins, Charles 04/28/64 04/30/64
Woodland, Elizabeth C. (Mrs.) died 05/06/65 05/08/65
Woodland, Georgeanna married Thomas, Josiah 03/01/63 03/03/63
Woodland, Ida Teagle died 04/04/64 04/05/64
Woodland, Laura A. married Ross, Anthony P. 02/16/63 02/17/63
Woodland, Susie F. married Magness, Thomas M. 04/14/65 04/18/65
Woodman, John married Ward, Martha 10/20/63 11/06/63
Woodman, Mary Ann (Mrs.) died 10/07/63 10/08/63
Woodruff, Jennie H. married Keller, Harry M. 04/13/64 04/19/64
Woodruff, S. S. married Fitzpatrick, Mary 10/25/64 12/03/64
Woods, Alexander Quarrier died 02/02/62 02/03/62
Woods, Alexander Quarrier died 02/02/62 02/06/62
Woods, Alfred Price died 05/22/65 05/31/65

```
Woods, Anna married Carroll, James 03/07/61  03/08/61
Woods, Catherine A. married Richter, G. H. 09/26/65  10/10/65
Woods, Daniel C. married Crane, Maria Louisa 11/23/65  11/28/65
Woods, Edward died 04/07/63  04/09/63
Woods, Edward Payson died 12/22/63  12/24/63
Woods, Edward Payson died 12/22/63  12/23/63
Woods, Ellen A. married Mercer, Thomas V. 01/31/61  02/02/61
Woods, Frank died 11/16/65  11/17/65
Woods, G. Darridge died 10/21/62  10/22/62
Woods, Harriet married Brohawn, William 01/16/65  01/24/65
Woods, Herbert died no date  07/12/65
Woods, Hiram died 03/15/62  03/17/62
Woods, Josephine married Butler, John 10/29/63  10/31/63
Woods, Laura J. married Amos, John H. 08/22/61  09/11/61
Woods, Lizzie D. married Crane, A. F. 06/08/64  06/09/64
Woods, Margaret Ann married Blackburn, Thomas F. 03/05/65  04/11/65
Woods, Mary Jane died 11/29/63  11/30/63
Woods, Sarah married Thompson, William P. 05/14/61  05/16/61
Woods, William died 05/16/64  07/04/64
Woods, William A. married Zinn, Emma Frances 06/23/64  06/28/64
Woods, William H. died 07/12/64  07/15/64
Woodside, Edmund L. married Porter, Margaret 04/15/62  04/21/62
Woodside, Eliza J. married Hoblitzell, Oliver 05/09/61  05/16/61
Woodside, James S. married Wilcox, Martie 11/10/63  11/17/63
Woodside, Robert Perter died 10/30/63  11/02/63
Woodward, A. G. married Anderson, Annie 12/19/61  12/30/61
Woodward, Annie L. married Price, John W. 01/06/63  01/14/63
Woodward, Estelle George died 03/20/62  03/21/62
Woodward, Francis Matilda died 11/17/61  11/19/61
Woodward, Frank M. married Tucker, Mary L. 10/27/65  11/01/65
Woodward, Laura J. married Ziegler, Daniel 01/14/64  01/26/64
Woodward, Mary Raborg died 08/10/65  08/12/65
Woodward, Minnieyetta died 10/16/63  10/20/63
Woodward, Rachel Ann died 10/06/65  10/12/65
Woodward, Rignal T. married Raborg, Mary 01/26/64  01/28/64
Woodward, Robert O. married Gillispie, Mary 09/10/64  09/13/64
Woodward, Susannah died 04/23/65  04/25/65
Woodward, Susannah (Mrs.) died 04/23/65  04/24/65
Woodward, Thomas died 03/24/65  03/25/65
Woolen, Benjamin C. died 01/04/65  01/06/65
Woolen, James R. married Horney, Mary Lizzie 06/24/62  06/25/62
Woolen, M. E. married Flynn, John T. 06/24/62  06/25/62
Woolen, William W. (Capt.) died 02/22/64  02/24/64
Woolford, Eliza Ann married Henry, Theodore A. V. 04/17/64  04/14/64
Woolford, Emily E. married Smoot, John B. 11/14/65  11/17/65
Woolford, Kate married Mace, John Wesley 01/14/62  01/21/62
Woolford, Littleton W. married Hughes, Johanna S. B. 12/28/65  12/30/6
Woolford, S. B. B. died 07/07/62  07/08/62
Woolford, Thomas S. (Cpt.) died 12/06/63  12/23/63
Woollen, Margaret Alma died 02/21/61  02/25/61
Woollen, Margeret Alma died 02/21/61  02/23/61
Woollen, Mary Ellen died 02/16/63  02/17/63
Woollen, Thomas died 12/26/65  12/27/65
Woolmer, Thomas died 08/04/62  08/05/62
Woolsey, Carey married Parks, Ida 10/19/65  11/07/65
```

Woolts, Catherine C. (Mrs.) died 08/07/64 08/16/64
Wooshe, Caroline (Mrs.) married Gibson, Henry 11/05/63 11/06/63
Wooten, John H. married Mitchell, Maggie E. 05/04/65 05/05/65
Wooters, James M. married Barton, Laura J. 09/01/64 09/03/64
Wooton, William T. (USA) died 06/18/63 07/30/63
Worcester, Sarah Sargent died 06/21/64 06/23/64
Wordsworth, Lucy died 09/05/62 09/06/62
Worick, Elizabeth Madora married Goodman, Marmaduke 06/19/65 07/14/65
Worick, George Thomas died 07/23/65 07/27/65
Work, Sallie J. married Berry, Alburtus D. 04/29/64 05/03/64
Work, Sarah Elizabeth died 02/16/65 02/18/65
Work, Virlinda married Perkins, Henry C. 08/10/65 08/12/65
Working, William M. married Patterson, Laura J. 09/10/61 09/17/61
Workington, Sarah (Mrs.) died 01/03/64 01/06/64
Works, Mary J. married Tull, Richard C. 04/10/65 04/12/65
Worm, Joshua W. died 03/04/64 03/05/64
Wormsley, Lucretia married Sloan, Pemperton 08/01/65 08/03/65
Worrell, Charles Thomas died 02/01/63 02/07/63
Worrell, Joseph T. died 02/12/61 02/14/61
Worthington, Annie H. married Love, Joseph H. 10/04/64 10/07/64
Worthington, C. Kate (Mrs.) died 09/23/63 09/29/63
Worthington, Charles L died 09/20/62 09/25/62
Worthington, Emma married Kennard, John 01/29/64 03/26/64
Worthington, Grace I. (Mrs.) died 05/19/63 05/20/63
Worthington, Harriet died 06/07/62 06/18/62
Worthington, J. Edward married Johnson, Libbie 01/17/65 01/25/65
Worthington, John died 05/08/62 05/10/62
Worthington, John G. died 07/08/62 07/14/62
Worthington, Kensey J. died 01/04/63 01/06/63
Worthington, Mary Elizabeth died 10/26/62 10/30/62
Worthington, Nicholas (Cpt.) married Dorsey, Nettie 05/15/62 05/16/62
Worthington, Otis A. married Dorsey, Nellie M. 11/16/65 11/20/65
Worthington, Rezin H. married Bernard, C. Kate 02/10/63 02/12/63
Woutissith, Leontine E. (Mrs.) died 03/11/64 03/12/64
Wren, Mary Jane married Moffet, George W. 05/01/64 05/16/64
Wright, (Mrs.) married Hollan, James 05/01/62 05/03/62
Wright, Amassa A. married Beringer, Cecilia 07/31/65 08/10/65
Wright, Ann E. (Mrs.) died 04/19/63 04/20/63
Wright, Buena V. died 03/03/61 03/05/61
Wright, Caroline married McGlanan, Thomas 05/14/65 05/18/65
Wright, Carrie A. married Frizell, John C. 10/08/61 10/15/61
Wright, Catharine (Mrs.) died 08/16/64 08/17/64
Wright, Charles Albert married Mitchell, Kate 04/19/63 04/23/63
Wright, Charles W. married Smith, Eliza A. 11/22/63 12/05/63
Wright, Charles W. (Capt.) died 06/12/62 06/13/62
Wright, Charlotte died 02/11/61 02/12/61
Wright, Edward S. Jr. died 01/02/63 01/20/63
Wright, Edwin C. died 12/06/63 12/08/63
Wright, Eliza (Mrs.) died 06/25/64 06/27/64
Wright, Elizabeth Ann married Verney, John J. 03/05/62 03/07/62
Wright, Elizabeth Peters died 02/02/63 02/05/63
Wright, Emily Marion Bell died 12/20/62 12/22/62
Wright, Eugenia H. married Sweeting, William Edward 05/30/61 06/05/61
Wright, Francis Scott died 04/16/64 04/18/64
Wright, George married Watkins, Georgeanna 09/12/61 09/14/61

Wright, Harriet E. married Hindes, Daniel B. 09/11/64 09/13/64
Wright, Henry V. married Welch, Eliza J. 08/12/63 08/21/63
Wright, Henry V. married Welch, Eliza J. (Mrs.) 08/12/63 08/22/63
Wright, Isabella married Poole, Thomas 02/19/62 02/26/62
Wright, Isabella died 07/27/65 07/29/65
Wright, J. L., Jr. married Rose, Annie E. 03/26/63 03/31/63
Wright, J. Thomas married Bond, Sallie A. 02/02/65 02/04/65
Wright, James died 02/01/63 02/02/63
Wright, James A. died 12/25/64 02/07/65
Wright, James B. married Grice, Charlotte E. 04/24/62 04/25/62
Wright, Joanna married Foige, Adolph 05/14/65 05/23/65
Wright, John died 10/02/61 10/04/61
Wright, John married Sowers, Ann 05/24/63 05/26/63
Wright, John married Jenkins, Jane 02/11/64 02/13/64
Wright, John A. married Grimes, Mary E. 06/18/65 07/21/65
Wright, John R. married Thompson, Mollie C. 02/17/64 02/25/64
Wright, Joseph H. married Harryman, Eliza J. 10/13/63 10/15/63
Wright, Josephine A. married Lilly, Alonzo, Jr. 10/12/64 10/13/64
Wright, Joshua J. died 08/10/63 09/15/63
Wright, Julia A. married Strett, Shadrach 01/02/63 01/03/63
Wright, Lorenzo A. died 01/16/64 01/18/64
Wright, Louisa died 06/16/65 06/23/65
Wright, Lydia married Hook, Thomas D. 01/11/65 02/16/65
Wright, Lydia Ann died 03/28/65 03/30/65
Wright, Lydia Jane died 11/22/64 11/24/64
Wright, Marcelline married Boggess, William B. F. 09/28/63 10/07/63
Wright, Margarette married Greenlee, John 04/25/61 04/27/61
Wright, Mary married Roberts, Henry 02/21/63 02/24/63
Wright, Mary A. died no date   11/27/62
Wright, Mary A. married Hubbard, Buran, 04/28/63 05/04/63
Wright, Mary Alice married Torney, Albert G. 03/03/64 03/29/64
Wright, Mary E. married Jones, John J. 06/10/62 06/12/62
Wright, Mathew U. married Purvis, Ann E. 04/14/64 04/16/64
Wright, Millie C. married Moale, George N. 04/14/62 04/16/62
Wright, Oliver Thomas died 08/27/64 08/29/64
Wright, Rebecca Jane (Mrs.) died 06/00/00 10/06/64
Wright, Reginald Norwood (Dr.) died 06/13/65 06/16/65
Wright, Robert died 05/14/64 05/16/64
Wright, Samuel D. died 08/08/63 08/10/63
Wright, Susan died 05/08/63 05/09/63
Wright, Susan (Mrs.) died 01/24/65 01/26/65
Wright, Susie Orrick died 06/08/62 06/10/62
Wright, Thomas married Augustus, Frances 12/22/64 12/24/64
Wright, W. B. (Rev.) married Johnson, L. C. 01/01/63 01/02/63
Wright, W. B. (Rev.) married Johnson, L. O. 01/01/63 01/03/63
Wright, Willard H. married Coath, Sallie E. 11/16/65 11/20/65
Wright, William E. died 02/18/63 02/21/63
Wright, William H. Decaucey died 03/25/64 03/26/64
Wright, William Latimer died 05/03/63 05/05/63
Wrighton, Sarah A. married Farren, Willis H. 01/11/64 01/19/64
Wrightson, Rebecca married Kemp, Joseph H. 11/01/65 11/18/65
Wrightson, Ulysses S. died 08/13/65 08/14/65
Wrinn, C. Virginia married Berry, J. I. 02/27/65 03/06/65
Wrisley, Sarah Jane died 04/29/61 04/30/61
Writeside, Ruth died 07/17/64 07/18/64

Wrixon, Sarah (Mrs.) died 04/25/64   04/26/64
Wroe, Marion Josephine married Watkins, Nicholas 12/16/62   12/23/62
Wroten, Benjamin died 12/22/63   12/24/63
Wroten, Elenor A. died 12/22/65   12/23/65
Wroten, Martie married Bridge, Stephen L. 09/25/62   10/06/62
Wroth, Edward W. married Clark, Louisa 09/21/65   09/30/65
Wroth, Mary died 03/09/61   03/11/61
Wroth, Mary Rebecca Potts died 10/31/63   11/03/63
Wudmuller, Eliza (Mrs.) married Ludwig, John 02/01/65   02/04/65
Wunsch, Xavier died 01/03/61   01/04/61
Wyant, Isaac L. married Adreon, Martha Ann 09/26/63   10/14/63
Wyant, William J. married Fields, Annie R. 02/17/61   03/06/61
Wyatt, Andrew married Hall, Emily Marion 12/31/60   01/11/61
Wyatt, Frances (Mrs.) died 11/09/63   11/11/63
Wyatt, Nancy A. married Freeman, William 07/26/65   09/19/65
Wyatt, Sallie Augusta died 01/17/62   01/18/62
Wyatt, Sallie Z. married Blew, Robert W. 01/10/61   01/12/61
Wyatt, Sallie Z. married Blew, Robert W. 01/10/61   01/11/61
Wyatt, Sophie Louise (Mrs.) died 11/01/64   11/03/64
Wyatte, William E. (Rev.) died 06/24/64   06/25/64
Wyeth, William N. married Maynard, Elenor 02/24/63   02/27/63
Wylie, George M. married Finley, Ella M. 03/08/64   03/10/64
Wylie, Robert married Magee, E. J. 09/30/63   10/02/63
Wylie, William J. died 05/07/62   05/08/62
Wyman, Elizabeth died 04/25/62   04/26/62
Wyman, Samuel died 03/29/65   03/31/65
Wyne, Ann (Mrs.) died 02/13/65   02/20/65
Wynkoop, Charles S. died 06/20/63   12/01/63
Wynn, Carrie H. died 04/21/64   04/23/64
Wyoming, Gertrude Sophia died 09/16/62   09/17/62
Wyse, Eliza died 05/04/62   05/06/62
Wyse, Frances Ida died 05/05/65   05/08/65
Wyse, John married Conkling, Caroline (Mrs.) 09/15/64   09/24/64
Wyse, John married Conkling, Caroline (Mrs.) 09/15/64   09/26/64
Wyvill, Margaret Frances died 11/05/61   11/07/61
Wyvill, Samuel A. died 03/23/63   03/24/63
Yagen, Elizabeth died 04/06/62   04/12/62
Yakel, Jerome N. died 12/30/62   01/01/63
Yam, Dorothea (Mrs.) died 10/02/64   10/04/64
Yater, Julia Beall died 06/27/64   06/28/64
Yates, Edmund L. (Col.) married Tilley, Hallie H. 04/29/61   05/06/61
Yates, Francis married Rooker, Sydney Virginia 06/25/63   08/13/63
Yates, Mary E. married Colein, William H. 06/09/64   06/16/64
Yeager, Amanda Geyer died 12/25/62   12/27/62
Yeager, Jessie H. married Smoot, Sallie E. 10/23/64   06/01/65
Yealdhall, Ellen died 01/14/64   01/20/64
Yealdhall, Sally died 03/26/63   04/02/63
Yeamans, Joseph N. married Salze, Caroline 02/18/64   02/27/64
Year, Sarah E. (Mrs.) died 08/27/63   09/05/63
Yearley, Annie J. died 02/16/63   02/17/63
Yearly, Ann (Mrs.) died 06/26/64   06/27/64
Yearly, Aquilla A. married Bowie, Sarah J. 07/12/65   08/24/65
Yearly, John T. married Cole, Matilda A. 03/12/65   03/17/65
Yearly, Ruth died 07/11/61   07/22/61
Yearsly, Albin married Taylor, Lizzie A. 06/22/65   06/28/65

Yeater, Antionette A. died 09/01/61   09/02/61
Yeates, Edward John married Grinville, Ellen Jane 08/16/64   08/18/64
Yeatman, James H. married Jarvis, Fanny 10/19/65   10/23/65
Yeatman, James H. married Jarvis, Fanny 10/19/65   10/25/65
Yeatman, John W. died 08/08/64   08/09/64
Yeatman, Joseph B. died 04/17/62   04/18/62
Yeaton, J. W. (Lt.) married Dove, Maggie V. 04/14/64   04/19/64
Yelhall, Irven married Heath, Margaret A. (Mrs.) 09/18/64   09/20/64
Yenrick, Mary E. married Posern, Theodore 01/04/64   01/12/64
Yent, Charles Augustus married Miskelly, Elizabeth Gorley 09/14/65   10/31/65
Yeo, Annie M. died 03/31/61   04/01/61
Yerby, Mary V. married Lusby, Henry 11/21/64   11/24/64
Yerkes, Fannie married Cornell, Mark J. 12/18/61   12/23/61
Yerkes, Sarah Lenora married Glenn, Samuel B. 03/31/63   04/02/62
Yewell, Elenora died 04/01/61   04/02/61
Yewell, John Thomas died 06/16/63   06/18/63
Yingling, Catharine D. died 12/15/63   12/24/63
Yingling, Henry married Pitt, Mary J. 10/05/65   10/06/65
Yingling, William married Metzger, Mary E. 09/15/64   09/27/64
Yoe, Alexander S. died 04/16/63   04/17/63
Yoe, Benjamin Rush married Riddle, Ariana Rebecca 05/16/61   05/30/61
Yoe, George A. (USN) married Weyforth, Elizabeth 09/07/65   09/09/65
Yoe, James Dall Norman died 01/07/62   01/10/62
Yoger, Andrew Jackson died 02/17/62   02/18/62
Yohe, Charles A. married Steiner, Bettie 12/30/62   12/31/62
Yong, McLintock married Mobberly, Louisa 06/19/62   06/28/62
York, Amelia C. married Mortimer, John H. 08/31/63   09/02/63
York, Frances Asbury died 06/02/62   06/07/62
York, Grace Eveline died 08/29/63   08/31/63
York, Rachel Ann died 12/04/63   12/05/63
Young, Alletha Virginia died 06/08/64   06/10/64
Young, Anna died 09/01/62   09/02/62
Young, Arthur M. married Neilson, Mary P. 09/21/64   09/26/64
Young, Bridget (Mrs.) died 12/21/65   12/22/65
Young, Caroline E. married Hartmeyer, Charles 06/29/65   07/08/65
Young, Catharine J. married Trott, Thomas G. (Cpt.) 02/13/62   03/14/62
Young, Charles H. died 12/19/65   12/21/65
Young, Charles Lewis married Philips, Hattie 06/05/62   06/09/62
Young, David F. married Webster, Cholotta 12/01/63   12/15/63
Young, Edward G. married Jones, Alice A. 03/03/63   03/09/63
Young, Edward Halbert died 12/27/64   12/29/64
Young, Edwin Franklin died 03/30/63   04/01/63
Young, Eliza died 01/06/65   01/07/65
Young, Elizabeth (Mrs.) died 03/10/63   03/14/63
Young, Elizabeth Paradise died 11/24/61   11/27/61
Young, Emma married Crothers, Samuel 01/11/64   01/13/64
Young, Emma Jane died 05/16/64   05/17/64
Young, Eugenia died 12/17/62   12/18/62
Young, Eugenia died 12/17/62   12/19/62
Young, Fanny Collins died 01/28/63   01/30/63
Young, Fanny G. married Scharff, Samuel R. 08/17/64   08/27/64
Young, Francis died 12/08/61   12/09/61
Young, George W. married Lewis, Elizabeth D. (Mrs.) 10/19/65   10/26/65
Young, George Washington married Smith, Georgeanna 12/30/62   01/01/63

Young, Grace died 01/26/64   01/27/64
Young, Harry M. died 04/23/63   04/25/63
Young, Harry M. died 04/23/63   04/30/63
Young, Hattie Virginia died 08/21/64   08/27/64
Young, Henrietta Maria died 01/13/62   01/14/62
Young, Henry M. died 03/11/64   03/12/64
Young, Howard Franklin died 04/30/64   05/03/64
Young, Isabella married Kauffman, J. C. 01/03/61   02/12/61
Young, James married Dickerson, Eugenia 09/22/62   09/24/62
Young, James married Gilmore, Nancy C. (Mrs.) 05/12/64   05/14/64
Young, James E. married Hooper, Annie E. (Mrs.) 03/28/64   07/06/64
Young, Jehu died 03/14/65   03/16/65
Young, Jimmy E. died 04/02/64   04/07/64
Young, John married Williams, Maggie A. 10/22/64   10/24/64
Young, John G. died 08/20/65   08/26/65
Young, John T. married Ingersoll, Sallie T. 01/01/62   01/04/62
Young, Joseph Simon married Gates, Barbara Ellen 02/06/62   02/07/62
Young, Josephine F. married Anderson, William H. 01/14/64   01/16/64
Young, Laura married Bonsail, R. F. 02/04/64   02/08/64
Young, Laura V. married Caulk, William J. 03/12/63   09/29/63
Young, Linnie married Glenville, W. Allen 09/26/61   10/08/61
Young, Louisa E. died 09/26/61   09/28/61
Young, Mary A. (Mrs.) died 04/08/64   04/09/64
Young, Mary Elizabeth married Hayden, Oscar G. 02/04/65   02/17/65
Young, Mary Frances died 10/04/64   10/06/64
Young, Mary Francis married Herpel, John H. 07/16/63   07/18/63
Young, Mary M. died 02/25/65   02/27/65
Young, Mary M. married Longridge, J. E. 08/08/64   08/16/64
Young, Mary R. married Cromwell, George W. 02/28/61   03/19/61
Young, Mary R. married Cromwell, George W. 02/28/61   03/18/61
Young, Oscar H. died 04/25/63   04/30/63
Young, R. W. married Jenkins, Mary E. 10/26/65   11/01/65
Young, Richard married Gilliard, Mary Ann 08/13/63   08/15/63
Young, Robert H. died 02/14/65   02/15/65
Young, Samuel married Brown, Ann Maria 10/30/62   11/01/62
Young, Sarah Ann (Mrs.) died 03/03/64   03/05/64
Young, Thomas died 05/02/64   05/03/64
Young, Thomas married Diffendarfer, Susanna 05/09/64   05/11/64
Young, Thomas J. married Murphy, Hettie V. 06/15/63   06/19/63
Young, William A. died 11/14/63   11/19/63
Young, William Edward died 02/18/65   02/20/65
Young, William H. died 06/22/64   06/24/64
Young, William H. Collins died 10/04/62   10/06/62
Young, William T. died 03/09/65   03/11/65
Younger, Anna E. died 07/01/64   07/04/64
Younger, Drusilla died 05/24/61   05/27/61
Younger, Eliza M. died 09/03/61   09/04/61
Younger, Maria died 07/18/65   07/19/65
Younger, William married Harford, Georgeanna A. 02/11/64   02/13/64
Youngman, Eliza J. married Birney, Charles 03/12/63   04/07/63
Youngman, Eliza Jane married Binney, Charles 03/12/63   03/27/63
Youngman, Mary A. died 01/13/65   01/18/65
Youse, Harry died 01/16/64   01/18/64
Youse, Henry W. married Musik, Lydia Ida 05/15/62   05/17/62
Youse, John P. died 01/13/63   01/14/63

Ysadora, Melvina married Leonard, Charles H. 06/10/64   06/11/64
Yundt, Joseph married Wheeler, Sarah 12/08/64   12/31/64
Zachary, Annie married Porteus, Robert L. 02/25/63   03/06/63
Zachary, Lizzie A. married Weigle, William H. (Lt.) 11/22/61   11/25/61
Zachary, Mary Olevia died 10/17/64   10/19/64
Zachary, Sarah L. married Miller, Lewis H. 10/22/62   03/23/63
Zeigler, Barbara died 01/09/65   01/11/65
Zeigler, Edward K. died 08/09/65   08/10/65
Zeigler, George W. married Henry, Susie 10/11/64   10/15/64
Zeigler, Sarah Lizzie married Penn, George W. 03/15/63   03/26/63
Zeitler, Augusta married Miller, George W. 06/05/64   06/06/64
Zell, Emma E. married Nicklas, George 04/20/65   04/21/65
Zell, Francis died 03/20/61   03/22/61
Zell, H. M. died 05/15/62   05/16/62
Zell, John Alburtes died 11/19/62   11/27/62
Zell, Louisa M. married Osborn, W. H. (Dr.) 01/06/63   01/12/63
Zell, Oliver C. married Selby, Fannie R. 10/23/62   10/24/62
Zell, Willie died 03/29/64   04/13/64
Zeneker, Susan A. died 09/26/65   09/27/65
Zentgraf, Adelbert married Guttle, Sophia 10/29/65   10/31/65
Zerckel, Thomas Hanson died 03/16/65   03/18/65
Zerweck, Elizabeth died 12/23/65   12/25/65
Zetzener, C. Daniel died 03/23/63   03/28/63
Ziegler, Catharine (Mrs.) died 04/02/64   04/04/64
Ziegler, Charles married Ohrenschall, Mary A. 03/13/65   03/14/65
Ziegler, Daniel married Woodward, Laura J. 01/14/64   01/26/64
Ziegler, Henry S. married Aler, Lucretia 08/29/65   09/05/65
Zile, Thirza Ann married Engel, Daniel 10/22/63   10/24/63
Zimmer, Charles Philip died 08/12/64   08/13/64
Zimmer, Oscar Summerville died 06/26/64   06/27/64
Zimmerman, Adelaide married Conrad, William 11/19/63   11/24/63
Zimmerman, Bolivar died 07/07/64   07/12/64
Zimmerman, Clara Christine died 10/02/63   10/03/63
Zimmerman, Corrilla married Keller, John H. 03/31/63   05/18/63
Zimmerman, H. S. married Zimmerman, M. Emma 10/03/65   10/10/65
Zimmerman, H. T. married Coombs, Fannie E. 05/04/65   05/06/65
Zimmerman, Isaac died 11/22/64   12/03/64
Zimmerman, Lizzie married Bennett, John E. 02/19/63   02/25/63
Zimmerman, M. Emma married Zimmerman, H. S. 10/03/65   10/10/65
Zimmerman, Mary died 03/21/61   03/25/61
Zimmerman, Roberto V. married Owens, Joseph R. (Dr.) 11/24/63   11/26/6
Zimmerman, Sarah Amelia died 08/02/61   08/03/61
Zimmerman, William F. died 03/29/63   04/02/63
Zimmerman, William Henry married Reed, Jennie Nelson 06/04/63   06/13/6
Zimmerman, William S. married Goldsborough, Gertrude 10/14/65   12/09/6
Zimmernam, Charles married Hoffmeister, Johanna 08/25/61   09/03/61
Zini, Leon died 03/20/61   03/22/61
Zink, Philip Frederick married Wissner, Christine 05/24/63   05/30/63
Zinkand, Henry died 06/04/64   06/10/64
Zinkaun, Leopold died 08/09/63   08/24/63
Zinkland, Mary E. married Cashmyer, Henry 10/18/64   10/21/64
Zinkler, Mary died 02/16/62   02/18/62
Zinn, Emma Frances married Woods, William A. 06/23/64   06/28/64
Zipp, Mary A. died 12/08/61   12/09/61
Zoeller, Mathias married Hoppy, Mary 05/21/61   06/12/61

Zolhnoffer, Fred married Keys, Mary Ann E. 07/18/62   07/21/62
Zollicoffer, Mary died 07/18/63   07/21/63
Zollinger, Fannie A. (Mrs.) died 08/01/64   08/02/64
Zollinhafer, George married Oltmans, Maria 10/25/64   11/22/64
Zorn, Eliza died 06/11/62   06/13/62
Zouck, Martha died 03/21/64   03/26/64
Zupp, Reuben married Hamilton, Sarah A. 03/26/63   04/07/63
Zurharst, E. (Mrs.) married Hosemann, Louis C. H. 08/14/64   08/29/64

www.ingramcontent.com/pod-product-compliance
Lightning Source LLC
Chambersburg PA
CBHW050423240426
43661CB00055B/2258